AMERICAN dissertations on Foreign Education

Doctor's Dissertations and Master's Theses Written at American Universities and Colleges Concerning Education or Educators in Foreign Countries and Education of Groups of Foreign Birth or Ancestry in the United States
1884-1958

Walter Crosby Eells

COMMITTEE ON INTERNATIONAL RELATIONS
National Education Association of the United States
Washington, D.C.   U.S.A.
1959

COPYRIGHT 1959

by

National Education Association of the United States
1201 Sixteenth Street, N. W.
Washington, D. C., U. S. A.

Library of Congress Catalog Card Number 59-12819

Printed in the United States of America

This publication is for sale at the following prices: Single copy, $5.75. Discounts for quantity orders: 2-9 copies, 10 per cent; 10-100 copies, 20 per cent; special discounts for quantities in excess of 100. To bookstores or other agencies for resale purposes: 20 per cent reduction. Orders not accompanied by remittance are subject to transportation charges. Make checks payable to the National Education Association, 1201 Sixteenth Street, Northwest, Washington 6, D. C.

FOREWORD

It is with considerable pleasure that the Committee on International Relations of the National Education Association presents this bibliography of dissertations in the field of Comparative Education. The growing interest in this area of study is evident on every hand as one sees the abundance of articles and studies which have appeared recently. And the establishment of the Comparative Education Society has given impetus and vigor to this significant endeavor in education.

This bibliography is of special importance in that many of the authors of the studies are nationals of the countries about which they are writing. They are also products of the educational systems which they describe and about which they have done their research. Many of these studies, at least in the form of published abstracts, are available in foreign countries. Places have been noted in the Introduction.

To Dr. Walter Crosby Eells credit must be given for his tireless and scholarly efforts in compiling and checking the entries in this book for which there has been a long-felt need. We hope that this will be a volume of use and value to the profession.

PAUL E. SMITH, Secretary
Committee on International Relations

CONTENTS

	Number	Page
FOREWORD		iii
INTRODUCTION		ix
Significance		ix
Usefulness		x
Studies Included		x
Criteria for Inclusion		xi
Geographical Classification, by Continents		xii
Geographical Classification, by Countries		xiii
Method of Compilation		xxi
Names of Authors		xxiv
Birth and Death Years		xxv
Institutions at Which Accepted		xxvi
Year of Acceptance		xxviii
Pagination		xxix
Topical Contents		xxx
Publication Data		xxx
Availability		xxxi
Acknowledgments		xxxiii
AVAILABILITY OF "DISSERTATION ABSTRACTS"		xxxiv
PRINCIPAL SOURCES		xxxvi
RELATED PUBLICATIONS		xxxviii
GENERAL	1	1-5
COMPOSITE	119	6-16
AFRICA	309	17-29
General	309	17
Composite	321	17
Algeria	331	18
Angola	338	18
Belgian Congo	342	19
Cameroons	357	19
Egypt	360	20
Ethiopia	429	23
Ghana	432	23
Kenya	436	23
Liberia	440	24
Nigeria	452	24
Nyasaland	479	25
Rhodesia	482	26
Sierra Leone	484	26
Sudan	495	27
Tanganyika	497	27
Togoland	498	27
Uganda	499	27
Union of South Africa	500	28

	Number	Page
AMERICA, NORTH	527	30-59
General		30
Composite	527	30
Bahama Islands	542	31
Bermuda	543	31
Canada	545	31
Costa Rica	840	44
Cuba	851	44
Dominican Republic	867	45
El Salvador	868	45
Guatemala	871	46
Haiti	876	46
Honduras	884	46
Mexico	887	47
Panama	1041	53
Puerto Rico	1044	53
Virgin Islands	1166	58
West Indies (British)	1168	58
AMERICA, SOUTH	1181	60-66
General	1181	60
Composite	1183	60
Argentina	1199	61
Bolivia	1212	61
Brazil	1217	62
Chile	1244	63
Colombia	1263	64
Ecuador	1270	64
Paraguay	1273	65
Peru	1274	65
Uruguay	1287	66
Venezuela	1290	66
ASIA	1293	67-137
General	1293	67
Composite	1297	67
Afghanistan	1323	68
Burma	1326	68
Ceylon	1347	69
Cyprus	1353	70
Formosa	1355	70
Hong Kong	1360	70
China	1362	71
India	1823	88
Indonesia	2134	100
Iran	2141	100
Iraq	2167	102
Israel	2200	103
Japan	2305	107
Jordan	2479	115
Korea	2481	115

	Number	Page
Lebanon	2542	117
Malaya	2553	118
Manchuria	2563	119
Pakistan	2564	119
Philippines	2580	120
Sarawak	2894	132
Syria	2895	132
Thailand	2901	133
Tibet	2956	135
Turkey	2957	135
Viet-Nam	2996	137
Yemen	2999	137
EUROPE	3001	138-211
General	3001	138
Composite	3068	140
Albania	3304	151
Austria	3305	151
Belgium	3312	152
Bulgaria	3324	152
Czechoslovakia	3328	153
Denmark	3352	154
Finland	3369	154
France	3374	155
Germany	3584	163
Great Britain	3848	173
Greece	4296	189
Hungary	4364	192
Iceland	4374	192
Ireland	4375	193
Italy	4402	194
Lithuania	4569	200
Netherlands	4572	200
Norway	4590	201
Poland	4607	202
Portugal	4624	203
Romania	4628	203
Spain	4630	203
Sweden	4662	205
Switzerland	4686	206
USSR (Union of Soviet Socialist Republics)	4723	207
Yugoslavia	4801	210
OCEANIA	4804	212-215
American Samoa	4804	212
Australia	4809	212
Guam	4837	213
New Guinea	4839	214
New Zealand	4840	214
Okinawa	4850	214
Pacific Islands	4854	215

	Number	Page
UNITED STATES OF AMERICA	4860	216-255
General	4860	216
Composite	4953	219
Albanian	5027	224
Arabian	5028	224
Armenian	5030	224
British	5031	224
Chinese	5032	225
Danish	5090	227
Dutch	5092	227
Filipino	5095	227
Finnish	5098	228
French	5100	228
German	5107	228
Greek	5113	229
Indian	5114	229
Iranian	5116	229
Irish	5117	230
Italian	5119	230
Japanese	5151	231
Latin-American	5207	234
Lithuanian	5654	251
Norwegian	5655	251
Polish	5655a	251
Portuguese	5658	252
Puerto Rican	5659	252
Scandinavian	5683	253
Slavic	5684	253
Swedish	5692	254
Syrian	5696	254
Turkish	5697	254
Welsh	5698	255
AUTHOR INDEX		256
GENERAL INDEX		277

INTRODUCTION

SIGNIFICANCE

Among the many methods available for developing international understanding and favorable attitudes between peoples of diverse races and cultures in different parts of the world, the exchange of information concerning school systems and educational problems and policies is by no means the least important since education plays such a basic role in the cultural and social development of any nation or people.

By common consent in the academic world, the doctor's degree, fitness for which is almost universally evidenced by the writing of a scholarly dissertation which must be the product of extended research, marks the completion of the highest level of formal scholarship in American institutions of higher education. Achievement of the doctorate normally requires three years or more of study beyond the level of the baccalaureate degree which marks the conclusion of a four-year course of study in the American college or university.

At a somewhat lower level of research stands the master's degree, normally secured after a single year of study beyond the baccalaureate level. Usually, but not always, the master's degree has required the preparation of a thesis, although not as extended or as scholarly a one as the doctor's dissertation. Master's theses vary considerably in extent and quality, but many of them contain original material of distinct value on a more restricted phase of a larger subject of study. Information regarding master's theses is much less widely known and more difficult to secure than that concerning doctor's dissertations. Very few of them have been published in full or even in abstract form. Thus they have been almost lost to the world of scholarship outside of the institutions at which they have been written.

During the past one hundred years, more than 150,000 doctor's degrees have been conferred by American universities and colleges; 98 percent of them in the twentieth century, almost half of them in the last ten years. Of this number more than 15,000 represent research in the professional field of education. During the same period approximately one and one-quarter million master's degrees have been conferred. During the past ten years 16 percent of the 74,000 doctor's degrees and 44 percent of the 577,000 master's degrees have been conferred in the field of education.

While most of these research studies in the educational field have dealt primarily with educational conditions and policies in the United States, it is significant of the interest in the international aspects of education that more than 5700 of them have been concerned with education or educators in foreign countries or with the education of foreign groups in the United States. It is the object of the present volume to present significant information concerning almost 1700 such doctor's dissertations and more than 4000 such master's theses.

USEFULNESS

It is hoped that the publication of this list of research studies with significant information concerning them and their availability will prove serviceable to a variety of scholars, administrators, and research workers. First of all, it should be useful to educational leaders in countries outside the United States of America who may wish to know the results of intensive research done by their own nationals while pursuing courses of advanced study in American graduate schools. Or they may be interested to learn the nature of advanced study of the educational problems of their various countries which have been made by American students.

It should also be useful to students of international education and of comparative education in the United States who may wish to compare and synthesize studies of a special topic in various countries, or to make an intensive investigation of educational policies and problems in a particular country or related group of countries. It should be particularly useful to graduate students, searching for suitable dissertation subjects in the international education field, helping them to avoid unnecessary duplication of topics already adequately studied, and aiding them in the selection of subjects which will profitably extend further the frontiers of knowledge in a particular field of interest or in a special section of the world.

And it should prove especially helpful to reference librarians in education libraries throughout the country in answering the numerous questions which come to them regarding sources of information in comparative education and related fields.

STUDIES INCLUDED

The present volume presents data concerning 1690 doctor's dissertations and 4026 studies which have been classified as master's theses, a total of 5716.[1] Included with the latter group, however, are 27 theses for the degree of Bachelor of Divinity, written at 16 different institutions. These institutions are all theological seminaries, usually requiring a baccalaureate degree for entrance, and conferring the bachelor of divinity degree after three years of study in advance of this entrance requirement. In substance and in quality, therefore, these

---

[1] The theses were numbered consecutively from 1 to 5698. After the numbering was completed, four duplications were found, caused by alternative spellings of the same name, while 22 new titles were found, making a net increase of 18 from 5698 to 5716. The inserted theses have been numbered 19a, etc.

particular theses probably represent a higher level of scholarship than the typical master's degree in other institutions. The identity of this group of theses and the institutions at which they were accepted can be found from the General Index under the entry "Bachelor of Divinity theses."

Most of the doctorates listed are the Doctor of Philosophy, but some of them are the early Doctor of Pedagogy or the more recent Doctor of Education, Doctor of Religious Education, and a few other designations. Most of the master's degrees represent the Master of Arts, but some are the Master of Science, Master of Science in Education, Master of Education, Master of Religious Education, and a few other designations. Most of the available published reference sources, listed later, do not distinguish between the particular type or designation of doctor's or master's degrees received, nor is it considered important for the purposes of the present reference list. No effort has been made, therefore, to include designation of the different types of doctor's or master's degrees which have been conferred by the various American institutions of higher education. Doctor's dissertations are reported separately from master's theses, however, in each of the countries listed, the arrangement in each group being alphabetical by authors.

CRITERIA FOR INCLUSION

The general criterion for inclusion in this volume was that a dissertation or thesis [2] should deal significantly with education or educators in a foreign country or with education of groups of foreign birth or ancestry in the United States. Frequently it was not possible to determine from the title alone whether a thesis included "education" or, if it did, whether it dealt with foreign education. Hundreds of original theses or abstracts of them were examined to determine their suitability for inclusion and their appropriate classification, by country and topic, if judged suitable.

A considerable number of theses have been written concerning missionary activities, both Protestant and Catholic, in foreign lands. Many of these include significant consideration of the educational activities and institutions, both colleges and schools, established by church groups as an integral part of their missionary activities. Missionary theses have not been included, however, on the basis of their titles alone. It was necessary to have definite evidence from the thesis, its abstract, or the testimony of a librarian, that consideration of educational activities was included in it. Doubtless a number of missionary theses have been omitted which would have been included if adequate information concerning their contents could have been secured.

---

[2] "Dissertation" is the term commonly used to indicate a doctor's study, "thesis" for a master's study; but "thesis" is frequently used as a generic term for both types of studies.

GEOGRAPHICAL CLASSIFICATION, BY CONTINENTS

Table I shows a geographical classification, by continents, of the doctor's dissertations and master's theses included in the present volume.

Table I. SUMMARY OF DOCTOR'S DISSERTATIONS AND MASTER'S THESES, BY CONTINENTS

CONTINENT	TOTAL Number	TOTAL Percent	DOCTORS Number	DOCTORS Percent	MASTERS Number	MASTERS Percent
General	119	2.1%	38	2.2%	81	2.0%
Composite	192	3.4	69	4.1	123	3.1
Africa	220	3.8	84	5.0	136	3.4
America, North	654	11.4	254	15.0	400	10.0
America, South	112	2.0	28	1.7	84	2.1
Asia	1718	30.1	570	33.7	1148	28.5
Europe	1803	31.5	493	29.2	1310	32.5
Oceania	57	1.0	23	1.4	34	0.8
United States of America . . .	841	14.7	131	7.7	710	17.6
TOTALS . . .	5716	100.0%	1690	100.0%	4026	100.0%

A word of explanation may be made concerning the three noncontinental groups in Table I -- General, Composite, and United States of America.

The "General" group, as its name indicates, includes titles so general in nature that they do not apply to education in any particular continent or country, such as "A Study of the Development and Underlying Principles of International Educational Organizations" (No. 9); "Trends in International Education from World War I through World War II" (No. 19); or "The Development of the Philosophy of UNESCO" (No. 21).

A much larger number of theses are classified as "Composite." These refer to theses which are studies of education in specific countries which are located in different continents. Examples of this group are "National Ministries of Education" (No. 119), which covers 55 countries on all continents; "A Comparative Study of the Secondary Education of Girls in England, Germany, and the United States, with a Consideration of the Secondary Education of Girls in Japan" (No. 148); or "A Documentary and Descriptive Analysis of the Administration of Educational Programs under Point Four in Brazil, Iran, and

Thailand" (No. 171). All such composite theses have been listed only once, but with full cross-references to them from each of the countries included in their content.

As to the third group, after a good deal of consideration, it was decided that it would be useful to include theses dealing with the education of groups of foreign birth or foreign parentage or descent in the United States. It was felt that many foreign educators, from Japan or Italy for example, as well as other students of international education, would often find it of distinct interest and value to have available information not only about education in Japan or Italy, but also concerning the education of Japanese or Italian groups in the United States. Examples are "A Study of the Educational Effects of Segregation upon Japanese Children in American Schools" (No. 5152); or "General Background Deficiencies of First Generation Italian Children of the Elementary School Level" (No. 5130).

The two examples just given refer to children of foreign parentage in the process of becoming Americanized. Quite a different type of thesis is also included in this classification involving mature students temporarily in the United States who expect to return or who have returned to their own countries upon completion of a period of advanced study in the United States, such as "A Study of the Problems of Foreign Students at the Berkeley Campus of the University of California" (No. 4975); or "A Study of the Professional Needs of Students from Other Lands Who Have Studied Home Economics in Colleges and Universities in the United States and Who Have Returned Home" (No. 4957).

GEOGRAPHICAL CLASSIFICATION, BY COUNTRIES

Table II shows a more detailed geographical classification by countries for each of the continents. The classification of countries is based, with minor modifications, upon that of the United Nations.[3]

---

[3] "Demographic Yearbook, 1957." Statistical Office of the United Nations, Department of Economic and Social Affairs, New York, 1957, p. 124-135. The chief change made in the classification plan of the United Nations is in the case of USSR which is there classified as separate from any continent. For the purposes of the present compilation the USSR has been placed in Europe, since most of the theses involved deal with European Russia.

Table II. **SUMMARY OF DOCTOR'S DISSERTATIONS AND MASTER'S THESES, BY CONTINENTS AND COUNTRIES**

CONTINENT AND COUNTRY	GRAND TOTAL	TOTAL Complete	TOTAL Partial	DOCTORS Complete	DOCTORS Partial	MASTERS Complete	MASTERS Partial
GENERAL	--	119	--	38	--	81	--
COMPOSITE	--	192	--	69	--	123	--
AFRICA	--	220	--	84	--	136	--
General	38	12	26	2	8	10	18
Composite	10	10	0	3	0	7	0
Algeria	15	7	8	1	1	6	7
Angola	5	4	1	2	0	2	1
Belgian Congo	20	15	5	4	0	11	5
Cameroons	6	3	3	1	1	2	2
Egypt	101	70	31	40	15	30	16
Ethiopia	5	3	2	1	1	2	1
Ghana	7	4	3	2	1	2	2
Kenya	8	4	4	0	0	4	4
Liberia	15	12	3	1	2	11	1
Nigeria	33	27	6	8	2	19	4
Nyasaland	4	3	1	1	0	2	1
Rhodesia	4	2	2	0	0	2	2
Sierra Leone	15	11	4	3	1	8	3
Sudan	3	2	1	0	0	2	1
Tanganyika	5	1	4	0	1	1	3
Togoland	2	1	1	0	0	1	1
Uganda	5	1	4	0	0	1	4
Union of South Africa	43	28	15	15	9	13	6
AMERICA, NORTH	--	654	--	254	--	400	--
General	26	0	26	0	3	0	23
Composite	15	15	0	10	0	5	0
Bahama Islands	1	1	0	0	0	1	0
Bermuda	3	2	1	1	0	1	1
Canada	325	296	29	135	12	161	17
Costa Rica	32	11	21	5	9	6	12
Cuba	35	16	19	2	7	14	12
Dominican Republic	14	1	13	0	4	1	9
El Salvador	18	3	15	2	6	1	9
Guatemala	25	5	20	3	10	2	10
Haiti	21	8	13	1	6	7	7
Honduras	21	3	18	0	7	3	11
Mexico	196	153	43	46	20	107	23
Panama	19	3	16	1	6	2	10
Puerto Rico	135	122	13	47	5	75	8
Virgin Islands	9	2	7	0	4	2	3
West Indies	16	13	3	1	2	12	1

Introduction

Table II. SUMMARY OF DOCTOR'S DISSERTATIONS AND MASTER'S THESES, BY CONTINENTS AND COUNTRIES – *Continued*

CONTINENT AND COUNTRY	GRAND TOTAL	TOTAL Complete	TOTAL Partial	DOCTORS Complete	DOCTORS Partial	MASTERS Complete	MASTERS Partial
AMERICA, SOUTH	--	112	--	28	--	84	--
General	29	2	27	0	4	2	23
Composite	16	16	0	7	0	9	0
Argentina	45	13	32	4	13	9	19
Bolivia	21	5	16	1	6	4	10
Brazil	49	27	22	2	10	25	12
Chile	51	19	32	3	13	16	19
Colombia	27	7	20	3	5	4	15
Ecuador	24	3	21	1	8	2	13
Paraguay	13	1	12	1	5	0	7
Peru	34	13	21	5	5	8	16
Uruguay	18	3	15	1	6	2	9
Venezuela	16	3	13	0	4	3	9
ASIA	--	1718	--	570	--	1148	--
General	24	4	20	1	7	3	13
Composite	26	26	0	7	0	19	0
Afghanistan	5	3	2	2	1	1	1
Burma	26	21	5	7	2	14	3
Ceylon	19	6	13	2	7	4	6
China	517	462	55	149	22	313	33
Cyprus	4	2	2	1	1	1	1
Formosa	8	5	3	1	1	4	2
Hong Kong	3	2	1	1	1	1	0
India	364	315	49	116	21	199	28
Indonesia	18	7	11	1	4	6	7
Iran	41	27	14	17	7	10	7
Iraq	56	34	22	26	9	8	13
Israel	148	105	43	36	16	69	27
Japan	216	174	42	52	19	122	23
Jordan	6	2	4	0	1	2	3
Korea	72	61	11	26	4	35	7
Lebanon	22	11	11	4	5	7	6
Malaya	16	10	6	2	3	8	3
Manchuria	2	1	1	0	1	1	0
Pakistan	20	16	4	6	2	10	2
Philippines	345	316	29	81	10	235	19
Sarawak	5	1	4	1	2	0	2
Syria	23	6	17	3	5	3	12
Thailand	67	56	11	19	7	37	4
Tibet	2	1	1	0	0	1	1
Turkey	59	39	20	8	11	31	9
Viet-Nam	4	3	1	1	0	2	1
Yemen	3	2	1	0	1	2	0

Table II. **SUMMARY OF DOCTOR'S DISSERTATIONS AND MASTER'S THESES, BY CONTINENTS AND COUNTRIES** – *Continued*

CONTINENT AND COUNTRY	GRAND TOTAL	TOTAL Complete	TOTAL Partial	DOCTORS Complete	DOCTORS Partial	MASTERS Complete	MASTERS Partial
UNITED STATES	--	841	--	131	--	710	--
(Foreign groups)							
General	94	94	0	17	0	77	0
Composite	74	74	0	23	0	51	0
Albanian	2	1	1	0	0	1	1
Arabian	4	2	2	2	2	0	0
Armenian	1	1	0	0	0	1	0
British	14	1	13	0	6	1	7
Chinese	83	58	25	19	12	39	13
Danish	9	2	7	0	6	2	1
Dutch	8	3	5	1	3	2	2
Filipino	15	3	12	0	8	3	4
Finnish	9	2	7	0	4	2	3
French	16	7	9	2	3	5	6
German	32	6	26	3	7	3	19
Greek	8	1	7	0	4	1	3
Indian	15	2	13	2	10	0	3
Iranian	5	1	4	0	3	1	1
Irish	9	2	7	0	0	2	7
Italian	58	32	26	7	7	25	19
Japanese	81	56	25	11	9	45	16
Latin-American	468	447	21	27	6	420	15
Lithuanian	8	1	7	0	0	1	7
Norwegian	11	1	10	1	5	0	5
Polish	23	3	20	1	5	2	15
Portuguese	6	1	5	0	3	1	2
Puerto Rican	28	24	4	9	3	15	1
Scandinavian	4	1	3	1	1	0	2
Slavic	24	8	16	0	5	8	11
Swedish	17	4	13	3	9	1	4
Syrian	4	1	3	0	3	1	0
Turkish	6	1	5	1	3	0	2
Welsh	1	1	0	1	0	0	0

An explanation of the brief terms "Complete" and "Partial" in the column headings of Table II may be needed. "Complete" refers to theses which deal completely or in a substantial part with education in the country named; "Partial" refers to theses, usually listed in the "Composite" group, which refer only in part to the country named, to which cross-reference is made in the lists in the text.

The meaning of these terms and of the entire table may be made clearer by an example, using Egypt for this purpose. The table shows that there are 101 theses which deal with education in Egypt in 70 of which Egyptian education is considered completely or substantially or is the major object of study, while in 31 others Egyptian education comprises only a part, perhaps a small part of the entire thesis. Of the doctoral dissertations (55 in number) dealing with education in Egypt, 40 deal with it completely or substantially, while 15 others deal with it only partially. Of the master's theses (46 in number) dealing with education in Egypt, 30 deal with it completely or substantially, while 16 others deal with it only partially. Entries for the other countries in Table II are to be read the same way.

The numbers shown in the second column of Table II which total 5716 refer to the dissertations and theses, full details of which are given consecutively in the body of the volume, classified by continents and countries in the same order as in the table. The 70 shown for Egypt, for example, in the second column are listed together as Nos. 360-428. If a thesis deals with education in more than one country (usually listed in the Composite group) it is cross-referenced to all countries to which it applies, such cross-referencing being indicated at the close of the doctor's and master's lists respectively.

In the case of several dozen smaller countries or other political subdivisions for which no complete thesis was found but which are considered in some of the entries in the Composite group, such as Aden, Crete, Danzig, Wales, or Zanzibar, no such cross-references are given in the body of the volume but they may be located from the appropriate entry in the General Index.

No totals are given for the first column of Table II, nor for the "Partial" columns, since so many duplications are involved from the Composite groups that such a total would have no meaning. The totals of "Complete" theses as given are those already used in Table I.

A different type of theses have been entered in the Composite groups in some continents -- those concerned with individuals whose significant educational activities and influence extended to more than one country, as for example D. F. Sarmiento in Argentina and Chile, or St. Thomas Aquinas in Italy and France.

Introduction

A question may be raised as to the inclusion as "foreign countries" of Puerto Rico, Virgin Islands, American Samoa, Guam, Okinawa, and some of the other Pacific Islands which are under American jurisdiction. In all of these territories the prevailing language is other than English. It was felt, therefore, that many of their educational problems were similar to those of other non-English-speaking countries which are more accurately termed "foreign" and therefore that it might prove helpful in many cases to have such theses available for reference also. With this criterion, theses regarding education in the Panama Canal Zone or Hawaii were excluded, since these are prevailingly English-speaking areas. The Philippines are included as a foreign country not only for theses written since 1946, when independence was achieved, but for the earlier period from 1898 to 1946 when this country was under the jurisdiction of the United States, but prevailingly Spanish-speaking. In all such cases the controlling factor was to make the compilation as useful as possible to a variety of potential users, not to limit it in all cases by strictly legalistic definitions of terms.

An examination of Table II shows 15 countries which are credited with 100 or more theses, as follows:

Great Britain	657	Italy	308
China	517	Japan	216
Germany	434	Mexico	196
France	421	Israel	148
India	364	Greece	139
Philippines	345	Puerto Rico	135
Canada	325	USSR	122
		Egypt	101

A consideration of the "Complete" theses credited to these countries in the second column of Table II shows that they account for considerably more than half of the total of 5716 theses; the first five countries account for more than a quarter of the entire number.

Table II also shows that of the theses devoted to education of foreign groups in the United States, the single Latin-American group accounts for more than half of the total number, but that there are substantial groups also devoted to education of Chinese, Japanese, Italians, and Puerto Ricans.

A rather surprising feature of the classification by continents shown in either Table I or II is the relatively small number of studies, either at the doctor's or master's levels, dealing with education in South America, less than 2 percent of the total number. This may be compared with the fact that approximately 12 percent of the 33,000 foreign students studying in the United States in 1954-55 were from South America.[4]

---

[4] Mary Irwin, Editor. "American Universities and Colleges," American Council on Education, Washington, D. C., 1956. Seventh edition. p. 92-93.

Figure 1

DISTRIBUTION BY CONTINENTS OF THESES DEALING WITH EDUCATION

N = 4564

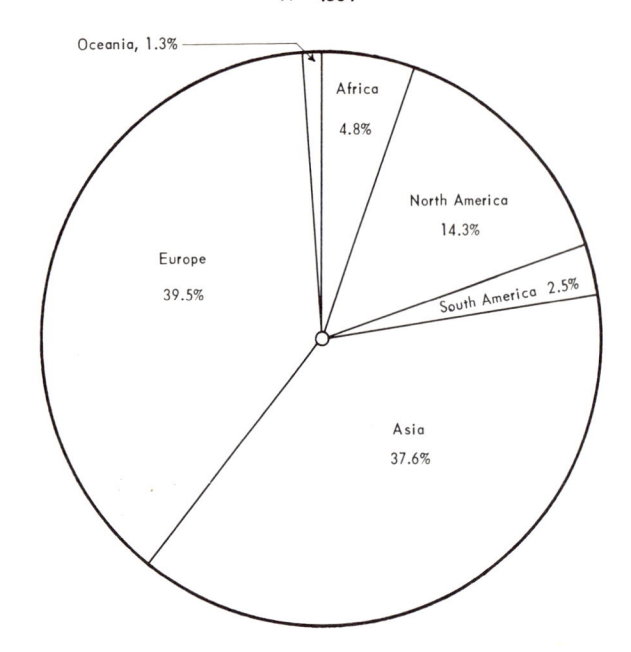

- Oceania, 1.3%
- Africa 4.8%
- North America 14.3%
- South America 2.5%
- Asia 37.6%
- Europe 39.5%

DISTRIBUTION BY CONTINENTS OF FOREIGN STUDENTS STUDYING IN THE UNITED STATES, 1954-55

N = 33,634

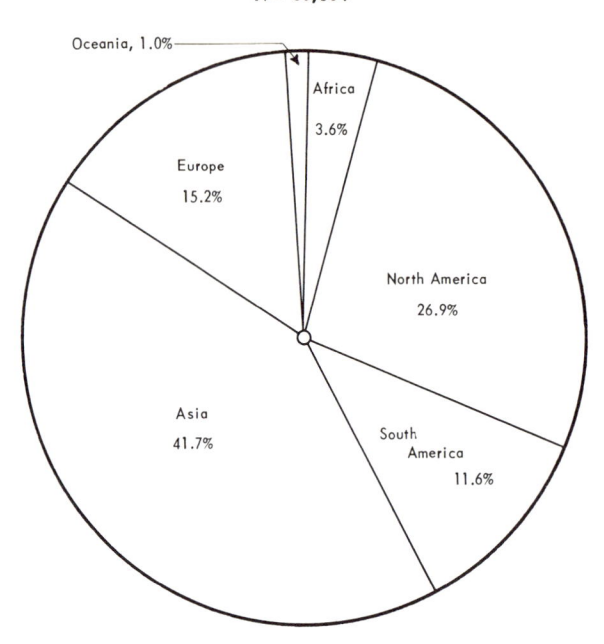

- Oceania, 1.0%
- Africa 3.6%
- Europe 15.2%
- North America 26.9%
- South America 11.6%
- Asia 41.7%

The relative number of theses dealing specifically with education in the six continental divisions (omitting the General, Composite, and United States classifications) is shown graphically in Figure 1. For comparison there is added the continental distribution of students studying in American institutions in 1954-55. [5]

Of course not nearly all of the foreign students studying in the United States have written theses concerning education in their own countries. Many of them have chosen topics concerned with natural sciences, social sciences, or humanities in their countries or in the United States.

On the other hand many American graduate students, some of whom have lived for a time in foreign countries as missionaries or under the recent Occupations of Japan, Germany, and Italy have selected thesis topics related to the educational practices and policies in the countries in which they have become especially interested.

---

[5] Loc. cit.

Introduction xxi

In spite of these varying influences, it might be expected that the proportion of theses would bear some general relation to the proportion of students who have come from the various continental areas to the United States for advanced study. A comparison of the two circle diagrams of Figure 1 shows such similarity among Asian, African, and Oceanic students and theses. For North American students (chiefly Latin-American and Canadian) the proportion of theses is more than half that of students, while for European students the proportion of theses is more than double that of students. South America is the only continent for which the proportion of theses is far smaller than the proportion of students -- less than one-fourth as great, in fact.

It is to be regretted that so few South American students, or graduate students from the United States, have shown much significant interest in studying the educational problems of the southern half of the Western hemisphere. Only about one-fourth of the theses concerning education in South America are by authors whose names are clearly recognizable as of Spanish or Portuguese type. As a matter of fact almost three times as many theses have been written concerning education in the Latin-American countries of North America as of South America. South America seems to be nearly the forgotten continent, educationally speaking, in terms of graduate dissertations.

It is noteworthy that more than a third of the theses classified by continents in Figure 1 (omitting the composite ones which deal with education in two or more continents) are devoted to education in Europe, and almost as many to education in Asia. These two continents account for more than three-quarters of the total number classified by continents.

METHOD OF COMPILATION

At intervals during the past five years, and intensively during most of 1958, the writer has accumulated the greater part of the information presented in this volume. This has been done in various libraries with the use of many printed and manuscript sources and by extensive correspondence. A list of the principal sources thus studied is given later.

Hundreds of original dissertations have been examined and other hundreds of abstracts read in order to determine the applicability and appropriate classification of many of the titles. The writer has also published a considerable number of articles in a variety of periodicals, in the United States and abroad, and corrections have been received from readers of them. For a list of these, see p. xxxviii.

The chief libraries in which intensive work has been done are: the library of the United States Department of Health, Education, and Welfare

NATIONAL EDUCATION ASSOCIATION OF THE UNITED STATES
1201 SIXTEENTH STREET, NORTHWEST, WASHINGTON 6, D. C.

Reference Librarian

Dear Sir or Madam:

At the request of the National Education Association, I am preparing for publication a volume, American Graduate Dissertations on Foreign Education. This will contain more than 4,000 entries of doctoral dissertations and master's theses which have been written in American colleges and universities about education and educators in foreign countries and education of foreign groups in the United States classified by countries. It will be distributed to the several hundred delegates who will attend the World Confederation of Organizations of the Teaching Profession to be held in Washington in August, 1959. It will also be available for libraries and scholars in the United States and abroad.

For each entry I am giving as far as possible the following information: (1) full name of author; (2) birth year and death year of author; (3) title of dissertation; (4) institution at which accepted; (5) year of acceptance; (6) pagination (Arabic numbers only for unpublished studies); (7) publication data, whether published in full, in part, in abstract, or by microfilm.

I have assembled as much of this information as possible from scores of different sources, primary and secondary, of widely varying reliability and degrees of completeness. In some cases I have found conflicting statements regarding the same thesis. I am sure you will agree with me as to the desirability of having such a permanently useful reference work as nearly complete and accurate as possible.

In order to insure this desired degree of accuracy and completeness I know of no way except to ask you to check carefully the entries for your institution, correct any errors, and furnish missing information. I know this is asking a good deal of you, but I hope you will be able to do it in the interests of sound scholarship and permanent usefulness to scholars in the field of international and comparative education and to fellow librarians throughout the country.

Accordingly I am enclosing carbon copies of the material for your institution, as now prepared for publication. It will be printed in this form, unless modified by you. I feel sure you will want your institution to be correctly represented. I can give you until July 1 to return these enclosures, with corrections made on them, if you need that long, although I should be glad to have them returned earlier, if convenient. You may disregard the guide lines at the top of each entry.

As a partial recognition of your services, I have arranged with the National Education Association to send you a complimentary copy of the volume as soon as it is published, probably late in 1958.

With appreciation for your cooperation,

Very truly yours,

Walter C. Eells

WCE:aa

Enclosures: [ ] Doctor's (yellow)   [ ] Master's (white)

Introduction

(incorporating the former library of the United States Office of Education); the Library of Congress; and the libraries of Catholic University of America, Teachers College of Columbia University, New York University, Princeton University, and Claremont Graduate School. As shown in a later paragraph, the first three university libraries named are at the three institutions which are credited with the largest number of theses in this volume, accounting for more than a quarter of the total number.

Early in 1958, when definite decision had been made by the National Education Association to publish the list, it became clear that there were many inconsistencies and inadequacies in the material which had been collected from so many different primary and secondary sources, varying widely in reliability and degrees of completeness. In particular, full names of authors, birth years, and numbers of pages in the theses were missing in many cases since the more extensive available lists did not give this information.

It was decided, therefore, to send carbon copies of the 4850 entries which had been accumulated up to that time to the reference librarians of the institutions at which these theses had been written. This was done in March and April 1958, accompanied by the letter of request which is reproduced on the opposite page.

The response to this request, sent to the librarians of almost three hundred institutions, was gratifying and fruitful. Only three or four failed to respond and many answered later letters asking for further information concerning certain theses. In this way scores of mistakes were corrected and additional information secured on hundreds of others. The librarians also furnished several hundred additional titles which had not been located in published sources or whose titles alone gave no indication that their content dealt with foreign education. On the other hand a few were rejected, such for example as ones whose titles indicated that they dealt with Canadian education and with education in Macedonia -- when the librarians reported that they referred to education in the towns of Canadian, Texas and Macedonia, Kentucky!

In a separate letter (not reproduced here) the librarians were asked also, following Commencement 1958, to send in lists of appropriate theses for individuals securing advanced degrees at that time, and many of them did so. Subsequently published lists of doctoral dissertations for 1957 and of master's theses for 1958 were checked, furnishing about one hundred additional titles. Unfortunately time did not permit sending these new titles to librarians for verification and additional information, particularly on pagination.

As a result of these methods of compilation, it is believed that the list herewith presented is reasonably complete and accurate through 1958, although doubtless some titles still have been overlooked which deserve inclusion and information is incomplete particularly on more recent titles.

It will be noted that librarians were asked to verify or give information, if possible, on (1) full names of authors, (2) birth and death years of authors, (3) institutions at which accepted, (4) year of acceptance, (5) pagination, and (6) publication data. Pertinent information concerning each of these topics is summarized in the following paragraphs.

NAMES OF AUTHORS

Many published lists, including the chief sources for doctor's dissertations, give only the initials of authors. These frequently result in errors or confusion and are insufficient for scholarly reference. Spanish names frequently suffer from such insufficiency of reporting.

It has been possible to secure full names for almost 90 percent of the authors, and to depend upon initials alone in the cases of a half dozen individuals only. [6]

There is no means of knowing accurately, without referring to original records of registrars in the various institutions, how many of the theses were the work of foreign authors, but in the cases of those concerned with education in South America, Africa, and Asia one can form a fairly reliable judgment from the non-English type of names of the individuals concerned that they were natives of the nations concerning which they had written. On this basis it appears that about 28 percent of the South American theses are by native authors, 40 percent of the African theses, and 62 percent, almost two-thirds, of the Asian theses.

An interesting feature, observable from the names of the authors, is the large number of theses on foreign education that have been written by women. As far as one can judge by the form of names, which are usually fairly clear as to sex, some 350, or 21 percent, of the doctor's dissertations and 1800, or 45 percent, of the master's theses were the work of women. In this connection it may be noted that less than 25 percent of the students from abroad studying in the United States in 1954-55 were women. [7]

---

[6] Two Americans failed to answer personal letters asking for their full names. Two from India (Nos. 1995 and 2074) failed to give more than their initials either on their theses or on the Commencement programs or registrars' records. Two others from Indonesia (No. 2139) and Pakistan (No. 2566) apparently have no first names.

[7] Mary Irwin, op. cit., p. 91.

Introduction

The proportions reported in the preceding paragraph may be compared with the fact that in the United States in the past 30 years only 11 percent of the total number of doctoral dissertations have been written by women. A fairer comparison, however, is in the field of "education." In the 10 years from 1948 to 1957 inclusive, a little more than one-sixth (17.6%) of the 11,800 American doctoral dissertations in education have been written by women. In the same period more than two-fifths (43.9%) of the 241,000 master's degrees in education have been conferred on women, although as indicated below, some of them, perhaps many of them, did not write theses. [8]

BIRTH AND DEATH YEARS

Library index cards usually give the birth year of the authors of doctor's dissertations, less frequently for authors of master's theses. It did not seem desirable to ask librarians to check with registrar's records for birth dates, although some of them did so voluntarily. Library of Congress cards usually give birth years for the relatively small number of published theses.

It was possible by these and occasional other means to secure birth years for almost three-quarters (73%) of the authors of doctoral dissertations, but for less than a quarter (23%) of the authors of master's theses.

Death years are harder to secure, since few librarians make any systematic effort to record them. Some Library of Congress cards contain them for published studies, but the number is not large. Therefore lists were made of all doctors whose birth years were known to be earlier than 1900 but for whom no death years were known. These were sent to alumni secretaries of the institutions concerned, with the request that they report death years, if available. Unfortunately alumni records regarding deaths, especially in the larger universities, are often incomplete, but in this way numerous additions to the record of death years were secured.

Death years have been found for 80 doctors (5%) and for 28 masters (0.7%). For most of the individuals for whom birth years prior to 1880 are given, the chances are strong that they are no longer living, although no specific information has been received concerning dates of death. Since a large proportion of the theses are the work of authors born in the twentieth century, it may be assumed that most of them are now living.

Information on birth years and death years, as far as known, are given immediately after the name of the author in the lists which follow.

---

[8] U. S. Office of Education, "Circulars," Nos 247, 262, 282, 333, 360, 380, 418, 461, 499, 527.

INSTITUTIONS AT WHICH ACCEPTED

Following is a summary of the number of doctor's dissertations accepted at the principal graduate schools in the country:

Columbia University	476
New York University	190
Harvard University	71
Stanford University	61
University of Chicago	60
Indiana University	46
University of Michigan	44
University of California	43
Catholic University of America	42
Cornell University	42
Yale University	41
Ohio State University	40
University of Southern California	29
University of Texas	26
Northwestern University	25
Fordham University	22
University of Washington	21
State University of Iowa	20
12 institutions, 10-19 each	169
18 institutions, 5-9 each	122
42 institutions, 1-4 each	100
90 institutions	1690

Names of all the institutions involved, their addresses, and dissertations written at them, may be found in the General Index.

Columbia University's record is outstanding for doctorates on foreign education, this institution being responsible for more than a quarter of the entire number. The first five institutions on the list above are responsible for more than half of the total number of doctor's dissertations.

Following is a similar summary of the number of master's theses accepted at American institutions:

Columbia University	389
Catholic University of America	253
University of Southern California	203
University of Chicago	178
University of Texas	127

Introduction

Boston University	114
Stanford University	113
Ohio State University	99
New York University	98
University of the Philippines	82
University of Washington	74
Texas College of Arts and Industries	67
Cornell University	62
College of the City of New York	58
George Peabody College for Teachers	58
University of California	55
4 institutions, 40-49 each	173
9 institutions, 30-39 each	312
19 institutions, 20-29 each	450
37 institutions, 10-19 each	507
184 institutions, 1-9 each	554
269 institutions	4026

Names of all the institutions involved, their addresses, and theses written at them, may be found in the General Index.

Columbia University also leads in number of master's theses, but not nearly so decisively as in the case of doctor's dissertations, being responsible for less than one-tenth of the total number. The 16 institutions named above are all that are required to account for half of the master's theses. The change in policy regarding requirement of a thesis for the master's degree, described later, affects the relative standing of several of the institutions listed above.

If doctor's dissertations and master's theses are combined in a single list, the following are the leading graduate schools in terms of total production of theses dealing with foreign education:

Columbia University	865
Catholic University of America	295
New York University	288
University of Chicago	238
University of Southern California	232
Stanford University	174
University of Texas	153
Ohio State University	139
Boston University	129
Cornell University	103

These ten institutions account for almost half (46%) of the total number of 5716 theses. Columbia University alone accounts for 15 percent of them.

YEAR OF ACCEPTANCE

Following is a summary, by five-year periods, of the years in which the doctoral dissertations and master's theses were accepted at the institutions summarized in the preceding section:

Years	Doctor's dissertations	Master's theses
1884-1889	1	0
1890-1894	7	1
1895-1899	8	7
1900-1904	8	21
1905-1909	21	51
1910-1914	37	60
1915-1919	37	101
1920-1924	56	234
1925-1929	86	388
1930-1934	153	655
1935-1939	164	600
1940-1944	171	440
1945-1949	202	364
1950-1954	387	579
1955-1958	352	525
	1690	4026

It may be noted that almost all of these theses in both groups are the product of twentieth century scholarship, less than one half of one percent having been accepted prior to 1900.

Half of the doctor's dissertations have been written during the past 12 years. A steady growth is shown in doctorates for each five-year period. If some of those probably missing for 1958 and those to be completed in 1959 were added, the number for the final five-year period, 1955-1959, would probably be more than 400.

The first doctor's dissertation on record, interestingly enough, was written by John Dewey at Johns Hopkins University in 1884, "Psychology of Kant"

Introduction

(No. 3601). The librarian of Johns Hopkins University reports that unfortunately no copy of this pioneer dissertation is on file in the university library.

Unlike the situation with reference to doctorates, the number of master's theses has shown a marked decline since their maximum in 1930-1934. This decline has been due in part to the conditions accompanying World War II, but more to a change of policy on the part of several of the leading graduate schools, such as Columbia University, University of Chicago, Stanford University, and others. In recent years these institutions have made the writing of a master's thesis optional instead of a requirement for the master's degree.

The number of master's <u>degrees</u> in education has increased from approximately 12,000 in 1948 to 31,000 in 1957, but the number of master's <u>theses</u> has shown no such proportional growth, chiefly because of the change of policy on the part of several institutions, just mentioned. The sheer bulk of the supervision of such a large number of candidates for the master's degree in the larger institutions has caused the abandonment of the policy, in some cases, in order that available time of professors may be given to the increasing number of candidates for the doctorate.

The result is that many candidates for the master's degree in these larger institutions now take additional courses as a substitute for a master's thesis -- an unfortunate development from the standpoint of potential research possibilities.

PAGINATION

Number of pages in the theses under consideration vary from less than a dozen pages to several hundred, with a few running more than a thousand pages each. The number of pages in such a study gives some indication of the extent and thoroughness of the research involved, as well as affording an idea of the cost if microfilm or other reproductions are to be secured.

Unfortunately neither of the current annual lists of doctor's dissertations or master's theses in education contain this information. For the most part it has been furnished by the librarians, and therefore is lacking for many of the 1957 and 1958 titles since time did not permit submitting them to the librarians for later additions. It will be found, however, that pagination is indicated for 93 percent of the doctor's dissertations and for 92 percent of the master's theses.

For 1263 unpublished doctoral dissertations for which information is available, the average number of pages of typewritten manuscript is 268, varying from 25 pages to 1281 pages. For 3686 unpublished master's theses, the average number of pages of typewritten manuscript is 101 varying from 4 pages to

791 pages. Thus the length of doctoral dissertations tend to be more than two and one half times that of master's theses.

TOPICAL CONTENTS

Students who may be interested in particular topics regarding education in different countries, rather than all theses which relate to a particular country, will find information in the General Index which will facilitate their locating many studies on specialized topics. In this way they may ascertain the theses dealing with elementary education, secondary education, or higher education; with adult education, rural education, or education of women; with particular subject matter fields such as art, chemistry, history, home economics, mathematics, or music; with religious education in general, or with Catholic, Protestant, Jewish and other types of religious education; with education of teachers and topics connected with teacher and student problems and welfare, et cetera.

They may also locate all theses dealing primarily with an individual educator, such as the 54 studies concerned with Rousseau and his influence on education, or the 29 studies related to Pestalozzi. The General Index, therefore, should be studied carefully to determine the resources of the complete group of theses reported in the body of the volume.

PUBLICATION DATA

Practice with reference to the publication of theses has varied greatly in the United States between different institutions and at different periods. Some dissertations have been published in their entirety. For others, abstracts only have been printed. Still others exist only in manuscript in the libraries of the institutions at which they were accepted. Many graduate schools formerly required the publication of their doctor's dissertations, but this became so expensive for the candidate, with advancing costs of printing and the development of the relatively inexpensive microfilm process, that the printing requirement has been dropped by most institutions. In recent years an increasing number of universities have arranged for reproduction of their dissertations at nominal cost by microfilm.

Obviously publication information concerning each thesis is desirable for the users of this bibliography, but it was not available in any single source and the assembly of it has involved much research in many sources. The extensive resources of the Library of Congress have been helpful but by no means sufficient.

Introduction

Information regarding the printed form (with publishers, date, and pagination) is given for almost two-fifths (38%) of the doctor's dissertations, but for only one-half of one percent of the master's theses. Information is given regarding publication of abstracts of another fifth (20%) of the doctor's dissertations and almost 10 percent of the master's theses. Thus some information is given on the printed form, if any, of almost three-fifths of the doctor's dissertations and of one-tenth of the master's theses. Addresses of periodicals which have published abstracts will be found in the General Index.

AVAILABILITY

Published dissertations, if still in print, may be secured from the publishers, whose names and addresses are given in connection with the publication data for each published study. If out of print, copies may be secured through dealers in second-hand books or can probably be found in the principal university and other reference libraries, both in the United States and in other countries.

Published abstracts, both of doctor's dissertations and master's theses, are found in numerous special abstract series issued by various institutions, also to be found in many reference libraries. Some of these, however, of many years duration have recently been discontinued, as for example those of Ohio State University and Stanford University, in favor of publication of abstracts in "Dissertation Abstracts." Others have been published in educational journals edited at the institutions where the studies have been made, such as "Teachers College Record" of Teachers College of Columbia University, or the "Catholic Educational Review" of Catholic University of America. Information concerning theses abstracted in these and similar publications will be found in the General Index.

By far the most comprehensive abstracting service for doctor's dissertations is provided by "Dissertation Abstracts," formerly "Microfilm Abstracts." More than 25,000 abstracts of dissertations in all fields have been printed in this journal in the past 20 years, a very large number of them in the field of education. The latest issue lists 93 American graduate schools which now cooperate with it in this form of publication, including most of the leading institutions of the country.

A partial list of university and other libraries outside the United States at which files of "Dissertation Abstracts" may be consulted is given immediately following this Introduction, pp. xxxiv-xxxv.

All dissertations thus abstracted by "Dissertation Abstracts" are available on microfilm from the publishers, Microfilm Abstracts, Ann Arbor,

Michigan at a cost of approximately one-half cent per page. Such microfilm copies, however, require the use of a special microfilm reading machine, electrically operated. For those who do not have access to such equipment, the same firm has recently developed the Xerox process by means of which they will furnish enlargements of the microfilm pages, approximately 5-1/2 x 8-1/2 inches (14 x 21 centimeters) in size, which can be read directly by eye. The cost is approximately 4-1/2 cents per page, with a minimum of $3. These prints are ordinarily supplied in roll form but can be cut and bound with spiral binding at a small additional cost.

References to the 280 doctoral dissertations listed in the present volume for which abstracts have been printed in "Dissertation Abstracts," and which are therefore available on microfilm, are given in the General Index. They are also indicated in connection with the listing of each dissertation so abstracted.

Special arrangements for microfilm reproduction of dissertations have been made by Colorado State College, Pennsylvania State University, University of Chicago, Catholic University of America, University of California, and perhaps other institutions. For the first two institutions, microfilm copies can be secured from University Microfilms, Ann Arbor, Michigan. The librarians of the other institutions can furnish information regarding microfilm availability of their dissertations.

Microfilm copies of all doctoral dissertations which have been abstracted in "Dissertation Abstracts" are available for use in the Microfilm Reading Room of the Library of Congress, Washington, D.C.

In the past two years the publishers of "Dissertation Abstracts" have inaugurated the publication of an annual index of all doctoral dissertations, compiled by the Association of Research Libraries. This supercedes the well-known "Doctoral Dissertations Accepted by American Universities" published by the H. W. Wilson Company of New York for 22 years. The latest volume of this index gives a list of 135 graduate schools in the United States which confer doctor's degrees and indicates for each whether printing of a dissertation is required, whether it accepts microfilming, whether it publishes abstracts, the number of manuscript copies supplied by the author to the library, and whether the library will loan either typed or printed copies.

Most university libraries have arrangements for interlibrary loan of theses of which more than one copy is in the library, if requested through another library. In general, if a user of this bibliography wishes to secure the use of any of the studies listed in it and finds none of the suggestions given above are applicable, he should write directly to the librarian of the institution at which the particular study was accepted for information regarding its availability.

ACKNOWLEDGMENTS

There remains the pleasant task of acknowledging, even if inadequately, the cooperation of many individuals who have rendered significant assistance in the compilation of this list of dissertations and theses concerning foreign education and in furnishing needed supplementary information concerning them.

Particular recognition should be given to the staff of the library of the United States Department of Health, Education, and Welfare (which now incorporates the former valuable Office of Education library) and especially to Miss Lora Brookley, Educational Reference Librarian, where the greater part of the work of compilation has been carried out. Also to the research staff of the Library of Congress, with its incomparable collections which supplement in many ways the more highly specialized collection made by the United States Office of Education.

Appreciation should also be expressed to the staffs of the libraries of the three institutions where the largest number of theses in the present compilation have been written -- Teachers College of Columbia University, New York University, and Catholic University of America -- who rendered much assistance during the many hours that the writer spent in working in their libraries and consulting theses in their collections.

Very great appreciation is due the almost three hundred reference librarians in the institutions in which the theses were written who responded so generously out of their busy lives and often, it is feared, at the expense of other pressing duties, to check the thousands of copies of thesis descriptions which were sent to them. The accuracy and completeness of the list in its present form is due in no small part to this professional service so freely given. It is hoped that they may feel compensated, at least in part, by the opportunity to use the volume in answering the many questions which are presented to them constantly in their positions.

Special thanks are due to Mrs. Florence O. Skuce, of the staff of the Publications Division of the National Education Association, for her careful editorial supervision in proofreading and in the innumerable details incident to seeing such a volume through the press.

It is, of course, too much to expect that the volume which is now published is entirely free from error. With the many thousand bits of information, in any of which mistakes are possible, some errors are inevitable. It is hoped that users will be charitable and will find that such errors as may be discovered will not affect significantly the basic usefulness of the volume for research scholars and other educators in all countries who may have occasion to refer to it. The undersigned, however, would appreciate having such errors as may be found called to his attention.

Washington, D. C.
May 1, 1959.

WALTER CROSBY EELLS

Availability of Dissertation Abstracts

The Association of Research Libraries of the United States has endorsed reproduction by microfilm and publication of abstracts in *Dissertation Abstracts* as a desirable means of making this scholarly material more widely available to scholars and research workers. Files of *Dissertation Abstracts* are available in many university, college, and research libraries in the United States. This publication also has more than 200 subscribers in foreign countries. Following is a list of the principal university and research libraries abroad at which files may be consulted.

AFRICA
Belgian Congo
Universtiteit van Belgisch-Congo en Ruanda-Urundi, Elisabethstad
Egypt
American University of Cairo, Cairo
Ghana
University College of Ghana, Achimota
Nigeria
University College of Nigeria, Ibadan
Northern Rhodesia
Central Technical Library, Kitwe
Union of South Africa
University of Cape Town, Cape Town
University of Witwatersrand, Johannesburg
Potchefstroom University, Potchefstroom
Department of Agriculture, Pretoria
University of Pretoria, Pretoria
University of Stellenbosch, Stellenbosch

AMERICA, NORTH
Canada
Memorial University of Newfoundland, St. Johns, Newfoundland
Agricultural Experimental Farm, Kentville, Nova Scotia
McGill University, Montreal, Quebec
University of Montreal, Montreal, Quebec
Ontario Agricultural College, Guelph, Ontario
Queen's University, Kingston, Ontario
University of Western Ontario, London, Ontario
National Library of Canada, Ottawa, Ontario
University of Ottawa, Ottawa, Ontario
University of Toronto, Toronto, Ontario
Assumption University of Windsor, Windsor, Ontario
University of Manitoba, Winnipeg, Manitoba
University of Alberta, Edmonton, Alberta
University of Saskatchewan, Saskatoon, Saskatchewan
University of British Columbia, Vancouver, British Columbia
Provincial Library, Victoria, British Columbia
Costa Rica
Inter-American Institute of Agricultural Science, Turrialba
Mexico
Nacional Financiera, S. A., Mexico, D. F.
Puerto Rico
University of Puerto Rico, Rio Piedras
West Indies
University College of the West Indies, Jamaica

AMERICA, SOUTH
Brazil
Instituto Brasileiro de Bibliografia e Documentacao, Rio de Janeiro
Centro Tecnico de Aeronautica, Sao Jose dos Campos

ASIA
India
Gujarat University, Ahmedabad
National Library of India, Calcutta
National Chemical Laboratory of India, Poona
Israel
Israel Institute of Technology, Haifa
Jewish National and University Library, Jerusalem
Israeli Institute for Biological Research, Ness-Zions
Weizmann Institute of Science, Rehovoth
Ministry of Defense, Tel Aviv
Japan
Hokkaido University, Sapporo
Genshiryoku Kenkyu-Sho, Tokyo
International Christian University, Tokyo
Korea
Korean Research Center, Seoul
Philippines
Institute of Public Administration, Manila
Philippine Union College, Manila
University of the Philippines, Quezon City
Singapore
University of Malaya, Singapore
Thailand
American Embassy, Bangkok

EUROPE
Austria
Buchandlung Franz Deuticke, Wien
Belgium
Societe Chimique de Belgique, Brussels
European Research Associates, Brussels
Librarie des Sciences, Brussels
University of Louvain, Louvain
Bulgaria
State Library, Sofia
Czechoslovakia
Orbis Newsagency, Praha
Denmark
Statsbiblioteket, Arhus
University of Copenhagen, Copenhagen
Atomenergikommissionens Bibliotek, Veddelev pr. Roskilde
Finland
Valtion Teknillinen, Helsinki
France
Centre Etudes Nucleaires, Fontenay-aux-Roses
Centre Etudes Nucleaires, Gif-Sur-Yvette
Centre Etudes Nucleaires du Grenoble, Grenoble
Bibliotheque Nationale, Paris
Universite a la Sorbonne, Paris
UNESCO Library, Paris
UCLAF Bibliotheque Scientifique, Paris

Germany
- Technischen Hochschule, Aachen
- Deutsche Staatsbibliothek, Berlin
- Gmelin Institute, Frankfort
- University of Göttingen, Göttingen
- Farbenfabriken Bayer, Leverkusen-Bayerwerk
- University of Muenster, Muenster
- Karl-Zink Buchhandlung, München

Great Britain
- National Library of Wales, Aberystwyth
- College of Technology, Birmingham
- University of Birmingham, Birmingham
- University of Cambridge, Cambridge
- University of Edinburgh, Edinburgh
- Royal Technical College, Glasgow
- Atomic Research Establishment, Harwell
- Hatfield Technical College, Hatfield
- University of Leeds, Leeds
- University of Liverpool, Liverpool
- British Museum, London
- National Central Library, London
- Queen Mary College, London
- Science Museum, South Kensington, London
- University of London, London
- College of Technology, Manchester
- Victoria University of Manchester, Manchester
- Bodleian Library, Oxford
- Radcliffe Science Library, Oxford
- Sheffield City Libraries, Sheffield

Italy
- Universita Cattolica del S. Cuore, Milan
- Libreria Natale Simonelli, Perugia
- Instituto di Chemica Generale, Pisa
- Biblioteca Apostolica Vativana, Rome
- United Nations Library, F. A. O., Rome
- Universita di Trieste, Trieste

Hungary
- Ku-Egyetemi Konyvtar, Budapest
- Ku-Kobanyai Gyogyszerarugyar, Budapest
- MTA Genetikai, Budapest

Netherlands
- Koninklijke-Shell-Laboratorium, Amsterdam
- Technische Hogeschool, Delft
- Bibliotheek der Staatsmijnen, Geleen
- International Federation for Documentation, The Hague
- Royal Library, The Hague
- N. V. Mij. Tot Exploitatie, Ijmuiden
- Burgersdijk & Niermans, Leiden

Norway
- Universitetet i Oslo, Oslo
- Universitetets Psykologiske Institute, Oslo
- Norges Tekniske Hogskole, Trondheim

Poland
- P. K. W. Z. "RUCH" Nr., Warszawa

Portugal
- Dr. Vincent Cocco, Coimbra

Spain
- Universidad de Madrid, Madrid

Sweden
- Chalmers Tekniska Hogskola, Goteborg
- Kungliga Tekniska Hogskolan, Stockholm
- Kungliga Biblioteket, Stockholm
- A. B. Lundequistska Bokhandeln, Uppsala

Switzerland
- Universitat Basel, Basel
- A. Francke Ltd. Co., Berne
- Herbert Lang & Cie., Berne
- Librairie Centrale, Lausanne
- Eidgenossische Technische Hochschule, Zurich

USSR
- Academy of Sciences of the USSR, Leningrad

Yugoslavia
- Jugoslovenska Knjiga, Beograd

OCEANIA

Australia
- University of Adelaide, Adelaide
- Commonwealth National Library, Canberra
- University of Western Australia, Nedlands
- Library Board of Western Australia, Perth
- University of Melbourne, Melbourne

New Zealand
- Department of Scientific and Industrial Research, Wellington

Principal Sources

Following is a list, with occasional supplementary notes, of the principal sources which have been used in compiling this bibliography;

1. *Doctoral Dissertations Accepted by American Universities.* New York: H. W. Wilson Co., 1934-1955, 22 volumes. (The most valuable single reference work for doctor's dissertations, but omits several hundred titles, especially from earlier volumes. Superseded for 1956 and later years by No. 2 below.)

2. *Index to American Doctoral Dissertations Combined with Dissertation Abstracts.* Ann Arbor, Michigan: University Microfilms. First two volumes, January 1957 and January 1958. Each volume is No. 13 of *Dissertation Abstracts.* (Includes titles and classifications formerly found in No. 1, above, and, in addition, references to all of them which have been abstracted in *Dissertation Abstracts* during the year.)

3. T. A. Lamke and H. M. Silvey. *Master's Theses in Education.* Cedar Falls, Iowa: Iowa State Teachers College. Lithoprinted by Edwards Brothers, Inc., Ann Arbor, Michigan. Seven annual volumes, 1951-52 to 1957-58. (The most valuable single reference work for master's theses in education since it began publication, following the suspension of No. 6 below. Latest volume contains titles of 2887 theses.)

4. *American Doctoral Dissertations Printed.* Washington: Library of Congress, 1912-1938, 27 volumes. (Limited to printed copies received by the Library of Congress, but with full bibliographical details concerning this limited group.)

5. Walter S. Monroe. *Titles of Masters' and Doctors' Theses in Education Accepted by American Colleges and Universities.* Urbana, Illinois: University of Illinois, Bureau of Educational Research, 1920 to 1928, six volumes. (A valuable early source, but incomplete, and sometimes inaccurate. The earliest such compilation made. Superseded by No. 6 below.)

6. Ruth Gray. *Bibliography of Research Studies in Education.* Washington: United States Office of Education, 1929 to 1941, 13 volumes. Continued in manuscript with some 4000 entries per year until 1951. (Includes both doctor's and master's theses, also other research studies, with frequent annotations regarding contents of many of the studies reported.)

7. Ruth Gray. *Doctors' Theses in Education.* Washington: United States Office of Education, Pamphlet No. 60, 1935. (Lists 797 dissertations, many of them in manuscript, deposited in the library of the U. S. Office of Education prior to September 1934.)

8. T. R. Palfrey. *Guide to Bibliography of Theses.* Chicago: American Library Association, 1936. (Valuable for early references to abstracts series of various institutions.)

9. Mary L. Lyda and Stanley B. Brown. *Research Studies in Education: A Subject Index, 1941-51.* Boulder, Colorado: University of Colorado, 1953. Continued as an annual series, under editorship of Stanley Elam, published by Phi Delta Kappa, Inc., Bloomington, Indiana. (Includes lists of doctoral studies in progress as well as completed dissertations.)

10. *Theses on Pan-American Topics Prepared by Candidates for Degrees in Universities and Colleges in the United States.* Washington: 1941. 170 p., mimeographed.

11. *Theses and Dissertations by Chinese Students in America.* New York: China Institute of America, 1927, 1928, 1934. (Three volumes covering theses written from 1902 to 1931.)

12. *Doctoral Dissertations on Japan Accepted by American Universities, 1912-1939.* New York: Japan Institute, Inc., 1940.

13. *List of Theses in Missions and Related Subjects Written during the Academic Year.* New York: Missionary Research Library, 3041 Broadway. Annual series for years 1949-50 to 1956-57.

14. *Doctoral Dissertations in the Field of Religion, 1940-1952.* New York: Columbia University Press, in cooperation with National Council on Religion in Higher Education. 1954. 194 p.

15. *Selected Graduate Series in Religious Education.* Chicago: International Council on Religious Education. Annual series, 1933 to 1942. (Later issues are entitled *Selected Doctoral Theses in Religious Education.*)

16. *Titles of Completed Theses in Home Economics and Related Fields in Colleges and Universities of the United States.* Washington: United States Department of Agriculture and United States Office of Education, 1944-1949, 1949-50, 1951-52, 1952-53, 1953-54.

17. *Dissertation Abstracts,* formerly *Microfilm Abstracts.* Ann Arbor, Michigan: University Microfilms. Vols. 1-19, 1938 to 1958. (The most important abstract journal available. Fully characterized in the Introduction.)

18. *Religious Education.* New York. (Beginning with 1950, the May-June issue of this journal has published a group of abstracts of doctor's dissertations in religious education for the previous year.)

19. *Teachers College Record.* New York: Teachers College, Columbia University. (This journal formerly published abstracts of doctor's dissertations written at Teachers College, but has discontinued the practice in recent years.)

20. *Teachers College Journal.* Terre Haute, Indiana: Indiana State Teachers College. (This journal publishes occasionally abstracts of master's theses written at the College.)

21. *Catholic Educational Review.* Washington: Catholic University of America. (This journal publishes in each issue abstracts of master's theses and occasionally of doctor's dissertations written at the University.)

22. Abstract series published by many institutions, especially those of Clark University, College of the City of New York, Cornell University, Fordham University, George Peabody College for Teachers, George

Washington University, Harvard University, New York University, Ohio State University, Pennsylvania State University, Stanford University, and Universities of Arizona, Chicago, Cincinnati, Colorado, Denver, Florida, Illinois, Pittsburgh, Southern California, Texas, and Washington.

23. Lists of dissertations in alumni directories and various specialized publications of individual institutions.

24. Files of College and University Catalogs. When other resources failed or discrepancies developed which needed to be resolved, recourse was had to the unique files of college catalogs, estimated at more than 90,000 in number, in the library of the United States Department of Health, Education, and Welfare. This is an invaluable collection for research purposes, not duplicated elsewhere in the country, many of the catalogues dating back to the establishment of the United States Office of Education in 1867. Many of them contain lists, especially in their earlier years, of names and dissertation titles for individuals upon whom the doctorate was conferred and some have similar information for recipients of master's degrees.

Related Publications

By Walter Crosby Eells

General

"American Doctoral Dissertations on Foreign Education." *Higher Education,* Vol. 12, p. 19-22. October 1955.

"Dissertations on Foreign Education Accepted by American Universities." *Journal of Educational Sociology,* Vol. 30, p. 147-156. November 1956. Reprinted in *Comparative Education: A Symposium,* William Brickman, editor. Monograph No. 4, Payne Educational Sociology Foundation, Inc., New York City, 1956.

Africa

"American Doctoral Dissertations on Education in South Africa." *Tydskrif vir Maatskaplike Navorsing* (Journal for Social Research), Pretoria, South Africa, Vol. 6, p. 43-44. June 1955.

America, North

"American Doctoral Dissertations on Education in Canada." *University of Toronto Quarterly,* Vol. 25, p. 249-258. January 1956.

"U. S. Dissertations on Education in Newfoundland." *N. T. A. Journal* (Official Organ of the Newfoundland Teachers Association), Vol. 49, p. 34-35. November 1957.

"Dissertations on Education in Nova Scotia." *Bulletin of the Nova Scotia Teachers' Union,* Vol. 34, p. 38-39. February 1958.

"United States Dissertations on Education in New Brunswick." *Educational Review* (Official Organ of the New Brunswick Teachers' Association), Vol. 72, p. 40-42. January-February 1958.

"United States Dissertations on Education in Canada." (Covers Ontario only.) *The Bulletin* (Published by the Ontario Secondary School Teachers' Federation), Vol. 38, p. 73-74, 105. March 31, 1958.

"United States Dissertations on Education in Manitoba." *The Manitoba Teacher,* Vol. 36, p. 32-34. January-February 1958.

"United States Dissertations on Education in Saskatchewan." *The Saskatchewan Bulletin* (Journal of the Saskatchewan Teachers' Federation), Vol. 33, p. 29-30. October 1957.

"U. S. Dissertations on Education in Alberta." *The ATA Magazine* (Official Organ of the Alberta Teachers Association), Vol. 38, p. 43-45. April 1958.

"U. S. Dissertations on Education in British Columbia." *The B. C. Teacher,* Vol. 38, p. 202-205. January 1959.

Asia

American Doctoral Dissertations on Education in Countries of the Middle East. Washington, D.C.: The Middle East Institute, September 1955. 28 p. mimeographed.

"American Doctoral Dissertations on Education in Countries of the Middle East." *Newsnotes on Education Around the World,* February 7, 1956. p. 4.

"American Graduate Dissertations on Jewish Education Outside the U.S.A." *Jewish Education,* Vol. 28, p. 61-63. Winter, 1957-58.

"American Doctoral Dissertations on Education in Iraq." *Al Muallin al Jadid* (The New Teacher), Baghdad, Iraq. Vol. 19, p. 481-482. June 1956. (In Arabic)

"American Doctoral Dissertations on Education in Iran." *Amuzesh wa Parvaresh Review,* Teheran, Iran. Aban 1336. November 1957. (In Persian)

"American Doctoral Dissertations on Education in Thailand." *Bangkok Post.* 1956.

"American Doctoral Dissertations on Education in the Philippines." *The Philippine Educator,* Manila. Vol. 10, p. 51-54. November 1955.

"American Essays on Japan Increasing." *Nippon Times,* Tokyo, June 22, 1955. p. 4.

"Dissertations on Japanese Education." *Phi Delta Kappan,* Vol. 36, p. 367-368. June 1955.

Europe

"Amerikanische Doktor-Dissertationem über Erziehung in Deutschland." *Bildung und Erziehung,* Frankfort, Vol. 8, p. 425-435. July 1955. (In German and English)

"Tesi Dottorali Negli Stati Uniti Sulla Pedagogia Italiana." *Scuola e Citta,* Florence, Vol. 7, p. 149-151. April 30, 1956.

Oceania

"American Doctoral Dissertations on Education in Australia." In Commonwealth Office of Education, Sydney, New South Wales, *Educational Research Being Undertaken in Australia,* 1955. p. 55-56.

Topical

"American Doctoral Dissertations on Adult Education in Foreign Countries." *Adult Education,* Vol. 6, p. 117-119. Winter 1956.

"American Doctoral Dissertations on the Education of Women in Foreign Countries." *Journal of the*

Introduction

National Association of Deans of Women, Vol. 19, p. 79-81. January 1956.

"American Doctoral Dissertations on Educational Psychology in Foreign Countries." *Journal of Educational Psychology,* Vol. 47, p. 133-136. March 1956.

"American Doctoral Dissertations on Health, Physical Education, and Recreation in Foreign Countries." *Research Quarterly of the American Association for Health, Physical Education, and Recreation,* Vol. 27, p. 119-121. March 1956.

"American Doctoral Dissertations on Personnel Problems and Procedures in Foreign Countries." *Personnel and Guidance Journal,* Vol. 34, p. 226-228. December 1955.

"American Doctoral Dissertations on Secondary Education in Foreign Countries." *Bulletin of the National Association of Secondary School Principals,* Vol. 40, p. 166-175. May 1956.

"Doctoral Dissertations on Social Studies in Foreign Countries." *Social Education,* Vol. 20, p. 23-26, 28. January 1956.

"American Doctoral Dissertations on Teacher Education in Foreign Countries." *Journal of Teacher Education,* Vol. 6, p. 301-304. December 1955.

GENERAL
(NOS. 1 – 118)

DOCTORS

1. ALLBEE, LEWIS, 1914- . *Education as an Implement of U.S. Foreign Policy, 1938-1948.* Yale University, 1948. Grand Rapids, Michigan: 270 p. Reproduced from typewritten copy. Available from the author at Grand Rapids High School, Grand Rapids, Michigan.

2. ALLEN, WARREN DWIGHT, 1885- . *Philosophies of Music History: A Comparison-Study of General Histories of Music in Chronological Order and with Reference to the Cultural Setting: Analysis of Basic Assumptions of the Uses of Analogy, and of Some Possibilities for New Comparison-Studies of Change and Continuity for Music Education and Musical Research.* Columbia University, 1939. New York: American Book Co., 1939. xxvi, 382 p.

3. BENNETT, ALVIN LE ROY, 1914- . *The Development of Intellectual Cooperation under the League of Nations and the United Nations.* University of Illinois, 1950. 299 p. ms. Abstract in *Abstracts of Completed Doctoral Dissertations for the Academic Year 1950-51*, (Department of State, External Research Staff, Office of Intelligence Research, Abstract Series No. 1, March 1952), p. 16-17. Abstract also in *Microfilm Abstracts* Vol. 11, No. 2, p. 154-155, 1951. Available on microfilm from University Microfilms, Ann Arbor, Michigan, as Publication No. 2,211.

4. CAMERY, LURA GERTRUDE, 1901- . *American Backgrounds of the UNESCO.* Stanford University, 1949. 457 p. ms. Abstract in Stanford University: *Abstracts of Dissertations . . . 1948-49*, p. 16-19. For master's thesis by same author, see No. 3361.

5. CANARY, PEYTON HENRY, Jr. *The Scriptural Teachings of the World's Living Religions on International Understanding and Goodwill.* Indiana University, 1933. 356 p. ms. Abstract in *Selected Graduate Theses in Religious Education*, 1934, p. 9-10. (Covers 11 living and 12 dead organized religions.)

6. CARSON, ARTHUR LEROY, 1896- . *A Study of Agricultural Missions: An Analysis of Philosophy, Program, and Personnel.* Cornell University, 1931. 594 p. ms. Published in part as *Agricultural Missions: A Study Based upon the Experience of 236 Missionaries and Other Rural Workers.* New York ?, 1933.? 107 p. photolithographed.

7. COFFIN, ERNEST WILLIAM. *On the Education of Backward Races.* Clark University, 1908. Published in *Pedagogical Seminary*, Vol. 15, p. 1-62, March 1908.

8. CORNETT, JOHN STANLEY. *Education in Early Christianity.* University of Chicago, 1925. 271 p. ms.

9. CRUM, CLYDE EUGENE. *A Study of the Development and Underlying Principles of International Educational Organizations.* University of Colorado, 1950. Abstract in University of Colorado: *Abstracts of Theses . . . 1951-52*, p. 56-58.

10. ECKERSLEY, ANNA L. *A Study of the Work, Development, and Functions of the International Society for Business Education.* Columbia University, 1957.

11. ELLIS, ALEXANDER CASWELL, 1871-1948. *History of the Philosophy of Education.* Clark University, 1897. Published in part as "Suggestions for a Philosophy of Education," *Pedagogical Seminary*, Vol. 5, p. 159-201, October 1897.

12. FENG, YEN-TSAI, 1923- . *An Analysis of the Impact of the Several Different Concepts of International Cultural Cooperation upon the Establishment and the Development of the United Nations Educational, Scientific, and Cultural Organization during Its First Six Years.* University of Denver, 1953. 469 p. ms.

13. FINK, THEODORE ROSS, 1903- . *United States Naval Policies on Education in Dependent Areas.* University of North Carolina, 1948. 290 p. ms. Abstract in *University of North Carolina Record*, No. 464, p. 84-85, October 1949.

14. FREEMAN, HARRY. *Principles and Procedures for Selecting and Adapting Literary Materials for Adults Learning English as a Second Language, with Illustrations from Modern American and British Short Stories.* Columbia University, 1957.

15. FREITAG, Mrs. HERTA TAUSSIG, 1908- . *The Use of the History of Mathematics in Its Teaching and Learning on the Secondary School Level.* Columbia University, 1953. 207 p. ms.

16. FUOSS, DONALD EUGENE, 1923- . *An Analysis of the Incidents of the Olympic Games for 1924 to 1948 with Reference to the Contribution of the Games to International Good Will and Understanding.* Columbia University, 1952. 297 p. ms.

17. HASCALL, THEODORUS BAILEY. *Christianity and the Pagan Schools of the First Three Centuries.* New York University, 1892. 88 p. ms.

18. HOLSINGER, CLYDE WILLIAM. *A History of Choral Conducting with Emphasis on the Time-Beating Techniques Used in Successive Historical Periods.* Northwestern University, 1954. (Methods of music teaching, from era of the Sumerians to present time.)

19. HYER, JUNE, 1920- . *Trends in International Education from World War I through World War II.* University of Texas, 1947. 337 p. ms.

19a. JEWELL, DANIEL WILLIAM. *Aspects of Authority in Christian Education in Historical Perspective.* Columbia University, 1957.

20. JOHNSON, GRANVILLE BRADBY, Jr. *An Experimental Analysis of the Origin and Development of Racial Attitudes with Special Emphasis on the Role of Bilingualism.* University of Colorado, 1949. 213 p. ms.

21. KARP, BASIL, 1923- . *The Development of the Philosophy of UNESCO.* University of Chicago, 1951. 206 p. ms. Available on microfilm: see index under "University of Chicago."

22. KENNY, Rev. ROBERT HUGH, 1917- . *A Sociological Analysis of the Conceptual Framework, Structure, and Operation of UNESCO.* St. John's University, 1955. 447 p. ms. Abstract in St. John's University: *Abstracts of Dissertations, 1953-1956*, p. 100-103.

23. LEVISON, MELVIN ERWIN. *The Ideas and Operation of the Cultural Activities Programme of*

UNESCO (1945-1952) in the Context of the UNESCO Programme as a Whole. Columbia University, 1958. 488 p. ms. Abstract in *Dissertation Abstracts*, Vol. 19, p. 161-162, July 1958. Available on microfilm from University Microfilms, Ann Arbor, Michigan, as Publication Mic. 58-2238.

24. LITTELL, HAROLD. *The Evolution of Educational Aims.* Indiana University, 1933. 488 p. ms. Abstract in Indiana University: *Abstracts of Theses and Dissertations in Education,* Vol. 7, p. 35-36. (Traces development from the earliest periods of civilization.)

25. MacKAY, VERA ALMA, 1912- . *Intercultural Education: An Historical Narrative and the Role of Indiana University.* Indiana University, 1954. 278 p. ms. Abstract in *Dissertation Abstracts,* Vol. 14, p. 1585, October 1954. Available on microfilm from University Microfilms, Ann Arbor, Michigan, as Publication No. 8,932. (Includes a historical review from the time of the ancient Greeks and study of intercultural activities of world's peoples in the twentieth century.)

26. O'BRIEN, MERCEDES ELLEN. *Education Viewed in the Light of Scholastic Philosophy.* Boston College, 1932. 174 p. ms.

27. RIDLEY, HARIETTE GOWER. *Music in the Life of Man.* New York University, 1942. (Discusses religious beliefs, social customs, and cultural achievements of man through the years as expressed in music, from ancient Greeks, through medieval period, and through 18th, 19th, and 20th centuries.)

28. ROTH, JULIAN BENEDICT, 1918- . *The Relationship of Scholasticism and Experimentation in Education.* Stanford University, 1955, 196 p. ms. Abstract in *Dissertation Abstracts,* Vol. 15, p. 2134-2135, November 1955. Available on microfilm from University Microfilms, Ann Arbor, Michigan, as Publication No. 12,348.

29. SINGER, EDGAR ARTHUR, 1873-1909. *The Content of Education, Historically Considered.* University of Pennsylvania, 1896.

30. STAATS, PAULINE GERTRUDE, 1901- . *A Study of the Educational Activities of the Intellectual Cooperative Organization of the League of Nations, 1920-1940: As Revealed in the Official Journals of the Council and the Records of the Assembly.* Stanford University, 1944. 188 p. ms. Abstract in Stanford University: *Abstracts of Dissertations . . . 1943-44,* p. 119-122.

31. STAINES, ROBERT GRAHAM, 1914- . *A History and Critique of the United Nations Information Program for Educational Institutions.* Columbia University, 1954. 517 p. ms. Abstract in *Dissertation Abstracts,* Vol. 14, p. 2268-2269, December 1954. Available on microfilm from University Microfilms, Ann Arbor, Michigan, as Publication No. 10,275.

32. STINE, DOROTHY PEARCE, 1912- . *The Role of the United States in the International Educational Exchange of Teachers and Students.* University of Houston, 1954. 367 p. ms. Abstract in *Dissertation Abstracts,* Vol. 14, p. 1609-1610, October 1954. Available on microfilm from University Microfilms, Ann Arbor, Michigan, as Publication No. 9,676.

33. STOB, GEORGE. *The Christian Reformed Church and Her Schools.* Princeton Theological Seminary, 1955. 469 p. ms. (Includes schools in various countries.)

34. STOUT, KENNETH DEANE. *International Teacher Exchange Programs under the Fulbright Act.* University of Tennessee, 1956. 187 p. ms.

35. TERMAN, EARLE LUTHER. *The Development and Application of National Educational Survey Techniques with Special Emphasis on Criteria for Measuring Intelligence Internationally.* New York University, 1930. 83 p. ms.

36. WILLIAMS, ROBERT EARL, 1920- . *The Relationship between Racial Evaluations and International Experiences.* University of Chicago, 1956. 133 p. ms. Available on microfilm: see index under "University of Chicago."

37. WORTHINGTON, RICHARD ALBERT, 1920- *A Review of Doctoral Dissertations in Music Education.* University of Illinois, 1956. 580 p. ms. Abstract in *Dissertation Abstracts*, Vol. 17, p. 537, March 1957. Available on microfilm from University Microfilms, Ann Arbor, Michigan, as Publication No. 19,888. (A detailed study of 391 dissertations from 39 American institutions. For each, a one- to two-page abstract is given stating problem, procedure, and conclusions, with publication data when available. Includes 16 dissertations on music education in foreign countries, all of which are included in the present bibliography.)

MASTERS

38. ADAMS, CLARENCE WIGTON, 1900- . *A Study of the Programs of Activity of Selected Missions of the Board of Foreign Missions of the Presbyterian Church in the U.S.A. in the Light of the Objectives of Christian Education.* Presbyterian Theological Seminary, 1932. 158 p. ms.

39. ANTTILLA, EARL URLO, 1914- *A Survey of the History of Education in the Vernacular.* University of Texas, 1943. 279 p. ms. (Deals with education "in various periods of history and various parts of the world".) For doctoral dissertation by same author, see No. 527.

40. ATHEARN, CLARENCE ROYALTY, 1895-1952. *A World Educational Association to Promote International Good Will.* Boston University, 1924.

41. BALDWIN, EDITH CORNELIA, 1893- . (Later Mrs. John L. Ruby.) *A Survey of Religious Education from the Earliest Times.* Boston University, 1926. 217 p. ms.

42. BALE, GEORGE WILBUR, 1927- . *School Discipline from Ancient Times to the Modern Day.* University of North Dakota, 1953. 115 p. ms. Abstract in University of North Dakota: *Abstracts of Doctoral Dissertations and Masters' Theses . . . 1953,* p. 30-31.

43. BARBANO, MARIE MARGUERITE, 1930- . *A Catholic Views UNESCO's Fundamental Education.* Boston College, 1952. 66 p. ms.

44. BIERER, DORA. *Intellectual Cooperation under the League of Nations.* Columbia University, 1946. 115 p. ms.

General

45. BORNE, CAROLINE MARIE. *The Problem of a Universal Language with Special Reference to Basic English.* Tulane University of Louisiana, 1945. 73 p. ms. Abstract in Tulane University of Louisiana: *Abstracts of Theses,* 1945, p. 8.

46. BROWN, ARTHUR MEADE. *History of the Art of Writing.* University of Southern California, 1927. 95 p. ms. (Covers the origin and development of the Roman alphabet in various countries.)

47. BROWN, SAMUEL R. *The Use of Audio-Visual Equipment in Modern Missionary Methods.* Nazarene Theological Seminary, 1952. (Thesis for degree of Bachelor of Divinity.)

48. BURKE, RICHARD DIGGINS, Jr., 1926- . *UNESCO and the American Teachers.* Clark University, 1950. 102 p. ms. Abstract in Clark University: *Abstracts of Dissertations and Theses . . .* 1950, p. 127-129.

49. BURNETT, ALTA HAZEL. *Historical Backgrounds of Current Educational Method.* University of Washington, 1933. 105 p. ms.

50. CEFKIN, J. LEO. *The Program of UNESCO.* Columbia University, 1949. 124 p. ms. (Includes educational program.)

51. CHAFFEE, MARY KOPER. *The Qualifications and Education of the Foreign Missionary Wife.* Biblical Seminary in New York, 1944. 122 p. ms.

52. CLARK, Sister MARY BORGIA. *The Educational Values of Music: Music's Place in Education in Early Times.* Catholic Sisters College of the Catholic University of America, 1913. 70 p. ms. (Covers ancient and medieval times, quoting philosophers of those periods.)

53. CLAYPOOLE, JACK O. *A Study of the Children of American YMCA Secretaries Raised Abroad.* George Williams College, 1958.

54. CLOPTON, REVEILLE ANN. *The Contributions of the Utopias to Modern Education.* Texas State College for Women, 1956. 170 p. ms.

55. COLLETT, WALTER A. *A Brief Study of Some of the Influences on Education in America, 1607-1900.* Agricultural and Technical College of North Carolina, 1958.

56. DODGE, NORMAN MAXUDIAN. *UNESCO's Contribution to Education.* Stanford University, 1949. 103 p. ms.

57. ENDRES, MILDRED SWANEY. *World Citizenship and the Role of the School in Its Development.* Allegheny College, 1951. 60 p. ms.

58. ERBACK, JOAN R. *An International Comparison of Physical Therapy Education.* New York University, 1958.

59. FAUSOLD, CHARLES DOTY. *The Parallel Development of History of Education and History of Civilization as Shown during Certain Periods, namely: Primitive, Ancient, Mediaeval.* Syracuse University, 1922. 87 p. ms.

60. FELDMAN, EDWIN. *UNESCO in Business Education.* University of Southern California, 1950. 76 p. ms.

61. FLEMING, WILLIAM COLEMAN. *Music in Cultural and Intellectual History: A Study in Historical Musicology.* Claremont College, 1941. 382 p. ms.

62. GOULTER, OSWALD JOHN. *Applied Christianity and World Missions.* Columbia University, 1937. 46 p. ms. (Includes consideration of religious education.) For another master's thesis by same author, see No. 1590.

63. GOWEN, MARY ELIZABETH. *A Study of the Nature and Role of the Student Volunteer Movement in Christian Missions.* Columbia University, 1950. 103 p. ms.

64. GREENE, OLIVE. *The Problem of the Article in the Teaching and Learning of English as a Foreign Language.* Kennedy School of Missions, 1957. 114 p. ms.

65. HAAS, FLORENCE L., 1893- . *Recreational Activities of Primitive and Tribal People.* Temple University, 1938. 161 p. ms.

66. HAUEISEN, ALLEN F., 1911- . *A Resume of the Second General Conference of UNESCO.* Arizona State College, Tempe, 1949. 172 p. ms.

67. HENDERSON, VINNIE LOUISE. *International Achievements through UNESCO.* Texas State College for Women, 1953. 144 p. ms.

68. HO, THOMAS C. K. *An Analysis of Current Concepts and Activities in International Education.* Catholic University of America, 1950. 56 p. ms. (Includes chapter on UNESCO and its educational programs, 1947 and 1948.)

69. JANNEY, ROBERT. *Agricultural Education on the Mission Field.* United Theological Seminary, Ohio, 1955. (Thesis for degree of Bachelor of Divinity.)

70. JONES, ROSALIE M. *A Study of the Literacy Movement.* San Francisco Theological Seminary, 1950.

71. KABAT, GLENNIS LUNDBERG, 1913- . *Educational Forerunners of the United Nations Educational, Scientific, and Cultural Organization.* University of Maryland, 1951. 158 p. ms.

72. KERN, CHARLOTTE HELEN. *Music in the Education of Primitive Racial Groups.* University of Washington, 1934. 136 p. ms.

73. KLAVON, Sister MARY VIOLA. *An Analysis of the Leiter International Performance Scale.* Catholic University of America, 1943. 41 p. ms.

74. LAMBIE, MARGARET. *International Treaties, Conventions, and Agreements Affecting the Practice of the Teaching Professions by Aliens.* American University, 1928. 130 p. ms.

75. LEBEQUE, DUANE E., 1922- . *A Survey of the Mechanical Skills and Knowledges Needed and Possessed by Missionaries Serving under the Faith Missionary Boards.* Stout State College, 1954. 175 p.

ms. Abstract in *Research in Industrial Education, 1930-1955.* p. 382.

76. LINSKEY, Rev. CHARLES J. *Objective Teaching in the Gospel and in the Early Church.* Catholic University of America, 1921. 30 p. ms.

77. LIT, MARK DAVID. *International Organizations with an Educational Program for World Peace.* University of Southern California, 1950. 89 p. ms.

78. LYON, SARAH S. *The Connection of the Foreign Division of the Young Women's Christian Association with Governments.* Columbia University, 1932. 58 p. ms. (Includes education.)

79. McRAE, WILLIAM ALEXANDER. *The Origin of Some Primitive Survivals in Modern Culture.* Columbia University, 1937. 26 p. ms. (Includes Christian education.)

80. MARK, LESLIE EARL. *The Problem of Education for the Children of Missionaries.* Gordon Divinity School, 1957. (Thesis for degree of Bachelor of Divinity.)

81. MINKLER, HELEN A. *Sources of Catechetical Instruction in the First Four Centuries of the Christian Church.* University of Pittsburgh, 1938. Abstract in University of Pittsburgh: *Abstracts of Theses . . .* Vol. 14, p. 374-375. (Thesis for Degree of Master of Arts.) For a thesis for the Degree of Master of Sacred Theology by same author, see No. 82.

82. MINKLER, HELEN A. *The Subject Matter of Christian Religious Education of the Early Church and the Present Day: A Comparison.* Western Theological Seminary, 1938. 102 p. ms. (Thesis for Degree of Master of Sacred Theology.) For a thesis for the Degree of Master of Arts by same author, see No. 81.

83. MOSHER, ALICE W. *An Exploratory Study of the Relationship of Dominant Interests, Values, and Motives to the Choice of Occupation of Missionaries and Technical Assistance Personnel.* Cornell University, 1958.

84. NETTINGS, DENA, 1900- *Projects that May Contribute to Christian Internationalism in High Schools under the Board of Foreign Missions of the Presbyterian Church in the United States of America.* Presbyterian College of Christian Education, 1938. 144 p. ms.

85. NUTT, MERLE CARO. *Education for International Understanding through Rotary International.* State University of Iowa, 1954. 266 p. ms. plus 64 p. of *Rotarian* and 32 p. of *Revista Rotaria.*

86. O'CONNELL, JOHN FRANCIS. *Jesuit Education.* Clark University, 1914. 53 p. ms.

87. OFFENKRANTZ, FREDERICK MILLMAN. *Activities of the Health Organization of the League of Nations, with Special Reference to Child Welfare.* Columbia University, 1934. 34 p. ms.

88. PATTERSON, VIRGINIA CATHERINE, 1931- *Case Histories of Missionary Children.* Columbia Bible College, 1956. 111 p. ms. (Covers family and school problems of 19 children of missionaries.)

89. PICKETT, DOUGLAS ROBINSON, 1929- . *Some Selected Principles of Understanding Human Behavior and Their Application to Program Development in Foreign Cultures.* Cornell University, 1958. 62 p. ms.

90. POWERS, FLORENCE J. *The History of Physical Education from Ancient to Modern Times.* Hunter College of the City of New York, 1940. 47 p. ms.

91. PUMPHREY, FRANKLIN. *The United Nations Educational, Scientific, and Cultural Organization: A Presentation of Two UNESCO Projects Emphasizing Education.* University of Maryland, 1954. 110 p. ms.

92. PUTNAM, BETTY JEAN, 1930- . *A Study of National and International Physical Education Associations.* Smith College, 1956. 109 p. ms.

93. RICE, ROBERT FRANKLIN. *Literacy Methods Used as a Medium for Personal Evangelism on the Foreign Mission Field.* Princeton Theological Seminary, 1949. 141 p. ms.

94. ROUB, CHARLES A. *The Place of Christian Education in Missions.* Bethel College and Seminary, 1952. (Thesis for degree of Bachelor of Divinity.)

95. ROWLETT, JOHN D. *A Study of the Craftsmen of Ancient and Medieval Civilizations to Show the Influence of Their Training on Our Present-Day Methods of Trade Education.* North Texas State College, 1950. 93 p. ms. Abstract in *Research in Industrial Education, 1930-1955,* p. 141.

96. SCHICK, SELMA. *Ideas of Educational Reform in Certain Utopias in the Sixteenth and Seventeenth Centuries.* New York University, 1939. 54 p. ms.

97. SCHMITTHENNER, SAMUEL W. *The Use of Audio-Visual Aids for Evangelism and Christian Education in Foreign Mission Fields.* Hood Theological Seminary, 1951. (Thesis for degree of Bachelor of Divinity.)

98. SCHRADER, ARTHUR F. *The International Institute as an Intercultural Educational Agency.* University of Buffalo, 1957. 115 p. ms.

99. SCHUETZ, Brother JOHN JOSEPH, 1874- *The Educational Activities of the Brethren of the Common Life.* Catholic University of America, 1916. 57 p. ms. For doctoral dissertation by same author, see No. 3125.

100. SELLERS, GERTRUDE H. *The United Nations Educational, Scientific, and Cultural Organization: Its Purpose, Structure, Accomplishments, and Plans.* Catholic University of America, 1948. 73 p. ms.

101. SHELDON, ALBERT BRADLEY. *The Development of International Education.* Columbia University, 1914. 37 p. ms. (Introductory outline names 32 countries studied.)

102. SIEVERT, JOHN. *Literacy, a Door for the Gospel. (A Study of the Laubach Method.)* Capital University, 1952. (Thesis for degree of Bachelor of Divinity.)

103. STOUT, MIRIAM ELIZABETH, 1928- . *The Value of Chemistry to the Foreign Missionary.* Colum-

bia Bible College, 1956. 39 p. ms. (Considers various contacts between chemistry and missionary work, notably in agriculture, medicine, teaching, and industry.)

104. TAYLOR, ELIZABETH MARGERY. *Daily Devotional Programs for Children in Mission Schools.* Berkeley Baptist Divinity School, 1942. 286 p. ms.

105. TEASDALE, RUTH HUDSON, 1908- . *The Attitudes and Methods Employed in Dealing with Adherents to the Ethnic Faiths.* Eastern Baptist Theological Seminary, 1939. 48 p. ms. Published as one of two theses in *Two Studies in Christian Missions* (Philadelphia: Eastern Baptist Theological Seminary, Contributions to Christian Education, 1939, No. 6, p. 15-22.)

106. TSAI, MILDRED, 1919- . *Fundamental Education: The Backbone of UNESCO.* Smith College, 1953. 87 p. ms.

107. VANGSNES, JOHANNES. *The United National Appeal for Children: An Experiment in International Organization.* Columbia University, 1949. 138 p. ms.

108. VERTANES, CHARLES AZNAKIAN. *The Capitalistic Orientation of Moral and Religious Instruction in Early Modern Times.* Union Theological Seminary, 1940. 59 p. ms.

109. VOIGHT, HENRY WILLIAM. *The Catechumenate in the Early Christian Church.* Yale University, 1923. 134 p. ms.

110. WALKWITZ, ROGER WILLIAM. *The Academic Education of Missionary Children.* Columbia Bible College, 1957. 85 p. ms. (Covers practice in foreign countries and in the homeland.)

111. WALLACE, EDWARD WILSON. *Problems in the Administration of Mission Education.* Columbia University, 1921.

112. WANG, TUNG. *A Study of the Application of Group Work Principles and Methods in the Student Christian Movements.* International YMCA College, 1941. 145 p. ms.

113. WARD, PHYLLIS ANNE. *The International Exchange of Students as a Project to Promote International Understanding.* Stanford University, 1947. 114 p. ms.

114. WEINER, MERVEYN M. *Leaves of Absence for Overseas Teaching.* San Francisco State College, 1958.

115. WHITE, WILLIAM BERRY. *A Student Travel Plan to Promote International Good Will.* Stanford University, 1947. 75 p. ms.

116. WILDER, GRACE EMMA, 1911- . *Religious Education on the Mission Field.* Andover Newton Theological School, 1937. 54 p. ms.

117. WILLIAMS, LIDA MYRTLE, 1877- . *Human Activities Approved in the Religious Literatures of the World.* University of Chicago, 1925. 92 p. ms.

118. YOUNG, BEULA LAVON, 1908- . *Building International Friendships through the Study of Intercultural Relationships.* New Jersey State College, Newark, 1958. 85 p. ms.

COMPOSITE

(NOS. 119 – 308)

Includes Titles Covering Countries Located in Two or More Continents. Cross-references are given in later sections for each country involved.

DOCTORS

119. ABEL, JAMES FREDERICK, 1878- *National Ministries of Education*. George Washington University, 1930. Washington: Government Printing Office, 1930. ix, 158 p. (U.S. Office of Education *Bulletin*, No. 12, 1930. Covers 55 countries including Afghanistan, Albania, Argentina, Austria, Belgium, Bolivia, Bulgaria, Chile, China, Colombia, Costa Rica, Cuba, Czechoslovakia, Danzig, Denmark, Dominican Republic, Ecuador, Egypt, El Salvador, Estonia, Finland, France, Great Britain, Greece, Guatemala, Haiti, Honduras, Hungary, Iran, Iraq, Ireland, Italy, Japan, Latvia, Liberia, Lithuania, Mexico, Netherlands, New Zealand, Nicaragua, Norway, Panama, Paraguay, Peru, Poland, Portugal, Rumania, Spain, Sweden, Thailand, Turkey, Union of South Africa, Uruguay, Venezuela, and Yugoslavia. Contains special chapters on France, Great Britain, and Mexico.)

120. ABOU-KHADRA, RAJAI. *UNESCO and the Arab Country*. University of Indiana, 1957. 382 p. ms. (Includes Egypt, Iraq, Jordan, Lebanon, Libya, Saudi Arabia, and Syria.)

121. ADAIR, J. B., 1913- . *The World Literacy Movement*. University of Texas, 1951. 228 p. ms. "J.B." is entire first name – Letter from author, Oct. 29, 1958. (Includes Philippines, USSR, Africa, Europe, South America.)

122. APPLETON, LILLA ESTELLE, 1858-1937. *A Comparative Study of the Play Activities of Adult Savages and Civilized Children, with the Pedagogical Deductions Therefrom*. University of Chicago, 1909. Published as *A Comparative Study of the Play Activities of Adult Savages and Civilized Children: An Investigation of the Scientific Basis of Education*. Chicago: University of Chicago Press, 1910. vii, 94 p. (Includes the Veddahs of Ceylon, the Central tribes of Australia, the Canoe Indians of Terra del Fuego (Argentina), the Bushmen of South Africa, and the Eskimo of Canada and Greenland.)

123. BISHOP, JULIUS IVYLOY, 1915- . *A Curriculum of Missionary Education through the Royal Ambassador Organization*. Southwestern Baptist Theological Seminary, 1955. 237 p. ms. (Missionary education organization in mission fields supported by Southern Baptists. Very active in Brazil and Mexico.)

124. BUASRI, SAROJ, 1916- . *A Study of Methods of Teaching Adults to Read as Developed for Literacy Campaigns by Some Members of UNESCO*. Ohio State University, 1951. 304 p. ms. Abstract in Ohio State University: *Abstracts of Dissertations* . . . No. 66, Spring Quarter, 1950-51, p. 29-34. (Compares five methods: (1) United States Office of Education, (2) UNESCO in Haiti, (3) Frank Laubach, (4) Brazilian, and (5) Thailand Literacy Campaign.)

125. BURTON, C. GRANT, 1916- *A Historical Study of the Concept of the Individual and Society in Educational Philosophy*. University of Southern California, 1954. 329 p. ms. Abstract in University of Southern California: *Abstracts of Dissertations*, 1954. p. 173-176. (Includes ancient Grecian, Jewish, and Roman concepts.)

126. CASANOVA, TEOBALDO, 1894- . *Educational Psychology and Some Aspects of Education in Latin America*. New York University, 1933. San Juan, Puerto Rico: Imprenta Venezuela, 1934. viii, 170 p. (But "Printed in U.S.A." Includes specific consideration of education in Argentina, Bolivia, Brazil, Chile, Colombia, Costa Rica, Cuba, Dominican Republic, Ecuador, El Salvador, Guatemala, Honduras, Mexico, Nicaragua, Panama, Paraguay, Peru, Uruguay, and Venezuela.)

127. CHEAVENS, SAM FRANK. *Vernacular Languages and Education*. University of Texas, 1957. 551 p. ms. Abstract in *Dissertation Abstracts*, Vol. 18, p. 921, March 1958. Available on microfilm from University Microfilms, Ann Arbor, Michigan, as Publication No. 25,185. (Includes many countries, with special emphasis on China, India, Mexico, Turkey, and USSR.)

128. CRESPI, ALBERTA R., 1891- . *Secondary School Teachers in the Territories and Possessions of the United States*. Fordham University, 1942. 320 p. ms. Abstract in Fordham University: *Dissertations Accepted for Higher Degrees* . . . 1943, p. 11-17. (Includes American Samoa, Guam, Philippines, Puerto Rico, and Virgin Islands.)

129. DeMAY, AMY JEANETTE. *Ancestry of Present Fraction Processes: The Romance of Fragments, 1600 B.C. to 1600 A.D.* New York University, 1941. 3 vols., 1082 p. ms. (Includes Egypt, France, Germany, Great Britain, India, Iraq, Italy, and the Netherlands.)

130. DORMAN, HARRY GAYLORD, Jr., 1906- *Toward Understanding Islam: Contemporary Apologetic of Islam and Missionary Policy*. Columbia University, 1947. New York: Bureau of Publications, Teachers College, Columbia University, 1948. x, 137 p. (Teachers College Contribution to Education, No. 940. Includes Asia in general, Middle East, and Egypt.)

131. FINLAY, PAUL RAYMOND. *A Comparative Study of Certain Ancient and Current Concepts of Religious Education in the Home*. New York University, 1958. 237 p. ms. Abstract in *Dissertation Abstracts*, Vol. 18, p. 2234, June 1958. Available on microfilm from University Microfilms, Ann Arbor, Michigan, as Mic. 58-1987. (Includes consideration of writing of the Hebrews and early Christians.)

132. FINLEY, ESTHER MARY, 1904- . *Factors Influencing Education for Nursing in the Near East*. Columbia University, 1955. 176 p. ms. (Includes Egypt, Iran, Iraq, Lebanon, Syria, and Turkey.)

133. FITZGERALD, DEAN TURNER, 1905- . *American Schools in Latin America*. University of Tulsa, 1954. vii, 201 p. ms. (Includes Argentina, Bolivia,

Brazil, Colombia, Costa Rica, Dominican Republic, Ecuador, El Salvador, Guatemala, Haiti, Honduras, Mexico, Nicaragua, Peru, and Venezuela.)

134. FOLEY, ROLLA, 1915- . *Work Songs of the Arabs.* Columbia University, 1956. 344 p. ms. (Includes folk songs from Arabs in Africa and Asia.)

135. FREEBURG, ROY EVERETT WALTER. *The Use of Musical Resources of the Pacific-Southwest Region for Elementary Education.* Stanford University, 1946. Abstract in Stanford University: *Abstracts of Dissertations . . . 1945-46,* p. 155-157. (Traces Mexican, Russian, and other European influences.)

136. GARBER, HELEN LISA. *A Comparative Study of Plato and Tagore in Relation to Aesthetic Education.* New York University, 1940. 310 p. ms. Abstract in New York University, School of Education: *Abstracts of Theses,* October 1939-June 1940, p. 169-172. (Greece, India.)

137. GELSTON-GELLES, ROBERT HANS, 1918- . *The Economic Development of Underdeveloped Countries and Education.* Columbia University, 1953. 257 p. ms. (Considers four broad geographic areas — "first, the vast areas of what is loosely termed East and Southeast Asia, India and China, countries with ancient civilizations, with half the population of the world; . . . secondly, the colonial and former colonial areas, especially Africa; thirdly, the Caribbean and parts of South America, another poor and largely overcrowded area; and fourthly, the Middle East.")

138. GILBERT, WILLIAM RALPH. *A Study of Teacher Programs on the Local, National, and International Levels, with Emphasis on the Seattle, Washington, Public School Exchange Program.* University of Washington, 1955. 350 p. ms. Abstract in *Dissertation Abstracts,* Vol. 15, p. 1560, September 1955. Available on microfilm from University Microfilms, Ann Arbor, Michigan, as Publication No. 12,984. (Based on questionnaires to teachers going from United States to foreign countries and 36 from foreign countries to the United States. Countries involved: Australia, Austria, Belgium, Burma, Canada, Ceylon, Denmark, Egypt, Finland, France, Germany, Great Britain, Greece, India, Indonesia, Iran, Iraq, Italy, Japan, Netherlands, New Zealand, Norway, Pakistan, Philippines, Sweden, Thailand, Turkey, and Union of South Africa.)

139. GOELMAN, ELAZAR, 1913- . *The Development of the Natural Method (Ivrit B'Ivrit) in the Teaching of Hebrew in Jewish Schools in Modern Times.* Dropsie College for Hebrew and Cognate Learning, 1953. 178 p. ms. Abstract in *Religious Education,* Vol. 49, p. 183-184, May-June 1954. (Covers Israel, Eastern Europe, and the United States.)

140. GOODEN, HERBERT BICKLING, 1911- . *A Causal—Comparative Approach to the Study of Secondary Education in Guatemala, Costa Rica, Ecuador, and Colombia, 1924-1944.* New York University, 1946. 235 p. ms. Abstract in *Microfilm Abstracts,* Vol. 7, No. 1, p. 36-38, 1946. Available on microfilm from University Microfilms, Ann Arbor, Michigan, as Publication No. 824.

141. HALNON, WILLIAM. *A Descriptive, Critical, and Constructive Study of the Control, Organization, and Administration of Training Elementary Teachers in England, Canada, and the United States.* Indiana University, 1925. 379 p. ms.

142. HAMMER, EUGENE LA VERNE, 1919- . *An International Study of Teachers Salaries.* Columbia University, 1953. 60 p. ms. Published in condensed form as *Teachers Salaries,* Washington: World Organization of the Teaching Profession, 1201 16th St., NW. 1953. v, 42 p. (Covers salaries in Australia, Austria, Bolivia, British West Indies, Canada, Ceylon, Cuba, Denmark, Germany, Great Britain, Haiti, Iceland, India, Ireland, Israel, Italy, Japan, Liberia, Malta, Netherlands, New Zealand, Norway, Philippines, Portugal, Spain, Switzerland, Turkey, and Union of South Africa.)

143. HANSOME, MARIUS, 1887- . *World Workers' Educational Movements: Their Social Significance.* Columbia University, 1931. New York: Columbia University Press; London: P.S. King & Son, Ltd., 1931. 596 p. (Studies in History, Economics, and Public Law, No. 338. Includes Australia, Austria, Belgium, Canada, China, Czechoslovakia, Denmark, Finland, France, Germany, Great Britain, India, Ireland, Israel, Japan, Mexico, Netherlands, New Zealand, Norway, Sweden, Switzerland, and USSR.)

144. HARVEY, McLEOD, 1862- . *The Pedagogy of Missions.* Clark University, 1911. Published, in part, in *Journal of Religious Psychology,* Vol. 7, p. 345-349, April 1915. (Treatment is primarily topical, not geographical, but contains numerous references to China, India, Israel, Japan, Korea, Pacific Islands, and Turkey.)

145. HAWES, HOMER HUGHES, 1916- . *A History of the Early Church and Christian Education from the Birth of Christ to the Council of Nicea, A.D. 1-325.* Michigan State College of Agriculture and Applied Science, 1954. 278 p. ms. Abstract in *Dissertation Abstracts,* Vol. 16, p. 61-62, January 1956. Available on microfilm from University Microfilms, Ann Arbor, Michigan, as Publication No. 14,275. (Includes Egypt, Israel, Italy, and Turkey.)

146. IYENGAR, N. SINGAMMAL, 1916- . *Workers Education: A Functional Approach.* Northwestern University, 1955. 228 p. ms. Abstract in *Dissertation Abstracts,* Vol. 15, p. 2424-2425, December 1955. Available on microfilm from University Microfilms, Ann Arbor, Michigan, as Publication No. 15,137. (Abstract shows Great Britain and Africa are included.)

147. JACK, HOMER ALEXANDER, 1916- . *The Biological Field Stations of the World: A Comparative and Descriptive Study.* Cornell University, 1940. 2 vols. 515 p; 486 p. Published as *Biological Field Stations of the World,* Waltham, Massachusetts: The Chronica Botanica Co.; New York: G. E. Stechert Co., 1945. 73 p. Abstract in Cornell University: *Abstracts of Theses . . . 1940,* p. 98-101. (*Chronica Botanica,* Vol. 9, No. 1, 1945. Covers several hundred stations in Algeria, Argentina, Australia, Belgium, Bermuda, Brazil, Bulgaria, Canada, Caroline Islands, Ceylon, Chile, China, Cuba, Czechoslovakia, Denmark, Egypt, Estonia, Finland, France, Germany, Great Britain, Greenland, Hungary, India, Indo-China, Indonesia, Ireland, Italy, Jamaica, Japan, Latvia, Manchukuo, Martinique, Mexico, Monaco, Netherlands, New Caledonia, New

Zealand, Norway, Panama, Philippines, Poland, Portugal, Rhodes, Roumania, Spain, Surinam, Sweden, Switzerland, Tunisia, Union of South Africa, and USSR.)

148. KASUYA, YOSHI, 1894- . *A Comparative Study of the Secondary Education of Girls in England, Germany, and the United States, with a Consideration of the Secondary Education of Girls in Japan.* Columbia University, 1933. New York: Teachers College, Columbia University, 1933. x, 211 p. (Teachers College Contribution to Education, No. 566.)

149. KELSEY, JOHN MARVIN, 1908- . *Study of Programs of Recreation in Selected Institutions of Higher Learning in North, Central, and South America.* State University of Iowa, 1956. 193 p. ms. Abstract in *Dissertation Abstracts,* Vol. 16, p. 1834-1835, October 1956. Available on microfilm from University Microfilms, Ann Arbor, Michigan, as Publication No. 18,543. (Covers countries and institutions as follows: Bolivia, 1; Canada, 7; Chile, 2; Cuba, 1; Mexico, 1; Panama, 1; and United States of America, 80.)

150. KNUDSON, EMMA R., 1899- . *Folk Music as a Tool in Inter-Cultural Education.* Northwestern University, 1946. 390 p. ms. Abstract in Northwestern University: *Summaries of Doctoral Dissertations . . .* Vol. 14, 1946, p. 133-138. (Studies 1198 folk songs from 84 countries, including 226 from the United States, 146 from England, 114 from France, 96 from Germany, 65 from various Latin-American countries, and 62 from Russia.)

151. LATHROP, JOHN CLARKE, 1909- . *Promotion of International Understanding through the Exchange of High School Students: A Project of the Metropolitan School Study Council Providing Exchange Visits between American, Latin-America, and Scandinavian Students.* Columbia University, 1948. 107 p. ms. (Covers 4 Canadian and 29 Latin-American students from 20 countries in 1947, 21 Scandinavian students in 1948, and 10 American students to Bolivia, Brazil, Chile, Ecuador, and Mexico in 1948.)

152. LEIBELL, *Sister* JANE FRANCES, 1877- (Secular name, Helen Dominica Leibell.) *Anglo-Saxon Education of Women from Hilda to Hildegarde.* Georgetown University, 1922. Washington: 1922. 176 p. (Includes also education of women in Egypt, France, Germany, Israel, and Italy.)

153. LEIS, *Sister* MARY de CHANTAL, 1902- *Utilization of Pagan Educational Facilities by the Early Christians from the Third to the Sixth Century.* University of Pittsburgh, 1934. 112 p. ms. Abstract in University of Pittsburgh: *Abstracts of Theses . . .* Vol. 10, 1934, p. 234-241. (Includes Egypt, Italy, and other countries of Europe.)

154. LING, PING, 1894- . *Public Schools and the War.* Clark University, 1919. Worcester, Massachusetts: 1919. 158 p. ("An endeavor to study the effect of the War upon schools in other countries and especially in the United States." Chiefly on the United States but also studies effects in Australia, France, Germany, and Great Britain.)

155. LIPP, SOLOMON. *The University Reform in Hispanic America.* Harvard University, 1949. 398 p. ms. (Includes Argentina, Chile, Colombia, Costa Rica, Cuba, Ecuador, Guatemala, Mexico, Panama, Paraguay, Peru, Uruguay, and Venezuela.)

156. LOPEZ, ROBERT SABATION, 1910- *State Colleges, Public Monopolies, and Regalia in the Roman and Byzantine Empires.* University of Wisconsin, 1942. 311 p. ms. Abstract in University of Wisconsin: *Summaries of Doctoral Dissertations,* Vol. 7, 1941-42, p. 144-146. (Italy, Turkey.)

157. LUNDEN, WALTER ALBIN, 1899- . *Changes in Mobility and Structure of Higher Education in the Western World since 1100 A.D.* Harvard University, 1934. 299 p. ms. Abstract in Harvard University: *Summaries of Ph.D. Theses,* 1934, p. 440-443. (Includes Austria, China, France, Germany, Great Britain, India, Italy, Japan, Poland, Portugal, Spain, USSR, and the United States.)

158. McCARTHY, *Sister* MARY KATHERINE. *Some Motives in Christian Education Compared with the Christian Ideal.* Catholic Sisters College of the Catholic University of America, 1914. Washington: Catholic University of America, 1914. 103 p. Published also in installments, complete except for bibliography, in *Catholic Educational Review,* as follows: Vol. 8, p. 161-175, September 1914; Vol. 8, p. 210-228, October 1914; Vol. 8, p. 341-351, November 1914; Vol. 8, p. 425-445, December 1914; Vol. 9, p. 43-56, January 1915; Vol. 9, p. 120-130, February 1915. (Greece, Israel, Italy.)

159. McINTOSH, LOIS, 1908- . *A Description and Comparison of Question Signals in Spoken English, Mandarin Chinese, French, and German for Teachers of English as a Second Language.* University of Michigan, 1953. 247 p. ms. Abstract in *Dissertation Abstracts,* Vol. 13, p. 341-342, 1953. Available on microfilm from University Microfilms, Ann Arbor, Michigan, as Publication No. 5,070.

160. MILLER, RICHARD IRIVIN, 1924- . *The United Nations Trusteeship System and Educational Advancement.* Columbia University, 1958. 287 p. ms. (Chap. III, "The Cameroons under French Administration," p. 31-99; Chap. IV, "New Guinea under Australian Administration," p. 100-158; Chap. V. "Tanganyika under United Kingdom Administration," p. 159-218.)

161. MOTTERSHEAD, NOEL FRANCIS, 1914- . *A Comparative Study of World Movements in Adult Education.* University of California, Berkeley, 1949. 436 p. ms. (Includes Australia, Austria, Belgium, Canada, Czechoslovakia, Denmark, Estonia, Finland, France, Germany, Great Britain, Hungary, Japan, Netherlands, New Zealand, Norway, Poland, South Africa, Spain, Sweden, Switzerland, and United States.)

162. MOYER, ELGIN SYLVESTER. *History of Missions in the Church of the Brethren.* Yale University, 1929. Published as *Missions in the Church of the Brethren: Their Development and Effect upon the Denomination.* Elgin, Illinois: Brethren Publishing House, 1931. 301 p. (Contains many references to educational work, especially in Africa, China, India, and Turkey.)

162a. MULDER, ROBERT LEONARD. *A Comparative Study of the Competence of Groups of Inter-National and Native Students in Aspects of Language that Hold Special Relevance to Speech.* Ohio State University, 1953. 221 p. ms. Abstract in *Dissertation Abstracts,* Vol. 19, p. 1863-1866, January 1959. Available on microfilm from University Microfilms, Ann Arbor, Michigan, as Mic. 58-7160. (Includes experiences with 20 native speakers of Spanish, 20 of Japanese, and 20 of English.)

163. NORDGAARD, MARTIN ANDREW, 1882-1952. *A Historical Survey of Algebraic Methods of Approximating the Roots of Higher Numerical Equations up to the Year 1819.* Columbia University, 1922. New York: Teachers College, Columbia University, 1922. vi, 64 p. (Teachers College Contribution to Education, No. 123. Includes consideration of mathematicians in China, Egypt, France, Great Britain, Greece, India, Babylon (Iraq), Italy, Japan, Netherlands, and Switzerland.)

164. PHILLIPS, CLIFTON JACKSON. *Protestant America and the Pagan World: The First Half Century of the American Board of Commissioners for Foreign Missions, 1810-1860.* Harvard University, 1954. 360 p. ms. (Includes Borneo, Ceylon, China, Cyprus, French Equatorial Africa, Greece, India, Iran, Israel, Liberia, Malta, Micronesia, Singapore, South Africa, Syria, Thailand, and Turkey, with educational activities in most of them.)

165. POUSSON, LEON BERNARD, 1913- . *The Totalitarian Philosophy of Education.* Catholic University of America, 1944. Washington: Catholic University of America Press, 1944. ix, 164 p. (Catholic University of America Philosophical Studies, Vol. 80. Includes study of situation in Germany, Italy, Japan, and the USSR.)

166. REID, CHARLES FREDERICK, 1898- . *Education in the Territories and Outlying Possessions of the United States.* Columbia University, 1941. New York: Bureau of Publications, Teachers College, Columbia University, 1941. xxv, 593 p. (Teachers College Contribution to Education, No. 825. Includes American Samoa, Guam, Puerto Rico, and the Virgin Islands.)

167. SAUSJORD, ROSA IGARZABEL, 1923- . *An Analysis of Primary Readers from Five Spanish-American Countries.* State University of Iowa, 1951. 731 p. ms. Abstract in State University of Iowa: *Doctor's Dissertations . . . 1949 through 1952,* p. 317-325. (Includes Argentina, Chile, Ecuador, Mexico, and Uruguay.)

168. SAYILI, AYDIN MEHMET. *The Institutions of Science and Learning in the Moslem World.* Harvard University, 1942. Abstract in Harvard University: *Summaries of Theses,* 1942, p. 226-228. (Author states intention to deal "more fully with the Eastern half of Islam, including Egypt." Covers Moslem countries of Asia, especially India.)

169. SAYMON, IGNATZ. *A Study in the Civilization and Education of Primitive Man.* New York University, 1911. 58 p. ms. (Primarily topical, not geographical, but considers primitive people in Arabia, China, India, Israel, Japan, Mexico, Pacific Islands, and Philippines.)

170. SCHERZER, ALFRED LEONARD. *Health Education in Public Health Programs for Underdeveloped Areas.* Columbia University, 1954. 291 p. ms. (Includes Burma, Ceylon, Formosa, Korea, Malaya, Pakistan, and Thailand.)

171. SHAW, LEANDER JERRY, 1906- . *A Documentary and Descriptive Analysis of the Administration of Educational Programs under Point Four in Brazil, Iran, and Thailand.* Pennsylvania State University, 1954. 151 p. ms. Abstract in *Penn State Review of Educational Research,* Vol. 6, December 1954, p. 13-15. Abstract also in Pennsylvania State University: *Abstracts of Doctoral Dissertations,* Vol. 17, 1954, p. 403. Available on microfilm from University Microfilms, Ann Arbor, Michigan, as Publication No. 11,763.

172. SMITH, FRANK WEBSTER, 1854-1943. *Studies in the Evolution of the Secondary School.* University of Nebraska, 1904. Various paging. Published as *The Historical Development of Secondary Education from Prehistoric Times to the Christian Era.* New York: Sturgis & Walton Co., 1916. iii, 172 p. (Contains brief consideration of secondary education in primitive times and among primitive tribes but concerned chiefly with secondary education in ancient Greece and Rome.)

173. SMUTS, MICHIEL NICOLAAS. *Modern Experimental Schools in Germany and Their Significance for South Africa.* New York University, 1926. 138 p. ms.

174. SPARKMAN, COLLEY FREDWARD, 1885- . *A History of Theories of Moral Education.* New York University, 1914. 183 p. ms. (Covers developments in China, Egypt, Germany, Greece, India, Iran, Israel, Italy, and Phoenicia (Lebanon, Syria); and the work of the Jesuits and Saracens.)

174a. STAMPER, ALVA WALKER. *A History of the Teaching of Elementary Geometry, with Reference to Present-Day Problems.* Columbia University, 1909. New York: Columbia University, 1909. x, 163 p. (Contribution to Education, Teachers College Series, No. 23. Includes Austria, Belgium, Bulgaria, Czechoslovakia, Denmark, Egypt, France, Great Britain, Greece, Netherlands, Norway, Sweden, Switzerland, and USSR.) For master's thesis by same author see No. 3062.

175. STOKER, SPENCER LONGSHORE, 1890- . *A Study of International Education.* Stanford University, 1931. Published as *The Schools and International Understanding,* Chapel Hill, North Carolina: University of North Carolina Press, 1933. xxvii, 243 p. Abstract in Stanford University, *Abstracts of Dissertations . . . 1930-31,* p. 60-65. (Covers activities in various countries including Austria, Belgium, Bulgaria, Czechoslovakia, Denmark, France, Germany, Great Britain, Greece, Hungary, Italy, Netherlands, Poland, Roumania, Spain, Switzerland, and Yugoslavia.)

176. STOUTEMYER, JOHN HOWARD, 1880- . *Religion and Race Education.* Clark University, 1910. 80 p. ms. Extensively reported under title "Religion and Race Education: A Study in Religious and Social Psychology," in *Journal of Religious Psychology,* Vol. 7, p. 273-322, April 1915. Also under title "Race Education in *Journal of Race Development,* Vol. 5, p. 438-466, April 1915. Also issued as separate monograph combining the above two publications and repaged. 80 p. (Primarily topical, but considers primitive groups in Canada, India, Indonesia, Nigeria, Paraguay, Philippines, Sierra Leone, and South Africa.)

177. TAPPERT, ESTHER ELIZABETH. (Later Mrs. Ralph Mortensen). *International Intellectual and Cultural Cooperation between Two Wars: A Study of the Development of the Concept and Its Propagation*

under the Auspices of the League of Nations. Yale University, 1946. 316 p. ms. (Includes special chapters on developments in France and Great Britain.)

178. TENG, TA-CHUN. *A Comparative Study of Teacher Education in China, England, France, and the United States.* University of Colorado, 1950. 378 p. ms. Abstract in University of Colorado: *Abstracts of Theses* . . . 1950-51, p. 37-39.

179. TODD, ARTHUR JAMES, 1878-1948. *The Family in Primitive Education.* Yale University, 1911. Incorporated in the author's *The Primitive Family as an Educational Agency,* New York: G. P. Putnam's Sons, 1913. ix, 251 p. (Primarily topical, not geographical, in treatment but refers to conditions in Africa, Australia, Borneo, Ceylon, China, Fiji Islands, India, Japan, Java, Malaya, New Guinea, Philippines, and Siberia.)

180. TOTAH, KHALIL ABDULLAH, 1886- *The Contributions of the Arabs to Education.* Columbia University, 1926. New York: Teachers College, Columbia University, 1926. v, 105 p. (Teachers College Contribution to Education, No. 231. Considers especially Arab contributions in Egypt, Iraq, Israel, Spain, and Syria. Contains special chapter on education of women.)

181. WEAR, ROBERT EDWARD, 1916- . *Physical Fitness and Performance of a Medically Healthy Group of Adult Males of Mongolian and Melanesian Racial Ancestry.* University of Michigan, 1955. 177 p. ms. Abstract in *Dissertation Abstracts,* Vol. 15, p. 1548, September 1955. Available on microfilm from University Microfilms, Ann Arbor, Michigan, as Publication No. 12,665. (China, India, Pacific Islands.)

182. WELLONS, RALPH DILLINGHAM, 1891- *The Organizations Set Up for the Control of Mission Union Higher Educational Institutions.* Columbia University, 1927. New York: 1927. vi, 138 p. (Includes institutions in China, India, Japan, Korea, and Mexico.) For master's thesis by same author, see No. 303.

183. WINTER, JOHN E. *The Development of Moral Education in Cyril, Jerome, Augustine, and Cassian.* University of Michigan, 1917. 143 p. ms. Abstract in University of Michigan: *Abstracts of Dissertations and Theses in Education, 1917-1931,* p. 1-3. (Africa, Asia, Europe.)

184. WISE, *Rev.* JOHN EDWARD, 1905- . *The Nature of the Liberal Arts.* Fordham University, 1946. Milwaukee, Wisconsin: Bruce Publishing Co., 1947. vii, 225 p. With Editor's Introduction by Francis M. Crowley. (The Catholic Education Series, No. 1) Abstract in Fordham University: *Dissertations Accepted for Higher Degrees . . .,* 1946, p. 55-59. (Contains chapters devoted to Plato, Cicero, Quintilian, St. Augustine, St. Thomas Aquinas, and Cardinal Newman. Greece, Italy, Tunisia, France, Great Britain.)

185. WOODHULL, ALICE SUMNER HAWLEY, 1893- . *Albert Schweitzer and Johann Wolfgang von Goethe: A Comparative Study of Their Contributions to the Field of Education.* University of Buffalo, 1954. 448 p. ms. (French Equatorial Africa, Germany.)

MASTERS

186. ALTER, SAMUEL NEALE. *Studies in the Psychology of Islam.* Hartford Seminary Foundation, 1928. 119 p. ms. (Africa, Asia.)

187. ANDREWS, GEORGE FRANKLIN, 1897-1949. *History of the Playground and Organization and Administration of Playgrounds.* International YMCA College, 1932. 248 p. ms. (Four chapters deal with America, Europe, Far East, and India. European: Belgium, France, Germany, Great Britain, Greece, Hungary, Israel, Italy, Poland, Turkey, and USSR. Far Eastern: China, Japan, Philippines.) For doctoral dissertation by same author, see No. 1826.

188. BAUMEISTER, *Sister* MARY GODFRIEDA. *Educational Influence at Work in the Realm of Charles V.* St. Scholastica's College, Philippines, 1928. 64 p. ms. (Refers to Charles V, Roman emperor and king of Spain. Includes Germany, Netherlands, Spain and briefly Mexico.)

189. BECKERLE, *Sister* MARY ROSE AGNES, 1915- *Roman Education as Reflected in the Confessions of St. Augustine.* St. Louis University, 1957. 48 p. ms. (Italy, Algeria.)

190. BENSON, WILLIAM MOBERG. *The Teaching of United States History in the Latin-American Republics.* Pennsylvania State College, 1946. 101 p. ms. (Includes Argentina, Bolivia, Brazil, Chile, Colombia, Costa Rica, Cuba, Dominican Republic, Ecuador, El Salvador, Guatemala, Haiti, Honduras, Mexico, Nicaragua, Panama, Paraguay, Peru, Uruguay, and Venezuela.)

191. BERNER, CARL WALTER. *A Historical Study of Education in the Christian Church from Paul to Augustine.* University of Southern California, 1934. 87 p. ms. (Asia, Europe.)

192. BLANK, EMANUEL. *The Teacher in the Territories and Outlying Possessions of the United States.* College of the City of New York, 1937. 148 p. ms. Abstract in College of the City of New York: *Abstracts of Theses . . . 1923-1939,* p. 97. (Includes American Samoa, Guam, Philippines, Puerto Rico, and the Virgin Islands.)

193. BLOUGH, JOHN HOWARD. *Methods and Scope of Work of Foreign Agricultural Christian Missions.* Iowa State College of Agriculture and Mechanic Arts, 1922. 74 p. ms. (Includes Africa, China, India, the Near East, and South America.)

194. BOARD, JOSEPH GREEN. *Comparison of Current Latin-American and United States History Texts.* George Peabody College for Teachers, 1938. 410 p. ms. (Includes 22 Latin-American textbooks from Argentina, Chile, Cuba, Ecuador, Mexico, and Uruguay.)

195. BOHRER, RICHARD W. *Education in Primitive Societies.* University of Southern California, 1956. 146 p. ms. (Includes 24 groups of primitive people, natives of Andaman Islands, Australia, Canada, Japan, Mexico, New Guinea, Peru, Samoa, Sierra Leone, Tanganyika, Uganda, and Central Asia.)

196. BOYLE, *Rev.* JOSEPH I. *A History of the Educational Work of the Augustinians of the United*

States. Catholic University of America, 1937. 98 p. ms. (Includes discussion of origin and spread throughout the world, especially in Mexico.)

197. BRENTLINGER, WILLIAM BROCK. *An Introduction to and Survey of the Field of Foreign Missionary Radio Broadcasting.* Indiana State Teachers College, 1951. 122 p. ms. Abstract in *Teachers College Journal,* Vol. 23, p. 52, November 1951. (Contribution of the Graduate School, No. 732. Covers educational programs used by stations in Costa Rica, Ecuador, Guatemala, Haiti, and Panama.)

198. BROWN, CLAUDE C. *An Exploratory Study of Biography in Relation to Educational Theory and Practice.* University of Colorado, 1935. 74 p. ms. Abstract in *University of Colorado Studies,* Vol. 23, No. 1, p. 8, November 1935. (Includes Mozart, Napoleon, Pasteur, and Gandhi; Austria, France, India.)

199. BROWN, EDNA B. *A Study on the Christian Education of National Women Leadership in Latin Lands.* Kennedy School of Missions, 1926. 79 p. ms. (North America, South America.)

200. BUCKLEY, Rev. WILLIAM D. *The Educational Work of the Oblates of St. Francis de Sales.* Catholic University of America, 1932. 51 p. ms. (Includes Austria, Brazil, Colombia, Ecuador, France, Germany, Great Britain, Greece, and Uruguay.)

201. BUTLER, MARY. *A Curriculum of Christian Education for Children in Latin America.* Berkeley Baptist Divinity School, 1951. 58 p. ms. (North America, South America.)

202. BUTTON, RENA FLORINA. *Visual Aids in Christian Education for Latin America.* Berkeley Baptist Divinity School, 1950. 84 p. ms. (North America, South America.)

203. CALLAHAN, Rev. EDMOND JOSEPH, 1897- *An Analysis of the Encyclical "Christian Education of Youth" in the Light of St. Augustine and St. Thomas.* St. Louis University, 1937. (Algeria, France, Italy.)

204. CAREY, JAMES EUGENE, 1925- . *Some Major Psychological Characteristics of Spanish-Speaking Peoples.* Arizona State College, Tempe, 1954. 71 p. ms. (North America, South America, Spain.)

205. CARTES, BRUNILDA. *Music Education in Latin America.* Northwestern University, 1946. 41 p. ms. (Includes Argentina, Bolivia, Brazil, Chile, Colombia, Costa Rica, Cuba, Dominican Republic, Ecuador, El Salvador, Guatemala, Haiti, Honduras, Mexico, Nicaragua, Panama, Paraguay, Peru, Uruguay, and Venezuela.)

206. CHAR, TIN-YUKE. *Legal Restriction on Chinese in English-Speaking Countries of the Pacific.* University of Hawaii, 1932. 134 p. ms. Published in *Chinese Social and Political Science Review,* Vol. 16, No. 4, p. 472-651, January 1933. (Includes consideration of conditions for entrance of students over 15 years of age. Covers Australia, Canada, and New Zealand.)

207. CHILDERS, LAURENCE MURRELL, 1892- *Education in California under Spain and Mexico, and under American Rule to 1851.* University of California, Berkeley, 1930. 237 p. ms. (Mexico, Spain.)

208. CHOI, EDNA. *Milton and Confucius: A Comparative Study of the Two Ethical Teachers.* Columbia University, 1947. 102 p. ms. (Great Britain, China.)

209. COBB, FRANCES TRUMAN. *Origin and Development of the Turnvereine.* George Peabody College for Teachers, 1936. 80 p. ms. (Covers activities in Germany and United States with brief consideration in 27 countries in all parts of the world.)

210. CORNISH-BOWDEN, ALTHEA. *The Sequential Development of Ideas Regarding the Intellectual Growth of Young Children: A Review of Representative Contributions from Comenius to the Present Day.* Tufts University, 1957. 136 p. ms. (Czechoslovakia, Europe.)

211. CRANDALL, JESSIE RUTH. (Later Mrs. Jessie R. Rung). *The Value of Educational Missions.* Boston University, 1926. 93 p. ms. (Includes Africa, China, India, and Korea.)

212. CRUM, MORRIS CHRISTIAN, 1924- . *United States Air Force Dependent Schools in Europe.* Colorado College, 1957. 53 p. ms. (Study of 17,534 students in Algeria, Canada, Denmark, France, Germany, Great Britain, Greece, Greenland, Iceland, Italy, Libya, Morocco, Netherlands, Norway, Saudi Arabia, Spain, and Turkey.)

213. DABROW, DAVID B., 1904- . *Historical Survey of Health Education.* Temple University, 1932. 146 p. ms. (Includes Belgium, Canada, China, Germany, Japan, Netherlands, USSR, and Union of South Africa.)

214. DANKERS, MARION E. *A Study of the Development of Inter-American Understanding: An Educational Challenge.* Claremont Graduate School, 1943. 94 p. ms. (North America, South America.)

215. DAVIS, VIVIAN LUCILLE, 1915- . *A Survey of Elementary Teaching Opportunities Outside the Continental United States.* University of North Dakota, 1956. 119 p. ms. Abstract in University of North Dakota: *Abstracts of Doctoral Dissertations and Masters' Theses . . . 1956,* p. 41-42. (Covers Arabia, Brazil, Colombia, Costa Rica, Ecuador, El Salvador, Guatemala, Nicaragua, West Africa, and territories and dependencies of the United States.)

216. DEADY, Rev. CARROLL MATTHEW. *An Historical Study of the Boy Scout Movement in England and United States.* Catholic University of America, 1928. 43 p. ms. (Includes educational aspects, with beginnings in India and South Africa.)

217. DELK, ROBERT CAMERON, 1920- . *The History and Influence of American Education in the Near East, 1823-1914.* Clark University, 1943. 271 p. ms. Abstract in Clark University: *Abstracts of Dissertation and Theses,* 1943, p. 64-66. (Includes Albania, Bulgaria, Egypt, Greece, Iraq, Israel, Syria, Turkey, and Yugoslavia. Separate chapters devoted to Constantinople Women's College, American University of Beirut, and Robert College.)

218. DEVLIN, Sister MARY RUTH. *The Inefficiency of Moral Education Without a Religious Basis.* The Teachers College (later the Catholic Sisters College) of the Catholic University of America, 1913. 53 p. ms. (Contains chapters on the problem in France, Germany, Great Britain, and Japan.)

219. DIVINE, JOHN WESLIE. *The History and Development of Wrestling in Our Educational System.* Oklahoma Agricultural and Mechanical College, 1937. 82 p. ms. (Traces development in Great Britain, Greece, Japan, and United States.)

220. DWYER, Sister MARY DAVIDE. *Historical Survey of the Jocist Inquiry Method as Exemplified in the Young Christian Students Movement in the United States.* Catholic University of America, 1955. 73 p. ms. (Includes Belgium, Canada, Costa Rica, and France.)

221. ENOS, LOUIS JOHN. *A Comparative Study of Educational Theory, Ancient and Modern.* Stanford University, 1936. 135 p. ms. (Includes China, Egypt, France, Greece, India, Israel, and Italy.)

222. FARRELL, ROBERT FRANCIS. *Apprenticeship Education in Medieval Europe and the United States.* Stanford University, 1940. 186 p. ms. (Includes Egypt, France, Great Britain, Greece, Israel, and Italy.)

223. FLANAGAN, THERESA ELIZABETH. *The Adolescent Characteristics of a Selected Group of Outstanding Men in History.* University of Oklahoma, 1933. 122 p. ms. Abstract in University of Oklahoma; *Abstracts of Theses . . . 1933,* p. 90. (Includes Simon Bolivar, Napoleon Bonaparte, and eight Americans; France, Bolivia.)

224. FLORES, DIEGO. *Las Ideas Educativas de Eugenio Maria de Hostos.* New York University, 1938. 53 p. ms. (Includes Chile, Dominican Republic, Puerto Rico, and Venezuela.)

225. FOLSOM, MORRILL GABRIEL. *Cultural Interrelations of India, Japan, and the West.* University of Denver, 1947. 97 p. ms. (Europe, North America.)

226. FOSTER, MARY NAOMI. *Postage Stamps as a Tool for the Religious Educator.* Hartford School of Religious Education, 1941. 125 p. ms. (Includes Aden, Abyssinia, Ethiopia, Afghanistan, Algeria, Argentina, Armenia, Austria, Belgium, Bolivia, Brazil, Bulgaria, Canada, Ceylon, China, Colombia, Congo, Costa Rica, Crete, Cuba, Cyprus, Czechoslovakia, Denmark, Dominican Republic, El Salvador, Ecuador, Egypt, Eritrea, Estonia, Finland, France, French Morocco, Great Britain, Greece, Guatemala, Haiti, Honduras, Hungary, Iceland, India, Indo-China, Indonesia, Iraq, Ireland, Italian East Africa, Italian Somaliland, Jamaica, Japan, Latvia, Lebanon, Libya, Lithuania, Malta, Mexico, Monaco, Morocco, Netherlands, New Zealand, Nicaragua, Nigeria, Norway, Palestine, Panama, Paraguay, Persia (Iran), Peru, Philippines, Poland, Portugal, Roumania, Russia, Siam, Spain, Straits Settlements, Sweden, Switzerland, Syria, Transjordan, Tunisia, Turkey, Union of South Africa, Uruguay, and Virgin Islands.)

227. FRANZ, ROBERT CARL. *A Study of the Health Problems of Latin America.* University of Southern California, 1950. 108 p. ms. (North America, South America.)

228. FRENZKEM, LUCILLE ELEANOR. *The Development of the Literacy Movement under Frank Laubach and Its Contribution to World Missions.* Biblical Seminary in New York, 1952. 101 p. ms. (Includes India, Philippines, Southern Asia, East Africa, and Latin America.)

229. GERATY, THOMAS SINCLAIR, 1914- . *A Comparative Investigation of the Mid-Century Status of Educational Ladders in the Middle East.* University of Southern California, 1957. 121 p. ms. (Includes Egypt, Iran, Iraq, Israel, Jordan, Lebanon, Syria, and Turkey). For doctoral dissertation by same author, see No. 1298.

230. GLATSTEIN, HARRY, 1894- . *Historical Survey of the Curriculum of the Jewish School.* Temple University, 1932. 31 p. ms. (Includes Germany, Greece, Iraq, Israel, Poland, Spain, and USSR.)

231. GOEDERTIER, JOSEPH M. *"The Relations between Dutch Learning and Confucianism and the Policy of the Bakafu toward Dutch Learning." Translated from the Japanese and Annotated.* Columbia University, 1950. 85 p. ms. (China, Japan, the Netherlands.)

232. GOSEN, Sister MARY DE SALES. *Faith and Understanding in the Religious Instruction Methods of the Fathers of the Church.* Catholic University of America, 1950. 56 p. ms. Abstract in *Catholic Educational Review,* Vol. 49, p. 194, March 1951. (Studies methods of three doctors of the Western church in Europe, and three of the Eastern church in Asia.)

233. GOTTSHALL, NEWTON TENNIS. *A Comparative Analysis of the Specified Literature of Mohammedanism, Buddhism, and Christianity with a View to Discovering the Common Elements upon Which a Program of Moral and Religious Education for a Mission School Enrolling Pupils from These Faiths Could Be Based.* Northwestern University, 1930. 149 p. ms. (Africa, Asia, Europe.)

234. HAGUE, DONALD WOOD. *Arts and Crafts of Egypt and Babylonia.* International YMCA College, 1932. 144 p. ms.

235. HARTZ, ANNA. *A Comparative Study of Home Economics Education in the English-Speaking Countries.* University of Southern California, 1933. 156 p. ms. (Includes Australia, Canada, Great Britain, Ireland, New Zealand, and South Africa.)

236. HAWKINS, EFFIE IZAH. *Recent Progress in Educational Reorganization in Selected World States.* Stanford University, 1923. 107 p. ms. (Includes China, Germany, Great Britain, Mexico, Peru, Uruguay, and USSR.)

237. HAZARD, ELIZABETH JANE, 1927- . *Education in Latin America: A Cultural and Historical Survey.* Cornell University, 1956. 124 p. ms. (Covers 20 republics of North and South America in a "broad" way.)

238. HEFFERNEN, Rev. ARTHUR JAMES. *An Evaluation of Ancient Educational Ideals.* Catholic

University of America, 1934. 43 p. ms. (Six chapters: (1) China and Japan; (2) India and Persia; (3) Egypt; (4) Babylonia, Assyria, Phoenicia, and Palestine; (5) Greece; (6) Rome.)

239. HELTIBRIDLE, MARY ELLEN, 1904- . *The Educational Possibilities of Dolls.* George Washington University, 1943. 91 p. ms. (Describes Japanese, Chinese, Korean, Indian, Javanese, Puerto Rican, Mexican, African, German, Italian, French, English, and American dolls and shows their educational possibilities.)

240. HENSEL, JOAN ELIZABETH, 1917- . *Inter-American Intellectual Cooperation.* Clark University, 1940. 194 p. ms. Abstract in Clark University: *Abstracts of Dissertations and Theses,* 1940, p. 89-91. (North America, South America.)

241. HESS, LELAH CHRISTINA. *Intellectual Cooperation between the United States and Latin America.* Ohio State University, 1938. 94 p. ms. (North America, South America.)

242. HOLDEN, GLADYS KEEN. *An Approach to a Problem of Initiating a Home Life Education Program among Rural Peoples in Latin-American Countries.* Texas Technological College, 1949. 90 p. ms. (Includes a lengthy chapter giving detailed description of the program in Bolivia. Other countries of North and South America considered more briefly.)

243. HOLMES, KENNETH LLOYD. *Religious Education in the Second Century.* Berkeley Baptist Divinity School, 1945. 52 p. ms. (Includes Assyria, Babylonia, Egypt, and Persia.)

244. HUME, MAUDE McPHERSON. *A Comparative Study of the Education of Women Prior to the Christian Era.* University of Southern California, 1931. 90 p. ms. (Covers Babylon, China, Egypt, Greece, Rome, and Palestine.)

245. HUTTENHAUER, HELEN GRAHAM, 1900- *Utopian Conceptions of Education as a Social Force.* Johns Hopkins University, 1936. (Considers Plato from Greece; More, Bacon, Harrington, Bulwer-Lytton, Butler, and Morris from Great Britain; Campanella from Italy; and Bellamy and Howells from United States.)

246. IM, YOUNG BIN, 1901- . *A Comparative Study of the Teachings of Jesus and Confucius.* Southern Methodist University, 1932. 68 p. ms. (Israel, China.)

247. JOHNSON, JAMES CURTIS. *Native Education in the Territories under the British Mandate.* University of Texas, 1930. 316 p. ms. (Includes Cameroons, Iraq, Israel, Jordan, Nauru, New Guinea, Tanganyika, Togoland, and Western Samoa.)

248. JONES, KATY MAE, 1905- . *Educational Activities of the Ancient and Medieval Periods.* Southern Methodist University, 1946. 165 p. ms. Abstract in Southern Methodist University: *Abstracts of Theses,* No. 12, 1946, 1947, p. 23. (Includes Egypt, Greece, Rome, the Saracens, and Europe in general.)

249. JONES, LENORE CULP. *Home Economics Outside the United States.* Oklahoma Agricultural and Mechanical College, 1937. 32 p. ms. (Includes Belgium, Canada, Czechoslovakia, Denmark, Finland, France, Germany, Great Britain, Ireland, Israel, Lithuania, Netherlands, Norway, Poland, Roumania, and Switzerland.)

250. KANE, Mrs. JULIA ISENSEE. *The Present Status in Laws and Practices in the Education of Women.* University of Arizona, 1930. 92 p. ms. (Includes China, Great Britain, India, Italy, Japan, Spain, and USSR.)

251. KEANEY, LUCY E., 1913- . (Mother Marie Fidelma) *The Educational Philosophy of the Religious of the Sacred Heart of Mary.* St. John's University, 1950. 69 p. ms. Abstract in St. John's University: *Abstracts of Dissertations, 1949-1950,* p. 50. (Founded in France. Includes "extent and nature of the Congregation's work throughout the two hemispheres." See also No. 290.)

252. KEE, LILLIAN SULLIVAN. *Latin-American Music: A Compendium of Bibliographical Aids for Teachers.* North Texas State Teachers College, 1944. 139 p. ms. (North America, South America.)

253. KELLY, DOROTHY KEATS BROWNING, 1919- . *The Major Trends in Latin-American Education from 1900 to the Present Time, with Special Emphasis on Elementary Education in Four Selected Republics.* University of Florida, 1945. 94 p. ms. (Includes Argentina, Costa Rica, Mexico, and Uruguay.)

254. KIEFER, OMER H. *Christ's Method of Teaching as Found in the Gospels, and the Socratic Method.* Catholic University of America, 1943. 47 p. ms. (Israel, Greece.)

255. LEAF, CURTIS TATE. *A Study of Representative History and Geography Textbooks Used in English-Speaking Countries Bordering on the Pacific.* University of Hawaii, 1927. 135 p. ms. (Includes Australia, Canada, and New Zealand.)

256. LINDEMAN, CARL V. *The Rise of Latin-American Trade Schools.* Iowa State College of Agriculture and Mechanic Arts, 1925. 141 p. ms. (Includes schools in Argentina, Bolivia, Brazil, Chile, Colombia, Cuba, Honduras, Mexico, Nicaragua, Panama, and Peru.)

257. LLOYD, EDITH, 1896- . (Later Mrs. Edith F. Malleis.) *A Survey of the Training and Certification of High School Commercial Teachers in the United States, Its Territories, and Dependencies.* Municipal University of Wichita, 1935. 121 p. ms. (Includes Philippines, Puerto Rico, and Virgin Islands.)

258. LUDDY, Sister MARY ANSELM. *Comparison between the Munich Method as Found in the Schorsch Religious Books and the Methods of Christ.* Catholic University of America, 1952. 48 p. ms. (Germany, Israel.)

259. McCLATCHY, VIVIENNE ROBINSON. *The Beginnings of Education.* University of Texas, 1920. 104 p. ms. (Discusses primitive education among such groups as American Indians, Polynesians, and Africans. One chapter on Chinese education.)

260. McCORKLE, FRANCES MARY. *Problems and Trends in Latin-American Education.* Southern Methodist University, 1946. 69 p. ms. Abstract in Southern Methodist University: *Abstracts of Theses,* No. 12, 1946, 1947, p. 29. (Includes Argentina, Bolivia, Brazil, Chile, Colombia, Costa Rica, Cuba, Dominican Republic, Ecuador, El Salvador, Guatemala, Haiti, Honduras, Mexico, Nicaragua, Panama, Paraguay, Uruguay, and Venezuela.)

261. McGRATH, ELLEN MARIE, 1908- . *Why International Organization for Education?* Boston University, 1949. 142 p. ms. (Concerned chiefly with UNESCO but considers also work of Comenius in Czechoslovakia, Julien in France, and general education in Germany before and after World War I.)

262. McMURRAY, HELEN B. *The Development of the Concept of Individual Differences in the Culture Patterns of the Ancient Civilizations of Babylonia, Egypt, Greece, and Rome.* Catholic University of America, 1955. 40 p. ms. Abstract in *Catholic Educational Review,* Vol. 54, p. 405, September 1956.

263. McMURTRY, ANNA. *History of Mathematics as Applied to the Teaching of Arithmetic, Algebra, and Geometry.* Columbia University, 1935. 28 p. ms. (Considers especially China, Egypt, Greece, and India.)

264. MAFRIGE, XENIA. *A Comparative Study of Non-Academic Education in England and Germany for a Proposed New System in Lebanon.* Columbia University, 1932. 64 p. ms.

265. MANSON, Rev. ALEXANDER MacLEOD. *The Work of the Protestant Churches for the Deaf in North America, 1815-1949.* Gallaudet College, 1949. Published in four installments in *American Annals of the Deaf,* Vol. 95, p. 265-279, May 1950; p. 387-433, September 1950; p. 461-485, November 1950; Vol. 96, p. 363-381, May 1951. (Considers also work of French and German schools for the deaf, and work in Canada, especially in the maritime provinces, under the United Church of Canada.)

266. MARSH, ISABEL THOMPSON. *The Inter-Relationship between Man's Political, Philosophical, and Religious Concepts and His Educational Theories and Practices.* University of Denver, 1933. 146 p. ms. (Includes Greece, Italy, and Europe during the Middle Ages.)

267. MASTER, ITHIEL VIRJIBHAI. *A Comparative Study of the Methodist Church in Gujarat, India, and the Church at Corinth.* Southwestern University, 1953. 123 p. ms. (India, Greece. Includes education.)

268. MEYERING, HARRY RALPH. *A Preliminary Study of Organization in American Board Schools.* University of Michigan, 1934. 80 p. ms. (Covers schools under auspices of the American Board of Commissioners for Foreign Missions as follows: China, 13; India, 11; Turkey, 5; Africa, 3; Ceylon, 3; Japan, 3; Mexico, 3; Greece, 3; Syria, 2. Special consideration of 7 schools in the Near East.)

269. MIMS, NELL RUTH. *Home Economics Development in Alaska, Hawaii, Puerto Rico, and the Philippines.* George Peabody College for Teachers, 1930. 63 p. ms.

270. MOSES, JASPAR TURNEY. *A Survey of Evangelical Education in Latin America.* University of Chicago, 1915. 63 p. ms. (Includes Cuba, Dominican Republic, Haiti, Mexico, Puerto Rico, Central America, and South America.)

271. OBER, ELSIE T. *Certain Art Cultures in Relation to Time, Race, and Space.* Columbia University, 1941. 74 p. ms. (Includes Aztecs, Eskimos, Florentines, and Gandas of the Congo.)

272. OCHSE, GEORGE HENRY, 1903- . *Nationality and Race Differences as Revealed through Objective Studies.* Temple University, 1937. 124 p. ms. (Covers Argentina, China; and Chinese, Japanese, Italians, and Mexicans in United States.)

273. OGDEN, RACHEL COUSINS. *Children's Literature Produced in Spanish America.* Columbia University, 1930. 54 p. ms. (Includes Argentina, Chile, Colombia, Cuba, and Mexico.)

274. PALEY, DIANE EVE, 1931- . *Comparative Survey of Philosophies and Psychology of Art Curriculums in the Elementary Schools of Various Countries.* Brooklyn College, 1956. 68 p. ms. (Includes Austria, Belgium, Czechoslovakia, Denmark, Finland, France, Germany, Great Britain, Japan, Netherlands, Norway, Spain, Sweden, Switzerland, and the USSR.)

275. PALMER, CLAIRE W. *Education among Primitive Peoples.* Colorado State Teachers College, 1933. 82 p. ms. (Includes Africa, Argentina, Australia, Caroline Islands, Ceylon, India, Indonesia, Malaya, Melanesia, Micronesia, New Guinea, Philippines, and South America.)

276. PEMBERTON, JAMES S., Sr. *Education in the Middle East.* Brown University, 1958. 150 p. ms. (Africa, Asia.)

277. PHILLEO, HELEN ISABELLE. *The Work of the Fourth, Fifth, Sixth, and Seventh Pan-American Conferences in the Economic, Social, and Intellectual Fields.* University of Wisconsin, 1938. 245 p. ms. (North America, South America.)

278. PYKE, LOUISE TAFT. *A Study of World Literacy in Its Relation to the Christian Movement: With Particular Emphasis on the Work of Y. C. James Yen and Frank C. Laubach.* Drew University, 1945. 102 p. ms. (China, Philippines.)

279. RAEPPEL, JOSEPHINE EUGENIA. *History of Libraries before the Invention of Printing.* New York University, 1937. 66 p. ms. (Includes Assyria-Babylonia (Iraq), China, Egypt, Greece, and Italy.)

280. RANDALL, DAISY FERDINA. *A Critical Analysis of the Youth Movement in the United States and in Certain Foreign Countries.* University of Southern California, 1940. 132 p. ms. (Includes China, Germany, Italy, and USSR.)

281. REDICK, JOSEPH PIERCE. *French Literature and the Literary Theories of Domingo Faustino Sarmiento.* University of Colorado, 1939. 92 p. ms. Abstract in *University of Colorado Studies,* Vol. 26, No. 2, p. 109, November 1939. (Shows that Sarmiento, representing especially Argentina and Chile, thought it necessary for the South American countries to accept

literary, political, and educational ideas from abroad, particularly from France.)

282. RULAND, DOROTHY ROBERTA. *A Survey of the Objectives and Procedures of the Music Education Programs in Fifty-Six Countries.* Ohio University, 1958. (Names of countries not available.)

283. SHUTLER, *Sister* MIRIA. *An Investigation of State Aid for Catholic Schools in Selected Countries Outside the United States.* St. John College of Cleveland, 1952. 102 p. ms. (Includes Australia, Brazil, Canada, Great Britain, Ireland, and the Netherlands.)

284. SIMMS, EDWARD PAUL, 1901- . *The Education of Saint Augustine.* Boston University, 1931. 89 p. ms. (Discusses the general characteristics of Roman education and the school experiences of Augustine in the elementary schools of Thagaste and Madaura, in present Algeria, and in the Rhetorical school of Carthage in present Tunisia.)

285. SOUDAH, PETER E. *The Work of Western Education in the Near East.* University of Michigan, 1933. (Africa, Asia.)

286. SPENCER, HOWARD N. *Contributions to Education from the World's Great Utopias.* Colorado State Teachers College, 1927. 114 p. ms. (Includes Saint Augustine from modern Algeria; More, Bacon, Harrington, Morris, and Wells from Great Britain; Plato from Greece; Campanella from Italy; and Bellamy from United States.)

287. SPRATT, MIRIAM CLARE. *The Uses of Rhythm in Education: Primitive and Modern.* University of Texas, 1941. 192 p. ms. (Many primitive groups mentioned, with special emphasis on North American Indians and African tribes.)

288. STEERE, JULIA. *The Woman Athlete: A Chronological Account of the Women in Athletic Sports from the Days of Ancient Egypt to 1900.* Colorado State College of Education, 1928. 131 p. ms. (Includes Belgium, Egypt, France, Great Britain, Iran, Iraq, Israel, Italy, Spain, and Syria.)

289. STEPHENS, MARY AGNES. *A Comparative Study of State Aid to Catholic Institutions in the United States and Selected Countries.* St. John College of Cleveland, 1953. 36 p. ms. (Selected countries were Canada, Great Britain, and the Netherlands.)

290. STEWART, *Mother* MARY VIANNEY, 1922- . (Secular name: Katherine P. Stewart) *A Brief History of the Religious of the Sacred Heart of Mary in the United States.* St. John's University, 1955. Abstract in St. John's University: *Abstracts of Dissertations, 1953-1956,* p. 245-246. (Includes founding of the Congregation in France and extension to Great Britain, Ireland, Italy, Portugal, Spain, Africa, North America, and South America.)

291. STORCH, *Sister* MARY FERDINAND. *A Comparison of the Teaching Methods of Christ and Socrates.* University of Notre Dame, 1931. 73 p. ms. (Israel, Greece.)

292. STREGE, ARTHUR H. *A History of Missouri Synod Work among the Japanese.* Concordia Seminary, 1952. (Includes educational work among Japanese in the United States, in China, and in other parts of the world. Thesis for degree of Bachelor of Divinity.)

293. STUECKLER, PAUL. *A Study of Schools Maintained Abroad by American Companies.* Texas Western College, 1954. 113 p. ms. (Includes schools in Aruba, Chile, Colombia, Cuba, Ecuador, Honduras, Peru, and Venezuela.)

294. TUOHY, JOHN W. *The "De Magistro" of St. Augustine and the "De Magistro" of St. Thomas Aquinas Compared.* Catholic University of America, 1937. 39 p. ms. (Algeria, France, Italy.)

295. TYER, MONA CROSS. *A Study of Children's Song Literature of Latin America, Including a Collection of Songs from the Countries of South America and Mexico: Also a Survey of the Cultural Background of These Countries.* Colorado State College of Education, 1942. 151 p. ms. (Includes Argentina, Brazil, Chile, Colombia, Ecuador, Mexico, Paraguay, Peru, Uruguay, and Venezuela.)

296. UNGER, SIDNEY EMANUEL. *Characteristics of Child Education as Reflected in the Educational Philosophy of Outstanding Periods — Ancient, Medieval, and Modern.* Temple University, 1939. 264+26 p. ms. (Includes Greece, Israel, Italy.)

297. VELASCO, MARIA DEL CARMEN. *La Cancion Folklorica Infantil el Mundo Espanol.* Texas State College for Women, 1951. 108 p. ms. (North America, South America.)

298. VLASSIS, GEORGE DEMETRIOS. *A Comparative Study of Secondary Education in the United States, Canada, and Greece: Administration and Curriculum.* University of Wisconsin, 1932. 62 p. ms.

299. VON WINNING, HASSO LEOPOLD. *Pre-Columbian Education among the Aztecs, Mayas, and Incas.* University of Southern California, 1954. 150 p. ms. (Mexico, Peru)

300. WALDMAN, MARK, 1873- . *The Influence of Graeco-Roman Schools on Koheleth or the Book of Ecclesiastes.* Columbia University, 1902. 56 p. ms. (Greece, Israel, Italy.) For doctoral dissertation by same author, see No. 2232.

301. WARREN, MARGARET WILSON. *Plays and Games of Other Nations and Races.* George Peabody College for Teachers, 1928. 138 p. ms. (Chapters are arranged by countries, including Greece and Rome, North America, South America, Mexico, Great Britain, Italy, Denmark, Turkey, Iran, Israel, China, India, Japan, Other Asiatic Countries, Africa, Borneo, and Philippines.)

302. WEBER, MADELYN ANNE. *The Relation of Government to Public and Private Education in Holland, Scotland, and Canada.* University of Detroit, 1954. 113 p. ms.

303. WELLONS, RALPH DILLINGHAM, 1891- . *The Control of Protestant Foreign Mission Colleges.* Indiana University, 1924. 106 p. ms. (Includes colleges in Ceylon, China, India, Japan, Korea, Philippines, and Turkey.) For doctoral dissertation by same author, see No. 182.

304. WENTWORTH, EVA. *Three Advanced Educational Reformers.* University of Southern California, 1931. 55 p. ms. (Covers Dewey in the United States, Sanderson in Great Britain, and Tagore in India.)

305. WILSON, BETTY ANN. *The Effect of Visual Auditory Stimulation on the Pronunciation Errors Made by Latin-American Teachers of English.* Indiana University, 1948. 112 p. ms. (North America, South America.)

306. WINSTON, MILDRED E. *The Development of the Culture of the Inter-Testament Period: A Study in the Background of the First Christian Century.* New York University, 1928. 55 p. ms. (Includes Egypt, Greece, Iran, Israel, Italy, and Syria.)

307. WULFECK, DOROTHY FORD. *A Survey of Commercial Education in Latin American Colleges and Universities.* Vanderbilt University, 1927. 131 p. ms. (Includes from one to 11 institutions each in Argentina, Bolivia, Brazil, Chile, Colombia, Costa Rica, Cuba, Dominican Republic, Ecuador, El Salvador, Guatemala, Honduras, Mexico, Nicaragua, Panama, Paraguay, Peru, Puerto Rico, Uruguay, and Venezuela.)

308. ZACOFSKY, WALTER J., 1916- . *A Cultural Study of Certain Basic Health Concepts of Selected Primitive Societies.* Boston University, 1951. 114 p. ms. (Studies many factors, including Education and Child Development and shows their significance for health education. Based on 36 primitive societies, including ones in Arabia, Assam, Australia, Burma, Canada (Eskimo), Ceylon, Colombia, Egypt, Formosa, India, Indo-China, Indonesia, Iraq, Israel, Japan, Madagascar, New Guinea, New Zealand, Pacific Islands, Panama, Philippines, Sudan, Syria, Turkey, USSR (Siberia), and Venezuela.)

AFRICA
(NOS. 309 – 526)
General
(NOS. 309 – 320)

DOCTORS

309. CARPENTER, GEORGE WAYLAND. *Church, State, and Society in Central Africa: Some Sociological Concomitants of Government and Missionary Policy in Central Africa, with Special Reference to Education.* Yale University, 1937. 308 p. ms.

310. RETIEF, MALCOLM WILHEIM. *A Program of Religious Education in Africa.* Southern Baptist Theological Seminary, 1930. 235 p. ms. (Considers all of Africa except extreme Northern and Southern coasts.)

See also Nos. 121, 130, 134, 137, 146, 162, 179, 183.

MASTERS

311. BICAISE, BANDELE ADELINE. *Needs of West African Families in Home and Family Life Education as a Basis for Curriculum Revision.* Pennsylvania State University, 1955. 56 p. ms.

312. BOOTH, Mrs. ESMA RIDEOUT. *Teaching the Bantu Child.* Kennedy School of Missions, 1936. 96 p. ms.

313. CLAAR, PHILIP D. *The Challenge of Literacy and Communism in French-Speaking Africa: A Plan of Action for Evangelicals.* Wheaton College, 1957. (Thesis for degree of Bachelor of Divinity.)

314. DAVIES, EVERETT SAMUEL, 1900- . *A Curriculum of Christian Religious Education for West Africa.* Yale University, 1930. 158 p. ms.

315. HARTZLER, OMAR LEE. *African Tribal Religious Education: A Study of the Way the Africans Teach Religion to Their Children.* Kennedy School of Missions, 1945. 402 p. ms.

316. LEASURE, Mrs. NETTIE NORRIS, 1893- . *Educational Adaptations to African Conditions.* Columbia University, 1934. 86 p. ms. For doctoral dissertation by same author, see No. 344.

317. MARSH, JOHN SAWYER, 1898- . *Bantu Initiation Rites.* Yale University, 1926. 160 p. ms.

318. OECHSNER DE CONINCK, EDOUARD GEORGAS: *The Use of Bantu Puberty Rites in Christian Education.* Union Theological Seminary, 1932. 82 p. ms. (East and South Africa.)

319. PARHAM, CATHERINE. *Christian Education for the Central African Community.* Hartford School of Religious Education, 1944. 130 p. ms.

320. ROSS, RUTH. *A Survey of Christian Missionary Activity in North Africa.* Columbia Bible College, 1958. (Includes education.)

See also Nos. 186, 193, 211, 215, 226, 228, 333, 239, 251, 259, 268, 275, 276, 285, 287, 290, 301, 330.

Composite
(NOS. 321 – 330)

DOCTORS

321. BETZ, ELIZABETH ANNE, 1916- . *Changing Methods of Social Control: A Study of Transitions in Techniques of Dealing with Youthful Deviancy in Selected Areas of West Africa.* New York University, 1956. (Covers Gold Coast, now Ghana, and Nigeria.)

322. DE MARCO, ROLAND REINALD, 1910- . *The Italianization of African Natives: Government Native Education in the Italian Colonies, 1890-1937.* Columbia University, 1942. New York: Teachers College, Columbia University, 1943. xvii, 150 p. (Teachers College Contribution to Education, No. 880. Covers Eritrea, Ethiopia, Libya, and Somaliland.)

323. KESSLER, JANE SARGENT. *Educating the Black Frenchman.* Harvard University, 1958. 243 p. ms. (Covers French West Africa, especially Dakar and Senegal.)

MASTERS

324. ALFORD, ROMEO JAMES. *Education in British West Africa: A Comparative Study.* University of Detroit, 1954. 72 p. ms. (Includes Gambia, Ghana, Nigeria, and Sierra Leone.)

325. CULVER, MAURICE EDWIN. *The Training of an African Christian Ministry in Relation to Certain Modern Forces Affecting African Life.* Kennedy School of Missions, 1944. 260 p. ms. (Includes Belgian Congo, Rhodesia, and South Africa.)

326. GAYLORD, MARY LOEW. *A Manual for Teaching the Fundamentals of Addition with Problems Adapted to the Social and Economic Life of Urundi, Uganda, and Kenya Colony.* University of Michigan, 1945.

327. GHORMLEY, NEWTON BAXTER. *The Genius of the Bantu: A Study of the Bantu Tribes in*

Africa. University of Southern California, 1918. Published as *The Land of the Heart of Livingstone; or, The Genius of the Bantu.* Published by author, 1920. 176 pp. Available from Woman's Foreign Missionary Society of Free Methodist Church, 1134 Washington Blvd., Chicago, Illinois. (Covers tribes in 38 geographical locations, including Angola, Belgian Congo, Cameroons, Gabun, German East Africa, Kenya, Natal, Portuguese East Africa, Spanish Guinea, Tanganyika, Uganda, Union of South Africa, and Zanzibar. Includes education.)

328. LA RUSSO, WILLIAM ANTHONY, 1931- . *Education in British East Africa: Kenya, Northern Rhodesia, Nyasaland.* New Jersey State College, Newark, 1958. 62 p. ms.

329. NELSON, NORMA KIRSCHSTEIN, 1906- . *Folklore of Western Africa.* New Jersey State Teachers College, Newark, 1957. 37 p. ms. (Covers Liberia and Nigeria.)

330. SHEA, EMMETT A., 1930- . *A Study of Educational Development in British Colonial Africa.* Boston University, 1956. 36 p. ms. (Includes British East Africa, British Central Africa, British West Africa, Gold Coast (Ghana), Nigeria, and Sierra Leone.)

Algeria
(NOS. 331 – 337)

DOCTOR

331. McCREADY, ROBERT H., -1929. *Augustine's Psychology.* New York University, 1893. 39 p. ms.

See also No. 147.

MASTERS

332. BARROWS, MARION, 1897- . *The Psychology of St. Augustine as Applied to Education.* New York State College for Teachers, Albany, 1923. 81 p. ms.

333. FELLENBAUM, Mrs. EDITH (HOLLINGER), 1898- . *Augustine Concerning Education.* Johns Hopkins University, 1957. 48 p. ms.

334. O'MEARA, Rev. DANIEL CHRISTOPHER. *Educational Aspects of St. Augustine's Life and Works.* Catholic University of America, 1921. 67 p. ms.

335. O'NEIL, ARTHUR J. *Evidences of Principles of Religious Guidance in the Possible Pertinent Works of St. Augustine.* Catholic University of America, 1944.

336. RONGIONE, Rev. LOUIS A. *St. Augustine's Pedagogical Principles on the Teaching of Religion as Presented in His "De Catechizandis Rudibus."* Catholic University of America, 1940. 72 p. ms.

337. SYNAN, Sister MARY BERNADETTE. *The Significance of St. Augustine's "De Magistro" for the Catholic Teacher.* Catholic Sisters College of the Catholic University of America, 1926. 27 p. ms.

See also Nos. 189, 203, 212, 226, 284, 286, 294.

Angola
(NOS. 338 – 341)

DOCTORS

338. BOOTH, Bishop NEWELL SNOW, 1903- . *Teaching a Bantu Community.* Kennedy School of Missions, 1936. 283 p. ms. (Refers to Angola.)

339. CHILDS, GLADWYN MURRAY, 1896- . *Umbundu Kinship and Character: Being a Description of the Social Structure and Individual Development of the Ovimbunda of Angola, with Observations Concerning the Bearing on the Enterprise of Christian Missions of Certain Phases of the Life and Culture Described.* Columbia University, 1950. London, New York, Toronto: Published for the International African Institute by Oxford University Press, and Witwatersrand University Press, 1949. xviii, 163 p.

MASTERS

340. McDOWELL, BESSIE CHERRY FONVIELLE. *Educational and Recreational Features of Umbundu Culture.* Kennedy School of Missions, 1931. 115 p. ms.

341. MALCOLM, FLORENCE CHRISTIAN. *Education of the Ovimbundu – Tribal, Formal, and Christian.* Kennedy School of Missions, 1934. 83 p. ms. (Ovimbundu inhabited Central Africa and Central Angola.)

See also No. 327.

Belgian Congo
(NOS. 342 – 356)

DOCTORS

342. BARDEN, JOHN GLENN, 1900- . *A Suggested Program of Teacher Training for Mission Schools Among the Batetela.* Columbia University, 1941. New York: Bureau of Publications, Teachers College, Columbia University, 1941. xi, 181 p. (Teachers College Contribution to Education, No. 853.)

343. DODSON, JAMES RICHARD, 1924- . *Some Proposals for the Development of the Educational Program of a Theological School in the Belgian Cango.* Union Theological Seminary, 1958; Columbia University, 1958. 233 p. ms. For Bachelor of Divinity thesis by same author, see No. 348.

344. LEASURE, Mrs. NETTIE NORRIS, 1893- . *Education for the BaKongo Village: Based Upon a Sociological Study of BaKongo Life.* Columbia University, 1939. North Manchester, Indiana: Private printing, 1939. xix, 241 p. With a Foreword by Mabel Carney. ("Limited to that portion of the Congo known as the BasCongo near the mouth of the Congo River.") For master's thesis by same author, see No. 316.

345. WOOD, LELAND FOSTER, 1885- . *Bobangi Life and Christian Education.* University of Chicago, 1923. 321 p. ms. Abstract in University of Chicago: *Abstracts of Theses, Humanistic Series,* Vol 1, 1922-23, p. 509-513.

MASTERS

346. BROWN, ARLEY R. *Baptist Educational Work in the Belgian Congo.* Berkeley Baptist Divinity School, 1951. (Thesis for degree of Bachelor of Divinity.)

347. BROWN, HENRY D. *A Suggested Program of In-Service Training for Elementary Teachers at Kimpese, Belgian Congo.* Seattle Pacific College, 1957.

348. DODSON, JAMES RICHARD, 1924- . *The Use of Loncundo Proverbs in Teaching Christianity to Congo Natives.* College of the Bible, 1950. (Thesis for degree of Bachelor of Divinity.) For doctoral dissertation by same author, see No. 343.

349. ENNS, KATHERINE M. ANN. *Problems of Adjustment of Missionaries' Children in the Central School, Belgian Congo.* Biblical Seminary in New York, 1954. 76 p. ms.

350. GUESS, BESSIE LORINE. *A Study of the Belgian Congo, with Special Interest in Christian Missions and Education.* University of Tennessee, 1954. 166 p. ms.

351. MERRILL, ALFRED FRANCIS. *A Study of Evangelistic Missionary Methods in the Belgian Congo in the Light of Some Modern Tendencies in Religious Education.* Columbia University, 1926. 66 p. ms.

352. MOON, SEYMOUR ELLSWORTH. *Educational Measurements in the Congo.* University of Minnesota, 1927. 89 p. ms. (The use of American standardized tests translated into Congo dialects and applied in mission schools.)

353. MOORE, IRA McLEES. *Teacher Education Problems of Protestant Missions in the Belgian Congo.* Furman University, 1952. 60 p. ms.

354. MOORE, LOREN ELLSWORTH, 1928- . *The Origin and Development of Christian Education in the Congo Belge.* Southern Baptist Theological Seminary, 1956. 81 p. ms.

355. STABELL, CLIFFORD CHRISTIAN. *Experimental Factors in the Adaptation of Curriculum Materials to Congo Culture.* Berkeley Baptist Divinity School, 1954. (Thesis for degree of Bachelor of Divinity.)

356. STEINER, RICHARD LEON. *An Historical Development of the Educational Program of the Congo Inland Mission in Its Belgian Congo Field.* Biblical Seminary in New York, 1957. (Thesis for degree of Bachelor of Divinity.)

See also Nos. 226, 271, 325, 326, 327

Cameroons
(NOS. 357-359)

DOCTOR

357. HORNER, NORMAN ASTE, 1913- . *Protestant and Roman Catholic Missions among the Bantus of Cameroun: A Comparative Study.* Hartford Seminary Foundation, 1955. 415 p. ms. Abstract in *Dissertation Abstracts,* Vol. 16, p. 808, April 1956. Available on microfilm from University Microfilms, Ann Arbor, Michigan, as Publication No. 16,105. (Includes education.)

See also No. 160

MASTERS

358. McGILLIARD, VIRGINIA DARE. *Concept of Experience Reading for Beginners and Its Application to the Native Children of Cameroun, North Africa.* Ohio State University, 1938. 156 p. ms. Abstract in Ohio State University: *Abstracts of Theses Presented*

by Candidates for the Master's Degree ... 1937-38, p. 68-69. (Abstracts of Masters' Degrees, No. 26.)

359. VOTAW, PAUL DEAN. *The Nevius Missionary Method and Its Application in the Cameroon Mission.* Princeton Theological Seminary, 1945. 127 p. ms.

See also Nos. 247, 327

Egypt
(NOS. 360-428)

DOCTORS

360. ABDALLA, ABDEL HAMID ELSAYED, 1920- . *Improving the Teaching of Social Studies in Egyptian Secondary Schools: Possible Adaptations of Practices in the United States.* Columbia University, 1955. 331 p. ms.

361. AFIFI, MOHAMED EL-HADI, 1923- . *An Analysis and Evaluation of Dr. William Heard Kilpatrick's Educational Theory with Special Reference to Education in Egypt.* Columbia University 1954. 277 p. ms.

362. AKHDARY, FAHEEN BOTROUS MIKHAIL ATTIA, 1909- . *A History of the Educational Emphases of the Major Religions of Egypt.* Boston University, 1955. 384 p. ms.

363. ALLAM, MOHAMED ABDEL KHALIK, 1921- . *A Recommended Health Education Program for the Preparatory Schools in Egypt.* Indiana University, 1955. 281 p. ms.

364. ASKAR, RIAD MOHAMED. *A Plan for the Education of Certain Types of Exceptional Children in Egypt.* Columbia University, 1941. 204 p. ms.

365. BAILEY, EWING MACREADY. *Problems in the Education of Teachers for Egypt with Special Reference to the American Mission.* Harvard University, 1934. 545 p. ms.

366. BASSIOUNY, MAHMOUD YOUSSEF el- , 1920- . *World Unity and Child Education with Special Reference to the Function of the Schema.* Ohio State University, 1949. 500 p. ms. Abstract in Ohio State University: *Abstracts of Dissertations* ... Autumn and Winter, 1949-50, p. 21-26. (Abstracts of Doctoral Dissertations, No. 62)

367. BLANKEMEYER, *Brother* FELIX, 1877- . *The Contribution of the Brothers of the Christian Schools to Education in Egypt.* Fordham University, 1934. 146 p. ms. Abstract in Fordham University: *Dissertations for Higher Degrees* ... 1935, p. 11.

368. BOKTOR, AMIR, 1896- . *School and Society in the Valley of the Nile.* Columbia University, 1936. Cairo: Elias Modern Press, 1936. xv, 269 p.

369. CROSE, KENNETH LAVERNE, 1915- . *Ahmad Amin and Lajnat Al-Ta'lif Wa Al-Tarjamah Wa Al-Nashr: A Study of Their Contribution to the Twentieth Century Renaissance of Egypt.* Hartford Seminary Foundation, 1955. 339 p. ms. Abstract in *Dissertation Abstracts,* Vol. 15, p. 1482, September 1955. Available on microfilm from University Microfilms, Ann Arbor, Michigan, as Publication No. 13,052.

370. el-ERIAN, MOHAMMED ALI, 1917- . *A Suggested Plan to Democratize the Educational Enterprize in Egypt.* Columbia University, 1952. 463 p. ms.

371. GALT, RUSSELL, 1889- . *The Effects of Centralization on Education in Modern Egypt.* Columbia University, 1936. Cairo: Department of Education, American University of Cairo, 1936. iii, 134 p.

372. GAUCHE, *Rev.* WILLIAM JOHN. *Didymus the Blind: An Educator of the Fourth Centruy.* Catholic University of America, 1934. Washington: Catholic University of America, 1934. 138 p. For master's thesis by same author, see No. 405.

373. HARRIS, CARL VERNON, 1922- . *Origen of Alexandria's Interpretation of the Teacher's Function in the Early Christian Hierarchy and Community.* Duke University, 1952. 277 p. ms.

374. HOWARD, C. WORTH, 1899- . *Literature in English for an American Institution in the Middle East.* New York University, 1946. 344 p. ms. (Refers to the American University at Cairo)

375. IBRAHIM, ABDELLATIF FOUAD, 1900- . *Social Studies in Egyptian Secondary Schools and the Professional Preparation of Teachers of These Studies, during the Period 1930-1947.* Columbia University, 1950. 216, 319 p. ms. Abstract in *Microfilm Abstracts* Vol. 10, No. 3, p. 68-69, 1950. Available on microfilm from University Microfilms, Ann Arbor, Michigan, as Publication No. 1,747.

376. ISTAVRIDIS, VASIL TOMA, 1925- . *Theological Education in the Alexandrian School.* Boston University, 1951. 220 p. ms.

377. KANDEEL, SAAD DIAB, 1920- . *The Democratic Concept of Supervision: Implications for Supervision in the Egyptian Public Secondary Schools.* University of Mississippi, 1956. 184 p. ms.

378. KANDIL, IBRAHIM HAMED, 1924- . *The Construction of a Tentative Physical Education Course of Study for Egyptian Secondary Schools.* Indiana Univeristy, 1954. 248 p. ms. La Crosse, Wisconsin: Northern Engraving and Manufacturing Co., 1954. 6 microcards. (Microprint copy of typescript)

379. KAZEM, MOHAMED IBRAHIM, 1928- . *Prominent Values of Egyptian and American Students as Determined by an Analysis of their Autobiographies, with Educational Implications.* University of Kansas, 1957. 187 p. ms. Abstract in *Dissertation Abstracts,* Vol. 17, p. 2187-2188, October 1957. Available on microfilm from University Microfilms, Ann Arbor, Michigan, as Publication No. 22,876.

380. KOTB, YUSEF SALAH EL-DIN, 1911- . *Science and Science Education in Egyptian Society.* Columbia University, 1951. New York: Bureau of Publications, Teachers College, Columbia University, 1951. xi, 250 p. (Teachers College Contribution to Education, No. 967)

381. LOTFI, MOHAMED KADRI, 1911- . *Changes Needed in Egyptian School Readers to Increase Their Value as Media of Instruction.* University of Chicago, 1948. 253 p. ms. Available on microfilm; see index under "University of Chicago."

382. MANSOURY, IBRAHIM MIKHAIL. *A Cooperative Farm Project for Village Education in Egypt.* Columbia University, 1942. Union Theological Seminary, 1942. 56 p. ms. For master's thesis by same author, see No. 414.

383. METAWEH, IBRAHIM ESMET, 1923- . *Improvement of Rural Teacher Education in Egypt.* University of Minnesota, 1954. 301 p. ms. Abstract in *Dissertation Abstracts,* Vol. 14, p. 2003, November 1954. Available on microfilm from University Microfilms, Ann Arbor, Michigan, as Publication No. 9,619.

384. el-NEGEHI, MOHAMED LABIB, 1923- . *Toward a Responsible Elite: A Study in Egyptian University Education.* Columbia University, 1958. 215 p. ms.

385. RADWAD, ABE AL-FUTUOH AHMED, 1910- . *Old and New Forces in Egyptian Educational Proposals for the Reconstruction of the Program of Egyptian Education in the Light of Recent Cultural Trends.* Columbia University, 1951. New York: Bureau of Publications, Teachers College, Columbia University, 1951. xiv, 192 p. (Teachers College Contributions to Education, No. 973.)

386. el-RIMAWI, QASIM MOHAMED, 1918- . *Education and the Challenge of Industrialization in Egypt.* Columbia University, 1956. 359 p. ms.

387. RIZK, RIZK GIRGIS, 1905- . *Evaluative Criteria for Academic Secondary Schools in Egypt.* University of Pennsylvania, 1956. 93 p. ms.

388. RUSSELL, CHARLES PARTRIDGE. *The Economic and Fiscal Requirements of Universal Education in the Kingdom of Egypt.* University of Chicago, 1923. 174 p. ms. Abstract in University of Chicago: *Abstracts of Theses, Humanistic Series,* Vol. 2, 1923-24, p. 115-118.

389. SALEM, MOHAMED MOKHLISS, 1907- . *The Training and Attitudes of Egyptian Biology Teachers and American Science Teachers.* Columbia University, 1951. 190 p. ms. plus 28-page appendix in Arabic.

390. SAMAAN, SADEK HALAKA, 1922- . *Egyptian Secondary Education: A Study in Philosophical Foundations.* Columbia University, 1953. Published as *Value Reconstruction and Egyptian Education: A Projection of a Cultural and Philosophical Foundation, with Reference to Secondary Schools.* New York: Bureau of Publications, Teachers College, Columbia University, 1955. 157 p. (Teachers College Studies in Education). Abstract in *Dissertation Abstracts,* Vol. 14, p. 1646-1647, October 1954. Available on microfilm from University Microfilms, Ann Arbor, Michigan, as Publication No. 8,820.

391. SAMAAN, WAHIB HILMY IBRAHIM. *Concerning Centralization in Education, with Special Reference to Egypt.* Harvard University, 1954. 379 p. ms.

392. SARHAN, EL-DEMERDASH ABDEL MEGUID, 1914- . *Interests and Culture: A Comparative Study of Interests, Concerns, Wishes, Likes, Dislikes, and Happiest Days of Egyptian and American Children.* Columbia University, 1951. New York: Bureau of Publications, Teachers College, Columbia University, 1950. x, 123 p. (Teachers College Contribution to Education, No. 959.)

393. SHALTOUT, ALI FAHIM MOHAMED, 1913- . *The Relation between Socio-Economic Status and Intelligence of Egyptian Pupils in Alexandria.* Wayne State University, 1955. 151 p. ms. Abstract in *Dissertation Abstracts,* Vol. 16, p. 286, February, 1956. Available on microfilm from University Microfilms, Ann Arbor, Michigan, as Publication No. 15,415.

394. SHEHAB, IBRAHIM KHALIL, 1923- . *Personal and Social Problems as Identified by Egyptian Adolescents.* Columbia University, 1953. 349 p. ms. Abstract in *Dissertation Abstracts,* Vol. 14, p. 1623-1624, October 1954. Available on microfilm from University Microfilms, Ann Arbor, Michigan, as Publication No. 8,830.

395. TANTAWI, AHMED MAHMOUD OSMAN, 1913- . *Upgrading the Egyptian Primary School Principalships.* Columbia University, 1950. 222 p. ms. Abstract in *Teachers College Record,* Vol. 52, p. 458, April 1951.

396. YOUSEF, MOHAMED FOUAD, 1924- . *Attitudes of the Egyptian Adolescent toward His Parents, His Peers, and Himself.* Columbia University, 1954. 130 p. ms.

397. ZAKI, ELSAYED GAMAL. *The Possible Role of Adult Education in Developing the Egyptian Rural Communities.* Indiana University, 1958. 331 p. ms. Abstract in *Dissertation Abstracts,* vol. 19, p. 1008-1009, November 1958. Available on microfilm from University Microfilms, Ann Arbor, Michigan as Mic. 58-5223. For Master's thesis by same author, see No. 428.

398. ZAKI, ELSAYED MAHMOUD, 1909- . *The Expansion of Adult Education in Egypt.* Columbia University, 1949. 177 p. ms. Abstract in *Teachers College Record,* Vol. 51, p. 380-381, March 1950.

See also Nos. 119, 120, 129, 130, 132, 138, 145, 147, 152, 153, 163, 168, 174, 174a, 180

MASTERS

399. AMIN, GHALI. *The Possible Role of Audio-Visual Materials in Egyptian Culture.* Indiana University, 1948. 226 p. ms.

400. ASFOUR, MOURAD GRANT. *The Leisure Time Activities of the Egyptian Secondary School Boys.* International YMCA College, 1939. 79 p. ms.

401. ATCHISON, ALDA BELLE. *The Study of the Development of Education in Modern Egypt.* University of Southern California, 1926. 204 p. ms.

402. ATTALLAH, FAHMY. *Education in Egypt.* University of Southern California, 1956. 126 p. ms.

403. DILLING, HULDA ADINA. *The History of the Education of Women in Egypt.* University of Chicago, 1930. 58 p. ms.

404. FAM, YACOUB, 1892- . *Character Education for Egyptian Boys.* Yale University, 1928. 161 p. ms.

405. GAUCHE, Rev. WILLIAM JOHN. *Didymus the Blind of Alexandria: An Educator of the Fourth Century.* Catholic University of America, 1932. 42 p. ms. For doctoral dissertation by same author, see No. 372.

406. GERAWI, NASSIM. *A Comparative Study of American and Egyptian Education.* University of Pittsburgh, 1925. 60 p. ms.

407. GREEN, EDITH JOSEPHINE. *A Study of Selected Areas of the Social Structures in Egypt as a Basis for Curriculum Planning in Nursing Education.* University of Washington, 1958.

408. HASSAN, NAZIRA MOHAMED, 1929- . *An Educational Program for Mentally Retarded Children in Egypt.* University of Maryland, 1958. 99 p. ms.

409. IBRAHIM, FATHIA SOLEIMAN. *A Study of Egyptian Secondary Education with Special Reference to the Preparation of Science Teachers.* Ohio State University, 1948. 106 p. ms.

410. KAMAL, MONA. *A Plan for an Audio-Visual Program to Be Carried Out in Egypt.* University of Southern California, 1955. 118 p. ms.

411. KILANI, SADIA F. *Art Education in Egypt.* Hunter College of the City of New York, 1957. 108 p. ms.

412. McELROY, PAUL S. *Egyptian Secondary Education.* Union Theological Seminary, 1931. 32 p. ms.

413. MAKARY, EL SOURIANY. *Ancient and Contemporary Education in the Coptic Church of Egypt.* Princeton Theological Seminary, 1955. 186 p. ms.

414. MANSOURY, IBRAHIM MIKHAIL. *A Settlement Project for Underprivileged Boys in Cairo.* International YMCA College, 1939. 57 p. ms. For doctoral dissertation by same author, see No. 382.

415. MIKHAIL, HILMY. *A Manual for Camping in Egypt, with an Introduction on the History and Philosophy of Modern Camping.* International YMCA College, 1941. 74 p. ms.

416. MORSI, SAYED ABDEL HAMID, 1918- . *Education and Social Guidance in the Egyptian Army.* George Washington University, 1955. 97 p. ms.

417. MOUSTAFA, MOHAMED FOUAD OMAR. *The Role of the Rural Community School in Egypt.* Ohio State University, 1957. 119 p. ms.

418. NAPIER, ALICE. *Alexandrian Mathematics of Interest to High School and College Students.* George Peabody College for Teachers, 1931. 33 p. ms.

419. NASSIM, GERGAWI. (Also listed as Gergawi, Nassim). *A Comparative Study of American and Egyptian Education.* University of Pittsburgh, 1925. 60 p. ms.

420. RIDHA, MOHAMMAD JAWAD. *Egyptian Education from English Sources, 1929-54.* University of Michigan, 1955. 105 p. ms.

421. ROSSITER, RICHARD DAVID. *Educational Theories and Principles of Clement of Alexandria, as Found in the "Paedagogus" and "Stromata."* Catholic University of America, 1947. 120 p. ms. Abstract in *Catholic Educational Review*, Vol. 46, p. 171, March 1948.

422. SABER, NEIMAT. *A Proposed Curriculum in Health, Physical Education, and Recreation for Training Men and Women Teachers in Egypt.* University of Wyoming, 1954. 39 p. ms.

423. SCHWARTZ, GROVER CLEVELAND. *The History of American Missions in Egypt.* Columbia University, 1922. 130 p. ms. (Includes education)

424. SNOW, LUCILLE JEANETTE. *Background Material for Use of Student and Teacher in the Study of Egypt, Including Bibliographies, Illustrative Material, and Creative Art Problems.* Columbia University, 1932. 41 p. ms.

425. STEARNS, VIRGINIA HARDIN. *Egyptain Education with Special Reference to Secondary Education.* University of Colorado, 1930. 93 p. ms. Abstract in *University of Colorado Studies*, Vol. 18, No. 1, p. 107-108, December 1930.

426. TAKLA, AIDA I. *An Analysis of Vocational Guidance with Implications for the Secondary Schools of Egypt.* University of California, Los Angeles, 1955. 84 p. ms.

427. THOMPSON, MARY CHRISTINE. *A Study of the Examination Systems of Egyptian Secondary Schools.* Stetson University, 1954. 71 p. ms.

428. ZAKI, ELSAYED GAMAL, 1923- . *The Possible Development of the Egyptian Community through Adult Education.* Indiana University, 1954. 130 p. ms. For doctoral dissertation by same author, see No. 397.

See also Nos. 217, 221, 222, 236, 229, 234, 238, 243, 244, 248, 262, 263, 279, 288, 306, 308

For Egyptian groups in the United States, *see* Nos. 4956, 4970, 4975, 4990

Ethiopia
(NOS. 429 – 431)

DOCTOR

429. ELLIOTT, DEAN ALEXANDER, 1922- . *Role of Agricultural Education in the Development of Agriculture in Ethiopia.* Iowa State College of Agriculture and Mechanic Arts, 1957. 394 p. ms. Abstract in *Dissertation Abstracts*, Vol. 17, p. 2903-2904, December 1957. Available on microfilm from University Microfilms, Ann Arbor, Michigan, as Publication No. 24,610.

See also No. 322

MASTERS

430. GEBRE-HIWET, MENGESHA. *A Study of Mass Literacy Programs with Special Emphasis on a Proposal for the Development of a Mass Literacy Program in Ethiopia.* Ohio State University, 1956. 84 p. ms. For doctor's dissertation by same author, see No. 3878a.

431. MURRAY, WILLIAM. *Agricultural Missions in Ethiopia.* Bethel College and Seminary, 1951. (Thesis for degree of Bachelor of Divinity.)

See also No. 226

Ghana
(NOS. 432 – 435)

DOCTORS

432. McELLIGOTT, THERESA ELIZABETH, 1907- . *Education in the Gold Coast Colony, 1920-1949.* Stanford University, 1950. 233 p. ms. Abstract in Stanford University: *Abstracts of Dissertations ...* 1949-50, p. 24-25. For master's thesis by same author, see No. 3236.

433. MORRISON, GRESHAM WYNTER. *Education for Nationhood: A Study in African National Education among the Negro Tribes of the Gold Coast.* Hartford School of Religious Education, 1923. 2 vols.

See also No. 321

MASTERS

434. ACQUAH, JOSEPH W. *A New Concept of Education for the Gold Coast, British West Africa.* Niagara University, 1951. 86 p. ms.

435. BOATENG, GEORGE AKUAMOA, 1924- . *An Analysis of the Major Efforts at Rural Development in the African Gold Coast, and Suggestions for Improving Their Effectiveness.* Cornell University, 1955. 199 p. ms.

See also Nos. 324, 330

Kenya
(NOS. 436 - 439)

MASTERS

436. HALL, JEWELL. *Attitudes of Pupils toward Teachers in Intermediate Schools in Kenya Colony, Africa.* Butler University, 1956.

437. ROGERS, FERN. *Creative Music for African Children.* University of Southern California, 1946. 257 p. ms. (Based on experience at Kavirondo school, Kenya.)

438. ROGERS, SIDNEY PHILO. *A Plan for a Course of Study among the Primitive Blacks in Africa: With Special Reference to the Kavirondo People of Kenya Colony, British East Africa.* State College of Washington, 1933. 85 p. ms.

439. STOUGHTON, Mrs. MINNIE VIRGINIA (BOOKAMER), 1914- . *Recent Trends in Teacher Education Applied to the Training of Native Teachers in Kenya Colony, British East Africa.* Indiana University, 1943. 95 p. ms.

See also Nos. 326, 327, 328, 330

Liberia
(NOS. 440 - 451)

DOCTOR

440. DALE, GILBERT RALSTON, 1893- . *The History of Education in Liberia.* University of Missouri, 1946. 452 p. ms.

See also Nos. 142, 164

MASTERS

441. BURGESS, Mrs. RUTH LONGSTAFF. *A Proposed Social Studies Book for Children of Liberia, West Africa.* Kennedy School of Missions, 1954. 135 p. ms.

442. DE GROAT, EMILY ROSE, 1895- . *Culture and Education in Liberia, West Africa.* New Jersey State Teachers College, Newark, 1955. 117 p. ms.

443. FAHNBULLEH, EDWIN OWEN, 1912- . *A Critical Appraisal of Recent Educational Programs with Special Emphasis on the Discovery of Bases for an Implementation In-Service Program in Liberia.* North Carolina College at Durham, 1955. 38 p. ms.

444. HARDING, MOTUBA ISRAEL, 1933- . *Improving Elementary School Principalships in Liberia.* Illinois State Normal University, 1957. 69 p. ms.

445. HOFF, EDWARD JULIUS, 1921- . *A Proposed Program for In-Service Teacher Education in Liberia.* Illinois State Normal University, 1957. 68 p. ms.

446. JENSEN, KNUD RASMUSSEN. *The Educational Aspect of the Lutheran Mission in Liberia.* New York University, 1927. 93 p. ms.

447. MAMULU, MOSES MAMMADI. *A Revised Program of Vocational Education for Booker T. Washington Agricultural and Industrial Institute, with Implications for Liberia.* Ohio State University, 1953. 111 p. ms. Abstract in *Research in Industrial Education, 1930-1955,* p. 66.

448. NORMAN, LAURA CECILIA, 1918- . *Criteria for Reorganization of Secondary-School Curriculum in Liberia.* Illinois State Normal University, 1957. 72 p. ms.

449. SPEARE, NEMA PUO TIDI ANNA, 1935- . *Organizing a Kindergarten Curriculum for Liberia.* Illinois State Normal University, 1958. 58 p. ms.

450. WEEFUR, MOSES KRONYANH, 1925- . *A Survey of Public School Finance in Liberia, 1826-1956.* Illinois State Normal University, 1957. 82 p. ms.

451. YANCY, MARY GERTRUDE, 1912- . *Developing a Reading Program for Liberia, Grades 1-4.* Illinois State Normal University, 1958. 71 p. ms.

See also No. 329

Nigeria
(NOS. 452 - 478)

DOCTORS

452. ADEGEBITE, JOSEPH ADEJUMOBI, 1918- . *Science Education and Developmental Tasks of Nigerian Youth: An Analysis of Some Crucial Developmental Tasks and Their Implications for the Improvement of Science Education in Nigeria.* Columbia University, 1953. 200 p. ms.

453. BITTENGER, DESMOND WRIGHT, 1905- . *An Educational Experiment in Northern Nigeria in Its Cultural Setting.* University of Pennsylvania, 1940. Published in full, Philadelphia: 1941. xvi, 343 p. Also published as *Black and White in the Sudan.* Elgin, Illinois: Brethren Publishing House, 1941. xvi, 343 p.

454. FAFUNWA, ALLIU BABATUNDE, 1923- . *An Historical Analysis of the Development of Higher Education in Nigeria.* New York University, 1955. 2 vols. 355 p. ms. Abstract in *Dissertation Abstracts,* Vol. 16, p. 905-906, May 1956. Available on microfilm from University Microfilms, Ann Arbor, Michigan, as Publication No. 13,604.

455. HELSER, ALBERT DAVID, 1897- . *Education of Primitive People: A Presentation of the Folklore of the Bura Animists with a Meaningful Experience Curriculum.* Columbia University, 1934. New York: Fleming H. Revell Co., 1934. 316 p. With Foreword by Mabel Carney.

456. OKEKE, UDUAROH, 1924- . *Educational Reconstruction in an Independent Nigeria: The Aims and Objectives of the Secondary School Curricula.* New York University, 1956. 291 p. ms. Abstract in *Dissertation Abstracts,* Vol. 16, p. 1387-1388, August 1956. Available on microfilm from University Microfilms, Ann Arbor, Michigan, as Publication No. 16,599.

457. OKONGWU, NNODU JOEL, 1919- . *History of Education in Nigeria, 1842-1942.* New York University, 1946. 195 p. ms. Abstract in *Microfilm Abstracts,* Vol. 7, No. 1, p. 46-48, 1946. Available on microfilm from University Microfilms, Ann Arbor, Michigan, as Publication No. 822. For master's thesis by same author, see No. 474.

458. UKEJE, ONYERISARA, 1927- . *Nigerian Needs and Nigerian Education: A Study of the Critical Needs of an Emergent Nation and the Role of Education in Meeting Them.* Columbia University, 1957. 548 p. ms.

459. UKPABY, ERNEST NNORUM, 1919- . *American Education: A Critical Analysis of Its Possible Implications for Nigerian Education.* Bradley University, 1956. 150 p. ms. Abstract in *Dissertation Abstracts*, Vol. 16, p. 2110, November 1956. Available on microfilm from University Microfilms, Ann Arbor, Michigan, as Publication No. 18,723.

See also Nos. 176, 321

MASTERS

460. AKPABIO, IBANGA UDO. *Suggestions for Improvement of Secondary Education in Nigeria.* Columbia University, 1942. 60 p. ms.

461. AYORINDE, JAMES TANIMOLA. *Christian Education in Nigeria: An Historical Study of Missions to Determine and Evaluate Their Educational Work.* Oberlin College, 1942. 145 p. ms.

462. DALLMAN, GLENN ROBERT. *An Evaluation of Educational Textbooks Used in Ibibio Teacher Training Schools.* Wisconsin State College, Milwaukee, 1954. 114 p. ms. plus appendix, 100 p.

463. DIEI, JOSEPH K. *Counting Systems of Ibo, Yoruba, and Hausa Peoples of Nigeria, West Africa.* Ohio State University, 1958.

464. DOWNING, LAWRENCE RICHARD. *Proposed Program of Teacher Training for Nigerian Training College.* University of Nebraska, 1952. 90 p. ms.

465. EKONG, EDEM UDO. *A Study of the History And Administration of Vocational Education in the United States as a Possible Basis for Establishing Vocational Education in Nigeria.* University of Washington, 1957.

466. FADIPE, N. ARINREMI. *A Yoruba Town: A Sociological Study of Abeokuta in the British Colony and Protectorate of Nigeria, West Coast of Africa.* Columbia University, 1931. 119 p. ms. (Includes education.)

467. GRAVES, ALMA NOREAN, 1907- . *Educational Trends and Potentialities in Nigeria.* University of North Carolina, 1945. 65 p. ms. Abstract in *University of North Carolina Record*, No. 429, p. 96, October 1946.

468. HARR, WILBER CHRISTIAN. *A Christian Approach to a Pagan People in Northern Nigeria.* Union Theological Seminary, 1940. 177 p. ms. (Includes education as one phase.)

469. HOESCH, ARMIN CHARLES, 1921- . *Development of Elementary Education in an Illiterate Society in Nigeria.* Trinity University, 1954. 90 p. ms.

470. IMOH, BEN UDO. *The Administration and Organization of Schools in Nigeria.* State University of Iowa, 1956. 90 p. ms.

471. McCORMICK, HUGH PENDLETON. *An Achievement Study of Nigerian Pupils in Standards Four and Five.* George Peabody College for Teachers, 1933. 41 p. ms.

472. MOZIA, PAUL AUENE AKOH, 1921- . *A Study of the Teacher Education Programme at the Baptist Teachers' Training College, Iwo, Nigeria, 1948-1952.* Tennessee Agricultural and Industrial University, 1954. 76 p. ms.

473. OGUNSANYA, JAMES O. *The Opinions of Some Nigerian Teachers on Some Socially Significant Issues: A Survey of Teachers Opinion and Its Implications for Nigerian Education.* Atlanta University, 1958.

474. OKONGWU, NNODU JOEL, 1919- . *Professional Education of Teachers in Nigeria.* Columbia University, 1943. 109 p. ms. For doctoral dissertation by same author, see No. 457.

475. OKONKWO, ONUZULIKE. *The Improvement of Education in Nigeria.* University of Nebraska, 1953. 188 p. ms.

476. RAPIER, CHRISTINE ELIZABETH. *Teaching of Efik Reading to Illiterate Adults and to First Grade Children.* Washington University, St. Louis, 1945. 156 p. ms. (Efik is a native dialect of Nigeria.)

477. ROTIMI, BARBABUNMI OSAYE, 1922- . *An Investigation into the General Administration and Organization of the Full Secondary Schools and the Higher Elementary Teacher Training Institutions in Western Nigeria.* Syracuse University, 1952. 211 p. ms.

478. UKA, NGWOBIA. *Education for Democratic Citizenship in Nigeria: A Critical Evaluation of the Scope and Content of Secondary Education in Nigeria.* Claremont Graduate School, 1953. 88 p. ms.

See also Nos. 226, 324, 329, 330

For Nigerian groups in the United States, see Nos. 4956, 4970

Nyasaland

(NOS. 479 - 481)

DOCTOR

479. STEYTLER, JOHN GEORGE, 1891-1944. *Educational Adaptations with Reference to Village Schools in Central Nyasaland.* Cornell University, 1937. Published in modified from as *Educational Adaptations with Reference to African Village Schools with Special Reference to Central Nyasaland.* London: The Sheldon Press, 1939. xxvii, 266 p. ("It has been necessary to make some considerable changes in the wording of the original text, and to add a new chapter on the training of the village teacher."-Author.) Abstract in Cornell University: *Abstracts of Theses . . . 1937*, p. 101-104.

MASTERS

480. CADWALLADER, EDWARD MILES. *Preparatory or Pre-Book Stage of Teaching English in Schools for Natives in British Tropical Africa.* University of Southern California, 1933. 134 p. ms.

481. YEARSLEY, RUTH ESTER, 1903- . *Missionary Activities in Nyasaland.* Temple University, 1941. 169 p. ms. (Includes educational activities.)

See also No. 328

Rhodesia
(NOS. 482 - 483)

MASTERS

482. DRYDEN, REGINALD NORMAN, 1911- . *How the Application of the Church's Right of Entry in Southern Rhodesia Public Schools can be Modified to the Enrichment of Religious Education.* Pacific School of Religion, 1951.

483. ROBINSON, GRACE ELLEN, 1919- . *A Fundamental Course in School Organization for First Year Teacher Education in Northern and Southern Rhodesia.* Pacific Union College, 1954. 115 p. ms.

See also Nos. 325, 328

Sierra Leone
(NOS. 484 - 494)

DOCTORS

484. CARR, ARTHUR TAYLOR. *Samuel Lewis: Educational and Social Reformer.* Western Reserve University, 1938. 234 p. ms.

485. COLESON, EDWARD PAUL, 1913- . *Educational Change in Sierra Leone.* University of Michigan, 1956. 349 p. ms. Abstract in *Dissertation Abstracts*, Vol. 16, p. 1395, August 1956. Available on microfilm from University Microfilms, Ann Arbor, Michigan, as Publication No. 17,426.

486. FITZJOHN, WILLIAM HENRY, 1915- . *Proposals for the Improvement of Teaching in the Elementary Schools of Sierra Leone Protectorate.* Columbia University, 1949. 161 p. ms.

See also No. 176

MASTERS

487. BRODERICK, SYLVESTER MODUPE. *North Carolina Suggestions for Education in Sierra Leone.* Columbia University, 1928.

488. CAULKER, RICHARD YELSAHA. *The Religious Implications of Education in West Africa.* Oberlin College, 1937. 152 p. ms. Abstract in *Selected Graduate Theses in Religious Education,* 1937. p. 12.

489. CAULKER, SOLOMON BROOKS. *The Integration of Religion within the Program of Secondary Schools in Sierra Leone.* University of Chicago, 1946. 84 p. ms.

490. JOHNSON, THOMAS WILLIAM DOSUMU. *A History of Sierra Leone, with Emphasis on Education.* Columbia University, 1936. 75 p. ms.

491. PEACOCK, AMYOGOLLO E. *Missionary Work in Sierra Leone.* Howard University, 1940. 75 p. ms. (Includes education.)

492. ROSSELOT, GLEN TAYLOR. *The Origin, Growth, and Development of the United Brethren in Christian Mission Schools in Sierra Leone, West Africa.* University of Chicago, 1936. 121 p. ms.

493. THOMAS, HARLAND HAYWARD. *Plans for Developing a Curriculum of Religious Education for Mission Schools in West Africa.* University of Kansas, 1931. 48 p. ms.

494. WARRATIE, SYLMADI. *Christian Literature in British West Africa.* United Theological Seminary, Dayton, 1955. (Considers problems and approaches to literacy in the area by a native of Sierra Leone. Thesis for degree of Bachelor of Divinity.)

See also Nos. 195, 324, 330

For a Sierra Leone group in the United States, see No. 4956

Sudan
(NOS. 495 – 496)

MASTERS

495. BERGMAN, VINCENT H., 1920- . *An Educational Analysis of the Illiteracy Problem in the Anglo-Egyptian Sudan.* Eastern Baptist Theological Seminary, 1949. 103 p. ms.

496. GROVE, ELSIE ELIZABETH. *Education of Women and Girls in the Anglo-Egyptian Sudan.* Kennedy School of Missions, 1931. 61 p. ms.

See also No. 308

Tanganyika
(NO. 497)

DOCTOR

See No. 160

MASTER

497. HESS, ANNA MARGARET, 1926- . (Later Mrs. Gene C. Lander). *The Missionary Meeting the Educational Needs of the Sukuma Tribe.* Eastern Baptist Theological Seminary, 1947. 91 p. ms.

See also Nos. 195, 247, 327

Togoland
(NO. 498)

MASTER

498. ADZANKU, ADOLF GUSTAV KODZO. *A Study of Discipline in the Middle Schools of Togoland under British Trusteeship.* Drake University, 1955. 53 p. ms.

See also No. 247

Uganda
(NO. 499)

MASTER

499. KALIBALA, ERNEST BALINTUMA. *Education for the Villages in Uganda, East Africa.* Columbia University, 1934. 79 p. ms.

See also Nos. 195, 326, 327, 330

Union of South Africa

(NOS. 500 – 526)

DOCTORS

500. AUCAMP, ANNA JACOBA, 1892- . *Bilingual Education and Nationalism, With Special Reference to South Africa.* Columbia University, 1926. Pretoria, Union of South Africa: J. L. Van Schaik, Ltd. 1926. 247 p.

501. BOEHMKE, MATHIAS JULIUS WILHELM. *The Rural School Problem in the Province of the Cape of Good Hope, South Africa.* Columbia University, 1919.

502. BRUECKNER, K. ROBERT. *Curriculum Implications from the Changing Culture and Civilization of the South African Native: With Particular Reference to Natal and Zululand.* Columbia University, 1933. 2 volumes. Vol. I, 247 p. ms. Vol. II, unpaged.

503. COOK, PETER ALAN WILSON, 1905- . *The Education of a South African Tribe.* Columbia University, 1934. Cape Town and Johannesburg, South Africa: Juta & Co. Ltd., 1934. viii, 95 p. (Deals with a Bantu tribe in Cape Province. Also contains a chapter, for comparative purposes, on education in Mexico.)

504. EYBERS, EBENEZER. *Educational Developments at the Cape of Good Hope (1652-1839), with Special Reference to the Period of Transition from Dutch to British Rule (1803-1839).* New York University, 1918. 133 p. ms.

505. FICK, MARTIN LAWRENCE, 1895- . *The Problem of Bilingual Instruction with Special Reference to Instruction in the Transvaal.* Harvard University, 1924. 146 p. ms.

506. GELDENHUYS, FRANS EDUARD. *Sociological Backgrounds and Agriculture in the Elementary and Secondary Schools of the Union of South Africa.* Cornell University, 1917. 574 p. ms. Published as *Landbouonderwys Deur die Skool,* Bloemfontein: Nasionale Pers Bpk, 1925. 232 p.

506a. HILL, KATHLEEN F. *Social Welfare Needs of Urban African Children.* Columbia University, 1958. 299 p. ms. Abstract in *Dissertation Abstracts,* Vol. 19, p. 1858-1859, January 1959. Available on microfilm from University Microfilms, Ann Arbor, Michigan, as Mic. 58-7038. (Based on information "obtained from responses of one thousand African school children in Johannesburg and from a group of adult Africans in training as social workers at the Jan H. Hofmeyer School of Social Work, also in Johannesburg.")

507. LORAM, CHARLES TEMPLEMAN, 1879-1940. *The Education of the South African Native.* Columbia University, 1915. London and New York: Longmans, Green & Co., 1917. xx, 340 p.

508. MALAN, JOHANNES ROSSOUW, 1887- . *The Reorganization of Rural Education in the Cape Province of the Union of South Africa.* Columbia University, 1922. 168 p. ms.

509. MALAN, WOUTER DE VOS, 1892- . *Tendencies in Secondary Education with Special Reference to the Situation in the Cape Province of the Union of South Africa: Present Status and Future Tendencies.* Columbia University, 1923. Wellington, Cape Province, Union of South Africa: Wellington Economic Press, 1923. 176 p.

510. MALHERBE, ERNST GIDEON, 1895- . *Education in South Africa, 1652-1922: A Critical Survey of the Development of Educational Administration in the Cape, Natal, Transvaal, and the Orange Free State.* Columbia University, 1926. Capetown and Johannesburg, Union of South Africa: Juta & Co., xxii, 521 p.

511. SMUTS, ADRIAAN JOSIAS, 1907- . *The Education of Adolescents in South Africa.* Columbia University, 1938. Capetown and Johannesburg, Union of South Africa: Juta & Co., Ltd., 1938. xiii, 283 p.

512. VAN GRAAN, LAMBERT RUDOLF, 1897- . *The Reorganization of Elementary Education in the Orange Free State to Meet the Needs of the Rural Schools.* Cornell University, 1931. 315 p. ms. Ithaca, New York: 1931. 4 p. Abstract of thesis.

513. VAN ZYL, ABRAHAM JOHANNES, 1911- . (Zyl, Abraham Johannes Van, in Library of Congress card catalog). *Mathematics at the Cross-Roads: A Critical Survey of the Teaching of Mathematics in the Secondary Schools of the Union of South Africa, with Suggestions for Reorganization.* Columbia University, 1940. Cape Town, South Africa: Meskew Miller, Ltd., 1942. ix, 239 p.

See also Nos. 119, 122, 138, 142, 147, 161, 164, 173, 176

MASTERS

514. DICK, MARY G. *The Establishment of a Mission, Being the Work of the American Board of Commissioners for Foreign Missions among the Zulus of South Eastern Natal, 1834-1860.* Columbia University, 1934. 68 p. ms. (Includes education)

515. JACOBS, STELLA VIRGINIA, 1924- . *The Development of Post-Primary Education for the Colored Child in the Cape Province, Union of South Africa.* Syracuse University, 1949. 98 p. ms.

516. KACHELHOFFER, SUSIE C. *Facing a New Day with the Native African Woman.* Vanderbilt University, 1930. Thesis for degree of Bachelor of Divinity. (Presents program for religious education of women and girls in South Africa.)

517. KETTLEY, DAISY LILLIAN MARY, 1893- . *The Supervision of African Schools.* Rutgers University, 1934. 86 p. ms. (South Africa only.)

518. LORAM, JOAN MARION. *Health and Physical Education in the Cape Province, Union of South Africa.* Columbia University, 1934. 73 p. ms.

519. LOVELL, ORMOND E. *Missionary Education and the South African Problem.* University of Chicago, 1919. 100 p. ms.

520. MOLEFE, GEORGE B. *A Religious Education Program for a Bantu Church School.* Columbia University, 1939; Union Theological Seminary, 1939. 87 p. ms. (For a school to be located in South Africa.)

521. NDAMSE, CURNICK MVELASE CURWENS. *Bantu Education in South Africa.* Kennedy School of Missions, 1956. (Thesis has been withheld from public use because of fear of reprisals.)

522. RAMAILA, HENRY SEGOME. *Christian Education Endeavors in a Culturally Changing South Africa.* Columbia University, 1955. Union Theological Seminary, 1955. 59 p. ms.

523. REASBY, HAROLD VELTON, 1931- . *A Study of the Sociological Implications of Racial Separation in South Africa.* Iowa State Teachers College, 1955. 105 p. ms. (Includes education.)

524. RUBENSTEIN, DAVID HARNLY. *A Critical Survey of Frustration and Frustration-Instigated Response and Application as a Counseling Tool for Work with Zulus.* University of Buffalo, 1953. 74 p. ms.

525. STERN, RENATE. *Selected Nutrition Education Programs of Central Ohio, with Proposals for Application in the Union of South Africa.* Ohio State University, 1956. 117 p. ms.

526. WAHL, C. ARNOLD. *The Training of European Teachers in the Province of the Cape of Good Hope.* Columbia University, 1920.

See also Nos. 213, 216, 226, 235, 325, 327

For South African groups in the United States, see Nos. 4956, 4957, 4970, 4975

AMERICA, NORTH
(NOS. 527 – 1180)

General

26 CROSS REFERENCES

DOCTORS

See Nos. 137, 150, 151

MASTERS

See Nos. 196, 199, 201, 202, 204, 214, 225, 227, 228, 237, 240, 241, 242, 251, 252, 259, 270, 277, 287, 290, 297, 301, 305

Composite
(NOS. 527 – 541)

DOCTORS

527. ANTTILLA, EARL URLO, 1914- . *United States Educational Policy in the Carribean.* University of Texas, 1953. 329 p. ms. (Includes Cuba, Dominican Republic, Haiti, Puerto Rico, and the Virgin Islands.) For master's thesis by same author, see No. 39.

528. BARTH, PIUS JOSEPH, 1908- . *Franciscan Education and the Social Order in Spanish North America, 1501-1821.* University of Chicago, 1945. Chicago: xi, 431 p. (Lithoprinted in a private edition. Contains 44 illustrations of old materials, many of them teaching materials. Includes Guatemala, Haiti, Honduras, Mexico, and Nicaragua.)

529. BELTRANENA-VALLADARES, LUIS, 1921- . *Attempts to Form a Union of Central America.* University of Notre Dame, 1947. Notre Dame, Indiana: Department of Political Science, 1947. x, 94 p. (Includes discussion of ambitious plan of education with organization of a Central American university. Covers Costa Rica, El Salvador, Guatemala, Honduras, and Nicaragua.)

530. ESPENDEZ NAVARRO, JUAN. *A Critical Appreciation of the Educational Programs of Central America.* Indiana University, 1941. 772 p. ms. (Includes Costa Rica, El Salvador, Guatemala, Honduras, and Nicaragua.) For master's thesis by same author, see No. 1111.

531. KARNES, THOMAS LINDAS, 1914- . *Attempts to Confederate the States of Central America.* Stanford University, 1953. 281 p. ms. Abstract in *Dissertation Abstracts*, Vol. 13, p. 221-222, February 1953. Available on microfilm from University Microfilms, Ann Arbor, Michigan, as Publication No. 4,673. (Includes consideration of attempts to found a University of Central America. Covers Costa Rica, El Salvador, Guatemala, Honduras, and Nicaragua.)

532. PETTIT, GEORGE ALBERT, 1901- . *Primitive Education in North America: Its Processes and Effects.* University of California, Berkeley, 1940. Berkeley and Los Angeles: 1946. 182 p. (University of California Publications in American Archaeology and Ethnology, Vol. 43, No. 1. Concerned chiefly with American Indians, but includes also Eskimos of Canada and Greenland.)

533. RODRIGUEZ BOU, ISMAEL, 1911- . *A Study of the Parallelism of English and Spanish Vocabularies.* University of Texas, 1944. Rio Piedras, Puerto Rico; Superior Educational Council of Puerto Rico, University of Puerto Rico, 1950. 313 p. (Educational Publication, Series 2, No. 9. An outgrowth of the Inter-American Tests. See No. 536.)

534. SPAULDING, SETH JOSEPH, 1928- . *An Investigation of Factors which Influence the Effectiveness of Fundamental Education Reading Materials for Latin-American Adults.* Ohio State University, 1953. 2 vols. (Primarily concerned with Costa Rica and Mexico.)

535. SPELL, Mrs. LOTA MAY HARRIGAN, 1885- . *Musical Education in North America during the Sixteenth and Seventeenth Centuries.* University of Texas, 1923. 167 p. ms. Published in part, as follows: (1) "The First Teacher of European Music in America," (Pedro de Gante who arrived at Vera Cruz, Mexico, August 30, 1523), *Catholic Historical Review*, Vol. 2, p. 373-378, October 1922; (2) Same, as translated by Rafael Heliodoro Valle, as "Hace Cuatro Siglos Llego a Veracruz Fray Pedro de Gante, el Primer Maestro de Musica Europea en America," *El Universal* (Mexico City), August 12, 1923; (3) "Musical Teaching in New Mexico in the Seventeenth Century," *New Mexico Historical Review*, Vol. 2, No. 1, January 1927; (4) Same reprinted in *Women Tell the Story of the Southwest*, by Mattie Lloyd Wooten, (San Antonio, Texas, 1940), p. 183-190; (5) "Aztec Music and Musicians," *Proceedings of the Music Teachers National Association*, 1925, p. 98-105; (6) Same, as translated by Francisco Olave, *Revista de Revistas*, March 20, 1927; (7) "The First Music Books Printed in America," *Musical Quarterly*, Vol. 15, p. 50-54, January 1929; (8) Same in *Boletin Latino-Americano de Musica*, Vol. 5, p. 195-200, 1941; (9) "Music in the Cathedral of Mexico in the Sixteenth Century," *Hispanic American Historical Review*, Vol. 26, p. 293-319, August 1946; (10) Same, as translated by Francisco Curt Lange, *Revista de Estudios Musicales*, Vol. 2, p. 217-255, August, 1950; (11) "The First Half-Century of European Music in America," *Atlanta* (London), Vol. 1, p. 158-162, July 1953; (12) "Music in New France in the Seventeenth Century," *Canadian Historical Review*, Vol. 7, p. 119-131, June 1927. (Chiefly concerned with Mexico, but two chapters trace the teaching of music, before 1700, in the French and English colonies.)

General, Composite, Bahama Islands, Bermuda, Canada

536. STOVAL, FRANKLIN LINDSAY. *A Study of Scaled Scores with Special Reference to the Inter-American Tests.* University of Texas, 1945. 250 p. ms. plus 50 p. of printed tests. (Highly statistical study of best methods of scoring the tests, based upon administration of experimental forms to some 20,000 school children in Puerto Rico, 6,000 in Mexico, and 7,500 in Texas. Tests were given at all levels and in all grades for which they were designed. The Spanish edition was given in Mexico, the English edition in Texas, and both editions in bilingual Puerto Rico.)

MASTERS

537. FRINK, LESTER MARTIN. *Educational Trends in Mexico, Central America, and the West Indies.* University of Southern California, 1940. 121 p. ms. (Includes Costa Rica, Cuba, Dominican Republic, El Salvador, Guatemala, Haiti, Honduras, Mexico, Nicaragua, and Panama.)

538. IOBST, ROBERT ALLEN, 1915- . *Teaching the Bible to Primitive People Particularly the Miskito and Sumu Indians of Nicaragua and Honduras.* Princeton Theological Seminary, 1947. 120 p. ms.

539. MARSH, THEODORE HENRY. *Protestant Missionary Education in Central America.* Dallas Theological Seminary and Graduate School of Theology, 1952. 111 p. ms. (Includes Costa Rica, El Salvador, Guatemala, Honduras, Nicaragua, and Panama.)

540. RECTENWALD, Brother JOHN W. *The Influence of Eugenio Maria Hostos in the Development of Democratic Citizenship in the Antilles through His Normal School and Educational Theory.* Catholic University of America, 1941. 74 p. ms. (Includes Cuba, Dominican Republic, and Puerto Rico.)

541. WEBBER, CHARLES LYLE. *Educational Influences in Central America.* University of Southern California, 1942. 90 p. ms. (Includes Costa Rica, El Salvador, Guatemala, Honduras, and Nicaragua.)

Bahama Islands
(NO. 542)

MASTER

542. BAKER, HELEN MARIE. *Introducing and Establishing Music Education in a School in the Bahamas.* Boston University, 1954.

Bermuda
(NOS. 543 – 544)

DOCTOR

543. ROBINSON, KENNETH ELLSWORTH. *Education in Bermuda.* Harvard University, 1952. 349 p. ms.

MASTER

544. GASCOIGNE, STANLEY, 1914- . *Education in Bermuda with Special Emphasis on the Supply of Teachers.* Boston University, 1953. 62 p. ms.

See also No. 147

Canada
(NOS. 545 – 839)

Classification by Provinces

NEWFOUNDLAND. Nos. 552, 599, 603, 647, 648, 717, 725, 764, 781, 807

NOVA SCOTIA. Nos. 549, 564, 578, 607, 608, 624, 627, 629, 636, 637, 639, 645, 662, 667, 693, 698, 700, 747, 750, 752, 753, 763, 796, 811, 817, 828, 834

PRINCE EDWARD ISLAND. Nos. 607, 624, 637, 640, 752, 804

NEW BRUNSWICK. Nos. 547, 559, 572, 585, 607, 624, 629, 633, 637, 683, 752, 753, 755, 768, 772

QUEBEC. Nos. 546, 555, 562, 576, 592, 596, 600, 607, 609, 615, 617, 629, 650, 668, 670, 686, 687, 690,

692, 695, 710, 718, 722, 733, 736, 743, 752, 753, 761, 800, 801, 807, 808, 815, 820, 825, 829, 832, 837

ONTARIO. Nos. 546, 550, 559, 560, 568, 569, 570, 571, 581, 583, 590, 604, 607, 619, 628, 642, 651, 658, 665, 670, 676, 688, 711, 714, 719, 721, 740, 741, 746, 752, 753, 754, 757, 775, 778, 783, 799, 800, 810, 813, 816, 822, 824, 830, 839

MANITOBA. Nos. 545, 554, 595, 622, 635, 678, 680, 685, 716, 728, 731, 752, 753, 773, 776, 784, 795

SASKATCHEWAN. Nos. 545, 554, 559, 561, 566, 589, 593, 620, 623, 635, 675, 697, 731, 752, 753, 766, 770, 773, 823, 838

ALBERTA. Nos. 545, 551, 554, 557, 559, 563, 573, 574, 579, 580, 587, 610, 626, 631, 635, 643, 646, 649, 652, 653, 654, 664, 672, 681, 696, 703, 704, 709, 712, 720, 730, 731, 735, 752, 753, 766, 767, 769, 773, 785, 786, 788, 790, 812, 835

BRITISH COLUMBIA. Nos. 545, 548, 554, 559, 588, 597, 598, 614, 630, 634, 635, 656, 663, 671, 673, 689, 701, 702, 706, 707, 724, 737, 742, 748, 751, 752, 753, 756, 758, 759, 771, 773, 774, 789, 791, 792, 793, 806, 814, 818, 821, 826, 836

DOCTORS

545. AIKENHEAD, JOHN DOUGLAS. *To Teach; Or Not to Teach.* University of Oregon, 1954. 191 p. ms. (Reports results of a questionnaire to students in last two years of high school and first two years of college in four western provinces asking whether or not they chose to become teachers.) For master's thesis by same author, see No. 680.

546. ALLEN, HOWARD CLARENCE. *The Organization and Administration of the Educational Systems of the Canadian Provinces of Quebec and Ontario.* Syracuse University, 1937. Syracuse, New York: 1937. 314 p. ms.

546a. ALOIA, ALEX DOMINIC. *The Organization of Student Recreation in Selected Large Institutions of Higher Learning.* University of Southern California, 1951. Abstract in University of Southern California: *Abstracts of Dissertations,* 1951, p. 131-134. (Based on 43 universities in the United States with enrollments of over 9,000 and the three largest Canadian universities.)

547. ANDERSON, AMOS McINTYRE. *The History of Elementary Education in the Province of New Brunswick.* New York University, 1940. 163 p. ms. Abstract in New York University, School of Education: *Abstracts of Theses,* 1940-41, p. 9-12.

548. ANDERSON, HENRIETTA ALEXANDRINA RAMAYA. *Supervision of Rural Schools in British Columbia: A Review of the Present System and a Plan for Reorganization.* University of Washington, 1931. 170 p. ms.

549. ARCHIBALD, JUANITA HELEN, 1915- . *A Nutrition Education Programme in Cape Sable Island.* Columbia University, 1952. 216 p. ms.

550. BAESZLER, Sister ST. ALFRED OF ROME, 1898- . *The Congregation of Notre Dame in Ontario and the United States: The History of Holy Angels Province.* Fordham University, 1944. 251 p. ms. Abstract in Fordham University: *Dissertations Accepted for Higher Degrees . . .* 1944, p. 32-35. For master's thesis by same author, see No. 687.

551. BAILEY, WARREN STEVENSON, 1920- . *The Influence of the Alberta Teachers' Association on Educational Legislation in Alberta, 1918-1948.* Stanford University, 1956. 204 p. ms. Abstract in *Dissertation Abstracts,* Vol. 17, p. 85, January 1957. Available on microfilm from University Microfilms, Ann Arbor, Michigan, as Publication No. 19,896.

552. BARNES, ARTHUR, 1866- . *The History of Education in Newfoundland.* New York University, 1917. 169 p. ms.

553. BEST, ERNEST MAURICE, 1880- . *Social Reconstruction in Canada.* New York University, 1920. (Includes education.)

554. BLACK, WILLIAM GRIFFITHS, 1898- . *The Development and Present Status of Teacher Education in Western Canada, with Special Reference to the Curriculum.* University of Chicago, 1936. 341 p. ms. Part of the dissertation (8 p. photolithographed) was distributed to libraries in the United States and abroad in 1936. For master's thesis by same author, see No. 699.

555. BLUM, WILLIAM DEMUTH, 1914- . *Opinion Toward Education in Montreal, Canada.* University of Wisconsin, 1946. 120 p. ms. Abstract in University of Wisconsin: *Summaries of Doctoral Dissertations,* Vol. 9, 1943-1947, p. 402-404.

556. BOON, HAROLD WATSON, 1910- . *The Development of the Bible College or Institute in the United States and Canada since 1880 and Its Relationship to the Field of Theological Education in America.* New York University, 1950. 204 p. ms. Abstract in New York University; School of Education: *Abstracts of Theses . . .* October 1949-June 1950, p. 169-173. Abstract also in *Religious Education,* Vol. 46, p. 164-165, May-June 1951.

557. BYRNE, TIMOTHY CLARKE. *The Historical Development and an Evaluation of Provincial Leadership in the Field of High School Instruction for the Province of Alberta.* University of Colorado, 1956. 426 p. ms. Abstract in *Dissertation Abstracts,* Vol. 18, p. 115-116, January 1958. Available on microfilm from University Microfilms, Ann Arbor, Michigan, as Publication No. 22,593.

558. CAMPBELL, PEARL READ, 1908- . *Speech Education in the English-Speaking Teacher Training Institutions of Canada.* University of Wisconsin, 1957. 198 p. ms. Abstract in *Dissertation Abstracts,* Vol. 17, p. 2084-2085, September 1957. Available on microfilm from University Microfilms, Ann Arbor, Michigan, as Publication No. 22,326.

559. CANN, MARJORIE MITCHELL. *An Historical Study of the Office of Coordinator of Teacher Education in the Canadian Provinces of New Brunswick, Ontario, Saskatchewan, Alberta, and British Columbia.* University of Maryland, 1957. 150 p. ms. Abstract in *Dissertation Abstracts,* Vol. 18, p. 1315, April 1958. Available on microfilm from University Microfilms, Ann Arbor, Michigan, as Mic. 58-890.

560. CARLTON, SYLVIA, 1913- . *Egerton Ryerson and Education in Ontario, 1844-1877.* University of Pennsylvania, 1950. 416 p. ms.

561. CARTER, ALFRED, 1906- . *The Life and Labors of the Rev. Robert Terrill Rundle, Pioneer Missionary to the Saskatchewan, Canada.* Boston University, 1952. 172 p. ms. Abstract in *Doctoral Dissertations in the Field of Religion, 1940-1952,* p. 30. (Includes his educational work with various Indian tribes.)

562. CARTER, MARY DUNCAN, 1896- . *A Survey of Montreal Library Facilities and a Proposed Plan for a Library System.* University of Chicago, 1942. 180 p. ms. Part of the dissertation (24 p. photolithographed) was distributed to libraries in the United States and abroad in 1945.

563. CHALMERS, JOHN WEST, 1910- . *Some Factors Conducive to Correspondence Teaching Success in Public Education in Alberta.* Stanford University, 1947. 387 p. ms. Abstract in Stanford University: *Abstracts of Dissertations . . . 1946-47,* p. 149-151.

564. CHANCE, NORMAN ALLEE. *Portsmouth: The Study of a Bi-Cultural Community under Stress.* Cornell University, 1957. 281 p. ms. Abstract in *Dissertation Abstracts,* Vol. 17, p. 2759-2760, December 1957. Available on microfilm from University Microfilms, Ann Arbor, Michigan, as Publication No. 24,756. (Refers to Portsmouth, Nova Scotia. Considers many factors, including education, in conflicts between populations of English and French descent.)

565. CHURCHLEY, FRANKLIN EUGENE, 1930- . *The Piano in Canadian Music Education.* Columbia University, 1958. 136 p. ms.

566. CLARKE, WILLIAM FRANCIS, 1918- . *The Volunteer Lay Leadership of the United Church of Canada in Rural Saskatchewan.* Columbia University, 1949. 168 p. ms. Abstract in *Teachers College Record,* Vol. 51, p. 484, April 1950. Abstract also in *Religious Education,* Vol. 45, p. 104-105, March-April 1950.

567. CLIMENHAGA, ASA W., 1889- . *Administrative Practices of the Educational Program of the Brethren in Christ Church of the United States and Canada.* Syracuse University, 1944. Published as *History of the Brethren in Christ Church.* Nappanee, Indiana: E. V. Publishing House, 1942. 390 p.

568. CLUBINE, GORDON LAVERNE, 1910- . *A Plan for the Improvement and Extension of Art Education in Ontario Secondary Schools.* Columbia University, 1952. 218 p. ms.

569. CLUBINE, IVAN WARD, 1906- . *Teacher Load in the Secondary Schools of Ontario.* New York University, 1944. 188 p. ms. Abstract in New York University, School of Education: *Abstracts of Theses,* 1943-44, p. 117-124.

570. CLUBINE, MARY HELEN, 1908- . *Effective Procedures in the Teaching of Art in Ontario Secondary Schools.* Columbia University, 1952. 218 p. ms.

571. COLEMAN, HERBERT THOMAS JOHN, 1872- . *Public Education in Upper Canada (Ontario), with Special Reference to the Period between 1791 and 1841.* Columbia University, 1907. Published as *Public Education in Upper Canada.* New York: Teachers College, Columbia University, 1907. 120 p. (Columbia University Contributions to Education, Teachers College Series, No. 15.)

572. COOK, JOHN THOMAS. *Teacher Training in the Province of New Brunswick: An Historical and Analytical Study of Its Evolution Together with Proposed Measures of Practical Reform.* Harvard University, 1940. 579 p. ms.

573. COOPER, ALVIN JOHN, 1910- . *The Development of a Department of Practical Theology at St. Stephen's College, Edmonton, Canada.* Columbia University, 1950. 88 p. ms. Abstract in *Religious Education,* Vol. 46, p. 168-169. May-June 1951.

574. COUTTS, HERBERT THOMAS, 1907- . *The Relation between the Reading Competence of Alberta's Ninth-Grade Pupils in Four Content Fields and Their Achievement in Those Fields.* University of Minnesota, 1951. 268 p. ms. (Covers English language and literature, mathematics, general science, and social studies.)

575. CRAGG, EDITH MARION CATHERINE, 1903- . *A Study of the Content of Literature Textbooks for English-Speaking Students in Canadian High Schools in Relation to International Understanding between the United States and Canada and Canadian Unity.* Northwestern University, 1950. 253 p. ms. Abstract in Northwestern University: *Summaries of Doctoral Dissertations . . .* Vol. 18, 1950, p. 235-241.

576. DALTON, ROY CLINTON, 1924- . *The History of the Jesuits' Estates, 1760-1888.* University of Minnesota, 1957. 386 p. ms. Abstract in *Dissertation Abstracts,* Vol. 18, p. 212, January 1958. Available on microfilm from University Microfilms, Ann Arbor, Michigan, as Publication No. 23,929. (Includes education.)

577. DAVIDSON, STEWART ALEXANDER, 1921- . *A History of Sports and Games in Eastern Canada Prior to World War I.* Columbia University, 1951. 168 p. ms.

578. DAVIS, DAVID GRAY. *Reorganization of Secondary Education in Nova Scotia.* Harvard University, 1927. 240 p. ms.

579. DEVERELL, ALFRED FREDERICK, 1908- . *Educational Needs of the Rocky Mountain Division, Alberta, Canada.* Stanford University, 1950. 207 p. ms. Abstract in Stanford University: *Abstracts of Dissertations . . . 1949-50,* p. 314-316.

580. DOUCETTE, ANDREW LEO, 1900- . *A Science Program for Alberta Schools Based on Student Interests.* Stanford University, 1950. 2 vols., 211 p. ms., 103 p. ms. Abstract in Stanford University: *Abstracts of Dissertations . . . 1949-50,* p. 323-329.

581. DUNLOP, FLORENCE SARA, 1896- . *Subsequent Careers of Non-Academic Boys.* Columbia University, 1935. Ottawa, Canada: 1935. 95 p. (Deals with boys in Ottawa schools.)

582. DYDE, WALTERS FARRALL, 1890- . *Public Secondary Education in Canada.* Columbia University, 1929. New York: Teachers College,

Columbia University, 1929. ix, 263 p. (Teachers College Contribution to Education, No. 345.)

583. ELLIOTT, CHARLES MARTYN, 1916- . *Proposals for the Improvement of the Instructional Leadership Provided by Elementary School Inspectors in Northern Ontario.* Columbia University, 1954. 119 p. ms.

584. ELLIS, EDWARD NORMAN, 1917- . *The Effectiveness of Culture-Free Tests in Measuring the Intellectual Characteristics of German Immigrants to Canada.* Oregon State College, 1956. 190 p. ms.

585. FAHS, LOIS S. *The Social Situation in Seven Rural Communities in New Brunswick Studied as the Basis for Planning a Program of General Recreation with Special Emphasis on Dancing.* Columbia University, 1941. 359 p. ms.

586. FERRIER, WILLIAM KENNETH, 1900- . *Programs for Alcohol Education in the United States and Canada.* Oregon State College, 1953. 189 p. ms. Available on microcards, Microcard No. 296.

587. FINN, THEOPHILUS GEORGE, 1907- . *The Social Studies Program in the Province of Alberta.* Stanford University, 1950. 170 p. ms. Abstract in Stanford University: *Abstracts of Dissertations . . .* 1949-50, p. 347-349.

588. FLATHER, DONALD McINTOSH, 1903- . *An Evaluation of the Science Program in the High Schools of British Columbia.* University of Washington, 1950. 423 p. ms.

589. FOSTER, JOHN EDWIN. *The Administrative Means of Extending the Use of Audio-Visual Materials in Saskatchewan.* Indiana University, 1950. 210 p. ms. Abstract in Indiana University: *Studies in Education,* 1950, p. 31-36. (Thesis Abstract Series, No. 2, January 1950.)

590. FOX, JAMES HAROLD, 1900- . *The Centralized Control of Secondary Education in the Province of Ontario: An Evaluation of the Administrative Control Exercised by the Central Educational Authority, with Suggestions Regarding Desirable and Practical Adjustments.* Harvard University, 1937. 554 p. ms.

591. FRASER, ARTHUR McNUTT, 1915- . *Music in Canadian Public Schools: A Survey and Recommendations.* Columbia University, 1951. 129 p. ms. Abstract in *Teachers College Record,* Vol. 53, p. 334-335, March 1952.

592. GIBSON, GEORGE DAVIS, 1906- . *Jesuit Education of the Indians in New France, 1611-1658.* University of California, Berkeley, 1940. 146 p. ms.

593. GILLESPIE, EDGAR DEAN, 1907- . *A Study of Some Emerging Practices in Larger School Units of Administration in Saskatchewan.* Columbia University, 1950. 157 p. ms.

594. GLAZIER, KENNETH MacLEAN, 1912- . *The Place of Religion in the History of the Non-Catholic Universities of Canada.* Yale University, 1944. 401 p. ms.

595. GLINZ, LESLIE ALBERT, 1896- . *The Development of Public Secondary Education in Manitoba.* Stanford University, 1931. 319 p. ms. Abstract in Stanford University: *Abstracts of Dissertations . . .* 1930-31, p. 50-55.

596. GRANT, HAROLD EMBREE, 1898- . *A Plan for a Guidance Program in the Montreal Protestant Central School System.* Columbia University, 1950. 183 p. ms.

597. GRANTHAM, HERBERT HARRIS, 1905- . *The Science Curriculum in British Columbia Schools with Emphasis upon the Secondary Levels.* Stanford University, 1951. 344 p. ms. Published in abreviated form as "Secondary School Science in British Columbia," *British Columbia Schools,* Secondary Edition, Vol. 6, Nos. 51-54, October 1951, March 1952, May 1952. Abstract in Stanford University: *Abstracts of Dissertations . . .* 1950-51, p. 9-14.

598. GROSS, CARL HENRY, 1911- . *Education in British Columbia, with Particular Consideration of the Natural and Social Factors.* Ohio State University, 1939. 355 p. ms. Abstract in Ohio State University: *Abstracts of Dissertations . . .* Summer 1939, p. 76-78. (Abstracts of Doctoral Dissertations, No. 31.) For master's thesis by same author, see No. 3197.

599. GUSHUE, WILLIAM JOSEPH. *The Acceptability of Certain Principles of Secondary Education and the Implications for Newfoundland Education.* Boston University, 1958. 199 p. ms. Abstract in *Dissertation Abstracts,* Vol. 19, p. 2025-2026, February 1959. Available on microfilm from Microfilm Abstracts, Ann Arbor, Michigan, as Mic. 58-7384.

600. HAMILTON, LORNE DANIEL. *The Issue of Public Aid to Catholic Parochial Schools in the United States, with Reference to Education in Quebec.* Harvard University, 1953. 203 p. ms.

601. HARRIS, RONALD SUTTON, 1919- . *The Place of English Studies in a University Program of General Education: A Study Based on the Practices of the English-Speaking Universities and Colleges of Canada in 1951-1952.* University of Michigan, 1953. 339 p. ms. Abstract in *Dissertation Abstracts,* Vol. 13, No. 3, p. 336, 1953. Available on microfilm from University Microfilms, Ann Arbor, Michigan, as Publication No. 5,041.

602. HAUCK, ARTHUR ANDREW, 1893- . *Some Educational Factors Affecting the Relation between Canada and the United States.* Columbia University, 1932. Easton, Pennsylvania: 1932. 100 p.

603. HICKMAN, GEORGE ALBERT, 1909- . *A Guide to the Improvement of the Pre-Service Programme of Teacher Education in Newfoundland.* Columbia University, 1954. 244 p. ms.

604. HIGH, NORMAN HERVEY, 1913- . *A Study of Educational Opportunity in the Provincially-Controlled Schools of Haldimand County, Ontario.* Cornell University, 1950. 250 p. ms.

605. HOWARD, JAMES WILLIS, 1899- . *A Study of Cadet Training in the Dominion of Canada.* Cornell University, 1936. 183, 191 p. ms. Ithaca, New York: 1936, 4 p. Abstract of Thesis.

606. HOWSAM, ROBERT BASIL, 1916- . *The City Superintendent of Schools in Canada.* University of California, Berkeley, 1956. 2 vols, 341 p. ms.

607. HUGHES, NORAH LOUISE, 1905- . *A History of the Development of Ministerial Education in Canada from Its Inception Until 1925 in Those Churches Which Were Tributary to the United Church of Canada in Ontario, Quebec, and the Maritime Provinces of Canada.* University of Chicago, 1945. 263 p. ms. Part of the dissertation (Chapter 8, "Uniting Three Curricula", p. 195-211) was reproduced for distribution to libraries in the United States and abroad.

608. HUNTER, JAMES JAMISON, Jr., 1911- . *The Organization and the Administration of the Public School System in the Province of Nova Scotia.* Syracuse University, 1942. 264 p. ms.

609. HUTTON, HARRY KELLY, 1908- . *French-Canadian Normal Schools: An Historical, Interpretive, and Evaluative Study.* Pennsylvania State College, 1952. 166 p. ms. Abstract in *Penn State Review of Educational Research,* Vol. 4, No. 1, p. 47-50, December 1952. Abstract also in Pennsylvania State College: *Abstracts of Doctoral Dissertations,* Vol. 15, p. 327-331, 1952. Available on microfilm from University Microfilms, Ann Arbor, Michigan, as Publication No. 4,784.

610. JONASON, JONAS CHRISTIAN, 1900- . *The Large Units of School Administration in Alberta.* University of Oregon, 1951. 185 p. ms.

611. JOYCE, LESTER DOUGLAS, 1917- . *A Guide for Teachers of Arithmetic in Canadian Elementary Schools.* Columbia University, 1949. 192 p. ms. Abstract in *Teachers College Record,* Vol. 51, p. 178-179, December 1949.

612. KENNEDY, WILLIAM FRANCIS RUSSELL, 1917- . *Health, Physical Education, and Recreation in Canada: A History of Professional Preparation.* Columbia University, 1955. 184 p. ms.

613. KIDD, JAMES ROBBINS, 1915- . *A Study to Formulate a Plan for the Work of the Canadian Citizenship Council.* Columbia University, 1947. 140 p. ms.

614. KING, HERBERT BAXTER, 1879- . *The Financing of Education in British Columbia.* University of Washington, 1936. Published in modified form as *School Finance in British Columbia,* Victoria, British Columbia: Charles F. Banfield, The King's Printer, 1935. x, 230 p.

615. KISTLER, RUTH BARTHOLD, 1904- . *Religion, Education, and Language as Factors in French-Canadian Cultural Survival.* New York University, 1947. 235 p. ms. Abstract in New York University, School of Education: *Abstracts of Theses,* October 1947 - June 1948, p. 29-34.

616. KRULEVITCH, WALTER KINGSON, 1916- *National School Broadcasts of the Canadian Broadcasting Corporation.* New York University, 1949. 357 p. ms. Abstract in *Microfilm Abstracts,* Vol. 10, No. 1, p. 40-41, 1950. Available on microfilm from University Microfilms, Ann Arbor, Michigan, as Publication No. 1,568. (*Note:* The degree was conferred on Walter Kingson *Krulevitch* but subsequently he changed his name to Walter Krulevitch *Kingson,* under which his publications are indexed in the Library of Congress.)

617. LAMBERT, PIERRE DE ROME, 1921- . *Contemporary Pattern of French-Canadian Education in the Province of Quebec.* State University of Iowa, 1954. 129 p. ms. Abstract in *Dissertation Abstracts,* Vol. 14, p. 2266, December 1954. Available on microfilm from University Microfilms, Ann Arbor, Michigan, as Publication No. 10,225.

618. LANCASTER, CHARLES FREDERICK. *Religious Education under the Church of England in Canada, with Special Application to the Sunday School.* Harvard University, 1923. 474 p. ms.

619. LANGFORD, HOWARD DAVID, 1896- . *Educational Service: Its Functions and Possibilities.* Columbia University, 1932. New York: Teachers College, Columbia University, 1931. 212 p. (Teachers College Contribution to Education, No. 509. "The descriptive material is drawn mainly from educational practice in the Province of Ontario, Canada." — Introduction.)

620. LANGLEY, GERALD JAMES, 1913- . *Saskatchewan's Separate School System: A Study of One Pattern of Adjustment to the Problem of Education in a Multi-Religious Democratic Society* Columbia University, 1951. 230 p. ms. Abstract in *Dissertation Abstracts,* Vol. 12, p. 29, January 1952. Available on microfilm from University Microfilms, Ann Arbor, Michigan, as Publication No. 3,356.

621. LARSON, VERNON CARL, 1923- . *A Survey of Short Course Programs Throughout the United States and Canada.* Michigan State University of Agriculture and Applied Science, 1955. 137 p. ms. Abstract in *Dissertation Abstracts,* Vol. 17, p. 1254-1255, June 1957. Available on microfilm from University Microfilms, Ann Arbor, Michigan, as Publication No. 20,212. (Includes 14 institutions in 6 Canadian provinces.)

622. LAW, NORMA RICHMOND, 1916- . *Problems of Older Permanently Appointed Winnipeg Teachers and Administrative Procedures to Meet These Problems.* Northwestern University, 1949. 228 p. ms. Abstract under title *Problems of Older Teachers in a Large City School System and Administrative Procedures to Meet These Problems,* in Northwestern University: *Summaries of Doctoral Dissertations . . .* 1949, p. 177-182.)

623. LORIMER, WESLEY CRAWFORD, 1913- . *The Improvement of Teacher Education in the Normal School of Saskatchewan.* Columbia University, 1948. 229 p. ms. Abstract in *Teachers College Record,* Vol. 50, p. 431, March 1949.

624. LOSIER, *Sister* ST. MICHAEL, 1907- . *An Evaluation of Education for Democracy in the Secondary Schools of the Maritime Provinces of Canada.* Fordham University, 1952. 265 p. ms.

625. MacARTHUR, ANNIE ISABEL, 1916- . *Factors Associated with the Satisfactions of Dietitians in Canada: What Implications for Recruitment?* Columbia University, 1952. 104 p. ms.

626. McCALL, HORACE FILLMORE, 1914- . *Organization and Procedures of Supervision in the Alberta Public Schools.* Oregon State College, 1956. 234 p. ms.

627. McCARTHY, JOSEPH PATRICK. *The Effectiveness of the Nova Scotia High School Curriculum in Preparing Urban High School Graduates for Vocations,*

for Citizenship, and for the Worthy Use of Leisure Time. Harvard University, 1945. 270 p. ms.

628. McCAW, WILLIAM RALPH, 1927- . *Non-Institutional Training of Retarded Children in Ontario.* Northwestern University, 1956. 165 p. ms. Abstract in *Dissertation Abstracts*, Vol. 17, p. 305, February 1957. Available on microfilm from University Microfilms, Ann Arbor, Michigan as Publication No. 19,020.

629. McCUTCHEON, WILFRED WHYTE, 1919- . *Some Factors for Consideration in the Establishment of Departments of Agriculture in the Protestant Rural Secondary Schools of Quebec and in the Rural Secondary Schools of New Brunswick and Nova Scotia.* Cornell University, 1951. 291 p. ms.

630. MacDOUGALL, JOHN INNES, 1913- . *An Investigation into the Subject and Grade Level Factors in Teacher Load, with Particular Reference to the Program of Studies for the High Schools of British Columbia.* University of Washington, 1945. 93 p. ms.

631. McDOUGALL, WILLIAM DEWAR, 1895- . *Suggestions for the Improvement of Elementary Teacher Education in the Province of Alberta.* Columbia University, 1946. 239 p. ms.

632. MacGREGOR, HUGH ALTON, 1893- . *A Proposal for Canadian Federal-Provincial Participation in Vocational Agriculture.* Oregon State College, 1951. 271 p. ms. For master's thesis by same author, see No. 769.

633. MacKENZIE, WILLIAM HOWARD. *A Plan of Procedures for the Reorganization of the School Administrative Units in the Province of New Brunswick.* Columbia University, 1942. 219 p. ms.

634. MacLAURIN, DONALD LESLIE, 1881- . *The History of Education in the Crown Colonies of Vancouver Island and British Columbia and in the Province of British Columbia.* University of Washington, 1937. 359 p. ms. Abstract in University of Washington: *Abstracts of Theses . . .* Vol. 2, 1937, p. 495-500.

635. McLEAN, Rev. DONALD ALEXANDER, 1886- . *Catholic Schools in Western Canada: Their Legal Status.* Catholic University of America, 1923. Toronto, Canada: The Extension Print, 1923. x, 162 p. Published also in installments, complete except for bibliography, in *Catholic Educational Review*, as follows: Vol. 19, p. 371-380, June 1921; Vol. 19, p. 458-463, September 1921; Vol. 19, p. 509-516, October 1921; Vol. 19, p. 571-579, November 1921; Vol. 19, p. 641-645, December 1921; Vol. 20, p. 35-41, January 1922; Vol. 20, p. 100-106, February 1922. For master's thesis by same author, see No. 773.

636. MacLEOD, NELSON BURGESS, 1901- . *A Plan for Teacher Education in Nova Scotia, with Emphasis on In-Service Education.* Columbia University, 1949. 240 p. ms. Abstract in *Teachers College Record*, Vol. 51, p. 388, March 1950.

637. MACHLIN, EVANGELINE LEWIS. *Educational Dramatics in the Maritime Universities in Canada.* Columbia University, 1942. 139, 109 p. ms.

638. MACMILLAN, CYRUS JOHN. *The Folk Songs of Canada.* Harvard University, 1909. 2 vols. 1101 p. ms.

639. MARSHALL, MORTIMER VILLIERS, 1898- . *An Evaluation of the Present Teacher-Training Program in Nova Scotia, with Recommendations for Improvement.* Harvard University, 1930. 343 p. ms.

640. MATTHEWS, JOHN CLARK, 1907- . *The Report of the Survey of the Public Schools of Charlottetown, Prince Edward Island.* Columbia University, 1954. 272 p. ms.

641. MEAGHER, JOHN WILLIAM, 1927- . *A Projected Plan for the Reorganization of Physical Education Teacher-Training Programs in Canada.* Pennsylvania State University, 1958. 174 p. ms. Abstract in *Dissertation Abstracts*, Vol. 19, p. 1299-1300, December 1958. Available on microfilm from University Microfilms, Ann Arbor, Michigan, as Mic. 58-7293.

642. MELVIN, ARTHUR GORDON, 1894- . *The Professional Training of Teachers for the Ontario Public Schools.* Columbia University, 1923. Published as *Professional Training of Teachers for the Canadian Public Schools as Typified by Ontario,* Baltimore, Maryland: Warwick & York, 1923. 212 p.

643. MILLER, HERBERT E., 1906- . *Scholarships for Alberta.* Columbia University, 1947. 50 p. ms.

644. MILLER, JAMES COLLINS, 1880-1940. *Rural Schools in Canada: Their Organization, Administration, and Supervision.* Columbia University, 1913. New York: Teachers College, Columbia University, 1913. xi, 236 p. (Teachers College, Contribution to Education, No. 61.) For master's thesis by same author, see No. 779.

645. MORRISON, ALLAN BRUCE, 1910- . *A Proposal for Reorganizing Intermediate Administrative Districts in the Province of Nova Scotia.* Columbia University, 1948. 204 p. ms.

646. MOWAT, GORDON LESLIE, 1916- . *A Plan for Reorganizing the Costs of Pupil Transportation in Alberta for Purposes of Equalization of Educational Opportunity.* Stanford University, 1953. 206 p. ms. Abstract in *Dissertation Abstracts*, Vol. 13, No. 5, p. 707-708, 1953. Available on microfilm from University Microfilms, Ann Arbor, Michigan, as Publication No. 5,772.

647. NEWCOMER, RICHARD SEYLER, 1910- . *The Administration of the Extension Courses of the University of Maryland at Harmon Air Force Base in Newfoundland, 1951-1952.* Duke University, 1953. 249 p. ms.

648. O'NEILL, FLORENCE MARY. *A Plan for the Development of an Adult Education Program for Rural Newfoundland.* Columbia University, 1944. 154 p. ms.

649. OVIATT, DELMER THOMAS, 1911- . *A Revision to the Program of Studies for the Elementary Schools of Alberta, Grades I-IV.* Stanford University, 1949. 333 p. ms. Abstract in Stanford University: *Abstracts of Dissertations . . .* 1948-49, p. 486-489. For master's thesis by same author, see No. 788.

650. PATTERSON, LAURENCE PRESCOTT, 1904- . *A Plan for the Reorganization of the Ad-*

ministrative Structure of Protestant Education in Greater Montreal. Columbia University, 1947. 227 p. ms.

651. PLEWES, DORIS WILLARD. *A Course of Study in Health, Physical Education, and Recreation, London, Ontario (Kindergarten — Grade XIII.)* Columbia University, 1943. 430 p. ms.

652. READ, EDWIN ALBERT. *Promotion Policies and Practices in the Schools of Alberta.* University of Oregon, 1956. 393 p. ms.

653. REES, ROBERT ELLSWORTH, 1907- . *Superintendents of Schools in Relation to School Division Boards in the Province of Alberta.* Northwestern University, 1947. 262 p. ms. Abstract in Northwestern University: *Summaries of Doctoral Dissertations,* Vol. 15, p. 142-146.

654. REEVES, ARTHUR WEIR, 1907- . *The Equalization of Educational Opportunity in the Province of Alberta.* Stanford University, 1949. 212 p. ms. Abstract in Stanford University: *Abstracts of Dissertations . . . 1948-49,* p. 500-503.

655. RICHARDSON, WILLIAM LEEDS, 1873- . *The Administration of Schools in the Cities of the Dominion of Canada.* University of Chicago, 1919. Toronto, Canada: J. M. Dent & Sons, Ltd., 1922. xxviii, 315 p.

656. RITCHIE, MYLES HOUSTON, 1911- . *An Investigation of Audio-Visual Education with Emphasis on British Columbia.* Oregon State College, 1943. 200 p. ms.

657. ROBERTSON, ELIZABETH IRENE, 1920- . *Person-Centered Teacher Training for Canadian Baptist Sunday Schools.* Southwestern Baptist Theological Seminary, 1958. 202 p. ms.

658. ROBINSON, GEORGE CARLTON, 1882- . *A Historical and Critical Account of Public Secondary Education in the Province of Ontario, Canada, 1792-1916.* Harvard University, 1918. 189 p. ms.

659. ROSE, MARY JEAN, 1905- . *A History of School Broadcasting in Canada.* Northwestern University, 1951. 398 p. ms. Abstract in Northwestern University: *Summaries of Doctoral Dissertations,* Vol. 19, 1951, p. 181-185.

660. ROSS, GEORGE JOHN, 1910- . *The Courts and the Canadian Public Schools.* University of Chicago, 1948. 246 p. ms.

661. ROWLES, EDITH CHILD, 1906- . *A Brief History of Some Early Canadian Developments in Home Economics.* Columbia University, 1956. 227 p. ms. Abstract in *Journal of Home Economics,* 50: 224, March 1958.

662. SHIPLEY, CHARLES MORTON, 1910- . *Proposals for Developing the Curriculum for a Two-Year Program in Nova Scotia's Provincial Normal College.* Columbia University, 1948. 195 p. ms.

663. SMITH, DENIS CHARLES, 1912- . *A Study of the Origin and Development of Administrative Organization in the Educational System of British Columbia.* University of California, Los Angeles, 1952. 257 p. ms.

664. SPARBY, HARRY THEODORE, 1906- . *History of the Alberta School System to 1925.* Stanford University, 1958. 236 p. ms. Abstract in *Dissertation Abstracts,* Vol. 19, p. 726. October 1958. Available on microfilm from University Microfilms, Ann Arbor, Michigan, as Mic. 58-3624.

665. SPENCE, RUTH ELIZABETH, 1890- . (Arndt, Mrs. Ruth Elizabeth Spence, in Library of Congress card catalog.) *Education as Growth: Its Significance for the Secondary Schools of Ontario.* Columbia University, 1925. Toronto, Canada: 1925. viii, 183 p.

666. STREVIG, JENNIE MAY. *A History of the Missionary Education Movement in the United States and Canada.* New York University, 1930. 157 p. ms.

667. THIBEAU, PATRICK WILFRED, 1892- . *Education in Nova Scotia before 1811.* Catholic University of America, 1922. Washington: 1922. 121 p. Published also in installments, covering first 74 pages only, in *Catholic Educational Review,* as follows: Vol. 21, p. 101-107, February 1923; Vol. 21, p. 166-171, March 1923; Vol. 21, p. 233-238, April 1923; Vol. 21, p. 294-300, May 1923; Vol. 21: p. 365-370, June 1923; Vol. 21, p. 425-430, September 1923; Vol. 21, p. 487-493, October 1923; Vol. 21, p. 552-558, November 1923; Vol. 21, p. 606-612, December 1923, Vol. 22, p. 38-43, January 1924; Vol. 22: p. 107-111, February 1924. February 1924 installment concludes "to be continued", but no further installments published.

668. TRUEMAN, GEORGE JOHNSTONE, 1872- . *School Funds in the Province of Quebec.* Columbia University, 1919. New York: Teachers College, Columbia University, 1920. iii, 158 p. (Teachers College Contribution to Education, No. 106.)

669. VAN VLIET, MAURICE LEWIS, 1913- . *A Guide to Administrative Policies for Physical Education in Canadian Public Schools, Grades One through Nine.* University of California, Los Angeles, 1950. 127 p. ms.

670. WAIDE, FREDERICK GORDON. *A History of Primary Education in Ontario and Quebec.* New York University, 1912. 106 p. ms.

671. WALES, BERTRAM EDWARDS, 1905- . *The Development of Adult Education in British Columbia.* Oregon State College, 1958. 235 p. ms. Abstract in *Dissertation Abstracts,* Vol. 19, p. 724, October 1958. Available on microfilm from University Microfilms, Ann Arbor, Michigan, as Mic. 58-3828.

672. WALKER, BERNAL ERNEST, 1911- . *Public Secondary Education in Alberta: Organization and Curriculum, 1889-1951.* Stanford University, 1953. 301 p. ms. Abstract in *Dissertation Abstracts,* Vol. 15, p. 1776-1777, October 1955. Available on microfilm from University Microfilms, Ann Arbor, Michigan, as Publication No. 13,294.

673. WEEKS, HAROLD LOUIS. *Organization, Administration, and Supervision of Business Education in British Columbia.* Harvard University, 1943. 298 p. ms.

674. WELLS, WARD M., 1911- . *An Evaluation of the Methods Either in Use or Proposed for Use to Determine Team Winners in Interscholastic and Intercollegiate Ski Competitions in the United States and Canada.* Indiana University, 1955. 179 p. ms.

675. WIGGIN, GLADYS ANNA, 1907- . *Agricultural Adult Education Programs in Saskatchewan.* University of Maryland, 1947. 233 p. ms. Abstract in University of Maryland: *Abstracts of Dissertations . . .* 1952, p. 45.

676. WILKINS, CECIL JAMES, 1898- . *An Administrative Plan for the Improvement of Reading in the Toronto Secondary Schools.* Columbia University, 1952. 181 p. ms.

677. WILSON, JOHN ABRAHAM ROSS, 1911- . *The Counselor in Canadian Secondary Schools.* Oregon State College, 1952. 293 p. ms.

678. WOODS, DAVIS SCOTT, 1884- . *Financing the Schools of Rural Manitoba.* University of Chicago, 1935. Chicago: 1935. xiii, 261 p. Photolithographed. Private edition distributed to libraries in the United States and abroad.

See also Nos. 122, 138, 141, 142, 143, 147, 149, 151, 161, 176, 532, 535

MASTERS

679. ADDISON, WINFORD DEWEY. *The Educational Activities of Kiwanis International.* University of Chicago, 1930. 200 p. ms. (Covers activities of clubs in Canada and the United States.)

680. AIKENHEAD, JOHN DOUGLAS. *Consolidated and Non-Consolidated Schools in Manitoba.* University of Chicago, 1930. 84 p. ms. For doctoral dissertation by same author, see No. 545.

681. ALDRIDGE, ATHELSTAN ARNOLD, 1902- . *A History of the Guidance Program for Schools of Alberta.* Oregon State College, 1954. 65 p. ms.

682. ALEXANDER, MARCELLE V., 1909- . (Later, Mrs. James E. Boren) *A Study of the Personnel, Status, and Activities of Directors of Religious Education in Local Protestant Churches of the United States and Canada.* Presbyterian College of Christian Education, 1938. 114 p. ms. Published under joint authorship of Otto Mayer and Marcelle Alexander Boren as *Directors of Religious Education and Their Profession,* Chicago: International Council of Religious Education, 1939. 56 p. (International Bulletins of Religious Education, Research Bulletin, No. 18). Abstract in *Selected Graduate Theses in Religious Education,* 1938, p. 5. (Includes replies from churches in Nova Scotia and Ontario.)

683. ALLEN, EDWIN G. *A Study in Educational Testing: A Comparison of American Standardized Tests and Canadian Standardized Tests as Given to Grade Six in the Ralph Waldo Emerson School, Newton, Massachusetts, U.S.A., and Grade Six of Devon School, Fredericton, New Brunswick.* Clemson Agricultural College, 1955.

684. ANDERSON, CARL ANTHONY, 1883- . *An Educational Index for the Provincial School Systems of Canada.* University of California, Berkeley, 1929. 35 p. ms.

685. ANDERSON, WILLIAM ABRAHAM. *A Study of Secondary School Examinations.* University of Chicago, 1928. 114 p. ms. (Manitoba)

686. ARMSTRONG, STEPHEN. *A Survey of Boys Physical Education in the English-Speaking Public High Schools of the City of Montreal and District.* Springfield College, 1954. 176 p. ms.

687. BAESZLER, Sister ST. ALFRED OF ROME, 1898- . *The Contributions of the Congregation of Notre Dame of Montreal to Education in the United States.* Fordham University, 1939. 96 p. ms. Abstract in Fordham University: *Dissertations Accepted for Higher Degrees,* 1940. p. 64. For doctoral dissertation by same author, see No. 550.

688. BAKER, LAURA. *The Clothing Purchases of High School Girls in Home Economics Classes of Toronto High School.* Colorado State College of Agriculture and Mechanic Arts, 1943. 99 p. ms.

689. BARBER, DAVID ALEXANDER. *The Educational System of British Columbia.* University of Washington, 1919. 81 p. ms.

690. BARRETTE, Rev. JOSEPH ARMOND. *The Teaching of Religion in the Primary Schools of the Province of Quebec.* Catholic University of America, 1928. 64 p. ms.

691. BASKERVILLE, DORIS RENWICK, 1924- . *A Survey of Student Personnel Services in English-Speaking Canadian Colleges and Universities with Particular Reference to the Role of the Dean of Women.* Syracuse University, 1953. 245 p. ms.

692. BASKINE, Mrs. GERTRUDE F. duTREMBLAY. *New France in Canada: Abstract of Education in the Province of Quebec, 1635-1759.* Columbia University, 1939. 57 p. ms.

693. BATES, Sister ANNE CATHERINE. *A Study of the Adult Education Movement in Nova Scotia.* Villanova College, 1941. 64 p. ms.

694. BELL, RALPH ROGERS, 1922- . *The History and Development of Agricultural Education in Secondary Schools of the United States, with Implications for a Program of Agricultural Education in Secondary Schools of Canada.* Oregon State College, 1949. 178 p. ms.

695. BERNIER, Rev. ADRIAN. *The Contributions of the Schools of Sainte-Anne-de-la-Pocatiere to Catholic Education in the Province of Quebec.* Catholic University of America, 1942. 115 p. ms.

696. BICKELL, DAVIL EARL. *The Organization of an Audio-Visual Bureau in the Calgary City School System.* University of Southern California, 1947. 54 p. ms.

697. BIE, ELIZABETH HYNDMAN. *A Study of the Health Knowledge of Grade Twelve Students in the Province of Saskatchewan, Canada.* University of Washington, 1938. 43 p. ms. Abstract in University of Washington: *Abstracts of Theses,* Vol. 4, 1939, p. 55-56.

698. BINNIE, RUTH. *In-Service Education of Home Economics Teachers in the Province of Nova Scotia: A Report of Supervision, with Emphasis on the Demonstration Technique.* Syracuse University, 1948. 173 p. ms.

699. BLACK, WILLIAM GRIFFITHS, 1898- . *A Comparative Study of the Public School Curricula of the Provinces of Canada.* University of Chicago, 1926. 123 p. ms. For doctoral dissertation by same author, see No. 554.

700. BROOKS, C. BERNADETTE. *A Study of the Occupational Interests and Motives of Certain High School Students in Nova Scotia.* Catholic University of America, 1958.

701. BROWN, CLIFTON GILBERT. *An Analytical Study of the Junior Matriculation Examinations of British Columbia.* University of Washington, 1935. 274 p. ms.

702. BROWN, DENIS WORSFOLD. *A Study of Special Needs and Problems in the Administration of an Audio-Visual Programme in a British Columbia School System.* University of Washington, 1957.

703. BROWN, MARJORY FRANCES. *A Study of the Public School Publicity in Selected Newspapers of Southern Alberta during 1955.* University of Washington, 1956. 107 p. ms.

704. BUXTON, EARL WILLIAM. *A Teacher's Guide to the Grade Eleven Literature Program in Alberta High Schools.* University of Washington, 1955. 258 p. ms.

705. CAMERON, JEAN S. *A Follow-up Study of Graduates and Non-Graduates of Certain Schools for Crippled Children in the United States and Canada during the Ten-Year Period 1944 through 1954.* Boston University, 1958.

706. CAMPBELL, CLAUDE LANE. *The British Columbia Teachers Federation.* University of Washington, 1930. 65 p. ms.

707. CAMPBELL, HAROLD LANE. *The Development of a Large Educational Administrative Area in British Columbia.* University of Washington, 1938. 110 p. ms. Abstract in University of Washington: *Abstracts of Theses*, Vol. 3, 1938, p. 65-71.

708. CAMPION, ANNA LOUISE, 1904- . *Education for Special Librarians in the United States and Canada in 1946 and 1952.* Drexel Institute of Technology, 1953. 37 p. ms.

709. CANTELON, HARTFORD ALEXANDER, 1918- . *A Study of the Religious Influence of State Junior Colleges in Alberta, Canada, and California in the Light of Church-State Relationships.* Pacific School of Religion, 1949.

710. CHARBONNEAU, M. L. GABRIELLE. *The History of the School of Public Health Nursing at the University of Montreal, Canada, 1925-1950.* Catholic University of America, 1956. 89 p. ms.

711. CHATTERS, HARRIETT. *Negro Education in Kent County, Ontario, up to 1890.* Howard University, 1956. 70 p. ms.

712. CHITTICK, RAE. *An Evaluation of the Social and Cultural Life of Teachers in Rural Communities in Alberta.* Stanford University, 1943. 116 p. ms.

713. CLARKE, HELEN. *A Study of Dietetic Courses for Pupil Nurses in Class "A" Hospitals in the United States and Canada.* Ohio State University, 1922. 21 p. ms.

714. CONNAUGHTON, Rev. EDWARD ANTHONY. *A Study of the Provisions Made for the Catholic Elementary Schools of the Province of Ontario.* Catholic University of America, 1940. 95 p. ms.

715. COPP, HAROLD WESLEY. *The History of Physical Education and Health in the Elementary and Secondary Schools of Ontario, Canada.* University of Michigan, 1933. 85 p. ms.

716. COSTANTINI, DOMINIC EURICO. *The Manitoba Training Program for Trade and Industrial Teachers Compared with Other Provinces and States.* Colorado Agricultural and Mechanical College, 1951. 440 p. ms. Abstract in *Research in Industrial Education, 1930-1955*, p. 21.

717. CRUMLISH, Brother MICHAEL LEO. *The Christian Brothers as Factor in the Development of Education in Newfoundland.* University of Notre Dame, 1932. 96 p. ms.

718. CYRILLA, Sister MARY. *Mary of the Incarnation: Pioneer Educator and Teacher of French Canada.* Mount St. Joseph Teachers College, 1956. 68 p. ms.

719. DAFOE, HELEN ISABEL. *Civic Education in Secondary Schools in Ontario.* Columbia University, 1919.

720. DANIELS, LEROI ALLISTER. *The History of Education in Calgary.* University of Washington, 1954. 215 p. ms.

721. DEAN, CHARLOTTE RUTH. *A Report of a Survey of the Graduates of the Dietitians Course from 1928 to 1933, Central Technical School, Toronto.* Columbia University, 1935. 21 p. ms.

722. DION, Sister RAYMOND DE JESUS, 1918- . *An Analysis of the Principles of Religious and Moral Guidance Applied in the Federation of Catholic Guides of the Province of Quebec.* Fordham University 1952. 145 p. ms.

723. DOLE, HARVEY PETER. *The Professional Training of Canadian Teachers.* Columbia University, 1908. 34 p. ms.

724. DUNN, ERIC JOHN. *Prediction of Freshman Success in the University of British Columbia.* University of Washington, 1939. 47 p. ms. Abstract in University of Washington: *Abstracts of Theses*, 1941, Vol. 5, p. 33-36.

725. DUNPHY, Sister MARY HILDEGARDE. *A Comparison of the Reading Achievement of Sixth Grade Urban and Non-Urban Pupils in the Catholic Schools of the Province of Newfoundland.* Catholic University of America, 1956. 29 p. ms.

726. EDLUND, RICHARD ARTHUR, 1924- . *Training and Eligibility Rules of High School Athletics in the United States and Canada.* University of North Dakota, 1954. 56 p. ms. Abstract in University of North Dakota: *Abstracts of Doctoral Dissertations and Masters' Theses* ... 1954, p. 47.

727. EVENSON, ARCHIBALD B. *The Length and Organization of the School Year in the United States and Canada.* Stanford University, 1954. 97 p. ms.

728. FERGUSON, RUTH HUNYCKE. *Home Background of Home Economics Students of the University of Manitoba as an Index to College Training for Family Living.* Iowa State College of Agriculture and Mechanic Arts, 1937. 84 p. ms.

729. FISCHETTE, Rev. ROBERT MATTHEW. *Father Bellisle's Philosophy of Education.* University of Detroit, 1943. 81 p. ms.

730. FISHER, OLIVE MARGARET. *The School Festival and Its Contribution to the Cultural Life of Alberta.* Stanford University, 1943. 136 p. ms.

731. FOREST, Sister JEANNE. *The Preparation of Survey Schedules for the Selection of the Facilities in Three Canadian Provinces for the Organization of a Collegiate Program in Nursing.* Catholic University of America, 1945. 111 p. ms. (Includes Alberta, Manitoba, and Saskatchewan.)

732. GEIL, MILTON GEORGE. *The Development of the Canadian Standard Efficiency Program.* North-Western University, 1928. 126 p. ms.

733. GERMANEY, RICHARD THOMAS HOWARD. *A Teaching Manual for Beginning Teachers of Boys' Physical Education in the Protestant High Schools of Montreal.* Springfield College, 1955. 241 p. ms.

734. GILMER, WILLIAM ERNEST. *Training for Church Membership in the United Church of Canada.* Oberlin College, 1958. 128 p. ms.

735. GISH, WALTER KUHNS. *An Examination of the Alberta High School Curriculum.* State College of Washington, 1944. 137 p. ms.

736. GORMLEY, Sister ST. FRANCIS FAVRIANO, 1907- . (Also given as Favriano, Sister St. Francis). *The Congregation de Notre Dame of Montreal and the Ideals of Catholic Education.* Fordham University, 1955. 89 p. ms.

737. GRAHAM, GEORGE ARTHUR, 1909- . *The Organization of Public Education in British Columbia.* State College of Washington, 1951. 78 p. ms.

738. GRAY, WILLIAM HENRY. *A Comparative Study of the Entrance Requirements of American and Canadian Universities.* University of Chicago, 1926. 120 p. printed.

739. GRYTE, CARL ANTONIUS. *An Analysis of the High School Curricula in the Provinces of Canada.* University of Chicago, 1927. 139 p. ms.

740. HEDGES, HENRY GEORGE. *An Analysis of the Attitudes Expressed in Press Comments on the Recommendations Pertaining to Grade Reorganization in the Report of the Royal Commission on Education in Ontario, 1950.* University of Michigan, 1952. 109 p. ms.

741. HUGHTON, CHARLES W. *A Study of the Problem of Guidance in the Central Collegiate Institute, Hamilton, Ontario.* University of Michigan, 1937. 49 p. ms.

742. HUNKIN, ARTHUR THOMAS. *A Remedial Reading Project in a British Columbia Junior High School* University of Washington, 1940. 90 p. ms. Abstract in University of Washington: *Abstracts of Theses*, Vol. 6, 1942, p. 62-63.

743. HUSSEY, Rev. JOHN M. *Catholic Action in the Schools and Colleges of Quebec.* Catholic University of America, 1937. 112 p. ms.

744. JENSEN, JOHN C., 1901- . *An Analysis of the Job Instructor Training Program in Canada during World War II.* Stout Institute, 1949. 92 p. ms. Abstract in *Research in Industrial Education, 1930-1955*, p. 512.

745. JOHNS, RICHARD JAMES. *Origin and Development of Technical Education in Canada.* Colorado State College of Agriculture and Mechanic Arts. 131 p. ms. Abstract in *Research in Industrial Education, 1930-1955*, p. 132.

746. JONES, FRANK ARTHUR. *Training of Teachers in the Province of Ontario, Canada.* University of Chicago, 1915. 86 p. ms.

747. KELLY, MARY GLENNA, 1909- . *The Cooperative Movement and Its Promotion by Catholic Leaders.* Boston University, 1940. 121 p. ms. (Includes consideration of St. Francis Xavier University, Nova Scotia.)

748. KENDRICK, ALBERT C. *To Make Recommendations for a Program of Industrial Arts Teacher Education with Special Reference to British Columbia.* Western Washington College of Education, 1958.

749. KING, DOROTHY. *Professional Training for Social Work in Canada.* New York University, 1944. 63 p. ms.

750. KING, KEITH VICTOR. *A Study to Determine the Relationship between Total Body Reaction Time and the Chronological Age of Boys.* International YMCA College, 1953. 48 p. ms. (Refers to boys in Nova Scotia.)

751. KNOTT, WALLACE WEDNELL DINSDALE. *The Junior College in British Columbia.* Stanford University, 1932. 114 p. ms. Abstract in *Junior College Journal*, 3: 114, November 1932.

752. LaFLAMME, Sister MADELEINE DE JESUS. *A Study of Educational Requirements as Stated in Acts Relating to the Registration of Nurses Passed in the Nine Provinces of Canada from 1910 to 1944.* Catholic University of America, 1947. 58 p. ms.

753. LAVIGNE, Sister DENISE MARGUERITE. *Present Status and Needs of Nurse Instructors in a Selected Group of Canadian Schools of Nursing.* Catholic University of America, 1952. 68 p. ms. (Covers 44 schools in British Columbia, Alberta,

Saskatchewan, Manitoba, Ontario, Quebec, New Brunswick, and Nova Scotia.)

754. LAWSON, ANNE M. *Problems of Teaching Family Relations in Secondary Schools, Ontario, Canada.* Iowa State College of Agriculture and Mechanic Arts, 1958.

755. LE BLANC, RENE. *An Evaluation of Provisions Made by the Secondary Schools of New Brunswick in the Preparation of French-Speaking Pupils for University Matriculation.* Catholic University of America, 1957. 48 p. ms.

756. LEDUC, ROBERT JOSEPH, 1930- . *The History and Present Status of Industrial Arts in the Public Schools of British Columbia.* Oregon State College, 1958. 148 p. ms.

757. LEE, MARGARET O. *A Study of the Needs of Students in Relation to the Adequacy of Courses in Social Understandings at the Toronto Teachers College.* Cornell University, 1958.

758. LEVIRS, FRANKLIN PARKER. *The Six-Year High School in British Columbia: A Status Study.* University of Idaho, 1941. 116 p. ms.

759. LISTER, FRASER. *First Steps in Curriculum Revision in British Columbia.* University of Washington, 1931. 98 p. ms.

760. LISTER, RALPH WILLIAM. *A Survey of Physical Education and Athletic Administration in Canadian Colleges and Universities.* International YMCA College, 1935. 155 p. ms.

761. LITTLE, ALEXANDER MILTON. *Religious Education in the Protestant State-Schools of the Province of Quebec.* Oberlin College, 1950, 109 p. ms.

762. LOOSLEY, ELIZABETH W. *The Home and School Association as a Socializing Agency in an Upper Middle-Class Canadian Community.* University of Chicago, 1952. 179 p. ms.

763. LYONS, Sister CLARE MARIE. *A Proposed Four-Year Curriculum Leading to a Baccalaureate Degree in Nursing in the Catholic Schools of Nursing in Nova Scotia.* Catholic University of America, 1951. 58 p. ms.

764. McCORMACK, Sister MARY BASIL. *The Educational Work of the Sisters of Mercy in Newfoundland.* Catholic University of America, 1956. 131 p. ms. Abstract in *Catholic Educational Review*, Vol. 55, p. 555, November 1957.

765. McDILL, WILLIAM ALEXANDER. *Apprenticeship in Canada and the Northeastern Border States.* Colorado Agricultural and Mechanical College, 1948. 663 p. ms. Abstract in *Research in Industrial Education, 1930-1955*, p. 494.

766. McEACHERN, AUBREY. *A Comparative Study of the Development of School Legislation in Alberta and Saskatchewan.* University of Minnesota, 1934. 193 p. ms.

767. McFARLANE, ADA BERNEICE, 1912- . *The Adequacy of the Alberta High School Fabrics and Dress Courses to Meet Student Needs.* Oregon State College, 1957. 72 p. ms.

768. MacFARLANE, ROBERT MANSON. *A Study of Commercial Education in New Brunswick, Canada.* Columbia University, 1935. 125 p. ms.

769. MacGREGOR, HUGH ALTON, 1893- . *An Evaluation of Existing Courses of Study in Pre-College Science in Terms of the Needs of Alberta, Canada.* Cornell University, 1934. 106 p. ms. For Doctoral dissertation by same author, see No. 632.

770. McKINNON, ALEXANDER. *A Supervisory Rural School in Saskatchewan: Present Defects and Suggested Improvements.* University of Washington, 1938. 66 p. ms. Abstract in *University of Washington: Abstracts of Theses*, Vol. 3, 1938, p. 93-95.

771. MacKINNON, GEORGE WATSON. *The Evolution of the School System of British Columbia.* University of Washington, 1920. 63 p. ms.

772. MacLATCHY, JOSEPHINE HARRIET. *The Legislative History of New Brunswick Education from 1802 to 1847.* University of Chicago, 1915. 73 p. ms.

773. McLEAN, Rev. DONALD ALEXANDER, 1886- . *Legal Status of Catholic Schools in Western Canada.* Catholic University of America, 1920. 70 p. ms. For doctoral dissertation by same author, see No. 635.

774. McLELLAN, FREDERICK ANDREW. *The Organization of a Visual Instruction Department in the Kitsilano High School, Vancouver, British Columbia.* University of Washington, 1934. 143 p. ms.

775. McQUEEN, JAMES. *The Development of the Technical and Vocational Schools of Ontario.* Columbia University, 1934. 64 p. ms.

776. MARTIN, FREDERICK D. *Jewelry, Lapidary, and Art Metal Work Equipment for the Winnipeg Technical-Vocational School.* Colorado Agricultural and Mechanical College, 1950. 118 p. ms.

777. MILES, GEORGE WILLIAM. *The Preparation of Industrial Arts Teachers in the United States and Canada.* Colorado State College of Education, 1950. 193 p. ms. Abstract in *Research in Industrial Education, 1930-1955*, p. 28.

778. MILLER, ERNEST ALLAN. *History and Development of the Question of Religion in the School System of Ontario, 1790-1841.* Columbia University, 1900. 73 p. ms.

779. MILLER, JAMES COLLINS, 1880-1940. *Rural Education in Canada.* Columbia University, 1911, 209 p. ms. For doctoral dissertation by same author, see No. 644.

780. MORRIS, RAYMOND PHILIP. *A Study of the Library Facilities of a Group of Representative Protestant Theological Seminaries in the United States and Canada.* Columbia University, 1933. 235 p. ms.

781. MULCAHY, Sister MARY NOLASCO. *An Analysis of Errors Made by Grade Eleven Students in Algebra in the Secondary Schools of Newfoundland.* Catholic University of America, 1957. 48 p. ms.

782. MURRAY, KENNETH HEMSLEY. *Anter-posterior Spinal Curves, Arch Angles, and Physical Fitness of High School Boys.* International YMCA College, 1935. 237 p. ms. (Refers to Canadian boys.)

783. NETHERCOTT, JAMES P. S. *A Project to Provide and Disseminate Suitable Occupational Information for the New Guidance Program, London, Ontario.* Columbia University, 1947. 12 p. ms.

784. NEUFELD, HERBERT VICTOR, 1930- . *The Larger School Unit: An Approach to the Problem in Manitoba.* University of Minnesota, 1956. 87 p. ms.

785. NEWTON, DONALD M. *A Study of Student Costs in Selected High Schools of Alberta, Canada.* Brigham Young University, 1958.

786. NISH, DALE LEROY, 1932- . *Early Identification of Dropouts in Rural Schools of Alberta, Canada.* Brigham Young University, 1958.

787. OLNEY, PETER, 1924- ; LAVERNVICH, ALPHONSE; and LEWIS, VERNON. *The Social Studies Taught in the Secondary Schools in Canada.* Boston University, 1951. 203 p. ms.

788. OVIATT, DELMER THOMAS, 1911- . *A Study of the Progress of Alberta High School Students Granted Conditional Promotion.* Stanford University, 1943. 154 p. ms. For doctoral dissertation by same author, see No. 649.

789. PECK, MIRIAM LOUISE. *The Development of a System of Progress Cards for Schools in British Columbia.* University of Washington, 1941. 124 p. ms. Abstract in University of Washington: *Abstracts in Theses,* Vol. 6, 1942, p. 72-74.

790. PETERSON, LELAND DEAN. *The School System of Alberta.* University of Idaho, 1940. 61 p. ms.

791. POTTER, WILLIAM SYDNEY. *A Study of the Position of the Principal and the Vice-Principal in the Administration of Secondary Schools of British Columbia.* University of Washington, 1952. 203 p. ms.

792. PRITCHARD, DONALD L. *A Comparative Study of Grade VIII Standards in Arithemetic.* University of Washington, 1945. 83 p. ms. (Based upon data from Kitsilano Junior High School, Vancouver, B. C.)

793. REID, WILLIAM DENNAN. *The Construction of a Mathematics Test for Use in Grade Eleven Classes of the Province of British Columbia.* University of Washington, 1951. 126 p. ms.

794. RICE, LETHA E. *A Study of the Status of Speech Correction in the Public Schools of the United States and Canada, with Suggestions and Exercises for Speech Correction in the Elementary School.* Kansas State Teachers College, Emporia, 1931. 200 p. ms.

795. RICHARD, ISABEL. *A Handbook for Speech and Hearing Therapists in the Winnipeg Public Schools.* Kent State University, 1953.

796. ROBB, JEAN ARCHIBALD. *A Course of Study in Home Economics for Grades Seven, Eight, and Nine in Halifax, Nova Scotia.* Syracuse University, 1934. 177 p. ms.

797. ROBERT, Sister FRANCOISE DE CHANTAL. *A Study of Advanced Programs in Teaching, Supervision, and Administration in Nursing Education Offered by Four Canadian Universities.* Catholic University of America, 1951. 46 p. ms. (Universities are not identified by name.)

798. ROGERS, RUTH AUDREY. *French-Canadian Folk Music.* Northwestern University, 1947. 115 p. ms.

799. ROLLS, Rev. ROBERT LAIDLAW. *Program for the Religious Education in the High Schools of the Province of Ontario.* Niagara University, 1957.

800. RYAN, JOHN DAVID, 1915- . *A Study of Canadian-American Commercial Secondary Education along the St. Lawrence River.* New York State College for Teachers, Albany, 1943. 109 p. ms.

801. RYAN, Rev. WILLIAM MICHAEL. *The Educational System of the Province of Quebec.* Catholic University of America, 1924. 46 p. ms. Published in part as "The Jews in the Schools of Quebec," *Catholic Educational Review,* Vol. 22, p. 201-208, April 1924.

802. SAUNDERS, ROBERT JAMES. *The Parallel Development of Art Education in Canada and the United States, with Emphasis on the History of Art Education in Canada.* Pennsylvania State College, 1954. 93 p. ms.

803. SCHAEFER, CHARLOTTE SKILLING. *Education in Canada.* Indiana University, 1939. 168 p. ms.

804. SHARKEY, CHARLES WILFRED, 1918- . *The History of Education in the Province of Prince Edward Island.* Boston University, 1948. 39 p. ms.

805. SHKLANKA, ELIAS. *A Comparative Study of the Content of American and Canadian Textbooks in English History.* University of Chicago, 1925. 71 p. ms.

806. SHOPLAND, STELLA. *Status of Married Women Teachers in the Province of British Columbia.* University of Washington, 1957.

807. SHUMAN, WILLIAM LAWRENCE. *The Organization and Administration of Public Education in Canada.* Ohio State University, 1929. 130 p. ms. Abstract in Ohio State University: *Abstracts of Theses Presented by Candidates for the Master's Degree,* August 1929, p. 160-161. (Abstracts of Master's Theses, No. 1. Contains separate chapters on Quebec and Newfoundland.)

808. SMITH, HERBERT FREDERICK A. *Student Reactions to the St. Johns, Quebec, High School.* University of Michigan, 1943. 84 p. ms.

809. SNIDER, WINIFRED D. *Extramural Library Service in Libraries and Extension Departments of Canadian Universities.* Columbia University, 1948. 64 p. ms.

Canada

810. SNOWDON, HERBERT ASHLEY. *A Comparative Study of Secondary Education in Ontario and Louisiana.* Tulane University of Louisiana, 1930. 75 p. ms.

811. SPICER, STANLEY THOMPSON. *A Graduated Program in Physical Education for the Rural Junior High Schools of Nova Scotia.* International YMCA College, 1947. 150 p. ms.

812. STANSELL, SIDNEY SMITH STOUT. *The Rise of Elementary Education in Alberta.* Stanford University, 1934. 126 p. ms.

813. STEWART, EDWARD EMSLIE. *The 1955 Status of Recommendations in the Report of the Royal Commission on Education in Ontario, 1950.* University of Michigan, 1956. 257 p. ms.

814. STEWART, JAMES ALBERT. *A Study of the Recipients of University Entrance to Royal Institute Scholarships in the Province of British Columbia.* University of Washington, 1954. 169 p. ms.

815. STUEVE, Rev. BERNARD C. *The Adaptation of the French-Canadian Jocist Movement to the Teaching of Religion.* Catholic University of America, 1943. 113 p. ms.

816. SWEENEY, Rev. JOHN AUSTIN. *Separate School Question in Ontario.* Niagara University, 1938. 31 p. ms.

817. TIMMONS, HERMAN P. *An Analysis of the Religio-Cultural Aspects of the Nova Scotia Adult Education Movement.* Catholic University of America, 1939. 49 p. ms.

818. TODD, HAROLD JAMES. *Financing of Extra-Curricular Activities: A Study of the Financial Practices Followed in the High Schools of British Columbia.* University of Washington, 1953. 166 p. ms.

819. TUPPER, LOIS A. *A Basic Leadership Education Course for Leaders of Adolescents in Church Programs in Canada.* Columbia University, 1948. 87 p. ms.

820. TURENNE, Sister MARY OF BETHLEHEM. *"Jeunesse Etudiante Catholique": Its Method of Incorporation in the Catholic Educational System of the Sisters of Saint Ann, Lachine, Quebec, Canada.* College of St. Rose, 1952. 94 p. ms.

821. TURNER, ALICE VERNA. *An Experimental Study of the Value of Readiness Testing in the Field of Grade Nine Algebra in British Columbia.* University of Washington, 1941. 147 p. ms. Abstract in University of Washington: *Abstracts of Theses,* Vol. 7, 1943, p. 67-68.

822. TWIST, FRANCIS JOHN, Jr., 1921- . *A Comparative Investigation of the Curricula and Methods of Secondary Mathematics in the Province of Ontario, Canada, and Western New York.* Canisius College, 1949. 98 p. ms.

823. UPRICHARD, ELIZABETH MURIEL, 1911- . *A Study Evaluating Objectives and Available Materials in the Social Studies for Grades 5 and 6 in the Public Schools of Saskatchewan, Canada, Accompanied by Three Chapters of a Supplementary Textbook.* Smith College, 1944. 163 p. ms.

824. VANDER WEELE, EDWARD JOHN. *A Study of the Control and Finance of Schools of Ontario, Canada, with Implications for the Organization of Private Schools.* Drake University, 1956. 57 p. ms.

825. WALKER, Mother MARY ROSANNA. *The Catholic Youth Movement in Quebec: Its Development and Social Significance.* Catholic University of America, 1938. 61 p. ms.

826. WALLACE, FRASER MELVIN. *A Statistical Analysis of the British Columbia Junior Matriculation Examination Marks and a Suggested Improvement in the Marking System.* University of Washington, 1930. 99 p. ms.

827. WALLENS, JOHN W. S. *Young People's Leadership Training in the United Church of Canada.* Columbia University, 1947. 30 p. ms.

828. WALSH, Sister FRANCIS XAVIER, 1914- . *The Evolution of the Catholic Public Schools in Nova Scotia.* Boston College, 1958. 110 p. ms.

829. WANG, MARY SCOTT. *Manual for the Correction of Speech Defects of French-Canadian Children.* University of Wisconsin, 1944. 92 p. ms.

830. WARD, ALMA VERNE. *Developing a Program to Meet Individual Differences in the Toronto Public Schools.* Ohio State University, 1943. 88 p. ms.

831. WARNER, LA VERNE ANTHONY, 1924- . *Service for Education in Family Management.* 116 p. ms. (Refers to schools in Canada.)

832. WEKEL, Sister MARY FELICITAS. *An Analysis of the R.N. Examinations in the Province of Quebec for a Twelve-Year Period.* Catholic University of America, 1953. 120 p. ms.

833. WHITE, AVICE. *Certain Aspects of the Teaching of English in the Secondary Schools of the Dominion of Canada.* University of Cincinnati, 1936. 127 p. ms.

834. WHITE, EDITH MURIEL. *A Community Survey: A Study of the Educational, Religious, and Social Needs of Wolfville, Nova Scotia.* Columbia University, 1953. 88 p. ms.

835. WHITELAW, JAMES AITKEN. *A Construction and an Evaluation of a Physical Education Program for Ninth-Grade Boys in Calgary Schools.* University of Southern California, 1950. 77 p. ms.

836. WHITTLE, HAROLD DOUGLAS. *Aspects of Body Size, Motor Performance, and Physical Fitness on a Sample of White School Boys, Ages Twelve to Eighteen Years at Nanaimo, British Columbia.* University of Oregon, 1952. 40 p. ms.

837. WILSON, HAROLD THOMAS, 1900- . *The Teaching of English in French-Canada.* Boston University, 1935. 39 p. ms.

838. WILSON, IRA CARRELL. *A Comparison of the Centralization in School Systems of Saskatchewan,*

Canada, and the State of Washington. Stanford University, 1923. 67 p. ms. plus bibliography.

839. WILSON, RUTH DANENHOWER. *Canadian Colonies of Descendants of American Slaves.* New York University, 1948. 71 p. ms. (Includes study of educational conditions, particularly at Dawn Institute, Ontario.)

See also Nos. 195, 206, 212, 213, 220, 226, 235, 249, 255, 265, 271, 283, 289, 298, 302, 308, 4719

For Canadian groups in the United States, see Nos. 4970, 4988

Costa Rica
(NOS. 840 – 850)

DOCTORS

840. ALERS-MONTALVO, MANUEL. *Cultural Changes in a Costa Rican Village.* Michigan State College of Agriculture and Applied Science. 1953. 185 p. ms. Abstract in *Dissertation Abstracts,* Vol. 14, p. 436, March 1954. Available on microfilm from University Microfilms, Ann Arbor, Michigan, as Publication No. 7,154. (Studies results of a special program of rural education.)

841. DEL RIO SEPULVEDA, FERNANDO, 1916- . *The Professional Needs of Costa Rican Extension Workers.* Cornell University, 1958. 264 p. ms.

842. DOBLES, MARGARITA, 1915- . *Identification of Youth Problems in Costa Rica.* Stanford University, 1958. 270 p. ms. Abstract in *Dissertation Abstracts,* Vol. 19, p. 2284, March 1959. Available on microfilm from University Microfilms, Ann Arbor, Michigan, as Mic. 58-3579.

843. GAMBOA, EMMA MARIA, 1901- . *Elementary Education in Costa Rica within the Interaction of Culture.* Ohio State University, 1951. 382 p. ms. For master's thesis by same author, see No. 846.

844. NELSON, WILTON MONS, 1908- . *A History of Protestantism in Costa Rica.* Princeton Theological Seminary, 1957. 413 p. ms. (Includes educational activities.)

See also Nos. 119, 126, 133, 140, 155, 529, 530, 531, 534

MASTERS

845. ARRIETA, ROMAN. *A Follow-up Study of High School Graduates and School-Leavers of El Liceo de Costa Rica High School, 1943-1947 Inclusive.* Catholic University of America, 1952. 76 p. ms.

846. GAMBOA, EMMA MARIA, 1901- . *An Evaluation of Elemetary and Teacher Education in Costa Rica.* Ohio State University, 1940. 77 p. ms. For doctoral dissertation by same author, see No. 843.

847. PAGES, CARMEN. *History of Education in Costa Rica.* University of Southern California, 1948. 128 p. ms.

848. WOODS, MARION F. *A Training Program for Methodist Preachers in the Pacific Zone of Costa Rica.* Scarritt College for Christian Workers, 1956.

849. ZEMEL, HARRY. *Education in Costa Rica.* University of Maryland. 1949. 75 p. ms.

850. ZUNIGA-TRISTAN, VIRGINIA, 1917- . *Music in the Schools of Costa Rica.* University of Kentucky, 1943. 155 p. ms.

See also Nos. 190, 197, 205, 215, 220, 226, 253, 260, 307, 537, 539, 541

For Costa Rican groups in the United States, see Nos. 4957, 4975

Cuba
(NOS. 851-866)

DOCTORS

851. READ, GERALD HOWARD, 1913- . *Civic-Military Rural Education in Cuba: Eleven Eventful Years, 1936-1946.* Ohio State University, 1950. 496 p. ms. Abstract in Ohio State University: *Abstracts of Dissertations . . .* Spring Quarter, 1949-50, p. 317-324. (Abstracts of Doctoral Dissertations, No. 63.) For master's thesis by same author, see No. 861.

852. SHEPHARD, WILLIAM HENDY, 1906- . *An Exploration of the Effectiveness of Denominational Influence upon Students of a Mission School in Cuba.* University of Maryland, 1955. 179 p. ms. Abstract in *Dissertation Abstracts,* Vol. 15, p. 1012-1013, June 1955. Available on microfilm from University Microfilms, Ann Arbor, Michigan, as Publication No. 12,091. (The mission school considered is the Colegio Adventista de las Antillas.)

See also Nos. 119, 126, 142, 147, 149, 155, 527

MASTERS

853. BARILLAS, MARIA YSABELL. *Desenvolvimiento de la Economica Domestica y el*

Trabajo Manual en la Republica de Cuba. University of Texas, 1952. 98 p. ms.

854. CEPEDA, RALPH, 1917- . *Satisfactions and Dissatisfactions with the Sunday Church School Lesson Materials Used in the Presbyterian Churches of Cuba.* Presbyterian College of Christian Education, 1944. 53 p. ms.

855. DAVIS, MERLE L. *The Educational System in Cuba.* Columbia University, 1927. 218 p. ms.

856. GARNISS, GEORGE WINSLOW. *The Physical Examination of the Cuban.* International YMCA College, 1920. 123 p. ms.

857. HILL, BENJAMIN OGILVIE, 1883- . *Foundations and Beginnings of Religious Education in Cuba.* Southern Methodist University, 1933. 188 p. ms. Abstract in Southern Methodist University, *Abstracts of Theses*, No. 2, 1934, p. 22.

858. HULL, FERN LANE, 1908- . *Rural Education in Cuba.* George Washington University, 1939. 71 p. ms.

859. LABOY, MARIA J. *Development of Home Economics in Latin America Through Project 39 of the Organization of American States: The Demonstration Area Approach in Cuba.* Cornell University, 1958.

860. LINARES, SILVIA MARGARITA. *La Ensenanza del Ingles en Cuba.* University of Texas, 1952. 85 p. ms.

861. READ, GERALD HOWARD, 1913- . *Cuban Education: A History and Contemporary Survey.* Ohio State University, 1938. 220 p. ms. For doctoral dissertation by same author, see No. 851.

862. REITHMEIER, AMANDUS, 1873-1954? *Public Education in the Republic of Cuba.* University of Florida, 1934. 158 p. ms.

863. ROSE, CHARLES RAYMOND. *A Study of Art Education in Cuba.* Ohio State University, 1953. 84 p. ms.

864. ROSS, DONALD L. *Social Studies in the Cuban Bachillerato.* Stanford University, 1950. 97 p. ms.

865. STEWART, CARL DEVOE, *An Educational Survey of the Isle of Pines and a Comparison of Its Schools with Those of Cuba and Denver.* University of Denver, 1938. 74 p. ms. Abstract in University of Denver: *Educational Research Bulletin*, Vol. 1, no. 21, p. 28.

866. VALLVE, GRACIELA. *Adult Education in the Evening Schools of Cuba and Texas.* University of Texas, 1952. 72 p. ms.

See also Nos. 190, 194, 205, 226, 256, 260, 270, 273, 293, 307, 537, 540

For Cuban groups in the United States, see Nos. •4957, 4969, 4975, 5530

Dominican Republic
(NO. 867)

DOCTORS

See Nos. 119, 126, 133, 527

MASTER

867. JEWEL, ELSIE FLOREINE. *The Development of Education and Culture in the Dominican Republic since American Occupation.* University of Southern California, 1931. 86 p.

See also Nos. 190, 205, 224, 226, 260, 270, 307, 537, 540

El Salvador
(NOS. 868 - 870)

DOCTORS

868. PENNER, EVA NELLY, 1902- . *Public School Music in El Salvador.* University of North Dakota, 1946. 136 p. ms.

869. PFROMMER, VIOLA GERTRUDE, 1909- . *Possible Areas of American Friends Service Committee Cooperation in the Integral Rural Demonstration Area of El Salvador.* Columbia University, 1953. 85 p. ms.

MASTER

870. THOMPSON, MACK SCOTT. *The Educational System of the Republic of El Salvador.* University of Colorado, 1943. 75 p. ms. Abstract in *University of Colorado Studies*, Vol. 27, No. 2, p. 38, December 1943.

See also Nos. 190, 205, 215, 226, 260, 307, 537, 539, 541

See also Nos. 119, 126, 133, 529, 530, 531

For Salvadorean groups in the United States, see Nos. 4969, 4975

Guatemala
(NOS. 871 - 875)

DOCTORS

871. ADEN, ROBERT CLARK, 1927- . *Teacher Training in Guatemala.* George Peabody College for Teachers, 1955. 195 p. ms. Abstract in *Dissertation Abstracts,* Vol. 15, p. 1791-1792, October 1955. Available on microfilm from University Microfilms, Ann Arbor, Michigan, as Publication No. 13,303.

872. NIBLO, WINFIELD PUTENNEY, 1912- . *An Experiment in the Teaching of Freedom -- A Report on the Development of the Guatemalan Citizenship Education Project.* Columbia University, 1958. 126 p. ms, plus 56 p. appendix of printed materials. (Circulation restricted.)

873. SAENZ DE SANTA MARIA, CARMELO. *A History of the Organization of Philosophical Studies in Guatemala, 1575-1769.* Georgetown University, 1953. 209 p. ms.

See also Nos. 119, 126, 133, 140, 155, 528, 529, 530, 531, 887

MASTERS

874. HESTER, MARIE GUEYDON, 1894- . *A Study of Recent Educational Progress in Guatemala.* Louisiana State University and State Agricultural and Mechanical College, 1943. 140 p. ms. Abstract in *Louisiana State University Bulletin,* Vol. 36, n.s., No. 1, p. 35-36, March 1944.

875. PHILLIPS, EUGENIA ALICE. *The Development of Modern Education in Guatemala.* University of Southern California, 1927. 110 p. ms.

See also Nos. 190, 197, 205, 215, 226, 260, 307, 537, 539, 541

For Guatemalan groups in the United States, *see* Nos. 4957, 4969, 4975

Haiti
(NOS. 876 - 883)

DOCTOR

876. PHIFER, JULIETTE VIRGINIA, 1905- . *Public Education in Haiti since 1934: Or a Survey of Education in the Republic of Haiti.* New York University, 1948. 259 p. ms.
See also Nos. 119, 124, 133, 142, 527, 528

MASTERS

877. DORSINVILLE, FRITZ. *A Critical Analysis of the Professional Education Course in the Normal Schools of Haiti.* Ohio State University, 1956. 123 p. ms.

878. DREYFUS, ROGER, 1905- . *The Improvement of Urban Life in Haiti through Education.* Yale University, 1940. 140 p. ms.

879. GAGNERON, MARIE. *Development of Education in Haiti.* Atlanta University, 1941. 77 p. ms.

880. HAWKE, JERRY RAYMOND. *Three Years of Vocational Industrial Education in Haiti, 1925-1928.* Pennsylvania State College, 1930. 136 p. ms. Abstract in *Penn State Studies in Education,* No. 2, p. 87-88, 1931. Abstract also in *Research in Industrial Education, 1930-1955,* p. 130.

881. HENEISE, HAROLD KENNETH. *The Adaptation of American Baptist Youth Materials for Haiti.* Berkeley Baptist Divinity School, 1956. 94 p. ms.

882. LOGAN, RAYFORD WHITTINGHAM. *The History of Education in Haiti.* Williams College, 1929. Published as "Education in Haiti," *Journal of Negro History,* Vol. 15, p. 401-460, October 1930.

883. ORJALA, PAUL RICHARD. *Some Implications of Haitian Culture for Leadership Education in the Evangelical Church in Haiti.* Kennedy School of Missions, 1956. 221 p. ms.

See also Nos. 190, 197, 205, 226, 260, 270, 537

For a Haitiian group in the United States, *see* No. 4970

Honduras
(NOS. 884 - 886)

DOCTORS

See Nos. 119, 126, 133, 528, 529, 530, 531

MASTERS

884. BROWN, BETTY ANN, 1929- . *A Week-Day Program for Junior and Intermediate Girls in Honduras.* Wheaton College, Illinois, 1954. 55 p. ms.

Guatemala, Haiti, Honduras, Mexico

885. MENDOZA, OFELIA. *Education of Teachers in Honduras.* Ohio State University, 1937. 196 p. ms.

886. VALLE, ARMANDO JOSE, 1924- . *Development of Extension Work through a Pilot Project Approach in Honduras.* Cornell University, 1958. 64 p. ms.

See also Nos. 190, 205, 226, 256, 260, 293, 307, 537, 538, 539, 541

For Honduran groups in the United States, see Nos. 4956, 4969, 4975

Mexico
(NOS. 887 - 1040)

Includes California, Arizona, New Mexico, and Texas during period when those areas or parts of them were under the jurisdiction of Mexico.

DOCTORS

887. ALISKY, MARVIN HOWARD, 1923- . *Educational Aspects of Broadcasting in Mexico.* University of Texas, 1953. 309 p. ms. (Concerned primarily with Mexico, but also considers nature and effect of official foreign programs broadcast from Great Britain, Guatemala, and the United States)

888. BARRANCO, MANUEL, 1884- . *Mexico: Its Educational Problems -- Suggestions for Their Solution.* Columbia University, 1914. New York: Teachers College, Columbia University, 1915. vii, 78 p. (Teachers College Contribution to Education, No. 73.)

889. BLAIR, EVELYN, 1902- . *Education Movements in Mexico, 1821 to 1836.* University of Texas, 1941. 348 p. ms.

890. BOOTH, GEORGE CLIVE, 1901- . *The Philosophy and Technique of the Mexican Socialist School.* University of Southern California, 1939. Published as *Mexico's School-Made Society.* Stanford University, California: Stanford University Press, 1941. xi, 175 p. Abstract in University of Southern California: *Abstracts of Dissertations,* 1939, p. 26-31.

891. CANFIELD, DELOS LINCOLN, 1903- . *Spanish Literature in Mexican Languages as a Source for the Study of Spanish Pronunciation.* Columbia University, 1934. New York: Columbia University, Instituto de las Espanas en los Estados Unidos, 1934. 257 p.

892. CASTANIEN, DONALD GARNER, 1914- . *A Seventeenth Century Mexican Library and the Inquisition.* University of Michigan, 1951. 296 p. ms. Abstract in *Microfilm Abstracts,* Vol. 11, No. 2, p. 344-345, 1951. Available on microfilm from University Microfilms, An Arbor, Michigan, as Publication No. 2,389.

893. DANIELS, BLAIR ELLSWORTH, 1896- . *Technical and Industrial Education in the Public Schools of Mexico City.* Temple University, 1937. Philadelphia: The Majestic Press, Inc., 1937. xi, 87 p.

894. DAVIS, JOE EDWARD, 1915- . *The Development of Justo Sierra's Educational Thought.* University of Texas, 1951. 413 p. ms.

895. DELMEZ, ALBERT JAURES, 1916- . *The History of the Cultural Missions in Mexican Education.* University of Missouri, 1949. 308 p. ms. Abstracts in University of Missouri: *Abstracts of Dissertations in Education . . . from 1946 through 1950,* p. 37-38. Abstract also in *Microfilm Abstracts,* Vol. 9, No. 3, p. 112-113, 1949. Available on microfilm from University Microfilms, Ann Arbor, Michigan, as Publication No. 1,463.

896. DIRKS, DEMPSTER PERRY, 1912- . *Social and Cultural Characteristics of La Paz, Mexico.* University of Southern California, 1955. 248 p. ms. Abstract in University of Southern California: *Abstracts of Dissertations,* 1955, p. 198-201.

897. DOSSICK, JESSE JOHN. *Education Among the Ancient Aztecs.* Harvard University, 1941. 494 p. ms.

898. EBAUGH, CAMERON DUNCAN, 1893-1949. *The National System of Education in Mexico.* Johns Hopkins University, 1931. Baltimore, Maryland: Johns Hoskins University Press, 1931. ix, 149 p. (Johns Hopkins University Studies in Education, No. 16)

899. ENGLISH, WILLIAM EMBREY, 1909- . *Fray Alonzo de la Veracruz in Mexican Colonial Education.* University of Texas, 1950. 159 p. ms.

900. ESTARELLAS RIPOLL, JUAN. (Also found as Ripoll, Juan Estarellas) *Cultural Foundations of Mexico: A Study of the Educational Aims, Institutions, and Practices of the Spanish Colonization in Sixteenth Century Central New Spain.* Harvard University, 1956. 326 p. ms.

901. ETHERIDGE, TRUMAN HARRISON, 1890- . *Education in the Republic of Texas.* University of Texas, 1942. 522 p. ms.

902. EVANS, HARRY LEO, 1907- . *Mexican Silversmithing: A Study of Historial and Contemporary Contributions Pertinent to Industrial Arts Education.* University of Florida, 1953. 358 p. ms. Abstract in University of Florida: *Abstracts of Doctoral Studies*

in *Education*, 1953, p. 16-20. Abstract also in *Research in Industrial Education, 1930-1955*, p. 125.

903. FISHER, GLEN HARRY, 1922- . *Programs of Directed Culture Change in Latin America: The Application of Modern Theories of Culture Change to an Analysis of the Mexican Pilot Project in Basic Education in Santiago, Nayarit, Mexico.* University of North Carolina, 1952. 334 p. ms. Published as *Directed Culture Change in Nayarit, Mexico: Analysis of a Pilot Project in Basic Education.* New Orleans, Louisiana: Middle American Research Institute, Tulane University of Louisiana, 1953. (Reprinted from Publication No. 17, p. 65-176). Abstract in *University of North Carolina Record*, No. 520, p. 280-281, October 1953.

904. FREDERICK, LAWRENCE MONT, 1921- . *Origin and Development of Industrial Education in New Mexico.* University of Missouri, 1955. 267 p. ms. Abstract in *Dissertation Abstracts*, Vol. 16, p. 494, March 1956. Available on microfilm from University Microfilms, Ann Arbor, Michigan, as Publication No. 14,947. (Chiefly concerned with education in New Mexico under United States control, but treats it also "while the territory was governed by Spain and Mexico.")

905. GARRARD, JAMES LATHROP, 1909- . *A Survey of the Education of the Indians of Mexico as a Factor in Their Incorporation into Modern Mexican Society.* University of Washington, 1956. 300 p. ms. Abstract in *Dissertation Abstracts*, Vol. 16, p. 2104-2105, November 1956. Available on microfilm from University Microfilms, Ann Arbor, Michigan, as Publication No. 18,496.

906. GILL, CLARK CYRUS. *The Role of the Federal Government in Public Education in Mexico.* University of Minnesota, 1948. 433 p. ms.

907. HALE, CHARLES ADAMS. *The Problem of Independence in Mexican Thought, 1821-1953.* Columbia University, 1957. 345 p. ms. Abstract in *Dissertation Abstracts*, Vol. 17, p. 1738, August 1957. Available on microfilm from University Microfilms, Ann Arbor, Michigan, as Publication No. 21,790.

908. HELMS, JAMES ERWIN, 1901- . *Origins and Growth of Protestantism in Mexico to 1920.* University of Texas, 1955. 575 p. ms. (Includes consideration of schools and other educational activities in ten denominational groups.)

909. JACOBSEN, JEROME VINCENT, 1894- . *Educational Foundations of the Jesuits in New Spain.* University of California, Berkeley, 1934. Published as *Educational Foundations of the Jesuits in Sixteenth Century New Spain.* Berkeley, California: University of California Press, 1938. xii, 292 p. With preface by Herbert Eugene Bolton.

910. LEVITZ, JACOB, 1912- . *The Jewish Community in Mexico: Its Life and Education.* Dropsie College of Hebrew and Cognate Learning, 1954. 224 p. ms. Summary as "Jewish Education in Mexico," in *Jewish Education*, Vol. 26, p. 35-41, Spring 1956.

911. LOGAN, LILLIAN MAY, 1909- . *Kindergarten Education in Mexico.* University of Wisconsin, 1952. 452 p. ms. Abstract in University of Wisconsin: *Summaries of Doctoral Dissertations*, Vol. 14, 1952-1953, p. 378-379.

912. LOGAN, VIRGIL GLEN, 1904- . *Speech Education in Mexico, D.F.* University of Wisconsin, 1951. 347 p. ms. Abstract in University of Wisconsin: *Summaries of Doctoral Dissertations*, Vol. 13, 1951-1952, p. 369-370.

913. MILOR, JOHN HENRY, 1900- . *Education in the State of Baja California.* University of California, Los Angeles, 1956. 395 p. ms.

914. MOONEY, GERTRUDE XAVIER. *Mexican Folk Dances for American Schools.* Columbia University, 1948.

915. MOYERS, ROBERT ARTHUR. *A History of Education in New Mexico.* George Peabody College for Teachers, 1941, 2 vols. Nashville, Tennessee: 1941. 6 p. Abstract of Contribution to Education, No. 302. (Includes education and Spanish schools when the area was part of Mexico from 1540 to 1846)

916. MULVIHILL, Father DANIEL JOSEPH, 1915- . *Juan de Zumarraga, First Bishop of Mexico.* University of Michigan, 1954. 324 p. ms. Abstract in *Dissertation Abstracts*, Vol. 14, p. 1209, August 1954. Available on microfilm from University Microfilms, Ann Arbor, Michigan, as Publication No. 8,387. (Covers his educational activities, including first recommendations for the establishment of a national university.)

917. PEDRAZA, ROBERTO, 1909- . *Creative Education for a Democratic Mexico: An Educational Study to Be Recommended as a Tentative Project to the Mexican Secretariat of Education.* University of Denver, 1951. 143 p. ms.

918. PICKARD, EDWARD E., 1902- . *A Survey of Commercial Education in Mexico City.* Rutgers University, 1934. 181 p. ms.

919. PORTER, EUGENE OLIVER, 1899- . *A History of Methodism in Mexico.* Ohio State University, 1939. 192 p. ms. Abstract in Ohio State University: *Abstracts of Dissertations . . .* Summer Quarter, 1939-40, p. 275-280. (Abstracts of Doctoral Dissertations, No. 31. Includes consideration of educational activities of the church.)

920. ROSADO, HUMBERTO, 1919- . *The Ejidatorios' View of the Extension Service in the State of Mexico.* Cornell University, 1957. 180 p. ms. Abstract in *Dissertation Abstracts*, Vol. 17, p. 2080-2081, September 1957. Available on microfilm from University Microfilms, Ann Arbor, Michigan, as Publication No. 22,208.

921. RUIZ, RAMON EDUARDO, 1921- . *Mexico's Struggle for Rural Education, 1910-1950.* University of California, Berkeley, 1954. 261 p. ms.

922. SCHEMEL, MARGARET CONSTANCE, 1893- *Present-Day Foreign Language Instruction in the Secondary Schools of Mexico in the Light of Its Historical Development.* Indiana University, 1944. 289 p. ms.

923. SMITH, CLEO DAWSON. *Education in Mexico.* University of Kentucky, 1947. 244 p. ms.

Mexico

924. SMITH, HAYDEN RICHARD. *The Effectiveness of Two Instructional Procedures in Comparative Education.* University of Michigan, 1957. 157 p. ms. Abstract in *Dissertation Abstracts*, Vol. 18, p. 1309-1310, April 1958. Available on microfilm from University Microfilms, Ann Arbor, Michigan, as Mic. 58-996. (Deals with film and lecture concerning UNESCO project at Patzcuaro, Mexico.)

925. SMITH, MATTHEW DINSDALE, 1891- . *Factors Contributing to the Development of Public Secondary Education in Mexico from 1867 to 1927.* University of California, Berkeley, 1930. 174 p. ms. Abstract in University of California: *Abstracts of Doctors' Theses in Education, 1898-1933*, p. 79-80.

926. STANLEY, JOSEPH WIGHT, 1906- . *"La Casa del Pueblo": Mexico's Experiment in Rural Education.* Stanford University, 1948. 313 p. ms. Abstract in Stanford University: *Abstracts of Dissertations . . . 1947-48*, p. 37-41.

927. TOWNSEND, EVERETT B. Jr., 1905- . *A Survey of Public Night Schools in Mexico City.* Rutgers University, 1951. 155 p. ms.

928. TRAINOR, JOSEPH CHARLES, 1905- . *A Critical Analysis of Recent Mexican Federal School Legislation.* University of Washington, 1941. 152 p. ms. Abstract in University of Washington: *Abstracts of Theses . . . 1940-41*, p. 255-257.

929. WALLS, FOREST WESLEY. *The Activities of Selected United Nations Specialized Agencies with Particular Reference to Field Projects in Mexico.* University of Washington, 1958.

930. WILLIAMS, RONALD IRVING, 1910- . *Art in Mexico: A Text Emphasizing the Techniques of Mexican Art for the College Art Teacher.* New York University, 1941. 163 p. ms.

931. WILSON, IRMA, 1895- . *Mexico: A Century of Educational Thought.* Columbia University, 1941. New York: Hispanic Institute in the United States, 1941. 376 p.

932. ZOOK, LESTER MARTIN, 1906- . *A Study of Agricultural Colonization with a View to a Particular Proposal for the Lower Mixteca Region in Southern Mexico.* Pennsylvania State University, 1954. 355 p. ms. Abstract in Pennsylvania State University: *Abstracts of Doctoral Dissertations . . .* Vol. 17, p. 74-79, 1954. Available on microfilm from University Microfilms, Ann Arbor, Michigan, as Publication No. 11,696. (Primarily a study in agricultural economics and rural sociology, but with some emphasis on related problems in agricultural education. Also contains brief treatment of education in the State of Oaxaca.)

See also Nos. 119, 123, 126, 127, 133, 135, 143, 147, 149, 151, 155, 167, 169, 182, 503, 528, 533, 534, 535, 536

MASTERS

933. ANDREWS, ALMA S. *A History of Education in Mexico since 1857.* College of the Pacific, 1933. 129 p. ms.

934. ARNOLD, Rev. WALTER A. *The Eidetic Image and the Mexican Child: A Study of Racial Peculiarity of the Eidetic Image in the Mexican Child.* Catholic University of America, 1934. 43 p. ms.

935. ASHLEY, MARY. *The Influence of Mexican Art upon the Home, Commercial, and School Life of Texas.* Colorado State College of Education, 1939. 286 p. ms.

936. AUSERE, AURELIO JOE, 1917- . *The Life and Works of Mariano Azuela.* Arizona State Teachers College, Tempe, 1953. 100 p. ms.

937. BARBOUR, LIZZIE MESSICK. *Federal Participation in Public Education in Mexico, 1934-1937.* University of Texas, 1939. 132 p. ms.

938. Omit. Error.

939. BENTHIEN, ELIZABETH MARGARET. *The Educational System of Mexico.* University of Washington, 1916. 54 p. ms.

940. BLAISDELL, JAMES BROOKS. *The Development of Education in Mexico.* University of Southern California, 1931. 84 p. ms.

941. BOSLET, Sister MARY ROSE GERTRUDE, 1901- . *The Educational Work Done by the Franciscans among the Indians of Mexico in the Sixteenth Century.* St. John's University, 1948. 44 p. ms. Abstract in St. John's University: *Abstracts of Dissertations*, 1946-1948, p. 28.

942. BUCKINGHAM, ELIZABETH, 1895- . *Mexican Schools: Past and Present.* University of California, Berkeley, 1929. 201 p. ms.

943. CADWELL, JACQUELINE LOIS, 1922- . *The Elementary Educational Program in the Rural Schools of Mexico.* Loyola University, 1954. 62 p. ms.

944. CADWELL, LOUISE MARION, 1922- . *The Initial Reading Program in Mexico.* Loyola University, 1954. 63 p. ms.

945. CAIN, HENRY L. *National Education in Mexico.* Baylor University, 1927.

946. CANDOR, ETHEL. *The Musical Talent of Mexican School Children.* University of Denver, 1933. 39 p. ms. Abstract in University of Denver: *Abstracts of Theses in Education, 1930-1938*, p. 29.

947. CARTER, EULA LEE. *The Educational Program of the Mexican Government, 1920-1924.* University of Texas, 1925. 150 p. ms.

948. CASTANEDA, JOSEPHINE E. *History of the Educational Work of the Spanish Missions in Texas.* Texas College of Arts and Industries, 1951.

949. CHERRYHOMES, RAWLINS, 1917- . *Factors Determining Protestant Missionary Policy in Mexico.* Texas Christian University, 1942. 126 p. ms. (Thesis for degree of Bachelor of Divinity. Includes educational policy.)

950. COOK, DIANE F., 1931- . *The Development of Secondary Education in Mexico.* Southern Methodist University, 1956. 151 p. ms.

951. CORBIN, CLARINDA, 1897- . *Past and Present School Activities and School Program of the Methodist Episcopal Church, South, in Seven Centers of Its Mexican Work.* University of California, Berkeley, 1922. 126 p. ms.

952. CRAWFORD, HELEN ROYSE. *The Contribution of Benito Juarez to Education.* University of Texas, 1938. 84 p. ms.

953. CROWLE, HAZEL ARAMINTA, 1894- . *An Interpretative Study of the Official Jarabe Tapatio, the National Dance of Old Mexico.* San Jose State College, 1952. 114 p. ms.

954. DANIELS, MARTHA JEANNETTE, 1889- . *The Separation of Church and State in Mexico and Its Effect on Evangelical Educational Effort.* Northwestern University, 1931. 119 p. ms.

955. DILLON, Rev. NOEL PATRICK. *Educational Efforts of the Missionaries in Upper California from 1810-1836.* Catholic University of America, 1925. 45 p. ms.

956. DOUGLAS, CATHERINE CHRISTINE. *Art Education of Young Children in Public Schools of Mexico.* George Peabody College for Teachers, 1937. 112 p. ms.

957. ESTRADA, GRACIELA ENPARZA. *Religious Education in Mexico.* Asbury Theological Seminary, 1951.

958. EVANS, MARIE PADGETT, 1919- . *Mexican Minatures: A Study of the Educational Contributions of Minatures in Revealing Customs, Habits, and Cultures of Mexico.* University of Florida, 1952. 98 p. ms.

959. FEEHAN, Rev. JOSEPH FRANCIS. *The Curriculum in the Franciscan Mission System of California.* Catholic University of America, 1927. 44 p. ms.

960. FODY, MICHAEL, Jr. *Hispanic Contributions to Education in the Southwestern United States.* State University of Iowa, 1953. 74 p. ms.

961. FURNIVALL, FRED. *A Proposed Program for the Teaching of Mexican-American Children Based upon a Survey of a Mexican Rural Community and a Mexican Urban Community.* Claremont Graduate School, 1948. 74 p. ms.

962. GARCIA, ENOS E. *History of Education in Taos County.* University of New Mexico, 1950. 120 p. ms. (Chapter 3: "Education During the Spanish and Mexican Occupations.")

963. GARCIA RUIZ, FEDERICO. *Proposal for a College of Tropical Agriculture in Mexico.* Iowa State College of Agriculture and Mechanic Arts, 1943. 102 p. ms.

964. GERHARDT, Mrs. HAIDIE WILLIAMS. *The History of the University of Mexico.* University of Texas, 1928. 90 p. ms.

965. GHENT, ELIZABETH CHURCH. *Educational Reorganization in Mexico.* University of Washington, 1952. 126 p. ms.

966. GIDDINGS, EDITH MAY. *The Modernization of Education in Mexico.* University of Southern California, 1935. 171 p. ms.

967. GONZALES, MARIA. *Some Aspects of Spanish-Language Folklore of the United States-Mexican Border.* Southwest Texas State Teachers College, 1957. 130 p. ms.

968. GONZALEZ, ADOLFO. *A Study on Mexico Minor Seminarians.* Catholic University of America, 1956. 27 p. ms. Abstract in *Catholic Educational Review,* Vol. 56, p. 613, December 1958.

969. HALL, MARJORIE BELLE. *An Evaluation of the New Keystone Course for Use in Mexico.* Berkeley Baptist Divinity School, 1943. 64 p. ms.

970. HAMILTON, THOMAS GNADY. *How Practical Arts Education Has Functioned in Mexico.* North Texas State Teachers College, 1938. 150 p. ms. Abstract in North Texas State Teachers College: *Abstracts of Theses, 1935-1940,* p. 62.

971. HANSON, EDITH JOSEPHINE. *A Study of Intelligence Tests for Mexican Children Based on English and Mexican Test Forms* University of Southern California, 1931. 78 p. ms.

972. HARRELL, MILDRED, 1899- . *Social Teachings in Mexican Secondary Schools* Southern Methodist University, 1945. 120 p. ms. Abstract in Southern Methodist University: *Abstracts of Theses,* No. 11, 1943, 1944, p. 11-12.

973. HAWKINS, ORIN RAYNOR. *A Study of the Educational System of the Republic of Mexico.* Allegheny College, 1937. 105 p. ms.

974. HAYDEN, JESSIE. *The La Habra Experiment in Mexican Social Education.* Claremont College, 1934. 202 p. ms.

975. HOOD, ANITA LOUISE. *The Reorganization of Secondary Education in Mexico since 1926.* University of Texas, 1955. 93 p. ms.

976. HUTCHISON, CORNELIA. *A Comparative Study of the Teaching Materials for Six-Year-Old Children in Mexico and Texas.* University of Texas, 1945. 133 p. ms.

977. INGRUM, DORA LOUVENIA. *Types of Mission Schools Needed in Mexico.* University of Missouri, 1925. 113 p. ms.

978. JAUCKENS, ANITA. *Mexican Readers as Instruments of the Socialist Program: A Critical Examination of Two Series of Mexican Urban Elementary Readers as Instruments of the Mexican Socialistic Program.* University of Louisville, 1940. 185 p. ms.

979. JENKINS, RUTH ELIZABETH. *An Historical Study of the Dances of the Mexicans in the Latter-Pre-Hispanic, Colonial, and Modern Periods of Mexico.* New York University, 1932. 41 p. ms.

980. KAMMERER, VIOLET GOULD. *Development of Public Education in Mexico since 1920.* University of Southern California, 1931. 59 p. ms.

Mexico

981. LEMON, HALLIE. *A Study of the Use of Radio in the Ministry of Education of the Republic of Mexico.* American University, 1934. 56 p. ms.

982. LEONARD, MARY JOAN, 1926- . *Anti-Illiteracy Campaign in Mexico, 1944-1946.* University of California, Berkeley, 1958.

983. LIEFIELD, MARTHA C. *Teacher Education in Mexico: A Mid-Century Study.* Kent State University, 1955.

984. LOPEZ, RUDOLPH MULLER. *History of Physical Education and Sports in Mexico.* Claremont Graduate School, 1953. 146 p. ms.

985. McCARTHY, Father EDWARD JAMES. *The Augustinians in Primitive Mexico, 1533-1572.* Catholic University of America, 1938. 112 p. ms. (Includes educational activities.)

986. McCOY, BERENICE BOWMAN, 1902- . *Secondary Education in Mexico,* George Washington University, 1934. 75 p. ms.

987. McHUGH, Rev. JAMES JOHN. *Educational Aspects of the Mission System in Upper California.* Catholic University of America, 1922. 31 p. ms.

988. McKAY, BETTY RILEY. *The UNESCO Fundamental Education Project at Patzcuaro, Michoacan, Mexico.* East Tennessee State College, 1953. 56 p. ms.

989. McKAY, WILLIAM CALVIN. *The New Education in Mexico.* Southern Methodist University, 1939. 120 p. ms. Abstract in Southern Methodist University: *Abstracts of Theses,* No. 7, 1940, p. 29-30.

990. McKINNEY, MARGARET GLADDIE, 1902- . *Vocabulary Study of Three Elementary Reading Texts, Approved for Use in Mexican Public Schools.* Southern Methodist University, 1931. 133 p. ms.

991. MACIAS, ARTURO CAMPIRANO. *The Rural School in Mexico.* University of Chicago, 1937. 84 p. ms.

992. MADDALUN, DANIEL ANTHONY, 1912- . *An Evaluation of Baptist Work in Mexico.* Texas Christian University, 1945. 232 p. ms. (Includes education.)

993. MICHAELS, LEILA. *A Report on the Latin-American Regional Fundamental Education Centre, CREFAL.* University of California, Los Angeles, 1956. 158 p. ms.

994. MOONEY, PATRICIA ANN. *Potential Educational Values of Current Mexican Proverbs.* East Texas State Teachers College, 1944. 358 p. ms.

995. MOORE, MOLLY ANN. *Mexican Church-State Relations in the Field of Education.* Stanford University, 1948. 154 p. ms.

996. MORKOVSKY, Rev. JOHN L. *Education among the Indians in the Spanish Missions of East and South Central Texas, 1690-1830.* Catholic University of America, 1942. 58 p. ms.

997. MORPHIS, JOHN WASHINGTON, 1912- . *History of the Educational Efforts of the Methodists in Mexico.* Texas Christian University, 1935. 125 p. ms.

998. MUNRO, Sister MARY GEORGIA. *A Study of the Growth of Catholic Education in the Diocese of El Paso from the Earliest Mission Era to the Present Time.* Catholic University of America, 1944. 76 p. ms.

999. MYERS, Mrs. MINNIE MOORE PORTER. *The Origin and Beginning of the University of Mexico, 1553 to 1580.* University of Texas, 1929. 108 p. ms.

1000. NEELY, MARGARET TERRELL. *The Reactions of a Group of Mexican School Children to Relatively Unfamiliar Vegetables.* Iowa State College of Agriculture and Mechanic Arts, 1931. 69 p. ms.

1001. NESBITT, PORTER BEASLEY. *Federal Provisions for Education in Mexico.* Miami University, 1952. 62 p. ms.

1002. NEWBERRY, JOSEPHINE. *Legends and Festivals Associated with Indigenous Dances of Mexico.* University of Texas, 1942. 98 p. ms.

1003. NICKSON, THOMAS BLAIR. *Development of Formal Education in Mexico.* University of Buffalo, 1949. 105 p. ms.

1004. NICOLL, MARION. *A Series of Original Dance Compositions Based upon Selected Phases of Mexican Life.* Texas State College for Women, 1951. 77 p. ms.

1005. O'HARA, OLIVE MARIE FUTCH. *The Community Aspects of the Rural School of Mexico since 1917.* University of California, Los Angeles, 1945. 123 p. ms.

1006. OJEDA, PERALES. *Building a Reference Collection for the National University of Mexico.* Kent State University, 1955.

1007. OROZCO, JOSE ENRIQUE. *A Normative Study of Health Examinations of Y. M. C. A. Members in Mexico City.* International YMCA College, 1941. 165 p. ms.

1008. PALM, RUFUS ATWOOD. *New Mexico Schools from 1581 to 1846.* 82 p. ms. Abstract in University of New Mexico: *Abstracts of Theses, 1929-1932,* p. 44-45 (Bulletin, Catalog series, Vol 55, No. 8. Covers the early period when the area of the present New Mexico was Mexican territory. Chapter 2: "The Spanish Period, 1581-1821," p. 8-37; Chapter 3: "The Mexican Period, 1821-1846," p. 38-55.)

1009. PALMER, Mrs. PHYLLIS BLAKE. *Rural Education in Mexico.* Boston University, 1944. 145 p. ms.

1010. PALMINTERI, PETER JOSEPH. *Influence of American Culture as Evidenced in the Curricula of Mexican Educational Institutions.* College of the City of New York, 1941. 105 p. ms.

1011. PERRY, ELSIE ADELE. *A Comparison of the Content Material in Mexican and United States Readers.* University of Texas, 1931. 443 p. ms.

1012. PORT, GEORGE EDWARD, Jr., 1930- . *Seventy-Five Years of Mexican Secondary Education, 1876-1951.* Boston College, 1952. 70 p. ms.

1013. POWER, HARRIET CLAIRE. *The Educational Growth of the Mexicans: Changing Concepts and Their Historical Background.* Hunter College of the City of New York, 1943. 47 p. ms.

1014. PUGH, GRACE THOMPSON. *Historical Background and Significance of Mexican Folk Dances.* Southwest Texas State Teachers College, 1945. 49 p. ms.

1015. RESUME, RHODA GERTRUDE. *Achievement of the Church in Education in Mexico from 1519 to 1821.* University of Detroit, 1935. 75 p. ms.

1016. RICCIARDI, MILDRED WATERS. *Post-Revolution Reform in Mexican Education.* Claremont Graduate School, 1936. 118 p. ms.

1017. ROBERTSON, THELMA AUTRY, 1907- . *Henry C. Rebsamen, the Reformer of Elementary Education in Mexico.* Texas Wesleyan College, 1955. 107 p. ms. (Translation from Spanish of book originally written in German by Edward Zollinger.)

1018. ROSENBLUTH, MATHILDE. *Elementary Education in Mexico.* Columbia University, 1924. 26 p. ms.

1019. ROYER, NENA SORENSEN. *A Study of Methods of Vocational Education in the Old Spanish Missions.* University of Southern California, 1926. 65 p. ms. (Covers California missions when the region was part of Mexico.)

1020. RYAN, SYLVIA NIGEL. *A Translation of Book I of the Chronicle of the Notable and Royal University of the City of New Mexico and New Spain, with Critical Notes.* University of Southern California, 1924. 294 p. ms.

1021. SHIVE, JAMES WILLIAM. *A Study Guide for an Educational Tour of Mexico.* Western Illinois State College, 1954. 81 p. ms. (Includes discussion of Mexican educational system, Chapter 5, p. 48-56.)

1022. SISTO, THOMAS J. *Justo Sierra, Modern Mexican Educator: An Analysis of the Ideas and Attitudes of Justo Sierra and His Contributions to Popular Education in Mexico.* Claremont Graduate School, 1950. 144 p. ms.

1023. SMITH, INA ELIZABETH. *A Study of Educational Progress in Mexico.* Yale University, 1920. 209 p. ms.

1024. SORAN, *Sister* MARY ROSE TERESA. *Lorettine Educational History in New Mexico.* University of New Mexico, 1949. 150 p. ms. (Chapter 2, "Pioneer Education in New Mexico," p. 10-19, summarizes educational efforts in the period when New Mexico was Mexican territory before the sisters entered the territory in 1852.)

1025. SPAULDING, DAVID MERRICK. *The Development of a National Program of Education in Mexico.* University of Southern California, 1928. 72 p. ms.

1026. SPEAS, GENEVA MAE, 1908- . *The Mexican Revolution of 1910 and the Peon: A Study in Rural Problems and Education.* University of California, Berkeley, 1933. 123 p. ms.

1027. STEED, EDITH MARNEY, 1904- . *The Effect of the Revolution of 1910 on Rural Education in Mexico.* Southern Methodist University, 1951. 78 p. ms. Abstract in Southern Methodist University: *Abstracts of Theses,* No. 14, 1950, 1951, p. 50.

1028. STEELE, ELIZABETH S. *Censorship of Books in Sixteenth Century Mexico.* University of New Mexico, 1950. 108 p. ms.

1029. TAYLOR, CHARLES RICHARD, 1921- . *A Follow-up Study of Mexican Union Training School Graduates.* Pacific Union College, 1955. 89 p. ms.

1030. TAYLOR, MARTHA R. *Rural Education in Mexico.* Southwest Texas State Teachers College, 1941. 74 p. ms.

1031. TORMAY, *Sister* MARY CYRILLA, 1893- . *Franciscan Pioneering in Higher Education in America.* Canisius College, 1940. 40 p. ms. (Covers Mexico and Southern United States.)

1032. ULREY, DOROTHY L. *The Federal Rural Schools in Mexico.* University of Southern California, 1938. 82 p. ms.

1033. WACKERBARTH, ALLIE MAE. *A Comparison of Spanish and English Primers.* University of Texas, 1932. 69 p. ms. (Spanish primers were those used in Mexico.)

1034. WALSH, *Sister* MARIE CATHERINE. *The Contributions of Junipero Serra to Christian Civilization in Mexico and the Californias.* St. Bonaventure University, 1958.

1035. WEBB, JAMES HENRY, Jr., 1906- . *A Study of Certain Social and Nationalistic Attitudes as Revealed in a Group of Mexican History Textbooks.* George Washington University, 1943. 96 p. ms. (Based on an analysis of seven textbooks.)

1036. WHITBY, HAROLD RUSSELL. *Industrial Arts Projects from Rural Mexico.* State University of Iowa, 1937. 98 p. ms.

1037. WHITE, LYMAN CROMWELL. *Mexico's Educational Advance.* Columbia University, 1929. 50 p. ms.

1038. WILLIAMS, NARBON B. *Some Significant Differences between American Education and that of Mexico.* North Texas State Teachers College, 1945. 43 p. ms. Abstract in North Texas State Teachers College: *Abstracts of Theses, 1941-1946,* p. 113. (Bulletin No. 191, January 1948.)

1039. WOLFE, ARTHUR WHITING. *Certain Factors Conditioning Curriculum Construction in Mexico.* University of Chicago, 1925. 242 p. ms.

1040. WRIGHT, MARGARITA. *An Experimental Course of Study in the School Sciences on the Basis of Activities Adapted to an Elementary School in Mexico Subject to State Requirements.* Claremont Graduate School, 1931. 115 p. ms.

Mexico, Panama, Puerto Rico

See also Nos. 188, 190, 194, 195, 196, 205, 207, 226, 236, 239, 253, 256, 260, 268, 270, 271, 273, 295, 299, 301, 307, 537, 5607

For Mexican groups in the United States, *see* Nos. 5207-5653

Panama
(NOS. 1041 – 1043)

DOCTOR

1041. CANTON, ALFREDO, 1916- . *The Beginnings of Panamanian National Education.* Washington University, 1949. 312 p. ms.

See also Nos. 119, 126, 147, 149, 155, 1073

MASTERS

1042. CEDENO, LUISA ELIDA, 1917- . *Reducing Failures in Panama Secondary Schools.* Drake University, 1945. 52 p. ms.

1043. DIAZ, CLEMENCIA. *An Elementary Teacher Education Program for Panama.* Bowling Green State University, 1950.

See also Nos. 190, 197, 205, 226, 256, 260, 307, 308, 537, 539

For Panamanian groups in the United States, *see* Nos. 4970, 4975

Puerto Rico
(NOS. 1044 – 1165)

DOCTORS

1044. ALMENAS DE VERGNE, AIDA, 1915- . *Improving In-Service Education for Beginning Elementary Teachers in Puerto Rico.* Columbia University, 1951. 130 p. ms.

1045. BERRIOS GONZALEZ, ELISEO, 1897- . *A Study of the Impact of Population Growth in Puerto Rico on Natural Resources, Including a Suggested Program for Improvement.* New York University, 1945. 151 p. ms. (Presents a program for education in agricultural practices.)

1046. BLANCO, COLON R. *Permanent Withdrawals from Grades Four, Five, and Six in Puerto Rico.* George Peabody College for Teachers, 1947.

1047. CACERES, JOSE ANTONIO, 1921- . *Proposed Modification of Courses in the Social Foundations of Education at the University of Puerto Rico.* Columbia University, 1956. 314 p. ms.

1048. CAFOUROS, Mrs. ANGELES PERELES. *The History of Elementary Education in Puerto Rico under the American Government, 1898-1951.* Indiana University, 1951. 121 p. ms.

1049. CANDELAS DE CRUZ, AIDA S., 1915- . *Linguistic Principles Underlying the Experiment in the Teaching of English as a Second Language in Puerto Rico.* Columbia University, 1953. 122 p. ms.

1050. CARRILLO DE CACERES, ANA MARIA, 1921- . *Group Activities in the Secondary Schools of Puerto Rico: A Handbook for Teachers.* Columbia University, 1957. 123 p. ms.

1051. CEBOLLERO, PEDRO ANGEL, 1896- . *Suggestions for a Language Policy for the Public Schools of Puerto Rico.* Columbia University, 1937. Published as *A School Language Policy for Puerto Rico -- English Edition*, San Juan: Imprenta Baldrich, 1945. 133 p. (Superior Educational Council of Puerto Rico, Educational Publications, Series 2, No. 1). Also as *La Politica Linguistica-Escolar de Puerto Rico*, San Juan de Puerto Rico: Imprenta Baldrich, 1945. 145 p. (Ensenanza de Puerto Rico, Publicaciones Pedagogicas, Ser. 2, Nom. 1.) For master's thesis by same author, see No. 1099.

1052. COLE, JAMES ELLIS, 1914- . *A Study of School Service Bureaus in Selected Colleges and Universities in the United States, Puerto Rico, and Hawaii.* University of Utah, 1952. 246 p. ms.

1053. GARCIA, MARION, 1915- . *The Guidance of the Normal School Student: Proposals for a Program of Staff Participation at the College of Education, University of Puerto Rico.* Columbia University, 1953. 227 p. ms.

1054. GOMEZ, LAURA, 1911- . *Suggestions for Improving the Work of the Principal in the Elementary Schools in Puerto Rico.* Columbia University, 1951. 129 p. ms.

1055. GONZALEZ DE DAVILA, CECELIA, 1912- . *A Proposal for Community Education in Selected Resettlements in Puerto Rico.* New York University, 1955. 224 p. ms. Abstract in *Dissertation Abstracts*, Vol. 16, p. 1009, May 1956. Available on microfilm from University Microfilms, Ann Arbor, Michigan, as Publication No. 12,206.

1056. HERNANDEZ, CARLOS. *The Spanish Revision of the S. R. A. Junior Inventory, Form A.* Purdue University, 1958. 134 p. ms. Abstract in *Dissertation Abstracts,* Vol. 19, p. 354-355, August 1958. Available on microfilm from University Microfilms, Ann Arbor, Michigan, as Mic. 58-1785. (For use in Puerto Rico in grades 4 to 7, ages 10 to 15 years.)

1057. HETH, EDWARD LEON, 1915- . *A Plan for Revising and Augmenting the Music Curriculum of the Polytechnic Institute of Puerto Rico.* Columbia University, 1950. 125 p. ms.

1058. KAVETSKY, JOSEPH, 1918- . *The Development of an English Reader for Puerto Rican Adults.* Columbia University, 1954. 61, 203 p. ms.

1059. MARTINEZ, JUAN N. *Attitudes and Concepts of Puerto Rican Professionals Regarding Mental Illness.* New York University, 1958.

1060. MARTINEZ-ACEVEDO, REINALDO I., 1913- . *A Comparison of the Attitudes of Educators toward the Future Development of Young and Adult Farmer Instruction in Vocational Agriculture in Puerto Rico.* Pennsylvania State University, 1955. 102 p. ms. Abstract in Pennsylvania State University: *Abstracts of Doctoral Dissertations,* Vol. 18, 1955, p. 23-25. Available on microfilm from University Microfilms, Ann Arbor, Michigan, as Publication No. 14,793. For master's thesis by same author, see No. 1135.

1061. MELLADO, RAMON ANTONIO, 1904- . *Culture and Education in Puerto Rico.* Columbia University, 1947. San Juan, Puerto Rico: Bureau of Publications, Puerto Rico Teachers Association, 1948. vii, 140 p. (Educational Monograph, No. 1.)

1062. MENDEZ, ADELE MARGUERITE, 1910- . *The Reorganization of the Basic Course in English at the University of Puerto Rico.* Columbia University, 1953. 212 p. ms.

1063. MENDOZA, ANTONIO CUESTA, 1873- . *Historia de la Educacion en Puerto Rico, 1512-1826.* Catholic University of America, 1937. Washington: Catholic University of America, 1937. xxvi, 191 p. (Studies in American Church History, Vol. 27). For master's thesis by same author, see No. 1138.

1064. MORENO MARRERO, JOSE AGAPITO, 1901- . *An Art Curriculum for the Junior High Schools of Puerto Rico.* University of Colorado, 1944. 227 p. ms. Abstract in University of Colorado: *Abstracts of Theses . . .* 1944, p. 55-56. For master's thesis by same author, see No. 1143.

1065. MUELLER, JOHN FREDERICK, 1911- . *A Survey of the Educational Program of Catholic Elementary and Secondary Schools in the San Juan Diocese of Puerto Rico.* Columbia University, 1953. 344 p. ms.

1066. MUNOZ, MARIA LUISA, 1905- . *Music in Puerto Rico.* Columbia University, 1958. 210 p. ms. (Music education.)

1067. MURPHY, MARCELINO, 1912- . *Educational and Social Action Programs in Governmental Sponsored Rural Communities in Puerto Rico.* Columbia University, 1953. 93 p. ms.

1068. NASH, WILLARD LEE, 1898- . *The Stated Aims and Purposes of the Departments of Military Science and Tactics and Physical Education in the Land-Grant Colleges of the United States.* Columbia University, 1934. New York: Teachers College, Columbia University, 1934. 129 p. (Teachers College Contribution to Education, No. 614. Includes consideration of the University of Puerto Rico.)

1069. NAZAZARIO DE LOPATEGUI, MIGUELINA, 1915- . *Needs and Problems of Puerto Rican High School Students Related to N Variables.* Purdue University, 1957. 116 p. ms. Abstract to be published in *Dissertation Abstracts.* Available on microfilm from University Microfilms, Ann Arbor, Michigan.

1070. OSUNA, JOHN JOSEPH, 1884- . (Osuna, Juan Jose, in Library of Congress card catalog). *Education in Porto Rico.* Columbia University, 1923. New York: Teachers College, Columbia University, 1923. viii, 312 p. (Teachers College Contribution to Education, No. 133). Second edition, in modified form, as *A History of Education in Porto Rico,* Rio Piedras, Puerto Rico: Editorial de la Universidad de Puerto Rico, 1949. xxiv, 657 p.

1071. PASTOR, ANGELES, 1905- . *Learning to Write through Experience: A Guide for Elementary School Teachers in Puerto Rico.* Columbia University, 1955. 326 p. ms.

1072. PLANADEBALL, MARTA JOSEPHINA, 1923- . *Problems in Reading English as a Second Language at the University of Puerto Rico, with Suggestions for Improvement.* Columbia University, 1955. 188 p. ms.

1073. PORRATA, OSCAR EMILIO, 1898- . *A Suggested Policy for the Administration and Control of Public Education in Puerto Rico.* Pennsylvania State College, 1947. 258 p. ms. Published in abbreviated form, under same title, Rio Piedras, Puerto Rico: Bureau of Publications, Puerto Rico Teachers Association, 1949. vii, 144 p. (Educational Monograph No. 2). Abstract in Pennsylvania State College: *Abstracts of Doctoral Dissertattions,* Vol. 10, 1947, p. 179-186. Abstract also in Pennsylvania State College: *Abstracts of Studies in Education and Psychology . . .,* No. 26, p. 22-24, 1951. Available on microfilm from University Microfilms, Ann Arbor, Michigan, as Publication No. 1,027. (Includes brief consideration also of education in American Samoa, Guam, Panama, the Philippines, and the Virgin Islands.) For master's thesis by same author, see No. 1151.

1074. QUINTERO, ANGEL GUILLERMO, 1916- . *A Critical Analysis of the General Studies Program of the University of Puerto Rico and a Plan for Its Development.* University of Chicago, 1949. 207 p. ms.

1075. RAMIREZ-LOPEZ, RAMON, 1910- . *A Comparative Study of the Values of Teachers, Students of Education, and Other University Students in Puerto Rico.* University of Texas, 1957. 242 p. ms. Abstract in *Dissertation Abstracts,* Vol. 17, p. 2503, November 1957. Available on microfilm from University Microfilms, Ann Arbor, Michigan, as Publication No. 23,018. For master's thesis by same author, see No. 3260.

1076. RICCIO, ROBERT ALBERY, 1927- . *A Proposed Course in Humanities for the College of Agriculture and Mechanic Arts of the University of Puerto Rico.* Columbia University, 1957. 143 p. ms.

1077. RODRIGUEZ, ANTONIO, 1897- . *The Second Unit and the Rural School Problem of Puerto Rico.* Indiana University, 1943. 291 p. ms. San Juan, Puerto Rico: Imprenta Venezuela, Inc., 1945. xv, 238 p.

1078. RODRIGUEZ, OSCAR, 1904- . *A Proposal for a Church Program of Education for Family Living in Puerto Rico.* Columbia University, 1952; Union Theological Seminary, 1952. 282 p. ms.

1079. RODRIGUEZ DIAZ, MANUEL, 1898- *Conceptions Involved in Re-Planning Rural Education in Puerto Rico* Cornell University, 1948. 309 p. ms. For master's thesis by same author, see No. 1155.

1080. RODRIGUEZ ROBLES, JUAN, 1908- *A Manual in Community Problems for Puerto Rican Schools.* New York University, 1950. 924 p. ms. Abstract in *Microfilm Abstracts,* Vol. 10, No. 4, p. 130-136, 1950. Available on microfilm from University Microfilms, Ann Arbor, Michigan, as Publication No. 1,931.

1081. ROJAS, PAULINE M. *A Critical Analysis of the Vocabulary of Three Standard Series of Pre-Primers and Primers in Terms of How the Words Are Used: With Special Reference to the Language Problem of the Spanish-Speaking Children of Puerto Rico.* University of Michigan, 1946. 285 p. ms. Abstract in *Microfilm Abstracts,* Vol. 7, No. 1, p. 64-66, 1946. Available on microfilm from University Microfilms, Ann Arbor, Michigan, as Publication No. 769.

1082. SAEZ, FLORENCIO, 1895- . *Democratizing Organization and Administration in the Evangelical Seminary of Puerto Rico.* Columbia University, 1947. 104 p. ms.

1083. SEDA, ANGEL LUIS. *Implications for Puerto Rico in a Study of the Hospital Chaplaincy in the United States.* Columbia University, 1958. 175 p. ms. (Includes guidance and religious education, with implications for a Puerto Rican training program.)

1084. TOSSAS DE IRIZARRY, LEILA VICTORIA, 1912- *Introducing a Program of Laboratory Experiences in the Basic Course in Elementary Education in the Inter-American University of Puerto Rico.* Columbia University, 1957. 154 p. ms.

1085. URGELL, FRANCISCO CARLOS, 1893- *The Development and Contemporary Problems of Vocational Education in Puerto Rico.* Pennsylvania State College, 1942. 292 p. ms. Abstract in Pennsylvania State College: *Abstracts of Doctoral Dissertations,* Vol. 5, 1942, p. 156-166. Abstract also in *Research in Industrial Education, 1930-1955,* p. 146. Available on microfilm from University Microfilms, Ann Arbor, Michigan, as Publication No. 530. For master's thesis by same author, see No. 1161.

1086. VARONA, Mrs. CARTADA LAUDALINA FERNANDEZ, 1910- . *Some Procedures for Using Pictures in Teaching English as a Second Language.* Columbia University, 1956. 124 p. ms.

1087. VAZQUEZ, HERMINIA, 1911- . *The Role of the College of Education in the Reorientation of Secondary Education in Puerto Rico.* Columbia University, 1953. 106 p. ms.

1088. VINCENTY, NESTOR ISAAC. *Racial Differences in Intelligence as Measured by Pictorial Group Tests with Special Reference to Porto Rico and the United States.* Harvard University, 1930. 202 p. ms.

1089. WELLMAN, COE RUSHFORD. *A Plan for In-Service Training of Teachers and Leaders in the Methodist Church Schools of Puerto Rico.* Columbia University, 1936. 101 p. ms.

1090. ZAPATA RIVERA, LUCILA, 1918- *Geography of the Commonwealth of Puerto Rico for Secondary Schools.* Columbia University, 1958. 155 p. ms.

See also Nos. 128, 166, 527, 533, 536

MASTERS

1091. ALBERTY-RUIZ, RAMON. *Bilingualism in Puerto Rico: Its Implications.* University of Nebraska, 1948. 81 p. ms.

1092. ALVAREZ DE CHOUDENS, EUNICE, 1923- *A Study of the Cooperative Office Practice Training Programs in the High Schools of Puerto Rico.* Boston University, 1953. 61 p. ms.

1093. BUXO-BENITEZ, ZULMA J., 1922- . *Foods and Nutrition Extension Work in the Southern United States and Puerto Rico.* Virginia Polytechnic Institute, 1948. 87 p. ms.

1094. CALLICUTT, Mrs. DOROTHY (HINDS). *A Study of the Socio-Economic Status of Puerto Rican School Children.* University of Texas, 1945. 92 p. ms.

1095. CALZADA, PATRIA. *A Study of the Mastery of Certain Mathematical Skills and Concepts by Puerto Rican Children in Seventh and Eighth Grades.* University of Michigan, 1935. 43 p. ms.

1096. CAPO CABALLERO, CARMELINA. *A Program for Student Teaching in Home Making in Puerto Rico.* Colorado State College of Agriculture and Mechanic Arts, 1939. 176 p. ms.

1097. CARRION, JUSTINA. *Social Conditions in Two Rural Communities of Puerto Rico and the Educational Implications of These Conditions.* Columbia University, 1940. 33 p. ms.

1098. CASELLAS JAVET, BONOSIO. *Trades and Industries Curriculum and Organization as a Part of the Vocational Education Program in Puerto Rico.* University of Texas, 1952. 139 p. ms.

1099. CEBOLLERO, PEDRO ANGEL, 1896- *A Study of the Teachers' Pension System of Porto Rico.* University of Chicago, 1929. 121 p. ms. For doctoral dissertation by same author, see No. 1051.

1100. CHICO, ROSARIO. *A Study of Living Conditions and Community Conditions as Related to the Teaching Satisfaction of Home Economics Teachers in Puerto Rico.* University of Tennessee, 1950. 91 p. ms.

1101. COPLEY, ELTON GILBERT. *Cause of Absence in Puerto Rican Senior High School and Suggested Remedial Measures.* University of Nebraska, 1944. 51 p. ms.

1102. CRESPO, CARMEN M. *Use of Time by Fifty-Three Puerto Rican Homemakers.* Cornell University, 1958.

1103. CRUZ APONTE, RAMON A., 1927- . *A Study of Personnel Policies and Practices in the School System of Puerto Rico.* University of Florida, 1957. 100 p. ms.

1104. DANN, JANET ANNE. *Application of Practices in Modern Reading Instruction to Bilingual Reading in Puerto Rico.* University of Michigan, 1939. 91 p. ms.

1105. DECLET, Sister AIDA MARIA. *An Analysis of the Admission Procedures in the Basic Professional Diploma Programs in Schools of Nursing in Puerto Rico.* Catholic University of America, 1956. 49 p. ms.

1106. DE LA LUZ, ANTONIO, 1921- . *A Program of Teacher Training in Business Education for Puerto Rico.* Montana State University, 1951. 140 p. ms.

1107. DEL PILAR, LUIS. *Vocational Education: A Need for Puerto Rico.* University of Cincinnati, 1953. 70 p. ms. Abstract in *Research in Industrial Education, 1930-1955,* p. 123.

1108. DE QUINONES, LAURA VAVQUEZ. *Preliminary Survey of the Needs and Interests of Adult Homemakers in the Rural and Urban Zones of Puerto Rico, 1955-56, with Implications for the Development of the Homemaking Program for Adults.* University of Tennessee, 1956. 142 p. ms.

1109. DOWNING, RONALD ALLEN. *Development of a School for Continentals at Ramey Air Force Base, Puerto Rico.* University of Cincinnati, 1954. 65 p. ms.

1110. EASTER, JANET LOUISE, 1929- . *A Study of the Program of Teacher Education in Puerto Rico.* Wayne University, 1956. 180 p. ms.

1111. ESPENDEZ NAVARRO, JUAN. *An Historic Development of Practical Arts and Vocational Education in the Island of Puerto Rico, 1898-1939.* Indiana University, 1940. 283 p. ms. Abstract in *Research in Industrial Education, 1930-1955,* p. 125. For doctoral dissertation by same author, see No. 530.

1112. FONT, RAFAEL OCTAVIO. *Improving Industrial Arts Education in Puerto Rico.* Pennsylvania State College, 1936. 99 p. ms.

1113. GANDARA, MARIA ANTONIA. *A Study of the Home Economics Program for Boys in Selected High Schools in Puerto Rico with Recommendation for Improvement.* University of Tennessee, 1951. 129 p. ms.

1114. GANDIA, Sister ROSA DEL CARMEN. *The Organization, Growth, and Development of the Hospital de Damas and Its School of Nursing in Ponce, Puerto Rico, 1863-1953.* Catholic University of America, 1956. 127 p. ms.

1115. GARCIA, GLORIA MODESTO DE. *A Study of the Effectiveness of the Home Experience Program in Puerto Rico.* University of Tennessee, 1955. 197 p. ms.

1116. GARCIA DEERE, CARMEN PILAR, *Home Experiences Suitable for Girls Enrolled in Home Economics II, Puerto Rico.* Iowa State College of Agriculture and Mechanic Arts, 1944. 94 p. ms.

1117. GARCIA-HERNANDEZ, LORENZO. *The Program of Agricultural Instruction for the Out-of-School Farm Youth in Puerto Rico.* Ohio State University, 1938. 110 p. ms.

1118. GARCIA-PALMIERI, RAFAEL A., 1926- . *The Development of a Measure of Father-Son Verbal Communication for Students of the Puerto Rican Senior High Schools.* George Washington University, 1954. 74 p. ms.

1119. GONZALEZ, WILLIAM. *In-Service Education on the Elementary Level in Representative School Districts in Puerto Rico.* Ohio University, 1955. 80 p. ms. Abstract in *Ohio University: Abstracts of Master's Theses . . . 1955,* p. 24-25.

1120. GONZALEZ DE GUEITS, FRANCISCA, 1907- . *A Study of the Child Development Program on the Secondary School Level in Texas and Its Implications to Puerto Rico.* University of Texas, 1946. 93 p. ms.

1121. HADDOCK, HORTENSIA. *A Vocational Home Economics Program for the Reorganized Secondary School in Guayama, Puerto Rico.* Colorado State College of Agriculture and Mechanic Arts, 1939. 89 p. ms.

1122. HERBANS, LAURA LETICIA. *A Comparison of the Attitudes toward Marriage of the Catholic and Non-Catholic Junior and Senior Students of the University of Puerto Rico.* Catholic University of America, 1957. 56 p. ms.

1123. HERNANDEZ, NIVEA M. *American Idioms and the Teaching of English in Puerto Rico.* University of Texas, 1954. 127 p. ms.

1124. IRIZARRY, JOSELINA Y. *Ten Years of Home Demonstration Work in Puerto Rico.* Florida State University, 1945. 199 p. ms.

1125. IRONS, HELEN MARIE CALVIN, 1918- *Evolution of Community Education in Puerto Rico.* University of Delaware, 1954. 171 p. ms.

1126. LANAUSSE, EVA Y. *Reactions to Four-Class Type of Homemaking Education in Puerto Rico.* Texas Technological College, 1958.

1127. LEDESMA, MOISES M. *Sociological Background of the Puerto Rican.* Columbia University, 1935. 41 p. ms. (Includes education as one aspect.)

1128. LOPES, SUSANA. *Recommendations for Equipping Home Economics Departments in Puerto Rico.* Iowa State College of Agriculture and Mechanic Arts, 1956. 114 p. ms.

1129. McELROY, RALPH LEE. *Administrative Aspects of an English Fluency Training Program for Puerto Rican Soldiers.* San Francisco State College, 1956. 95 p. ms.

1130. MARCHESE, ANTHONY H., 1916- . *A History of the School System of Puerto Rico, 1898-1951.* University of Scranton, 1953. 137 p. ms.

1131. MARSH, VIVIAN. *Public Education in the Elementary and Secondary Schools of Puerto Rico.* Hunter College of the City of New York, 1939. 63 p. ms.

1132. MARTIN, AMERICA Q. *The Development of an Improved Curriculum for a Junior High School in Puerto Rico.* University of Michigan, 1953. 322 p. ms.

1133. MARTINEZ, ANA L. REYES DE. *A Study of the Effectiveness of the Homemaking Program in Puerto Rico, with Implications for Needed Changes in the Curriculum.* University of Tennessee, 1953. 178 p. ms.

1134. MARTINEZ, ISABEL WALKER DE. *Professional Attitudes and School Conditions Affecting Home Economics Teachers in Puerto Rico.* Iowa State College of Agriculture and Mechanic Arts, 1948. 99 p. ms.

1135. MARTINEZ-ACEVEDO, REINALDO I., 1913- . *A Study of Former Students of Vocational Agriculture in Puerto Rico.* Pennsylvania State College, 1953. 80 p. ms. For doctoral dissertation by same author, see No. 1060.

1136. MASSO, GILDO, 1891- . *The Growth of the School System of Porto Rico under the American Administration.* University of Chicago, 1922. 249 p. ms. For doctoral dissertation by same author, see No. 3108.

1137. MENDEZ, NICOLAS, 1903- . *A Plan for Improving the Supervised Farming Program for Vocational Education in Agriculture in Puerto Rico.* Virginia Polytechnic Institute, 1937. 130 p. ms.

1138. MENDOZA, Rev. ANTONIO CUESTA, 1873- . *Historia de la Educacion en Puerto Rico, 1509-1700.* Catholic University of America, 1932. 106 p. ms. For doctoral dissertation by same author, see No. 1063.

1139. MILLER, ELMA MAE. *A History of Education in Porto Rico.* College of the Pacific, 1928. 115 p. ms.

1140. MOLINARY, SAMUEL. *The District as a Unit for the Administration and Supervision of Vocational Agriculture in Puerto Rico.* Pennsylvania State College, 1944. 47 p. ms.

1141. MOORE, BARBARA GIRLANDINE. *The Teaching of English in a Bilingual Country.* Ohio State University, 1942. 119 p. ms. (Refers to Puerto Rico.)

1142. MORALES RIVERA, MANUEL. *The Status of Industrial Arts in Puerto Rico.* Colorado State College of Education, 1946. 208 p. ms. Abstract in *Research in Industrial Education, 1930-1955,* p. 393-394.

1143. MORENO MARRERO, JOSE AGAPITO, 1901- . *An Art Curriculum for the Elementary Schools of Puerto Rico.* Colorado State College of Education, 1940. 281 p. ms. For doctoral dissertation by same author, see No. 1064.

1144. MORTON, CLEMENT MANLY. *Principles Underlying the Development of a Program of Religious Education for Porto Rico.* Hartford School of Religious Education, 1928. 136 p. ms.

1145. MUERMAN, JOHN CHARLES, 1865-1935. *The Public Schools of Porto Rico.* George Washington University, 1916. 101 p. ms.

1146. MULHEARN, Rev. JAMES JOSEPH. *Present Day Catholic Education in Puerto Rico.* Catholic University of America, 1933. 40 p. ms.

1147. MUNIZ, ALFREDO C. *An Evaluation of the Commercial Curriculum of Puerto Rican High Schools.* New York University, 1935. 121 p. ms.

1148. ORLANDI, LILY ESTHER. *The Preparation of a Suggested Plan for a Pre-School Laboratory at the University of Puerto Rico Based on a Survey of the Various Problems on the Island Affecting the Development of Children.* Pennsylvania State College, 1945. 94 p. ms.

1149. PEREZ, SILVIA LOPEZ. *Problems in the Handicraft Program of the Extension Service in Puerto Rico, with Recommendations for Solution.* Iowa State College of Agriculture and Mechanic Arts, 1954. 66 p. ms.

1150. PONCE, JOSE A. *Technical Training Needs of Teachers of Vocational Agriculture in Puerto Rico.* Agricultural and Mechanical College of Texas, 1946. 70 p. ms.

1151. PORRATA, OSCAR EMILIO, 1898- . *Retardation in the Elementary Urban Schools of Porto Rico.* University of Chicago, 1934. Rio Piedras, Puerto Rico: University of Puerto Rico, 1939. 63 p. (University of Puerto Rico *Bulletin,* Series 10, No. 1, September 1939). For doctoral dissertation by same author, see No. 1073.

1152. RAMIREZ, MARIA MERCEDES. *Aspects of the Teaching of Algebra, with Particular Reference to Puerto Rico.* University of Texas, 1934. 87 p. ms.

1153. RAMOS, Mrs. GLORIA C. *The Teaching of English in Puerto Rico: A Brief Account of Policies, Plans, and Programs in Connection with the Language Problem of Education.* Columbia University, 1942. 48 p. ms.

1154. RIVERA, ZAIDA NYDIA. *Opinions of a Selected Group of Teachers and Supervisors Concerning the Homemaking Education Program for Adults in Puerto Rico.* Pennsylvania State College, 1954. 113 p. ms.

1155. RODRIGUEZ DIAZ, MANUEL, 1898- . *The Rural Schools in Puerto Rico.* Cornell University, 1942. 162 p. ms. For doctoral dissertation by same author, see No. 1079.

1156. SEDA, JOSE I., 1905- . *Playgrounds and Non-Commercialized Recreation in Puerto Rico: A*

Survey and Program. New York University, 1943. 112 p. ms.

1157. TORREGROSA RIVERA, FELICIO MIGUEL, 1913- . *A Study of Certain Phases of Physical Education for Boys in the Public High Schools of Puerto Rico.* Syracuse University, 1938. 89 p. ms.

1158. TRAINA, SALVADOR. *The Growth and Progress of Public Education in Puerto Rico since the American Occupation.* Columbia University, 1925. 53 p. ms.

1159. TRILLO DE GARRIGA, ANA MARIA. *The Place of the English Language in the Public Educational System of Puerto Rico, 1898-1956.* University of Texas, 1957. 104 p. ms.

1160. TUCK, DOROTHY ISABELLE, 1902- . *The History of the Educational System of Puerto Rico.* Boston University, 1925. 49 p. ms.

1161. URGELL, FRANCISCO CARLOS, 1893- . *The Evolution of Industrial Arts Education in Puerto Rico.* Pennsylvania State College, 1938. 175 p. ms. Abstract in *Research in Industrial Education, 1930-1955*, p. 146. For doctoral dissertation by same author, see No. 1085.

1162. VAZQUEZ-TORRES, ERNESTO. *The All-Day Program of Vocational Agriculture Education of the Island of Puerto Rico: A Study of the History, Development, and Present Status of the All-Day Program with a View to Suggesting Plans to Improve Its Effectiveness.* Pennsylvania State College, 1939. 163 p. ms.

1163. VEGA BRAU, IVAN. *Industrial Arts in Puerto Rico: Its Status and Projection.* Ohio State University, 1948. 166 p. ms. Abstract in Ohio State University: *Abstracts of Masters' Theses*, No. 57, p. 142.

1164. WILSON, ROBERT NEWTON. *A History of the Educational Policy of the United States in Porto Rico: A Phase of Our Later Colonial Policy.* University of Texas, 1924. 103 p. ms.

1165. WINTRUP, MARJORIE, 1910- . *Trends in Education in Puerto Rico from 1898 to 1953.* University of Delaware, 1954. 200 p. ms.

See also Nos. 192, 224, 239, 257, 269, 270, 307, 540.

For Puerto Rican groups in the United States, *see* Nos. 5659-5682.

United States of America

For education of foreign groups, in the United States, see Nos. 4860-5698.

Virgin Islands

(NOS. 1166 – 1167)

DOCTORS

See Nos. 128, 166, 527, 1073

MASTERS

1166. BURNET, AMINTA C. NATHALIA. *Education in the Virgin Islands under Denmark and the United States.* College of the City of New York, 1940. 130 p. ms.

1167. McDONOUGH, OTTO GEORGE. *Education in the Virgin Islands.* University of Washington, 1928. 107 p. ms.

See also Nos. 192, 226, 257

For a group of Virgin Islanders in the United States, *see* No. 4970

West Indies (British)

(NOS. 1168 – 1180)

Also known as West Indies Federation, formerly British West Indies. Includes Grenada, Jamaica, and Trinidad

DOCTOR

1168. JAMES, ERIC GEORGE, 1910- . *Administrative Institutions and Social Change in Jamaica, British West Indies: A Study of Cultural Adaptation.* New York University, 1956. 2 vols. 625 p. ms. (Includes brief consideration of administration of education.)

See also Nos. 142, 147

MASTERS

1169. FRANCIS, CYRIL A. *The Development of Vocational Education in Jamaica since 1936.* Fisk University, 1953.

1170. GRANT, INEZ M. *Development of Introductory Reading Material with Adaptations for Jamaica.* Ohio State University, 1958.

1171. GREEN, BERYL A. *Folk Music in Jamaica, British West Indies.* Wayne University, 1951.

1172. HARRISON, GLADYS M. *Re-Designing a Curriculum for the Jamaican Schools.* Columbia University, 1948. 108 p. ms.

1173. HENRY, ARTHUR I. *A Comparative Analysis of the Training of Personnel in Agricultural Education in Jamaica and the United States.* Cornell University, 1958.

1174. MILLS, HERMAN ADOLPHUS, 1924- . *Toward a More Functional Curriculum for Jamaican Youth.* San Diego State College, 1955. 98 p. ms.

1175. PHILIP, DORIS V. *A Suggested Programme for Providing Farm Experience for High School Students in Jamaica.* Cornell University, 1958.

1176. PHILIPS, DUDLEY JONATHAN, 1916- . *A Comparative Analysis of the Extension Services in Jamaica, B.W.I. and the United States of America.* Cornell University, 1956. 115 p. ms.

1177. PITT, MARTHA LOUISE. *Survey of Libraries in Grenada, B.W.I.* Catholic University of America, 1951. 70 p. ms.

1178. ROCHESTER, VIVIAN WILBERFORCE, 1921- . *An Approach to Program Planning and Coordination in Extension Service of Jamaica, B.W.I.* Cornell University, 1958. 115 p. ms.

1179. WELLER, EGBERT DOUGLAS-HAIG. *Educational Measures for Agrarian Reform in Jamaica.* Iowa State College of Agriculture and Mechanic Arts, 1952. 113 p. ms.

1180. YOUNG, CONSTANCE I. *New Methods of Personnel Counseling in Relation to Work with Girls in Trinidad.* Columbia University, 1930. 39 p. ms.

See also No. 226

For West Indian (British) groups in the United States, *see* Nos. 4970, 4975

AMERICA, SOUTH
(NOS. 1181 – 1292)
General
(NOS. 1181 – 1182)

DOCTORS

See Nos. 121, 137, 150, 151

MASTERS

1181. HUFF, ELLA MARIE. *Roman Catholic Ideals and Methods of Religious Education.* Kennedy School of Missions, 1930. 100 p. ms. (Chapter IV: "How It Worked in South America".)

1182. KILLELEA, MARY E. *Simon Bolivar's Dream of Solidarity for the Americas.* Massachusetts State Teachers College, Fitchburg, 1942. 62 p. ms. (Includes consideration of "Education and Morals as Basis for Government".)

See also Nos. 193, 196, 199, 201, 202, 204, 214, 227, 228, 237, 240, 241, 242, 251, 252, 270, 275, 277, 281, 290, 297, 301, 305

Composite
(NOS. 1183 – 1198)

DOCTORS

1183. ANDRESS, PAUL, 1899- . *An Educational Approach to the Work of the Protestant Church in Latin America.* Columbia University, 1951. 264 p. ms. Abstract in *Teachers College Record,* Vol. 53, p. 458-459, May 1952. (Covers work in Argentina, Brazil, and Chile extensively with incidental references to work in 20 other countries.)

1184. BARAGER, JOSEPH RUFUS, 1914- . *Sarmiento and the United States.* University of Pennsylvania, 1951. 301 p. ms. Abstract in *Abstracts of Completed Doctoral Dissertations for the Academic Year 1950-1951.* (Department of State, External Research Staff, Office of Intelligence Research, Abstract Series No. 1, March 1952, p. 53. Argentina, Chile.)

1185. HALL, ROBERT KING, 1912- . *Federal Control of Secondary Education in the ABC Republics.* University of Michigan, 1941. 480 p. ms. Abstract in *Microfilm Abstracts,* Vol. 4, No. 1, p. 19-20, 1942. Available on microfilm from University Microfilms, Ann Arbor, Michigan, as Publication No. 387. (Argentina, Brazil, Chile.) For master's thesis by same author, see No. 1204.

1186. KRUMTUM, JAMES CHARLES MALOY, 1884- *Domingo Faustino Sarmiento, The Horace Mann of Argentina.* University of Oklahoma, 1936. 260 p. ms. Abstract in *University of Oklahoma Bulletin, Abstracts of Theses Issue,* New series, No. 760, p. 3-16, January 1, 1939. (Argentina. Chile.)

1187. SCHUTTER, CHARLES HENRY, 1905- . *The Development of Education in Argentina, Chile, and Uruguay.* University of Chicago, 1943. Chicago: 1943. v, 165 p. Lithoprinted in a private edition for distribution to libraries in the United States and abroad.

1188. TAVEL, DAVID Z. *A Comparative Study of Secondary School Social Studies in Peru and Chile.* Boston University, 1958. 229 p. ms. Abstract in *Dissertation Abstracts,* Vol. 19, p. 2035, February 1959. Available on microfilm from University Microfilms, Ann Arbor, Michigan, as Mic. 59-442.

1189. YORKE, GERTRUDE CUSHING, 1895- . *Some Effects of the Compulsory Use of Metric Weights and Measures: A Study of the Results of Compulsory Use of Metric Weights and Measures in Brazil, Argentina, Uruguay, and Paraguay.* Boston University, 1942. 344 p. ms. (Considers the effect on the curriculum and on children of learning a dual system of weights and measures.)

MASTERS

1190. BATTERSON, FRANK JOHN. *The Educational Ideals of Domingo F. Sarmiento.* Ohio State University, 1929. 79 p. ms. Abstract in Ohio State University: *Abstracts of Theses Presented by Candidates for the Master's Degree,* August 1929, p. 9-10. (Abstracts of Masters Theses, No. 1. Argentina, Chile.)

1191. CHRISTENSEN, CARL DONALD. *A Partial Evaluation of the Seventh-Day Adventist Secondary Mission Schools in Peru and Bolivia.* University of Nebraska, 1940. 92 p. ms.

1192. DUNN, NORMAN WILLIAM, 1896- . *Seventh-Day Adventist Education in South America.* Southern Methodist University, 1946. Abstract in Southern Methodist University: *Abstracts of Theses . . . No. 12,* 1947. p. 14. (Limited to Argentina, Brazil, Chile, and Peru as "other countries have similar systems".)

1193. HERSHEY, PHARES ROBERT. *D. F. Sarmiento, Apostle of Civilization.* Northwestern University, 1930. 81 p. ms. (Argentina, Chile.)

1194. HOLDEN, JESSIE FERN. *The Educational Views of Domingo Faustino Sarmiento in Relation to His Life and Times.* University of Colorado, 1939. 83 p. ms. Abstract in *University of Colorado Studies,* Vol. 26, No. 2, p. 73, November 1939. (Argentina, Chile.)

1195. INGENHUETT, ARTHUR HILMER. *La Influencia de Horacio Mann en la Obra de Domingo Faustino Sarmiento.* University of Texas, 1926. 113 p. ms. (Argentina, Chile.)

1196. KAIN, CATHERINE M. *Advanced Foreign Preparation for Faculty Members of Selected Schools of Nursing in South America: A Study of Its Effectiveness.* Catholic University of America, 1953. 70 p. ms. (Includes eleven schools in Brazil, Chile, Colombia, Ecuador, Peru, and Venezuela.)

1197. MAHOOD, MILDRED HAYBURN. *Mathematics in the Educational Programs of Certain Countries of South America.* University of Florida, 1952. 89 p. ms. (Includes Chile, Colombia, and Peru.)

1198. SANDY, GERALD HERBERT. *An Account of the National Libraries of Spanish South America.* University of Illinois, 1932. 109 p. ms. (Note: Author's name as Sanjurgo, Gerald Herbert, by Pan American Union, Washington, D.C., in *Theses on Pan American Topics,* Bibliographical Series No. 5, December 1941, p. 103, No. 1350. Includes Argentina, Bolivia, Chile, Colombia, Ecuador, Paraguay, Peru, Uruguay, and Venezuela.)

Argentina

(NOS. 1199 – 1211)

DOCTORS

1199. FAUST, AUGUSTUS F., 1918- . *The Public School System of Argentina.* University of Utah, 1950. 284 p. ms.

1200. HOWELL, JOHN MARION. *Federal Support and Control of Education in the United States of America and in the Argentine Republic.* University of Nebraska, 1942. 160 p. ms. Abstract in *University of Nebraska: Abstracts of Doctoral Dissertations,* 1942, p. 132-138.

1201. MADDOCK, SAYRE PAUL, 1891- . *An Attempt to Achieve Needed Changes in the Argentine Secondary School (Colegio Nacional) through the Influence of a New Program of Study in the American School, Buenos Aires.* Columbia University, 1937. 278 p. ms.

1202. MOORE, DONALD EDWIN, 1917- . *The Educational Philosophy of Juan Mantovani.* University of California, Los Angeles, 1957. 256 p. ms. For master's thesis by same author, see No. 1289.

See also Nos. 119, 122, 126, 133, 147, 155, 157, 1183, 1184, 1185, 1186, 1187, 1189

MASTERS

1203. GRAEFE, EDWARD WALTER, 1916- *Education for Argentine Youth Through the Institutions of the Protestant Church.* Princeton Theological Seminary, 1949. 247 p. ms.

1204. HALL, ROBERT KING, 1912- . *The Secondary School in Argentina.* University of Chicago, 1936. 94 p. ms. For doctoral dissertation by same author, see No. 1185.

1205. HEWATT, VIVIAN ELIZABETH. *History of Education in Argentina through Sarmiento's Administration.* University of Colorado, 1942. 119 p. ms. Abstract in *University of Colorado Studies,* Vol. 27, No. 1, p. 33-34, November 1942.

1206. HUNTINGTON, SUSAN DICKINSON. *The Public Elementary School System of the Argentine Republic.* Columbia University, 1908. 45 p. ms.

1207. LLORENS, JAMES. *The English-Speaking People in Argentina: A Study of Their Social and Cultural Influences.* Columbia University, 1930. 66 p. ms. (Includes educational influences.)

1208. MAHDESIAN, ROXIE. *The Development of Education in Argentina.* University of Southern California, 1941. 103 p. ms.

1209. MARCIANO, LEONARD P., 1918- . *The History and Development of the Argentine Public Schools to 1951.* University of Scranton, 1953. 97 p. ms.

1210. POPE, RAQUEL VAN DER POLL. *A Comparative Study of the Training of Secondary School Teachers in the United States of America and in Argentina.* University of Georgia, 1956. 142 p. ms.

1211. TAYLOR, GEORGE BENJAMIN. *The Influence of Domingo Faustino Sarmiento on the Development of Public Instruction in Argentina.* Stanford University, 1936. 111 p. ms.

See also Nos. 190, 194, 205, 226, 253, 256, 260, 272, 273, 275, 281, 295, 307, 1190, 1192, 1193, 1194, 1196, 1198

For Argentinian groups in the United States, see Nos. 4969, 4970, 4975

Bolivia

(NOS. 1212 – 1216)

DOCTOR

1212. BECK, BESSIE DUNN, 1891- *A Study of Changing Social Attitudes in the American Institutes of Bolivia.* University of Chicago, 1935. 374 p. ms. Part of the dissertation (18 p. lithoprinted) was distributed to libraries in the United States and abroad in 1935.

See also Nos. 119, 126, 133, 142, 149, 151

MASTERS

1213. ANIBARRO-PONCE DE LEON, DELINA. *A Proposed Plan for the Reorganization of the Secondary School System in Bolivia.* Ohio State University, 1952. 97 p. ms.

1214. BURNS, RAY G. *The American Institute of La Paz, Bolivia.* Oklahoma Agricultural and Mechanical College, 1938. 51 p. ms.

1215. GUARDIA, LUIS RAMON, 1912- . *The Extension Service in Bolivia: Its Origin, Development, Accomplishments, and Projections.* Cornell University, 1958. 135 p. ms.

1216. RICHARDS, MARY. *Education in Bolivia.* Adams State College, 1958.

See also Nos. 190, 205, 223, 226, 242, 256, 260, 307, 1191, 1198

For a Bolivian group in the United States, *see* No. 4975

Brazil

(NOS. 1217 – 1243)

DOCTORS

1217. HAWKINS, DORINE COBB, 1916- . *The Development and Influence of the Woman's Missionary Training Schools in Brazil.* Southwestern Baptist Theological Seminary, 1957. 25 p. ms.

1218. PIERSON, ROBERT DONALD, 1900- . *A Study of Racial and Cultural Adjustment in Bahia, Brazil.* University of Chicago, 1939. 245 p. ms. Published as *Negroes in Brazil: A Study of Race Contact at Bahia.* Chicago: University of Chicago Press, 1942. xviii, 392 p. (University of Chicago Sociological Series). With Introduction by Robert E. Park. (Chiefly sociological, but includes section on ethnic composition of the schools, both students and teachers, p. 187-191.)

See also Nos. 123, 124, 126, 133, 147, 151, 171, 1183, 1185, 1189

MASTERS

1219. ALBANO, JOAO PITANGUY. *Rural Education and Its Special Problems in Brazil and in the United States.* University of Wisconsin, 1946. 128 p. ms.

1220. BAKER, MATTIE ALIDA. *A Vocabulary Study of the Primers Adopted in Sao Paulo, Brazil.* George Peabody College for Teachers, 1931. 164 p. ms.

1221. BRITO CUNHA, RENATO M. G. *Guides for the Reorganization of the Physical Education Program in the Public Secondary Schools of Brazil.* Springfield College, 1956. 91 p. ms.

1222. BROWN, MARY SUE. *The Development of Secondary Education in Brazil.* University of Texas, 1935. 98 p. ms.

1223. CHAVES, DERLY DE AZEVEDO, 1895- . *A Curriculum Project for the School of Theology of Granbery College, Brazil.* Emory University, 1928. 71 p. ms.

1224. DAWSON, SARAH M. *The Story of a School for Young Children: The Pre-Primary School of Colegio Bennett, Rio de Janeiro, Brazil.* Columbia University, 1954. 127 p. ms.

1225. DE MATTOS, DOM XAVIER. *The Elementary Public Schools in Brazil from 1759 to 1827.* Catholic University of America, 1931. 83 p. ms.

1226. DOS SANTOS, Sister MARY LEONILDA. *Twentieth-Century Development of Secondary Education in Brazil.* Catholic University of America, 1958.

1227. ELLIS, JAMES ELIJAH. *The Development of Education in Brazil.* Emory University, 1922. 39 p. ms. (Thesis for degree of Bachelor of Divinity.)

1228. FOSBRINK, RALEIGH HARMON, 1917- . *A Study of Agricultural Institutions in the State of Minas Gerais, Brazil.* Cornell University, 1958. 108 p. ms.

1229. FRANKLIN, MARLINE ROSE. *The Role of Protestant Mission Schools in Brazil.* Biblical Seminary in New York, 1955.

1230. FREITAS, WILLIAM JOHN. *History of the Brazilian Naval Academy, 1808 to 1948.* Stanford University, 1948. 109 p. ms.

1231. GAMMON, WILLIS HUMPHREYS. *Contributions of American Evangelical Schools to the Development of Education in Brazil.* Drew University, 1940. 119 p. ms.

1232. HINN, HENRY THEODORE. *The Strategy of Christian Education in the Evangelistic Mission in Santa Calarina, Brazil.* Princeton Theological Seminary, 1944. 117 p. ms.

1233. HURST, GEORGE HOWARD. *Problem: To Lay Down a Working Plan for Making the First Steps in the Training of Leaders of Religious Education in the West Brazil Mission.* Louisville Presbyterian Theological Seminary, 1929. 78 p. ms.

1234. LANGMACK, CLARA JOHANNE, 1915- . *A Study of Brazilian Singing Games.* George Washington University, 1943. 95 p. ms. (Considers singing games and dances for use in school and community programs.)

1235. McKINNEY, RUTH ELIZABETH. *Evangelization of the Teen Age Brazilian Girl in the Program of Mission Schools.* Biblical Seminary in New York, 1950. 79 p. ms.

Bolivia, Brazil, Chile

1236. MOORE, JESSIE MARIE. *Woman's Work in Brazil of the Methodist Episcopal Church, South.* George Peabody College for Teachers, 1930. 146 p. ms. (Includes consideration of schools and colleges.)

1237. NEUBAUER, GERHARDT W., 1915- . *A Summary of Available Literature in the English Language on the Historical Development and Present Status of Education in Brazil.* Stout Institute, 1944. 113 p. ms. Abstract in *Research in Industrial Education, 1930-1955,* p. 476.

1238. NOVAES, INES ROMEU, 1916- . *A Proposed Course in Corrective Physical Education for the Teacher Training Institution at Sao Paulo, Brazil.* Smith College, 1950. 76 p. ms.

1239. PITHON PINTO, ANTONIO, 1911- . *Education in Brazil.* University of North Carolina, 1943. 237 p. ms. Abstract in *University of North Carolina Record,* No. 429, p. 116-117, October 1946.

1240. REASONER, ELLEN MAE. *The Study and Evaluation of the Primary Program of the New Curriculum of the Presbyterian Church, U.S.A., with a View to Possible Translation and Adaptation for a Rural Brazilian Situation.* Biblical Seminary in New York, 1950. 88 p. ms.

1241. TERRY, ZULA. *State Control of Education in Brazil during the Empire, 1822-1899.* University of Texas, 1932. 139 p. ms.

1242. VERNON, VANCE ORAE, 1921- *Illiteracy in Brazil.* Southern Baptist Theological Seminary, 1951. 59 p. ms.

1243. WILLIAMS, LOIS MARIETTA. *The Application of a Specific Group Principle and Techniques to an Administration Problem in the Public Educational System of the Federal District of Brazil.* Northwestern University, 1940. 137 p. ms.

See also Nos. 190, 200, 205, 215, 226, 256, 260, 283, 295, 307, 1192, 1196

For Brazilian groups in the United States, see Nos. 4970, 4975, 4988

Chile
(NOS. 1244 – 1262)

DOCTORS

1244. SALAS-DIAZ, DARIO ENRIQUE, 1881-1941. *A Comparative Study of the Normal Schools of the United States and Chile.* New York University, 1907. 88 p. ms.

1245. SALAS SILVA, IRMA, 1903- . *The Socio-Economic Composition of the Secondary School Population of Chile.* Columbia University, 1930. Santiago, Chile: 1930. xiii, 144 p.

1246. SEGUEL, LEOPOLDO F. *Proposals for the Foundations of a State Program of Instructional Improvement in the Elementary Schools of Chile.* Columbia University, 1942. 78 p. ms.

See also Nos. 119, 126, 147, 149, 151, 155, 167, 1183, 1184, 1185, 1186, 1187, 1188

MASTERS

1247. ALONSO, M. PAULINA, 1896- . *Civic Education in Chile.* University of California, Berkeley, 1923. 144 p. ms.

1248. ARMS, PAUL RAY. *Secondary Education in Chile during the Nineteenth and Twentieth Century.* State University of Iowa, 1954. 128 p. ms.

1249. BERND, CLARK B. *The Reform of Secondary Education in Chile from 1945.* University of California, Los Angeles, 1950. 94 p. ms.

1250. GONZALEZ, EMA LASTENIA. *Development of Normal Schools in Chile, with a Brief History of the National System of Education.* Ohio State University, 1933. 120 p. ms. Abstract in Ohio State University: *Abstracts of Theses Presented by Candidates for the Master's Degree . . . 1933,* p. 104-105. (Abstracts of Master's Theses, No. 13.)

1251. KOHL, MICHAEL JOHN. *A Study of the Gradual Reorganization of Secondary Education in the Republic of Chile, 1945-1949.* University of Washington, 1953. 138 p. ms.

1252. MANOSALVA, MARIE MERCEDES. *A Comparison of Elementary Education in Chile with that of the United States.* University of Wisconsin, 1921.

1253. OATES, MARION DAVIS, 1922- . *A History of the Baptist Mission in Chile.* Southern Baptist Theological Seminary, 1950. (Includes educational activities.)

1254. ORELLANA, MARINA, 1918- . *Possible Contributions of Educational Thought and Practice in America to Vocational Education in Chile.* Smith College, 1942. 148 p. ms.

1255. PEET, ALICE LIDA. *The Use of Speech and Drama in the Teaching of English as a Foreign Language at Santiago College, Santiago de Chile.* University of Wisconsin, 1952. 111 p. ms.

1256. PERADA OVIEDO, ARMANDO. *The History and Development of Secondary Education in Chile.* Tufts College, 1942. 89 p. ms.

1257. RAMIREZ, HERNAN. *Adult Education in Chile.* Columbia University, 1944. 46 p. ms.

1258. RIOS-CASTRO, RIGOBERTO, 1910- *A Health Education Program for Chile.* Massachusetts Institute of Technology, 1941. 295 p. ms.

1259. SEEL, EDWARD GEORGE. *The Teaching of English in Chile.* Columbia University, 1926. 71 p. ms.

1260. TURK, LAUREL H., 1903- . *Andres Bello: Educator and Scholar.* University of Kansas, 1926. 86 p. ms.

1261. UDICK, BERNICE. *Gabriela Mistral: A Study of One of the Great Women of Today.* Colorado State Teachers College, 1929. 95 p. ms.

1262. WATT, MARIA ELENA. *A Study of the Methods of Teaching English in the United States and in Chile.* Florida State University, 1942. 164 p. ms.

See also Nos. 190, 194, 205, 224, 256, 260, 273, 281, 293, 295, 307, 1190, 1192, 1193, 1194, 1195, 1196, 1197, 1198

For Chilean groups in the United States, see Nos. 4957, 4970, 4975, 4990

Colombia

(NOS. 1263 - 1269)

DOCTORS

1263. BARNEY, MARIA INES, 1904- . *Planning for Colombian Youth.* Columbia University, 1948. 131 p. ms.

1264. FILELLA, *Rev.* JAMES FERRER, 1927- . *Educational and Sex Differences in the Organization of Abilities in Technical and Academic Students in Colombia, South America.* Fordham University, 1957. 178 p. ms.

1265. VALENCIA-VASQUEZ, HECTOR GLAUCO, 1920- . *Theories and Practices of Secondary School Organization and Administration in the Republic of Colombia.* Ohio State University, 1953. 280 p. ms. Abstract in *Dissertation Abstracts,* Vol. 19, p. 1993-1996, February 1959. Available on microfilm from University Microfilms, Ann Arbor, Michigan, as Mic. 58-718.

See also Nos. 119, 126, 133, 140, 155

MASTERS

1266. EGGER, *Sister* MARY SEFERINA. *The Development of the Primary and Secondary School Systems in Colombia, South America, 1886-1949.* Catholic University of America, 1951. 104 p. ms.

1267. PARKER, LYDIA EDITH. *Public Education in Colombia, South America.* University of Texas, 1931. 243 p. ms.

1268. RIVERA, RODOLFO OSVALDO, 1901- . *Education in Colombia: Its Historical Development and Present Status.* Duke University, 1929. 196 p. ms.

1269. SMILEY, VIRGINIA BELL. *Survey of the History and Missionary Background of Colombia, South America.* Columbia Bible College, 1952. 117 p. ms. (Includes brief section on education in the country and more fully the educational work of missionary societies.)

See also Nos. 190, 200, 205, 215, 226, 256, 260, 273, 293, 295, 307, 308, 1196, 1197, 1198

For Colombian groups in the United States, see Nos. 4956, 4969, 4975, 4990, 5229

Ecuador

(NOS. 1270 - 1272)

DOCTOR

1270. ABLEN, BEATRICE P., 1901- . *A Reading Readiness and Pre-Primer Manual for the Teaching of Beginning Reading in the Urban Primary Schools of Ecuador, South America.* New York University, 1953. 37, 39, 96 p. ms. Abstract in *Dissertation Abstracts,* Vol. 14, p. 316, February 1954. Available on microfilm from University Microfilms, Ann Arbor, Michigan, as Publication No. 7,123.

See also Nos. 119, 126, 133, 140, 151, 155, 167, 1276

MASTERS

1271. DAVID, MURIEL GRACE. *A Plan for a School for Girls in Ecuador.* Biblical Seminary in New York, 1936. 158 p. ms.

1272. RUIZ, CRISTOBAL, 1913- . *The Extension Service in Ecuador: Its Past, Its Present Accomplishments, and Its Future.* Cornell University, 1958. 87 p. ms.

See also Nos. 190, 194, 197, 200, 205, 215, 226, 260, 293, 295, 307, 1196, 1198

For an Ecuadorean group in the United States, see No. 4975

Paraguay
(NO. 1273)

DOCTOR

1273. ELLIOTT, ARTHUR ELWOOD, 1888- . *Paraguay — A Case Study in Missionary Education.* Columbia University, 1931. Published as *Paraguay: Its Cultural Heritage, Social Conditions, and Educational Problems.* New York: Bureau of Publications, Teachers College, Columbia University, 1931. xiv, 210 p. (Teachers College Contribution to Education, No. 473.)

See also 119, 126, 155, 176, 1189

MASTERS

See Nos. 190, 205, 226, 260, 295, 307, 1198

For a Paraguayan group in the United States, *see* No. 4957

Peru
(NOS. 1274 — 1286)

DOCTORS

1274. DALE, WILLIAM PRATT II., 1909- . *The Cultural Revolution in Peru, 1750-1820.* Duke University, 1941. 322 p. ms. (Includes education as one phase of culture.)

1275. ESPINOZA-LLANOS, NICEFORO ENRIQUE, 1915- . *Exploratory Analysis on Some Key Influences on Children in Southern Indian Communities of Peru with Implications for Education in Rural Schools.* University of Maryland, 1953. 227 p. ms. Abstract in University of Maryland: *Abstracts of Dissertations . . . 1953-54*, p. 46.

1276. GAMARRA, TEOFILA VIOLETA, 1925- *Recommendations for the Administration of Audio-Visual Materials and Equipment in Peru.* Indiana University, 1952. 426 p. ms. Abstract in Indiana University, School of Education: *Studies in Education*, 1952. p. 121-127. (Thesis Abstract Series, No. 4. Includes also "Suggestions for the Organization of an Audio-Visual Department in Quito, Ecuador" (in Spanish), by Hagen Hasselbalch.)

1277. NOTHDURFT, IVAN HENRY, 1917- . *A Proposed Plan of Religious Education in the Victoria Mission Program of Lima, Peru.* Columbia University, 1951; Union Theological Seminary, 1951. 191 p. ms.

1278. TIBESAR, ANTOINE SEVERIN, 1909- *The Colegios de Missiones in Peru.* Catholic University of America, 1952. Published as *Franciscan Beginnings in Colonial Peru*, Washington: Catholic University of America, 1952. viii, 277 p. Also published, same title, Washington: Academy of American Franciscan History, 1953. xviii, 162 p. (Monograph Series, Vol. 1.) With Introduction by Victor a Belaunde. Also issued by Catholic University of America on microfilm cards, No. BX 3,614.

See also Nos. 119, 126, 133, 155, 1188

MASTERS

1279. CARTER, ERNEST N. *A Historical Study of Physical Education and Athletics in Peru for the Purpose of Discovering Pertinent Problems and to Recommend Solutions.* Claremont Graduate School, 1952. 80 p. ms.

1280. CASTRO-POZO, CARMEN. *Reorganizing the Secondary Schools of Peru to Provide for Work Experience.* Ohio State University, 1944. 120 p. ms.

1281. GOLDFINGER, MARY, 1904- . *Social and Intellectual Life in Viceregal Peru, as Revealed in "Tradiciones Peruanas" by Ricardo Palma.* Colorado State Teachers College, 1931. 92 p. ms.

1282. JIBIYA, PEDRO FLAVIO. *An Adaptation of American Education and Institutions to the Needs of the Republic of Peru.* University of Southern California, 1925. 115 p. ms.

1283. KOCH, ALVERNA M. *An Historical Study of the Commercial Department of Lima High School, Lima, Peru, and a Survey of Graduates from 1919 through 1945.* Bowling Green State University, 1948.

1284. MURPHY, CLARA MAY. *A Report on a Study of the Family in Relation to Its Place in the Curriculum of Home Economics in Lima High School, Lima, Peru.* Columbia University, 1937. 23 p. ms.

1285. TAMAYO, MARIA LUISA. *A Proposed Plan for Reorganizing Secondary Education in the Republic of Peru.* Ohio State University, 1952. 231 p. ms.

1286. TEJADA, MARIA CARMELA. *A Manual for Peruvian Students on Choosing a Career.* University of Maryland, 1947. 88 p. ms.

See also Nos. 190, 194, 195, 205, 226, 236, 256, 293, 295, 299, 307, 1191, 1192, 1196, 1197, 1198

For Peruvian groups in the United States, *see* Nos. 4957, 4970, 4975, 4990

Uruguay
(NOS. 1287 – 1289)

DOCTOR

1287. PONTEROTTO, ITALO LOUIS, 1917- . *Jose Pedro Varela and His Contribution to Education in Uruguay.* New York University, 1951. 3 vols. 524 p. ms. Abstract in *Dissertation Abstracts,* Vol. 12, No. 4, p. 521-522, 1952. Available on microfilm from University Microfilms, Ann Arbor, Michigan, as Publication No. 3,703.

See also Nos. 119, 126, 155, 167, 1187, 1189

MASTERS

1288. CROSS, LILLY. *Cultural Development of Uruguay.* Oklahoma Agricultural and Mechanical College, 1945. 61 p. ms. (Includes education.)

1289. MOORE, DONALD EDWIN, 1917- . *The Development of Public Primary Education in Uruguay.* University of California, Los Angeles, 1948. 111 p. ms. For doctoral dissertation by same author, see No. 1202.

See also Nos. 190, 200, 226, 236, 253, 260, 295, 307, 1198

For an Uruguayan group in the United States, see No. 4957

Venezuela
(NOS. 1290 – 1292)

DOCTORS

See Nos. 119, 126, 133, 155

MASTERS

1290. BLACK, HARRIET MAE. *The Education of the Child of the American National in Venezuela.* University of Hawaii, 1939. 70 p. ms.

1291. RUDE, PEARL. *A Survey of the Cultural Developments of Venezuela.* Oklahoma Agricultural and Mechanical College, 1945. 53 p. ms. (Shows that the wealth of the country is being utilized to improve the cultural and educational phases of life.)

1292. TREVINO, EMMA. *Concern with the Concepts and Life and Ideals in the United States as Presented in Portions of the Venezuelan Course of Study for Elementary Schools.* University of Texas, 1956. 171 p. ms.

See also Nos. 190, 224, 260, 293, 295, 307, 308, 1196, 1198

For Venezuelan groups in the United States, see Nos. 4969, 4975, 4988

ASIA
(NOS. 1293 – 3000)

General
(NOS. 1293 – 1296)

DOCTOR

1293. RANDALL, HERBERT M. *American Baptist Mission among Primitive Peoples in Southeast Asia.* Northern Baptist Theological Seminary, 1957. (Includes education.)

See also Nos. 18, 130, 134, 137, 168, 174, 183

MASTERS

1294. BORNCAMP, FRED FOSTER. *The Mental Development of Orientals.* Stanford University, 1920. 92 p. ms.

1295. KINBERG, HJAALMAR HENNINGSSON. *"The Adulteration of Knowledge" by Muhammed ibn Ahmed al-Dhahabi.* Columbia University, 1935. 26 p. ms.

1296. RANASINGHE, Rev. V. S. ALEX. *The Philosophy of Man in Buddhism and Its Educational Implications.* Catholic University of America, 1956. Abstract in *Catholic Educational Review*, Vol. 55, p. 553, November 1957.

See also Nos. 186, 191, 193, 195, 228, 232, 233, 248, 276, 278, 285, 301, 1320

Composite
(NOS. 1297 – 1322)

DOCTORS

1297. CHOW, TIMOTHY YU-HSI, 1914- . *A Comparison of Jesus and Confucius as Teachers.* Boston University, 1952. 317 p. ms. (Israel, China.)

1298. GERATY, THOMAS SINCLAIR, 1914- . *An Investigation of Higher Education in Iran, Iraq, and Lebanon.* University of Southern California, 1958. 416 p. ms. For master's thesis by same author, see No. 229.

1299. HOBART, KENNETH GRAY. *A Comparative History of the East China and South China Missions of the American Baptist Foreign Mission Society, 1833-1935.* Yale University, 1937. Published in part as *Early American Baptist Missions to the Chinese*, Shanghai, Privately printed, 1939. (Includes educational activities in Hong Kong, Singapore, and Thailand, as well as in China.)

1300. LEE, SOOKNEY, 1923- . (Yi, Sung Nyo in Library of Congress card catalog). *Primary Arithmetic Textbooks in Korea, Japan, China, and the United States.* State University of Iowa, 1954. 398 p. ms. Abstract in *Dissertation Abstracts*, Vol. 14, p. 1584, October 1954. Abstract also in W. C. Eells, *The Literature of Japanese Education 1945-1954*, p. 89-90. Available on microfilm from University Microfilms, Ann Arbor, Michigan, as Publication No. 9,586.

1301. NAGLE, JAMES STEWART, 1889-1952. *The Educational Needs of the Straits Settlements and the Federated Malay States.* Johns Hopkins University, 1926. Baltimore, Maryland: 1928. 194 p.

1302. PARKER, LINDSAY. *Gautama Buddha and Jesus Christ as Moral Teachers.* New York University, 1893. 52 p. ms. (India, Israel.)

1303. REED, CASS ARTHUR. *Problems of American Education in the Near East.* Harvard University, 1921. 523 p. ms. (Deals with a dozen American-founded institutions in the old Ottoman Empire of 1900, including American University of Beirut and various institutions in the present Turkey.)

MASTERS

1304. BRONSON, BERTRAM BETHUEL, 1891- . *The Educational Principles and Methods of the Philippine School System and Their Adaptability to the Present Needs of Siam.* University of California, Berkeley, 1921. 73 p. ms. (Philippines, Thailand.)

1305. EKDAHL, NAOMI MARGUERITE GOLDTHWAITE. *The Psychology of Buddhism.* Syracuse University, 1923. 98 p. ms. (Includes Burma, Ceylon, China, India, Indonesia, Korea, Thailand, and Tibet.)

1306. FENN, WILLIAM P. *The Use of Schools for American Children in the Far East for Education in Internationalism.* New York University, 1928. 90 p. ms. (Includes schools in China, Japan, and Korea.)

1307. JEHA, ADMA MICHAEL, 1924- . *Educational Guidance in the American Public Senior High School and Its Potentialities for the Public Secondary Schools of Syria and Lebanon.* Smith College, 1948. 155 p. ms.

1308. KHOURI, HANNA ANDY, 1913- . *A Plan of Reconstruction for Rural Syria and Lebanon.* Cornell University, 1947. 56 p. ms. (Includes education.)

1309. LING, HO-TEE, 1925- . *Leadership Training for Chinese Churches in Malaya and Sarawak, Borneo.* Pacific School of Religion, 1956.

1310. LUTZ, MARTHA LUCILE. *A Comparative Study of the Chinese and Japanese Abaci.* Ohio State University, 1956. 89 p. ms. (China, Japan.)

1311. McGUFFIN, RICHARD LAWRENCE, 1898- . *The Teaching of English to Syrian and Palestinian Arabs.* Boston University, 1925. 150 p. ms.

1312. McLEES, WILLIE. *American Schools in Certain Outposts of Western Civilization.* University of Cincinnati, 1937. 65 p. ms. (Includes schools in China, India, Japan, Philippines, and Syria.)

1313. MAASS, ERNEST. *The Problem of Establishing Official Languages in New States, with Reference to Pakistan and Indonesia.* New York University, 1956.

1314. MARTYN, FLORENCE HARRIETTE. *A Critically Selected, Annotated Bibliography Which May Be Used in Developing and Evaluating a Plan of Organization and Administration of Nursing in Pakistan and India.* Catholic University of America, 1950. 251 p. ms. (Contains 400 references, many on nursing education and related topics. Fully indexed.)

1315. MENON, KUNNATH APPUNNI. *The Educational Policy of the British in India as Compared with the American Policy in the Philippines.* Syracuse University, 1920. 170 p. ms.

1316. NICHOLAS, CATHERINE KATE. *A Brief Study of the Development of Some of the Educational Enterprizes Existing Today in India, Including Burma.* University of Southern California, 1931. 97 p. ms.

1317. OVERZET, CLARENCE. *The Army Education Program in the Far East.* San Francisco State College, 1956. 71 p. ms. (Includes Formosa and Japan.)

1318. ROGERS, Sister MARY JAMES. *Elements of Musical Study in the Missionary School and in Some Missions Afar.* Catholic University of America, 1938. 99 p. ms. (Includes Maryknoll missions in China, Japan, and Korea.)

1319. RONQUILLO, BEATRIZ PABLO. *A Comparative Study of the Education of Oriental Women.* University of Chicago, 1935. 162 p. ms. (Includes China, India, Japan, Korea, and Philippines.)

1320. SACKS, MAXWELL LAWRENCE. *Fundamental Issues in Jewish and Buddhistic Education: A Comparative Study of the Essential Phases of Judaism and Buddhism.* New York University, 1925. 55 p. ms.

1321. VU, YEN THI, 1923- . *Some Aspects of Compulsory Education in the Philippines, Thailand, and Viet-Nam.* Loyola University, 1956.

1322. WOODRING, ETHEL O. *Education in the Philippines and in the Dutch East Indies.* Columbia University, 1927. 65 p. ms.

Afghanistan
(NOS. 1323 – 1325)

DOCTORS

1323. KAYEUM, ABDUL, 1919- . *Recommendations for Improvement of the Instruction in the Social Sciences for Schools in Afghanistan Based on a Cultural Study of Afghans.* University of Denver, 1947. 235 p. ms.

1324. TARAKI, MOHAMED RASAL, 1915- . *A Proposed Functional Training Program for Elementary School Teachers in Afghanistan.* Cornell University, 1945. 183 p. ms. Abstract in Cornell University: *Abstracts of Theses* . . . 1945, p. 63-67.

See also No. 119

MASTER

1325. GHIIZAI, GHULAM FARUA. *Teachers' Education in Afghanistan.* San Francisco State College, 1957. 55 p. ms.

See also No. 226

For Afghanistani groups in the United States, *see* Nos. 4972, 4975

Burma
(NOS. 1326 – 1346)

DOCTORS

1326. JOSIF, GEORGE DEMETRIUS. *A More Adequate and Integrated Program of Education for the American Baptist Mission in Burma.* Columbia University, 1935. 48 p. ms. For master's thesis by same author, see No. 1341.

1327. SEMMENS, LINDSAY ALFRED, 1895-1947. *A History of the Development of Education under British Administration in Burma to 1886.* University of Southern California, 1938. 373 p. ms. Abstract in University of Southern California: *Abstracts of Dissertations,* 1938, p. 83-86.

1328. TAN, GWAN LEONG, 1905- . *Bilingual Education and Its Inherent Problems, with Special Reference to Burma.* University of California, Berkeley, 1947. 223 p. ms.

1329. TAW, FLORENCE MAY, 1914- . *Proposals for Curriculum Change in the Secondary Schools of Burma.* Columbia University, 1954. 256 p. ms.

1330. TAYLOR, NORMAN PETER, 1918- . *A Suggested Course of Study for General Science in Urban Schools in the Union of Burma.* Columbia University, 1954. 508 p. ms.

1331. THAUNG, MAUNG B., 1916- . *A Guide for Reorganizing the Curriculum for Elementary Schools of the Union of Burma.* University of Denver, 1950. 173 p. ms.

1332. WOLF, FRANK EDWARD, 1920- . *The Cultural Surrogate in International Relations: A Case Study of the Role of a Fulbright Teacher of Science Education from the United States in Bassein, Burma, for a One-Year Program.* New York University, 1956. 212 p. ms. Abstract in *Dissertation Abstracts,* Vol. 17, p. 2889-2890, December 1957. Available on microfilm from University Microfilms, Ann Arbor, Michigan, as Publication No. 20,007.

See also Nos. 138, 170

MASTERS

1333. BOYLES, JAMES R. *A Program of Adult Education for Twante, Burma.* University of Denver, 1938. 88 p. ms. Abstract in University of Denver: *Educational Research Bulletin,* Vol. 1, p. 11. (Includes also Denmark and India.)

1334. DAVIS, BERTHA ETTIE. *Adaptability of the Old Testament to the Religious Education of the Burmese* University of Chicago, 1915. 32 p. ms.

1335. HACKETT, PAUL RICHMOND. *Religious Education of Burman Buddhists.* University of Chicago, 1921. 62 p. ms.

1336. HATTERSLEY, LINN WHEELER. *Baptist Mission Schools for Burmans.* University of Chicago, 1919. 55 p. ms.

1337. HINTON, HERBERT ERNEST. *Problems of Education in Burma.* University of Cincinnati, 1927. 163 p. ms.

1338. HOBBS, CECIL CARLTON. *Christian Education and the Burmese Family.* Colgate Rochester Theological Seminary, 1942. 259 p. ms.

1339. HUNT, ETHEL LEORA. *Education in Burma.* University of Washington, 1926. 86 p. ms.

1340. JOHNSON, CECILIA LOUISE. *A History of the Development of Education in Burma under the Auspices of the American Baptist Foreign Mission Societies.* University of Chicago, 1920. 223 p. ms.

1341. JOSIF, GEORGE DEMETRIUS. *The Burmese System of Teacher Training.* University of Chicago, 1919. 71 p. ms. For doctoral dissertation by same author, see No. 1326.

1342. LINDER, ELIZABETH, 1926- , and LING, PATRICIA, 1931- . *A Program for Youth Camps in Burma.* Eastern Baptist Theological Seminary, 1955. 187 p. ms.

1343. OLMSTEAD, CLARENCE EUGENE. *The Curriculum of a Theological School in Burma.* Northwestern University, 1922. 85 p. ms.

1344. SI, MA KYIN, 1915- . *A Proposed Corrective Physical Education Program for the Elementary Schools of Burma.* Smith College, 1948. 71 p. ms.

1345. THWE, MA KHIN. *Family Centered Home Economics Education for Burma.* Ohio State University, 1955. 112 p. ms.

1346. TINT, MAUNG SAN, 1926- . *An Investigation into the Study of the Educational System in the Kayah State, Burma.* Syracuse University, 1953. 104 p. ms.

See also Nos. 308, 1305, 1316

For Burman groups in the United States, see Nos. 4956, 4957, 4970, 4975

Ceylon
(NOS. 1347 – 1352)

DOCTORS

1347. MILLER, CHARLES WINTHROP. *Education and the Family among the Jaffnese of Ceylon: A Survey from the Standpoint of Religious Education of the Factors Involved in Reconstructive Methods in a Hindu Society.* Columbia University, 1923. 244+19 p. ms.

1348. STRAUS, MURRAY ARNOLD, 1926- . *Child Training and Child Personality in a Rural and Urban Area of Ceylon.* University of Wisconsin, 1956. 229 p. ms. Abstract in *Dissertation Abstracts,* Vol. 16, p. 2230-2231, November 1956. Available on microfilm from University Microfilms, Ann Arbor, Michigan, as Publication No. 18,446.

See also Nos. 122, 138, 142, 147, 164, 170, 179

MASTERS

1349. ARASARATNAM, JESUTHASON GEORGE, 1911- . *Religious Education in Ceylon.* Princeton Theological Seminary, 1954. 104 p. ms.

1350. NILAM, NITA, 1917- . *The Significance of Home Economics Education in Ceylon and Some Suggestions for the Improvements of the Existing Program.* Cornell University, 1955. 109 p. ms.

1351. PEEK, EVA MABEL. *A Critical Examination of Adaptations in Missionary Work to Ceylonese Culture.* Columbia University, 1941. 95 p. ms.

1352. ROSA, ALFRED CHRISTOPHER. *Leadership in Christian Education in Buddhist Ceylon.* Columbia University, 1952; Union Theological Seminary, 1952. 39 p. ms.

See also Nos. 226, 268, 275, 303, 308, 1305

Cyprus
(NOS. 1353 – 1354)

DOCTOR

1353. WEIR, WILLIAM WILBUR, 1893- . *Education in Cyprus: Some Theories and Practices in Education in the Island of Cyprus since 1878.* Columbia University, 1952. Cyprus: Cosmos Press, 1952. 312 p.

See also No. 164

MASTER

1354. KAZAMIAS, ANDREAS MICHAEL. *Educational Theories and Curriculum Aspects of American and Cyprus Secondary Schools.* Fort Hays Kansas Stat College, 1954. 211 p. ms. For doctoral dissertation by same author, see No. 3896.

See also No. 226

Formosa
(NOS. 1355 – 1359)

DOCTOR

1355. RODD, WILLIAM G. *A Cross-Cultural Study of Taiwan's Schools.* Western Reserve University, 1958. 500 p. ms. approx. Summarized, in part, as "Mathematics and Science Ability in Taiwan Schools," *School and Society,* Vol. 86, p. 284-286, June 21, 1958.

See also No. 170

MASTERS

1356. CHENG, LILLIAN LI-LING. *The Educational Program of the Chinese Nationalist Government in Formosa.* American University, 1953. 95 p. ms.

1357. LEUNG, FLORENCE YU. *Application of Audio-Visual Aids to Secondary Education in Formosa: Problems and Possibilities.* American University, 1953. 66 p. ms.

1358. NEE, NELSON VEN-CHUNG. *A Program of Vocational Industrial Education in Taiwan, Republic of China.* University of Tennessee, 1958. 117 p. ms.

1359. TZENG, JENN. *Charting Educational Philosophy for Free China.* De Paul University, 1956. 98 p. ms.

See also Nos. 308, 1317

Hong Kong
(NOS. 1360 – 1361)

DOCTOR

1360. LAU, KWAI-CHEUK. *The Formation of a Plan to Be Proposed to the Faculty in Lingnam Middle School, Hong Kong, for the Improvement of Extra-Curricular Activities in the School and for the Guidance of Pupil Participation in These Activities.* Columbia University, 1940. 210 p. ms.

See also No. 1299

MASTER

1361. DOME, ARTHUR EDMOND. *Growth of Cantonese School Boys (Being a Study of the Height, Weight, Vital Capacity, and Strength of Grip of Cantonese Boys in the Schools of Hong Kong).* International YMCA College, 1926. 155 p. ms.

For a Hong Kong group in the United States, see No. 4956.

China
(NOS. 1362 – 1822)

DOCTORS

1362. AI, JOSEPH WEI, 1891- . *An Analysis of the Factors Involved in Learning the Chinese Language.* George Washington University, 1925. 148 p. ms. Abstract in George Washington University: *Summaries of Doctoral Dissertations,* 1925-28, p. 3-5.

1363. ALLEN, WALTER POWELL, 1917- . *Selecting Reading Materials for Chinese Students: A Technique for Selecting Reading Materials which Provide Cultural Background for Learning English at Huachung University.* Columbia University, 1948. 103 p. ms. Published in modified form as *Selecting Reading Materials for Foreign Students: A Technique for Selecting Reading Materials which Provide Cultural Background for Learning English.* Washington: Washington Publications, 1955. 73 p.

1364. ANDERSON, ELAM JONATHAN, 1890-1944. *An Investigation of the Factors Conditioning Success in Teaching English as a Foreign Language to Students in Educational Institutions in China.* University of Chicago, 1924. 129 p. ms. Published in modified form, with Introduction by E. W. Wallace, as *English Teaching Efficiency in China,* Shanghai: The Commercial Press, 1925. xviii, 182 p. Abstract in University of Chicago: *Abstracts of Theses: Humanistic Series,* Vol. 2, 1923-24, p. 53-57.

1365. ANDERSON, MARY RALEIGH, 1878- . *Protestant Mission Schools for Girls in South China (1827 to the Japanese Invasion).* Columbia University, 1943. Mobile, Alabama: Heiter-Starke Printing Co., 1943. xxvii, 365 p. (Note: Manuscript prepared in 1936.) For master's thesis by same author, see No. 1511.

1366. ARENS, RICHARD, 1912- . *The Impact of Communism on Education in China, 1949-50.* University of Chicago, 1952. 255 p. ms. Available on microfilm: see index under "University of Chicago."

1367. ATTERBURY, MARGUERITE, 1896- . *A Study of Some Phases of Chinese-American Cooperation in Promoting China's Agricultural Extension.* Columbia University, 1954. 401 p. ms. Abstract in *Dissertation Abstracts,* Vol. 14, p. 1274, August 1954. Available on microfilm from University Microfilms, Ann Arbor, Michigan, as Publication No. 8,600.

1368. BUSCH, HEINRICH, 1912- . *The Tung-lin Academy and Its Political and Philosophical Significance.* Columbia University, 1953. 246 p. ms. Abstract in *Dissertation Abstracts,* Vol. 14, p. 93-94, January 1954. Available on microfilm from University Microfilms, Ann Arbor, Michigan, as Publication No. 6,587.

1369. CHAN, FOOK-TIM, 1911- . *An Experience in Cultural Education.* Columbia University, 1946. 389 p. ms. (Part I covers visits of Chinese teachers to the United States. Part II covers conditions in China — Historical, Geographical, Political, Economic, Social, Religious, Educational, Dramatic, and Literary.)

1370. CHAN, KAI-PING. *A Proposed Program for Religious Education for Lingnan University in China.* Columbia University, 1940. 91 p. ms.

1371. CHAN, SHAU-YI. (Ch'en, Shou-i in Library of Congress card catalog.) *The Influence of China on English Culture during the Eighteenth Century.* University of Chicago, 1928. 225 p. ms. Abstract in University of Chicago: *Abstracts of Theses, Humanities Series,* Vol. 8, p. 537-541.

1372. CHAN, YING, 1916- . *The Development of Parallel Reading Comprehension Examinations in English and Chinese at the Graduate Level.* Columbia University, 1953. 25 p. ms. For master's thesis by same author, see No. 5055.

1373. CHANDLER, HORACE EDWARD, 1884- . *The Work of the American Presbyterian Mission, from 1918 to 1941, toward the Lessening of Adult Illiteracy in Shantung Province, China.* University of Pittsburgh, 1943. 192 p. ms. Abstract in University of Pittsburgh: *Abstracts of Theses . . .,* Vol. 19, 1944, p. 46-55.

1374. CHANG, CHERRY Y. K., 1914-   *A Program of Christian Education in Baptist Churches in China.* Southwestern Baptist Theological Seminary, 1955. 306 p. ms.

1375. CHANG, CHUNG-YUAN, 1907- . *A Study of the Relative Merits of the Vertical and Horizontal Lines in Reading Chinese Print.* Columbia University, 1942. New York: 1942. 64 p. (*Archives of Psychology,* No. 276.) For master's thesis by same author, see No. 1534.

1376. CHANG, HWEI-LAN, 1898- . *A Colligation of Facts and Principles Basic to Sound Curriculum Construction for Physical Education in China.* State University of Iowa, 1944. 99 p. ms. Abstract in State University of Iowa: *Doctoral Dissertations: Abstracts and References, 1942-1948,* Vol. 5, p. 720-721; also in State University of Iowa: *Series on Aims and Progress of Research,* No. 75, November 15, 1944, unpaged.

1377. CHANG, JEN-CHI. 1903- . *Certain Relationships of School Administration and the Rural Community of China.* University of North Dakota, 1952. 124 p. ms.

1378. CHANG, PE-CHIN, 1899- . *The Administrative Reorganization of the Educational System of a County in China — Based on the Analysis of Cheng Ting-Hsien.* Cornell University, 1935. 124 p. ms. Ithaca, New York: 1935. 10 p. Abstract of thesis.

1379. CHANG, PENG-CHUN, 1892- . *Education for Modernization in China: A Search for Criteria of Curriculum Construction in View of the Transition in National Life, with Special Reference to Secondary Education.* Columbia University, 1923. New York: Teachers College, Columbia University, 1923. iii, 92 p. (Teachers College Contribution to Education, No. 137.)

1380. CHAO, FREDERICK PU-HSIA, 1903- . *Education for a Democratic China.* Columbia University, 1946. 330 p. ms.

1381. CHAO, SANKEY C. 1921- . *The Teaching of English to Cantonese Students: A Critical Study of Some Cultural and Linguistic Problems.* Columbia University, 1953. 153 p. ms.

1382. CHEN, CHING-SZU, 1907- . *The Significance for Religious Education of Modern Educational Trends in China.* State University of Iowa, 1940. 199 p. ms. Abstract in *Selected Doctors' Theses in Religious Education,* No. 8, 1940. p. 5. Abstract also in *Doctoral Dissertations in the Field of Religion, 1940-1952,* p. 186.

1383. CHEN, SIH-KONG. *A Plan for Adult Education in China Based on the Experiences of Major Experiments of Adult Education, the Resources of the Social Conditions in China, and the History of Chinese Education in the Last Eighty Years.* Columbia University, 1942. 168 p. ms.

1384. CHEN, WEI-LUN. *A Sociological Foundation of Adult Education in China.* New York University, 1935. 100 p. ms.

1385. CHEN, WILLIAM JUN-TUNG, 1915- . *Some Controversies on Chinese Education and Culture.* Columbia University, 1951. 345 p. ms. Abstract in *Microfilm Abstracts,* Vol. 11, No. 3, p. 651-653, 1951. Available on microfilm from University Microfilms, Ann Arbor, Michigan as Publication No. 2,526.

1386. CHENG, ANDREW CHIH-YI, 1898- . *Hsuntzu's Theory of Human Nature and Its Influence on Education and Government in China.* Columbia University, 1935. Peking, China: Privately Printed, 1928. iii, 84 p.

1387. CHENG, RONALD YU-SOONG, 1903- . (Ch'en, Yu Sung in Library of Congress card catalog.) *The Financing of Public Education in China: A Factual Analysis of Its Major Problems of Reconstruction.* Columbia University, 1935. Shanghai: Commercial Press, Ltd., 1935. xvi, 300 p.

1388. CHI, KUANG-TOU. *The Problem of Developing an Indigenous Program for the Village Church in North China.* Drew University, 1950. 229 p. ms. (Includes consideration of program of religious education.)

1389. CHIANG, MON-LIN. *A Study in the Chinese Principles of Education.* Columbia University, 1917. Shanghai: Commercial Press, Ltd., 1918. 187 p.

1390. CHIANG, WEN-HAN. *The Ideological Background of the Chinese Student Movement.* Columbia University, 1948. New York: King's Crown Press, 1948. x, 176 p. By Kiang, Wen-han.

1391. CHOU, FU-CHUAN. *China's Need for Universal Education.* Syracuse University, 1921. 170 p. ms.

1392. CHOU, WO-MIN. *An Historical and Statistical Survey of the Recent Development of Chinese Education.* New York University, 1920.

1393. CHU, DON-CHEAN, 1910- . *Tao Hsing-chin and Chinese Education.* Columbia University, 1953. 254 p. ms.

1394. CHU, PING-CHIEN, 1915- . *A Proposed Administrative Pattern of the Hsien (County) School System in China.* Columbia University, 1947. 231 p. ms.

1395. CHU, SAMUEL C. *Chang Chien, Pioneer Industrialist, Educator, and Conservationist of Modern China (1853-1926).* Columbia University, 1958. 349 p. Abstract in *Dissertation Abstracts,* Vol. 19, p. 307-308, August 1958. Available on microfilm from University Microfilms, Ann Arbor, Michigan, as Mic. 58-2677.

1396. CHU, SHIH-YING. *The Problem of Life and the Problem of Education as Viewed by Ancient Chinese Thinkers — with Constructive Analyses and Suggestions Towards a Philosophy of Education.* Harvard University, 1926. 226 p. ms.

1397. CHU, YU-KUANG, 1902- . *Some Problems of a National System of Education in China: A Study in the Light of Comparative Education.* Columbia University, 1933. Shanghai: Commercial Press, Ltd., 1933. xiii, 394 p.

1398. CHUANG, CHAI-HSUAN, 1895- . (Chuang, Tse-hsuan in Library of Congress card catalog.) *Tendencies Toward a Democratic System of Education in China.* Columbia University, 1922. Shanghai: Commercial Press, Ltd., 1922. xvi, 176 p.

1399. CREIGHTON, JOHN WILLIS. *The Chinese Mind: A Study in Race Psychology.* University of Missouri, 1917. 84 p. ms. (Includes mental tests, association tests, and discussion of memory and other qualities.)

1400. DeFRANCIS, JOHN FRANCIS, 1911- . *Nationalism and Language Reform in China.* Columbia University, 1950. Princeton, New Jersey: Princeton University Press, 1950. xi, 306 p.

1401. DJUNG, LU DZAI, 1899- . (Chung, Lu-Chai in Library of Congress card catalog.) *Democratic Tendencies in the Development of Modern Education in China.* Stanford University, 1930. 277 p. ms. Published as *A History of Democratic Education in Modern China.* Shanghai: Commercial Press, Ltd., 1934. xxxiii, 258 p. Abstract in Stanford University: *Abstracts of Dissertations . . . 1930-31,* p. 182-188.

1402. ESTES, CHARLES SUMNER, 1858-1934. *Christian Missions in China.* Johns Hopkins University, 1895. Baltimore: 1904. 62 p. (Includes education.)

1403. FAN, CHUNG-TEH, 1913- . *Curriculum Reorganization in Rural China.* Columbia University, 1948. 230 p. ms.

1404. FAN, IH-CHI, 1914- . *A Study of the Problem of Audio-Visual Education for Teacher Education in China, 1930-1949.* Indiana University, 1952. 465 p. ms. Abstract in Indiana University, School of Education: *Studies in Education, 1952.* (Thesis Abstract Series No. 4, 1953), p. 103-109.

1405. FAN, TSEN-CHUNG. *Chinese Culture in England: Studies from Sir William Temple to Oliver Goldsmith (1685-1760).* Harvard University, 1931. 408 p. ms. Abstract in Harvard University: *Summaries of Ph.D. Theses,* 1931, p. 223-226.

1406. FANG, TUNG-YUAN, 1900- . *An Improved Program of Secondary Education in Postwar China.* University of Pennsylvania, 1947. 201 p. ms. Philadelphia: 1948. 37 p. Essential portion.

1407. FOO, THOONG-SIEN, 1910- . *Method in Moral Judgment — An Intercultural Analysis.* Columbia University, 1950. 153 p. ms. Abstract in *Microfilm Abstracts,* Vol. 10, No. 3, p. 69-70, 1950. Available on microfilm from University Microfilms, Ann Arbor, Michigan, as Publication No. 1,848. (Compares stress on practical intelligence of Confucianism with educational theories of four modern American authors.)

1408. FORD, EDDY LUCIUS, 1879-1936. *The History of the Educational Work in the Methodist Episcopal Church in China: A Study of Its Development and Present Trends.* Northwestern University, 1936. Foochow, China: Christian Herald Mission Press, 1938. ii, 294 p. Abstract in Northwestern University: *Summaries of Doctoral Dissertations,* Vol. 4, 1936, p. 82-86.

1409. FUGH, PAUL CHEN. *Reconstruction of the Chinese Elementary School Curriculum to Meet Rural Needs of China.* Cornell University, 1924. 346 p. ms. Ithaca, New York: 1924. 8 p. Abstract of thesis.

1410. GAGE, BROWNELL, 1874-1945. *The American Colleges in the Orient as Exemplified by the College of Yale-in-China.* Yale University, 1924. 203 p. ms.

1411. GALT, HOWARD SPILMAN, 1872-1948. *The Historical Development of the Theory of Education in China to the Close of the Han Dynasty, 220 A.D.* Harvard University, 1927. 210 p. ms. Published as *The Development of Chinese Educational Theory: The Historical Development of the Theory of Education in China to the Close of the Han Dynasty, A.D. 220.* Shanghai: Commercial Press, 1929. vii, 180 p. ms.

1412. GENG, GEORGE YUEN-HSIOH, 1905- . *The Promotion of the Economic Welfare of the Chinese People through the Protestant Churches of China.* Columbia University, 1951. 244 p. ms. (Includes chapter on Adult Education, and consideration of education in other chapters.)

1413. GREGG, ALICE HENRIETTA, 1893- . *China and Educational Autonomy: The Changing Role of the Protestant Educational Missionary in China, 1807-1937.* Columbia University, 1945. Syracuse, New York: Syracuse University Press, 1946. xvi, 285 p.

1414. GUO, LOIS RUJEN WANG. *A Critique of Proposals for Educational Reconstruction in China.* University of Michigan, 1944. 255 p. ms.

1415. HAN, CHING-LIEN. *A Comparative Study of Administration of Publicly Supported Higher Education in the United States and China.* University of Minnesota, 1941. 453 p. ms. Abstract in University of Minnesota: *Summaries of Ph.D. Theses,* Vol. 4, 1949, p. 79-82.

1416. HIGHBAUGH, IRMA, 1891- . *A Family-Centered Program in Rural Reconstruction in West China, with Special Reference to the Preschool Child.* Cornell University, 1945. Published in modified form as *Family Life in West China,* New York: Agricultural Missions, Inc., 1948. xi, 240 p. Abstract in Cornell University: *Abstracts of Theses . . . 1945,* p. 239-242.

1417. HOCKIN, KATHARINE BOEHNER, 1910- *A Method and Plan of Work for Developing a Program in Religious Education for Christian Secondary Schools in Szechuan, China.* Columbia University, 1948. 338 p. ms. Abstract in *Teachers College Record* Vol. 50, p. 129, November 1948. Abstract also in *Religious Education,* Vol. 45, p. 176-177, May-June 1950. For master's thesis by same author, see No. 1597.

1418. HOH, YAM TONG, 1898- . *The Boxer Indemnity Remissions and Education in China: Being an Historical and Analytical Study of the China Indemnity of 1901 as Remitted to China by the United States of America, Great Britain, France, Belgium, Italy, Soviet Russia, and the Netherlands, and the Application of These Remissions to Educational and Cultural Purposes, Together with a Chapter on Japan's Use of Her Share "for Cultural Work in China."* Columbia University, 1933. 485 p. ms. For master's thesis by same author, see No. 1599.

1419. HOLDEN, REUBEN ANDRUS, 4th., 1918- . *An Educational Experiment in China: The Story of the Development of Yale-in-China.* Yale University, 1951. 307 p. ms.

1420. HSIAO, THEODORE ENCHENG. *A History of Modern Education in China.* New York University, 1925. 113 p. ms. Peiping: Peking University Press, 1932. xiv, 164 p.

1421. HSIEH, CHING-SHENG. *Rural Reconstruction in China: A Study of Problems and Methods, with Suggested Policies for the Chinese Government and for the Christian Church.* Drew University, 1944. 2 vols, ms. (Includes consideration of educational policies.)

1422. HSU, JENNIE, 1904- . *A Study of Certain Problems in the Higher Institutions for Women in China.* Columbia University, 1931. Tientsen, China: 1931. 133 p.

1423. HU, CHANG HO JIUGOW. *A General Outline on the Reorganization of the Chinese Educational System.* New York University, 1917. 250 p. ms.

1424. HU, I. (I is first name, not an initial.) *An Experimental Study of the Reading Habits of Adult Chinese.* University of Chicago, 1928. 141 p. ms. Abstract in University of Chicago: *Abstract of Theses, Humanistic Series,* Vol. 7, 1928-29, p. 113-116. For master's thesis by same author, see No. 1614.

1425. HU, SHIH, 1891- . (Also as Shih, Hu, in Library of Congress card catalog). *The Development of Logical Methods in Ancient China.* Columbia University, 1917. Shanghai: Oriental Book Co., 1922. x, 187 p.

1426. HUANG, CHING-SZE, 1897- *Elementary Supervision on a County Basis by Specialized Agents in Selected States: Professional Supervision of Instruction in Selected States on a County Basis, with Application to China.* Columbia University, 1927. Peking: Peiping Cultural Association, 1927. iii, 177 p.

1427. JUAN, KANG-CHENG. *An Educational Program for China in Transition.* Columbia University, 1940. 300 p. ms.

1428. KIANG, YING-CHENG, 1913- . *The Geography of Higher Education in China.* Columbia University, 1955. 282 p. ms. Abstract in *Dissertation Abstracts,* Vol. 15, p. 1359, August 1955. Available on microfilm from University Microfilms, Ann Arbor, Michigan, as Publication No. 12,310. For master's thesis by same author, see No. 1638.

1429. KUH, KOH-NIE, 1898- . *A Musicological Study of the Important Tonal Systems of the T'ang Dynasty (A.D. 619-907).* New York University, 1942. 271 p. ms.

1430. KUO, PING-WEN, 1879- . *The Chinese System of Public Education.* Columbia University, 1914. New York: Teachers College, Columbia University, 1915. xii, 209 p. (Teachers College Contribution to Education, No. 64.) For master's thesis by same author, see No. 1646.

1431. LACY, CREIGHTON BOUTELLE. *Protestant Missions in Communist China.* Yale University, 1953. 670 p. ms. (One chapter concerns educational institutions and property.)

1432. LEE, PAO-CHEN, 1907- . (Li, Pao-ch'en in Library of Congress card catalog). *A Proposed Plan for the Education of Music Teachers at Peiping National Teachers College.* Columbia University, 1948. 143 p. ms. For master's thesis by same author, see No. 1661.

1433. LEE, PETER HSING-HSIEN, 1903- . *A Study of Progressive Christian Education in the Light of the Needs of China.* Southern Baptist Theological Seminary, 1950. 259 p. ms.

1433a. LEE, WILLIAM CHENG-CHIAN. *The Opinions of American Professional Educators about Chinese Education from 1895-1945.* University of California, Los Angeles, 1957.

1434. LEFFORGE, ROXY, 1888- . *Some Guiding Principles for Christian Education in China Today.* Boston University, 1933. 457 p. ms.

1435. LEGER, SAMUEL HOWARD, 1891- . *Education of Christian Ministers in China: An Historical and Critical Study.* Columbia University, 1925. Shanghai, China: 1925. xi, 118 p.

1436. LEW, TIMOTHY TING-FANG, 1891- . (Liu, Ting-fang in Library of Congress card catalog). *The Psychology of Learning Chinese: A Preliminary Analysis by Means of Experimental Psychology of Some of the Factors Involved in the Process of Learning Chinese Characters.* Columbia University, 1920. Peking: 1924. Published as a special monograph by *Chinese Social and Political Science Review.* 377 p.

1437. LEWIS, IDA BELLE, 1887- . *Some Phases of the Education of Chinese Women.* Columbia University, 1919. Published as *The Education of Girls in China,* New York: Teachers College, Columbia University, 1919. v, 92 p. (Teachers College Contribution to Education, No. 104.)

1438. LI, CHIEN-HSUN, 1884- *Some Phases of Popular Control of Education in the United States: An Analytical Study of Legal Status Relating to State Control of Education.* Columbia University, 1928. Shanghai: Commercial Press, 1927. xvi, 256 p. (Extensive section, "Application to the Needs of China," p. 200-245.)

1439. LI, MEI-YUN, 1906- . *An Analysis of Social, Economic, and Political Conditions in Peng-Shan Hsien, Szechuan, China, Looking toward Improvement of Educational Program.* Cornell University, 1945. Abstract in Cornell University: *Abstracts of Theses . . .* 1945, p. 55-58.

1440. LI, YUNTIN CHENG. *A Study of the Organization of the American One-Teacher School, with Suggestions for Possible Adaptation to the Chinese Village School.* Columbia University, 1929. Shanghai: Chung Hua Book Co., 1929. viii, 174 p.

1441. LIN, EN-CHIN, 1911- . *Educational Changes in China since the Establishment of the People's Republic and Some Steps Leading to Them.* University of Pennsylvania, 1955. 131 p. ms.

1442. LIN, JEN-SU, 1912- . *English Pronunciation Practices of Amoy Students.* Columbia University, 1955. 203 p. ms.

1443. LIN, Mrs. SAN-SU CHEN, 1916- . *Practice Materials on the Use of the English Article: A Supplementary Textbook for Chinese Students Learning English.* Columbia University, 1953. 152 p. ms.

1444. LIU, HERMAN CHAN-EN, 1896-1938. *Non-Verbal Intelligence Tests for Use in China.* Columbia University, 1922. New York: Teachers College, Columbia University, 1922. viii, 84 p. (Teachers College Contribution to Education, No. 126.)

1445. LIU, HSIAO-CHUAN, 1919- . *Introducing English Poetry to Chinese College Students.* Columbia University, 1954. 172 p. ms.

1446. LIU, PAO-CHIN. *The Improvement of Education in Kiangsi Province, China.* New York University, 1927. 165 p. ms.

1447. LO, REN-YEN, 1890- . *The Social Teaching of Confucius.* Syracuse University, 1914. For master's thesis by same author with same title, see No. 1682.

1448. LOH, LING-SU, -1924. *The Status of Primary Education in China.* University of Chicago, 1922. 224 p. ms. Abstract in University of Chicago: *Abstracts of Theses: Humanities Series,* Vol. 1, 1922-23, p. 119-126. For master's thesis by same author, see No. 1685.

1449. LUND, RENVILLE CLIFTON, 1923- . *The Imperial University of Peking.* University of Washington, 1957. 358 p. ms. Abstract in *Dissertation Abstracts*, Vol. 17, p. 1321, June 1957. Available on microfilm from University Microfilms, Ann Arbor, Michigan, as Publication No. 21,207.

1450. LUNG, CHIENG-FU, 1906- . *The Evolution of Chinese Social Thought.* University of Southern California, 1935. 396 p. ms. Los Angeles: University of Southern California Press, 1941. 40 p. Extract from thesis. (University of Southern California Social Science Series, No. 23.) For master's thesis by same author, see No. 1689.

1451. LUTZ, JESSIE GREGORY, 1925- . *The Role of the Christian Colleges in Modern China before 1928.* Cornell University, 1955. 375 p. ms. Abstract in *Dissertation Abstracts*, Vol. 16, p. 327-328, February 1956. Available on microfilm from University Microfilms, Ann Arbor, Michigan, as Publication No. 15,498.

1452. McCAIN, PEARLE. *A Plan for Developing a Functional Curriculum in the Bible Teachers Training School in Nanking in the Postwar Era.* Columbia University, 1946; Union Theological Seminary, 1946. 174 p. ms. For master's thesis by same author, see No. 1690.

1453. McMULLEN, ROBERT JOHNSTON. *Co-operation among East China Colleges: A Project to Prepare a Plan which Will Enable the Six Mission Colleges in East China to Make a More Significant Contribution to Education in China by Coordinating Their Programs of Instruction, Research, Public Service, and Administration.* Columbia University, 1937. 107 p. ms. For master's thesis by same author, see No. 1693.

1454. MATHIS, MARCIAN JOSEPH, 1918- . *The Constitution and Supreme Administration of Regional Seminaries Subject to the Sacred Congregation for the Propagation of the Faith in China: A Historical Synopsis and a Commentary.* Catholic University of America, 1953. Washington: Catholic University of America Press, 1952. x, 172 p. (Canon Law Studies, No. 331.)

1455. MENSENDIEK, CHARLES W. *The Protestant Missionary Understanding of the Chinese Situation and the Christian Task, 1890-1911.* Union Theological Seminary, 1958. (Includes education.)

1456. MIAO, CHU-SENG, 1894- . *The Value of Confucianism for Religious Education in China.* University of Chicago, 1923. 109 p. ms. Abstract in University of Chicago: *Abstracts of Theses: Humanistic Series,* Vol. 1, 1922-23, p. 505-508. For master's thesis by same author, see No. 1704.

1457. MOK, POON-KAN, 1905- . *The History and Development of the Teaching of English in China.* Columbia University, 1951. 286 p. ms. Abstract in *Microfilm Abstracts,* Vol. 11, No. 3, p. 594-595, 1951. Available on microfilm from University Microfilms, Ann Arbor, Michigan, as Publication No. 2,546.

1458. MORRIS, JOHN GLENN, 1918- . *Christianity and Social Change in China, 1912-1942.* Southern Baptist Theological Seminary, 1946. 175 p. ms. (Considers relation of government to Christian schools.)

1459. NASH, MARY ROOKER. *A Source Book in Individual Development and Guidance for Students in Yenching University, Peiping, China.* Columbia University, 1938. Unpaged.

1460. NELSON, LINNEA A. *A Proposed Curriculum for a Selected Senior Middle School in China.* University of California, Berkeley, 1946.

1461. O'YANG, SIANG, 1899- . *Reconstruction of Teacher Training in China on the Elementary Level.* Ohio State University, 1935. 273 p. ms. Abstract in Ohio State University: *Abstracts of Dissertations . . .* Spring Quarter, 1935, p. 313-321. (Abstracts of Doctoral Dissertations, No. 18.) For master's thesis by same author, see No. 1714.

1462. PEAKE, CYRUS HENDERSON, 1900- . *Nationalism and Education in Modern China.* Columbia University, 1932. New York: Columbia University Press, 1932. xiv, 240 p. ("A digest of textbooks used in the mass education movement and the most popular textbooks used in the primary and middle schools of China from 1905-1929.") For master's thesis by same author, see No. 2438.

1463. PRICE, FRANK WILSON, 1895- . (Price, Francis Wilson, in Library of Congress card catalog). *The Rural Church in China: A Survey.* Shanghai: Kelly & Walsh, 1941. First edition. (The first edition was never distributed due to the burning of the entire stock during the Japanese Occupation, except for one copy in the hands of the author.) New York: Agricultural Missions, 1948. Second edition. xi, 274 p. (Studies in the World Mission of Christianity, No. 9.) With Foreword by S. W. Chen. Second edition has an added chapter: "The Rural Church in China During and After the War." (Deals extensively with religious education.)

1464. RINDEN, ARTHUR OWEN, 1900- . *Christian Education of Adults in China.* Yale University, 1941. 406 p. ms. Abstract in *Selected Doctoral Theses in Religious Education,* 1941, p. 15.

1465. RUGH, ARTHUR DOUGLAS, 1907- . *American Influence in China's Changing Education.* University of Washington, 1940. 207 p. ms. Abstract in University of Washington: *Abstracts of Theses,* Vol. 6, 1942, p. 253-254.

1466. SETO, YAU S. *The Problem of Missionary Education in China: Historical and Critical.* New York University, 1927. 106 p. ms.

1467. SHAO, LUTHER CHING-SAN, 1901- . *Religious Liberty and Christian Education in China.* Yale University, 1934. 612 p. ms. Abstract in *Selected Graduate Theses in Religious Education,* 1934. p. 59-60.

1468. SHEN, WEI-CHIH, 1896- . *The Role of Education in Postwar China.* University of Pennsylvania, 1948. Philadelphia: 1948. iii, 39 p. Essential portion of thesis. ("Chapter V . . . Chapter VI . . . and Recommendations were chosen as the essential portion of the thesis to be published. Two microfilm copies of the whole manuscript have been deposited in the library of the University of Pennsylvania.")

1469. SHEN, YE. *A Proposed Program for a Chinese Junior High School in Respect to Gifted Children as Compared with Other Children.* Columbia University, 1936. 69 p. ms. (The high school was located in Shanghai.)

1470. SMITH, CHARLES STANLEY, 1890- . *Protestant Theological Education in China.* Yale University, 1938. 496 p. ms.

1471. SMITH, HAROLD FRED, 1885- . *Elementary Education in Shantung, China: A Study of the Reorganization of the Curriculum of the Elementary Schools of Rural Shantung, and Plans for the Preparation of Teachers for These Schools.* Columbia University, 1930. Nashville, Tennessee: Amessu, 1931. vi, 159 p. Published also in abridged form as *Elementary Education in Shantung, China: A Study of the Reorganization of the Curriculum to Relate it to Rural Life and in Connection with this, a Course of Education for Teachers.* New York, 1930. 32 p.

1472. STOWE, EVERETT McKINLEY. *Character and Religious Education in Christian Middle Schools in China.* Columbia University, 1937. 119 p. ms.

1473. STUART, WARREN HORTON, 1879- . *The Use of Material from China's Spiritual Inheritance in the Christian Education of China's Youth: A Guide and Source Book for Christian Teachers in China.* Yale University, 1932. Shanghai: Kwang Hsueh Publishing House, Oxford University Press, China Agency, 1932. ix, 202 p. With Introduction by Robert Seneca Smith.

1474. SU, TING. *A Functional Program of Organization and Administration for the Public Schools of Suiyuen Province, China.* Indiana University, 1940. 264 p. ms.

1475. SUN, HUAI-CHIN. *A Study of Chinese Secondary Education with a Suggested Program for Reorganization.* University of Colorado, 1949. 431 p. ms. Abstract in University of Colorado: *Abstracts of Theses* . . . 1948-49, p. 105-107.

1476. SUNG, KE, 1905- . *A Study of Secondary School Curriculum in Kansu, China, with a Suggested Reorganization of the Program.* Cornell University, 1940. 165 p. ms. Abstract in Cornell University: *Abstracts of Theses* . . . 1940, p. 114-117. For master's thesis by same author, see No. 1747.

1477. TAAI, WAI-KING. *Adolescent Education in China.* New York University, 1940. 171 p. ms. Abstract in New York University, School of Education: *Abstracts of Theses,* 1939-40, p. 145-148.

1478. TAAM, CHEUK-WOON, 1900- . (T'an, Cho-yuan in Library of Congress card catalog.) *The Development of Chinese Libraries under the Ching Dynasty, 1644-1911.* University of Chicago, 1933. Shanghai: The Commercial Press, Ltd., 1935. ix, 107 p. A private edition was distributed to libraries in the United States and abroad in 1935.

1479. TAI, CHEN-HWA, 1914- . *A Critical Study of the Resolutions of the Chinese Federation of Educational Associations, 1915-1926.* Columbia University, 1954. 206 p. ms.

1480. TAI, CHIN-HSIEO. *The Life and Work of Tsai Yuan-Pei.* Harvard University, 1952. 208 p. ms.

(Subject of the dissertation was Chinese Minister of Education, 1911-12, and Chancellor of National Peking University, 1916-26.)

1481. TAN, JEN-MEI, 1904- . *The History of Modern Chinese Secondary Education.* University of Pennsylvania, 1940. 248 p. ms.

1482. TAYLOR, PAUL VIVIAN, 1892- . *Philosophy of Values in Education Revealed in the Work of Religious Education Conducted by the Reformed Church in the U.S. in China.* Kennedy School of Missions, 1929. 328 p. ms.

1483. THOM, ELEANOR WAI-CHUN, 1904- . *A Plan for the Organization and Administration of a Proposed Private Secondary School for Girls in Canton, China.* Columbia University, 1946. 217 p. ms.

1484. TSAI, Rev. MARK, 1908- . (Tsai, Jen-yu in Library of Congress card catalog). *Vital Problems in Modern Chinese Education, 1862-1945.* Fordham University, 1951. 265 p. ms. Abstract in Fordham University: *Dissertations Accepted for Higher Degrees* . . . 1951, p. 100-194.

1485. TSANG, CHIU-SAM, 1901- . *Nationalism in School Education in China since the Opening of the Twentieth Century.* Columbia University, 1933. Hong Kong: South China Morning Post, Ltd., 1933. iii, 241 p.

1486. TSENG, TSO-CHUNG, 1899- . *Nationalism and Pragmatism in Modern Education with Special Application to Post-Revolutionary Chinese Conditions.* University of Washington, 1934. 165 p. ms. Abstract in University of Washington: *Abstracts of Theses* . . . Vol. 2, 1937, p. 513-517. For master's thesis by same author, see No. 1762.

1487. TU, HORACE TSOU-CHOW, 1898- . *The Effects of Different Arrangements of the Chinese Language upon Speed and Comprehension of Silent Reading.* State University of Iowa, 1924. 180 p. ms. Published in part in *Pedagogical Seminary,* Vol. 38, p. 321-337, December 1930. Also offprint of same, Worcester, Massachusetts, 1930. For master's thesis by same author, see No. 1765.

1488. TUAN, RENDER D. S. *A Proposed Program in Radio Education for the University of Cheeloo.* University of Denver, 1952. 274 p. ms.

1489. TWISS, GEORGE RANSOM, 1863-1944. *Science and Education in China: A Survey of the Present Status and a Program for Progressive Improvement.* Columbia University, 1926. Shanghai: Commercial Press, 1925. ix, 361 p. (Published under the auspices of the Chinese National Association for the Advancement of Education.)

1490. VAN PUTTEN, JAMES DYKE, 1899- . *Christian Higher Education in China: A Survey of the Historical Developments and Its Contributions to Chinese Life.* University of Chicago, 1934. 472 p. ms. Part of the dissertation (66 p. photolithographed) was distributed to libraries in the United States and abroad in 1937.

1491. WANG, FENG-GANG, 1903- . *Japanese Influence on Educational Reform in China from 1895 to 1911.* Stanford University, 1931. 185 p. ms. Abstract in Stanford University: *Abstracts of Dissertations* . . .

1930-31, p. 66-70. For master's thesis by same author, see No. 1777.

1492. WANG, FUNG-CHIAI, 1906- . *An Experimental Study of Eye-Movements in the Silent Reading of Chinese.* University of Chicago, 1933. 172 p. ms. Part of the dissertation (38 p. lithographed) was distributed to libraries in the United States and abroad in 1934.

1493. WANG, TE-CHUNG, 1904- . *The Reorganization of Chinese Education to Meet the Needs of the Present Emergency Situation.* Cornell University, 1939. 233 p. ms. Abstract in Cornell University: *Abstracts of Theses . . .* 1939, p. 88-91.

1494. WANG, TSI-CHANG. *The Youth Movement of China.* University of Chicago, 1925. Published in modified form, New York: New Republic, 1927. xv, 245 p. Abstract in University of Chicago: *Abstracts of Theses, Humanistic Series,* Vol. 4, p. 231-235.

1495. WANG, TUNG-CHI. *Educational Ideas of Dr. Sun Yat Sen.* Washington University, St. Louis, 1952. 96 p. ms.

1496. WANG, YI-CHU. *Foreign Educated Chinese, 1872-1948.* University of Chicago, 1957. Available on microfilm: see index under "University of Chicago."

1497. WEBSTER, JAMES B. *Motives, Ideals, and Values in Christian Education in China: A Comparative Study of Western and Chinese Education to Determine Educational Needs and Values.* Hartford School of Religious Education, 1917. 405 p. ms.

1498. WEE, KOK ANN, 1897- . *Physical Education in Protestant Christian Colleges and Universities in China.* Columbia University, 1937. New York: 1937. vii, 105 p.

1499. WEI, WILSON SHIH-SHENG. *The History of Educational Philosophy in China.* New York University, 1934. 240 p. ms. For master's thesis by same author, see No. 1786.

1500. WEI, YUNG-CHING. *A Plan for the Preparation of Secondary School Teachers in Hopei Province, China.* Columbia University, 1943. 150 p. ms.

1501. WIANT, BLISS MITCHELL. *The Character and Function of Music in Chinese Culture.* George Peabody College for Teachers, 1946. 325 p. ms. Abstract in George Peabody College for Teachers: *Abstracts of Dissertations . . .* 1946, p. 125-133. (Peabody Contributions to Education, No. 376. Considers educational aspects of music in Chinese culture.)

1502. WILLIAMS, MELVILLE OWENS, Jr. *A Plan for Developing the Religious Quality of Life in and through Significant Areas of Student Experience at Soochow University, China.* Columbia University, 1936. 158 p. ms.

1503. WONG, FLORENCE FUNG-YEE, 1918- . *Music Education in Modern Chinese Schools.* Columbia University, 1952. 189 p. ms.

1504. WONG, PEARL HUI. *A Comparative Study of Four Social Movements in China from 1912 to 1942.* University of Southern California, 1946. 430 p. ms. Abstract in University of Southern California: *Abstracts of Dissertations,* 1946, p. 67-70. (Studies the Mass Education Movement, Woman's Movement, New Life Movement, and Chinese Industrial Cooperation Movement. Discusses seven trends resulting from them and 14 sociological implications.)

1505. WU, CHIH-KANG. *The Role of the YMCA in the Development of Physical Education in China.* University of Michigan, 1957. 211 p. ms. Abstract in *Dissertation Abstracts,* Vol. 18, No. 4, p. 1333-1334, April 1958. Available on microfilm from University Microfilms, Ann Arbor, Michigan, as Mic. 58-1019.

1506. WU, KWANG-TSING. *Scholarship, Book Production, and Libraries in China (618-1644).* University of Chicago, 1944. 291 p. ms. Available on microfilm: see index under "University of Chicago."

1507. YANG, LIANG KUNG. *A Study of the Organization, Functions, and Duties of Boards of Control of State Universities in the United States, and the Application from Such Study to the Similar Institutions in China.* New York University, 1928. 174 p. ms. For master's thesis by same author, see No. 1807.

1508. YANG, SHU-HSUIN, 1918- . *Practice Materials in the Pronunciation of American English with Special Reference to the Problems of Speakers of Mandarin Chinese.* Columbia University, 1951. 155 p. ms.

1509. YIN, CHILLING, 1897- . *The Reconstruction of Modern Educational Organizations in China.* New York University, 1923. Shanghai: Commercial Press, Ltd., 1924. xviii, 171 p. Title also in Chinese characters. For master's thesis by same author, see No. 1813.

See also Nos. 119, 127, 137, 143, 144, 147, 157, 159, 162, 163, 164, 169, 174, 178, 179, 181, 182, 1297, 1299, 1300, 2500, 2911

MASTERS

1510. ALEXANDER, MARY CHARLOTTE. *Education in China during the First Quarter of the Twentieth Century.* University of Texas, 1927. 165 p. ms.

1511. ANDERSON, MARY RALEIGH, 1878- . *Christian Education of Girls in China.* George Peabody College for Teachers, 1919. 169 p. ms. plus 26 p. appendix. For doctoral dissertation by same author, see No. 1365.

1512. ARNOLD, JOHN WILLIAM, 1924- . *Pioneer Protestant Educational Missions in China, 1807 to 1857.* Yale University, 1948. 177 p. ms.

1513. ATWELL, RUTH ELIZABETH. *Supervision of Instruction in Homes of Missionaries in China.* University of Tennessee, 1938. 110 p. ms.

1514. BACON, ROBERT LEONARD. *Foundations for a Christian Approach to Chinese Students.* Columbia University, 1942. 71 p. ms.

1515. BEATTY, MABEL A., 1886-1927. *Present Educational Tendencies in China.* Boston University, 1917. 31 p. ms.

1516. BECK, KARL HERBERT. *A Socio-Educational Study of the Chinese People.* Pennsylvania State College, 1936. 173 p. ms.

1517. BENJAMIN, HERMAN REBER STERRET. *The Function of the Christian Secondary School in China Today.* University of Chicago, 1933. 118 p. ms.

1518. BIH, MARION HAO RING. (Later Mrs. Howson Lee). *A Suggested Program of Religious Education for a Christian High School in China.* Eastern Baptist Theological Seminary, 1940. 126 p. ms.

1519. BLACKMAN, GLADYS YATES. *Notes on Carlyle's "Signs of the Times" Prepared for Chinese College Students.* Columbia University, 1931. 64 p. ms.

1520. BRETHORST, MARIE. *The Educational System of China.* University of Washington, 1921. 66 p. ms.

1521. BROKAW, ABEAM COVERT. *The Sunday School in the Protestant Christian Churches of China.* University of Chicago, 1924. 57 p. ms.

1522. BROKAW, ADAH HOLLOWAY. *Union School Movements for Higher Education in China.* University of Chicago, 1924. 54 p. ms.

1523. BRYAN, FLORENCE HORN. *A Survey of China's Program of Education for Unification.* University of Southern California, 1938. 188 p. ms.

1524. BUCK, FRANK CORNELIUS. *Moral Value of the Chinese Classical Educational System, Including an Estimate of the Civil Service Examinations.* University of Chicago, 1917. 56 p. ms.

1525. BULLOCK, AMASA ARCHIBALD. *The Old Chinese Educational Institutions: An Estimation of Their Values, with a Brief Survey of Their Development.* University of Chicago, 1909. 50 p. ms.

1526. BUMGARDNER, ALICE CHIALING, 1923- *Emphasis on Scholarship as One of the Most Important Factors Underlying China's Backwardness in Economic Life.* Cornell University, 1949. 51 p. ms.

1527. BYSTED, LOUIS CHRISTIAN. *The Contribution of Mo Ti to a Program of Religious Education for Hunan Province, China.* Hartford School of Religious Education, 1927. 75 p. ms.

1528. CARLYLE, ELIZABETH MARGARET. *The Development of Nursing Education in China.* University of Washington, 1933. 111 p. ms.

1529. CARTER, CAMERON A. *Preliminary Study of Chinese Education.* University of Maryland, 1928. 111 p. ms.

1530. CASSELMAN, FRANCIS RAYMOND. *Curricula and Textbooks for Christian Religious Education in China.* Columbia University, 1915. 77 p. ms.

1531. CHAN, LAN-CHING, 1899- . *Psychological Analysis and Evaluation of Ten Selected Series of American and Chinese Elementary Readers.* Albion College, 1935. 274 p. ms.

1532. CHANG, CHANG-YU. *The Immediate Demands of Chinese Education.* University of Idaho, 1927. 66 p. ms.

1533. CHANG, CHEN-CHIN. *A Course of Citizenship for Chinese Public Schools.* Columbia University, 1922.

1534. CHANG, CHUNG-YUAN, 1907- *A Study of the Vocabulary of the First Grade in the Chinese Elementary School.* University of Michigan, 1936. 74 p. ms. For doctoral dissertation by same author, see No. 1375.

1535. CHANG, SENG. *The Educational System in Modern China.* University of Michigan, 1936. 112 p. ms.

1536. CHANG, YA-KUN. *Lessons for China from the Development of Public School Support in the United States of America.* University of Michigan, 1938. 75 p. ms.

1537. CHANG, YAO-CHIANG. *Factors Affecting the Speed and Clearness of Reading Chinese.* Columbia University, 1919. 63 p. ms.

1538. CHANG, ZAH-LING. *The Administration of Public Education in Kiangsu Province, Covering a Period of Five Years from November 1911 to December 1916.* Columbia University, 1918. 20 p. ms.

1539. CHAO, EUNICE H. L. *A Suggested Music Program to Fit the Needs of the Students of a Chinese Secondary Religious School.* Ohio University, 1952. 65 p. ms.

1540. CHAO, HSI-FAN. *A Proposed Child Development and Child Welfare Program for Hopei Province, China, with Special Reference to Yen Shan County.* Iowa State College of Agriculture and Mechanic Arts, 1932. 129 p. ms.

1541. CHEN, ANTHONY K. C. *The Philosophy of Education of Communist China as Applied to Secondary and Higher Education.* De Paul University, 1957. 149 p. ms.

1542. CHEN, CHIN-CHANG. *A Course of Citizenship for Chinese Public Schools.* Columbia University, 1923. 48 p. ms.

1543. CHEN, CHIN-TAO. *A History of Chinese Mathematics: A Comparative Study.* University of California, Berkeley, 1902. 28 p. ms.

1544. CHEN, ELLEN HSI-YIN. *A Proposal for Improved Elementary Teaching in China.* University of Southern California, 1950. 75 p. ms.

1545. CHEN, LI-YE. *A General Concept of the Chinese Elementary and Secondary School System.* Indiana University, 1934. 167 p. ms.

1546. CHEN, MARY CHUH-CHIUN. *Christian Religious Education for Juniors in a Chinese Church.* Oberlin College, 1934. 166 p. ms.

1547. CHEN, PIN-SWAN. *Social Phases of Education in China.* Michigan State College of Agriculture and Applied Science, 1931. 109 p. ms.

1548. CHEN, RUEY-TZU, 1909- . *A Description and Evaluation of the Christian Education of Youth in the Methodist Church in China, and a Suggested Program for Future Work.* Emory University, 1949. 122 p. ms.

1549. CHEN, SHIH-CHIEH. *A Brief Study of Public Education in China.* Allegheny College, 1938. 100 p. ms.

1550. CHEN, WILLIAM YUAN-LUNG, 1894- . *Social Value of Vocational Education for China.* Syracuse University, 1919. 79 p. ms.

1551. CHEN, WILSON WEI-SING, 1919- . *The Prospect of Student Christian Work in Communist China.* Andover Newton Theological School, 1950. 103 p. ms.

1552. CHEN, YERK-KUN. *The Development of China's Educational System, with a Comparative Study of Its Social Significance.* Drake University, 1940. 149 p. ms.

1553. CHENG, CHI-PAO. *The Training of Teachers in China, with Special Reference to the Normal Schools.* University of Chicago, 1922. 68 p. ms.

1554. CHENG, CHIH-TIEN. *The Scope, Organization, and Program of the Christian School in China.* Boston University, 1925. 104 p. ms.

1555. CHENG, DAVID CHIN-TE. *On the Mathematical Significance of the Chinese Ho-T'u and Lo-Shu and the Use of Computing Rods in China.* Columbia University, 1925. 25 p. ms.

1556. CHENG, MOU-TA, 1922- . *Improving the Administration of the Public Secondary School in China.* Pacific University, 1952. 178 p. ms.

1557. CHENG, NAI-WEN. *The Training of Teachers in China.* University of Chicago, 1917. 64 p. ms.

1558. CHENG, YU-CHE. *Oriental and Occidental Thought Contrasted.* Stanford University, 1936. 288 p. ms.

1559. CHIA, LIN-PING. *New Education for Young China.* Oberlin College, 1929. 113 p. ms.

1560. CHIANG, HSIU-FENG, 1888- . *The Curriculum of Religious Education in the Junior and Senior Middle Schools of China.* Boston University, 1925. 106 p. ms.

1561. CHING JU, *Sister* ANTSILA YAO. *The Elementary Arithmetic Curriculum in China.* De Paul University, 1952. 116 p. ms.

1562. CHOU, *Sister* MARY ADOLPH. *The Chinese Translation of "The Highway to Heaven" Series.* Marquette University, 1939. 156 p. ms.

1563. CHOU, SIEGEN K. *Legibility of Chinese Characters: Influence of Reading Direction and Character Position upon the Speed of Reading Chinese by Means of a New Quadrant Tachistoscope.* Stanford University, 1928. 136 p. ms.

1564. CHOW, KWANG-TING. *Elementary Education in China under the Republic, 1911-1943.* Stanford University, 1946. 131 p. ms.

1565. CHOW, LUCINA YU-YING. *The Work of the Public School Principal in China.* Syracuse University, 1925. 97 p. ms.

1566. CHOW, SHUI-CHANG. *Correlations of Marks of Students in the Nanking Y.M.C.A. High School.* University of Chicago, 1928. 67 p. ms.

1567. CHU, JOB BENJAMIN. *The Opportunity in China for Religious Education.* University of Chicago, 1925. 72 p. ms.

1568. CHU, MIN-LIU. *The Idea of Moral Character as Presented in Chu Hsi's "Hsiao Hsueh" (Primary Education).* Catholic University of America, 1950. 73 p. ms.

1569. CHU, MU-HSIANG. *A Program for Freshman English in Chinese Colleges.* Stanford University, 1942. 117 p. ms.

1570. CHUNG, MEI-LIEN. *The History and Use of Music in Chinese Christian Schools.* Boston University, 1923.

1571. CLEVELAND, MARION ELINOR. *Lay Leadership Training for Rural Women of the China Inland Mission in West Szechwan.* Biblical Seminary in New York, 1939. 106 p. ms.

1572. CRAIG, JEAN FRANCIS. *Meeting the Conditions of Worship for Students in a Chinese Middle School.* Columbia University, 1942. 88 p. ms.

1573. DECKER, WILLIAM M. *The Foundations and Growth of Shantung Christian University, 1864-1917.* Columbia University, 1948. 130 p. ms.

1574. DICKINSON, FRANK, 1884- . *The Teaching of Agriculture in the Junior High Schools of the Province of Szechwan, West China.* Cornell University, 1929. 110 p. ms.

1575. DIXON, EDWARD EVERETT, Jr. *Village-Centered Christian Education in North China: Outline of a Search for Constructive Hypotheses to Be Further Tested.* Columbia University, 1937. 113 p. ms.

1576. DIXON, ESTHER McCRACKEN. *The Use of Chinese Pictures in Religious Education in China.* Boston University, 1928. 66 p. ms.

1577. DJAO, CHWANG CHIA. *The Growth of Teachers in Service in Chinese Middle Schools.* Colorado State College of Education, 1937. 142 p. ms.

1578. DJENG, BEATRICE. *The Leisure-Time Activities of Chinese High School Students in North China.* University of Michigan, 1935. 69 p. ms.

1579. DROUGHT, *Rev.* JAMES MATTHEW. *Twenty Five Years of Modern Systematized Education in China.* Catholic University of America, 1924. 50 p. ms.

1580. DSANG, LING GAO. *Materials for the Religious Education of Children from Six to Twelve in China.* Northwestern University, 1921. 124 p. ms.

1581. EDWARDS, MARGARET JANE. *A Course of Bible Studies for Use in Teaching Christian Women of Rural South China.* Biblical Seminary in New York, 1937. 137 p. ms.

1582. EIDE, MARY, *The Development of Secondary Education in China.* Drake University, 1927. 63 p. ms.

1583. EO-YANG, YU-CHING, 1894- . *A Proposed Program of Religious Education for the Evangelical Church in Hunan.* Yale University, 1928. 144 p. ms.

1584. EWAN, JAMES DOUGLAS. *The Student Influence in the Revolutionary Movement in China.* University of Southern California, 1928. 123 p. ms.

1585. FAIRFIELD, WYNN COWAN. *The Bearing of the Theory and Practice of Vocational Education in Europe and America upon the Problem of Vocational Education in Senior High Schools in China.* Oberlin College, 1926. 74 p. ms.

1586. FENG, HAN-YI, 1902- *The Lolo of China: Their History and Cultural Relations.* University of Pennsylvania, 1934. 47 p. ms.

1587. FENG, RICHARD TSU-YING. *The Educational Policy of the Nationalist Party in China.* Syracuse University, 1933. 71 p. ms.

1588. FIELD, Mrs. ELIZABETH B. *A Study of the Judgment by American White Students of the Facial Expression of Chinese and White Men Students.* Columbia University, 1934. 28 p. ms.

1589. GOODRICH, LUTHER C. *American Catholic Missions in China.* Columbia University, 1927. 67 p. ms. (Includes education activities.)

1590. GOULTER, OSWALD JOHN. *A History of Education in China since 1905.* Yale University, 1922. 155 p. ms. For another master's thesis by same author, see No. 62.

1591. GRAYBILL, HENRY BLAIR. *The Educational Reform in China.* Columbia University, 1907. 108 p. ms.

1592. HARRIS, GERTRUDE G. *Some Elements in My Philosophy of Religious Education as an Outgoing Missionary.* Columbia University, 1931. 17 p. ms. (Refers to China.)

1593. HEININGER, ALFRED DIXON. *Religious Education for Christian Middle Schools in China.* Kennedy School of Missions, 1925. 57 p. ms.

1594. HERNDON, Mrs. SCIOTO McADOW, 1891- *The Influence of Western Culture on China.* Drake University, 1926. 95 p. ms. (Includes education.)

1595. HO, DUANE PING-DUAN, 1911- . *A Syllabus for Teaching New Testament Greek in Chinese.* Pacific Union College, 1949. 120 p. ms.

1596. HO, YEN-SUN. *Chinese Education from the Western Viewpoint.* Northwestern University, 1913. 51 p. ms.

1597. HOCKIN, KATHARINE BOEHNER, 1910- . *Christian and National Influences in the Development of Modern Chinese Education, with Special Reference to the Secondary Field.* Columbia University, 1947. 112 p. ms. For doctoral dissertation by same author, see No. 1417.

1598. HOH, DAISY LAW. *A Practical Course in Parental Education for Chinese Mothers.* Stanford University, 1929. 184 p. ms.

1599. HOH, YAM TONG, 1898- *A Proposed System of Public Education for the City of Chung Shan, a Hypothetical City.* Stanford University, 1929. 197 p. ms. For doctoral dissertation by same author, see No. 1418.

1600. HOLLER, MARY ONI. *Ideas on Teaching Spoken English as Applicable to Chinese Schools.* George Peabody College for Teachers, 1933. 79 p. ms.

1601. HORNING, MARY EMMA. *Religious Education in a Chinese Village.* University of Chicago, 1928. 109 p. ms.

1602. HOUSEHOLDER, ETHEL. *The Training of Teachers for the Girls' Christian Schools of West China.* Boston University, 1920.

1603. HOY, GERTRUDE, 1892- . *The Course in Arithmetic for a Six-Year Primary School in China.* University of Pennsylvania, 1926. 131 p. ms.

1604. HSIA, JUI-CHING, 1899- *Significant Activities in Chinese Life as Revealed through an Analysis of Chinese Encyclopedias, Newspapers, and Periodicals.* University of Chicago, 1925. 85 p. ms.

1605. HSU, CHIA-PI. *An Inquiry into the Chinese National Library Act Relating to Public Libraries: An Historical, Analytic Study with Practical Suggestions for Its Future Development.* Columbia University, 1949. 135 p. ms.

1606. HSU, CONSTANCE JEN, 1923- . *Development of Modern Education and Guidance Work in Chinese Secondary Schools, and Organizing a Scientific Guidance Program.* Syracuse University, 1951. 102 p. ms.

1607. HSU, HELEN LEI, 1933- . *Some Difficulties Encountered by the Chinese in Learning English.* Furman University, 1957. 78 p. ms.

1608. HSU, MARIAN. *A Program of Studies for Junior Grades of the First High School in Foochow City, China.* New York University, 1929. 44 p. ms.

1609. HSU, PRINCETON SUNG-SHIH. *America's Contribution to the New Education of China.* George Peabody College for Teachers, 1930. 79 p. ms.

1610. HSU, TUNG-YEH, 1909- . *A Survey of Chinese Culture in American College Education.* Arizona State Teachers College, Tempe, 1943. 135 p. ms.

1611. HSUEH, HUNG-CHIH. *Secondary Education in China: A Statistical Presentation.* Stanford University, 1931. 137 p. ms.

1612. HSUNG, YA-NA, 1919- *A Study of the Family Life of Preschool Children in a Chinese Rural Town.* Cornell University, 1947. 229 p. ms.

1613. HU, CHING-WEN. *Selected Aspects of Rural Adult Education in the United States and Some Suggestions for Training Student Leaders for Mass Education in China.* University of Michigan, 1945. 69 p. ms.

China

1614. HU, I. (I is first name, not an initial.) *A Study of Perception Span in Reading the Chinese Language.* University of Chicago, 1926. 51 p. ms. For doctoral dissertation by same author, see No. 1424.

1615. HUA, Sister ARNOLDA CHANG-TSUI. *The Elementary Science Curriculum in China.* De Paul University, 1952. 110 p. ms.

1616. HUANG, CAROL SHU-NGO, 1913- . *Aspects of Religious Education in China with Particular Reference to Developments in the Hinghwa Annual Conference.* Emory University, 1948. 129 p. ms.

1617. HUANG, JAMES CHIONIN. *A Critical Study of the Present Educational System of China.* University of the Philippines, 1932.

1618. HUANG, SHU-FAN. *The Curriculum in Western Literature for the English Department of the Chinese College.* Stanford University, 1937. 172 p. ms.

1619. HUANG, TIEN-CHUAN. *A Short Survey of the Cultural Development in China.* Columbia University, 1927. 160 p. ms. (Includes education.)

1620. HUBBARD, Mrs. MABEL (ELLIS). *An Experiment in Teaching the Christian Religion by Life Situations in Fan Village, China.* Oberlin College, 1938. 87+33 p. ms. Abstract in *Selected Graduate Theses in Religious Education*, 1938, p. 22.

1621. HUMMEL, WILLIAM FREDERICK. *The Home Life of Chinese Children as a Basis for Religious Education.* Columbia University, 1916. 28 p. ms.

1622. HUMPHREY, LOREN RHODES. *Development of Professional and Lay Leadership in the Methodist Church in South China.* Union Theological Seminary, 1946.

1623. HUNG, KO-WONG. *New Emphases for the Chinese Elementary School: A Study of Increasing School Efficiency.* Stanford University, 1931. 234 p. ms.

1624. HUNG, MARJORIE ELLA. *Democratic Education for China.* Syracuse University, 1921. 119 p. ms.

1625. HUNG, WILLIAM. *The Annals of Confucius and Its Influence upon the Intellectual History of the Chinese.* Columbia University, 1919. 66 p. ms.

1626. HWANG, FU. *The New Educational Organization of China.* Stanford University, 1920. 162 p. ms.

1627. HWANG, WEN YU. *A Course of Religious Training for Girls of the Middle School Grade in China.* Hartford School of Religious Education, 1927. 71 p. ms.

1628. ING, ZAUNG TEH. *Education for the Masses in China.* Columbia University, 1913. 230 p. ms.

1629. JACQUET, MYRA ANNA. *China's Unrest: The Problem Presented and the Solution Proposed through Christian Education.* Boston University, 1923.

1630. JEN, NANCY YI-YING. *A Study of Some Selected Problems in Teaching English to Chinese Students.* Furman University, 1955. 53 p. ms.

1631. JEN, PEI-TAO, 1908- . *The Educational System of China from 1903 to 1933.* Municipal University of Wichita, 1933. 97 p. ms.

1632. JOHNSON, WILLIAM R. *A Suggested Plan for Rural Reconstruction Work under Christian Auspices in Kiangsi Province, China.* Columbia University, 1937. 44 p. ms. (Includes consideration of education.)

1633. JONES, ULRIC ROBERT. *Biology in the Educational System of China.* Columbia University, 1910. 41 p. ms.

1634. KAO, CHUN-CHE. *American Social Work in View of Its Applicability to China.* New York University, 1940. 112 p. ms.

1635. KAO, WEN-CHEN. *Chinese Education in Evolution.* Oberlin College, 1930. 181 p. ms.

1636. KEYS, JAMES NOEL, 1893-1948. *The Development of an Opposites Vocabulary Test as a Measure of English Attainment in Chinese Middle Schools.* University of Chicago, 1921. 63 p. ms.

1637. KIANG, WALLACE. *Present School System in China.* State University of Iowa, 1920. 72 p. ms.

1638. KIANG, YING-CHENG. *The Teaching of Geography in the Middle Schools of China.* Stanford University, 1945. 131 p. ms. For doctoral dissertation by same author, see No. 1428.

1639. KILLINGSWORTH, MYRA LOUISE. *A Study of Methods and Materials for Teaching English to Chinese.* George Peabody College for Teachers, 1937. 124 p. ms.

1640. KING, RUTH PYE. *The Development of Secondary Education in China.* George Peabody College for Teachers, 1927. 49 p. ms. Abstract in *Bulletin of the Department of Secondary School Principals of the National Education Association*, No. 43, p. 85-86, December 1932.

1641. KING, SHU CHUANG LU. *The Methods of Psychiatric Social Work in America and Their Application to Modern China.* University of Oregon, 1950. 109 p. ms.

1642. KOO, DANIEL CHIN, 1903- . *A Practical Program for Character Training in Yuth Dzae Academy.* Andover Newton Theological School, 1935. 56 p. ms.

1643. KUAN, MEI-JUNG. *Women's Future Development and Christian Work in China.* Oberlin College, 1934. 153 p. ms. Chapters 1 and 2 deal with woman's status in Chinese teaching; Chapter 4 with education as a factor in the changing status of Chinese women.)

1644. KUAN, TSUI-CHEN. *The Problems of Christian Parent Education in China.* Hartford School of Religious Education, 1934. 71 p. ms.

1645. KUNG, PU-SHENG. *The Student Christian Movement in War-Time China, 1937-1941.* Columbia University, 1942. 36 p. ms.

1646. KUO, PING-WEN, 1879- . *Teachers for Modern Schools of China.* Columbia University, 1912. 67 p. ms. For doctoral dissertation by same author, see No. 1430.

1647. KWEI, JOHN C. B. *An Historical Survey of Chinese Libraries.* Columbia University, 1928. 44 p. ms.

1648. KWEI, MARY TEH-HUA, 1892- . *Recent Education Tendencies in China.* University of North Carolina, 1932. 103 p. ms. Abstract in *University of North Carolina Record,* No. 282, p. 32, October 1932.

1649. KWOH, YU-YU, 1901- . *The Monitorial System in Relation to Popular Education in China.* University of Kentucky, 1932. 146 p. ms.

1650. LACY, CARLETON. *Jesus for Chinese Youth.* Columbia University, 1938. 24 p. ms. (Christian education.)

1651. LEAVELL, ULLIN WHITNEY. *Some Phases of the Administration of Christian Education for Boys in China.* George Peabody College for Teachers, 1921. 109 p. ms.

1652. LEE, BEATRICE DZUN, 1898- . (Also given as Li, Che-Min.) *Confucian Conception of Education.* Syracuse University, 1950. 86 p. ms. For another master's thesis by same author, see No. 4130.

1653. LEE, LING-AYI. *Mass Education Movement in China.* Columbia University, 1930. 33 p. ms.

1654. LEE, MAVIS SHOA-LING. *A Collection of Hymns for Use in Chinese Churches, Centers, and Schools in China.* Berkeley Baptist Divinity School, 1951. 207 p. ms.

1655. LEI, STEPHEN CHIANG, 1900- . *A Religious Curriculum for Christian Schools in China.* Yale University, 1930. 159 p. ms.

1656. LI, ANTHONY C. *The History of Privately Controlled Higher Education in the Republic of China.* Catholic University of America, 1955. 315 p. ms. Washington: Catholic University of America Press, 1954. xvii, 157 p. ("The following pages contain an abstract . . . The Introduction and Chapters III, V, and VI are published in full. Only the summaries of Chapters I, II, and IV are published."-Preface. Chapter I deals with nondenominational institutions, Chapter II with Protestant institutions, Chapter III with Catholic institutions.)

1657. LI, AUGUSTINE FONG-FU. *Financing of Chinese Public Libraries.* Columbia University, 1936. 93 p. ms.

1658. LI, CHING-LIEN. *The Renaissance in China in the Twentieth Century, Especially with Reference to Education and Religion.* Hartford School of Religious Education, 1930. 125 p. ms.

1659. LI, GWAN-FANG, 1896- . *Chinese Literature and Chinese Religous Education.* Boston University, 1926. 81 p. ms. (Thesis for degree of Master of Arts.)

1660. LI, GWAN-FANG, 1896- . *The Contribution of Religious Education to the Democratization of China.* Boston University, 1927. 153 p. ms. (Thesis for degree of Master of Religious Education.)

1661. LI, PAO-CHEN. *The Training of Music Teachers in China.* Oberlin College, 1945. 181 p. ms. For doctoral dissertation by same author, see No. 1432.

1662. LI, TINLIK LEWIS. *Some Social Effects of the Student and Youth Movement upon Present-Day China.* University of Southern California, 1931. 111 p. ms.

1663. LIAO, PAI-KI. *The Six Arts in China.* Stanford University, 1944. 299 p. ms. (Includes education.)

1664. LIDE, JANE W. *Considerations Underlying Education for Women in Shantung.* Hartford School of Religious Education, 1919. 178 p. ms.

1665. LING, CHEN-LING. *The Modern Objective Techniques in Supervision as Related to the Improvement of Instruction, with Special Reference to the Chinese Primary and Secondary Schools.* Northwestern University, 1930. 155 p. ms.

1666. LING, HAN-DAH. *A Study of English Textbooks Used in China from 1900 to 1937.* University of Colorado, 1938. 130 p. ms. Abstract in *University of Colorado Studies,* Vol. 26, No. 1, p. 12, November 1938.

1667. LIU, CHEN-EN. *Program of Religious Education for the "Lower Primary Division" of the Chinese Mission School.* Northwestern University, 1921. 96 p. ms.

1668. LIU, CHI-HUNG. *A Study of Modern Education in Kiangsu Province, China.* University of Washington, 1932. 124 p. ms.

1669. LIU, CHING-FU. *The Professional Preparation of Teachers for Junior Middle Schools in China.* Columbia University, 1925. 44 p. ms.

1670. LIU, I HSIN. *An Educational Program for Young Adults Adaptable to the Christian Churches in China.* University of Southern California, 1954. 269 p. ms.

1671. LIU, KATHERINE Y. CH., 1907- . *The Chinese Church School: A Guide for Leaders and Supervisors.* Drew University, 1943. 181 p. ms.

1672. LIU, KING-SHU. *Prolegomena to a Study of the Development of Chinese Thought.* Northwestern University, 1913. 126 p. ms.

1673. LIU, LUCRETIA CHUTAN. *A Comparison of the Curricula of the Private Middle Schools of Three Chinese Cities.* University of Michigan, 1932. 64 p. ms. Abstract in University of Michigan: *Abstracts of Dissertations and Theses in Education,* 1931-32, p. 72-73.

1674. LIU, MING-YUEN. *Chinese Education under "The Three Principles of the People."* Stanford University, 1931. 139 p. ms.

1675. LIU, PEI-CHANG, 1921- . *The Organization and Administration of Religious Education in the Student Department of the Y. W. C. A. for China.* Boston University, 1940.

1676. LIU, PING SHENG, 1914- . *The Motivational Interests in Recreation for College Girls in China.* Louisiana State University and State Agricultural and Mechanical College, 1940. 91 p. ms. Abstract in *Lousiana State University Bulletin*, Vol. 33, n.s., No. 1, p. 173, January 1941.

1677. LIU, SAO DSI. *Extra-Class Activities of Pupils in a Junior High School in China.* University of Chicago, 1930. 81 p. ms.

1678. LIU, SNOWPINE. *The Needs of China in Physical Education.* International YMCA College, 1931. 201 p. ms. For another master's thesis by same author, see No. 1679.

1679. LIU, SNOWPINE. *Proposed Organization of Physical Education for Chinese Colleges.* University of Southern California, 1933. 147 p. ms. For another master's thesis by same author, see No. 1678.

1680. LIU, YU-CHEN, 1905- . *An Adaptation of Parent Education Methods to Meet the Needs of the Changing Status of Chinese Familities.* Oregon State College, 1940. 77 p. ms.

1681. LO, HUAN. *Reorganizing the Administrative System of Education in China.* Cornell University, 1924. 79 p. ms.

1682. LO, REN-YEN, 1890- . *The Social Teaching of Confucius.* Syracuse University, 1912. 94 p. ms. For doctoral dissertation by same author with same title, see No. 1447.

1683. LO, TIMOTHY CHUNG-ZEN. *The Challenge of Modern Chinese Youth to Christianity and Christian Education.* Oberlin College, 1932. 135 p. ms.

1684. LO, YEUK-IU. *The Status of Physical Education and Health Education in China.* University of Southern California, 1933. 93 p. ms.

1685. LOH, LING-SU, -1924. *The Organization of Vocational Education in China.* University of Chicago, 1920. 87 p. ms. For doctoral dissertation by same author, see No. 1448.

1686. LOH, WAH-PING, 1904- . *Some Suggestions for the Use of Visual Education in Teaching Illiterate Chinese Parents.* Oregon State College, 1935. 138 p. ms.

1687. LU, HUI-CHING. *A Comparison of the Posture of Chinese and American Girls on the Basis of the MacEwan Method of Objective Grading.* Wellesley College, 1940. 84 p. ms. (First part of study done at Wellesley; second part after return to China.)

1688. LU, PAUL CHI-CHEN. *The Most Economical Method to Teach and to Learn the Chinese Phonetics.* Columbia University, 1921. 41 p. ms.

1689. LUNG, CHIENG-FU, 1906- . *Social Thought of Four Principal Thinkers of Ancient China.* University of Southern California, 1932. 115 p. ms. For doctoral dissertation by same author, see No. 1450.

1690. McCAIN, PEARLE. *An Educational Approach to the Task of the Christian Worker in China.* Union Theological Seminary, 1944. For doctoral dissertation by same author, see No. 1452.

1691. McCANDLISS, TIRZAH ROBERTS. *Program of Religious Education for Pre-School Children of Working Class Parents in Canton, China.* Kennedy School of Missions, 1930. 54 p. ms.

1692. McKIBBEN, CHARLES ROY. *A History of the Educational Development of China.* Emory University, 1922. 33 p. ms. (Thesis for degree of Bachelor of Divinity.)

1693. McMULLEN, ROBERT JOHNSTON. *The Christian College Confronts Chinese Culture: A Study of the Cultural Obstacles to Participation in the Religious Program of a Mission College in China with Suggestions as to How to Overcome Them.* Columbia University, 1936. 51 p. ms. For doctoral dissertation by same author, see No. 1453.

1694. MA, FREDERICK. *Chemical Terms in the Chinese Language.* George Peabody College for Teachers, 1933. 107 p. ms.

1695. MA, KWANG-YUNG. *The Influence of Western Culture on China.* New York University, 1933. 106 p. ms. (Includes educational influence.)

1696. MA, TEH-YIN, 1903- . *Village Life in North China: With Special Emphasis upon the Work of the Methodist Church and a Suggested Program for Post-War Rural Reconstruction.* Drew University, 1943. 157 p. ms. (Includes educational program.)

1697. MA, YI-YING, 1909- . *The Development of a National System of Education under the Chinese Republic, 1912-1938.* Smith College, 1939. 114 p. ms. For doctoral dissertation by same author, see No. 5045.

1698. MAO, PAO-HENG. *Chinese Secondary Education.* Butler College, 1925.

1699. MARK, STEPHEN GUM. *A Proposed Curriculum for the Canton Union Theological College.* Columbia University, 1935; Union Theological Seminary, 1935. 32 p. ms. For another master's thesis by same author, see No. 1700.

1700. MARK, STEPHEN GUM. *The Teaching of Confucius: A Systematic Treatment and Criticism.* Columbia University, 1945. For another master's thesis by same author, see No. 1699.

1701. MEEBOLD, LOUISE. *The Struggle Over the Control of Mission Schools in China.* University of Chicago, 1931. 110 p. ms.

1702. MEI, CHIN-YIN. *An Historical Study of Chinese Education and Its Changing Causes.* Syracuse University, 1917. 64 p. ms.

1703. MELROSE, ANNE MARIE, 1923- . *Some Aspects of Chinese Popular Religion as they Indicate Missionary and Educational Method.* Princeton Theological Seminary, 1947. 74 p. ms.

1704. MIAO, CHU-SENG, 1894- . *Materials of Ethical Instruction in Chinese Government Schools.*

University of Chicago, 1921. 58 p. ms. For doctoral dissertation by same author, see No. 1456.

1705. MIAO, ESTELLE. *A Survey of Religious Education in Chinese Christian Middle Schools.* Berkeley Baptist Divinity School, 1950. 70 p. ms.

1706. MO, EDWARD CHI-WEI. *A Syllabus of Physical Education Activities for Senior High School Boys in China.* International YMCA College, 1948. 278 p. ms.

1707. MONTEIRO, MARGARET KEAN. *American Elementary School Methods and Their Use in Chinese Schools.* University of Pittsburgh, 1925. 56 p. ms.

1708. MURPHY, ALICE EUGENIA. *The Training of Laymen for Christian Service in North China.* Kennedy School of Missions, 1938. 123 p. ms.

1709. NI, HSIAO RANG-YANG. *Recreation for Modern Chinese Women.* University of Southern California, 1938. 140 p. ms.

1710. NILSEN, FRIDA R., 1894- . *The Present Status of Secondary Education for Girls in China.* University of North Dakota, 1927. 78 p. ms.

1711. NINNEMAN, WESLEY DWIGHT. *A Comparison and Appraisal of Ten Gwayen Textbooks in Current Use by English-Speaking Students.* University of Southern California, 1947. 62 p. ms.

1712. OLIVE, LUCIUS BUNYAN. *Government Control of Christian Schools in China.* George Peabody College for Teachers, 1927. 68 p. ms.

1713. OSGOOD, RUSSELL GORDON, 1899- . *The Apperceptive Basis of Religious Education in China.* Yale University, 1924. 142 p. ms.

1714. O'YANG, SIANG, 1899- *Guidance Program in Chinese Elementary Schools.* Ohio State University, 1931. 110 p. ms. Abstract in Ohio State University: *Abstracts of Theses Presented by Candidates for the Master's Degrees . . . 1931-32,* p. 52-53. (Abstracts of Master's Theses, No. 8.) For doctoral dissertation by same author, see No. 1461.

1715. PAN, WEN TSAI-SUNG. *A Suggested Reorganization of the Secondary School Curriculum in China.* Stanford University, 1939. 106 p. ms. plus bibliography.

1716. PEASE, KINGSLEY EUGENE. *The American Penetration of Old China and the Democratic Drift in Education under the Empire.* University of Southern California, 1934. 144 p. ms.

1717. PERKINS, ELIZABETH SARAH. *Mores and Education in South China.* Columbia University, 1922. 47 p. ms.

1718. POTTS, ANNA HORTENSE. *The Religious Education of Youth in the New China.* University of Chicago, 1927. 76 p. ms.

1719. ROGERS, BURTON BRUSH, 1909- . *The Teaching of the English Language in China.* Yale University, 1937. 271 p. ms.

1720. ROLLAND, WILLIAM ALFRED. *Administration of Schools in China under Control of the Methodist Episcopal Church.* Ohio State University, 1927. 143 p. ms.

1721. RONNING, ELLA GRYTING. *A Study of the Experiences of Chinese Children and Their Implications for Religious Education.* Kennedy School of Missions, 1947. 147 p. ms.

1722. SEC, FONG-FOO. *The Problem of Teaching English to the Chinese.* Columbia University, 1906. 33 p. ms.

1723. SEECK, MARGARET, 1891- . *The Problem of Vocational Education and Vocational Guidance of Girls in the Mission Schools of China.* Boston University, 1923. 107 p. ms.

1724. SEITZ, ROBERT WILCOX. *English in Chinese Education.* Columbia University, 1922. 46 p. ms.

1725. SENN, PAULINE POY LING. *A Program for Moral and Religious Education Suitable for Elementary Schools in Rural China.* Boston University, 1926. 100 p. ms.

1726. SHAW, ERNEST T. *A Religious Education Program for Yu Ying Boys Junior High School, Peking, China.* Columbia University, 1926. 49 p. ms.

1727. SHAW, JOB CHIA-KWANG, 1895- . *A Study of the History, Development, and Progress of Education in the Empire and the Republic of China.* Syracuse University, 1948. 101 p. ms.

1728. SHAW, JOEL CHIA-KWEN. *The Social Ethics of Confucius.* Northwestern University, 1921. 138 p. ms.

1729. SHEW, LYNNE LEE, 1890- . *The Administration of Girls' Normal Schools for Primary and Secondary Teachers in China.* University of California, Berkeley, 1917. 156 p. ms.

1730. SHIH, CHAO-KUEI. *A Proposed Plan of Supervision for the Improvement of Common Education in China.* Stanford University, 1931. 144 p. ms.

1731. SHIH, PETER S. T. *The Making of a Curriculum for Chinese Elementary Schools.* George Peabody College for Teachers, 1922. 122 p. ms.

1732. SHRADER, RALPH RAYMOND. *Some Adjustment Problems of Chinese High School Students.* University of Chicago, 1933. 229 p. ms.

1733. SMITH, DOROTHEA MARGARET. *The Development of Some Significant Phases in Religious Education in China since 1930.* Columbia University, 1942. 41 p. ms.

1734. SMITH, FLORENCE WILSON. *The Use of the Bible with Chinese Christian Youth.* Union Theological Seminary, 1945. 40 p. ms.

1735. SMITH, HELEN HUNTINGTON. *The Reconstructive Process among Christian Youth in China.* Columbia University, 1935. 50 p. ms.

1736. SMITH, MADORAH ELIZABETH. *Teaching of Geography in China: A Course of Study.* State University of Iowa, 1918. 49 p. ms.

1737. SONNACK, IVER ARTHUR, 1922- . *The Development of Protestant Higher Education in China.* Yale University, 1951. 153 p. ms.

1738. SOO-HOO, CLARA, 1892- . (Name changed to Clara Soo-Hoo Ling, September 1932). *The Development of Education in Modern China.* University of California, Berkeley, 1915. 79 p. ms.

1739. SPEER, MARGARET BAILEY. *Notes on "Oliver Twist" for Chinese Students.* Columbia University, 1931. 43 p. ms.

1740. SPEERS, JAMES M., Jr. *A Study of the Problems Incurred in the Establishment of a Health Protection Program in China.* New York University, 1931. 59 p. ms.

1741. STANNARD, ELY MARTIN. *Social Implications of the Teaching of Agriculture in the Mission Schools of China.* University of Chicago, 1925. 77 p. ms.

1742. STEVEN, WALTER T. *The Role of Religion in Chinese Education under the Manchus, 1644 A.D. to 1908 A.D.* New York University, 1927. 55 p. ms.

1743. STRONG, NERISSA BROWN. *Curricular Adaptations in a Chinese Rural School.* Cornell University, 1943.

1744. SUN, EDITH CHIA-YING, 1910- . *A Plan for Adapting Nursery Schools to Existing Educational Centers in China.* Oregon State College. 1937. 98 p. ms.

1745. SUN, PAI-FAN. *Secondary Schools in Honan Province, China.* University of Washington, 1934. 92 p. ms.

1746. SUNG, DAVID NGAUH-NYEN. *Friendship Experience: A Course of Cooperative Thinking for Boys in China.* University of Chicago, 1929. 157 p. ms.

1747. SUNG, KE, 1905- . *The Development of a More Effective Type of Rural Education in Kankoo County, Kansu Province, China.* Cornell University, 1938. 83 p. ms. For doctoral dissertation by same author, see No. 1476.

1748. TAI, SHWANG-CHOW, 1896- . *An Analysis of Reading Curricula in Chinese Elementary Schools.* University of Chicago, 1924. 74 p. ms.

1749. TAN, SHULIN LINCOLN. *A Survey of the Ministry of Education in China.* Stanford University, 1924. 88 p. ms. plus bibliography.

1750. TANG, CHUNGHSUAN. *Modern Education in China.* University of Chicago, 1911. 87 p. ms.

1751. TANG, MARY RIGGAN. *The Influence of Christianity upon the Student Life of China.* Boston University, 1925. 95 p. ms.

1752. TANG, TSEKING WILLIAM. *Modern Religious Education in China.* Syracuse University, 1925. 112 p. ms.

1753. THOMAS, Mrs. RUTH MARGARET (HATCHER), 1901- . *Curricular Adaptations in a Chinese Rural School.* Cornell University, 1943. 95 p. ms.

1754. THOMSON, MARGARET COOK. *A Project in Adult Religious Education for a Group of Educated Chinese Women.* Columbia University, 1942. 29 p. ms.

1755. TIEN, SIN-KEN. *Y.M.C.A. Neighborhood Work in 23 American Cities.* International YMCA College, 1940. 156 p. ms. (Studies the philosophy and practice of the community approach to boys' work in American cities with a view to applying it to the YMCA Movement in China.)

1756. TING, IHSING. *A Proposed Program for Teaching of European History in the Chinese Teacher Preparatory Institutions.* Ohio State University, 1927. 74 p. ms.

1757. TONG, SHIK-FAN. *Recommended Educational Provisions for the Constitutions of China.* University of Southern California, 1927. 106 p. ms.

1758. TSANG, JEE-WOO. *How to Create a Felt Need of Physical Education in China.* New York University, 1935. 119 p. ms.

1759. TSANG, YALE-YIH. *An Experimental Study of the Effect of Vertical and Horizontal Alignment and of the Use of Punctuation Marks upon the Rate of Reading of the Chinese Language.* University of Washington, 1926. 72 p. ms.

1760. TSAO, JAMES TSUN-KAI. 1911- . *A Translation of Treatises on the Improvement of Instruction in the Secondary School.* Pacific Union College, 1953. 129 p. ms.

1761. TSENG, MARK H. S. *Chinese Cataloguing Principles and Practices in the Ching Dynasty, 1644-1900.* Columbia University, 1938. 53 p. ms.

1762. TSENG, TSO-CHUNG, 1899- . *Influence of the Direction of Writing upon the Speed of Writing Chinese Characters.* University of Washington, 1931. 45 p. ms. For doctoral dissertation by same author, see No. 1486.

1763. TSEU, TERESA MARGARET. *The Philosophy of Education According to Confucianism.* De Paul University, 1953. 136 p. ms.

1764. TSU, YU-HO. *Problems and Methods of Religious Education in a Chinese Christian Family.* Boston University, 1925. 99 p. ms.

1765. TU, HORACE TSOU-CHOW. *A Comparison of Reading Ability of American and Chinese Children.* State University of Iowa, 1923. 94 p. ms. For doctoral dissertation by same author, see No. 1487.

1766. TU, TIEN-HSIANG. *A Critical Study of Secondary Education in China.* Ohio State University, 1949. 96 p. ms.

1767. TUAN KWEI, MARY CHEN. *Rural Youth in Contemporary China.* Drew University, 1950. 154 p. ms. (Includes consideration of education.)

1768. TUNG, DANIEL CHI-TAC. *The Reorganization of Schools in the United States, and the Adaptation of the Plan to Conditions in China.* Northwestern University, 1920.

1769. TUNG, TEH-FU, 1899- . *The Technique of Curriculum Construction for Chinese Secondary Schools on the Basis of the Seven Objectives of Education.* University of California, Berkeley, 1928. 124 p. ms.

1770. TUTTLE, LELIA JUDSON. *An American School in China.* Columbia University, 1924. 62 p. ms.

1771. TWINEM, JESSIE MARGUERITE. *Toward a Religious Program for Youth in North China.* Kennedy School of Missions, 1938. 103 p. ms.

1772. VAN, AMBER LURRAINE. *The Development of Indigenous Leadership for Youth Work in China.* Union Theological Seminary, 1946.

1773. VAN HOOK, JOSEPH O. *A Decade of Educational Developments in the Republic of China.* Universiyt of Kentucky, 1926. 107 p. ms.

1774. VEE, LING-NYI. *The Mass Education Movement in China.* Columbia University, 1931. 32 p. ms.

1775. WALDRON, ROSE EDITH. *Contemporary Practices in Music Education and Their Application to the Mission Schools in China.* Claremont Graduate School, 1936. 146 p. ms.

1776. WANG, BESSIE PI-YUN. *An Analytical Study of the Difficulty of Reading Materials in Chinese Textbooks.* Claremont Graduate School, 1935. 88 p. ms.

1777. WANG, FENG-GANG, 1903- . *A Pyschological Study of the Process of Teaching the Chinese Written Language.* Stanford University, 1928. 54 p. ms. For doctoral dissertation by same author, see No. 1491.

1778. WANG, KEH-REN. *An Analysis of the History Curriculum in Chinese Elementary Schools.* University of Chicago, 1924. 68 p. ms.

1779. WANG, LILIAN YU-LU. *The Core Curriculum Theory and the Chinese Secondary Schools.* Stanford University, 1949. 99 p. ms.

1780. WANG, PENG-YUN. *Political Significance of the Chinese Student Movement from 1915 to 1925.* Syracuse University, 1928. 76 p. ms.

1781. WANG, PERCY HUNG-FANG. *Higher Education in Communist China.* University of Washington, 1953. 149 p. ms.

1782. WANG, SAMUEL C. *Student Life in Chinese Secondary Schools.* University of Southern California, 1926. 91 p. ms.

1783. WANG, SHU-KAI. *The Modernization of Education in China.* University of Southern California, 1922. 108 p. ms.

1784. WANG, YU-KA. *A Comparison of the School Systems in China and the United States.* University of Southern California, 1935. 93 p. ms.

1785. WANG, ZEALIN. *An Introduction to Character Education for China.* International YMCA College, 1933. 164 p. ms.

1786. WEI, WILSON SHIH-SHENG. *The Education of Women in Modern China.* Stanford University, 1927. 166 p. ms. For doctoral dissertation by same author, see No. 1499.

1787. WEI, YOEN-TU. *Educational Problems in China.* University of Richmond, 1945. 129 p. ms.

1788. WELCH, MARY MILDRED, 1898- . (Later Mrs. Earl Cranston). *The Organization and Content of the Curriculum of Religious Education in Protestant Christian Women's Colleges in West China.* Boston University, 1923. 98 p. ms.

1789. WEN, LIEN-CHUNG. *Changing Ideals in Chinese Education.* Ohio State University, 1929. 95 p. ms. Abstract in Ohio State University: *Abstracts of Theses Presented by Candidates for the Master's Degree . . . 1929-30,* p. 39-40. (Abstracts of Master's Theses, No. 2.)

1790. WEST, ANNA MAY, 1886-1942. *A Program for Girls' Junior High School (Mission) in Shanghai, China.* Boston University, 1927. 82 p. ms.

1791. WHITE, PHOEBE WIDDIFIELD. *The Role of the Missionary in the Introduction and Popularization of Western Learning in China in the Nineteenth Century.* Columbia University, 1941. 69 p. ms.

1792. WHITE, RALPH MANSON. *Private Education in the New Nationalism in China.* Columbia University, 1937. 57 p. ms.

1793. WILLIS, JESSIE LILLIAN. *Government Education in China.* Clark University, 1910. 72 p. ms.

1794. WILSON, SADIE MAI. *Principles of Educacational Missions in China.* New York University, 1924. 106 p. ms.

1795. WINTER, CHARLES EDWARD. *The Registration of Mission Schools in China.* University of Chicago, 1926. 58 p. ms.

1796. WOLFE, ALAN D. *The Development of Modern Education in China, 1898-1912.* Columbia University, 1950. 115 p. ms.

1797. WONG, GRACE D., 1900- *The Junior High School Problem in China.* Syracuse University, 1927. 129 p. ms.

1798. WONG, HONG-KWUN. *A Comparison between Some Speech Elements in the Cantonese Dialect of the Chinese Language and the English Language.* University of Hawaii, 1942. 57 p. ms.

1799. WONG, SANFORD CHANG-PING. *The Problem of Selecting Occidental Reference Books for Chinese College Libraries.* Columbia University, 1935. 68 p. ms.

1800. WONG, VI-LIEN. *A Study of Chinese Library Personnel.* Columbia University, 1936. 77 p. ms.

1801. WONG, WENSAN. *The Municipal Reference Libraries in the United States of America: A Study of Their Present Status, Activities, and Methods of Administration, with Suggestions for the Creation of a Municipal Reference Library at Peking, China.* Columbia University, 1928. 69 p. ms.

1802. WOO, GEE YONG. *Teaching Beginning English to Chinese Students.* Colorado State Teachers College, 1922. 67 p. ms.

1803. WRIGHT, ELEANOR M. *The Student Movement and Social Change in China.* Columbia University, 1933. 95 p. ms.

1804. WU, WILLIS CHIH-JEN. *A Comparison of the Professional Curriculum in Physical Education at the National Central University, China, and at the University of Southern California.* University of Southern California, 1949. 85 p. ms.

1805. YANG, CHU I. *The Pre-Adolescent Religious Education in China.* Oberlin College, 1934. 94 p. ms.

1806. YANG, ELLWOOD HSIN-PAO. *A Rural Extension Program for a Christian College in China Based on a Selective Study of Agricultural Extension and General University Extension in the United States of America.* Drew University, 1940. 244 p. ms.

1807. YANG, LIANG-KUNG. *The Reorganization of the Chinese High School Curriculum.* Stanford University, 1924. 123 p. ms. For doctoral dissertation by same author, see No. 1507.

1808. YANG, SZU-CHIEH. *The Development of the Primary and Middle School Curriculum in China.* University of the Philippines, 1937. 114 p. ms.

1809. YANG, THADDEUS WEN-HSIEN. *Development of Education in China.* De Paul University, 1951. 187 p. ms.

1810. YAUKEY, JESSE B. *Methods of Developing Native Christian Leadership in China.* Columbia University, 1930. 29 p. ms.

1811. YEN, WEN-YU. *"The Four Treasuries Library" and Its Influence upon Chinese Culture: A Historical and Critical Study.* Columbia University, 1932. 124 p. ms.

1812. YIEH, TSUNG-KAO, 1906- . *Adaptation of the American Character Education Methods to Chinese Schools.* Northwestern University, 1932. 118 p. ms. For doctoral dissertation by same author, see No. 5049.

1813. YIN, CHILING, 1897- . *The Problem of Training Teachers under the Compulsory Universal Education Requirement of China.* Columbia University, 1922. 42 p. ms. For doctoral dissertation by same author, see No. 1509.

1814. YING, KAI-SHIH, 1899- . *Administration and Supervision of the Christian Middle School in China.* Yale University, 1932. 157 p. ms.

1815. YOH, PETER LIANG-MU. *American Methods of Public Library Extension and Their Possible Application in China.* Columbia University, 1937. 119 p. ms.

1816. YOST, JOHN WYCLIFFE. *The Teaching of Reading in Chinese.* Columbia University, 1912. 38 p. ms.

1817. YOUNG, SAMUEL SUNG. *Chinese Education — Old and New.* Columbia University, 1905. 68 p. ms.

1818. YU, CHANG-FENG. *Religious Education for High Schools of the Methodist Episcopal Central China Conference.* Hartford School of Religious Education, 1930. 78 p. ms.

1819. YU, SOO-TSING, 1904- . *The Educational Crisis in China: A Critical Study of the Report by the League of Nations' Mission of Educational Experts, "The Reorganization of Education in China."* Smith College, 1933. 164 p. ms.

1820. YUAN, PAE-YEO, 1897- . *A Comparative Study of Chinese and American Secondary Education.* University of Pennsylvania, 1924. 91 p. ms.

1821. ZIA, ZONG-KAO, 1895- . *The Confucian Theory of Moral and Religious Education and Its Bearing on the Future Civilization of China.* Boston University, 1922. 120 p. ms.

1822. ZIMMER, SYLVIA RUTH. *Education: A Translation of Chapter Five of Ting Hsien by Franklin C. Lee.* Kennedy School of Missions, 1942. 101 p. ms.

See also Nos. 187, 193, 206, 208, 211, 213, 221, 226, 231, 236, 238, 239, 244, 246, 250, 259, 263, 268, 272, 278, 279, 280, 292, 301, 303, 1305, 1306, 1310, 1312, 1318, 1319, 1361, 2893

For Chinese groups in the United States, *see* Nos. 5032-5089

See also Formosa, 1355-1359

Cyprus

See Nos. 1353-1354

Formosa

See Nos. 1355-1359

Hong Kong

See Nos. 1360-1361

India

(NOS. 1823 – 2133)

DOCTORS

1823. ADISESHIAH, HELEN ESTHER MARY, 1909- . *A Teacher Training Program for the Children of Independent India.* New York University, 1953. 328 p. ms. Abstract in *Dissertation Abstracts,* Vol. 13, No. 6, p. 1030. Available on microfilm from University Microfilms, Ann Arbor, Michigan, as Publication No. 6,261.

1824. AKESON, MERLE ALDO, 1927- . *Intentions of Village and Government Subcultures in the Promotion of Rural Education in India.* Stanford University, 1957. 219 p. ms. Abstract in *Dissertation Abstracts,* Vol. 18, No. 2, p. 462-463, February 1958. Available on microfilm from University Microfilms, Ann Arbor, Michigan, as Publication No. 25,344.

1825. ALTER, D. EMMET, 1891- . *Organization, Support, and Administration of Mission Schools in India.* University of California, Berkeley, 1937. 158 p. ms.

1826. ANDREWS, GEORGE FRANKLIN, 1897-1949. *Physical Education for Boys in the Secondary Schools in India: A Critical Study with Suggestions for Reconstruction.* Columbia University, 1936. New York: (but "Printed by the Jupiter Press, Madras," India) 1934. xiv, 219 p. Also published as *Physical Education for Boys in Indian Schools,* Madras, India: Little Flower Co., 1935. 213 p. For master's thesis by same author, see No. 187.

1827. BANKER, PERIN KAIKHUSHROO. *A Plan for the Revision of Teacher Education for the Rural Girls' Schools of the Chhattisgargh Area, Central Provinces, India.* Columbia University, 1949. 158 p. ms. Abstract in *Teachers College Record,* Vol. 51, p. 176-177, December 1949.

1828. BHAGWAT, PRABHAKAR GOVIND. *The Theory of Education of Protestant Mission High Schools in India: A Critical Analysis.* New York University, 1935. 165 p. ms.

1829. BHATT, RAMANBHAI GANPATRAM, 1917- . *The Role of Vocational and Professional Education in the Economic Development of India, from 1918 to 1951.* Columbia University, 1957. 235 p. ms.

1830. BRAISTED, PAUL JUDSON, 1903- . *Indian Nationalism and the Christian Colleges.* Columbia University, 1935. New York: Association Press, 1935. xii, 171 p. For master's thesis by same author, see No. 1950.

1831. BROCK, EARL EARNEST, 1890- . *A Suggested Program for the Improvement of Education in the Village Schools in Assam, India.* University of Colorado, 1947. Abstract in University of Colorado: *Abstracts of Theses . . . 1946-47,* p. 5-7.

• 1832. BUCHANAN, M. EDITH M., 1905- . *A Study Guide in Nursing for Indian Nursing Students.* Columbia University, 1953. 674 p. ms. (Preface is signed only "Edith Buchanan.")

1833. CAMA, KATAYUN HORMUSJI, 1908- *A Study of the Native Hindustani Melody Pattern and the Acquired English Melody Pattern with Special Reference to the Teaching of English in India.* University of Michigan, 1938. 110 p. ms. Resume published in *Archives Neerlandaises de Phonetique Experimentale,* Tome XV, p. 103-110, 1939. (The Hague, Netherlands.)

1834. CHAMBERLAIN, WILLIAM ISAAC, 1862-1937. *Education in India.* Columbia University, 1899. New York: The Macmillan Co., 1899. vii, 107 p. (Columbia University Contributions to Philosophy, Psychology, and Education, Vol. 7, No 3.)

1835. CHAUBE, SARAYU PRASAD, 1919- . *A More Adequate Foundation of Secondary Education for Indian Democracy.* Indiana University, 1952. 308 p. ms. Abstract in Indiana University, School of Education: *Studies in Education, 1952,* p. 83-87. (Thesis Abstract Series, No. 4, 1953.)

1836. CHAURASIA, GULABCHANDRA SHARDAPRASAD, 1922- . *Suggestions for In-Service Education of Secondary School Teachers in India, with Special Reference to the State of Madhya Pradesh.* Columbia University, 1950. 259 p. ms.

1837. CHINNAPPA, SHANLAPPA PAUL, 1880- *The British System of Education in India.* Columbia University, 1934. Bangalore City, South India: Printed at Radha Power Printing Press, 1934. 315 p. (*Note:* Copy in Library of Congress says on cover and on title page: "Submitted in partial fulfilment of the requirements for the Degree of Doctor of Philosophy, Columbia University, 1915." No publication date given, but Library of Congress index card, printed in 1935, says "1934?" and "Thesis, Ph.D. – Columbia University, 1934." Author's *Vita* says he "studied at the University of Chicago July 1913-August 1914, and took his M.A. and did part of the work for the Ph.D. in Education. He studied in the Teachers College, Columbia University, New York, in 1914-15." Degree was conferred in 1934.)

1838. CHITAMBAR, JOHN BENEDICT, 1920- *A Study of Contacts and Changes among Different Groups of Rural People Served by Different Types of Extension Workers in a Program of Rural Development in North India.* Cornell University, 1958. 363 p. ms.

1839. CHOPRA, OM KRISHNA, 1911- . *A Plan for the Development of Evaluative Criteria for the Secondary Schools of the Punjab, India.* Columbia University, 1954. 165 p. ms.

1840. COELHO, GEORGE VICTOR. *Acculturative Learning: A Study of Reference Groups.* Harvard University, 1956. 315 p. ms.

1841. CORNELIUS, JOHN JESUDASON, 1886- . *Rabindranath Tagore, India's School Master: A Study of Tagore's Experiment in the Indianization of Education in the Light of India's History.* Columbia University, 1930. New York: (But printed by Methodist Publishing House, Madras, India) 1928 (i. e. 1930). v, 222 p. *(Note:* Cornelius is the name under which the degree was granted, but later the author used the name Jagadisan Mohandas Kumarappa, under which his publications, including this dissertation, are indexed in the Library of Congress.)

1842. CORNELIUS, MERCY. *Some Trends in Selected Aspects of Personnel Service in American Higher Education with Implications for Women's Colleges in India.* University of Michigan, 1946. 314 p. ms.

1843. CUTTS, ELMER HENRY. *British Educational Policy in India under the East India Company.* Harvard University, 1940. 419 p. ms. Abstract in Harvard University: *Summaries of Ph.D. Theses,* 1940, p. 173-176.

1844. DABOO, JER DOSABHAI, 1920- . *The Need for Providing an Organized Program of Guidance Services for the High Schools of Urban India.* University of Michigan, 1955. 323 p. ms. Abstract in *Dissertation Abstracts,* Vol. 15, p. 2082-2083, November 1955. Available on microfilm from University Microfilms, Ann Arbor, Michigan, as Publication No. 12,562.

1845. DAS, PARIMAL, 1904- . *Foundations for Guidance in Indian Philosophical and Social Thought.* Columbia University, 1948. 261 p. ms. Abstract in *Microfilm Abstracts,* Vol. 10, No. 3, p. 52-53, 1950. Available on microfilm from University Microfilms, Ann Arbor, Michigan, as Publication No. 1,840.

1846. DAVE, INDU, 1920- . *A Proposed Training Program for Indian School Counselors.* University of Georgia, 1956. 302 p. ms. Abstract in *Dissertation Abstracts,* Vol. 17, p. 102, February 1957. Available on microfilm from University Microfilms, Ann Arbor, Michigan, as Publication No. 20,010.

1847. DESAI, LALITA MANIBHAI, 1914- . *Proposals for the Development of Education in India Derived from a Synthesis of Occidental and Oriental' Sources.* University of Michigan, 1948, 258 p. ms. Abstract in *Microfilm Abstracts,* Vol. 9, No. 1, p. 35-37, 1949. Available on microfilm from University Microfilms, Ann Arbor, Michigan, as Publication No. 1,099.

1848. De SOUSA, *Rev.* HERBERT ALOYSIUS, 1918- . *Educational Issues of India, 1947-1954.* Fordham University, 1955. 189 p. ms.

1849. DEULKAR, DURGA, 1914- . *A Study of Teaching Techniques Practiced by Ten Selected Elementary School Teachers in New York State and the Formulation of Concepts for the Potential Adaptation of These Techniques in the Basic Schools of India.* Cornell University, 1958. 187 p. ms. For master's thesis by same author, see No. 1976. Abstract in *Dissertation Abstracts,* Vol. 19, p. 2266, March 1959. Available on microfilm from University Microfilms, Ann Arbor, Michigan, as Mic. 59-122. For master's thesis by same author, see No. 1976.

1850. DHAIRYAM, DESARAJ. *Personality Differences Between a Hindu and an American Group.* Columbia University, 1956. 138 p. ms. Abstract in *Dissertation Abstracts,* Vol. 16, p. 1281, July 1956. Available on microfilm from University Microfilms, Ann Arbor, Michigan, as Publication No. 16,803. (Compares 50 Tamil Brahmins studying in Madras, with 50 American Protestants studying in the United States.)

1851. DUKEWITS, WALTER CARL, 1904- . *A Plan for a Private College in South India.* Columbia University, 1949. 68 p. ms. Abstract in *Teachers College Record,* Vol. 52, p. 63-64, October 1950.

1852. DUTT, BEULAH MALL, 1923- . *Teacher Education in India.* University of Oklahoma, 1954. 132 p. ms.

1853. EAPEN, CHAVADIYIL THOMAS. *The Problem of Mass Education in India.* New York University, 1925. 125 p. ms. For master's thesis by same author, see No. 1981.

1854. EDWARDS, JOYCE. *A Philosophy of Education for Federated India.* New York University, 1929. 205 p. ms.

1855. EDWARDS, SETH JASON. *An Educational Program of Physical Education for Schools and Colleges of the United Provinces, Agra and Oudh, India.* New York University, 1931. 203 p. ms.

1856. ELLIOTT, VIDA COE, 1901- . *The Education of Hindu Women from Ancient Days with Its Bearing on the Preparation of the Hindu Woman for Her Place in Society.* Hartford Seminary Foundation, 1947. 436 p. ms.

1857. FISHMAN, ALVIN TEXAS. *Madigas in South India under Christian Guidance.* Yale University, 1941. Published as *Culture and the Underprivileged: A Study of Madigas in South India under Christian Guidance,* Madras, etc., India: The Christian Literature Society for India, 1941. viii, 207 p. (Chapter 3, "Education" p. 24-57.)

1858. FRENCH, CLARA MINNIE, 1903- . *A Study of the Work and Preparation of the Missionary in India: An Aid in Selecting, Preparing, and Placing the New Recruit.* Columbia University, 1953. 147 p. ms.

1859. GEORGE, KANICHUKATTIL KURIEN, 1916- . *Problems Confronting Christian Education in the Mar Thoma Syrian Church, and Indicated Solutions.* Princeton Theological Seminary, 1950. 283 p. ms. Abstract in *Religious Education,* Vol. 46, p. 170-171, May-June 1951.

1860. GIDEON, SINCLAIR SAMWORTH, 1901- . *A Plan to Modify the Policy, Organization, and Program of Ewing Christian College, Allahabad, India, with a View to Emphasizing a Democratic View of Life.* Columbia University, 1949. 122 p. ms. Abstract in *Religious Education,* Vol. 45, p. 105-106, March-April 1950.

1861. HAMDANI, MOHSIN SAIYEDI TAHER, 1912- . *A Plan to Develop an Educational Plan for Social Living in Elementary Schools of Bombay Province.* New York University, 1952. 200 p. ms. Abstract in *Dissertation Abstracts,* Vol. 13, No. 1, p. 69-70, 1953. Available on microfilm from University Microfilms, Ann Arbor, Michigan, as Publication No. 3,677.

1862. HAZARIKA, BHUPENDRA KUMAR, 1926- . *Proposals for Preparing India's Basic Education to Use Audio-Visual Techniques in Adult Education.* Columbia University, 1953. 180 p. ms.

1863. HEIN, NORVIN JACOB, 1914- . *The Vaishnava Dramatic Traditions of Mathura and Vrindaban.* Yale University, 1951. 431 p. ms. Abstract in *Doctoral Dissertations in the Field of Religion, 1940-1952,* p. 64. (Describes some of the non-scholastic instruments of religious education in orthodox Hindu society.)

1864. HOWARD, ARTHUR WESLEY, 1912- . *A Program of Physical Education for India.* University of Michigan, 1952. 171 p. ms. Abstract in *Dissertation Abstracts,* Vol. 12, No. 4, p. 513, 1952. Available on microfilm from University Microfilms, Ann Arbor, Michigan, as Publication No. 3,767.

1865. HUDLI, VISHWANATH JEEWANRAS. *A Program for Vocational Agriculture in India.* University of Minnesota, 1958. 376 p. ms. Abstract in *Dissertation Abstracts,* Vol. 19, p. 711-712, October 1958. Available on microfilm from University Microfilms, Ann Arbor, Michigan, as Mic. 58-2152. (Studies the political, cultural, educational, and agricultural conditions with special reference to agricultural education.)

1866. JACOB, THOTTUNGAL NINAN, 1894- . *The Reconstruction of the Curriculum of the Elementary Schools of India,* Columbia University, 1933. Calcutta: Association Press, YMCA, 1932. ix, 206 p. (The Education of India Series.)

1867. JHA, SHAMBLU NATH. *A Critical Study of Secondary Education in India, Particularly with Reference to Uttar Pradesh.* University of Oregon, 1955. 271 p. ms.

1868. JIVANAYAKAM, DANIEL, 1891- . *Training Teachers for English Schools in Travancore.* Columbia University, 1932. New York: (but "Printed at the V.V. Press, Trivandrum, India"), 1931. ii, 163 p.

1869. JOHN, THARAYIL THARIYAN, 1910- . *A Program of Christian Education for India (with Reference to the Mar Thoma Church.)* Hartford School of Religious Education, 1955. 473 p. ms. Abstract in *Dissertation Abstracts,* Vol. 15, p. 2109, November 1955. Available on microfilm form University Microfilms, Ann Arbor, Michigan, as Publication No. 13,823. For master's thesis by same author, see No. 2015.

1870. KALATHIVEETIL, TERESA K., 1928- . *A Guide to the Teaching of Civics in the High Schools of Kerala State, India, Based on a Critical Survey of Civics Curricula in Selected School Systems in the United States.* Loyola University, 1958. For master's thesis by same author, see No. 2017.

1871. KAUL, JAGAN NATH, 1920- . *Dissertations in the Social Sciences by Indian Doctoral Scholars, 1933-1953.* University of Michigan, 1955. 403 p. ms. Abstract in *Dissertation Abstracts,* Vol. 15, p. 2063-2064, November 1955. Available on microfilm from University Microfilms, Ann Arbor, Michigan, as Publication No. 12,598. (Analysis of 61 dissertations, including many in education and psychology.) For master's thesis by same author, see No. 2019.

1872. KHAIR, GAJANAN S. *Reconstruction of the Secondary School Curriculum in India with Specific Reference to Bombay Presidency.* New York University, 1933. 195 p. ms.

1873. KHAN, MOHAMMED IKRAM, 1916- . *A Proposed Teachers Training Program for Rural Universities in India.* Columbia University, 1954. 206 p. ms.

1874. KINI, KULAI NARAYANA, 1891- . *Proposals for a Program of Vocational Education for Mysore (India) Based upon Experience in Mysore and in the United States of America.* Columbia University, 1934. Bangalore City, India: The Bangalore Press, 1933. viii, 205 p.

1875. KITCHEN, LEWIS CLAYTON, 1896- . *Character Education among the Santals.* Kennedy School of Missions, 1936. 253 p. ms.

1876. KLINE, FRANK JOSHUA. *A Plan of Community Education for Rural Berar, India.* Columbia University, 1944. 222 p. ms.

1877. KRISHNAYYA, STEPHEN GANUGAPATI, 1898- . *A Study of the Community Aspects of Certain American Schools, with Special Reference to the Needs of Rural India.* Columbia University, 1932. Published as *The Rural Community and the School: The Message of Negro and Other American Schools for India.* Calcutta: Association Press, YMCA, 1932. xxii, 161 p. (The Education of India Series.)

1878. LAL, PREM CHAND, 1891- . *Reconstruction and Education in Rural India in the Light of the Programme Carried Out at Sriniketan, the Institute of Rural Reconstruction Founded by Rabindranath Tagore.* Columbia University, 1932. London: G. Allen & Unwin, Ltd., 1932. 262 p. With an introduction by Rabindranath Tagore.

1879. LAWRENCE, HARRIS SAM SAHAYAM, 1923- . *A Plan for the In-Service Education of High School Teachers in the State of Madras, India.* Columbia University, 1950. 161 p. ms.

1880. McCULLY, BRUCE TIEBOUT, 1904- . *English Education and the Origins of Indian Nationalism.* Columbia University, 1940. New York: Columbia University Press; London: P. S. King & Sons, Ltd., 1940. 418 p. (Studies in History, Economics, and Public Law, Edited by the Faculty of Political Science of Columbia University, No. 473.)

1881. McGAVRAN, DONALD ANDERSON, 1897- . *Education and the Beliefs of Popular Hinduism: A Study of the Beliefs of Secondary School Boys in Central Provinces, India, in Regard to Nineteen Major Beliefs of Popular Hinduism.* Columbia University, 1936. Jubbulpore, C.P., India: 1935. ii, 179 p.

1882. McKEE, WILLIAM JOHN, 1885- . *A Method of Procedure for Constructing a Curriculum for Rural Elementary Schools, Punjab, India.* Columbia University, 1931. Published as *New Schools for Young India: A Survey of Educational, Economic, and Social Conditions in India with Special Reference to More Effective Education.* Chapel Hill, North Carolina: University of North Carolina Press, 1930. xxi, 435 p. Published also in India as *Developing a Project Curriculum for Village Schools in India.* Calcutta: Association Press. (Incomplete information on Calcutta edition, taken from Chapel Hill edition, p. iv.)

1883. MAJUMDER, KUMUD BONDHU, 1911- . *The Development and the Adaptation to Bengal of American Methods and Techniques for Making a School Survey.* Cornell University, 1949. 383 p. ms.

1884. MALIK, ANAND KUMAR, 1924- . *Suggestions for Supervision and Curriculum Improvement in the Schools of India, with Special Reference to Basic Education and Social Education.* Columbia University, 1955. 154 p. ms.

1885. MANIKAM, RAJAH BHUSHANAM, 1897- . *Missionary Collegiate Education in the Presidency of Madras, India: A Study of the Historical Development, the Contributions, and the Religious Educational Program of Mission Colleges in the Presidency.* Columbia University, 1928. Lancaster, Pennsylvania: Conestoga Publishing Co., 1929. vii, 158 p.

1886. MATHEW, CHERUVATHUR CHERU, 1899- . *A Study of the American Agricultural Extension Work and Its Application to the Villages of the Native State of Cochin, India.* Columbia University, 1931. Ernakulan, India: Liberty Press, 1931. 165 p.

1887. MATHEW, MARIAM, 1905- . *Preschool Education in South India: Pyschological and Sociological Foundations.* Columbia University, 1950. 161 p. ms. For master's thesis by same author, see No. 2040.

1888. MILLER, ERNEST EDGAR. *The Problem of Literacy in Central Provinces and Berar, India.* New York University, 1939. 209 p. ms. Abstract in New York University, School of Education: *Abstracts of Theses,* October 1939-June 1940, p. 53-58. For master's thesis by same author, see No. 2045.

1889. MOFFATT, ELBERT MARSTON, 1884- . *Universities of India.* University of Washington, 1940. 250 p. ms. Abstract in University of Washington: *Abstracts of Theses . . .* Vol. 5, 1941, p. 265-269.

1889a. MAHANTY, GOURI SHYAM. *The Common Multi-Purpose School in the Democratic Republic of India: Its Issues and Problems.* Columbia University, 1957.

1890. MONE, SURENDRA SHANTARAM, 1911- . *Reorganization of Secondary Education in Bombay Province, India.* Columbia University, 1950. 169 p. ms.

1891. MOOMAW, IRA WILBUR, 1894- . *Farm Organization and Certain Aspects of Life among Depressed Class Farmers of Broach District, India.* Ohio State University, 1940. 243 p. ms. Abstract in Ohio State University: *Abstracts of Dissertations . . .* Spring Quarter, 1939-40, p. 191-198. (Abstracts of Doctoral Dissertations, No. 33. Includes study of student apprentices operating small farms in connection with the Vocational Training School at Anklesvar.)

1892. MUKERJI, SHRIDHAR NATH, 1909- . *The Role of Higher Education in Rural Development in Free India.* Columbia University, 1954. Published as *Higher Education and Rural India,* Baroda, India: Acharya Book Depot, 1956. 342 p.

1893. NATESH, ARCOT MANICKA. *The Educational and Vocational Rehabilitation of the Visually and Acoustically Handicapped of Mysore, India.* Columbia University, 1941. 132 p. ms.

1894. NAUGLE, HAZEL EDNA, 1913- . *Materials for a Christian Education Program for Pre-Literates in India: A Source Book Prepared for the Use of Indian Lay Leaders Concerned with the Village Work of the Andhra Evangelical Lutheran Church in South India.* New York University, 1954. 90, 144 p. Abstract in *Dissertation Abstracts,* Vol. 15, p. 635-636, April 1955. Available on microfilm from University Microfilms, Ann Arbor, Michigan, as Publication No. 10,675.

1895. NELSON, FLORA BINA, 1913- . *A Philosophical Approach to the Development of Physical Education Programs for Women in India.* New York University, 1950. 221 p. ms. Abstract in *Microfilm Abstracts,* Vol. 11, No. 1, p. 145-147, 1951. Available on microfilm from University Microfilms, Ann Arbor, Michigan, as Publication No. 2,191.

1896. NORONHA, GEORGE ERIC, 1904- . *Backgrounds in the Education of Indian Girls.* Catholic University of America, 1940. Washington: Catholic University of America (but printed in India by Glasgow Printing Co., Howrah), 1939. 237 p. (Note: "The present dissertation was completed in 1936. Its printing was delayed to enable the author, after his return to India, to study conditions at first hand and to make such revisions as seemed advisable.")

1897. OLCOTT, MASON, 1893- . *Village Schools and Teachers in India.* Columbia University, 1926. Calcutta: Association Press, 1926. xi, 235 p. Also published as *Village Schools in India: An Investigation, with Suggestions.* With Foreword by Daniel Johnson Fleming. Calcutta: Association Press, 1926. xi, 235 p. Also published as *Better Village Schools: A Program of Action, Being a Third Edition of Village Schools in India, Completely Rewritten.* Calcutta: YMCA Publishing House, 1937. v, 224 p. (The Education of India Series.)

1898. OSGOOD, WILLIAM CYRIL, 1902- . *An Adult Education Program for Orissa, India.* Oregon State College, 1947. Corvallis, Oregon: 1950. vi, 118 p. (Oregon State Monographs: Studies in Education and Guidance, No. 4.) For master's thesis by same author, see No. 2058.

1899. PANDYA, THAKORLAL RANCHHODLAL, 1881-1918. *Education in Baroda.* Columbia University, 1916. Bombay: Printed by Maneckjee Nowrojee and Published by T. R. Pandya, near Kothi, Raopura, Baroda, 1915. xxvi, 179 p. For master's thesis by same author, see No. 2063.

1900. PARIKH, ARVIND KUMAR, 1925- . *The Role of Craft in Basic Education in India.* Indiana

University, 1958. 129 p. ms. Abstract in Indiana University: *Studies in Education*, 1958 (Thesis Abstract Series, No. 10, 1959), p. 63-70. Abstract also in *Dissertation Abstracts*, Vol. 19, p. 2297, March 1959. Available on microfilm from University Microfilms, Ann Arbor, Michigan, as Mic. 58-5211.

1901. PAUL, MANUEL DEVAVARAM, 1913- . *Proposals for the Improvement of the Preparation of Teachers for Secondary Schools of the State of Madras, with Special Reference to the Teachers College, Saidapet.* Columbia University, 1951. 189 p. ms.

1902. PAVAMANI, VICTOR GEORGE MARTIN. *Community Colleges for India.* University of Washington, 1957. 459 p. ms. Abstract in *Dissertation Abstracts*, Vol. 17, p. 1943-1944, September 1957. Available on microfilm from University Microfilms, Ann Arbor, Michigan, as Publication No. 22,181.

1903. QURAISHI, RUKNUDDIN AHMAD, 1910- . *An Application to Hyderabad State of Certain Principles and Practices in the Preparation and Certification of School Administrators in the United States.* Cornell University, 1948. 313 p. ms.

1904. RAICHUR, SUNDERRAJ SATHIANATHAN, 1908- . *Religion in Public Education in India.* Boston University, 1949. 240 p. ms. Abstract in Council on Graduate Studies in Religion: *Doctoral Dissertations in the Field of Religion, 1940-1952*, p. 150. Abstract also in *Religious Education*, Vol. 45, p. 112-113, March-April, 1950.

1905. RIBEIRO, LYRA deRANGEL. *Mass Adult Education for a Rural India.* Harvard University, 1945. 234 p. ms.

1906. ROCKEY, CLEMENT DANIEL. *A Curriculum for Village Christians of the Western Part of the United Provinces, India.* University of Chicago, 1929. 378 p. ms. Abstract in University of Chicago: *Abstracts of Theses, Humanistic Series*, Vol. 8, 1929-30, p. 573-576. For master's thesis by same author, see No. 2083.

1907. ROY, BINAPINI. *The Philosophical Problem of Modern Indian Higher Education.* Harvard University, 1949. 223 p. ms.

1908. SALDANHA, MARY AGNES, 1908- . *The Widening of Higher Educational Opportunity in India in the Light of American Theory and Practice.* Syracuse University, 1957. 189 p. ms. Abstract in *Dissertation Abstracts*, Vol. 19, p. 2031-2032, February 1959. Available on microfilm from University Microfilms, Ann Arbor, Michigan, as Mic. 58-2307.

1908a. SANDHU, JAGJIT KAUR. *Implications for the Punjab State Found in Selected Professional Education Programs for the Preparation of Secondary School Teachers in the United States.* Ohio State University, 1958. 271 p. ms. Abstract in *Dissertation Abstracts*, 19: 2291-2292, March 1959. Available on microfilm from University Microfilms, Ann Arbor, Michigan, as Mic. 59-421.

1909. SATVEDI, HAMILTON GOVINDJI, 1916- . *A Comparative Study of Certain Phases of Basic Education in India and Elementary Education in the United States.* Ohio State University, 1956. 2 vols. 491 p. ms. Abstract in *Dissertation Abstracts*, Vol. 17, p. 1012-1013, May 1957. Available on microfilm from University Microfilms, Ann Arbor, Michigan, as Publication No. 20,717.

1910. SHAH, LALIT KUMAR. *Education and National Consciousness in India.* University of Chicago, 1928. 270 p. ms. Abstract in University of Chicago: *Abstracts of Theses* . . . Vol. 7, 1929, p. 669-673. For master's theses by same author, see No. 2095 and 2096.

1911. SHANNON, WINIFRED. *A Euthenics Program Suitable for the Junior-Senior Level of Women's Colleges in India and for the B.A. Requirements of the Board of Examiners of Lucknow University, United Provinces.* Columbia University, 1941. 284 p. ms.

1912. SHANTHAMALLAPPA, BASAVA LINGAIA, 1918- . *A Plan for the Development of Vocational Education in the State of Mysore, India.* University of Michigan, 1950. 208 p. ms. Abstract in *Microfilm Abstracts*, Vol. 10, No. 2, p. 54-55, 1950. Abstract also in *Research in Industrial Education, 1930-1955*, p. 69-70. Available on microfilm from University Microfilms, Ann Arbor, Michigan, as Publication No. 1,585.

1913. SHARMA, GYAN CHAND, 1901- . *Early Brahminic Education: An Historical Monograph on the Ancient Indian Education.* University of Notre Dame, 1926. 59 p. ms.

1914. SHEPHERD, FLORENCE MILDRED, 1916- . *English Written Usage in Selected High Schools in India and America.* George Peabody College for Teachers, 1949. Nashville, Tennessee: George Peabody College for Teachers, 1951. ix, 80 p. (George Peabody College for Teachers, Contributions to Education, No. 421.)

1915. SHILOTRI, PRABHAKER S., 1883- . *Indo-Aryan Thought and Culture and Their Bearing on Present Day Problems of India: An Argument from the Standpoint of a Native of That Country.* Columbia University, 1913. New York: Evening Post Job Printing Office, 1913. 81 p.

1916. SHRIDEVI, SRIPATI, 1912- . *The Development of Women's Higher Education in India.* Columbia University, 1954. 380 p. ms. Abstract in *Dissertation Abstracts*, Vol. 14, p. 1989-1990, November 1954. Available on microfilm from University Microfilms, Ann Arbor, Michigan, as Publication No. 10,184. ("This dissertation was completed and approved in 1949. The number of affiliated colleges for women has increased materially since then." — Author)

1917. SHRIMALI, KALULAL, 1909- . *The Wardha Scheme: The Gandhian Plan of Education for Rural India.* Columbia University, 1950. Udaipur, Rajasthan, India: Vidya Bhawan Society, 1949. xviii, 308 p.

1918. SIDDALINGAIYA, MOOGANAYKANKOTE, 1895- . *Reconstructing Elementary Education in Mysore, India.* Columbia University, 1935. Mysore City, India: Mysore Section, The New Education Fellowship, Wesley Press and Publishing House, 1935. xv, 211 p. With Foreword by N. S. Subra Rao, Director of Public Instruction, Mysore. Also published in Mysore City, India: Crown Electric Press, 1932, 158 p. with title in English and Kanarese, but text in Kanarese.

India

1919. SIDHANTA, RANJANA, 1924- . *A Study of Basic Concepts Relating to India.* State University of Iowa, 1950. 299 p. ms. Abstract in State University of Iowa: *Doctors Dissertations . . . 1949 through 1952,* p. 328. (Studies concepts of India as found in 70 social studies textbooks recommended by 90 Indian, British, and American scholars.)

1920. SIDHU, HITWANT, 1927- . *A Two-Year Undergraduate Professional Physical Education Curriculum for a Proposed College of Physical Education for Men in India.* Indiana University, 1957. 222 p. ms.

1921. SINGH, RAM KARAN. *Communal Educational Institutions in India and Their Influence.* Harvard University, 1939. 482 p. ms.

1921a. STEVDI, HAMILTON GOVINDIJI. *A Comparative Study of Certain Phases of Basic Education in India and Elementary Education in the United States.* Ohio State University, 1957.

1921b. SUDERSHANAN, RATNA. *A Study of In-Service Teacher Education of Secondary School Teachers in Andra Pradesh State, India.* Indiana University, 1958. Abstract in Indiana University: *Studies in Education,* 1958 (Thesis Abstract Series, No. 10, 1959), p. 321-326.

1922. TAKHT SINGH, PRITAM, 1904- . *An Experience-Based Teacher Education Programme: An Educational Experiment of India.* Columbia University, 1954. 154 p. ms.

1923. TANEJI, VIDYA BHUSHAN, 1917- . *The Construction and Standardization of an Achievement Test in Algebra for Ninth Grade Students in the High Schools of the Punjab State, India.* Columbia University, 1955. 156 p. ms.

1924. THOBURN, ISABELLA. *Reconstructing Education in India.* Western Reserve University, 1941. 210 p. ms.

1925. ULLAH, SALAMAT, 1913- . *A Scheme for the Reorganization of the Examination System of Elementary and Secondary Schools in India.* Columbia University, 1948. 134 p. ms.

1926. UPADHYAY, SHAMBHU NATH. *The Reconstruction of Teacher Education in Uttar Pradesh.* Harvard University, 1955. 235 p. ms.

1927. VAKHARIA, PARIN HORMASJI, 1923- . *Some Problems of Child Care in India: The Influence of Cultural and Social Conditions on Indian Children.* New School for Social Research, 1950. 156 p. ms.

1928. VARKI VARKI, KODIYAT, 1915- . *The Reorganization of Physical Education in the Secondary Schools of India.* Columbia University, 1951. 192 p. ms.

1929. VINCENT, ANTONIO MANSING. *A Comparative Study of Secondary Education in India and the United States of America from 1900 to 1956.* University of Texas, 1957. 350 p. ms. Abstract in *Dissertation Abstracts,* Vol. 18, p. 460-461, February 1958. Available on microfilm from University Microfilms, Ann Arbor, Michigan, as Publication No. 25,181.

1930. WALTER, GLADYS, 1910- . *Education of Girls in India under the Methodist Church.* Columbia University, 1950. 191 p. ms. Abstract in *Teachers College Record,* Vol. 52, p. 386-387, March 1951.

1931. WARDWELL, WAYNE DORAN, 1897- . *An Educational Program for Technical High Schools in India.* Ohio State University, 1950. 358 p. ms. Abstract in Ohio State University: *Abstracts of Dissertations . . . Spring Quarter, 1949-50,* p. 369-374. (Abstracts of Doctoral Dissertations, No. 63). Abstract also in *Research in Industrial Education, 1930-1955,* p. 71.

1932. WILLIAMS, FREDERICK GLADSTONE. *Foundations of a Functional Curriculum for Rural Schools in Western Bengal.* Columbia University, 1937. 362 p. ms.

1933. YALE, JOHN RICHARD, 1913- . *The Guru Principle in Indian Education.* University of Southern California, 1952. 336 p. ms. Abstract in University of Southern California: *Abstracts of Dissertations,* 1952, p. 310-314.

1934. ZELLNER, AUBREY ALBERT JOHN, 1910- . *A History of Education in the Lower Ganges River Area of India from 1858 to 1948.* State University of Iowa, 1948. 343 p. ms. Abstract in State University of Iowa: *Doctors Dissertations . . . 1942 through 1948,* p. 352-356. For master's thesis by same author, see No. 2132.

See also Nos. 127, 129, 136, 137, 138, 142, 143, 144, 147, 157, 162, 163, 164, 168, 169, 174, 176, 179, 181, 182, 1302

MASTERS

1935. ADAMS, EDWARD BRADFORD. *British Administration of Education in India.* Columbia University, 1905. 33 p. ms.

1936. AMOLIK, KUMARI VASANTIKA. *Developing Good Citizenship Education in High Schools in India.* George Peabody College for Teachers, 1954. 157 p. ms.

1937. ANDREWS, LOIS LENORE. *A History of Education in the Bombay Presidency, India, under the British Administration.* University of Chicago, 1925. 189 p. ms.

1938. ARUNACHALAM, KANDASWAMY. *School and Community Relations in the United States with Implications for Education in India.* State University of Iowa, 1952. 56 p. ms.

1939. BALLENGER, MAURICE GUILD. *Housing the Boys' Community Middle School in Arrah, India.* University of Southern California, 1928. 73 p. ms.

1940. BARPUTE, HARI V. *A Program of Physical Education for the Elementary Schools in India.* International YMCA College, 1950. 200 p. ms.

1941. BARPUTE, MIRA. *Professional Training in Physical Education for Women in India.* International YMCA College, 1950. 116 p. ms.

1942. BENJAMIN, CHELIKUZHIEL THOMAS. *The Christian College Teacher of English Literature in India: A Study in Background and Role.* Princeton Theological Seminary, 1957. 98 p. ms.

1943. BERNHEISEL, MARY LOUISE. *British Influence in the Development of Indian Education, 1813-1858.* University of Wisconsin, 1943. 73 p. ms.

1944. BHAGAT, KANTILAL PREMCHAND. *Religion on the Campus of Ahmednagar College.* Andover Newton Theological School, 1952. 60 p. ms. (Thesis for degree of Bachelor of Divinity.)

1945. BHAMBAL, REBECCA, 1914- . *A Study of Some Selected Programs in the United States of America in Parent Education with Special Reference to Their Usefulness to India.* Syracuse University, 1956. 145 p. ms.

1946. BHUSARI, INDUMATI. *Use of Films in Physical Education and an Athletic Film Guide of U.S.A. Films, Suitable for Secondary Schools in India.* International YMCA College, 1950. 123 p. ms.

1947. BIDDLE, LOIS GRACE, 1923- . *A Training Program in the Teaching of Health and Sanitation for Village Church Workers in India.* Cornell University, 1955. 186 p. ms.

1948. BOSE, AROTI. *The Position of Hindu Women in Bengal Today.* Columbia University, 1948. 79 p. ms. (Includes position in education.)

1949. BOSE, GUNENDRA NATH. *A Study of the Program for Vocational Rehabilitation of the Deaf in the United States and a Tentative Outline of a Similar Program for the Deaf in India.* Gallaudet College, 1952. 70 p. ms.

1950. BRAISTED, PAUL JUDSON, 1903- . *Alexander Duff as an Educator.* New York University, 1927. 73 p. ms. For doctoral dissertation by same author, see No. 1830.

1951. BRANDON, NANCY ADDALINE. *Changing Aspects of Rural Education in the Punjab.* Kennedy School of Missions, 1939. 141 p. ms.

1952. BRAUER, RICHARD HENRY. *Trends in Secondary Education of the Madras Presidency, Southern India.* University of Oklahoma, 1932. 107 p. ms. Abstract in University of Oklahoma: *Abstracts of Theses . . . 1932.* p. 53-54.

1953. BRUCE, CLARA HARDING. *The Place of Christian Education in the Development of the Indian Woman.* University of Chicago, 1916. 65 p. ms.

1954. CAMPBELL, MARY. *Education of Girls in India.* University of Washington, 1927. 85 p. ms.

1955. CASSADY, MELVIN A. *A Proposed Guidance Services Program for Use in Irwin Christian High School, Kolhapur, India.* University of Tennessee, 1956. 140 p. ms.

1956. CHAKRAVARTY, HARMANTI. *Establishment and Growth of British Education in Bengal.* Howard University, 1949. 120 p. ms.

1957. CHANDRA, SHYAM. *The Development of Physical Education in India.* International YMCA College, 1949. 95 p. ms.

1958. CHEPPANALIL, A. GEORGE. *Education in India as Related to the Needs of the Community.* Rutgers University, 1958.

1959. CLARK, ROBERT MAURICE. *The Use of Non-Christian Terms in Christian Teaching in the Primitive Church and in the Present Day Church in India.* Columbia University, 1942. 198 p. ms.

1960. CLEVELAND, ROZALINE JEAN. *Problems and Progress in the Development of Girls' Education in India.* Butler University, 1952.

1961. CLINTON, EMMA LAHUNA. *A Study of the Vocabulary of Written Work in Government and Mission High Schools in India.* State University of Iowa, 1925. 154 p. ms.

1962. COLONY, LUCILE. *A Proposed Program for the Teaching of Health in Elementary Schools in India.* State University of Iowa, 1929. 87 p. ms.

1963. COOMARASWAMY, DONA LUISA, 1905- . *A Summary of Values in Hindu Education and Philosophy.* Boston University, 1951. 104 p. ms.

1964. CROUSE, MARGARET DIBERT, 1876- . *The Significance for Mission Schools of the Educational Policy of the Indian Provincial Councils.* Boston University, 1922. 67 p. ms.

1965. CUMMINGS, JAMES BEVERIDGE. *Teaching Bible to the Non-Christian College Students of the Punjab.* New York University, 1930. 132 p. ms.

1966. CURRIE, ANNE ELIZABETH. *Standards for Short Term Schools for Christian Women of the Villages of the Punjab Province, India.* University of Washington, 1939. 89 p. ms. Abstract in University of Washington: *Abstracts of Theses,* Vol. 4, 1939, p. 65.

1967. CURRIMBHOY, ALLAN EBRAHIM. *The Production and Distribution of Educational Films in India.* Columbia University, 1948. 87 p. ms.

1968. DANTYAGI, SUSHEELA. *An Exploration of Factors to Be Considered in Developing a Post-Graduate Program of Teacher Education in Home Science in the Lady Irwin College, New Delhi, India.* University of Tennessee, 1958.

1969. DAS, RADHA CHARAN, 1925- . *Some Basic Considerations for the Development of Industrial Education in Orissa, India.* Cornell University, 1948. 127 p. ms. Abstract in *Research in Industrial Education, 1930-1955,* p. 362.

1970. DASKAWIE, M. ABDUL QAYYAM. *Nationalism and Education in India.* New York University, 1931. 162 p. ms.

1971. DAVIES, HILDA JOAN, 1911- . *Christian Education for Village Women in Central India.* Eastern Baptist Theological Seminary, 1948. 86 p. ms.

1972. DEASE, MARGARET EVELYN. *Christian Education in the Province of Agra and Oudh.* University of Chicago, 1920. 29 p. ms.

1973. DEB, MAYA, 1929- . *Education for Elementary Teachers in India, with Recommendations Based on Trends in Teacher Education in the United States.* Smith College, 1950. 141 p. ms.

1974. DESAI, MADHURI. *A Proposed Plan for Secondary Schools in India.* San Francisco State College, 1957. 79 p. ms.

1975. DE SOUZA, Rev. ANTHONY PASCAL. *A Critical Study of Mahatma Gandhi's Educational Theories.* Catholic University of America, 1954. 75 p. ms. Abstract in *Catholic Educational Review*, Vol. 54, p. 192, March 1956.

1976. DEULKAR, DURGA, 1914- . *An Approach to Teaching in the Basic Schools of India with Special Reference to Home Economics.* Syracuse University, 1956. 192 p. ms. For doctoral dissertation by same author, see No. 1849.

1977. DEVADAS, RAJAMMEL PACKIYANATHAN. *Proposals for a Four-Year Teacher Education Program in Home Economics for India.* Ohio State University, 1949. 213 p. ms.

1978. DHAR, VIOLET CHANDRAVATI. *The Pupil-Teacher Relationships with Special Reference to India.* George Peabody College for Teachers, 1952. 88 p. ms.

1979. DONALD, SHALINI SALVE. *Some Proposals for Changing Secondary Education in India to Promote Democracy.* Ohio State University, 1954. 140 p. ms.

1980. DUEWEL, WESLEY LUELF. *The Implications of the Socio-Economic Background of the Christian Community in India for the Non-Theological Course Offerings in the Allahabad Bible Seminary.* University of Cincinnati, 1949. 171 p. ms.

1981. EAPEN, CHAVADIYIL THOMAS. *Nationalization of Indian Education.* New York University, 1924. 45 p. ms. For doctoral dissertation by same author, see No. 1853.

1982. EMBREE, AINSLIE THOMAS. *The Distinctive Contribution of the Christian Colleges in India.* Columbia University, 1947. 78 p. ms.

1983. EMBREE, SUZANNE HARPOLE. *Social Mobility in India: A Study of the Caste Origins of the Educational Elite in Northern India, in 1927 and 1952.* Columbia University, 1956. 135 p. ms.

1984. ENGEBRECHT, NORBERT RICHARD. *A Study of the Administrative Aspects of Primary Education for Boys in British India, 1917-1937.* Washington University, 1946. 92 p. ms.

1985. EWING, RAYMOND HOOD. *India — Its Educational System and the Educational Policy of the American Baptist Foreign Missionary Society.* University of Chicago, 1921. 49 p. ms.

1986. FAIRBANK, Mrs. MARIE LIVELY. *Study of Religious Education in India.* Kennedy School of Missions, 1926. 65 p. ms.

1987. FAWELL, WILLIAM CROSDALE. *A Plan of Secondary Education for Boys in India, Based on the Present Status of Secondary Education, the Social and Economic Factors Involved, and on Educational Experiments that Have Met with Some Success in India and in America.* University of Nebraska, 1926. 108 p. ms.

1988. FELT, NETTIE MAUDE. *The Education of the Aboriginal Tribes and Depressed Classes of India.* University of Southern California, 1913. 42 p. ms.

1989. FERNANDO, SINGARAYER. *Secondary Education in India and in the United States.* De Paul University, 1956. 129 p. ms.

1990. FORBES, JOSEPH MORRIS. *The Principles and Techniques for Developing a Curriculum for Christian Leaders in Assam, India.* University of Southern California, 1937. 91 p. ms.

1991. FORD, EDITH MARION. (Later Mrs. Asa Wright Melliger.) *The Education of Indian Women.* Boston University, 1923. 48 p. ms.

1992. GALE, ESTHER. *Education in India: A Discussion of the Problem of Universal, Compulsory, Free Education in the Light of the History and Religion of the Indian People.* Yale University, 1920. 159 p. ms.

1993. GERSHOM, BENJAMIN SMITH. *A Manual for Secondary School Dormitory Managers in India.* University of Southern California, 1953. 124 p. ms.

1994. GETTY, ORVILLE MITCHELL. *Agricultural Missions and Evangelism in India.* Berkeley Baptist Divinity School, 1954.

1995. GHOSH, P. K. *A Study of the American Student Y.M.C.A. and Proposed Adaptation to India.* George Williams College, 1955.

1996. GOGATE, RAJARAM VINAYAK, 1895- . *Caste as an Educational Problem.* University of California, Berkeley, 1922. 189 p. ms.

1997. GOOD, MARY MAGDALENE. *A Tentative Program of Study for the Garjan Memorial School.* George Peabody College for Teachers, 1936. 101 p. ms.

1998. GORDON, DEVAPRIAM S. *Educational Reconstruction in South India.* Columbia University, 1930. 33 p. ms.

1999. GORDON, WILFRED ERNEST. *The Moral Training of the Hindu Boy.* University of Chicago, 1918. 36 p. ms.

2000. GRIFFITHS, WALTER GERALDSON. *An Evaluation of the Indian Scriptures in Their Relation to Selected Principles of Mental Hygiene.* New York University, 1931. 109 p. ms.

2001. GUPTA, PROMILA. *The Role of Schools in the Present and Future Progressive Society of Punjab, India.* University of Illinois, 1958.

2002. HALDER, RAS MOHUN, 1905- . *Education as Guidance for Blind Boys in Bengal (Calcutta School for Blind Children, Calcutta, Bengal, India).* Boston University, 1933. 131 p. ms.

2003. HANNUM, ROBERT HENRY. *The Christian Message to the Educated Classes of India.* University of Chicago, 1928. 69 p. ms.

2004. HARI-NARAIN, ANUGRAH, 1900- . *Curriculum Revision in American Schools with Special*

Applications to the Schools of India. Smith College, 1929. 79 p. ms.

2005. HARPER, IRENE MASON. *New Emphases for Religious Education in Christian Elementary Schools in India.* Columbia University, 1924. 44 p. ms.

2006. HAZLETT, CALVIN HOFFMAN. *A Study of Composition and Grammar Needs in Ewing Christian College, Allahabad, India.* University of Pittsburgh, 1932. 65 p. ms. Abstract in University of Pittsburgh: *Abstracts of Theses . . .* Vol. 8, 1932, p. 335-336.

2007. HEINS, CONRAD PHILIP. *A Study of the Application of Progressive Education Principles in Three Educational Experiments in India.* Columbia University, 1942. 57 p. ms.

2008. HILL, THOMAS BENJAMIN. *Progress of Education in India.* Clark University, 1918. 197 p. ms.

2009. HODSON, JANET EDNA. *A Partial Survey of Adult Education in America and Some Principles of Adult Education for India.* Kansas State Teachers College, Emporia, 1938. 126 p. ms.

2010. HOFFMEISTER, MILDRED, 1903- . *Primary Education in the Punjab Province of India.* Southern Methodist University, 1938. 210 p. ms. Abstract in Southern Methodist University: *Abstracts of Theses,* No. 6, 1939, p. 14-15.

2011. HOLLAND, OPAL L. *A Course of Study in Arithmetic for the First Three Standards in the Gadra, India, Primary Schools.* University of Southern California, 1948. 100 p. ms.

2012. HOLLOWOOD, MARGARET FRANCES, 1914- . *A Vacation School Course for Intermediates in Buram, Assam, Bengal-Orissa, South India.* Eastern Baptist Theological Seminary, 1940. 186 p. ms.

2013. ISAIAH, SUGANTHY. *The Reorganization of Rural Education in India.* Columbia University, 1940. 58 p. ms.

2014. JAMES, ELLEN JEMINA. *The Development of Science Instruction in the Secondary Schools of Madras Presidency, South India, from 1920 to the Present Day.* Ohio State University, 1953. 167 p. ms.

2015. JOHN, THARAYIL THARIYAN, 1910- . *Christian Education in India: How to Make It More Effective.* Columbia University, 1952. 35 p. ms. For doctoral dissertation by same author, see No. 1869.

2016. JOSEPH, KALAPPURAKAL DAVID, 1916- . *Developing Public Understanding about the Social and Educational Problems of the Blind in India.* Boston University, 1956. 81 p. ms.

2017. KALATHIVEETIL, THERESA K., 1928- . *An Analysis of the Problem of Illiteracy in India.* Loyola University, 1954. 115 p. ms. For doctoral dissertation by same author, see No. 1870.

2018. KANDARADALLY, JOSEPH. *A Program of Guidance for the Typical Catholic Secondary School in Kerala State, India.* Marquette University, 1958.

2019. KAUL, JAGAN NATH, 1920- . *The Place of Craft and Self-Sufficiency in Indian Basic Education.* University of Michigan, 1953. 85 p. ms. For doctoral dissertation by same author, see No. 1871.

2020. KEANS, LENA ALBERTA. *A Unit of Study for Telugu Adolescents.* Hartford School of Religious Education, 1936. 72 p. ms.

2021. KENNEDY, CATHERINE DAVIDSON. *Macaulay and Western Education in India.* Columbia University, 1927. 63 p. ms.

2022. KHANNA, SUNANDAN. *Basic Education in India.* American University, 1957. 46 p. ms.

2023. KIMBALL, Mrs. LORNA JEAN (THOMAS). *A Critical Evaluation of Curricula in Use among Primary Age Children in the Marathi Mission Area of Western India.* Oberlin College, 1953. 136 p. ms.

2024. KING, BETTY MARIE. *Secondary and Higher Education for Women in India.* University of Southern California, 1937. 266 p. ms.

2025. KNOX, PUTTU LAL. *Policies Recommended for the Selection of Teachers in America and Their Application to India.* George Peabody College for Teachers, 1954. 113 p. ms.

2026. KOENIG, JOHN CHARLES. *A Comparative Study of the Vocabularies of Hindi Readers.* Washington University, 1934. 156 p. ms.

2027. KOILPILLAI, ROBINSON, 1923- . *The Impact of National Awakening on Primary and Secondary Education in India.* Pacific Union College, 1955. 87 p. ms.

2028. KUZHANDAVELU, KANDASWAMY. *Planning an Audio-Visual Center for a College of Education in India.* Ohio State University, 1954. 93 p. ms.

2029. LARSON, HELEN RUTH. *Materials for a Course in Child Psychology to Be Used for Teachers in the Mission Schools of India.* University of Nebraska, 1934. 125 p. ms.

2030. LEETE, WILLIAM ROOKWELL. *The Relation of Mysticism to Education in India.* Columbia University, 1912. 63 p. ms.

2031. LIDDLE, HARRY VICTOR, 1920- . *Rural Life in the Doon Valley.* Drake University, 1953. 82 p. ms. (Includes education.)

2032. LINDSEY, ELIZABETH PRENTISS, 1917- . *Education in India: A Study of Secondary and Higher Education of Women.* George Washington University, 1939. 77 p. ms.

2033. LYALL, JONATHAN CHARLES. *The Production and Use of Filmstrips in Fundamental Education in India.* Ohio State University, 1953. 128 p. ms.

2034. LYNGDOH, HOLLANDO, 1923- . *Toward a New Curriculum for the Khasi People.* Pacific University, 1952. 61 p. ms.

2035. McHENRY, WILLIAM JOSHUA, 1916- . *An Analysis of Four First-Year Marathi Reading Programs.* Pacific Union College, 1955. 106 p. ms.

2036. MAJUMDAR, PRASANTA SANKAR, 1923- *An Analytical Study of the Training Program of an Extension Training School in West Bengal, India, and Suggestions for Its Improvement.* Cornell University, 1956. 119 p. ms.

2037. MANGUM, RUTHA MYRTLE. *The Contribution of American Protestant Missions to Higher Education among the Women in India.* University of Southern California, 1925. 85 p. ms.

2038. MANIKAM, DOSS J. *Nationalism and Education in India.* Columbia University, 1930. 62 p. ms.

2039. MANLEY, MYRL OTIS, 1913- . *A Brief History of the Origin, Growth, and Organization of Seventh-Day Adventist Schools in the Northeast India Union.* Pacific Union College, 1948. 234 p. ms.

2040. MATHEW, MARIAM, 1905- . *The Problem of Women's Education in India.* New York University, 1932. 214 p. ms. For doctoral dissertation by same author, see No. 1887.

2041. MEHRA, LAL CHAND, 1897- . *The Arya Samaj as an Educational Movement.* University of California, Berkeley, 1925. 135 p. ms.

2042. MENON, N. PARAMESWARA. *A Program of Physical Education Activities for Senior High School Boys in Travancore, India.* International YMCA College, 1948. 394 p. ms.

2043. MENZEL, EMIL WOLFGANG. *A Tentative Standardization of the Goodenough Intelligence Test for Central Provinces, India.* Washington University, 1934. 94 p. ms.

2044. MIALIL, Rev. KURIAKOSE. *A Study of the Guidance Program in a Selected Number of Catholic Secondary Schools, with Special Reference to the Applicability of the Principles and Techniques to the Secondary Schools of the Travancore-Cochin State, India.* Catholic University of America, 1955. 90 p. ms. Abstract in *Catholic Educational Review*, Vol. 55, p. 554-555, November 1957.

2045. MILLER, ERNEST EDGAR. *The Problem of National Education in India.* New York University, 1929. 127 p. ms. For doctoral dissertation by same author, see No. 1888.

2046. MILLER, LOUISA A. *A Study of the Vocabulary of Beginning Readers in the Telegu Language.* State University of Iowa, 1928. 72 p. ms.

2047. MOFFAT, CODY S. *The Western Influence of Physical Education in India.* International YMCA College, 1950. 149 p. ms.

2048. MOOS, HOMAI JAL. *A Proposed Program for Using Audio-Visual Materials in Education in the State of Bombay, India.* Ohio State University, 1955. 127 p. ms.

2049. MOTT, IRENE. *An Outcaste Hindu Village, Its People and Problems and a Suggested Educational Program.* Columbia University, 1927. 203 p. ms.

2050. MOW, ANETTA CORDULA. *The Adaptation of Primary Missionary Education to the Needs of the Indian Village (with Special Reference to Baroda State.)* University of Chicago, 1932. 104 p. ms.

2051. MUKERJEE, RANO KANTO. *An Investigation into the Use of Mass Media for Religious Education in Rural India.* Ohio State University, 1952. 102 p. ms.

2052. NADKARNI, VATSALA MAHADEO. *A Functional Syllabus in Health for Secondary Schools in Bombay.* University of Southern California, 1951. 164 p. ms.

2053. NEGI, LAKSHMI SINGH. *Teaching for International Understanding between India and the United States.* University of Southern California, 1952. 77 p. ms.

2054. NELSON, CAROLINE CHRISTINE. *Superstitions and Fears of East Indian School Children.* University of Nebraska, 1930. 64 p. ms. (Based on twelve city schools in the United Provinces and Rajputana.)

2055. NICHOLS, EDWARD GENUNG. *Religious Education in Rural Churches in South India.* Union Theological Seminary, 1939. 90 p. ms.

2056. NICHOLSON, ELMER SAMUEL. *The Preparation of Elementary Teachers in Telugu Mission Schools.* University of Chicago, 1926. 80 p. ms.

2057. NOLTING, EDWARD L. *A Survey of the Academic and Voluntary Activities of the American College, Madura, India, with Suggestions for Further Developments.* Columbia University, 1933; Union Theological Seminary, 1933. 42 p. ms.

2058. OSGOOD, WILLIAM CYRIL, 1902- . *A Study of Some of the Problems Related to the Training of Elementary School Teachers in India.* Oregon State College, 1936. 202 p. ms. For doctoral dissertation by same author, see No. 1898.

2059. PALLIKUNNEN, EMMANUEL. *General Education and the New Indian Social Order.* De Paul University, 1958.

2060. PALMER, PEARL EDITH. *Real Education for Rural India.* Columbia University, 1941. 46 p. ms.

2061. PANDIT, HARSHIDA RAMU. *A Critical Appreciation of the Educational Philosophy of Mahatma Gandhi.* University of Southern California, 1957. 75 p. ms.

2062. PANDIT, KUMUDINI SADASHIVE. *Home Economics in the College Program in India.* Ohio State University, 1948. 141 p. ms.

2063. PANDYA, THAKORLAL RANCHHODLAL, 1881-1918. *Secondary Education in India.* Columbia University, 1910. 61 p. ms. For doctoral dissertation by same author, see No. 1899.

2064. PARDESHI, MANDAKINI G. *Major Problems of Secondary Education in the State of Bombay, India.* Ohio State University, 1954.

2065. PARKS, VERA ECHO. *A Course of Study in Home Economics for the Lal Bagh Girls High*

School, Lucknow, India. Purdue University, 1937. 154 p. ms.

2066. PATIAL, MAY EDITH, 1909- . *A Proposed Plan for the Organization and Administration of a Department of Audio-Visual Education in the Town of Lahore, India.* Boston University, 1949. 79 p. ms.

2067. PHILLIPS, LILY MOBLEY, 1928- . *American Baptist Missions in Bengal-Orissa.* Andover Newton Theological School, 1956. 101 p. ms. (Thesis for the degree of Bachelor of Divinity. Includes education.)

2068. PIMPALKHARE, MORESHWAR HARI. *A Study of the Guidance Procedures in the Secondary Schools of Bombay State, India.* Ohio State University, 1955. 117 p. ms.

2069. PRASAD, RAM L. *A Scientific Basis for Physical Education in Bihar, India.* University of Utah, 1958.

2070. PRECISE, ANNE ETHEL PEARL. *The History and Development of the Education for Girls and Women in North India under the Auspices of the Methodist Episcopal Church.* Boston University, 1922. 101 p. ms.

2071. PRENTICE, JOHN WILBUR. *A Financial Accounting System for Christian Colleges in India.* University of Chicago, 1933. 140 p. ms.

2072. PUSHPANATHAN, MIRABAI. *A Comparative Study of the Science Programmes in the Elementary Grades of the Practising Elementary Schools of the St. Christopher Training College, Madras, and the University School, Ohio State University.* Ohio State University, 1956. 69 p. ms.

2073. RAI, DORIS MONGOL, 1912- . *A Study of the Primary and Elementary Education in India.* George Washington University, 1946. 57 p. ms.

2074. RAJAMANICKAM, I. J., 1912- . *Reorganization of Secondary School Systems in Madras, South India.* Ohio State University, 1953. 195 p. ms. For another master's thesis by same author, see No. 2075.

2075. RAJAMANICKAM, I. J., 1912- . *The Curriculum of Religious Education in the Churches of the United States of America and of South India.* Drew University, 1954. 129 p. ms. For another master's thesis by same author, see No. 2074.

2076. RAMANJULU, VIOLET, 1921- . *Higher Education and Christian Leadership in the Telegu Baptist Area of South India.* Eastern Baptist Theological Seminary, 1950. 59 p. ms.

2077. RAMASESHAN, PADMINI HANNAH, 1926- *Secondary Education in the Madras State with Emphasis on Home Economics Education.* University of Kansas, 1955. 138 p. ms.

2078. RAVAL, SUSHILA N. *Basic Education in Modern India: A Critique of Gandhian Educational Philosophy.* American University, 1958. 67 p. ms.

2079. RAYMOND, Rev. STEPHEN P. *A Catholic Evaluation of Rabindranath Tagore's Educational Philosophy.* Catholic University of America, 1949. 73 p. ms.

2080. REDDY, DELICIA, 1908- . *Development of a Program of Home Economics Education for Mysore State, India.* Syracuse University, 1949. 285 p. ms.

2081. REDDY, EPHRAIM CHANNA, 1895- . *Suggestions for a Plan of Civic Education in the Secondary Schools of India.* Boston University, 1933. 113 p. ms.

2082. RICHARDS, GLADYS PEARL. *Suggestions for the Guidance of Teachers in Basic Schools of India.* George Peabody College for Teachers, 1954. 70 p. ms.

2083. ROCKEY, CLEMENT DANIEL. *A Course of Lessons for the Primary Department of a City Sunday School in India.* Northwestern University, 1921. 61 p. ms. For doctoral dissertation by same author, see No. 1906.

2084. ROGERS, MIRIAM EMMA. *The Charterhouse Program of Religious Education with Reference to Its Use in Sholapur, India.* Union Theological Seminary, 1945.

2085. ROYER, MARY NEUHOUSER. *Education of Village Children in a Central Province Mission, India.* George Peabody College for Teachers, 1931. 96 p. ms.

2086. SAGAR, WINNIE. *The Place of Christian Education in Changing India.* Asbury Theological Seminary, 1951.

2087. SAHAI, PREM NATH, 1928- . *Arithmetic Competences Possessed by Prospective Elementary Teachers of India.* Iowa State Teachers College, 1958. 72 p. ms.

2088. SAKSENA, BHUMIJA. *Achievement and Progress in Social (Adult) Education in India from 1947 to 1955.* American University, 1957.

2089. SAMUEL, GETSIE RATNABAI. *A Handbook on Human Relations for Teachers in South India.* University of Southern California, 1952. 109 p. ms.

2090. SANDHU, SURINDERJEET. *Developing a Guidance Program in India under the Leadership of Guidance Bureaus.* Fresno State College, 1957.

2091. SANFORD, ARTHUR LLOYD. *Christian Education for Youth in Bengal-Orissa.* Berkeley Baptist Divinity School, 1953. 101 p. ms.

2092. SAPRA, KRISHNA, 1925- . *A Proposed Program of Physical Education for the Women's Colleges of Delhi, India.* Smith College, 1955. 107 p. ms.

2093. SATAKOPOCHARI, PADMA. *A Study of Home and Community Practices of Pupils in Four High Schools in Tanjore, India, as a Basis for an Evaluation of the Home Science Curriculum.* Drexel Institute of Technology, 1952. 49 p. ms.

2094. SHAFI, RAFAT SAEED, 1923- . *A Plan for the Removal of Illiteracy through the Broad Use of Audio-Visual Education in Delhi State: A Preliminary Study for a Five-Year Program.* Boston University, 1955. 120 p. ms.

2095. SHAH, LALIT KUMAR. *Rural Education in India.* Butler College, 1925. For doctoral dissertation by same author, see No. 1910. For another master's thesis by same author, see No. 2096. For doctor's thesis by same author, see No. 1910.

2096. SHAH, LALIT KUMAR. *The Place of Education in Rural Economy in India.* University of Chicago, 1927. 199 p. ms. For doctoral dissertation by same author, see No. 1910. For another master's thesis by same author, see No. 2095. For doctor's thesis by same author, see No. 1910.

2097. SHANTAPPA, BABANNA, 1915- . *A Suggested Program of Guidance for Vijaya Vidyalaya, Deccan, India.* Boston University, 1949. 69 p. ms.

2098. SHANTHAPPA, PREMALATHA, 1925- . *Development of a Program for Home and Family Life Education for Hyderabad State, India.* Syracuse University, 1952. 221 p. ms.

2099. SHASTRY, SHOMINATH, 1903- . *The Development of a Suggested Elementary School Curriculum for Village Schools of Bengal, India.* Southern Methodist University, 1934. 56 p. ms. Abstract in Southern Methodist University: *Abstracts of Master's Theses,* No. 3, 1936, p. 20-21.

2100. SHAW, AGNES. *Adapting American Reading Techniques to Teaching English in India.* George Peabody College for Teachers, 1952. 791 p. ms.

2101. SHAW, GEORGE JACOB. *The Educational Outlook for India.* Syracuse University, 1922.

2102. SHELDON, MABEL. *Vitalizing the Primary School Curriculum in the Village Schools of India.* Kansas State Teachers College, Pittsburg, 1934. 193 p. ms.

2103. SHIPSTONE, CLARICE. *Parent-Teacher Education for India.* George Peabody College for Teachers, 1954. 135 p. ms.

2104. SHODHAN, NEELA G. *A Study of the UNESCO Program in Fundamental Education with Specific Reference to its Implications for India.* University of California, Los Angeles, 1952. 138 p. ms.

2105. SIMONS, LAO GENEVRA. *Characteristics of Hindu Education and the Bearing of These on Hindu Mathematics.* Columbia University, 1912. 38 p. ms.

2106. SINGH, HARINDER KAPUR. *A Guide-Education of Women in the Punjab, India.* Adelphi College, 1955. 43 p. ms.

2107. SLEETH, EULA HUTCHISON. *The History of the Educational Work of the Presbyterian Church of America in India.* University of Chicago, 1921. 114 p. ms.

2108. SLIFER, LUTHER WALTER. *The Work of the American Evangelical Lutheran Mission of Guntur, India.* Columbia University, 1922. 25 p. ms.

2109. SOLOMON, GNANAMANI. *The Value of the Popular Literature of India for Religious Education.* University of Chicago, 1925. 95 p. ms.

2110. SOLOMON, REGIBURT J. *The Distinctive Tasks of the YMCA in India.* George Williams College, 1954.

2111. SOURI, JAYARAJAH D. *The Village Teaching-Catechist in India: His Task in Adult Education* Columbia University, 1941. 38 p. ms.

2112. STEEVES, JOHN MILTON. *The Present Status of Education in the United Provinces of Agra and Oudh in British India.* University of Washington, 1936. 73 p. ms. Abstract in University of Washington: *Abstracts of Theses,* Vol. 2, August 1937, p. 97-99.

2113. STONER, SUSAN LAVINIA. *An Evaluation of, and Suggestions for, an Integrated Program of Religious Education for Woodstock School, Mussourie, U.P., India.* University of Southern California, 1935. 131 p. ms.

2114. STOVER, WILBUR BRENNAN. *An Historical Study of the Curriculum in the Elementary Schools of Bombay Presidency, India.* Northwestern University, 1922. 102 p. ms.

2115. STRANLER, MILTON WEBSTER. *Reorganization of Elementary Education in India.* University of Chicago, 1922. 68 p. ms.

2116. SUBBUKRISHNAIYA, EPPAGUNTA. *The Significance of Trends in Modern Religious Education for the Hindus.* University of Chicago, 1933. 89 p. ms.

2117. SUGANTHY, ISAIAH. *The Reorganization of Rural Education in India.* Columbia University, 1940. 61 p. ms.

2118. TAIT, MARION JESSIE. *A Survey of the Education of Women in Assam, India.* University of Chicago, 1929. 113 p. ms.

2119. UPADHYAYA, HARCHARAN LAL. *The Significance of Vocational and Apprenticeship Training in the Industrialization of India.* University of Wisconsin, 1956. 158 p. ms.

2120. VAN DOREN, ALICE B. *Teacher Training and Extension Work for Village Schools in India.* Columbia University, 1930. 40 p. ms.

2121. VARNEY, W. DREW. *Enriching the Program of the American Baptist Mission Training School, Bapatla, India.* Columbia University, 1938. 52 p. ms.

2122. VEDANAGAGAM, EDITH. *A New Set-up of Guidance and Testing Program for High Schools in Madras State, India.* University of Redlands, 1958.

2123. VENUGOPAL, KALIDOSS, 1908- . *Development of a Course of Study in Extension Education for Undergraduates at the Osmania Agricultural College, Hyderabad, India.* Cornell University, 1957. 195 p. ms.

2124. VICKLAND, ELLEN ELIZABETH. *The Nationalization of Education in India.* University of Chicago, 1934. 179 p. ms.

2125. VISHNOI, SHANKER LAL, 1909- . *An Analysis of Current Research in Major Phases of Extension Education in the United States of America, with Suggested Application in Madhya, India.* Cornell University, 1955. 188 p. ms.

2126. WAGNER, MABEL BURDETTE. *The North Indian Village and the New Missions.* Drew University, 1937. 210 p. ms. (Includes consideration of education.

2127. WARNER, MARIAN. *The Preparation of a Handbook for Housefathers and Matrons of Boarding School Hostels in India.* State University of Iowa, 1943. 133 p. ms.

2128. WHITING, ETHEL LUTITIA. *A Study of the Factors Influencing the Development of Schools for Girls in British India, from the Beginning of Western Influence to the Present Time.* University of Nebraska, 1926. 82 p. ms.

2129. WHITTLE, MARY ATKINSON. *British Educational Policy in India since 1858.* Columbia University, 1917. 47 p. ms.

2130. WINDHAM, MILTON E. *Agricultural Missions and Reconstruction: A Survey and a Tentative Program for Assam.* Berkeley Baptist Divinity School, 1953. (Thesis for degree of Bachelor of Divinity.)

2131. WOODS, BEULAH MAE. *An Application to Rural India of Methods of Educating Backward Peoples Developed at Hampton Institute and in the Philippines.* University of Chicago, 1923. 85 p. ms.

2132. ZELLNER, AUBREY ALBERT JOHN, 1910- . *Backgrounds for a Study of Education in the Lower Ganges River Valley of India.* State University of Iowa, 1947. 141 p. ms. For doctoral dissertation by same author, see No. 1934.

2133. ZIMMERMAN, CHRISTIE ELEANOR. *A Study of Worship in the Higher Elementary Schools of the United Lutheran Church Mission in India, with Suggestions for Its Improvement.* Biblical Seminary in New York, 1936. 144 p. ms.

See also Nos. 193, 195, 198, 211, 216, 221, 225, 226, 228, 238, 239, 250, 263, 267, 268, 275, 301, 303, 304, 308, 1305, 1312, 1314, 1315, 1316, 1319, 1320, 1333

For Indian groups in the United States *see* Nos. 5114-5115

Indonesia
(NOS. 2134 – 2140)

DOCTOR

2134. EDWARDS, WILLARD MARSH McILVAIN. *A Concentrated Educational Program to Facilitate the Transition of Technology for Officials of an Underdeveloped Country.* University of Colorado, 1954. 339 p. ms. (Refers to Indonesia.)

See also Nos. 138, 147, 176, 179

MASTERS

2135. BERTRAM, LEON HENRY, 1928- . *The Movement for Independence in the Republic of Indonesia.* Texas College of Arts and Industries, 1956. 116 p. ms. (Includes education.)

2136. CHOW, MOSES C. B. *Education in the New Republic of Indonesia.* Columbia Bible College, 1958.

2137. DENYES, MARY ELIZABETH. *Racial Characteristics and Social Conditions Fundamental in a Program of Religious Education for the Pakag Batlaks of Sumatra.* Northwestern University, 1922. 88 p. ms.

2138. LOMMEN, HENRY L. *A Critical Analysis of the Official Indonesian Government Program for the Training of Secondary School Teachers.* Catholic University of America, 1958.

2139. MARDIAH, 1918- . *Proposals for In-Service Training of Home Economics Teachers in Indonesia.* Syracuse University, 1958. (No first name given in vita included with the thesis.)

2140. NASUTION, SORIMUDA. *Suggestions for the Improvement of the Elementary School Curriculum in Indonesia.* Ohio State University, 1956. 152 p. ms.

See also Nos. 226, 239, 275, 308, 1305, 1313, 1322

Iran
(NOS. 2141 – 2166)

DOCTORS

2141. ABADI, AHMAD KHAN ALI. *Higher Education in Iran: Its Evolution, Its Trends, and Plans for Its Improvement.* New York University, 1939. 155 p. ms. Abstract in New York University, School of Education: *Abstracts of Theses*, October 1938-June 1939, p. 101-105.

2142. AFZAL, MANUCHEHR, 1920- . *The Cultural Setting of the Problems of Teacher Training in Iran.* Columbia University, 1956. 354 p. ms. Abstract in *Dissertation Abstracts*, Vol. 16, p. 1234, July 1956. Available on microfilm from University Microfilms, Ann Arbor, Michigan, as Publication No. 16,797.

2143. BANAI, HOSSEIN, 1911- . *The Formulation and Validation of Operational Principles for a National Program of Physical Education for Iran.* New York University, 1953. 4 vols. 761 p. ms. Abstract in *Dissertation Abstracts*, Vol. 14, p. 294-295, February 1954. Available on microfilm from University Microfilms, Ann Arbor, Michigan, as Publication No. 7,125.

2144. BOYCE, ARTHUR CLIFTON, 1884- . *The Comparison of Two Forms of Persian Writing by Means of Scales Constructed and Standardized for the Purpose.* University of Chicago, 1933. 81 p. ms. A private edition (81 p. photolithographed) was distributed to libraries in the United States and abroad in 1933.

2145. EKRAMI, ABBAS M., 1912- . *A Program for the Improvement of Elementary Education in Iran.* University of Minnesota, 1953. 423 p. ms. Abstract in *Dissertation Abstracts,* Vol. 14, p. 488-489, March 1954. Available on microfilm from University Microfilms, Ann Arbor, Michigan, as Publication No. 7,224.

2146. FARYAR, ABDOLLAH, 1910- . *A Suggested Policy for Administrative Reorganization of Rural Education in Iran.* Columbia University, 1956. 286 p. ms.

2147. HARDING, Mrs. PARVIN KHALATBARI, 1922- . *A Plan for In-Service Education of Teachers in Iran.* Columbia University, 1949. 183 p. ms.

2148. HOOSHMAND, FATOOLLAH AMIR, 1903- (Amir-Hushmand, Aath-Allah in Library of Congress card catalog). *An Analysis of Child Welfare and Training in Iran, with Proposals for Their Development.* University of Pittsburgh, 1939. 216 p. ms. Abstract in University of Pittsburgh: *Abstracts of Theses . . .* Vol. 15, 1939, p. 120-124.

2149. JALALI-SHIRAZI, MEHDI, 1909- . *Education in Iran and Some Suggestions for Its Betterment.* University of Pittsburgh, 1938. 222 p. ms. Abstract in University of Pittsburgh: *Abstracts of Theses . .* Vol. 14, 1938, p. 160-169.

2150. KANI, ALI, 1906- . *The Reconstruction of Persian Education.* University of North Carolina, 1939. 230 p. ms. Abstract in *University of North Carolina Record,* No. 347, p. 60-61, October 1939.

2151. KASIR, DAOUD SULEIMAN, 1892- . *The Algebra of Omar Khayyam.* Columbia University, 1929. New York: Teachers College, Columbia University, 1931. iv, 126 p. (Teachers College Contribution to Education, No. 385.)

2152. NAKOSTEEN, MEHDI KHAN, 1904- . *The Development of Persian Education and Learning.* Cornell University, 1933. 417 p. ms. Ithaca, New York: 1953. 5 p. Abstract of thesis.

2153. NEYSARI, SALIM, 1920- . *Comparative Method of Teaching Persian as the Mother Tongue and as a Foreign Language, with Special Reference to the Work of Beginners.* Indiana University, 1954. 135 p. ms. Abstract in *Dissertation Abstracts,* Vol. 14, p. 1964-1965, November 1954. Available on microfilm from University Microfilms, Ann Arbor, Michigan, as Publication No. 10,154.

2154. SADIQ, ISSA KHAN. (Sadiq, 'Isa in Library of Congress card catalog). *Modern Persia and Her Educational System.* Columbia University, 1931. New York: Teachers College, Columbia University, 1931. ix, 125 p. (Studies of the International Institute of Teachers College, Columbia University, No. 14.)

2155. SASSANI, ABUL HASSAN KHAN, 1911- . *The Development of the Control of Education in Iran.* University of Missouri, 1940. 240 p. ms. Abstract in University of Missouri: *Abstracts of Dissertations in Education . . . 1939-1946,* p. 68-69. Abstract also in *Microfilm Abstracts,* Vol. 3, No. 1, p. 13-14, 1941. Available on microfilm from University Microfilms, Ann Arbor, Michigan, as Publication No. 221.

2155a. SHARIFY, NASSER. *A Code for the Cataloguing of Persian Publication.* Columbia University, 1958. 157 p. ms. Abstract in *Dissertation Abstracts,* Vol. 19, p. 1765-1766, January 1959. Available on microfilm from University Microfilms, Ann Arbor, Michigan, as Mic. 58-2714.

2156. VAFA, JAVAD, 1924- . *Liberal Nationalism and Educational Policies in Iran.* Indiana University, 1956. 371 p. ms. Abstract in *Dissertation Abstracts,* Vol. 18, p. 126-127, January 1958. Available on microfilm from University Microfilms, Ann Arbor, Michigan, as Publication No. 22,713.

See also Nos. 119, 132, 138, 164, 171, 174, 1298

MASTERS

2157. ADJOODANI, MAHMOOD. *A Study of Previous Achievement and a Plan for Broadening Teacher Training in Iran-Daneshara.* American University, 1958. 48 p. ms.

2158. ADJOODANI, SHAHRENAZ. *The Development of Public High Schools in Iran: Their History, Present Status, and Future Growth.* American University, 1958. 59 p. ms.

2159. BENEDUM, Mrs. GRACE COVENTRY, 1928- . *A Descriptive Study of Iran: Shiite Islam.* Columbia Bible College, 1956. 126 p. ms. (A survey of work of missionary institutions.)

2160. DIDEBAN, ZAHRA. *The Role of the Teacher in Iran.* George Peabody College for Teachers, 1954. 137 p. ms.

2161. GAGON, GLEN SCOTT, 1920- . *A Study of the Development and Implementation of a System of Elementary Education for the Ghasghi and Basseri Nomadic Tribes of Fars Ostan, Iran.* Brigham Young University, 1957. 184 p. ms.

2162. LARUDY, FEIZOLLAH, 1920- . *Christian Education in Iran.* Princeton Theological Seminary, 1954. 139 p. ms.

2163. RASCOLI, JOSEPH M. *Modern Education in Persia.* Oberlin College, 1933. 50 p. ms.

2164. SAHBA, HOMA. *Higher Education in Iran.* San Francisco State College, 1957. 63 p. ms.

2165. WRIGHT, EDWIN M. *The Background of Present Moslem Education in Persia.* Columbia University, 1930. 46 p. ms.

2166. YOUNG, HERRICK BLACK. *Educational Theories of Sa'di, the Persian.* Columbia University, 1928. 27 p. ms.

See also Nos. 226, 229, 238, 243, 288, 301, 306

For Iranian groups in the United States, see Nos. 4956, 4970, 4975, 4977, 5116

Iraq
(NOS. 2167 – 2199)

DOCTORS

2167. AKRAWI, MATTA, 1901- . *Curriculum Construction in the Primary Schools of Iraq in the Light of a Study of the Political, Economic, Social, Hygenic, and Educational Conditions and Problems of the Country, with Some Reference to the Education of Teachers.* Columbia University, 1942. New York: 1942. viii, 257 p. Reproduced from typewritten copy.

2168. el-BUSTANI, AFIFA ISMAIL, 1916- . *Problems Facing a Selected Group of Iraqi Women.* Columbia University, 1956. 172 p. ms. (Includes section on education of Iraqi women and consideration of the social issues involved in their education.)

2169. ELIAS, TAHA HAJ, 1923- . *A Program for Preparing Secondary School Principals in Iraq.* University of Maryland, 1958. 220 p. ms.

2170. FARGO, ADEEB F., 1927- . *Compatibility of the Cultural Heritage and Education in Iraq.* University of Maryland, 1956. 314 p. ms. Abstract in *Dissertation Abstracts*, Vol. 17, p. 530-531, March 1957. Available on microfilm from University Microfilms, Ann Arbor, Michigan, as Publication No. 19,675.

2171. al-HAFIDH, NURI ABDUL SALAM, 1913- *A Plan for the In-Service Education of Teachers in Iraq.* Columbia University, 1951. 316 p. ms.

2172. el-HASHIMI, KHALID MAHMOOD, 1908- *Reconstruction of Teacher Education in Iraq with Special Reference to Arab-Muslim Culture.* Ohio State University, 1941. 161 p. ms. Abstract in Ohio State University: *Abstracts of Dissertations . . .* Autumn Quarter, Winter Quarter, 1941-42, p. 47-49. (Abstracts of Doctoral Dissertations, No. 38.)

2173. al-HASSUN, ABDUR-RAHMAN ISA, 1920- *The Social Studies Programs in the Iraqi Public Secondary Schools.* Stanford University, 1956. 153 p. ms. Abstract in *Dissertation Abstracts*, Vol. 17, p. 262-263, February 1957. Available on microfilm from University Microfilms, Ann Arbor, Michigan, as Publication No. 19,894.

2174. ISMAIL, SUAD KHALIL, 1928- . *A Study of Basic Factors in Curriculum Development in the Public Schools of Iraq.* University of California, Berkeley, 1955. 228 p. ms.

2175. JAFAR, NOURI, 1914- . *The Philosophy of Boyd H. Bode, with Especial Consideration of Its Meaning for Education in Iraq.* Ohio State University, 1949. 237 p. ms. Abstract in Ohio State University: *Abstracts of Dissertations . . .* Summer Quarter, 1949-50, p. 211-215. (Abstracts of Doctoral Dissertations, No. 61.)

2176. al-JALILI, ABDUL RAZZAK, 1921- . *A Study of Public Education in Iraq, with Suggestions for Its Reorganization.* University of Southern California, 1954. 263 p. ms. Abstract in University of Southern California: *Abstracts of Dissertations*, 1955, p. 135-137.

2177. JAMALI, MOHAMMED FADHEL, 1902- . *The New Iraq: Its Problem of Bedouin Education.* Columbia University, 1934. New York: Teachers College, Columbia University, 1934. xi, 160 p. (Studies of the International Institute of Teachers College, Columbia University, No. 16.)

2178. KADHIM, ABDUL HAMID, 1912- . *A Plan for the Reconstruction of Teacher Education in Iraq.* Columbia University, 1947. 125 p. ms.

2179. KHADDOURI, ROSE KHADDOURI, 1915- . *Suggestions for the Improvement of Instruction in the Urban Primary Schools of Iraq.* Columbia University, 1951. 158 p. ms. Abstract in *Teachers College Record*, Vol. 53, p. 407-408, April 1952.

2180. KHALID, ABDUL RAHMAN MOHAMED, 1919- . *Science Education in Iraqi Society.* Columbia University, 1954. 294 p. ms. Abstract in *Dissertation Abstracts*, Vol. 14, p. 2008-2009, November 1954. Available on microfilm from University Microfilms, Ann Arbor, Michigan, as Publication No. 10,178.

2181. KOURY, ENVER M. *Iraq in Transition.* American University, 1958. 294 p. ms. Abstract in *Dissertation Abstracts*, Vol. 19, p. 558-559, September 1958. Available on microfilm from University Microfilms, Ann Arbor, Michigan as Mic. 58-2813. (Includes consideration of education as one factor.)

2182. MAJID, HAMMOUDI ABDUL, 1912- . *Guide for the Improvement of Teacher Education in Iraq.* Columbia University, 1953. 303 p. ms.

2183. NASIR, MOHAMMAD, 1910- . *Proposals for the Reorganization of Post-Secondary Education in Iraq in the Light of Recent Trends and Practices in Higher Education.* Columbia University, 1955. 255 p. ms.

2184. QADRY, HIND TAHSIN, 1924- . *Problems of Women Teachers in Iraq.* Stanford University, 1957. 197 p. ms. Abstract in *Dissertation Abstracts*, Vol. 18, p. 476-477, February 1958. Available on microfilm from University Microfilms, Ann Arbor, Michigan, as Publication No. 25,357.

2184a. al-QAYSI, ABDUL WAHHAB ABBAS. *The Impact of Modernization of Iraqi Society during the Ottoman Era: A Study of Intellectual Development in Iraq, 1869-1917.* University of Michigan, 1958. 238 p. ms. Abstract in *Dissertation Abstracts*, Vol. 19, p. 2072, February 1959. Available on microfilm from University Microfilms, Ann Arbor, Michigan, as Mic. 58-3631.

2185. al-RAHEEM, AHMED HASAN. *Curriculum Development in the High Schools of Iraq.* University of Tennessee, 1954. 222 p. ms.

2186. STRUCK, JOHN WARREN, 1922- . *A Survey of the Vocational Industrial Education Needs of Baghdad, Iraq, and Its Service Area.* Pennsylvania State University, 1956. 244 p. ms. Abstract in *Penn State Review of Educational Research*, Vol. 8, p. 30-

31, November 1956. Abstract also in *Dissertation Abstracts*, Vol. 17, p. 286-287, February 1957. Available on microfilm from University Microfilms, Ann Arbor, Michigan, as Publication No. 19,347.

2187. al-TOMA, SALIH JAWAD. *The Teaching of Classical Arabic to Speakers of the Colloquial in Iraq: A Study of the Problem of Linguistic Duality and Its Impact on Language Education.* Harvard University, 1957. 301 p. ms.

2188. TOMA, STEPHEN, 1912- . *The Cultural Challenge to Education in the Arab World, with Special Reference to Teacher Education in Iraq.* Ohio State University, 1939. 204 p. ms. Abstract in Ohio State University: *Abstracts of Dissertations . . . Summer Quarter,* 1939-40, p. 333-334. (Abstracts of Doctoral Dissertations, No. 31.)

2189. YASIN, MOHAMMED HUSSAIN, 1913- . *Education for All Iraqi Youth: Reorganization of Secondary Education in Iraq.* Columbia University, 1947. 238 p. ms.

2190. YOUNIS, HAMDI, 1924- . *A Study of the Teaching of English as a Foreign Language with Special Reference to Iraqi Secondary Schools.* University of Maryland, 1957. 372 p. ms. Abstract in *Dissertation Abstracts,* Vol. 17, p. 1716, August 1957. Available on microfilm from University Microfilms, Ann Arbor, Michigan, as Publication No. 21,541.

2191. al-ZOBAIE, ABDUL JALIL, 1925- . *Intelligence Test Development with Special Reference to a Test for Use in Iraq.* University of Southern California, 1954. 326 p. ms. Abstract in University of Southern California: *Abstracts of Dissertations,* 1955, p. 308. For master's thesis by same author, see No. 2199.

See also Nos. 119, 120, 129, 132, 138, 163, 180, 1298, 2213

MASTERS

2192. ADIBE, Mrs. NESRINE ALI. *A Synthesis of Subject Matter Material in Science for Use in the Elementary Schools of Iraq.* University of Michigan, 1952.

2193. AZIZ, AZIZ SHALLAL. *A Proposed Program for Utilizing Radio in Education in Iraq.* Ohio State University, 1953. 201 p. ms.

2194. al-BASSAM, HASSAN KADHUM, 1928- . *The Extension Service of Iraq and Some Suggestions for Its Improvement.* Cornell University, 1957. 147 p. ms.

2195. al-BASSAM, NOURI ABDUL AMEER. *Curriculum and Teaching of Mathematics in the Intermediate Schools of Iraq.* University of Texas, 1954. 108 p. ms.

2196. al-HAKKAK, HASSAN J., 1927- . *A Comparative Study of Accounting and Business Practices in the United States and Iraq.* Northeast Missouri State Teachers College, 1955. 60 p. ms.

2197. al-RAWI, MUSARI HASSAN. *Analysis of Pedagogical Methods Used in the Schools of Iraq.* University of Illinois, 1955. 63 p. ms.

2198. TATNALL, EDITH COMFORT. *The Education of Scribes in Relation to the Temple in Ancient Mesopotamia in the Second and Third Milleniums, B.C.* Columbia University, 1953. 134 p. ms.

2199. al-ZOBAIE, ABDUL JALIL, 1925- . *A Handbook for Students in Primary Teachers' Training Schools in Iraq.* University of Southern California, 1952. 85 p. ms. For doctoral dissertation by same author, see No. 2191.

See also Nos. 217, 226, 229, 230, 234, 238, 243, 244, 247, 262, 279, 288, 308

For Iraqi groups in the United States, see Nos. 4956, 4970, 4975, 4977, 4990

Israel

(NOS. 2200 – 2304)

DOCTORS

2200. BARDIN, SHLOMO, 1898- . *Pioneer Youth in Palestine.* Columbia University, 1932. New York: Bloch Publishing Co., 1932. x, 182 p.

2201. BAVLY, SARAH, 1900- . *Family Food Consumption in Palestine: Comparison of Consumption of Jewish Urban Population in 1943 and in 1946 and a Study of Methods Conducive to Improvement of Food Selection.* Columbia University, 1947. New York: Bureau of Publications, Teachers College, Columbia University, 1949. viii, 107 p. (Teachers College Contribution to Education, No. 946. Suggests sound films for use in nutrition education.) For master's thesis by same author, see No. 2238.

2202. BERG, WILLIAM VANDERVEER. *The Creative Imagination of Jesus.* New York University, 1933. 118 p. ms. (Gives applications to various aspects of religious education.)

2203. BERLIN, LEWIS LEON, 1908- . *The Health Teachings and Practices Derived from the Hebrew Bible.* New York University, 1953. 381 p. ms. Abstract in *Dissertation Abstracts,* Vol. 14, p. 263-264, February 1954. Available on microfilm from University Microfilms, Ann Arbor, Michigan, as Publication No. 7,088.

2204. BLOUNT, LOUISE FOREMAN, 1899- . *An Examination of Some of the Teaching Practices of Jesus in the Light of Principles of Group Dynamics.* Eastern Baptist Theological Seminary, 1951. 177 p.

ms. Abstract in *Religious Education*, Vol. 47, p. 209-210, May-June 1952.

2205. BORTNIKER, ELIJAH, 1910- . *The Multiple Trends in Israel's Jewish Elementary School System: An Investigation into the Origin, Development, and Present Status of Israel's School System and Its Political Subdivisions Known as "Trends."* New York University, 1953. 370 p. ms. Abstract in *Dissertation Abstracts*, Vol. 14, p. 2249-2250, December 1954. Available on microfilm from University Microfilms, Ann Arbor, Michigan, as Publication No. 7,089.

2206. BRAWER, CHAIM ISAAC, 1918- . *Suggestions for Improving the Israeli Urban High School.* Columbia University, 1954. 130 p. ms.

2207. CARPENTER, JAMES WALTER. *The Jewish Educational System in Palestine during the Time of Jesus.* American University, 1958. 276 p. ms. Abstract in *Dissertation Abstracts*, Vol. 19, p. 478, September 1958. Available on microfilm from University Microfilms, Ann Arbor, Michigan as Mic. 58-2806.

2208. COMISH, ALLEN B. *The Leadership Characteristics of Moses.* Southwestern Baptist Theological Seminary, 1956. 202 p. ms. Abstract in *Religious Education*, Vol. 52, p. 182, May 1957.

2209. DRAZIN, NATHAN, 1906- . *History of Jewish Education from 515 B.C.E. to 220 C.E. (During the Periods of the Second Commonwealth and the Tannaim).* Johns Hopkins University, 1937. Baltimore, Maryland: Johns Hopkins Press, 1940. x, 161 p. (Johns Hopkins University Studies in Education, No. 29.)

2210. EBNER, ELIEZER, 1912- . *Elementary Jewish Education in Palestine during Tannaitic Times.* Dropsie College for Hebrew and Cognate Learning, 1949. Published as *Elementary Education in Ancient Israel during the Tannaitic Period (10 - 220 C.E.)* New York: Bloch Printing Co., 1956. 128 p. Abstract in *Religious Education*, Vol. 45, p. 174-175, May-June 1950.

2211. FINEBERG, SOLOMON ANDHIL, 1896- . *Biblical Myths and Legends in Jewish Education: The Presentation of Biblical Myths and Legends in Books for Jewish Religious Schools.* Columbia University, 1932. New York: Behrman's Jewish Book House, 1932. vi, 156 p.

2212. FRITCHLEY, NEWTON HORACE, 1916- *Present-Day Uses of Jesus' Method of Teaching.* Boston University, 1948. 234 p. ms.

2213. GOLDMAN, *Rabbi* LEO Y. *Jewish Philosophy of Education.* Wayne State University, 1957. 304 p. ms. Abstract in *Dissertation Abstracts*, Vol. 18, p. 1300, April 1958. Available on microfilm from University Microfilms, Ann Arbor, Michigan, as Mic. 58-1188. (Covers Jewish history from 1400 B.C., including Babylonian Exile and dispersion in Europe.)

2214. HAKLAI, MICHAEL D., 1901- . *Mizrachi Education in Israel.* Yeshiva University, 1954. 203 p. ms. (Written in Hebrew.)

2215. HANCOCK, THOMAS, -1929. *Psychology of the Ethics of Jesus.* Clark University, 1918.

2216. JIGGETTS, J. IDA. *A Study of the Absorption and Integration of the Yemenite Jew in the State of Israel.* New York University, 1957. 178 p. ms. Abstract in *Dissertation Abstracts*, Vol. 17, p. 2705, November 1957. Available on microfilm from University Microfilms, Ann Arbor, Michigan, as Mic. 57-4351. (Includes study of schools attended in Israel by Yemenite Jews. "Offers significant data to social scientists and educators concerned with problems of cultural adaptability, education for community living, and the correlation of skin color with social prejudice and discrimination.")

2217. KANG, THOMAS JUNGSON. *The Philosophy of the Apostle Paul.* New York University, 1938. 326 p. ms. Abstract in *Selected Doctoral Theses in Religious Education*, 1939, p. 13.

2218. KING, JAMES. *The Psychology of St. Paul.* Clark University, 1918. 126 p. ms.

2219. KNELLER, HERBERT SAMUEL, 1925- . *Israeli Youth Education Today and Tomorrow: An Administrative Plan for the Introduction of an Experience-Centered Curriculum into Israeli Education.* Columbia University, 1953. 85 p. ms.

2220. KOKHBA, MOSHEH, 1900- . *Interest-Patterns in Compositions of Fifth Grade Pupils in American and Palestinian Elementary Schools.* Columbia University, 1936. Jerusalem, Israel: Central Press, 1936. v, 56 p.

2221. KUIST, HOWARD TILLMAN, 1895- . *The Pedagogy of St. Paul.* New York University, 1924. New York: George H. Doran Co., 1925. xiii, 169 p.

2222. McKOY, CHARLES FRANCIS, 1878- . *The Art of Jesus as a Teacher.* New York University 1929. Philadelphia and Boston: The Judson Press, 1950. xi, 185 p.

2223. MALLER, JULIUS BERNARD, 1901- . *A Psychological Study of Talmudic Folklore with Comparisons between the Babli and Yerushalmi.* Jewish Theological Seminary of America, 1927.

2224. MAYNARD, JOHN ALBERT FONSEGRIVE 1884- . *A Survey of Hebrew Education.* New York University, 1919. Milwaukee, Wisconsin: Morehouse Publishing Co., 1924. xx, 65 p. (Biblical and Oriental Series, S.A.B. Mercer, General Editor.)

2225. NARDI, NOACH, 1902- . *Zionism and Education in Palestine.* Columbia University, 1934. New York: Teachers College, Columbia University, 1934. ix, 99 p. (Teachers College Contribution to Education, No. 629.)

2226. NORMAN, Mrs. JEAN SCHIFFER, 1904- . *Working Together for Better Schools in Israel.* Columbia University, 1954. 178 p. ms.

2227. PYATT, CHARLES LYNN, 1886- . *The Moral Teachings of the Jews at the Time of Christ.* Harvard University, 1916. 286 p. ms.

2228. ROTH, ALVIN SYDNEY, 1917- *Rabbinic Foundations of Jewish Education as Reflected in Talmudic Literature, 10 C.E. to 499 C.E.* Northwestern University, 1957. 166 p. ms. Abstract in *Dissertation Abstracts,* Vol. 17, p. 3106, December 1957. Available on microfilm from University Microfilms, Ann Arbor, Michigan, as Publication No. 23,539. Abstract also in *Religious Education,* Vol. 53, p. 276-277, May-June 1958.

2229. SHAPIRO, *Rabbi* JOSEPH, 1905- . *Education among Early Hebrews with Emphasis upon Talmudic Period.* University of Pittsburgh, 1938. 164 p. ms. Abstract in University of Pittsburgh: *Abstracts of Theses . . .* Vol. 14, 1938, p. 249-254.

2230. SHUMSKY, ABRAHAM, 1921- . *An Analysis of the Ethnic Group Problem in Israel with Implications for the Role of the School.* Columbia University, 1954. Published as *The Clash of Cultures in Israel: A Problem for Education.* New York: Bureau of Publications, Teachers College, Columbia University, 1955. xi, 170 p. (Teachers College Studies in Education.)

2231. TADMOR, SHLOMO, 1926- . *Adult Education in Israel: Problems and Principles for Future Development.* Columbia University, 1958. 164 p. ms.

2232. WALDMAN, MARK, 1873- . *Ideal View of Pre-Exilic Education as Introductory to the Talmudic, the Medieval, and the Modern Era.* New York University, 1910. For master's thesis by same author, see No. 300.

2233. WALDSTEIN, DANIEL, 1921- . *East European Jews in Israel Society: An Official Study.* Columbia University, 1951. 361 p. ms. Abstract in *Teachers College Record,* Vol. 53, p. 345, March 1952. (Discusses how the educational institutions of Israel could diminish the intensity of conflicting modes of behavior exhibited by East European Jews.)

2234. YOUSUF, ABDULQADIR MOHAMMAD, 1920- . *The British Educational Policy in the Arab Public Schools of Palestine during the Mandate.* Indiana University, 1956. 371 p. ms. Abstract in *Dissertation Abstracts,* Vol. 16, p. 1821, October 1956. Available on microfilm from University Microfilms, Ann Arbor, Michigan, as Publication No. 17,991.

2235. ZELIGS, DOROTHY F. *Psychoanalysis and the Bible: A Psychoanalytic Study of Six Biblical Personalities in the Early History of Israel.* Columbia University, 1957. 368 p. ms.

See also Nos. 125, 131, 139, 142, 143, 144, 145, 152, 158, 164, 169, 174, 180, 1297, 1302, 3639

MASTERS

2236. ANDERSON, HERMAN. *The Influence of the Historical Environment upon the Teaching and Activity of the Prophets from B.C. 700 to B.C. 570.* Northwestern University, 1919. 86 p. ms.

2237. BAUMEL, MORRIS. *Philo Judaeus: His Educational Significance.* New York University, 1932. 78 p. ms.

2238. BAVLY, SARAH, 1900- . *Outline of Projected Work as Supervising Dietitian of the Hadassah Medical Organization in Palestine.* Columbia University, 1929. 88 p. ms. For doctoral dissertation by same author, see No. 2201.

2239. BERGMAN, ROBERT, 1921- . *Educational Principles of Kibbotrim.* Hebrew Union College-Jewish Institute of Religion, 1955. 115 p. ms.

2240. BLANTON, JOHN HOMER. *The Educational Principles and Practices of Jesus.* Southwest Texas State Teachers College, 1941. 25 p. ms.

2241. BOWER, GLADICE, 1897- . *Jesus, the Counselor.* Syracuse University, 1945. 114 p. ms.

2242. BOYD, JOSEPH. *The Use of Theology in Religious Education as Exemplified by Paul in His Epistles to the Churches.* Columbia University, 1941. 109 p. ms.

2243. BRICK, OLLIE AMELIA. *Blind Men: A Study of Interpretations of Jesus.* Columbia University, 1936. 93 p. ms. (Includes Christian education.)

2244. CHAMBERLAIN, ROBERT S. *Jesus and the New Education.* New York University, 1928. 55 p. ms.

2245. CHERTOFF, ESTHER B. *Origin and Development of the Modern School in Israel.* College of the City of New York, 1956. 53 p. ms.

2246. COXHEAD, MARY, 1902- . *The Place of the Hexateuch in Religious Education.* Pacific School of Religion, 1936. 45 p. ms.

2247. DARST, MINNIE ANNA, 1864- . *The Education of the Hebrew Child in Early and Later Biblical Times, and Its Significance in the Present.* University of California, Berkeley, 1911. 69 p. ms.

2248. DOWNING, WILLIAM LEANDER. *The Bible in Education, Considered Historically and Constructively.* University of Texas, 1927. 118 p. ms.

2249. FISCHBACHER, THEODORE. *The Place of Jesus Christ in the History of Education.* University of California, Los Angeles, 1958.

2250. FRANKLIN, LEO M., 1870-1948. *Education among the Jews in Biblical and Talmudic Times.* Hebrew Union College-Jewish Institute of Religion, 1892. 148 p. ms.

2251. FRAWLEY, *Rev.* JOHN JOSEPH. *The Pedagogical System of Christ as Found in the Gospels.* University of Notre Dame, 1943. 72 p. ms.

2252. GREENBERG, GERTRUDE I. *Mathematics among the Ancient Hebrews.* College of the City of New York, 1928. 28 p. ms.

2253. HAVERKAMP, FREDERICK WILLIAM. *The Book of Proverbs as a Source of Moral Instruction.* George Peabody College for Teachers, 1939. 66 p. ms.

2254. HEALY, *Sister* MARY MARGARET IRENE. *Christ's Method in Training the Apostles.* De Paul University, 1954. 68 p. ms.

2255. HEATON, CHARLOTTE L. *Jesus in Religious Education for the Beginner.* Columbia University, 1933. 46 p. ms.

2256. HOFFMAN, Rev. MEINRAD LOUIS. *The Educational Values of the Psalms.* University of Notre Dame, 1930. 52 p. ms.

2257. HOWARD, NORBERT CLIFTON. *Certain Principles of Guidance in the Epistles of Saint Paul Compared to the Principles of Guidance of Ten Modern Authors.* Catholic University of America, 1956. 64 p. ms. Abstract in *Catholic Education Review*, Vol. 56, p. 262, April 1958. (The ten modern authors are all Americans.)

2258. ITZKOWITZ, BENJAMIN. *Education and the Labor Movement in Palestine.* College of the City of New York, 1933. 96 p. ms. Abstract in College of the City of New York: *Abstracts of Theses . . . 1923-1939.* p. 59.

2259. KIDESS, ATTALLAH ALEXANDER. *Health Education as Related to Physical Education.* International YMCA College, 1935. 140 p. ms. (Designed to meet the needs of Palestinian educators giving them a body of scientific knowledge upon which to base their thinking and understanding of this topic.)

2260. KIEFER, Sister MARY PAULETTE. *Educational Theories in the Letters of St. Jerome.* Creighton University, 1951. 72 p. ms.

2261. LATEEF, NASSIR ABED. *Analysis of the Institutions in Ein Yabroad Village, Palestine.* University of Tennessee, 1949. 174 p. ms. (Includes section on the rural school and education.)

2262. LEHRMAN, IRVING. *Early Sources for Jewish Education: Talmud Torah as Found in the Pesiktadi Rab Kohana.* Hebrew Union College-Jewish Institute of Religion, 1942.

2263. LEIPZIGER, EMIL WILLIAM, 1877- . *Talmudic Education.* Hebrew Union College-Jewish Institute of Religion, 1900. 187 p. ms.

2264. LIMPER, HENRY WILLIAM. *The Social Teaching of the Hebrew Prophets of the Eighth Century, B.C.* Northwestern University, 1909. 117 p. ms.

2265. McCARTY, GRACE. *A Study of the Technique in Discovering Ideals as Taught by Jesus.* University of Pittsburgh, 1925. 156 p. ms.

2266. McKENNA, DAVID L. *An Inductive Study of Jesus' Qualifications, Principles, and Techniques as a Personal Counselor.* University of Michigan, 1955. 176 p. ms.

2267. MacLEOD, ALEXANDER BENJAMIN, -1934. *Jesus as Teacher and Hygienist.* Clark University, 1922. 158 p. ms.

2268. MAVIS, W. CURRY. *The Religious Pedagogy of S. John.* New York University, 1934. 74 p. ms.

2269. MELCONIAN, VARTAN DIKRAN. *The Pedagogy of the Pentateuch, with Especial Reference to Moses as an Educational Leader.* New York University, 1927. 90 p. ms.

2270. MILLER, NETTIE BELLE. *Methods Jesus Used in Training His Twelve Disciples.* Hartford School of Religious Education, 1933. 133 p. ms.

2271. MORTON, HENRY ALSTON, 1896- . *The Scholarship of Jesus.* Boston University, 1932. 101 p. ms. (Includes a study of Jewish schools at time of Jesus, his own home life and school training, and his qualities as a critical scholar.)

2272. MOSES, ISADOR E. *Post-Exilic Hebrew Schools.* New York University, 1918. 32 p. ms.

2273. MOSSTON, MOSHE. *The Attitudes of the Jewish People towards Physical Activities during the Period from the Patriarchs to the Maccabees.* College of the City of New York, 1954. 52 p. ms.

2274. NAOR, ZIPORA SHAPIRO. *A Comparative Study of Methods of Teaching Arithmetic in the First Grade in Louisville Public Schools and in the Reali Schools, Haifa, Israel.* University of Louisville, 1952. 124 p. ms.

2275. NAPAHA, SHRAGA, 1890- . *The Philosophy of the European Double and the American Single Educational Ladder and Its Bearing on the Zionist Educational System in Palestine.* Yale University, 1931. 77 p. ms.

2276. NELSON, SAMUEL FERDINAND. *The Background of the Ethical Teachings of Jesus.* Berkeley Baptist Divinity School, 1935. 82 p. ms.

2277. NIR, AMOS, 1922- . *A Suggested Program for Organizing Pupil Personnel Services in the Elementary Schools in Israel.* University of Maryland, 1952. 147 p. ms.

2278. PACKER, BOYD KENNETH, 1924- . *An Evaluation of the Teaching of Jesus in Terms of Selected Principles of Education.* Utah State Agricultural College, 1953. 56 p. ms.

2279. PEARCE, CLARENCE SPENCE. *The Education of Hebrew Youth from the Earliest Times to the Maccabean Period.* University of Cincinnati, 1930. 62 p. ms.

2280. PHELEY, GORDON EDWARD. *The Development of Education in Palestine under the British Mandate.* University of Southern California, 1937. 83 p. ms.

2281. PLUMB, CECIL. *Education and the Words of Jesus.* Auburn Theological Seminary, 1938.

2282. RANDELL, Mrs. ANNE RAGLAND. *The Pedagogy of Jesus.* University of Denver, 1932. 68 p. ms.

2283. RIEGER, ELIEZAR LIBER. *Selection of a Hebrew Spelling Vocabulary in Hebrew.* University of Chicago, 1931. 129 p. ms.

2284. ROSENBERG, MEYER JOSHUA. *The Historical Development of Hebrew Education from Ancient*

Times to 135 A.D. New York University, 1926. 111 p. ms.

2285. RUSSELL, Rev. WILLIAM HENRY. *St. Jerome as an Educator.* Catholic University of America, 1921. 24 p. ms.

2286. SCHROEDER, RUTH JONES, 1915- . *Principles of Teaching as Revealed by the Teaching Ministry of Jesus.* Eastern Baptist Theological Seminary, 1939. Philadelphia: Eastern Baptist Theological Seminary, 1939. (Contributions to Christian Education, No. 14, p. 4-28.)

2287. SCHULTE, Sister MARY GEORGIANA. *Saint Jerome's Educational Theories and Principles as Presented in "Ad Laetum de Institutione Filiae" and in "Ad Pacatulam."* Catholic University of America, 1945. 57 p. ms.

2288. SEGAL, ALEXANDER. *Jewish Education in the Period of Transition Following Mendelssohn.* Hebrew Union College-Jewish Institute of Religion, 1918. 23 p. ms.

2289. SMITH, BLANCHE AWILDA. *A Background Study of the Social Teachings of St. Paul.* Hartford School of Religious Education, 1939. 92 p. ms.

2290. SORSCHER, LUCILLE. *The Place of Religion in the Public School System of Israel.* Hunter College of the City of New York, 1956. 32 p. ms.

2291. STRIGHT, HAYDEN LEROY, 1898- . *Teaching Value of the Legends and Myths of Israel.* Boston University, 1929. 65 p. ms.

2292. SUCHOFF, LIBBIE. *The Education and Social Status of the Jewish Woman of the Past.* Columbia University, 1915. 34 p. ms.

2293. SUMMERS, GEORGE EDWIN. *The Place of St. Cyril of Jerusalem in the Development of Religious Education in the Early Church.* Emory University, 1924. 40 p. ms. (Thesis for degree of Bachelor of Divinity.)

2294. TSAKOVA, VICTORIA IVANOVA, 1905- . *The Social Teachings of the Eighth Century Prophets.* Boston University, 1932. 86 p. ms.

2295. TUCKER, FLORENCE INDIANA. *Jesus — the Modern Teacher.* University of Washington, 1936. 98 p. ms. Abstract in University of Washington: *Abstracts of Theses,* Vol. 2, 1937, p. 102.

2296. WALES, LOLA FAE. *Jesus Christ as an Educator.* Texas Technological College, 1932. 142 p. ms.

2297. WEBB, ARNOLD HENRY, 1886- . *Hebrew Education.* University of Kentucky, 1945. 70 p. ms.

2298. WELTY, FREDERICK ARTHUR. *Changing Emphasis of Music in the Bible.* University of Pittsburgh, 1936. 49 p. ms. Abstract in University of Pittsburgh: *Abstracts of Theses . . .* Vol. 12, 1936, p. 329-330.

2299. WHATLEY, ALLAN. *An Investigation into the Teaching Methods of Jesus.* New York University, 1929. 53 p. ms.

2300. WILBUR, ETHEL MARGARET. *A Study of the Epistle to the Hebrews for Its Pedagogical Implications.* Biblical Seminary in New York, 1937. 77 p. ms.

2301. WILSON, MARTHA ELIZABETH. *Jesus as a Leader in Relation to the Christian Education of Youth.* Biblical Seminary in New York, 1937. 95 p. ms.

2302. WINGARD, EILEEN SCHIFF. *Music Education in Israel.* University of California, Los Angeles, 1954.

2303. WINTERS, ALTON, 1927- . *Elementary Education as Reflected in the Talmud.* Hebrew Union College-Jewish Institute of Education, 1947.

2304. ZECHMAN, HARRY WILLIAM. *Educational Values in the New Testament.* Union Theological Seminary, 1946.

See also Nos. 187, 217, 221, 222, 226, 229, 230, 238, 244, 246, 247, 249, 254, 258, 288, 291, 296, 300, 301, 306, 308, 1311, 1320, 1334, 1650, 3000, 3553

For Israeli groups in the United States, see Nos. 4956, 4957, 4970, 4975, 4977

Japan

(NOS. 2305 – 2478)

DOCTORS

2305. ANDERSON, PAUL SEWARD, 1913- . *The Reorientation Activities of the Civil Education Section of the Osaka Civil Affairs Team: A Case Study in Educational Change.* University of Wisconsin, 1954. 437 p. ms. Abstract in University of Wisconsin: *Summaries of Doctoral Dissertations . . .* Vol. 15, 1953-54, p. 510-512.

2306. ANTHONY, DAVID FORSYTH, 1919- . *The Administration of Hokkaido under Kuroda Kiyotaka, 1870-1882.* Yale University, 1951. 156 p. ms. Abstract in *Microfilm Abstracts,* Vol. 11, No. 1, p. 154-155, 1951. Available on microfilm from University Microfilms, Ann Arbor, Michigan, as Publication No. 2,211. Abstract in *Abstracts of Completed Doctoral Dissertations for the Academic Year 1950-51* (Department of State, External Research

Staff, Office of Intelligence Research, Abstract Series No. 1, March 1952), p. 16-17. Also in W. C. Eells: *The Literature of Japaneses Education, 1945-1954*, p. 6. (One chapter deals with organization of Sapporo Agricultural College now Hokkaido University.)

2307. AOKI, HIDEO, 1920- . *The Effect of American Ideas upon Japanese Higher Education.* Stanford University, 1957. 363 p. ms. Abstract in *Dissertation Abstracts*, Vol. 17, p. 1506, July 1957. Available on microfilm from University Microfilms, Ann Arbor, Michigan, as Publication No. 21,563.

2308. ASHMEAD, JOHN Jr. *The Idea of Japan, 1853-1895: Japan as Described by American and Other Travellers from the West.* Harvard University, 1951. 2 vols. 631 p. ms. Abstract in *Abstracts of Completed Doctoral Dissertations for the Academic Year 1950-51* (Department of State, External Research Staff, Office of Intelligence Research, Abstract Series No. 1, March 1952), p. 350-352. (Includes consideration of education as characterized by missionaries and other foreign teachers.)

2309. BLUMHAGEN, HERMAN HERBERT. *Nationalistic Policies and Japanese Public Education.* Rutgers University, 1957. 314 p. ms. Abstract in *Dissertation Abstracts*, Vol. 18, p. 1708-1709, May 1958. Available on microfilm from University Microfilms, Ann Arbor, Michigan, as Publication No. 22,566.

2310. BOLLER, PAUL FRANKLIN, Jr., 1916- . *The American Board and the Doshisha, 1875-1900.* Yale University, 1947. 299 p. ms.

2311. BRAIBANTI, RALPH J. D., 1920- . *The Occupation of Japan: A Study in Organization and Administration.* Syracuse University, 1949. 970 p. ms. Published in part as "The Administration of Military Government at the Prefectural Level in Japan," *American Political Science Review*, Vol. 43, p. 250-275, June 1949; and as "The Role of Administration in the Occupation of Japan," *Annals of the American Academy of Political and Social Science*, Vol. 267, p. 154-163, January 1950. (Includes Administration of Education.)

2312. CHAPMAN, JOHN GRIFFEN, 1900- . *The Re-Education of the Japanese People.* University of Houston, 1954. 269 p. ms. Abstract in *Dissertation Abstracts*, Vol. 14, p. 1988-1989, November 1954. Abstract also in W. C. Eells, *The Literature of Japanese Education, 1945-1954*, p. 21. Available on microfilm from University Microfilms, Ann Arbor, Michigan, as Publication No. 9,847.

2313. COHEN, JEROME BERNARD, 1915- . *The Japanese War Economy. 1937-1945.* Columbia University, 1949. Minneapolis, Minnesota: University of Minnesota Press, 1949. 416 p., 41 p. (With Foreword by Sir George Simpson). Also published as *Japanese Economy in War and Reconstruction.* Minneapolis, Minnesota: University of Minnesota Press, 1949. xix, 545 p. (First six chapters identical with above. Chapter 7, "The Economy under Occupation," has nothing on education). Abstract in W. C. Eells, *The Literature of Japanese Education, 1945-1954*, p. 24-25.

2314. COPELAND, EDWIN LUTHER, 1916- . *The Crisis of Protestant Missions in Japan, 1889-1900.* Yale University, 1949. 386 p. ms. Chapter III (p. 100-168), with only minor variations, published as "The Japanese Government and Protestant Christianity, 1889-1900" in *Contemporary Japan*, Vol. 22, p. 650-671, Numbers 10-12, 1953; and Vol. 23, p. 101-126, Numbers 1-3, 1954. Abstract in W. C. Eells, *The Literature of Japanese Education, 1945-1954*, p. 27-28. (Discusses discrimination against Christian teachers in the schools and limitations imposed on Christian schools.)

2315. CROSS, EDMOND, 1912- . *Japanese Education, 1868-1953, with Emphasis on Various Phases of Education in Aomori Prefecture.* Columbia University, 1954. 302 p. ms.

2316. DOI, JAMES ISAO. *Educational Reform in Occupied Japan: A Study of Acceptance of and Resistance to Institutional Change.* University of Chicago, 1953. 390 p. ms. Available on microfilm: see index under "University of Chicago."

2317. FEELY, GERTRUDE MARIE, 1903- . *A Program for Youth in Oita, Japan.* Columbia University, 1949. 142 p. ms. Abstract in *Teachers College Record*, Vol. 52, p. 189, December 1950. Abstract also in W.C. Eells, *The Literature of Japanese Education, 1945-1954*, p. 42-43.

2318. GILLETT, CLARENCE SHERMAN. *To Formulate an Appropriate Philosophy of Mission Work and to Determine for Work with Students of High School Age, in What Strategic Areas and in What Ways the American Board Missionary of Sendai, Japan, Can Make His Best Contribution.* Columbia University, 1936. 80 p. ms.

2319. GRIFFITH, HARRY ELMER, 1908- . *Japanese Normal School Education.* Stanford University, 1950. 392 p. ms. Abstract in Stanford University: *Abstracts of Dissertations . . . 1949-50*, p. 364-369. Abstract also in W. C. Eells, *The Literature of Japanese Education, 1945-1954*, p. 50.

2320. HIROSE, HAMAKO, 1905- . *A Guide for Curriculum Development for Religious Education Department of Seiwa Woman's College in Nishinomiya, Japan.* Columbia University, 1950. 90 p. ms.

2321. HOFFSOMER, WALTER EDWARD, -1922. *The Middle School as the Place in Japan Where the Civilization of the East and West Can Best Be Amalgamated.* Columbia University, 1918. "Dr. Hoffsomer died [November 1922] before his manuscript was published. His degree was awarded and the requirement governing publication was waived. The manuscript copy is the only one on record." — Columbia University *Register of Doctoral Dissertations.* The Columbia University library (Teachers College) has two manuscripts, each titled *The Japanese Middle School* — a preliminary edition, dated at Meiji Gakuin, Tokyo, Japan, 1919, 93 p. ms.; and a final edition, not dated but including a letter from the author, dated January 14, 1922, submitting it, 159 p. ms.

2322. HUDDLE, BENJAMIN PAUL, 1916- . *History of the Lutheran Church in Japan.* Temple University, 1956. 270 p. ms. (Includes educational activities.)

2323. IBANEZ, DALMYRA MONTGOMERY. *A Study of the Cultural Background of Japanese Education.* University of Southern California, 1948. 307 p. ms. Abstract in University of Southern California: *Abstracts of Dissertations,* 1948, p. 243-244. Abstract also in W. C. Eells, *The Literature of Japanese Education, 1945-1954,* p. 59-60.

2324. IGLEHART, CHARLES WHEELER. *The Japanese Spirit as a Conditioning Factor in the Further Integration of the Christian Movement in Japan: A Study in Education.* Drew University, 1934. 211 p. ms. Abstract in *Selected Graduate Theses in Religious Education,* 1934, p. 36-37.

2325. IKE, NOBUTAKA, 1916- . *The Beginnings of Political Democracy in Japan.* Johns Hopkins University, 1949. Baltimore, Maryland: Johns Hopkins Press, 1950. xvi, 246 p. "Issued under the auspices of the International Secretariat, Institute of Pacific Relations, and the Hoover Institute and Library on War, Revolution, and Peace." Abstract, with references to two reviews, in W. C. Eells, *The Literature of Japanese Education, 1945-1954,* p. 61. (Considers the influence of education in the development of democracy.)

2326. ISHIZAKA, MASANOBU, 1861-1934. *Christianity in Japan, 1859-1883.* Johns Hopkins University, 1895. Baltimore, Maryland: 1895. 35 p. (Brief consideration of education.)

2327. KAWACHI, RISAKU, 1901- . *An Analytical Study of the Reorganization Movements and Their Underlying Philosophies of the Teacher Training School System of Nippon.* University of Southern California, 1935. 415 p. ms. (Makes comparisons with systems of France, Germany, Great Britain, Italy, and the United States.) For master's thesis by same author, see No. 2400.

2328. KERLINGER, FREDERICK NICHOLS, 1910- . *The Development of Democratic Control in Japanese Education: A Study of Attitude Change in Shikoku, 1948-1949.* University of Michigan, 1953. 242 p. ms. Abstract in *Dissertation Abstracts,* Vol. 13, p. 722-723, October 1953. Abstract also in W. C. Eells, *The Literature of Japanese Education, 1945-1954,* p. 80-81. Available on microfilm from University Microfilms, Ann Arbor, Michigan, as Publication No. 5,686.

2329. KLEINJANS, EVERETT. *A Descriptive-Comparative Study Predicting Interference for Japanese in Learning English Noun-Head Modification Patterns.* University of Michigan, 1958. 205 p. ms. Abstract in *Dissertation Abstracts,* Vol. 19, p. 1306, December 1958. Available on microfilm from Microfilm Abstracts, Ann Arbor, Michigan as Mic. 58-7743. ("Tests were sent to Japan for administration to junior and senior high school students.")

2330. McGOVERN, JAMES RICHARD. 1928- . *American Christian Missions to Japan, 1918-1941.* University of Pennsylvania, 1957. 267 p. ms. Abstract in *Dissertation Abstracts,* Vol. 17, p. 2994-2995, December 1957. Available on microfilm from University Microfilms, Ann Arbor, Michigan, as Publication No. 23,614. (Considers influence of State Shinto in education and the educational work of missionaries.)

2331. MARUYAMA, KAZUTERU. *A Study of the Ideals of Japanese Children as Determined by Social Environment.* New York University, 1920. 130 p. ms.

2332. MATSUMOTO, TORU, 1913- . *A Proposed Program of Voluntary Religious Education at Meiji Gakuen, Tokyo, Japan.* Columbia University, 1949; Union Theological Seminary, 1949. 224 p. ms. Abstract in *Teachers College Record,* Vol. 52, p. 125-126, November 1950. Abstract also in W. C. Eells, *The Literature of Japanese Education, 1945-1954,* p. 827. For master's thesis by same author, see No. 2415.

2333. MESHIZUKA, TETSUO, 1921- . *A Program of Professional Training in Physical Education for Colleges and Universities in Japan.* State University of Iowa, 1956. 168 p. ms. Abstract in *Dissertation Abstracts,* Vol. 16, p. 2087-2088, November 1956. Available on microfilm from University Microfilms, Ann Arbor, Michigan, as Publication No. 18,548.

2334. MITA, SETSUKO, 1906- . *A Comparative Study of the Preparation of School Music Teachers in Japan and in the United States.* Michigan State University of Agriculture and Applied Science, 1957. 281 p. ms. Abstract in *Dissertation Abstracts,* Vol. 18, p. 250, January 1958. Available on microfilm from University Microfilms, Ann Arbor, Michigan, as Publication No. 23,468.

2335. MURRAY, ROBERT ALLEN, 1929- . *Education as an Instrument of Japanese Governmental Policy, 1918-1945.* Kansas State College of Agriculture and Applied Science, 1956. 87 p. ms.

2336. NAOI, JOHN YUTAKA, 1906- . *The Educational Reformation in Japan after World War II.* Catholic University of America, 1955. 305 p. ms. Abstract in W. C. Eells, *The Literature of Japanese Education, 1945-1954,* p. 104. Abstract also in *Catholic Educational Review,* Vol. 53, p. 621-622, December 1955. For master's thesis by same author, see No. 2426.

2337. NELSON, JOHN MONNINGER, 1916- . *The Adult Education Program in Occupied Japan, 1946-1950.* University of Kansas, 1954. 2 vols. 448 p. ms.

2338. NISHIYAMA, SEKUJI. *The Educational History of Japan.* New York University, 1910.

2339. ORR, MARK TAYLOR, 1914- . *Education Reform Policy in Occupied Japan.* University of North Carolina, 1954. 278 p. ms. Abstract in *University of North Carolina Record,* No. 548, p. 231-232, October 1955. Abstract also in W. C. Eells, *The Literature of Japanese Education, 1945-1954,* p. 109.

2340. OTAKE, MASUKO, 1911-1955. *Education for Leadership in the Christian Colleges of Japan.* Yale University, 1951. 410 p. ms. Published in part, under same title in *Japan Christian Quarterly,* Vol. 19, p. 9-21, Winter 1953. Abstract in *Religious Education,* Vol. 47, p. 222-223, May-June 1952.

2341. OTOMO, SHIGERU. *An Experimental Study of the Eye Movements Made by Various Persons in the Reading of Japanese Texts of Different Forms.* University of Chicago, 1924. 148 p. ms. Abstract in University of Chicago: *Abstracts of Theses, Humanistic Series,* Vol. 3, 1924-25, p. 75-80. For master's thesis by same author, see No. 2434.

2342. POOS, FREDERICK WILLIAM, 1921- . *Kawakami Hajime (1879-1946): An Intellectual Biography.* Stanford University, 1957. 169 p. ms. Abstract in *Dissertation Abstracts,* Vol. 17, p. 2586, November 1957. Available on microfilm from University Microfilms, Ann Arbor, Michigan, as Publication No. 23,212. (Subject of the dissertation was a prominent professor of economics at Kyoto University.)

2343. RYDER, STEPHEN WILLIS, 1880- . *A Historical-Educational Study of the Japan Mission of the Reformed Church in America.* Columbia University, 1935. York, Pennsylvania: York Printing Co., 1935. 172 p. Chapters I–III published also as Chapters I–III of the author's *A Historical Sourcebook of the Japan Mission of the Reformed Church in America (1850-1930),* Same publishers, 1935. 156 p.

2344. SAITO, MITSUKO, 1925- . *Speech Education in Japan in the Latter Half of the Nineteenth Century.* Northwestern University, 1957. 330 p. ms. Abstract in *Dissertation Abstracts,* Vol. 18, p. 698-699, February 1958. Available on microfilm from University Microfilms, Ann Arbor, Michigan, as Publication No. 24,921.

2345. SCHROER, GILBERT WILLIAM. *A Religious Education Program for the Nihon Kirisuto Kyokwai for Iwate Prefecture.* Hartford School of Religious Education, 1938. 258 p. ms. For master's thesis by same author, see No. 2443.

2346. SCHWANTES, ROBERT SIDNEY. *American Influence in the Education of Meiji Japan, 1868-1912.* Harvard University, 1950. 373 p. ms. Incorporated in greatly changed form in Chapter 4, "New Education for Japan" of *Japanese and Americans: A Century of Cultural Relations,* New York: Harper & Bros, 1955. xi, 380 p. With Foreword by John D. Rockefeller, 3rd. Published in part as "Christianity Versus Science: A Conflict of Ideas in Meiji Japan," *Far Eastern Quarterly,* Vol. 12, p. 123-132, February 1953; and as "Results of Study Abroad: Japanese Students in America, 1865-1885," *School and Society,* Vol. 72, p. 375-376, December 9, 1950. Abstract in W. C. Eells, *The Literature of Japanese Education, 1945-1954,* p. 124.

2347. SKILLMAN, JOHN HAROLD, 1927- . *A Study of the Relationship between Participation in Various Types of Extra-Class Activities and Academic Achievement in Three Private Japanese Schools.* Syracuse University, 1958. 116 p. ms. Abstract in *Dissertation Abstracts,* Vol. 19, p. 1958, February 1959. Available on microfilm from University Microfilms, Ann Arbor, Michigan, as Mic. 58-7242. (Refers to Aoyama Gakuin, Joshi-sei Gakuin, and Meiji Gakuin, all in Tokyo.)

2348. SONG, UN SUN, 1917- . *A Sociological Analysis of the Value System of Pre-War Japan as Revealed in the Japanese Government Elementary School Textbooks, 1933-1941.* University of Maryland, 1958. 289 p. ms.

2349. SPAE, JOSEPH JOHN. *Ito Jinsai, a Philosopher, Educator, and Sinologist of the Tokugawa Period.* Columbia University, 1948. Peiping, China: Catholic University of Peiping, 1948. xv, 278 p. (Monumenta Nipponica, Monograph Series No. 12.)

2350. SUH, DOO SOO, 1907- . (So, Tu-su in Library of Congress card catalog.) *The Struggle for Academic Freedom in Japanese Universities before 1945.* Columbia University, 1953. 462 p. ms. Abstract in *Dissertation Abstracts,* Vol. 13, No. 2, p. 201, 1953. Abstract also in W. C. Eells, *The Literature of Japanese Education, 1945-1954,* p. 134. Available on microfilm from University Microfilms, Ann Arbor, Michigan, as Publication No. 4,901.

2351. TAKAYAMA, KIYOSHI. *Fundamental Considerations Underlying the Reconstruction of the School Curriculum in Japan: A Sociological Search for Criteria of the Reconstruction of the Public Elementary School Curriculum in View of the Modern Transition in the National Life of Japan, Especially since 1918.* New York University, 1928. 240 p. ms.

2352. THOMAS, WINBURN TOWNSEND, 1906- . *A History of Protestant Christianity in Japan, 1883-1889.* Yale University, 1942. 218 p. ms. Abstract in *The United States, 1865-1900: A Survey of Current Literature with Abstracts of Unpublished Dissertations.* Vol. 1, September 1941-August 1942. p. 156-157. (Includes educational activities of missionaries.)

2353. TSURU, HARUO, 1923- . *Japanese Universities in a Changing Society: A Study of Some Historical, Sociological, and Psychological Bases of Student Personnel Work in Japanese Universities.* Columbia University, 1958. 449 p. ms.

2354. WEBB, HERSCHEL F. *The Thought and Work of the Early Mito School.* Columbia University, 1958. 306 p. ms. Abstract in *Dissertation Abstracts,* Vol. 19, p. 316, August 1958. Available on microfilm from University Microfilms, Ann Arbor, Michigan, as Mic. 58-2719.

2355. WUNDERLICH, HERBERT JOHN, 1906- . *The Japanese Textbook Problem and Solution, 1945-1946.* Stanford University, 1953. 382 p. ms. Abstract in Stanford University: *Abstracts of Dissertations . . . 1951-52,* p. 726-727. Abstract also in W. C. Eells, *The Literature of Japanese Education, 1945-1954,* p. 175.

2356. YOSHINO, IKURO ROGER, 1920- . *Selected Social Changes in a Selected Japanese Village, 1935-1953.* University of Southern California, 1955. 188 p. ms. Abstract in University of Southern California: *Abstracts of Dissertations,* 1955, p. 218-219. (Includes education.)

See also Nos. 119, 138, 143, 144, 147, 148, 157, 161, 162a, 163, 165, 169, 179, 182, 1300, 1418, 1491, 2482, 2911.

MASTERS

2357. ALLEN, THOMASINE. *The Religious Educational Value of Japanese Folklore.* University of Chicago, 1928. 126 p. ms.

2358. ARMOUR, JANE. *The Higher Education of Women in Japan.* University of Chicago, 1940. 62 p. ms.

2359. BISSELL, THOMAS TAYLOR, 1928- . *Elementary and Secondary Education Reforms in Japan since 1945.* Cornell University, 1957. 59 p. ms.

Japan

2360. BLAIR, MARY GILLET. *A Study of Gotama as a Teacher with Reference to Christian Education in Japan.* Biblical Seminary in New York, 1936. 124 p. ms.

2361. BROWN, HOMER GRANT. *Development of Education in Japan.* Columbia University, 1913. 46 p. ms.

2362. CARTER, THOMAS J. *Religious Education a Guarantee of Peace with Japan.* Emory University, 1925. 72 p. ms.

2363. CASHEN, GEORGE BERNARD, 1884- . *History and Psychology of the Jesuit Missionaries in Japan.* Clark University, 1910. 59 p. ms.

2364. CHIBA, Mrs. SHIN. *Audio-Visual Aids in Leadership Education for the Churches of Japan.* Berkeley Baptist Divinity School, 1953. 110 p. ms.

2365. CHINIAN, JACK. *Text Material and Its Influence on Japanese Education in a Period of Transition.* Massachusetts State Teachers College at Boston, 1954. 66 p. ms.

2366. COUCH, HELEN. *Outline Course for Student Teachers in Japan.* Columbia University, 1931. 21 p. ms.

2367. COVELL, JAMES HOWARD. *An Evaluation of a Course in Shushin Used in Japanese Middle Schools.* University of Chicago, 1928. 52 p. ms.

2368. DAILY, MAURICE CECIL, 1910- . *The Major Contributions of Toyohiko Kagawa as a Religious Educator.* Emory University, 1934. 87 p. ms. Abstract in *Selected Graduate Theses in Religious Education,* 1934, p. 14. (Thesis for degree of Bachelor of Divinity.)

2369. DEMPSEY, Rev. ARTHUR FRANCIS. *Elementary Education in Japan.* Catholic University of America, 1929. 61 p. ms.

2370. DRLICA, KARL FRANCIS, 1917- . *The Teachers' Union in a Typical Prefecture in Japan.* Oregon State College, 1952. 203 p. ms. (Deals with Miyagi Prefecture.)

2371. DURHAM, JOANNA BELLE. *A Study of the Development and Application of the United States Postwar Educational Policy in Japan.* University of Southern California, 1949. 277 p. ms.

2372. ENGLEBERT, MERLE. *A Study of Indoctrination in the Schools of Japan as Revealed by a Survey of the Literature, 1890-1940.* University of Kansas, 1949.

2373. ETTER, CARL LEO. *Preliminary Study of the Influence of Christian Schools and Teachers upon the Socio-Ethical Standards of Japan.* University of Southern California, 1928. 68 p. ms.

2374. FOOTE, FRANCIS P., Jr. *Adapting Bonsai — Japanese Art of Miniature Plant Growth — to Secondary Agriculture Education.* Arizona State College, Flagstaff, 1954. 70 p. ms.

2375. FRANK, ROGER CHESTER, Jr., 1921- . *Allied Control Machinery for Japan.* Texas College of Arts and Industries, 1949. 100 p. ms. (Includes section on educational reform, p. 61-66.)

2376. FUJIKAWA, FUMIKO MARIA CHRISTINI, 1931- . *The Educational Contents of "The Education of Our Girls" by Dr. Thomas Edward Shields.* Catholic University of America, 1958. 54 p. ms. (Refers to work of Sisters of Notre Dame de Namur in Japan.)

2377. FUJIMOTO, EMIKO. *A Study of Teaching English to Japanese Students at the Secondary Level.* Southwestern University, 1955. 137 p. ms.

2378. FUKUDA, HANAKO, 1906- . *New Goals for the Music Teacher in Post-War Japan.* San Diego State College, 1954. 203 p. ms.

2379. FULTZ, MARY CATHERINE. *The Missionary's Use of the Bible in Teaching English in the Japanese Junior College.* Biblical Seminary in New York, 1955. 102 p. ms.

2380. GARDNER, DOROTHY ALINE. *Mental Fatigue of Japanese Children.* University of Denver, 1929. 124 p. ms.

2381. GOOD, MARY ELIZABETH SALOME. *Moral Education in Japan.* University of Washington, 1926. 189 p. ms.

2382. GWINN, ALICE ELIZABETH. *Women in Japan.* University of Washington, 1937. 171 p. ms. Abstract in University of Washington: *Abstracts of Theses,* Vol. 2, 1937, p. 229-236. (Includes education of women.)

2383. HALL, MARION ERNEST. *A Study of Japan's Culture in Its Relation to Her Modern Educational Problems.* Columbia University, 1931. 35 p. ms.

2384. HANSELL, SARAH GLOVER. *The Problem of Secondary Education of Women in Japan.* George Peabody College for Teachers, 1918. 67 p. ms.

2385. HARA, MEGUMI. *A Study of Protestant Christian Broadcasting in Japan.* Ohio State University, 1956. 239 p. ms.

2386. HARING, DOUGLAS GILBERT, 1894- . *Propaganda in Elementary School Readers in Japan: A Study in Social Control.* Columbia University, 1924. 74 p. ms.

2387. HASE, HELEN Y. *Christian Social Welfare Work in Japan.* San Francisco Theological Seminary, 1950.

2388. HASEGAWA, SHINICHIRO. *Indebtedness of Japan to the Netherlands.* University of Southern California, 1912. 75 p. ms. (Includes educational and cultural indebtedness.)

2389. HIROTA, DENZO. *Moral Teaching in the Public Schools of Japan.* Colorado State Teachers College, 1923. 93 p. ms.

2390. HOFFMAN, BENJAMIN PHILIP. *The Place of Religious Education in the Making of Modern Japan.* University of Southern California, 1934. 127 p. ms.

Abstract in *Selected Graduate Theses in Religious Education,* 1934. p. 32.

2391. HONJO, TOMOKO. *A Study of Learning and Teaching English as a Foreign Language from the Japanese Point of View.* University of Oregon, 1958. 80 p. ms.

2392. HORNER, LAYTON. *The American Occupation of Japan at the Prefectural Level.* University of Denver, 1949. 212 p. ms. (Includes consideration of education.)

2393. HOUSTON, NEAL BRYAN. *A Survey of Thought in Postwar Japanese Education.* University of Texas, 1954. 78 p. ms.

2394. HUNT, ROBERT B. *A Report on the Modern Japanese Educational System.* College of Idaho, 1958.

2395. INOMATA, HENRY BUNJI. *The Personal Problems of Japanese High School Students and Their Implications for Guidance.* Catholic University of America, 1953. 124 p. ms. Abstract in *Catholic Educational Review,* Vol. 52, p. 264, April 1954. Abstract also in W. C. Eells, *The Literature of Japanese Education, 1945-1954,* p. 61-62. (Based on study of almost 2,000 students in four Japanese senior high schools.)

2396. INOUYE, ISAAC, 1889- . *The Development of Religious Education in Japan.* Emory University, 1922. 55 p. ms. (Thesis for degree of Bachelor of Divinity.) For another master's thesis by same author, see No. 2397.

2397. INOUYE, ISAAC, 1889- . *The Development of Religious Education in Japan.* Boston University, 1924. 63 p. ms. (Thesis for degree of Master of Religious Education.) For another master's thesis by same author, see No. 2396.

2398. IOKI, TOSHI. *The Physical and Mental Basis of Ancient Japanese Civilization.* Columbia University, 1909. 80 p. ms.

2399. KANO, MICHIO. *A Manual of Program Resources for Boys' Work Leaders in the YMCA of Japan.* George Williams College, 1955.

2400. KAWACHI, RISAKU, 1901- . *A Comparative Study of the Administration of Compulsory Attendance in the United States and Japan.* University of Southern California, 1934. 213 p. ms. For doctoral dissertation by same author, see No. 2327.

2401. KIMURA, YUKIKO. *The Evaluation of the Programs for Character Training of the Early and Middle Adolescent Boys and Girls in Japan, Based on the Diagnosis of Adolescence and Its Problems.* Oberlin College, 1937. 377 p. ms. Abstract in *Selected Graduate Theses in Religious Education,* 1937, p. 30.

2402. KITAJIMA, TSUYA. *Development and Influence of Christian Educational Institutions for Women in Japan.* Boston University, 1926. 87 p. ms.

2403. KLEINAS, JACK. *Educational Reforms in Japan.* University of Southern California, 1954. 197 p. ms.

2404. KNUDTEN, RUTH CRUM. *Use of Play and Pageantry for the Encouragement of Patriotism and Religion in Japan.* University of Chicago, 1928. 97 p. ms.

2405. KUMANO, KICHIJIRO. *The Japanese High School.* University of Illinois, 1917. 91 p. ms. Abstract in Russell Taaffe Gregg: *Annotated Bibliography of Graduate Theses in Education at the University of Illinois,* 1931. p. 44. (Bureau of Educational Research, Bulletin No. 55.)

2406. LEE, CHANG-HEI. *Chemical Instruction in Japanese Secondary Schools.* George Peabody College for Teachers, 1935. 57 p. ms.

2407. LINDSAY, OLIVE C. *An Introduction to Christian Ethics for Teachers in Japan.* Union Theological Seminary, 1932. 95 p. ms.

2408. LIPTZIN, SOLOMON. *Lafcadio Hearn, the Teacher.* Columbia University, 1922. 47 p. ms.

2409. LOOMIS, CLARA DENISON. *Japan's Educational System.* Columbia University, 1901. 49 p. ms.

2410. LUBEN, BARNERD MAURICE. *American Influence in Early Modern Japanese Education.* University of Chicago, 1937. 98 p. ms.

2411. LUHMER, Rev. NICHOLAS. *Philosophy of the New Education in Japan.* University of Detroit, 1952. 91 p. ms.

2412. McELHANEY, JAMES HAROLD. *Educational Reform in Japan at a Regional Level, 1946-1948.* Ohio State University, 1949. 321 p. ms.

2413. MANNING, JAMES JOSEPH. *Education in Occupied Japan.* University of Illinois, 1951. 96 p. ms.

2414. MATSUMIYA, KAZUYA. *A Comparative Study of Certain Religious Ideas among Japanese and American Children.* Hartford School of Religious Education. 1929. 280 p. ms.

2415. MATSUMOTO, TORU, 1913- . *The Policy of Religious Education in the Christian Middle Schools in Japan.* Union Theological Seminary, 1938. For doctoral dissertation by same author, see No. 2332.

2416. MATTHEWSON, MILDRED E. *Christian Education in Japan: A Study of the Contribution of Protestant Christian Schools to Girls' Secondary Education in Japan.* University of Buffalo, 1955. 52 p. ms.

2417. MIKAMI, KAORU, 1900- . *A Proposed Religious Education Program for a Girls' High School in Japan.* Pacific School of Religion, 1934.

2418. MIZUNO, TSUNEKICHI. *The Effect of Kindergarten Training upon the Physical, Mental, and Moral Traits of Japanese School Children.* University of Illinois, 1916. 50 p. ms. Abstract in Russell Taaffe Gregg: *Annotated Bibliography of Graduate Theses in Education at the University of Illinois,* 1931, p. 50. (Bureau of Educational Research, Bulletin No. 55.)

2419. MOCHIZUKI, KENJI. *Horace Bushnell's Theory of Christian Education and Its Influence in Japan.* Oberlin College, 1958. 77 p. ms.

2420. MONIKURA, SAKUSUKE. *The Development of the State Educational System in Japan under Western Influence.* Columbia University, 1909. 35 p. ms.

2421. MOTOMIYA, ISAAC YAHEI. *The Construction of a Church School Curriculum with Special View to the Situation in Japan.* Yale University, 1920. 100 p. ms.

2422. MUKOYAMA, KIYO. *The Outline of a Bible Course for Hiroshima Girl's School.* George Peabody College for Teachers, 1927. 74 p. ms.

2423. NAGANO, SATOKO. *A Study in the Development of Criteria for the Selection of Reading Materials in English for Teaching English to Japanese Senior High School Students.* Claremont Graduate School, 1956. 104 p. ms.

2424. NAKAMURA, TAIRA. *A Comparative Study of Public Elementary School Curricula of the United States and Japan.* Columbia University, 1906. 80 p. ms.

2425. NAKANO, AIKO, 1917- . *Modification of the Japanese Grammar to Fit the Needs of the Japanese Students.* Arizona State Teachers College, Tempe, 1939. 38 p. ms.

2426. NAOI, JOHN YUTAKA, 1906- . *Postwar Educational Reorganization in Japan and the Influence of American Education.* Catholic University of America, 1952. 112 p. ms. Abstract in W. C. Eells, *The Literature of Japanese Education, 1945-1954,* p. 104. Abstract also in *Catholic Educational Review,* Vol. 51, p. 336-337, May 1953. For doctoral dissertation by same author, See No. 2336.

2427. NISHIMOTO, MITOJI. *Vocational Guidance in Osaka, Japan.* Columbia University, 1925. 92 p. ms.

2428. NISHIMURA, SEIICHIRO. *Kaibara Ekken (1631-1716), a Pioneer of Elementary Education in Japan.* Columbia University, 1911. 34 p. ms.

2429. NOGUCHI, HIROSHI. *Teachers in Japan: An Appraisal of the Educational Reform in Post-War Japan.* University of Minnesota, 1952. 57 p. ms.

2430. OBAMA, SHIGESHI. *The Fundamental Characteristics of Moral Education in Japan.* New York University, 1932. 89 p. ms.

2431. OBARA, KUNI. *The Place of the Japanese Family in Religious Education.* New York University, 1930. 94 p. ms.

2432. OLTMANS, SARAH CLARK. *The Japanese System of Education.* University of Kentucky, 1942. 90 p. ms.

2433. OTANI, YOSHIO. *Sociological Analyses of Elementary Curricula in Japan.* Columbia University, 1932. 94 p. ms.

2434. OTOMO, SHIGERU. *The Training of Teachers in Japan.* University of Chicago, 1923. 190 p. ms. For doctoral dissertation by same author, see No. 2341.

2435. OZAKI, TAKAKO CATHERINE. *The Educational Work of the Sisters of Notre Dame de Namur in Japan.* Catholic University of America, 1956. 76 p. ms. Abstract in *Catholic Educational Review,* Vol. 56, p. 613, December 1958.

2436. PATTERSON, VERNON K. *Lafcadio Hearn, the Teacher in Japan.* University of Southern California, 1946. 90 p. ms.

2437. PAWLEY, ANNABELLE. *The Development of Education for Women in Japan.* New York University, 1929. 76 p. ms.

2438. PEAKE, CYRUS HENDERSON. *The Influence of Japan upon European Thought, as Revealed in Books Written by Europeans, 1800-1890.* Columbia University, 1925. 42 p. ms. For doctoral dissertation by same author, see No. 1462.

2439. PLACE, PAULINE ALLEN, 1888- . (Later Mrs. Charles Rowland.) *The Educational Bearing of the Recent Industrial Changes upon the Women of Japan.* Boston University, 1923. 51 p. ms.

2440. ROOT, WILLIAM DARWIN. *The Problem of English in the Government Middle Schools of Japan.* Columbia University, 1906. 42 p. ms.

2441. SANO, CHIYE. *Problems Peculiar to Japanese Language Teaching.* State University of Iowa, 1953. 115 p. ms.

2442. SCHROER, CORNELIA RODEHEFFER. *An Enterprise in Homemaking for Young Persons Fifteen to Seventeen Years of Age in Morioka Christian Education Center.* Hartford School of Religious Education, 1938. 63 p. ms.

2443. SCHROER, GILBERT WILLIAM. *The Educational Evangelization Program of the Church of Christ in North Japan.* Hartford School of Religious Education, 1930. 100 p. ms. For doctoral dissertation by same author, see No. 2345.

2444. SHAW, ANITA HYGATE. *A Historical Review of Education for Girls in Japan.* American University, 1956. 103 p. ms.

2445. SHIDLER, WILLIAM LAWRENCE. *The Present Educational System of Japan.* University of Washington, 1927. 61 p. ms.

2446. SHIMAMURA, YAMA. *Evaluation of Shushin Text Books for Grades One to Three.* University of Chicago, 1927. 56 p. ms.

2447. SHIVELY, BENJAMIN FRANKLIN. *An Examination of a Japanese Sunday School Curriculum.* Columbia University, 1914. 71 p. ms.

2448. SMITH, PERCY ALMERIN. *Education in Old Japan.* University of Illinois, 1912. 307 p. ms. Abstract in Russell Taaffe Gregg: *Annotated Bibliography of Graduate Theses in Education at the University of Illinois,* 1931, p. 63. (Bureau of Educational Research, Bulletin No. 55.)

2449. SMITH, ROBERT KREITER. *An Experimental Study of the Teaching of English to Japanese Secondary School Students.* Ohio State University, 1954. 101 p. ms.

2450. SODEN, Brother ALOYSIUS M. *The Present Status of the Catholic Institutions of Higher Learning in Japan, 1945-1956.* Catholic University of America, 1957. 90 p. ms.

2451. SPENCER, DORIS LOUISE. *The Christian Education of Women and Children in Japan.* Central Baptist Theological Seminary, 1951.

2452. STARMER, GARRETT LUDLOW. *The Adolescent Japanese Mind.* Stanford University, 1944. 188 p. ms.

2453. STOWE, GRACE HANNAH. *A Critical Survey of English Used by Students of Kobe College, Japan.* University of Chicago, 1932. 79 p. ms.

2454. SWANSON, EDWIN, 1917- . *Presenting the Gospel to Young Japanese Converts.* Boston University, 1956. 149 p. ms. (A report on methods of Christian education.)

2455. TAJIMA, MATSUE HARADA. *The Religion of Pre-Adolescent Children in Japan.* Oberlin College, 1933. 115 p. ms.

2456. TAKAYAMA, WILLIAM KIYOSHI. *Some Fundamental Factors and Principles Underlying Education in Nationalism and Internationalism in Japan.* Columbia University, 1918. 62 p. ms.

2457. TAKENAKA, JIRO. *A Historical Study of Western Influence on Japanese National Education.* Columbia University, 1934. 67 p. ms. (Includes both American and European influences, the latter English, French, and German.)

2458. TAKEUCHI, Mrs. MEI MATSUMOTO. *Religious Education in Japan: With Special Reference to Protestant Christian and Buddhist Sunday Schools.* Oberlin College, 1929. 199 p. ms.

2459. TANAKA, JITSUKO. *Christian Education for Older Youth in Japan.* Berkeley Baptist Divinity School, 1956. 98 p. ms.

2460. TAYLOR, DOROTHY MAY, 1908- . *The Administration of the Christian Schools of Japan Related to Members of the Interboard Committee in the Decade 1947-1956.* Johns Hopkins University, 1956. 79 p. ms.

2461. TOGASHI, TOMOKAZEN, 1928- . *Educational Vacuum: A Critical Study of the Japanese Blind Education.* Phillips University, 1957. 79 p. ms.

2462. TREMAIN, MARTEL A. *Leadership in Religious Education in Ishikawa Prefecture, Japan.* Columbia University, 1933. 12 p. ms.

2463. TSUNEKAWA, YOHOI. *Religious and Moral Education in Japan.* University of Chicago, 1909. 42 p. ms.

2464. TUCKER, ARTHUR RANDOLPH. *Nationalism in the Educational System of Japan.* University of Washington, 1939. 81 p. ms. Abstract in University of Washington: *Abstracts of Theses,* Vol. 5, 1941, p. 60-62.

2465. TUNG, LOU HISAKO WATANABE. *Library Developments and Status of National Bibliography in Japan.* University of Chicago, 1952. 193 p. ms. Available on microfilm. See index under "University of Chicago."

2466. UESUGI, SUMIO. *Contribution of Western Athletics to Japanese Education.* University of Chicago, 1916. 40 p. ms.

2467. WATSON, HAZEL TUNSTEAD, 1919- . *A School for English-Speaking Children, Miyazaki, Japan.* New Jersey State Teachers College, Newark, 1956. 46 p. ms.

2468. WEIBLE, GERALDINE M. *A Study of Teacher Preparation in Japan between 1920 and 1945.* Catholic University of America, 1948. 153 p. ms. Abstract in W. C. Eells, *The Literature of Japanese Education, 1945-1954,* p. 171-172.

2469. WEST, RALPH ELLSWORTH. *A Constructive Program of Religious Education for Aoyama Gakuin.* New York University, 1931. 61 p. ms.

2470. WILLISTON, HORACE, Jr. *General Araki's Contribution to Japanese Militarism and Ultra-Nationalism in the 1930's.* University of California, Berkeley, 1951. 174 p. ms. (General Araki was Japanese Minister of Education before World War II.)

2471. WOODARD, WILLIAM. *A Leadership Training Program for Teachers in Church Schools in Hokkaido, Japan.* University of Chicago, 1929. 89 p. ms.

2472. YAMAGATA, RURIKO. *Christian Girls' High Schools in Japan.* George Peabody College for Teachers, 1933. 82 p. ms.

2473. YAMAMOTO, SHEILA PATRICIA ANNE, 1928- . *A Survey of Japanese Educators' Opinions towards the Influence of the American Mission of Education since 1946.* Boston College, 1953. 43 p. ms.

2474. YOKOGAWA, YOSOHACHI, -1941. *The Education of Japanese Women.* Clark University, 1917. 71 p. ms.

2475. YOSHIKAWA, TETSUTARO. *Social Change and Educational Theory and Practice in Japan.* University of Southern California, 1930. 60 p. ms.

2476. YOSOHACHI, YOKAGAWA. *The Education of Japanese Women.* Clark University, 1917.

2477. YOUNG, Mrs. DOROTHY TROY. *Lafcadrio Hearn's Tokyo Lectures.* Columbia University, 1943. 155 p. ms. (Given at Tokyo Imperial University.)

2478. ZISCHKE, JAMES BRADEN. *JAPOC — the First Year of the Occupation of Japan.* Stanford University, 1947. 147 p. ms. (Includes discussion of educational changes and prefectural investigations of education.)

See also Nos. 187, 195, 213, 218, 219, 225, 226, 231, 238, 239, 250, 268, 274, 301, 303, 308, 1306, 1310, 1312, 1317, 1318, 1319, 4841

For Japanese groups in the United States, see Nos. 5151-5206.

Jordan
(NOS. 2479-2480)

DOCTOR

See No. 120

MASTERS

2479. KHURY, LAILA, 1929- . *Some Projections of Teaching Mathematics in the Secondary Schools of Jordan.* University of North Carolina, 1957. 41 p. ms.

2480. TAHER, MUHAMMAD TAHER. *Proposals for the Reconstruction of the Program of Education in the Secondary Schools of Jordan with Particular Reference to Student Non-Academic Activities.* Ohio State University, 1954. 206 p. ms.

See also Nos. 226, 229, 247

Korea
(NOS. 2481-2541)

DOCTORS

2481. ADAMS, DONALD KENDRICK, 1925- . *Education in Korea, 1945-1955.* University of Connecticut, 1956. 318 p. ms. Abstract in *Dissertation Abstracts,* Vol. 16, p. 1630, September 1956. Available on microfilm from University Microfilms, Ann Arbor, Michigan, as Publication No. 18,314.

2482. AUH, PAUL. *Education as an Instrument of National Assimilation: A Study of the Policy of Japan in Korea.* Columbia University, 1931. 246 p. ms. For master's thesis by same author, see No. 2509.

2483. BAICK, DAI HYEN. *Pasture Establishment and Management for Students of Vocational Agriculture in Korea.* Louisiana State University and State Agricultural and Mechanical College, 1956. 146 p. ms. Abstract in *Dissertation Abstracts,* Vol. 18, p. 723, March 1958. Available on microfilm from University Microfilms, Ann Arbor, Michigan, as Publication No. 18,728.

2484. CHEY, SOON-JU. *A Suggested Commercial Curriculum for the Chosen Christian College in Korea.* New York University, 1930. 271 p. ms.

2485. CHO, SEUNG HAK, 1903- . *A Study of the Korean Elementary School Curriculum.* University of Wisconsin, 1937. 200 p. ms. Abstract in University of Wisconsin: *Summaries of Doctoral Dissertations,* Vol. 2, 1936-37, p. 243-244.

2486. CHOY, YOUNG-HO. *Reorganization of Private Education in Korea, with Special Emphasis on the Rural Secondary Phase.* Indiana University, 1930. 139 p. ms. Abstract in Indiana University: *News Letter of Alpha Chapter* (of Phi Beta Kappa), April 1931, p. 9.

2487. CHUN, SUNG-CHUN, 1913- . *Schism and Unity in the Protestant Churches of Korea.* Yale University, 1955. 214 p. ms. (Principal basis for schism was policy on education.)

2488. CHUNG, KEI WON, 1900- . (Chong, Ki-won in Library of Congress card catalog.) *The Origins of the Korean Alphabet.* Princeton University, 1938. 123 p. ms. Available on microfilm from University Microfilms, Ann Arbor, Michigan, as Publication No. 2,928.

2489. CLARK, CHARLES ALLEN, 1878- . *The National Presbyterian Church of Korea as a Test of the Validity of the Nevius Principles of Missionary Method.* University of Chicago, 1929. Published as *The Korean Church and the Nevius Methods.* New York: Fleming H. Revell Co., 1930. 278 p. Abstract in University of Chicago: *Abstracts of Theses, Humanistic Series,* Vol. 7, p. 647-652. (Includes consideration of religious education.)

2490. COOPER, BERNARR. *Radio Broadcasting to Chinese and Korean POW's: A Rhetorical Analysis.* Stanford University, 1957.

2491. DIETZ, Mrs. ELISABETH HOFFMAN WARNER, 1908- . *Normal School Education in the Republic of Korea, 1952-53.* New York University, 1955. 345 p. ms. Abstract in *Dissertation Abstracts,* Vol. 16, p. 501-502, March 1956. Available on microfilm from University Microfilms, Ann Arbor, Michigan, as Publication No. 15,541.

2492. FISHER, JAMES EARNEST, 1886- . *Democracy and Mission Education in Korea.* Columbia University, 1928. New York: Teachers College, Columbia University, 1928. xiii, 187 p. (Teachers College Contribution to Education, No. 306.)

2493. KIM, HELEN KITEUK, 1899- . *Rural Education for the Regeneration of Korea.* Columbia University, 1931. 124 p. ms.

2494. KIM, HYUN CHUL, 1901- . *History of Education in Korea.* American University, 1931. 291 p. ms.

2495. LAH, KIHOUGH H. 1895- . *Geography of Korea,* Columbia University, 1957. 204 p. ms. ("This project is a text on Korean geography suitable for the South Korean secondary schools . . . . They need a modern geography of Korea with emphasis on human elements and the world peace.")

2496. LEE, SUNG-HWA. *The Social and Political Factors Affecting Korean Education, 1885-1950.* University of Pittsburgh, 1958. 235 p. ms. Abstract in *Dissertation Abstracts,* Vol. 19, p. 1284-1285, December 1958. Available on microfilm from University Microfilms, Ann Arbor, Michigan, as Mic. 58-5619.

2497. PAIK, HYUNG KI, 1928- . *Designing Country Cooperative Service for the Improvement of the School and Community in the Rural Areas of Korea, with Special Attention to Audio-Visual Service.* Columbia University, 1956. 246 p. ms.

2498. PAIK, LARK-JUNE GEORGE, 1895- . *The History of Protestant Missions in Korea, 1832-1910.* Yale University, 1927. Pyeng Yang, Korea: Union Christian College Press, 1929. ix, 438 p. With Foreword by K. S. Latourette. (Includes the educational work of the missions.)

2499. RIM, HAN YOUNG, 1917- . *The Development of Higher Education in Korea during the Japanese Occupation (1910-1945).* Columbia University, 1952. 246 p. ms.

2500. ROE, CHUNGIL YHAN. *The True Function of Education in Social Adjustment: A Comparative Estimate and Criticism of the Educational Teachings of Confucius and the Philosophy of John Dewey, with a View to Evolving a Project for a System of National Education Which Will Meet the Needs of Korea.* University of Nebraska, 1928. Lincoln, Nebraska: University of Nebraska Press, 1927. 60 p.

2501. SMITH, MELTON VERN. *Self Representations of American and Korean Youth.* University of Texas, 1958. 154 p. ms. Abstract in *Dissertation Abstracts*, Vol. 18, No. 6, p. 2065. Available on microfilm from University Microfilms, Ann Arbor, Michigan, as Mic. 58-1670.

2502. SUHR, MYONG WON. *Together We Live: A Proposed Civics Textbook for the Elementary Schools in the New Korea.* George Peabody College for Teachers, 1953. 168 p. ms. (Contribution to Education, Second series, No. 20.) Abstract in George Peabody College for Teachers: *Abstracts of Dissertations . . . 1953,* p. 205-213.

2503. UNDERWOOD, HORACE HORTON, 1890-1951. *An Outline History of Modern Education in Korea.* New York University, 1926. Published as *Modern Education in Korea,* New York: International Press, 1926. xv, 336 p. For master's thesis by same author, see No. 2539.

2504. VAN LIEROP, PETER. *The Development of Schools under the Korea Mission of the Presbyterian Church in the U. S. A., 1919-1950.* University of Pittsburgh, 1955. 265 p. ms. Abstract in *Dissertation Abstracts,* Vol. 16, p. 170, January 1956. Available on microfilm from University Microfilms, Ann Arbor, Michigan, as Publication No. 15,109.

2505. WASSON, ALFRED WASHINGTON, 1880- . *Factors in the Growth of the Church in Korea.* University of Chicago, 1931. Published as *Church Growth in Korea,* New York: International Missionary Council, 1934. xii, 175 p. (Studies in the World Mission of Christianity, No. 1). With Introduction by John R. Mott and Foreword by Kenneth S. Latourette. Reprint of above distributed to libraries in the United States and abroad in 1934. (Includes consideration of educational work of the Methodist Episcopal Church, South.)

2506. YOO, HYUNG JIN. *An Intellectual History of Korea from Ancient Times to the Impact of the West, with Special Emphasis on Education.* Harvard University, 1958. 300 p. ms.

See also Nos. 144, 170, 182, 1300

MASTERS

2507. AHN, WHAYOUNG CHUNG. *Development of a Piano Course in Colleges in Korea.* Illinois Wesleyan University, 1951.

2508. ANDERSON, SARA MAY. *The Use of Korean Folk Songs in School Music.* University of Rochester, Eastman School of Music, 1940.

2509. AUH, PAUL. *A Suggested Plan for Industrial Education in the Schools of Korea.* Northwestern University, 1927. 154 p. ms. For doctoral dissertation by same author, see No. 2482.

2510. BAY, JUNG H. *A Suggested Application of United States Standardized Tests in Elementary Mathematics in Korea.* Texas State College for Women, 1957. 112 p. ms.

2511. CHAN, WHA CHIEN. *A Proposal for a Guidance Program in the Secondary Schools of Korea.* West Texas State College, 1958.

2512. CHANG, UN PYO. *A Proposed Audio-Visual Program for the Teacher Training Institutions in Korea.* Ohio State University, 1958.

2513. CHOI, E. SOON, 1912- . *A Plan for Adapting Principles of Child Development to Meet the Needs of Korean Children.* Oregon State College, 1938. 144 p. ms.

2514. CHU, YOSEI. *Elementary Education in Korea.* Stanford University, 1928.

2515. CHYUNG, TAI-CHIN. *Korean Youths: Their Major Difficulties and Proposed Solutions.* Columbia University, 1931. 52 p. ms.

2516. CONROW, MARION LANE, 1894- . *A Program for the Teaching of English in the Ewha Woman's College, Seoul, Korea.* Boston University, 1929. 103 p. ms.

2517. GOODWIN, MIRIAM FULLER. *The Possibilities of Religious Education in Korea.* Hartford School of Religious Education, 1929. 81 p. ms.

2518. HO, CHAI SOOK. *The Audio-Visual Handbook for the Teachers in Korea.* University of Southern California, 1958.

2519. KIM, HELEN. *Historical Development of Religious Education in the Methodist Church in Korea.* Emory University, 1953. (Written in School of Theology under Prof. Arva C. Floyd. Not available in University library. Librarian states name is Pauline Kim.)

2520. KIM, INN SYE. *Propose the Supervisory Program for Korean Secondary Schools.* San Francisco State College, 1957. 96 p. ms. (Note: Librarian states that title was probably intended to be "A Proposed Supervisory Program," etc.)

2521. KIM, SUN JAI, 1917- . *Education for Korean Students, with Emphasis on the Interrelationship of Reading and Speaking.* Boston University, 1950. 113 p. ms.

2522. KNECHTEL, EARL AARON. *The Task of Religious Education in the United Church of Canada Territory of the Korean Presbyterian Church.* Columbia University, 1935. 59 p. ms.

2523. LEE, KEITH CHUN, 1910- . *A Historical Survey of Korean Education from the Close of the Yi Dynasty to the Reestablishment of an Independent State (1883-1948).* University of Delaware, 1950. 136 p. ms.

2524. LEE, KYU H. *A Study of Education of Women in Korea since 1910.* University of Washington, 1957.

2525. LEE, KYU YONG, 1892- . *A Proposed Plan for the Training of Leaders for the Program of Religious Education in the Protestant Churches of Korea.* Presbyterian Theological Seminary, 1931. 146 p. ms.

2526. LEE, YUN SHIG SYNN. *A Proposed Plan of Christian Nuture for Pre-School Children in the Korean Home.* Biblical Seminary in New York, 1955. 96 p. ms.

2527. LEE, YUNG DUG. *A Study of a Proposed Guidance Program for the Public Schools of Korea.* Ohio State University, 1956. 221 p. ms.

2528. LYON, WILLIAM BARKLEY. *History of the Sunday School Work of the Chosen (Korea) Mission of the Presbyterian Church in the U.S.A.* Northwestern University, 1930. 122 p. ms.

2529. MIN, CHAN HO. *A Study of the History of Education in Modern Korea.* University of Southern California, 1917. 50 p. ms.

2530. PAK, MARIA HOWELL. *An Outline of a Program of Religious Education for Ewha College.* George Peabody College for Teachers, 1932. 127 p. ms.

2531. PEERMAN, ERNEST LESLIE. *Religious Education in Korea.* Hartford School of Religious Education, 1922. 77 p. ms.

2532. REINER, RALPH OLIVER. *The Organization and Administration of Modern Public Education in Korea.* University of Southern California, 1931. 243 p. ms.

2533. SHEN, YUNG-CHEN. *Secondary Education in Korea.* Stanford University, 1928. 80 p. ms.

2534. SHIPP, FREDERIC THOMAS. *A Christian Education Program for the Korean Y.M.C.A.* Stanford University, 1931. 86 p. ms. plus bibliography.

2535. SUH, WHA SOOK, 1919- . *A Critique of Proposed Programs of Reorganization in Korea in the Light of Her Twentieth Century History and Culture.* Texas Christian University, 1952. 192 p. ms. (Includes education.)

2536. TRESCHMAN, HELENE FREDERICKA. *A Program of Religious Education for Mission Centers in Korea.* Northwestern University, 1924.

2537. TROXEL, MONETA JEAN. *A Study of the Nature Experiences of Korean College Students.* University of Chicago, 1932. 119 p. ms.

2538. UNDERWOOD, ETHEL VAN WAGENER. *A Tentative Program of Health Education for Korea.* New York University, 1925. 59 p. ms.

2539. UNDERWOOD, HORACE HORTON, 1890-1951. *A Comparison of the Relative Efficiency for Reading, Writing, and Comprehension of the Mixed Script and the Vernacular in Korean.* New York University, 1924. 87 p. ms. For doctoral dissertation by same author, see No. 2503.

2540. YOO, YUN SOOK. *A Study of Some Selected Teaching Aids and Techniques for College Level Secretarial Office Practice Courses in Korea.* University of Southern California, 1958.

2541. YOON, STANLEY SUNG SOON. *A Study of the Teachers in Certain Private High Schools of Korea in 1928.* University of Minnesota, 1929. 90 p. ms. Abstract in University of Minnesota: *Abstracts of Masters' and Doctors' Theses in Education . . .* July 1, 1929 to July 1, 1930, p. 14.

See also Nos. 211, 239, 303, 1305, 1306, 1318, 1919

For Korean groups in the United States, see Nos. 4956, 4970, 4972, 4979, 5013

Lebanon

(NOS. 2542-2552)

DOCTORS

2542. GHALIB, HANNA. *A Suggested Plan for Improving Teacher Education in the Republic of Lebanon.* Ohio State University, 1957. 237 p. ms. Abstract in *Dissertation Abstracts,* Vol. 18, p. 2069, June 1958. Available on microfilm from University Microfilms, Ann Arbor, Michigan, as Mic. 58-2068. For master's thesis by same author, see No. 2550.

2543. NAJARIAN, PERGROUHI HAROUTUN, 1918- . *Toward a Theory of Human Nature and Growth: A Basis for a Philosophy of Education for Lebanon.* Cornell University, 1952. 329 p. ms. For master's thesis by same author, see No. 2552.

2544. NAJJAR, FARID JIBRAIL, 1909- . *Guides to the Improvement of Teacher Education in Lebanon.* Columbia University, 1957. 166 p. ms.

2545. NASR, RAJA TEWFIK, 1929- . *The Phonological Problems Involved in the Teaching of American English to Native Speakers of Lebanese Arabic.* University of Michigan, 1955. 163 p. ms. Abstract in *Dissertation Abstracts.* Vol. 15, No. 9, p. 1617, September 1955. Available on microfilm from University Microfilms, Ann Arbor, Michigan, as Publication No. 12,628.

See also Nos. 120, 132, 174, 1298, 1303

MASTERS

2546. BAROODY, WADAD B., 1933- . *Planning for the Blind in Lebanon.* Boston University, 1956. 67 p. ms.

2547. BOCK, DOROTHY ADELE. *The Selection of Students at the American University of Beirut.* University of Chicago, 1932. 55 p. ms.

2548. DAVIS, EDITH CELESTE, 1914- . *An Elementary Education Curriculum for Middle East College.* Pacific Union College, 1950. 89 p. ms.

2549. FLOWER, BETTY EILEEN. *Christian Education in Lebanon, a Moslem Frontier.* Princeton Theological Seminary, 1955. 89 p. ms.

2550. GHALIB, HANNA. *Guides for the Establishment of Professional Laboratory Experiences for Students of Teachers Colleges in Lebanon.* Ohio State University, 1956. 131 p. ms. For doctoral dissertation by same author, see No. 2542.

2551. KHOURY, JOSEPH FARJALLAH, 1935- . *The Lebanon Rural Community Organization and Education.* University of Maryland, 1958. 102 p. ms.

2552. NAJARIAN, PERGROUHI HAROUTUN, 1918- . *The Educational Frontiers in Lebanon and John Dewey's Philosophy of Education.* Cornell University, 1950. 167 p. ms. For doctoral dissertation by same author, see No. 2543.

See also Nos. 226, 229, 238, 264, 1307, 1308

For Lebanese groups in the United States see Nos. 4957, 4970, 4975, 4977

Malaya
(NOS. 2553-2562)

DOCTORS

2553. HENDERSHOT, VERNON EDWARDS, 1895- . *A Historical Critique of the School System of British Malaya.* University of Southern California, 1941. 190 p. ms. Abstract in University of Southern California: *Abstracts of Dissertations,* 1941, p. 34-36. For master's thesis by same author, see No. 4337.

2554. HO, SENG ONG, 1898- . *An Evaluation of the Educational System of British Malaya with Special Reference to Need for Unity in Its Plural Society.* University of Denver, 1949. Published as *Education for Unity in Malaya: An Evaluation of the Educational System of Malaya with Special Reference to Need for Unity in Its Plural Society,* Penang, Malaya: Malayan Teachers Union, 1952. ix, 209 p. (Educational Research Series, No.1.)

See also Nos. 170, 179, 1301

MASTERS

2555. BELL, PERCY BAILEY. *Education in Malaya.* University of Washington, 1953. 107 p. ms.

2556. BUNCE, THIRZZ ELEANOR. *A Study of Moral and Religious Education in British Malaya.* Indiana State Teachers College, 1932. 67 p. ms. Abstract in *Teachers College Journal,* Vol. 3, p. 289-290. July 1932, Section 2. (Contributions of the Graduate School, No. 63.)

2557. HAINES, JOSEPH HARRY. *A History of the Methodist Church in Malaya.* Princeton Theological Seminary, 1956, 119 p. ms. (Includes educational activities.)

2558. HALL, CLYDE JESSE. *A Program of Religious Education for an Anglo-Chinese Day School of Malaysia.* Northwestern University, 1921. 74 p. ms.

2559. HAMEL, ALBERT, 1925- . *History of Methodist Education in Malaysia.* Emory University, 1949. 332 p. ms.

2560. PETERSON, HERBERT HENRY. *The Development of English Education in British Malaya.* University of Denver, 1942. 167 p. ms.

2561. SUMMERS, GERALD VAUGHN. *The Teaching of Beginning Reading to Non-English-Speaking Children.* University of Nebraska, 1934. 67 p. ms. ("The results of the study are to be applied in teaching in the English schools of Malaya where three racial groups dominate, Chinese, Malays, and Tamils.")

2562. SWIFT, ROBERT DEAN. *A Theological Curriculum for British Malaysia.* Northwestern University, 1922. 100 p. ms.

See also Nos. 226, 275, 1309

Manchuria

(NO. 2563)

DOCTOR

See No. 147

MASTER

2563. KIM, DAVID SUK CHIN. *An Area Study of Manchuria: An Opening Study of Trends in Manchurian Education and Factors Influencing Them between 1932 and 1945.* State University of Iowa, 1953. 118 p. ms.

Pakistan

(NOS. 2564-2579)

DOCTORS

2564. BALOCH, NABI BAKHSH KHAN ALIMUHAMMAD KHAN, 1917- . *Proposals for the Education of Teachers in Pakistan for the New National System of Education.* Columbia University, 1949. 371 p. ms. Abstract in *Teachers College Record,* Vol. 51, p. 386, March 1950.

2565. CHOUDHURY, MUMTAZ UDDIN, 1921- . *A Plan of Adult Education for Eastern Pakistan.* Cornell University, 1949. 374 p. ms.

2566. FEROZE, 1923- . *The Use of Audio-Visual Materials in Fundamental Education in Pakistan.* Ohio State University, 1953. 242 p. ms. (No first name given. Autobiography begins: "I, Feroze, was born in Delhi . . .")

2567. JAFFERI, GHULAM HUSSAIN ALLAH OBAHIO KHAN, 1905- . *A Suggestive Plan for Operating the Rural Schools in Sind (Pakistan) as Community Schools.* Cornell University, 1950. 627 p. ms.

2568. QURAISHI, ZAHIDA, 1922- . *Suggestions and Resource Materials for the Development of a Home Economics Curriculum at the College Level in Pakistan Based on the Study of Home Economics Curricula of Four Colleges in New York State.* Cornell University, 1953. 305 p. ms.

2569. RASHID, RIFAT JAHAN, 1922- . *The Reorganization of Physical Education in Institutions of Higher Learning in Pakistan.* Columbia University, 1952. 235 p. ms.

See also Nos. 138, 170

MASTERS

2570. ALI, KHWAJA SAGHIR. *Possible Impacts of Secondary Education in America on Secondary Education in Pakistan.* Chico State College, 1955. 93 p. ms.

2571. ASAF, MUHAMMAD RAFIQ. *Teaching of English in Pakistan Schools and Suggestions for Improvements.* Southwestern University (Master of Arts degree), 1953. 171 p. ms. For another master's thesis by same author, see No. 2572.

2572. ASAF, MUHAMMAD RAFIQ. *Causes of Mass Illiteracy in Pakistan and a Suggested Program of Adult Education.* Southwestern University (Master of Education degree), 1952. 180 p. ms. For another master's thesis by same author, see No. 2571.

2573. CHAUDRY, NAZIR AHMED, 1907- . *A Recommended Audio-Visual Program for the Punjab, Pakistan, Based upon a Critical Analysis of the Literature and Research Dealing with Audio-Visual Education.* Indiana University, 1953. 312 p. ms.

2574. MALL, WILLIAM K., 1912- . *Education in Pakistan.* Temple University, 1955. 96 p. ms.

2575. MASSEY, SADIG GHULAM. *A Critical Study of the Teaching of History in Punjab (Pakistan) Schools and Suggestions for Improvement in the Light of American Progressive Education.* Southwestern University, 1953. 172 p. ms.

2576. NEEMUCHWALA, NADIR P. *A Proposed Program of Education for Pakistan.* Emerson College, 1958.

2577. NESA, AZIZ UN, 1920- . *Improved Methods of Evaluating the Progress of Students at the Secondary School Level in East Pakistan.* Arizona State Teachers College, Tempe, 1954. 59 p. ms.

2578. SIDDIQUE, HARIBA. *A Translation of the Wechsler-Bellevue Intelligence Scale for Children, with Adaptations Suitable to West Pakistan.* Claremont Graduate School, 1956. 102 p. ms.

2579. ZAFAR, SHOUKAT, 1933- . *A Study of Areas of Interest in Family Financial and Economic Education in Four Colleges in Pakistan.* Cornell University, 1958. 41 p. ms.

See also Nos. 1313, 1314

For Pakistani groups in the United States, see Nos. 4956, 4957, 4964, 4967, 4970, 4977, 5026

Philippines
(NOS. 2580-2893)

Includes theses written at the University of the Philippines and at three other institutions (one thesis each) before July 1946 while these institutions were under the jurisdiction of the United States.

DOCTORS

2580. ADRIANO, PAZ VERNUZ, 1917- . *A Study of the Conditions Affecting the Interests, Attitudes, Ideals, and Problems of Adolescent Girls in Catholic and Public Schools in the Philippines.* Fordham University, 1956.

2581. ALDANA, BENIGNO V., 1898- . *Developing a Defensible Financial Program for the Public Schools of the Philippines.* University of California, Berkeley, 1956. 113 p. ms. For master's thesis by same author, see No. 2666.

2582. BAUTISTA, JOSEPHA, 1900- . *A Critical Analysis of the Centralized Public Education System in the Philippines with Emphasis on Secondary Education.* Indiana University, 1958. 261 p. ms.

2583. BENNETT, GEORGE HENRY, 1910- . *Guidance and Counseling in the Philippines, and Procedures for Vitalizing Its Function in the Public Schools.* New York University, 1954. 179 p. ms. Abstract in *Dissertation Abstracts,* Vol. 15, p. 205-206, January 1955. Available on microfilm from University Microfilms, Ann Arbor, Michigan, as Publication No. 10,657.

2584. BOBBITT, JOHN FRANKLIN, 1876-1956. *The Growth of Philippine Children.* Clark University, 1909. Published in part, with same title, in *Pedagogical Seminary,* vol. 16, p. 137-168, June 1909. Also as a reprint of the above, Worcester, Massachusetts: 1909. 34 p. ms.

2585. BORLONGAN, DEOGRACIAS. *The Significance of Vocational Choices of Philippine High School Seniors.* University of Michigan, 1941. 233 p. ms. Abstract in *Microfilm Abstracts* Vol. 3, No. 2, p. 27-28, 1941. Available on microfilm from University Microfilms, Ann Arbor, Michigan, as Publication No. 284. For master's thesis by same author, see No. 2700.

2586. BUCKISCH, WALTER GERARD MARTIN, 1888- . *The Relation between Private Education and the State in the Philippines, 1924-1933.* Sanford University, 1935. 289 p. ms. Abstract in Stanford University: *Abstracts of Dissertations . . . 1934-35,* p. 169-173.

2587. CALIMQUIM, AURORA AGUSTIN, 1922- . *The History of Elementary Education in the Philippines, 1898-1941.* University of California, Berkeley, 1955. 199 p. ms.

2588. CALIP, Monsignor OSMUNDO ARCE, 1911- . *The Administration of the Constitutional Provisions Related to Religious Instruction in the Public Schools in the Philippines.* University of Notre Dame, 1956. 131 p. ms. Abstract in *Dissertation Abstracts,* Vol. 16, p. 2345-2346, December 1956. Available on microfilm from University Microfilms, Ann Arbor, Michigan, as Publication No. 18,073.

2589. CARLOS, CARMEN BALDERRAMA, 1925- . *A Study of Some Basic Guiding Principles in Teaching Selected Aspects of Elementary Arithmetic with Implications for Educational Practice and Teacher Education in the Philippines.* Indiana University, 1958. 279 p. ms. Abstract in Indiana University: *Studies in Education,* 1958 (Thesis Abstract Series, No. 10, 1959), p. 63-70.

2590. CARREON, MANUEL LINGAD. *The Determination of the Degree of Applicability of Educational Measurements and Psychological Tests in America to the Philippines.* University of Minnesota, 1923. Published as *Applicability of Standard Tests to the Filipino,* Yonkers-on-Hudson, New York: World Book Co., 1926. xiv, 175 p. Also published as *Philippine Studies in Mental Measurement,* with an Introduction by Arthur S. Otis. Yonkers-on-Hudson, New York: World Book Co., 1926; and Manila: Philippine Book Co., 1926. xiv, 175 p. For master's thesis by same author, see No. 2709.

2591. CATEDRAL, ALFREDO PERLA, 1910- . *A Plan for Developing an Organized Guidance Program at the Central Philippine College, Iloilo City, Philippines.* Columbia University, 1949. 236 p. ms. Abstract in *Teachers College Record,* Vol. 51, p. 322-323, February 1950.

2592. CHAMBERS, R. FRED, 1902- . *Central Philippine College: An Historical Study in the Light of Philippine Historical and Cultural Background.* University of Colorado, 1949. 347 p. ms. Abstract in University of Colorado: *Abstracts of Theses . . . 1948-49,* p. 122-124.

2593. CLEMENTE, TITO AGCAOILE, 1892- . *A Comparative Study of the Vocabularies of Philippine and American Readers for the First Grade.* Columbia University, 1937. Manila: Printed at Carmelo & Bauermann, Inc., 1937. iv, 117 p. For master's thesis by same author, see No. 2721.

2594. CORPUS, SEVERINO FERMIN. *Social Change in the Philippines during the Independence Movement, 1898-1935.* University of Southern California, 1951. 646 p. ms. Abstract in University of Southern California: *Abstracts of Dissertations* . . . 1951, p. 227-230. Abstract also in *Abstracts of Completed Doctoral Dissertations for the Academic Year 1950-51* (Department of State, External Research Staff, Office of Intelligence Research, Abstract Series No. 1, March 1952), p. 367-370.

2595. CUIZON, ERLINDA ASUNCION, 1924- . *An Analysis of the Bureau of Private Schools of the Department of Education of the Philippine Republic.* Indiana University, 1956. 303 p. ms. Abstract in Indiana University: *Studies in Education 1956.* (Thesis Abstract Series No. 8, 1957), p. 71-78. Abstract also in *Dissertation Abstracts,* Vol. 16, p. 1823, October 1956. Available on microfilm from University Microfilms, Ann Arbor, Michigan, as Publication No. 17,764.

2596. DANDOY, MAXIMA ANTONIO, 1910- . *Student Teaching in Public Teacher Education Institutions of the Philippines.* Sanford University, 1952. 357 p. ms. Abstract in Stanford University: *Abstracts of Dissertations* . . . 1951-52, p. 498-501.

2597. ELEQUIN, ELEANOR TENGONCIANG, 1927- . *A Study of the Effectiveness of the Student Personnel Services and Adequacy of Guidance and Related Course Offerings for Teacher Training at Philippine Normal College.* Michigan State College of Agriculture and Applied Science, 1954. 245 p. ms. Abstract in *Dissertation Abstracts,* Vol. 14, p. 952-953, June 1954. Available on microfilm from University Microfilms, Ann Arbor, Michigan, as Publication No. 8,067.

2598. ENVERGA, TOBIAS Y, 1917- . *The Comparative Role Expectations of Filipino and American Teachers with Regard to the Administrator.* University of Chicago, 1954. 262 p. ms. Available on microfilm: see index under "University of Chicago." For master's thesis by same author, see No. 2730.

2599. ESTACIO Y CALANOG, CEFERINA IRENEA. *Design of an Approach to the Teaching of English in the Philippines.* Harvard University, 1956. ("This thesis is not yet available. The author apparently still must make some revisions, though the degree was granted in due order in 1956. She has not yet deposited her work with the Harvard University Archives." – Librarian, December 1958.

2600. FACTORA, AGAPITO QUEVEDEO, 1898- . *A Critical Examination of the American School System in the Philippine Islands.* University of Southern California, 1940. 48 p. ms. Abstract in University of Southern California: *Abstracts of Dissertations,* 1940, p. 41-42.

2601. FERRER, ADINA RIGOR, 1919- . *Procedures for Reconstructing the Course of Study in Physical Education for Elementary Schools in the Philippines.* State University of Iowa, 1956. 172 p. ms. Abstract in *Dissertation Abstracts,* Vol. 16, p. 1632-1633, September 1956. Available on microfilm from University Microfilms, Ann Arbor, Michigan, as Publication No. 17,471.

2602. FOX, HENRY FREDERICK, 1912- . *Official Spanish Policy Concerning Elementary Education in the Philippines from 1863 to 1898, Compared with Official American Policy from 1900 to 1935.* University of Chicago, 1953. 395 p. ms. Available on microfilm: see index under "University of Chicago."

2603. GEMARINO, Sister ROSALIA GARINGALAO, 1910- . *Student Problems in Extracurricular Activities: A Study of the Daughters of Charity Schools in the Philippines.* Fordham University, 1957. 345 p. ms. Abstract in *Religious Education,* Vol. 53, p. 268-269, May-June, 1958.

2604. GONZALEZ, EVA BEATRICE. *The Educational Philosophy of Teachers of Home and Family Courses in the Public General Secondary Schools of Luzon, Philippines.* Cornell University, 1958. 141 p. ms. Abstract in *Dissertation Abstracts,* Vol. 19, p. 69-70, July 1958. Available on microfilm from University Microfilms, Ann Arbor, Michigan, as Mic. 58-2443.

2605. GOSS, GEORGE EDWARD, 1886-1936. *The Development of Organized Physical Education in the Philippine Islands.* New York University, 1932. 170 p. ms. For master's thesis by same author, see No. 3034.

2606. GRAVES, SAMUEL MONROE, 1878-1943. *Education in the Philippine Islands.* Harvard University, 1913. 324 p. ms.

2607. GUIANG, PEDRO GARAZA, 1898- . *The Service Load of Secondary School Teachers in the Philippines.* University of Washington, 1935. 119 p. ms. Abstract in University of Washington: *Abstracts of Theses . . .* Vol. 2, 1937, p. 461-466. For master's thesis by same author, see No. 2757.

2608. HABITO, CELESTINE PABELLO. *Development of an Adult-Farmer Education Program for the Philippines.* University of Minnesota, 1958. 380 p. ms. Abstract in *Dissertation Abstracts,* Vol. 19, p. 722, October 1959. Available on microfilm from University Microfilms, Ann Arbor, Michigan, as Mic. 58-3534.

2609. HEFLIN, CLYDE EVERETTE, 1888- . *Teacher Education for Philippine Democracy: Plans to Be Used as a Guide in Developing at Silliman University a Program Designed to Educate Teachers for Leadership in the Movement to Make the Schools of the Philippines Better Serve the Needs of Their Communities.* Columbia University, 1946. 227 p. ms.

2610. HUDSON, VANAVERY DON, 1902- . *The Legislative History of Philippine Independence Legislation.* State University of Iowa, 1936. 420 p. ms. Abstract in State University of Iowa: *Programs Announcing Candidates for Higher Degrees . . .* 1936. Abstract also in *Bulletin of the Northeast Missouri State Teachers College,* Kirksville, Missouri, Vol. 37, No. 10, November 1937, 30 p. (Includes consideration of development of education.)

2611. ISIDRO Y SANTOS, ANTONIO, 1901- . (Also listed as Santos, Antonio Isidro y). *The Development of Written English Expression of Filipino Children.* University of Chicago, 1934. 208 p. ms. Part of the dissertation (42 p. photolithographed) was distributed to libraries in the United States and abroad in 1937. For master's thesis by same author, see No. 2765.

2612. JESENA, FLORINDA M., 1928- . *A Study of the Problems and Guidance Needs of Adolescent*

Girls Attending Catholic Boarding Schools in the Philippines. Fordham University, 1956. 433 p. ms.

2613. JIMINEZ, CARMEN TOMBO, 1910- . *A Proposed Student Personnel Program for the Philippine Women's College, Iloilo City, Philippines.* Columbia University, 1951. 283 p. ms.

2614. JURADO, LEONARDA MARTINEZ, 1912- . *Group Work as an Effective Approach for the Improvement of In-Service Education of Teachers in the Philippines.* Cornell University, 1953. 304 p. ms.

2615. LACUESTA Y GASCON, MANUEL. *The History of the Preparation of High School Teachers in the Philippines, 1901-1941.* Columbia University, 1958. 440 p. ms. Abstract in *Dissertation Abstracts*, Vol. 19, p. 1284, December 1958. Available on microfilm from University Microfilms, Ann Arbor, Michigan, as Mic. 58-2693.

2616. LARDIZABAL, AMPARO SANTAMARIA, 1908- . *Pioneer American Teachers and Philippine Education.* Stanford University, 1956. 336 p. ms. Abstract in *Dissertation Abstracts*, Vol. 16, p. 1834, October 1956. Available on microfilm from University Microfilms, Ann Arbor, Michigan, as Publication No. 17,726.

2617. LEAR, ELMER NORTON, 1917- . *Collaboration, Resistance, and Liberation: A Study of Society and Education in Leyte, the Philippines, under Japanese Occupation.* Columbia University, 1951. 719 p. ms. Abstract in *Dissertation Abstracts*, Vol. 12, p. 340-341, March 1952. Available on microfilm from University Microfilms, Ann Arbor, Michigan, as Publication No. 3,358.

2618. LIMCACO, ESPERANZA RUIZ, 1920- . *The Guidance Needs of Students at the University of the Philippines.* Stanford University, 1955. 135 p. ms. Abstract in *Dissertation Abstracts*, Vol. 16, p. 51, January 1956. Available on microfilm from University Microfilms, Ann Arbor, Michigan, as Publication No. 15,348.

2619. MACALINAO-SOLIS, MIGUELA, 1908- . *Organization and Administration of Elementary Teacher Education in the Philippines.* Stanford University, 1955. 428 p. ms. Abstract in *Dissertation Abstracts*, Vol. 15, p. 754, May 1955. Available on microfilm from University Microfilms, Ann Arbor, Michigan, as Publication No. 11,165.

2620. MANALAYSAY, RAQUEL SALTING, 1921- . *An Appraisal of Selected Aspects of the Teacher Education Program at Philippine Union College.* Indiana University, 1957. 320 p. ms. Abstract in *Dissertation Abstracts*, Vol. 18, p. 513, February 1958. Available on microfilm from University Microfilms, Ann Arbor, Michigan, as Publication No. 25,161.

2621. MARIANO, PABLO PINEDA, 1902- . *Guides to Developing a Four-Year Pre-Service Educational Program for the Preparation of Elementary School Teachers in the Philippines.* Columbia University, 1952. 245 p. ms.

2622. MARTIN, DALMACIO, 1903- . *The Potentialities of the Cooperative Work-Experience Program for General Secondary Education in the Philippines.* Ohio State University, 1954. 437 p. ms. For master's thesis by same author, see No. 2795.

2623. MARTINEZ Y MALAYA, JESUS ISABELO, 1907- . *Guides for Developing Graduate Division Curricula at the Philippine Normal College.* Columbia University, 1953. 212 p. ms.

2624. MARTIN-VALDES, MATILDE. *An Exploratory Study of Reported Personal Problems of a Group of Women Students in the College of Education, University of the Philippines.* University of Buffalo, 1954. 222 p. ms.

2625. MENDEZ, PAZ POLICARPIO, 1903- . *Family Relations: A Test for Filipino High School and College Youth.* Columbia University, 1951. 364 p. ms.

2626. MEURMAN, JOHN CHARLES, 1865-1935. *The Philippine Schools under the Americans.* George Washington University, 1922. 157 p. ms.

2627. NOGUERA, REMEDIOS, 1902- . *A Proposal for a Student Personnel Program for the Philippine Women's University.* Indiana University, 1954. 236 p. ms. Abstract in *Dissertation Abstracts*, Vol. 14, p. 618-619, April 1954. Abstract also in Indiana University, School of Education: *Studies in Education*, 1954, p. 147-150. Available on microfilm from University Microfilms, Ann Arbor, Michigan, as Publication No. 7,908.

2628. OCAMPO, PATROCINIO SISON, 1914- . *In-Service Education Practices in Selected Secondary Schools and Their Implications for the Improvement of Teaching Faculties in the Philippines.* University of Minnesota, 1956. 349 p. ms. Abstract in *Dissertation Abstracts*, Vol. 16, p. 1094-1095, June 1956. Available on microfilm from University Microfilms, Ann Arbor, Michigan, as Publication No. 16,561.

2629. PABLEO, DONATO BERNARDEZ, 1908- . *A Proposal for Curricular Expansion in Philippine Vocational and Technological Colleges.* University of Kentucky, 1955. 173 p. ms. For master's thesis by same author, see No. 2812.

2630. PERALTA, CRESCENCIO GUIDOTE, 1907- . *Teacher Education for Rural Philippine Life.* Stanford University, 1952. Published in part as *Current Issues in Philippine Education*, Manila: Silangan Publishing House, 1955. 203 p. Abstract in Stanford University: *Abstracts of Dissertations* . . . 1951-52, p. 665-667.

2631. PERALTA, MARIA CID Y ADIARTE DE, 1906- . *An Analysis of Procedures for Improving Curriculum Development in the Philippines.* University of Chicago, 1952. 347 p. ms. Available on microfilm: see index under "University of Chicago."

2632. PEREZ, PRESENTACION T., 1906- . *Problems of Employed Women in Certain Professional Groups in the Philippines and Their Educational Implications.* University of Minnesota, 1955. 288 p. ms. Abstract in *Dissertation Abstracts*, Vol. 15, p. 359-360, March 1955. Available on microfilm from University Microfilms, Ann Arbor, Michigan, as Publication No. 11,113.

2633. PINEDA, JULIANA CRUZ, 1897- . *A Critical Study of the Supervisory Program and Practices in the Philippines in the Light of Certain Democratic Principles of Supervision.* Indiana University, 1951. 160 p. ms. Abstract in Indiana University, School of

Education: *Studies in Education,* 1951, p. 107-112. For master's thesis by same author, see No. 2828.

2634. PINERO, FLORA NAVE, 1912- . *Democratic Educational Administration for the Philippine Educational System.* Indiana University, 1952. 392 p. ms. Abstract in Indiana University, School of Education: *Studies in Education,* 1952, p. 257-261.

2635. POLICARPIO-MENDEZ, PAZ. *Family Relations: A Test for Filipino High School and College Youth.* Columbia University, 1951.

2636. PRIEST, BILL JASON, 1917- . *Philippine Education in Transition, 1941-1946.* University of California, Berkeley, 1947. 287 p. ms.

2636a. PRUDENCIADO, Mrs. SOFIA LOZANO, 1919- . *A Proposed Audio-Visual Program for the Philippine Normal College.* Indiana University, 1955. 372 p. ms. Abstract in *Dissertation Abstracts,* Vol. 15, p. 1563-1564, October 1955. Available on microfilm from University Microfilms, Ann Arbor, Michigan, as Publication No. 13,225.

2637. PUTONG, CECILIO, 1891- . *Specific Objectives and Contents of Vocational Education in Agriculture in the Philippine Islands Rice Culture.* University of Chicago, 1937. 177 p. ms. Part of the dissertation (22 p. lithoprinted) was distributed to libraries in the United States and abroad in 1939.

2638. QUIRANTE, LUCENO L., 1913- . *A Study of the Policy of Centralization of Education in the Philippines, 1898-1953.* University of Maryland, 1953. 116 p. ms. Abstract in University of Maryland: *Abstracts of Dissertations . . . 1952-1953 and 1953-1954,* p. 52.

2639. RAMIREZ, EMILIANO CASTRO, 1905- . *Activities and Procedures of Some Community Schools in the United States and Their Implications for the Philippines.* Ohio State University, 1953. Published as *Some Community-School Practices in the United States and Their Implications for the Philippines,* Pasay City, Philippines: National Publishing House, 1954. xvi, 386 p.

2640. ROSARIO, OSEAS A. DEL, 1913- . (Also given as Del Rosario.) *A Proposed Audio-Visual Program for Schools and Colleges in the Philippines.* Indiana University, 1956. 199 p. ms. Abstract in Indiana University: *Studies in Education,* 1956 (Thesis Abstract Series, No. 8), p. 105-112.

2641. ROTZ, HENRY WELTON, 1911- . *A Study of the Recruitment, Training, Support, and Performance of Church Leaders in Three Protestant Denominations in the Philippine Federation of Christian Churches.* Cornell University, 1955. 442 p. ms. Abstract in *Dissertation Abstracts,* Vol. 16, p. 1525-1526, August 1956. Available on microfilm from University Microfilms, Ann Arbor, Michigan, as Publication No. 15,620.

2642. RUTLAND, LOLITA GARCIA, 1920- . *The History of Teacher Education in the Philippines to 1955.* University of Florida, 1955. 113 p. ms. Abstract in University of Florida: *Abstracts of Doctoral Studies in Education,* 1955, p. 119-122. Abstract also in *Dissertation Abstracts,* Vol. 15, p. 2463, December 1955. Available on microfilm from University Microfilms, Ann Arbor, Michigan, as Publication No. 14,328.

2643. SABELLA, RICARDO HICETA, 1895- . *American Educational Policy in the Philippines, 1898-1935: With Special Reference to the Growth of the Public Schools and the Progress Attained by the Filipinos for Self Government.* American University, 1935. 357 p. ms.

2644. SACAY, FRANCISCO MONTALBO, 1904- . *A Survey and Evaluation of Vocational Education in Agriculture in the Philippines.* Cornell University, 1931. 460 p. ms. For master's thesis by same author, see No. 2848.

2645. SAMONTE, SOLEDAD ESPEJO, 1905- . *The Program and Supervision of Elementary Student Teaching in Three Mid-Western Teacher Educating Institutions and Their Implications for Teacher Education in the Philippines.* University of Minnesota, 1953. 452 p. ms. Abstract in *Dissertation Abstracts* Vol. 13, No. 5, p. 729, 1953. Available on microfilm from University Microfilms, Ann Arbor, Michigan, as Publication No. 5,367.

2646. SANGUINET, EDWIN NEIHZE, 1892- . *An Approach to Curriculum Construction Based on a Child Activity Survey in the Philippine Islands.* Columbia University, 1934. Manila: Philippine Teachers Digest, 1934. iv, 87 p.

2647. SANTIAGO, ALICIA ALEJO, 1930- . *A Study of the In-Service Education of Public Secondary School Teachers in Manila, Philippines.* Indiana University, 1957. 362 p. ms. Abstract in *Dissertation Abstracts,* Vol. 18, p. 515, February 1958. Available on microfilm from University Microfilms, Ann Arbor, Michigan, as Publication No. 24,838.

2648. SORIANO, DOMINGO GONZALES, 1906- . *A Plan to Promote Adaptability in the Division of Zamboango, Philippines.* Columbia University, 1953. 101 p. ms. (Includes educational adaptability.)

2649. SORIANO, Mrs. LICERIA BRILLANTES, 1906- . *Planning the Development and Administration of Science Programs for Philippine Community Schools.* Columbia University, 1958. 186 p. ms.

2650. STUART, HARLAND FRANCIS. *The Improvement of Vocational Education in the Philippine Islands.* Harvard University, 1933. 547 p. ms. Available on microfilm, Library of Congress No. Mic. 57-5068.

2651. TADENA, TOMAS P., 1908- . *A Proposed Audio-Visual Program for the University of the Philippines.* Indiana University, 1956. 258 p. ms. Abstract in Indiana University: *Studies in Education,* 1956, p. 315-322. (Thesis Abstract Series, No. 8.) Abstract also in *Dissertation Abstracts,* Vol. 17, p. 83, January 1957. Available on microfilm from University Microfilms, Ann Arbor, Michigan, as Publication No. 19,284.

2652. TIRO, AURELIO AMORES, 1918- . *Existing Guidance Practices in Selected Elementary Schools of the United States and Their Implications for the Philippines.* University of Denver, 1956. 158 p. ms.

2653. TORRANCE, ARTHUR FREDERICK. *The Philippine Moro: A Study in Social and Race Pedagogy.* New York University, 1917. 202 p. ms. Available on microfilm, Library of Congress No. Micro. 57-5073.

2654. TUMBAGAHAN, TIBURCIO JAMORA, 1913-
The First Forty Years: A History of Silliman University from 1901 to 1941. Stanford University, 1949. 107 p. ms. Abstract in Stanford University: *Abstracts of Dissertations . . .* 1948-49, p. 558-561.

2654a. TY, EUFEMIA FORMENTO. *A Proposed Program of Guidance Services for the Rural Schools of the Philippines.* University of Colorado, 1957.

2655. UNTALAN, PELAGIA PACINOY, 1900- . *A Study of Student Teaching Programs in Elementary Education in the Light of Selected Principles, with Special Emphasis Being Given to the Student Teaching Program in the Philippine Normal College.* Indiana University, 1954. 406 p. ms. Abstract in Indiana University: *Studies in Education,* 1954, p. 229-235. Abstract also in *Dissertation Abstracts,* Vol. 15, p. 769-770, May 1955. Available on microfilm from University Microfilms, Ann Arbor, Michigan, as Publication No. 11,211.

2656. VELASQUEZ, MAXIMINIANO ASPIRAS, 1910- . *Development of Principles for In-Service Improvement of Teachers in the Philippines, with Special Reference to Sulu Province.* University of Illinois, 1953. 300 p. ms. Abstract in *Dissertation Abstracts,* Vol. 14, p. 313-315, February 1954. Available on microfilm from University Microfilms, Ann Arbor, Michigan, as Publication No. 6,992.

2657. VILLARIBA, CESAR ARENETA, 1922- . *A Plan for Vocational Education in Four Private High Schools in Quezon Province, Philippines.* Columbia University, 1955. 142 + 96 p. ms.

2658. WHITWELL, CHARLES GARLAND, 1903- *Spanish Educational Policy in the Philippines.* University of Texas, 1940. 258 p. ms. For master's thesis by same author, see No. 2889.

See also Nos. 121, 124, 128, 138, 142, 147, 169, 176, 179, 1073

MASTERS

Note on Availability. "Please note that a number of the entries for the theses from the University of the Philippines from 1918 to 1935 lack pagination. This is due to the fact that most of the copies of the prewar theses were lost when our entire library was destroyed by the Japanese in February 1945, and the lists of theses salvaged from the damaged archives of the University do not include the number of pages of each of these theses." — Acting Librarian.

2659. ADAMS, FERN BURNETT. *A Psychological Study of Filipino-American Children.* University of the Philippines, 1941. 94 p. ms.

2660. AGATEP, CANDIDO PASCUA. *Student Activities Plan for the Rural High Schools of the Philippines.* University of Southern California, 1958.

2661. AGLIAM, ROSARIO TOLENTINO. *Trends of Vocational Education in the Philippine Islands as Revealed by Reports of the Director of Education.* University of Nebraska, 1934. 211 p. ms.

2662. AGUSTIN, SIMEON MUNSAYAC. *An Analysis of the Composition Interests of Pupils in the Intermediate Grades of the Public Schools of the City of Manila.* University of the Philippines, 1940. 205 p. ms.

2663. ALARILLA, LUIS M. *The Difficulties of Students in Beginning College Physics in the University of the Philippines.* University of the Philippines, 1941. 74 p. ms.

2664. ALBA, ROQUE S. *An Analysis and Evaluation of the Desirable Characteristics of the Textbooks in Reading and Social Science for Intermediate Grades.* University of the Philippines, 1939.

2665. ALDABA, ESTEFANIA JULIAN. *Girls' Juvenile Delinquency in the Philippines.* University of the Philippines, 1938. 296 p. ms.

2666. ALDANA, BENIGNO V., 1898- . *The Evolution of the Primary and the General Curriculum of the Public School System.* University of the Philippines, 1933. For doctoral dissertation by same author, see No. 2581.

2667. ALDECOA, VENANCIO. *An Experimental Study of the Effect of Written Preparation of Achievement in General Science.* Silliman University, 1941. 97 p. ms.

2668. ALEJO, ALEJANDRO. *An Analytical Study of the Load of Teachers in Sixty-six Elementary Schools in Bulacan and Its Implications.* University of Manila, 1927. 115 p. ms.

2669. ALONSO, AGUSTIN S. *The Psychology of Feeling.* University of the Philippines, 1922.

2670. ALZONA, ENCARNACION. *The Development of the School Education of Women in the Philippines.* University of the Philippines, 1918.

2671. ANDERSON, RONALD ELMER. *Contributions of Protestant Missions to Agriculture in the Philippine Islands.* Iowa State College of Agriculture and the Mechanic Arts, 1956. 59 p. ms.

2672. ANG, JOSEPHINE. *Audio-Visual Aids to Enrich the Secondary Schools in the Philippines.* San Francisco State College, 1956. 52 p. ms.

2673. ANGELES, FRANCISCO DELOR M., 1928- *Beginnings of the American Educational Work in the Philippines, 1898-1904.* University of Florida, 1953. 135 p. ms.

2674. ANNAGUEY, ELENO D. *A Course in Practical Biology for the Secondary Schools in the Philippines.* University of Southern California, 1951. 111 p. ms.

2675. ANTONIO Y MENDOZA, SYLVESTRE. *The Administration and Supervision of Student Teaching.* Colorado State Teachers College, 1930. 123 p. ms. (Includes application to the Philippines.)

2676. ARANETA, REBECCA YULO. *Education of Philippine Church School Teachers of Preschool Children.* Berkeley Baptist Divinity School, 1958. 114 p. ms.

2677. ARELLENO, MAGDELENO GARCIA, 1907- *A Study of Some Aspects of the Organization and*

Philippines

Administration of Public Education in the Philippines under the American Regime. University of Kansas, 1936. 140 p. ms.

2678. ARIZABAL Y LUCIANO, PAULA. *The Evolution of the Division of Normal Institutes in Relation to the In-Service Training of Elementary School Teachers.* University of the Philippines, 1937.

2679. ASCANO, ANTONIO FRANCISCO. *The Training of Teachers in the Philippine Islands.* University of Chicago, 1923. 126 p. ms.

2680. AUTAJAY, LEONARD CUEVAS. *Youth Work in the Convention of Philippine Baptist Churches.* Berkeley Baptist Divinity School, 1954. 84 p. ms.

2681. AZCUETA, FELIX A. *The Development of Secondary Education in the Philippines under American Rule.* State University of Iowa, 1934. 126 p. ms.

2682. BAJA, TIBURCIO C. *An Analysis of the Language Textbooks Now in Use in the Public Elementary Schools of the Philippines Islands.* University of the Philippines, 1934.

2683. BALTAZAR Y CRUZ, TOMAS. *The Organization, Functions, and Supervision of Educational Research in the Philippine Public Schools.* University of the Philippines, 1935.

2684. BARD, HARRY ERWIN. *The Cost of Public Education in the Philippine Islands.* Columbia University, 1907. 50 p. ms.

2685. BARLAHAN Y VALERA, BIBIANA. *Difficulties of Student Teachers in Grade IV and in the Intermediate Grades of the Training School of the Philippine Normal School.* University of the Philippines, 1932.

2686. BARRION, Sister MARY CARIDAD. *Elementary and Secondary Education in Philippine Private Schools during the Japanese Occupation, 1942-1945.* Creighton University, 1947. 156 p. ms.

2687. BARTOLOME, CANDIDO CONCEPCION. *Observation in Anthropometry and Physical Examination of the Students in the University of the Philippines.* University of the Philippines, 1926. For another master's thesis by same author, see No. 2688.

2688. BARTOLOME, CANDIDO CONCEPCION. *Physical Measurements of Freshmen Filipino Students in the University of the Philippines.* International YMCA College, 1929. 164 p. ms. For another master's thesis by same author, see No. 2687.

2689. BATOON, MARIA ALBANO. *A Course of Study in Physical Education for Girls in Philippine High Schools.* Colorado State College of Education, 1941. 130 p. ms.

2690. BAUTISTA, ADELAIDA TEVES. *Family Life Education for High School Seniors in the Philippines.* San Francisco State College, 1955. 125 p. ms.

2691. BAUTISTA, FERNANDO G. *A Study of Pupil Failures in the Intermediate Classes of the Public Schools in the City of Manila.* University of the Philippines, 1936. 114 p. ms.

2692. BENITEZ, CONRADO. *A Study of Primary Education in the Philippines during Spanish Domination.* University of Chicago, 1911. 70 p. ms.

2693. BERMEJO, FERNANDO V., 1893-1927. *Education in the Philippines under the American Regime.* University of Kansas, 1922. 163 p. ms.

2694. BERNARDINO, VITALIANO. *A Survey of the Philippine Textbooks from the Point of View of Nationalism.* University of the Philippines, 1938.

2695. BERNARDO, LIBRADA. *A Study of the Intelligence of 100 Inmates of the City Boys Reformatory.* University of the Philippines, 1923.

2696. BLACK, GLADYS HELEN. *A Manual for Leaders of Girls' Clubs in the Philippine Islands.* University of Southern California, 1932. 137 p. ms.

2697. BLAKE, OWN ANDREW. *An Effective Accounting System for Seventh-day Adventist Academies and Colleges.* University of the Philippines, 1934.

2698. BOLICH, GEORGE HENRY KRICK. *The Transition from the Spanish to the American System of Education in the Philippine Islands, 1898-1903.* Pennsylvania State College, 1933. 57 p. ms.

2699. BOLLMAN, MARIE ANTOINETTE. *Secondary Education in the Philippines.* University of Washington, 1925. 43 p. ms.

2700. BORLONGAN, DEOGRACIAS. *Classroom Difficulties of Student Teachers in the University High School.* University of the Philippines, 1930. 152 p. ms. For doctoral dissertation by same author, see No. 2585.

2701. BUENO, RAMON, 1906- . *A Study of the Program in the Development of Education in the Philippine Islands.* University of South Dakota, 1930. 85 p. ms.

2702. CABANATAN, SATURINO INVEWCION. *Vocabulary Burden of Eighth Grade English Textbooks in the Public High Schools of the Philippine Islands.* University of Michigan, 1932. 145 p. ms.

2703. CABANOS, JUAN A. *The Training, Compensation, and Emoluments of Filipino Teachers.* University of the Philippines, 1924. 172 p. ms.

2704. CANAVE, JUAN C. *Correlation Between Standings in the Intermediate School and Later Standings in the High School.* University of the Philippines, 1924.

2705. CARINO, ALVARO. *A Brief Survey of the History and Problems of Education in the Philippines and Their Bearing on Mission Work.* Concordia Seminary, 1952. (Thesis for degree of Bachelor of Divinity.)

2706. CARINO, FRANCISCO. *A Suggested Program of Religious Education for Filipino High School Students, Based on a Study of Five Church Programs in Evanston, Illinois.* Northwestern University, 1927. 81 p. ms.

2707. CARINO, OLIVA PALAFOX. *The Easel Age Scale with Philippine and American School Children.* University of Nebraska, 1957. 48 p. ms.

2708. CARPIO, REMIGIA D. *A Study of the Philippine Pensionado System Abroad.* University of the Philippines, 1934.

2709. CARREON, MANUEL LINGAD. *The Role of Standardized Tests in Philippine Public School Administration.* University of Minnesota, 1921. 79 p. ms. For doctoral dissertation by same author, see No. 2590.

2710. CARSWELL, MACKY KENION. *The Education of the Igorots.* Wake Forest College, 1928. 81 p. ms.

2711. CASIM, CANUTO P. *The Service Load of Elementary School Teachers in the City of Manila.* University of the Philippines, 1936. 122 p. ms.

2712. CASTAÑEDA, DEOGRACIAS B. *An Analysis of Philippine Arithmetic (Third Grade): A Study on Curriculum Building.* University of the Philippines, 1932.

2713. CASTILLEJO, LINO JUAN, 1891- . *Industrial Education in the Philippines.* George Washington University, 1920. 96 p. ms.

2714. CASTRO, JOSE S. DE. *A History of Volleyball in the Philippines.* Springfield College, 1954. 99 p. ms.

2715. CASTRO, PROCESO C. *Activities of Elementary School Principals for the Improvement of Instruction.* University of the Philippines, 1936.

2716. CASTRO Y GUICO, ILUMINADO DE. *A Survey of the Behavior Problems of School Children in the Elementary Grades of the City School.* University of the Philippines, 1935.

2717. CATOY, FAUSTO PANGILINAN. *The Development of Public Education in the Philippine Islands from 1898 to 1933.* University of Oregon, 1936. 203 p. ms.

2718. CAULKINS, GLENN WHITMAN. *Public Education in Mindanao-Sulu, Philippine Islands, under the American Regime.* University of Washington, 1934. 110 p. ms.

2719. CERVINI, THERESE MARIE, 1914- . *Educational Work of the American Jesuits in the Philippine Islands.* Fordham University, 1938. 83 p. ms. Abstract in Fordham University: *Dissertations Accepted for Higher Degrees . . .* 1939, p. 77.

2720. CHARLES, Mrs. CAROLINE (LAMBERT). *Development of the Philippine Public School System.* Kennedy School of Missions, 1941. 78 p. ms.

2721. CLEMENTE, TITO AGCAOILE, 1892- . *A Critical Analysis of the Vocabularies of Philippine Primary School Readers.* University of Kansas, 1927. 71 p. ms. For doctoral dissertation by same author, see No. 2593.

2722. CRUZ, ARMEN E. *A Study of the Scholarship of Students Engaged in Extra-Curricular Activities at the University of the Philippines.* University of the Philippines, 1937. 95 p. ms.

2723. CRUZ Y ENRIQUEZ, LOURDES. *A Study of the Scholarship Status of Athletes in the University of the Philippines from 1910 to 1932.* University of the Philippines, 1935.

2724. DANNUG, LEON BURGOS. *The Status of the High School Principal in the Philippines.* University of Washington, 1931. 130 p. ms.

2725. DEVERA, ANDRES BAUTISTA. *The Development of Public High Schools in the Philippine Islands.* University of Chicago, 1929. 103 p. ms.

2726. DIAZ, FLORA E. *A Constructive Study of of the Curriculum of Religious Education in the College Department of Silliman Institute.* State University of Iowa, 1934. 63 p. ms.

2727. DIZON, ERLINDA SILAS, 1933- . *Problems in Teaching English to Tagalog Children.* Northeast Missouri State Teachers College, 1953. 39 p. ms.

2728. DOLE, MARY JANE, 1922- . *The Secular Educational Efforts of the Presbyterian and Protestant Episcopal Churches in the Philippine Islands, 1899-1941.* Smith College, 1945. 212 p. ms.

2729. EDRALIN, MARIE S., 1905- . *Spelling Problems Peculiar to Philippine Students.* Northeast Missouri State Teachers College, 1953. 37 p. ms.

2730. ENVERGA, TOBIAS Y., 1917- . *The Purpose of the Luzonian Colleges.* University of Chicago, 1952. 68 p. ms. For doctoral dissertation by same author, see No. 2598.

2731. ESCALANTE, PASTOR. *Student Self-Government in Philippine Secondary Schools.* University of the Philippines, 1931.

2732. ESCARRILLA, MANUEL T. *The Organization and Administration of Philippine Schools Before and During the American Regime.* University of Wisconsin, 1929. 117 p. ms.

2733. ESTRELLAS, ANGEL RIVERA. *A Comparative Evaluation of the Public School Systems of the United States and of the Philippines.* University of Arizona, 1930. 108 p. ms.

2734. FELDSTEIN, LILLIAN KATHERINE. *Education in the Philippine Islands.* University of Buffalo, 1945. 102 p. ms.

2735. FELICIANO Y ROMAS, JOSE. *A Critical and Descriptive Study of the Teachers' Pension System in the Philippine Islands.* University of the Philippines, 1934.

2736. FIERRO, VITO N. DEL. *An Analytical Study of Written Composition Interest of Students in the High School.* University of the Philippines, 1934.

2737. FLORES, MARIANO SOMERA. *The Development of Public Elementary Schools in the Philippine Islands.* University of Chicago, 1933. 114 p. ms.

2738. FLORES, RODOLFO W. *Physical and Health Education in the Philippines.* University of the Philippines, 1925.

2739. FLORES, TOMAS W. *A Comparative Study of the Educational Achievements of Different Major Groups of the College of Education.* University of the Philippines, 1933. 107 p. ms.

2740. FLOREZA, FRANCISCO ARCIAGA. *A Study of the Development of Education in the Philippines.* University of Southern California, 1935. 105 p. ms.

2741. FORES-GANZON, GUADALUPE. *A Study of the Socio-Economic Status of the Secondary School Population in Manila.* University of the Philippines, 1940. 100 p. ms.

2742. FRANCISCO, FLORENCIA VILLA, 1931- . *An Exploratory Study on Child Rearing Practices and Personality Adjustment in Two Socio-Economic Classes in the Philippines.* Cornell University, 1956. 66 p. ms.

2743. FUENTES, FERNANDO SOLIDUM, 1894- . *Statistical Study of the Progress of the Philippine Public Schools, 1910-1921.* University of California, Berkeley, 1922. 81 p. ms.

2744. GALANG, RICARDO C. *Citizenship Concepts: a Study on Citizenship Traits, Attitudes, Duties and Obligations, and Rights and Privileges Based on Editorials and Basal Texts in Elementary Civics and Character and Conduct.* University of the Philippines, 1938. 171 p. ms.

2745. GAMBLE, JOHN CHAMBERS. *A Study of the Technical Errors in Filipino Students' Written English Composition.* University of Pittsburgh, 1933. 104 p. ms. Abstract in University of Pittsburgh: *Abstracts of Theses . . .* Vol. 9, 1933, p. 373-374.

2746. GARCIA, AQUILINO S. *A Study of the Supplementary Readers Used in the Public Elementary Schools, Manila.* University of the Philippines, 1938. 124 p. ms.

2747. GARCIA, FELICITAT A. *A Tentative Curriculum Guide for Nursery School Teachers in the City of Manila.* Iowa State Teachers College, 1958.

2748. GARCIA, LOLITA C. *The History of Nursing and Nursing Education in the Philippines during the Years 1906 to 1932, Inclusive.* Catholic University of America, 1949. 85 p. ms.

2749. GILITO, DAVID. *The Development of Teacher Training in the Philippine Islands.* University of Southern California, 1934. 138 p. ms.

2750. GIRON-TUPAS, ANASTACIA. *History of Nursing in the Philippines.* University of the Philippines, 1935. Manila: Published by the author, 1952. 216 p. (Includes nursing education.)

2751. GLORIA, PAZ M. *Correlation of the Binet-Simon Intelligence Test with the School Graduates.* University of the Philippines, 1922.

2752. GODUCO, ANTONIA MENDOZA. *The Education of the Filipino Woman: An Historical Study.* Stanford University, 1949. 123 p. ms.

2753. GONZALES, MARCELO UBANDO. *A Proposed Type of Vocational School for Filipino Rural Education.* University of Oregon, 1941. 129 p. ms. Abstract in *Research in Industrial Education, 1930-1955*, p. 63.

2754. GONZALEZ, ALFREDO QUIMBIONG, 1896- . *A Suggested Program of Studies for Philippine Public High Schools.* Boston University, 1921. 46 p. ms.

2755. GOYENECHEA, FLORA CASTUERAS. *A Critical Study of the Distributive Education Program in the Philippine College of Commerce.* Ohio State University, 1956. 165 p. ms.

2756. GREGORIO, HERMAN CRUZ, 1905- . *The Growth of Agricultural Schools in the Philippines, 1914-1928.* University of Kansas, 1930. 62 p. ms.

2757. GUIANG, PEDRO GERAZA, 1898- . *An Analysis of the Major Aspects of Secondary Education in the Philippines.* University of Washington, 1927. 119 p. ms. For doctoral dissertation by same author, see No. 2607.

2758. GUINID, MARTIN N. *A Psychological Study of the Customs, Mores, and Taboos of the Ifugao People.* University of the Philippines, 1941. 265 p. ms.

2759. GULLEY, ELSIE ELIZABETH. *The Social and Educational Policy of the United States in the Philippines.* Syracuse University, 1914. 174 p. ms.

2760. HAYNES, ALBERT. *On the Philippine School System.* University of Oklahoma, 1923. 33 p. ms.

2761. IBALLO, AURORA L. *A Study of the Entrance Examination to the Philippine Normal School.* University of the Philippines, 1933.

2762. IBANEZ, JUANITA CONTRERAS. *An English Language Arts Program for Philippine High Schools.* Ohio State University, 1953. 146 p. ms.

2763. IDAO, LOLITA. *A Study of the Curriculum of the Philippine Secondary Schools.* Mills College, 1952. 66 p. ms.

2764. IMPERIAL, BENEDICTO M. *Education in the Philippines.* College of the City of New York, 1928. 94 p. ms. Abstract in College of the City of New York: *Abstracts of Theses . . . 1923-39*, p. 18-19.

2765. ISIDRO Y SANTOS, ANTONIO, 1901- . *Moral Education in the Philippines.* University of the Philippines, 1928. 368 p. ms. For doctoral dissertation by same author, see No. 2611.

2766. JOVER, AUREA M. *A Study of the Difficulties in High School Mathematics.* University of the Philippines, 1927.

2767. JUAN, VIRGINIO CASTILLO. *The Educational Attainment, Service Status, and In-Service Training Needs of Agriculture Teachers in the Philippines.* Pennsylvania State University, 1955. 67 p ms.

2768. JULIANO, JORGE PATRIARCA, 1930- . *The Technical Training of Teachers of Vocational Agriculture in the Philippines.* Pennsylvania State University, 1954. 69 p. ms.

2769. KOLK, Rev. RAYMOND F. *Educational Activities of the Society of the Divine Word in the Philippines.* De Paul University, 1955. 226 p. ms.

2770. LAROCO, GUILLERMO LAUDENCIA. *Historical Exposition of the American Educational System of the Philippine Islands.* University of Utah, 1925. 58 p. ms.

2771. LAUREL, MIMI. *The Development of the Public School System under the Philippine Republic, 1946-1956.* Catholic University of America, 1957. 150 p. ms.

2772. LAYA, JUAN CABREROS. *The Extent to Which High School Students of the City of Manila Use English Outside School.* University of the Philippines, 1938. 225 p. ms.

2773. LAYAGUE, ELMIRA CASTELLANO. *A Proposal for Vocational Guidance Counseling in Philippine Schools.* Ohio University, 1954. 46 p. ms.

2774. LAZARO, FELICIDAD M. *A Collection of Unpublished Dances of the Philippines.* Springfield College, 1955. 62 p. ms.

2775. LIVELY, MORRIS UBERTA. *Philippine Education Prior to Magellan.* University of Louisville, 1925. 64 p. ms.

2776. LUIS, ANDRES N. *A Practical High School Course in Biology for the Philippines.* University of Southern California, 1948. 100 p. ms.

2777. MacDONALD, HELEN ELIZABETH. *A Study of the Development and Usage of Christian Education Curricula in the Philippine Evangelical Church.* San Francisco Theological Seminary, 1952.

2778. McKINLEY, JAMES FRANKLIN. *Foundations and a Suggested Program for Supervising Student Teaching in Village Sunday Schools in Connection with the Program of Field Work at the College of Theology, Silliman University, Dumaguete, P.I.* Union Theological Seminary, 1937; Columbia University, 1937. 41 p. ms.

2779. McNUTT, THEODOSIA EVA. *History of Education in the Philippine Islands for 1558-1939.* East Texas State Teachers College, 1942. 162 p. ms.

2780. MACEDA, CORAZON. *Philippine Folk Songs in Music Education.* University of Rochester, Eastman School of Music, 1948. 119 p. ms.

2781. MACEDA, DELFINA SALVADOR. *Home Food Situations and Food Selection of Girls Enrolled in Home Economics at Rizal High School, Rizal, Philippines.* Iowa State College of Agriculture and Mechanic Arts, 1949. 75 p. ms.

2782. MACEDA, WILFREDO. *A Comparative Study of the Achievements of the Various Groups of the College of Education, University of the Philippines, Based on the Entrance Tests, Type A (1926-1929.)* University of the Philippines, 1934.

2783. MADRIÑAN, CEFERINO MADRIGAL. *A Comparative Study of the Intelligence Level of Students Enrolled in the Different Types of Schools.* University of the Philippines, 1941. 170 p. ms.

2784. MAGBANUA, FACIFICO R. *A Study of the Social and Economic Status of the Elementary School Teachers in the Province of Rizal.* University of the Philippines, 1931.

2785. MAGLEO Y GALECIA, RICARDO. *A Comparative Study of the Academic Achievements of Fourth Grade Boys and Girls in San Carlos, Pangasinan.* University of the Philippines, 1935.

2786. MAGSARILI, MERCEDES REYES, 1916- . *A Tentative Guide to Teaching Exploratory Business Education in the Public Schools in the Philippines.* Iowa State Teachers College, 1955. 93 p. ms.

2787. MAGTIRA Y CLEMENTE, CIRILO. *A Study on the Mathematics Needed in High School Physics Widely Used in the Philippine Public Schools.* University of the Philippines, 1933.

2788. MALONEY, MARY VIRGINIA. *Education and the Social Order in the Philippines.* De Paul University, 1953. 84 p. ms.

2789. MANACOP, CARLOS, 1903- . *Development, Organization, and Administration of Public Schools in the Philippines.* Syracuse University, 1949. 124 p. ms.

2790. MANALO, ISABELO. *Critical Evaluation of the Bureau of Education Primary Mental Ability Tests With Particular Reference to Their Reliability and Their Predictive Value.* University of the Philippines, 1941. 53 p. ms.

2791. MANGAHIS Y CARO, ERNESTO. *Juvenile Delinquency in the Philippines.* University of the Philippines, 1935. 199 p. ms.

2792. MANITI, VIRGINIA R., 1923- . *An Evaluation of Group-Graded Church School Lesson Materials for Children in the Philippines.* Drew University, 1955. 145 p. ms.

2793. MARIANO Y ROMEROSO, HONESTO. *Correlation Between Standings in the High School and Later Standings in the University.* University of the Philippines, 1923.

2794. MARIANO Y TIONGCO, ANDREA. *Correlation of Efficiency in Secondary Mathematics and Efficiency in Other High School Branches.* University of the Philippines, 1920.

2795. MARTIN, DALMACIO, 1903- . *Education and Propaganda in the Philippines during the Japanese Occupation.* Stanford University, 1953. 481 p. ms. For doctoral dissertation by same author, see No. 2622.

2796. MARTINEZ-ALVARADO, MARIA, 1918- . *The Influence of Education on Filipino Family Life During the Spanish and American Regimes.* St. Louis University, 1956. 62 p. ms.

2797. MELEGRITO, GREGORIO G., 1916- . *A Survey of the Socio-Economic Offerings of American Secondary Technical Schools With a Critical Analysis of their Usability in Philippine Secondary Technical Schools.* Northeast Missouri State Teachers College, 1957. 131 p. ms.

2798. MERCADO, GLORIA SORIANO, 1930- . *The Significance of Extension Work in the Philippines and*

Its Implications on the Proposed Home Economics Extension Education Curriculum for Filipino Students. Cornell University, 1956. 78 p. ms.

2799. MOE, KILMER OSCAR, 1882-1949. *Education as a Factor in the Social and Economic Progress of the Philippine Islands.* University of Hawaii, 1935. 144 p. ms.

2800. MONLEON, Rev. PEDRO OLMEDO. *Early Education in the Philippines.* Catholic University of America, 1927. 90 p. ms.

2801. MONTANA, EDUARDO FAUSTO. *Secondary Education in the Philippine Islands under the Spanish Regime and Up to the Present Time.* Stanford University, 1931. 200 p. ms.

2802. MONTEMAYOR-MAGSANOC, BALDOMERA. *Homemaking Activities as Basis for the Construction of the Secondary Home Economics Curriculum in the Philippines.* University of the Philippines, 1941. 89 p. ms.

2803. MOTOMAL, JOSE T. *A Comparative Study of the Educational Philosophy of Dr. José Rizal.* University of the Philippines, 1931.

2804. NAVAL Y ISRAEL, MACARIO GONZALO. *Teacher Training in the Philippines.* Stanford University, 1926. 169 p. ms.

2805. NAVALES, FLORENCIA C. *An Evaluation of the University of the Philippines Womens' Physical Education Program in Terms of Selected Criteria.* Utah State University of Agriculture and Applied Science, 1958. 54 p. ms.

2806. NOBLEZA, EVANGELINA MONOTILLA. *Strengths and Weaknesses of the Home Economics Education Program of Silliman University.* Pennsylvania State University, 1955. 66 p. ms.

2807. OCA, ANGELA S. *A Personal, Educational, Vocational Guidance and Counseling Program for the Filipino Blind.* San Francisco State College, 1956. 57 p. ms.

2808. OLIVAR, CELIA BOCOBA. *The Development of Physical Education in the Philippines.* University of Oregon, 1952. 85 p. ms.

2809. ORDONA, ALFREDO OBUNGEN, 1905- . *The Philippine Public Secondary School Curricula from 1920 to 1934 in Terms of Two Criteria -- The Seven Cardinal Objectives of Secondary Education and Philippine Conditions.* University of Kansas, 1935. 100 p. ms.

2810. ORDONEZ, DAVID ESPIRITU. *A Proposed Plan of Junior High School for the Province of Pangasinan, Philippines.* State University of Iowa, 1921. 105 p. ms.

2811. OSBORNE, CRESENCIA BUNDA, 1923- . *Elementary Education in the Philippine Islands.* New Jersey State Teachers College, Newark, 1957. 64 p. ms.

2812. PABLEO, DONATO BERNARDEZ, 1908- . *An Economics Curriculum for Philippine Institutions of Higher Learning Based upon Recent Surveys of Socio-Economic Conditions.* Northeast Missouri State Teachers College, 1953. 62 p. ms. For doctoral dissertation by same author, see No. 2629.

2813. PABLO, SERGIA VARILLA. *An Audio-Visual Instructional Program for the City Schools of Manila.* University of California, Los Angeles, 1951. 148 p. ms.

2814. PACANA, CAYETANO, Jr. *History of Educational Legislation in the Philippine Islands under American Rule, 1898-1930.* University of Chicago, 1934. 104 p. ms.

2815. PADOLINA, PRISCILLA FAJARDO, 1925- . *Some General Principles of Education and Their Application to Rural Extension Work in the Philippines.* Cornell University, 1957. 53 p. ms.

2816. PAGTANAC, JOSEFINA GUTIERREZ. *Improving a Community High School in the Philippines.* Ohio State University, 1953. 90 p. ms.

2817. PALACPAC, LEONCIO ASEO. *A Handbook for Filipino Teachers.* University of Southern California, 1948. 104 p. ms.

2818. PALMER, BLANCHE SHAFRER. *Biblical Allusions in the Reading Textbooks of the Philippine Elementary Schools.* University of the Philippines, 1935. 244 p. ms.

2819. PANGANIBAN, FRANCISCO COSTA, 1903- . *A Study of the Major Difficulties Encountered by Extension Workers in the Philippines.* Cornell University, 1956. 94 p. ms.

2820. PANLASIGUI, ASUNCION GIRON. *A Study on the Elimination of Students in the University of the Philippines.* University of the Philippines, 1940. 104 p. ms.

2821. PAREDES, LORENZO BENEDICTO. *A Study of Administrative Problems and Practices in the Philippine Public High Schools.* University of Illinois, 1930. Abstract in Russell Taaffe Gregg: *Annotated Bibliography of Graduate Theses in Education at the University of Illinois, 1931, p. 55.* (Bureau of Educational Research, Bulletin No. 55.)

2822. PASCAUL, MARIANO C., 1905- . *Folk Tales as Materials for Philippine Textbooks.* University of Florida, 1955. 268 p. ms.

2823. PASCUA, ELEUTERIO GABRIEL. *A Program of Religious Education for High School and College Students under the Auspices of the Methodist Church in the Philippines.* University of Denver, 1934. 87 p. ms.

2824. PAULINO, SANCHO. *Organization and Functions of School Supervision in the Philippine Public Schools.* University of the Philippines, 1941. 168 p. ms.

2825. PEARCE, GERALDINE M. *History and Problems of Vocational Education in Philippine Public Schools Since 1898.* University of the Philippines, 1941. 184 p. ms.

2826. PERRON, DONALD FERDINAND, 1903- . *Religious Education on a Baptist Foreign Mission*

Field. Andover Newton Theological School, 1937. 86 p. ms.

2827. PETERSON, BERNDT OSCAR. *A Program of Religious Education for a Philippine Community.* Northwestern University, 1922. 129 p. ms.

2828. PINEDA, JULIANA CRUZ. *Vocabulary Building in English in the Primary Grades of the Public Schools in Manila.* University of the Philippines, 1940. 131 p. ms. For doctoral dissertation by same author, see No. 2633.

2829. PINGA, ESTELA GUEVARA. *Tentative Proposals for Teaching the English Language in Philippine Secondary Schools.* Ohio State University, 1956. 171 p. ms.

2830. POBLADOR, HONORIO GONZAGA, 1887- . *Organization and Administration of American Public Education in the Philippines.* University of California, Berkeley, 1913. 77 p. ms.

2831. POWERS, MAURICE. *Public Schools in the Philippines.* Columbia University, 1923. 42 p. ms.

2832. PRUDENCIO Y BENITEZ, CARMEN. *A Preliminary Survey of the Child Guidance Clinics in Certain Philippine Public Schools.* University of the Philippines, 1941. 348 p. ms.

2833. RAMORAN, QUIRINO. *The Development of the Educational System in the Philippines.* University of Oregon, 1933. 83 p. ms.

2834. RAMO, AURELIO C. *Comparative Study of the Native Intelligence of Filipino Youth.* University of the Philippines, 1922.

2835. RAQUEL, MARCIANO REBOROZO. *A Study of Guidance for Filipino Prospective Teachers in the University of Washington.* University of Washington, 1936. 92 p. ms.

2836. RAQUEÑO, PEDRO GONZALES. *A Study of the Types of Errors in English Written Composition of Filipino High School Students in 1926 and 1936.* University of the Philippines, 1940. 154 p. ms.

2837. RAQUIZA, PRAXEDES FORONDA, 1933- . *A Suggested Program of Philippine Physical Education for Girls in the Secondary School.* Northeast Missouri State Teachers College, 1958.

2838. RAYOS, BLAS F. *Correlation of Motor Sensory Reactions with Intelligence and Academic Grades.* University of the Philippines, 1924.

2839. REYES, FRANCISCA S. *Philippine Folk Dances and Games.* University of the Philippines, 1926.

2840. RHOTEN, WALTER GLENN. *An Analysis of the Agricultural Schools in the United States, Territories, and Insular Possessions Compiled into a Guidance Manual to Be Used by Prospective Agricultural Students.* Ohio State University, 1933. 501 p. ms. (Includes Alaska, Hawaii, and Philippines, but not Puerto Rico or Virgin Islands.)

2841. RODIL Y REYES, DEOGRACIAS. *A Corrective Physical Education Program for the University of the Philippines.* International YMCA College, 1948. 143 p. ms.

2842. ROSALES, VICENTE Z. *The Araneta Institute of Agriculture: Its Role in Philippine Nationalism.* Cornell University, 1958.

2843. ROSE, GERTRUDE HAZELTON. *American Public Education in the Philippines.* Columbia University, 1918. 35 p. ms.

2844. ROTH, RUSSELL DORING. *The Attempts by the United States Government to Establish Systems of Education and Sanitation in the Philippine Islands, 1898-1907.* Bucknell University, 1951. 127 p. ms.

2845. RUIZ, VICENTE B. *Status of Working Children in Manila.* University of the Philippines, 1931.

2846. RUIZ Y BUENO, MACARIO. *Status of Filipino Elementary School Principals.* University of the Philippines, 1932. 135 p. ms.

2847. RYAN, ARCHIE LOWELL. *A Study of the Organization and Activities of the Philippine Islands Sunday School Union.* Northwestern University, 1927. 209 p. ms.

2848. SACAY, FRANCISCO MONTALBO, 1904- . *A Study of the Agriculture of the Philippines as a Basis for Building a Program of Agricultural Education.* Cornell University, 1930. 236 p. ms. For doctoral dissertation by same author, see No. 2644.

2849. SAN AGUSTIN, LUCIA ROBLEDO. *The Effectiveness of the Home Economics Program in the Public Schools of the Philippines.* Pennsylvania State College, 1953. 70 p. ms.

2850. SANCHEZ, CONCORDIA. *A Survey of Philippine Public Elementary School Libraries.* University of the Philippines, 1940. 139 p. ms.

2851. SAN DIEGO, SERAPIO MILARE, 1901- . *A Vocabulary Study of "New Elements of Biology" -- a Philippine Text.* University of Kansas, 1929. 49 p. ms.

2852. SANTOS, ALFONSO PABLO. *Rizal's Educational Achievements and Influence in Philippine Education.* University of Southern California, 1938. 265 p. ms.

2853. SANTOS, FELICISMO ASUNCION, 1903- . *The History of Teacher Training in the Philippine Islands.* George Washington University, 1933. 88 p. ms.

2854. SANTOS, PATROCINIO VALENZUELA, 1928- . *Research Needs in School Administration and Finance in the Philippines.* Cornell University, 1958. 191 p. ms.

2855. SARTHOU-AGONCILLO, FE. *An Exploratory Study of the Oral Method of Teaching Poetry in the Filipino High School.* San Francisco State College, 1956. 52 p. ms.

2856. SEBASTIAN, MAXIMO PAULINO. *A Study of the School System of the Philippine Islands.* University of Idaho, 1941. 125 p. ms.

Philippines

2857. SEMILLA, FEDERICO DE JESUS. *A Study on the Senior Teacher Examination Given by the Bureau of Civil Service.* University of the Philippines, 1941. 136 p. ms.

2858. SEVILLA, GERGORIO J. *Salaries, Experience, and Training of Teachers in Philippine Schools that Give Vocational Instruction, 1940-1941.* Wayne University, 1941. 80 p. ms.

2859. SIAN, RICHARDA S. *A Comparative Study of Both Public and Private High Schools Based on the Scholarship Grades attained by their Graduates in the University of the Philippines.* University of the Philippines, 1926.

2860. SILOS, DOLORES G. *What Are the Classroom Difficulties of the Public Primary School Teachers of Manila?* University of the Philippines, 1935. 207 p. ms.

2861. STUMP, LAWRENCE M. *Present Tendencies in the Teaching of Religion in the Public Schools.* University of the Philippines, 1933. 203 p. ms.

2862. TAN, FRANCISCO CRUZ. *A Proposed Program for the Education of the Deaf in the Philippines.* Washington University, 1945. 158 p. ms.

2863. TANGCO, CRISANTA GONZALES. *Physically Handicapped Children in the Public Elementary Schools in the City of Manila.* University of the Philippines, 1941. 150 p. ms.

2864. THORNTON, EVERETT WHITFIELD. *The Development of the Curriculum in the Philippine Public Schools.* University of Chicago, 1927. 196 p. ms.

2865. TIOJANCO, LUIS. *Accrediting Private Educational Institutions in the Philippines.* University of the Philippines, 1941. 150 p. ms.

2866. TIRONA, RAMONA S. *A Survey of Juvenile Delinquency in the Philippines.* University of the Philippines, 1919.

2867. TOLEDO, MELECIO. *Elementary School Supervision in the Philippines.* University of Washington, 1934. 93 p. ms.

2868. TORRIJAS, FERNAND, 1915- . *The Development of Elementary Education in the Philippine Islands.* Southern Methodist University, 1940. 96 p. ms. Abstract in Southern Methodist University: *Abstracts of Theses,* No. 8, p. 34-35.

2869. TRINIDAD, TOMAS MERCADO. *A Survey of the Ability of Children in Grades V to VII of the Public Schools of Manila to Read and Write in Tagalog Without Previous Instruction in This Vernacular.* University of the Philippines, 1940. 76 p. ms.

2870. TRINIDAD, VENANCIO. *Current Tendencies in Teacher Training and Their Bearing upon the Professional Education of Teachers in the Philippines.* Columbia University, 1928. 115 p. ms.

2871. TROTH, DENNIS CLAYTON. *The Development of American Educational Policies in the Philippine Islands.* University of Washington, 1920. 111 p. ms.

2872. TUASON, ROMAN CRESPO. *A Study of Retarded Pupils in the Training Department of the Philippine Normal School.* University of the Philippines, 1940. 237 p. ms.

2873. UY, JUAN TUAN-UAN. *A Brief Survey of the Chinese Educational System in the Philippines.* Columbia University, 1925. 70 p. ms.

2874. VALLEJOS, GERTRUDIS YABES. *Evaluation of Audio-Visual Materials for Home Economics Education for the Philippines.* University of Idaho, 1953. 95 p. ms.

2875. VAN WINKLE, HAROLD, 1906- . *A History of Public Education in the Philippines During the American Regime, 1901-1941.* Indiana University, 1948. 180 p. ms.

2876. VARIAS, JOSEFINA ROMEROSO. *A Study of the Guidance Program in Philippine Universities.* University of Texas, 1954. 91 p. ms.

2877. VARONA, Rev. ANTHONY. *Dominican Education in the Philippines.* Catholic University of America, 1926. 58 p. ms.

2878. VELASCO, VICTORIO ACOSTA. *The Underlying Philosophy of Public Education in the Philippines.* University of Washington, 1942. 139 p. ms. Abstract in University of Washington: *Abstracts of Theses . . .* Vol. 7, 1943, p. 69-70.

2879. VELORIA Y FERNANDEZ, POLICARPO. *Health Vocabulary for Grade Seven Texts in Health and Supplementary Health Materials.* University of the Philippines, 1936.

2880. VERGARA, FELICIDAD C. *Duplication of the Objectives in the Courses of Study and of the Content of Textbooks in the Philippine Elementary Schools.* University of the Philippines, 1941. 190 p. ms.

2881. VERGARA, JOSE RIVERA. *The Extent of Staff Participation in the Administration and Supervision of the Technical Education Program of the Philippine School of Arts and Trades.* Ohio State University, 1952. 104 p. ms. Abstract in *Research in Industrial Education, 1930-1955,* p. 8.

2882. VIADO-TUAZON, REMEDIOS. *The Adjustment of Problem Children in the Training Department of the Philippine Normal School.* University of the Philippines, 1941. 199 p. ms.

2883. VICENTE, JOSEFINA A. *The Development of a Proposed Science Curriculum for the Philippine Normal College.* Iowa State Teachers College, 1956. 210 p. ms.

2884. VILLACORTA Y LUNA, EXEQUIEL. *A Study of the Nature and the Demand and Supply of Secondary Teachers in the Public Schools.* University of the Philippines, 1937. 134 p. ms.

2885. VILLANUEVA, PATERNO C., 1899- . *The Status of Psychology in the Schools of the Philippine*

Islands. George Washington University, 1927. 63 p. ms.

2886. VIOLANDA, FLORA T. *A Teacher's Guide on Physical Education for the Primary Grades of the Bureau of Public Schools, Philippines.* Springfield College, 1955. 138 p. ms.

2887. VIRAY, BONIFACIO V. *A Survey of the Book Collections of Four Private Universities in Manila, Philippines.* University of the Philippines, 1940. 117 p. ms. (Names of institutions are intentionally omitted.)

2888. WALSH, *Rev.* THOMAS STEPHEN. *The Present Status of Elementary Education in the Philippine Islands.* Catholic University of America, 1928. 68 p. ms.

2889. WHITWELL, CHARLES GARLAND, 1903- . *The Development of the Curricula in the Public Schools of the Philippine Islands.* University of Texas, 1938. 96 p. ms. For doctoral dissertation by same author, see No. 2658.

2890. WRIGHT, HOWARD EMERY. *An Analysis of Results with Certain Tests of Interests and Attitudes.* Ohio State University, 1933. 69 p. ms. (Refers to results in the Philippines.)

2891. YAP, DIOSDADO MAURILLO, 1907- . *Secondary Education in the Philippines.* George Washington University, 1931. 96 p. ms.

2892. YLAGAN, FELISA RIZALINA OROSA, 1928- . *A Study of Day Care Centers in the United States with a Feasible Plan for Its Introduction in Manila, Philippines.* Cornell University, 1954. 95 p. ms.

2893. YOUNG, JOSEPH. *Survey of the Overseas Chinese in the Philippines with a Suggested Program of Evangelism.* Columbia Bible College, 1958. (Includes education.)

See also Nos. 187, 192, 226, 228, 257, 269, 275, 278, 301, 303, 308, 1304, 1312, 1315, 1319, 1321, 1322, 2131, 4858

For Filipino groups in the United States, see Nos. 5095-5097

Sarawak
(NO. 2894)

DOCTOR

2894. CHOU, IVY SU-TENG, 1917- . *Planning a Leadership Training Program for the Theological School in Sarawak, Borneo.* Columbia University, 1955. 219 p. ms.

See also Nos. 164, 179

MASTERS

See Nos. 301, 1309

For a Sarawak group in the United States, see No. 4956

Syria
(NOS. 2895 – 2900)

DOCTORS

2895. HURBLI, ABDUSSAMI, 1911- . *The Improvement of Teacher Education in Syria.* Columbia University, 1950. 187 p. ms.

2896. KOUATLY, MARZIA ABDUL HAMID EL-, 1919- . *A Study of Selected Curriculum Practices in American Secondary Education which May Have Significance for the Taghiz School for Girls in Damascus.* New York University, 1951. 228 p. ms. Abstract in *Dissertation Abstracts,* Vol. 12, No. 4, p. 515-516, 1952. Available on microfilm from University Microfilms, Ann Arbor, Michigan, as Publication No. 3,702.

2897. WHITE, FRANK LAURENCE. *Religious Education in the Senior High Schools of the Presbyterian Mission in Syria.* Columbia University, 1942. 195 p. ms.

See also Nos. 120, 132, 164, 174, 180

MASTERS

2898. DOOLITTLE, MARGARET, 1891- . *Problems of the Mission Schools in Syria.* Yale University, 1925. 130 p. ms.

2899. HOWRANI, RAJA FARIS. *The Proposed National School of Damascus.* Columbia University, 1930. 20 p. ms.

2900. STOLTZFUS, WILLIAM ALFRED. *The North Syria School, 1927-1937, Aleppo, Syria: An Adaptation of General Education to the Needs of Syrian Youth.* University of Minnesota, 1938. 102 p. ms.

Philippines, Sarawak, Syria, Thailand

See also Nos. 217, 226, 229, 238, 268, 288, 306, 308, 1307, 1308, 1311, 1312

For Syrian groups in the United States, *see* Nos. 4956, 4970, 4975, 5696

Thailand

(NOS. 2901 – 2955)

DOCTORS

2901. BHAOPICHITR, KAMOL. *Education and Life in Thailand.* Columbia University, 1941. 198 p. ms.

2902. BHARNURATNA, SAI, 1914- . *Application of a Theory of Communication to Problems of Supervision of Primary Extension Schools in Thailand.* University of Florida, 1956. 241 p. ms. Abstract in *Dissertation Abstracts,* Vol. 16, p. 1639, September 1956. Available on microfilm from University Microfilms, Ann Arbor, Michigan, as Publication No. 17,542.

2902a. CHAIKOSI, BOONCHOM. *The Utilization of Instructional Resources in Teacher Education Programs, with Implications for Teacher Education in Thailand.* Indiana University, 1958. 430 p. ms. Abstract in *Dissertation Abstracts,* Vol. 19, p. 2014-2015, February 1959. Abstract also in Indiana University: *Studies in Education,* 1958 (Thesis Abstract Series, No. 10, 1959.), p. 87-92.

2903. DHANAGOM, DAVIRASHMI, 1917- . *The Role of Home Economics in Democratic Family Living with Reference to Child Well-Being and Proposals for Furthering Such Education in Thailand.* Ohio State University, 1954. 311 p. ms.

2904. DHARMGRONGARTAMA, SANOH, 1913- . *Proposals for Reorganizing the Curriculum of the Secondary Schools of Thailand.* University of Michigan, 1954. 381 p. ms. Abstract in *Dissertation Abstracts,* Vol. 14, p. 623, April 1954. Available on microfilm from University Microfilms, Ann Arbor, Michigan, as Publication No. 7,637. For master's thesis by same author, see No. 2925.

2905. EKASAGDI, KAMOLKAN, 1922- . *A Proposed Plan for the Implementation of Professional Laboratory Experience in the Pre-Service Secondary Student Teaching Program of the Division of Education, Royal University, Bangkok.* Columbia University, 1953. 204 p. ms.

2906. ISARASENA, TASNIYA, 1922- . *The Development of Elementary Education in Thailand.* University of Wisconsin, 1953. 175 p. ms. Abstract in University of Wisconsin: *Summaries of Doctoral Dissertations,* Vol. 14, 1952-53, p. 377.

2907. KINGSHILL, KONRAD, 1923- . *Ku Daeng, The Red Tomb: A Village Study in Northern Thailand.* Cornell University, 1957. 545 p. ms. Abstract in *Dissertation Abstracts,* Vol. 17, p. 1867-1868, September 1957. Available on microfilm from University Microfilms, Ann Arbor, Michigan, as Publication No. 22,200. (Includes a chapter on education.)

2908. KRUATRACHUE, FUANGFOONG, 1917- . *Conception of a Public Elementary School Curriculum Appropriate for the Children of Thailand, with Suggested Procedures for Curriculum Development in Thailand.* Columbia University, 1956. 314 p. ms.

2909. LANDON, KENNETH PERRY, 1903- . *Modern Trends in Siamese Culture.* University of Chicago, 1938. Part of the dissertation (p. 230-264) was distributed to libraries in the United States and abroad in 1942. (One chapter deals with education. Others give consideration to the education of monks. and other educational topics.)

2910. LAO SUNTHARA, SUDCHAI, 1916- . *A Study of the Current Status of Teacher Personnel in the Secondary and Vocational Schools of Bangkok, Thailand, with a View to Program Improvement.* Indiana University, 1955. 189 p. ms. Abstract in *Dissertation Abstracts,* Vol. 15, p. 1759, October 1955. Available on microfilm from University Microfilms, Ann Arbor, Michigan, as Publication No. 13,223.

2911. MEESOOK, AMBHORN JAYAPANI, 1919- . *The Educational System of Siam: A Study in the Light of Comparative Education.* Radcliffe College, 1947. 288 p. ms. (Includes consideration also of education in China, France, Great Britain, and Japan.)

2912. MENDIONES, RUCHIRA CHINNAPONGSE, 1918- . *Teacher Training and the Improvement of Living Conditions in Thailand.* University of Illinois, 1957. 152 p. ms. Abstract in *Dissertation Abstracts,* Vol. 17, p. 2528-2529, November 1917. Available on microfilm from University Microfilms, Ann Arbor, Michigan, as Publication No. 23,355.

2913. MOON, CHANG-WOOK, 1905- . *American Relations with Siam: Diplomatic, Commercial, Religious, and Educational.* University of Southern California, 1936. 327 p. ms. Abstract in University of Southern California: *Abstracts of Dissertations,* 1936, p. 73-77.

2914. PANISH, KAW SWASDI, 1922- . *A Reading Program for First Grade Children in Thailand Schools.* University of California, Berkeley, 1953. 159 p. ms.

2915. PRATOOMRATHA, ZENG VIZIZ, 1911- . *A Physical Education Curriculum for the Teachers College of Thailand.* New York University, 1944. 170 p. ms. Abstract in New York University, School of Education: *Abstracts of Theses,* 1943-44, p. 209-216.

2916. RATANAKUL, SUCHART, 1927- . *A Study of Mathematics Education in Thailand.* Columbia University, 1958. 241 p. ms.

2917. SARADATTA, LAMAIMAS, 1916- . *Proposed Policies and Procedures for the In-Service Education of* the *Public Primary School Teachers of Thailand.* Columbia University, 1952. 127 p. ms.

2918. Omit. Error.

See also Nos. 119, 124, 138, 164, 170, 171, 1299

MASTERS

2919. ARAWAROP, BOONSOOM. *A Study of the Development of Childhood Education in Thailand.* University of Georgia, 1955. 170 p. ms.

2920. BOONSAITH, BOONNAM. *A Comparison of Elementary Education in the United States and Thailand with Suggestions for Curriculum Development in Thailand.* University of California, Los Angeles, 1955. 58 p. ms.

2921. BRININSTOOL, KEITH EARL. *The Training of Leaders for the Christian Church in Thailand.* Berkeley Baptist Divinity School, 1955. (Thesis for degree of Bachelor of Divinity.)

2922. BUNNAG, NONGLAK, 1916- . *The Teaching of English in Thailand.* Indiana University, 1957. 88 p. ms.

2923. BURR, WINNIE A. (Later, Mrs. Herbert W. Stewart.) *An Analysis of the Teachings Found in Selected Government-Approved Textbooks on Ethics Used in Dara Academy and Suggestions for a Program of Worship.* Presbyterian College of Christian Education, 1939. 84 p. ms.

2924. CHAVALITDAMRONG, BOONSIRI. *A Proposed System of Cumulative Records for the Thai Commerical School.* Ohio State University, 1956. 104 p. ms.

2925. DHARMGRONGARTAMA, SANOH, 1913- . *The Comparison of the American and the Siamese Secondary Schools.* Southwest Texas State Teachers College, 1949. 127 p. ms. For doctoral dissertation by same author, see No. 2904.

2926. DURR, THOMAS ANTRIM, 1929- . *The Culture and the Curriculum of Secondary Education in Thailand.* Cornell University, 1956. 214 p. ms.

2927. ELDER, NEWTON CARL. *A Study to Determine a Workable Program for the Training of Leaders for Service in the Church of Christ in Siam.* Oberlin College, 1938. 122 p. ms.

2928. IAMSAKUN, PHUANG P. *A Four-Year Program of Teacher Preparation for the Department of Education, Chulalongkorn University, Thailand.* Bank Street College of Education, 1957.

2929. ISARABHAKDI, RONGRATANA. *Development of Supervisory Services in Thailand.* San Francisco State College, 1957. 73 p. ms.

2930. KAMALANATHAN, GODAVARI SINGARAVEL, 1926- . *A Study of Dental Status in a Thai Village.* Cornell University, 1956. 67 p. ms.

2931. KARUNYAVANIJ, LA OR, 1920- . *Suggested Programs of Teaching Social Studies in the Elementary School in Thailand.* Indiana University, 1956. 123 p. ms.

2932. KUSUMA NA AGUDHYA, TUAK. *Recommendations for Organizing Guidance Program in a Boys' Secondary School in Thailand.* Ohio State University, 1953. 85 p. ms. Abstract in Ohio State University: *Abstracts of Theses Presented by Candidates for the Master's degree . . . 1939,* p. 104. (Abstracts of Master's Theses, No. 73.)

2933. McCALL, LEWIS EDMUND. *An Introduction to the New Era of Education in Thailand for the Christian Educator.* Southeastern Baptist Theological Seminary, 1956. 93 p. ms.

2934. MAKARASARA, CHALUAY KIANGSIRI. *A Follow-up Study of the 1948-1953 Graduates of the Faculty of Commerce and Accountancy, Chulalongkorn University, Thailand.* Ohio State University, 1955. 108 p. ms.

2935. MAVISES, SUTHIRA. *A Workbook for Improving the Oral English of Junior-High School Pupils in Thailand.* Boston University, 1958. 63 p. ms.

2936. MILLINDRA, CHAROON, 1928- . *Measuring and Reporting Pupil Progress in Thai Language at the Elementary Level.* Indiana University, 1957.

2937. MONGKOLLUGSANA, CHUTIKA. *The Improvement of Teaching Elementary Statistics in Thailand through the Use of Audio-Visual Aids.* Ohio State University, 1954. 81 p. ms.

2938. NANNAR, BOON THANG, 1926- . *Occupational Choices Compared with Occupational Opportunities of Selected Students from Cholburi.* Indiana University, 1957.

2939. NILGDOM, WANIDA, 1918- . *Appraisal of Pupil Progress in Arithmetic at Prathom IV Level in Amphur Muang, Cholburi, Thailand.* Indiana University, 1957.

2940. PHABHAVI-VADHANA, PADA. *A Study of Western Influence on the Educational System of Thailand.* American University, 1957. 98 p. ms.

2941. POONPANICH, RUANG RAI, 1916- . *The Development and Application of a Reading Comprehension Test in Thai Language for Prathom IV to Mathyom III, in Amphur Muang, Cholburi, Thailand.* Indiana University, 1957.

2942. POSHAKRISHNA, TONGPOONARI. *History of Education in Thailand.* American University, 1955. 56 p. ms.

2943. RATIKANOKE, THIN, 1910- . *History of Education in Thailand.* Texas College of Arts and Industries, 1957. 66 p. ms.

2944. RESANONTHA, PORN, 1927- . *A Study of Vocational Agriculture in the United States of America, with Suggested Adaptations for Thailand.* Utah State Agricultural College, 1956. 78 p. ms.

2945. SAKDAPOLRAK, BOONCHUAN, 1928- . *Proposals for the Improvement of School Health Education in Thailand.* Smith College, 1957. 95 p. ms.

2946. SATHRANON, SOMPOCHPAN, 1916- . *An Analysis of Factors in Reading Ability in English Language at the Secondary Level in Amphur Muang, Cholburi.* Indiana University, 1957.

2947. SCHAEFER, ALICE HELEN. *The Development and Contribution of Christian Education in Siam.* Biblical Seminary in New York, 1937. 96 p. ms.

2948. SEHAPAYAK, SOMBOON. *A Plan for Improving the Teaching of Elementary Chemistry in Thailand.* Iowa State Teachers College, 1957. 78 p. ms.

2949. SEMPRASAT, AREEYA. *Teaching English to Non-English-Speaking Pupils in Siam.* University of Southern California, 1951. 39 p. ms.

2950. SINGHABHANDHU, SNONG, 1916- . *A Survey of Elementary School Enrollments and Government Elementary School Building Needs of Amphur Cholburi, Cholburi Province, Thailand.* Indiana University, 1957.

2951. SITASUWANA, RABIL. *A Proposed Plan for Improving and Evaluating the Instruction in Elementary Mathematics in Thailand.* Ohio State University, 1954. 111 p. ms.

2952. SMITHANANDA, PHANOM, 1911- . *Prospective Curriculum for Training Extension Workers at College Level for the Kingdom of Thailand.* Cornell University, 1958. 106 p. ms.

2953. SRITANYARATANA, SOMCHITT. *Recommendations for Improving the Secondary Schools of Thailand.* University of Cincinnati, 1954. 87 p. ms.

2954. VIJAYA, SUPHAT. *The Development of Education in Thailand.* University of Illinois, 1954. 64 p. ms.

2955. XUTO, PHAVA. *A Proposed Plan for Using Radio in Education in Thailand.* Ohio State University, 1954. 149 p. ms.

See also Nos. 226, 1304, 1305, 1321

For Thai groups in the United States, see Nos. 4956, 4957, 4970, 4977, 4990

Tibet
(NO. 2956)

MASTER

2956. MILLER, MARGARET EVELYN, 1915- . *The Influence of the Lama Training on Tibetan Concepts of Education.* Kennedy School of Missions, 1955. 133 p. ms.

See also No. 1305

Turkey
(NOS. 2957 – 2995)

DOCTORS

2957. GORMLEY, CHARLES LUTHER, 1911- . *The Development of Byzantine Higher Education.* Stanford University, 1950. 219 p. ms. Abstract in Stanford University: *Abstracts of Dissertations . . .* 1949-50, p. 357-359.

2958. LANZA, ANTHONY ROBERT, 1925- . *Business Education in the Republic of Turkey: A Guide to Its Further Reorganization, Administration, and Future Planning, with Emphasis on Secondary Education.* New York University, 1957. 439 p. ms. Abstract in *Dissertation Abstracts,* Vol. 18, p. 905-906, March 1957. Available on microfilm from University Microfilms, Ann Arbor, Michigan, as Publication No. 25,024.

2959. MARKHAM, REUEL FINNEY, 1891- . *The Mission School in Turkey.* Columbia University, 1946; Union Theological Seminary, 1946. 218 p. ms. For master's thesis by same author, see No. 2979.

2960. OZDIL, ILHAN, 1920- . *A Causative-Diagnostic Analysis of Turkey's Main Problems and a Communication Approach to Their Solution (Democratic Planning and Mass Communication.)* Ohio State University, 1954. 333 p. ms. (Includes education.)

2961. POLADIAN, TERENIG VARTAPET, 1914- . (See note below on *Vartapet.*) *The Educational Role of the Armenian Church.* New York University, 1944. 202 p. ms. Abstract in New York University, School of Education: *Abstracts of Theses,* October 1943-June 1944, p. 157-161. (*Note:* "Vartapet" is evidently an error for "Vartabed" as given for various publications of the author in the Library of Congress. *Vartabed,* however, is not a given name but a title in the Armenian Church, analogous to *Bishop.* Publications of 1939 and 1941 are listed in the Library of Congress as by Poladian, Terenig Vartabed. Publications of 1943 and 1953, however, are listed as by Poladian, Terenig, *vartabed.* The 1953 publication according to the title page is by "Bishop Perenig Poladian." The correct use of *vartabed* as a title rather than a given name was evidently not known to the earlier cataloguer of the Library of Congress.)

2962. SARAFIAN, KEVORK AVEDIS, 1889- . *History of Education in Armenia.* University of Southern California, 1929. La Verne, California: Press of the La Verne Leader, 1930. xi, 320 p. With Introductions by Lester B. Rogers and Rt. Rev. Bishop Karekin.

2963. SAVI, BANU PERIHAN, 1923- . *Adult Education in the Democratic State of Turkey.* Indiana University, 1954. 248 p. ms.

2964. TAN, HASAN, 1922- . *A Proposal for a Program of Guidance Services for Turkey, within a Framework of Pupil Personnel Services.* University of Maryland, 1958. 257 p. ms. Abstract in *Dissertation Abstracts*, Vol. 19, p. 91-92, July 1958. Available on microfilm from University Microfilm, Ann Arbor, Michigan, as Publication No. Mic. 58-2224. For master's thesis by same author, see No. 2993.

See also Nos. 119, 127, 132, 138, 142, 144, 145, 156, 162, 164, 1303

MASTERS

2965. ANTOINETTE, Sister MARIE. *An Educational Anthology from the Writings of St. Chrysostom.* Catholic Sisters College of the Catholic University of America, 1914. Published in three installments in *Catholic Educational Review*, as follows: Vol. 9, p. 193-205, March 1915; Vol. 9, p. 319-327, April 1915; Vol. 9, p. 436-444, May 1915.

2966. AVIGDOR, ROSETTE. *A Study of the Influence of the School System on Moral Attitudes of Turkish Children.* Columbia University, 1948. 54 p. ms.

2967. BASMADJIAN, YERVANT HETOOM. *Educational Systems in Turkey.* University of Chicago, 1918. 74 p. ms.

2968. BEHA, VEDIDE HAKKI. *Selection of Material for a Non-Language Mental Test for Turkish Children.* University of Chicago, 1930. 52 p. ms.

2969. FUKUYAMA, YOSHIO. *The American Board in Turkey.* Chicago Theological Seminary, 1950. (Includes educational activities. Thesis for degree of Bachelor of Divinity.)

2970. HALIM, BELKIS, 1908- . *Textbooks in Nature Study for Use in the Elementary Schools of Turkey.* Smith College, 1938. 222 p. ms.

2971. HAYES, Rev. JOHN J. *The Educational Principles in the Great Catechism of St. Gregory of Nyssa.* Catholic University of America, 1934. 52 p. ms.

2972. IRWIN, HARRY NEWTON. *The Schools of Turkey.* University of Chicago, 1910. 41 p. ms.

2973. KEMAL, ALI. *Social and Educational Growth in Turkey, 1908-1928.* New York University, 1929. 50 p. ms.

2974. KHAULI, BULUS KUZMA. *Education in Turkey.* Columbia University, 1905. 106 p. ms.

2975. KUNDAK, SUAT SAADET, 1921- . *Factors Related to the Use of Time in the Homemaking Activities by Selected Turkish Housewives.* Purdue University, 1958. 54 p. ms.

2976. KUTLUG, BILAL RIZA. *A Study of Educational and Vocational Guidance in United States Secondary Schools and a Suggested Guidance Program for Turkish Life.* University of Michigan, 1937. 106 p. ms.

2977. LEVONIAM, LEON JOHN K. *A Study of Educational Problems in Turkey.* Columbia University, 1909. 90 p. ms.

2978. LOBOYKO, GENE J. *Elements of a Philosophy of Education in the Writings of St. John Chrysostom.* De Paul University, 1958.

2979. MARKHAM, REUEL FINNEY, 1891- . *Adapting Education in Missionary Schools to the New Conditions in Turkey.* Columbia University, 1928. 84 p. ms. For doctoral dissertation by same authority, see No. 2959.

2980. MIKAELIAN, LUCIA. *A Course for First Year Primary in Religious Education in Turkey.* Hartford School of Religious Education, 1924. 87 p. ms.

2981. MOSES, JOSEPH. *The Foundations of Education in the Cappodocian Fathers.* Columbia University, 1909. 47 p. ms.

2982. MYERS, WALTER F., 1900- . *Religious Education in the Byzantine Empire.* Yale University, 1929. 146 p. ms.

2983. NILSON, PAUL EMANUEL. *Moral Education in American Schools in Turkey.* University of Chicago, 1926. 86 p. ms.

2984. NOSSER, MARION ANTIONETTE. *Educational Policies of the American Board of Commissioners for Foreign Missions in Turkey, 1823 - 1923.* University of Chicago, 1924. 123 p. ms.

2985. O'CONNOR, Sister MARY JOSEPH. *The Educational Ideals of St. Basil.* Catholic Sisters College of the Catholic University of America, 1915. 42 p. ms.

2986. OGUZKAN, ABDULBAKI TURHAN. *Recent Trends and Practices in Adult Education in the Turkish Republic: An Appraisal and Recommendations.* Ohio State University, 1953. 146 p. ms.

2987. ORVIS, SUSAN WEALTHY. *Religious Education in the American Schools in the Ottoman Empire.* University of Chicago, 1915. 105 p. ms.

2988. PIERCE, LILLIAN ELIZABETH. *The Christian Educator Looks at Turkey.* Andover Newton Theological School, 1953. 35 p. ms.

2989. REJEBIAN, SAMUEL MINAS. *Education in the Reconstruction of Armenia.* Yale University, 1920. 29 p. ms.

2990. SMITH, ALAN HARVEY. *An American College on the Bosporus.* Columbia University, 1951. 250 p. ms.

2991. SULEYMAN, ZEKIYE, 1908- . *A Study of the History and Development of Education in Turkey with Special Emphasis upon the Influence of American Education.* Smith College, 1934. 87 p. ms.

2992. SWANSON, AUDREY McCARRON. *Education in Turkey.* Tulane University of Louisiana, 1947. 104 p. ms. Abstract in Tulane University of Louisiana: *Bulletin,* Series 48, No. 11, p. 15-16, September 1947. (Makes comparisons with recent educational advances in Mexico. Considers also education in China and the USSR.)

2993. TAN, HASAN, 1922- . *A Survey of Student Problems with the "Mooney Problem Check List" in a Secondary School in Istanbul, Turkey.* University of Maryland, 1953. 158 p. ms. For doctoral dissertation by same author, see No. 2964.

2994. TATEOSSIAN, ADRIENNE. *A Suggested Program of Studies for Armenian Girls' Orphanages.* University of Wisconsin, 1926. 69 p. ms.

2995. VARIS, FATMA, 1927- . *A Critical Study of the Turkish Elementary Teacher Education Program.* University of Florida, 1953. 89 p. ms.

See also Nos. 187, 212, 217, 226, 229, 268, 301, 303, 308

For Turkish groups in the United States, See Nos. 4970, 4972, 4975, 4977, 4988, 5030, 5697

Viet-Nam
(NOS. 2996 – 2998)

DOCTOR

2996. DUONG, DUU. *The Confucian Tradition in the History of Vietnamese Education.* Harvard University, 1958. 133 p. ms.

MASTERS

2997. PHAN, Rev. FRANCIS TRANNGOE. *A History of Catholic Education in Vietnam, Indo-China.* Canisius College, 1953. 42 p. ms.

2998. VU, ICH TAM, 1923- . *A Historical Survey of Educational Development in Viet Nam.* University of Kentucky, 1957. 203 p. ms.

See also No. 1321

Yemen
(NOS. 2999 – 3000)

DOCTOR

See No. 2216

MASTERS

2999. BEREZNER, AVIVA. *The Sociocultural Institutions of the Jewish Community in Yemen.* New School for Social Research, 1956.

3000. REICH, SIGMUND. *A Yemen Textbook for the Instruction of the Jewish Child: A Manuscript in the Library of Columbia University Described by Sigmund Reich.* Columbia University, 1900. 50 p. ms.

EUROPE
(NOS. 3001 – 4803)

General
(NOS. 3001 – 3067)

DOCTORS

3001. ABELSON, PAUL, 1878-1953. *The Seven Liberal Arts: A Study in Mediaeval Culture.* Columbia University, 1906. New York: Teachers College, Columbia University, 1906. viii, 150 p. (Teachers College Contribution to Education, No. 11.)

3002. ANDERSON, LEWIS FLINT, 1866-1932. *The Development of the Non-Professional School in Europe before the Renaissance.* Clark University, 1907. Published in part as "A Study of the Protypes of the Modern Non-Professional School among the Greeks and Romans," *Pedagogical Seminary,* Vol. 14, p. 1-38, March 1907; and "A Study of Mediaeval Schools and Schoolwork," *Pedagogical Seminary,* Vol. 14, p. 223-282, June 1907.

3003. BARNES, EUGENE BURDETTE, Jr., 1917- *The International Exchange of Knowledge in Western Europe, 1680-1689.* University of Chicago, 1947. 151 p. ms.

3004. BULLOUGH, VERN LEROY, 1928- . *Medical Education in Western Europe during the Thirteenth and Fourteenth Centuries.* University of Chicago, 1954. 222 p. ms. Available on microfilm: see index under "University of Chicago."

3005. BURCH, VELLA JANE, 1911- . *Baptist Youth Work in Europe.* Southwestern Baptist Theological Seminary, 1954. 289 p. ms.

3006. CAMAJANI, GIOVANNI, 1910- . *Cantus Planus: The Experimental Didactics and Philosophic Aspects of Medieval Monody: A Genetic, Comparative, and Expository Study of the Contemporary Music Study.* New York University, 1945 197 p. ms.

3007. CAMPBELL, ANNA MONTGOMERY, 1888- *The Black Death and Men of Learning.* Columbia University, 1931. New York: Columbia University Press, 1931. xii, 210 p. (History of Science Society Publications, New Series, No. 1.) For master's thesis by same author, see No. 3447.

3008. ESCHER, ERWIN. *The Direct Method of Studying Foreign Languages: A Contribution to the History of Its Source and Development.* University of Chicago, 1928. 336 p. ms. Abstract in University of Chicago: *Abstracts of Theses, Humanistic Series,* Vol. 7, p. 463-469. (Deals with methods of language study in the Middle Ages.) For master's thesis by same author, see No. 3032.

3009. MATHIS, WILLIAM STEPHEN. *Thirty-Six Choral Works of the Sixteenth Century Adapted and Annotated for Performance by Non-Professional Choral Groups.* Florida State University, 1952. 316 p. ms. Abstract in *Dissertation Abstracts,* Vol. 12, No. 5, p. 632, 1952. Available on microfilm from University Microfilms, Ann Arbor, Michigan as Publication No. 4,295.

3010. ROCHESTER, LORETTO MARIE. *The Educational System of the Jesuits.* New York University, 1902. 93 p. ms. (Includes brief theoretical discussion of the Ratio Studiorum.)

3011. STUERM, FRANCIS H. *American Interest in European Education from 1865 to 1914 as Shown by the Content of Educational Magazines.* New York University, 1934. 315 p. ms.

3012. THOMPSON, KENNINGTON LEANING. *School Punishments from the Renaissance to the Present: An Historical Experimental Investigation.* New York University, 1915. 348 p. ms.

3013. THORNDIKE, EVERETT LYNN, 1882- . *The Place of Magic in the Intellectual History of Europe.* Columbia University, 1905. 110 p. ms. For master's thesis by same author, see No. 3064.

3014. TOOKER, DU BOIS. *The "Ratio Studiorum" of the Jesuits and Its Relation to Their Constitution.* New York University, 1914. 129 p. ms.

3015. WELDER, ELI, 1925- . *The Teaching of the Bible in the Jewish Schools of Europe during the Fifteenth and Sixteenth Centuries.* Johns Hopkins University, 1952. 174 p. ms. Abstract in *Religious Education,* Vol. 49, p. 199-200, May-June 1954. (Author classifies the schools as Italian, and the Ashkenazic schools of Central and Eastern Europe.)

See also Nos. 27, 28, 121, 131, 135, 139, 153, 174, 183, 2213, 2233, 4307, 4405

MASTERS

3016. ALEXIA, *Sister* MARY. *Education in the Benedictine Monasteries of the Early Middle Ages.* Catholic Sisters College of the Catholic University of America, 1919. 42 p. ms.

3017. BARKDULL, MARIAN LUCILLE. *The Role of Medieval Christianity in Health Education and Medical Practices.* Stanford University, 1949. 78 p. ms.

3018. BARR, JOSIAH HENRY. *The Church and the Origin of the University Movement.* State University of Iowa, 1909.

3019. BRONARS, *Rev.* JOSEPH C., 1925- . *An Analysis of the Treatment of the Church and Catholic Contributions to Education before the Protestant Revolt in Selected Histories of Education.* Catholic University of America, 1955. 147 p. ms. Abstract in *Catholic Educational Review,* Vol. 54, p. 335-336, May 1956. (The nine histories analyzed are all of American authorship.) For doctoral dissertation by same author, see No. 4607.

3020. BROOKE, *Sister* MARY ANGELE. *Educational Aspects of the Mediaeval Craft Guilds.* Catholic Sisters College of the Catholic University of America, 1918. 35 p. ms.

General

3021. BYRNS, LOIS ELIZABETH ANNE. *Educational Opportunity Offered by the Medieval Church to the Lower Classes.* University of Wisconsin, 1931. 67 p. ms.

3022. CAMPBELL, VINCENT DE PAUL. *Benedictine Monachism and Its Contribution to Education, Past and Present.* College of William and Mary, 1942. 163 p. ms.

3023. CARR, CORNELIUS JOHN, 1920- . *Case Studies in the Use of Prelection of the Jesuit "Ratio Studiorum."* Fordham University, 1949. 153 p. ms.

3024. COHEN, SUMNER HUGH, 1932- . *A Preliminary Analysis of Resources in Europe for the Training and Care of the Handicapped Child.* Boston University, 1955. 117 p. ms.

3025. COSTELLO, Rev. PAUL. *The Baccalaureate Degree in Medieval Universities.* Catholic University of America, 1916. 27 p. ms.

3026. COTE, ARTHUR BASIL, 1885- . *The Dominicans and Education.* Catholic University of America, 1925. 27 p. ms. For doctoral dissertation by same author, see No. 4410.

3027. CRINER, RUSSELL LEE. *History of Education in the Middle Ages.* East Texas State Teachers College, 1950. 179 p. ms.

3028. DAVIS, GENEVA K. *An Evaluation of Selected Aspects of Two Educational Tours to Europe Offered by Chico State College.* Chico State College, 1958.

3029. DAVIS, GEORGE EMERSON. *Education in the American Expeditionary Force with the 90th Division Program in Detail.* State University of Iowa, 1920. 147 p. ms.

3030. DEVLIN, EUGENE J., 1920- . *A Study of the Psychological Principles of Character Formation as Contained in the Ratio Studiorum of the Society of Jesus.* Fordham University, 1952. 137 p. ms.

3031. ELISE, Sister MARY. *The History of Science Education in the Seventeenth Century.* Mount St. Joseph's Teachers College, 1956. 218 p. ms.

3032. ESCHER, ERWIN. *Essay on the Sources and the History of the Direct Method of Teaching Modern Languages until Its Establishment in France and Germany.* University of Chicago, 1919. 127 p. ms. For doctoral dissertation by same author, see No. 3008.

3033. FREEHILL, Rev. ALPHONSE MICHAEL. *Physical Culture and Recreation in the Middle Ages.* Catholic University of America, 1931. 29 p. ms.

3034. GOSS, GEORGE EDWARD, 1886-1936. *Some Contributions of the American Young Men's Christian Association to Physical Education in Europe from 1918 to 1928.* New York University, 1931. 138 p. ms. For doctoral dissertation by same author, see No. 2605.

3035. HASTINGS, Sister MARY PARACLETA. *The Educational Value of the Scholastic Commentary.* Catholic Sisters College of the Catholic University of America, 1921. 37 p. ms.

3036. HILLIS, MARY CARROLL. *A Study of the Origin of Certain European Folk Dances and Singing Games.* State University of Iowa, 1940. 186 p. ms.

3037. HORAN, WILLIAM C. *Analysis of the Treatment of the Church and Catholic Contributions to Education since the Protestant Revolt in Selected Histories of Education.* Catholic University of America, 1956. 87 p. ms. (The nine histories used are all of American authorship.)

3038. KEARNEY, Sister MARY AUGUSTA. *Provision for the Education of Women in the Early Christian Centuries.* New York State College for Teachers, Albany, 1921. 67 p. ms.

3039. KELLEHER, ELEANOR. *Origin and Influence of the Jesuit Ratio of 1599.* Massachusetts State Teachers College, North Adams, 1940. 50 p. ms.

3040. KREINER, LILLIAN MAY. *The Sixteenth Century Conception of an Educated Gentleman.* Columbia University, 1913. 31 p. ms.

3041. LENNON, MARCUS LAFAYETTE, 1881- . *Scholasticism: Its Rise and Decline.* George Washington University, 1919. 25 p. ms.

3042. LEOPOLD, Brother. *The Liberal Arts Course in the Cathedral Schools before the Rise of the Universities.* Catholic University of America, 1918. 32 p. ms.

3043. LEWIS, JOSEPH LEONARD. *A Study of the Craft Guilds of the European Middle Ages and Their Contribution to Industrial Arts Education.* North Texas State College, 1950. 197 p. ms. Abstract in *Research in Industrial Education, 1930-1955,* p. 135.

3044. LOUGHERY, Sister MARY BERNARD FRANCIS. *St. John's Program: Instructional Elements Comparable with Medieval University Education.* Catholic University of America, 1948. 74 p. ms. (Refers to St. John's College, Annapolis, Maryland. Contains chapters on curriculum and on teaching techniques in medieval universities.)

3045. McCONAUGHY, GERALDINE, 1900- . *An Historico-Critical Study of Legislation Concerning Education in Colonial Times.* Fordham University, 1935. 97 p. ms. Abstract in *Fordham University: Dissertations Accepted for Higher Degrees ... 1936,* p. 45. (Includes consideration of background conditions in Europe.)

3046. McGRATH, Sister PAUL OF THE CROSS. *Chivalry as an Educational Movement.* Catholic Sisters College of the Catholic University of America, 1919. 34 p. ms.

3047. McHUGH, HELEN VIRGINIA. *Anglo-Saxon Scholars on the Continent in the Seventh, Eighth, and Ninth Centuries.* Stanford University, 1945. 107 p. ms.

3048. MARSHALL, THOMAS FRANKLIN. *The Schools of Western Europe from the Time of Charlemagne to Abelard.* Columbia University, 1908. 74 p. ms.

3049. MATTHEWS, WILLIAM CALVIN. *The Development of Vocational Education in Europe and America.* Stanford University, 1927. 32 p. ms.

3050. MILLER, MARGARET ELIZABETH, 1905- . *The Educational Work of the Society of Jesus in the First Hundred Years of Its Existence.* Boston University, 1929. 79 p. ms.

3051. NEIL, LANTHA-DALE. *The Influence of European Educators on School Music Education in the United States.* University of Illinois, 1941. 122 p. ms.

3052. OBERST, Sister MARY SABINA. *An Estimate of the Teaching Office in Catholic Times.* Catholic Sisters College of the Catholic University of America, 1920. 50 p. ms.

3053. PATTERSON, HELLINE M. *An Historical Survey of the Changing Educational Aims and Attitudes in Relation to Cultural Changes Following the Renaissance.* University of Southern California, 1932. 56 p. ms.

3054. RICHTER, Sister MARY ANGELINA. *The Education of a Prince in the Middle Ages.* Catholic University of America, 1938. 52 p. ms. ("The purpose of this paper is to show that the sons of noblemen received a thorough classical education.")

3055. RIEBE, CHARMETTA. *UNESCO and Intercultural Music Education: Folk Music Teaching in Europe and in the United States under UNESCO Teacher-Exchange Basis.* University of Michigan, 1950.

3056. RUSSELL, Sister MARY CLARA. *The Clausura of Religious Women and Its Relation to Education.* Catholic Sisters College of the Catholic University of America, 1916. 38 p. ms.

3057. RUTHERFORD, SYBIL. *American Education in Occupied Europe.* Sul Ross State College, 1955.

3058. SCHERRER, Brother GEORGE. *Artisans and Teachers in the Middle Ages (Thirteenth Century).* Catholic University of America, 1942. 62 p. ms.

3059. SCHREIBER, Rev. RONIN G. *The Teaching of Catechism at the Eve of the Reformation as Seen from a Critical Study of the "Tabula Christianae Religionis."* Catholic University of America, 1950. 67 p. ms. Abstract in *Catholic Educational Review*, Vol. 49, p. 43, January 1951.

3060. SHANLEY, MARY J. *The Relation of the Modern University to the Mediaeval University.* Creighton University, 1924.

3061. STADER, AUGUST MARTIN. *The Ratio Studiorum of the Society of Jesus: Its History and Contemporary Applications.* Adelphi College, 1955. 97 p. ms.

3062. STAMPER, ALVA WALKER. *A History of the Teaching of Geometry with Particular Reference to the Period Beginning with the Thirteenth and Ending with the Sixteenth Century.* Columbia University, 1905. 126 p. ms. For doctoral dissertation by same author, see No. 174a.

3063. STONE, MARY EILEEN and YOUNGS, JOSEPH PATRICK, Jr. *Catholic Education of the Deaf in the United States, 1837-1948.* Gallaudet College, 1948. Reprinted from the *American Annals of the Deaf*, Vol. 93, p. 411-510, November 1948. (Includes consideration of European background of education of the deaf.)

3064. THORNDIKE, EVERETT LYNN. *The Study of Magic in Medieval Universities.* Columbia University, 1903. 95 p. ms. For doctoral dissertation by same author, see No. 3013.

3065. VERMALD, VIANNEY FRANCIS, 1918- . *Grammar of the Trivium of the Liberal Arts.* St. Bonaventure University, 1952. 82 p. ms.

3066. WATSON, Mrs. HELEN VICTORIA ROCKWELL. *A Study of the Physical Recreation Activities of Selected European Countries.* University of Southern California, 1938. 131 p. ms.

3067. WYNN, CRYSOSTOM. *Catholic Higher Education of the Thirteenth Century and Its Relation to Systems Today.* Creighton University, 1920.

See also Nos. 191, 210, 225, 232, 233, 248, 266, 1585, 1959, 2275, 2438, 2457, 3202, 3278, 4355, 4456, 4543, 4563

Composite
(NOS. 3068 – 3303)

DOCTORS

3068. ALEXANDER, RICHARD THOMAS, Jr., 1917- . *Foreign Study in Teacher Education: An Evaluation Study of the 1953-54 Adelphi College Foreign Study Experience.* University of Tennessee, 1956. 288 p. ms. (Foreign study was carried out in Lyon and Strasbourg, France; Goettingen, Heidelberg, Koln, and Tubingen, Germany; Perugia, Italy; Edinburgh, Scotland; and Fribourg and Geneva, Switzerland. Winter headquarters was in Freiburg, Germany.)

3069. BARRETT, Sister MARY CONSTANCE, 1895- . *An Experimental Study of the Thomistic Concept of the Faculty of Imagination.* Catholic University of America, 1941. Washington: Catholic University of America Press, 1941. 51 p. (Catholic University of America: Studies in Psychology and Psychiatry, Vol. 5, No. 3. Reports an experiment with 234 pupils in grades four to eight. France, Italy.)

3070. BEAN, MARY VERNACE. *Development of the Ph. D. Program in the United States in the Nineteenth Century.* Ohio State University, 1953. 344 p. ms. Abstract in *Dissertation Abstracts*, Vol. 18, p. 1325-1328, April 1958. Available on microfilm from University Microfilms, Ann Arbor, Michigan, as Publication No. 25,429. (Includes European backgrounds, especially at Universities of Bologna, Paris, Oxford, Cambridge, Halle, and Berlin.)

General, Composite

3071. BEDDIE, JAMES STUART. *Libraries in the Twelfth Century.* Harvard University, 1928. 536 p. ms. Abstract in Harvard University: *Summaries of Ph. D. Theses,* 1928, p. 64-65. (Includes libraries in France, Germany, Great Britain, Italy, the Netherlands, and Spain.)

3072. BOARDMAN, ROGER CRAGER, 1914- . *A History of Theories of Teaching Piano Technic.* New York University, 1954. 229 p. ms. Abstract in *Dissertation Abstracts,* Vol. 15, p. 272-273, February 1955. Available on microfilm from University Microfilms, Ann Arbor, Michigan, as Publication No. 10,621. (Covers teachers of music in various European countries, including Austria, Germany, Hungary, Italy, and Poland.)

3073. BOYCE, GRAY COWAN, 1899-1952. *The English Nation in the University of Paris during the XIII and XIV Centuries.* University of California, Berkeley, 1925. Published as *The English-German Nation in the University of Paris during the Middle Ages.* Bruges, Belgium: Saint Catherine Press, Ltd., 1927. 232 p. (France, Germany, Great Britain.)

3074. BRENNAN, *Sister* ROSE EMMANUELLA, 1902- . *The Intellectual Virtues According to the Philosophy of St. Thomas.* Catholic University of America, 1941. Washington: Catholic University of America Press, 1941. xii, 188 p. (Catholic University of America, Philosophical Studies, Vol. 59. France, Italy.)

3075. CANNON, MARY AGNES, 1870- . *The Education of Women during the Renaissance.* Catholic Sisters College of the Catholic University of America, 1916. Washington: National Capital Press, 1916. 182 p. Published also in installments, complete except for bibliography, in *Catholic Educational Review,* as follows: Vol. 12, p. 32-43, June 1916; Vol. 12, p. 109-121, September 1916; Vol. 12, p. 211-230, October 1916; Vol. 12, p. 318-340, November 1916; Vol. 12, p. 401-423, December 1916; Vol. 13, p. 25-36, January 1917; Vol. 13, p. 136-150, February 1917; Vol. 13, p. 225-239, March 1917; Vol. 13, p. 311-326, April 1917; Vol. 13, p. 408-429, May 1917. (Contains separate chapters on Italy, Spain and Portugal, England, France, and Northern Europe – Germany and the Netherlands.)

3076. CARPENTER, NAN COOKE, 1919- . *Music in the Medieval and Renaissance Universities.* Yale University, 1948. 581 p. ms. (Includes universities in Czechoslovakia, France, Germany, Great Britain, Italy, the Netherlands, Poland, Spain, Sweden, and Switzerland.)

3077. COLEMAN, ROBERT J. *The Development of Informal Geometry.* Columbia University, 1942. New York: Bureau of Publications, Teachers College, Columbia University, 1942. xii, 178 p. (Contains 5 chapters on development in German schools; 2 chapters on developments in English schools.)

3078. DASGUPTA, DEBENDRA CHANDRA, 1901- . *The Place of Vocational Education in Modern Educational Theory from the Sixteenth to the Twentieth Century.* University of California, Berkeley, 1932. 224 p. ms. (Study of writing of 14 educational leaders: four British, one Czechoslovakian, three French, three German, one Spanish, one Swiss, and one American.)

3079. DEMIASHKEVICH, MICHAEL JOHN, 1891-1938. *The Activity School: New Tendencies in Educational Method in Western Europe Critically Examined.* Columbia University, 1926. New York: J. J. Little & Ives Co., 1926. vi, 151 p. (Includes France, Germany, and Great Britain.)

3080. DRISCOLL, GLEN ROBERT, 1920- . *Seventeenth Century Science as a Product of European Universities.* University of Minnesota, 1952. 362 p. ms. Abstract in *Dissertation Abstracts,* Vol. 13, No. 2, p. 219, 1953. Available on microfilm from University Microfilms, Ann Arbor, Michigan, as Publication No. 4,852. (Includes universities in Belgium, France, Germany, Great Britain, Italy, and the Netherlands.)

3081. EFRON, ALEXANDER, 1897- . *The Teaching of Physical Sciences in Secondary Schools of the United States, France, and Soviet Russia.* Columbia University, 1937. New York: Teachers College, Columbia University, 1937. vii, 296 p. (Teachers College Contribution to Education, No. 725.)

3082. FLACK, HOWARD WATSON. *Totalitarianism and Physical Education.* George Peabody College for Teachers, 1940. 433 p. ms. Nashville: George Peabody College for Teachers, 1940. 6 p. (Abstract of Contribution to Education, No. 272. Includes Germany and Italy.)

3083. FRANZBLAU, ROSE NADLER, 1905- . *Race Differences in Mental and Physical Traits Studied in Different Environments.* Columbia University, 1935. New York: Columbia University, 1935. 44 p. (Archives of Psychology, No. 177. Covers Italian children in Italy, Danish children in Denmark, and Danish-American and Italian-American children in America.)

3084. FRENCH, LAWRENCE HENRY. *The Educational Validity of Preparation for Confirmation in the Lutheran and Anglican Churches.* New York University, 1934. 148 p. ms. (Germany, Great Britain.)

3085. GAMORAN, EMANUEL, 1895- . *Changing Conceptions of Jewish Education.* Columbia University, 1924. New York: Macmillan Co., 1924. 2 volumes. xiii, 239 p. and viii, 186 p. Vol. I. "Jewish Education in Russia and Poland." Vol. II. "Principles of the Jewish Curriculum in America."

3086. GARDNER, ELEANOR ADELAIDE. *A Comparative Study of the Educational and Related Theories of Plato and Rousseau.* New York University, 1923. 191 p. ms. (Greece, France.)

3087. GILL, BARBARA JUNE, 1916- . *A Comparative Study of Physical Education for Women in England and Germany, with Special Emphasis on the Period from 1933 to 1940.* State University of Iowa, 1950. 399 p. ms.

3088. GUINAN, *Sister* ANGELICIA. *Freedom and Authority in Education.* Catholic University of America, 1936. Washington: Catholic University of America, 1936. xiii, 117 p. (Contains chapter on French and German influences on academic freedom in the universities.)

3089. HALBERT, ANNA EVELYNA. *Problems of Self-Activity in Modern Educational Theory, with Special Reference to Rousseau, Harris, Dewey, and Montessori.* New York University, 1925. 185 p. ms. (France, Italy.) For master's thesis by same author, see No. 3200.

3090. HEINRICH, Sister MARY PIA. *The Canonesses and Education in the Early Middle Ages.* Catholic Sisters College of the Catholic University of America, 1924. Washington: 1924. v, 218 p. (Includes schools of canonesses in Belgium, France, Germany, Great Britain, and Ireland.)

3091. HINTZ, CARL WILLIAM EDMUND, 1907- . *Internationalism and Scholarship: A Comparative Study of the Research Literature Used by American, British, French, and German Botanists.* University of Chicago, 1952. 175 p. ms.

3092. HOBAN, JAMES HENRY. *The Thomistic Concept of Person and Some of Its Social Implications.* Catholic University of America, 1939. Washington: Catholic University of America Press, 1939. viii, 97 p. (Catholic University of America, Philosophical Studies, Vol. 43. Includes a chapter, "The Person in the Philosophy of Education." France, Italy.)

3093. HOLMES, CHESTER WINFIELD, 1894- . *The Disciplinary Class: A Survey of the Status and Administration of Disciplinary Schools and Classes for Grades 7-12 in Large Cities in the United States with a Suggested Program for the Reorganization of the Disciplinary Classes in Washington, D.C.* George Washington University, 1936. 207 p. ms. (Includes comparisons with large cities of France, Germany, and Great Britain--England and Scotland.)

3094. JACKSON, LAMBERT LINCOLN, 1870-1952. *The Educational Significance of Sixteenth Century Arithmetic, from the Point of View of the Present Time.* Columbia University, 1906. New York: Teachers College, Columbia University, 1906. 232 p. (Teachers College Contribution to Education, No. 8. Primarily topical in treatment, but considers textbooks of France, Germany, Great Britain, Italy, and the Netherlands.)

3095. JANSSEN, ANNA MAE, 1923- . *The Guilds of Rhetoric in the Low Countries during the Fifteenth and Sixteenth Centuries.* Northwestern University, 1957. 203 p. ms. Abstract in *Dissertation Abstracts,* Vol. 17, p. 3122-3125, December 1957. Available on microfilm from University Microfilms, Ann Arbor, Michigan, as Publication No. 23,517. (Belgium, the Netherlands.)

3096. KAJAVA, KALEVI SIMO, 1909- . *The Traditional European School and Experiments in the New Education.* Columbia University, 1951. 233 p. ms. Abstract in *Microfilm Abstracts,* Vol. 11, No. 3, p. 577-578, 1951. Available on microfilm from University Microfilms, Ann Arbor, Michigan, as Publication No. 2,539. (Includes Belgium, Germany, and Great Britain.)

3097. KASMAN, SAUL, 1905- . *A Comparative Study of the Russian and German Philosophies of Education.* Northwestern University, 1942. 303 p. ms. Abstract in Northwestern University: *Summaries of Doctoral Dissertations,* Vol. 10, 1942, p. 138-144.

3098. KATZIN, SAMUEL. *A Comparative Study of the Problem of Control in the Administration of Higher Education in the United States and Europe.* New York University, 1931. 200 p. ms. (Includes Belgium, France, Germany, Great Britain, Italy, and Poland.)

3099. KEHOE, Sister THERESA REGINA. (Secular name: Catherine Theresa Kehoe.) *The Work of the Nuns in Education during the Middle Ages.* Boston College, 1938. 227 p. ms. (Includes France, Germany, and Great Britain.)

3100. KLOYDA, Sister MARY THOMAS A KEMPIS. *Linear and Quadratic Equations, 1550-1660.* University of Michigan, 1935. Ann Arbor, Michigan: Edwards Brothers, Inc. 1938. xii, 141 p. (Covers early textbooks as used in Belgium, France, Germany, Great Britain, Italy, the Netherlands, and Spain.)

3101. LEE, DAVID RUSSELL, 1869-1933. *The Parent-Child Relationship in Plautus.* University of Wisconsin, 1907. Published as *Child-Life, Adolescence, and Marriage in Greek New Comedy and in the Comedies of Plautus: A Study of the Relations Existing between Parents and Their Children.* Madison, Wisconsin: 1919. x, 76 p. (Greece, Italy.)

3102. LEWIS, LEW J. *The Violin Family in Music Education.* Stanford University, 1951. (Includes France, Germany, Great Britain, and Italy.)

3103. LIEN, MARIE ELIZABETH, 1911- . *The Scandanavian Organizations for the Promotion of Home Industries in Arts and Crafts.* Columbia University, 1941. Published in modified form as *Norwegian National Organizations for the Promotion of Home Arts and Crafts (Husflid),* Oslo: Fabritius & Sonner, 1946. 135 p. (Contains chapter, "Education and Husflid," p. 51-77. Includes Denmark, Finland, Norway, and Sweden.)

3104. LOCK, ETHEL DOUGLAS, 1886- . *Education and the Democratic Ideal in the Eighteenth Century with Emphasis on the Contribution of Switzerland.* University of Kansas, 1940. 341 p. ms. Abstract in University of Kansas: *Abstracts of Doctoral Dissertations in Education,* 1940, p. 44-53. (Includes Germany, Great Britain, and expecially France, as well as Switzerland.)

3105. McCAIN, REA. *Travel in Italy as Part of the Education of the English Gentleman during the Renaissance.* New York University, 1931. 195 p. ms.

3106. McCORMICK, PATRICK JOSEPH, 1880-1953. *Education of the Laity in the Middle Ages.* Catholic University of America, 1911. Washington; 1912. 65 p. Published also in installments, complete except for preface and bibliography, in *Catholic Educational Review,* as follows: Vol. 2, p. 805-815, November 1911; Vol. 3, p. 13-21, January 1912; Vol. 3, p. 114-125, February 1912; Vol. 3, p. 385-394, May 1921; Vol. 4, p. 3-12, June 1912. (Primarily a treatment by centuries, not by countries, but includes much concerning education in France, Germany, Great Britain, Italy, Ireland, and Spain.) For master's thesis by same author, see No. 4517.

3107. MAHER, CHRISTOPHER HENRY, 1877- *Youth Movements in Various Countries.* New York University, 1942. 211 p. ms. (Includes Austria, Czechoslovakia, Germany, Great Britain, and USSR.)

3108. MASSO, GILDO, 1891- . *Education in Utopias.* Columbia University, 1927. New York: Teachers College, Columbia University, 1927. vii, 200 p. (Teachers College Contribution to Education, No. 257. Includes France, Germany, Great Britain, and Greece.) For master's thesis by same author, see No. 1136.

3109. MENSING, Rev. CYPRIAN FLORIAN, 1894- . *An Acitivity Analysis of the Four Cardinal Virtues Suggested by the Writings of St. Thomas.* Catholic University of America, 1929. Washington: 1929. 143 p. ("Our analysis has yielded a fundamental list of activities, such as is needed in the preliminary stages of curriculum making." France, Italy.)

3110. MISAWA, TADASU. *Modern Educators and Their Ideals.* Clark University, 1908. New York: D. Appleton & Co., 1909. vi, 304 p. (Includes Comenius from Czechoslovakia; Rousseau from France; Basedow, Fichte, Froebel, Herbart, Hegel, and Kant from Germany; Locke from Great Britain; Pestalozzi from Switzerland; and Harris and Hall from the United States of America.)

3111. MUELLER, WILLIAM A. *A Critical Analysis of Karl Barth's "Theology of Crisis" and Its Implications for an Evangelical Pedagogy.* New York University, 1933. 224 p. ms. (Germany, Switzerland.)

3112. MUUSS, ROLF EDUARD HELMUT, 1924- . *Theories of Adolescence: An Analysis of Selected American and European Positions.* University of Illinois, 1957. 318 p. ms. Abstract in *Dissertation Abstracts,* Vol. 18, p. 500-501, February 1958. Available on microfilm from University Microfilms, Ann Arbor, Michigan, as Publication No. 25,258. (Principal analysis deals with three American and three Central European positions, represented by Freud, Gesell, Lewin, Mead, Remplein, and Spranger. Also considers earlier theories of Plato, Aristotle, Locke, and Rousseau. Austria, France, Greece, Great Britain.)

3113. NEMETZ, MIRIAM GROSSMAN, 1902- . *Child Psycho-Analysis of Melanie Klein and of Anna Freud: A Comparative Study of Their Theories and Methods.* New York University, 1953. 296 p. ms. Abstract in *Dissertation Abstracts,* Vol. 14, p. 634-635, April 1954. Available on microfilm from University Microfilms, Ann Arbor, Michigan, as Publication No. 7,105. (Great Britain, Austria.)

3114. NYQUIST, FREDRIK VICKSTROM. *A Comparative Study of Drawing Methodology in London, Paris, and Vienna on the Higher Levels of Art Education.* Harvard University, 1937. 294 p. ms.

3115. PALMER, MARY EWEN. *The Development of Characteristic Patterns of Adult Education in the United States, England, Denmark, and Germany.* Harvard University, 1946. 216 p. ms.

3116. PASCHANG, Rev. JOHN LINUS, 1895- . *The Popes and the Revival of Learning.* Catholic University of America, 1927. Washington: 1927. iii, 146 p. (Reports attitudes of 17 popes (1417-1527) toward prominent scholars of the time, the Vatican library, the Roman University, and other institutions of learning in various countries, including Austria, Belgium, Denmark, France, Germany, Ireland, Italy, Portugal, Scotland, Spain, and Switzerland.)

3117. PAYNE, BRUCE RYBURN, 1874-1937. *Public Elementary School Curricula: A Comparative Study of Representative Cities of the United States, England, Germany, and France.* Columbia University, 1905. New York: Silver, Burdett & Co., 1905. 200 p.

3118. POST, GAINES. *The Papacy and the Rise of the Universities.* Harvard University, 1931. 445 p. ms. Abstract in Harvard University: *Summaries of Ph.D. Theses,* 1931, p. 107-110. (Includes universities in France and Italy.)

3119. RESSING, CLINTON PHILIP, 1912- . *Public Relations of Medieval Universities.* University of Buffalo, 1956. 139 p. ms. (Covers Universities of Oxford, Paris, Bologna, and Salerno.)

3120. RICHARD, ERNST, 1859-1914. *Education in Great Britain and Ireland.* New York University, 1894. 59 p. ms.

3121. RILEY, MAURICE WINTON, 1911- . *The Teaching of Bowed Instruments from 1511 to 1756.* University of Michigan, 1954. 449 p. ms. Abstract in *Dissertation Abstracts,* Vol. 14, p. 1089, July 1954. Available on microfilm from University Microfilms, Ann Arbor, Michigan, as Publication No. 8,236. (Includes teachers and teaching methods in France, Germany, Great Britain, and Italy.)

3122. ROGERS, JAMES CLARKSON. *Pansophic Ideas of the Seventeenth Century with Special Reference to England.* New York University, 1908. 58 p. ms. (Includes considerable discussion of Comenius.)

3123. ROYAL, R. FLETCHER, 1903- . *The Contribution of Christian Education to the Reformation.* Southwestern Baptist Theological Seminary, 1949. 163 p. ms. (Includes Belgium, Czechoslovakia, France, Germany, Great Britain, the Netherlands, and Switzerland.)

3124. SCAFATI, GEORGE DOMINIC, 1909- . *Mario Casotti and the Activity School: A Presentation of Adolph Ferriere's Activity-School Principles and Program Analyzed in the Light of the Theory and Practice of Christian Education as Enumerated by Mario Casotti.* New York University, 1943. 230 p. ms. (Belgium, Italy, Switzerland.)

3125. SCHUETZ, Brother JOHN JOSEPH, 1874- . *The Origin of the Teaching Brotherhoods.* Catholic University of America, 1918. Washington: 1918. 104 p. (Includes activities in Belgium, France, Ireland, and the Netherlands.) For master's thesis by same author, see No. 99.

3126. SOUTHWOOD, HOWARD DENE, 1920- . *Adult Education in Scandinavia: A Study in Democracy and Its Meaning for Continuing Education in the United States, Especially as It Pertains to the Community College.* 157 p. ms. Abstract in University of Florida: *Abstracts of Doctoral Studies in Education,* 1956, p. 23-30. Abstract also in *Dissertation Abstracts,* Vol. 16, p. 1096-1097, June 1956. Available on microfilm from University Microfilms, Ann Arbor, Michigan, as Publication No. 16,362. (Includes Denmark, Norway, and Sweden.)

3127. SPENCER, MARGARET. *Traits of Notable Educators.* New York University, 1938. 213 p. ms. (Includes Comenius from Czechoslovakia; Rouseeau from France; Herbart and Froebel from Germany; Spencer from Great Britain; Plato and Aristotle from Greece; Quintilian from Italy; Pestalozzi from Switzerland; and James from the United States.)

3128. STENIUS, ARTHUR CHARLES, 1904- . *Radio Education in Europe: A Critical Examination of School Broadcasting in Ten European Countries, 1939-40.* Ohio State University, 1942. 454 p. ms. Abstract in Ohio State University: *Abstracts of Dis-*

sertations . . . Summer 1941, p. 263-270. (Abstracts of Doctoral Dissertations, No. 37. Includes Belgium, Denmark, France, Germany, Great Britain, Italy, the Netherlands, Norway, Sweden, and Switzerland.)

3129. STOB, RALPH. *Platonism in English Educators and Theologians: Educators of the Sixteenth and Theologians of the Sixteenth and Seventeenth Centuries.* University of Chicago, 1930. 240 p. ms. Abstract in University of Chicago: *Abstracts of Theses, Humanistic Series,* Vol. 8, 1929-30, p. 335-341. (Greece, Great Britain.)

3130. SUTTON, ROBERT BENJAMIN, 1914- . *European and American Backgrounds of the American Concept of Academic Freedom, 1500-1914.* University of Missouri, 1950. 327 p. ms. Abstract in *Microfilm Abstracts,* Vol. 10, No. 3, p. 91, 1950. Abstract also in University of Missouri: *Abstracts of Dissertations in Education . . . from 1946 through 1950,* p. 135-137. Available on microfilm from University Microfilms, Ann Arbor, Michigan, as Publication No. 1,802. (Considers especially developments in universities of Germany and the Netherlands.)

3131. THURBER, CHARLES H., 1864-1938. *The Principles of School Organization: A Comparative Study Chiefly Based on the Systems of the United States, England, Germany, and France.* Pedagogical Seminary, vol. 8, p. 351-394, September 1901. Also Worcester, Massachusetts: Press of O. B. Woods, 1901. 72 p.

3132. TWERSKY, JACOB, 1920- . *The American War Blind as Aided by the Federal Government.* New York University, 1947. 211 p. ms. (Contains chapters on conditions in France, Germany, and Great Britain.)

3133. VON MOHRENSCHILDT, DIMITRI SERGIUS, 1902- . *Russia in the Intellectual Life of Eighteenth-Century France.* Columbia University, 1936. New York: Columbia University Press, 1936. x, 325 p. (Columbia University Studies in English and Comparative Literature, No. 124.)

MASTERS

3134. ADAIR, ARTHUR EUGENE. *Historical Insights of Christian Education and Some Modern Applications.* Columbia University, 1943. 37 p. ms. (Includes consideration of France and Great Britain.)

3135. ALLEN, WILLIE. *Spenser, Lucretius, and the New Science.* University of Texas, 1935. 230 p. ms. (Great Britain, Italy.)

3136. APPERSON, CORNELIUS JONES, 1900- . *The Secondary School Teacher in France, Germany, and the United States: A Comparison.* University of Virginia, 1929. 67 p. ms.

3137. ARCHDEACON, Brother JOHN PHILIP. *St. Thomas Aquinas, and the Problem Method.* Catholic University of America, 1924. 40 p. ms. (France, Italy.)

3138. ARMSTRONG, MARION CAROLYN, 1900- . *A Comparison of the Religious Educational Work of John Wesley with the Religious Educational Work of Heinrich Pestalozzi.* Boston University, 1934. 87 p. ms. (Great Britain, Switzerland.)

3139. ATKINSON, MINNIE, 1900- . *Intercollegiate Sports and Physical Education: An Historical Study.* University of North Carolina, 1931. 168 p. ms. Abstract in *University of North Carolina Record,* No. 276, p. 29-30, October 1931. (Includes Germany, Great Britain, Greece, and Sweden.)

3140. AUBREY, RUTH HOWELL. *A Comparative Study of the Teaching Methods of Leopold, Mozart, and Auer.* University of Texas, 1953. 71 p. ms. (Austria, Hungary, USSR.)

3141. BARNARD, JUSTIN FRED. *Great Educators We Should Know and Teach.* Colorado State Teachers College, 1933. 101 p. ms. (Lists 24 individuals: Comenius from Czechoslovakia, Rousseau from France, Froebel and Herbart from Germany, Plato and Socrates from Greece, Pestalozzi from Switzerland, and 17 from the United States.)

3142. BARRY, WILLIAM RICHARD. *Schools in Scandanavia.* International YMCA College, 1952. 109 p. ms. (Includes Denmark, Finland, Norway, and Sweden.)

3143. BEATTY, HARRY MILLARD. *A Comparative Study of the Educational Views of John Locke and Jean Jacques Rousseau.* Ohio State University, 1917. 88 p. ms. (Great Britain, France.)

3144. BERMAN, EDWARD. *A Comparative Study of Education in Present Day Italy, Germany, and Russia.* University of Hawaii, 1936. 86 p. ms.

3145. BIZZLE, EDNA EARL. *Contrasts between Certain Attitudes toward Education in the Sixteenth and Twentieth Centuries.* Oklahoma Agricultural and Mechanical College, 1935. 49 p. ms. (Compares attitudes in England in 16th century with those in France and United States in 20th century.)

3146. BOHRER, ELIZABETH ANNE SPENCER. *The Educational Views of Luther and Rousseau and Their Relation to Theory Today.* University of Southern California, 1956. 114 p. ms. (Germany, France.)

3147. BOWIE, ARTHUR. *The Curricula of the New Schools, Here and Abroad: A Comparative Study.* New York University, 1931. 52 p. ms. (Includes Belgium, Germany, and Russia.)

3148. BRAND, PHILIP. *A Comparative Study of the Treatment of the Causes of the World War in Secondary School Textbooks of England, Germany, Neutral Powers, and the United States.* College of the City of New York, 1935. 161 p. ms. Abstract in College of the City of New York: *Abstracts of Theses . . . 1923-1939,* p. 84. (Great Britain, Germany, Denmark, the Netherlands, Norway, Sweden.)

3149. BREDESTEGE, Rev. FRANCIS JOSEPH, 1892-1939. *The Extent of Rousseau's Dependence on Locke as an Educational Philosophical Author.* University of Cincinnati, 1926. 212 p. ms. (France, Great Britain.) For doctoral dissertation by same author, see No. 4404.

3150. BREED, VICTOR THADDIUS. *The Scholae Cantorum in the Early Middle Ages.* Catholic University of America, 1930. 89 p. ms. (Includes schools in France, Germany, and Great Britain.)

3151. BROWER, GEORGE GRISWOLD. *John Sturm and English Education.* Columbia University, 1899. 27 p. ms. (Germany, Great Britain.)

3152. BROWN, EPHENOR ADRASTUS. *Relative Bearing of the Philosophy of Plato and Spencer on Education.* Columbia University, 1910. 37 p. ms. (Greece, Great Britain.)

3153. BROWN, MYRTLE CYRENA. *Recent Changes in the Teaching of Geometry in the Continental Countries.* University of Texas, 1915. 78 p. ms. (Inclues France, Germany, Great Britain, and Italy.)

3154. BRUTON, MARIE JOSEPHINE, 1896- . *Religion and Modern Social Trends.* Boston University, 1938. 118 p. ms. (Includes education in Germany, Italy, and USSR.)

3155. BYLES, Mother MARY, 1913- . *Hugo of Saint Victor and the Pursuit of Leanring in the Twelfth Century.* Fordham University, 1947. 99 p. ms. (Includes France and Germany.)

3156. CAHILL, Rev. EDWARD JAMES. *The Education of the Medieval Apprentice.* Catholic University of America, 1924. 59 p. ms. (Treats apprenticeship in France and Great Britain.)

3157. CAHILL, EMMA A. *The Comparative Views of Locke and Rousseau on History.* New York University, 1936. 85 p. ms. (Great Britain, France.)

3158. CALLON, Mrs. BLANCHE. *Secondary Education for Girls in Western Europe.* University of Cincinnati, 1933. 96 p. ms. (Includes Denmark, France, Germany, Great Britain, Italy, Norway, and Sweden.)

3159. CARLSON, RICHARD HOWARD. *A Comparative Study of the Educational Philosophy of Rousseau's "Emile" and in Three British Novels.* University of Hawaii, 1954. 231 p. ms. (France, Great Britain.)

3160. CARPENTIER, MARIUS A. *Rousseau and Spencer on Education as a Preparation for Life.* New York University, 1911. 34 p. ms. (France, Great Britain.)

3161. CATES, LILLIAN DOROTHY. *Youth Movements of Germany and Russia: Their Educational Implications.* University of California, Los Angeles, 1947. 101 p. ms.

3162. CLARK, Sister MARY EILEEN. *A Comparative Study of the Opinions of Vives and Fenlon on the Education of Women.* Catholic University of America, 1940. 135 p. ms. (Spain, France.)

3163. CLYMER, PAUL. *A Comparison of the Requirements of the Last Years of Secondary Schools of France, England, and Germany with the Academic Requirements of the United States Junior College.* Columbia University, 1935. 44 p. ms.

3164. COOK, EVA McCONNELL. *A Survey of Adult Education in Northern Europe since the World War.* College of the Pacific, 1933. 133 p. ms. (Includes Denmark, Great Britain, Norway, and Sweden.)

3165. COX, CHARLES MANDES. *The Early Literary and Educational Activities of the Jesuits.* Columbia University, 1917. 34 p. ms. (Includes France, Germany, Italy, Portugal, and Spain.)

3166. CRETCHER, MARY WOOTON, 1904- . *A Study of the Beontes in the Light of Nineteenth Century Educational Problems in England and Belgium.* Illinois State Normal University, 1947. 106 p. ms. Abstract in Illinois State Normal University: *Abstracts of Theses, 1945-1947,* p. 18-19.

3167. CROWLEY, ROSE MARIE, 1905- . *A Comparative Study of Three Established Methods of Educating Children in the Kindergarten and Primary Grades.* St. John's University, 1943. 62 p. ms. Abstract in St. John's University: *Abstracts of Dissertations, 1942-1945,* p. 33-34. (Study of the Froebelian, the Montesorri, and the Activity methods.)

3168. CUMMINGS, ROBERT ALEXANDER. *Nineteenth Century Educational Ideals, and Their Reaction on Religion in the United States.* University of Illinois, 1910. 45 p. ms. Abstract in Russell Taaffe Gregg: *Annotated Bibliography of Graduate Theses in Education at the University of Illinois, 1931.* p. 24. (Bureau of Educational Research, Bulletin No. 55.) (Includes Comenius, Rousseau, Froebel, Alcuin, Bacon, Erasmus, Locke, Milton, Aristotle, Plato, Cicero, Quintilian, and Pestalozzi in Czechoslovakia, France, Germany, Great Britain, Greece, Italy, and Switzerland.)

3169. CURTIN, DANIEL F. *The Virtue of Religion According to St. Thomas Aquinas and Its Relation to Religious Education.* Catholic University of America, 1950. 86 p. ms. (France, Italy.)

3170. DASELER, JACK EUGENE. *A History and Description of the United States Army Dependent Schools Program in Europe since the End of World War II.* College of the Pacific, 1956. 104 p. ms. (Includes France and Germany.)

3171. DAVIES, ELIZABETH. *The Teaching of History in France, Germany, England, and the United States.* University of Washington, 1927. 121 p. ms.

3172. DAVIS, MARINITA. *A Study of Tolstoi and H. G. Wells as Educators.* Stanford University, 1929. 96 p. ms. (USSR, Great Britain.)

3173. DEHNERT, EDMUND JOHN. *An Analysis of the Nature of Esthetic Music Appreciation According to the Principles of Thomistic Psychology and Metaphysics.* De Paul University, 1957. 29 p. ms. (France, Italy.)

3174. DIGGINS, Rev. JOHN P. *Freedom and Authority in Education.* Catholic University of America, 1933. 50 p. ms. (Includes Rousseau, Basedow, Froebel, and Pestalozzi in France, Germany, and Switzerland.)

3175. DOLLIVER, EDITH NICHOLSON, 1903- . *The Treatment of International Ethics in Some Recent Textbooks on Ethics.* Boston University, 1930. 196 p. ms. (Covers 10 textbooks, including one each British, German, and Russian.)

3176. DONOHUE, JOHN WALDRON, 1917- . *The Teaching-Learning Process According to St. Thomas and Henry C. Morrison.* St. Louis University, 1944. 147 p. ms. (France, Italy.)

3177. DRYER, LLOYD LEE. *A Comparison of Athletic Sports in Homer and Malory.* Oklahoma Agricultural and Mechanical College, 1935. 37 p. ms. (Greece, Great Britain.)

3178. DUNN, DAISYBELLE. *Cataloging Entries for Four Selected Governmental Agencies of England, Wales, Scotland, and Ireland.* Columbia University, 1941. 205 p. ms. (Agencies are Health, Agriculture, Education, and Geological Survey.)

3179. DWYER, MADELINE THERESA, 1915- . *Character Education through Biography.* Boston University, 1938. 102 p. ms. (Studies lives and characteristics of six women, including Elizabeth Barrett Browning and Florence Nightingale in Great Britain; and Joan of Arc in France.)

3180. ELDRIDGE, IRENE. *Democratic Tendencies in the Education of Certain Countries.* Beloit College, 1924. 4 p. ms. (Includes France, Germany, Great Britain, and USSR.)

3181. ENGELHARDT, ROSE. *Landerziehungsheime -- Historical Development and Critical Discussion of the Country Home Schools in Germany, Switzerland, and France.* College of the City of New York, 1932. 71 p. ms. Abstract in College of the City of New York: *Abstracts of Theses . . . 1923-1939.* p. 42.

3182. ESTRIDGE, MARCELLA PITSCH. *National Youth Movements in Representative Countries with Reference to Christian Education.* Biblical Seminary in New York, 1936. 84 p. ms. (Germany, Italy, USSR.)

3183. FASTENBERG, RASHELLE. *Les Idees Pedagogiques de Jean-Jacques Rousseau et de Leon Tolstoi.* Columbia University, 1921. (France, USSR.)

3184. FENTON, Rev. EZRA J. *Educational Theories in the "De Regimine Principium" of Aegidius Colonna.* Catholic University of America, 1939. 97 p. ms. (Includes France and Italy.)

3185. FILBECK, ORVAL. *John Calvin and Jean Jacques Rousseau: A Contrast and Comparison of Their Philosophies.* East Texas State Teachers College, 1938. 88 p. ms. Abstract in East Texas State Teachers College: *Graduate Studies (Abstracts), 1937-38,* p. 14. (Switzerland, France.)

3186. FOLEY, Rev. FREDERICK CLEMENT. *An Explanation of the Rite of the Mass by St. Thomas Aquinas: A Source in the Realization of the Liturgical Movement in Colleges.* Catholic University of America, 1934. 70 p. ms. (France, Italy.)

3187. FRANEY, JOHN T. *The Application of St. Thomas Aquinas' Principles of Self-Activity in the Religious Education in the Minor Seminary.* Catholic University of America, 1944. 88 p. ms. (France, Italy.)

3188. FRAZIER, ANNIE CROMARTIE MURPHY. *Attitudes toward Child Life as Revealed in Letters to Children.* George Peabody College for Teachers, 1930. 174 p. ms. (Includes discussion of letters from Locke in England and Rousseau in France.)

3189. FREIVOGEL, ESTHER EMMA, 1895- . *A Comparison of the "Mother School" of Comenius with the "Kindergarten" of Froebel.* Boston University, 1930. 103 p. ms. (Czechoslovakia, Germany.)

3190. GALZ, ANNE. *Piano Technique and Pedagogy through Two Centuries of the Development of the Instrument and Its Literature.* University of Rochester, Eastman School of Music, 1944. 50 p. ms. (Includes Austria, Germany, and Great Britain.)

3191. GATES, WAYLAND DUNN. *The Relation of Ethics to Education, with Special Reference to Spencer and Kant.* Columbia University, 1907. 25 p. ms. (Great Britain, Germany.)

3192. GEOFFREY, JACOB REUBEN. *A Comparative Study of the Training of Secondary School Teachers in the United States, France, and Germany.* Harvard University, 1924. 100 p. ms.

3193. GERDINE, CORINNE, 1890- . *The History of Method since Rousseau.* Emory University, 1931. 92 p. ms. (Includes consideration of Rousseau, Herbart, and Pestalozzi in France, Germany, and Switzerland.)

3194. GIBSON, ALICE SCHIEFFELIN. *Matthew Arnold's Studies in French and German Education.* Columbia University, 1902. 30 p. ms. (Great Britain, France, Germany.)

3195. GIRARD, RUTH STODGILL. *Early Development of Twelve Eminent Musicians.* University of Cincinnati, 1944. 186 p. ms. (Stresses their educational development and implications for education. Includes Schubert in Austria; Sibelius in Finland; Berlioz, Debussy, Franck, and Ravel in France; Brahms and Schumann in Germany; Chopin in Poland; Tschaikowsky in USSR; and Foster and McDowell in the United States of America.)

3196. GRIEBLING, FAYE GLADYS. *A Comparison of the Educational Opportunities in Mohammedan Spain and Catholic Europe in the Tenth Century.* Columbia University, 1926. 62 p. ms. (Includes France, Germany, Great Britain, Italy, and Spain.)

3197. GROSS, CARL HENRY, 1911- . *German and German-Swiss Influences on American Elementary Education, 1800-1860.* University of Oregon, 1935. 98 p. ms. For doctoral dissertation by same author, see No. 598.

3198. GRZYBOWSKA, ZOFIA. *A Study of the Destruction of European Libraries by Totalitarian Aggressors in World War II.* Catholic University of America, 1954. 87 p. ms. (Includes Belgium, Czechoslovakia, Denmark, Finland, France, Greece, Great Britain, Italy, Luxembourg, Netherlands, Norway, Poland, and Yugoslavia.)

3199. GUTERL, LESTER FRANCIS XAVIER, 1907- *The Classical Program and Method of the "Ratio Studiorum" of 1586, 1591, and 1599.* St. Louis University, 1937. 71 p. ms. (Concerned with Jesuit activity in Belgium, France, Germany, Italy, Portugal, and Spain.)

3200. HALBERT, ANNA EVELYNA. *Interest, a Factor in Education, with Special Reference to Rousseau and Pestalozzi, with Some Modern Comparisons.* New York University, 1919. 62 p. ms. (France, Switzerland.) For doctoral dissertation by same author, see No. 3089.

3201. HALL, ROGER SCHULTZ. *The Influence of Xenophon upon the Educational Principles of Roger Ascham, as Shown in "Toxaphilas" and the "Schoolmaster."* Columbia University, 1940. 38 p. ms. (Greece, Great Britain.)

3202. HALPIN, Sister MARY JOSELLA. *The Medieval College as a Distinct Element in Medieval University Life.* Boston College, 1937. 176 p. ms. (Covers Western Europe generally with special emphasis on the universities of Bologna, Paris, and Oxford.)

3203. HANNAN, Rev. JAMES E. *An Investigation of the Applicability of St. Thomas Aquinas' Treatment of the Gifts of the Holy Ghost to High School Religion Courses.* Catholic University of America, 1945. 88 p. ms. (France, Italy.)

3204. HARBOURT, JOHN AMBROSE. *Treatment of the World War in Secondary Texts of Germany, France, England, and the United States.* University of Chicago, 1929. 83 p. ms.

3205. HENDERSON, ANNA LOUISE. *The Recognition of Individual Differences as Expressed in the Educational Philosophies of Certain Educators from Plato to Dewey.* University of Utah, 1937. 186 p. ms. (Includes Plato from Greece; Comenius from Czechoslovakia; Locke from Great Britain; Rousseau from France; Pestalozzi from Switzerland; Froebel and Herbart from Germany; and Dewey from United States of America.)

3206. HOFER, MARI R. *The Recreations of the Greeks and Romans Shown in Records of Their Plays, Games, Festivals, and Physical Training.* University of Southern California, 1928. 255 p. ms.

3207. HOYE, ELIZABETH G. *The Role of Theology in the Educational Ideas of Maritain, Gilson, and Newman.* Manhattanville College of the Sacred Heart, 1955. 40 p. ms. (Belgium, France, Great Britain.)

3208. HRVOL, ANNA EMILY. *A Comparison of Czechoslovakian and American Latin Textbooks.* George Peabody College for Teachers, 1936. 120 p. ms. (Includes consideration of classical education in Austria, France, Germany, Great Britain, Hungary, and Italy.)

3209. HUGHES, LILLIAN, 1910- . (Later, Mrs. Inshup). *English Education as Shown by the English Novel of the Eighteenth Century.* New York State College for Teachers, Albany, 1932. 147 p. ms. Abstract in New York State College for Teachers: *Masters Theses* (Official Register, Vol. 17, No. 3), p. 26. (Includes study of influence of Locke from England and Rousseau from France.)

3210. HUNT, MATE GRAYE. *A Historical Survey of Children's Literature.* Southern Methodist University, 1938. 145 p. ms. Abstract in Southern Methodist University: *Abstracts of Theses,* No. 6, 1939, p. 16-17. (Includes Denmark, France, Germany, Great Britain, Italy, Netherlands, and Switzerland.)

3211. JACKSON, BESSIE. *The Use of Biography in Education.* Southern Methodist University, 1947. 74 p. ms. Abstract in Southern Methodist University: *Abstracts of Theses . . .* No. 12, 1946, 1947, p. 20-21. (Includes Rousseau in France, Boswell and Pepys in Great Britain, Plutarch in Greece, and Celleni in Italy.)

3212. JOHNSON, ETHEL WENTWORTH. *Physical Exercises as Practiced among the Early Greeks and Romans.* George Peabody College for Teachers, 1928. 80 p. ms.

3213. KAHN, HANS PETER, 1921- . *Either Or — or Both And: A Modern Interpretation of the Aesthetic Education Described by Kierkegaard and Schiller.* New York University, 1952. (Denmark, Germany.)

3214. KEARNEY, Sister MARY WINIFRED. *The Growth of Democracy in Education in France and Germany since the World War.* Loyola University, 1931. 82 p. ms.

3215. KEENAN, Sister MARY ELLEN. *French Teaching Communities and Early Convent Education in the United States, 1727-1850.* Catholic University of America, 1934. 70 p. ms. (Includes origins of five teaching orders in France and Italy.)

3216. KENNEDY, NORA. *Implications for Education from the Lives of Sixteen Eminent Women.* Ohio State University, 1942. 117 p. ms. (Includes Sarah Bernhardt and Rosa Bonheur from France; George Eliot, Julia Marlowe, Florence Nightingale, and Christine Rosetti from Great Britain; Marie Curie from Poland; Jenny Lind from Sweden; and eight from the United States.)

3217. KEOWN, SALLY FRANCES. *Business Education in Selected European Countries.* University of Tennessee, 1941. 231 p. ms. (Includes France, Germany, Great Britain, and Italy.)

3218. KINGMAN, GERRISH DAVID, 1908- . *The Religious Educational Values of Karl Barth's Teachings.* Boston University, 1934. 85 p. ms. (Germany, Switzerland.)

3219. KOCHANSKI, STANLEY WALTER, 1911- . *A Study of Certain Factors Influencing Height of French and Swedish Males.* Boston University, 1949. 42 p. ms.

3220. KOONS, MARTHA LUCILE. *The Rise of Educational Philosophy Relating to Methods of Teaching.* University of Colorado, 1938. 104 p. ms. Abstract in *University of Colorado Studies,* Vol. 26, No. 1, p. 83, November 1938. (Includes Italy, France, Germany, Great Britain, and Greece.)

3221. KOWALSKI, Rev. ADALBERT N. *Contributions of Certain Educators to the Development of Selected Aspects of Sensory Education.* St. John's University, 1942. 54 p. ms. Abstract in St. Johns University: *Abstracts of Dissertations, 1942-1945,* p. 40. (Includes Comenius from Czechoslovakia; Montaigne and Rabelais from France; Froebel, Herbart, and Ratke from Germany; Bacon from Great Britain; Pestalozzi from Switzerland; and Dewey from the United States of America.)

3222. KRAEMER, DELPHINE. *Educational and Vocational Guidance in European Countries.* Rutgers University, 1932. 72 p. ms. (Includes Austria, Belgium, Czechoslovakia, Denmark, France, Germany, Great Britain, Italy, Poland, Spain, Sweden, Switzerland, and USSR.)

3223. KU, P. S. YUEH-CHUNG. *Selected Aspects of School Finance in the United States, England, France, and Germany.* Stanford University, 1946. 182 p. ms.

3224. KURKE, GEORGE S. *What Phases of the Educational Philosophy of Plato, Aristotle, Quintilian, Comenius, Locke, and Rousseau Are Applicable to the Junior High School?* New York University, 1933. 103 p. ms. (Greece, Italy, Czechoslovakia, Great Britain, France.)

3225. LAUER, J. QUENTIN, 1917- . *The Art of Teaching According to the Principles of St. Thomas.* St. Louis University, 1943. 88 p. ms. (France, Italy.)

3226. LeBLANC, ESTELLE. *Platonism in Rousseau's "Theory of Education."* Oklahoma Agricultural and Mechanical College, 1933. 80 p. ms. (Greece, France.)

3227. LECKIE, GEORGIA WILSON, 1907- . *Pragmatism, Associationism, Gestalt, and Aristotle: A Comparison.* University of Kentucky, 1937. 94 p. ms. (Germany, Greece.)

3228. LE FEVER, LELOY. *The Reputation of Jean Jacques Rousseau in England from 1750 to 1850.* Kansas State Teachers College, Emporia, 1938. 69 p. ms. (France, Great Britain.)

3229. LESZYNSKY, HATTIE L. *A Comparison of Secondary Education in Germany, England, and the United States.* University of California, Berkeley, 1901. 63 p. ms.

3230. LEXAU, KONRAD JOHN. *The Development of the International Vocational Guidance Association.* Chico State College, 1956. 130 p. ms. (Includes Belgium, France, Germany, Great Britain, Italy, the Netherlands, and Norway.)

3231. LIEB, THOMAS J. *To Show the Comparative Value of the American System of Physical Education and Other Systems, Notably the German and Swedish.* University of Notre Dame, 1926. 31 p. ms.

3232. LINEBERGER, ERNEST ROBINSON. *Educational Tendencies of the Reformation.* University of South Carolina, 1925. 42 p. ms. (Includes France, Germany, Great Britain, Italy, and Switzerland.)

3233. LINEHAN, Sister MARY ST. PAUL, 1920- . *The Thomistic Theory of Knowledge Contrasted with that of John Dewey.* St. Louis University, 1957. 116 p. ms. (France, Italy.)

3234. LODGE, MABEL. *Rousseau and the Educational Novel in England.* Columbia University, 1914. 49 p. ms. (France, Great Britain.)

3235. LYNCH, RAWLEY FRANCIS. *A Survey of Present Day Compulsory School Attendance in France, England, and the United States.* Niagara University, 1947. 58 p. ms.

3236. McELLIGOTT, THERESA ELIZABETH, 1907- . *The Extent to Which Classics Were Taught in Schools for Girls in the Middle Ages.* Stanford University, 1946. 107 p. ms. (Includes France, Germany, Great Britain, Italy, and Spain.) For doctoral dissertation by same author, see No. 432.

3237. McFARLAND, CATHERINE GEIS. *An Essay toward a History of Women in Education.* Gonzaga University, 1957. 63 p. ms. (Includes France, Germany, Great Britain, Greece, Ireland, and Italy.)

3238. McGLYNN, JOHN FRANCIS, 1914- . *The Influence of France upon Erasmus.* St. John's University, 1938. 42 p. ms. (Includes section on Erasmus as a teacher in the Netherlands and Great Britain.)

3239. MANN, LAWRENCE THOMPSON. *Evolution of Ideas and Practices with Respect to Corporal Punishment.* Ohio State University, 1932. 64 p. ms. Abstract in Ohio State University: *Abstracts of Theses Presented by Candidates for the Master's Degree* ... 1932, p. 181-182. (Abstracts of Masters' Theses, No. 10. Includes France, Great Britain, Greece, and Switzerland.)

3240. MASCARINO, MARIO CHANOUX. *A Comparative Study of the Training of Modern Foreign Language Secondary School Teachers in the United States and Europe.* Loyola University, 1931. 66 p. ms. (Includes France, Germany, Great Britain, and Italy.)

3241. MAYER, HENRY. *A Study of the Practical Aspects of Vocational Guidance in Germany, England, and Scotland.* College of the City of New York, 1926. 79 p. ms. Abstract in College of the City of New York: *Abstracts of Theses* ... 1923-1939, p. 11.

3242. MAYER, MARY HELEN, 1902- . *An Exposition on the Philosophy of Teaching Proposed by Saint Thomas Aquinas in His "De Magistro" with a Translation of the Text Appended.* Marquette University, 1928. Milwaukee: Bruce Publishing Co., 1928. 40 p. (France, Italy.)

3243. Omit. Error.

3244. MOONEY, AURELIUS AINSWORTH. *Secondary Mathematics of France, Germany, England, and the United States.* George Peabody College for Teachers, 1934. 215 p. ms.

3245. MOWER, ANN PEDLAR. *Rousseau's Theories of Education as Influenced by Pestalozzi.* Sacramento State College, 1957. 93 p. ms. (France, Switzerland.)

3246. MUELLER, CORNELIA ANNA. *Rousseauistic Ideas in the Educational Novel of Eighteenth Century England.* Washington University, 1942. 165 p. ms. (France, Great Britain.)

3247. MUNROE, Rev. JOHN FRANCIS. *St. Thomas and the Student.* Catholic University of America, 1933. 42 p. ms. (France, Italy.)

3248. MURRAY, WILLIAM EARL. *A Study of the Life and Work of Four Eminent Scientists.* Ohio State University, 1932. 115 p. ms. Abstract in Ohio State University: *Abstracts of Theses Presented by Candidates for the Master's Degree* ... 1932, p. 154-157. (Abstracts of Masters' Theses, No. 9. Covers Newton, Pasteur, Faraday, and Darwin in France and Great Britain. Includes chapter on use of history of science in teaching.)

3249. NEUMAN, SAMUEL. *A Study of Jean Jacques Rousseau and His Influence on Johann Gottfried Herder as Evidenced in a Selection of Herder's Written Works.* Massachusetts State College, 1937. 90 p. ms. (France, Germany.)

3250. NORTH, Rev. WILLIAM E. *The Influence of the Town on the Gown in the Middle Ages.* Catholic University of America, 1934. 65 p. ms. (Contains sections on Universities of Oxford, Paris, and Bologna.)

3251. OLSON, ALBERT HENRY. *The Educational Philosophy of Thomas Aquinas.* Stanford University, 1948. 155 p. ms. (France, Italy.)

3252. PARISI, ATTILIO GRAZIETT. *A Comparative Study of the New Italian and Russian Systems of Education.* University of California, Los Angeles, 1935. 116 p. ms.

3253. PATRICE, Sister ANNE. *A Study of the Calasanctian Method of Education and Its Continuance by the Piarist Fathers.* Mount St. Joseph Teachers College, 1957. 98 p. ms. (Includes Italy, Spain, and the United States.)

3254. PEFFER, THOMAS GEORGE. *A Study of Plato's "Republic" and Quintilian's "Institutes" in the Light of Twentieth Century Progressive Education.* College of the Pacific, 1929. (Greece, Italy.)

3255. PFLAUM, GEORGE RAYMOND ROY, 1895- *The Voice Training of the Orators in Antiquity up to the Time of Quintilian: A Translation of "Die Stimmbildung der Redner im bis auf die Zeit Quintilian von Dr. Armin Krumbacher."* Cornell University, 1924. 150 p. ms. (Includes orators only in Greece and Rome.)

3256. PITTS, RALPH SHAW. *A Survey of the Development and Meanings of Degrees.* University of Denver, 1931. 44 p. ms. (Includes institutions in France, Germany, and Great Britain.)

3257. POWERS, KATHLEEN ELIZABETH GROGAN, 1903- . *The Treatment of Adolescence by Certain Educational Writers from the Seventeenth to the Twentieth Century.* Johns Hopkins University, 1929. 61 p. ms. (Writers were from France, Germany, Great Britain, and United States.)

3258. PRATT, EDITH CORNELL, 1916- . *The Migration of Italian Students to German Universities.* Cornell University, 1940. 112 p. ms.

3259. PUDERER, FREDERICA CHARLOTTE. *A Comparison of John Locke's "Thoughts Concerning Education" with Jean Jacques Rousseau's "Emile."* Tulane University of Louisiana, 1945. 71 p. ms. Abstract in Tulane University of Louisiana: *Abstracts of Theses,* 1945, p. 11. (Great Britain, France.)

3260. RAMIREZ-LOPEZ, RAMON, 1910- . *A Comparative Study of Plato and Unamuno.* New York University, 1936. 73 p. ms. (Greece, Spain.) For Doctoral dissertation by same author, see No. 1075.

3261. RIESE, RENEE ISABELLE. *Rousseau's "Emile" and Some English Educational Novels of the Late Eighteenth Century.* Columbia University, 1946. 128 p. ms. (France, Great Britain.)

3262. RIVERA, VICENTE LAROCO. *A Comparative Study of the Educational Systems of the United States, Germany, and England.* University of Michigan, 1939. 144 p. ms.

3263. ROBINSON, JANE MOLLIE. *The Education of the Prince: A Comparative Study of Machiavelli, Fenelon, and Wieland.* Stanford University, 1938. 188 p. ms. Abstract in Stanford University: *Abstracts of Dissertations* ... 1938-39, p. 60-65. (France, Germany, Italy.)

3264. ROCHE, MAXINE LANE, 1914- . *A Historical Survey of Vocal Teaching.* University of Kansas, 1939. 199 p. ms. (Includes France, Great Britain, and Italy.)

3265. ROCKETT, RICHARD HENRY, 1902- . *Predicting Pupil Success in Various Subject-Matter Fields by Reference to Teachers' Marks.* Boston University, 1938. 104 p. ms. (Includes discussion of teaching of the Classics in France, Germany, and Great Britain.)

3266. RODUTSKEY, Rev. JOHN ALOYSIUS. *Some Aspects of the Teaching of St. Thomas Aquinas on Social Justice.* University of Notre Dame, 1936. 115 p. ms. (France, Italy.)

3267. RUEFF, MARIE ELIZABETH. *The Classical Ideal of Culture and the Educational Implications.* Ohio State University, 1933. 81 p. ms. Abstract in Ohio State University: *Abstracts of Theses Presented by Candidates for the Master's Degree* ... 1933. p. 244-245. (Abstracts of Masters' Theses, No. 13. Greece, Italy.)

3268. RUNKEL, VIOLET MARIE. *The Teaching of History in the Secondary Schools of England, France, and Germany.* University of Wisconsin, 1927. 62 p. ms.

3269. SAIDLA, LEO ERVAL. *The Rhetoric of the Seven Arts.* Columbia University, 1925. 47 p. ms. (Includes Ancient Rome and Medieval England.)

3270. SANBORN, MILDRED LOUISE. *Madame de Genlis as an Educator and Her Relations with Her Contemporaries in England.* Columbia University, 1931. 49 p. ms. (France, Great Britain.)

3271. SEEMAN, Rev. LESTER W. *The Educational Theories of Some Modern Idealists.* Catholic University of America, 1934. 75 p. ms. (Concerned chiefly with H. H. Horne of the United States, but discusses also ideas of R. R. Rusk of University of Glasgow, G. H. Thomson of University of Edinburgh, and G. Gentile of Italy.)

3272. SHANAHAN, Sister ST. JOHN, 1909- . *The Language Courses in the Secondary Schools of the Thirteenth Century as Measured by Twentieth Century Standards.* Fordham University, 1938. Abstract in Fordham University: *Dissertations Accepted for Higher Degrees,* 1939, p. 67-68. (Includes France, Great Britain, and Italy.)

3273. SHAW, Brother STEPHEN C., 1929- . *Toward a Thomistic Learning Theory.* Immaculate Heart College, 1956. 94 p. ms. (France, Italy.)

3274. SHEFFIELD, BARBARA NEVINS. *Formal Education in the Ideal State: A Critique of Certain Famous Utopias and Their Implications for Modern Education.* Stanford University, 1945. 141 p. ms. (Considers eight Utopias by authors in Austria, Great Britain, Greece, Italy, Sweden, and the United States.)

3275. SHEPPARD, DAVID IRVING. *A Study of the Resemblances between the Educational Ideas of John Dewey, and Those of Rousseau, Herbart, and Froebel.* University of California, Los Angeles, 1942. 97 p. ms. (France, Germany.)

3276. SHORES, LOUIS S. *A Survey of the Municipal University: Its Origin, Development, and Present Status.* College of the City of New York, 1928. 80 p. ms. Abstract in College of the City of New York:

Abstracts of Theses ... 1923-1939, p. 21. (Treats nine municipal universities in the United States and their European counterparts in England and Germany.)

3277. SLEDD, GLADYS. *Secularization of the Elementary School as Revealed in Theory and Practice since the Time of Comenius.* Wake Forest College, 1930. 85 p. ms. (Includes Czechoslovakia, France, Germany, Great Britain, and Switzerland.)

3278. SLEVEN, Sister NORBERTA. *A Comparative Study of the Medieval Apprenticeship System and the Modern Trade School System in the United States.* University of Notre Dame, 1929. 70 p. ms. (Considers Europe in general, with special treatment of England and France.)

3279. SMITH, FRANCES EMILY. (Later Mrs. Walter Scott Athearn.) *Educational Implications in a Comparison of the Teachings of John Calvin and Jean Jacques Rousseau.* Boston University, 1928. 102 p. ms. (Switzerland, France.)

3280. SMITH, JULIA ANNA. *A Comparative Study of Physical Education for Girls in the Secondary Schools of the United States, Germany, and England.* University of Southern California, 1935. 135 p. ms.

3281. SNYDER, M. ELIZABETH. *A Comparative Study of Music Instruction in the Free Elementary Schools of Certain European Countries and the United States.* University of Pittsburgh, 1935. 115 p. ms. Abstract in University of Pittsburgh: *Abstracts of Theses* ... Vol. 11, 1935, p. 301-302. (Includes France, Germany, Great Britain, and Switzerland.)

3282. SPALDING, Sister MARY ROSE. *St. Thomas' Theory of Knowledge from a Pedagogical Viewpoint.* Catholic Sisters College of the Catholic University of America, 1921. 46 p. ms. (France, Italy.)

3283. STRYKER, RUSSELL FOOTE. *The Teaching of Latin in France and England.* Columbia University, 1913. 32 p. ms.

3284. SUN, CLARA. *St. Thomas on Teaching: A Study of the "De Magistro" (De Veritate, q. XI) and Related Texts.* Marquette University, 1952. 89 p. ms. (France, Italy.)

3285. SYKES, NORMAN JOHN. *The Ideas of Thomas Day and Their Kinship to Those of Rousseau, Including a Short Biography of Day.* Columbia University, 1929. 74 p. ms. (Great Britain, France.)

3286. TAYLOR, WARREN SWAN. *The Twentieth Century Development of European Education.* Pennsylvania State College, 1928. 87 p. ms. (Includes Denmark, France, Germany, Great Britain, and Sweden.)

3287. THOMAS, RUTH MARIE. *A Comparison of the Views of Plato and Rousseau Concerning the Education of Women.* New York University, 1930. 65 p. ms. (Greece, France.)

3288. THOMPSON, SAMUEL HENRY. *The Vocational School in Germany and England.* Columbia University, 1908. 37 p. ms.

3289. THURSTON, HOLLIS HENDRIX. *Democratization of European Schools.* University of Missouri, 1906. 105 p. ms. (Includes schools in France, Germany, and Great Britain.)

3290. TORRE, CAMILLA ALLISON. *The Art of Letter Writing in the Middle Ages.* Tulane University of Louisiana, 1943. 62 p. ms. Abstract in Tulane University of Louisiana: *Abstracts of Theses*, 1943, p. 12. (Considers a subject which was prominent in medieval schools. Includes France, Great Britain, and Italy.)

3291. TYRRELL, Sister MARY IGNACITA. *A Comparison of the Ideas of Jules Payot and Johann Lindworsky on the Training of the Will.* Catholic University of America, 1940. 68 p. ms. (France, Germany.)

3292. UTZINGER, ANITA DENISE, 1929- . *A Contribution to the History of the Education of Deaf-Blind Children in Europe.* Boston University, 1957. 38 p. ms. (Includes Belgium, Finland, France, Germany, Great Britain, Greece, Hungary, Italy, the Netherlands, Norway, Spain, Sweden, Switzerland, and USSR.)

3293. VANDERBIE, JAN HENRY. *An Evaluation of the Principles Underlying European Systems of Physical Education According to Selected American Criteria.* International YMCA College, 1949. 142 p. ms. ("It was the purpose of this thesis to determine how far the theory of the Swedish system, the Austrian system as practiced in Holland, and the French system of physical education agree with the selected American criteria.")

3294. WADE, HERBERT ALFRED. *The Youth Movement and Hostel System in Germany and Their Repercussions in Certain European Countries.* University of Hawaii, 1934. 123 p. ms. (The certain countries were Austria, Belgium, Denmark, Great Britain, the Netherlands, Norway, Sweden, and Switzerland.)

3295. WALKER, ELITA. *Melvida von Meysenbug and the Liberal Intellectual of the Nineteenth Century.* Claremont Graduate School, 1942. 167 p. ms. (Includes her activities in France, Germany, Great Britain, and Italy.)

3296. WALLACE, CORA JEANNETTE. *Educational Opportunities for Crippled Children in England, France, Germany, and the United States.* University of Cincinnati, 1933. 155 p. ms.

3297. WARNER, KIDD PHILLIPS. *A Study of Contemporary Physical Recreation for the Adolescent Girl in Russia, Italy, Germany, England, and the United States.* Louisiana State University and State Agricultural and Mechanical College, 1939. 72 p. ms. Abstract in *Louisiana State University Bulletin*, Vol. 32, n.s., No. 1, p. 177-178, January 1940.

3298. WATTAWA, VIRGINIA. *Gerbert — The Scholar and Teacher.* University of Wisconsin, 1926. 62 p. ms. (Includes France, Italy, and Spain.)

3299. WEIL, TRUDA THERESA. *Creative Education in Contrasted European and American Schools.* New York University, 1930. 50 p. ms. (Includes France, Germany, and Switzerland.)

3300. WILLIAMS, CHARLES SHELDON, 1903-1954. *A Comparative Study of the Schools for Secondary Instruction in Europe and America.* Boston University, 1928. 132 p. ms. (Includes Denmark, France, Germany, England, Scotland, and Switzerland.)

3301. WILLIAMS, SARAH HOLBROOK. *The Conception of the Individual in Rousseau and Froebel.* Columbia University, 1907. 62 p. ms. (France, Germany.)

3302. WINSTED, HULDAH LUCILE. *The Open Air School Movement.* University of Minnesota, 1912. 53 p. ms. (Includes Germany, Great Britain, and the United States.)

3303. WOODFORD, BURTON HADLEY, 1871-1954. *Trends in Latin from the Early Middle Ages to 1931.* Municipal University of Wichita, 1931. 166 p. ms. (Includes France, Germany, and Great Britain.)

Albania
(NO. 3304)

DOCTOR

See No. 119

MASTER

3304. COSTA, NICHOLAS JAMES. *The Effect of Cultural and External Forces upon the Growth and Development of the Albanian Educational System.* Boston University, 1958. 99 p. ms.

See also No. 217

For Albanian groups in the United States, see Nos. 5001, 5027

Austria
(NOS. 3305-3311)

DOCTORS

3305. LAHEY, HELEN CONSTANCE, 1913- . *The Development of Teacher Education in Austria.* Fordham University, 1949. 2 vols. 939 p. ms. Abstract in Fordham University: *Dissertations Accepted for Higher Degrees* ... 1949, p. 43-47.

3306. LEVITT, MORTON, 1920- . *Freud and Dewey: A Comparative Study of Their Psychological Systems.* University of Michigan, 1956. 200 p. ms. Abstract in *Dissertation Abstracts,* Vol. 16, p. 2386, December 1956. Available on microfilm from University Microfilms, Ann Arbor, Michigan, as Publication No. 18,618.

3307. PARKER, BERYL, 1893- . *The Austria B. E. A. or Bundeserziehungsanstalten (Austrian Federal Boarding Schools.)* Columbia University, 1931. Published as *The Austrian Educational Institutes,* Vienna and Leipzig: Austrian Federal Publisher for Education, Science, and Art, 1931. 174 p.

3308. SCHOENCHEN, GUSTAV G. *Eduard Burger and John Dewey: A Comparative Study of Burger's "Arbeitsschule" and Contemporary American Activity Schools as Representative of Dewey's Philosophy.* New York University, 1939. 428 p. ms. Published, in modified form, as *The Activity School: A Basic Philosophy for Teachers,* New York and London: Longmans Green & Co., 1940. x, 359 p. (Longman's Education Series.)

3309. SIEGL, Mrs. MAY HOLLIS, 1892- . *Reform of Elementary Education in Austria.* Columbia University, 1933. New York: 1933. 145 p.

See also Nos. 119, 138, 142, 143, 157, 161, 175, 3072, 3107, 3112, 3113, 3114, 3116, 174a.

MASTERS

3310. HARRIS, IRWIN J. *Changes in the Secondary Schools of Austria Brought About by the Revolution of February 1934.* College of the City of New York, 1937. 71 p. ms. Abstract in College of the City of New York: *Abstracts of Theses* ... 1923-1939, p. 99.

3311. RAAB, LUELLA. *A Critical Analysis of Methods of Teaching Figure Drawing to Children in Austrian Schools.* State University of Iowa, 1937. 61 p. ms.

See also Nos. 198, 200, 226, 274, 3140, 3190, 3195, 3208, 3222, 3274, 3293, 3294

For Austrian groups in the United States, see Nos. 4959, 4963, 4975, 4985, 5001, 5020, 5083

Belgium

(NOS. 3312-3323)

DOCTORS

3312. DePAUW, GOMMER ALBERT LEO JULIAAN, 1918- . *The Educational Rights of the Church and Elementary Schools in Belgium.* Catholic University of America, 1953. Washington: Catholic University of America Press, 1953. xiv, 148 p. (Catholic University of America, Canon Law Studies, No. 336.)

3313. FROST, HENRY HOAG, 1907- . *The Functional Sociology of Emile Waxweiler, Director (1902-1916) of the Institut de Sociologie Solvay of Brussels, Belgium.* University of California, Berkeley, 1934. 276 p. ms.

3314. KIRK, Sister ROSE GERTRUDE. *The Belgian Method of Educating the Deaf.* Niagara University, 1938. 255 p. ms.

3315. MADISON, BERNICE QUATEMAN, 1910- . *Education for Social Work in Belgium.* University of Chicago, 1952. 349 p. ms. Available on microfilm: see index under "University of Chicago."

3316. MARIQUE, PIERRE JOSEPH, 1872- . *Vocational Education in Belgium.* New York University, 1912.

3317. THENO, E. CHARLES. *A Study of Orlando di Lasso's Choral Works with Reference to School Performance.* University of Oregon, 1954. 167 p. ms.

See also Nos. 119, 138, 143, 147, 161, 175, 1418, 3080, 3090, 3095, 3096, 3098, 3100, 3116, 3123, 3124, 3125, 3128, 174a.

MASTERS

3318. DE BEVERE, *Rev.* PAUL M. *Church-State Relationships in Education in Belgium.* Catholic University of America, 1950. 101 p. ms.

3319. HASELDEN, JANE, 1903- . *Ovide Decroly: Psychologist and Educator.* University of Kentucky, 1940. 312 p. ms.

3320. HUERTAS, *Sister* MARY CLARA, 1913- . *The Educational Works of Cardinal Mercier.* Fordham University, 1945. 157 p. ms.

3321. RENSON, *Rev.* RAYMOND POLYDORE, 1925- . *The Educational Work and Theory of Frans De Hovre.* Loyola University, 1954. 83 p. ms.

3322. STERCK, *Rev.* LEO CLEMENT. *The Infant School and the System of Notre Dame of Namur in Belgium.* Catholic University of America, 1927. 38 p. ms.

3323. TJOLLE, *Brother* ROGER. *The Influence of Father Poppe on Religious Instruction in the Elementary Schools of Belgium.* Catholic University of America, 1950. 77 p. ms.

See also Nos. 187, 213, 220, 226, 249, 274, 288, 3147, 3166, 3198, 3199, 3207, 3222, 3230, 3292, 3294.

For Belgian groups in the United States, *see* Nos. 4957, 4970, 4975.

Bulgaria

(NOS. 3324-3327)

DOCTOR

3324. HALL, WILLIAM WEBSTER, Jr. *The American Board Mission in Bulgaria, 1878-1918.* Yale University, 1937. Published as *Puritans in the Balkans: The American Board Mission in Bulgaria, 1878-1918: A Study in Purpose and Procedure,* Sofia, Bulgaria: 1938. xx, 280 p. (Studia Historico-Philologia Serdicensia, Supplementi Vol. 1. Treatment is primarily chronological, not topical, but each of the seven chapters includes some consideration of educational activities and problems.)

See also Nos. 119, 147, 174a, 175.

MASTERS

3325. BORIKOVA, ELENA STEFANOVA, 1910- (Later Mrs. Bradford North Craven.) *Education in Bulgaria from the First Kingdom, 865 A.D. to the Liberation, 1878 A.D.* Boston University, 1934. 73 p. ms.

3326. FURNADJIEFF, VASIL DEMETRIUS. *The Religious Education of Youth in Bulgaria.* Union Theological Seminary, 1932. 80 p. ms.

3327. LONG, MABEL ELIZA. *Education in Bulgaria.* Columbia University, 1931. 33 p. ms.

See also Nos. 217, 226.

Czechoslovakia

(NOS. 3328-3351)

DOCTORS

3328. ANDIC, VOJTECH ERVIN, 1910- . *A Comparative Study of Education in Czechoslovakia for the Periods of 1918 to 1938 and 1948 to 1953.* New York University, 1954. 315 p. ms. Abstract in *Dissertation Abstracts,* Vol. 14, p. 777, May 1954. Available on microfilm from University Microfilms, Ann Arbor, Michigan, as Publication No. 7,995.

3329. HAY, FLORENCE HUNTLEY, 1913- . *Apparent Reflections of Comenius' Philosophy in Contemporary Education.* Michigan State University of Agriculture and Applied Science, 1955. 271 p. ms. Abstract in *Dissertation Abstracts,* Vol. 15, p. 2462-2463, December 1955. Available on microfilm from University Microfilms, Ann Arbor, Michigan, as Publication No. 14,276.

3330. MEYER, HENRY HERMAN, 1874-1951. *The Religious-Educational Theory and Practice of Count Ludwig Nicholaus von Zinzendorf.* Yale University, 1927. Published as *Child Nature and Nurture According to Nicholaus von Zinzendorf.* New York: The Abingdon Press, 1928. 229 p.

3331. TEHIE, JOHN TICHY, 1917- . *T. G. Masaryk: An Intellectual in Social and Political Action.* Columbia University, 1954. 459 p. ms. Abstract in *Dissertation Abstracts,* Vol. 14, p. 1648, October 1954. Available on microfilm from University Microfilms, Ann Arbor, Michigan, as Publication No. 8,844.

See also Nos. 119, 143, 147, 161, 175, 3076, 3078, 3107, 3110, 3122, 3123, 3127, 174a.

MASTERS

3332. ANGELOVIC, Sister MARIA INNOCENTA. *Education in Slovakia.* De Paul University, 1950. 133 p. ms.

3333. BORN, PAUL H., 1898- . *The Educational Ideas of John Amos Comenius with Special Reference to His Aims.* Marquette University, 1945. 94 p. ms.

3334. BURES, MARGARET ELIZABETH. *John Amos Comenius: The Forces that Influenced Him and His Contributions to Education.* Adelphi College, 1956. 68 p. ms.

3335. DINDA, JOHN PAUL. *Education in Czechoslovakia, with Emphasis on Urban and Secondary Schools.* Western Reserve University, 1931. 63 p. ms.

3336. DOUGLAS, JAMES LEONARD. *Education in Czechoslovakia.* New York University, 1931. 40 p. ms.

3337. GORDON, GERTRUDE R. *The Cizek Method and Its Influence on Art Education.* New York University, 1931. 67 p. ms.

3338. HESS, CHARLOTTE. *Education in Czechoslovakia: A Survey of Education in Czechoslovakia of Three Periods: The Republic, The War Period of Nazi Rule, Communist Czechoslovakia.* Allegheny College, 1955. 136 p. ms.

3339. JAHODA, GRACE. *Higher Education in Czechoslovakia.* Hunter College of the City of New York, 1932. 79 p. ms.

3340. JIRA, JAROSLAV. *Legal Basis and Development of Communal Public Libraries in the Czechoslovakian Republic from 1918 to 1945.* Catholic University of America, 1956. 256 p. ms.

3341. KAYSER, ELMER LOUIS, 1896- . *The Exodus of the Germans from the University of Prague.* George Washington University, 1918. 29 p. ms.

3342. McKINNEY, EVA RUTH. *The History of the Educational Progress in Czechoslovakia.* University of Southern California, 1925. 72 p. ms.

3343. MOSTOCKY, VACLAV. *Library Organization and Policies in Czechoslovakia from 1945 to 1954: With a Historical Introduction.* Catholic University of America, 1954. 90 p. ms.

3344. NIEBUHR, HAROLD EMIL. *Comenian Elements in Progressive Education.* Southwest Texas State Teachers College, 1940. 58 p. ms.

3345. ORR, WALTER TRUMAN. *Comenius as an Educator.* Indiana University, 1909. 86 p. ms.

3346. PERRY, GERTRUDE VEACH. *History and Development of the Sokol Movement of Czechoslovakia.* George Peabody College for Teachers, 1936. 44 p. ms.

3347. ROUCEK, JOSEPH SLABEY. *The Development of Sociology in Czechoslovakia.* New York University, 1937. 46 p. ms.

3348. TURECHEK, ALMA ALICE. *Problems Involved in Arranging a Selected Group of Czech Folk Songs for Educational Purposes.* State University of Iowa, 1941. 45 p. ms.

3349. TURNER, HELEN. *The Influence of Comenius in an Elementary School.* University of South Carolina, 1934. 102 p. ms.

3350. VASA, VLADIMIR, 1901- . *The Development of the Teaching of Social Studies in the Secondary Schools of Czechoslovakia.* George Washington University, 1944. 62 p. ms.

3351. VON WENCK, KATHERINE. *A Critical Evaluation of Czechoslovakian Folk Dances for Use in American School Situations.* New York University, 1933. 123 p. ms.

See also Nos. 210, 226, 249, 261, 274, 3141, 3168, 3189, 3198, 3205, 3208, 3221, 3222, 3224, 3277

For Czechoslovakian and other Slavic groups in the United States, see Nos. 5683-5691

Denmark
(NOS. 3352-3368)

DOCTORS

3352. ANDREASEN, PAUL JOHN. *Grundtvig as an Educator, with Special Reference to the Folk High School Movement.* New York University, 1936. 132 p. ms.

3353. BLOETJES, MARY K. *A Study of the Professional Work of, and the Training Program for Danish Hospital Dietitians.* Cornell University, 1954.

3354. HEGLAND, MARTIN, 1880- . *The Danish Peoples School, Including a General Account of the Educational System of Denmark.* Columbia University, 1915. Washington: Government Printing Office, 1915. 182 p. (U. S. Bureau of Education Bulletin 1915, No. 45.)

3355. JORGENSEN, SIGURD, 1898- . *The Danish Folk High School with Emphasis upon the "Living Word," Folk Song, and Gymnastics.* Ohio State University, 1945. 334 p. ms. Abstract in Ohio State University: *Abstracts of Dissertations ... Spring Quarter, 1944-1945,* p. 31-38. (Abstracts of Doctoral Dissertations, No. 48.)

3356. LARSON, PAUL MELVILLE, 1903- . *A Rhetorical Study of Bishop Frederick Severin Grundtvig.* Northwestern University, 1942. 392 p. ms. Abstract in Northwestern University: *Summaries of Doctoral Dissertations,* Vol. 10, p. 66-71. (Discusses Bishop Gruntvig's influence on the educational system of Denmark.)

3357. OLSON, DAVID. *The Life and Educational Influence of Nicholai Frederik Severin Grundtvig.* Western Reserve University, 1931. 277 p. ms.

3358. OZER, CHARLES L., 1910- . *Naphtali Herz Wesseley: A Study of the Educator and the Poet.* Dropsie College for Hebrew and Cognate Learning, 1944. 272 p. ms.

3359. THOMTE, REIDAR, 1902- . *The Significance of the Philosophy of Soren Kierkegaard for Religious Education.* New York University, 1945. 321 p. ms. Abstract in New York University, School of Education: *Abstracts of Theses ... October 1944- June 1945,* p. 149-154. For master's thesis by same author, see No. 3368.

See also Nos. 119, 138, 142, 143, 147, 151, 161, 175, 3083, 3103, 3115, 3116, 3126, 3128, 4417, 174a.

MASTERS

3360. BAILEY, HELEN LIVINGSTON, 1897- *Hoffding's Theory of Religious Value and Its Relation to Education.* Boston University, 1922. 63 p. ms.

3361. CAMERY, LURA GERTRUDE, 1901- . *The Danish Folk High Schools and Their Significance for American Education.* Claremont Graduate School, 1940. 117 p. ms. For doctoral dissertation by same author, see No. 4.

3362. CAMPBELL, JACK KENAGY. *Kierkegaard's Existential Contributions to Education.* University of Illinois, 1957. 129 p. ms.

3363. ELLGAARD, THEODORE JESSEN. *A Comparative Study of the American Physical Training and Sir Niels Bukh's "Primitiv Gymnastik."* State University of Iowa, 1936. 39 p. ms. (Bukh's volume was published in Copenhagen in 1924.)

3364. ESTERLY, VIRGINIA JUDY, 1882-1946. *The Higher Education of Women in Denmark.* University of California, Berkeley, 1930. 228 p. ms.

3365. FILIPINO, RALPH FRANCIS, 1928- . *An Explanation of the Danish Folk Schools.* Boston College, 1953. 48 p. ms.

3366. KROLIKOWSKI, WALTER PHILIP, 1923- . *The Educational Implications of Kierkegaad's Theory of Communication.* St. Louis University, 1953. 126 p. ms.

3367. THOMSON, MARJORIE UTTER. *The Origin and Development of the Danish Folk High School, with Some Implications for American Education.* University of Southern California, 1930. 62 p. ms.

3368. THOMTE, REIDER, 1902- . *The Formative Years of Soren Kierksgaard,* New York University, 1939. 199 p. ms. For doctoral dissertation by same author, See No. 3359.

See also Nos. 212, 226, 249, 274, 301, 1166, 1333, 3142, 3148, 3158, 3164, 3198, 3210, 3213, 3222, 3286, 3294, 3300

For Danish groups in the United States, see Nos. 5090-5091

Finland
(NOS. 3369-3373)

DOCTOR

3369. HIPPAKA, THOMAS AUGUST. *A Survey of Education in Finland, 1800 to 1825.* University of Wisconsin, 1938. 176 p. ms. Published in modified form, with Foreword by Charles E. Friley, as *Indomitable Finland: Educational Background,* Washington: The Daylion Co., 1940, 199 p. By Thomas A. Hippaka, Ph. D. (Tri: Toivo Augusti Hiipakka.) Abstract in University of Wisconsin: *Summaries of Doctoral Dissertations,* Vol. 3, 1937-38, p. 261-263.

See also Nos. 119, 138, 143, 147, 151, 161, 3103, 4417

MASTERS

3370. HOBSON, GRACE RUGGELS. *A Study of Education in Finland.* University of Southern California, 1934. 118 p. ms.

3371. HUSSONG, HERBERT LEIGH. *Physical Measurements of Finnish School Children: A Discussion as to the Relation of Physical Development to Pedagogical Classification.* University of Oregon, 1918. 35 p. ms.

3372. ORAVINEN, LAURI OLAVI, 1919- . *Religious Education in Elementary and Secondary Schools in Finland.* Clark University, 1950. 136 p. ms. Abstract in Clark University: *Abstracts of Dissertations and Theses,* 1950, p. 143-144.

3373. SEPPI, RUDOLPH HENRY. *The Educational System of Finland.* Stanford University, 1936. 152 p. ms.

See also Nos. 226, 249, 274, 3142, 3195, 3198, 3292

For Finnish groups in the United States, see Nos. 5098-5099

France
(NOS. 3374-3583)

DOCTORS

3374. BARALL, MILTON, 1911- . *The Contribution of Emile Blais De Sauze to the Teaching of Modern Foreign Languages.* New York University, 1948. 328 p. ms. (Chief work was in America, but considers also his early work in France.)

3375. BASKIN, WADE. *Ferdinand de Saussure's Course in General Linguistics.* Columbia University, 1957.

3376. BAYM, MAX ISAAC. *The French Education of Henry Adams.* Columbia University, 1951. New York: Columbia University Press, 1951. xiv, 358 p.

3377. BERGKAMP, JOSEPH URBAN, 1900- . *Dom Jean Mabillon and the Benedictine Historical School of Saint-Maur.* Catholic University of America, 1928. Washington: Catholic University of America, 1928. vii, 123 p.

3378. BONHOMME, *Mother* MARY BERNARD. *Educational Implications of the Philosophy of Henri Bergson.* Catholic University of America, 1944. Washington: Catholic University of America Press, 1944. xv, 208 p. Abstract in *Catholic Educational Review,* Vol. 45, p. 615-616, December 1947.

3379. COOPER, SONOMA, 1893- . *The Development of the Medical School at Montpellier.* University of California, Berkeley, 1938. 234 p. ms.

3380. DIELMANN, RETA HAZEL, 1892- . *Dramatic Representation as a Means of Popular Instruction in the French Revolution, 1789-1794.* Cornell University, 1924. 121 p. ms.

3381. ELWELL, CLARENCE EDWARD, 1904- . *The Influence of the Enlightenment on the Catholic Theory of Religious Education in France, 1750-1850.* Harvard University 1938. Cambridge, Massachusetts: Harvard University Press 1944. x, 335 p. (Harvard Studies in Education, Vol. 29.) Abstract in Harvard University: *Summaries of Ph.D. Theses . . . 1938,* p. 80-84.

3382. FARRINGTON, FREDERIC ERNEST, 1872-1930. *The Public Primary School System of France: With Specific Reference to the Training of Teachers.* Columbia University, 1904. New York: Teachers College, Columbia University, 1906. 303 p. (Teachers College Contribution to Education, No. 7.) For master's thesis by same author, see No. 4474.

3383. FREE, LINCOLN FORREST. *The Philosophical and Educational Views of Henri Bergson.* New York University, 1939. 155 p. ms. Abstract in New York University, School of Education: *Abstracts of Theses,* 1939-40, p. 37-42.

3384. FRIEDENBERG, JANICE. *The Teacher in the Modern Theater in France.* Columbia University, 1934. Paris: Les Presses Modernes, 1934. 182 p.

3385. GAUDIN, ALBERT CHARLES, 1887- . *The Educational Views of Charles Rollin.* Columbia University, 1939. New York: 1939. xii, 151 p.

3386. GRAF, RICHARD M. 1926- . *The Cultural Services of the French Embassy: Their History and Educational Importance.* Columbia University, 1952. 136 p. ms.

3387. GRAVES, FRANK PIERREPONT, 1869-1956. *Peter Ramus and the Educational Reformation of the Sixteenth Century.* Columbia University, 1912. New York: The Macmillan Co., 1912. xi, 227 p.

3388. GROSSMAN, MORDECAI, 1897- . *The Philosophy of Helvetius: With Special Emphasis on the Educational Implications of Sensationalism.* Columbia University, 1926. New York: Teachers College, Columbia University, 1926. iii, 181 p. (Teachers College Contribution to Education, No. 210.)

3389. GUINDON, FRANCIS XAVIER. *The Educational Philosophy and Influence of John Gerson.* Harvard University, 1949. 207 p. ms.

3390. HALLOWAY, FRED. *Objectives in Education According to Rousseau: A Study of the Educational Ends and Aims Advanced by Jean Jacques Rousseau.* Columbia University, 1931. 23 p. ms.

3391. HATCHER, MATTIE LOUISE. *Nationalism in the Curricula of the Public School System of France.* New York University, 1937. 238 p. ms.

3392. HUEBSCH, ARTHUR. *Jean Jacques Rousseau and John Dewey: A Comparative Study and a Critical Estimate of Their Philosophical and Their Educational and Related Theories and Practices.* New York University, 1930. 2 vols. 321 p. ms.

3393. KABAT, GEORGE JULE, 1912- . *The Preparation of Teachers in France.* University of Maryland, 1947. 236 p. ms. Abstract in University of Maryland: *Abstracts of Dissertations* . . . 1952, p. 42-43.

3394. LA FONTAINERIE, FRANCOIS DE, 1877- *French Liberalism and Education in the Eighteenth Century: The Writings of La Chalotais, Turgot, Diderot, and Condorcet on National Education.* Columbia University, 1931. New York and London: McGraw-Hill Co., 1932. ix, 385 p.

3395. LANG, ROBERT ALFRED, 1918- . *The Development of Rhetorical Theory in French Colleges, 1550-1789: With Indications of Other Available Rhetorics.* Northwestern University, 1950. 321 p. ms. Abstract in Northwestern University: *Summaries of Doctoral Dissertations* . . . Vol. 18, p. 137-141.

3396. LENAWAY, Sister MARY ALBERT. *Principles of Education According to Bishop Dupanloup.* Catholic University of America, 1942. 169 p. ms. Abstract in *Catholic Educational Review,* Vol. 45, p. 361, June 1947.

3397. LERNER, RUTH SPERO. *Dr. Alfred Binet's Contriubtion to Experimental Education.* New York University, 1933. 297 p. ms.

3398. LEVINE, ALBERT JULIUS. *Moral Education in the French Public Primary Schools under the Third Republic: The Efficiency of Moral Instruction as Exemplified by Civic-Moral Instruction in France.* New York University, 1920. 125 p. ms.

3399. LIBBY, MARGARET ROBERTS SHERWOOD, 1898- . *The Attitude of Voltaire to Magic and the Sciences.* Columbia University, 1935. New York: Columbia University Press; London: P. S. King & Son, Ltd., 1935. 299 p. (Studies in History, Economics, and Public Law of the Faculty of Politcal Science, No. 408.)

3400. LOZIER, GILBERT C. *A Translation of Jouvancy's "Method of Learning and Teaching" with Historical Significance.* University of Cincinnati, 1957. 191 p. ms. Abstract in *Dissertation Abstracts,* Vol. 17, p. 2930, December 1957. Abstract also in *Religious Education,* Vol. 52, p. 191, May-June 1957. Available on microfilm from University Microfilms. Ann Arbor, Michigan, as Publication No. 24,299.

3401. McLAUGHLIN, MARY M., 1919- . *Intellectual Freedom and Its Limitation in the University of Paris, Thirteenth and Fourteenth Centuries.* Columbia University, 1954. 429 p. ms. Abstract in *Dissertation Abstracts,* Vol. 15, p. 1052-1053, June 1915. Available on microfilm from University Microfilms, Ann Arbor, Michigan, as Publication No. 10,271.

3402. McMURRY, RUTH EMILY, 1892- . *The Training of Modern Foreign Language Teachers for the French Secondary Schools.* Columbia University, 1929. 163 p. ms. Published in McMurry, R.E., Mueller, Max; and Alexander, Thomas, *Modern Foreign Languages in France and Germany: The Training of Teachers and Methods of Instruction.* New York: Teachers College, Columbia University, 1930. viii, 516 p. (Studies of the International Institute of Teachers College, Columbia University, No. 9.) Miss McMurry's dissertation constitutes Part. I, p. 1-159.

3403. MALIN, WILLIAM EDWARD, 1916- *The Idea of Progress through Education in Eighteenth Century French Philosophy.* University of California, Berkeley, 1954. 321 p. ms.

3404. MERAS, EDMOND ALBERT, 1896- . *Francois Gouin, Teacher and Educational Reformer.* New York University, 1937. 254 p. ms.

3405. MILES, DONALD WILFRED, 1913- . *Recent Reforms in French Secondary Education, with Certain Implications for French and American Education.* Columbia University, 1953. New York: Bureau of Publications, Teachers College, Columbia University, 1953. x, 163 p. (Teachers College Studies in Education.)

3406. MOORMAN, RICHARD HERBERT. *Some Educational Implications of Descartes' Synthesis of Mathematics and Philosophy.* George Peabody College for Teachers, 1940. 381 p. ms. Nashville: George Peabody College for Teachers, 1940. 8 p. (Abstract of Contribution to Education, No. 278.)

3407. NESTICO, RALPH FRANK. *A Comparative Study of Selected Aspects of Vocational Guidance in France and the United States.* University of Connecticut, 1958. 198 p. ms. Abstract in *Dissertation Abstracts,* Vol. 19, p. 991, November 1958. Available on microfilm from University Microfilms, Ann Arbor, Michigan, as Mic. 58-3927.

3408. NOTHOMB, Mother MARY ELIZABETH, 1913- . *The Education Theory of Jacques Maritain.* University of California, Berkeley, 1953. 185 p. ms.

3409. RECTOR, LIZZIE ELIZA, 1866–1955. *Montaigne.* New York University, 1895. 127 p. ms. Published in modified form as *Montaigne: The Education of Children: Selected, Translated, and Annotated by L. E. Rector, Ph.D.* With an Introduction by William T. Harris. New York: D. Appleton & Co., 1899. xxviii, 191 p. (International Education Series: Edited by W.T. Harris. Vol. 46.)

3410. REDMOND, Sister CATHERINE FRANCES. *The Convent School of French Origin in the United States, 1727 to 1843.* University of Pennsylvania, 1936. Philadelphia: 1936. 246 p. (Includes considerations of origins in France.)

3411. REDMOND, Sister JUSTINE. *Laicism in the Schools of France.* Catholic University of America, 1932. Washington: Catholic University of America, 1932. x, 79 p.

3412. ROBERTS, Mrs. EUNICE (CARMICHAEL), 1902- . *The Educational Ideals of Anatole France.* University of Illinois, 1940. 200 p. ms. Urbana, Illinois: 1940. 15 p. (Abstract of Thesis.)

3413. ROCHEDIEU, CHARLES ALFRED EMMANUEL, 1892- . *A Contribution to the Study of Jean Jacques Rousseau.* George Peabody College for Teachers, 1934. Nashville: George Peabody College for Teachers, 1934. 7 p. (Abstract of Contribution to Education, No. 182.)

3414. RUTTENBERG, JOSEPH. *Discussion and Legislation on Public Instruction and National Education by the French Constituent and Legislative Assemblies and by the National Convention, 1791-1795.* Cornell University, 1926. 314 p. ms. Ithaca, New York: 1927. 20 p. Abstract of thesis.

3415. SCARPITTO, MICHAEL. *Guidance and Student Personnel Services in French Secondary Schools.* University of Chicago, 1955. 277 p. ms. Available on microfilm: see index under "University of Chicago."

3416. SHANE, MILTON LANNING, 1899- . *France in the Letters of Prosper Merimee, 1826-1870.* George Peabody College for Teachers, 1938. 421 p. ms. Nashville: George Peabody College for Teachers, 1930 (i.e. 1938) 8 p. (Abstract of Contribution to Education, No. 214.)

3417. SHELEY, CURTIS FRANKLIN. *The Role of the Fable in Present Day French Education.* George Peabody College for Teachers, 1942. 400 p. ms. (Contribution to Education No. 324). Abstract in George Peabody College for Teachers: *Abstracts of Dissertations* . . . 1942, p. 83-93.

3418. SHERESHEVSKY, ESRA, 1915- . *Rashi as a Teacher, Interpreter of Text, and Molder of Character.* Dropsie College for Hebrew and Cognate Learning, 1957. 180 p. ms. Abstract in *Religious Education,* Vol. 53, p. 277-278, May-June 1958.

3419. SIDES, ARTHUR CLEMENT. *The Influence of the French Revolution on Education in France.* New York University, 1913. 208 p. ms.

3420. SKELTON, JAMES WILLIAM, 1913- . *An Analysis of the Philosophy of Jacques Maritain in Respect to Its Implications for Democratic Education.* Ohio State University, 1947. 160 p. ms. Abstract in Ohio State University: *Abstracts of Dissertations* . . . Spring Quarter, 1946-47, p. 341-345. (Abstracts of Doctoral Dissertations, No. 54.)

3421. TOMPKINS, ADA ECKERT. *The Educational Contributions of Charlemagne.* New York University, 1911. 42 p. ms.

3422. WALKER, EVELYN, 1874–1953. *A Study of the "Trait des Indivisibles" of Giles Personne de Roberval, with a View to Answering, insofar as Is Possible, the Two Questions: Which Propositions Contained Therein Are His Own, and Which Are Due to His Predecessors or Contemporaries? And What Effect, if Any, Had this Work on His Successors?* Columbia University, 1930. New York: Teachers College, Columbia University, 1932. vi, 272 p. (Teachers College Contribution to Education, No. 446.)

3423. WILDE, ARTHUR HERBERT, 1865-1944. *The Administration of the Schools of Gaul from the Fourth Century to the Reforms of Charlemagne.* Harvard University, 1901. 170 p. ms. Published in part as "Decadence of Learning in Gaul in the Seventh and Eighth Centuries as Viewed Especially in the Lives of the Saints," *American Journal of Theology,* Vol. 7, p. 443-451, July 1903.

3424. WILLIAMS, JOHN ROBERT. *The Schools of Laon in the Twelfth Century.* Harvard University, 1927. 351 p. ms. Abstract in Harvard University: *Summaries of Ph.D. Theses,* 1927, p. 96-99.

3425. WILLIAMS, LESLIE PEARCE, 1927- . *Scientific Education in France during the Revolutionary and Imperial Periods, 1789-1815.* Cornell University, 1952. 227 p. ms.

3426. WILLIAMS, LOUISE, 1885- . *A Cultural Survival from the Old Regime.* Stanford University, 1936. 170 p. ms. Abstract in Stanford University: *Abstracts of Dissertations* . . . 1935-36, p. 80-83. (Includes consideration of education as one aspect of cultural survival.)

See also Nos. 119, 129, 138, 143, 147, 150, 152, 154, 157, 159, 160, 161, 163, 175, 177, 178, 184, 1418, 2327, 2911, 3032, 3048, 3068, 3069, 3070, 3071, 3073, 3074, 3075, 3076, 3078, 3079, 3080, 3081, 3086, 3088, 3089, 3090, 3091, 3092, 3093, 3094, 3098, 3099, 3100, 3102, 3104, 3106, 3108, 3109, 3110, 3112, 3114, 3116, 3117, 3118, 3119, 3121, 3123, 3125, 3127, 3128, 3131, 3132, 3233, 4417, 174a.

MASTERS

3427. ADRIAN, Brother FRANCIS. *An Historical Study of the Use of the Vernacular as an Instrument of Instruction in the Education of Boys in Seventeenth-Century France.* Loyola College, 1955.

3428. AGATHO, Brother. *The Social Influence of St. John Baptist de la Salle.* Catholic University of America, 1925. 38 p. ms.

3429. AGATSTEIN, MICHAEL. *Syndicalism and the French Elementary School Teacher.* College of the City of New York, 1936. 67 p. ms. Abstract in College of the City of New York: *Abstracts of Theses* . . . 1923-1939, p. 91.

3430. ALBRIGHT, SARA CELESTE. *Education in the French National Assembly.* Vanderbilt University, 1939. 148 p. ms. Abstract in Vanderbilt University: *Bulletin of Vanderbilt University,* Vol. 39, No. 10, p. 59.

3431. ANDERSON, WILLIAM JAMES. *A Study of the Philosophy of Rousseau concerning the Practical Arts and His Influence on the Philosophy of Industrial Arts in the Secondary Schools of the United States.* North Texas State College, 1950. 55 p. ms. Abstract in *Research in Industrial Education, 1930-1955,* p. 470-471.

3432. ANDRIOT, Sister MARY MADELEINE, 1914- . *Catholic Teachings in the Novels of Francois Mauriac.* Fordham University, 1947. 174 p. ms.

3433. BADANES, SAUL. *August Compte's Theory and Practice of Education.* Columbia University, 1902. 26 p. ms.

3434. BARRAS, GABRIEL JOSEPH, 1901- . *The Technique of Character Training of Pere Antonin Eymiue, S.J.* St. Louis University, 1937. 71 p. ms.

3435. BELLINFANTE, JOSEPH, 1898- . *Fenelon as an Educator.* Temple University, 1930. 97 p. ms.

3436. BENOIT, DOLIVE. *Lakanal et le Collège d'Orléans.* Louisiana State University and State Agricultural and Mechanical College, 1938. 57 p. ms. Abstract in *Louisiana State University Bulletin,* Vol. 31, n.s., No. 1, January 1939.

3437. BERNIQUE, GEORGES MAURICE. *What Theories of Rabelais, Montaigne, and Rousseau Are Incorporated in Modern Education?* Massachusetts State College, 1937. 105 p. ms.

3438. BISHOP, JOSEPH A., 1916- . (Brother Gilroy.) *A Chain of French Literary Contributions to Education from the Renaissance to the Eighteenth Century.* St. John's University, 1946. 83 p. ms. Abstract in St. John's University: *Abstracts of Dissertations,* 1946-48, p. 67.

3439. BLAIR, JOHN ALVIN, 1883- . *Historic Influence of History Study as Illustrated by the French Revolution.* University of Kansas, 1918. 163 p. ms.

3440. BOSANKO, PAUL. *Une Etude Raisonee de la Trilogie Catholique de J. K. Huysmans.* Colorado State Teachers College, 1922. 69 p. ms. (J.K. Huysmans is pseudonym of Charles Marie G. Huysmans.)

3441. BOSWORTH, STANLEY A. *Pierre Janet: A Bibliographic Study.* New York University, 1958.

3442. BRADY, Rev. WILLIAM OTTERWELL IGNATIUS. *Religious Education in the Schools of the Port Royalists.* Catholic University of America, 1924. 50 p. ms.

3443. BRAUCH, Sister MARIE SUZANNE. *A Comparison of Fenelon's and Dupanloup's Ideas on Education of Girls.* Catholic University of America, 1938. 66 p. ms.

3444. BRAZELTON, HELEN KATHRYN, 1910- *Some French Educational Philosophies of the Eighteenth Century.* University of Arizona, 1933. 120 p. ms. Abstract in University of Arizona: *Abstracts of Theses for Higher Degrees,* 1933, p. 8-9.

3445. BRITT, ESTHER LEE, 1900- . *French Influences on Educational Practices in the United States.* Emory University, 1932. 119 p. ms.

3446. BUCK, KATHRYNE ELIZABETH. *Educational Aspects of Barat Catholic Action Center.* St. Louis University, 1943. 104 p. ms.

3447. CAMPBELL, ANNA MONTGOMERY, 1888- *Evidences of a Spirit of Nationalism in the University of Paris in the Late Middle Ages.* Columbia University, 1924. 42 p. ms. For doctoral dissertation by same author, see No. 3007.

3448. CARVEN, AGNES MARY, 1899- . *The Influence of Rousseau on Modern Education.* Boston University, 1922. 20 p. ms.

3449. CHAO, CHING-HUI. *French Libraries in the Fifteenth and Sixteenth Centuries.* Columbia University, 1941. 61 p. ms.

3450. CHILSON, JOHN BARRETT. *A Study of Rousseau's System of Education as Developed in His "Emile."* Syracuse University, 1916. 31 p. ms.

3451. CINQ-MARS, Sister MARY ANNUNCIATA. *The Educational Bearings of the Social Philosophy of Frederic Ozanam.* Catholic University of America, 1936. 90 p. ms. Abstract in Catholic University of America: *Summaries of Dissertations, June 1935-June 1936,* p. 33.

3452. CLAIRE, Sister MARIE. *"For Christ's Little Ones."* Translated from the French *"Pour les Tout-Petits des Jardins d'Enfants,"* by Quinet. Rivier College, 1956. 156 p. ms.

3453. CLARK, Rev. B. ALBERT. *Religious Education Principles of Saint John Baptist de la Salle.* Catholic University of America, 1953. 46 p. ms.

3454. COLLINS, Sister ELIZABETH ANN. *A Study of Educational Theories and Practices as Found in the Life and Works of Saint Vincent De Paul.* Villa Nova College, 1949. 62 p. ms.

3455. COLLINS, JOSEPH. *The Educational Opportunities Afforded American Permissionaries in the Leave Areas of France.* University of Michigan, 1935.

3456. CONNOLY, Rev. JAMES LOUIS. *The Catechitical Method of St. Sulpice.* Catholic University of America, 1924. 51 p. ms.

3457. CONWAY, JOSEPH GERARD. *La Morale Laique in the French Schools.* Catholic University of America, 1930. 88 p. ms.

3458. COX, ANNA McMULLIN, 1915- *Rousseau's Contribution to the Modern Progressive School.* University of Kentucky, 1941. 126 p. ms.

3459. CRAUSAZ, ROBERT MARTIN. *The Educational Ideas of Anatole France.* Ohio State University, 1928. 70 p. ms. Abstract in Ohio State University: *Abstracts of Theses Presented by Candidates for the Master's Degree,* August 1929, p. 37-38. (Abstracts of Masters' Theses, No. 1.)

3460. CROFTS, HARRY, 1927- . *A Critical Study of the Teaching Methods Used in the French "Classes Nouvelles" with Particular Reference to the Teaching of Languages.* Northeastern University, 1954. 109 p. ms.

3461. CRUMLY, EMILE. *The Ecole Unique Reform in French Education.* University of Southern California, 1940. 102 p. ms.

3462. CRYIER, Sister ALPHONSUS LIGUORI. *Developments in Church-State Educational Relations in France between the Two World Wars.* Catholic University of America, 1950. 59 p. ms.

3463. CUDMORE, MURIEL FRANCES, 1920- . *Madame de Maintenon and the Education of Girls in Seventeenth Century France.* Fordham University, 1945. 149 p. ms.

3464. CYR, Rev. GUY JOSEPH, 1912- . *Father Jean-Claude Colin's Contribution to Education.* Boston College, 1954. 69 p. ms.

3465. DEA, ROMALA M. *Charlemagne's Influence on Education.* Creighton University, 1922.

3466. DERHAM, MARY TERESA. *Charlemagne's Palace School.* Stanford University, 1936. 64 p. ms.

3467. DeVINEAU, Rev. CHARLES EMILE. *Bishop Dupanloup's Philosophy of Education.* Catholic University of America, 1930. 35 p. ms. Washington: Catholic University of America, *Educational Research Bulletin*, Vol. 4, No. 10, December 1929.

3468. DONNELLY, EDWARD McTAMMANY, 1893- . *The Education of Francois Rebelais and Its Effect upon His Educational Ideal of the "Complete Man."* New York State College for Teachers, Albany, 1935. 71 p. ms.

3469. DOOLEY, MARGARET M. *The Influence of Rousseau's Educational Theories on Modern Educational Theories.* New York University, 1936. 73 p. ms.

3470. DOON, Sister MARY LEO. *Educational Contributions of St. John De La Salle.* New York State College for Teachers, Albany, 1916. 45 p. ms.

3471. DOWD, WINIFRED ADRIAN. (Later, Mrs. John Mahoney.) *Rebelais — His Educational Theories.* Boston University, 1922. 32 p. ms.

3472. DUPONT, Rev. JOSEPH ALOYSIUS. *Rabanus Maurus, Educator of the Clergy in the Ninth Century.* Catholic University of America, 1904. 92 p. ms.

3473. EDEN, ROYAL KREBS. *Grammar and Grammarians in France, 1 A.D. — 1500 A.D. as Revealed in the "Historie Litteraire de la France."* University of Illinois, 1925. 47 p. ms. Abstract in Russell Taaffe Gregg: *Annotated Bibliography of Graduate Theses in Education at the University of Illinois,* 1931, p. 26-27. (Bureau of Educational Research, Bulletin No. 55.)

3474. ELLMAN, SHEPARD S. *Francois Vetable, First Professor of Hebrew in the College de France (c. 1495-1547.)* Columbia University, 1938. 71 p. ms.

3475. ENDSLOW, Rev. BARTHOLOMEW S. (On thesis title page, Rev. Bart Endslow). *The Educational Theories of Jacques Maritain.* Catholic University of America, 1951. 77 p. ms. Abstract in *Catholic Educational Review,* Vol. 50, p. 191-192, March 1952.

3476. FALDWELL, Sister MARY PHILIP. *Montaigne as an Educational Realist.* Catholic Sisters College of the Catholic University of America, 1922. 39 p. ms.

3477. FERRIGNO, JAMES MOSES, 1910- . *Moliere and the Education of Women.* Boston University, 1934.

3478. FRANKE, VIRGINIA. *The Attitude of the Sorbonne Toward the "New Learning" of the Sixteenth Century.* Columbia University, 1923. 27 p. ms.

3479. FREDERICK, LILA RAE. *The Foreign Language Textbooks of France and the United States.* Colorado State College of Education, 1937. 50 p. ms.

3480. FREEMAN, WILLIAM F. *Public Education in France during the Revolution.* Columbia University, 1939. 26 p. ms.

3481. FRENOY, FORTUNE C. *A Comparative Study of the Educational Philosophies of Jacques Maritain and Robert M. Hutchins.* Tulane University of Louisiana, 1957. 66 p. ms.

3482. FRIEDRICH, RUTH. *The Educational Policy of the French National Convention.* State University of Iowa, 1932. 112 p. ms.

3483. GELINAS, Sister MARIE DE LIESSE, 1886- . *Madame de Maintenon's Educational Methods in the Light of Present Day Terminology.* Boston College, 1934. 80 p. ms.

3484. GILLMAN, VERNALD. *The Educational Ideas and Ideals of Condorcet.* College of the City of New York, 1932. 102 p. ms. Abstract in College of the City of New York: *Abstracts of Theses...* 1923-1939, p. 43.

3485. GLAHN, Sister MAUREEN. *A Study of the Educational Philosophy of Jacques Marie Morsabre as Exemplified in His Discourses and Panagyriques.* Catholic University of America, 1948. 61 p. ms.

3486. GLYNN, Sister MARY AGNETA. *Mother Catherine McAuley, Foundress of the Sisters of Mercy, an Eminent Catholic Humanist.* St. John's University, 1946. Abstract in St. John's University, *Abstracts of Dissertations, 1946-1948,* p. 29.

3487. GOEHEGEN, GRACE. *The Educational Theories of Rousseau and Dewey.* Birmingham-Southern College, 1933. 140 p. ms.

3488. GOTTLEIB, Mrs. JEAN G. *The Education of Louis XIV.* Columbia University, 1939.

3489. GRAHAM, MARY ALICE. *The Ideas of Madame de Maintenon, Fenelon, and Moliere on the Education of Women.* University of Pittsburgh, 1932. 52 p. ms. Abstract in University of Pittsburgh: *Abstracts of Theses...* Vol. 8, 1932, p. 448-449.

3490. GREER, VIRGINIA DELL, 1910- . *Comparison and Evaluation of the Secondary School Systems of France and the United States.* Texas Christian University, 1931. 98 p. ms.

3491. GREGORY, MARY ALEXANDER, 1890- . *The Emergence of Secular Education in France.* George Washington University, 1935. 40 p. ms.

3492. GUALANDRIS, PETER JOHN. *The Educational Contents and Implications of the "De Disciplina Scholarium" of Pseudo-Boethius.* Catholic University of America, 1957. 131 p. ms.

3493. HAMEL, Brother ALBERT, 1896- . *Father Champagnat, One of the Great Educators of the Nineteenth Century.* Fordham University, 1937. 78 p. ms. Abstract in Fordham University: *Dissertations Accepted for Higher Degrees,* 1938, p. 52

3494. HAMMERMAN, DOROTHY. *The Educational Activities of the Confederation Generale du Travail.* Hunter College of the City of New York, 1939. 99 p. ms.

3495. HARRIS, ISABELLE B. *Montaigne's Educational Ideals.* University of Pittsburgh, 1932. 63

p. ms. Abstract in University of Pittsburgh: *Abstracts of Theses...* Vol. 8, 1932, p. 388-389.

3496. HARTMAN, Rev. JOSEPH. *A Critical Study of the Educational Theories and Principles of Michel de Montaigne.* Catholic University of America, 1948. 59 p. ms. Abstract in *Catholic Educational Review,* Vol. 47, p. 683, December 1949.

3497. HARVEY, THOMAS M., 1914- . *The "Metalogicus" of John of Salisbury: A Medieval Humanist's Theory of Education.* St. Louis University, 1939. 137 p. ms. (France and Great Britain.)

3498. HEGARTY, Sister MARY EUGENE. *A Comparison of Fenelon's Ideas on the Education of Girls with Those of Janet Stuart.* Catholic University of America, 1949. 82 p. ms.

3499. HEMPFLING, Sister MARY LORETTA. *The Educational Theories and Principles of Madame Henriette Genest Campan.* Catholic University of America, 1945. 107 p. ms.

3500. HENGEHOLD, Rev. ROGER. *Early Franciscans at Paris.* Catholic University of America, 1929. 48 p. ms.

3501. HENNESSEY, Sister MARY OF ST. PETER OF ALCANTARA, 1905- . *Evaluation of the Philosophy of Education of Francois Fenelon.* Fordham University, 1944. 72 p. ms.

3502. HOULNE, Sister ANTOINETTE MARIE. *Abbe Lanne as a Christian Educator.* Catholic University of America, 1938. 71 p. ms.

3503. JANNUZI, LEDA FLORA. *The Child and Child Education in Anatole France.* Columbia University, 1931. 54 p. ms.

3504. JARRETT, ELIZABETH AGNES. *Theory of Education of Madame de Maintenon.* Stanford University, 1946. 111 p. ms.

3505. JOB, CORDELIA CRAFTS. *Education in France: Its Organization and Institutions.* Wellesley College, 1934. 370 p. ms.

3506. KAMBER, FLORENCE REBECCA. *A Study of the Movement for the Education of Girls in France from Fenelon to Rousseau.* Ohio State University, 1929. 105 p. ms.

3507. KEELAN, JAMES A. *The Educational Principles of Father Jean-Claude Colin, S. M.* Catholic University of America, 1957. 63 p. ms.

3508. KILLEEN, Rev. SYLVESTER M. *History of Premonstratensian Educational Institutions in the United States.* Catholic University of America, 1936. 55 p. ms. (Includes history of such institutions in France.)

3509. KIRKPATRICK, LEONARD HENRY. *The Single School Movement in France.* Stanford University, 1935. 106 p. ms.

3510. KNECHT, AMANDA L. *The New Education in France with a Tentative Curriculum for Classes in French in American Schools.* Colorado State Teachers College, 1924. 82 p. ms.

3511. KNOX, ANTOINETTE. *The Napoleonic School System.* Columbia University, 1924. 64 p. ms.

3512. KROLL, FLORENCE IRENE, 1909- . *Comparison of the Content of Certain French and American First Year Algebra Textbooks.* University of North Dakota, 1930. 75 p. ms.

3513. LANDON, MARY AUGUSTA. *The Plan of Graduate Study Offered by Teachers College in Cooperation with the University of Paris to Candidates for the Degree of Master of Arts Specializing in the Teaching of French.* Columbia University, 1929. 32 p. ms.

3514. LARRABEE, HARRIET CLARA, 1908- . *The Relation of the French Cathedral Schools to the Rise of the University of Paris.* Boston University, 1937. 61 p. ms.

3515. LEHMAN, Sister MARY MAGNA. *Fenelon's Curriculum for the Education of the Girl.* Catholic Sisters College of the Catholic University of America, 1923. 52 p. ms.

3516. LENNON, GRACE, 1907- . (Later Mrs. William R. Terry.) *The Influence of French Education on American Education during the Nationalistic Period.* New York State College for Teachers, Albany, 1930. 88 p. ms.

3517. LEVIT, MARTHA ANNE. *The Education of Girls in Eighteenth Century France.* College of the City of New York, 1941. 98 p. ms.

3518. LLOYD, EVERETT T. *The Place of International Student Correspondence in Modern Language Teaching.* College of the City of New York, 1937. 128 p. ms. Abstract in College of the City of New York: *Abstracts of Theses... 1923-1939,* p. 100. (Includes correspondence with French students.)

3519. LYON, EVERETT STANLEY, 1893- . *Rousseau and Modern Education.* Dartmouth College, 1924. 109 p. ms.

3520. McCARTHY, Sister DE CHANTAL. *Saint Vincent de Paul's Concept of the Care of the Sick Applied to Objectives in Nursing Education.* Catholic University of America, 1938. Washington: Catholic University of America, 1938. viii, 40p. (Studies in Nursing Education, Vol. 3, Fasc. 1.)

3521. McCAULEY, JAMES A. *The "Expositie Super Canonem Missae," with an Analysis, and Modern Studies on the Same Subject.* Catholic University of America, 1955. 38 p. ms.

3522. MacDONALD, JESSIE LOUISE. *French Influence on Higher Education in the United States.* New York University, 1941. 74 p. ms.

3523. McPARLAN, FRANCIS CLARK, 1907- . *The Training of Teachers in France for the Public Primary and Secondary Schools from 1875 to 1925.* Fordham University, 1938. 88 p. ms. Abstract in Fordham University: *Dissertations Accepted for Higher Degrees,* 1939, p. 64.

3524. MacRURY, NORMA OLIVE. *Theories on the Education of Women in France.* Boston University, 1928. 70 p. ms.

3525. MAHONE, LENA LOUISA. *A Translation of Durkheim's "Education et Sociologie," with Introductory Chapter.* University of Washington, 1933. 141 p. ms.

3526. MARKET, Rev. JOHN C. *A Critical Study of the Educational Tenets of Jean Jacques Rosseau and John Dewey in the Light of Catholic Doctrine on Original Sin and the Supernatural Destiny of Man.* Catholic University of America, 1950. 92 p. ms.

3527. MARSHALL, EDWARD ARMSTRONG. *An Educator's Guide to French Travel.* University of Southern California, 1951. 66 p. ms.

3528. MASON, DOROTHY EVELYN. *Condorcet: A Study of His Educational Views and Activities Accompanied by a Translation of the "Rapport."* Ohio State University, 1931. 188 p. ms. Abstract in Ohio State University: *Abstracts of Theses Presented for the Master's Degree. . .* 1931, p. 123-125.

3529. MINOR, MICHAEL M., 1914- . *De La Salle's Place in the History of Education.* University of Scranton, 1955. 104 p. ms.

3530. MOLPHY, ROSEMARY THERESE, 1919- . (Sister Teresa Elizabeth.) *Fenelon, Madame de Maintenon, and the Education of Women.* St. John's University, 1955. 58 p. ms. Abstract in St. John's University: *Abstracts of Dissertations, 1953-1956,* p. 281-282.

3531. MONTGOMERY, CORA MAY. *Plan and Program of Study in the French Elementary Schools: A Translation.* Stanford University, 1935. 164 p. ms.

3532. MOORE, Sister MARY ELLEN. *History of the Educational Activities of the Congregation of the Sisters of the Holy Humility of Mary.* University of Cincinnati, 1943. 125 p. ms.

3533. MULLEN, Rev. MICHAEL F. *The Contribution of St. Vincent de Paul to the Establishment of Seminaries in France.* Catholic University of America, 1945. 97 p. ms.

3534. MUNRO, NORA GERALDINE, 1907- . *Abelard's Place in Christian Education.* Boston University, 1933. 76 p. ms.

3535. MURPHY, Rev. JOHN X. *The Pedagogical Methods of the University of Paris during the Middle Ages.* Catholic University of America, 1914. 74 p. ms.

3536. NEYHOUSE, DOROTHY AYAHR. *A Comparison of the Theory of Education Found in the "Philosophical Dictionary" and "Letters to Frederick the Great of Prussia" of Voltaire, and the Modern Theory of Education.* Indiana State Teachers College, 1935. 42 p. ms. (Contribution of the Graduate School, No. 226.) Abstract in Teachers College Journal, Vol. 7, p. 116, July 1936.

3537. NICE, MARJORIE DUNCAN. *Academic Freedom at the University of Paris in the Thirteenth Century.* Columbia University, 1934. 48 p. ms.

3538. NOONAN, WILLIAM MICHAEL, 1910- . *The Contribution of the French to the Development of the History of Mathematics.* Boston College, 1934. 33 p. ms.

3539. OREN, FRANCINE F. *Some Sex and Social Status Differences in Personality at the Kindergarten Level in Paris, France.* Kent State University, 1955.

3540. OSATO, TIMOTHY. *Nationalism and the Reforms in French Primary Education, 1879-1882.* Columbia University, 1950. 108 p. ms.

3541. PELLETIER, Rev. TIMOTHY JOHN. *The Monastic Schools of Bec.* Catholic University of America, 1931. 40 p. ms.

3542. PHILLIPS, BETTY LOU. *An Annotated Index of Subject Matter Pertaining to Language in "Revue Generale De L'Enseignement Des Sourde-Muet", 1923-1951.* Gallaudet College, 1952. 85 p. ms.

3543. PIETERS, MAURICE. *Some Aspects of the Renaissance of the French Religious Spirit.* Clark University, 1919. 22 p. ms. (Considers the Renaissance in politics, religion, and education.)

3544. POWELL, LINDSAY JAMES. *Education in the French Legislative Assembly, 1791-1792.* Vanderbilt University, 1939. 81 p. ms. Abstract in Bulletin of Vanderbilt University, Vol. 40, No. 10, p. 67.

3545. PRESINGER, Rev. CHARLES V. *The French Revolution and Elementary Schools.* Catholic University of America, 1934. 99 p. ms.

3546. PURTELL, Mother AILEEN, 1906- . *The Teacher Ideal of St. Madeleine Sophie Barat.* Marquette University, 1939. 81 p. ms.

3547. RAMSAY, Mrs. MATHILDE P. *Comparison of Elementary Education in France and Tennessee.* University of Tennessee, 1924. 215 p. ms.

3548. RAMSEY, KATHERINE HOLBROOK. *Comparative Study of the Educational Theories of Rousseau and John Dewey.* Texas Technological College, 1931. 77 p. ms.

3549. REINERT, PAUL CLARE, 1910- . *Rousseau's Educational Theories regarding Civic, Moral, and Religious Indoctrination.* St. Louis University, 1934. 148 p. ms.

3550. RICE, BESSIE LILLIAN. *La Chalotais, Condorcet, and Jefferson on National Education.* Johns Hopkins University, 1943. 55 p. ms.

3551. ROBINSON, MAYME SUE. *Montaigne on the Education of the Gentry.* University of Texas, 1940. 102 p. ms.

3552. ROSENBERG, LEON W. *The Organization of American Student Life in Paris.* College of the City of New York, 1939. 92 p. ms. Abstract in College of the City of New York: *Abstracts of Theses . . . 1923-1939,* p. 108.

3553. RUTLAND, Brother DENIS. *The Role of Jesus in the Teacher-Training Program of Saint John Baptist de la Salle.* Catholic University of America, 1941. 56 p. ms.

3554. SAUTE, ALFRED E. *Significance of the Educational Principles of Rabelais, Fenelon, and Rousseau to Current Thought.* Rhode Island College of Education, 1956.

3555. SCHILLE, Rev. NICHOLAS JOHN. *Lanfranc, the Educator.* Catholic University of America, 1927. 20 p. ms.

3556. SCHOOFF, Rev. RAPHAEL LEONARD. *The Educational Contents of the "De Eruditione Filiorum Nobilium" by Vincent of Beauvais.* Catholic University of America, 1942. 87 p. ms.

3557. SHAVER, FRANCES ELIZABETH. *Twentieth Century Reorganization of the French Secondary School.* George Peabody College for Teachers, 1938. 100 p. ms.

3558. SHERWOOD, MARGARET ROBERTS. *The Sorbonne and the Early Days of the Reformation in France.* Columbia University, 1923. 51 p. ms.

3559. SINGER, LILLIAN M. *A Survey of the Salient Advances in the Secondary School System of France since the World War (1920-1930.)* College of the City of New York, 1931. 126 p. ms. Abstract in College of the City of New York: *Abstracts of Theses . . . 1923-1939,* p. 39.

3560. SKULY, JOSEPH A. *Christian Principles of Educational Supervision According to the Venerable William Joseph Chaminade.* Catholic University of America, 1943. 100 p. ms.

3561. SMITH, ETHANNE. *Jean-Baptiste de la Salle.* Boston University, 1958.

3562. SPADARO, LOUIS. *Fifty Years of the Alliance Francaise (1883-1933.)* College of the City of New York, 1933. 213 p. ms. Abstract in College of the City of New York: *Abstracts of Theses . . . 1923-1939,* p. 67.

3563. SPEER, Sister MARY RAPHAEL. *The Contribution of St. Jane Frances to Religious Education.* Catholic University of America, 1942. 63 p. ms.

3564. STOAKS, CHARLES E. *Educational Legislation in France during the Revolution and the Napoleonic Era.* Columbia University, 1932. 50 p. ms.

3565. SULLIVAN, MARGARET ANN. *French Influence in American Education.* University of Texas, 1931. 141 p. ms.

3566. SWEENEY, MARILYN. *French Primary Education, 1850-1870.* Columbia University, 1950. 103 p. ms.

3567. TAFFEL, ABRAM. *Jules Ferry and the Reform of the French Elementary Primary Schools.* College of the City of New York, 1936. 105 p. ms. Abstract in College of the City of New York: *Abstracts of Theses . . . 1923-1939, p. 96.*

3568. TEFFT, LLOYD GORDON, 1917- . *The University of Paris in the Middle Ages.* St. Bonaventure University, 1946. 76 p. ms.

3569. TERNER, HYMAN. *The Problem of L'Ecole Unique in France, by Jean-Albert Bede: A Translation from the French, with an Introduction.* College of the City of New York, 1933. 157 p. ms. Abstract in College of the City of New York: *Abstracts of Theses . . . 1923-1939, p. 68.*

3570. TOMLINSON, LEONORA LUCAS. *Rousseau and His French Predecessors in the Field of Pedagogy.* Northwestern University, 1922. 38 p. ms.

3571. UHL, CLARA AUGUSTA, 1902- . *The Influence of Jean Jacques Rousseau on Modern Theory and Practice in Education.* Southern Methodist University, 1947. 87 p. ms. Abstract in Southern Methodist University: *Abstracts of Theses,* No. 12, 1946, 1947, p. 41.

3572. UNDERWOOD, HARRIET, 1871- . *The Binet-Simon Tests.* George Washington University, 1917. 25 p. ms.

3573. VAN REETH, Sister MARIE ELISE. *A Study of France through the Realia of Selected Texts.* University of Cincinnati, 1933. 62 p. ms.

3574. VARON, EDITH JUDITH, 1909- . *The Development of Alfred Binet's Psychology.* Cornell University, 1934. Princeton, New Jersey: Psychological Review Co., 1935. 129 p. (*Psychological Review Publications.* No. 207. Vol. 46, No. 3.)

3575. WALBERGER, KATHERINE LILLIAN. *Jules Ferry and French Education.* University of Wisconsin, 1946. 103 p. ms.

3576. WALSH, Sister JULIA. *Concepts of Administration of Saint Vincent de Paul Related to Modern Criteria for Democratic Administration in Nursing Education.* Catholic University of America, 1956. 44 p. ms.

3577. WALT, EVA B., 1888- . *The Educational Ideas of La Chalotais.* Temple University, 1931. 100 p. ms.

3578. WEBSTER F. CHAMPLIN, Jr., 1905- . *Secondary Education in France since the World War.* Boston University 1932. 131 p. ms.

3579. WEITZEL, Brother EUGENE J. *The Educational Principles and Contributions of Pere Louis Querbes.* De Paul University, 1953. 107 p. ms.

3580. WHEATON, DOROTHY DOYLE. *The Treatment of the Professor in Modern French Literature.* Stanford University, 1934. 98 p. ms.

3581. WITTENBERG, MARY EDNA. *A Study of the Ideas of Madame de Sevigne on the Education of Women.* Stanford University, 1931. 42 p. ms.

3582. WOLLSTEIN, ROSE HEYLBUT. *The French Girl of Good Family as Seen by Three Educators of 1686-1687: Fenelon, Fleury, and Mme. de Maintenon.* Columbia University, 1921.

3583. WRIGHT, Sister ELLEN ST. JOHN. *The Principles of Religious Guidance According to Blessed Julie Billiart.* Catholic University of America, 1948. 102 p. ms.

See also Nos. 187, 198, 200, 203, 212, 218, 220, 221, 222, 223, 226, 239, 249, 251, 261, 265, 274, 281, 288, 290, 294, 2457, 3032, 3134, 3136, 3137, 3141, 3143, 3145, 3146, 3149, 3150, 3153, 3155, 3156, 3157, 3158, 3159, 3160, 3162, 3163, 3165, 3168, 3169, 3170, 3171, 3173, 3174, 3176, 3179, 3180, 3181, 3183, 3184, 3185, 3186, 3187, 3188, 3192, 3193, 3194, 3195, 3196,

3198, 3199, 3200, 3202, 3203, 3204, 3205, 3207, 3208,
3209, 3210, 3211, 3214, 3215, 3216, 3217, 3219, 3220,
3221, 3222, 3223, 3224, 3225, 3226, 3228, 3230, 3232,
3233, 3234, 3235, 3236, 3237, 3238, 3240, 3242, 3243,
3244, 3245, 3246, 3247, 3248, 3249, 3250, 3251, 3256,
3257, 3259, 3261, 3263, 3264, 3265, 3266, 3268, 3270,
3272, 3273, 3275, 3277, 3278, 3279, 3281, 3282, 3283,
3284, 3285, 3286, 3287, 3289, 3290, 3291, 3292, 3293,
3295, 3296, 3298, 3299, 3300, 3301, 3303, 4153, 4580.

For French groups in the United States, see Nos. 5100-5106.

Germany

(NOS. 3584 – 3847)

DOCTORS

3584. ALEXANDER, THOMAS, 1887- . *The Prussian Elementary Schools.* Columbia University, 1918. New York: The Macmillan Co., 1918. viii, 571 p. (Textbook Series in Education.)

3585. ANDRESS, JAMES MACE, 1881-1942. *Johann Gottfried Herder as an Educator.* Clark University, 1916. New York: G. E. Steckert & Co., 1916. 316 p.

3586. BASON, CECILIA HATRICK, 1887- . *Study of the Homeland and Civilization in the Elementary Schools of Germany, with Special Reference to the Education of Teachers.* Columbia University, 1937. New York: Teachers College, Columbia University, 1937. iv, 165 p. (Teachers College Contribution to Education, No. 710.)

3587. BECKWITH, HOLMES, 1884-1921. *German Industrial Education and Its Lessons for the United States.* Columbia University, 1913. Washington: Government Printing Office, 1913. 154 p. (U.S. Bureau of Education, Bulletin, 1913, No. 19.)

3588. BRICKMAN, WILLIAM W. *The Contribution of Herman Lietz to Education.* New York University, 1938. 382 p. ms. Abstract in New York University, School of Education: *Abstracts of Theses,* 1938-39, p. 1-4.

3589. BUCHTERKIRCHEN, ERICH KARL, 1899- . *Hitler's Psychological, Sociological, and Philosophical Principles of Education in the Third Reich.* Niagara University, 1936. 146, 49 p. ms.

3590. CAEMMERER, RICHARD RUDOLPH. *The Education of Representative German Princes in the Sixteenth Century.* Washington University, 1944. 320 p. ms.

3591. CANNON, ALLEN E. *The Pedagogic Value of the Six Sonatas for Violin and Piano by George Frederic Handel.* Chicago Musical College of Roosevelt University, 1954.

3592. CERF, JAY HENRY, 1923- . *Political Indoctrination and Control of Students in East Germany.* Yale University, 1958.

3593. CHISHOLM, Mrs. HULDA (HEPPERLE), 1900- . *Wilhelm von Humboldt's Ideal of Humanity and Its Relation to American Education.* University of Washington, 1939. 175 p. ms.

3594. COCHRAN, EMORY ELLSWORTH, 1890- . *The Experimental Didactics of Ernst Otto.* New York University, 1941. 250 p. ms. Abstract in New York University, School of Education: *Abstracts of Theses,* 1941-42, p. 13-16.

3595. COLE, PERCIVAL RICHARD, 1879- . *Herbart and Froebel: An Attempt at Synthesis.* Columbia University, 1907. New York: Teachers College, Columbia University, 1907. 116 p. (Columbia University Contributions to Education, Teachers College Series, No. 14.)

3596. COLODNER, SOLOMON, 1908- . *Jewish Education in Nazi Germany.* Dropsie College for Hebrew and Cognate Leaning, 1954. 206 p. ms. Abstract in *Religious Education,* Vol. 50, p. 169-170. May-June 1955.

3597. CONNOR, ALICE MARY, 1883- . *A Comparative Study of the Social Theories of Education of Otto Willman and John Dewey.* New York University, 1944. 200 p. ms.

3598. COSTRELL, EDWARD STANLEY, 1913- . *Reforming the German People: German Education and the American Occupation, 1945-1949.* Clark University, 1950. 353 p. ms. Abstract in Clark University: *Abstracts of Dissertations and Theses,* 1949, p. 75-78.

3599. DAMBACH, JOHN ISADOR, 1896- . *Physical Education in Germany.* Columbia University, 1937. New York: Teachers College, Columbia University, 1937. 116 p. (Teachers College Contribution to Education, No. 731.)

3600. DAY, MARY SARILDA, 1890- . *Scheubel as an Algebraist: Being a Study of Algebra in the Middle of the Sixteenth Century, Together with a Translation of and a Commentary upon an Unpublished Manuscript of Scheubel's Now in the Library of Columbia University.* Columbia University, 1926. New York: Teachers College, Columbia University, 1926. 168 p. (Teachers College Contribution to Education, No. 219.)

3601. DEWEY, JOHN, 1859-1952. *Psychology of Kant.* Johns Hopkins University, 1884. (Copy not deposited in the University library.)

3602. DINGMAN, ERWIN, 1910- . *A History of Vocational Education and Vocational Guidance in Hesse, Germany, during the United States Occupation, May 1945 to January 1948, with Backgrounds Forward from the Roman Occupation.* New York University, 1949. 476 p. ms. Abstract in *Research in Industrial Education,* 1930-1955, p. 123-124.

3603. EBY, SAMUEL L, 1878- . *German Educational Practice in the Eighteenth Century.* Yale University, 1913. 221 p. ms.

3604. ECKOFF, WILLIAM JULIUS, 1853-1908. *Educational Views of Goethe.* New York University, 1891. 53 p. ms.

3605. EDWARDS, MORRIS OSWALD. *A Case Study of Military Government in Germany during and after World War II.* Georgetown University, 1957. (Includes education.)

3606. EHRENFELD, ABRAHAM. *The Mannheim School System: An Ideal Municipal Experiment in Germany.* New York University, 1936. 372 p. ms.

3607. ELLISON, ALFRED. *The Composer under Twentieth Century Political Ideologies.* Columbia University, 1950. (Educational implications in National Socialist Germany, Soviet Union, and the United States.)

3608. ENGELBRECHT, HELMUTH CAROL, 1895-1939. *Johann Gottlieb Fichte: A Study of His Political Writings with Special Reference to His Nationalism.* Columbia University, 1933. New York: Columbia University Press, 1933. 221 p. (Studies in History, Economics, and Public Law, No. 383. Includes Fichte's idea on education and nationalism, education and the state, and his plans for education.)

3609. ERICKSON, HAROLD BARTELL, 1914- . *An Analysis of Some Aspects of Secondary Education in East Germany.* University of California, Berkeley, 1954. 376 p. ms.

3610. GOERNER, WALTER JOHN, 1883- . *The Contributions of August Herman Francke and His Followers to Modern Education.* University of Texas, 1950. 297 p. ms.

3611. GUNDERSHEIMER, ERNEST M., 1918- . *Samson Raphael Hirsch as an Educator.* Dropsie College for Hebrew and Cognate Learning, 1957. 176 p. ms. Abstract in *Religious Education,* Vol. 53, p. 259. May-June 1958.

3612. GUNKEL, NATALIE LOUISE. *The Origin and Content of the Pedagogy of Georg Kerschensteiner in Relation to Contemporary Experimental and Progressive Education.* New York University, 1939. 399+50 p. ms. Abstract in New York University, School of Education: *Abstracts of Theses,* 1938-39, p. 149-154. For master's thesis by same author, see No. 3734.

3613. HAGENHOFF, *Sister* MARY PELAGIA, 1878- . *The Educational Philosophy of Friedrich Wilhelm Foerster.* Catholic University of America, 1946. Washington: Catholic University of America Press, 1946. xiii, 256 p. Abstract in *Catholic Educational Review,* Vol. 46, p. 43-44, January 1948.

3614. HAHN, WALTER, 1913- . *German Secondary Education, with Emphasis on Problems of the Postwar Period.* University of Utah, 1950. 264 p. ms.

3615. HARTSHORNE, EDWARD YARNELL, 1912-1946. *The German Universities and National Socialism.* University of Chicago, 1938. 143 p. ms. Published in four forms, as follows: (1) As *The German Universities and National Socialism,* London: G. Allen & Unwin, Ltd., 1937. 184 p. (2) Same title, Cambridge, Massachusetts: Harvard University Press, 1937. 184 p. (3) In part, as *The German Universities and the Government,* Philadelphia, 1938. 25 p. Distributed by University of Chicago to libraries in the United States and abroad. (4) In part, same content as No. 3 above, in *Annals of the American Academy of Political and Social Science,* Vol. 200, p. 210-234, November 1938. Same issue of the *Annals* contains review of No. 1, above, by E. J. Gumbel, p. 307.

3616. HARTUNG, HELENE. *Paul Natarp as Philosopher and Educator.* New York University, 1935. 170+38 p. ms.

3617. HERKNESS, WALTER WEAVER, Jr., 1902- . *A Comparative Study of the Teaching of a Modern Foreign Language in the Secondary Schools of the United States and Germany.* Temple University, 1934. Philadelphia: 1934. iii, 169 p.

3618. HILL, CHARLES LEANDER, 1906- . *An Exposition and Critical Estimate of the Philosophy of Philip Melanchthon.* Ohio State University, 1938. 230 p. ms. Abstract in Ohio State University: *Abstracts of Dissertations . . . Winter Quarter 1937, Winter Quarter 1938,* p. 85-92. (Abstracts of Doctoral Dissertations, No. 26. Includes consideration of Melanchthon's theory of education and of his activities as "creator of the system of higher education in Germany.")

3619. HOLADAY, BEVERLY ELI, 1910- . *Educational Psychology in the Third Reich.* Ohio State University, 1937. 312 p. ms. Abstract in Ohio State University: *Abstracts of Dissertations . . . Summer Quarter, 1937,* p. 153-160. (Abstracts of Doctoral Dissertations, No. 25.)

3620. HOUGHTON, ALCINA BURRILL. *The Struggle for the Einheitsschule in Germany.* New York University, 1936. 125 p. ms.

3621. JELLINEK, HARRY JACOB. *The Work of Rudolph Schulze in Experimental Education.* New York University, 1937. 153 p. ms.

3621a. JI, WON YONG. *The Concept of Education in the Light of the Theology of Martin Luther.* Concordia Theological Seminary, 1957. 252 p. ms. Abstract in *Religious Education,* vol. 53, p. 263-264.

3622. JOHNSTON, DORA BELLE. *A Comparison of the Philosophies of Hegel and Brightman with Implications for Education.* New York University, 1937. 233 p. ms.

3623. KANDEL, ISAAC LEON, 1881- . *The Training of Elementary School Teachers in Germany.* Columbia University, 1910. New York: 1910. 137 p. (Columbia University Contributions to Education, Teachers College Series, No. 31.)

3624. KELLEY, WILLIAM ARMOND, 1924- . *The Relationship of the Early Lutheran Hymns to Certain Features of Martin Luther's Theories of Religious Education.* New York University, 1957. 332 p. ms. Abstract in *Dissertation Abstracts,* Vol. 18, p. 1511, April 1958. Available on microfilm from University Microfilms, Ann Arbor, Michigan, as Mic. 58-653.

3625. KETTELKAMP, GILBERT CLARENCE, 1903- . *Jean Paul and His Relationship to the Pedagogical Theories of His Day.* University of Illinois, 1941. 273 p. ms. Urbana, Illinois: 1941. 18 p. Abstract of Thesis. (Jean Paul is the pseudonym of Jean Paul Friedrich Richter. Given in card catalog of Library of Congress as Johann Paul Friedrich Richter.)

3626. KLAEGER, MAX LUDWIG, 1925- . *A Comparative Study of the Preparation of Art Teachers for American and German Secondary Schools.* University of Minnesota, 1956. 169 p. ms. Abstract in *Dissertation Abstracts,* Vol. 17, p. 569-570, March 1957. Available on microfilm from University Microfilms, Ann Arbor, Michigan, as Publication No. 18,937.

3627. KNELLER, GEORGE FREDERICK, 1908- . *The Educational Philosophy of the Third Reich.* Yale University, 1940. 481 p. ms.

3628. KOHAKE, CLETUS PAUL, 1915- . *The Life and Educational Writings of Rabanus Maurus.* Cornell University, 1948. 188, 183 p. ms.

3629. KRAFT, MILTON EDWARD, 1909- . *A Study of the Governmental Decrees Regulating the Preparation and Certification for Certain of the Learned Professions in Germany.* University of Illinois, 1934. 233 p. ms. Urbana, Illinois: 1934. 25 p. (Abstract of Thesis.)

3630. LANDSCHOOF, JOSEPH AUBREY. *Life and Work of Johann Bernard Basedow.* New York University, 1933. 279+32 p. ms.

3631. LEARNED, WILLIAM SETCHEL, 1876-1950. *The Development of the Professional and Social Organization of Secondary Teachers in Germany.* Harvard University, 1912. Published as *The Oberlehrer: A Study of the Social and Professional Evolution of the German Schoolmaster.* Cambridge, Massachusetts: Harvard University Press, 1914. xiv, 150 p. (Harvard Studies in Education, No. 1.)

3632. LIEBMAN, REBEKAH RUTLEDGE, 1907- . *Herbartianism as a Factor in American Education.* Johns Hopkins University, 1948. 173 p. ms.

3633. LIGHT, JEREMIAH KREIDER, 1863-1928. *Kant's Influence on German Pedagogy.* Yale University, 1893. Lebanon, Pennsylvania: Report Publishing Co., 1893. 195 p.

3634. LILGE, FRITZ. *Ideas and Problems in the Philosophy of German Higher Learning, 1810-1933.* Harvard University, 1941. 285 p. ms. Abstract in Harvard University: *Summaries of Ph.D. Theses,* 1941, p. 152-156. 285 p. ms.

3635. LOGAN, CARRIE ELIZABETH, 1876- . *The Psychology of Schooenhauer in Its Relation to His System of Metaphysics.* New York University, 1902. Brooklyn, New York: 1903. 103 p.

3636. LUQUEER, FREDERIC LUDLOW. *Hegel as Educator.* Columbia University, 1896. New York: Macmillan & Co., 1896. x, 185 p. (Columbia University Contribution to Philosophy, Psychology, and Education, Vol. 2, No. 1.)

3637. McMURRY, DOROTHY, 1899- . *Herbartian Contributions to History Instruction in American Elementary Schools.* Columbia University, 1945. New York: Teachers College, Columbia University, 1946. viii, 172 p. (Teachers College Contribution to Education, No. 920.)

3638. MAGYAR, FRANCIS. *The Contribution of Paul Ranschburg to Experimental Education.* New York University, 1936. 192 p. ms.

3639. MARGOSHES, SAMUEL, 1887- . *The Curriculum of the Jewish Schools in Germany from the Middle of the Seventeenth to the Middle of the Nineteenth Century.* Jewish Theological Seminary, of America, 1917.

3640. MARTIN, CLYDE VINCENT. *A Comparative Study of the Concept of Interest in the Educational Philosophies of Johann Friedrich Herbart and John Dewey.* University of Southern California, 1952. 226 p. ms. Abstract in University of Southern California: *Abstracts of Dissertations,* 1952, p. 107-110.

3641. MAYER, LYLE VERNON, 1916- . *A Study of German Universities in the American Zone of Occupation, 1945 to 1953.* University of Maryland, 1954. 233 p. ms. Abstract in University of Maryland: *Abstracts of Dissertations . . .* 1955, p. 49-50.

3642. MEYER, ADOLPHE ERICH, 1897- . *William Stern: His Contribution to Experimental Education.* New York University, 1926. 104 p. ms.

3643. MEYER, WILLIAM THEODORE, 1907- . *The Ideas of Race and Nationality in the Education of National Socialist Germany.* State University of Iowa, 1937. 329 p. ms. Published in part as "Reorganization of the Secondary Schools of Germany," *School Review,* Vol. 47, p. 37-43, January 1939.

3644. NABHOLZ, JOHANNES. *The History of the Faculty of Arts in German Universities.* New York University, 1936. 136 p. ms. For master's thesis by same author, see No. 3783.

3645. NEUENSCHWANDER, MILO HUGO, 1889-1946. *Johann Georg Sulzer: Philosopher-Educator and Aesthetician.* Ohio State University, 1941. 404 p. ms. Abstract in Ohio State University: *Abstracts of Dissertations . . .* Summer 1941, p. 157-165. (Abstracts of Doctoral Dissertations, No. 37.)

3646. NYBERG, PAUL. *The Educational Implications of Karl Mannheim's Sociology.* Harvard University, 1957.

3647. OKTAVEC, FRANK LEOPOLD, 1897- . *Professional Education of Special Men Teachers of Physical Education in Prussia.* Columbia University, 1929. New York: Teachers College, Columbia University, 1929. vi, 112 p. (Teachers College Contribution to Education, No. 369.)

3648. OSSWALD, EDITH, 1902- . *Children's Books Printed in the United States Zone of Germany, 1945-1947.* Yale University, 1950. 283 p. ms.

3649. PERLOW, BERNARD DAVID, 1920- . *Institutions for the Education of the Modern Rabbi in Germany during the Nineteenth Century.* Dropsie College for Hebrew and Cognate Leaning, 1954. 210 p. ms. Abstract in *Religious Education,* Vol. 50, p. 181-182, May-June 1955.

3650. RANDELS, GEORGE BASIL, 1876-1942. *The Doctrines of Herbart in the United States.* University of Pennsylvania, 1909. Philadelphia: 1909. 67 p.

3651. ROBBINS, CHARLES LEONIDAS, 1876-1938. *Teachers in Germany in the Sixteenth Century: Conditions in Protestant Elementary and Secondary Schools.* Columbia University, 1912. New York: Teachers College, Columbia University, 1912. 126 p. (Teachers College Contribution to Education, No. 52.)

3652. SANDERS, WILLIAM JOSEPH, 1907- . *Evidences of the Hegelian Dialectic in the Educational Philosophy of John Dewey.* Yale University, 1935. 218 p. ms. Published in part as "The Logical Unity of John Dewey's Educational Philosophy," *Ethics,* Vol. 50, p. 424-440, July 1940.

3653. SAWIN, PHILIP QUIGLEY, 1908- . *Nationalism and the Control of Education in Prussia, 1800-1871.* University of Wisconsin, 1954. 189 p. ms. Abstract in University of Wisconsin: *Summaries of Doctoral Dissertations,* Vol. 15, 1953-54, p. 549-551.

3654. SCHACHT, FRANK EUGENE. *"Levana," A Philosophy of Education by Jean Paul Friedrich Richter.* Harvard University, 1958. 285 p. ms.

3655. SCHMID, ROBERT CARL, 1916- . *German Youth Movements: A Typological Study.* University of Wisconsin, 1941, 299 p. ms. Abstract in University of Wisconsin: *Summaries of Doctoral Dissertations,* Vol. 7, 1941-42, p. 167-169.

3656. SCHMITZ, MATTHIAS FRED. *Der Dichter-Paedagoge Gottfried Keller.* Harvard University, 1933. 327 p. ms. Abstract in Harvard University: *Summaries of Ph.D. Theses,* 1933, p. 304-307.

3657. SCHMULLER, ALLEN MARK, 1913- . *The Role of Education in the Rehabilitation of the Prussian Empire.* University of Southern California, 1949. 327 p. ms. Abstract in University of Southern California: *Abstracts of Dissertations,* 1949, p. 52-54.

3658. SCHUBERT, JOHN VOLLMER. *Modern German Social Pedagogy.* New York University, 1916.

3659. SEIP, WILLIAM H. 1895-1939. *Science Teaching in Secondary Schools of Prussia since the Reorganization.* Temple University, 1932.

3660. SHERMAN, CHARLES LESTER, 1880- . *The Relation of Kant's Pedagogy to His Philosophy.* New York University, 1912. 90 p. ms. Dissertation for degree of Doctor of Pedagogy. For dissertation for degree of Doctor of Philosophy, see No. 3934.

3661. SIEGMEISTER, WALTER. *Theory and Practice of Dr. Rudolf Steiner's Pedagogy.* New York University, 1932. 320 p. ms. For master's thesis by same author, see No. 4795.

3662. SILBERBERG, IRMA LOUISE. *The School of Wisdom: An Experiment in Adult Education.* New York University, 1932. 217 p. ms. (Devoted to the school of Count Hermann Keyserling in Darmstadt, Germany.)

3663. SISSON, EDWARD OCTAVIUS, 1869-1949. *The Protestant Religious Instruction in Prussian Schools.* Harvard University, 1905. 179 p. ms. Portions, revised, published as follows: (1) "The Content of Religious Instruction in German Protestant Schools," *Education,* Vol. 27, p. 150-163, November, 1906; (2) "The Spirit and Value of Prussian Religious Education," *American Journal of Theology,* Vol. 11, p. 250-268, April, 1907; (3) "Religious Instruction and Religiousness in Germany," *Religious Education,* Vol. 1, p. 101-105, April, 1906; (4) "German Religious Instruction: Illustrative Translations," *Religious Education,* Vol. 2, p. 144-150, August 1907.

3664. SMITH, ABRAHAM. *Ernst Meumann as the Founder of Experimental Pedagogy: A Comparative Critical Historical Study.* New York University, 1922. 256 p. ms.

3665. SNOWDEN, ALBERT ALEXANDER. *The Industrial Improvement of Schools of Wuertemberg.* Columbia University, 1908. First 72 pages published originally in *Teachers College Record,* Vol. 8, No. 5, p. 1-88, November 1907. With foreword by Henry S. Pritchett. Published separately, New York: 1908. 88 p. ("The present monograph is an abridgement of the chapters on industrial training in a work on *The Schools of Wuertemberg* to be issued at another time." No record of promised volume found in card catalog of Library of Congress.)

3666. STAFFORD, DOUGLAS KENTWORTH. *The Mind of Herbart.* Harvard University, 1956. 296 p. ms.

3667. STRATEMEYER, CLARA, 1905- . *Supervision in German Elementary Education, 1918-1933.* Columbia University, 1938. New York: Teachers College, Columbia University, 1938. vi, 172 p. (Teachers College Contribution to Education, No. 734.)

3668. TAYLOR, JOHN WILKINSON, 1906- . *Youth Welfare in Germany: A Study of Governmental Action Relative to Care of the Normal German Youth.* Columbia University, 1936. Nashville, Tennessee: Baird-Ward Co., 1936. iv, 259 p.

3669. TOEWS, EMIL OTTO, 1902- . *The Life and Professional Works of Georg Michael Kerschensteiner (1854-1932.)* University of California, Los Angeles, 1955. 248 p. ms. ("The reputation and influence of Georg Kerschensteiner extended beyond the boundaries of his native Germany and contributed to the development of education in several foreign countries, notably in the United States." —Introduction.)

3670. WATSON, GENEVIEVE MARGARET. *The Educational Philosophy of Froebel and Dewey Compared and Evaluated.* New York University, 1931. 140 p. ms.

3671. WYLIE, JOYCE FYFE, 1916- . *Karl Mannheim's Social Theory and Concept of Education.* University of Illinois, 1956. 197 p. ms. Abstract in *Dissertation Abstracts,* Vol. 16, p. 1643-1644, September 1956. Available on microfilm from University Microfilms, Ann Arbor, Michigan, as Publication No. 18,214.

3672. ZEIDERS, CLOYD ELIAS. *Herbart's Metaphysical Concept of the Ego and Its Consequences for His Pedagogics.* University of Cincinnati, 1925. 45 p. ms.

See also Nos. 129, 138, 142, 143, 147, 148, 150, 152, 154, 157, 159, 161, 165, 173, 174, 175, 185, 584,

Germany

2327, 3032, 3057, 3068, 3070, 3071, 3072, 3073, 3075, 3076, 3077, 3078, 3080, 3082, 3084, 3087, 3088, 3090, 3091, 3093, 3094, 3096, 3097, 3098, 3099, 3100, 3102, 3104, 3106, 3107, 3108, 3110, 3111, 3115, 3116, 3117, 3121, 3123, 3127, 3128, 3130, 3131, 3132, 4417, 174a

MASTERS

3673. AMDUR, IRVING. *A Critical Study of the Development of the School Organization and Pedagogical Philosophy of George Kerschensteiner.* College of the City of New York, 1936. 179 p. ms. Abstract in College of the City of New York: *Abstracts of Theses . . . 1923-1939*, p. 91.

3674. ANDREWS, LEILA MAE. *A Study of Education for Nationalism during Three Periods of the German Empire.* University of Southern California, 1935. 214 p. ms.

3675. ANGELA, Sister MARY. *Rhabanus Maurus, Early Medieval Educator.* Catholic University of America, 1928. 34 p. ms.

3676. ARAKAKI, JACQUELINE SHIGENO, 1927- . *The Educational Theory of Rabanus Maurus.* St. Louis University, 1952. 80 p. ms.

3677. AUS, GEORGE. *Schleiermacher as an Educational Philosopher.* New York University, 1929. 140 p. ms.

3678. BADER, Sister MARY HILARY. *Friedrich Wilhelm Foerster's Theory of Character Education.* University of Texas, 1936. 128 p. ms.

3679. BAHR, EHRHARD. *A Study of Nietzsche's Educational Philosophy from the Point of View of Democratic Education.* University of Kansas, 1958.

3680. BANKS, RICHARD GRIFFIN, 1912- . *The Development of Education in Württemberg-Baden under United States Military Government.* University of Virginia, 1949. 293 p. ms.

3681. BAVER, EDMUND LEON. *Expressed Feelings toward Germans of American High School Students after Given Periods of Residence in Germany.* Springfield College, 1956. 83 p. ms.

3682. BERMAN, ABRAHAM A. *A Comparison of the Content and Amount of Reading Material in Modern Foreign Language Work in the American and German Secondary Systems.* College of the City of New York, 1930. 73 p. ms. Abstract in College of the City of New York: *Abstracts of Theses . . . 1923-1939*, p. 27.

3683. BERMAN, NELLIE. *Current Educational Practice and Herbartian Theory.* Ohio State University, 1926. 85 p. ms.

3684. BERNKOPF, ANNA. *Johann Joachim Becher as Educator.* Columbia University, 1916. 37 p. ms.

3685. BIECKER, THOMAS CYRIL, 1909- . *The Educational System of Johann Frederick Herbart: Its Moral Aspect.* St. Louis University, 1934. 62 p. ms.

3686. BIRKNER, ELSA MARIE. *The Educational Reforms in Prussia during the Period of Regeneration with Special Reference to the Work of Wilhelm von Humboldt.* Columbia University, 1922.

3687. BLAIR, RUTH MARGARET, 1933- . *The System of Education in Germany for the American Exchange Teacher.* Oregon State College, 1954. 98 p. ms.

3688. BLUMBERG, ALBERT A. *Gerhart Hauptmann and Education.* Stanford University, 1935. 53 p. ms.

3689. BONNIN, GUNTHER MAURICE. *Intellectual and Moral Incentives in the Munich Student Revolt of 1943.* Stanford University, 1948. 81 p. ms.

3690. BORNEMANN, Sister ANGELA. *Rhabanus Maurus, Early Mediaeval Educator.* Catholic Sisters College of the Catholic University of America, 1928. 34 p. ms.

3691. BRANDAUER, FREDERICK WILLIAM. *Philip Melanchthon as an Educator.* New York University, 1935. 68 p. ms.

3692. BREUNING, LOTHAR, 1908- . *Friedrich Wilhelm Foerster's Theory of Direct Moral Instruction.* St. Louis University, 1941. 67 p. ms.

3693. BROWN, MARY GERALDINE. *A Comparative Study of the Educational Philosophy and Methods of Republican and Nazi Germany.* University of Southern California, 1946. 266 p. ms.

3694. BROWNE, ROBERT BELL. *The Present Status of Herbartianism in the United States.* University of Illinois, 1929. 52 p. ms. Abstract in Russell Taaffe Gregg, Annotated Bibliography of Graduate Theses in Education at the University of Illinois, 1931, p. 18. (Bureau of Educational Research Bulletin No. 55.) (Includes life and teachings of Herbart.)

3695. BRUGGMAN, Sister MARY AMBROSE, 1890- . *The Training of the Germanic Child and Youth Prior to 400 A. D.* St. Louis University, 1929. 64 p. ms.

3696. BURNS, ZED HOUSTON. *A Consideration of Herbart's Philosophy with Some of Its Influence upon Modern Educational Thought.* Alabama Polytechnic Institute, 1929.

3697. BURRITT, BAILEY BARTON. *A Comparison of Hegel's and Herbart's Theories of the Mind, with Some Educational Implications.* Columbia University, 1903. 23 p. ms.

3698. BURTON, JOHN STEVENS. *A Study of Alfred Adler's Theory and Practice of Individual Psychology Applied to Adolescent Boys.* Columbia University, 1938. 60 p. ms.

3699. BURTON, ROBERT ALFRED, 1910- . *Martin Luther's Influence on Education.* Southern Methodist University, 1946. 94 p. ms. Abstract in Southern Methodist University: *Abstracts of Theses. . . . No. 12, 1946*, 1947, p. 9.

3700. CARPENTER, DOROTHY HEARTWELL. *Herbart's Theory of Character Education.* Boston University, 1939. 97 p. ms.

3701. CATE, DONALD FRANCIS, 1920- . *Democracy as Exemplified by Western Powers and by the Soviet Union in the Reorientation of Youth in Occupied Germany.* Oregon State College, 1951. 185 p. ms.

3702. CHAMBERLAIN, RAYMOND. *The Influence of the Epistemology of Kant upon the Theory of Education.* Columbia University, 1902. 58 p. ms.

3703. CISLER, LILLIAN ELEDA, 1902- . *Martin Luther's Ideas Concerning Religious Education, with a Discussion of Parallels in Present Practice in the United Lutheran Church.* Northwestern University, 1927. 70 p. ms.

3704. CLAMON, BENJAMIN. *Trends of Secondary Education in Germany.* Brown University, 1933. 49 p. ms.

3705. CLARKE, MARTHA ANN, 1894-1953. *The Contribution of Luther to Religious Education.* Boston University, 1929. 60 p. ms.

3706. CLASGENS, Sister MARY GONZALES, 1894- . *St. Peter Canisius and the Founding of Jesuit Colleges.* Boston College, 1939. 89 p. ms.

3707. CLAY, DOROTHY NELL. *The Reconstruction of Elementary Education in the United States Zone of Western Germany, 1945-1955.* University of Southern California, 1957. 182 p. ms.

3708. COMSTOCK, ADA LOUISE. *The Development of Aim in the Teaching of the Mother Tongue in Germany.* Columbia University, 1899. 42 p. ms.

3709. CROYLE, HARLEY IRWIN. *The Influence of the Lutheran Reformation on Educational Theory and Practice.* Columbia University, 1915. 39 p. ms.

3710. DEWITT, CHARLES MAURICE, 1918- . *An Historical and Critical Analysis of the Abitur.* Drake University, 1951. 75 p. ms.

3711. DIETEL, WILLIAM. *The Development of the German Realschule.* University of Texas, 1914. 221 p. ms.

3712. DOMANDI, MARIO. *The Youth Movement and Its Place in German Culture.* Columbia University, 1952. 91 p. ms.

3713. DUGSTAD, RICHARD ANDREW, 1928- . *The Role of the Hitler Youth in Nazi Education.* Iowa State Teachers College, 1955. 156 p. ms.

3714. ECKHART, RUTH ALMA, 1890- . *The Characterology of Edward Spranger as a Contribution to a Philosophy of Education.* American University, 1933. 411 p. ms.

3715. ENGEL, LAWRENCE E. *The Rise of Hitlerism as a Lesson for Democracy.* Columbia University, 1942. 87 p. ms. (Includes education.)

3716. EPPINGER, ANNA MARIE, 1892- . (Later, Mrs. Anna Arve.) *German Children's Literature.* Boston University, 1931. 106 p. ms.

3717. FENG, PANG-YEN. *A Comparative Study of German and American Public School Education after the World War.* Municipal University of Wichita, 1932. 83 p. ms.

3718. FERGUSON, ELVA CLAIRE D. *Education of German Youth under the American Occupation.* Stanford University, 1949. 160 p. ms.

3719. FERRING, CLARENCE AUGUSTINE. *Friedrich Wilhelm Foerster, Character Educator.* Catholic University of America, 1930. 73 p. ms.

3720. FITE, GEORGE KERSE. *A Historical Study of Frederic Froebel and His Contribution to World Education.* East Texas State Teachers College, 1950. 98 p. ms.

3721. FOSTER, CLARKE LESLIE. *Johann Bernhard Basedow and the Philanthropinists: A Study of Their Origins and Their Effects on Education.* Ohio State University, 1932. Abstract in Ohio State University, 1932. Abstract in Ohio State University: *Abstracts of Theses Presented by Candidates for the Master's Degree. . .* 1932, p. 55-56. (Abstracts of Masters' Theses, No. 9.)

3722. FRANKE, CLARA ELSA. *An Estimate of Paulsen's Contributions to Education.* Columbia University, 1908.

3723. FREEDMAN, ALICE E. *Der Wandervogel: Its History and Influence.* University of Southern California, 1932. 102 p. ms. (A study of the first organization of the youth movement in Germany.)

3724. FREITAG, Sister MARY CHRISTIANA. *A Study of the Educational Principles and Influence of Lorenz Kellner.* Catholic University of America. 1945. 75 p. ms.

3725. FRIEDLAND, DIEPOLD KINDLE, 1900- . *Social Studies in Secondary Schools in Western Germany after World War II.* Boston University, 1957. 39 p. ms.

3726. FRIEDMANN, ERIC MARTIN, 1930- . *The Influence of German Educational Ideas, Practices, and Institutions on American Educational Development, with Particular Application to Clark University.* Clark University, 1955. 148 p. ms. Abstract in Clark University: *Dissertations and Theses,* 1955, p. 9.

3727. FRIESENHEHN, Sister MARY HOPE. *Johann Ignaz Von Felbiger, Educational Reformer and Pedagogical Writer.* Catholic Sisters College of the Catholic University of America, 1916. 92 p. ms.

3728. FYNES, HELEN MARSHALL, 1903- . (Later, Mrs. Robert Johnson.) *The Relation of the Educational Activities of Martin Luther and Philip (Schwartzerd) Melanchthon.* Boston University, 1933. 126 p. ms.

3729. GEORGE, RAYMOND CONRAD, 1891- . *The Development of Chemistry in German High Schools.* Syracuse University, 1930. 50 p. ms.

3730. GIFFORD, WALTER JOHN. *The Philosophy of Friedrich Schiller: Its Development in Relation to Kantian Thought, and Its Contributions, with Their Bearings on Education.* Columbia University, 1911. 67 p. ms.

3731. GOETZINGER, HERMANN. *Problems of School Reform in the United States Occupation Zone in Germany.* Claremont Graduate School, 1951. 119 p. ms.

3732. GREEN, ARTHUR S. *An Evaluation of Froebelian Literature.* De Paul University, 1952. 140 p. ms.

3733. GREENE, ANTOINETTE. *August Boeckh's Theory of Scholarship, with Illustrations from the Study of English.* Cornell University, 1907. 148 p. ms.

3734. GUNKEL, NATALIE LOUISE. *The Arbeitschule as a New Deal in Education, with Special Reference to the Controversy between Kerschensteiner and Gaudig.* New York University, 1936. 277 p. ms. For doctoral dissertation by same author, see No. 3612.

3735. HAAKE, HELEN BERTHA, 1910- . *The Educational Theories Expressed by Goethe in His Autobiography and Selected Works.* New York State College for Teachers, Albany, 1938. 38 p. ms.

3736. HAMILTON, JOHN MAURICE, 1918- . *Luther's Philosophy of Education.* Eastern New Mexico University, 1952. 103 p. ms.

3737. HANSEN, CANUTE. *The Significance of Experimental Pedagogy of Rudolf Steiner with Special Reference to Teeth.* New York University, 1932. 203 p. ms. (Describes stages in development of dentistry.)

3738. HARLOW, REX FRANCIS. *The Educational Implications of the Theories of Value of Nicolai Hartmann and John Dewey.* University of Texas, 1935. 97 p. ms.

3739. HATCH, WILLABELLE MARY. *A Study of Personality Traits in Four Selected Leaders in Education: Froebel, Mann, Barnard, and Paulsen.* University of Southern California, 1942. 129 p. ms.

3740. HAU, GEORGE WILLIAM. *Herder as Educator.* Columbia University, 1909. 82 p. ms.

3741. HAWES, VINCENT LAWRENCE, 1925- . *The Reconstruction of German Education in the United States Zone of Occupation, 1945-1949.* Boston College, 1952. 100 p. ms.

3742. HAYNES, ALICE FENTON. *The Influence of Fichte, Krause, and Schelling upon Froebel.* Columbia University, 1910. 38 p. ms.

3743. HERAK, MARY HELEN, 1914- . *Education, Democracy, and Germany.* University of Arizona, 1948. 109 p. ms.

3744. HOFFMAN, THOMAS MICHAEL, 1910- . *An Annotated Bibliography of Untranslated Books in German on Education in the Library of Congress.* George Washington University, 1938. 59 p. ms.

3745. HOLZSCHUH, ALMA. *The Treatment of Juvenile Delinquency in Germany.* University of Southern California, 1933. 112 p. ms.

3746. HOPMAN, ABRAHAM NATHAN, 1917- . *A Study of Adult Education in the United States Zone of Germany, 1945-1947.* George Washington University, 1948. 44 p. ms.

3747. HOWARD, JOHN GORDON. *Martin Luther as an Educator.* New York University, 1927. 141 p. ms.

3748. JACKMAN, CHARLES FREDERICK. *The Influence of Hegelian Pedagogy on the Elementary Course of Study.* Indiana University, 1907.

3749. JACKSTEIT, BERTHOLD. *Lessing's Educational Ideals.* University of Pittsburgh, 1940. 54 p. ms.

3750. JONES, GERTRUDE MARTHA. *Physical Education Aspects of the German Youth Movement.* George Peabody College for Teachers, 1936. 143 p. ms.

3751. KAHAN, NORBERT N. *A Translation of George Kerschensteiner's "Charakterbegriff und Charakterziehung" with a Translator's Introduction on the Application of George Kerschensteiner's Conception of Character Training by Modern Progressive Schools in Germany.* College of the City of New York, 1934. 178 p. ms. Abstract in College of the City of New York: *Abstracts of Theses. . . 1923-1939*, p. 77.

3752. KAHN, ROBERT I., 1910- . *Jewish Academic Ideals in Germanic Lands during the 17th and 18th Centuries.* Hebrew Union College - Jewish Institute of Religion, 1935. 73 p. ms.

3753. KAINER, Sister MARY CELINE. *A Critical Study of Johann Friederich Flattich's Principles of Education and Guidance.* Catholic University of America, 1942. 44 p. ms.

3754. KALLIO, REINO ILMARI, 1915- . *Martin Luther as an Educator.* Clark University, 1953. 169 p. ms. Abstract in Clark University: *Dissertations and Theses*, 1953, p. 26.

3755. KARBE, WOLFGANG WILHELM HANS KARL, 1921- . *Sports from 1933 to 1956 in East and West Germany.* University of California, Berkeley, 1958.

3756. KENNEY, CHARLES BLASE, 1912- . *The History of Mathematics in Germany.* Boston College, 1934. 77 p. ms.

3757. KIDDER, JONATHAN EDWARD. (1) *The Place of Religion in State Education.* 16 p. ms. (2) *Ritschl's Philosophy of Education.* 15 p. ms. University of Pittsburgh, 1926.

3758. KINGSLEY, EDITH HALLIDAY, 1893- . *Herman Hesse's Interpretation of Adolescent Boyhood.* Boston University, 1932. 55 p. ms.

3759. KINNEAR, EDNA LUCETTA. *German Influence upon Educational Institutions in the United States and Its Effects.* Syracuse University, 1919. 53 p. ms.

3760. KLASEK, CHARLES BERNARD. *Reconstruction of the German Public Secondary School under British and American Occupation, 1945-1948.* University of Nebraska, 1956. 197 p. ms.

3761. KNAUER, JAMES ERVIN. *Some Aspects of the Problem of Rebuilding Education in the American Zone of Germany.* University of California, Los Angeles, 1948. 190 p. ms.

3762. LAINE, IVER, 1915- . *The "Activity" Principle in the Educational Theories of Froebel and Dewey.* Clark University, 1937. 73 p. ms. Abstract in Clark University: *Abstracts of Dissertations and Theses*, 1937, p. 145-147.

3763. LAMBE, BARBARA MARIE. *Johann Sebastian Bach as an Educator.* Stanford University, 1948. 101 p. ms.

3764. LANGSAM, KURT HELMUTH. *A Comparative Study of Fine Arts Education in the Secondary Schools of the City of New York and Prussia.* College of the City of New York, 1931. 64 p. ms. plus special supplement. Abstract in College of the City of New York: *Abstracts of Theses . . . 1923-1939,* p. 45.

3765. LANGSAM, WALTER CONSUELO. *Nationalism and Patriotism in Prussian Elementary School History Instruction, 1888-1914.* Columbia University, 1926. 77 p. ms.

3766. LEAVELL, ADDIE LETA. *The Pedagogical Ideas of the Youthful Herder.* Columbia University, 1915. 40 p. ms.

3767. LEUCHS, FREDERICK ADOLPH HERMAN. *The "Erziehung des Menschengeschlechts" of Gotthold Ephraim Lessing.* Columbia University, 1908. 48 p. ms.

3768. LINDEMANN, ELIZABETH. *Review of German Legislation (1888-1914) Affecting Child Welfare.* Columbia University, 1917. 50 p. ms.

3769. LIVINGSTON, PAUL Y. *The Educational Principles of the German Protestant Reformers.* New York University, 1932. 69 p. ms. (Includes Luther, Bugenhagen, Melanchthon, Sturm, and Duke Ernest.)

3770. LUEBECK, BRUNO HERMANN. *An Analysis of Religious Education in Germany since the Year 1919.* University of Chicago, 1931. 100 p. ms.

3771. LUSE, EVA MAY. *The Application of the Herbartian Formal Steps of Instruction to the Teaching of Elementary Grammar.* State University of Iowa, 1910. 109 p. ms.

3772. MALOVICH, BLANCHE. *Hugo Gaudig: The Philosophy of Education as Typified by His Writings.* College of the City of New York, 1933. 48 p. ms. Abstract in College of the City of New York: *Abstracts of Theses . . . 1923-1939,* p. 61.

3773. MARKS, LOUIS. *Certain Inconsistencies in the Educational Doctrines of Herbart.* Columbia University, 1905. 57 p. ms.

3774. MASCORD, ELIZABETH FRANCES. *The Social Theories of Froebel.* Columbia University, 1908. 50 p. ms.

3775. MATTHEWS, ALBERT PETERS, 1921- . *A Study of Physical Education in the German Boys' High Schools during the National Socialist Era and the Federal Republic Era.* Appalachian State Teachers College, 1957. 37 p. ms.

3776. MEFORT, CARLTON JAY. *Physical Education in Germany under Hitler.* Ohio State University, 1937. 81 p. ms.

3777. METZGER, DELLA ELIZABETH. *Goethe's Educational Ideas.* State University of Iowa, 1909. 42 p. ms.

3778. MIKUS, Rev. FRANK P. *An Inquiry into the Educational Philosophy of Otto Willmann.* Catholic University of America, 1946. 93 p. ms. Abstract in *Catholic Educational Review,* Vol. 46, p. 108, February 1948.

3779. MITCHELL, CAROLINE TILDEN. *Development of Aim in History Teaching in Germany.* Columbia University, 1899. 72 p. ms.

3780. MITCHELL, MILDRED JANET. *An Evaluation of Mysticism in the Educational Philosophy of Friedrich Froebel.* New York University, 1933. 78 p. ms.

3781. MONTIER, EARL WOODSON, 1926- . *Fulbright Program for German Youth.* Texas College of Arts and Industries, 1953. 60 p. ms.

3782. MOORE, FREDERIC. *Herbartianism.* West Virginia University, 1898. 33 p. ms.

3783. NABHOLZ, JOHANNES. *The Organization and Administration of German Universities.* New York University, 1931. 77 p. ms. For doctoral dissertation by same author, see No. 3644.

3784. NAFTZINGER, HERMAN JACOB. *Frederick Augustus Rauch, Pioneer Psychologist and Educator.* University of Pittsburgh, 1949. 112 p. ms.

3785. NAUER, HENRY LUDGER. *Catholic Resources in Germany as Potential Factors for Its Re-Education.* Catholic University of America, 1944. 103 p. ms.

3786. NAUMANN, THEODOR, 1918- . *Problems of German Youth Since World War I.* Oregon State College, 1954. 107 p. ms.

3787. NICHOLSON, JANE HERBERT. *Froebel's Conception of the Kindergarten Gifts.* Columbia University, 1909. 63 p. ms.

3788. NIEBUHR, ARTHUR. *A Translation of Wilhelm Rein's "Outline of Pedagogy."* Southwest Texas State Teachers College, 1940. 132 p. ms.

3789. NORMAN, ALBERT, 1914- . *The Media of Public Education in Postwar Germany: A Year of United States Military Government, 1945-46.* Clark University, 1949. 138 p. ms. Abstract in Clark University: *Abstracts of Dissertations and Theses,* 1949, p. 139-141.

3790. NORMINGTON, LOUIS WATSON, 1914- . *The Educational Philosophy of Martin Luther.* Pacific Union College, 1950. 88 p. ms.

3791. OECHSNER, Sister MARIA LAURELIA. *A Comparison between German and American Views of Christocentrism in Religious Education.* Catholic University of America, 1947. 78 p. ms.

3792. OPPE, HUBERT WILHELM, 1924- . *The German Youth Movement: A Sociological Analysis.* University of California, Berkeley, 1957. 116 p. ms. (Includes sections on education.)

3793. OVERMAN, Sister MARY LOYOLA. *The Educational Theories of Right Reverend Franz X.*

Eggersdorfer. Catholic University of America, 1938. 69 p. ms.

3794. PANCHAUD, FRANCES LEE. *Hugo Gaudig: His Contribution to Modern German Education.* New York University, 1932. 48 p. ms.

3795. PECK, JOHN SCHUYLER, Jr., 1905- . *The Influence of Germany on the Study and Teaching of History in the United States, 1914-1930.* New York State College for Teachers, Albany, 1935. 125 p. ms.

3796. PETERSON, RUSSELL ARTHUR. *Education for the Masses: A Study of Martin Luther as an Educator.* State University of Iowa, 1947. 55 p. ms.

3797. PFEFFER, Sister MARY LOUISE. *A Critical Evaluation of the "Neubau des Katholischen Religionsunterrichtes" of Heinrich Kautz.* Catholic University of America, 1933. 42 p. ms.

3798. PIETSCH, DOROTHEA JOHANNA SOPHIE. *Goethe's Paegagogik.* Northwestern University, 1909. 117 p. ms.

3799. PIHLBLAD, MARIE. *A Study of the German Romantic Composers of the Nineteenth Century in Relation to Political and Cultural Trends, as a New Technique in Teaching Music Appreciation.* University of Southern California, 1938. 145 p. ms.

3800. PLANTINGA, CORNELIUS A., 1908- . *The Personalistic Philosophy and Psychology of William Stern and Their Applications to Education.* Duke University, 1942. 134 p. ms.

3801. POVISH, KENNETH J. *The Educational Content and Implications of the "De Institutione Clericorum" of Rhabanus Maurus.* Catholic University of America, 1950. 67 p. ms. Abstract in *Catholic Educational Review,* Vol. 50, p. 122, February 1952.

3802. PREECE, WARREN E. *George Tichnor at Harvard: The First Phase of the Germanic Influence in American Education.* Columbia University, 1947. 86 p. ms.

3803. RAMRAS, JOSEPH. *A Descriptive Study of the Berlin Abendgymnasium.* College of the City of New York, 1932. 116 p. ms. Abstract in College of the City of New York: *Abstracts of Theses . . . 1923-1939,* p. 48.

3804. REARDON, PAULINE ANNETTE, 1912- . *The Educational Ideas of Friedrich Froebel.* Southern Methodist University, 1943. 117 p. ms. Abstract in Southern Methodist University: *Abstracts of Theses,* No. 11, 1943, 1944, 1945. p. 17.

3805. ROBERTSON, MARY B. *Martin Luther's Contribution to American Education.* Trinity University, 1958.

3806. RODNEY, THOMAS CLARENCE, 1926- . *Educational Principles and Practices of Martin Luther and the Schools of the Lutheran Church — Missouri Synod: A Comparative Analysis.* Loyola College, 1956 100 p. ms.

3807. ROSE, HILDEGARD. *Education in Modern Germany.* New York University, 1931. 113 p. ms.

3808. ROSEN, LEAH. *Moses Mendelssohn as Educator.* College of the City of New York, 1933. 55 p. ms. Abstract in College of the City of New York: *Abstracts of Theses . . . 1923-1939,* p. 84.

3809. ROSSER, FRANK. *A Study of Herbart in Modern Education.* Kansas State Teachers College, Emporia, 1945. 90 p. ms.

3810. ROSVALL, TOIVO DAVID, 1913- . *The Philosophy of Education in Nazi Germany.* Clark University, 1938. 41 p. ms. Abstract in Clark University: *Abstracts of Dissertations and Theses,* 1938, p. 157-159.

3811. ROWNTREE, Mrs. MILDRED L. *Cultural Potential of German Folk Music in Modern Teaching.* Sul Ross State College, 1954.

3812. RYAN, Sister MARY BRIGITTINE. *Blessed Albert the Great as an Educator.* Catholic Sisters College of the Catholic University of America, 1920. 69 p. ms.

3813. SAMPSON, ABRAHAM HARRY, 1896- . *An Expository Outline of Frederick Nietzsche's Educational Theories.* Temple University, 1934. 93 p. ms. For doctoral dissertation by same author, see No. 3932.

3814. SCHNEPEL, EMIL PAUL. *The Life and Work of Friedrich Ludwig Jahn.* Ohio State University, 1935. 122 p. ms.

3815. SCHWARTZ, EMANUEL. *"Kindesmundart," Child Speech by Berthold Otto and His Pedagogical Philosophy: A Critical Translation.* College of the City of New York, 1933. 131 p. ms. Abstract in College of the City of New York: *Abstracts of Theses... 1923-1939,* p. 65-66.

3816. SCHWEHM, ERHARD FREDERICK, 1921- . *U. S. Army Dependent Schools: Europe — Germany.* New Jersey State College, Newark, 1958. 41 p. ms.

3817. SEAGO, EARL BERTRAM. *Physical Education for Boys of the Seventh and Eighth Grades in Pestalozzi School, Bremerhaven, Germany.* University of Texas, 1956. 58 p. ms.

3818. SHANNON, KENNETH COLEMAN. *A Survey of Physical Education in the Germany of Today.* George Peabody College for Teachers, 1931. 80 p. ms.

3819. SHAPLEIGH, MAUDE. *Germany's Struggle to Liberate the Public Schools from the Control of the Church.* Columbia University, 1936. 37 p. ms.

3820. SHEN, KUAN-CHUN. *German Secondary Education under the Nazi Regime.* Stanford University, 1946. 210 p. ms.

3821. SMITH, AUTREY. *Principles Underlying a Program of Education for Nazi Germany.* North Texas State Teachers College, 1945. 48 p. ms. Abstract in North Texas State Teachers College: *Abstracts of Theses, 1941-1946,* p. 81.

3822. SPOCK, MARJORIE. *Teaching as an Art: An Introduction to the Educational Methods of Dr. Rudolph Steiner.* Columbia University, 1942. 194 p. ms.

3823. STAPPERT, Sister MARY PATRICIA. *The Development of Catholic Secondary Schools for Boys in Prussia from 1800 to 1933.* Catholic University of America, 1935. 88 p. ms. Abstract in Catholic University of America: *Summaries of Dissertations,* June 1935-June 1936, p. 37.

3824. STAYER, JESSE LEE, 1893- . *The Control of Education in the German Empire.* University of Pennsylvania, 1931. 44 p. ms.

3825. STEINHART, HANS, 1903- . *Hrabanus Maurus, 776-856: An Historical Study of Some Aspects of Medieval Education.* Boston University, 1956. 84 p. ms.

3826. STEPHAN, LUTHER VICTOR. *Luther as an Educator.* Oklahoma Agricultural and Mechanical College, 1937. 88 p. ms.

3827. STRELOW, TIMOTHY PHILETUS. *Confessional Implications of Luther's Small Catechism for Christian Education.* Southern Methodist University, 1956. 95 p. ms.

3828. SUGGS, WILLIAM ALBERT, 1922- . *The Comparative Influence of Herbartism and Deweyism upon the Objectives of Twentieth Century Education.* Tennessee Agricultural and Industrial State University, 1957. 68 p. ms.

3829. THOMPSON, MARY ALICE. *The Foundation Philosophy of Froebel and the Kindergarten.* Oglethorpe University, 1940. 78 p. ms.

3830. TRACEY, HELEN AGNES, 1913- . *Secondary Schools and Secondary School Teachers in the German Republic.* Boston University, 1935. 140 p. ms.

3831. TREICK, EDWARD L. *The United States Dependents Schools in Germany.* Central Washington College of Education, 1958.

3832. TRUMMER, Father WILLIAM. *The Philosophy of German Education from 1794 to 1940.* University of Cincinnati, 1951. 167 p. ms.

3833. URNAUER, Sister MARIA FRANCESCA. *Hoelderlin the Educator.* University of Pittsburgh, 1929. 128 p. ms.

3834. VANCE, FANNYE. *The Influence of Herbart on Education in the United States.* Southern Methodist University, 1937. 72 p. ms. Abstract in Southern Methodist University: *Abstracts of Theses,* No. 5, 1938, p. 20.

3835. VIAULT, BIRDSALL S. *Similarities to and Deviations from the Marxian Theory of History as Presented in Certain Textbooks and a Teacher's Manual Prepared in the Soviet Union for Use in East Germany.* Adelphi College, 1956. 110 p. ms.

3836. WARREN, LURENE ZARIFA. *A Comparison of the Wiener Schulreife Tests with Other Tests of School Readiness.* Oberlin College, 1937. 120 p. ms.

3837. WEISS, DAVID. *German Contributions to the Study of Reasoning.* College of the City of New York, 1936. 104 p. ms. Abstract in College of the City of New York: *Abstracts of Theses . . . 1923-1939,* p. 96.

3838. WEITZDORFER, RUDIGER. *Recreation and Aesthetic Culture of Youth in Germany.* International YMCA College, 1933. 164 p. ms.

3839. WESTPHAL, MARGARET E. *"Wilhelm Meisters Lehrjahre" and "Der Gruene Heinrich" as Educational Novels.* Columbia University, 1939. 58 p. ms.

3840. WIKSTEN, FRANK ALFRED. *A Historical Study of the American Dependents' Secondary Schools Functioning in Germany from 1946 to 1955.* University of Washington, 1957. 51 p. ms.

3841. WILKINSON, RALPH C. *The Influence of Herbart on American Education.* Drake University, 1958.

3842. WILLIAMS, MARY LODGE. *A Study of Some of the Influences of the Bauhaus Theories on Art Education in the United States Today.* Ohio University, 1939. 64 p. ms. Abstract in Ohio University: *Abstracts of Master's Theses . . . 1939,* p. 69.

3843. WILWERS, Rev. NICOLAUS. *"Lebensschule" of Modern Germany.* Catholic University of America, 1926. 57 p. ms.

3844. WINICOV, WILLIAM R., 1897- . *August Herman Francke as an Educator.* Temple University, 1933. 87 p. ms.

3845. WITTENBRINK, BONIFACE LEO. *The Educational Contents and Implications of the "Didascalicon de Studio Legendi" of Hugh of St. Victor.* Catholic University of America, 1948. 59 p. ms.

3846. ZIEROTH, EDWARD HENRY. *The Hitler Youth and the German Schools under the Nazi Regime.* University of California, Berkeley, 1934.

3847. ZIMMERER, Sister MARY FORTUNATA. *A Critical Evaluation of Otto Willmann's Contributions to Catholic Education.* Catholic University of America, 1936. 50 p. ms.

See also Nos. 187, 188, 200, 209, 212, 213, 218, 230, 236, 239, 249, 258, 261, 264, 265, 274, 280, 2457, 3032, 3136, 3139, 3141, 3144, 3146, 3147, 3148, 3150, 3151, 3153, 3154, 3155, 3158, 3161, 3163, 3165, 3167, 3168, 3170, 3171, 3174, 3175, 3180, 3181, 3182, 3189, 3190, 3191, 3192, 3193, 3194, 3195, 3196, 3197, 3199, 3204, 3205, 3208, 3210, 3213, 3214, 3217, 3218, 3220, 3221, 3222, 3223, 3227, 3229, 3230, 3231, 3232, 3236, 3237, 3240, 3241, 3244, 3249, 3256, 3257, 3258, 3262, 3263, 3265, 3268, 3275, 3276, 3277, 3280, 3281, 3286, 3288, 3289, 3291, 3292, 3295, 3296, 3297, 3299, 3300, 3301, 3302, 3303, 3341, 3536, 4563, 4719

For German groups in the United States, see Nos. 5107-5112

Great Britain

(NOS. 3848—4295)

Includes England, Wales, Scotland, and Northern Ireland

DOCTORS

3848. ALECK, ADOLPH WILLIAM, 1899- . *The Essentials of Mental Hygiene in the History of Education to Herbert Spencer.* New York University, 1931. vi, 229 p. ms.

3849. BACHMAN, FRANK PUTERBAUGH, 1871-1934. *The Elementary School Curriculum of England.* Columbia University, 1902. (No copy in Columbia University library.)

3850. BENJAMIN, HAROLD RAYMOND WAYNE, 1893- . *An Inquiry into the Origin and Administration of the 1918 Education Act in England.* Stanford University, 1927. 199 p. ms. Abstract in Stanford University: *Abstracts of Dissertations* . . . 1927-28, p. 15-19.

3851. BERDAHL, ROBERT OLIVER, 1926- . *English Universities and the State.* University of California, Berkeley, 1958. 386 p. ms.

3852. BLISS, LUCY R. *A History of the Monastic Schools of Great Britain from the Fourth to the Twelfth Century.* New York University, 1902.

3853. BOYER, JAMES ALEXANDER, 1909- . *Thomas Henry Huxley and His Relation to the Recognition of Science in English Education.* University of Michigan, 1949. 288 p. ms. Abstract in *Microfilm Abstracts*, Vol. 9, No. 3, p. 58-59, 1950. Available on microfilm from University Microfilms, Ann Arbor, Michigan, as Publication No. 1,295.

3854. BRITTON, WEBSTER EARL. *The Educational Purpose of Smollett's Fiction.* University of Michigan, 1945. 373 p. ms.

3855. BRODERICK, *Sister* MARY JOHN, 1885- . (Secular name, Mary F. Broderick.) *The Status of Catholic Schools in England.* Catholic University of America, 1936. Published as *Catholic Schools in England.* Washington: Catholic University of America, 1936. xi, 187 p. Abstract in Catholic University of America: *Summaries of Dissertations* . . . June 1935-June 1936, p. 2-3.

3856. BURNETT, JOE RAY, 1908- . *The Educational Philosophy of Alfred North Whitehead.* New York University, 1958. 395 p. ms. Available on microfilm from University Microfilms, Ann Arbor, Michigan, as Mic. 58-1985.

3857. BUTLER, JAMES DONALD, 1908- . *The Philosophy of Andrew Martin Fairbairn.* New York University, 1937. 284 p. ms.

3858. BUYS, WILLIAM ERNEST, 1919- . *Speech Education of the English Gentleman in Tudor Behavior Books.* University of Wisconsin, 1952. 555 p. ms. Abstract in University of Wisconsin: *Summaries of Doctoral Dissertations*, Vol. 14, 1952-53, p. 400-402.

3859. CHAPMAN, ARTHUR d'ARCY EUGENE. *The Study of Geography in Schools, with Special Reference to Its Organization and Teaching in England.* Harvard University, 1922. 496 p. ms.

3860. CHIU, CHUN. *Educational Theories of the Utilitarians.* Columbia University, 1924. 210 p. ms.

3861. CLARKE, FRANCES MARGUERITE, 1903- . *The Influence of Thomas Simpson on the Progress and Development of Mathematics in England during the Century Following the Death of Newton.* Columbia University, 1929. Published as *Thomas Simpson and His Times.* New York: 1929. x, 215 p.

3862. CLIPPINGER, FRANK WARREN, 1895- . *Ruskin's Ideas on Education in Relation to Twentieth Century Educational Reform.* University of Illinois, 1941. 259 p. ms. Urbana, Illinois: 1941. 8 p. (Digest of thesis.)

3863. CLYMER, WAYNE KENTON, 1917- . *Some Implications in the Thought of William Temple for a Philosophy of Christian Education.* New York University, 1950. 293 p. ms. Abstract in *Religious Education*, Vol. 45, p. 172-173, May-June 1950. Abstract also in *Microfilm Abstracts*, Vol. 10, No. 3, p. 165-166, 1950. Available on microfilm from University Microfilms, Ann Arbor, Michigan, as Publication No. 1,804.

3864. CORBY, *Rev.* EDMUND, 1892- . *John Colet: The Man and the Educator.* Fordham University, 1936. 169 p. ms. Abstract in Fordham University: *Dissertations Accepted for Higher Degrees*, 1936. p. 11-12.

3865. CUFF, *Sister* MARY LOUISE. *The Limitations of the Educational Theory of John Locke Especially for the Christian Teacher.* Catholic Sisters College of the Catholic University of America. Washington: 1920. 148 p. Published also in installments, complete except for bibliography, in *Catholic Educational Review*, as follows: Vol. 19, p. 39-50, January 1921; Vol. 19, p. 99-109, February 1921; Vol. 19, p. 167-180, March 1921; Vol. 19, p. 338-348, May 1921; Vol. 19, p. 398-412, June 1921; Vol. 19, p. 474-483, September 1921; Vol. 19, p. 533-551, October 1921; Vol. 19, p. 592-606, November 1921; Vol. 19, p. 660-666, December 1921; Vol. 20, p. 43-50, January 1922; Vol. 20, p. 107-111, February 1922; Vol. 20, p. 173-179, March 1922; Vol. 20, p. 230-238, April 1922.

3866. DAVIES, FRANK JOSEPH JOHN, 1894- . *Matthew Arnold and Education.* Yale University, 1934. 449 p. ms.

3867. DEALY, *Sister* MARY BONAVENTURE, 1887- . *Catholic Schools in Scotland.* Catholic University of America, 1945. Washington: Catholic University of America Press, 1945. xii, 305 p. Abstract in *Catholic Educational Review*, Vol. 45, p. 108-109, February 1947.

3868. DEWEY, CHARLES SHERMAN, 1905- . *Some Concepts of Vocational Education and Guidance in England from 1600 to 1760.* Stanford University: 1944. 461 p. ms. Abstract in Stanford University: *Abstracts of Dissertations* . . . 1945-46, p. 94-98.

3869. DICKINSON, THOMAS HERBERT, 1877- *Schools, Scholars, and Scholarships in Elizabethan Drama.* University of Wisconsin, 1906. 181 p. ms.

3870. DOWNS, NORTON, 1918- . *Thomas Smith: Scholar.* University of Pennsylvania, 1950. 159 p. ms. Abstract in *Dissertation Abstracts,* Vol. 14, p. 1367-1368, September 1954. Available on microfilm from University Microfilms, Ann Arbor, Michigan, as Publication No. 8,917.

3871. DuCHEMIN, RODERIC CLARK, 1920- *Aspects of the Philosophies of John Dewey and Bertrand Russell and Their Relation to Education.* Ohio State University, 1953. 386 p. ms. Abstract in *Dissertation Abstracts,* Vol. 19, p. 1612-1615, January 1959. Available on microfilm from University Microfilms, Ann Arbor, Michigan, as Mic. 58-7196.

3872. DUDLEY, FRED ADAIR, 1901- . *Matthew Arnold and Science.* State University of Iowa, 1939. 76 p. ms. New York: Modern Language Association of America, 1942. p. 275-294 (Summary of thesis.) Abstract in State University of Iowa: *Series on Aims and Progress of Research,* No. 63.

3873. DUNN, ROBERT ELBERT, 1928- . *A Descriptive Analysis of Administrative Practices and Techniques in English Secondary Schools, with Implications for American Secondary Schools.* University of Connecticut, 1955. 293 p. ms. Abstract in *Dissertation Abstracts,* Vol. 15, p. 1530-1531, September 1955. Available on microfilm from University Microfilms, Ann Arbor, Michigan, as Publication No. 12,720.

3874. EDGAR, FREDERICK RUSSELL, 1911- . *A Study of John Wesley from the Point of View of the Educational Methodology Used by Him in Fostering the Wesleyan Revival in England.* Columbia University, 1952. 171 p. ms. Abstract in *Dissertation Abstracts,* Vol. 13, No. 1, p. 130, 1953. Available on microfilm from University Microfilms, Ann Arbor, Michigan, as Publication No. 4,567.

3875. EDMONDSON, ERNEST MORTON, 1891- *Church-State Relationship in England, 1800-1840, and Its Implications for Public Education.* New York University, 1952. 300 p. ms. Abstract in *Dissertation Abstracts,* Vol. 12, No. 3, p. 288, 1952. Available on microfilm from University Microfilms, Ann Arbor, Michigan, as Publication No. 3,612.

3876. EGINTON, DANIEL PETER, 1899- . *A Comparison between Some Principles of Control of Education in England and New Jersey as a State in the United States.* Columbia University, 1933. New York: 1933. iii, 128 p.

3877. EVANS, PATRICIA MORFORD. *Oral Interpretation in Anglo-Saxon England.* Northwestern University, 1957. 322 p. ms. Abstract in *Dissertation Abstracts,* Vol. 18, p. 1145-1146, March 1958. Available on microfilm from University Microfilms, Ann Arbor, Michigan, as Publication No. 24,903.

3878. EYLER, MARVIN HOWARD, 1920- . *Origins of Some Modern Sports.* University of Illinois, 1956. 406 p. ms. Abstract in *Dissertation Abstracts,* Vol. 16, p. 907, May 1956. Available on microfilm from University Microfilms, Ann Arbor, Michigan, as Publication No. 16,392.

3878a. GEBRE-HIWET, MENGESHA. *Contrasting Philosophies of Education: Nunn and Dewey.* Ohio State University, 1958. 103 p. ms. Abstract in *Dissertation Abstracts,* Vol. 19, p. 2293, March 1959. Available on microfilm from University Microfilms, Ann Arbor, Michigan, as Mic. 59-377. For master's thesis by same author, see No. 430.

3879. GILBERT, AMY MARGARET, 1895- . *The Work of Lord Brougham for Education in England.* University of Pennsylvania, 1922. Chambersburg, Pennsylvania: Franklin Repository, 1922. ii, 127 p.

3880. GLOYN, CYRIL KENNARD, 1906- . *The Church and the Social Order: A Study of Anglican Social Theory from Coleridge to Morris.* Columbia University, 1941. Forest Grove, Oregon: Pacific University, 1942. 201 p. (Includes consideration of education.)

3881. GOWIN, LAWRENCE ERNEST, 1920- . *Pre-Fabricated Primary School Buildings in Great Britain.* University of California, Berkeley, 1955. 331 p. ms.

3882. HAAR, EVA CORNELIA, 1900- . *Education in the Eighteenth Century English Novel.* Johns Hopkins University, 1942. 361 p. ms.

3883. HAGSTOLZ, HILDA BOETTCHER. *The Educational Theories of John Ruskin.* University of Nebraska, 1940. Lincoln, Nebraska: University of Nebraska Press, 1942. xi, 294 p.

3884. HAMNER, HERMAN NICHOLAS, 1922- . *The Political Significance of the Religious Factor in the Reform of Elementary Education as Formulated in the Parliamentary Act of 1902.* Ohio State University, 1957. 303 p. ms. Abstract in *Dissertation Abstracts,* Vol. 18, p. 1023, March 1958. Available on microfilm from University Microfilms, Ann Arbor, Michigan, as Mic. 58-533. For master's thesis by same author, see No. 4076.

3885. HART, JOHN RICHARD, 1907- . *The Influence of Herbert Spencer's Evolutionary Naturalistic Philosophy on American Education.* Fordham University, 1942. 209 p. ms. Abstract in Fordham University: *Dissertations Accepted for Higher Degrees* . . . 1943, p. 18.

3886. HELLER, HOBART FRANKLIN. *Concerning the Evolution of the Topic of Factoring in the Textbooks on Elementary Algebra Published in England and the United States from 1631 to 1890.* Columbia University, 1940. Published in full, Berwick, Pennsylvania: 1940. 165 p.

3887. HIGGINSON, JAMES JACKSON, 1884-1919. *Spencer's "Shephard's Calendar" in Relation to Contemporary Affairs.* Columbia University, 1912. 365 p. ms. (Contains a section on academic disputes in University of Cambridge, 1569-1576, p. 30-38.)

3888. HIGHLAND, HARRY JOSEPH. *Utopian Education: A Study of the Ideal Worlds from Sir Thomas More to H. G. Wells.* New York University, 1942. 354 p. ms.

Great Britain

3889. HILL, ALFRED TUXBURY, 1908- . *The Emergency Training Scheme for Teachers in England and Wales.* Columbia University, 1949. 294 p. ms. Abstract in *Microfilm Abstracts,* Vol. 10, No. 2, p. 44-46, 1950. Available on microfilm from University Microfilms, Ann Arbor, Michigan, as Publication No. 1,649.

3890. HODGEN, MARGARET TRABUE, 1890- . *Workers' Education in England and the United States.* University of California, Berkeley, 1925. London: K. Paul, Trench, Trubner & Co., Ltd.; New York: E. P. Dutton & Co., 1925. xiii, 312 p.

3891. HOWARD, PALMER PECKHAM, 1901- . *Educational Policies of the National Union of Teachers, 1920-1939.* Yale University, 1943. 276 p. ms.

3892. HOYT, NATHANIEL DEMING. *Church-State Relations and Education in England since 1900.* Harvard University, 1953. 400 p. ms.

3893. JENNINGS, HENRIETTA COOPER, 1899- . *The Political Theory of State-Supported Education in England, 1750-1833.* Bryn Mawr College, 1927. Lancaster, Pennsylvania: Lancaster Press, 1927. vii, 159 p.

3894. JONES, DORSEY DEE, 1898- . *Edwin Chadwick and the Early Public Health Movement in England.* State University of Iowa, 1929. Iowa City, Iowa: State University of Iowa, 1931. 160 p. (University of Iowa, Studies in the Social Sciences, Vol. 9, No. 3.)

3895. KAISER, ARTHUR L. *Aspects of English Education from an American Viewpoint.* University of Buffalo, 1950. 213 p. ms.

3896. KAZAMIAS, ANDREAS MICHAEL. *The New Prospect in Education: Changes in the Conception of English Secondary Education.* Harvard University, 1958. 490 p. ms. For master's thesis by same author, see No. 1,354.

3897. KENDRICK, ISABEL WITTE. *The University of Edinburgh, 1660-1717: A Study in the Transformation of Teaching Methods and Curriculum.* Bryn Mawr College, 1957.

3898. KILCOYNE, FRANCIS PATRICK, 1902- . *The Emergence and Growth of the Social and Political Expression in the Works of John Galsworthy.* New York University, 1945. 221 p. ms. (Includes consideration of Galsworthy's judgments on British education.)

3899. KIMBALL, ELSA PEVERLY, 1889- . *Sociology and Education: An Analysis of the Theories of Spencer and Ward.* Columbia University, 1932. New York: Columbia University Press; London: P. S. King & Son, Ltd., 1932. 323 p. (Studies in History, Economics, and Public Law, Columbia University, No. 369.)

3900. KNAGGS, GEORGE AUGUSTUS, 1917- . *A Study of the Historical Development of Physical Education in English Schools to 1945.* University of Houston, 1957. 2 vols. 568 p. ms. Abstract in *Dissertation Abstracts,* Vol. 17 p. 1509, August 1957. Available on microfilm from University Microfilms, Ann Arbor, Michigan, as Publication No. 21,411.

3901. LARIMORE, EDDA REES. *The Ideas of Francis Bacon on Education.* University of Nebraska, 1944. 224 p. ms. Abstract in University of Nebraska: *Abstracts of Doctoral Dissertations,* 1944, p. 112-121.

3902. LeSOURD, GILBERT QUINN. *The Place of Thomas Henry Huxley in Nineteenth Century Education.* New York University, 1917.

3903. LINGENFELTER, LYNWOOD SAMUEL, 1905- . *A Bibliography of Pedagogy in English Fiction, 1750-1825.* Pennsylvania State College, 1941. 759 p. ms. Abstract in Pennsylvania State College: *Abstracts of Doctoral Dissertations,* Vol. 4, 1941, p. 237-242. Available on microfilm from University Microfilms, Ann Arbor, Michigan, as Publication No. 343.

3904. LINK, SEYMOUR GORDDEN, 1907- . *Matthew Arnold's "Sweetness and Light" in America, 1848-1938.* George Peabody College for Teachers, 1938. 396 p. ms. Nashville, Tennessee: George Peabody College for Teachers, 1938. 12 p. (Abstract of Contribution to Education No. 209.)

3905. McDERMOTT, JOHN CHARLES, 1901- . *The Educational Philosophy of Matthew Arnold.* Fordham University, 1937. 226 p, ms. Abstract in Fordham University: *Dissertations Accepted for Higher Degrees,* 1938, p. 15-17.

3906. McELROY, HOWARD CLIFFORD, 1898- . *Bentham's Educational Policies.* University of Pittsburgh, 1939. 194 p. ms. Abstract in University of Pittsburgh: *Abstracts of Theses . . .* Vol. 15, 1939, p. 216-223.

3907. McMAHON, CLARA PATRICIA, 1910- . *Education in Fifteenth-Century England.* Johns Hopkins University, 1942. Baltimore, Maryland: Johns Hopkins Press, 1947. ix, 181 p. (Johns Hopkins University Studies in Education, No. 35.)

3908. McPHERSON, ROBERT GRIER. *The Evolution of Liberal Education in Oxford and Cambridge, 1800-1877.* Johns Hopkins University, 1957.

3909. MACK, EDWARD CLARENCE, 1904- . *Public Schools and British Opinion, 1780 to 1860: An Examination of the Relationship between Contemporary Ideas and the Evolution of an English Institution.* Columbia University, 1938. London: Methuen & Co., Ltd., 1938. 432 p.

3910. MARDER, LOUIS, 1915- . *Aspects of Shakespeare's Education.* Columbia University, 1950. 279 p. ms. Abstract in *Microfilm Abstracts,* Vol. 10, No. 4, p. 219-220, 1950. Available on microfilm from University Microfilms, Ann Arbor, Michigan, as Publication No. 1,880. For master's thesis by same author, see No. 4,154.

3911. MARSH, ROBERT CHARLES. *Bertrand Russell's Philosophy of Education.* Harvard University, 1951. 260 p. ms.

3912. MARSHALL, DANIEL WAITE. *England's Plans for County Colleges: A Critical Study of the Nation's Efforts to Provide the Continuation Schools Required by the Education Act, 1944.* Harvard University, 1952. 294 p. ms.

3913. MATTHEWS, RODERIC DONALD, 1899- . *Post-Primary Education in England: A Study of the*

Relation of the Board of Education to the Provision for Post-Primary Education in England, 1902-1929. University of Pennsylvania, 1931. Published in full, Philadelphia: 1932. 235 p.

3914. MATTINGLY, ALETHEA SMITH, 1904- . *The Mechanical School of Oral Reading in England, 1761-1821.* Northwestern University, 1955. 350 p. ms. Abstract in *Dissertation Abstracts,* Vol. 14, p. 2439, December 1954. Available on microfilm from University Microfilms, Ann Arbor, Michigan, as Publication No. 10,310.

3915. MEADER, Mrs. EMMA BLAKELY GRANT. *Teaching Speech in the Elementary School: A Comparative Study of Speech Education in the Elementary Schools of England and of the United States.* Columbia University, 1928. New York: Teachers College, Columbia University, 1928. vi, 129 p. (Teachers College Contribution to Education, No. 317.)

3916. MINOGUE, WILLIAM JOHN DESMOND, 1920- *The Educational Philosophies of John Dewey and Alfred North Whitehead.* Ohio State University, 1950. 338 p. ms. Abstract in Ohio State University: *Abstracts of Dissertations . . . Autumn Quarter, Winter Quarter,* 1950-51, p. 219-226. (Abstracts of Doctoral Dissertations, No. 65.)

3917. MOORHEAD, SYLVESTER ANDREW, 1920- *The Dalton Plan in the United States and England.* Stanford University, 1950. 288 p. ms. Abstract in Stanford University: *Abstracts of Dissertations . . .* 1949-50, p. 26-27.

3918. MORLAN, GEORGE KOLMER, 1904- . *America's Heritage from John Stuart Mill.* Columbia University, 1936. New York: Columbia University Press, 1936. viii, 209 p. (Includes a chapter on liberal education.) For master's thesis by same author, see No. 4170.

3919. NEWTON, MILDRED EMILY, 1901- . *Florence Nightingale's Philosophy of Life and Education.* Stanford University, 1949. 266 p. ms. Abstract in Stanford University: *Abstracts of Dissertations . . .* 1949-50, p. 444-450.

3920. NORMAN, JAMES WILLIAM, 1884- . *A Comparison of Tendencies in Secondary Education in England and the United States.* Columbia University, 1920. New York: Teachers College, Columbia University, 1920. x, 186 p. (Columbia University Contributions to Education, Teachers College Series, No. 119.)

3921. NUTTALL, ANNA RUTH, 1898-1952. *The Contributions of Alfred the Great to Religious Education.* Boston University, 1938. 259 p. ms. Abstract in *Selected Graduate Theses in Religious Education,* 1938, p. 23.

3922. OLIVER, EARL LESTER, 1920-1946. *The Grammar School Background of Christopher Marlowe.* University of Illinois, 1945. 245 p. ms. Urbana, Illinois: 1945. 9 p. (Abstract of thesis.)

3923. PFEIFER, EDWARD JUSTIN. *Reception of Darwinism in the United States, 1859-1880.* Brown University, 1957. 219 p.ms. Abstract in *Dissertation Abstracts,* Vol. 18, p. 1024-1025, March 1958. Available on microfilm from University Microfilms, Ann Arbor, Michigan, as Publication No. 23,451.

3924. PRINCE, JOHN WESLEY, 1892- . *The Religious-Educational Theory of John Wesley.* Yale University, 1924. Published as *Wesley on Religious Education: A Study of John Wesley's Theories and Methods of the Education of Children in Religion.* New York: Methodist Book Concern, 1926. 164 p.

3925. RATCLIFFE, RUSSELL SPENCE, 1907- . *A Comparison of Agricultural Education and Advisory Services Provided for Rural-Urban Fringe Families in Selected Areas of the United States and Great Britain.* University of Maryland, 1955. 214 p. ms. Abstract in *Dissertation Abstracts,* Vol. 16, p. 63-64, January 1956. Available on microfilm from University Microfilms, Ann Arbor, Michigan, as Publication No. 15,303.

3926. REX, MILLICENT BARTON, 1905- . *University Representation in England, 1604-1690.* Columbia University, 1952. 654 p. ms. Abstract in *Dissertation Abstracts,* Vol. 12, No. 4, p. 545, 1952. Available on mocrofilm from University Microfilms, Ann Arbor, Michigan, as Publication No. 3,913.

3927. RICE, GEORGE P. Jr., 1910- . *Speakers and Speeches in Tudor and Stuart History: A Study of Personalities in Politics.* Cornell University, 1944. 298 p. ms. Abstract in Cornell University: *Abstracts of Theses . . .* 1944, p. 63-66. (Includes consideration of education of the speakers studied.)

3928. RIDDICK, MORFORD LOUIS, 1907- . *An Appreciation of Sir John Adams and His Contributions to Modern Education.* University of Southern California, 1942. 281 p. ms. Abstract in University of Southern California: *Abstracts of Dissertations,* 1942, p. 34-38.

3929. RIDER, LLOYD ALMY. *The Educational Philosophy of John Stuart Mill.* New York University, 1926. 116 p. ms.

3930. ROSS, MARY ALICE, 1925- . *St. Paul's School in London: Its Relationship to English Renaissance Education.* University of Chicago, 1954. 288 p. ms. Available on microfilm: see index under "University of Chicago."

3931. RYAN, JOHN JOSEPH. *John Scotus Erigena: Philosopher and Educator.* New York University, 1931. 231 p. ms.

3932. SAMPSON, ABRAHAM HARRY, 1896- . *The Philosophy of John Scott Haldane with Special Reference to Education.* Temple University, 1938. 161 p. ms. For master's thesis by same author, see No. 3813.

3933. SANDIFORD, PETER, 1882-1941. *The Training of Teachers in England and Wales.* Columbia University, 1910. New York: Teachers College, Columbia University, 1910. xiv, 168 p. (Teachers College Contribution to Education, No. 32.)

3934. SHERMAN, CHARLES LESTER, 1880- . *The Relation between Herbert Spencer's Social and Educational Philosophy.* New York University, 1913. Dissertation for degree of Doctor of Philosophy. For Dissertation for degree of Doctor of Pedagogy, see No. 3660.

3935. SHROPSHIRE, OLIVE ESTIL, 1884- . *The Teaching of History in English Schools.* Columbia

University, 1936. New York: Teachers College, Columbia University, 1936. viii, 189 p. (Teachers College Contribution to Education, No. 671.)

3936. SIES, RAYMOND WILLIAM, 1878-1922. *Teachers Pension Systems in Great Britain.* Columbia University, 1913. Washington: Government Printing Office, 1913. 88 p. (U.S. Bureau of Education, Bulletin, 1913, No. 34.)

3937. SIMONDS, CHARLES A. *Alfred the Great as an Educator.* New York University, 1913. 27 p. ms.

3938. SINGER, Mrs. FANNY K. *The Contribution of Cecil Reddie to the New School Movement.* New York University, 1939. 358 p. ms.

3939. SOLIS-COHEN, Mrs. ROSEBUD TESCHNER, 1903- . *A Comparative Study of the History Program in English and American Secondary Schools.* University of Pennsylvania, 1939. Published in full, Philadelphia: 1939. xii, 198 p.

3939a. SPECTON, SAMUEL H. *The Educational and Social Philosophy of George Bernard Shaw.* Wayne University, 1957.

3940. SPROTT, SAMUEL ERNEST, 1919- . *Tom Browne's School Days: A Study of the Education of Sir Thomas Browne at Winchester College.* Columbia University, 1954. 295 p. ms. Abstract in *Dissertation Abstracts*, Vol. 14, p. 1731, October 1954. Available on microfilm from University Microfilms, Ann Arbor, Michigan, as Publication No. 8,837.

3941. STABLER, ERNEST. *London Education, 1890-1910, with Special Reference to the Work of Sidney and Beatrice Webb.* Harvard University, 1951. 312 p. ms.

3942. STOWE, ANCEL ROY MONROE, 1882-1952. *English Grammar Schools in the Reign of Queen Elizabeth.* Columbia University, 1909. New York: Teachers College, Columbia University, 1908. 200 p. (Columbia University Contributions to Education, Teachers College Series, No. 22.)

3943. THOMPSON, DONNA FAY, 1882- . *Professional Solidarity among the Teachers of England.* Columbia University, 1927. New York: 1927. 339 p. (Columbia University Studies in History, Economics, and Public Law, No. 288.)

3944. TOVEY, GEORGE VERNON, 1920- . *Francis Bacon, the Reformer of Learning.* Columbia University, 1950. 134 p. ms. Abstract in *Microfilm Abstracts*, Vol. 10, No. 3, p. 179-180, 1950. Available on microfilm from University Microfilms, Ann Arbor, Michigan, as Publication No. 1755.

3945. TRAUGER, WILMER KOHL. *Pedagogues and Pupils: A Study in Eighteenth Century Fiction.* Harvard University, 1940. 426 p. ms. Abstract in Harvard University: *Summaries of Ph.D. Theses*, 1940, p. 373-378.

3946. TURNER, IVAN STEWART, 1903- . *The Training of Mathematics Teachers for Secondary Schools in England and Wales and in the United States.* Columbia University, 1939. New York: Teachers College, Columbia University, 1939. xiii, 231 p. Published also as *Fourteenth Yearbook of the National Council of Teachers of Mathematics*, 1939. Same publishers and pagination. With Preface by W. D. Reeve.

3947. USDANE, WILLIAM MILLER, 1914- . *A Comparative Study of Vocational Rehabilitation Legislation for the Severely Handicapped Orthopedic Civilian in Great Britain and in the United States.* New York University, 1955. 436 p. ms. Abstract in *Research in Industrial Education, 1930-1955*, p. 524. Abstract also in *Dissertation Abstracts*, Vol. 16, p. 1011-1012, May 1956. Available on microfilm from University Microfilms, Ann Arbor, Michigan, as Publication No. 12,243.

3948. VAN CAMP, RUTH. *The National Union of Teachers in England: Its History and Present Status.* Western Reserve University, 1945. 222 p. ms.

3949. VAN ZYL, HENRY, 1883- . *The Struggle about State Aid to Voluntary Elementary Schools in Great Britain.* University of Michigan, 1932. 243 p. ms. Abstract in University of Michigan: *Abstracts of Dissertations and Theses in Education, 1931-32*, p. 8-10. Abstract also in *Microfilm Abstracts*, Vol. 3 No. 2, p. 43, 1941. Available on microfilm from University Microfilms, Ann Arbor, Michigan, as Publication No. 321. For master's thesis by same author, see No. 4587.

3950. VANDRAEGEN, DANIEL E. 1906- . *The Natural School of Oral Reading in England, 1748-1828.* Northwestern University, 1949. 273 p. ms. Abstract in Northwestern University: *Summaries of Doctoral Dissertations*, Vol. 17, 1949, p. 126-131.

3951. WADE, NEWMAN ATKINSON, 1894- . *Post-Primary Education in the Primary Schools of Scotland, 1872-1936.* Columbia University, 1939. London: University of London Press, Ltd., 1939. xvi, 275 p.

3952. WALCOTT, FRED GEORGE. *Matthew Arnold and the Growth of Democratic Education in England.* University of Michigan, 1945. 358 p. ms.

3953. WATERFALL, EDITH ANNA, 1880- . *The Day Continuation School in England: Its Function and Future.* Columbia University, 1923. London: G. Allen & Unwin, Ltd., 1923. 221 p.

3954. WEIR, EVANGELINE GENEVA, 1896- . *The Vernacular Sources of the Middle English Plays of the Blessed Virgin Mary: A Study of the Marian Elements in the Homilies and Other Works of Religious Instruction from 1200 to 1500 in Relation to the Mary Plays.* Stanford University, 1942. 2 Vols. 786 p. ms. Abstract in Stanford University: *Abstracts of Dissertations . . . 1941-42*, p. 46-51.

3955. WOELFEL, Brother LA SALLE. *A Comparative Study of Certain Accounting Institutions and Practices in England and the United States.* University of Texas, 1957. 282 p. ms. Abstract in *Dissertation Abstracts*, Vol. 19, p. 702-703, October 1959. Available on microfilm from University Microfilms, Ann Arbor, Michigan, as Publication No. 25,187. (Includes comparisons of professional education and professional examinations.)

3956. WOOD, NEAL NORMAN, 1922- . *Communism and the British Intellectual.* University of California, Berkeley, 1958. 410 p. ms.

3957. WOOLCOCK, CYRIL WILLIAM, 1910- . *A Study of the Implications of the New Education for the Revision of the Curriculum of Secondary Schools in England.* Ohio State University, 1940. 276 p. ms. Abstract in Ohio State University: *Abstracts of Dissertations* . . . 1940-41, p. 659. (Abstracts of Doctoral Dissertations, No. 34.)

3958. WOOTON, FLAUD CONAROE, 1893- . *The Transfer of the Local Control of Education in Scotland from the Educational Authorities to the County and Town Councils.* Stanford University, 1931. 307 p. ms. Abstract in Stanford University: *Abstracts of Dissertations* . . . 1931-32, p. 46-49.

3959. YOUNG, FRANCIS ALFRED. *The Life and Work of Samuel Wilderspin: A Study in the History of Popular Education.* Harvard University, 1949. 375 p. ms.

3960. YUHAS, THEODORE FRANK, 1916- . *The Educational Work of Sir John Adams in the United States.* University of California, Los Angeles, 1953. 302 p. ms. (Includes his early life and work in England.)

See also Nos. 14, 119, 129, 138, 141, 142, 143, 146, 147, 148, 150, 154, 157, 160, 161, 163, 175, 177, 178, 184, 420, 887, 1405, 1418, 1837, 1843, 1880, 1919, 2327, 2560, 2911, 3068, 3070, 3071, 3073, 3075, 3076, 3077, 3078, 3079, 3080, 3084, 3087, 3090, 3091, 3093, 3094, 3096, 3098, 3099, 3100, 3102, 3104, 3105, 3106, 3107, 3108, 3110, 3112, 3113, 3114, 3115, 3116, 3117, 3119, 3120, 3121, 3122, 3123, 3127, 3128, 3129, 3130, 3131, 3132, 4417, 4578, 174a.

MASTERS

3961. ABBOT, FLORENCE ARVIDSON, 1917- . *Thomas Davidson and His Educational Ministry.* Clark University, 1948. 185 p. ms. Abstract in Clark University: *Abstracts of Dissertations and Theses.* 1948, p. 121-122.

3962. ACKERMAN, WILLIAM ALFRED. *Roger Ascham and His Relation to Education.* Columbia University, 1898. 59 p. ms.

3963. AKIN, AUGUSTA HOPLEY. *Defoe's Theory of Education.* Columbia University, 1908. 32 p. ms.

3964. ALVORD, THOMAS HOPKINS. *John Milton's Educational Theories in the Light of Seventeenth Century Conditions.* Columbia University, 1915. 45 p. ms.

3965. ASH, WILLOUGHBY ROSS. *A Comparative Study of the English Public Schools and the American Public High Schools.* University of Cincinnati, 1934. 115 p. ms.

3966. ASHFORD, GUY WILLARD. *A Survey of the Educational Letters of Lord Chesterfield to His Son and Godson.* University of Texas, 1943. 165 p. ms.

3967. BAILEY, DOROTHY M. *Some Aspects of Education in the English Novel of the Nineteenth Century.* Loyola University, 1938. 152 p. ms.

3968. BAILLIE, GORDON STUART. *Educational Ideas of H. G. Wells.* Washington University, 1939. 109 p. ms.

3969. BALL, MARGUERITE DOROTHY. *Sir Thomas More and English Education.* Niagara University, 1940. 85 p. ms.

3970. BALLANTINE, MARGARET WINTHROP, 1889- . *Dickens as an Educational Reformer.* Yale University, 1932. 159 p. ms.

3971. BARBER, HARRIET LOUISA. *Hannah More and Her Work in Education.* Columbia University, 1912. 24 p. ms.

3972. BASTIAN, HATTIE BELLE. *Educational Ideals in "The Parnassus Plays."* Columbia University, 1922.

3973. BEAUCAGE, Mother MARY CONRAD. *A Study of the Influence of the Ratio Studiorum on Mother Cornelia Connelly's System of Education as Embodied in the Book of Studies.* Gonzaga University, 1953. 127 p. ms.

3974. BEDWELL, FRIEDA. *A Study of the Background Scenes in the Life of John Milton.* Indiana State Teachers College, 1945. 80 p. ms. (Contributions of the Graduate School, No. 516. Includes consideration of Milton's educational theories and methods of educating his daughters.)

3975. BEERS, ELSA LOLITA. *Herbert Spencer's Philosophy of Art.* New York University, 1934. 69 p. ms. (Includes consideration of educational significance and implications.)

3976. BERNIKOW, MARY. *Lady Mary Wortley Montagu and the Educational Theories of Her Time.* New York University, 1938. 60 p. ms.

3977. BERO, Sister MARY MONICA, 1902. *Milton's "Tractate on Education" and Locke's "Thoughts Concerning Education:" A Comparative Study.* Fordham University, 1938. 59 p. ms. Abstract in Fordham University: *Dissertations Accepted for Higher Degrees,* 1939. p. 65.

3978. BERREMAN, GEORGE CURTIS. *Educational Philosophy of Herbert Spencer: A Critique.* University of Oregon, 1933. 75 p. ms.

3979. BLACKWELL, WILLIAM ALBERT. *English Spelling in the Fourteenth Century.* State University of Iowa, 1907. 37 p. ms.

3980. BLAIR, FRANK OSCAR. *The Social and Economic Theories of John Ruskin in the Light of Modern Industrial Relations.* University of Wyoming, 1931. 181 p. ms. (Contains one chapter on education.)

3981. BLINCOE, MARY NERINX. *Education of Women in England during the Renaissance.* Creighton University, 1924.

3982. BLUE, JOHN HENRY. *A Bibliographical Sketch of Joseph Priestly, Educator and Scientist.* University of Detroit, 1933. 52 p. ms.

3983. BOLIN, ERNESTINE. *Educational Ideas of Herbert Spencer.* Southern Methodist University, 1938.

103 p. ms. Abstract in Southern Methodist University: *Abstracts of Theses*, No. 6, 1939, p. 7-8.

3984. BOOKMAN, REBECCA. *Matthew Arnold and Education.* New York University, 1931. 57 p. ms.

3985. BOREN, ELIZABETH. *The Educational Views of Daniel Defoe.* University of Texas, 1931. 147 p. ms.

3986. BOTKIN, BENJAMIN ALBERT. *The Early Life of Thomas Edward Brown, His Race, Family, Boyhood, School and College Days: An Introduction to the Study of the Letters and Poems.* Columbia University, 1921.

3987. BOUDREAU, Rev. STEPHEN J., 1910- . *The Miltonic Theory of Education.* Fordham University, 1941. 108 p. ms.

3988. BOUNDY, CHARLES MILBURN. *A Comparative Study of English and American Adult Education.* University of Washington, 1927. 141 p. ms.

3989. BOYER, CARL WRIGHT. *The Educational Theories of H. G. Wells.* New York University, 1924. 77 p. ms.

3990. BOYLE, GEORGE KIMMET. *Oxford University and the Reformation.* Catholic University of America, 1931. 38 p. ms.

3991. BREADY, JOHN WESLEY. *The History of Theological Study in Sixteenth Century England.* Columbia University, 1918.

3992. BRENNAN, Sister THOMAS MARIE, 1905- . *An Inquiry into the Secondary Education of Girls in England and in the United States in the Nineteenth Century.* Fordham University, 1934. 115 p. ms.

3993. BRIGGS, MARGARET BURNET. *Cambridge University from 1785 to 1815 with Special Reference to Wordsworth, Coleridge, and Byron.* Columbia University, 1930. 85 p. ms.

3994. BRITTAIN, WILLIAM MacKELLAR. *British National Training Schools for Boys.* Columbia University, 1907. 45 p. ms.

3995. BROSE, OLIVE J. *How the British State Became Involved in Education.* Columbia University, 1949. 120 p. ms.

3996. BROWN, HAZEL. *Charles Kingsley as an Educational Critic.* Columbia University, 1913. 40 p. ms.

3997. BROWN, LOUISE. *A Study of the Educational Concepts of Certain English Writers during the Victorian Period.* University of Cincinnati, 1934. 68 p. ms.

3998. BRYANT, HELEN WINIFRED. *The Educational Ideas of George Eliot.* Columbia University, 1911. 35 p. ms.

3999. BULLOCK, FLORENCE WINGFIELD. *Opposition in England to State Aid for Education (1800-1870.)* Columbia University, 1914. 52 p. ms.

4000. BUNCH, GEORGE ALBERT, 1923- . *The Influence of John Locke's Philosophy on Benjamin Franklin's Academy.* University of Kansas, 1956. 79 p. ms.

4001. BURD, CHARLES GILLETTE. *Dr. Isaac Watts as an Educator.* Columbia University, 1912. 30 p. ms.

4002. BURKE, Sister MARY MARTINA. *The Educational Principles of Richard Mulcaster.* Oklahoma Agricultural and Mechanical College, 1940. 56 p. ms.

4003. BURKHALTER, MARY ALICE. *Chesterfield and Johnson on Education.* University of Tennessee, 1937. 144 p. ms.

4004. BURLINGAME, JANE. *The Relation of Matthew Arnold and Thomas Arnold.* University of Chicago, 1930. 56 p. ms.

4005. CAHILL, ANITA RUTH, 1899- . *A Survey of the Philosophy of Education of Charles Dickens.* University of Akron, 1942. 93 p. ms.

4006. CAINE, JAMES PATRICK, 1904- . *A Study of Newman's Theory of Higher Education.* St. Louis University, 1932. 57 p. ms.

4007. CALHOUN, GEORGE NELSON, 1904- . *Benjamin Jowett as an Educator.* Temple University, 1931. 61 p. ms.

4008. CARPENTER, JOHN HALL, 1903- . *The Educational Influence of Thomas Henry Huxley.* Southern Methodist University, 1938. 102 p. ms. Abstract in Southern Methodist University: *Abstracts of Theses*, No. 6, 1939, p. 10-11.

4009. CASSELS, ROLAND B., 1894- . *Educational Philosophy of Simon Somerville Laurie (1829-1909.)* Temple University, 1931. 92 p. ms.

4010. CASSILETH, FAY H. *Adult Labor Education in England.* College of the City of New York, 1929. 125 p. ms. Abstract in College of the City of New York: *Abstracts of Theses . . . 1923-1939*, p. 23.

4011. CHACHERE, MARVIN LANCELOT, 1927- . *The Oxford Reform Controversy of 1810-1811.* Boston College, 1953. 48 p. ms.

4012. CHANG, YIN-LIN. *Comparative Study of the Ethical Theories of G. E. Moore and John Dewey.* Stanford University, 1932. 95 p. ms.

4013. CHIANG, JOANNA M. TSE-YU. *A Philosophy of Social Education According to John Henry Newman and John Dewey.* Manhattanville College of the Sacred Heart, 1955. 75 p. ms.

4014. CLARK, CYNTHIA ANNE, 1908- . *English Lower School in the Late Seventeenth and Early Eighteenth Centuries.* Northwestern University, 1930. 95 p. ms.

4015. CLARK, EGBERT B. Jr. *Recent Developments in British Education.* Stanford University, 1923. 100 p. ms.

4016. CLARKE, VIRGINIA FRANKIE. *Wordsworth on Education.* Columbia University, 1946. 64 p. ms.

4017. CLEVELAND, NELLIE OPHELIA. *William Blake's Treatment of Childhood.* Columbia University, 1920.

4018. COHEN, LOUIS. *A Comparative Study of the Teaching of Plane Trigonometry in the Secondary Schools of England and the United States.* College of the City of New York, 1934. 105 p. ms. Abstract in College of the City of New York: *Abstracts of Theses . . . 1923-1939,* p. 73-74.

4019. CONKEY, LEIGHTON EDGAR. *The Educational Philosophy of Charles Dickens and Its Bearing upon Present Day Public Education in the United States.* Ohio State University, 1935. 195 p. ms.

4020. COOK, ELSIE M. *Educational Views Expressed in Wordsworth's Poetry.* New York University, 1929. 79 p. ms.

4021. COOPER, ALAN. *The Place of Education in Matthew Arnold's Criticism.* Columbia University, 1954. 126 p. ms.

4022. CRAGIN, EMMA. *Children in Dickens.* Columbia University, 1920.

4023. CRAMER, MARY EVA. *The Influence of Oxford and Cambridge Universities on New England Culture.* Columbia University, 1903. 26 p. ms.

4024. CRANDALL, FRANK BYRON. *The Rationalistic Element in Locke's Theory of Knowledge.* Cornell University, 1907. 49 p. ms.

4025. CROFTON, WALTER M. *The Influence of John Knox on Formal Education in Scotland.* University of South Carolina, 1927. 67 p. ms.

4026. CULL, ALAN CLIVE KENYON, 1920- . *A History and Exposition of a Student International Exchange Project between Central School, Yankton, South Dakota, and Caversham Secondary Modern School, Reading, England.* University of South Dakota, 1955. 270 p. ms.

4027. CUNEO, EDWARD JOHN, 1913- . (Name changed legally to Edward John Booth.) *A Study of John Napier of Merchiston and of His Contributions to the Science of Mathematics.* Boston College, 1937. 33 p. ms.

4028. CUSTER, DONALD M. *The Educational Plan of Matthew Arnold.* University of Colorado, 1934. 54 p. ms. Abstract in *University of Colorado Studies,* Vol. 22, No. 1, p. 15, November 1934.

4029. DARROW, DOROTHY HESPER. *Education in England in the Nineteenth Century as Portrayed by Charles Dickens.* State University of Iowa, 1937. 89 p. ms.

4030. DAVIES, ORA MILDRED. *Thomas Henry Huxley on Education.* Temple University, 1932. 89 p. ms.

4031. DECKROSH, VERN LEWIS. *The Democratization of Secondary Education in England in the Twentieth Century.* Ohio State University, 1933. 114 p. ms. Abstract in Ohio State University: *Abstracts of Theses Presented by Candidates for the Master's Degree . . . 1933,* p. 64-65. (Abstract of Masters' Theses, No. 13.)

4032. DOORES, MAURINE WANDA. *Mrs. Gaskell's Attitude towards Education and Social Morality.* University of Colorado, 1937. 48 p. ms. Abstract in *University of Colorado Studies:* Vol. 25, No. 1, p. 37-38, November 1937.

4033. DOUGHERTY, Sister MARY EUNICIA. *A Comparative Study of the Educational Philosophies of Robert Maynard Hutchins and John Cardinal Newman.* University of Notre Dame, 1941. 151 p. ms.

4034. DUNSON, CHARLES EDWARD. *An Investigation of Teacher Adjustment to Exchange Positions between the United States and Great Britain.* University of Southern California, 1951. 118 p. ms.

4035. EDELSON, LEO. *Thomas Arnold, Educator.* College of the City of New York, 1931. 40 p. ms. Abstract in College of the City of New York: *Abstracts of Theses . . . 1923-1939,* p. 35-36.

4036. EICKELBERGER, THOMAS J. *A Comparison of Principles of English Physical Education with Selected Principles Underlying American Physical Education.* International YMCA College, 1952. 134 p. ms.

4037. EILBERG, HERMAN. *Joseph Priestley — His Educational Philosophy.* Temple University, 1930. 119 p. ms.

4038. EISEMAN, MILDRED. *A Comparison of the Teaching Profession in England and the United States.* Butler University, 1940. 73 p. ms.

4039. ELSON, HERMAN. *Bertrand Russell's Views on Mathematics in Education.* New York University, 1936. 68 p. ms.

4040. ESSAME, ENID MARY. *A Comparative Study of the Aims and Methods in American and in British Education for Girls.* American University, 1935. 130 p. ms.

4041. EVANS, OVA MONA. *An Analytical Study of Courtesy as Exemplified by Spencer's "Sir Calidere."* Oklahoma Agricultural and Mechanical College, 1936. 92 p. ms.

4042. EVERETT, CHARLES WARREN. *The Education of Jeremy Bentham.* Columbia University, 1924. 34 p. ms.

4043. FARR, HELEN L. K. *Early and Contemporary Didactic Drama Showing the Importance of Education of Children.* Columbia University, 1946. 69 p. ms.

4044. FATH, Rev. JOSEPH JOHN. *The Social Philosophy and Educational Ideas of Benjamin Kidd.* Catholic University of America, 1937. 63 p. ms.

4045. FENTON, DOROTHY MAIE. *Biographical Dictionaries and Directories of English Colleges and Universities: A Study of Their Importance in Biographical Research.* Columbia University, 1931. 63 p. ms.

4046. FENTON, ELIZABETH LAWRENCE. *A Study and Comparison of the Aims, Textbooks, and Methods Used in the Teaching of the First Two Years of Latin in England and the United States.* University of Illinois, 1926. 110 p. ms. Abstract in Russell Taaffe Gregg: *Annotated Bibliography of Graduate Theses in Education at the University of Illinois,*

1931, p. 29. (Bureau of Educational Research, Bulletin No. 55.)

4047. FINE, EARL M. *An Investigation of the Teaching of Religion in the Primary Schools of England.* Kansas State Teachers College, Emporia, 1956. 81 p. ms.

4048. FINLEY, GEORGIA ELIZABETH. *English Elementary Educational Legislation, 1906-22, as Related to Standards of Child Care in the Home.* University of Chicago, 1922. 149 p. ms.

4049. FITZPATRICK, DOROTHY. *Education in the Writings of Samuel Butler.* Columbia University, 1949. 83 p. ms.

4050. FITZSIMONS, ISABELLE. *The Condition of Public and Private Schools in Dickens' Time.* Columbia University, 1920.

4051. FLANAGAN, Sister MARY MARGUERITE, 1907- . *An Anthology: Chesterton's Ideas on Education.* Boston College, 1953. 476 p. ms.

4052. FLOCKHART, LOLILA L. W. *Dickens and Education.* New York University, 1931. 102 p. ms.

4053. FOLLMER, MARJORIE ELIZABETH. *John Lyly's School Learning.* Stanford University, 1936. 55 p. ms.

4054. FRANZ, NELLIE ALDEN. *The Opening of the Professions to English Women: A Study of the Movement toward Sex Equality during the Past Hundred Years.* Columbia University, 1934. 102 p. ms.

4055. FREEMAN, ALICE TALBOT, 1885- . *Milton's Educational Theory.* Boston University, 1923. 38 p. ms.

4056. FRENCH, WILLIAM HENRY, Jr., 1902- . *The Educational Philosophy of Thomas Davidson.* Temple University, 1936. 169 p. ms.

4057. FROST, FRANK HAROLD. *A Study of Athletics in England's Secondary Schools and Universities.* George Peabody College for Teachers, 1932. 54 p. ms. Abstract in *Bulletin of the Department of Secondary School Principals of the National Education Association,* No. 43, p. 82-85, December 1932.

4058. GABBARD, AGNES. *Child Characters in Shakespeare and His Predecessors.* University of Tennessee, 1935. 142 p. ms.

4059. GARGLE, IRMA N. *A Comparative Study of the Treatment of the War of 1812 in English and American Secondary School History Textbooks.* College of the City of New York, 1933. 100 p. ms. Abstract in College of the City of New York: *Abstracts of Theses . . . 1923-1939,* p. 55-56.

4060. GIBSON, CHRISTINE M. *The Teaching of English in the United States and England, with Special Reference to Secondary Schools.* Columbia University, 1932. 47 p. ms.

4061. GILLILAND, ALICE MABEL. *Mathematics in the Great Public Schools of England.* Columbia University, 1903. 71 p. ms.

4062. GODARD, LAUREN FRANCIS, 1920- . *Selected Phases of England's Arts and Crafts Program Applied to Industrial Arts in the United States.* Oregon State College, 1952. 147 p. ms. Abstract in *Research in Industrial Education, 1930-1955,* p. 196.

4063. GOEDEKER, Sister MARY LUVINA, 1908- . *The Educational Theories of Arnold, Huxley, and Newman.* St. Louis University, 1939. 58 p. ms.

4064. GOLDMAN, CHARLOTTE RUTH. *Education under the Governess System of Victorian England.* Columbia University, 1942. 59 p. ms.

4065. GOODNOUGH, RUTH LEAH, 1913- . (Later Mrs. Steven J. Ryan.) *Robert Raikes: His Work for Education and Social Betterment.* Boston University, 1934. 77 p. ms.

4066. GRAVES, RUTH, 1907- . *The Educational Influence of Matthew Arnold.* Southern Methodist University, 1936. 153 p. ms. Abstract in Southern Methodist University: *Abstracts of Theses,* No. 4, 1937, p. 11-12.

4067. GREEN, ALICE EVANGELINE. *The Educational Theories of Matthew Arnold.* University of Southern California, 1930. 53 p. ms.

4068. GRIMES, EDWIN T. *Materials for a History of Austin Friars at Oxford, 1400-1500.* Catholic University of America, 1937. 53 p. ms.

4069. GRUENER, JENNETTE ROWE. *A Study in Educational Method: Methods of Teaching Algebra in the Latter Part of the Eighteenth Century in Relation to Certain Modern Methods of Teaching Algebra.* Wellesley College, 1925. 191 p. ms. (Based on analysis of one American and several British textbooks.)

4070. GULENTZ, AMELITIA BERYL, 1910- . *Music Courses in England and the United States.* George Washington University, 1934. 69 p. ms.

4071. GUSTAFSON, GUSTAF JOSEPH. *Influence of Darwin on Education.* Catholic University of America, 1936. 108 p. ms. Abstract in Catholic University of America: *Summaries of Dissertations,* June 1935-June 1936, p. 35.

4072. GUYER, CLYDE ROYAL. *The Educational Philosophy of Sir Thomas More in Relation to Contemporary Educational Theory.* University of Southern California, 1932. 81 p. ms.

4073. GWYNN, IRENE ROGERS. *Charles Dickens' Criticism of the English School System as Implied in His Novels.* Massachusetts State Teachers College, Boston, 1953. 75 p. ms.

4074. HAINLINE, MARGARET LOUISE. *The Place of Cambridge University in Nineteenth Century Thought as Reflected in Representative Nineteenth Century Novels.* Columbia University, 1930. 75 p. ms.

4075. HALL, ELIZABETH SEAY. *Education of Harriet Martineau.* Columbia University, 1921.

4076. HAMNER, HERMAN NICHOLAS, 1922- . *The Religious Factor in the Education Reform in England under King Edward VII.* Emory University,

1948. 109 p. ms. For doctoral dissertation by same author, see No. 3884.

4077. HANDLOSER, EMMA. *Educational Theories in English Prose of the Seventeenth Century.* University of Pittsburgh, 1930. 97 p. ms. Abstract in University of Pittsburgh: *Abstracts of Theses . . .* Vol. 6, p. 280-281, November 1930.

4078. HANDY, SYDNEY SPEIDEN. *Educational Theories of Matthew Arnold.* Columbia University, 1919.

4079. HARADA, MICHAEL FRANCIS MITSUN, 1922- . *A Comparative Study of Some Aspects of the Pragmatism of Sir Francis Bacon and John Dewey.* Occidental College, 1957. 126 p. ms.

4080. HARDY, BERTHA A. *John Wesley as an Educator.* New York University, 1928. 74 p. ms.

4081. HARRINGTON, GERALD ALEXANDER. *A Comparison of the Views of John Henry Newman and Thomas Henry Huxley as Published in "The Idea of a University" (New York, 1902), and "Science and Education" (New York, 1899.)* Columbia University, 1928. 10 p. ms.

4082. HART, NINA. *The Educational Theories of Matthew Arnold.* Columbia University, 1906. 27 p. ms.

4083. HARVEY, HELEN BRANDEBURG. *A Study of the Education and Intelligence of Shakespeare's Women.* Marshall College, 1941.

4084. HAWVER, CARL F. *Aldous Huxley's Theory of Education.* Bowling Green State University, 1938. 40 p. ms. Abstract in Bowling Green State University: *Abstracts of Masters' Theses, 1935-1940,* p. 38.

4085. HAZLETT, WILLIAM W. Jr., 1900- . *The Educational Philosophy of the Reverend Robert Herbert Quick.* Temple University, 1931. 167 p. ms.

4086. HEAD, WILFRED OLDHAM. *W. E. Forster and the English Education Act of 1870.* Tulane University of Louisiana, 1952. 110 p. ms.

4087. HEASLEY, JUSTINE ISABELLE. *Upper and Lower Class Schools as Reflected in Some Victorian Novels.* Columbia University, 1928. 76 p. ms.

4088. HEAVIN, ALBERT WILLIAM. *The Professional and Social Status of Teachers in England and Wales as Evidenced by Their Training, Working Conditions, Remuneration, Tenure and Retirement, Solidarity, and Social Prestige.* Indiana University, 1930. 233 p. ms.

4089. HERNDON, CLARA ALICE. *A Study of Certain Educational Implications in the Life and Works of Robert Browning.* University of Southern California, 1932. 70 p. ms.

4090. HEYMAN, KATE SELMA. *The Child in English Poetry in Relation to the Educational and Social Background of the Times from Chaucer to the Present.* College of the City of New York, 1930. 130 p. ms.

4091. HINES, JESSIE MAY. *A Study of Dickens' Treatment of Children in Certain of His Novels.* Oklahoma Agricultural and Mechanical College, 1942. 74 p. ms.

4092. HOLLAR, E. CLEVELAND. *A Study of the Educational Writings of John Locke.* University of Missouri, 1923. 59 p. ms.

4093. HOLZWARTH, WILLIAM G. *A Comparative Study of Certain Educational and Corrective Institutions in the United States and in Northern Ireland.* Bowling Green State University, 1949.

4094. HOOLEY, MARY E. *Tennyson's "Princess": The Education of Woman, and Mary Wollstonecraft's "Vindication of the Rights of Woman."* Columbia University, 1926. 38 p. ms.

4095. HOOVER, MERLE VINCENT, 1920- . *Aphoristic Opinions of Physicists Concerning Education.* George Washington University, 1946. 43 p. ms. (Concerned with 7 British and 5 American physicists.)

4096. HUME, LAURABEL NEVILLE. *The Academical Learning in Sidney's "Arcadia."* Stanford University, 1935.

4097. HUNTER, ROBERT VINCENT. *Roger Ascham and His Philosophy of Education.* New York State College for Teachers, Albany, 1934. 88 p. ms.

4098. HUTCHINS, MARGARET. *History and Practice of Inter-Library Loans in British Libraries, with a List of Printed Aids for the Location of Books in the British Isles.* Columbia University, 1931. 55 p. ms.

4099. INWRIGHT, HULDA MAY. *Some Theories of Higher Education in Arnold, Mill, and Newman.* Columbia University, 1918.

4100. JACKIEWICZ, Sister MARY AMBROSIA, 1909- . *Sir William Temple as a Critic of Learning.* Fordham University, 1943. 169 p. ms.

4101. JENKINS, WESLEY EDGAR. *A Study of Apprenticeship in the English Woodworking Guilds.* Ohio State University, 1934. 103 p. ms. Abstract in Ohio State University: *Abstracts of Theses Presented by Candidates for the Master's Degree,* Summer Quarter, 1934, p. 129-130. (Abstracts of Master's Theses, No. 16.)

4102. JOHNSON, BOYD WILLIAM. *Alcuin's Influence on Christian Education.* Southern Methodist University, 1935. 61 p. ms. Abstract in Southern Methodist University: *Abstracts of Theses,* No. 3, 1933-1935, p. 7.

4103. JOHNSON, LAURA ELIZABETH. *John Locke as a Religious Educator.* New York University, 1931. 81 p. ms.

4104. JOHNSON, THOMAS COVINGTON. *The Financial Support of Medieval English Schools.* Indiana University, 1928. 65 p. ms.

4105. JOHNSTON, CHARLOTTE HUGHES. *Treatment of School Life in Some English Novels of the Nineteenth Century.* Columbia University, 1939. 208 p. ms.

Great Britain

4106. JONES, DAVID JOHN. *Welsh Education from 1840 to 1881.* University of Oregon, 1924. 104 p. ms.

4107. JONES, EARL ROBERTSON. *A Study of Allegorical Manuals of Religious Instruction in Middle English.* University of Tennesee, 1936. 96 p. ms.

4108. JUDD, ADAH RICHARD, 1894- . *Mr. H. G. Wells' Views on Education since the World War.* Smith College, 1938. 63 p. ms.

4109. KAVANAGH, ROBERT VINCENT. *A Critical Examination of the Work of Burt, Spearman, Thorndike, and Tilton with Regard to the Concept and Testing of the Higher Mental Processes.* University of Southern California, 1928. 46 p. ms.

4110. KEARNEY, MARYADELLE. *Matthew Arnold as an Educator.* State University of Iowa, 1934. 86 p. ms.

4111. KEITHAHN, RALPH RICHARD, 1898- . *The "Religious Difficulty" and the English Elementary Education Act of 1870.* Yale University, 1926. 226 p. ms.

4112. KELLEY, Mrs. RHODA SACHSE, 1902- . *Educational Ideas of John Locke.* Southern Methodist University, 1937. 86 p. ms. Abstract in Southern Methodist University: *Abstracts of Theses,* No. 5, 1938, p. 9-10.

4113. KELLY, LOIS A. *Child Characters in Charles Dickens.* Columbia University, 1923. 35 p. ms.

4114. KELLY, MAE ELIZABETH, 1906- . *A Comparative Study of English as Taught in the Secondary Modern Schools of Birmingham, England, and the Upper Elementary Grades of Bridgeport, Connecticut.* University of South Dakota, 1951. 71 p. ms.

4115. KENNEDY, GEORGE. *Vocational Education in England for Boys.* University of Pittsburgh, 1936. 118 p. ms. Abstract in University of Pittsburgh: *Abstracts of Theses . . .* Vol. 12, 1936, p. 305-306.

4116. KIMMEL, HERBERT. *The Educational Implications of the Philosophy of Locke.* University of Chicago, 1909. 22 p. ms.

4117. KING, DOROTHY ANNE, 1927- . *Thomas Day, Author of "Sandford and Merton": An Experiment in Education.* Fordham University, 1949. 99 p. ms.

4118. KIRKWOOD, KENNETH MUNN. *Classical Studies in the English Universities, 1400-1535.* Claremont Graduate School, 1940. 63 p. ms.

4119. KOBUSKI, AGNES MARIE. *Wordsworth's Theory of Education.* Cornell University, 1921. 90 p. ms.

4120. KOENIG, VERNON HENRY, 1921- . *John Alcuin's Contribution to Learning.* Pacific Union College, 1955. 42 p. ms.

4121. KOSH, MIRIAM. *Vindicia Presbyterorum: Being the Life and Works of the Reverend Thomas Hall, B.D., Presbyterian Prophet, Teacher, and Preacher.* Columbia University, 1939. 77 p. ms.

4122. KOSMAK, KATHARINE. *Greek in Nineteenth Century Education: Its Defense and Its Defenders.* Columbia University, 1934. 103 p. ms.

4123. KUEHNER, RAYMOND LOWELL. *An Appraisal of Federal Aid to Education in the Light of the British National System.* Ohio State University, 1953. 71 p. ms.

4124. LANE, LILA SCHECHTMAN, 1926- . *The Effect of Recent Legislation on Government Provided Primary Schools in England.* New Jersey State Teachers College, Newark, 1955. 62 p. ms.

4125. LARMORE, JOHN CLEMENT. *Thomas More and English Education.* Columbia University, 1922. 37 p. ms.

4126. LATSHAW, MARY LEWERS, 1903- . *Interchange of Teachers.* George Washington University, 1938. 122 p. ms. (Interchange of American teachers primarily with those of Great Britain and American possessions.)

4127. LAURIE, ETHEL E. *A Study of Post-War Tendencies in English Education.* Hunter College of the City of New York, 1932. 70 p. ms.

4128. LeCOMTE, Sister MARY VIOLA. *The Limitations of L. P. Jacks' Theory of Education for Leisure.* Catholic University of America, 1946. 50 p. ms. Abstract in *Catholic Educational Review,* Vol. 46, p. 170-171, March 1948.

4129. LEE, ANNIE. *Wordsworth's Theory of Natural Education.* Columbia University, 1917. 66 p. ms.

4130. LEE, BEATRICE DZUN, 1896- . *The Religious Educational Work of John Wesley.* Boston University, 1930. 102 p. ms. For another master's thesis by same author, see No. 1652.

4131. LEECH, LAURA MILLICENT SPROSTON. *Secondary Education in England Today.* University of Pittsburgh, 1936. 73 p. ms. Abstract in University of Pittsburgh: *Abstracts of Theses . . .* Vol. 12, 1936, p. 308-309.

4132. LEMMO, CHRISTINE ELIZABETH, 1898- . *Joseph Payne and His Educational Ideals.* Temple University, 1931. 72 p. ms.

4133. LEO, Brother VINCENTIUS. *English Gild Schools.* Catholic University of America, 1918. 36 p. ms.

4134. LEOPOLD, MICHAEL, 1898- . *Educational Ideals of Robert Owen.* Temple University, 1930. 98 p. ms.

4135. LICARI, JOSEPH J. *Matthew Arnold's Philosophy of Secondary and Higher Education.* College of the City of New York, 1934. 66 p. ms. Abstract in College of the City of New York: *Abstracts of Theses . . . 1923-1939,* p. 79-80.

4136. LINDEL, BERTHA NEOLA. *A Study of the Poems of Robert Browning with the Object of Finding Ideas Contributory to the Educational Theory of John Dewey.* University of Southern California, 1934. 60 p. ms.

4137. LYNCH, JAMES J. *Chaucer, the Religious Teacher.* State University of Iowa, 1936. 84 p. ms.

4138. McBRIDE, RUSSELL WHITNEY, ?- 1950. *The Educational Philosophy of Alexander Bain.* Temple University, 1931. 134 p. ms.

4139. McCAFFERY, ELEANOR MARIE, 1905- *The Teaching of History in the English Secondary Schools during the Nineteenth and Twentieth Centuries.* Boston University, 1928. 68 p. ms.

4140. McCORMICK, JAMES WILLIAM. *Thomas Moore: Educator and Humanist.* Catholic University of America, 1924. 44 p. ms.

4141. McCUE, GEORGE SUTHERLAND. *Humanistic and Modern Educational Theory in "The Scholemaster."* University of Colorado, 1935. 82 p. ms. Abstract in *University of Colorado Studies,* Vol. 23, No. 1, p. 39, November 1935.

4142. McDONALD, BLANCHE. *The Education of Women in the Time of Queen Elizabeth.* Columbia University, 1927. 30 p. ms.

4143. McDONOUGH, JOSEPH ANDREW, 1925- . *The Education Acts of Great Britain, 1944-1948.* Boston College, 1954. 46 p. ms.

4144. McDOWELL, M. R. COULTER. *A Mathematics Curriculum for the Sixth Form in a Northern Ireland Grammar School.* Columbia University, 1954. 46 p. ms.

4145. McGEHEE, ELISE, 1911- . *Education in Certain English Literature of the Eighteenth Century.* University of North Carolina, 1941. 142 p. ms. Abstract in *University of North Carolina Record,* No. 371, p. 55, October 1941.

4146. McGIVERN, ELIZABETH DOROTHY. *Dickens and the New Education.* New York State College for Teachers, Albany, 1936. 130 p. ms.

4147. McLARTY, MARY ADELAIDE, 1925- . *Elementary Education in England during the Middle Ages, 500 to 1600 A. D.* University of North Carolina, 1949. 115 p. ms. Abstract in *University of North Carolina Record,* No. 478, p. 160, October 1950.

4148. McMAHON, CORNELIA ALICE, 1903-1928. *The Educational Philosophy of John Henry Newman.* Trinity College, 1924. 50 p. ms.

4149. MAGUIRE, DOROTHY CARROLL. *Secondary Education in England.* Brown University, 1926. 105 p. ms. (Not available at Brown University. Copy may be obtained from author, 64 Brightside Street, Cranston, Rhode Island.)

4150. MAGUIRE, Mother MARY IMMACULATA. *The Educational Philosophy of Alfred North Whitehead.* Catholic University of America, 1941. 67 p. ms.

4151. MALONEY, CORNELIUS LEO. *The "Disputatio Puerorum per Interrogeticnes et Responses" of Alcuin.* Catholic University of America, 1943. 97 p. ms.

4152. MANESS, M. MAE. *The Influence of Cambridge University upon Tennyson.* Columbia University, 1934. 64 p. ms.

4153. MANLEY, MICHAEL FRANCIS, 1904- *Locke's Theory of Primary and Secondary Qualities as a Development of Cartesian Psychology.* St. Louis University, 1933. 44 p. ms.

4154. MARDER, LOUIS, 1915- . *The Education of Shakespeare: Being a Summary of the Opinions in the Rise and Progess of the Controversy from the Year 1592 to 1766, the Age of Rationalization.* Columbia University, 1947. 211 p. ms. For doctoral dissertation by same author, see No. 3910.

4155. MARKS, THERESA. *English Men of Letters in Their Relation to the Workingmen's College.* Columbia University, 1932. 50 p. ms.

4156. MARSHALL, HELEN. *Education in the Poetical and Prose Writings of William Wordsworth.* Ohio State University, 1918. 61 p. ms.

4157. MARTZ, ETHELWYN. *The Advantages of the Oxford Summer School for American Teachers of English.* Columbia University, 1936. 38 p. ms.

4158. MAXWELL, ALMA BALDWIN. *Children in the Novels of Charles Dickens.* Columbia University, 1920.

4159. MAYER, Sister MARY MARCIANA. *Twentieth-Century Trends in Church-State Educational Relations in the United States and in England.* Catholic University of America, 1951. 95 p. ms. Abstract in *Catholic Educational Review,* Vol. 50, p. 264-265, April 1952.

4160. MEEHAN, CHARLES RICHARD, 1919- . *The Further Education and Training Scheme in England.* Boston College, 1953. 72 p. ms.

4161. MEHOK, WILLIAM JOSEPH, 1913- . *The Historical and Philosophical Basis of Newman's "Idea of a University" in the Light of Catholic Tradition.* St. Louis University, 1938. 89 p. ms.

4162. MENDES, LUCIA NORWOOD. *The Education of Young Women in the Early English Renaissance.* Columbia University, 1954. 57 p. ms.

4163. MEREDITH, BERNICE HUFF, 1908- . (Later, Mrs. Donald G. Wright.) *An Interpretation of the Educational Theories of John Locke in Contrast to the Theory of Formal Discipline.* Syracuse University, 1934. 104 p. ms.

4164. MIESTER, ANNABELLE ROBERTSON. *British Views of American Education, 1800-1860.* Tulane University of Louisiana, 1937. 89 p. ms.

4165. MILLER, GEORGE ALBERT, 1910- . *John Ruskin on Education.* Temple University, 1935. 60 p. ms.

4166. MILLER, GRADY CROMER. *John Wesley as an Educator.* Chicago Lutheran Theological Seminary, 1925. 17 p. ms.

4167. MILLER, LEOTA AGNES. *The Pursuit of Classical Learning by a Lady of the Nobility in the*

Age of Elizabeth. University of Southern California, 1933. 101 p. ms.

4168. MITCHELL, IAN WATSON, 1924- . *The Application of Certain Aspects of the Cooperative Extension Service of the United States to the Scottish Agricultural Advisory Service.* Cornell University, 1955. 124 p. ms.

4169. MOORE, THOMAS GILBERT. *Samuel Butler's Ideas of Education.* Washington University, 1940. 110 p. ms.

4170. MORLAN, GEORGE KOLMER, 1904- . *John Stuart Mill's Educational Psychology.* Columbia University, 1931. 50 p. ms. For doctoral dissertation by same author, see No. 3918.

4171. MORRIS, BETTY JANE. *Speech Education in Postwar Great Britain.* University of Wisconsin, 1954. 93 p. ms.

4172. MURPHY, BESSIE MYRTLE. *The Case of Magdalen College, 1687-88.* Washington University, 1940. 121 p. ms.

4173. NEIDER, MARK. *The Educational Views of Samuel Johnson, 1709-1784.* College of the City of New York, 1951. 67 p. ms.

4174. NEWTON, MARGARET MARY, 1902- . *Educational Ideas Expressed by Thomas Arnold and Cardinal Newman: Comparison and Contrast.* Boston University, 1938. 91 p. ms.

4175. NILSON, MARGERY. *The Religious Education of the Victorian Child.* Columbia University, 1929. 103 p. ms.

4176. NOBIS, GEORGIA ELIZABETH. *British Education in English Literature, A. D. 673 to A. D. 1744.* New York University, 1923. 124 p. ms.

4177. O'NEIL, MAUD E., 1892- . *The Educational Ideas of Thomas Elyot, as Revealed in "The Governour" (1531.)* University of California, Los Angeles, 1944. 95 p. ms.

4178. OPDYCKE, JOHN BAKER. *The English Education Act of 1902.* Columbia University, 1906. 136 p. ms.

4179. OSGOOD, STELLA MORRIS. *Education in the British Islands from the Introduction of Christianity to the Death of Alfred the Great.* Boston University, 1915. 65 p. ms.

4180. OVERMYER, BERNICE BUTLER, 1917- . *Opinions on the Education of Women as Expressed in English Literature, 1660-1750.* Louisiana State University and State Agricultural and Mechanical College, 1942. 152 p. ms. Abstract in *Louisiana State University Bulletin,* Vol. 35, n. s., No. 1, January 1943.

4181. Omit. Error.

4182. PAIEWSKY, ISIDORE. *A Comparative Study of the Treatment of the American Revolution and Its Causes in the History Textbooks of England and of the United States.* College of the City of New York, 1931. 80 p. ms. Abstract in College of the City of New York: *Abstracts of Theses . . . 1923-1939,* p. 37-38. (28 textbooks studied.)

4183. PAOLUCCI, HENRY. *The Education of James Thompson (1834-1882.)* Columbia University, 1948. 202 p. ms.

4184. PARKER, ALICE VIRGINIA. *Matthew Arnold and Modern Educational Theory.* Indiana State Teachers College, 1936. 63 p. ms. (Contributions of the Graduate School, No. 281.) Abstract in *Teachers College Journal,* Vol. 8, p. 76-77, July 1937.

4185. PARKER, RUTH LOUISE. *Early English Teachers: Grocyn, Linacre, and Colet.* Columbia University, 1905. 24 p. ms.

4186. PAUL, HELEN HEDWIG. *The Metamorphosis of the Circle Singing Game in England.* University of Pittsburgh, 1935. 108 p. ms. Abstract in University of Pittsburgh: *Abstracts of Theses . . .* Vol. 11, 1935, p. 290-291.

4187. PAVLAK, Sister MARY CONCEPTA. *The Educational Philosophy of Michael E. Sadler.* Catholic University of America, 1941. 71 p. ms.

4188. PERPETUA, Sister MARY A. *A Study of the Dual System of Education in England with Emphasis on Catholic Schools.* Mount Saint Joseph Teachers College, 1958.

4189. PERRY, IRENE GLADYS, 1912- . *The Effect on Education of the Dissolution of the Monasteries in England.* University of Arizona, 1951. 69 p. ms.

4190. PETERSON, CLARENCE STEWART. *Adult Education in England and the United States.* Columbia University, 1928. 32 p. ms.

4191. PHEMISTER, BRUCE BRANDON. *William Cowper on Education.* Columbia University, 1946. 71 p. ms.

4192. PITTARD, MARY. *The Education of Women in Tudor Pedagogical Literature.* University of Texas, 1932. 109 p. ms.

4193. PLUMMER, ROBERT NEWCOMB. *Milton's and Locke's Educational Theories Compared with Seventeenth Century Practices.* George Peabody College for Teachers, 1936. 105 p. ms.

4194. POLLOCK, MARY DELPHINE. *The Value for Character Education of Certain Poems by Robert Browning: A Course for the High School.* Arizona State Teachers College, Flagstaff, 1938. 88 p. ms.

4195. POPLOFSKY, SOLOMON. *A Comparative Study of Elementary and Intermediate Algebra as Taught in the Schools of England and the United States.* College of the City of New York, 1932. 88 p. ms. Abstract in College of the City of New York: *Abstracts of Theses . . . 1923-1939,* p. 48.

4196. POWELL, LOUISE SHELLEY. *A Comparative Study of the Treatment of the American Revolution in 1776 in Some Secondary School History Textbooks Used Currently in England and in the United States of America.* University of Louisville, 1937. 160 p. ms.

4197. POWERS, LOULIE KNOX. *The Educational Reforms of Dickens.* Columbia University, 1910. 22 p. ms.

4198. PRUDELL, Rev. HAROLD O. *The Educational Theories of Sir Richard Winn Livingstone.* Catholic University of America, 1954. 109 p. ms. Abstract in *Catholic Educational Review,* Vol. 54, p. 335, May 1956.

4199. RADNER, SANFORD R. *George Meredith and Late Victorian Education.* Columbia University, 1954. 63 p. ms.

4200. RAINBOW, EDWARD LOUIS, 1929- . *A Comparative Study of Selected Seventeenth and Eighteenth Century String Methods Published in England.* Iowa State Teachers College, 1956. 117 p. photoprinted.

4201. RAINWATER, Mrs. VERA BAUMGARTNER. *Renaissance Background of Milton's "Of Education".* Indiana University, 1941. 71 p. ms.

4202. RAPPAPORT, MITCHELL ERIK. *Robert Burton and the "Anatomy of Melancholy" as a Psychological Source Book.* Columbia University, 1933. 85 p. ms.

4203. RAUWOLF, Rev. HUGH L. *Spencer's Educational Theories.* Catholic University of America, 1928. 49 p. ms.

4204. REGENSTREIF, IRENE. *The Schoolmaster in Some Victorian and Contemporary Fiction.* Columbia University, 1945. 80 p. ms.

4205. REILMAN, ANTHONY HERMAN. *John of Salisbury: A Study of His Life and Contributions to Educational Thought.* Ohio State University, 1935. 158 p. ms.

4206. RENTSCH, HELEN J. *Michael Ernest Sadler: Man and Educator* University of California, Los Angeles, 1957. 189 p. ms.

4207. RICHARD, Brother. *A Study of the Monastic Schools of England, from the Seventh Century to the Twelfth.* Catholic University of America, 1915. 67 p. ms.

4208. RIGER, LESTER DAVID, 1913- . *The Development of the Teaching of History in the Public High Schools of Washington, D. C.* George Washington University, 1938. 80 p. ms. (Includes study of the teaching of history in England from 1623 to the eighteenth century.)

4209. RILEY, VIRGINIA LEE. *Joseph Lancaster: The Educational System He Devised and the Lancasterian Schools in the United States.* University of Maryland, 1941. 189 p. ms.

4210. RITTER, DECKARD. *The Educational Philosophy of John Ruskin.* New York University, 1927. 43 p. ms.

4211. RIVES, FANNY V. *The Education of the Canterbury Pilgrims.* University of Cincinnati, 1933. 109 p. ms.

4212. RODEWIG, FLORENCE. *The Educational Theories of Mary Wollstonecraft.* Columbia University, 1912. 24 p. ms.

4213. ROGAN, MARIE JOSEPH. *The Value of Book Reviews of English and American Literature for College Library Book Selection.* Columbia University, 1942. 100 p. ms.

4214. ROLLINS, WILLIAM BERT, Jr. *The Exchange of Teachers Between the United States and Great Britain, 1946-47.* University of California, Los Angeles, 1949. 86 p. ms.

4215. ROWLAND, WILMINA MALTBIE, 1908- . *The Contribution of Ruth Rouse to the World's Student Christian Federation.* Yale University, 1937. 281 p. ms. Abstract in *Selected Graduate Theses in Religious Education,* 1937, p. 45.

4216. ROYSTER, SALIBELLE. *The Value of Travel in England to Teachers of English.* Columbia University, 1939. 72 p. ms.

4217. RUSSELL, JANE LILLIAN. *A Study of Business Education in the Secondary Schools of England and Wales.* Boston University, 1958. 63 p. ms.

4218. SALZMAN, SAMUEL. *A Comparison of the Educational Theories of John Dewey and Bertrand Russell.* New York University, 1930. 100 p. ms.

4219. SATUREN, PAUL I., 1897- . *The Educational Philosophy of H. G. Wells.* Temple University, 1934. 110 p. ms.

4220. SCHATNIZKY, SAM. *Samuel Richardson as Educator.* College of the City of New York, 1936. 157 p. ms. Abstract in College of the City of New York: *Abstracts of Theses . . . 1923-1939,* p. 95.

4221. SCHNAPER, MIRIAM, 1926- . *Occupational Mobility of Oxford and Combridge Students between 1752 and 1886.* University of Kentucky, 1948. 93 p. ms.

4222. SCHREIBER, MORRIS. *The Schoolmaster in English Literature of the Nineteenth Century.* College of the City of New York, 1939. 135 p. ms. Abstract in College of the City of New York: *Abstracts of Theses . . . 1923-1939,* p. 108.

4223. SCHUSTER, ELDON BERNARD. *Bertrand Russell's Philosophy of Education.* Catholic University of America, 1937. 96 p. ms.

4224. SCIFRES, MARY LOUISE. *Wordsworth's Views on Education.* Indiana University, 1946. 39 p. ms.

4225. SCOWINS, Mother MARY ELIZABETH, 1895- . *A Study of the Psychological Principles of Character Training in the Book of Studies and the System of Character Training of Mother Cornelia Connelly.* Fordham University, 1945. 147 p. ms.

4226. SHANAHAN, Sister ST. THOMAS OF CANTERBURY, 1897- . *A Historical Study of Some Monastic Contributions in English Medieval Art Education.* Fordham University, 1943. 63 p. ms.

4227. SHEEVERS, HARRY P. *A Study of the Evidences of Change in the Secondary Schools of Post War England and Wales.* University of New Mexico, 1950. 84 p. ms.

4228. SHERMAN, Sister MARY FRANCISCA. *An Analysis of Newman's Idea of a University in the Light of Contemporary Problems on Education.* University of Cincinnati, 1943. 62 p. ms.

4229. SIBLEY, HOMER. *Dean Swift and His Educational Program.* University of Oregon, 1933. 130 p. ms.

4230. SILVA, WILLIAM HIRSH. *A Critical Interpretation of Herbert Spencer's "Synthetic Philosophy".* University of Tennessee, 1939. 96 p. ms.

4231. SIMPSON, HUGH FRANCIS. *The Teaching of Duns Scotus on the Primacy of Christ as Motivation for a High School Religious Course.* Catholic University of America, 1942. 79 p. ms.

4232. SIMPSON, MABEL A. *A Comparison of the Social Theories of Joseph Addison with the Ideas of Modern Frontier Thinkers in Education.* University of Oregon, 1934. 111 p. ms.

4233. SLATTERY, Sister CLEMENTINE JOSEPHINE. *The Educational Ideals of John Ruskin.* University of Southern California, 1926. 75 p. ms.

4234. SMITH, ANNE MILDRED, 1897- . *The Educational Philosophy of Thomas Carlyle.* Temple University, 1930. 248 p. ms.

4235. SMITH, CATHERINE ATKINSON. *The Educational Principles and Theories of Richard Mulcaster.* Catholic University of America, 1956. 55 p. ms. Abstract in *Catholic Educational Review,* Vol. 55, p. 555, November 1957.

4236. SMITH, CHARLES RUGGLES. *Macaulay's College Days: A Biographical Study.* Columbia University, 1922. 84 p. ms.

4237. SMITH, EDWARD NELSON, 1895- . *The School Teachers in the Novels of Charles Dickens: Their Significance and Their Prototypes.* University of Virginia, 1941. 238 p. ms.

4238. SMITH, GORDON B. *A Comparative Study of the Principles and Methods in Business Education between the United States and England.* American University, 1958. 115 p. ms.

4239. SMITH, PHILIP. *Matthew Arnold's Philosophy of Elementary Education.* College of the City of New York, 1933. 100 p. ms. Abstract in College of the City of New York: *Abstracts of Theses . . . 1923-1939,* p. 67.

4240. SNODGRASS, CLARE BERKLEY. *Some American Adaptations of the English House Plan.* Ohio State University, 1932. 117 p. ms. Abstract in Ohio State University: *Abstracts of Theses Presented by Candidates for the Master's Degree . . .* 1932, p. 272-273.

4241. SOKALSKA, Sister MARY ANTONIA. *Professional Opinions in England Concerning the Education of Women during the Renaissance.* Catholic University of America, 1945. 98 p. ms.

4242. SONN, MARIE. *Educational Implications in the Life and Poetry of William Morris.* New Jersey State Teachers College, Montclair, 1934. 78 p. ms.

4243. SOUTHWORTH, JOHN VAN DUYN. *The Use of the Radio for Formal Education in Great Britain and the United States, with Special Emphasis on the Teaching of History.* Columbia University, 1936. 119 p. ms.

4244. SPENCER, EDWIN ROLLIN. *Daniel Defoe's Contributions to Education.* University of Illinois, 1914. 66 p. ms. Abstract in Russell Taaffe Gregg: *Annotated Bibliography of Graduate Theses in Education at the University of Illinois,* 1931, p. 64. (Bureau of Educational Research, Bulletin No. 55.)

4245. SPERRY, MARY GRAHAM. *The Contribution of John Locke to Christian Education.* Biblical Seminary in New York, 1937. 104 p. ms.

4246. STACK, JAMES H. *The Educational Views of George Eliot.* New York University, 1933. 134 p. ms.

4247. STANTON, GLADYS ESTHER, 1895- . *The Educational Ideas of Matthew Arnold.* Yale University, 1932. 97 p. ms.

4248. STANTON, VIRGINIA KEYS, 1919- . *Education in Chaucer's Time.* University of Maryland, 1952. 40 p. ms.

4249. STEVENS, WESLEY ADDISON. *The Contributions Made to Mathematics by the British School during the Seventeenth Century.* Columbia University, 1925. 48 p. ms.

4250. STRICKLAND, ARVARH EUNICE. *Keynesian Economic Theory in Social Studies Textbooks for Grades Nine through Twelve: A Content Analysis.* University of Illinois, 1953. 92 p. ms.

4251. SUMNER, Mrs. MARGARET LIPPINCOTT. *The Schoolmaster in the Eighteenth Century Novel.* Columbia University, 1939. 70 p. ms.

4252. TALBOTT, GRACE ANN. *John Milton and His Relation to Modern Philosophy of Education.* Indiana State Teachers College, 1933. 94 p. ms. (Contributions of the Graduate School, No. 118.) Abstract in *Teachers College Journal,* Vol. 4, p. 319-320, July 1933.

4253. TELLER, JAMES DAVID. *The Educational Views and Influence of Thomas Henry Huxley.* Ohio State University, 1935. 276 p. ms.

4254. TEN BRINKE, DIRK PIETER. *Science Teaching in London Secondary Schools.* University of Minnesota, 1954. 139 p. ms.

4255. THEARLE, BEATRICE JUNE. *Educational Opinion in England during the Seventeenth Century.* University of Maryland, 1945. 70 p. ms.

4256. THOMAS, DAN F., 1916- . *A Study of the Changing Emphasis in the English School System.* Utah State Agricultural College, 1952. 77 p. ms.

4257. TOBEY, CAROLYN S. *The Influence of the War on Education in England.* Columbia University, 1917.

4258. TOBIN, MARIE AGNES. *The Educational Philosophy of John Ruskin.* Loyola University, 1931. 79 p. ms.

4259. TOLBERT, GERTRUDE. *Huxley's Relation to Education.* Columbia University, 1926. 62 p. ms.

4260. TOLMAN, LORRAINE ENID. *A Comparative Study of the Educational Philosophies of John Milton and John Henry Newman.* University of Southern California, 1948. 103 p. ms.

4261. TURNER, ANNIE R. 1895- . *Milton and the Puritan Influence in Education.* Southern Methodist University, 1917. 127 p. ms. Abstract in Southern Methodist University: *Abstracts of Theses,* No. 12, 1946, 1947, p. 40.

4262. TYLER, BEULAH B. *Educational Implications in the Poetry of William Wordsworth.* Colorado State Teachers College, 1932. 102 p. ms.

4263. UHLENKOTT, Sister MARY SCHOLASTICA. *A Comparative Study of the Educational Philosophies of Hutchins and Newman.* Gonzaga University, 1956. 74 p. ms.

4264. VELDER, MILTON, 1927- . *Charlotte Bronte and Education.* University of Maryland, 1952. 76 p. ms.

4265. VEVIER, ERSULL IDA, 1910- . *The Educational Theories of Robert Owen and Their Applications to the New Lanark School.* St. Louis University, 1944. 83 p. ms.

4266. VIETS, WALLACE TROWBRIDGE. *John Wesley's Theories of Education as Revealed in His Writings.* Hartford Theological Seminary, 1950. 117 p. ms.

4267. WALCH, HARVEY JOHN, 1907- . *Elementary Educational Reform in England, 1900-1923.* University of North Dakota, 1933. 66 p. ms.

4268. WALKER, LALLA ALMEDA. *The Philosophy of Character Education in the English Public Schools.* George Peabody College for Teachers, 1941. 101 p. ms.

4269. WALKER, T. ASHLEY. *The Philosophy of Character Education in English Public Schools as Portrayed in Some Representative English Novels.* Columbia University, 1938. 56 p. ms.

4270. WALSH, Rev. WILLIAM J. *The Dual System in England and Its Desirability in the United States.* Catholic University of America, 1927. 45 p. ms.

4271. WATTS, ANNABELLE. *A Critical Study of the Curriculum for the Elementary Schools in England.* Ohio State University, 1927. 94 p. ms.

4272. WEBB, ALLIE MARGUERITE. *Some Social Studies in Anthony Trollope.* Columbia University, 1929. 32 p. ms.

4273. WEBB, ROBERT K. *Harriet Martineau and the Movement for the Diffusion of Knowledge.* Columbia University, 1949. 136 p. ms.

4274. WEIR, Sister MARY BEATA, 1919- . *A Comparative Analysis of the Concept of a Liberal Education as Expressed in Newman's Idea of a University and in the Harvard Report.* Immaculate Heart College, 1952. 109 p. ms.

4275. WELLWORTH, Sister MARY GONZAGA. *A Comparative Study of Locke and Spencer.* New York State College for Teachers, Albany, 1916. (Studied as educators.)

4276. WELSHEIMER, EDITH L. *The Literature of Education of the Sixteenth Century.* University of New Mexico, 1934. 135 p. ms. Abstract in University of New Mexico: *Abstracts of Theses, 1933-1937.* p. 112-113 (Publications, Miscellaneous Series, No. 1.)

4277. WHITE, GEORGINA MARY. *The Place of Dr. Richard Busby in the Seventeenth Century Scheme of Education.* State University of Iowa, 1941. 66 p. ms.

4278. WHITE, GOODRICH COOK. *The Ethical Psychology of Herbert Spencer.* Columbia University, 1911. 37 p. ms.

4279. WHITELEY, BERNICE REESE. *English Spelling Reform.* East Texas State Teachers College, 1940. 111 p. ms. Abstract in East Texas State Teachers College: *Graduate Studies,* 1940, p. 83-84. (Studies modifications made since the invention of printing.)

4280. WHITSETT, MAY BELLE. *Cambridge University in the Works of Charles Kingsley.* Columbia University, 1931. 58 p. ms.

4281. WILL, FREDERICK LUDWIG. *A Study of Bertrand Russell from the Point of View of Education.* Ohio State University, 1931. 110 p. ms. Abstract in Ohio State University: *Abstracts of Theses Presented by Candidates for the Master's Degree . . . 1931,* p. 332-334. (Abstracts of Master's Theses, No. 7.)

4282. WILLIAMS, WILLIAM HAROLD. *The Educational Views of Thomas Carlyle.* Stanford University, 1935. 154 p. ms.

4283. WILSON, HELEN ABINA, 1901- . *John Henry Cardinal Newman: His Theory of Education.* Boston University, 1924. 32 p. ms.

4284. WITUCKI, Sister MARY ALBENSIA. *Tennyson's Idea of Higher Education of Women as Expressed in "The Princess."* Catholic Sisters College of the Catholic University of America, 1926. 36 p. ms.

4285. WOOD, MARGARET LOUISE. *T. B. Macauley's Theory of Public Speaking.* State University of Iowa, 1938. 136 p. ms.

4286. WOODRUFF, HAROLD ELBORT. *The Significance of Bertrand Russell's Philosophy for the Curriculum.* University of Cincinnati, 1940. 136 p. ms.

4287. WRIGHT, Mrs. SUSIE THOMPSON, 1902- . *Education in the Writings of Dickens.* Southern Methodist University, 1933. 86 p. ms. Abstract in Southern Methodist University, *Abstracts of Theses,* No. 2, 1927-1933, p. 11.

4288. WUKITSCH, Rev. EPHREM OTTO. *The Educational Contents and Implications of Roger Bacon's "Opus Tertium."* Catholic University of America, 1942. 96 p. ms.

4289. WYATT, MARJORIE. *Secondary Educational Reconstruction in England and Wales.* University of Buffalo, 1950. 46 p. ms.

4290. YOUNG, RALPH ELLSWORTH. *Techniques of Experimentation in the United States and Great Britain.* University of Colorado, 1932. 96 p. ms. Abstract in *University of Colorado Studies,* Vol. 20, No. 1, p. 110, November 1932.

4291. YOUNG, WESLEY GEORGE, ?-1922. *An Interpretation of Recent Tendencies in English Education.* University of Washington, 1921. 68 p. ms.

4292. ZABRISKIE, EDWARD CORNELL. *Ruskin's Theory of Art, with Its Educational Implications.* Columbia University, 1911. 33 p. ms.

4293. ZACHAR, IRWIN J. *Samuel Butler versus His Education.* College of the City of New York, 1936. 80 p. ms. Abstract in College of the City of New York: *Abstracts of Theses . . . 1923-1939,* p. 96.

4294. ZEARING, SUSAN F. *A Study of Free Secondary Education in England since 1440.* Oberlin College, 1932. 77 p. ms.

4295. ZOLLO, RICHARD P. *Resources in the British Isles of Interest to Language Arts and Dramatic Teachers.* Boston University, 1958.

See also Nos. 187, 200, 208, 212, 218, 219, 222, 226, 235, 236, 239, 245, 249, 250, 251, 264, 274, 283, 286, 288, 289, 290, 301, 302, 304, 1315, 2084, 2280, 2457, 3047, 3134, 3135, 3138, 3139, 3143, 3145, 3148, 3149, 3150, 3151, 3152, 3153, 3156, 3157, 3158, 3159, 3160, 3163, 3164, 3166, 3168, 3171, 3172, 3175, 3177, 3178, 3179, 3180, 3188, 3190, 3191, 3194, 3196, 3198, 3201, 3202, 3204, **4305**, 3207, 3208, 3209, 3210, 3211, 3216, 3217, 3220, 3221, 3222, 3223, 3224, 3228, 3229, 3230, 3232, 3234, 3235, 3236, 3237, 3238, 3239, 3240, 3241, 3244, 3246, 3248, 3250, 3256, 3257, 3259, 3261, 3262, 3264, 3265, 3268, 3269, 3270, 3271, 3272, 3274, 3276, 3277, 3278, 3280, 3281, 3283, 3285, 3286, 3288, 3289, 3290, 3292, 3294, 3295, 3296, 3297, 3300, 3302, 3303, 3497, 3498.

For British groups in the United States, see Nos. 4957, 4959, 4963, 4970, 4975, 4978, 4985, 4989, 5006, 5013, 5020, 5025, 5031, 5698.

Greece

(NOS. 4296–4363)

DOCTORS

4296. ANTONAKAKI, Mrs. KALLINIKI DENDRINOU, 1908- . *Greek Education: Reorganization of the Administrative Structure.* Columbia University, 1954. New York: Bureau of Publications, Teachers College, Columbia University, 1955. xiii, 274 p. (Teachers College Studies in Education.)

4297. BURRAGE, DWIGHT GRAFTON, 1873- . *Educational Progress in Greece during the Minoan, Mycenaeum, and Lyric Periods.* University of Nebraska, 1920. Omaha, Nebraska: Cockle Printing Co., 1920. iii, 68 p.

4298. CATSIOULAS, EVANGELOS JOHN, 1910- . *Changing Influence on Greek Education, 1821-1951.* University of Michigan, 1953. 148 p. ms. Abstract in *Dissertation Abstracts,* Vol. 13, No. 3, p. 332-333, 1953. Available on microfilm from University Microfilms, Ann Arbor, Michigan, as Publication No. 5,018.

4299. CHINNOCK, EUGENIE. *Plato's Educational Views: A Comparative Study of "The Republic" and "The Laws."* New York University, 1940. 195 p. ms. Abstract in New York University, School of Education: *Abstracts of Theses,* 1939-40, p. 109-112.

4300. CLAROS, THOMAS STAVROS. *The Curriculum of the Greek Gymnasium.* University of Connecticut, 1958. 176 p. ms. Abstract in *Dissertation Abstracts,* Vol. 19, p. 999-1000, November 1958. Available on microfilm from University Microfilms, Ann Arbor, Michigan, as Mic. 58-3907.

4301. DAVISON, JEAN MARGARET. *A Study of Attic Geometric Workshops.* Yale University, 1957.

4302. GOLDAT, GEORGE DAVID, 1928- . *The Early Medieval Traditions of Euclid's Elements.* University of Wisconsin, 1956. 411 p. ms. Abstract in *Dissertation Abstracts,* Vol. 17, p. 1319, June 1957. Available on microfilm from University Microfilms, Ann Arbor, Michigan, as Publication No. 20,236.

4303. GORMAN, Sister MARY ROSARIA. *The Nurse in Greek Life.* Catholic Sisters College of the Catholic University of America, 1917. Boston: Foreign Languages Print Co., 1917. 51 p. By Sister Mary Rosaria. (Includes consideration of the place of the nurse in education.)

4304. LAVELL, CECIL FAIRFIELD, 1872-1948. *The Evolution of Greek Moral Education.* Columbia University, 1911. Published as *Greek Moral Ideals: A Study in Evolution,* Kingston, Canada: Jackson Press, 1911. 97 p.

4305. MICHAELIDES, GEORGE PETER. *The Religious Teachings and Influence of Koraes, Kairis, and Macrakis: A Study of the History of the Church in Greece during the Nineteenth Century.* Hartford Theological Seminary, 1938. 479 p. ms.

4306. MICHAELIDES-NOUAROS, ANDREW, 1922- . *Current Problems in Secondary Education in Greece.* Indiana University, 1952. 335 p. ms.

4307. MOORE, ERNEST CARROLL, 1871-1955. *Relation of Education to Philosophy in Greece and Early Christianity.* University of Chicago, 1898.

4308. MUNRO, KATHLEEN. *The Role of Music in the Development of Educational Thought among the Early Classical Greeks.* University of Washington, 1937. 189 p. ms. Abstract in University of Washington: *Abstracts of Theses* . . . Vol. 2, p. 503-507.

4309. RABUS, MAXIMILLIAN. *The Fine Arts in the Education of Hellenic Boys.* New York University, 1926. 5 volumes, 614 p. ms.

4310. REPP, ARTHUR CHRISTIAN. *Educational Philosophy of John Chrysostom.* Washington University, St. Louis, 1951. 258 p. ms.

4311. SAVVIDIS, ANTONIOS PANAYOTOU. *An Expository, Critical, and Constructive Study of Education in Modern Greece.* Harvard University, 1917. 490 p. ms.

4312. SHUTE, CLARENCE WILLIAM, 1903- . *The Psychology of Aristotle: An Analysis of the Living Being.* Columbia University, 1941. New York: Columbia University Press, 1941. xiv, 148 p. (Columbia Series in Philosophy, No. 1.)

4313. SMITH, JOHN MILTON, 1910- . *A Comparison and Criticism of the Educational Philosophies of Plato and John Dewey.* State University of Iowa, 1941. 164 p. ms. Abstract in State University of Iowa: *Doctoral Researches* . . . Vol. 4, 1940, 1941, p. 278-283.

4314. TZOVAS, CONSTATINOS, 1915- . *An Emerging Role of the Elementary School Teacher in Greece.* Columbia University, 1957. 154 p. ms.

4315. WILCOX, GEORGE MILO, 1890- . *Education in Modern Greece.* Columbia University, 1933. Tiffin, Ohio: Commercial Printing Co., 1933. 113 p.

See also Nos. 27, 119, 125, 136, 138, 158, 163, 164, 172, 174, 175, 184, 3002, 3086, 3101, 3108, 3112, 3127, 3129, 174a.

MASTERS

4316. AERY, WILLIAM ANTHONY. *The Educational Theory of Plato: An Outline of His Psychology and His Social Philosophy.* Columbia University, 1905. 24 p. ms.

4317. ANASTASSOPOULOS, PANAYOTHIS A. *Curriculum and Supervision Problems Underlying Greek Education.* Columbia University, 1956. 180 p. ms.

4318. ARMSTRONG, ANN VERONICA. *Health and Related Topics in the "Republic" and "Timaeus" of Plato.* New York University, 1943. 53 p. ms.

4319. ARNEST, Sister MARY THOMAS. *A Comparative Study of Education in Ancient Greece with that in the United States Today.* University of Notre Dame, 1932. 61 pp. ms.

4320. ATHANASSIADOU, IRENE MENELAOU. *The Needs of Greek Families in Home and Family Life Education as a Basis for Curriculum Construction.* Pennsylvania State College, 1954. 91 p. ms.

4321. BARTO, ELIZABETH, 1902- . *The Ethical Teachings in the Extant Greek Dramas.* Wittenberg College, 1941. 202 p. ms.

4322. BLACKWELL, LIZZIE LENA. *A Study of Absolutism: Plato as an Absolutist and His Influence on Modern Education.* North Texas State Teachers College, 1945. 33 p. ms. Abstract in North Texas State Teachers College: *Abstracts of Theses, 1941-1946*, p. 37-38.

4323. BRANDL, Sister MARY INNOCENT. *Mathematics of Aristotle.* St. Bonaventure University, 1958.

4324. BRUNE, IRVIN HENRY. *Greek Mathematics and Modern Teaching.* Ohio State University, 1933. 174 p. ms. Abstract in Ohio State University: *Abstracts of Theses Presented by Candidates for the Master's Degree* . . . No. 12, 1933. p. 32-33. (Abstracts of Master's Theses, No. 12.)

4325. CANOY, Sister MARY ZENO, 1907- . *Stoicism in Modern Educational Theory and Practice.* St. Louis University, 1957. 133 p. ms.

4326. CASSELL, STAFFORD HENDRICKS. *A Comparative Study of American and Spartan Physical Education.* Pennsylvania State College, 1940. 93 p. ms.

4327. CLEVELAND, TREADWELL. *Greek Psychology before Aristotle.* Columbia University, 1898. 49 p. ms.

4328. DALTON, SIDNA POAGE. *A Critical Review of the Theory of Education in Plato's Republic.* University of Missouri, 1914. 61 p. ms.

4329. DIAMANTIDES, DIAMANDES GEORGE. *Grecian Physical Education, 1834-1934.* International YMCA College, 1934. 151 p. ms.

4330. DORLAND, GEORGE WILLIAM. *The Relation of Aristotle's Psychology, Ethics, and Politics to His Educational Theory.* Columbia University, 1905. 26 p. ms.

4331. GAREY, WALTER FRANCIS. *Implications of Plato's Philosophy to Physical Education.* Ohio State University, 1953. 90 p. ms.

4332. GIADRIDES, GEORGE ELIAS. *Modernity of Educational Ideas of Adamandios Coraes (Koraes), 1748-1833, a Greek Scholar, Educator, and Patriot.* New York University, 1928. 74 p. ms.

4333. GIFFORD, RUTH, 1899- . *A Comparative Study of Certain Phases of the Educational Theories of Plato and John Dewey.* Syracuse University, 1931. 53 p. ms.

4334. GLAVAS, CHRISTOS B. *Secondary Mathematical Education in Greece and a Contrast to Its Counterpart in the U. S. A.* Columbia University, 1954. 50 p. ms.

4335. GRUESER, Sister FRANCOSIE THERESE. *The Educational Theories and Principles of Saint John Chrysostom as Presented in His "De Liberis Educandis."* Catholic University of America, 1945. 45 p. ms.

4336. HEFLEY, JESSE LEHMANOWSKY. *Evolution of the Laws of Learning.* University of Oklahoma, 1930. 62 p. ms. Abstract in University of Oklahoma: *Abstracts of Theses* . . . 1930, p. 24. (Begins with Socrates.)

4337. HENDERSHOT, VERNON EDWARDS, 1895- . *A Comparative Study of the Educational Philosophies of Plato and Dewey.* University of Southern California, 1927. 73 p. ms. For doctoral dissertation by same author, see No. 2553.

4338. INGRAM, DESSIE BROWN. *Contrasting Concepts of Aristotelian and Modern Science.* George Peabody College for Teachers, 1937. 147 p. ms.

4339. JOHNSON, HAROLD LLEWELLYN. *Influence of Plato's Environment on the Educational Doctrines of the "Republic."* University of Southern California, 1934. 139 p. ms.

4340. KAKOURIS, NICHOLAS K. *Teacher Training in Hellas.* University of Pittsburgh, 1930. 100 p. ms. Abstract in University of Pittsburgh: *Abstracts of Theses* . . . Vol. 6, 1930, p. 304-305.

4341. KASER, LAWRENCE SINELE. *Pythagoras, His Life and Works.* Peabody College for Teachers, 1933. 45 p. ms.

4342. KEIM, CHARLES ZANE, 1907- . *Isocrates as an Educator.* University of Pittsburgh, 1930. 28 p. ms. Abstract in University of Pittsburgh: *Abstracts of Theses* . . . Vol. 6, 1930, p. 307.

4343. LITTLE, DWIGHT R. *Plato's Ideas on Education Based on the "Republic."* New York University, 1904. 11 p. ms.

4344. McCORKLE, THOMAS SMITH, 1898-1955. *Music in Greek Life and Some of Its Educational Implications.* Southern Methodist University, 1936. 97 p. ms. Abstract in Southern Methodist University: *Abstracts of Theses*, No. 4, 1937, p. 14-15.

4345. McGRAW, JOHN LAWRENCE. *Development of Education and the Democracy in Ancient Athens.* University of Colorado, 1938. 79 p. ms. Abstract in *University of Colorado Studies*, Vol. 26, No. 1, p. 94, November 1938.

4346. MAKRIS, ARISTIDES JOHN. *A Program in Agricultural Education for Young Farmers in Macedonia, Greece.* Rutgers University, 1939. 91 p. ms.

4347. MAUCH, Rev. EUGENE ANTHONY. *Criticisms of Plato's Educational Theories from the Christian Standpoint.* Catholic University of America, 1927. 66 p. ms.

4348. MAYNE, MABEL DeLILLIAN. *A Parallel Study of Ancient and Classical Greek Dance and Music.* George Peabody College for Teachers, 1938. 121 p. ms.

4349. MITCHELL, THEODORE CLARENCE. *The Treatment of Education in the "Clouds" of Aristophanes.* Columbia University, 1901. 47 p. ms.

4350. MOFFATT, RUTH JENNINGS. *The Dance in the Life of the Early Greeks.* George Peabody College for Teachers, 1932. 62 p. ms.

4351. MOUSSOUROS, BASIL GEORGE, 1904- . *Developing Programs of Continuation Education for Rural Populations in Greece.* Cornell University, 1947. 114 p. ms.

4352. NARDELLI, WALTER, 1912- . *Aristotle, the Modern Philosopher of Education.* Boston College, 1941. 72 p. ms.

4353. PAUL, GEORGE CASE, 1897- . *A Comparison of the Educational Philosophy of Plato and John Dewey.* Temple University, 1929. 111 p. ms.

4354. RIGGENBACH, JOHN B., 1921- . *Plato's Philosophy of Education in the Early Dialogues.* Boston University, 1951. 340 p. ms.

4355. SMITH, EARL KENNETH, 1919- . *Platonic Influences upon Christian Education in the First Three Centuries.* Pacific Union College, 1951. 91 p. ms.

4356. STRIKER, EDITH PARKER. *The Change in Plato's Ideas of Education between the "Republic" and the "Laws".* Columbia University, 1900. 67 p. ms.

4357. TARROU, DEMETRIOS IOANNOU. *The Political and Economic Influences on Greek Education from 1935 to 1948.* Ohio State University, 1952. 132 p. ms.

4358. THIBAULT, Sister MARTHA OF BETHANY. *A Study of the Contrasts and Similarities in Educational Problems in Athens after the Persian War with the Problems in the United States after the World War.* University of Notre Dame, 1931. 82 p. ms.

4359. TOBIN, FRANCIS ALOYSIUS. *A Study of Sophistic Education.* Clark University, 1913. 62 p. ms.

4360. TRIANTAFYLLOU, TRIANTAFYLLOS T., 1920- . *A Program for Improving Education of the Mentally Retarded Children in the Elementary Schools of Greece.* New York University, 1956.

4361. VOIGHT, WALTER W. *A Criticism of Plato's Theory of Education in the "Republic."* Columbia University, 1913. 25 p. ms.

4362. WILLIAMS, MAMIE. *The Educational Implications of the Platonic and Pragmatic Concepts of the Good.* North Texas State Teachers College, 1941. 80 p. ms. Abstract in North Texas State Teachers College: *Abstracts of Theses, 1941-1946*, p. 84.

4363. WINGER, OTHO. *Applications in Education of Aristotle's Theory of Katharsis.* Indiana University, 1907.

See also Nos. 187, 200, 212, 217, 219, 221, 222, 226, 230, 238, 244, 245, 248, 254, 262, 263, 266, 267, 268, 279, 286, 291, 296, 298, 300, 301, 306, 3139, 3141, 3152, 3168, 3177, 3198, 3201, 3205, 3206, 3211, 3212, 3220, 3224, 3226, 3227, 3237, 3239, 3254, 3255, 3260, 3267, 3274, 3287, 3292.

For Greek groups in the United States, *see* Nos. 4954, 4956, 4957, 4975, 4982, 4985, 5006, 5113.

Hungary

(NOS. 4364 – 4373)

DOCTORS

4364. DAVIS, Mrs. MAXINE COUCH, 1912- . *Analytical Study of the Mikrokosmos of Bela Bartok.* Columbia University, 1957. 330 p. ms.

4365. HORAN, Mother MARY ANNUNCIATA. *The Mikrokosmos of Bela Bartok: Description and Analysis of the Problems Encountered in Form, Rhythm, Harmony, Melody, and Expressive Elements – Its Use in Teaching.* Boston University, 1957.

4366. KEREKES, JOHN, 1913- . *Relationship of Protestant Education to State Education in Hungary.* University of Pittsburgh, 1943. Abstract in University of Pittsburgh: *Abstracts of Theses* . . . Vol. 19, 1944, p. 127-134.

4367. REARICK, ELIZABETH CHARLOTTE, 1899- . *Dances of the Hungarians: A Study of the Dances Found Today in Hungary, Together with a Description of Some of the Peasant Festivities.* Columbia University, 1939. New York: Teachers College, Columbia University, 1939. viii, 151 p. (Teachers College Contribution to Education, No. 770.)

See also Nos. 119, 147, 161, 175, 3072, 3688.

MASTERS

4368. FERNANDEZ, Rev. MANUEL. *Professional Opinions of Tihamer Toth Concerning the Religious Education of Youth.* Catholic University of America, 1950. 93 p. ms.

4369. KARDOS, LILLIAN ILONA. *Education in Hungary Before and After the World War.* University of Southern California, 1931. 75 p. ms.

4370. PALLAY, MARY ELIZABETH. *The Teaching of Art in the Elementary Schools of Hungary.* Ohio University, 1940. 128 p. ms. Abstract in Ohio University: *Abstracts of Master's Theses* . . . 1940, p. 39-40.

4371. SCHANZER, LYDIA B. *The Language Reform in Hungary, 1770-1870.* Columbia University, 1950. 63 p. ms.

4372. SCHUETZ-HARKANYI, AUGUSTA. *A Proposed Course of Study for the Training of Deans of Women and Other Personnel Officers at the University of Budapest, Based on a Study of Training Offered in the United States.* University of Pittsburgh, 1933. 262 p. ms. Abstract in University of Pittsburgh: *Abstracts of Theses* . . . Vol. 9, 1933, p. 449-450.

4373. SZABO, STEPHEN. *The Presentation of English to College Youth in Hungary Using the Mediation of Latin.* University of Pittsburgh, 1929. 110 p. ms.

See also Nos. 187, 226, 3140, 3208, 3292.

For Hungarian groups in the United States, *see* Nos. 4970, 4975, 4980, 4981, 4985, 4992, 5014, 5020, 5021.

Iceland

(NO. 4374)

DOCTOR

See No. 142.

MASTERS

4374. JONSDOTTIR, ASA, 1919- . *Secondary Education in Iceland.* University of North Dakota, 1947. 57 p. ms.

See also Nos. 212, 226.

For an Icelandic Group in the United States, *see* No. 4975.

Ireland

(NOS. 4375 – 4401)

DOCTORS

4375. GALLAGHER, Sister ANTHONY MARIE, 1903- . *Education in Ireland. (Eire.)* Catholic University of America, 1948. Washington: Catholic University of America Press, 1948. xi, 315 p. Abstract in *Catholic Educational Review*, Vol. 46, p. 452-453, September 1948.

4376. MERONEY, GERALDINE MARIE. *The Celtic Origin of the Institutions of Christian Learning in Ireland.* University of Oregon, 1954. 296 p. ms.

4377. SIMON, LOUIS, 1908- . *The Educational Theories of George Bernard Shaw.* New York University, 1956. 395 p. ms. Abstract in *Dissertation Abstracts*, Vol. 16, p. 2069-2070, November 1956. Available on microfilm from University Microfilms, Ann Arbor, Michigan, as Publication No. 17,673.

4378. THOMPSON, FRANCIS JOHN. *Fenianism and the Celtic Renaissance.* New York University, 1941. 3 vols. 1281 p. ms.

See also Nos. 119, 142, 143, 147, 3090, 3106, 3116, 3120, 3125.

MASTERS

4379. CARMODY, IMELDA. *Records of the Charter School System in the Eighteenth Century as Exemplified at Clonmel.* St. Louis University, 1936. 52 p. ms.

4380. CLAYTON, HELEN TERESA, 1917- . *The Influence of the Arts and Education on Ireland and Its People.* Boston College, 1939. 79 p. ms.

4381. CORSBERG, MYRTLE MARIE. *A Survey of the Present Educational Situation in the Irish Free State.* University of Southern California, 1933. 100 p. ms.

4382. CURTIS, MICHAEL SEBASTIAN. *The Significance of the Work of Edmond Ignatius Rice as a Pioneer in the Field of Primary Education in Ireland, 1802-1844.* University of Notre Dame, 1928. 56 p. ms.

4383. DAWSON, WILLIAM ROBERT. *Education in the Irish Free State, 1922-1930.* Stanford University, 1931. 132 p. ms.

4384. DICKSON, ANNA MOORE. *Maria Edgeworth's Ideas on the Training of Children.* Columbia University, 1913. 9 p. ms.

4385. DILLON, DAVID GIBSON, 1905- . *Irish Monastic Schools and Scholars.* Boston College, 1931. 73 p. ms.

4386. EGAN, Brother CHARLES AMBROSE, 1901- . *Patrick H. Pearse: Artist, Educator, and Poet.* Fordham University, 1938. 75 p. ms. Abstract in Fordham University: *Dissertations Accepted for Higher Degrees*, 1939, p. 20-21.

4387. GLYNN, ELIZABETH VERONICA, 1903- . (*Sister Mary Agneta.*) *Mother Catherine McAuley, Foundress of the Sisters of Mercy, an Eminent Catholic Humanist.* St. John's University, 1946. 104 p. ms. Abstract in St. John's University: *Abstracts of Dissertations, 1946-48*, p. 29.

4388. GRAHAM, HUGH. *Early Irish Monastic Schools.* University of Minnesota, 1919. 156 p. ms.

4389. HAGGERTY, RUTH LOUISE. *Children's Literature in Ireland.* Massachusetts State Teachers College, Boston, 1953. 53 p. ms.

4390. HASTINGS, Sister MARY BORGIA. *Nano Nagle, Heroine of Irish Education.* Boston College, 1933. 42 p. ms.

4391. JOHNSON, EDWARD ROBERT. *The Irish University Question.* University of Detroit, 1956. 104 p. ms.

4392. KIRWAN, ELIZABETH JOSEPHINE, 1906- . *The Mission of the Jesuits in Ireland under the Tudors.* Fordham University, 1936. 154 p. ms. Abstract in Fordham University: *Dissertations Accepted for Higher Degrees*, 1937, p. 56. (Includes consideration of Jesuit schools.)

4393. LANIGAN, EDMUND MURRAY. *Celtic Monasticism and Education.* Boston College, 1934. 51 p. ms.

4394. McCARTY, Sister MARY BENECIO. *Padraic Henry Pearse and Education in the Gaelic Tradition.* Marquette University, 1939. 165 p. ms.

4395. McGEEHAN, MARY ELLEN, 1925- . *The Contributions of Catherine McAuley to Education.* University of Maryland, 1956. 90 p. ms.

4396. MacMAHON, Brother CORNELIUS. *The Irish Christian Brothers as a Factor in the National and Educational Life of Ireland, 1802-1924.* University of Notre Dame, 1928. 59 p. ms.

4397. MULHERN, JAMES ANTHONY, 1890- . *A Comparative Study of Irish and American Secondary Education.* University of Pennsylvania, 1925. 144 p. ms.

4398. O'BRIEN, Sister MARY CATALDUS. *The Irish Lyric in the Development of Christian Character in the Catholic High School.* Boston College, 1937. 61 p. ms.

4399. O'CONNELL, Rev. GEOFFREY. *The Educational Significance of the Gaelic Language Revival.* Catholic University of America, 1933. 82 p. ms.

4400. O'DONNELL, Brother CHARLES AELRED. *The Contribution of the Monastic Schools of Ireland to Education.* Gonzaga University, 1957. 86 p. ms.

4401. ROWLAND, EUGENIA. *Education in the Golden Age of Ireland.* University of Southern California, 1942. 168 p. ms.

See also Nos. 226, 235, 249, 251, 290, 3178, 3237, 4231.

For Irish groups in the United Stated, *see* Nos. 5117-5118.

Italy
(NOS. 4402-4568)

DOCTORS

4402. BATTISTINI, LAWRENCE HENRY, 1907- . *Italian Education under Fascism.* Yale University, 1947. 549 p. ms.

4403. BORGHI, LAMBERTO, 1907- . *Education and Authority in Modern Italy.* New School for Social Research, 1950. Published as *Educazione e Autorita nell'Italia Moderna.* Firenze (Florence), Italy: Al Nuova Italia, 1951. x, 342 p. (Storici Antichi e Moderni. Nuova Serie, 2.)

4404. BREDESTEGE, Rev. FRANCIS JOSEPH, 1892-1939. *The Educational Philosophy of Antonio Rosmini-Serbati.* University of Cincinnati, 1932. 333 p. ms. Abstract in University of Cincinnati: *Graduate Theses in Education, 1931-36,* p. 1-23. For master's thesis by same author, see No. 3149.

4405. BRENNAN, MARGARET VIRGINIA, 1911- . *A Study of the Influence of Quintilian on the Teaching of Speech from the Renaissance to the Nineteenth Century.* Stanford University, 1940. 124 p. ms. Abstract in Stanford University: *Abstracts of Dissertations* . . . 1939-40, p. 184-188.

4406. CARTER, JANE GRAY, 1875- . *Quintilian's Didactic Metaphors.* New York University, 1910. 63 p. ms.

4407. CAVELL, MATTHEW CIAVARELLA. *Giovanni Gentile's Reform of Education in Italy.* New York University, 1932. 179 p. ms.

4408. CERONI, VITTORIO FEDERICO, 1894- . *Pedagogical Principles Enunciated in the Works of Dante.* New York University, 1932. 133 p. ms.

4409. COSTA-MINNECI DI VILLAREAL, JOYCE. *The Montessori Elementary Curriculum Content and the Corresponding American Curriculum Content: A Cross-Cultural Study.* American University, 1958. For master's thesis by same author, see No. 4463.

4410. COTE, ARTHUR BASIL, 1885- . *Blessed Giovanni Dominici: Regola del Governo di Cura Familiare, Parte Quarta. On the Education of Children: Translation and Introduction.* Catholic University of America, 1927. Washington: Catholic University of America, 1927. 71 p. For master's thesis by same author, see No. 3026.

4411. COVELLO, LEONARD, 1887- . *The Social Background of the Italo-American School Child: A Study of the Southern Italian Family Mores and Their Effect on the School Situation in Italy and America.* New York University, 1944. 3 vols. 758 p. ms.

4412. DI FRANCO, JOSEPH, 1917- . *A Suggested Advisory Program for Rural Italy.* Columbia University, 1958. 116 p. ms. (Deals with extension education.)

4413. DUEY, PHILIP A. *Bel Canto in Its Golden Age: A Study of Its Teaching Concepts.* Columbia University, 1950.

4414. FANNING, Sister MARIA WALBURG. *"Maphei Vegii Laudensis de Educatione Liberorum et eorum Claris Moribus, Libri Sex:" A Critical Text of Books I-III.* Catholic University of America, 1934. Washington: Catholic University of America, 1933. xxv, 127 p. (Studies in Medieval and Renaissance Latin, Vol. 1. See also Sullivan, A.S. No. 4437.)

4415. GORMAN, Sister MARY JANE THOMAS, 1904- . *Tertiary Franciscan Missionary Sisters of the Sacred Heart and Catholic Education in the United States.* Fordham University, 1946. 383 p. ms. Abstract in Fordham University: *Dissertations Accepted for Higher Degrees* . . . 1946, p. 30-33. (Considers also the origin and work of the order in Italy.)

4416. GUERRA, EMILIO LEWIS, 1909- . *The Contributions of Guiseppe Lombardo-Radice to Education.* New York University, 1942. 278 p. ms.

4417. HAWKES, LOUISE RESTIEAUX. *Before and After Pinocchio: A Study of Italian Children's Books.* Columbia University, 1933. 207 p. ms. (Chapter 8: "Development of Children's Literature in England, France, Germany, Scandinavia, Spain, and Russia".)

4418. HISSONG, Mrs. MARY CHAMPE, 1907- . *The Philosophical Bases of Italian Educational Reform.* Ohio State University, 1940. 260 p. ms. Abstract in Ohio State University: *Abstracts of Dissertations* . . . Summer 1940, p. 221-229. (Abstracts of Doctoral Dissertations, No. 34.)

4419. HOFFMAN, MARTHA WILSON. *The Membership of the Four Major Colleges of Priests from 44 B.C. to 37 A.D.* Bryn Mawr College, 1951. 181 p. ms. Abstract in *Dissertation Abstracts,* Vol. 12, No. 1, p. 44-45, 1952. Available on microfilm from University Microfilms, Ann Arbor, Michigan, as Publication No. 3,208.

4420. HORKAN, VINCENT JOSEPH, 1915- . *Educational Theories and Principles of Maffeo Vegio.* Catholic University of America, 1953. Washington: Catholic University of America Press, 1953. viii, 229

p. Abstract in *Catholic Educational Review*, Vol. 51, p. 687, December 1953. For master's thesis by same author, see No. 4583.

4421. KEYES, GORDON LINCOLN, 1920- . *Studies in Roman Education.* Princeton University, 1944. 117 p. ms. Abstract in *Dissertation Abstracts,* Vol. 12, No. 3, p. 256, 1952. Available on microfilm from University Microfilms, Ann Arbor, Michigan, as Publication No. 2,989.

4422. KNOFLACH, AUGUSTIN. *Education in Italy.* New York University, 1894. 87 p. ms.

4423. KOPF-SEITZ, CAROLA E. *Don Giovanni Bosco as an Educator.* Catholic Sisters College of the Catholic University of America, 1926. Washington: Catholic University of America Press, 1926. 78 p.

4424. LA MALFA, JOACHIM J., 1915- . *Educational Psychology in Italy.* University of Michigan, 1949. 265 p. ms. Abstract in *Microfilm Abstracts,* Vol. 9, No. 2, p. 81-83, 1949. Available on microfilm from University Microfilms, Ann Arbor, Michigan, as Publication No. 1,203.

4425. LA RUSSO, DOMINIC A. *Rhetoric and the Social Order in Italy, 1450-1600.* Northwestern University, 1957. 320 p. ms. Abstract in *Dissertation Abstracts,* Vol. 17, p. 433-434, February 1957. Available on microfilm from University Microfilms, Ann Arbor, Michigan, as Publication No. 19,572.

4426. MERIDETH, DOROTHY McCLURE. *Social Origins of the Humanist Educational System in Renaissance Italy.* University of Minnesota, 1948. 271 p. ms.

4427. MONICA, Sister MARY, 1892- . *The Teaching Idea of Angela Merici, 1474-1540.* University of Notre Dame, 1926. Published as *Angela Merici and Her Teaching Idea, 1474-1540.* New York: Longmans Green & Co., 1927. xvii, 429 p. With introduction by Most Rev. J. F. Regis Canevin.

4428. NELSON, Brother JOEL STANISLAUS. *The "De Liberorum Educatione" of Aeneas Silvius Piccolomini: A Translation with an Introduction.* Catholic University of America, 1940. Washington: Catholic University of America Press, 1940. xi, 231 p.

4429. O'REILLY, CHARLES TERRANCE. *Race Prejudice among Catholic College Students in the United States and Italy: A Comparative Study of the Role of Religion and Personality in Inter-Group Relations.* University of Notre Dame, 1954. 236 p. ms. Abstract in *Dissertation Abstracts,* Vol. 16, p. 1008, May 1956. Available on microfilm from University Microfilms, Ann Arbor, Michigan, as Publication No. 15,676.

4430. ROEDER, WILLIAM SAMUEL. *Roman Civic Education as Revealed in the Literature of the "Golden Age" (70 B.C. - 25 A.D.)* New York University, 1933. 241 p. ms.

4431. ROSSI, MARGUERITE AIMEE, 1892- . *How Fascista Italy Educates Her Youth: A Study of Italian Thought on the Education of Italians.* Stanford University, 1941. 420 p. ms. Abstract in Stanford University: *Abstracts of Dissertations . . . 1940-41,* p. 50-52.

4432. RYAN, Rev. J. JOSEPH, 1915- . *An Operative Account of Christian Education from the Papal Encyclicals of the Past Century.* Fordham University, 1952. 207 p. ms.

4433. SANTAYANA, SILVIO GEORGE, 1899- . *Two Renaissance Educators: Alberti and Piccolomini.* New York University, 1928. Boston: Meador Publishing Co., 1930. 125 p.

4434. SANTI, EMANUELE. *Liberal Religious Education in a Protestant Orphanage in Italy: A Discussion of Suggested Improvements in Religious Education at Casa Materna, Portici, Italy.* Columbia University, 1939. 76 p. ms.

4435. STARR, JAMES MARION, 1913- . *The Educational Philosophy and Method of Marcus Fabius Quintilian.* University of Washington, 1952. 250 p. ms.

4436. STEIN, HENRY FREDERICK ANDREW. *Quintilian's System of Rhetoric and Tribute to Caesar.* New York University, 1914.

4437. SULLIVAN, Sister ANNE STANISLAUS. *Maphei Vegii Laudensis de Educatione Liberorum et eorum Claris Moribus, Libri Sex: A Critical Text of Books IV-VI.* Catholic University of America, 1937. Washington: Catholic University of America, 1936. xxxii, 129-249. (Studies in Medieval and Renaissance Latin, Vol. 1. Text is paged in continuation of the text of Books I-III, edited by Sister Maria Walburg Fanning as a doctoral dissertation in 1933. See No. 4414.)

4438. TARCHER, MARTIN, 1921- . *The Italian Institute for Community Centers — A Social Experiment in Italy.* Columbia University, 1958. 242 p. ms. (Social foundations of education.)

4439. THOMPSON, MERRITT MOORE, 1884- . *The Educational Philosophy of Giovanni Gentile.* University of Southern California, 1930. Los Angeles: University of Southern California Press, 1934. ix, 217 p. (Southern California Educational Monographs . . . 1933-34 Series, No. 1.) For master's thesis by same author, see No. 4944.

4440. ZANFAGNA, Sister MARY LAURENTANA. *Educational Theories and Principles of Cardinal Silvio Antoniano.* Catholic University of America, 1940. Washington: Catholic University of America Press, 1940. viii, 134 p.

See also Nos. 119, 125, 129, 138, 142, 145, 147, 152, 153, 156, 157, 158, 163, 165, 172, 174, 175, 184, 1418, 2327, 3002, 3015, 3068, 3069, 3070, 3071, 3072, 3074, 3075, 3076, 3080, 3082, 3083, 3089, 3092, 3094, 3098, 3100, 3101, 3102, 3105, 3106, 3109, 3116, 3118, 3119, 3121, 3124, 3127, 3128, 3130.

MASTERS

4441. ARGY, Mother MARY PASCAL, 1930- . *The Ursuline Plan of Education Viewed in the Light of the Writings of Pope Pius XII.* Boston College, 1952. 76 p. ms.

4442. AVALLONE, Rev. PAUL PETER, 1921- . *Don Bosco and His Preventive Technique in Education.* St. John's University, 1956. 95 p. ms. Abstract in St.

John's University: *Abstracts of Dissertations, 1953-56*, p. 151-152.

4443. AYERS, DONALD MURRAY. *Contemporary Roman Criticism of Rhetorical Education in the First Century, A. D.* Stanford University, 1947. 97 p. ms.

4444. BALLETTA, AURORA JOSEPHINE. *Leon Battista Alberti and His Concept of Education.* Columbia University, 1939. 67 p. ms.

4445. BARKLEY, DAVID WRIGHT. *The Concept of History in the Philosophy of Benedetto Croce.* University of Southern California, 1934. 146 p. ms.

4446. BECK, Sister MARY HILARY. *Saint Albert, the Great Science Teacher.* University of Houston, 1946. 121 p. ms.

4447. BISSEN, Rev. PETER ALOYSIUS. *The Roman Rhetorical School.* Catholic University of America, 1927. 55 p. ms.

4448. BITTENZ, FRANCIS ALOYSIUS, 1909- . *A Discussion of the Influence of Cusa and Copernicus on the Pantheistic Teaching of Giordano Bruno.* St. Louis University, 1933. 41 p. ms.

4449. BLOXOM, BLANCHE. *The Status of the Doctor and the Lawyer in Rome.* University of Colorado, 1937. 149 p. ms. Abstract in *University of Colorado Studies*, Vol. 25, No. 1, p. 40-41, November 1937. (Includes consideration of their educational preparation.)

4450. BOURLAND, MINNIE LEIGH. *Quintilian as a Modern Teacher.* University of Washington, 1933. 139 p. ms.

4451. BRUEWER, Sister MARY BERTRAND. *Don John Bosco's Philosophy of Education.* University of Cincinnati, 1944. 74 p. ms.

4452. BRUNO, LOUISE ELIZABETH. *A Comparison of Elementary School Organization in Italy and the United States.* New York University, 1930. 46 p. ms.

4453. BUCKLEY, ARTHUR ROBERT, 1919- . *An Analysis of Roman Educational Theory and Practice Based on the "Institutio Oratorio" of M. Fabius Quintilianus.* Boston University, 1934. 57 p. ms.

4454. BUONGIORNO, ROSE. *New Ideals and Practices in the Public Instruction of Modern Italy.* New York University, 1930. 83 p. ms.

4455. BURKE, MARGARET LORETTA, 1913- . *Don Bosco, Originator of the Youth Guidance Movement.* Boston College, 1952. 82 p. ms.

4456. CANNON, Rev. EDMUND JOSEPH. *The Educational Influence of Boethius in the Middle Ages.* Catholic University of America, 1925. 30 p. ms.

4457. CARLESI, NICHOLAS P., 1918- . *Don Bosco, Great Christian Educator.* University of Scranton, 1954. 85 p. ms.

4458. CASEY, Sister MARY ROSE ELLEN. *A Study of the Educational Principles Contained in the Encyclicals of Pope Leo XIII.* Creighton University, 1952. 101 p. ms.

4459. CASSIDY, Rev. THOMAS VINCENT. *Quintilian — Roman Educator.* Catholic University of America, 1923. 37 p. ms.

4460. CESARIO, Sister CARMELA, 1901- . *St. John Bosco's Application of the Preventative Method to Character Education.* Fordham University, 1935. 73 p. ms. Abstract in Fordham University: *Dissertations Accepted for Higher Degrees . . .* 1936, p. 41-42.

4461. CHIODO, THERESA M. *A Brief History of Early Italian Education.* Niagara University, 1950. 67 p. ms.

4462. COHEN, JOSEPH. *Dynamic Sociology and Social Education, with Special Reference to the Works of Lester F. Ward and Savario de Dominicis.* New York University, 1912. 79 p. ms.

4463. COSTA-MINNECI DI VILLAREAL, JOYCE. *Methods and Materials of the Montessori System: An Interpretation.* American University, 1957. 72 p. ms. For doctoral dissertation by same author, see No. 4409.

4464. CRADDOCK, ELIZABETH CODA. *Educational Theories and Ideals of Cicero.* George Peabody College for Teachers, 1936. 66 p. ms.

4465. DAMON, JOSEPH K. *The Youth Movement in Italy.* College of the City of New York, 1934. 29 p. ms. Abstract in College of the City of New York: *Abstracts of Theses . . . 1923-1939*, p. 74.

4466. DE CHELLO, Sister MARY RITA. *A Translation of Book One "Dell' Educatione Christiana Dei Figliuoli" by Silvio Antoniano, from Sixteenth Century Italian.* St. John College of Cleveland, 1954. 163 p. ms.

4467. DESMOND, JOHN T. *The Educational Contents and Implications of the Institutiones of Cassiodorus.* Catholic University of America, 1956. Abstract in *Catholic Educational Review*, Vol. 55, p. 121, February 1957.

4468. DONOVAN, EGBERT H. *The Educational Implications in the Rule of Saint Benedict.* Catholic University of America, 1946. 82 p. ms.

4469. DRISKILL, RUTH ALICE. *Progressive Educational Ideals: Lectures and Demonstrations by Marcus Fabius Quintilianus.* George Peabody College for Teachers, 1932. 61 p. ms.

4470. DRURY, HARRY PATRICK. *Vittorino da Feltre, the Man and his Teaching.* University of California, Los Angeles, 1955. 68 p. ms.

4471. DUDINE, Rev. CHARLES. *Educational Psychology and the Rule of St. Benedict: A Comparative Study.* University of Notre Dame, 1929. 63 p. ms.

4472. ELLISON, LOUISE. *A Study of Maria Montessori's Theory of Discipline through an Examination of Her Principles and Practices and an Experiment with Pre-School Children.* Tufts University, 1957. 378 p. ms.

4473. FARRELL, Sister ROSE ANGELA, 1907- . *Benedictine Influence on Modern Education.* Immaculate Heart College, 1953. 120 p. ms.

Italy

4474. FARRINGTON, FREDERIC ERNEST, 1872-1930. *Cicero's Educational Ideals.* Columbia University, 1902. 20 p. ms. For doctoral dissertation by same author, see No. 3382.

4475. FAY, THOMAS PATRICK. *Don Bosco: His Contribution to Boys Work.* University of Notre Dame, 1933. 50 p. ms.

4476. FINNAN, *Mother* MARY ROSE, 1895- . *St. Angela and the Objectives of Ursuline Education.* Fordham University, 1943. 98 p. ms.

4477. FLEMING, WILLIAM J. *A Critical Analysis of Principles of Democratic Administration Found in the Writings of Pope Leo XIII.* Catholic University of America, 1958.

4478. FOWLER, *Mrs.* FRANCESCA SAVINI. *Intellectual Activities of Perugia in the Thirteenth and Fourteenth Centuries.* Columbia University, 1930. 49 p. ms.

4479. FOX, JOHN THOMAS, 1925- . *Remedial Reading: An Adaptation of the Montessori Method.* Illinois State Normal University, 1951. 31 p. ms. Abstract in Illinois State Normal University: *Abstracts of Theses,* June 1951–August 1951, p. 24.

4480. FRABBITO, PAUL FRANCIS. *A Critical Evaluation of Madame Montessori's Pedagogy.* New York University, 1917. 81 p. ms.

4481. GENOVA, VINCENT OCTAVUS. *The Catholic University of the Sacred Heart at Milan.* Catholic University of America, 1928. 57 p. ms.

4482. GIRARD, *Sister* MARY MARSILE. *Contributions Made by America from 1930 to 1950 Toward Development of the Concept of Christian Education as Outlined and Decreed by Pope Pius XI in "Christian Education of Youth."* Catholic University of America, 1955. 115 p. ms. Abstract in *Catholic Educational Review,* Vol. 55, p. 49, January 1957.

4483. GLASS, MARCUS ROBERT. *Arts and Medicine at the University of Bologna 1370-1513: With Charts of the Faculty Based on the "Rotuli" of Umberto Dallari.* Columbia University, 1930. 55 p. ms.

4484. GLYNN, *Sister* MARY VERA, 1908- . *Don Bosco: Modern Educator.* Immaculate Heart College, 1953. 66 p. ms.

4485. GOOZEE, EFFIE SHERWOOD. (Later, Mrs. Edward Everett Martin.) *Roman Education under the Early Empire.* Boston University, 1923. 29 p. ms.

4486. GORMAN, *Rev.* NICHOLAS. *The Educational Philosophy of Mario Casotti.* Catholic University of America, 1958.

4487. GUILD, *Sister* MARY FRANCINE. *A Comparison and Evaluation of the Educational Treatises of Vergerio and Sadoleto.* St. Louis University, 1930. 67 p. ms.

4488. GRAY, DOROTHY. *Cicero's Ideas Concerning Education.* Butler University, 1937. 18 p. ms.

4489. GRAZIANI, GUIDO. *Physical Education under the Fascist Regime.* International YMCA College, 1931. 110 p. ms.

4490. GREINER, *Rev.* WILFRED EDWARD. *The Ascetism of St. Francis as an Educational Motive.* Catholic University of America, 1927. 31 p. ms.

4491. GRILLO, FRANK CHARLES, 1929- . *Secondary Education in Italy.* Boston University, 1933. 92 p. ms.

4492. HALL, JOSEPH S. *The Influence of Early Christian Philosophy upon the Educational System of Rome.* University of Tennessee, 1957. 88 p. ms.

4493. HAMAN, *Sister* MARY HARRIET. *Implications for Education in the Encyclical Writings of Pope Leo XIII.* Catholic University of America, 1958.

4494. HASKINS, FLEETA HUDSON. *The Mathematical Aspects of Early Roman Geography.* George Peabody College for Teachers, 1939. 70 p. ms.

4495. HEALY, *Sister* EDWARD EMMANUEL. *Vittorino De Feltre, a Great Christian Humanist Teacher.* Villanova University, 1954. 65 p. ms.

4496. HEH, GERALDINE PERPETUA, 1911- . (*Sister* Mary Maurice) *A Comparative Study of the Preventative System of Education of St. John Bosco and of the Educational Opportunities Afforded Dependent Girls in the Convent of Mercy Home.* St. John's University, 1947. 78 p. ms. Abstract in St. John's University: *Abstracts of Dissertations, 1946-1948,* p. 30.

4497. HOGAN, EDWARD WILLIAM. *The Training for Citizenship in Ancient Rome.* Catholic University of America, 1921. 31 p. ms.

4498. HOLBROOK, SARA VAN VLECK. *The New Education in Italy: A Social Study.* New York University, 1938. 33 p. ms.

4499. HOYO, PEARL. *Comparative Study of the Views of Maria Montessori and Susan E. Blow on the Training of Children.* Catholic University of America, 1944. 70 p. ms.

4500. HUBER, *Sister* MARY ADRIA. *Correlation of the Pronouncements of Pius XII and the Aims of Education in Guiding Growth in Christian Social Living.* St. John College of Cleveland, 1953. 70 p. ms.

4501. JACKSON, MYRA BARRY. *Roman Books and Libraries.* George Peabody College for Teachers, 1940. 66 p. ms.

4502. JONATA, *Sister* CATERINA. *L'Educazione nel Concetto di Machiavelli.* Columbia University, 1935. 23 p. ms.

4503. KAROBLIS, *Rev.* ANDREW K. *An Analysis of the Encyclical Letters of the Last Five Popes in Reference to Seminary Training.* Catholic University of America, 1958.

4504. KEANE, HELEN. *Study and Practice in Quintilian's Theory of Oratorical Training.* Cornell University, 1925. 71 p. ms.

4505. KENNY, JOHN P. *Education in the Encyclicals and Allocutions of the Last Four Popes.* Catholic University of America, 1940. 56 p. ms.

4506. KINNEY, MARIE A. *Philosophy of Education Deduced from Selected Writings of Saint Bonaventure.* De Paul University, 1953.

4507. KIRBY, Mother COLUMBA. *The Educational Viewpoints of Marie de St. Jean Martin Regarding Preparation for Christian Marriage and Motherhood.* Catholic University of America, 1954. 107 p. ms.

4508. KIRKPATRICK, WILLIAM. *Catholic Education and Fascism in Italy.* State University of Iowa, 1942. 81 p. ms.

4509. LANCIONE, ANTONIO M. *Educational Structure of Italy after the Advent of Mussolini.* University of Buffalo, 1948. 116 p. ms.

4510. LAWLER, Sister MARY IMELDIS. *The Contribution of St. Francis of Assizi to Religious Education.* Catholic University of America, 1944. 73 p. ms.

4511. LENHART, Sister MARY ST. MICHAEL. *Saint Charles Borromeo as an Educator.* Catholic Sisters College of the Catholic University of America, 1916. 32 p. ms.

4512. LEWIS, LOUISE BRUNN. *A Comparative Study of Fascism and the Italian Schools.* New York University, 1940. 64 p. ms.

4513. LUKER, HELEN G., 1898- . *Roman Education and Its Influence on Christianity.* Marquette University, 1940. 130 p. ms.

4514. LYNN, Rev. JOHN FINBAR. *The Philosophy of Education of Giovanni Gentile.* Fordham University, 1942. 62 p. ms.

4515. McAULLIFFE, JOHN OLIVER. *The Influence of Fascism on Italian Education.* Catholic University of America, 1935. 58 p. ms.

4516. McCANTS, Sister MARY DOROTHEA. *The Educational Contents of Books One to Six of the "De Educatione Liberorum" of Maffeo Vegio.* Catholic University of America, 1941. 179 p. ms.

4517. McCORMICK, PATRICK JOSEPH, 1880-1953. *Vittorino da Feltre and Guarino da Verona: An Educational Study of the Fifteenth Century.* Catholic University of America, 1906. 76 p. ms. For doctoral dissertation by same author, see No. 3106.

4518. McGOVERN, DOROTHY ANN. *Changes Effected by the Allied Occupation on the Italian Educational System.* De Paul University, 1955. 70 p. ms.

4519. McGRATH, Mother MARY MECHTILDE. *English-Speaking National Colleges in Rome.* Villanova College, 1946. 135 p. ms.

4520. McKENNA, Rev. BERNARD ALOYSIUS. *Cassiodorus: An Educational Study of the Sixth Century.* Catholic University of America, 1905. 51 p. ms.

4521. McLERAN, RUTH LOUISE. *An Analysis of the "Divinatio in Caecilium" of Cicero with Respect to Its Pedagogical Value.* State University of Iowa, 1941. 35 p. ms.

4522. MARKHAM, LEONORA C., 1903- . (Sister Regina Catherine). *St. John Bosco: Ideal Christian Teacher and Counselor of Orphans.* St. John's University, 1948. 62 p. ms. Abstract in St. John's University: *Abstracts of Dissertations, 1946-1948*, p. 31.

4523. MARRARO, HOWARD R. *Contemporary Italian Educational Ideals.* Columbia University, 1925. 275 p. ms.

4524. MASON, Sister MARY PAUL. *A Synthesis of the Rights of the Family in the Education of the Child as Defined by the Last Five Popes in Their Encyclicals and Allocations.* Catholic University of America, 1950. 71 p. ms. Abstract in *Catholic Educational Review*, Vol. 49, p. 123, February 1951.

4525. MILMOE, MARY F. *Saint John Bosco: Exponent of Character Education.* St. John's University, 1942. Abstract in St. John's University: *Abstracts of Dissertations, 1942-1945*, p. 42.

4526. MORELLI, CARRIE A. *Secondary Education in Italy.* Hunter College of the City of New York, 1934. 74 p. ms.

4527. MURDOCK, MARION LIPPITT. *Professional and Vocational Education in the Roman Empire.* Columbia University, 1944. 109 p. ms.

4528. MURPHY, Sister MARY JUDITH. *Benedictine Principles of Education Applied in Secondary Schools.* De Paul University, 1953. 151 p. ms.

4529. MUSELLA, GEMMA. *The Gentile Elementary School Reform and Its Subsequent Modifications.* Columbia University, 1938. 83 p. ms.

4530. NOVELLI, FRANK. *A Comparative Study of the Educational Systems in Italy and in the United States.* University of Cincinnati, 1935. 133 p. ms.

4531. NUGENT, JAMES IRVINE. *The Educational Principles of Pope Pius XII.* Catholic University of America, 1957. 188 p. ms.

4532. NUXOLL, Sister MARY ILDEPHONSE. *"Monte Cassino": Its Influence on Education.* University of Idaho, 1947. 120 p. ms.

4533. O'HERN, EDWARD PHILIP. *The Montessori Method: Its Value for Teaching Religion and Morals in the Catholic School.* Catholic University of America, 1927. 76 p. ms.

4534. O'NEIL, JOHN F. *C. E. Craig's Adaptation of the Montessori Methods at the Rhode Island College of Education.* Catholic University of America, 1937. 39 p. ms.

4535. Error. Omit.

4536. PAOLINO, VIRGIL AMERICO. *The Philosophy of Actual Idealism in the Italian Educational Life.* University of Southern California, 1942. 80 p. ms.

4537. PARDI, CAROLINE FLORIANA. *Pietro Bachi, the First Italian to Teach His Native Tongue at Harvard University.* Columbia University, 1947. 35 p. ms.

4538. PAVDA, Sister MARY JOSEPH. *Social Teachings as Contained in Papal Documents as a Guide for Catholic Social Studies.* St. John College of Cleveland, 1953. 153 p. ms.

4539. REICHMANN, LILLY DOERFLER, 1919- . *Public Education in Italy: Elementary and Secondary Education.* Cornell University, 1958. 108 p. ms.

4540. REID, ARTHUR WAUCHAP. *Roman Education as Seen in Pliny's Letters.* Indiana University, 1933. 63 p. ms.

4541. REO, CLOTHILDE ELIZABETH, 1917- . *Analysis of the Encyclical of Pope Pius XI on the "Christian Education of Youth," and Subsequent Catholic Educational Thought in the United States.* Smith College, 1941. 90 p. ms.

4542. RICHARDSON, MARY FAISON. *The Relationship of the Montessori Method of Pre-School Education to Current Nursery School Theory and Practice in America.* Vassar College, 1940. 68, 37 p. ms.

4543. RICHMOND, SIDNEY ALBERT, 1902- . *Educational Provisions in the Canon Law from the Earliest Times to 1484.* University of California, Berkeley, 1928. 206 p. ms.

4544. ROEBROCKS, PETER JOSEPH, 1909- . *Giovanni Gentile: A Critical Analysis of His Actual Idealism and His Educational Philosophy.* St. Louis University, 1936. 137 p. ms.

4545. RONIGER, Mother STELLA MARIS, 1887- . *Contributions of the Missionary Sisters of the Sacred Heart to Education in Italy and the United States.* Fordham University, 1938. 77 p. ms. Abstract in Fordham University: *Dissertations Accepted for Higher Degrees . . . 1939,* p. 68.

4546. ROQUE, WARREN PAUL. *Quintilian — Ancient and Modern Educator.* Brown University, 1956. 61 p. ms.

4547. ROSEMAN, NORMAN. *The Education of Charles V.* Columbia University, 1951. 55 p. ms.

4548. ROSS, NANNIE FAE. *Quintilian's Principles and Practices of Education Compared with Modern Views.* George Peabody College for Teachers, 1930. 81 p. ms.

4549. RYAN, Rev. THOMAS ANTHONY, 1904- . *The Tridentine Seminary, an Institution Exclusively for the Training of Men for the Roman Catholic Priesthood: Its Antecedents and Its Immediate Origin in the Sixteenth Century.* Fordham University, 1940. 71 p. ms.

4550. SCHUMACHER, Sister MARY IRMA. *The Attitude of Augustus Toward Social Life, Education, and Religion.* Catholic Sisters College of the Catholic University of America, 1916. 56 p. ms.

4551. SERRANO, Rev. JOHN T. *The Concept of Authority in Papal Encyclicals and Its Implications for Education.* Catholic University of America, 1953. 150 p. ms. Abstract in *Catholic Educational Review,* Vol. 53, p. 335-336, May 1955.

4552. SHEALY, KUMA, 1889- . *Roman Education as Revealed in the Satirical Writings of Horace and Juvenal.* Louisiana State University and State Agricultural and Mechanical College, 1939. 167 p. ms. Abstract in *Louisiana State University Bulletin,* Vol. 32, n.s., No. 1, p. 117, January 1940.

4553. SHERRY, Sister MARY EUSTOLIA. *Cicero, the Educator.* New York State College for Teachers, Albany, 1921. 89 p. ms.

4554. SMITH, JEAN LOUISE. *The Decorations of the Sistine Chapel as Illustrative Material in Religious Education.* University of Chicago, 1936. 82 p. ms.

4555. SPEAR, WILTON DAY, 1902- . *A Comparison of the Work of Vittorino da Feltre and the Principles of the Progressive School of Today.* Cornell University, 1936. 91 p. ms.

4556. SPEICHER, Rev. NORMAN FRANCIS. *Sadoleto on the Education of Boys.* Catholic University of America, 1930. 48 p. ms.

4557. SPICER, EVA ADALINE. *The Attitude of the Romans toward Children.* Syracuse University, 1920.

4558. STRUB, Rev. HERMAN. *Some Changes in College Religious Texts Necessitated by the Papal Encyclicals, "Mystici Corporis," and "Mediator Dei."* Catholic University of America, 1950. 69 p. ms.

4559. TARASKA, Sister MARY IRMINA. *The Education of a Prince in the Early Renaissance.* Catholic University of America, 1941. 69 p. ms. (Reports education in Mantuan Court School of Vittorino da Feltre and in Court School of Guarino da Verona at Ferrara.)

4560. TIERNEY, Sister MARY CONSTANCE, 1903- . *The Application of Franciscan Ideals to Secondary Education.* Immaculate Heart College, 1956. 195 p. ms.

4561. TINSLEY, ANNA IRENE. *Educational Practice as Found in the Works of Quintilian.* Oklahoma Agricultural and Mechanical College, 1934. 42 p. ms.

4562. TRZEBIATOWSKI, Sister MARY WILHELMINE. *The Educational Principles of Pope Leo XIII.* Catholic University of America, 1943. 66 p. ms.

4563. WALLING, Mrs. LOIS ELAINE (MONOSMITH). *The Influence of Writers upon Roman Education upon the Educational Ideas during the Renaissance.* University of Texas, 1935. 127 p. ms. (Purpose: "To show how far Cicero and Quintilian, through their writings on education, influenced the educational ideas of . . . Desiderius Erasmus, Juan Vives, and John Sturm.")

4564. WALSH, Mother MARY FLORENCE. *Religious Guidance According to Saint Angela Merici.* Catholic University of America, 1944. 66 p. ms.

4565. WARE, Mrs. WENONAH ROACH. *Subject-Matter and Method as Proposed by Certain Leaders of the Italian Renaissance.* University of Texas, 1932. 80 p. ms.

4566. WHITE, RUTH F., 1928- . *Secondary Education in Italy under Fascism.* Wayne State University, 1956. 188 p. ms.

4567. ZANELLI, LOUIS J. *Italian Model Schools.* College of the City of New York, 1931. 42 p. ms. Abstract in College of the City of New York: *Abstracts of Theses . . . 1923-1939*, p. 40.

4568. ZIMPFER, DAVID GEORGE. *Quintilian, the Educator, Ancient and Modern.* University of Buffalo, 1953. 74 p. ms.

See also Nos. 187, 189, 203, 212, 221, 222, 238, 239, 244, 245, 248, 250, 251, 262, 266, 271, 279, 280, 284, 286, 288, 290, 294, 296, 300, 301, 306, 3135, 3137, 3144, 3153, 3154, 3158, 3165, 3167, 3168, 3169, 3173, 3176, 3182, 3184, 3186, 3187, 3196, 3198, 3199, 3202, 3203, 3206, 3208, 3210, 3211, 3212, 3215, 3217, 3220, 3222, 3224, 3225, 3230, 3232, 3233, 3236, 3237, 3240, 3242, 3243, 3247, 3250, 3251, 3252, 3253, 3254, 3255, 3258, 3263, 3264, 3266, 3267, 3269, 3271, 3272, 3273, 3274, 3282, 3284, 3290, 3292, 3295, 3297, 3298, 4324

For Italian groups in the United States, *see* Nos. 5119-5150

Lithuania
(NOS. 4569 – 4571)

DOCTOR

See No. 119

MASTERS

4569. ERINGIS, STEPHEN ANTHONY. *Education as a Cultural Agency in Lithuania.* University of Washington, 1932. 67 p. ms.

4570. KONCEVICIUS, Rev. JOSEPH B. *Education in Lithuania under the Russian Government.* Catholic University of America, 1925. 64 p. ms. Published in installments in *Catholic Educational Review*, as follows: Vol. 24, p. 76-84, February 1926; Vol. 24, p. 163-172, March 1926.

4571. SIMONAITIS, JOSEPH JOHN, 1897- . *The Lithuanian School and Its Service for Good Citizenship.* Fordham University, 1933. 61 p. ms.

See also No. 226, 249

For Lithuanian groups in the United States, *see* Nos. 4985, 4987, 4992, 4993, 5000, 5003, 5020, 5653

Netherlands
(NOS. 4572 – 4589)

DOCTORS

4572. ALTENA, JULIANA ELISABETH VON REGTEREN, 1899- . *A Comparative Study of Education in the Netherlands and the United States of America.* Columbia University, 1947. 600 p. ms.

4573. GINSBURG, HARVEY HILLSON, 1922- . *The Struggle for the Control of Primary Education in the Netherlands, 1848-1917.* Yale University, 1952. 333 p. ms.

4574. HOLTROP, WILLIAM FRANS, 1908- . *The Development and Present Status of Vocational Education in the Netherlands.* University of California, Los Angeles, 1948. 297 p. ms. Published as *Vocational Education in the Netherlands*, Berkeley, California: University of California Press, 1951. vii, 31-158 p. (University of California Publications in Education, Vol. 11, No. 2.) Abstract in *Research in Industrial Education, 1930-1955*, p. 274.

4575. JAARSMA, CORNELIUS RICHARD, 1897- . *The Educational Philosophy of Herman Bavinck: A Textbook in Education.* New York University, 1934. Grand Rapids, Michigan: William B. Erdmams Publishing Co., 1935. 242 p.

4576. KRAMER, KLAAS, 1916- . *A Comparison of Objectives, Methods, and Achievement in Arithmetic in the United States and in the Netherlands.* State University of Iowa, 1957. 376 p. ms. Abstract in *Dissertation Abstracts*, Vol. 17, p. 2881, December 1957. Available on microfilm from University Microfilms, Ann Arbor, Michigan, as Publication No. 23,760. For master's thesis by same author, see No. 4584.

4577. RABENORT, WILLIAM LOUIS, 1870-1938. *Spinoza as Educator.* New York: Teachers College, Columbia University, 1911. vi, 87 p. (Teachers College Contribution to Education, No. 38.)

4578. SHEPPARD, ALBERT. *Erasmus as an Educator.* New York University, 1931. 146 p. ms.

See also Nos. 119, 129, 138, 142, 143, 147, 161, 163, 175, 1418, 3071, 3075, 3076, 3080, 3094, 3095, 3100, 3123, 3125, 3128, 3130, 174a

MASTERS

4579. BULLER, FRANCIS PAUL, 1892- . *Educational Implications of the Theology of Menno Simons.* Yale University, 1923. 108 p. ms.

4580. DEDGE, RENE. *Religious Education among French-Speaking Protestants in the Netherlands up to 1685.* Union Theological Seminary, 1925. 51 p. ms.

4581. DE VETTE, WILLIAM ANTON. *Educational Aspects of the Dutch Craft Gilds.* University of Pittsburgh, 1931. Abstract in University of Pittsburgh: *Abstracts of Theses* ... Vol. 7, 1931, p. 263-264.

4582. FRASER, HUGH GUNN. *Erasmus' Position in Renaissance Education.* University of Pittsburgh, 1929. 63 p. ms.

4583. HORKAN, Rev. VINCENT JOSEPH, 1915- . *The Educational Theories and Principles of Erasmus as Set Forth in His "De Civilitate Morum Puerilium."* Catholic University of America, 1947. 68 p. ms. Abstract in *Catholic Educational Review,* Vol. 46, p. 108, February 1946. For doctoral dissertation by same author, see No. 4420.

4584. KRAMER, KLAAS, 1916- . *A Comparison of the Educational Systems in the United States and in the Netherlands.* Drake University, 1945. 74 p. ms. For doctoral dissertation by same author, see No. 4576.

4585. RANDALL, JULIA DAVENPORT. *Common Sense of Erasmus Applied to Social Education.* University of Chicago, 1913. 62 p. ms.

4586. RANDEN, GRIETJE VAN, 1929- . *Application to the Netherlands of Selected Housing Research in Home Economics Undertaken in the United States.* Cornell University, 1957. 303 p. ms.

4587. VAN ZYL, HENRY, 1883- . *The History of Pensioning of the Elementary Teachers in the Netherlands.* University of Chicago, 1926. 107 p. ms. For doctoral dissertation by same author, see No. 3949.

4588. VERINGA, GERHARD HEINRICH, 1924- . *From General to Special Prevention: The Development of Child Legislation in the Netherlands.* Fordham University, 1947. 71 p. ms.

4589. WARMER, GEORGE ALBERT, 1910- . *Religious Educational Values in Thomas a Kempis' Life and Teachings.* Boston University, 1934. 89 p. ms.

See also Nos. 188, 212, 213, 226, 231, 249, 274, 283, 289, 302, 2388, 3148, 3198, 3210, 3230, 3238, 3292, 3293, 3294, 4563

For Dutch groups in the United States, see Nos. 5092-5094.

Norway

(NOS. 4590 - 4606)

DOCTORS

4590. ANDERSON, DAVID ALLEN, 1874- . *The School System of Norway.* State University of Iowa, 1912. Boston: The Gorham Press, 1913. 232 p. For master's thesis by same author, see No. 4595.

4591. ARENT, EMMA, 1881- . *The Relation of the State to Private Education in Norway: A Study of the Historical Development of State Regulations Governing the Various Types of Private Education in Norway.* Columbia University, 1926. New York: Bureau of Publications, Teachers College, Columbia University, 1926. ix, 94 p. (Teachers College Contribution to Education, No. 235.)

4592. BARTON, ALLEN H. *Sociological and Psychological Problems of Economic Planning in Norway.* Columbia University, 1957. 617 p. ms. Abstract in *Dissertation Abstracts,* Vol. 18, p. 1529-1530, April 1958. Available on microfilm from University Microfilms, Ann Arbor, Michigan, as Mic. 58-1331. (Based on study of the problem at University of Oslo.)

4593. HANSEN, ROBERT EUGENE. *The Democratization of Norwegian Education.* Harvard University, 1952. 236 p. ms.

4594. JENSEN, ARNE SIGURD, 1886- . *The Rural Schools of Norway.* University of Washington, 1927. Boston: The Stratford Co., 1928. 280 p.

See also Nos. 119, 138, 142, 143, 147, 151, 161, 3103, 3126, 3128, 4417, 174a.

MASTERS

4595. ANDERSON, DAVID ALLEN, 1874- . *The School System of Norway: A Preliminary Survey of the Educational Provisions Made for the People of Norway.* State University of Iowa, 1910. 64 p. ms. For doctoral dissertation by same author, see No. 4590.

4596. BERGLUND, RUTH, 1921- . *A Course of Study in "Principles of Education" for Onsrud Mission School.* Pacific Union College, 1950. 186 p. ms.

4597. DORRUM, ELEANOR VALBORG. *A Study of Selected Norwegian Folk Songs with Special Reference to the Adaptation for High School Mixed Chorus.* State University of Iowa, 1942. 62 p. ms.

4598. FJELD, KOLBJORN. *Rural Libraries in Norway.* Columbia University, 1930. 98 p. ms.

4599. HAUG, ARNE. *A Study of the Education of Administrators in Norway and in Southern California.* Claremont Graduate School, 1954. 149 p. ms.

4600. HINDAL, BERTHOLD. *A History of the Y.M.C.A.'s Boy's Work in Norway.* International YMCA College, 1940. 69 p. ms.

4601. JANSEN, TRYGVE DEIRK. *Elementary Teacher Education in Norway: A Descriptive Historical Study.* University of California, Los Angeles, 1957. 147 p. ms.

4602. JENSSEN, HANS. *Building the Book Collection of the Institute of Economics at the University at Oslo.* Columbia University, 1937. 55 p. ms.

4603. KINDEM, INGEBORG ECKHOFF. *A Study of the Practices of Music Teaching in the Secondary Schools of Norway.* University of Southern California, 1949. 172 p. ms.

4604. STAUTLAND, SIGURD. *A Comparative Study of the Selective Recruitment of Elementary School Teachers in the United States and Norway.* College of the Pacific, 1956. 98 p. ms.

4605. THOMAS, MARY ETTA. *A Study of Children in Ibsen's Drama.* George Peabody College for Teachers, 1922. 32 p. ms.

4606. TRONVOLD, HELEN L., 1915- . *A Comparative Study of First Grade Reading in Two Communities, One in Minnesota and One in Norway.* Minnesota State Teachers College, Mankato, 1958. 125 p. ms.

See also Nos. 212, 226, 249, 274, 3142, 3148, 3158, 3164, 3198, 3230, 3292, 3294.

For Norwegian groups in the United States, see Nos. 4957, 4963, 4970, 4971, 4975, 4978, 4985, 4988, 5023, 5025, 5655, 5683.

Poland
(NOS. 4607 – 4623)

DOCTORS

4607. BRONARS, Rev. JOSEPH C., 1925- . *Higher Education in Poland: Some Aspects of Its Sovietization.* Catholic University of America, 1957. 374 p. ms. Washington: Catholic University of America Press, 1957. 13 p. (Abstract). Abstract also in *Catholic Educational Review*, Vol. 55, p. 482-483, October 1957. For master's thesis by same author, see No. 3019.

4608. DROBKA, Rev. FRANK JOSEPH, 1898- . *Education in Poland: Past and Present.* Catholic University of Armerica, 1927. Washington: 1927. viii, 131 p. Published in part as "School Reform in Poland," *Catholic Educational Review*, Vol. 24, p. 284-290, May 1926; and as "Elementary Schools in Poland," *Catholic Educational Review*, Vol. 26, p. 81-87, February 1928.

4609. EISENSTEIN, MIRIAM, 1922- . *Jewish Schools in Poland, 1919-1939: Their Philosophy and Development.* Columbia University, 1948. New York: King's Crown Press, 1950. 112 p.

4610. FURIE, WILLIAM BENJAMIN, 1913- . *A History of Jewish Education in Poland before 1765.* Boston University, 1939. 215 p. ms.

4611. JARACZ, Sister MARY DOLORIA, 1912- . *Group Experiences in Polish Education.* Fordham University, 1949. 101 p. ms.

4612. KAR, ANTHONY LOUIS, 1907- . *The Response of the People to the Use of Formal Education in the Attempted Denationalization of Poland, 1795-1914.* University of Michigan, 1955. 199 p. ms. Abstract in *Dissertation Abstracts*, Vol. 15, p. 1542-1543, October 1955. Available on microfilm from University Microfilms, Ann Arbor, Michigan, as Publication No. 12,597.

4613. Error. Omit.

4614. PRZEDPELSKI, BOLESLAW JOZEF, 1896- . *Agricultural Extension Education in Poland, 1918-1939.* Columbia University, 1948. Published as *A Study of Agricultural Extension Education in Poland between Two World Wars, 1918-1939*, New York: King's Crown Press, 1948. x, 139 p.

4615. WOJCICKI, ANTONI B., 1906- . *Adult Education in Poland during the Nineteenth and Twentieth Centuries.* Columbia University, 1949. Cambridge, Massachusetts: 1951. xiv, 141 p.

See also Nos. 119, 147, 157, 161, 175, 3072, 3076, 3085, 3098.

MASTERS

4616. CZERWINSKI, Brother VICTOR. *Evolution and Status of Education in Poland.* University of Notre Dame, 1933. 88 p. ms.

4617. FODOR, RENEE. *Psychological Observations of the Jewish Family during the German Occupation of Poland.* College of the City of New York, 1955. 106 p. ms.

4618. GRAJEWSKI, HENRY C. *The Founding of the Polish School System, the First Universal Public School Program in Europe.* Marquette University, 1947. 96 p. ms.

4619. HARRIS, PATRICIA. *A Comparison of the Linguistic Formulations of John Dewey and Alfred Korzybski.* Arizona State College, Tempe, 1954. 35 p. ms.

4620. JURCZAK, CHESTER ARTHUR, 1918- . *Age-Sex Categories Related to Youth in Polish Rural Society.* Fordham University, 1948. 99 p. ms.

4621. LITTLETHUN, CLARA CHRISTINE. *Educational Progress and Development in Modern Poland.* University of Southern California, 1928. 52 p. ms.

4622. LOYES, Sister MARY EDMUND. *Preschool Education in Poland.* Catholic University of America, 1934. 66 p. ms.

4623. MARCZYNSKI, Brother RAPHAEL. *Health Education in Poland.* University of Notre Dame, 1936. 119 p. ms.

See also Nos. 187, 226, 230, 249, 3195, 3198, 3216, 3222.

For Polish groups in the United States, see Nos. 5655a-5657.

Portugal
(NOS. 4624 – 4627)

DOCTOR

4624. SHERIDAN, Mrs. LEORA JAMES, 1886- . *The Origin and Development of Secondary Education in Portugal.* University of Pennsylvania, 1940. 274 p. ms. Essential portion published as *Secondary Education in Portugal: Its Origin and Development.* Philadelphia: University of Pennsylvania, 1941. 63 p. For master's thesis by same author, see No. 4626.

See also Nos. 119, 142, 147, 157, 3075, 3116

MASTERS

4625. BETTENCOURT E AVILA, Rev. JOSE MARIA. *Religious Instruction in the Schools of Portugal from 1772 to 1911.* Catholic University of America, 1938. 54 p. ms.

4626. SHERIDAN, Mrs. LEORA JAMES, 1886- . *The Recent Reform in Secondary Education in Portugal.* Claremont Graduate School, 1937. 199 p. ms. For doctoral dissertation by same author, see No. 4624.

4627. STEWART, CHARLES TODD. *The Background of Portuguese Education.* University of Maryland, 1951. 169 p. ms.

See also Nos. 226, 251, 290, 3165, 3199

For Portuguese groups in the United States, see Nos. 4965, 4968, 4975, 4991, 5013, 5658.

Romania
(NOS. 4628 – 4629)

DOCTORS

See Nos. 119, 147, 175, 4364, 4365

MASTERS

4628. COMICESCU, CORNELIA. *A Criticism of Roumanian Elementary Education and Some Remedies Through an American Influence.* Columbia University, 1934. 39 p. ms.

4629. COMICESCU, GHEORGHE. *Some American Educational Practices Available for the Actual System of Education in Roumania.* Columbia University, 1934. 41 p. ms.

See also Nos. 226, 249

For Romanian groups in the United States, see Nos. 4956, 4963, 4970, 4975.

Spain
(NOS. 4630 – 4661)

DOCTORS

4630. BAXTER, EDWARD JOACHIM. *The Educational Thought of Juan Luis Vives.* Harvard University, 1943. 471 p. ms. Abstract in Harvard University: *Summaries of Ph.D. Theses,* 1943-1945, p. 164-168.

4631. DALY, Rev. WALTER ALOYSIUS, 1883- . *The Educational Psychology of Juán Luis Vives.* Catholic University of America, 1924. Washington: 1924. 71 p.

4632. MARTEL, JOSE. *Ferrer's Experimental School as a Symbol of Modern Progressive Educational Development.* New York University, 1933. 281 p. ms.

4633. MECREDY, MARY FLORENCE. *The Socio-Educational Significance of the Revival of Interest in Juan Luis Vives.* University of Southern California, 1942. 310 p. ms. Abstract in University of Southern California: *Abstracts of Dissertations,* 1942, p. 30-33.

4634. PERZ, JOHN RAYMOND, 1896- . *Secondary Education in Spain.* Catholic University of America, 1935. Washington: The Catholic University of America, 1934. xii, 179 p.

4635. STEELE, CHARLES WILLIAM. *The Literary Expression of Educational Attitudes and Ideas in the Novels of Perez Galdos.* Ohio State University, 1957. 257 p. ms. Abstract in *Dissertation Abstracts,* Vol. 18, p. 2150, June 1958. Available on microfilm from University Microfilms, Ann Arbor, Michigan, as Mic. 58-2110.

See also Nos. 119, 142, 147, 157, 161, 175, 180, 904, 3071, 3075, 3076, 3078, 3100, 3106, 3116, 4417, 162a

MASTERS

4636. BARRETT, JOHN GERALD, 1915- . *Juan Luis Vives' Views on Education for Social Effectiveness.* Boston College, 1938. 47 p. ms.

4637. BENABARRE, Rev. BENIGNO. *Adequacy of Preparatory Function of Spanish Academic Secondary School.* Catholic University of America, 1950. 76 p. ms.

4638. CARMODY, NORA, 1887- . *The Social Motive in the Educational Theories of Juan Luis Vives.* St. Louis University, 1931. 71 p. ms.

4639. DORCAS, HERBERT CLIFFORD. *Juan Luis Vives as an Educator.* Columbia University, 1903. 110 p. ms.

4640. EMPEY, LOUENA JEANETTE. *Spanish Folk Music as Source Material for Religious Education.* University of Chicago, 1931. 119 p. ms.

4641. GARCIA, Rev. DOLSE A., 1900- . *Don Andres Manjon — Educator, 1846–1923.* Catholic University of America, 1934. 63 p. ms.

4642. HINE, MARIE. *A Study in the History of Spanish Education to 1900: Based upon a Translation of "The History of Spanish Pedagogy," by Eugenio Garcia y Barbarin.* University of Washington, 1940. 267 p. ms. Abstract in *University of Washington: Abstracts of Theses,* Vol. 6, 1942, p. 58-59.

4643. JACKSON, GABRIEL. *The Problems of Land Reform, the Church, and Education in Republican Spain, 1931-1933.* Stanford University, 1950. 122 p. ms.

4644. KIMBALL, LILIAN EMMA. *La Educacion de la Mujer Segun Juan Luis Vives y Fray Luis de Leon.* Columbia, 1920.

4645. KUSTOFF, ABRAHAM PHILIP, 1913- . *Elementary Education in the Spanish Republic.* George Washington University, 1936. 107 p. ms.

4646. McELROY, AMANDA P., 1886- . *A Study of Unamuno's Philosophy of Life.* Temple University, 1927. 45 p. ms.

4647. MOSKOWITZ, LOUIS. *Current Tendencies in Education in the Primary Schools of Madrid, 1933-1934.* College of the City of New York, 1935. 117 p. ms.

Abstract in College of the City of New York: *Abstracts of Dissertations . . . 1923-1939,* p. 89.

4648. NEWMAN, BERNARD. *The Changes in Spanish Primary Education under the New Republic.* College of the City of New York, 1936. 57 p. ms. Abstract in College of the City of New York: *Abstracts of Theses . . . 1923-1939,* p. 94.

4649. NIEHOFF, Sister MARGUERITE ANN. *The Educational Theories and Principles of Juan Luis Vives as Presented in His "De Ratione Studii Puerilis" (for the Girl and for the Boy.)* Catholic University of America, 1948. 54 p. ms. Abstract in *Catholic Educational Review,* Vol. 47, p. 544, October 1949.

4650. NUSBAUM, AGNES STRICKLAND. *El Castellano como un Medio de Cultura.* Colorado State Teachers College, 1924. 148 p. ms. (Discusses influence of Spanish culture on America education.)

4651. ORTINEZ, Rev. JAMES. *A Comparison between St. Joseph Calasanctius and John Dewey.* Immaculate Heart College, 1958.

4652. POUSSON, Sister ROSE OF LIMA. *The Principles of Moral Education of Ramon Ruiz Amado de Contreras.* Catholic University of America, 1947. Abstract in *Catholic Educational Review,* Vol. 46, p. 171-172, March 1948.

4653. RAMIREZ, MARIA del CARMEN. *A Critical Evaluation of Jose Ortega y Gasset's Philosophy of Education.* Catholic University of America, 1955. 84 p. ms. Abstract in *Catholic Educational Review,* Vol. 54, p. 552, November 1956.

4654. REED, ANNIE MARTHA. *The Educational Ideas of Galdos.* Columbia University, 1922. 42 p. ms.

4655. REINEMUND, GRETCHEN. *The Literature, Art, and Education in Spain as Seen by Jose Ortega y Gasset.* Stanford University, 1939. 144 p. ms.

4656. ROTHSTEIN, BLANCHE. *Francisco Giner de Los Rios: His Educational Ideals and Contributions.* College of the City of New York, 1936. 57 p. ms. Abstract in College of the City of New York: *Abstracts of Theses . . . 1923-1939,* p. 95.

4657. SANCHES, Brother EVERGISTO BAZACO. *The School in Spain.* Catholic University of America, 1926. 40 p. ms.

4658. SCHEWEL, HENRY H. *Miguel de Cervantes Laovedra: A Study of the Student and Education in the "Nouvelas Ej Emplares" and "Don Quixote."* Columbia University, 1950. 121 p. ms.

4659. SCIARILLO, LEWIS PATRICK. *Luis Vives: A Study Tracing the Similarities between His Methods and Modern Methods.* Gonzaga University, 1957. 95 p. ms.

4660. SULLIVAN, VERA FAYE. *El Ideal de Gregorio Martinez Sierra Acerca de la Mujer Espanola.* Colorado State Teachers College, 1922. 76 p. ms.

4661. WALRATH, PHILIP LEON. *Francisco Ferrer as an Educator.* New York University, 1919. 25 p. ms.

See also Nos. 188, 204, 207, 212, 226, 230, 250, 251, 274, 288, 290, 3162, 3165, 3196, 3199, 3222, 3236, 3253, 3260, 3292, 3298, 4241, 4547, 4563.

For Spanish groups in the United States, *see* Nos. 5013, 5417, 5547, 5592.

Sweden

(NOS. 4662 – 4685)

DOCTORS

4662. BOGOSLOVSKY, Mrs. CHRISTINA MARIA ELIZABETH STAEL VON HOLSTEIN, 1888- . *The Educational Crisis in Sweden in the Light of American Experience.* Columbia University, 1932. New York: Columbia University Press, 1932. xiv, 301 p.

4663. BORGESON, FRITHIOF CAROL, 1899- . *Administration of the Elementary and Secondary Education in Sweden.* Columbia University, 1927. New York: Teachers College, Columbia University, 1927. viii, 231 p. (Teachers College Contribution to Education, No. 278.)

4664. BROTEN, GEORGE ARTHUR. *An Exploration of Swedish Physical Education.* University of Southern California, 1957.

4665. FAWCETT, KATHLEEN, 1921- . *A Study of Publicly Supported Summer Educational Services for Children in Sweden.* New York University, 1954. 2 vols. 294 p. ms. Abstract in *Dissertation Abstracts,* Vol. 14, p. 1639-1640, October 1954. Available on microfilm from University Microfilms, Ann Arbor, Michigan, as Publication No. 9,305.

4666. KILANDER, HOLGER FREDERICK, 1900- . *Science Education in the Secondary Schools of Sweden: A Comparative Study of Sweden and the United States.* Columbia University, 1931. New York: Teachers College, Columbia University, 1931. vi, 166 p. (Teachers College Contribution to Education, No. 463.)

4667. OSTERGREN, DAVID LAWRENCE, 1897- . *The Folk High Schools of Sweden.* Columbia University, 1952. 168 p. ms. Abstract in *Dissertation Abstracts,* Vol. 13, No. 1, p. 55-56, 1953. Available on microfilm from University Microfilms, Ann Arbor, Michigan, as Publication No. 4,587.

4668. PETERSON, AXEL GEORGE, 1898- . *The Training of Elementary and Secondary Teachers in Sweden.* Columbia University, 1933. New York: Teachers College, Columbia University, 1934. vi, 110 p. (Teachers College Contribution to Education, No. 575.)

4669. REHNSTROM, AUGUST EDWIN ARTHUR, 1895- . *An Interpretation of the Histroy of Religious Education in Sweden.* Boston University, 1945. 336 p. ms. Abstract in Council on Graduate Studies in Religion: *Doctoral Dissertations in the Field of Religion, 1940-1952,* p. 132-133.

4670. TEGNER, OLAF HERMAN, 1918- . *Adult Education in Sweden: Its Administration and Organization, with Implications for Adult Education in California.* University of Southern California, 1958, 311 p. ms.

4671. WESTERBERG, IWAR SIGURD. *The School System of Sweden.* University of Washington, 1923. 184 p. ms.

See also Nos. 119, 138, 143, 147, 151, 161, 3076, 3103, 3126, 3128, 4417, 174a.

MASTERS

4672. BROWN, EBBA CORNELIA JOHNSON. *Educational System of Sweden.* Stanford University, 1941. 122 p. ms.

4673. CARLSON, JOEL SEBASTIAN. *The People's High School Movement in Sweden.* Brown University, 1934. 45 p. ms.

4674. ENGBERG, GRETA. *A Comparison of Elementary Education in the United States and Sweden, with Suggested Application of Principles and Practices of American Education to Swedish Schools.* University of California, Los Angeles, 1950. 93 p. ms.

4675. ENGLEBREKTSON, SUME, 1923- . *Sloyd: The Foundation of Industrial Arts Education.* New York University, 1949. 119 p. ms. Abstract in *Research in Industrial Education, 1930-1955,* p. 473.

4676. GODDARD, ISAAC, 1878- . *Gustaf Larsson, and the Sloyd Training School.* Boston University, 1936. 79 p. ms.

4677. JOHNSON, EMIL LUTHER, 1929- . *The Role of Foreign Languages in Swedish Education.* Clark University, 1951. 166 p. ms. Abstract in Clark University: *Abstracts of Dissertations and Theses,* 1951, p. 168-169.

4678. LARSEN, Rev. JOSEPH EINER ALFRED, 1888- . *Some Aspects of Social Welfare Work in Sweden.* Fordham University, 1935. 53 p. ms. Abstract in Fordham University: *Dissertations Accepted for Higher Degrees . . . 1936,* p. 69. (Includes child welfare.)

4679. LUCAS, JOHN APOSTAL. *An Analysis of American and Swedish Long-Distance Running and a Suggested Program for the American College Track Team.* University of Southern California, 1952. 127 p. ms.

4680. NELSON, LILLIAN MATHILDE. *Modern Trends in Swedish Education.* University of Southern California, 1928. 130 p. ms.

4681. NORMAN, EBBA ANNA SOFIA. *Problems of Training for Leadership in Religious Education in Sweden.* Boston University, 1924. 57 p. ms.

4682. OHBERG, HJORDIS GLAD. *A Comparative Study of Selected Types of Organized Camping in Sweden and the United States.* University of Michigan, 1946. 109 p. ms.

4683. OSTMAN, KARIN. *Physical Education in the Secondary Schools of Sweden.* University of Michigan, 1937. 96 p. ms.

4684. PALSSON, KLAS FILIP. *Dental Education in Sweden: Its Origin and Development with Due Regard to Its Present Actual Problems.* Northwestern University (Dental School), 1932. 58 p. ms.

4685. PATTON, WILMA BLANCHE, 1904- . *A Comparative Study of the Characteristics of Low Readers with a Control Group in East Whittier, California, and in Stockholm, Sweden.* Whittier College, 1957. 78 p. ms.

See also Nos. 226, 274, 3139, 3142, 3148, 3158, 3164, 3216, 3219, 3222, 3231, 3274, 3286, 3292, 3293, 3294.

For Swedish groups in the United States, see Nos. 5683, 5692-5694.

Switzerland

(NOS. 4686 – 4722)

DOCTORS

4686. AVERILL, LAWRENCE AUGUSTUS, 1891- . *The Contribution of Pestalozzi.* Clark University, 1915.

4687. BOERSMA, CLARENCE, 1906- . *The Educational Ideal in the Major Works of Hermann Hesse.* University of Michigan, 1949. 308 p. ms. Abstract in *Microfilm Abstracts*, Vol. 9, No. 2, p. 125-126, 1949. Available on microfilm from University Microfilms, Ann Arbor, Michigan, as Publication No. 1,186.

4688. CAUGHEY, FRANK McCLURE, 1887- . *The Sources of the Thought and Teaching of John Calvin.* University of Pittsburgh, 1937. 208 p. ms. Abstract in University of Pittsburgh: *Abstracts of Theses . . .* Vol. 13, 1937, p. 46-51.

4689. HAYES, ELOISE DE LAY, 1914- . *Pestalozzianism, a Foundation of the Public School System in the United States.* University of North Carolina, 1954. 394 p. ms. Abstract in *University of North Carolina Record*, No. 534, p. 66-68, October 1954.

4690. JONES, JAMESON MILLER, 1916- . *The Problem of Faith and Reason in the Thought of John Calvin.* Duke University, 1942. 276 p. ms. Abstract in *Doctoral Theses in Religious Education*, 1942, p. 14.

4691. MINSKY, HENRI S. *Ernest Bloch and His Music.* George Peabody College for Teachers, 1945. (Treats the composer "as a man, musician, educator, and philosopher.")

4692. WALCH, *Sister* MARY ROMANA, 1905- . *Pestalozzi and the Pestalozzian Theory of Education: A Critical Study.* Catholic University of America, 1953. Washington: Catholic University of America Press, 1952. xiii, 218 p. Abstract in *Catholic Educational Review*, Vol. 51, p. 686-687, December 1953.

See also Nos. 142, 143, 147, 161, 163, 175, 3068, 3076, 3078, 3104, 3110, 3111, 3116, 3123, 3124, 3127, 3128, 3612, 174a.

MASTERS

4693. ALT, *Sister* MARY ROSALIA. *Pestalozzi's Anschuung in Theory and Practice.* Catholic Sisters College of the Catholic University of America, 1917. Published in *Catholic Educational Review*, Vol. 14, p. 16-41, June 1917.

4694. BEIFELD, MINNIE MARGARET. *"My Investigations into the Course of Nature in the Development of the Human Race" — Pestalozzi.* Columbia University, 1905. 56 p. ms.

4695. BILLICA, WILLARD C. *Calvin and Education.* Pittsburgh-Xenia Theological Seminary, 1950. 83 p. ms.

4696. BYERS, BENJAMIN HOWARD. *The Life, Work and Influence of Pestalozzi.* Pennsylvania State College, 1929. 59 p. ms.

4697. CONLIN, *Rev.* EDWARD F. *Pedagogical Values of the Asceticism of St. Francis De Sales.* Catholic University of America, 1933. 41 p. ms.

4698. DOANE, FRANCES CUMMINGS, 1898- . *The Influence of Pestalozzianism upon Lowell Mason's Work in Music Education.* University of Vermont and State Agricultural College, 1937. 71 p. ms.

4699. DONAHUE, *Rev.* JAMES C. *The Contributions of the Oblates of St. Francis De Sales to Education in the United States.* Catholic University of America, 1958.

4700. EDELMAN, NATHAN. *A Translation of J. L. Claparede's "The Teaching of History and the International Spirit," with a Translator's Introduction on the Bearing of the International Spirit on History Instruction.* College of the City of New York, 1934. 140 p. ms. Abstract in College of the City of New York: *Abstracts of Theses . . . 1923-1939*, p. 75.

4701. HALLIDAY, EDGAR. *Pestalozzi, His Life and Principles.* Columbia University, 1902. 144 p. ms.

4702. HILL, WALTER BENTON. *The Influence of Calvinism on Education.* Western Theological Seminary, 1945.

4703. HUBER, Sister MARY CECELIA. *Post-War Changes in Education in Switzerland.* Loyola University, 1931. 125 p. ms.

4704. HUFFERT, ANTON M. *The Teaching of English "Kulturkunde" in the "Stadtisches Gymnasium" of Berne.* College of the City of New York, 1935. 132 p. ms. Abstract in College of the City of New York: *Abstracts of Theses . . . 1923-1939,* p. 87.

4705. JARVIS, JOHN A. *John Henry Pestalozzi: His Contribution to Education.* Wayne University, 1941. 27 p. ms.

4706. JORDAN, THOMAS F. *Philipp Emanuel von Fellenberg: A Catholic Educator and Philanthropist.* Catholic University of America, 1939. 65 p. ms.

4707. KAUFFMAN, ALFRED EZRA. *The Educational Practices of Pestalozzi.* University of Detroit, 1935. 88 p. ms.

4708. KAY, LELAND OLIVER. *An Analysis of the Works of Pestalozzi in Education and His Philosophy Concerning Practical Arts.* North Texas State College, 1950. 59 p. ms. Abstract in *Research in Industrial Education, 1930-1955,* p. 475.

4709. LOEWENHEIM, FELICE S. *Pestalozzianism in the United States.* Hunter College of the City of New York. 1929. 62 p. ms.

4710. MacLENNAN, DUNCAN GEORGE. *The Influence of John Calvin on Education.* University of Denver, 1924. 66 p. ms.

4711. MAAS, Rev. ANDREW HUBERT. *Pere Girard: Swiss Educational Reformer.* Catholic University of America, 1930. 111 p. ms. Published as *Pere Girard, Educator,* New York: J. F. Wagner, Inc., 1931. x, 59 p. (Franciscan Studies, No. 9, May 1931.)

4712. MALEFYT, PAUL, 1893- . *The Influence of Calvin upon Our Educational Institutions.* New York State College for Teachers, Albany, 1931. 50 p. ms.

4713. MAYO, JESSIE NORRIS. *The Aims of Education and Modes of Instruction in the Modern Elementary School which Are Due to the Influence of the Work of Pestalozzi.* University of Washington, 1932. 162 p. ms.

4714. RATHBURN, LOIS MERCEDES, 1914- . *The Dalcroze Theory of Eurhythmics in Education.* Smith College, 1938. 140 p. ms.

4715. SCHMERLER, SAMUEL. *The Teaching of English at the Municipal Gymnasium of Berne.* College of the City of New York, 1935. 105 p. Abstract in College of the City of New York: *Abstracts of Theses . . . 1923-1939,* p. 89-90.

4716. SCHMID, WERNER DAVID. *Religious Education in Switzerland.* Union Theological Seminary, 1932. 50 p. ms.

4717. SCHUELER, HERBERT. *The Bilingual Situation in Bienne, Switzerland.* College of the City of New York, 1935. 61 p. ms. Abstract in College of the City of New York: *Abstracts of Theses . . . 1923-1939,* p. 91.

4718. SIMPSON, Mrs. CLEMENCE M. *Pestalozzi and His Influence in the United States.* Southern Methodist University, 1926. 97 p. ms. Abstract in Southern Methodist University: *Abstracts of Master's Theses,* No. 1, 1915-1916, p. 16-17.

4719. WALLIS, EVA SMITH. *A Comparison of Pestalozzi's Educational Principles and Practices with Those of Some Leading Modern Educators.* Florida State University, 1946. 155 p. ms. (All of the modern educators are American except Peter Sandiford of Canada, and Kurt Lewin, who was born in Germany but taught in United States, 1933-1947.)

4720. WELLS, GRACE A. *John Henrich Pestalozzi, 1747-1827, a Social Educator of the Conservative School.* St. Bonaventure University, 1947. 50 p. ms.

4721. WHELAN, JAMES FRANCIS. 1899- . *Dominic Yenni, a Jesuit Teacher and Grammarian (1810-1888.)* St. Louis University, 1936. 93 p. ms.

4722. WILLINGHAM, DORA ANN. *John Henry Pestalozzi: His Educational Principles and Methods.* University of Texas, 1927. 135 p. ms.

See also Nos. 226, 249, 274, 3138, 3141, 3168, 3174, 3181, 3185, 3193, 3197, 3200, 3205, 3210, 3218, 3221, 3222, 3232, 3239, 3245, 3277, 3279, 3281, 3292, 3294, 3299, 3300.

For Swiss groups in the United States, see Nos. 4957, 4959, 4970, 4975.

USSR (Union of Soviet Socialist Republics)

(NOS. 4723 – 4800)

DOCTORS

4723. BABEY, ANNA MARY, 1911- . *Americans in Russia, 1776-1917: A Study of the American Travelers in Russia from the American Revolution to the Russian Revolution.* Columbia University, 1938. New York: Comet Press, 1938. xiv, 175 p. (Chapter 6, "Education," p. 91-105.)

4724. COGER, LESLIE IRENE, 1912- . *A Comparison for the Oral Interpreter of Teaching Methods of Curry and Stanislavsky.* Northwestern University, 1952. 223 p. ms. Abstract in Northwestern University: *Summaries of Doctoral Dissertations,* Vol. 20, 1952. p. 92-97.

4725. DONIGER, SIMON. *Children's Literature in the Soviet Union as a Method in Social Education.* New York University, 1938. 281 p. ms. Abstract in New York University, School of Education: *Abstracts of Theses*, February-June 1938, p. 85-90.

4726. DRAKEFORD, JOHN WILLIAM, 1914- . *The Implications of Communism for Religious Education.* Southwestern Baptist Theological Seminary, 1956. 240 p. ms. Abstract in *Religious Education*, Vol. 52, p. 183-184, May-June 1957.

4727. FOURNADJIEFF, KONSTANTIN ZAHAKIEV, 1901- . *Early Childhood Education in the Soviet Union.* Yale University, 1948. 378 p. ms.

4728. FREITAG, CHARLES ROBERT, 1922- . *Biological Science Teaching at the Secondary School Level in the United States of America and the Union of Soviet Socialist Republics: A Comparative Study.* Cornell University, 1955. 472 p. ms. Abstract in *Dissertation Abstracts*, Vol. 15, p. 1214-1215, July 1955. Available on microfilm from University Microfilms, Ann Arbor, Michigan, as Publication No. 12,278.

4729. HETLER, LOUIS. *The Influence of the Stanislavsky Theories of Acting on the Teaching of Acting in the United States.* University of Denver, 1957.

4730. JOHNSON, WILLIAM HERMAN ECKART, 1907- . *The Russian Educational Heritage: A Brief History of Education in the Russian Empire, 1600-1917, with Particular Emphasis on the Training of Teachers.* Columbia University, 1949. Published as *Russia's Educational Heritage*, Pittsburgh, Pennsylvania: Carnegie Press, 1950. xvi, 451 p. Authorized Distributing Agent, Rutgers University Press, New Brunswick, New Jersey. Also published as *Russia's Educational Heritage: Teacher Education in the Russian Empire, 1600-1917*, same publishers.

4731. KRAMER, RICHARD, 1923- . *Practical Morality Taught to Soviet Children, as Illustrated in Four Official Soviet Periodicals, 1937-1951.* Columbia University, 1954. 374 p. ms. Abstract in *Dissertation Abstracts*, Vol. 14, p. 1111, July 1954. Available on microfilm from University Microfilms, Ann Arbor, Michigan, as Publication No. 8,337.

4732. LEARY, DANIEL BELL, 1886-1946. *Education and Autocracy in Russia from the Origins to the Bolsheviki.* Columbia University, 1919. Buffalo, New York: University of Buffalo, College of Arts and Sciences, 1919. 127 p. (Buffalo University Studies No. 1.)

4733. LEVIT, MARTIN, 1918- . *Education in Soviet Political and Social Theory.* University of Chicago, 1949. 138 p. ms. Available on microfilm; see index under "University of Chicago."

4734. PAELIAN, GARABED HAGOP, 1880- . *Nicholas Roerich's Contribution to Modern Life and Education.* New York University, 1936. 219 p. ms.

4735. PILCH, JUDAH, 1902- . *The Heder Metukan (The Modern Hebrew School in Russia of Pre-World War I.)* Dropsie College for Hebrew and Cognate Learning, 1952. 151 p. ms.

4736. POOLE, CHARLES PINCKNEY, 1893- . *Two Centuries of Education in Alaska.* University of Washington, 1948. 267 p. ms. (Includes the earlier period when Alaska was under Russian jurisdiction, to which an entire chapter is devoted.)

4737. ROCKOFF, GARSON. *A Supplementary Reader on a Boy's Life in Russia, 1902-1911, and His Growing Up in America, 1911-1938.* New York University, 1938. 60 p. ms.

4738. ROSENBAUM, MAURICE WILLIAM, 1912- . *Ivan Alexandrovich Goncharov and the Sociological Novel in Russia.* New York University, 1946. 236 p. ms. (Contains a chapter on Goncharov's life at the University of Moscow, 1831-1834.)

4739. SHORE, MAURICE JOSEPH, 1898- . *The Marxian Theory of Education.* Johns Hopkins University, 1940. Published in modified form as *Soviet Education: Its Psychology and Philosophy*, New York: Philosophical Library, Inc., 1947. xxii, 346 p. ("The substance of this work was conceived in 1937, while at Johns Hopkins University. The basic materials were then laid down for a work, *The Marxian Theory of Education* - - - - Swift moving events on the world scene shook the setting and the inner sinews. . . . Some materials of the old work were discarded or shifted, while others were shortened or enlarged."—*Forethought*. Note: Author's *vita* included with his dissertation gives 1898 as his birth year. His sketch in *Who's Who in America* gives 1901. Library of Congress used 1898 earlier but has changed to 1901. Letter to author asking for explanation is unanswered.)

4740. TANDLER, Mrs. FREDRIKA MOREHOUSE, 1909- . *The Workers' Faculty (Rabfak) System in the U.S.S.R.* Columbia University, 1955. 338 p. ms. Abstract in *Dissertation Abstracts*, Vol. 15, p. 1343-1344, August 1955. Available on microfilm from University Microfilms, Ann Arbor, Michigan, as Publication No. 12,476. (Treats a special type of adult school.)

See also Nos. 121, 127, 135, 143, 147, 150, 157, 165, 179, 1418, 3081, 3085, 3097, 3107, 3133, 3606, 4417, 174a.

MASTERS

4741. ANDERSON, HOBSON DEWEY. *Historic Development and Present Status of Physical Culture in Russia.* Stanford University, 1930. 176 p. ms.

4742. BACKUS, GRACE W. *The Influence of the Government in the Educational System of the Soviet Union.* Claremont Graduate School, 1934. 85 p. ms.

4743. BENDIX, DOROTHY. *Adult Education and Popular Libraries in the Soviet Union and in the United States.* Columbia University, 1926. 77 p. ms.

4744. BERKE, OBERT, 1910- . *Russian Migration to the United States.* University of North Dakota, 1946. 90 p. ms. (Contains a chapter on education in Russia.)

4745. BEST, WILLIAM McNEELY, 1918- . *The Philosophy and Practice of Modern Soviet Primary and Secondary Education.* Southern Methodist University, 1958. 82 p. ms.

4746. BISHOP, COSTELLO J. *The Availability of Education in the Soviet Union.* Claremont Graduate School, 1950. 192 p. ms.

4747. BOLLIG, Rev. RICHARD JOSEPH. *The German Catholic Schools in (Southern) Russia.* Catholic University of America, 1929. 37 p. ms.

4748. BOOKER, JAMES OAKLEY. *Polytechnical Aspects of Soviet Education.* Stanford University, 1941. 143 p. ms.

4749. BROSNAN, MARY HELEN. *Education in Soviet Russia, 1918 to 1932.* University of Idaho, 1934. 24 p. ms.

4750. BURG, BERNARD B. *Vocational Education in Russia.* Columbia University, 1918.

4751. BYRD, MYRTLE DELLA. *Tolstoi's Theories of Education.* Southern Methodist University, 1932. 120 p. ms.

4752. CHRISTOFF, ATHANASIUM TOLLEFF. *The School System in Soviet Russia.* State University of Iowa, 1926. 295. p. ms.

4753. CHYUNG, NAM-CHYU. *The Educational Practice of Soviet Russia.* University of Southern California, 1933. 76 p. ms.

4754. DAWKINS, JOAN. *Russian Communism: Its Significance and Challenge for the Christian Educator.* Columbia University, 1948. 71 p. ms.

4755. DE VINNEY, GEORGE H. *Education in the Soviet Union.* University of Buffalo, 1953. 71 p. ms.

4756. DICKERSON, WINIFRED SMITH. *The Physical Education Program in Soviet Russia.* Ohio State University, 1945. 78 p. ms.

4757. EHRENBURG, ANATOLE FRANCE. *The Educational Ideas of the Leaders of Communism and Their Application in the Soviet Union.* University of Colorado, 1934. 74 p. ms. Abstract in *University of Colorado Studies,* Vol. 22, No. 1, p. 20-21, November 1934.

4758. EMERSON, MARK FARLEY, 1903- . *Education as a Means of Social Reconstruction in the Soviet Union.* Dartmouth College, 1934. 99 p. ms.

4759. FINLEY, ROBERTA JANE. *Education in Russia.* University of Illinois, 1940. 84 p. ms.

4760. FLAHERTY, PAUL FREDERICK. *Communism versus Democracy: A Comparsion of the Governmental Principles of Communism, as in the Union of Soviet Socialist Republics, with Democracy, as in the United States.* Massachusetts State Teachers College, Fitchburg, 1938. 97 p. ms. (Includes study of education in the USSR.)

4761. FORD, EUDORA LORENE. *Character Education in Russia since 1917.* University of Colorado, 1936. 76 p. ms. Abstract in *University of Colorado Studies,* Vol. 24, No. 1, p. 26-27, November 1936.

4762. GILBERT, ELMO EDISON. *Health Education Program in Soviet Russia.* George Peabody College for Teachers, 1936. 88 p. ms.

4763. GRAY, GIBSON. *The Basis of Self-Expression of the Student of Soviet Higher Education.* Columbia University, 1950. 142 p. ms.

4764. GREENSPOON, BERT. *Education in the USSR.* New York University, 1935. 108 p. ms.

4765. HARSKY, JOSEPH EDWARD. *Development of Physical Education in Schools of Soviet Russia from 1919 to 1931.* University of Pittsburgh, 1932. 98 p. ms. Abstract in University of Pittsburgh: *Abstracts of Theses . . .* Vol. 8, 1932. p. 332.

4766. HORTON, ARTHUR G. *A Study in Sociological Integration.* Columbia University, 1930. 114 p. ms. (Includes consideration of education as one factor in social integration.)

4767. HUTCHISON, STELLA BELLE. *Trends in Education in the Soviet Union since 1895, and Their Philosophical Bases.* University of Maryland, 1950. 54 p. ms.

4768. JUVILER, PETER H. *The Aims and Organization of Soviet Education, 1928-1932.* Columbia University, 1954. 119 p. ms.

4769. KELLY, KATHERINE L. *Technical Education in Soviet Russia.* Texas State College for Women, 1933. 83 p. ms.

4770. KIBITZ, ADOLPH. *Primary Education in Russia in the Period of the Third Duma.* Columbia University, 1940. 88 p. ms.

4771. KIPPES, Sister MARY ETHEL. *The Educational Philosophy of Michael John Demiashevich.* Catholic University of America, 1941. 53 p. ms.

4772. LEEDY, FREDERICK A. *National Defense and Revolutionary Expansion in the Political Education of the Red Army, 1939-1941: A Study of Krasnaia Zvezda.* Columbia University, 1952. 84 p. ms.

4773. LEVITAS, ARNOLD. *Methods of Education and Training in the Union of Soviet Socialist Republics.* New York University, 1934. 66 p. ms.

4774. LUBOVICH, GEORGE VLADIMIR. *A Defense of Soviet Education in the Light of Cultural Development.* University of Colorado, 1947. 295 p. ms. Abstract in *University of Colorado Studies,* Vol. 28, Nos. 2, 3, p. 84, June 1949.

4775. LYNN, Rev. WILLIAM CARMEL, 1908- . *The Application of the Marxian Materialism to Education in Soviet Russia during the Early Years of the Revolution.* Fordham University, 1936. 57 p. ms. Abstract in Fordham University: *Dissertations Accepted for Higher Degrees,* 1937, p. 46-47.

4776. McCARTHY, MADELINE HELEN, 1909- . *Metamorphis of Dr. George S. Counts' Thinking Relative to the Soviet and to Education.* Boston College, 1953. 76 p. ms.

4777. MATH, HELEN M. *Social Studies as a Vehicle of Propaganda in the Schools of Russia and the United States.* New Jersey State Teachers College, Upper Montclair, 1935. 71 p. ms.

4778. MAURIN, Mrs. RAISSA BLOCH, 1909- . *A Survey of Soviet Literature in Library Science, 1948-1952.* Catholic University of America, 1954. 149 p. ms.

4779. MODELL, DAVID A. *Tolstoy's Educational Theories, Together with a Translation of His Essay on Public Education.* Columbia University, 1909. 67 p. ms.

4780. MORRIS, EDNA NIXON. *A Historical Study of the Russian Educational System with Particular Reference to the Elementary Level.* Sul Ross State College, 1951. 102 p. ms.

4781. MUDGE, RICHARD BACHELDER. *The Social Studies in Pre-Soviet Russian Education.* Stanford University, 1947. 102 p. ms.

4782. OSEPOFF, VASIL GABRIEL, 1901- . *Atheism through Education in Soviet Russia.* Emory University, 1934. 190 p. ms.

4783. PIDDUCK, HARRIET EMMA. *A Study of the Relationship between the Political and Social Conditions in Russia from 1850 to 1910 and the Music of the Russian "Fives."* University of Southern California, 1940. 133 p. ms. ("The problem is one suggested by the newer aspects of the teaching of music appreciation."—Introduction.)

4784. POCKROSE, FANNIE M. *New Developments In Methods of Teaching Modern Foreign Languages in the Schools of Soviet Russia.* New York University, 1932. 53 p. ms.

4785. RABUKA, MIKE M., 1903- . *Elementary Education of the Soviets.* Western State College of Colorado, 1943. 51 p. ms.

4786. REED, GORDON S. *Soviet Education as Reflected in Post World War II Literature.* University of Wisconsin, 1955. 107 p. ms.

4787. REESE, SHERWOOD RAY. *A Study of Education in the Union of Socialist Soviet Republics.* University of Southern California, 1933. 183 p. ms.

4788. REYNOLDS, JAMES P. *Soviet Influence on the Russian Educational System.* Massachusetts Agricultural College, 1934.

4789. SALEMI, A. RICHARD. *Systems of Education in Russia and in the United States: A Comparative Study.* University of Buffalo, 1947. 129 p. ms.

4790. SANDLER, Mrs. JANET MODRY. *References in Drawing in the Case of Moscow Children.* Columbia University, 1935. 34 p. ms.

4791. SAVRAN, WILLIAM S. 1899- *Education in the United Socialist Soviet Republics as Revealed by Official Documents.* Temple University, 1936. 98 p. ms.

4792. SCALISI, VICTOR F. *Tolstoy's Philosophical and Educational Views.* New York University, 1929. 94 p. ms.

4793. SCHWARTZ, BERNICE GOLIGER. *Development of Higher Education in Soviet Russia.* Hunter College of the City of New York, 1937. 42 p. ms.

4794. SEIDLIN, JOSEPH. *An Inside View of the Russian School System, Including Mr. Kondratier's Report on "Gymnazia of Russia": An Essay.* Columbia University, 1916. 30 p. ms.

4795. SIEGMEISTER, WALTER. *The New Educational System of Soviet Russia.* New York University, 1931. For doctoral dissertation by same author, see No. 3661.

4796. SIMON, JOHN RICHARD. *The Teacher in Russian Education: The Investigation of Soviet Education Pointed toward a Description of the Teacher and His Position as an Educator.* Ohio State University, 1956. 113 p. ms.

4797. SMITH, SAMUEL. *Educational Experimentation in Soviet Russia: Causes, Methods, and Results.* New York University, 1932. 227 p. ms.

4798. SOSIN, GENE. *Plays for the Soviet Children's Theatre as a Medium of Communist Education, 1925-1948.* Columbia University, 1949. 182 p. ms.

4799. UDIN, SOPHIE ADA. *The Book Trade under the Soviets and Its Relationship to Higher Institutes of Learning,* Columbia University, 1929. 77 p. ms.

4800. WINN, ROWENA HUDSON, 1892- . *The Preschool in the System of Elementary Education in the Union of Socialist Soviet Republics.* Smith College, 1935. 144 p. ms.

See also Nos. 187, 213, 226, 230, 236, 250, 280, 308, 3140, 3144, 3147, 3154, 3162, 3172, 3175, 3180, 3182, 3183, 3195, 3222, 3252, 3292, 3297, 3701, 3835, 4570.

For Russian (Soviet) groups in the United States, see Nos. 4963, 4970, 4975, 4978, 4985, 4987, 5001, 5013, 5015, 5017, 5020, 5021, 5024.

Yugoslavia

(NOS. 4801 – 4803)

DOCTORS

See No. 119, 175

MASTERS

4801. CHESAREK, ELEANOR. *A Study of Slovenia and Its Folk Music with Representative Selections*

Suitable for Use in American Schools. University of Southern California, 1949. 164 p. ms.

4802. MILANOVICH, ANTHONY. *A Collection of Serbian Folk Tales.* Indiana State Teachers College, 1942. 126 p. ms. (Contributions of the Graduate School, No. 483. Contains 12 tales, five in Serbian with English translations, seven in English only.)

4803. RATKOVICH, MILO M., 1905- . *The Educational Significance of the Heroic Ballads of Serbia.* University of Akron, 1945. 89 p. ms.

See also Nos. 217, 3198.

For Slavic groups in the United States, *see* Nos. 5684-5691.

OCEANIA
(NOS. 4804 – 4859)

American Samoa
(NOS. 4804 – 4808)

DOCTORS

4804. SANCHEZ, PEDRO CRUZ, 1925- . *Education in American Samoa.* Stanford University, 1956. 242 p. ms. Abstract in *Dissertation Abstracts*, Vol. 16, p. 705, April 1956. Available on microfilm from University Microfilms, Ann Arbor, Michigan, as Publication No. 16,009.

4805. SHAHAN, JAMES BUHL, 1908- . *American Colonial Administration in the Western Pacific: A Study in Civil-Military Relations.* Ohio State University, 1950. 335 p. ms. Abstract in Ohio State University: *Abstracts of Dissertations . . .* Summer Quarter, 1950-51, p. 481-486. (Abstracts of Doctoral Dissertations, No. 64. Includes Philippines, Guam, Samoa, and Trust Territories, but discusses education for Samoa only.)

See also Nos. 128, 166, 1073.

MASTERS

4806. McTAGGART, EARL LINTON. *Agricultural Education in American Samoa.* University of Hawaii, 1936. 189 p. ms. Available on microfilm.

4807. MITCHELL, DONALD DEAN. *Education in American Samoa, with Special Reference to Health Problems.* University of Hawaii, 1936. 204 p. ms.

4808. SUTHERLAND, MARK MONROE. *A Study of Teacher Training in American Samoa.* University of Hawaii, 1941. 301 p. ms.

See also Nos. 192, 195.

Australia
(NOS. 4809 – 4836)

DOCTORS

4809. ALLSOP, JOAN WINIFRED. *An Appraisal of the Discussion Group Scheme of the University of Sydney, Australia, 1937-1956, with Recommendations Regarding Future Developments.* Columbia University, 1957. 171 p. ms.

4810. BALSON, MAURICE, 1927- . *A Suggested Guidance Program for High Schools of Victoria, Australia.* University of California, Los Angeles, 1958. 276 p. ms.

4811. COOK, PHILIP HALFORD, 1912- . *The Theory and Technique of Child Guidance, with Special Reference to Australian Conditions.* University of Kansas, 1941. 255 p. ms.

4812. CRAMER, JOHN FRANCIS. *Financing Public Education in Australia.* University of Oregon, 1937. 131 p. ms. For master's thesis by same author, see No. 4828.

4812a. GORDON, LES McKENZIE JAMES. *Improving the Program of Citizenship Education through the Social Studies in New South Wales Schools.* Stanford University, 1958. 400 p. ms. Abstract in *Dissertation Abstracts*, Vol. 19, p. 2267-2268, March 1959. Available on microfilm from University Microfilms, Ann Arbor, Michigan, as Mic. 59-238.

4813. HEPWORTH, TOM STANLEY. *Religion and Education in the Queensland Social Order: A History of the Development of a System of Public Education in Queensland, with Special Reference to the Relationship between Church and State Throughout This Development.* Harvard Univesity, 1953. 346 p. ms.

4814. McDOWELL, ERNEST GORDON, 1907- . *An Approach to the Reorganization of the Rural Secondary School Program in Tasmania.* Columbia University, 1948. 238 p. ms.

4815. MacKENZIE, THOMAS FINDLAY. *Social Forces Influencing the Evolution of a State Educational System in New South Wales, with Special Reference to the Period of Australia's Incipient Nationalism.* New York University, 1933. Published as *Nationalsim and Education in Australia, with Special Reference to the State of New South Wales.* London: P. S. King & Son, Ltd., 1935. xi, 148 p.

4816. NEAL, WALTER DOUGLAS, 1920- . *An Analysis of Selected Problems in Personnel Relationships in the Public Secondary Schools of Western Australia.* Columbia University, 1957. 147 p. ms.

4817. POULTER, MAXWELL WILLIAM, 1913- . *Socio-Economics for Australian Secondary Schools: A Guide for Teachers.* Columbia University, 1950. 201 p. ms.

4818. RAYNER, SAMUEL ALAN, 1921- . *The Administration of Pupil Personnel Services: A Comparative Study of Services in the United States and Queensland, Australia.* University of Illinois, 198 p. ms. Abstract in *Dissertation Abstracts*, Vol. 15, p. 72-73, January 1955. Available on microfilm from University Microfilms, Ann Arbor, Michigan, as Publication No. 10,535.

4819. ROBINSON, HAROLD C. S., 1907- . *The Significance of Philosophy in the Development of Australian Educational Policies.* University of Kentucky, 1948. 185 p. ms.

4820. WESTERMAN, WILFRED ALAN. *A Plan for the Reorganization of Secondary Education in New South Wales.* Columbia University, 1947. 409 p. ms.

4821. WHEEN, GEORGE ALFRED, 1912- . *The Training of Christian Youth Leaders in New South Wales, Australia: A Plan for the Training of Youth Leaders in the Methodist Church in New South Wales, Australia, Based upon an Approach to the Process of Religious Education New to Those Who Will Participate in the Plan. This Plan to Include a War-Memorial Youth Center in Sydney for Training Leaders and a Full-Time Program Developed through District and Local Supervision.* Columbia University, 1948. 116 p. ms.

4822. WHITFORD, RICHARD LESLIE, 1915- . *A Framework of Reference for the Determination of Policy with Respect to the Organization of Education in Tasmania.* Columbia University, 1956. 239 p. ms.

4823. WRIGHT, CLIFFORD JOHN, 1910- . *A Philosophy and Outline for the Educational Programme of the Australian Methodist Church.* Columbia University, 1953. 173 p. ms. Abstract in *Religious Education*, Vol. 49, p. 201-202, May-June 1954.

4824. WYETH, EZRA ROBERT HARDING, 1910- . *Some Implications of the Queensland Proposal to Raise the School Leaving Age.* University of California, Berkeley, 1948. 184 p. ms.

See also Nos. 122, 138, 142, 143, 147, 154, 160, 161, 179.

MASTERS

4825. ARCHER, ERNEST WALLACE, 1898- . *The Private and Church Schools of Victoria.* Yale University, 1931. 202 p. ms.

4826. BARRY, Sister MARY BRIAN. *Present Status of Catholic Education in Australia.* Catholic University of America, 1958.

4827. COLLINS, ALAN KEITH, 1921- . *An Instructor's Manual in Executive Counseling at Vacuum Oil Company, Melbourne, Australia.* Cornell University, 1955. 122 p. ms.

4828. CRAMER, JOHN FRANCIS. *A Comparative Study of Educational Expenditures in the State of Oregon and in the State of Victoria.* University of Oregon, 1932. 51 p. ms. For doctoral dissertation by same author, see No. 4812.

4829. DYSTER, COLIN McKENZIE, 1905- . *A Study of the Curriculum of St. Andrews Theological Hall, Sydney, New South Wales, Australia.* Pacific School of Religion, 1948. 106 p. ms.

4830. McCLOUGHAN, EVELYN. *A History of the Development of Physical Education in the Public School System of New South Wales, Australia, 1788-1954.* Ohio State University, 1956. 173 p. ms.

4831. REID, JOAN INNES. (Later, Mrs. Metal) *The Dependent Child in New South Wales.* University of Chicago, 1940. 158 p. ms.

4832. REILLY, JAMES JOSEPH, 1913- . *A Study of Australian Education Together with a Consideration of the United States Relation to It.* Boston College, 1941. 48 p. ms.

4833. ROBINSON, CLARICE MAURINE, 1897- . *A Comparative Study of the Educational Systems of Australia.* Indiana University, 1938. 251 p. ms.

4834. SADLER, DOUGLAS G. *A Case for Reform of General Education in New South Wales Secondary Schools, with Particular Reference to Junior High Schools.* Columbia University, 1954. 94 p. ms.

4835. WHYTE, JEAN PRIMROSE. *Education for Librarianship in the United States and in Australia: A Comparison.* University of Chicago, 1956. 232 p. ms.

4836. WOLFE, JOHN ROBERT MATHER, 1929- . *Selected Principles of Extension Education and Their Implications in Advisory Work for Queensland, Australia.* Cornell University, 1958. 88 p. ms.

See also Nos. 195, 206, 235, 255, 275, 283, 308.

For Australian groups in the United States, *see* Nos. 4956, 4957.

Guam
(NOS. 4837 – 4838)

DOCTORS

See Nos. 128, 166, 1073.

MASTERS

4837. LINTNER, MARY C. *An Exploratory Study of Certain Phases of the Teaching of Reading in the Territory of Guam.* Virginia Polytechnic Institute, 1955. 93 p. ms.

4838. RIOS, ALBERT JAMES. *A High School Biology Course for Guam.* University of Southern California, 1952. 88 p. ms.

See also No. 192.

New Guinea
(NO. 4839)

DOCTORS

See Nos. 160, 179.

MASTERS

4839. MAGER, JOHN FREDERICK. *Education and Social Change in a New Guinea Society.* University of Chicago, 1937. 92 p. ms.

See also Nos. 195, 247, 275, 308.

New Zealand
(NOS. 4840 – 4849)

DOCTORS

See Nos. 119, 138, 142, 143, 147, 161.

MASTERS

4840. BLAIR, ROBERT. *A Contribution towards a Proposed System of Moral and Religious Education for New Zealand.* Boston University, 1928. 240 p. ms. (Thesis for degree of Master of Religious Education.) For another master's thesis by same author, see No. 4841.

4841. BLAIR, ROBERT. *A History of Religious Education in New Zealand.* Boston University, 1928. 144 p. ms. (Thesis for degree of Master of Arts.) For another master's thesis by same author, see No. 4840.

4842. BRAMLEY, VIOLET EUGENIE. *Post-Primary Education in New Zealand.* University of Michigan, 1937. 113 p. ms.

4843. CAMPBELL, EDWARD HARVEY. *Public Service for Teachers in New Zealand and the Implications for Such a System in Oregon.* University of Oregon, 1939. 58 p. ms.

4844. CLINE, ROBERT CARLYLE, 1890- . *The Educational and Social Development of New Zealand.* George Washington University, 1925. 29 p. ms.

4845. KELLY, EDWARD JAMES. *The History of Education in New Zealand as a Resultant of Culture Pattern and Surroundings.* State University of Iowa, 1948. 165 p. ms.

4846. MATHER, ARCHIBALD JENNINGS. *The Educational System of New Zealand.* University of Washington, 1927. 76 p. ms.

4847. NEWICK, CYNTHIA ROBIN. *A Creative Dance Programme for New Zealand.* University of Utah, 1957. 264 p. ms.

4848. RUSSELL, DONALD STEPHEN. *Vocational Education and Guidance in the Schools of New Zealand.* University of Southern California, 1947. 98 p. ms. Abstract in *Research in Industrial Education, 1930-1945*, p. 93.

4849. STONE, MABEL. *A Comparative Study of Secondary Education in New Zealand and Selected States.* Stanford University, 1934. 77 p. ms.

See also Nos. 206, 226, 235, 255, 308.

For New Zealand groups in the United States, see Nos. 4957, 4975.

Okinawa
(NOS. 4850 – 4853)

DOCTOR

4850. MARETZKI, THOMAS WALTER, 1921- . *Child Rearing in an Okinawan Community.* Yale University, 1957. 525 p. ms.

MASTERS

4851. GILL, ELVA PERRY, 1900- . *Okinawan Adaptations to Life.* New Jersey State Teachers College, Newark, 1957. 89 p. ms. (Chapter 9, "Adaptations to Education," p. 58-65.)

4852. TOMOYOSE, EIICHIRO, 1927- . *The Development of the Educational System of Okinawa, 1879 to 1954.* Northeast Missouri State Teachers College, 1955. 157 p. ms.

4853. WRIGHT, VIOLA K. *Handbook for New Teachers in the American Dependents Schools on Okinawa.* Drake University, 1958.

Pacific Islands
(NOS. 4854 – 4859)

DOCTORS

4854. FISCHER, ANN. *The Role of the Trukese Mother and Its Effect on Child Training.* Radcliffe College, 1957.

4855. MANN, CECIL WILLIAM, 1895- . *The Educational System of the Colony of Fiji.* Stanford University, 1938. 447 p. ms. Published in part as "A Test of General Ability in Fiji," *Pedagogical Seminary,* Vol. 54, p. 435-454, June 1939. Much of the background and data of the dissertation were published as *Education in Fiji,* Melbourne: Melbourne University Press, 1935. 137 p. (Australian Council for Educational Research.) Abstract in Stanford University: *Abstracts of Dissertations* . . . 1937-38, p. 129-131.

4856. MUKAIDA, SAMUEL NOZOMI, 1919- . *A Proposal to Improve Audio-Visual Education and Establish a Productive Center to Serve Hawaii and Neighboring Islands.* Columbia University, 1952. 165 p. ms. (Includes consideration of the Trust Territory of the Pacific Islands, formerly the Japanese Mandated Islands, consisting of 96 distinct clusters of islands, the most important being Saipan, Palaus, Yap, Truk, Ponape, and Majuro.)

See also Nos. 144, 147, 164, 169, 181.

MASTERS

4857. HILEMAN, ESTHER MAY, 1922- . *Ancient Polynesian Life and Customs as a Basis for Modern Dance Composition.* Illinois State Normal University, 1948. 64 p. ms. Abstract in Illinois State Normal University, *Abstracts of Theses,* 1948, p. 25.

4858. MOE, KILMER OSCAR, Jr. *The Influence of the Hilo Boarding School on Agricultural Education in the Pacific.* University of Hawaii, 1953. 77 p. ms. (Includes Fiji Islands, Marquesas Islands, Micronesia, and Philippines.)

4859. YOUNG, DONALD E. *A Historical Study of the Sports Activities of Natives in the Western Pacific Islands.* University of Wyoming, 1954. 79 p. ms. (Covers Caroline, Gilbert, Mariana, and Marshall Islands.)

See also Nos. 195, 247, 259, 275, 308.

UNITED STATES OF AMERICA

General

(NOS. 4860 - 4952)

DOCTORS

4860. ALLAWAY, WILLIAM HARRIS, 1924- . *Development of International Understanding in Foreign Students at the University of Kansas.* University of Denver, 1957. 466 p. ms.

4861. ATZMAN, EZRI. *The Impact of Educational Programs on the Acculturation of Adult Jewish Immigrants in Metropolitan Detroit (1949-1955).* University of Michigan, 1958. 264 p. ms. Abstract in *Dissertation Abstracts,* Vol. 19, p. 477, September 1958. Available on microfilm from University Microfilms, Ann Arbor, Michigan, as Mic. 58-3633.

4862. BERGER, MORRIS ISAIAH. *The Settlement, the Immigrant, and the Public School: A Study of the Influence of the Settlement Movement and the New Migration upon Public Education, 1890-1924.* Columbia University, 1956. 196 p. ms. Abstract in *Dissertation Abstracts,* Vol. 16, p. 1230-1231, July 1956. Available on microfilm from University Microfilms, Ann Arbor, Michigan, as Publication No. 16,798.

4863. BOHN, RALPH CARL. *An Evaluation of the Educational Program for Students from Foreign Countries: With Emphasis upon Orientation Procedures, Individual Problems, and Psychological Variables.* Wayne State University, 1957. 361 p. ms. Abstract in *Dissertation Abstracts,* Vol. 18, p. 1344, April 1958. Available on microfilm from University Microfilms, Ann Arbor, Michigan, as Mic. 58-1174.

4864. CIESLAK, EDWARD CHARNWOOD, 1917- . *A Study of the Administrative and Guidance Practices for Students from Abroad in Representative Collegiate Institutions of the United States.* Wayne University, 1953. Published as *The Foreign Student in American Colleges: A Survey and Evaluation of Administrative Problems and Practices,* Detroit, Michigan: Wayne University Press, 1955. x, 175 p. ("Originally a thesis ... it has been completely rewritten for publication." – Preface.) Abstract in *Dissertation Abstracts,* Vol. 14, p. 944-948, June 1954. Available on microfilm from University Microfilms, Ann Arbor, Michigan, as Publication No. 8,167.

4865. DARCY, NATALIE TERESA, 1909- . *The Effect of Bilingualism upon the Measurement of the Intelligence of Children of Pre-School Age.* Fordham University, 1945. 164 p. ms. Abstract in Fordham University: *Dissertations Accepted for Higher Degrees* ... Vol. 12, 1945, p. 11-15.

4866. DUNLAP, JACK WILBER, 1902- . *Race Differences in the Organization of Numerical and Verbal Abilities.* Columbia University, 1931. New York, 1931. 72 p. (*Archives of Psychology,* No. 124)

4867. HAYDEN, JAMES RICHARD, 1909- . *An Analysis of the Personal-Social Problems Considered Important by the Junior-High-School Adolescent According to Sex, Grade, Age, Intelligence Quoitent, and Bilingualism.* Boston University, 1956. 2 Vols. 670 p. ms. Abstract in *Dissertation Abstracts,* Vol. 17, p. 275, February 1957. Available on microfilm from University Microfilms, Ann Arbor, Michigan, as Publication No. 18,763.

4868. HUFFMAN, VONCILE B. *Beginning Reading Materials for Bilingual Children.* University of Denver, 1957.

4869. HUTCHINS, BRAHNA CHALEFMAN. *Counseling Programs as Related to Foreign Students in Ten Institutions of Higher Education in New York: An Exploratory Survey.* Columbia University, 1955.

4870. LOUGHEED, VIRGIL ROBERT, 1908- . *A Study of Administrative, Counseling, and Social Practices Affecting Foreign Students at an Urban University.* Wayne University, 1956. 287 p. ms. Abstract in *Dissertation Abstracts,* Vol. 16, p. 1625, September 1956. Available on microfilm from University Microfilms, Ann Arbor, Michigan, as Publication No. 17,161.

4870a. NEARY, JOHN BERNARD. *Problems Indigenous to Large Cities Arising from Immigrants and In-migrants as Related to a State. Correction Index.* Columbia University, 1958.

4871. REAMAN, GEORGE ELMORE, 1889- . *A Method of Teaching English to Foreigners.* Cornell University, 1920. Toronto, Canada: T. H. Best Printing Co., Ltd., 1921. 64 p.

4872. REMPEL, AVERNO MILTON, 1919- . *Studies of the Role of the State University of Iowa in World Affairs: I. Foreign Student Relationships; II. Certain Variables Involved in the Development of International Understanding.* State University of Iowa, 1954. 388 p. ms. Abstract in *Dissertation Abstracts,* Vol. 15, p. 519-520, April 1955. Available on microfilm from University Microfilms, Ann Arbor, Michigan, as Publication No. 7,012.

4873. SEMMES, Sister CATHERINE. *The Teaching of English to Foreign-Born Students.* Fordham University, 1931.

4874. TOUCHSTONE, MADELAINE MAUDE, 1913- . *The Administration of Foreign Student Affairs in Colleges and Universities of the United States.* University of Missouri, 1949. 301 p. ms. Abstract in *Microfilm Abstracts,* Vol. 9, No. 3, p. 84-86, 1950. Abstract also in University of Missouri: *Abstracts of Dissertations in Education ... from 1946 through 1950,* p. 140-142. Available on microfilm from University Microfilms, Ann Arbor, Michigan, as Publication No. 1,379.

4875. WYBURN, MARJORY ADA, 1915- . *Proposals for Improving the Clothing and Textile Educational Experiences of Home Economics Students from Other Lands.* Columbia University, 1958. 145 p. ms.

MASTERS

4876. AHMED, MOHSEN ABD ELHAMID. *Educational and Social Adjustment of Foreign Students*

General

at Washington University, St. Louis, Missouri, Fall 1952. Washington University, 1953. 159 p. ms.

4877. ALBERTS, LOIS CANNON. *An Experimental Study of the Relationship between Speech Sound Discrimination Ability and Intelligibility of the Speech of Students with Foreign Accents.* Bowling Green State University, 1953.

4878. ALE, IDA G. *The English Situation as a Background in Meeting the Needs of Foreign Children.* New York University, 1927. 113 p. ms.

4879. ALLEN, HARLAND H., 1889- . *Educating the Immigrant for Citizenship.* Colorado State Teachers College, 1917. 73 p. ms.

4880. ASCOLILLO, JEANETTE. *Americanization, Emphasizing Social and Educational Phases.* Columbia University, 1924. 29 p. ms.

4881. BADOIAN, MARTIN J. *A Study and Correlation of Marks of Two Distinct Groups: Students of Foreign-Born Parents and Students of Non-Foreign-Born Parents in a Particular High School.* American International College, 1954.

4882. BALLETTI, LINDA MADELINE, 1904- . *The Need of Adult Education in a Changing Civilization.* Boston University, 1934. 98 p. ms. (Includes education of foreign groups in the United States.)

4883. BARRETT, CHARLES B. *The Mathematical Achievement of Eighth Grade Pupils from the Standpoint of Racial Ancestry.* University of Hawaii, 1939. 83 p. ms.

4884. BARTON, HILDA I. *The School as a Factor in the Adjustment of Second Generation Children of the Foreign Born.* Massachusetts State Teachers College, Hyannis. 1944. 81 p. ms. (Institution closed in 1944. Library consolidated with that of Massachusetts State Teachers College, Bridgewater.)

4885. CAMPBELL, JOHN BERCHAMANS. *The Progress that Children of Foreign Parents Make in Silent Reading by the Use of Remedial Measures in Grades Five and Six of the Exeter Borough Schools.* Pennsylvania State College, 1933. 31 p. ms.

4886. COMBATALADE, AIMEE MARIE. *A Comparison of Children of Foreign-Born Parents with Those of Native Parents in the Mechanics of Junior High School English Composition.* Stanford University, 1936. 40 p. ms. (Considers chiefly children of North European parentage.)

4887. COOK, FLORA. *Education of the Foreign-Born for Citizenship through Instruction in the English Language.* University of Buffalo, 1950. 103 p. ms.

4888. CRAMER, BEATRICE ESTELLE, 1897- *Promoting Desirable Attitudes among National and Racial Groups in Junior High Schools through the Medium of Work on Immigration.* New York State College for Teachers, Albany, 1938. 242 p. ms. (Considers Jewish, Negro, and mixed foreign groups.)

4889. DALVEN, Mrs. RAE (NEGRIN.) *An Objective Study of the Backgrounds of Foreign-Born Children with the View to Vitalization of English Teaching in the Classroom.* New York University, 1928. 70 p. ms.

4890. DARLING, MARY REBECCA. *Americanization of the Foreign-Born in Greeley, Colorado.* Colorado State Teachers College, 1932. 156 p. ms.

4891. DAVIS, MARGARET MORTON, 1891- . *The Vocabularies of Two Direct-Method Elementary Texts for Teaching English to Foreigners.* University of Alabama, 1932. 83 p. ms.

4892. DEAN, ALICE E. *A Comparative Study of the Academic Achievement and the Physical Conditions of Sons of Foreign-Born Parents and Sons of American-Born Parents.* West Virginia University, 1937. 18 p. ms.

4893. DE SMIDT, MARGENE ESTHER, 1929- . *A Study of a Four-Day Community Program for Entertaining Foreign Students.* Cornell University, 1954. 104 p. ms.

4894. DONLON, THOMAS WELLER. *A Study in Free Reading among Foreign-Born Children.* University of Southern California, 1934. 54 p. ms.

4895. DRISCOLL, ANNE MARIE, 1901- . *A Comparison of the Silent Reading Ability of a Group of Pupils of Foreign-Speaking Parents with a Group of Pupils of English-Speaking Parents.* Smith College, 1934. 86 p. ms.

4896. ESTAVILLE, LAWRENCE ERNEST. *A Comparison of Bilinguals in the United States and a Study of State Recommended Bilingual Education Programs.* University of Southern California, 1956. 102 p. ms. (Determines percentage of bilingualism in each state and status of state programs.)

4897. FISHER, ALICIA. *A Study of the Migrant Situation in the United States with Special Reference to Christian Education.* Biblical Seminary in New York, 1936. 111 p. ms.

4898. FRANCK, GUY PAUL. *The Attitude of Certain Foreign-Born Nationality Groups toward the Public School.* University of Wyoming. 1937. 74 p. ms.

4899. FRANKLIN, SAMUEL PETTY. *A Correlation of Visual and Auditory Memory with Scholarship of 1,000 Foreign Fifth-Grade Children of the Public Schools of Chicago.* Northwestern University, 1921. 39 p. ms.

4900. GATES, ISABELLE MERRITT. *The Church School and Racial Education.* Berkeley Baptist Divinity School, 1935. 61 p. ms.

4901. GAUTHIER, EDWARD HAINES. *Tests and Drills for the Writing Program in Americanization Classes for Beginners.* Brown University, 1936. 180 p. ms.

4902. GEIS, GILBERT L. *A Study of Racial Attitudes and Problems in the Educational Program, Provo City, Utah.* Brigham Young University, 1949. 169 p. ms.

4903. GONZALEZ, TERESITA FELICIANO. *Personality and Academic Adjustment of Foreign Students to Ohio University Campus.* Ohio University, 1951. 43 p. ms. Abstract in Ohio University: *Abstracts of Master's Theses . . . 1951,* p. 99.

4904. GRAHAM, CHESTER ARTHUR. *Some Basic Considerations in Formulating a Course of Study for Adult Immigrant Education.* University of Illinois, 1926. 103 p. ms. Abstract in Russell Taaffe Gregg: *Annotated Bibliography of Graduate Theses in Education at the University of Illinois,* 1931, p. 31. (Bureau of Educational Research, Bulletin No. 55.)

4905. GRAY, ROBERT FLOYD, 1894- . *Americanization in the Evening School.* University of California, Berkeley, 1920. 217 p. ms.

4906. GREENE, HARRY HORTON. *Comparison of Scholastic Achievement of Native-Born and Foreign-Born Ninth-Grade Pupils in Marion County, West Virginia.* West Virginia University, 1934. 37 p. ms.

4907. HOPKINS, THOMAS FRANCIS. *A Program of Study for Teaching American-English Speech to Non-Native Students.* Colorado State College of Education, 1954. 74 p. ms.

4908. HOPPER, WILLIAM RILEY. *A Comparison of the Educational Achievement of Migratory and Non-Migratory Pupils of the Intermediate and Junior High Grades of Aurora Public Schools.* Colorado State College of Education, 1940. 54 p. ms.

4909. JAMES, H. MARGUERITE. *Immigrant Education.* New York State College for Teachers, Albany, 1915. 104 p. ms.

4910. KARLSEN, BJÖRN. *Attitudes of Foreign Students at the University of Nebraska towards Personnel and Practices at the University.* University of Nebraska, 1951. 98 p. ms.

4911. KEARNEY, Brother ROGATUS. *A Study of the Eidetic Ability in Boys of Different Nationalities.* Catholic University of America, 1933. 29 p. ms. (Covers American-born boys.)

4912. KORB, ERNEST ALEXANDER. *The Writing Abilities of Elementary School Children of American and Foreign Parentage.* University of Pittsburgh, 1932. 30 p. ms. Abstract in University of Pittsburgh: *Abstracts of Theses . . .* Vol. 8, 1932, p. 344-345. (Children of foreign parentage grouped only as Central European and South European.)

4913. LAWLER, MARY CLAIRE, 1914- . *Problems Presented by Foreign-Speaking Children and Suggestions for Overcoming Them.* Boston College, 1942. 63 p. ms.

4914. LAZENBY, JOHN CLINTON. *Non-English Home Conditions and Their Effect on School Work.* University of Chicago, 1923. 50 p. ms.

4915. LEE, TERESA. *The Use of the Flannelgraph in Promoting Reading Readiness in Non-English-Speaking Children.* Arizona State College, Flagstaff, 1954. 74 p. ms.

4916. LEVINE, VIOLET. *The Foreign Student at Stanford University.* Stanford University, 1949. 32 p. ms. (Considers students from 45 countries.)

4917. LOWREY, SARAH GOODWIN. *An Evaluation of Beginning English Texts for Non-English-Using Adults.* University of Pittsburgh, 1930. 40 p. ms. Abstract in University of Pittsburgh: *Abstracts of Theses . . .* Vol. 6, 1939, p. 324-325.

4918. McCLIMANS, GRACE BELL. *The Program of the United States Government for the Interchange of Students.* Stanford University, 1949. 67 p. ms.

4919. McCOOEY, DOROTHY LEMBACH. *The Educational Implications for the Chicago Public Schools of the Geographic Redistribution of Seven Ethnic and Racial Groups.* De Paul University, 1955. 150 p. ms.

4920. McGOLDRICK, KATHLEEN ATTRACTA. *The Effects of Bilingualism on Achievement in Foreign Languages.* Loyola University, 1954. 78 p. ms.

4921. MARKOWSKI, ADAM JOHN, 1915- . *The Effect of Bilingualism upon the Reading Habits of Sixth Grade Children.* Syracuse University, 1939. 32 p. ms.

4922. MASSARI, GLORIA C. *A Case Study of the Speech Difficulties of Twenty Adults with Foreign Dialect.* Boston University, 1958.

4923. MATTSON, OSCAR FREDRICK. *A Course of Instruction for Nationalization.* University of Wisconsin, 1925. 28 p. ms.

4924. MORGAN, GLENN. *A Study of the Interests and Accomplishments of the Different Nationalities Who Graduated from the Clinton, Indiana, High School in the Years 1922 to 1935.* Indiana State Teachers College, 1939. 83 p. ms. Abstract in *Teachers College Journal,* Vol. 11, p. 150-151, July 1940. (Covers 1268 graduates of 18 nationalities.)

4925. MULVEHILL, WILLIAM. *An Americanization Course for Children of Foreign Parentage.* University of Southern California, 1950. 102 p. ms.

4926. O'BRIEN, JULIA ROSE, 1880- . *The Adaptation of the Boston Fourth, Fifth, and Sixth Grade Courses of Study in English to the Children of Foreign Districts.* Boston University, 1927. 81 p. ms.

4927. O'DONNELL, JOSEPH DUGAN. *The Treaty Making Power of the United States and the Right of the United States Government by a Treaty to Regulate Education and Prevent Segregation of Aliens in a State.* Northwestern University, 1908. 68 p. ms.

4928. POLICASTRO, SUSAN. *Survey: The Scholastic Data on Refugee Pupils in the Secondary Schools of Newark, New Jersey, June 1949.* Hunter College of the City of New York, 1949. 75 p. ms.

4929. POND, ELSIE ADA. *Americanization and Education of Adult Immigrants in California.* Stanford University, 1920. 138 p. ms. (Covers 500 individuals representing 29 nationalities.)

4930. POPKIN, DOROTHY J. *A Guide for Newly Assigned English Teachers of Foreign Speaking Adult Students.* University of Southern California, 1958.

4931. REID, PEARL M. *Bilingualism as a Factor in Achievement in Reading and Arithmetic.* De Paul University, 1956.

4932. RICHARDSON, FANNY ELIZABETH. *A Survey of the Education of the Foreign-Born in Hennapin County.* University of Minnesota, 1942. 341 p. ms.

4933. RONTOS, KATHERINE. *A Study of the Development of the Americanization Program of the Chicago Board of Education.* De Paul University, 1957.

4934. SHIBLES, BURLEIGH HAROLD. *Measurement of the Size of English Understanding of Pupils in Grade One in Relation to Measured Intelligence and Bilingualism.* University of Maine, 1957. 86 p. ms.

4935. SINCLAIR, CRAWFORD CLARK. *Bi-Lingual Influence of School Progress.* Rutgers University, 1931. 99 p. ms.

4936. SOMERS, ELIZABETH A. *A Comparison of Personality Adjustments and Intelligence Quotients of Children of American Parents and Children of Foreign-Born Parents in the Westville Township High School, Westville, Illinois.* Indiana State Teachers College, 1939. 47 p. ms. (Contributions of the Graduate School, No. 403). Abstract in *Teachers College Journal,* Vol. 11, p. 149, July 1940.

4937. SPURGIN, ERNESTINE CONNER. *Teaching Music to Foreign Language Groups in Elementary School.* University of Redlands, 1940. 59 p. ms.

4938. STAVRIDOU, HELEN PERICLES. *A Study of Identification of Foreign Students at Ohio University and Adelphi College.* Ohio University, 1954. 56 p. ms.

4939. STEPHENS, SARA. *A Comparison of the Achievement in English of the Pupils in Whose Homes English is the Only Language Spoken with Those in Whose Homes a Foreign Language is also Spoken.* Kansas State Teachers College, Pittsburg, 1930.

4940. STIDHAM, KATHRYN HEALEY. *The Foreign Student in an American Metropolis.* University of Chicago, 1929. 127 p. ms.

4941. STOCKDALE, HOMER I. *A Study of Intelligence and Achievement among Children of Foreign Parentage and American Children of Grades Five to Eight in the Columbus School.* Indiana State Teachers College, 1929. 37 p. ms. (Contributions of the Graduate School, No. 378). Abstract in *Teachers College Journal,* Vol. 11, p. 137, July 1940.

4942. TAYLOR, Mrs. JULIA HAMILTON (ROBINSON). *A Critical Review of the Literature of Teaching English to Foreign-Home-Language Children.* University of Texas, 1956. 97 p. ms.

4943. THOMAS, ANNA M. *A Vocabulary for Non-English-Speaking Children.* New Mexico Western College, 1953.

4944. THOMPSON, MERRITT MOORE, 1884- . *The Teaching of English to Foreigners.* University of Southern California, 1923. 90 p. ms. For doctoral dissertation by same author, see No. 4439.

4945. TRAUTWEIN, MARY CUNLIFFE. *A History of the Development of Schools for Foreign-Born Adults in Los Angeles.* University of Southern California, 1928. 157 p. ms.

4946. WERNER, EMMI ELISABETH. *Social Distances between Various Ethnic and Religious Groups and Students in Lincoln, Nebraska.* University of Nebraska, 1951. 61 p. ms.

4947. WEST, Mrs. NELLIE ELIZABETH DALY, 1895- . *The Motivation of Adult Education for Americanization.* University of Arizona, 1944. 196 p. ms. Abstract in University of Arizona: *Abstracts of Theses for Higher Degrees,* 1943, 1944, p. 29.

4948. WEST, ROSCOE LAMBERT. *A Nationality and Age-Grade Study of the Schools of Trenton, New Jersey.* Harvard University, 1923. 82 p. ms.

4949. WILSON, FLORENCE. *The Work of the Schools for the Foreign Element in New Orleans.* Tulane University of Louisiana, 1925. 114 p. ms. (Covers over 40 nationalities.)

4950. WONG, HELEN WEN-CHUAN, 1904- . *Assistance in English for Foreign Students: A Critical Study of Provisions for Special Assistance in English for Foreign Students in Liberal Arts Colleges, Especially Barnard, Mt. Holyoke, Radcliffe, Smith, Vassar, and Wellesley.* Smith College, 1950. 180 p. ms.

4951. YOWELL, WILLIAM MERCER. *The Educational Problems Involved in the Americanization of the Foreigners in the United States of America.* University of Texas, 1921. 201 p. ms.

4952. ZIPRICK, ELSIE HELENE. *Methods of Orienting the Foreign Student to Life and Education in the United States through the American University.* University of Washington, 1952. 146 p. ms.

Composite

(NOS. 4953 - 5026)

DOCTORS

4953. ARJONA, ADORACION QUIJANO, 1925- . *An Experimental Study of the Adjustment Problems of a Group of Foreign Graduate Students and a Group of American Graduate Students at Indiana University.* Indiana University, 1956. 164 p. ms. Abstract in Indiana University: *Studies in Education,* 1956 (Thesis Abstract Series No. 8), p. 11-18; also in *Dissertation Abstracts,* Vol. 16, p. 1838, October 1956. Available on microfilm from University Microfilms, Ann Arbor, Michigan, as Publication No. 17,757. (Includes 62 foreign students from Asia, Europe, and Latin America.)

4954. BARDIS, PANOS DEMETRIUS, 1924- . *Dating Attitudes and Patterns among Foreign Students at Purdue University.* Purdue University, 1955. (Principal groups were from China, Greece, India, Philippines, Scandinavia, and Latin America.)

4955. BERE, MAY. *A Comparative Study of the Mental Capacity of Children of Foreign Parentage.* Columbia University, 1924. New York: Teachers College, Columbia University, 1924. ix, 105 p.

(Teachers College Contribution to Education, No. 154. Covers 379 South Italians, 366 East Europeans, and 100 Bohemians.)

4956. CAJOLEAS, LOUIS PETER, 1921- . *The Academic Record, Professional Development, and Return Adjustment of Doctoral Students from Other Lands: A Study of Teachers College Alumni, 1946-1955.* Columbia University, 1958. 280 p. ms. Abstract in *Dissertation Abstracts*, Vol. 19: p. 250-251, August 1958. Available on microfilm from University Microfilms, Ann Arbor, Michigan, as Publication No. 58-2611. (Covers 156 students, 114 men, 42 women, from 30 countries: 29 from China, 24 from India, 19 from Egypt, 14 from Puerto Rico, and smaller numbers from Australia, Burma, Colombia, Finland, Germany, Greece, Hong Kong, Honduras, Iran, Iraq, Israel, Japan, Korea, Netherlands, Nigeria, Pakistan, Philippines, Poland, Puerto Rico, Rumania, Sarawak, Sierra Leone, Sweden, Syria, Thailand, and Union of South Africa.)

4957. GEPHART, MARY LOUISE, 1913- . *A Study of the Professional Needs of Students from Other Lands Who Have Studied Home Economics in Colleges and Universities in the United States and Who Have Returned Home.* Columbia University, 1954. 221 p. ms. (Based on data received from 58 students, who studied in 16 American institutions, from the following 28 countries: Australia, Belgium, Burma, Chile, Costa Rica, Cuba, Denmark, Finland, Germany, Great Britain, Greece, Guatemala, India, Israel, Japan, Lebanon, the Netherlands, New Zealand, Norway, Pakistan, Paraguay, Peru, Philippines, Sweden, Switzerland, Thailand, Union of South Africa, and Uruguay.)

4958. GRAHAM, GRACE, 1910- . *Foreign Students in an American University.* Stanford University, 1952. 269 p. ms. Abstract in Stanford University: *Abstracts of Dissertations* . . . 1951-52, p. 563-565. (Covers 194 foreign students at "Lowlands University." "The Japanese and Chinese [students] have the highest number of problems.")

4959. HARPER, HEBER REECE, 1885- . *What European and American Students Think on International Problems: A Comparative Study of the Worldmindedness of University Students.* Columbia University, 1931. 255 p. ms. New York: Teachers College, Columbia University, 1931. xiii, 255 p. (Studies of the International Institute of Teachers College, Columbia University, No. 12. Includes students from Austria, Czechoslovakia, Denmark, France, Germany, Great Britain, and Switzerland.)

4960. HOPKINS, THOMAS W. *Educational Standardization and the "Foreign Child."* New York University, 1933. 276 p. ms. (Chiefly Polish children, but also includes Chinese, Filipino, Italian, Japanese, and Slavic groups.)

4961. HOUNTRAS, PANOS TIMOTHY, 1927- . (First name has since been legally changed from Panos to Peter.) *Factors Associated with the Academic Achievement of Foreign Graduate Students at the University of Michigan from 1947 to 1949.* University of Michigan, 1955. 136 p. ms. Abstract in *Dissertation Abstracts*, Vol. 15, p. 762-763, May 1955. Available on microfilm from University Microfilms, Ann Arbor, Michigan, as Publication No. 11,297. (Based on study of 587 students, as follows: China, 226; India, 98; and 53 other countries.)

4962. IRVINE, WILLIAM BAY, 1893- . *A Study of Relative Participation of the Children of Foreign-born, Native, and Mixed Parentage in Eight Recreational and Religious Agencies of Sharon, Pennsylvania.* University of Pittsburgh, 1938. Abstract in University of Pittsburgh: *Abstracts of Theses* . . . Vol. 14, 1938, p. 150-159. (Czechoslovakian and Italian groups ranked first and second in size among the children of foreign-born parents.)

4963. JORDAN, RIVERDA HARDING, 1873-1950. *The Relationship between Nationality and School Progress.* University of Minnesota, 1919. Published as *Nationality and School Progress: A Study in Americanization,* Bloomington, Illinois: Public School Publishing Co., 1921. 105 p. (School and Home Education Monographs, No. 4. Covers Austrian, British, Danish, Finnish, German, Italian, Norwegian, Polish, Roumanian, Russian, and Swedish groups.)

4964. KIELL, NORMAN TENESE, 1916- . *A Study of Attitudes of Indian and Pakistani Students: A Study of Attitudes of Indian and Pakistani Students in the United States toward America and American Democracy and the Responsibility of American Educational Institutions toward Exchange Students.* Columbia University, 1949. 189 p. ms.

4965. LARRY, ETTA CYNTHIA, 1903- . *A Study of the Sounds of the English Language as Spoken by Five Racial Groups in the Hawaiian Islands.* Columbia University, 1942. New York: Columbia University, 1942. 79 p. Reproduced from typewritten copy. (Includes Chinese, Filipino, Hawaiian, Japanese, and Portuguese groups.)

4966. LEITER, RUSSELL GRAYDON, 1901- . *A Comparative Study of the General Intelligence of Caucasian, Chinese, and Japanese Children, as Measured by the Leiter International Performance Scale.* University of Southern California, 1938. 618 p. ms. Abstract in University of Southern California: *Abstracts of Dissertations,* 1938, p. 25-29.

4967. LEVAI, BLAISE, 1919- . *A Study of Group Discussions among Indian Students on a Controversial Subject.* University of Michigan, 1952. 87 p. ms. Abstract in *Dissertation Abstracts*, Vol. 12, No. 3, p. 273-274, 1952. Available on microfilm from University Microfilms, Ann Arbor, Michigan, as Publication No. 3,586. (Based on opinions expressed by 120 graduate students from India and Pakistan in four American universities on the question: "Future of India and Pakistan: United or Disunited?")

4968. LUKE, ORRAL STANFORD, 1903- . *Differences in Musical Aptitude in School Children of Different National and Racial Origin.* University of California, Berkeley, 1939. 149 p. ms. (Includes 168 northern Europeans, 109 Italians, 130 Chinese, 55 Japanese, and 31 Spanish and Portuguese.)

4969. MARTIN, RICHARD PANTALL, 1913- . *The Adjustment of Latin-American Male Students in Selected Private Secondary Schools in the United States.* Northwestern University, 1954. 312 p. ms. Abstract in *Dissertation Abstracts,* Vol. 14, p. 1605-1606, October 1954. Available on microfilm from University Microfilms, Ann Arbor, Michigan, as Publication No. 9,253. (Includes students from Argentina, Aruba, Colombia, Cuba, El Salvador, Guatemala, Honduras, Mexico, Puerto Rico, and Venezuela. Twenty-five were students at Pennington School, New Jersey; 27 at Western Military Academy, Illinois.)

4970. MIERZWA, DOROTHY ROSE, 1924- . *A Study of Some of the Problems of Adjustment Experienced in the Non-Academic Areas by International Students in Teachers College.* Columbia University, 1953. 133 p. ms. (Includes 217 students from 46 countries: 37 from Canada, 19 from China, 19 from Philippines, 12 from India, 11 from Brazil, 11 from Egypt, and smaller numbers from Arabia, Argentina, Belgium, British West Indies, Burma, Chile, Czechoslovakia, Denmark, Finland, France, Germany, Great Britain, Haiti, Hungary, Iran, Iraq, Israel, Japan, Korea, Lebanon, Nicaragua, Nigeria, Norway, Pakistan, Panama, Peru, Poland, Puerto Rico, Romania, Sweden, Switzerland, Syria, Thailand, Turkey, Union of South Africa, USSR, Virgin Islands, Yugoslavia.)

4971. MOORE, FORREST GURNEY, 1916- . *Factors Affecting the Academic Success of Foreign Students in American Universities.* University of Minnesota, 1953. 565 p. ms. Abstract in *Dissertation Abstracts,* Vol. 14, p. 492-493, March 1954. Available on microfilm from University Microfilms, Ann Arbor, Michigan, as Publication No. 7,486. (Covers 516 students from China, India, and Norway.)

4972. SANMANN, MADGE STEWART, 1899- . *A Study of the Experiences of Selected Oriental Students in Colleges and Universities in the United States and Implications for Higher Education.* Northwestern University, 1948. 424 p. ms. Abstract in Northwestern University: *Summaries of Doctoral Dissertations,* Vol. 16, 1948, p. 251-255. (Includes students from Afghanistan, China, India, Japan, Korea, Philippines, and Turkey.)

4973. SCOTT, Mrs. ADELINE STAILEY WHITE, 1890- . *A Comparative Study of Responses of Children of Different Nationalities and Environments in Intelligence and Achievement Tests.* Columbia University, 1929. New York: Bureau of Publications, Teachers College, Columbia University, 1929. iii, 30 p. (Teachers College Contribution to Education, No. 367. Studies groups of children of German, Mexican, and American parentage in Texas.)

4974. SCULLY, GRACE MARY, 1915- . *An Exploratory Study of Students from Abroad Who Do Not Expect to Return to Their Home Country.* Columbia University, 1956. 217 p. ms. (Based on extensive personal interviews with 22 students of 15 institutions in the Greater New York area, from the Far East, Middle East, Southern Europe, Northern Europe, Africa, and South America. "Identity of the interviewees, institutions, and cultures has been concealed in the writing of the cases.")

4975. VASWANI, HARI VALIRAM, 1923- . *A Study of the Problems of Foreign Students at the Berkeley Campus of the University of California.* University of California, Berkeley, 1950. 165 p. ms. (Based on all foreign students, 599 in number, on student visas in spring of 1949, grouped as follows: Asia, exclusive of India and China, 207; India, 77; China, 100; Latin America, 87; Europe, 115; Stateless, 13. Asiatic group included Afghanistan, Burma, Egypt, Iran, Iraq, Israel, Lebanon, Malaya, Philippines, Saudi Arabia, Syria, and Turkey. Latin-American group included Argentina, Bolivia, Brazil, Chile, Colombia, Costa Rica, Cuba, Ecuador, El Salvador, Guatemala, Honduras, Jamaica, Mexico, Panama, Peru, Trinidad, and Venezuela. European group included Austria, Belgium, Cyprus, Czechoslovakia, Denmark, France, Germany, Great Britain, Greece, Hungary, Iceland, Italy, Latvia, the Netherlands, New Zealand, Norway, Poland, Portugal, Rumania, South Africa, Sweden, Switzerland, and USSR.)

MASTERS

4976. ARCHANGEL, Sister MARY. *Bilingualism and Achievement in Grades Four and Six.* Mt. St. Joseph's Teachers College, 1956. 63 p. ms. (Considers especially groups of Italian and Polish children.)

4977. ARIDI, BASHER, 1927- . *Attitude of the Asiatic Students Attending the Utah State Agricultural College toward the United States, Logan, and the U. S. A. C.* Utah State Agricultural College, 1953. 45 p. ms. (Covers 54 students, distributed as follows: Iraqi, 20; Iranian, 11; Israeli, 8; Chinese, 4; Lebanese, 3; Thai, 3; Indian, 3; Pakistani, 1; Turkish, 1.)

4978. BARTLETT, KATHERINE. *A Racial Classification of College Students.* University of Denver, 1930. 115 p. ms. (Includes British, French, German, Irish, Italian, Norwegian, Russian, and Swedish students.)

4979. BUTZBACH, ARTHUR GRAHAM. *The Segregation of Orientals in the San Francisco Schools.* Stanford University, 1928. (Includes Chinese, Japanese, and Koreans.)

4980. CARTER, RUTH CORBIN, 1896- . *Problems of Adult Education Classes among the Hungarians and Italians in Tangipahoa and Livingston Parishes.* Louisiana State University and State Agricultural and Mechanical College, 1935. 66 p. ms.

4981. CLARFIELD, ALBERT BORIS. *The Americanization of the Foreign-Born in Duluth: A Typical American Community.* University of Minnesota, 1920. 121 p. ms. (Considers chiefly Finns, Hungarians, Scandanavians, and Slavs.)

4982. DOI, HELEN NOBUKO. *A Study of the Elementary Grade Children Attending the Greek and the Japanese Language Schools.* University of Utah, 1954. 166 p. ms.

4983. ELLZEY, ROSE C., 1908- . *A Comparative Study of the Reading Ability of French-Speaking and Spanish-Speaking Pupils in the Elementary Grades.* Louisiana State University and State Agricultural and Mechanical College, 1937. 81 p. ms. Abstract in *Louisiana State University Bulletin,* Vol. 30, n.s., No. 3, p. 34-35, March 1938.

4984. ELY, PHILIP LLOYD. *The Status of Pupils of Different Foreign Ancestry in the Valley Wheel Schools.* Massachusetts State College, 1938. 55 p. ms. (Chief groups: Polish, Southern European, Northern European.)

4985. ENEBOE, ROSE ADELAIDE. *The Musical Aptitude of 740 High School Students of Different Nationalities.* Northwestern University, 1933. 53 p. ms. (Includes Austrian, British, Czech, Danish, Dutch, French, German, Greek, Hungarian, Irish, Italian, Lithuanian, Norwegian, Russian, Slavic, and Swedish groups.)

4986. ENOCHS, JAMES BYRON. *Language Peculiarities in a Mining Town, Jerome, Arizona.* University of Colorado, 1937. 34 p. ms. Abstract in *University of Colorado Studies,* Vol. 25, No. 1, p. 62, November 1937. (Includes German, Irish, Italian, Mexican, and Slavic groups.)

4987. EPSTEIN, MAX. *A Comparative Study of the Intelligence of Children of Foreign Parentage.* College of the City of New York, 1928. 105 p. ms. (Includes German, Irish, Italian, Lithuanian, Polish, and Russian groups.)

4988. FORSTAT, REISHA ELAINE. *Problems of Foreign Students at Purdue University.* Purdue University, 1950. 79 p. ms. Published in part as "Adjustments of International Students," *Sociology and Social Research,* Vol. 36, p. 25-30, September-October 1951. (Based on study of 182 students from 37 countries, including Canada, 34; China, 34; Turkey, 18; India, 14; Norway, 10; Venezuela, 9; and Brazil, 6.)

4989. GARDNER, ANNA ELIZABETH, 1887- *A Study of Certain Phases of Musical Ability in Young Children of Different Nationalities.* New York State College for Teachers, Albany, 1930. 38 p. ms. (Includes British, German, Irish, Italian, Scandanavian, and Slavic groups.)

4990. GUKICH, DOROTHY. *A Survey of the Adjustments of Graduate International Students in Education at the Ohio State University.* Ohio State University, 1948. 119 p. ms. (Includes students from Chile, China, Colombia, Egypt, Iraq, Peru, and Thailand.)

4991. HALE, HARRY MORGAN. *A Study of the Music Talents of Hawaiian, Filipino, and Portuguese Children.* University of Hawaii, 1936. 68 p. ms.

4992. HAVEN, SETH EDSON. *The Relative Effort of Children of Native Versus Foreign-Born Parents.* Ohio State University, 1929. 36 p. ms. (Foreign-born include French, German, Hungarian, Lithuanian, and Polish groups.)

4993. HOLDEN, Sister MARY AMATA. *The Relation between the Intelligence of Pupils of Different Nationalities and the Accomplishments of These Same Individuals of Different Levels of Mental Ability.* Indiana State Teachers College, 1942. 109 p. ms. Abstract in *Teachers College Journal,* Vol. 14, p. 135-136, July 1943. (Contributions of the Graduate School, No. 490. Includes groups of 200 children each of German, Italian, Lithuanian, and Polish parentage.)

4994. HOLLEY, TOM, 1904- . *The Educational Status of the Public Schools in Karnes, Jim Wells, and Brooks Counties of Texas.* Southern Methodist University, 1937. 124 p. ms. Abstract in Southern Methodist University: *Abstracts of Theses,* No. 5, 1938, p. 9. (Considers Bohemian, German, Mexican, and Polish groups.)

4995. HUGHES, RUTH CAROL. *Educational Implications of Civil Rights Practices with Minority Groups in a Local Community.* Stanford University, 1949. 127 p. ms. (Considers Chinese-American and Japanese-American groups.)

4996. HYDE, HELEN IRENE. *A Comparison of the Physical Characteristics of American, Japanese, and Mexican School Children.* University of Southern California, 1928. 126 p. ms.

4997. JOHNSON, FLORENCE BOOCO. *A Comparative Study of the Basic Music Talents of Three Racial Groups — Chinese, Japanese, and Part Hawaiian.* University of Hawaii, 1933. 95 p. ms.

4998. KAY, GRACE MARION, 1893- . *Personality Differences in Children of Polish, Italian, Jewish, and American-Born Parents.* New York State College for Teachers, Albany, 1938. 40 p. ms.

4999. KELTY, OMA B. *A Comparison of Reading Abilities of First Grade Children from English-Speaking Homes with Those from Non-English-Speaking Homes in East Chicago.* Indiana State Teachers College, 1936. 25 p. ms. (Contributions of the Graduate School, No. 269.) Abstract in *Teachers College Journal,* Vol. 8, p. 70, July 1937. (Includes study of 99 Mexican children and 97 Polish children.)

5000. KEYSER, EDITH. *An Experimental Study of Overstatement among Different Races.* University of Southern California, 1932. 105 p. ms. (Based on Japanese, Mexican, Negro, and White students in the United States.)

5001. KIERNAN-VASA, HELEN COGAN, 1882- *Language Errors of Adult Foreign-Born Students.* George Washington University, 1939. 78 p. ms. (Includes Albanian, Austrian, Chinese, German, Italian, Lithuanian, Mexican, and Russian groups.)

5002. KNUDSON, RUTH BLANCHARD. *Attitudes of International Students toward Their Experiences at Iowa State College.* Iowa State College of Agriculture and Mechanic Arts, 1956. 85 p. ms. (Largest group was from Latin-American countries with considerable number from Far East.)

5003. LINDQUIST, RUTH MARY. *An Experiment in Teaching a Group of Foreign-Born Homemakers.* University of Chicago, 1922. 74 p. ms. (Group consisted of 19 Lithuanians and Poles.)

5004. MARSHALL, EMILY LEORA. *A Study of the Achievement of Chinese and Japanese Children in the Public Schools of Honolulu.* University of Hawaii, 1927. 75 p. ms.

5005. MASON, MARY ELEANOR. *A Comparison of the Cole and Vincent Group Intelligence Test for School Entrants and the Stanford Revision of the Binet-Simon Test for English-Speaking Foreign Children.* University of Colorado, 1923. 78 p. ms. (Includes Mexican and Italian children in Kentucky and Colorado.)

5006. MITCHELL, M. MAXINE. *A Further Comparison of the Adjustment to Syracuse University of Students Whose Parents Are Foreign-Born with a Controlled Group of Students Whose Parents are American-Born.* Syracuse University, 1943. 115 p. ms. (Each group consisted of 113 women students. The foreign consisted of groups of several students each from Austria, Germany, Great Britain, Greece, Italy, and Poland, with one or two each from a score of other countries in Asia and South America as well as Europe.)

5007. MOORE, JOHN ABE. *A Comparative Study of the School Progress of Certain Language Groups in the Rural Schools of Texas.* University of Texas, 1936. 78 p. ms. (Principal groups were Czechs, Germans, and Spanish-Americans.)

5008. NEELY, ANNA ELIZABETH. *The Foreign Student on the American Campus.* University of Chicago, 1922. 60 p. ms. (Chiefly students from China, Japan, and the Phillipines.)

5009. OLESEN, ELISABETH WALCOTT, 1919- . *The Adjustment of a Group of Children to Life on a Refugee Boat.* Cornell University, 1943. 99 p. ms. ("Based on the writer's experience during the month of January, 1943, as a member of a group which brought 35 refugee children from Portugal to the United States." —Introduction, The children were French, German, and Polish.)

5010. PARKS, HUGH AUGUSTUS. *Giving Non-English-Speaking Germans and Japanese a Basic Speaking Ability in English through Using Only English in the Classroom.* North Texas State Teachers College, 1946. 86 p. ms. Abstract in North Texas State Teachers College: *Abstracts of Theses, 1941-1946,* p. 106.

5011. PERRY, NEAL CLIFFORD. *An Investigation of Certain Aspects of the Social, Economic, and Educational Status of Second-Generation Chinese and Japanese Graduates of the High Schools of Fresno, California.* University of Southern California, 1938. 141 p. ms.

5012. PETERSON, ARTHUR ELLIOTT, 1884- . *Religious Education and the Oriental in the Pacific Coast States.* Pacific School of Religion, 1924. (Chinese, Japanese.)

5013. POTTER, ROBERT ELMER. *The Backgrounds and Development of Physical Education in Hawaii.* Ohio University, 1948. Abstract in Ohio University: *Abstracts of Master's Theses . . . 1948,* p. 22. (Covers groups of foreign parentage or descent including British, Chinese, Filipino, German, Japanese, Korean, Portuguese, Puerto Rican, Russian, and Spanish.)

5014. PREDMORE, ROYAL LIONEL. *Bi-Lingualism and the First Year of School.* Rutgers University, 1931. 100 p. ms. (Includes Hungarian and Slavic children.)

5015. ROGERSON, JESSIE BROWNE. *A Case Study of the Socialization of Foreign Children through Instruction in Home Economics.* University of Southern California, 1935. 99 p. ms. (Covers American-born daughters of Italian, Japanese, Mexican, Russian, and Slavic parents in San Pedro, California.)

5016. ROLLS, HARRIET MAUD, 1895- . *A Comparative Study of Mistakes Made in Written Composition by Children of Slavic, Italian, and American Parentage.* New York State College for Teachers, Albany, 1934. 57 p. ms.

5017. SHUWARGER, MICHAEL. *Case Studies of Educational Problems of Iron Curtain Immigrants.* University of Southern California, 1954. 58 p. ms. (Includes six Russians and Ukrainians and one German.)

5018. SOHNS, HAROLD WILLIAM. *Achievement of Seventh Grade Pupils of American and Foreign Parentage in the Public Schools of Trinidad, Colorado.* University of Colorado, 1938. 46 p. ms. Abstract in *University of Colorado Studies,* Vol. 26, No. 1, p. 134, November 1938. (Children were chiefly of Spanish-American and Italian parentage.)

5019. SOWERS, LLOYD ELLSWORTH. *A Comparative Study of the Reading Ability of Mexican, Japanese, and American Children.* University of Southern California, 1942. 114 p. ms.

5020. STACKHOUSE, DAISY MARIE. *Foreign Foods: A Project in Teaching Foods to Foreign Students in Bedford, Ohio.* Ohio State University, 1936. 205 p. ms. (Includes Austrian, British, Croatian, Czechoslovakian, German, Hungarian, Irish, Italian, Lithuanian, Polish, Russian, Serbian, and Slovak students.)

5021. STUBBINS, DONALD GEORGE, 1902- . *A Comparison of the Scholastic Difficulties of Immigrant and Native American Children in the Schools of Mott, Hottinger County, North Dakota.* University of North Dakota, 1936. 79 p. ms. (Immigrant children distributed as follows: German, 48 per cent; German-speaking section of Russia, 36 per cent; Hungarian, 16 per cent.)

5022. SULLIVAN, MARY, 1900- . *A Comparison of the Errors in English Usage of a Group of Senior High School Pupils of Non-English-Speaking Parents with a Group of Senior High School Pupils of English-Speaking Parents.* Smith College, 1935. 106 p. ms. (Principal groups were French and Polish speaking.)

5023. VEGHER, MARY ROSE. *A Comparative Study of Children of Foreign Parentage and American Parentage in Attaining the Dominant Objectives of the Social Studies.* University of Southern California, 1930. 117 p. ms. (Compares 119 foreign and 119 American children. Foreign children were of Austrian, Finnish, Norwegian, Swedish, and Yugoslavian parentage.)

5024. VOELLER, JOSEPH B., 1901- . *The Origin of the German-Russian People and Their Role in North Dakota.* University of North Dakota, 1940. 114 p. ms. (Includes many educational factors and recommendations.)

5025. WILCOX, ALFRED CHURCHILL. *A Study of the Relative Progress Made in an American School by Pupils Representing Various European Nationalities.* State University of Iowa, 1927. 51 p. ms. (Study of Eveleth, Minnesota, schools with British, Czech, Danish, Dutch, Finnish, German, Irish, Italian, Norwegian, Polish, Serbian, Slavonic, and Swedish children.)

5026. WOELLNER, ALBERTA LEE. 1930- . *A Phonetic Study of the Pronunciation of General American English Spoken by Selected Foreign Students from India and Pakistan.* University of Kansas, 1957. 93 p. ms.

Albanian
(NO. 5027)

MASTER

5027. ADAMS, PHILIP S. *Problems of A Group of Adolescents of Albanian Immigrant Parentage.* Catholic University of America, 1950. 61 p. ms. (Includes chapter on role of the secondary school.)

See also No. 5001.

Arabian
(NOS. 5028 - 5029)

DOCTORS

5028. AINSWORTH, LABAN LINTON, Jr., 1925- *An Exploratory Study of the Academic Achievement of Arab Students.* University of Texas, 1957. 140 p. ms. Abstract in *Dissertation Abstracts*, Vol. 17, p. 1702-1703, August 1957. Available on microfilm from University Microfilm, Ann Arbor, Michigan, as Publication No. 21,027. (Covers 148 Arab students at University of Texas.)

5029. DIAB, LUTFY N. *Authoritarianism and Prejudice in Near-Eastern Students Attending American Universities.* University of Oklahoma, 1956. 59 p. ms. Abstract in *Dissertation Abstracts*, Vol. 17, p. 419, February 1957. Available on microfilm from University Microfilms, Ann Arbor, Michigan, as Publication No. 19,487.

See also Nos. 4970, 4975.

Armenian
(NO. 5030)

MASTER

5030. JANES, HATTIE ELIZABETH. *A Comparative Study of the Achievement of American and Armenian Children in the Same School System.* Stanford University, 1932. 84 p. ms.

British
(NO. 5031)

DOCTORS

See Nos. 4957, 4959, 4963, 4970, 4975, 5698.

MASTER

5031. EUSDEN, RAY ANDERSON. *The Educational Work of the Church of England in the American Colonies, 1700-1776.* University of Chicago, 1916. 65 p. ms.

See also Nos. 4978, 4985, 4989, 5006, 5013, 5020, 5025.

Chinese

(NOS. 5032 - 5089)

DOCTORS

5032. CHANG, FRANCIS YOUNG, 1903- . *A Study of the Movement to Segregate Chinese Pupils in the San Francisco Public Schools up to 1885.* Stanford University, 1936. 404 p. ms. Abstract in Stanford University: *Abstracts of Dissertations* . . . 1935-36, p. 185-188.

5033. CHU, JENNINGS PINK-WEI, 1895- . *Chinese Students in America: Qualities Associated with Their Success.* Columbia University, 1922. New York: Teachers College, Columbia University, 1922. iii, 55 p. (Teachers College Contribution to Education, No. 127.)

5034. DJANG, HISANG LAN. *The Adjustment in American Culture of the Chinese Children in Chinatown, Chicago, and Its Educational Implications.* Northwestern University, 1940. 240 p. ms.

5035. HAO, PETER TE-YUAN, 1915- . *An Analysis of Certain Learning Difficulties of Chinese Students in New York City.* New York University, 1955. 373 p. ms. Abstract in *Dissertation Abstracts,* Vol. 15, p. 1551, October 1955. Available on microfilm from University Microfilms, Ann Arbor, Michigan, as Publication No. 12,218.

5036. HO, PERRY YEWTON. *A Comparative Study of the Ingenuity of American and Chinese Students.* University of Southern California, 1926. 58 p. ms.

5037. HUANG, LUCY, 1920- . *Dating and Courtship Innovations of Chinese Students in America.* University of Chicago, 1954. 480 p. ms. Available on microfilm: see index under "University of Chicago."

5038. KAO, LIN-YING, 1918- . *Academic and Professional Attainments of Native Chinese Students Graduating from Teachers College, Columbia University, 1909-1950.* Columbia University, 1951. 153 p. ms.

5039. KUNG, SAMUEL SHI-SHIN, 1915- . *Personal and Professional Problems of Chinese Students and Former Students in the New York Metropolitan Area.* Columbia University, 1955. 186 p. ms.

5040. KWOH, EDWIN SIH-UNG. *Chinese Students in American Universities.* Columbia University, 1946. 220 p. ms.

5041. LI, PEI-CHAO, 1917- . *A Study of the Heterosexual Social Life of Single Male Chinese College Students in New York City.* Columbia University, 1955. 165 p. ms.

5042. LIU, CHING-HO, 1913- . *The Influence of Cultural Background on the Moral Judgment of Children.* Columbia University, 1950. 101 p. ms. Abstract in *Microfilm Abstracts,* Vol. 10, No. 4, p. 319-321, 1950. Available on microfilm from University Microfilms, Ann Arbor, Michigan, as Publication No. 1,869. (Compares 52 Chinese-American children with 52 White-American children.)

5043. LIU, FU-JU. *A Comparative Demographic Study of Native-Born and Foreign-Born Chinese Populations in the United States.* Michigan State College of Agriculture and Applied Science, 1953. 278 p. ms. Abstract in *Dissertation Abstracts,* Vol. 14, p. 203-204, January 1954. Available on microfilm from University Microfilms, Ann Arbor, Michigan, as Publication No. 5,925. (Includes educational factors.)

5044. LIU, YUNG-SZI, 1902- . *The Academic Achievement of Chinese Graduate Students at the University of Michigan, 1907-1950.* University of Michigan, 1956. 169 p. ms. Abstract in *Dissertation Abstracts,* Vol. 16, p. 2380, December 1956. Available on microfilm from University Microfilms, Ann Arbor, Michigan, as Publication No. 18,620.

5045. MA, YI YING, 1909- . *Effects of Attendance at Chinese Language Schools upon San Francisco Children.* University of California, Berkeley, 1945. 87 p. ms. For master's thesis by same author, see No. 1,697.

5046. PORTER, RAYMOND WILLIS, 1889-1950. *A Study of the Musical Talent of Chinese Attending Public Schools in Chicago.* University of Chicago, 1931. 167 p. ms. Abstract in University of Chicago: *Abstracts of Theses, Humanistic Series:* Vol. 9, p. 81-86.

5047. SHEN, EUGENE, 1900- . (Shen, Yu-Kan in Library of Congress card catalog). *The Reading of Chinese in Vertical and Horizontal Axes: An Experimental Study by Means of Photographic Recording of Eye Movements.* Stanford University, 1926. 139 p. ms. Abstract in Stanford University: *Abstracts of Dissertations* . . . 1926-27, p. 244-247.

5048. SHIH, HSIEN-JU, 1904- . *The Social and Vocational Adjustment of the Second Generation Chinese High School Students in San Francisco.* University of California, Berkeley, 1937. 152 p. ms.

5049. YIEH, TSUNG-KAO, 1906- . *The Adjustment Problems of Chinese Graduate Students in American Universities.* University of Chicago, 1934. Chicago: 1924. ii, 127 p. Private edition, distributed to libraries in the United States and abroad in 1934. For master's thesis by same author, see No. 1,812.

5050. YU, SIU-WEN. *A Guidance Program for Chinese Youth in the Chinese Christian Center, New York City.* Columbia University, 1940. 131 p. ms.

See also Nos. 1369, 4954, 4956, 4958, 4960, 4961, 4965, 4966, 4968, 4970, 4971, 4972.

MASTERS

5051. ADAMS, FLORA A. *Chinese Student Life at the University of Southern California.* University of Southern California, 1935. 117 p. ms.

5052. BROWN, SALLY ANN. *Adult Education in a Chinese-American Community.* Stanford University, 1949. 72 p. ms.

5053. BRUGGER, FLORENCE. *The Chinese-American Girl: A Study in Cultural Conflicts.* New York University, 1935. 265 p. ms.

5054. CASEY, THERESA AGNES. *A Study of the Difficulties in English Usage Encountered by American-Born Chinese Children.* Stanford University, 1940. 100 p. ms.

5055. CHAN, YING, 1916- . *Remedial Reading Problems and Techniques for Chinese Students in the United States.* University of Southern California, 1950. 58 p. ms. For doctoral dissertation by same author, see No. 1372.

5056. CHANG, Rev. JAMES ALOYSIUS, 1922- . *Survey of the Educational Needs of Boston Chinese.* Boston College, 1953. 73 p. ms.

5057. CHANG, TAO-PIN. *The Rural School House and Equipment with Special Reference to Cochise and Pinal Counties, Arizona, and Their Adaptation to Chinese Conditions.* University of Arizona, 1923. 52 p. ms.

5058. CHEN, EUGENIA VIOLA. *Survey of Chinese Youth and Student Clubs in New York City.* University of Michigan, 1945. 145 p. ms.

5059. CHEO, YUAN-CHEN. *The Cultural and Social Activities of the Chinese Students in the State of California.* Stanford University, 1929. 156 p. ms.

5060. CHIN, DOROTHY FONG. *Vocational Guidance of Chinese Students at Commerce High School, San Francisco, Spring 1948.* Stanford University, 1948. 92 p. ms.

5061. CHIN, ETTIE LEN-TOY. *Leisure-Time Activities of the Chinese Students of the University of Michigan.* University of Michigan, 1937. 87 p. ms.

5062. CHINN, FLORENCE WORLEY. *Religious Education in the Chinese Community of San Francisco.* University of Chicago, 1920. 59 p. ms.

5063. CHOW, LILLIAN WAI-CHUEN. *A Study of the Height and Weight of Chinese School Children in Some Northern California Cities.* College of the Pacific, 1944. 30 p. ms.

5064. CHRISTENSON, EDITH JULIA. *English Difficulties of Chinese Pupils in the Haines Elementary School, Chicago.* University of Chicago, 1934. 51 p. ms.

5065. CHUE, KING-HO, 1905- . *The Education of Chinese Children in Washington, D. C.* George Washington University, 1939. 47 p. ms.

5066. CHUN, ELINOR YUK-LIN. *A Study of the Use of Sentences by the Bilingual Child of Chinese Ancestry in Hawaii.* University of Hawaii, 1935. 77 p. ms.

5067. COSSUM, WILFORD WELLS. *A Study of Relative Reading Efficiency in English and Chinese.* University of Chicago, 1920. 38 p. ms.

5068. DUNBAR, AGNES MARY. *The Second-Generation Chinese in New York City's Chinatown, and Especially the Vocational Problems of the American-Born Females in that Community.* Columbia University, 1937. 146 p. ms.

5069. DUSEL, JOHN PAUL. *The Adjustment of American-Chinese Students in a California High School.* Stanford University, 1946. 101 p. ms.

5070. GIN, DZI-SHI. *Food for Children, with Special Reference to Dietaries for Chinese Children.* College of the Pacific, 1934. 163 p. ms.

5071. GRAALFS, MARILYN. *A Sociometric Study of Chinese Students in a Polytechnic High School.* University of Washington, 1949. 61 p. ms.

5072. INGLE, PHYLLIS SOUTHARD. *The Presentation of American-English to Cantonese-American Bilingual Students.* San Francisco State College, 1952. 97 p. ms.

5073. LAI, KUM-PUI. *The Natural History of the Chinese Language School in Hawaii.* University of Hawaii, 1935. 169 p. ms.

5074. LEE, MABEL SAM. *The Recreational Interests and Participation of a Selected Group of Chinese Boys and Girls in Los Angeles, California.* University of Southern California, 1939. 90 p. ms.

5075. LEE, MARY BO-TZE, 1896- . *Problems of the Segregated School for Asiatics in San Francisco.* University of California, Berkeley, 1922. 41 p. ms.

5076. LEE, SARAH DOCFON, 1898- . (Name changed to Sarah Lee Cheuk, September 1937). *A Comparative Study of the Intelligence of Normal Chinese and American School Children.* University of California, Berkeley, 1921. 57 p. ms.

5077. LI, SYLVIANNE FEI-AI. *A History of the Education of the Chinese in Hawaii.* Oberlin College, 1940. 64 p. ms.

5078. LOWE, ERLINE ROCHELLE. *The Growth of Cantonese Boys in the United States.* State University of Iowa, 1941. 48 p. ms.

5079. MOTOYAMA, ELSIE CHING. *A Study of the Growth in Vocabulary of Young Bilingual Children of Chinese Ancestry Before and After a Year of Kindergarten Instruction.* University of Hawaii, 1940. 92 p. ms.

5080. PAU, RUTH MUI-KUANG. *A Study of the Characteristics of Chinese Children from Three to Six Years of Age in a Kindergarten in New York City and Some Comparisons with American Children of Pre-School Age.* New York University, 1929. 62 p. ms.

5081. PIAN, JUNA HSUEH-CHUN. *A Comparative Study of the Daily Time Distribution of Chinese and American Junior High School Pupils.* University of Michigan, 1932. 120 p. ms. Abstract in University of Michigan: *Abstracts of Dissertations and Theses in Education,* 1931, 1932, p. 94-95.

5082. POTT, JAMES HAWKS. *The Measurement of Attitudes of Chinese Students at the University of Michigan toward Americans.* University of Michigan, 1933. 76 p. ms.

5083. ROSSI, VICTOR LUCIEN. *The Reading Vocabulary Proficiency of Bilingual American-Chinese Children.* Stanford University, 1949. 70 p. ms.

5084. SOONG, RUTH JOAN. *A Survey of the Education of Chinese Children in Chicago.* University of Chicago, 1931. 121 p. ms.

5085. TAAM, TSO-TIN, 1903- . *A Proposed Program of Christian Education for the Chinese Churches in the San Francisco Bay Region.* Pacific School of Religion, 1934.

5086. TSOU, GEORGE YU-CHIEH. *The Chinese Organizations in New York City: A Social Study of the Cultural, Educational, Social, and Welfare Organizations in New York City.* New York University, 1938. 102 p. ms.

5087. WONG, Mrs. CORINNE HONG-SLING. *The Christian Education Program of Chinese Protestant Churches of Chinatown in New York.* Biblical Seminary in New York, 1954.

5088. YEE, ALYCE AKO. *A Study of the Development of Language among Bilingual Children of Chinese Ancestry in the City of Honolulu as Measured by Their Use of English and Chinese Words.* University of Hawaii, 1935. 83 p. ms.

5089. YEUNG, KWOK-TSUEN. *The Intelligence of Chinese Children in San Francisco and Vicinity.* Stanford University, 1921. 64 p. ms.

See also Nos. 272, 4977, 4979, 4988, 4990, 4995, 4997, 5001, 5004, 5008, 5011, 5012, 5013.

Danish
(NOS. 5090 – 5091)

DOCTORS

See Nos. 3083, 4957, 4959, 4963, 4970, 4975.

MASTERS

5090. GRANTHAM, GRACE CONE, 1901- . *The Danes in Wharton County.* Texas College of Arts and Industries, 1947. 42 p. ms. (Includes consideration of education.)

5091. JORGENSEN, PETER. *The Determination of the Spelling Difficulty for Pupils from Danish-Speaking Homes of Those Phonetic Elements of the English Language which Are Not Found in Danish.* State University of Iowa, 1924. 51 p. ms.

See also No. 5025. See also Scandinavian.

Dutch
(Nos. 5092 – 5094)

DOCTOR

5092. STEGENGA, PRESTON JAY, 1924- . *Hope College in Dutch-American Life, 1851-1951.* University of Michigan, 1952. Published as *Anchor of Hope: The History of an American Denominational Institution, Hope College.* Grand Rapids, Michigan: Eerdmans, 1954. 271 p. Abstract in *Dissertation Abstracts*, Vol. 12, No. 4, p. 528, 1952. Available on microfilm from University Microfilms, Ann Arbor, Michigan, as Publication No. 3,806.

See also Nos. 4956, 4957, 4975.

MASTERS

5093. HAAN, LEONARD RALPH. *Non-Public Schools among the Hollanders in Iowa.* State University of Iowa, 1941. 149 p. ms.

5094. LOBINGIER, JOHN LESLIE, 1884- . *Colonial Education under the Dutch Reformed Church.* University of Chicago, 1916. 72 p. ms.

See also Nos. 4985, 5025.

Filipino
(NOS. 5095 – 5097)

DOCTORS

See Nos. 4954, 4956, 4957, 4960, 4965, 4970, 4972, 4975.

MASTERS

5095. NOLASCO, DOMINGO F., 1906- . *A Study of Filipino Graduates in California High Schools.* University of California, Berkeley, 1933. 42 p. ms.

5096. REYES, JOSE, 1902- . *Filipino Students in the United States: A Survey of Conditions in the States of Oregon, California, Washington, Idaho, Montana, and Wyoming.* Reed College, 1930. 200 p. ms.

5097. RUIZ, LEOPOLDO TEODOSIO. *Filipino Students in the United States.* Columbia University, 1924. 78 p. ms.

See also Nos. 2659, 4991, 5008, 5013.

Finnish
(NOS. 5098 – 5099)

DOCTORS

See Nos. 4956, 4957, 4963, 4970.

MASTERS

5098. BRANSTATOR, HILDA GOERIG. *A Study of the Finnish Children in Astoria, Oregon.* Stanford University, 1933. 123 p. ms.

5099. LARSON, KATHRYN ELIZABETH. *A Study of Language Achievements and Difficulties of Children of Finnish-Born Parentage.* University of Cincinnati, 1939. 62 p. ms.

See also Nos. 4981, 5023, 5025. See also Scandinavian

French
(NOS. 5100 – 5106)

DOCTORS

5100. LAPATI, *Rev.* AMERICO DOMENICO, 1924- . *A History of Catholic Education in Rhode Island.* Boston College, 1958. (Deals with French-speaking groups.)

5101. PORTRE-BOBINSKI, MARCELLE ANDREE GERMAINE, 1898- . *French Civilization and Culture in Natchitoches.* George Peabody College for Teachers, 1940. New Orleans, Louisiana: T. H. Harvey Press, 1941. iv, 120 p. (Contribution to Education, No. 310. Includes study of educational factors.)

See also Nos. 4959, 4970, 4975.

MASTERS

5102. BARRE, *Rev.* AIME JOSEPH. *The History and Present Status of Religious Education among the Franco-American Population of Fall River.* Catholic University of America, 1938. 46 p. ms.

5103. CYR, *Sister* MARY ST. PAUL, 1922- . *Comparative Study of Scores Obtained by Bi-Linguals on French and English Intelligence Tests.* Boston College, 1954. 63 p. ms.

5104. EVANS, GLADYS MARY. *Causes of Failure of French-Speaking Children.* George Peabody College for Teachers, 1939. 80 p. ms.

5105. GUYETTE, GEORGE FRANCIS. *A Study of the Survival of Certain Neologisms and 17th Century French Words and Expressions among Pupils of French-Canadian Descent in the Woonsocket High School, Rhode Island, with a View to Determining Whether or Not This Survival Warrants Remedial Teaching.* University of Maine, 1941. 56 p. ms.

5106. HOUDE, *Sister* MARY OF ST. JOSEPH ARMAND, 1901- . *An Analysis of Spelling Errors in the Transcription Work of French-English Bilingual Students.* Boston University, 1953. 150 p. ms.

See also Nos. 4978, 4983, 4985, 4992, 5009, 5022.

German
(NOS. 5107 – 5112)

DOCTORS

5107. GATES, GUNTHER G. *A Study of the Achievement and Adjustment of German-Jewish Refugee Students in American Public High Schools in the San Francisco Bay Area.* University of California, Berkeley, 1955.

5108. MOORE, JEAN SARAH. *Religious Education among German Inhabitants of Colonial Pennsylvania.* Hartford School of Religious Education, 1925. 167 p. ms.

5109. NASON, CHARLES DICKENS, 1874-1901. *The Schools of the Society for the Propagation of*

Christian Knowledge among the Germans of Pennsylvania. University of Pennsylvania, 1899. 115 p. ms.

See also Nos. 4956, 4957, 4959, 4963, 4970, 4973, 4975.

MASTERS

5110. HOFFMAN, BERYL MAY. *German Education in Louisiana.* Tulane University of Louisiana, 1939. 85 p. ms. Abstract in Tulane University of Louisiana: *Abstracts of Theses,* 1939, p. 22-24.

5111. NOWLAN, IVAN SEYMOUR. *Educational Work of the German Reformed and Lutheran Churches in Pennsylvania During the Colonial Period.* University of Chicago, 1916. 74 p. ms.

5112. REARY, HILDA SCHWENCK. *A Study of the Speech Needs of High School Students in a Pennsylvania German Community.* University of Maine, 1941. 261 p. ms.

See also Nos. 4978, 4985, 4986, 4987, 4989, 4992, 4993, 4994, 5001, 5006, 5007, 5009, 5010, 5013, 5017, 5020, 5021, 5024, 5025.

Greek
(NO. 5113)

DOCTORS

See Nos. 4954, 4956, 4957, 4975.

MASTER

5113. PARAS, FRANK G., 1913- . *The Assimilation of the Greek Population in Milwaukee.* Marquette University, 1945. 78 p. ms. (Includes education as one factor.)

See also Nos. 4982, 4985, 5006.

Indian
(NOS. 5114 – 5115)

DOCTORS

5114. DeSOUSA, Rev. HERMAN JOSEPH, 1915- . *The Adjustment Problems of Indian Graduate Students in American Universities.* Fordham University, 1956. 380 p. ms.

5115. FLEMING, ROBERT L., 1905- . *Adjustment of Missionaries' Children in America.* University of Chicago, 1947. 276 p. ms. Summary in *Educational Administration and Supervision,* Vol. 33, p. 349-360, October 1947. Available on microfilm: see index under "University of Chicago." (A study of 88 children of missionaries who had attended Woodstock School in Mussrie, United Provinces, India.)

See also Nos. 4954, 4956, 4957, 4961, 4964, 4967, 4970, 4971, 4972, 4975.

MASTERS

See Nos. 4977, 4988, 5026.

Iranian
(NO. 5116)

DOCTORS

See Nos. 4956, 4970, 4975.

MASTER

5116. BUSCH, RUTH CHIPMAN, 1931- . *The Iranian Student in Logan: An Exploratory Study of Foreign Student Social Experience and Adjustment.* Utah State Agricultural College, 1955. 74 p. ms. Abstract in Utah State Agricultural College: 1955. 74 p. ms. Abstract in Utah State Agricultural College: *Abstracts of Theses,* 1955, p. 20.

See also No. 4977.

Irish
(NOS. 5117 - 5118)

MASTERS

5117. HEWITT, IRVING J. *The Irish Schoolmaster in America.* Catholic University of America, 1917. 27 p. ms.

5118. PURCELL, CLARA FICK. *Pioneer Irish Teachers in America.* Catholic University of America, 1932. 82 p. ms.

See also Nos. 4978, 4985, 4986, 4987, 4989, 5020, 5025.

Italian
(NOS. 5119 - 5150)

DOCTORS

5119. ARSENIAN, SETH, 1902- . *Bilingualism and Mental Development: A Study of the Intelligence and the Social Background of Bilingual Children in New York City.* Columbia University, 1937. New York: Teachers College, Columbia University, 1937. vi, 164 p. (Teachers College Contribution to Education, No. 712. Devoted chiefly to children of Italian parentage.)

5120. CONCISTRE, MARIE JOSEPHINE, 1887- . *Adult Education in a Local Area: A Study of a Decade in the Life and Education of the Adult Italian Immigrant in East Harlem, New York City.* New York University, 1943. 2 vols. 531 p. ms.

5121. HEINRICH, DESDEMONA LOUISA. *Dietary Habits of Elementary School Children: An Evaluation of the Quantitative and Qualitative Adequacy of the Daily Food Intake of 463 Elementary School Children of American, Jewish, and Italian Parents Living in Urban and Suburban New York City.* New York University, 1932. 144 p. ms.

5122. HILL, HARRY SEGNER, 1898- . *The Effect of Bilingualism on the Measured Intelligence of Elementary School Children of Italian Parentage.* Rutgers University, 1935. 220 p. ms.

5123. REED, DOROTHY, 1900- . *Leisure Time of Girls in a "Little Italy": A Comparative Study of the Leisure Interests of Adolescent Girls of Foreign Parentage Living in a Metropolitan Community, to Determine the Presence or Absence of Interest Differences in Relation to Behavior.* Columbia University, 1931. Portland, Oregon: Privately printed by the author, 1932. vi, 69 p.

5124. TAIT, JOSEPH WILFRID, 1896- . *Some Aspects of the Effect of the Dominant American Culture upon Children of Italian-Born Parents.* Columbia University, 1942. New York: Teachers College, Columbia University, 1942. ix, 74 p. (Teachers College Contribution to Education, No. 866.)

5125. ULIN, RICHARD OTIS. *The Italo-American Student in the American Public School: A Description and Analysis of Differential Behavior.* Harvard University, 1958. 212 p. ms.

See also Nos. 3083, 4955, 4960, 4962, 4963, 4968, 4975.

MASTERS

5126. BOLTON, BERNIECE. *A Program of Religious Education for the Elementary Division of the Church School, with Special Reference to the First Italian Church, Chicago.* Northwestern University, 1923. 102 p. ms.

5127. BUCK, RUTH HELEN. *Worship in the Junior Department of the Church School with Special Reference to the First Italian (M.E.) Church, Chicago.* Northwestern University, 1922. 120 p. ms.

5128. BUTERA, JOSEPHINE BETTY. *Study of an Italo-American Dialect: Adaptations into the Italian Language or Dialects for the Purpose of Adjustment in an Italo-American Environment.* New York University, 1941. 52 p. ms.

5129. CATALOZZI, MARIE CARMELA. *The Use of the Dialogue as an Aid to Students of Italian Extraction in Learning Italian.* Brown University, 1938. 47 p. ms.

5130. CORCORAN, VERNA H. *General Background Deficiencies of First Generation Italian Children of the Elementary School Level.* University of Buffalo, 1938. 140 p. ms.

5131. DE FRANCESCO, DOMENIC. *The First Generation of Italians in American Institutions, with a Comparative Study of Intelligence.* University of Rochester, 1930. 131 p. ms.

5132. DONOFRIO, ANTHONY FRANCIS, 1916- . *The Relationship between Level of Aspiration and Self-Confidence in the Jewish and Italian High School Students.* Fordham University, 1942. 45 p. ms.

5133. ELIACH, EZEKIAL. *The Influence of Bilingualism on the Intelligence Test Scores of School Children.* Columbia University, 1937. 25 p. ms. (Refers to Italian children.)

5134. ETTENSON, RUBELLE J. *A Comparative Study of the Language Ability of the Colored and Italian Children in the Second, Third, and Fourth Grades.* College of the City of New York, 1926. Abstract in College of the City of New York: *Abstracts of Theses . . . 1923-1939,* p. 10.

Irish, Italian, Japanese

5135. JONES, CHARLES HENRY, 1886-1939. *Reliability of Group Intelligence Tests Administered to Children from Foreign Language Homes.* New York State College for Teachers, Albany, 1930. 53 p. ms. (Homes represented were all Italian.)

5136. KELSEY, RUTH MARIE. *The Comparison of Scholastic Standing among Children of Native-Born Parents with Those of Foreign-Born Parents.* University of Denver, 1932. 159 p. ms. (Concerned chiefly with those of Italian parentage.)

5137. KEMPER, HOLLIS DUVAL. *An Intensive Study of Twenty Lower East Side Italian Boys, 13, 14, and 15 Years of Age.* Columbia University, 1925. 40 p. ms.

5138. KLINEBERG, NETTYE V. *Bilingualism and Intelligence in Ten-Year-Old Italian Girls.* Columbia University, 1932. 26 p. ms.

5139. LATONA, LOUISE. *A Study of the Scholastic Achievement of Children of Italian Parentage in Buffalo Public Schools.* University of Buffalo, 1933. 69 p. ms.

5140. LONDON, RIVA ESTHER, 1915- . *The Attitudes of Jewish and Italian Parents toward the Behavior Problems of Their Children.* Smith College, 1938. 93 p. ms. Abstract in Smith College: *Studies in Social Work,* Vol. 9, p. 146-148.

5141. MEAD, DOROTHY ELLEN. *A Program of Religious Education among Italians.* Northwestern University, 1921. 91 p. ms. (Refers to Italians in Chicago.)

5142. NOCE, LILLIAN. *South Italians in American Schools.* Colorado State Teachers College, 1922. 122 p. ms.

5143. PETERS, FLORENTINE. *Difficulties of Italian Children in Beginning Reading.* Columbia University, 1928. 51 p. ms.

5144. PUGH, THOMAS BRYAN, 1888- . *A Study of Graduates of the Independence High School.* Louisiana State University and State Agricultural and Mechanical College, 1939. 30 p. ms. Abstract in *Louisiana State University Bulletin,* Vol. 32, n.s., No. 1, p. 146, January 1940. (Compares the scholastic records of students of American and of Italian parentage.)

5145. ROMANOW, CAROL. *A Phonetic Analysis of the Articulation of Twenty Children of Italian Descent.* Boston University, 1958.

5146. SALANDRA, FELICIA. *Factors and Techniques Involved in the Effective Teaching of English to Italian Bilingual Children of a Fifth Grade.* New York University, 1941. 173 p. ms.

5147. SANDERCOCK, GRACE AMELIA, 1915- . *Culture Conflict and the Behavior Difficulties of Adolescent Italian Boys.* Smith College, 1939. 70 p. ms. Abstract in Smith College: *Smith College Studies in Social Work,* Vol. 10, p. 159-160.

5148. SCHAEFFER, GOLDIE E. *The Nature Concepts of Children of Italian Parentage in Second-Year Elementary School.* College of the City of New York, 1933. 76 p. ms.

5149. SCUDDER, EDNA DRAKE. *Suggestions on Methods of Work and the Course of Study for Italian Children.* Columbia University, 1912. 48 p. ms.

5150. WALLACK, SIMON I. *A Comparison of the Achievements of Pupils of Jewish Parentage with Pupils of Italian Parentage in the Various Subjects of the Curriculum.* Temple University, 1926. 91 p. ms.

See also Nos. 272, 4976, 4978, 4980, 4985, 4986, 4987, 4989, 4992, 4993, 4998, 5001, 5005, 5006, 5015, 5016, 5018, 5020, 5025.

Japanese
(NOS. 5151 - 5206)

DOCTORS

5151. AKAMATSU, ALFRED SABURO, 1904- . *The Function and Type of Program of a Japanese Minority Church in New York City.* Columbia University, 1948. 268 p. ms. Abstract in *Religious Education,* Vol. 45, p. 101-102, March-April 1950.

5152. BELL, REGINALD, 1894- . *A Study of the Educational Effects of Segregation upon Japanese Children in American Schools.* Stanford University, 1933. Published in modified form as *Public School Education of Second-Generation Japanese in California.* Stanford University Press, 1935. 116 p. (Stanford University Publications, University Series, Education-Psychology, Vol. 1, No. 3.) For master's thesis by same author, see No. 5162.

5153. CAUDILL, WILLIAM ABEL, 1920- . *Japanese-American Personality and Acculturation.* University of Chicago, 1950. 364 p. ms. Published in abridged form in *Genetic Psychology Monographs,* Vol. 45, First Half, p. 3-102, February 1952. Available on microfilm: see index under "University of Chicago."

5154. DARSIE, MARVIN LLOYD, 1887-1940. *The Mental Capacity of American-Born Japanese Children.* Stanford University, 1924. 201 p. ms. Baltimore, Maryland: Williams & Wilkins Co., 1926. 89 p. (Comparative Psychology Monographs, Vol. 3, Serial No. 15.)

5155. IGA, MAMORU. *Acculturation of Japanese Population in Davis County, Utah.* University of Utah, 1955.

5156. KUKI, BASIL ICHIZO. *The Anthropological Study of the Japanese in the United States of America.* New York University, 1914. 165 p. ms.

5157. LIGHT, JEROME THOMAS, 1903- . *The Development of a Junior-Senior High School Program in a Relocation Center for People of Japanese Ancestry during the War with Japan.* Stanford University, 1947. 2 vols. Vol. 1, 594 p. ms. Vol. 2, appendix. Abstract in Stanford University: *Abstracts of Dissertations* . . . 1946-47, p. 184-187.

5158. ROSS, VERNE RALPH, 1885-1931. *The Relation between Intelligence, Scholastic Achievement, and Musical Talent of Three Racial Groups.* University of Southern California, 1931. 285 p. ms. Published in abridged form as *Relationship between Intelligence, Achievement, and Musical Talent.* Claremont, California: California Bureau of Juvenile Research, 1937. ix, 37 p. (One of the three racial groups was composed of 365 Japanese-American children who were compared with 427 American Indian and 1541 White American children.)

5159. SMITH, MILDRED JOAN, 1915- . *Backgrounds, Problems, and Significant Reactions of Relocated Japanese-American Students.* Syracuse University, 1949. 230 p. ms.

5160. TAKAKI, TORI, 1918- . *The Treatment of Japan and the Peoples of Japanese Descent in Senior High School American History Textbooks.* University of Michigan, 1954. 288 p. ms. Abstract in *Dissertation Abstracts,* Vol. 14, p. 626, April 1954. Available on microfilm from University Microfilms, Ann Arbor, Michigan, as Publication No. 7,744.

5161. THOMSON, RUTH HAINES, 1896- . *Events Leading to the Order to Segregate Japanese Pupils in the San Francisco Public Schools.* Stanford University, 1931. 176 p. ms. Abstract in Stanford University: *Abstracts of Dissertations* . . . 1931-32, p. 44-45.

See also Nos. 4956, 4957, 4958, 4960, 4965, 4966, 4968, 4970, 4972.

MASTERS

5162. BELL, REGINALD, 1894- . *A Study of Certain Phases of the Education of Japanese in Central California.* Stanford University, 1928. 131 p. ms. For doctoral dissertation by same author, see No. 5152.

5163. BELL, WARD HORTON, 1896- . *A Comparative Study between Japanese War Location Authority Secondary Schools and Secondary Public Schools.* Arizona State College, Tempe, 1946. 105 p. ms.

5164. CHANSLER, HORACE F. *The Assimilation of the Japanese in and around Stockton.* College of the Pacific, 1932. 67 p. ms.

5165. CROFT, CARMA HUNSAKER. *Comparative Scholastic Achievements of Japanese-American Students and Caucasian Students of the University of Utah for the Academic Year, 1942-43.* University of Utah, 1944. 84 p. ms.

5166. DARBY, HAROLD E. *The General Intelligence of American-Born Japanese Children in California as Measured by the Leiter International Performance Scale.* University of Southern California, 1940. 144 p. ms.

5167. EDDY, SARA. *The Adaptation of Japanese Games as a Unit in the Junior High School.* University of Southern California, 1937.

5168. FREEMAN, GEORGE HAYWARD. *A Comparative Investigation of the School Achievement and Socio-Economic Background of the Japanese-American Students and the White American Students of Gardena High School.* University of Southern California, 1938. 92 p. ms.

5169. FUJIYOSHI, DONALD HIROSHI. *A Study of the Educational Program of the Church School of the Japanese Christian Church and Institute of Los Angeles.* University of Southern California, 1942. 101 p. ms.

5170. GEORGE, ROBERT CHIPMAN LEE. *The Granada (Colorado) Relocation Center Secondary School.* University of Colorado, 1944. 134 p. ms. Abstract in *University of Colorado Studies,* Vol. 27, No. 3, p. 45, November 1945.

5171. GOULARD, STANLEY ELLSWORTH. *The General Intelligence of American-Born Japanese Children in California Measured by the Leiter International Performance Scale.* University of Southern California, 1940. 118 p. ms.

5172. HARADA, KOICHI GLENN. *A Survey of Japanese Language Schools in Hawaii.* University of Hawaii, 1934. 165 p. ms.

5173. HAYASHIDA, AKIYOSHI. *Japanese Moral Instruction as a Factor in the Americanization of Citizens of Japanese Ancestry.* University of Hawaii, 1933. 45 p. ms.

5174. HAYES, ROBERT W. *A Phonological Study of the English Speech of Selected Japanese Speakers in Hawaii.* University of Hawaii, 1958. 243 p. ms.

5175. HERTZLER, VIRGINIA BEAZLEY. *A Sociometric Study of Japanese Students in a Polytechnic High School.* University of Washington, 1949. 84 p. ms.

5176. HIRABAYASHI, GORDON KIYOSHI. *A Sociometric Study of University of Washington Students of Japanese Ancestry.* University of Washington, 1948. 65 p. ms.

5177. HOPKINSON, SHIRLEY LOIS. *An Historical Account of the Evacuation, Relocation, and Resettlement of the Japanese in the United States, 1941-1946.* Claremont Graduate School, 1951. 264 p. ms. (Includes a full description of the school systems established for over 30,000 pupils in 10 relocation centers, pp. 95-106.)

5178. HOUSE, HAZELLE LORINDA. *A Study of the Japanese in Pasadena, California, to Determine the Extent of Their Americanization.* Colorado State Teachers College, 1930. 111 p. ms. (Considers the value of the Americanization programs in schools.)

5179. JOHNSON, DONALD ORVILLE. *The War Relocation Authority School of Tule Lake, California.* Stanford University, 1947. 97 p. ms.

5180. JOHNSTON, PETRA B. *Analysis of the Vocabulary Achievement of Japanese Children.* Stanford University, 1923. 34 p. ms.

5181. KAAPU, MYRTLE KING. *A Study of the Influence of Japanese Syntax and Idiom upon the Spoken and Written English of a Group of Ninth-Grade Pupils.* University of Hawaii, 1937. 108 p. ms.

5182. KAMBARA, ALICE HIROKO. (Later, Mrs. Alice Hiroko Higashiuchi). *A Religious Education Program for the Young People of the Japanese Methodist Churches on the Pacific Coast.* Pacific School of Religion, 1936. 69 p. ms.

5183. KASHIWA, YOSHIKO IRENE. *A Study into the Attitudes of Some Children of Japanese Descent toward the Chinese and the Japanese during the Sino-Japanese War.* University of Hawaii, 1940. 111 p. ms.

5184. KONO, AYAKO. *Language as a Factor in the Achievement of American-Born Students of Japanese Ancestry.* University of Hawaii, 1934. 98 p. ms.

5185. KOSAKI, MILDRED DOI. *The Culture Conflicts and Guidance Needs of Nisei Adolescents.* University of Hawaii, 1949. 161 p. ms.

5186. LINDERFELT, FLORENCE MARGARET. *A Comparative Study of the Rorschach Protocols of Japanese and Caucasian College Students.* University of Hawii, 1949. 81 p. ms.

5187. McKNIGHT, ROBERT KELLOGG. *The Adjustment of Japanese Students to American University Life.* Ohio State University, 1954. 364 p. ms.

5188. MISAKI, HISAKICHI. *The Effect of Language Handicap on Intelligence Tests of Japanese Children.* Stanford University, 1928. 110 p. ms. plus appendix.

5189. MIYAMOTO, SHICHIRO. *A Study of Japanese Language Ability of the Second and Third Generation Japanese Children in a Honolulu Japanese School.* University of Hawaii, 1937. 113 p. ms.

5190. MORIMOTO, SHIZUKO. *A Study of Oral English Usage among Pupils of Japanese Ancestry Attending Public Schools in Hawaii.* University of Hawaii, 1939. 67 p. ms.

5191. MORISHITA, SUMI E. *A Program of Religious Education for the Japanese Children and Youth of Berkeley, California.* Pacific School of Religion, 1929.

5192. OHNO, KAZUO, 1926- . *Obstacles in Teaching English to Japanese High School Students.* Whittier College, 1957. 129 p. ms.

5193. OKA, WILFRED MITSUJI. *A Study of Japanese Social Institutions in Hawaii.* International YMCA College, 1935. 132 p. ms. (Includes study of Japanese language school, p. 59-74.)

5194. ONISHI, KATSUMI. *A Study of the Attitudes of the Japanese in Hawaii toward the Japanese Language Schools.* University of Hawaii, 1943. 291 p. ms.

5195. POWERS, MYRON ELGIN. *Telic Attempts of Two Racial Groups to Retain Their Social Inheritances.* University of Washington, 1932. 82 p. ms. (Japanese and Jewish groups.)

5196. PRICE, CORA NATALIE, 1903- . *A Study of the Attitudes of Japanese-American and of Native American High School Freshmen toward Discipline.* Oregon State College, 1940. 87 p. ms.

5197. PUGH, WILLIAM RICHARD. *A Study of the Growth of Japanese Boys from 42 Northern California High Schools over a Five-Year Period.* Stanford University, 1938. 64 p. ms.

5198. RICHARDSON, JOHN MILLS. *A Comparative Study of Japanese and Native American White Children.* University of Southern California, 1937. 116 p. ms.

5199. RYCHLAK, JOSEPH FRANK. *Personality Correlates of the Social Adjustment of Japanese Students in America.* Ohio State University, 1954. 60 p. ms.

5200. SANJUME, JISCO. *An Analysis of the New Americans Conferences from 1927 to 1938.* University of Hawaii, 1939. 93 p. ms. Privately printed in Honolulu by Take Okumura, 1939. 51 p. (Considers the Americanization campaign for young Japanese-Americans.)

5201. SERISAWA, KOKO. *A Comparison of the American and Japanese Pupils in the Same High School.* University of Southern California, 1935. 62 p. ms.

5202. SHIKAMURA, ALICE HARUKO. *The Vocational Intentions of Second Generation Japanese Students in Three California Universities.* Stanford University, 1948. 134 p. ms. (University of California, San Jose State College, and Stanford University.)

5203. UNOURA, KOJIRO, 1891- . *The Religious Education of the Japanese in California.* Pacific School of Religion, 1918.

5204. WILLIAMS, GRACE PREVOST. *The Effect of High School Home Economics Instruction on Food Habits of a Group of Japanese Girls in Southern California.* Iowa State College of Agriculture and Mechanic Arts, 1939. 60 p. ms.

5205. YANAGIMACHI, NOBUKO, 1909- . *Curriculum for Japanese Methodist Episcopal Churches on the Pacific Coast.* Pacific School of Religion, 1934.

5206. ZANGLE, FRANCES LORENE. *A Study of English Language Difficulties of Japanese Children of Los Angeles City.* University of California, Berkeley, 1935. 47 p. ms.

See also Nos. 272, 292, 4979, 4982, 4995, 4996, 4997, 5000, 5008, 5010, 5011, 5012, 5013, 5015, 5019, 5075.

Latin-American

(NOS. 5207 – 5653)

Prevailingly Mexican-American, but includes other unspecified Latin-Americans and Spanish-Americans, except Puerto Ricans. For Puerto Ricans, see Nos. 5659 – 5682.

DOCTORS

5207. BACA, FIDEL GARCIA, 1916- . *Bilingual Education in Certain Southwest School Districts.* University of Utah, 1956. 180 p. Abstract in *Dissertation Abstracts*, Vol. 17, p. 1016-1017, May 1957. Available on microfilm from University Microfilms, Ann Arbor, Michigan, as Publication No. 20,041.

5208. BROOM, PERRY MORRIS, 1908- . *An Interpretative Analysis of the Economic and Educational Status of Latin-Americans in Texas, with Emphasis upon the Basic Factors Underlying the Approach to an Improved Program of Occupational Guidance, Training, and Adjustment for Secondary Schools.* University of Texas, 1942. 499 p. ms.

5209. CARROW, Sister MARY ARTHUR. *A Comparative Study of the Linguistic Functioning of Bilingual Spanish-American Children and Monolingual Anglo-American Children at the Third-Grade Level.* Northwestern University, 1956. 211 p. ms. Abstract in *Dissertation Abstracts*, Vol. 16, p. 400, February 1956. Available on microfilm from University Microfilms, Ann Arbor, Michigan, as Publication No. 15,122.

5210. CLINCHY, EVERETT ROSS, Jr., 1919- . *Equality of Opportunity for Latin-Americans in Texas: A Study of the Economic, Social, and Educational Discrimination against Latin-Americans in Texas, and the Efforts of the State Government on Their Behalf.* Columbia University, 1954. 221 p. ms. Abstract in *Dissertation Abstracts*, Vol. 14, p. 1245, August 1954. Available on microfilm from University Microfilms, Ann Arbor, Michigan, as Publication No. 8,633.

5211. CORONA, BERT CHARLES, 1921- . *A Study of Adjustment and Interpersonal Relations of Adolescents of Mexican Descent.* University of California, Berkeley, 1955. 226 p. ms. (Based on study of adolescents in a California junior high school.)

5212. DICKINSON, JAMES H., 1916- . *The Supervision of Religious Education in Latin-American Baptist Missions in Texas.* Southwestern Baptist Theological Seminary, 1951. 210 p. ms. Abstract in *Religious Education*, Vol. 47, p. 214-215, May-June 1952.

5213. HANSON, Mrs. RITA MOHLER, 1902- . *Educating Elementary School Children of Seasonal Migrant Agricultural Workers in the San Joaquin Valley.* Stanford University, 1950. 202 p. ms. Abstract in Stanford University: *Abstracts of Dissertations . . .* 1949-50, p. 382-387.

5214. HERR, SELMA ERNESTINE, 1904- . *The Effect of Pre-First Grade Training upon Reading Readiness and Reading Achievement among Spanish-American Children in the First Grade.* University of Texas, 1945. 323 p. ms.

5215. HOULE, BETTIE ECKHARDT TOTTEN, 1919- . *Some Significant Characteristics Associated with Popularity in American and Mexican Elementary School Children.* University of Chicago, 1953. 117 p. ms. Available on microfilm: see index under "University of Chicago."

5216. HUGHES, Mrs. MARIE MORRISON, 1900- . *The English Language Facility of Mexican-American Children Living and Attending School in a Segregated Community.* Stanford University, 1952. 302 p. ms. Abstract in Stanford University: *Abstracts of Dissertations . . .* 1951-52, p. 591-593. For master's thesis by same author, see No. 5422.

5217. JOHNSON, VALLEY LOU, 1915- . *Survey of Spanish-Speaking Scholastics in Brewster County, Texas.* Colorado State College of Education, 1950. 182 p. ms.

5218. KNIGHT, JAMES, 1895- . *A Laboratory Study of the Reading Habits of Spanish-Speaking Children.* University of Texas, 1931. 179 p. ms.

5219. LADO, ROBERT, 1915- . *Measurement in English as a Foreign Language with Special Reference to Spanish-Speaking Adults.* University of Michigan, 1950. 274 p. ms. Abstract in *Microfilm Abstracts*, Vol. 10, No. 4, p. 114-115, 1950. Available on microfilm from University Microfilms, Ann Arbor, Michigan, as Publication No. 1,983. For master's thesis by same author, see No. 5459.

5220. LOOMIS, NELLIE HOLMES, 1908- . *Spanish-Anglo Cleavage in a New Mexican High School.* Michigan State University of Agriculture and Applied Science, 1956. 98 p. ms. Abstract in *Dissertation Abstracts*, Vol. 15, p. 2595, December 1955. Available on microfilm from University Microfilms, Ann Arbor, Michigan, as Publication No. 14,297.

5221. LYNN, KLONDA, 1915- . *A Phonetic Analysis of the English Spoken by Mexican Children in the Elementary Schools of Arizona.* Louisiana State University and State Agricultural and Mechanical College, 1940. 307 p. ms. Abstract in *Louisiana State University Bulletin*, Vol. 33, n.s., No. 1, p. 29-30, January 1941.

5222. McNIEL, GUY BRETT. *A Pre-First-Grade Oral-English Program as Related to the Scholastic Achievement of Spanish-Speaking Children.* University of Colorado, 1958. 130 p. ms.

5223. PUTNAM, HOWARD L., 1909- . *The Relation of College Programs of Community Services to the Needs of the Spanish-Speaking People.* University of Texas, 1956. 317 p. ms. (Refers to 16 counties in South Texas.)

5224. RENNER, RICHARD ROY, 1927- . *Some Characteristics of Spanish-Name Texans and Foreign Latin-Americans in Texas Higher Education.* University of Texas, 1957. 449 p. ms. Abstract in *Dissertation Abstracts,* Vol. 17, p. 2471, November 1957. Available on microfilm from University Microfilms, Ann Arbor, Michigan, as Publication No. 23,059.

5225. REX, FREDERICK J. *A Plan for the Development of a Latin-American Institute at the Horace Mann-Lincoln School of Teachers College.* Columbia University, 1943. 75 p. ms.

5226. SAENZ, ALFREDO N., 1912- . *A Field Study of Two Programs Designed for Preparing the Resident, Non-English-Speaking Child of Spanish Culture to Meet First-Grade Requirements in One Year.* University of Houston, 1957. 156 p. ms. Abstract in *Dissertation Abstracts,* Vol. 18, p. 125, January 1958. Available on microfilm from University Microfilms, Ann Arbor, Michigan, as Publication No. 21,734.

5227. SANCHEZ, GEORGE ISIDORE, 1906- . *The Education of Bilinguals in a State School System.* University of California, Berkeley, 1934. 161 p. ms. (Based on study of 49,751 Spanish-speaking children in New Mexico.) For master's thesis by same author, see No. 5577.

5228. SANCHEZ, LUISA GUERRERO, 1921- . *The Latin-American of the Southwest: Backgrounds and Curricular Implications.* University of Texas, 1954. 257 p. ms.

5229. SCHUITEMAN, ROBERT ALLEN. *A Study of Colombian Nationals Who Attended Collegiate Institutions in the United States.* University of Michigan, 1957. 261 p. ms. Abstract in *Dissertation Abstracts,* Vol. 18, No. 4, p. 1308-1309, April 1918. Available on microfilm from University Microfilms, Ann Arbor, Michigan as Mic. 58-986. (Deals with 116 students from Colombia.)

5230. VILLAREAL, JESSE J., 1913- . *A Test of the Aural Comprehension of English for Native Speakers of Spanish.* Northwestern University, 1947. 250 p. ms. Abstract in Northwestern University: *Summaries of Doctoral Dissertations,* Vol. 15, 1947, p. 77-82.

5231. WACHS, WILLIAM, 1910- . *A Study of the Extent to Which Textbooks Teaching English to Foreign-Born Hispanic Adults in New York City Help Them to Comprehend the Daily English Newspaper They Read.* New York University, 1946. 305 p. ms. Abstract in New York University: *Abstracts of Theses,* 1945-46, p. 83-86.

5232. WILLIAMS, HENDLEY V., Jr., 1903- . *Socio-Economic Status of Transient and Non-Transient Pupils on the Elementary Level.* Colorado State College of Education, 1943. 123 p. ms. Field Study No. 1. Available on microfilm from University Microfilms, Ann Arbor, Michigan, as Publication No. 778. (See note under No. 5233.)

5233. WILLIAMS, HENDLEY V., Jr., 1903- . *Leisure Activities of a Selected Sample of Spanish-American High School Seniors.* Colorado State College of Education, 1946. 197 p. ms. Abstract in Colorado State College of Education: *Abstracts of Field Studies for the Degree of Doctor of Education,* Vol. 8, 1946. Available on microfilm from University Microfilms, Ann Arbor, Michigan, as Publication No. 884. (Note: Dr. Williams submitted two different dissertations "in partial fulfillment of the requirement for the degree of Doctor of Education".)

See also Nos. 4953, 4954, 4969, 4973, 4974, 4975, 162a.

MASTERS

5234. ACEVEDO, JOE RODRIGUEZ, 1909- . *Mental Hygiene Guidance for the Spanish-Culture Home Preschool Children Problems.* Texas College of Arts and Industries, 1949. 101 p. ms.

5235. AIMONE, VIRGINIA MEYER. *A Program in English for Spanish-Speaking Children in the Third Grade.* Texas Western College, 1953. 358 p. ms.

5236. AJUBITA, MARIA LUISA. *Language in Social Relations, with Special Reference to the Mexican-American Problem.* Tulane University of Louisiana, 1943. 65 p. ms. Abstract in Tulane University of Louisiana: *Abstracts of Theses,* 1943, p. 10.

5237. AKERY, NICHOLAS. *An Exploratory Study of the Education of Spanish-Speaking Children in the Primary Grades in Edinburg, Texas.* University of Texas, 1956. 103 p. ms.

5238. ALCORN, BEATRICE WARNER. *Educational Implications of Food Habits of Spanish-American Families.* Colorado State College of Agriculture and Mechanic Arts, 1944. 108 p. ms.

5239. ALLSTROM, ERIK W. *A Program of Social Education for a Mexican Community in the United States.* University of Arizona, 1929. 48 p. ms.

5240. ANDERSON, AMELIA BROOKS. *The Number Abilities and Concepts of Spanish-Speaking Children When They Enter Grade One in an English-Speaking School.* Texas School of Mines and Metallurgy, 1944. 90. p. ms.

5241. APODACA, ANACLETO GARCIA, 1919- . *Major Difficulties Encountered by County Extension Agents in Reaching Spanish-Speaking People in New Mexico.* George Washington University, 1949. 59 p. ms.

5242. ARMACK, CLIFFORD M. *A Comparative Survey of the Educational Achievement of the Mexican and the English-Speaking Children in the Williams, Arizona, Public Schools for the Years 1932-33 to 1936-37.* Arizona State Teachers College, Flagstaff, 1938. 86 p. ms. Abstract in Arizona State Teachers College: *Abstracts of Masters' Theses,* 1938-1942, p. 2-3.

5243. ARMSTRONG, LORENE. *Health Services, Southgate Elementary School, Corpus Christi, Texas, 1950-1951.* Texas College of Arts and Industries, 1951. 74 p. ms. (School consists predominantly of Spanish-culture children.)

5244. ARREDANDO, SANTOS TORRES. *A Survey of Special Methods and Procedures for Teaching*

English to Spanish-Speaking Children. Southwest Texas State Teachers College, 1943. 60 p. ms.

5245. BAIRD, DELILA, 1908- . *A Comparison of Spanish-Speaking Children on the Basis of Parents' Ability to Speak the English Language.* West Texas State Teachers College, 1943. 111 p. ms. Abstract in West Texas State Teachers College: *Abstracts of Master's Theses, 1932-1944,* p. 31-32.

5246. BAIRD, FLORA. *A Study of the Language Handicap of the First Grade Mexican Child.* Arizona State College, Flagstaff, 1953. 68 p. ms.

5247. BAKER, DOUGLAS CLARK. *A Two Culture Study of School Progress: Santa Rosa, Texas, 1947-1948.* Texas College of Arts and Industries, 1949. 52 p. ms.

5248. BAKER, ESTHER VALE, 1905- . *A Proposed Curriculum for the Primary and Intermediate Grades of Six Common School and Two Independent Reorganized Districts.* Texas College of Arts and Industries, 1952. 68 p. ms. (Majority of school population in each area is of Spanish-culture parentage.)

5249. BAKER, GILLESPIE PARISH, 1900- . *A Proposed Plan for the Reorganization of Six Common School Districts and Two Independent Districts.* Texas College of Arts and Industries, 1952. 59 p. ms. (Covers same schools as No. 5248.)

5250. BALL, CHARLES CLYDE. *Comparison of Mexican and White Children of the Washington Irving Junior High School of San Antonio, Texas, on the Basis of the Stanford Achievement Test, the Terman Group Tests of Mental Ability, and the National Intelligence Test.* State University of Iowa, 1924. 55 p. ms.

5251. BALLARD, JOSEPHINE GALLOWAY. *Planning a Curriculum Which Is Conducive to the Optimum Organismic Development of the First Grade Non-English-Speaking Mexicans.* Southwest Texas State Teachers College, 1956. 82 p. ms.

5252. BARBARICK, HENRY ARTHUR, Jr. *Relation of Neuro-Muscular Coordination of Spanish-American and Anglo-American Boys Fourteen Years Old.* Arizona State College, Flagstaff, 1955. 91 p. ms.

5253. BARFELL, LAWRENCE OTTO. *A Study of the Health Program among Mexican Children with Special Reference to the Prevalence of Tuberculosis and Its Causes.* University of Southern California, 1937. 103 p. ms.

5254. BARRON, JOHN F., 1909- . *A Study of Educational Efficiency of Schools of Cameron County, Texas, of Less than 500 Scholastics.* Texas College of Arts and Industries, 1938. 54 p. ms. (Predominantly Spanish-culture area.)

5255. BARROWS, RANSELAER. *Norms for Detroit First Grade Intelligence Tests for Spanish-Speaking Children.* University of Arizona, 1925. 23 p. ms.

5256. BAUGH, LILA. *A Study of the Pre-School Vocabulary of Spanish-Speaking Children.* University of Texas, 1933. 129 p. ms. (Refers to children in Texas.)

5257. BEARD, E. ALICE. *A Study of the Mexican Pupils in the Fremont Junior High School, Pomona, California, 1940-41.* Claremont Graduate School, 1941. 68 p. ms.

5258. BISHOP, HAZEL PECK CAMPBELL. *A Case Study of the Improvement of Mexican Homes through Instruction in Home Making.* University of Southern California, 1937. 131 p. ms.

5259. BLACKBURN, BEATRICE BRAY, 1906- . *Survey of the Reading Habits of Spanish-Speaking Children from the Seventh through the Twelfth Grades of Certain Schools in New Mexico, Arizona, and Texas.* Eastern New Mexico University, 1952. 78 p. ms.

5260. BLACKMAN, ROBERT D. *The Language Handicap of Spanish-American Children.* University of Arizona, 1940. 58 p. ms. Abstract in University of Arizona, *Abstracts of Theses for Higher Degrees,* 1939, 1940, p. 10-11.

5261. BLASINGAME, CHARLES THOMAS. *Causes for Absenteeism among Children Enrolled in the Austin Elementary School, 1949-50, Corpus Christi, Texas.* Texas College of Arts and Industries, 1950. 66 p. ms. (School has majority of Spanish-culture students.)

5262. BOX, WILLIAM JENNINGS, 1908- . *To Determine the Factors Influencing the Attendance of Spanish-Culture Children in Raymondville Elementary Schools.* Texas College of Arts and Industries, 1952. 52 p. ms.

5263. BRAND, CORA OWENS, 1907- . *An Attempt to Show that the Activities Program Contributes to the Developmental Growth of Beginning Latin-American Children in Austin Elementary School, Corpus Christi, Texas, 1949-1950.* Texas College of Arts and Industries, 1950. 150 p. ms.

5264. BRAND, ERWIN INGRAM. *A Study of the Outstanding Problems of Beginning Latin-American Children in the Falfurrias Elementary School, Texas, 1939-40.* North Texas State Teachers College, 1941. 99 p. ms. Abstract in North Texas State Teachers College: *Abstracts of Theses, 1941-1946,* p. 89-90. (Bulletin No. 191, January 1948.)

5265. BROSAM, EMMA LOUISA, 1890- . *Some Comparisons with the Written Vocabularies of English-Speaking and Non-English-Speaking Pupils from Grade Four through Grade Seven of Jerome, Arizona.* University of Arizona, 1939. 27 p. ms. Abstract in University of Arizona: *Abstracts of Theses for Higher Degrees,* 1939, 1940, p. 13.

5266. BROWN, FLORINE HART. *Experiments in Social Living, Grade Four, Southgate Elementary School, Corpus Christi, Texas, 1952-53.* Texas College of Arts and Industries, 1953. 117 p. ms. (Predominantly Spanish-culture pupils.)

5267. BROWN, HARIETTE LOUISE. *A Study of the Home Practice Facilities of Latin-American Girls Enrolled in the Home Economics Classes of the Brownsville, Texas, High School.* Colorado State College of Agriculture and Mechanic Arts, 1936. 117 p. ms.

5268. BROWN, LILLIAN WARD. *A Description and Evaluation of the Pupil Attendance Program,*

Sidney Lanier High School, San Antonio, Texas. Texas College of Arts and Industries, 1937. 76 p. ms. (Predominantly Spanish-culture area.)

5269. BROWN, WILLIE LEONZO. *Knowledge of Social Standards among Mexican and Non-Mexican Children.* University of Texas, 1934. 76 p. ms.

5270. BRYANT, KATHERINE FAGAN, 1900- . *A Homemaking Program for Spanish-Culture Girls of Kleberg County.* Texas College of Arts and Industries, 1945. 35 p. ms.

5271. BRYANT, VERNA LEONA. *A Study of the Mathematical Vocabulary of English-Speaking and Spanish-Speaking Children in the Junior High School.* University of Texas, 1942. 124 p. ms.

5272. BUCHEN, BAYARD K. *A Survey of Male Juvenile Delinquency in Corpus Christi, 1936-38.* Texas College of Arts and Industries, 1939. 92 p. ms. (Studies school data and other factors for 48 boys of whom 15 were Spanish-American.)

5273. BUCK, JAMES T., 1911- . *The Child-Study Program of the Evans-Heath Elementary Schools, Corpus Christi, Texas.* Texas College of Arts and Industries, 1945. 131 p. ms. (Case studies of 10 Latin-American children.)

5274. BUCKNER, HERMAN A. *A Study of Pupil Elimination and Failure among Mexicans in the United States.* University of Southern California, 1935. 159 p. ms.

5275. BUNDY, WILLIAM WILSON. *The Mexican Minority Problem in Otero County, Colorado.* University of Colorado, 1940. 113 p. ms. Abstract in *University of Colorado Studies,* Vol. 26, No. 3, p. 24, November 1940. (Shows need of elementary education adapted to needs of Spanish-Speaking American and Mexican citizens; special emphasis on program of adult education.)

5276. BURGESS, NONA, 1903- . *A Survey of the Education of the Latin-Americans in the Abilene Public Schools.* Hardin-Simmons University, 1950. 87 p. ms.

5277. BURKHALTER, ROBERT EDWIN. *A New Articulation Test Applied to a Selected Group of Children Living in the State of New Mexico.* University of New Mexico, 1953. 62 p. ms. (For children who had not learned English before entering school.)

5278. BURNS, MALCOLM EDWARD, 1911- . *A Study of Spanish-Americans in the Greeley Public Schools.* Colorado State College of Education, 1947. 179 p. ms.

5279. CAJERO, MANUEL. *A Study of the Causes of Certain Spelling Difficulties among Spanish-Speaking Children.* Arizona State Teachers College, Flagstaff, 1938. 62 p. ms. Abstract in Arizona State Teachers College: *Abstracts of Master's Theses, 1938-1942,* p. 1-2.

5280. CALDWELL, HENRY BOHON, Jr., 1920- . *Problems in the Education of Spanish-Speaking Children in the Southwestern United States.* Colorado College, 1955. 74 p. ms.

5281. CALLOWAY, ESTHER ALMA. *A Proposed Program of Moral Instruction for Mexican Children in the Intermediate Grades.* University of Arizona, 1932. 150 p. ms.

5282. CAMPA, JUSTA C. *Christian Education in the Mexican Baptist Churches in the U. S. A.* Berkeley Baptist Divinity School, 1951. 83 p. ms.

5283. CAMPBELL, PAUL COPELAND. *A Practical Curriculum for the Latin-American Elementary School.* Texas Technological College, 1940. 49 p. ms.

5284. CANTU, AURORA PONCE, 1921- . *Rejected Children.* Texas College of Arts and Industries, 1949. 80 p. ms. (Children considered are all Latin-American.)

5285. CARLSON, HARRY J. *A Study of Causes of Retardation of Spanish-American Children in a Small Junior High School in New Mexico.* New Mexico Western College, 1956. 21 p. ms.

5286. CARNES, HUBERT MILTON. *A Program of Health Education and Sanitation for the Latin-American Population of the Lytle School District.* Southwest Texas State Teachers College, 1945. 45 p. ms.

5287. CARSON, BYRTA BEA. *Clothing Construction Handbook for Latin-American Pupils in Junior High School.* Colorado Agricultural and Mechanical College, 1945. 341 p. ms.

5288. CAUDILL, MILLARD E., 1908- . *Spanish-Culture Withdrawals, Sixth Grade Level, Texas Public Schools, Fremont, Texas.* Texas College of Arts and Industries, 1939. 67 p. ms.

5289. CHAMBERLIN, LUCE ROSE. *Low Sixth Grade, Laredo, Texas, Age and Achievement Retardation with Possible Causes.* Texas College of Arts and Industries, 1937. 91 p. ms. (Concerned principally with Spanish-culture children.)

5290. CHAMNES, EMMETT EARL, 1884- . *A Comparison of the Educational Achievements of Mexican and American Children in Weslaco, Texas.* Southern Methodist University, 1930. 87 p. ms.

5291. CHAPMAN, JAMES ROY. *Administrative Problems Created by School Attendance of Migratory Pupils.* University of Texas, 1956. 86 p. ms.

5292. CHAVEZ, DAVID JULIAN. *Civic Education of the Spanish-American.* University of Texas, 1923. 143 p. ms.

5293. CHERNOSKY, ADELMA SHIRLEY. *Educational Enrichment for Spanish-Speaking Children in the Third Grade and Its Effect on Intelligence and Achievement Scores.* University of Texas, 1956. 146 p. ms.

5294. CLARK, CLARENCE CHARLES, 1916- . *A Study of Factors which Contribute to High School Failures.* Texas College of Arts and Industries, 1951. 97 p. ms. (Prevailingly Spanish-culture students.)

5295. CLARK, DANIEL HENDRICKS. *A Comparison of the Factors Related to Success in Problem Solving in Mathematics for Latin-American and Anglo-American Students in the Junior High School.* University of Texas, 1938. Abstract in University of Texas:

Abstracts of Masters' and Doctors' Theses in Education, p. 13. (Bulletin No. 1.)

5296. CLARK, GEORGE. *A Study of the Achievement of the Spanish-Speaking Child.* University of Texas, 1956. 130 p. ms.

5297. CLARK, MADELINE MARGUERITE. *A Preliminary Survey of the Employment Possibilities of the Spanish-American Girls Receiving Commercial Training in the San Antonio Secondary Schools.* University of Texas, 1936. 97 p. ms.

5298. CLARK, NETTIE. *The Reading Problem of the Spanish-American Child in the Primary Grades.* University of Southern California, 1950. 50 p. ms.

5299. CLAUSEWITZ, EDITH LINDHOLM, 1908- *Analysis of the Needs of a Latin-American School.* Trinity University, 1953. 127 p. ms. (Refers to school in San Antonio, Texas.)

5300. COAN, BARTLETT E. *A Comparative Study of the American and Mexican Children in the Big Bend Area for 1935-1936.* University of Texas, 1936. 47 p. ms.

5301. COAN, MARY WRIGHT. *The Language Difficulty in Measuring the Intelligence of Spanish-American Students.* University of New Mexico, 1927. 56 p. ms. Abstract in University of New Mexico: *Abstracts of Master's Theses, 1917-1918*, p. 12-13. (Bulletin, Catalog series, Vol. 42, No. 2.)

5302. COBB, ALBERT FOLSOME. *A Comparative Study of the Athletic Ability of Latin-American and Anglo-American Boys on a Junior High School Level.* University of Texas, 1952. 59 p. ms.

5303. COERS, WALTER CLARENCE. *Comparative Achievement of White and Mexican Junior High School Pupils.* George Peabody College for Teachers, 1933. 40 p. ms.

5304. CONDIT, ELEANOR DAILY. *An Appraisal of Certain Methods of Treating Bilingualism in the Claremont Elementary School.* University of Southern California, 1947. 97 p. ms. (Considers only Mexican children.)

5305. COOLE, Mrs. RUTH MUSGRAVE. *A Comparison of Anglo-American and Latin-American Girls in Grades Five to Eleven, with Reference to Their Vocational and Academic Preferences and Aversions.* University of Texas, 1937. 63 p. ms. Abstract in University of Texas: *Abstracts of Masters' and Doctors' Theses in Education* (Bulletin No. 1.) 1941, p. 14-16.

5306. COOPER, ELIZABETH KEYSER, 1908- . *Attitudes of Children and Teachers toward Mexican, Negro, and Jewish Minorities.* University of California, Los Angeles, 1945. 91 p. ms.

5307. COOPER, RITA S. *Material Useful in Working with Spanish-Speaking Children in a Day Nursery.* Bank Street College of Education, 1958.

5308. CORNELIUS, JOHN SCOTT. *The Effect of Certain Changes of Curriculum and Methods on the School Achievement of Mexican Children in a Segregated School.* University of Southern California, 1941. 154 p. ms.

5309. CRAIG, ANNE LUCILE. *The Performance of Mexican Children on the Leiter International Performance Scale.* University of Southern California, 1938. 146 p. ms. (Refers to Mexican children in California.)

5310. CRAIG, EDNA L. *An Integrated Art Program for the Pre-Primary Mexican Child, Williams, Arizona.* Arizona State Teachers College, Flagstaff, 1940. 108 p. ms. Abstract in Arizona State Teachers College: *Abstracts of Master's Theses, 1938-1942*, p. 56-57.

5311. CRENSHAW, TROY CLAY. *A Basic English Vocabulary for Spanish-Speaking Students.* Colorado State Teachers College, 1928. 47 p. ms.

5312. CRON, HELEN CARVER. *Auditory Implementation of the Primary Reading Program.* Texas College of Arts and Industries, 1957. 68 p. ms. (Prevailingly Spanish-culture pupils.)

5313. CRONIN, Sister EILEEN MARIE. *An Analysis of the Reading Interests of Mexican-American Children.* Catholic University of America, 1954. 74 p. ms. Abstract in *Catholic Educational Review*, Vol. 53, p. 187, March 1955. (Based on study of 930 children in 19 California schools.)

5314. CRUZ, MARIA ANGELITA. *Spanish-Speaking Children's Expressed Attitudes toward Money Values.* University of Texas, 1943. 49 p. ms.

5315. CUMMINGS, CATHERINE L. *A Bilingual List of General Reference Books for Artesia, New Mexico.* Kent State University, 1955.

5316. CURRAN, HARRIET EDGAR, 1893- . *A New Approach to Health and Physical Education Instruction for Mexican Children.* Southern Methodist University, 1940. 70 p. ms. Abstract in Southern Methodist University: *Abstracts of Dissertations . . .* No. 8, 1941, p. 10.

5317. CURRIE, MONA BOYD. *Problems of Teaching Spanish to Spanish-Speaking Students in California.* Claremont Graduate School, 1950. 145 p. ms.

5318. DALY, MARY ANN. *The Educational Problem of the Mexican Migrants of Texas with Specific Reference to Average Daily Attendance.* Southwest Texas State College, 1955. 51 p. ms.

5319. DAUCHY, NORMA MEYERS. *A Social Living School Program for Beginner Spanish-Speaking Children Emphasizing Experiences with Language.* Southwest Texas State Teachers College, 1955. 103 p. ms.

5320. DAVENPORT, ANE JOHNSON. *A Study to Determine a Program to Aid in the Instruction and Social Integration of Latin-American and Anglo-American Pupils in the Secondary Schools of Texas.* North Texas State College, 1953. 223 p. ms.

5321. DAVENPORT, EVERARD LEE. *A Comparative Study of Mexican and Non-Mexican Siblings.* University of Texas, 1931. 59 p. ms. (Refers to Mexicans in the United States.)

Latin-American

5322. DAVIS, EDDITH MANTOOTH. *Socio-Economic Status and Problems of Anglo-American and Latin-American High School Girls.* North Texas State College, 1955. 37 p. ms.

5323. DAVIS, RICCA FRIEDLANDER. *A Study of the Special Methods and Techniques Used by Public School Systems of the United States in Teaching Spanish-Speaking Beginners to Speak and Read the English Language.* Southwest Texas State Teachers College, 1942. 65 p. ms.

5324. DEAL, GERALD V. *A Study of the Vocational Opportunities in Pomona Valley for Mexican-Americans: A Study in Counseling.* Claremont Graduate School, 1951. 142 p. ms.

5325. DELAGADO, Sister JOSEPHINE. *Some Administrative Factors Related to the Education of Spanish-Speaking Children.* Immaculate Heart College, 1956. 133 p. ms.

5326. DELMET, DON THOMAS. *A Study of the Mental and Scholastic Abilities of Mexican Children in the Elementary School.* University of Southern California, 1928. 106 p. ms. (Based on tests administered to 371 Mexican children in the United States.)

5327. DENLAY, RAYMOND EMERY. *A Study of Height and Weight of Mexican Children.* Stanford University, 1940. 58 p. ms. (Children were in the United States.)

5328. DIAS, ROSARIO SIMON. *A Vocabulary of California Spanish Words of English Origin Used by the First Generation Spaniards of California.* Stanford University, 1942. 131 p. ms.

5329. DICKS, CATHERINE. *Food Management Practices and Food Habits of Anglo-American and Spanish-American Girls in New Mexico.* Colorado State College of Agriculture and Mechanic Arts, 1944. 145 p. ms.

5330. DIENST, LILLIAN H. *Education for Better Intercultural Relationships in the Schools of Grant County, New Mexico.* New Mexico Western College, 1952. 56 p. ms.

5331. DOBBS, MARGARET. *A Proposed Handbook for the Improvement of Beginning Reading for Spanish-Speaking Children.* University of Wyoming, 1955. 81 p. ms.

5332. DODD, ELMER CECIL. *A Comparison of Spanish-Speaking and English-Speaking Children in Brownsville, Texas.* University of Texas, 1930. 111 p. ms.

5333. DOERR, MARVIN FERDINAND. *Problem of the Elimination of Mexican Pupils from School.* University of Texas, 1938. 76 p. ms.

5334. DORSEY, GEORGIA LEE. *A History of the Education of Spanish-Speaking People in Texas.* North Texas State Teachers College, 1941. 133 p. ms.

5335. DOUGLASS, HAROLD R. *Intelligence Quotients and Achievement of Mexican-American Children in Grades One through Twelve.* Stanford University, 1949. 112 p. ms.

5336. DRAKE, ROLLEN HARRISON. *A Comparative Study of the Mentality and Achievement of Mexican and White Children.* University of Southern California, 1927. 68 p. ms.

5337. DRENNAN, DAVY DEOLECE. *The Progress in Reading of Fourth Grade Spanish-Speaking and English-Speaking Pupils.* University of Texas, 1937. 130 p. ms.

5338. DRENNAN, ORLENA PINK. *The Progress in Reading of Second Grade Spanish-Speaking and English-Speaking Pupils.* University of Texas, 1939. 115 p. ms. Abstract in University of Texas: *Abstracts of Masters' and Doctors' Theses in Education,* No. 1, 1942, p. 16-17.

5339. DUFFEY, ELLEN LOUISE, 1937- . *Spanish-American Culture in the Colonial Period.* Boston University, 1928. 80 p. ms. (Includes education, p. 27-38.)

5340. EAST, MARY ELIZABETH. *A Comparison of the Reading Achievement of Mexican and American Children on the Gates Silent Reading Tests.* University of Southern California, 1943.

5341. EBEL, CLARA PETERSON, 1908- . (Later name, Clara Ebel Forbes.) *Developing an Experience Curriculum in a Mexican First Grade.* Arizona State Teachers College, Tempe, 1940. 111 p. ms. (Mexican first grade in Eighth Street School, Tempe.)

5342. ELLIOTT, JAMES ALTON, 1904- . *The Language Handicap in Spanish-American Children in Intelligence and Achievement.* University of Arizona, 1942. 31 p. ms. Abstract in University of Arizona: *Abstracts of Theses for Higher Degrees,* 1941, 1942, p. 21-22.

5343. ELLIS, CHRISTINE EVANGELINE. *The Relation of Socio-Economic Status to the Intelligence and School Success of Mexican Children.* University of Texas, 1932. 81 p. ms. (Refers to children in San Antonio, Texas.)

5344. ELLIS, PHYLLIS, 1907- . *A Comparative Study of Two Methods of Teaching Retarded First-Grade Mexican Children to Read English.* Southern Methodist University, 1938. 147 p. ms. Abstract in Southern Methodist University: *Abstracts of Theses,* No. 6, 1939, p. 12-13.

5345. EMERSON, RALPH WADDELL, 1890- . *Education of the Mexican in Texas.* Southern Methodist University, 1929. 59 p. ms.

5346. ESPARZA, DANIEL. *An Exploratory Study of the Mental Ability and Scholastic Achievement of a Group of Spanish-Speaking Pupils according to Extent of Bilingualism.* University of Southern California, 1956. 62 p. ms.

5347. ESPEN, ETHEL M. *Special Education for the Spanish-Speaking Child in Texas.* Sul Ross State College, 1949. 69 p. ms.

5348. ESTAVILLO, FRANCISCO H. *A Study of the Effect of the Use of Spanish in Teaching English to Spanish-Speaking Children.* Arizona State Teachers College, Flagstaff, 1943. 36 p. ms.

5349. EZELL, PAUL HOWARD, 1913- . *A Racial Comparison of Pre-Adolescent White, Mexican, and Negro Boys.* University of Arizona, 1939. 98 p. ms. Abstract in *University of Arizona Record*, Vol. 34, p. 25.

5350. FARMER, WILLIAM ANDREW. *The Influence of Segregation of Mexican and American Children upon the Development of Social Attitudes.* University of Southern California, 1937. 112 p. ms.

5351. FAUNCE, LEO WARRINGTON, 1902- . *An Analysis of the Vocational and Avocational Pursuits of Mexican Men.* University of Arizona, 1941. 171 p. ms. Abstract in University of Arizona: *Abstracts of Theses for Higher Degrees*, 1941, 1942. p. 23. (Indicates need of courses in industrial arts for Mexican boys.)

5352. FERGES, MILDRED LOUISE, 1920- . *Music, an Essential in Teaching Non-English-Speaking First-Grade Children.* Texas College of Arts and Industries, 1952. 139 p. ms.

5353. FITZPATRICK, DOROTHA CHAFFEE, 1903- . *Mexican Crafts in Relation to Related Arts in the Calexico Public Schools.* Oregon State College, 1939. 89 p. ms.

5354. FLORES, ZELLA K. JORDAN. *The Relation of Language Difficulty to Intelligence and School Retardation in a Group of Spanish-Speaking Children.* University of Chicago, 1926. 96 p. ms.

5355. FRECH, FLORENCE PAGE. *Spanish Culture: Supplementary Elementary Curriculum Material.* Texas College of Arts and Industries, 1950. 103 p. ms.

5356. FRENZEL, RUFUS EMIL. *Factors that Contribute to Non-Attendance in Schools of Latin-American Children and to Withdrawal after Entering the Ninth Grade in the Big Wells Independent School District.* Southwest Texas State Teachers College, 1951. 58 p. ms.

5357. FRERICHS, RUTH MARY. *The Interests and Attitudes of Mexican Parents toward Education in an Elementary School.* Trinity University, 1951. 68 p. ms. (Refers to parents in San Antonio, Texas.)

5358. FRITZ, JOHN CAROLUS, 1916- . *A Comparison of Musical Capacity and Musical Achievement of Spanish-American and American Pupils in Morenci Junior High School.* University of Arizona, 1940. 42 p. ms. Abstract in University of Arizona: *Abstracts of Theses for Higher Degrees*, 1939, 1940, p. 28.

5359. FULLWOOD, REVELLA J. *A Comparative Study of Selected Groups of Anglo- and Latin-American Slow Learners.* Texas Woman's University, 1958.

5360. FUSSELL, WILLIAM DURWOOD. *Comparable Norms for Anglo-American and Latin-American Pupils on a Scholastic Aptitude Test.* University of Texas, 1940. 62 p. ms.

5361. GALLOWAY, BERNICE OZETA. *A Study of the Artistic Abilities of Natively Spanish-Speaking Children and Natively English-Speaking Children.* University of New Mexico, 1939. 78 p. ms.

5362. GANT, LONELLA SCRUGGS. *A Study of Music as a Contributing Factor in Teaching Latin-American Children in Grades One, Two, and Three of Martindale School.* Southwest Texas State Teachers College, 1956. 88 p. ms.

5363. GARNER, Mrs. VELDRON BERDEAN (ROZELL). *Developmental Tasks and Television Choices of Latin-American and Anglo-American School Children.* University of Texas, 1957. 97 p. ms.

5364. GARNETT, Mrs. HATTIE MAE (BRYAN). *Boy-Girl Relationships of Latin-American Children as Shown in Anecdotal Records by Teachers.* University of Texas, 1954. 164 p. ms.

5365. GARRETSON, OLIVER KELLEAM. *Causes of Retardation of Mexican Children in American Schools.* University of Texas, 1926. 174 p. ms.

5366. GARZA, EDWARD DANIEL. *LULAC (League of United Latin-American Citizens).* Southwest Texas State Teachers College, 1951. 64 p. ms. (Includes education.)

5367. GARZA, GEORGE J. *Social and Economic Status of Mexicans in San Marcos and Its Bearings upon the Education of Mexican Children.* Southwest Texas State Teachers College, 1940. 59 p. ms.

5368. GARZA, Mrs. MARIA AZCUNIA. *Teaching of English to Spanish-Speaking Beginners.* University of Texas, 1953. 97 p. ms.

5369. GAUT, GERTRUDE FLINN. *Relative Efficiency of the Direct and Indirect Method of Teaching English Vocabulary to Spanish-Speaking Children at Kindergarten Age.* New Mexico Normal University, 1930. 111 p. ms.

5370. GIBSON, MARY ELLEN, 1913- . *Some Important Problems in Teaching Spanish-Culture Children.* Texas College of Arts and Industries, 1940. 125 p. ms.

5371. GIBSON, WELDON G. *A Program of Health Education for Southgate Elementary School.* Texas College of Arts and Industries, 1940. 129 p. ms. (Predominantly Spanish-culture children.)

5372. GILBERT, FRANCES GABRILLA, 1918- . (Later, Mrs. William B. Fawcett.) *An Evaluation of the Religious Education Curriculum Materials Used Most Frequently with Junior Age Spanish-Speaking Children in the Southwest.* Presbyterian College of Christian Education, 1943. 74 p. ms.

5373. GILL, MARY SODD. *The Child of Foreign Parentage.* North Texas State Teachers College, 1944. 38 p. ms. Abstract in North Texas State Teachers College: *Abstracts of Theses*, 1941-1946, p. 72-73.

5374. GILLETTE, GEORGE CURTISS. *A Diagnostic Study of the Factors Affecting the Low Scores of Spanish-Speaking Children on Standardized Tests.* University of Southern California, 1941. 302 p. ms.

5375. GLADNEY, KATIE MARGARET. *Arithmetic Achievement Tests for Six Weeks Periods for the First Grade of the Stephen F. Austin School in Kingsville.* Texas College of Arts and Industries, 1942. 49 p. ms. (Predominantly Spanish-culture children.)

Latin-American

5376. GOLDEN, MARTHA ELOISE, 1903- . *Spanish-American Education in the Public Schools of the City of El Paso, Texas.* Southern Methodist University, 1929. 89 p. ms.

5377. GOMEZ, LUCY R. 1915- . *Instructional Problems of Teachers with First Graders from the Non-English Speaking Home.* San Jose State College, 1957. 111 p. ms.

5378. GONZALES, AURORA MARJORIE. *A Study of the Intelligence of Mexican Children in Relation to Their Socio-Economic Status.* University of Texas, 1932. 45 p. ms.

5379. GONZALEZ DE LOS SANTOS, MARIA DE JESUS. *Factors Affecting the Education of Twenty-Five Migrant Spanish-Speaking Children.* University of Texas, 1952. 79 p. ms.

5380. GORE, WALTER ROOSEVELT, 1900- . *A Comparison of Reading, English, and Arithmetic Achievements of Pupils of Spanish-American Descent and other American-Born Pupils in the Washington School.* University of Denver, 1940. 81 p. ms.

5381. GOTT, MARGARET ELLA, 1907- . *Teaching Reading to Spanish-Speaking Children.* San Diego State College, 1956. 277 p. ms.

5382. GOULD, BETTY. *Methods of Teaching Mexicans.* University of Southern California, 1932. 131 p. ms.

5383. GRAHAM, LEON R., 1904- . *A Comparison of the English-Speaking and Latin-American Students in the Mercedes, Texas, Schools.* Southern Methodist University, 1938. 93 p. ms. Abstract in Southern Methodist University: *Abstracts of Theses,* No. 6, 1939, p. 13-14.

5384. GROSS, STUART MURRAY. *A Vocabulary of New Mexico Spanish.* Stanford University, 1936. 78 p. ms.

5385. GROUT, PAUL ASBURY, 1906- . *Trends in Scolastics, Enrollment, Average Daily Attendance, and Age-Grade Distribution of Spanish-American Pupils in Lyford, Texas, Public Schools, 1933-1938.* Texas College of Arts and Industries, 1938. 66 p. ms.

5386. GRUSENDORF, ARTHUR AUGUST. *A Study of Latin and Spanish Students of the Waco High School.* Baylor University, 1925.

5387. GUNN, EWING LEYTON. *An Eye-Movement Study of the Reading Habits of Spanish-American Children.* University of Texas, 1935. 116 p. ms.

5388. HABERMACHER, ANDREW LEE, 1914- . *Physical Development of Anglo- and Spanish-Culture School Boys and Girls, Ages 13 to 18 Inclusive.* Texas College of Arts and Industries, 1940. 79 p. ms.

5389. HAMILTON, EMMA FRANCES, 1920- . *A Comparison of Scores Made on College Entrance Examination by "Latin" and "Anglo" Students.* Texas College of Arts and Industries, 1957. 33 p. ms.

5390. HAMILTON, OLIVE F. *Improvement of Dietary Practices and Housing Conditions of Spanish-Speaking People through Homemaking Education.* Colorado State College of Agriculture and Mechanic Arts, 1942. 104 p. ms.

5391. HAMMER, HENRY BURTON, 1922- . *Problems in Educating Migrant Children.* Sul Ross State College, 1957. 95 p. ms.

5392. HANCOOK, MILDRED. *Teaching Numbers in the Range from One to Six to Latin-American Beginners.* Southwest Texas State Teachers College, 1951. 83 p. ms.

5393. HARBIN, TILGHMAN A. *Financial Inequalities of the Schools of Willacy County, 1952.* Texas College of Arts and Industries, 1952. 52 p. ms. (All schools have high proportion of Spanish-American students.)

5394. HARKINS, BUTLER STERLING. *Methods of Teaching Creative Writing to Mexican Children of the Elementary Grades.* University of Southern California, 1944. 131 p. ms. (Refers to Mexican children in Oxnard, California.)

5395. HARREL, BILLYE JONES, 1925- . *A Study of Some Attitudes Regarding Society and the World of Work of Four Groups of Sophomore Students.* Texas College of Arts and Industries, 1957. 57 p. ms. (Concerned with the Latin-American Anglo-American dichotomy. Class studied was one third Latin-American.)

5396. HARRIS, JAMES KILBOURNE. *A Sociological Study of a Mexican School in San Antonio, Texas.* University of Texas, 1927. 98 p. ms.

5397. HARRIS, SHIRLEY, 1920- . *Protestant Christian Education Among the Spanish-Speaking People in Northern New Mexico.* Princeton Theological Seminary, 1949. 122 p. ms.

5398. HARRISON, DAVID CALDWELL. *A Survey of the Administrative and Educational Policies of the Baptist, Methodist, and Presbyterian Churches among the Mexican-American People in Texas.* University of Texas, 1953. 153 p. ms.

5399. HARRISS, VESTA McDANIEL, 1912- . *A Study of Reading Readiness of Latin-American Children in Looney Ward School, Brownwood, Texas.* Hardin-Simmons University, 1952. 62 p. ms.

5400. HART, ROBERT NEWTON. *A Comparison of the Academic Achievements of Mexican-American Children with Those of Anglo-American Children in the Fourth, Fifth, and Sixth Grades of Chino Elementary Schools.* Claremont Graduate School, 1949. 88 p. ms.

5401. HELMKE, WILLARD RICHARD. *The Effect of English Language Handicap on the IQ's of Spanish-American Children.* University of Colorado, 1937. 55 p. ms. Abstract in *University of Colorado Studies,* Vol. 25, No. 1, p. 69, November 1937.

5402. HENRY, RALPH FREDERICK. *"Yo Quisiera Hablar Ingles" — An English Course for Spanish-Speaking Adults.* University of Southern California, 1950. 111 p. ms.

5403. HERNANDEZ, ARCADIA. *A Study of Retarded Spanish-Speaking Children in the Second Grade.* University of Texas, 1938. 143 p. ms.

5404. HERRON, FRANK HOWARD, Jr. *The Settlement: Its Contribution towards the Americanization of the Mexican Boy.* University of Notre Dame, 1935. 47 p. ms.

5405. HIDALGO, J. THOMAS. *A Study of Words of English Origin Used by the Kansas Mexican.* Kansas State Teachers College, Emporia, 1937. 52 p. ms.

5406. HIGLEY, JOSEPH KENT. *Two Methods of Teaching English to Mentally Subnormal Mexican Children.* University of Southern California, 1942. 134 p. ms.

5407. HILL, BERA BROWN, 1910- . *Teaching Non-English-Speaking Beginners: A Supervisor's Study.* Texas College of Arts and Industries, 1956. 142 p. ms.

5408. HILL, JOE WARREN, 1908- . *An Administrator's Study of the Yancey School.* Texas College of Arts and Industries, 1941. 71 p. ms. (Chapter 5: "Problem of Spanish-Speaking Child." Chapter 7: "Course of Study for Spanish-Speaking Child.")

5409. HILL, MARGUERITE W. *A Proposed Guidance Program for Mexican Youth in the Junior High School.* Claremont Graduate School, 1945. 108 p. ms.

5410. HILLSEN, HENRY HARTLEY. *A Comparative Study of the Intelligence Quotient Scores and the Reading Achievement Scores of Spanish-Speaking Children in Redlands Elementary Schools, Redlands, California.* University of Redlands, 1953. 95 p. ms.

5411. HINES, BEN BARNES, 1899- . *The Present Status of Education in Kaufman and Van Zandt Counties.* Southern Methodist University, 1936. 145 p. ms. Abstract in Southern Methodist University: *Abstracts of Theses,* No. 4, 1937, p. 12-13.

5412. HODGES, LYDIA HERRERA. *A Study of the Reading Ability of Mexican Children in Relation to Their Socio-Economic Status.* Southwest Texas State Teachers College, 1938. 37 p. ms.

5413. HOGAN, MILO ARTHUR VAN VORMAN. *A Study of the School Progress of Mexican Children in Imperial County.* University of Southern California, 1935. 94 p. ms.

5414. HOLCOMBE, WALTER MERTON. *An Inquiry into the Length of Recitation in the Case of Mexican Children.* University of Denver, 1929. 151 p. ms.

5415. HOLDER, HELEN LEE. *Family Resemblances in the Intelligence Quotients of Mexican Children and Their Socio-Economic Status.* Southwest Texas State Teachers College, 1940. 78 p. ms.

5416. HOLMES, KATHLEEN. *The Contribution and Use of Marionettes Particularly with Reference to Spanish-American Elementary School Children.* University of Texas, 1938. 101 p. ms.

5417. HOWARD, DONALD STEVENSON. *A Study of the Mexican, Mexican-American, and Spanish Population in Pueblo, Colorado.* University of Denver, 1930. 81 p. ms. (Includes education.)

5418. HOWARD, MAXINE D., 1911- . *A Study of the Brownsville High School Business Administration and Its Contribution to the Needs of Brownsville, Texas.* Texas College of Arts and Industries, 1951. 92 p. ms. (Includes 170 Latin-American students.)

5419. HOWARD, RAYMOND GLENN. *Acculturation and Social Mobility among Latin-Americans in Resaca City.* University of Texas, 1952. 136 p. ms. (Education considered as one phase of acculturation.)

5420. HOWE, ANNA LYNN. *Proposals for the Organization and Administration of a Program of Special Education to Improve the English Speech of Certain Spanish-Speaking Pupils, Eagle Pass, Texas.* University of Texas, 1953. 134 p. ms.

5421. HUGHES, Mrs. LOIS SPEARS. *A Comparative Study of the Intelligence of Mexican and Non-Mexican Children.* University of Texas, 1928. 78 p. ms.

5422. HUGHES, Mrs. MARIE MORRISON, 1900- *Rate of Acquisition of an English-Speaking Vocabulary by Spanish-Speaking Children.* University of Chicago, 1935. 123 p. ms. For doctoral dissertation by same author, see No. 5216.

5423. HURST, WALTER JOSEPH, 1903- . *The Pupil Personnel Program in the Pharr-San Juan-Alamo Schools.* Texas College of Arts and Industries, 1952. 67 p. ms. (Very large Spanish-culture enrollment.)

5424. IRISH, BETTY H. *The Concurrent Development of Oral and Reading English Vocabularies with Mexican First Grade Children.* Arizona State Teachers College, Flagstaff, 1938. 132 p. ms. Abstract in Arizona State Teachers College: *Abstracts of Masters' Theses, 1938-1942,* p. 3-4.

5425. IVEY, ALFRED JOE. *A Study of the Vocabulary of Newspapers Printed in the Spanish Language in Texas.* University of Texas, 1927. 137 p. ms.

5426. JACKSON, DORIS ELAINE GOFORTH. *Educational Status of Mexican Children in a Texas Elementary School.* University of Texas, 1953. 71 p. ms.

5427. JACKSON, Mrs. LUCILE PRIM. *An Analysis of the Language Difficulties of the Spanish-Speaking Children of the Bowie High School, El Paso, Texas.* University of Texas, 1938. 170 p. ms.

5428. JAMES, HELEN NANCY. *How Health, Social Conditions, and Educational Opportunities of the Mexican Children in the Sonora Independent School May Be Improved.* North Texas State Teachers College, 1941. 84 p. ms. Abstract in North Texas State Teachers College: *Abstracts of Theses, 1941-1946,* p. 99.

5429. JENSEN, CARL ROBERT. *A Study of the Spanish-American Normal School at El Rito.* University of New Mexico, 1939. 78 p. ms.

5430. JENSEN, JAMES MAURICE. *The Mexican-American in an Orange County Community.* Claremont Graduate School, 1947. 113 p. ms. (Includes one chapter on the Mexican-American in school.)

5431. JERDEN, CECIL M., 1908- . *A Study of Racial Differences in the El Paso Public Schools.* Southern Methodist University, 1939. 75 p. ms. Abstract in Southern Methodist University: *Abstracts of Theses,* No. 7, 1940, p. 23.

5432. JIRON, MARY J. *Procedures for Teaching English to Bilingual Children as a Basis for Reading Practices.* Adams State College, 1956.

5433. JOHNS, CRYSTINE GORDON. *A Program of Education to Fit the Needs of the Mexican Children in Wichita Falls, Texas.* North Texas State Teachers College, 1938. 63 p. ms. Abstract in North Texas State Teachers College: *Abstracts of Theses, 1935-40,* p. 46-47. (Bulletin No. 142, December 1941.)

5434. JOHNSON, CORAL GILMORE. *The Effectiveness of Sight Singing Instruction for Mexican and Negro Children.* University of Southern California, 1938. 85 p. ms.

5435. JOHNSON, HARPER DANIELS. *The Intelligence and Achievement of Mexican Children as Determined by the Otis Classification Tests.* University of Denver, 1929. 43 p. ms.

5436. JOHNSON, MAUREEN MILDRED. *A Comparison of Public and Private Education of Bilingual Children of Certain Cities of New Mexico.* Brigham Young University, 1943. 92 p. ms.

5437. JOHNSON, ROBERTA MURIEL. *History of the Education of Spanish-Speaking Children in Texas.* University of Texas, 1932. 121 p. ms.

5438. JOHNSON, TOMMIE JEWEL. *Remedial Reading for Seventh, Eighth, and Ninth Grades in the Petronila School: A Means for Reducing Failures.* Texas College of Arts and Industries, 1949. 83 p. ms. (Large Spanish-American enrollment. One Spanish-American case study.)

5439. JONES, HUBERT LEDYARD, 1915- . *A Comparison of Physical Skill and Intelligence of Negro and Spanish-American Boys of Junior High School Age.* University of Denver, 1940. 33 p. ms.

5440. JONES, KATHERINE GREENAWALT, 1917- . *A Program for First Grade Spanish-American Children on Language Experiences.* Arizona State Teachers College, Tempe, 1945. 96 p. ms.

5441. JONES, WILLIAM C. *Educational Offerings to Mexicans and Americans in Big Bend County, Texas.* George Peabody College for Teachers, 1928. 130 p. ms.

5442. KADERLI, ALBERT TURNER. *The Education Problem in the Americanization of the Spanish-Speaking Pupils of Sugar Land, Texas.* University of Texas, 1940. 71 p. ms.

5443. KADERLI, JAMES NICHOLAS. *A Study of Mexican Education in Atascosa County with Special Reference to Pleasanton Elementary School.* University of Texas, 1938. 77 p. ms.

5444. KEELE, Mrs. JEWEL HELEN (STANLEY). *A Study of the Varieties and Misspellings by Anglo-American and Spanish-American Children.* University of Texas, 1953. 118 p. ms.

5445. KEEN, MARVIN SPRUCE. *A Comparative Study of the Motor-Ability of Latin-American and Anglo-American Boys.* University of Texas, 1941. 82 p. ms.

5446. KELLEY, CLARA AMANDA. *An Investigation of Some Aspects of Hispanic-American Culture.* University of Idaho, 1939. 43 p. ms. (Chiefly devoted to education.)

5447. KENEFICK, RUTH MAUREEN. *The Power and Position of the Spanish and Mexican Folk Dance in Southern California.* Claremont Graduate School, 1936. 69 p. ms.

5448. KENNEDY, RUBY LUCILE IMLAY, 1904- . *The Collateral Reading Program in the Bilingual High Schools of South Texas.* Texas College of Arts and Industries, 1956. 111 p. ms.

5449. KENT, JAMES L. *Segregation of Mexican School Children in Southern California.* University of Oregon, 1940. 89 p. ms.

5450. KILFOYLE, JOHN GRANT. *Educational Differences of Mexican-American Children.* University of Utah, 1955. 80 p. ms.

5451. KINDARD, EUNICE WALKER. *Strengthening English for Latin-American Pupils.* Sul Ross State College, 1957. 95 p. ms.

5452. KING, ESTHER MARTIN. *Reading Achievement of Spanish-American Children in the First Grade, Monte Vista, Colorado.* Colorado State College of Education, 1941. 110 p. ms.

5453. KING, GWENDOLYN NOON, 1908- . *Musical Experiences to Aid Mexican Bilingual Children in Correcting Speech Defects.* University of Arizona, 1946. 73 p. ms. Abstract in University of Arizona: *Abstracts of Theses for High Degrees, 1945-46,* p. 18.

5454. KING, JOHN RANDLE. *An Inquiry into the Status of Mexican Segregation in Metropolitan Bakersfield.* Claremont Graduate School, 1946. 89 p. ms. (Includes study of attitudes of Mexican and American students in the schools, pp. 58-66.)

5455. KINSEY, LURA, 1892- . *A Comparison of the Achievement of American and Mexican Seventh- and Eighth-Grade Pupils.* University of Arizona, 1937. 33 p. ms. Abstract in University of Arizona: *Abstracts of Theses for Higher Degrees, 1937, 1938,* p. 34.

5456. KNOPF, ARTHUR CARLYLE. *Some Mexican Characteristics and Their Educational Significance.* University of Southern California, 1943. 86 p. ms. (Based on study of Mexican children in Riverside, California.)

5457. KRAMME, CLYDE IRA, 1913- . *A Comparison of Anglo-Culture with Spanish-Culture Elementary Students in Physical Development as Determined by Height, Weight, and Vital Capacity Measurements.* Texas College of Arts and Industries, 1939. 89 p. ms.

5458. KROPF, LOUISE IRMA. *Making the School for Latin-Americans from Mexico a Functional Community Center.* Texas State College for Women, 1944. 79 p. ms.

5459. LADO, ROBERT, 1915- . *A Study of the Use of Motion Pictures in Teaching Spanish-Speaking Adults to Read.* University of Texas, 1944. 115 p. ms. For doctoral dissertation by same author, see No. 5219.

5460. LA GRONE, EMMA RUTH. *Activities to Help Second Grade Latin-American Children Understand and Use a Second Grade Basic Reading Vocabulary.* Southwest Texas State Teachers College, 1951. 80 p. ms.

5461. LANE, IRENE C. *Special Reading Program for Retarded Spanish-Speaking Children.* Sul Ross State College, 1954. 104 p. ms.

5462. LEHMAN, VICTOR BOYD. *A Study of the Social Adjustment of the Mexican-Americans in Chino and a Proposed Program of Community Action under School Leadership.* Claremont Graduate School, 1947. 179 p. ms.

5463. LEIS, WARD WILLIAM. *The Status of Education for Mexican Children in Four Border States.* University of Southern California, 1932. 78 p. ms.

5464. LIGHTON, EDWARD WILLIAM. *Language Difficulty and Its Measurement among Spanish-American Junior High School Students.* Stanford University, 1931. 53 p. ms. plus appendix.

5465. LINTHICUM, JOHN BUREN. *The Classification of Spanish-American Beginners in an Albuquerque Public School.* University of Southern California, 1920. 73 p. ms.

5466. LLERA, ALTALUZ. *A Guide for Teaching Early California History to Mexican Children.* University of Southern California, 1951. 74 p. ms.

5467. LLOMBART, ROSA MARIA CHIQUES DE. *A Minimum Vocabulary List for Use in Teaching an Intensive Course in American English to Latin-American Students.* University of Michigan, 1946. 71 p. ms.

5468. LOFTIN, JAMES OTIS. *Mexican Secondary Education as Developed in the Sidney Lanier Junior School.* Colorado State Teachers College, 1927. 118 p. ms.

5469. LOGAN, LILLIAN PARK, 1905- *A Working-Reading Program for the Spanish-Speaking Children of the Primary Grades of O'Brien Elementary School of O'Brien, Texas.* Hardin-Simmons University, 1949. 85 p. ms.

5470. LOPEZ, MARIA SALDANA, 1912- . *A Study of Ten Retarded Eighth Grade Pupils in the Hebronville Junior High School.* Texas College of Arts and Industries, 1953. 78 p. ms. (All ten were Spanish-Americans.)

5471. LOPEZ, MARY LOUISE. *The Relationship of Kindergarten Experience to the Learning of English by the Spanish-Speaking Child.* Southwest Texas State Teachers College, 1956. 78 p. ms.

5472. LOZANO, AMPARO AUGUSTA. *An Experiment in Teaching Spanish and English to Spanish-Speaking Children.* University of Texas, 1932. 48 p. ms.

5473. LUJAN, JUAN ROBERTO. *Fourteen-Year-Old Spanish-Named Drop-Outs in the Harlingen School System.* University of Texas, 1956. 116 p. ms.

5474. LUNT, OLAS ARNOLD. *Withdrawals of Spanish-Speaking Students from an Arizona School System and Implications Derived Therefrom.* Arizona State Teachers College, Flagstaff, 1942. 100 p. ms. Abstract in Arizona State Teachers College: *Abstracts of Master's Theses, 1938-1942,* p. 89-90.

5475. LYON, LAURA LUCILE. *Investigation of the Problem for the Adjustment of Mexican Girls to the High Schools of the San Fernando Valley.* University of Southern California, 1933. 74 p. ms.

5476. McCALIB, REFUGIO D. *Pupil Personnel and Adjustment Services as Related to Improving School Attendance in Bruni Elementary School, Laredo, Texas.* Texas College of Arts and Industries, 1950. 60 p. ms. (Large proportion of students of Spanish-cultural background. Considers problem of migratory Mexican-Americans.)

5477. McCAMMON, ELEANOR LOUISE, 1910- . *A Scale for the Measurement of Attitudes toward Mexicans.* University of California, Berkeley, 1934. 88 p. ms.

5478. McCLEAN, VELMA P. *A Study of Audio-Visual Aids for Language Improvements of Mexican-Americans.* University of Southern California, 1958.

5479. McCRAINIE, JOSEPHINE. *A Study of Four Inter-American Tests Applied to High School Seniors.* University of Texas, 1944. 80 p. ms.

5480. McCULLOUGH, VIVIAN TALLANT, 1909- . *Some Educational Problems of Spanish-Speaking Pupils in the Elementary Grades.* San Jose State College, 1955. 239 p. ms.

5481. McDANIEL, GERTRUDE DOROTHY. *The Use of Visual Aids in Teaching the Mexican Beginner to Read.* University of Texas, 1937. 91 p. ms.

5482. McDANIEL, OPAL. *Achievement of Mexican Pupils in Certain Non-Segregated and Segregated Junior High Schools.* University of Oregon, 1942. 45 p. ms.

5483. McGEHEE, LORINE V. *Training for Household Employment in a Large Mining Community in Arizona.* Colorado State College of Agriculture and Mechanic Arts, 1940. 131 p. ms. (Reports interviews with 100 housekeepers employing Mexican girls and with 71 Mexican household workers.)

5484. McGREGOR, RUTH PRINCE. *The Elimination of Eighth-Grade Graduates among the Mexicans from the High Schools of a Certain Small City in California.* University of Southern California, 1940. 67 p. ms.

5485. McLENNAN, LeROY. *A Comparison of the Spanish-Speaking and English-Speaking Children in Nine Schools over a Five-Year Period.* University of Texas, 1936. 55 p. ms.

5486. MACEL, *Sister* MARY GABRIEL. *Reading Interests of Latin-American Children.* Catholic University of America, 1947. 91 p. ms. Abstract in

Catholic Educational Review, Vol. 46, p. 172, March 1948.

5487. MADDUX, HAZEL. *Some Conditions Which Influence the Mexican Children in Greeley, Colorado, and Its Vicinity.* Colorado State Teachers College, 1932. 69 p. ms.

5488. MADKIN, NORMA HILLARY. *Modifying a Reading Program to Meet the Needs of Spanish-Speaking Children.* University of Southern California, 1951. 64 p. ms.

5489. MALMS, CHESTER W. *A Study of the Music Background of 308 Sixth Grade Students in Four Corpus Christi Elementary Schools, May 1952.* Texas College of Arts and Industries, 1953. 55 p. ms. (Compares Latin-American and Anglo-American students.)

5490. MANN, LOUISE MANSON. *A Comparison of the Achievement of Spanish and English Children in Algebra.* University of Southern California, 1937. 69 p. ms. (Based on students in schools of Albuquerque, New Mexico.)

5491. MANZO, RICARDO, 1906- . *Difficulties of Spanish-Speaking Children in the Fundamental Number Combinations.* University of Arizona, 1939. 112 p. ms.

5492. MARSHALL, FLOYD LESLIE, 1914- . *History and Present Status of Latin-American Education in Melvin, Texas.* Hardin-Simmons University, 1950. 97 p. ms.

5493. MARTIN, GERTRUDE RUNYAN. *A Study of Oral Language Activities Used in Teaching Vocabulary and Concepts to Pre-First Grade Spanish-Speaking Children in the Reading Readiness Program in the Pre-First Grade.* New Mexico Western College, 1954. 159 p. ms.

5494. MARTINEZ, ARMULFO SIMEON. *A Study of the Scholastic Census of the Spanish-Speaking Children of Texas.* University of Texas, 1944. 105 p. ms.

5495. MARTINEZ, DOMINGO. *A Comparative Study of the Academic Achievement of the Mexican-American Students in the Wilson Junior High School, Oxnard, California.* Claremont Graduate School, 1956. 85 p. ms.

5496. MARX, MEYER. *The Problem of Bilingualism among Spanish-Groups in the United States: A Review of the Literature.* University of Southern California, 1954. 86 p. ms.

5497. MATZIGKEIT, WESLEY WINFRED. *The Influence of Six Mexican Cultural Factors on Group Behavior.* University of Southern California, 1947. 120 p. ms.

5498. MAYER, LENA C. *A Critique of Fifty American Poems Found in Spanish Translation.* Colorado State Teachers College, 1928. 272 p. ms.

5499. MAYERS, VERA. *The Migratory Child in California: His Mode of Life and the Attempt Made to Better His Situation.* University of Chicago, 1938. 160 p. ms.

5500. MELLEIN, *Sister* MIRIAM FIDELIS. *A Survey of the Effectiveness of the Elementary and Secondary Education of Latin-American Children.* Catholic University of America, 1950. 50 p. ms. (Covers 1949 pupils in "a city in the Rio Grande Valley, the name of which has been withheld for obvious reasons.")

5501. MELLENBRUCH, Mrs. JULIA IDA (KLATTENHOFF). *Teaching Spanish-Speaking Students in Texas High Schools.* University of Texas, 1955. 91 p. ms.

5502. MENDENHALL, WARREN O. *A Comparative Study of Achievement and Ability of the Children in Two Segregated Mexican Schools.* University of Southern California, 1938. 90 p. ms. (Schools in Orange County, California.)

5503. MERCER, ORENE RAY. *A Check List Analysis of Methods Used by the Pre-Primer Teachers of Non-English-Speaking Children.* Southwest Texas State Teachers College, 1941. 61 p. ms.

5504. MERCHANT, LAWRENCE KEY, 1907- . *Bishop, Texas: School Transportation, Its Development and Problems.* Texas College of Arts and Industries, 1949. 81 p. ms. (Considers the problems of the separate Spanish-American school.)

5505. MERRYWEATHER, ROSE. *A Study of the Comparative Ability of the Mexican and American Children in the Upper Elementary Grades.* University of Southern California, 1933. 83 p. ms.

5506. MICHEA, CLAUDE ANGUS. *The Intelligence of Nine- and Ten-Year-Old Mexican Children Measured by the Leiter International Performance Scale.* University of Southern California, 1942. 150 p. ms.

5507. MILLER, Mrs. BONNIE BELLE (MOORE). *Meeting the Need of the Spanish-Speaking Migrant in the Coahoma Elementary School, Howard County, Texas, 1950-1953 Inclusive.* University of Texas, 1953. 67 p. ms.

5508. MILLIGAN, CARMEN IRENE. *An Integration of Instructional Methods for Teaching Children of Latin-American Descent.* Southwest Texas State Teachers College, 1945. 75 p. ms.

5509. MILLIGAN, ROLAND WILLIAM. *A Case Study of Benevides High Graduates, 1923-38.* Texas College of Arts and Industries, 1941. 83 p. ms. (Over half of graduates were Latin-Americans.)

5510. MILLS, HELEN RISINGER. *Home-School Cooperation for Child Development in the Latin-American Primary School.* Southwest Texas State Teachers College, 1951. 93 p. ms.

5511. MITCHELL, ARTHUR J. *The Effect of Bilingualism in the Measurement of Intelligence.* University of Colorado, 1936. 56 p. ms. Abstract in *University of Colorado Studies*, Vol. 24, No. 1, p. 48-49, November 1936.

5512. MITCHELL, FREDERIC FRANCIS, 1917- . *Shortcomings in the Written English of Spanish-Speaking Ninth Grade Pupils in the Schools of Tucson, Arizona.* University of Arizona, 1943. 63 p. ms. Abstract in *University of Arizona: Abstracts of Theses for Higher Degrees*, 1943, 1944, p. 21.

5513. MITCHELL, QUINCY BRADY, 1876-1939. *The Comparative Achievement of White, Mexican, and Colored Children in Elementary Public Schools.* University of Kansas, 1928. 97 p. ms.

5514. MOORE, BEATRICE McCURDY. *Adult Educational Opportunities in Corpus Christi, Texas, and Uses Made of Them by Latin-American Women.* Texas State College for Women, 1952. 138 p. ms.

5515. MORAN, MATTIE BELLE SAUER. *A Study of the Oral and Reading Vocabularies of Beginning Spanish-Speaking Children.* University of Texas, 1940. 109 p. ms.

5516. MORGAN, ELIZABETH ANNELIES, 1914- . *The English Language Background of the Latin-American Students at the University of Florida.* University of Florida, 1951. 75 p. ms.

5517. MORRISON, CHARLOTTE AMOS. *A Comparison of the Achievement of Mexican Pupils in Learning English in a Segregated School and in a Non-Segregated School.* University of Oregon, 1944. 52 p. ms.

5518. MORTON, MARGARET MARION. *A Study of the Results of Administration of Verbal and Non-Verbal Intelligence Tests to Mexicans.* University of Denver, 1933. 127 p. ms.

5519. MOWRY, MARY DAVIS. *Objective versus Essay Examinations for Spanish-American Pupils in Mixed Classes.* New Mexico State Teachers College, 1933. 193 p. ms.

5520. MUNOZ, ROSALIO FLORIAN, 1913- . *The Relation of Bilingualism to Verbal Intelligence and Social Adjustment among Mexican Children in the Salt River Valley, Arizona.* Arizona State Teachers College, Tempe, 1938. 81 p. ms.

5521. NANNY, ORVAL EDMOND. *The Effectiveness of the Transportation System of Riviera Independent School District.* Texas College of Arts and Industries, 1951. 47 p. ms. (Studies effect of the Spanish-American worker problem on school transportation.)

5522. NELSON, GWENDOLYN. *The Use of Music Activities with Retarded Latin-American Children.* North Texas State College, 1953. 67 p. ms.

5523. NICHOLS, GARRETT C. *Agricultural Influences on the Mexican Residents of the Coachella Valley as Particularly Related to Education.* Claremont Graduate School, 1955. 94 p. ms.

5524. NICOLA, PETRA CASTRO. *The Educational Problem of the Mexican Migrants of Texas, with Specific Reference to San Marcos, Texas.* Southwest Texas State Teachers College, 1952.

5525. NICOLL, JAMES STEWART. *A Comparison of the Physical Development, Motor Capacity, and Strength of Anglo-American and Spanish-American Boys.* University of Southern California, 1943. 57 p. ms.

5526. NICOLL, JOHN. *A Study of the Self and Social Adjustment Patterns of Equated Mexican-American Groups Entering Excelsior High School, Norwalk, California, from Both Mixed and Segregated Elementary Schools.* Claremont Graduate School, 1949. 85 p. ms.

5527. NIEMEYER, ERNESTINE HELENA, 1896- . *A Manual for Teaching Elementary English to First-Grade Spanish-Speaking Children.* George Washington University, 1934. 132 p. ms.

5528. NOLD, DOROTHY STUBBS. *Arts and Crafts in the Corpus Christi Junior High Schools, 1933-1949.* Texas College of Arts and Industries, 1949. 67 p. ms. (Two of the six case studies are of Latin-Americans.)

5529. O'BRIEN, MARY ROSE. *A Comparison of the Reading Ability of Spanish-Speaking Pupils with Non-Spanish-Speaking Pupils in Grade 6A of the Denver Public Schools.* University of Denver, 1937. 58 p. ms.

5530. O'BRYANT, HORACE. *The Cuban Child in Division Street School, Key West, Florida.* University of Florida, 1932. 85 p. ms.

5531. OCHOA, HERMELINDA. *Linguistic Errors Made by Spanish-Speaking Children in Written English.* University of Texas, 1942. 85 p. ms.

5532. ODENTHAL, JOSEPH WILLIAM, 1916- . *A Survey of the Articulation Errors of a Group of Spanish-Speaking Children.* San Diego State College, 1955. 134 p. ms.

5533. OLIPHINT, HOWARD LEE, 1913- . *A Comparison of English and Latin-American Students in the Kingsville, Texas, High School.* Sam Houston State Teachers College, 1942. 44 p. ms.

5534. OSWALD, EDWARD H. *A Comparison of the Achievement of Mexican Children on an Intelligence Test Administered both in English and in Spanish.* Arizona State Teachers College, Flagstaff, 1940. 82 p. ms. Abstract in Arizona State Teachers College: *Abstracts of Master's Theses, 1938-1942,* p. 38-39.

5535. PAGE, GWEN ALLISON. *A Comparative Study of Spelling Errors for Third and Sixth Grade Children of Anglo and Bilingual Backgrounds.* Texas Western College, 1956. 108 p. ms.

5536. PALACE, ARTHUR LAWRENCE. *A Comparative Description of Anglo-White and Mexican-White Boys Committed to Pacific Colony.* University of Southern California, 1950. 103 p. ms.

5537. PARADA, STELLA GARZA. *School Attendance of Southside School (Latin-American), San Marcos, Texas.* Southwest Texas State Teachers College, 1945. 43 p. ms.

5538. PARK, YONG HAK, 1907- . *A Study of the Methodist Mexican Mission in Dallas.* Southern Methodist University, 1936. 133 p. ms. Abstract in Southern Methodist University: *Abstracts of Theses,* No. 4, 1937, p. 40-41. (Includes religious educational activities.)

5539. PARKE, Mrs. FANDEE YOUNG. *A Study of the Musical Talents of the Negro, Mexican, and White Children in the Public Schools of San Marcos, Texas.* Southwest Texas State Teachers College, 1938. 60 p. ms.

5540. PARKER, VILAS WILLIAM, 1900- . *Transiency and Its Relation to the Progress of Pupils.* University of

Arizona, 1941. 93 p. ms. Abstract in University of Arizona: *Abstracts of Theses for Higher Degrees, 1941,* 1942, p. 53.

5541. PARR, EUNICE ELVIRA. *A Comparative Study of Mexican and American Children in the Schools of San Antonio, Texas.* University of Chicago, 1926. 70 p. ms.

5542. PARR, JESSE BURNS, 1915- . *Some Mechanisms of Adjustment Found in Corpus Christi Elementary School Children.* Texas College of Arts and Industries, 1947. 102 p. ms. (One of the five case studies is of a Spanish-American. Occupies 14 pages.)

5543. PARRY, ESTHER LOUISE. *A Comparison of the Abilities of Spanish-Speaking and English-Speaking Children in Ninth Grade Algebra.* University of Texas, 1933. 62 p. ms.

5544. PEAK, GEORGE JOSEPH. *Relative Achievement of English-Speaking and Spanish-Speaking Children,* University of Arizona, 1931. 55 p. ms.

5545. PEBWORTH, VIRGINIA M. *English Without Accent for Spanish-Speaking Children.* New Mexico Western College, 1956. 72 p. ms.

5546. PENINGER, NOAMA. *A Comparison of Some Social and Recreational Activities of Anglo-American and Spanish-American Vocational Homemaking Students in New Mexico.* Colorado State College of Agriculture and Mechanic Arts, 1942. 104 p. ms.

5547. PEREZ, OCTAVIE ELI, 1911- . *Some Spanish Folklore for the Elementary School.* Texas College of Arts and Industries, 1943. 68 p. ms.

5548. PETERS, MARY M. *The Segregation of Mexican American Children in the Elementary Schools of California — Its Legal and Administrative Aspects.* University of California, Los Angeles, 1948. 192 p. ms.

5549. PETERSEN, CLARENCE EUGENE. *Characteristics of Migrant Children in Fresno County, California.* Stanford University, 1947. 217 p. ms.

5550. PETERSON, INEZ. *Reading Readiness of Bilingual Children.* University of Chicago, 1941. 63 p. ms. (Refers to Mexican-American children in California.)

5551. POLAND, ETHEL BURGESS, 1916- . *Amount of Parental Education Compared with the Child's School Attendance: A Statistical Study.* Texas College of Arts and Industries, 1947. 35 p. ms. (Covers school for Spanish-culture children.)

5552. PONCEL, JOSEPH ALEXANDER. *The Socio-Economic Background and Educational Preparation of Adolescent Boys and Girls of Certain Spanish-American Villages in Northeastern New Mexico: Implications for a Junior High School Curriculum.* State University of Iowa, 1937. 86 p. ms.

5553. PORTER, LUCY. *Occupations and Educational Needs of Latin-American Girls Who Formerly Attended Lanier High School.* Colorado State College of Agriculture and Mechanic Arts, 1940. 105 p. ms.

5554. POWELL, SADIE RAY GRAHAM. *How to Increase Attendance in a Mexican School.* Southwest Texas State Teachers College, 1943. 58 p. ms.

5555. RAINBOLT, HAZEL. *Housing Conditions of Anglo-American and Spanish-American Girls in Vocational Homemaking Classes in New Mexico, 1938-39.* Colorado State College of Agriculture and Mechanic Arts, 1942. 80 p. ms.

5556. RAMIREZ, SARA LEONIL. *The Educational Status and Socio-Economic Backgrounds of Latin-American Children in Waco, Texas.* University of Texas, 1957. 102 p. ms.

5557. RAMSEY, LUCILE SIVLEY, 1901- . *A Comparative Study of the Reading Ability of the Anglo- and Latin-Americans in the Eighth Grade of Edgewood Elementary School.* Trinity University, 1952. 61 p. ms.

5558. RANDALS, EDWYNA HENRIETTA. *A Comparative Study of the Intelligence of Mexican and Negro Children in Two Elementary Schools.* University of Southern California, 1929. 65 p. ms.

5559. RANDEL, MAGGIE COFFEE. *A Study of the Intelligence of Anglo-American and Spanish-American Pupils in Grade Eight as Revealed by an Error Analysis of the Hennon-Nelson Tests of Mental Ability, Grades Seven to Twelve.* Sul Ross State College, 1941. 171 p. ms.

5560. RASCO, LILY SPIVEY, 1902- . *Providing High School Education for Rural Children in Cameron County, Texas.* Texas College of Arts and Industries, 1952. 40 p. ms. (Area considered is prevailingly Spanish-American.)

5561. RAVEN, Mrs. LILLIAN MARGARET (LEISSNER). *A Comparative Study of Sociometric Status and Athletic Ability of Anglo-American and Latin-American Sixth Grade Boys.* University of Texas, 1952. 97 p. ms.

5562. RAWLINSON, KENNETH. *A Comparative Study of Aggression in Caucasian, Mexican, and Negro Delinquent Boys as Measured by the Rorschach and the Thematic Apperception Tests.* Claremont Graduate School, 1953. 80 p. ms.

5563. REAM, GLEN ORVILLE, 1894- . *Spanish-Speaking Pupils in the High School at Albuquerque, N. M.* Yale University, 1930. 87 p. ms.

5564. REED, MARY DEETTE. *A Study of the Effect of a Balanced Reading Program on Third-Grade Mexican Children.* State University of Iowa, 1929. 195 p. ms.

5565. REEVES, GRACE ELIZABETH. *Adult Mexican Education in the United States.* Claremont Graduate School, 1929. 166 p. ms.

5566. REEVES, WILLIAM AUBREY, 1914- . *A Study of Refugio County Schools.* Texas College of Arts and Industries, 1951. 55 p. ms. (County has large and early Spanish-culture population. Studies the conflict with later Anglo-culture population.)

5567. REUTHINGER, HORTENSE. *A Comparative Study of Two Methods of Theory Instruction for Latin-American Girls.* University of Texas, 1956. 54 p. ms.

5568. RICE, THEODORE DAVENPORT, 1904- . *Some Contributing Factors in Determining the Social*

Adjustment of the Spanish-Speaking People in Denver and Vicinity. University of Denver, 1932. 160 p. ms.

5569. RIGGINS, RACHEL THOMPSON, 1908- . *Factors in Social Background which Influence the Mexican Child in School as Revealed in a Study of Twenty-Five Mexican Families in Tucson.* University of Arizona, 1947. 190 p. ms.

5570. ROACH, JAMES WALLIS. *Repeaters and Financial Cost in the Alice Public Schools, 1936-1941.* Texas College of Arts and Industries, 1941. 54 p. ms. (Comparative figures from Spanish-culture and Anglo-culture elementary schools.)

5571. ROBERTSON, CLYDE REEVES. *A Comparative Study of the Progress of American and Mexican Pupils in Certain Elementary Schools in Texas.* University of Texas, 1935. 46 p. ms.

5572. RODEN, Mrs. PAULA (BEGNAUD). *A Study of Relationships among Various Intelligence Test and Reading Test Results Obtained with Latin-American Second-Grade Children.* University of Texas, 1955. 43 p. ms.

5573. ROGERS, MARJORIE KATHERINE. *A Study of the Pronunciation Difficulties of Spanish-Culture Beginners.* Texas College of Arts and Industries, 1940. 48 p. ms.

5574. ROLLINS, E. L., 1914- . *A Snellen Chart Technique Study of Visual Acuity of the Spanish-Culture Pupils in the Stephen F. Austin Public Elementary School, Kingsville, Texas.* Texas College of Arts and Industries, 1937. 70 p. ms.

5575. ROOTS, FLOY EULA. *Methods and Materials for Teaching Spanish to Spanish-Speaking Students in Texas High Schools.* University of Texas, 1936. 175 p. ms. Abstract in University of Texas: *Abstracts of Masters' and Doctors' Theses in Education,* p. 34-35. (Bulletin No. 1.)

5576. SAENZ, ESTELA PINA. *Methods for Teaching Spanish to the San Diego Eighth Graders.* Texas College of Arts and Industries, 1947. 41 p. ms. (Methods for teaching Spanish-speaking pupils.)

5577. SANCHEZ, GEORGE ISADORE, 1906- . *A Study of the Scores of Spanish-Speaking Children on Repeated Tests.* University of Texas, 1931. 74 p. ms. For doctoral dissertation by same author, see No. 5227.

5578. SAUNDERS, Mrs. MAXINE (PLEYDELL-PEARCE). *Some Educational Problems of Spanish-Speaking Children on the Intermediate Grade Level.* University of Texas, 1952. 102 p. ms.

5579. SAYLER, THELMA. *A Study of the Language Development of Spanish-Speaking Children.* Arizona State Teachers College, Tempe, 1945. 183 p. ms.

5580. SCAIFE, DOROTHY PAGE. *A Study of Pre-Reading Instruction for Spanish-American Pupils in Grade One.* Sul Ross State College, 1942. 99 p. ms.

5581. SCHNEIDER, VIRGINIA. *A Comparative Study of the Abilities of White and Mexican Children as Shown by the Rational Learning Test.* University of Southern California, 1931. 93 p. ms.

5582. SCHROFF, RUTH. *A Study of Social Distance between Mexican Parents and American Teachers in San Bernardino, California.* University of Southern California, 1936. 108 p. ms.

5583. SCHUETTE, MARGARETE, 1924- . *A Study of the Most Common Linguistic Errors in English Made by Spanish-Speaking Students in the Eighth Grade of Sidney Lanier High School and Suggestions of Methods and Techniques of Overcoming These Errors.* Colorado State College of Education, 1949. 116 p. ms.

5584. SHELDON, WILLIAM HERBERT, Jr. *A Comparison of the Intelligence of Mexican and White Children.* University of Colorado, 1923. 142 p. ms.

5585. SIMA, BERNICE. *A Case Study Investigation of the Relationship between the English Speech Sounds Produced by Mexican Children of Spanish-Speaking Parents and Proficiency in the English Language Arts.* Bowling Green State University, 1954. 108 p. ms.

5586. SION, ALVIN PETER. *Mentally Deficient Mexican-American Delinquent Boys Who Made Good after Institutional Care: An Analysis of Six Cases.* University of Southern California, 1951. 73 p. ms.

5587. SLAVITCHEK, MARTHA GLADYS WILLIAMS. *Orientation Methods and Techniques Used in Elementary Schools in the Lower Rio Grande Valley with Latin-American Beginners.* North Texas State College, 1956. 77 p. ms.

5588. SMITH, Mrs. AVIS (DOWIS). *A Comparative Study of Some Attitudes and Interests of Latin-American and Anglo-American Boys.* University of Texas, 1940. 82 p. ms.

5589. SMITH, EVALEEN CARTEN. *Willacy County, Texas, Second Graders: A Study of Ages and Achievements.* Texas College of Arts and Industries, 1949. 47 p. ms. (Compares Anglo-culture and Spanish-culture pupils.)

5590. SMITH, IDA GAFFORD, 1907- . *An Evaluation of the Latin-American Ward School in Coleman, Texas.* Hardin-Simmons University, 1949. 139 p. ms.

5591. SMITH, SUE IDA, 1903- *Three Case Studies of Retarded Spanish-Culture Beginners, Edinburg, Texas, 1946-47.* Texas College of Arts and Industries, 1947. 85 p. ms.

5592. SMULKER, FREDA. *The Language Handicaps of Bilinguals.* Columbia University, 1937. 49 p. ms. (Considers especially Mexican, Spanish, and Jewish bilinguals.)

5593. SPARKS, GAYLE THRELKELD. *Placement of Out-of-School Spanish-American Girls in Domestic Service in Phoenix, Arizona.* Colorado State College of Agriculture and Mechanic Arts, 1941. 92 p. ms. (Studies the factors in school training which proved effective in stability of employment.)

5594. SPRINKLE, EUNICE CARLINE. *A Comparative Investigation of the Reading Interests of Mexican and White Children.* University of Southern California, 1941. 142 p. ms.

Latin-American

5595. STEVENS, JOHN HENRY. *A Study of the Status of Spanish-Speaking Migrant Children in the Outlook (Sunnyside, Washington) Elementary School in Relation to Guidance Practices Followed by Selected Yakima Valley Elementary Schools in the Adjustment of Such Children.* University of Washington, 1955. 75 p. ms.

5596. STEWARD, ADDIE KATHLEEN. *The Indigenous Development of the Learning-Teaching Process in the Christian Education of Spanish-Speaking Groups in the United States.* Auburn Theological Seminary, 1933. (Available at library of Union Theological Seminary.)

5597. STOHL, Mrs. DARTHULA (DAVIS). *A Study Treating the Teaching of Language Skills through Music to Spanish-Speaking Children.* University of Texas, 1954. 77 p. ms.

5598. STOLZ, ALBERTA LOUISE. *A Comparative Study of the Art Judgment of Spanish-Speaking and English-Speaking Children.* University of Texas, 1931. 57 p. ms.

5599. SUMMERS, HELEN. *An Evaluation of Certain Procedures Used in Teaching the Non-English-Speaking Mexican Child.* University of California, Los Angeles, 1939. 65 p. ms.

5600. SWALESTUEN, ESTHER D. *A Comparative Study of the Mexican and White Child in Ninth-Grade Algebra with Respect to a Language Handicap.* University of Southern California, 1933. 60 p. ms.

5601. TACK, MELVA PAULINE, 1911- . *Typical Spanish Folk Songs of North New Mexico Adapted and Arranged for Use in a Program of Music Education.* University of Kansas, 1948. 91 p. ms.

5602. TAIT, ROBERT R., 1911- . *A Proposal for a Program of Education for the Slow Learning and Educationally Retarded Students in the Secondary Schools of Harlingen, Texas.* Texas College of Arts and Industries, 1957. 100 p. ms. (55 per cent of students are Latin-American.)

5603. TATA, LORRAINE POWERS. *A Comparative Study and Measurement of Inate Musical Abilities of Mexican and American White Children.* Arizona State Teachers College, Tempe, 1940. 103 p. ms.

5604. TAYLOR, HARRY FRANKLIN. *The Musical Abilities of Spanish-American Children.* University of Denver, 1934. 42 p. ms. Abstract in University of Denver: *Abstracts of Theses in Education, 1930-1938,* p. 28.

5605. TAYLOR, JAUNITA FAYE. *A Comparison of First and Second Generation Mexican Parents.* University of Southern California, 1944.

5606. TAYLOR, MERL COBB. *Retardation of Mexican Children in the Albuquerque Schools.* Stanford University, 1927. 203 p. ms.

5607. THOMAS, ROBERT LYLE, 1902- . *Tip-Top Island: A Pleasure Type Reader for Language Handicapped Fifth Grade Pupils.* University of Arizona, 1946. 88 p. ms. Abstract in University of Arizona: *Abstracts of Theses for Higher Degrees, 1945-46,* p. 26. (Attempts to determine the qualities of a book which will tempt Mexican children to select and read it. Checks the reactions of Mexican-American children to books read in their free reading periods.)

5608. TINDER, CHARLES ELSTON, 1915- . *A Study of Spanish-American Children in the Public Schools of Hutchinson, Kansas.* Colorado State College of Education, 1948. 143 p. ms.

5609. TODDHUNTER, LAWRENCE EDMUND. *A Comparative Study of the Achievement of American and Mexican Children in an Elementary School.* Stanford University, 1936. 84 p. ms.

5610. TRAMEL, LUCILE. *Play Interests of Pre-School Mexican Children.* Southwest Texas State Teachers College, 1941. 33 p. ms.

5611. TREFF, SIMON LUDWIG. *The Education of Mexican Children in Orange County.* University of Southern California, 1934. 144 p. ms.

5612. TRIPLETT, WILLIAM GRADY, 1901- . *A Critical Vocabulary Comparison of Texas 1938-39 Adopted Readers, the Preprimer to the Second Reader, Inclusive.* Texas College of Arts and Industries, 1939. 189 p. ms. (Recommendations made with reference to Spanish-speaking children.)

5613. TUBBS, LOWELL LESTER. *A Survey of the Problems of the Migratory Mexicans.* University of Texas, 1952. 117 p. ms. (Chapter 3: "Educational Problems.")

5614. ULMER, FEMLEE M. *The Problem of the Education of the Migrant Child of Texas.* Sul Ross State College, 1957. 119 p. ms.

5615. UNDERWOOD, Mrs. MARION LUNDAY. *A Study of the Homes of One Hundred Latin-American Girls in Corpus Christi to be Used as a Basis for a Homemaking Education Program in the Elementary Schools.* University of Texas, 1937. 91 p. ms.

5616. VEGA, MARGUERITE DE LA. *Some Factors Affecting Leadership of Mexican-Americans in a High School.* University of Southern California, 1952. 65 p. ms.

5617. VETTERS, Mrs. ANNA (HILL). *Speech Correction among Spanish-American Children in an Elementary School.* University of Texas, 1942. 71 p. ms.

5618. VINCENT, HENRIETTA HATHAWAY. *A Study of the Performance of Spanish-Speaking Pupils on Spanish Tests.* New Mexico State Teachers College, 1933. 93 p. ms.

5619. WAGER, CLINTON E. *A Study of Certain Peculiarities of Syntax Common to Spanish-Speaking Students of Jerome Junior-Senior High School.* Arizona State Teachers College, Flagstaff, 1945. 44 p. ms.

5620. WAITS, LOGAN ABNER. *The Education of the Mexican in Texas.* Columbia University, 1930. 61 p. ms.

5621. WALLACE, Mrs. MARGARET ADELLE (LONG). *Creative, Dramatic, Graphic, and Craft Activities in an Enriched Program for the Primary*

Spanish-Speaking Child. University of Texas, 1954. 130 p. ms.

5622. WAY, ROBERT VES. *Adapting the Curriculum of an Elementary School to Serve the Language Needs of Spanish-Speaking Children.* University of Southern California, 1950. 68 p. ms.

5623. WEATHERBY, LELA, 1902- . *A Study of the Early Years of the Presbyterian Work with the Spanish-Speaking People of New Mexico and Colorado and Its Development from 1850 to 1920.* Presbyterian College of Christian Education, 1942. 101 p. ms. (Includes educational work.)

5624. WEATHINGTON, DOROTHY THOMPSON. *Socially Maladjusted Children, Lamar School, Corpus Christi.* Texas College of Arts and Industries, 1951. 89 p. ms. (School is predominantly Spanish-American.)

5625. WEBB, REBECCA FRANCES. *The Relative Achievement of Mexican and American Children in the Elementary School.* Stanford University, 1931. 89 p. ms.

5626. WEIBUSCH, MARGARET. *An Effective Method of Teaching English to Spanish-Speaking Children in One Fourth Grade in Nogales, Arizona.* Arizona State College, Flagstaff, 1954. 127 p. ms.

5627. WEITZEL, TOM R. *Change in Mental Ability of Spanish-Speaking Children Over a Period of Two Years.* Arizona State Teachers College, Flagstaff, 1941. 37 p. ms. Abstract in Arizona State Teachers College: *Abstracts of Master's Theses, 1938-1942,* p. 74-75.

5628. WELLS, GLADYS, 1908- . *Factors Influencing the Assimilation of the Mexicans in Texas.* Southern Methodist University, 1941. 68 p. ms. Abstract in Southern Methodist University: *Abstracts of Theses,* No. 9, 1942, p. 17-18.

5629. WEST, GUY ASHLEY. *Racial Attitudes among Teachers of New Mexico.* Chico State Teachers College, 1934. (Compares attitudes of American and Spanish teachers.)

5630. WESTERGAARD, HENRY CHRISTEN. *A Study of the Transient Mexican Children in the Granger, Washington, Public Schools.* University of Washington, 1952. 65 p. ms.

5631. WETZEL, MARION L., 1917- *Factors Influencing the Attendance of Latin-American Children in West Ward, Looney, and Central Ward Schools, Brownwood, Texas.* Hardin-Simmons University, 1950. 73 p. ms.

5632. WHALEN, JANICE. *Adapting the Curriculum of the First Year in School to the Needs of the Beginning Non-English-Speaking Mexican-Americans.* University of Southern California, 1952. 112 p. ms.

5633. WHITE, ALFRED EUGENE, 1899- . *The Apperceptive Mass of Foreigners as Applied to Americanization: The Mexican Group.* University of California, Berkeley, 1923. 131 p. ms.

5634. WHITE, CHARLES F. *The Problem of Retarded Mexican Pupils in Texas Border Schools with Recommendations for Solution.* Sul Ross State College, 1942. 93 p. ms.

5635. WHITE, MARVIN IRVING. *The Administration of an Elementary School in the Mexican-American Area of East Los Angeles: Its Problems and Some Suggested Recommendations.* University of Southern California, 1957. 88 p.ms.

5636. WHITED, HAZEL COTTRELL, 1897- . *Adaptation of Instruction to First and Second Grade Pupils in the Dwight W. Morrow School.* West Texas State Teachers College, 1941. 112 p. ms. Abstract in West Texas State Teachers College: *Abstracts of Master's Theses, 1932-1944,* p. 138. (School is for Mexican children in Amarillo, Texas.)

5637. WHITWELL, INEZ MARGARET. *A Homemaking Program for Mexican Girls Who Will Be Unable to Attend High School.* University of Southern California, 1938. University of Southern California, 1938. 88 p. ms. (Girls were in Arizona.)

5638. WICKS, ROBERT HAROLD. *Group Formation in a Fifth Grade.* Texas College of Arts and Industries, 1956. 121 p. ms. (Largely concerned with the Anglo-American Latin-American dichotomy.)

5639. WILLIAMS, CHARLES HOWARD. *A Study of the Adjustment of Students from Latin-America at the University of Texas.* University of Texas, 1956. 219 p. ms.

5640. WILLIAMS, JAMES HESTER. *A Proposed Plan for Reorganization of Public Schools of Willacy County, Texas.* Texas College of Arts and Industries, 1942. 33 p. ms. (Area is predominantly Spanish-American.)

5641. WILLIAMS, LUELLA DANIELLS. *Story-Telling as an Aid to Teaching English to Latin-American Children.* Southwest Texas State Teachers College, 1945. 79 p. ms.

5642. WILLIAMS, WILTON EDWARD, 1906- *Problems Involved in Meeting the Needs of Male Latin-American Scholastics of Area X for Instruction in Vocational Agriculture.* Agricultural and Mechanical College of Texas, 1939. 26 p. ms.

5643. WILSON, JOE HARVEY. *Secondary School Drop-Outs, with Special Reference to Spanish-Speaking Youth in Texas.* University of Texas, 1953. 244 p. ms.

5644. WINN, JOHN C., 1908- . *A Comparative Study of the Mexican-Indian Students in the Carbon County Schools.* Utah State Agricultural College, 1955. 93 p. ms.

5645. WITHERS, CHARLES DINNIJES. *Problems of Mexican Boys.* University of Southern California, 1942. 132 p. ms. (Boys were in Los Angeles schools.)

5646. WITHERSPOON, ROBERT PAUL, 1923- . *A Comparison of the Problems of Certain Anglo- and Latin-American Junior High School Students.* Trinity University, 1952. 58 p. ms. (In San Antonio, Texas.)

5647. WUENSCH, OLIVE ALBERT. *Causes for Failure in General Mathematics in Hebronville Junior High School.* Texas College of Arts and Industries,

1952. 161 p. ms. (22 of the 27 students studied were of Spanish-culture background.)

5648. YATES, BYRON F. *A Proposed Course of Study for Latin-American Students of First-Term Mechanical Drawing in the Joel Chandler Harris Junior High School, San Antonio, Texas.* Southwest Texas State Teachers College, 1945. 104 p. ms.

5649. YBARRA, JESSE R., 1916- . *A Study to Determine Why Spanish-Speaking Children Drop Out of School in Junior and Senior School in a Particular Community in San Antonio, Texas.* Trinity University, 1955. 86 p. ms.

5650. YEAGER, Mrs. BARBARA ANN (STONE). *Meeting the Educational Needs of Migrant Children.* University of Texas, 1957. 92 p. ms. (Children were chiefly Mexican.)

5651. YOUNG, ALMA. *How Some of the Problems Connected with the Teaching of Reading to Spanish-American Children Are Being Met by Schools of the Southwest.* North Texas State Teachers College, 1937. 62 p. ms. Abstract in North Texas State Teachers College: *Abstracts of Theses . . . 1935-1940*, p. 58-59.

5652. YOUNG, MARY WINKLE. *A Proposed Program of Supervision for Teaching Non-English-Speaking Six-Year-Old Beginners in Edinburg School.* Texas College of Arts and Industries, 1953. 74 p. ms.

5653. ZEIGER, CARL EVERETTE, 1912- . *The Problem of Educating the Spanish-American Child in the Public Schools.* Colorado College, 1942. 130 p. ms.

See also Nos. 272, 961, 4983, 4986, 4994, 4996, 4999, 5000, 5001, 5002, 5005, 5007, 5015, 5018, 5019.

Lithuanian
(NO. 5654)

MASTER

5654. YURGUTIS, Sister MARY ALOYSIA, 1898- *Measuring and Improving the Reading Ability of Lithuanian Children.* Fordham University, 1933. 67 p. ms.

See also Nos. 4985, 4987, 4992, 4993, 5001, 5003, 5020.

Norwegian
(NO. 5655)

DOCTOR

5655. EIDBO, OLAV ELLING, 1918- . *Songs of the Norwegian Folk in Culture and Education in the United States.* University of North Dakota, 1956. 354 p. ms. Abstract in University of North Dakota: *Abstracts of Doctoral Dissertations and Masters' Theses . . . 1956*, p. 3-5.

See also Nos. 4957, 4963, 4970, 4971, 4975.

MASTERS

See 4978, 4985, 4988, 5023, 5025. *See also* Scandinavian.

Polish
(NOS. 5655a – 5657)

DOCTOR

5655a. WYTRWAL, JOSEPH ANTHONY. *The Role of Two American Polish Nationality Organizations in the Acculturation of Poles in America.* University of Michigan, 1958. 227 p. ms. Abstract in *Dissertation Abstracts*, Vol. 19, p. 1285, December 1958. Available on microfilm from University Microfilms, Ann Arbor, Michigan, as Mic. 58-7806.

See also Nos. 4956, 4960, 4963, 4970, 4975.

MASTERS

5656. FUSS, JOSEPH. *A Comparative Study of Silent Reading Comprehension of Pupils in Monolingual and Bilingual Schools.* Catholic University of America, 1952. 25 p. ms. (Covers pupils in four

Polish bilingual schools and two monolingual schools, all Catholic parochial schools in Connecticut.)

5657. OETJEN, CLARA E. *Problems in the Teaching of English to Polish Children in the Seventh, Eighth, and Ninth Grades.* Wayne University, 1932. 78 p. ms.

See also Nos. 4976, 4984, 4987, 4992, 4993, 4994, 4998, 4999, 5003, 5004, 5006, 5009, 5020, 5022, 5025.

Portuguese
(NO. 5658)

DOCTOR

See Nos. 4965, 4968, 4975.

MASTER

5658. McINNES, JOSEPH R., 1914- . *The Brava and His Educational Problems in Marion, Massachusetts.* Boston University, 1942. 126 p. ms.

See also Nos. 4991, 5013.

Puerto Rican
(NOS. 5659 – 5682)

DOCTORS

5659. ARRECHE, PAQUITA R., 1916- . *Vocational Needs of the Puerto Rican Migrant in New York City.* Fordham University, 1946. Abstract in Fordham University: *Dissertations Accepted for Higher Degrees* . . . Vol. 13, 1946, p. 26-30. (Considers educational needs of 3,024 workers from Puerto Rico.)

5660. DRUSINE, LEON, 1912- . *Some Factors in Anti-Negro Prejudice among Puerto Rican Boys in New York City.* New York University, 1956. 125 p. ms.

5661. JENKINS, SHIRLEY. *Intergroup Empathy: An Exploratory Study of Negro and Puerto Rican Groups in New York City.* New York University, 1957.

5662. KREIDLER, CHARLES WILLIAM. *A Study of the Influence of English on the Spanish of Puerto Ricans in Jersey City, New Jersey.* University of Michigan, 1958. 190 p. ms. Abstract in *Dissertation Abstracts*, Vol. 19, p. 527-528, September 1958. Available on microfilm from University Microfilms, Ann Arbor, Michigan, as Mic. 58-3691.

5663. MAYANS, FRANK, Jr., 1919- . *Puerto Rican Migrant Pupils in New York City Schools: A Comparison of the Effects of the Methods of Intellectual Grouping on English Mastery and Attitudes.* Columbia University, 1953. 73 p. ms.

5664. ROBINSON, GERTRUDE ASKEY, 1909- . *A Case Study of Puerto Rican Children in Junior High School No. 65, Manhattan, New York City.* New York University, 1956. 485 p. ms. Abstract in *Dissertation Abstracts*, Vol. 19, p. 264-265, August 1958. Available on microfilm from University Microfilms, Ann Arbor, Michigan, as Publication No. 20,291.

5665. ROSENTHAL, ALAN GERALD, 1927- *Pre-School Experience and Adjustment of Puerto Rican Children.* New York University, 1955. 176 p. ms. Abstract in *Dissertation Abstracts*, Vol. 15, p. 1205, July 1955. Available on microfilm from University Microfilms, Ann Arbor, Michigan, as Publication No. 12,232.

5666. RYAN, LOUISE T., 1897- . *Common Errors in English Usage Made by Spanish-Speaking Pupils: A Teaching Experience for the Correction of the Common Language Errors in Junior High School 101, Manhattan, and a Manual for Teachers.* New York University, 1950. 160 p. ms.

5667. SANGUINETTI, Mrs. CARMEN SACARELLO-BALS, 1912- . *Adapting Science Instruction in New York City Junior High Schools to the Needs of Puerto Rican Background Pupils.* Columbia University, 1956. 163 p. ms.

See also Nos. 4956, 4969, 4970.

MASTERS

5668. CARPENTIER, MARIE L., 1924- . *Some of the Needs of Puerto Rican Children and the Work of Settlements in Meeting These Needs.* Brooklyn College, 1952. 67 p. ms. (Refers to children in New York.)

5669. DARBEN, CHRISTINE ANDREWS. *A Free Reading Program for the Puerto Rican Child in the United States.* New Jersey State College, 1958. 63 p. ms.

5670. DUNKLIN, LAURA DOLAN. *A Study of the Intelligence of Some Puerto Rican Immigrant Children in a First Grade of a New York City School.* Columbia University, 1935. 33 p. ms.

5671. DWYER, ANN, 1928- . *Practices in Teaching English to Fourth Grade Puerto Rican Children.* Brooklyn College, 1953.

5672. EIMERMANN, ROBERT MONROE. *The Development of a Program for Teaching Non-English-Speaking Puerto Rican Children at the Thomas Jefferson School, Milwaukee.* University of Wisconsin, Milwaukee Campus, 1957. 102 p. ms.

5673. ENGLAND, JOAN T. *The Puerto Ricans: Melrose School and Community, New York City.* Hunter College of the City of New York, 1958.

5674. KIRSCHENBAUM, DEBORAH. *The Non-English Speaking Puerto Rican Child in the New York City Public School System.* Bank Street College of Education, 1958.

5675. LEVIN, NORMAN BALFOUR. *Language Arts for a Mixed Racial Group in a New York High School.* University of Texas, 1956. 92 p. ms. (Refers primarily to Puerto Ricans.)

5676. LODGE, HELEN MARY, 1913- . *Developmental Trends and Group Differences in Moral Judgment in Children.* Fordham University, 1938. 53 p. ms. Abstract in Fordham University: *Dissertations Accepted for Higher Degrees . . .* 1939, p. 97. (Compares American and Puerto Rican children in New York City.)

5677. MASON, MILDRED GRAHAM, 1932- . *A Guide to Teaching the Puerto Rican Child in Our Schools.* New Jersey State Teachers College, Newark, 1957. 46 p. ms.

5678. MIRANDA, CARMEN M. *A Study of the Acculturation Process and Its Effects on Two Hundred Puerto Rican Children Born and Brought Up in New York City.* Columbia University, 1948. 64 p. ms.

5679. TOUHEY, MARY ELIZABETH. *Some Problems Facing Certain Puerto Rican Children Coming into New York City as Seen by the Child.* Adelphi College, 1957. 45 p. ms.

5680. VERNO, CATHERINE A, 1927- . *A Study of the Placement and Adjustment of Puerto Rican Pupils in a Junior High School.* Fordham University, 1956. 94 p. ms.

5681. WEBER, DAISY A. *Changes in the Education Program in Public School 8, Manhattan, Resulting from Influx of Perto Rican Children.* New York University, 1955.

5682. WINBAUM, LAURA L. *Attitudes of Puerto Rican Migrants toward the Public Schools in New York City.* College of the City of New York, 1958.

See also No. 5013.

Scandinavian
(NO. 5683)

DOCTOR

5683. DAVIDSEN, OLUF MEJER, 1924- . *Visting Scandinavian Students at the University of Wisconsin, 1952-1954: A Study in Cross Cultural Education.* University of Wisconsin, 1956. 254 p. ms. Abstract in *Dissertation Abstracts*, Vol. 16, p. 2381, December 1956. Available on microfilm from University Microfilms, Ann Arbor, Michigan, as Publication No. 17,305. (Students were from Denmark, Norway, and Sweden but are treated as a single group.)

See also No. 4954.

MASTERS

See Nos. 4981, 4989. *See also* Danish, Finnish, Norwegian, and Swedish.

Slavic
(NOS. 5684 – 5691)

DOCTORS

See Nos. 4959, 4960, 4962, 4970, 4975.

MASTERS

5684. GREGOROVIC, Sister MARY CONSUELA. *The Contribution of the Rev. Mathew Jankola to Slovak Catholic Education in the United States.* Catholic University of America, 1944. 87 p. ms.

5685. JENSEN, ALFRED R. *European Background Influences on Education in the Milligan Public Schools.* University of Nebraska, 1952. 62 p. ms. ("A recent study showed that only 25 out of the village population of 1367 were of non-Czech origin".)

5686. MARCELLA, CHARLES. *Why Relatively Few Students of Yugoslav Parentage Have Gone to College: A Study of the Yugoslavs in Mountain View, California.* Stanford University, 1941. 89 p. ms.

5687. MURPHY, MARY MARTHA. *A Comparison of the Attainment of Slavic-Speaking Children and English-Speaking Children in the First Grade.* University of Chicago, 1938. 54 p. ms.

5688. PLACH, MARYROSE. *American Intergroup Education in a Czechoslovakian Neighborhood.* De Paul University, 1955. 62 p. ms.

5689. SNAPP, CHARLES ROSS. *Language Inhibitions of the Slovak-Speaking Child in Learning to Read English.* University of Chicago, 1930. 119 p. ms.

5690. STEFAN, Sister MARIA LEOCADIA. *The Role of Reverend Stephen Furdek in Education among the Slovaks in America from 1882 to 1915.* Catholic University of America, 1952. 52 p. ms.

5691. WHITFILL, ANDREW LINTON. *A Comparative Study of the Intelligence and Achievement in School of American and Czech Children.* Southern Methodist University, 1940. 37 p. ms. Abstract in Southern Methodist University: *Abstracts of Theses,* No. 8, 1941, p. 36.

See also Nos. 4981, 4985, 4986, 4989, 5007, 5014, 5015, 5016, 5020, 5023, 5025.

Swedish
(NOS. 5692 – 5695)

DOCTORS

5692. DOWIE, JAMES IVERNE. *Luther Academy, 1883 to 1903: A Facet of Swedish Pioneer Life in Nebraska.* University of Minnesota, 1957. 367 p. ms. Abstract in *Religious Education,* Vol. 53, p. 255, May-June 1958. (Use restricted. To be released June 1, 1959.)

5693. PERSON, PETER PER. *A History of Higher Education among the Swedish Immigrants in America.* Harvard University, 1941. 124 p. ms.

5694. WHYMAN, HENRY CARL. *The Conflict and Adjustment of Two Religious Cultures — the Swedish and the American, as Found in the Swede's Relation to American Methodism.* New York University, 1937. 254 p. ms. Abstract in *Selected Graduate Theses in Religious Education,* 1937, p. 51.

See also Nos. 4956, 4957, 4963, 4970, 4975, 4978, 4985, 5023, 5025.

MASTER

5695. LYRNER, ANITA and LYRNER, PER JOHAN. *What a Year in America and at Glen Maples Has Meant for Two Swedes.* Putney Graduate School of Teacher Education, 1956. 40 p. ms.

See also Nos. 4978, 4985, 5023, 5025. See also Scandinavian.

Syrian
(NO. 5696)

DOCTORS

See Nos. 4956, 4970, 4975.

MASTER

5696. ABLAHAT, RHODA BERTHA, 1910- . (Later Mrs. R. S. Ganja.) *An Analysis of the Background, Experiences, and Needs of the Assyrian Presbyterians of Chicago with a View toward Building a More Adequate Program of Religious Education for the Carter Memorial Church.* Presbyterian College of Christian Education, 1937. 59 p. ms.

Turkish
(NO. 5697)

DOCTOR

5697. GREEN, ELEANOR KUHLMAN, 1908- . *A Study of the Structure and Interaction of a Group of Turkish Students at the University of Florida, October 1952 to June 1953.* University of Florida, 1956. 649 p. ms. Abstract in University of Florida: *Abstracts of Doctoral Studies in Education,* 1956, p. 56-63. Abstract also in *Dissertation Abstracts*, Vol. 16, p. 2096-2097, November 1956. Available on microfilm from University Microfilms, Ann Arbor, Michigan, as Publication No. 17,551.

See also Nos. 4970, 4972, 4975.

MASTERS

See Nos. 4977, 4988.

Welsh

(NO. 5698)

DOCTOR

5698. CROCKER, BERTRAM. *A Study of the Cultural Integration of a Welsh Community with Its American Enrivonment.* Columbia University, 1952. 128 p. ms. (Considers role of education in integration of Welsh in Radnor, Ohio, with one chapter on "Formal Education.")

5716. After the consecutive numbering of titles was completed through No. 5698, four duplications were discovered and 22 new titles were added, the latter being indicated as 162a, etc. Thus the total number of titles listed is not 5698 but 5716.

AUTHOR INDEX

Includes names of all authors of dissertations and theses, and authors of introductory materials in published editions of them.

All references are to numbered theses, not to pages.

A

Abadi, A. K. A., 2141
Abbot, F. A., 3961
Abdalla, A. H. E., 360
Abel, J. F., 119
Abelson, P., 3001
Ablahat, R. B., 5696
Ablen, B. P., 1270
Abou-Khadra, R., 120
Acevedo, J. R., 5234
Ackerman, W. A., 3962
Acquah, J. W. 434
Adair, A. E., 3134
Adair, J. B., 121
Adams, C. W., 38
Adams, D. K., 2481
Adams, E. B., 1935
Adams, F. A., 5051
Adams, F. B., 2659
Adams, P. S., 5027
Addison, W. D. 679
Adegebite, J. A., 452
Aden, R. C. 871
Adibe, N. A., 2192
Adiseshiah, H. E. M., 1823
Adjoodani, M., 2157
Adjoodani, S., 2158
Adrian, F., 3427
Adriano, P. V., 2580
Adzanku, A. G. K., 498
Aery, W. A., 4316
Afifi, M. E., 361
Afzal, M., 2142
Agatep, C. P., 2660
Agatho, Bro., 3428
Agatstein, M., 3429
Agliam, R. T., 2661
Agneta, M., 4387
Agustin, S. M., 2662
Ahmed, M. A. E., 4876
Ahn, W. C., 2507
Ai, J. W., 1362
Aikenhead, J. D., 545, 680
Aimone, V. M., 5235
Ainsworth, L. L., 5028
Ajubita, M. L., 5236
Akamatsu, A. S., 5151
Akery, N., 5237
Akeson, M. A., 1824
Akhary, F. B. M. A., 362
Akin, A. H., 3963
Akpabio, I. U., 460
Akrawi, M., 2167
Alarilla, L. M., 2663
Alba, R. S., 2664
Albano, J. P., 1219
al-Bassam, H. K., 2194
al-Bassam, N. A. A., 2195
Alberts, L. C., 4877
Alberty-Ruiz, R., 1091
Albright, S. C., 3430
Alcorn, B. W., 5238

Aldaba, E. J., 2665
Aldana, B. V., 2581, 2666
Aldecoa, V., 2667
Aldridge, A. A., 681
Ale, I. G., 4878
Aleck, A. W., 3848
Alejo, A., 2668
Alers-Montalvo, M., 840
Alexander, M. C., 1510
Alexander, M. V., 682
Alexander, R. T., 3068
Alexander, T., 3402, 3584
Alexia, M., 3016
Alford, R. J., 324
al-Hafidh, N. A. S., 2171
al-Hakkak, H. J., 2196
al-Hassun, A. R. I., 2173
Ali, K. S., 2570
Alisky, M. H., 887
al-Jalili, A. R., 2176
Allam, M. A. K., 363
Allaway, W. H., 4860
Allbee, L., 1
Allen, E. G., 683
Allen, H. C., 546
Allen, H. H., 4879
Allen, T., 2357
Allen, W., 3135
Allen, W. D., 2
Allen, W. P., 1363
Allsop, J. W., 4809
Allstrom, E. W., 5239
Almenas de Vergne, A., 1044
Aloia, A. D., 546a
Alonso, A. S., 2669
Alonso, M.P., 1247
al-Raheem, A. H., 2185
al-Rawi, M. H., 2197
Alt, M. R., 4693
Altena, J. E. V. R., 4572
Alter, D. E., 1825
Alter, S. N., 186
al-Toma, S. J., 2187
Alvarez de Choudens, E., 1092
Alvord, T. H., 3964
al-Zobaie, A. J., 2191, 2199
Alzona, E., 2670
Amdur, I., 3673
Amin, G., 399
Amir-Hushmand, A. A., 2148
Amolik, K. V., 1936
Anastassopoulos, P. A., 4317
Anderson, A. B., 5240
Anderson, A. M., 547
Anderson, C. A., 684
Anderson, D. A., 4590, 4595
Anderson, E. J., 1364
Anderson, H., 2236
Anderson, H. A. R., 548
Anderson, H. D., 4741
Anderson, L. F., 3002
Anderson, M. R., 1365, 1511
Anderson, P. S., 2305

Anderson, R. E., 2671
Anderson, S. M., 2508
Anderson, W. A., 685
Anderson, W. J., 3431
Andic, V. E., 3328
Andreason, P. J., 3352
Andress, J. M., 3585
Andress, P., 1183
Andrews, A. S., 933
Andrews, G. F., 187, 1826
Andrews, L. L., 1937
Andrews, L. M., 3674
Andriot, M. M., 3432
Ang, J., 2672
Angela, M., 3675
Angeles, F. D. M., 2673
Angelovic, M. I., 3332
Anibarro-Ponce de Leon, D. 1213
Annaguey, E. D., 2674
Anthony, D. F., 2306
Antoinette, M., 2965
Antonakaki, K. D., 4296
Antonio y Mendoza, S., 2675
Anttilla, E. U., 39, 527
Aoki, H., 2307
Apodaca, A. G., 5241
Apperson, C. J., 3136
Appleton, L. E., 122
Arakaki, J. S., 3676
Araneta, R. Y., 2676
Arasaratnam, J. G., 1349
Arawarop, B., 2919
Archangel, M., 4976
Archdeacon, J. P., 3137
Archer, E. W., 4825
Archibald, J. H., 549
Arelleno, M. G., 2677
Arens, R., 1366
Arent, E., 4591
Argy, M. P., 4441
Aridi, B., 4977
Arizabal y Luciano, P., 2678
Arjona, A. Q., 4953
Armack, C. M., 5242
Armour, J., 2358
Arms, P. R., 1248
Armstrong, A. V., 4318
Armstrong, L., 5243
Armstrong, M. C., 3138
Armstrong, S., 686
Arndt, R. E. S., 665
Arnest, M. T., 4319
Arnold, J. W., 1512
Arnold, W. A., 934
Arreche, P. R., 5659
Arredando, S. T., 5244
Arrieta, R., 845
Arsenian, S., 5119
Arunachalam, K., 1938
Arve, A., 3716
Asaf, M. R., 2571, 2572
Ascano, A. F., 2679

Ascolillo, J., 4880
Asfour, M. G., 400
Ash, W. R., 3965
Ashford, G. W., 3966
Ashley, M., 935
Ashmead, J., 2308
Askar, R. M., 364
Atchison, A. B., 401
Athanassiadou, I. M., 4320
Athearn, C. R., 40
Athearn, W. S., 3279
Atkinson, M., 3139
Attallah, F., 402
Atterbury, M., 1367
Atwell, R. E., 1513
Atzman, E., 4861
Aubrey, R. H., 3140
Aucamp, A. J., 500
Auh, P., 2482, 2509
Aus, G., 3677
Ausere, A. J., 936
Autajay, L. C., 2680
Avallone, P. P., 4442
Averill, L. A., 4686
Avigdor, R., 2966
Ayers, D. M., 4443
Ayorinde, J. T., 461
Azcueta, F. A., 2681
Aziz, A. S., 2193

B

Babey, A. M., 4723
Baca, F. G., 5207
Bachman, F. P., 3849
Backus, G. W., 4742
Bacon, R. L., 1514
Badanes, S., 3433
Bader, M. H., 3678
Badoian, M. J., 4881
Baeszler, St. A. of R., 550, 687
Bahr, E., 3679
Baick, D. H., 2483
Bailey, D. M., 3967
Bailey, E. M., 365
Bailey, H. L., 3360
Bailey, W. S., 551
Baillie, G. S., 3968
Baird, D., 5245
Baird, F., 5246
Baja, T. C., 2682
Baker, D. C., 5247
Baker, E. V., 5248
Baker, G. P., 5249
Baker, H. M., 542
Baker, L., 688
Baker, M. A., 1220
Baldwin, E. C., 41
Bale, G. W., 42
Ball, C. C., 5250
Ball, M. D., 3969

AUTHOR INDEX

Ballantine, M. W., 3970
Ballard, J. G., 5251
Ballenger, M. G., 1939
Balletta, A. J., 4444
Balletti, L. M., 4882
Baloch, N. B. K. A. K., 2564
Balson, M., 4810
Baltazar y Cruz, T., 2683
Banai, H., 2143
Banker, P. K., 1827
Banks, R. G., 3680
Barager, J. R., 1184
Barall, M., 3374
Barbano, M. M., 43
Barbarick, H. A., 5252
Barber, D. A., 689
Barber, H. L., 3971
Barbour, L. M., 937
Bard, H. E., 2684
Barden, J. G., 342
Bardin, S., 2200
Bardis, P. D., 4954
Barfell, L. O., 5253
Barillas, M. Y., 853
Barkdull, M. L., 3017
Barkely, D. W., 4445
Barlahan y Valera, B., 2685
Barnard, J. F., 3141
Barnes, A., 552
Barnes, E. B., 3003
Barney, M. I., 1263
Baroody, W. B., 2546
Barpute, H. V., 1940
Barpute, M., 1941
Barr, J. H., 3018
Barranco, M., 888
Barras, G. J., 3434
Barre, A. J., 5102
Barrett, C. B., 4883
Barrett, J. G., 4636
Barrett, M. C., 3069
Barrette, J. A., 690
Barrion, M. C., 2686
Barron, J. F., 5254
Barrows, M., 332
Barrows, R., 5255
Barry, M. B., 4826
Barry, W. R., 3142
Barth, P. J., 528
Bartlett, K., 4978
Barto, E., 4321
Bartolome, C. C., 2687, 2688
Barton, A. H., 4592
Barton, H. I., 4884
Baskerville, D. R., 691
Baskin, W., 3375
Baskine, G. F. T., 692
Basmadjian, Y. H., 2967
Bason, C. H., 3586
Bassam, H. K. al-, 2194
Bassam, N. A. A. al-, 2195
Bassiouny, M. Y., 366
Bastian, H. B., 3972
Bates, A. C., 693
Batoon, M. A., 2689
Batterson, F. J., 1190
Battistini, L. H., 4402
Baugh, L., 5256
Baumeister, M. G., 188
Baumel, M., 2237
Bautista, A. T., 2690

Bautista, F. G., 2691
Bautista, J., 2582
Baver, E. L., 3681
Bavly, S., 2201, 2238
Baxter, E. J., 4630
Bay, J. H., 2510
Baym, M. I., 3376
Bean, M. V., 3070
Beard, E. A., 5257
Beatty, H. M., 3143
Beatty, M. A., 1515
Beaucage, M. C., 3973
Beck, B. D., 1212
Beck, K. H., 1516
Beck, M. H., 4446
Beckerle, M. R. A., 189
Beckwith, H., 3587
Beddie, J. S., 3071
Bedwell, F., 3974
Beers, E. L., 3975
Beha, V. H., 2968
Beifeld, M. M., 4694
Belaunde, V., 1278
Bell, P. B., 2555
Bell, R., 5152, 5162
Bell, R. R., 694
Bell, W. H., 5163
Bellinfante, J., 3435
Beltranena-Valladares, L., 529
Benabarre, B., 4637
Bendix, D., 4743
Benedum, G. C., 2159
Benitez, C., 2692
Benjamin, C. T., 1942
Benjamin, H. R. S., 1517
Benjamin, H. R. W., 3850
Bennett, A. L. R., 3
Bennett, G. H., 2583
Benoit, D., 3436
Benson, W. M., 190
Benthien, E. M., 939
Berdahl, R. O., 3851
Bere, M., 4955
Berezner, A., 2999
Berg, W. V., 2202
Berger, M. I., 4862
Bergkamp, J. U., 3377
Berglund, R., 4596
Bergman, R., 2239
Bergman, V. H., 495
Berke, O., 4744
Berlin, L. L., 2203
Berman, A. A., 3682
Berman, E., 3144
Berman, N., 3683
Bermejo, F. V., 2693
Bernardino, V., 2694
Bernardo, L., 2695
Bernd, C. B., 1249
Berner, C. W., 191
Bernheisel, M. L., 1943
Bernier, A., 695
Bernikow, M., 3976
Bernique, G. M., 3437
Bernkopf, A., 3684
Bero, M. M., 3977
Berreman, G. C., 3978
Berrios Gonzalez, E., 1045
Bertram, L. H., 2135
Best, E. M., 553
Best, W. M., 4745

Bettencourt e Avila, J. M., 4625
Betz, E. A., 321
Bhagat, K. P., 1944
Bhagwat, P. G., 1828
Bhambal, R., 1945
Bhaopichitr, K., 2901
Bharnuratna, S., 2902
Bhatt, R. G., 1829
Bhusari, I., 1946
Bicaise, B. A., 311
Bickell, D. E., 696
Biddle, L. G., 1947
Bie, E. H., 697
Biecker, T. C., 3685
Bierer, D., 44
Bih, M. H. R., 1518
Billica, W. C., 4695
Binnie, R., 698
Birkner, E. M., 3686
Bishop, C. J., 4746
Bishop, H. P. C., 5258
Bishop, J. A., 3438
Bishop, J. I., 123
Bissell, T. T., 2359
Bissen, P. A., 4447
Bittenger, D. W., 453
Bittenz, F. A., 4448
Bizzle, E. E., 3145
Black, G. H., 2696
Black, H. M., 1290
Black, W. G., 554, 699
Blackburn, B. B., 5259
Blackman, G. Y., 1519
Blackman, R. D., 5260
Blackwell, L. L., 4322
Blackwell, W. A., 3979
Blair, E., 889
Blair, F. O., 3980
Blair, J. A., 3439
Blair, M. G., 2360
Blair, R., 4840, 4841
Blair, R. M., 3687
Blaisdell, J. B., 940
Blake, O. A., 2697
Blanco, C. R., 1046
Blank, E., 192
Blankemeyer, F., 367
Blanton, J. H., 2240
Blasingame, C. T., 5261
Blincoe, M. N., 3981
Bliss, L. R., 3852
Bloetjes, M. K., 3353
Blough, J. H., 193
Blount, L. F., 2204
Bloxom, B., 4449
Blue, J. H., 3982
Blum, W. D., 555
Blumberg, A. A., 3688
Blumhagen, H. H., 2309
Board, J. G., 194
Boardman, R. C., 3072
Boateng, G. A., 435
Bobbitt, J. F., 2584
Bock, D. A., 2547
Boehmke, M. J. W., 501
Boersma, C., 4687
Bogoslovsky, C. M. E. S. V. H., 4662
Bohn, R. C., 4863
Bohrer, E. A. S., 3146
Bohrer, R. W., 195

Boktor, A., 368
Bolich, G. H. K., 2698
Bolin, E., 3983
Boller, P. F., 2310
Bollig, R. J., 4747
Bollman, M. A., 2699
Bolton, B., 5126
Bonhomme, M. B., 3378
Bonnin, G. M., 3689
Bookamer, M. V., 439
Booker, J. O., 4748
Bookman, R., 3984
Boon, H. W., 556
Boonsaith, B., 2920
Booth, E. J., 4027
Booth, E. R., 312
Booth, G. C., 890
Booth, N. S., 338
Boren, E., 3985
Boren, J. E., 682
Borgeson, F. C., 4663
Borghi, L., 4403
Borikova, E. S., 3325
Borlongan, D., 2585, 2700
Born, P. H., 3333
Borncamp, F. F., 1294
Borne, C. M., 45
Bornemann, A., 3690
Bortniker, E., 2205
Bosanko, P., 3440
Bose, A., 1948
Bose, G. N., 1949
Boslet, M. R. G., 941
Bosworth, S. A., 3441
Botkin, B. A., 3986
Boudreau, S. J., 3987
Boundy, C. M., 3988
Bourland, M. L., 4450
Bower, G., 2241
Bowie, A., 3147
Box, W. J., 5262
Boyce, A. C., 2144
Boyce, G. C., 3073
Boyd, J., 2242
Boyer, C. W., 3989
Boyer, J. A., 3853
Boyle, G. K., 3990
Boyle, J. I., 196
Boyles, J. R., 1333
Brady, W. O. I., 3442
Braibanti, R. J., 2311
Braisted, P. J., 1830, 1950
Bramley, V. E., 4842
Brand, C. O., 5263
Brand, E. I., 5264
Brand, P., 3148
Brandauer, F. W., 3691
Brandl, M. I., 4323
Brandon, N. A., 1951
Branstator, H. G., 5098
Brauch, M. S., 3443
Brauer, R. H., 1952
Brawer, C. I., 2206
Brazelton, H. K., 3444
Bready, J. W., 3991
Bredestege, F. J., 3149, 4404
Breed, V. T., 3150
Brennan, M. V., 4405
Brennan, R. E., 3074
Brennan, T. M., 3992
Brentlinger, W. B., 197
Brethorst, M., 1520

Breuning, L., 3692
Brick, O. A., 2243
Brickman, W. W., 3588
Briggs, M. B., 3993
Brininstool, K. E., 2921
Brito Cunha, R. M. G., 1221
Britt, E. L., 3445
Brittain, W. M., 3994
Britton, W. E., 3854
Brock, E. E., 1831
Broderick, M. J., 3855
Broderick, S. M., 487
Brokaw, A. C., 1521
Brokaw, A. H., 1522
Bronars, J. C., 3019, 4607
Bronson, B. B., 1304
Brooke, M. A., 3020
Brooks, C. B., 700
Broom, P. M., 5208
Brosam, E. L., 5265
Brose, O. J., 3995
Brosnan, M. H., 4749
Broten, G. A., 4664
Brower, G. G., 3151
Brown, A. M. 46
Brown, A. R., 346
Brown, B. A., 884
Brown, C. C., 198
Brown, C. G., 701
Brown, D. W., 702
Brown, E. A., 3152
Brown, E. B., 199
Brown, E. C. J., 4672
Brown, F. H., 5266
Brown, H., 3996
Brown, H. D., 347
Brown, H. G., 2361
Brown, H. L., 5267
Brown, L., 3997
Brown, L. W., 5268
Brown, M. C., 3153
Brown, M. F., 703
Brown, M. G., 3693
Brown, M. S., 1222
Brown, S. A., 5052
Brown, S. R., 47
Brown, W. L., 5269
Browne, R. B., 3694
Bruce, C. H., 1953
Brueckner, K. R., 502
Bruewer, M. B., 4451
Brugger, F., 5053
Bruggman, M. A., 3695
Brune, I. H., 4324
Bruno, L. E., 4452
Bruton, M. J., 3154
Bryan, F. H., 1523
Bryant, H. W., 3998
Bryant, K. F., 5270
Bryant, V. L., 5271
Buasri, S., 124
Buchanan, M. E. M. B., 1832
Buchen, B. K., 5272
Buchterkirchen, E. K., 3589
Buck, F. C., 1524
Buck, J. T., 5273
Buck, K. E., 3446
Buck, R. H., 5127
Buckingham, E., 942
Buckisch, W. G. M., 2586
Buckley, A. R., 4453
Buckley, W. D., 200

Buckner, H. A., 5274
Bueno, R., 2701
Buller, F. P., 4579
Bullock, A. A., 1525
Bullock, F. W., 3999
Bullough, V. L., 3004
Bumgardner, A. C., 1526
Bunce, T. E., 2556
Bunch, G. A., 4000
Bundy, W. W., 5275
Bunnag, N., 2922
Buongiorno, R., 4454
Burch, V. J., 3005
Burd, C. G., 4001
Bures, M. E., 3334
Burg, B. B., 4750
Burgess, N., 5276
Burgess, R. L., 441
Burke, M. L., 4455
Burke, M. M., 4002
Burke, R. D., 48
Burkhalter, M. A., 4003
Burkhalter, R. E., 5277
Burlingame, J., 4004
Burnet, A. C. N., 1166
Burnett, A. H., 49
Burnett, J. R., 3856
Burns, M. E., 5278
Burns, R. G., 1214
Burns, Z. H., 3696
Burr, W. A., 2923
Burrage, D. G., 4297
Burritt, B. B., 3697
Burton, C. G., 125
Burton, J. S., 3698
Burton, R. A., 3699
Busch, H., 1368
Busch, R. C., 5116
Bustani, A. I. el-., 2168
Butera, J. B., 5128
Butler, J. D., 3857
Butler, M., 201
Button, R. F., 202
Butzbach, A. G., 4979
Buxo-Benitez, Z. J., 1093
Buxton, E. W., 704
Buys, W. E., 3858
Byers, B. H., 4696
Byles, M., 3155
Byrd, M. D., 4751
Byrne, T. C., 557
Byrns, L. E. A., 3021
Bysted, L. C., 1527

C

Cabanatan, S. I., 2702
Cabanos, J. A., 2703
Caceres, J. A., 1047
Cadwallader, E. M., 480
Cadwell, J. L., 943
Cadwell, L. M., 944
Caemmerer, R. R., 3590
Cafouros, A. P., 1048
Cahill, A. R., 4005
Cahill, E. A., 3157
Cahill, E. J., 3156
Cain, H. L., 945
Caine, J. P., 4006
Cajero, M., 5279

Cajoleas, L. P., 4956
Caldwell, H. B., 5280
Calhoun, G. N., 4007
Calimquim, A. A., 2587
Calip, O. A., 2588
Callahan, E. J., 203
Callicutt, D. H., 1094
Callon, B., 3158
Calloway, E. A., 5281
Calzada, P., 1095
Cama, K. H., 1833
Camajani, G., 3006
Cameron, J. S., 705
Camery, L. G., 4, 3361
Campa, J. C., 5282
Campbell, A. M., 3007, 3447
Campbell, C. L., 706
Campbell, E. H., 4843
Campbell, H. L., 707
Campbell, J. B., 4885
Campbell, J. K., 3362
Campbell, M., 1954
Campbell, P. C., 5283
Campbell, P. R., 558
Campbell, V. D. P., 3022
Campion, A. L., 708
Canary, P. H., Jr., 5
Canave, J. C., 2704
Candelas de Cruz, A. S., 1049
Candor, E., 946
Canfield, D. L., 891
Cann, M. M., 559
Cannon, A. E., 3591
Cannon, E. J., 4456
Cannon, M. A., 3075
Canoy, M. Z., 4325
Cantelon, H. A., 709
Canton, A., 1041
Cantu, A. P., 5284
Capo Caballero, C., 1096
Carey, J. E., 204
Carino, A., 2705
Carino, F., 2706
Carino, O. P., 2707
Carlesi, N. P., 4457
Carlos, C. B., 2589
Carlson, H. J., 5285
Carlson, J. S., 4673
Carlson, R. H., 3159
Carlton, S., 560
Carlyle, E. M., 1528
Carmody, I., 4379
Carmody, N., 4638
Carnes, H. M., 5286
Carney, M., 344, 455
Carpenter, D. H., 3700
Carpenter, G. W., 309
Carpenter, J. H., 4008
Carpenter, J. W., 2207
Carpenter, N. C., 3076
Carpenter, M. A., 3160
Carpentier, M. L., 5668
Carpio, R. D., 2708
Carr, A. T., 484
Carr, C. J., 3023
Carreon, M. L., 2590, 2709
Carrillo de Caceres, A. M., 1050
Carrion, J., 1097
Carrow, M. A., 5209
Carson, A. L., 6
Carson, B. B., 5287

Carswell, M. K., 2710
Carter, A., 561
Carter, C. A., 1529
Carter, E. L., 947
Carter, E. N., 1279
Carter, J. G., 4406
Carter, M. D., 562
Carter, R. C., 4980
Carter, T. J., 2362
Cartes, B., 205
Carven, A. M., 3448
Casanova, T., 126
Casellas Javet, B., 1098
Casey, M. R. E., 4458
Casey, T. A., 5054
Cashen, G. B., 2363
Casim, C. P., 2711
Cassady, M. A., 1955
Cassell, S. H., 4326
Casselman, F. R., 1530
Cassels, R. B., 4009
Cassidy, T. V., 4459
Cassileth, F. H., 4010
Castaneda, D. B., 2712
Castaneda, J. E., 948
Castanien, D. G., 892
Castillejo, L. J., 2713
Castro, J. S. D., 2714
Castro, P. C., 2715
Castro-Pozo, C., 1280
Castro y Guico, I. D., 2716
Catalozzi, M. C., 5129
Cate, D. F., 3701
Catedral, A. P., 2591
Cates, L. D., 3161
Catherine, R., 4522
Catoy, F. P., 2717
Catsioulas, E. J., 4298
Caudill, M. E., 5288
Caudill, W. A., 5153
Caughey, F. M., 4688
Caulker, R. Y., 488
Caulker, S. B., 489
Caulkins, G. W., 2718
Cavell, M. C., 4407
Cebollero, P. A., 1051, 1099
Cedeno, L. E., 1042
Cefkin, J. L., 50
Cepeda, R., 854
Cerf, J. H., 3592
Ceroni, V. F., 4408
Cervini, T. M., 2719
Cesario, C., 4460
Chachere, M. L., 4011
Chaffee, M. K., 51
Chaikosi, B., 2902a
Chakravarty, H., 1956
Chalmers, J. W., 563
Chamberlain, R., 3702
Chamberlain, R. S., 2244
Chamberlain, W. I., 1834
Chamberlin, L. R., 5289
Chambers, R. F., 2592
Chamness, E. E., 5290
Chan, F. T., 1369
Chan, K. P., 1370
Chan, L. C., 1531
Chan, S. Y., 1372
Chan, W. C., 2511
Chan, Y., 1372, 5055
Chance, N. A., 564
Chandler, H. E., 1373
Chandra, S., 1957

AUTHOR INDEX

Chang, C. C., 1533
Chang, Chang-yu, 1532
Chang, Chung-yuan, 1375, 1534
Chang, C. Y. K., 1374
Chang, F. Y., 5032
Chang, H. L., 1376
Chang, J. A., 5056
Chang, J. C., 1377
Chang, Pe-chin, 1378
Chang, Peng-chun, 1379
Chang, S., 1535
Chang, T. P., 5057
Chang, U. P., 2512
Chang, Y. C., 1537
Chang, Y. K., 1536
Chang, Y. L., 4012
Chang, Z. L., 1538
Chansler, H. F., 5164
Chao, C. H., 3449
Chao, E. H. L., 1539
Chao, F. P. H., 1380
Chao, H. F., 1540
Chao, S. C., 1381
Chapman, A. D. E., 3859
Chapman, J. G., 2312
Chapman, J. R., 5291
Char, T. Y., 206
Charbonneau, M. L. G., 710
Charles, C. L., 2720
Chatters, H., 711
Chaube, S. P., 1835
Chaudry, N. A., 2573
Chaurasia, G. S., 1836
Chavalitdamrong, B., 2924
Chaves, D. D. A., 1223
Chavez, D. J., 5292
Cheavens, S. F., 127
Chen, A. K. C., 1541
Chen, C. C., 1542
Chen, C. S., 1382
Chen, C. T., 1543
Chen, E. H. Y., 1544
Chen, E. V., 5058
Chen, L. Y., 1545
Chen, M. C. C., 1546
Chen, P. S., 1547
Chen, R. T., 1548
Chen, S. C., 1549
Chen, S. I., 1371
Chen, S. K., 1383
Chen, W. J. T., 1385
Chen, W. L., 1384
Chen, W. W. S., 1551
Chen, W. Y., 1463
Chen, W. Y. L., 1550
Chen, Y. K., 1552
Chen, Y. S., 1387
Cheng, A. C. Y., 1386
Cheng, C. P., 1553
Cheng, C. T., 1554
Cheng, D. C. T., 1555
Cheng, L. L. L., 1356
Cheng, M. T., 1556
Cheng, N. W., 1557
Cheng, R. Y. S., 1387
Cheng, Y. C., 1558
Cheo, Y. C., 5059
Cheppanalil, A. G., 1958
Chernosky, A. S., 5293
Cherryhomes, R., 949
Chertoff, E. B., 2245
Chesarek, E., 4801

Cheuk, S. L., 5076
Chey, S. J., 2484
Chi, K. T., 1388
Chia, L. P., 1559
Chiang, H. F., 1560
Chiang, J. M. T. Y., 4013
Chiang, M. L., 1389
Chiang, W. H., 1390
Chiba, S., 2364
Chico, R., 1100
Childers, L. M., 207
Childs, G. M., 339
Chilson, J. B., 3450
Chin, D. F., 5060
Chin, E. L. T., 5061
Ching Ju, A. Y., 1561
Chinian, J., 2365
Chinn, F. W., 5062
Chinnappa, S. P., 1837
Chinnock, E., 4299
Chiodo, T. M., 4461
Chisholm, H. H., 3593
Chitambar, J. B., 1838
Chittick, R., 712
Chiu, C., 3860
Cho, S. H., 2485
Choi, E., 208
Choi, E. S., 2513
Chopra, O. K., 1839
Chou, F. C., 1391
Chou, I. S. T., 2894
Chou, M. A., 1562
Chou, S. K., 1563
Chou, W. M., 1392
Choudhury, M. U., 2565
Chow, K. T., 1564
Chow, L. W. C., 5063
Chow, L. Y. Y., 1565
Chow, M. C. B., 2136
Chow, S. C., 1566
Chow, T. Y. H., 1297
Choy, Y. H., 2486
Christensen, C. D., 1191
Christenson, E. J., 5064
Christoff, A. T., 4752
Chu, D. C., 1393
Chu, J. B., 1567
Chu, J. P. W., 5033
Chu, M. H., 1569
Chu, M. L., 1568
Chu, P. C., 1394
Chu, S. C., 1395
Chu, S. Y., 1396
Chu, Y., 2514
Chu, Y. K., 1397
Chuang, C. H., 1398
Chue, K. H., 5065
Chun, E. Y. L., 5066
Chun, S. C., 2487
Chung, K. W., 2488
Chung, M. L., 1570
Churchley, F. E., 565
Chyung, N. C., 4753
Chyung, T. C., 2515
Cieslak, E. C., 4864
Cinq-Mars, M. A., 3451
Cisler, L. E., 3703
Claar, P. D., 313
Claire, M., 3452
Clamon, B., 3704
Clarfield, A. B., 4981
Clark, B. A., 3453
Clark, Charles Allen, 2489
Clark, Cynthia Anne 4014

Clark, C. C., 5294
Clark, D. H., 5295
Clark, E. B., 4015
Clark, G., 5296
Clark, M. B., 52
Clark, M. E., 3162
Clark, M. M., 5297
Clark, N., 5298
Clark, R. M., 1959
Clarke, F. M., 3861
Clarke, H., 713
Clarke, M. A., 3705
Clarke, V. F., 4016
Clarke, W. F., 566
Claros, T. S., 4300
Clasgens, M. G., 3706
Clausewitz, E. L., 5299
Clay, D. N., 3707
Claypoole, J. O., 53
Clayton, H. T., 4380
Clemente, T. A., 2593, 2721
Cleveland, M. E., 1571
Cleveland, N. O., 4017
Cleveland, R. J., 1960
Cleveland, T., 4327
Climenhaga, A. W., 567
Clinchy, E. R., 5210
Cline, R. C., 4844
Clinton, E. L., 1961
Clippinger, F. W., 3862
Clopton, R. A., 54
Clubine, G. L., 568
Clubine, I. W., 569
Clubine, M. H., 570
Clymer, P., 3163
Clymer, W. K., 3863
Coan, B. E., 5300
Coan, M. W., 5301
Cobb, A. F., 5302
Cobb, F. T., 209
Cochran, E. E., 3594
Coelho, G. V., 1840
Coers, W. C., 5303
Coffin, E. W., 7
Coger, L. I., 4724
Cohen, J., 4462
Cohen, J. B., 2313
Cohen, L., 4018
Cohen, S. H., 3024
Cole, J. E., 1052
Cole, P. R., 3595
Coleman, H. T. J., 571
Coleman, R. J., 3077
Coleson, E. P., 485
Collett, W. A., 55
Collins, A. K., 4827
Collins, E. A., 3454
Collins, J., 3455
Colodner, S., 3596
Colony, L., 1962
Combatalade, A. M., 4886
Comicescu, C., 4628
Comicescu, G., 4629
Comish, A. B., 2208
Comstock, A. L., 3708
Concistre, M. J., 5120
Condit, E. D., 5304
Conkey, L. E., 4019
Conlin, E. F., 4697
Connaughton, E. A., 714
Connoly, J. L., 3456
Connor, A. M., 3597

Conrow, M. L., 2516
Conway, J. G., 3457
Cook, D. F., 950
Cook, Elsie M., 4020
Cook, Eva McConnell, 3164
Cook, F., 4887
Cook, J. T., 572
Cook, P. A. W., 503
Cook, P. H., 4811
Coole, R. M., 5305
Coomaraswamy, D. L., 1963
Cooper, A., 4021
Cooper, A. J., 573
Cooper, B., 2490
Cooper, E. K., 5306
Cooper, R. S., 5307
Cooper, S., 3379
Copeland, E. L., 2314
Copley, E. G., 1101
Copp, H. W., 715
Corbin, C., 951
Corby, E., 3864
Corcoran, V. H., 5130
Cornelius, J. J., 1841
Cornelius, J. S., 5308
Cornelius, M., 1842
Cornett, J. S., 8
Cornish-Bowden, A., 210
Corona, B. C., 5211
Corpus, S. F., 2594
Corsberg, M. M., 4381
Cossum, W. W., 5067
Costa, N. J., 3304
Costa-Minneci di Villareal, J., 4409, 4463
Costantini, D. E., 716
Costello, P., 3025
Costrell, E. S., 3598
Cote, A. B., 3026, 4410
Couch, H., 2366
Coutts, H. T., 574
Covell, J. H., 2367
Covello, L., 4411
Cox, A. M., 3458
Cox, C. M., 3165
Coxhead, M., 2246
Craddock, E. C., 4464
Cragg, E. M. C., 575
Cragin, E., 4022
Craig, A. L., 5309
Craig, E. L., 5310
Craig, J. F., 1572
Cramer, B. E., 4888
Cramer, J. F., 4812, 4828
Cramer, M. E., 4023
Crandall, F. B., 4024
Crandall, J. R., 211
Cranston, E., 1788
Crausaz, R. M., 3459
Craven, B. N., 3325
Crawford, H. R., 952
Creighton, J. W., 1399
Crenshaw, T. C., 5311
Crespi, A. R., 128
Crespo, C. M., 1102
Cretcher, M. W., 3166
Criner, R. L., 3027
Crocker, B., 5698
Croft, C. H., 5165
Crofton, W. M., 4025
Crofts, H., 3460
Cron, H. C., 5312

Cronin, E. M., 5313
Crose, K. L., 369
Cross, E., 2315
Cross, L., 1288
Crouse, M. D., 1964
Crowle, H. A., 953
Crowley, F. M., 184
Crowley, R. M., 3167
Croyle, H. I., 3709
Crum, C. E., 9
Crum, M. C., 212
Crumlish, M. L., 717
Crumly, E., 3461
Cruz, A. E., 2722
Cruz, M. A., 5314
Cruz Aponte, R. A., 1103
Cruz y Enriquez, L., 2723
Cryier, A. L., 3462
Cudmore, M. F., 3463
Cuff, M. L., 3865
Cuizon, E. A., 2595
Cull, A. C. K., 4026
Culver, M. E., 325
Cummings, C. L., 5315
Cummings, J. B., 1965
Cummings, R. A., 3168
Cuneo, E. J., 4027
Curran, H. E., 5316
Currie, A. E., 1966
Currie, M. B., 5317
Currimbhoy, A. E., 1967
Curtin, D. F., 3169
Curtis, M. S., 4382
Custer, D. M., 4028
Cutts, E. H., 1843
Cyr, G. J., 3464
Cyr, M. S. P., 5103
Cyrilla, M., 718
Czerwinski, V., 4616

D

Daboo, J. D., 1844
Dabrow, D. B., 213
Dafoe, H. I., 719
Daily, M. C., 2368
Dale, G. R., 440
Dale, W. P., 1274
Dallman, G. R., 462
Dalton, R. C., 576
Dalton, S. P., 4328
Dalven, R. N., 4889
Daly, M. A., 5318
Daly, W. A., 4631
Dambach, J. I., 3599
Damon, J. K., 4465
Dandoy, M. A., 2596
Daniels, B. E., 893
Daniels, L. A., 720
Daniels, M. J., 954
Dankers, M. E., 214
Dann, J. A., 1104
Dannug, L. B., 2724
Dantyagi, S., 1968
Darben, C. A., 5669
Darby, H. E., 5166
Darcy, N. T., 4865
Darling, M. R., 4890
Darrow, D. H., 4029
Darsie, M. L., 5154
Darst, M. A., 2247
Das, P., 1845

Das, R. C., 1969
Daseler, J. E., 3170
Dasgupta, D. C., 3078
Daskawie, M. A. Q., 1970
Dauchy, N. M., 5319
Dave, I., 1846
Davenport, A. J., 5320
Davenport, E. L., 5321
David, M. G., 1271
Davidsen, O. M., 5683
Davidson, S. A., 577
Davies, E., 3171
Davies, E. S., 314
Davies, F. J. J., 3866
Davies, H. J., 1971
Davies, O. M., 4030
Davis, B. E., 1334
Davis, D. G., 578
Davis, E. C., 2548
Davis, E. M., 5322
Davis, G. E., 3029
Davis, G. K., 3028
Davis, J. E., 894
Davis, M., 3172
Davis, M. C., 4364
Davis, M. L., 855
Davis, M. M., 4891
Davis, R. F., 5323
Davis, V. L., 215
Davison, J. M., 4301
Dawkins, J., 4754
Dawson, S. M., 1224
Dawson, W. R., 4383
Day, M. S., 3600
Dea, R. M., 3465
Deady, C. M., 216
Deal, G. V., 5324
Dealy, M. B., 3867
Dean, A. E., 4892
Dean, C. R., 721
Dease, M. E., 1972
Deb, M., 1973
De Bevere, P. M., 3318
De Chello, M. R., 4466
Decker, W. M., 1573
Deckrosh, V. L., 4031
Declet, A. M., 1105
Dedge, R., 4580
DeFrancis, J. F., 1400
De Francisco, D., 5131
De Groat, E. R., 442
Dehnert, E. J., 3173
Delagado, J., 5325
De La Luz, A., 1106
Delk, R. C., 217
Delmet, D. T., 5326
Delmez, A. J., 895
Del Pilar, L., 1107
Del Rio Sepulveda, F., 841
Del Rosario, O. A., 2640
De Marco, R. R., 322
De Mattos, D. X., 1225
De May, A. J., 129
Demiashkevich, M. J., 3079
Dempsey, A. F., 2369
Denlay, R. E., 5327
Denyes, M. E., 2137
DePauw, G. A. L. J., 3312
De Quinones, L. V., 1108
Derham, M. T., 3466
Desai, L. M., 1847
Desai, M., 1974

De Smidt, M. E., 4893
Desmond, J. T., 4467
De Sousa, H. A., 1848
De Sousa, H. J., 5114
De Souza, A. P., 1975
Deulkar, D., 1849, 1976
Devadas, R. P., 1977
Devera, A. B., 2725
Deverell, A. F., 579
De Vette, W. A., 4581
DeVineau, C. E., 3467
DeVinney, G. H., 4755
Devlin, E. J., 3030
Devlin, M. R., 218
Dewey, C. S., 3868
Dewey, J., 3601
Dewitt, C. M., 3710
Dhairyam, D., 1850
Dhanagom, D., 2903
Dhar, V. C., 1978
Dharmgrongartama, S., 2904, 2925
Diab, L. N., 5029
Diamantides, D. G., 4329
Dias, R. S., 5328
Diaz, C., 1043
Diaz, F. E., 2726
Dick, M. G., 514
Dickerson, W. S., 4756
Dickinson, F., 1574
Dickinson, J. H., 5212
Dickinson, T. H., 3869
Dicks, C., 5329
Dickson, A. M., 4384
Dideban, Z., 2160
Diei, J. K., 463
Dielmann, R. H., 3380
Dienst, L. H., 5330
Dietel, W., 3711
Dietz, E. H. W., 2491
Di Franco, J., 4412
Diggins, J. P., 3174
Dilling, H. A., 403
Dillon, D. G., 4385
Dillon, N. P., 955
Dinda, J. P., 3335
Dingman, E., 3602
Dion, R. D. J., 722
Dirks, D. P., 896
Divine, J. W., 219
Dixon, E. E., 1575
Dixon, E. M., 1576
Dizon, E. S., 2727
Djang, H. L., 5034
Djao, C. C., 1577
Djeng, B., 1578
Djung, L. D., 1401
Doane, F. C., 4698
Dobbs, M., 5331
Dobles, M., 842
Dodd, E. C., 5332
Dodge, N. M., 56
Dodson, J. R., 343, 348
Doerr, M. F., 5333
Doi, H. N., 4982
Doi, J. I., 2316
Dole, H. P., 723
Dole, M. J., 2728
Dolliver, E. N., 3175
Domandi, M., 3712
Dome, A. E., 1361
Donahue, J. C., 4699
Donald, S. S., 1979

Doniger, S., 4725
Donlon, T. W., 4894
Donnelly, E. M., 3468
Donofrio, A. F., 5132
Donohue, J. W., 3176
Donovan, E. H., 4468
Dooley, M. M., 3469
Doolittle, M., 2898
Doon, M. L., 3470
Doores, M. W., 4032
Dorcas, H. C., 4639
Dorland, G. W., 4330
Dorman, H. G., 130
Dorrum, E. V., 4597
Dorsey, G. L., 5334
Dorsinville, F., 877
Dos Santos, M. L., 1226
Dossick, J. J., 897
Doucette, A. L., 580
Dougherty, M. E., 4033
Douglas, C. C., 956
Douglas, J. L., 3336
Douglass, H. R., 5335
Dowd, W. A., 3471
Dowie, J. I., 5692
Downing, L. R., 464
Downing, R. A., 1109
Downing, W. L., 2248
Downs, N., 3870
Drake, R. H., 5336
Drakeford, J. W., 4726
Drazin, N., 2209
Drennan, D. D., 5337
Drennan, O. P., 5338
Dreyfus, R., 878
Driscoll, A. M., 4895
Driscoll, G. R., 3080
Driskill, R. A., 4469
Drlica, K. F., 2370
Drobka, F. J., 4608
Drought, J. M., 1579
Drury, H. P., 4470
Drusine, L., 5660
Dryden, R. N., 482
Dryer, L. L., 3177
Dsang, L. G., 1580
DuChemin, R. C., 3871
Dudine, C., 4471
Dudley, F. A., 3872
Duewel, W. L., 1980
Duey, P. A., 4413
Duffey, E. L., 5339
Dugstad, R. A., 3713
Dukewits, W. C., 1851
Dunbar, A. M., 5068
Dunklin, L. D., 5670
Dunlap, J. W., 4866
Dunlop, F. S., 581
Dunn, D., 3178
Dunn, E. J., 724
Dunn, N. W., 1192
Dunn, R. E., 3873
Dunphy, M. H., 725
Dunson, C. E., 4034
Duong, D., 2996
Dupont, J. A., 3472
Durham, J. B., 2371
Durr, T. A., 2926
Dusel, J. P., 5069
Dutt, B. M., 1852
Dwyer, A., 5671
Dwyer, M. D., 220
Dwyer, M. T., 3179

Dyde, W. F., 582
Dyster, C. M., 4829

E

Eapen, C. T., 1853, 1981
East, M. E., 5340
Easter, J. L., 1110
Edbaugh, C. D., 898
Ebel, C. P., 5341
Ebner, E., 2210
Eby, S. L., 3603
Eckersley, A. L., 10
Eckhart, R. A., 3714
Eckoff, W. J., 3604
Eddy, S., 5167
Edelman, N., 4700
Edelson, L., 4035
Eden, R. K., 3473
Edgar, F. R., 3874
Edlund, R. A., 726
Edmondson, E. M., 3875
Edralin, M. S., 2729
Edwards, J., 1854
Edwards, M. J., 1581
Edwards, M. O., 3605
Edwards, S. J., 1855
Edwards, W. M. M., 2134
Efron, A., 3081
Egan, C. A., 4386
Egger, M. S., 1266
Eginton, D. P., 3876
Ehrenburg, A. F., 4757
Ehrenfeld, A., 3606
Eickelberger, T. J., 4036
Eidbo, O. E., 5655
Eide, M., 1582
Eilberg, H., 4037
Eimermann, R. M., 5672
Eiseman, M., 4038
Eisenstein, M., 4609
Ekasagdi, K., 2905
Ekdahl, N. M. G., 1305
Ekong, E. U., 465
Ekrami, A. M., 2145
el-Bassiouny, M. Y., 366
el-Bustani, A. I., 2168
Elder, N. C., 2927
Eldridge, I., 3180
Elequin, E. T., 2597
el-Erian, M. A., 370
el-Hashimi, K. M., 2172
Eliach, E., 5133
Elias, T. H., 2169
Elise, M., 3031
Elizabeth, T., 3529
el-Kouatly, M. A. H., 2896
Ellgaard, T. J., 3363
Elliott, A. E., 1273
Elliott, C. M., 583
Elliott, D. A., 429
Elliott, J. A., 5342
Elliott, V. C., 1856
Ellis, A. C., 11
Ellis, C. E., 5343
Ellis, E. N., 584
Ellis, J. E., 1227
Ellis, P., 5344
Ellison, A., 3607
Ellison, L., 4472
Ellman, S. S., 3474

Ellzey, R. C., 4983
el-Negehi, M. L., 384
el-Rimawi, Q. M., 386
Elson, H., 4039
Elwell, C. E., 3381
Ely, P. L., 4984
Embree, A. T., 1982
Embree, S. H., 1983
Emerson, M. F., 4758
Emerson, R. W., 5345
Empey, L. J., 4640
Endres, M. S., 57
Endslow, B. S., 3475
Eneboe, R. A., 4985
Engberg, G., 4674
Engebrecht, N. R., 1984
Engel, L. E., 3715
Engelbrecht, H. C., 3608
Engelhardt, R., 3181
England, J. T., 5673
Englebert, M., 2372
Englebrektson, S., 4675
English, W. E., 899
Enns, K. A., 349
Enochs, J. B., 4986
Enos, L. J., 221
Enverga, T. Y., 2598, 2730
Eo-Yang, Y. C., 1583
Eppinger, A. M., 3716
Epstein, M., 4987
Erback, J. R., 58
Erian, M. A. el-, 370
Erickson, H. B., 3609
Eringis, S. A., 4569
Escalante, P., 2731
Escarrilla, M. T., 2732
Escher, E., 3008, 3032
Esparza, D., 5346
Espes, E. M., 5347
Espendez Navarro, J., 530, 1111
Espinoza-Llanos, N. E., 1275
Essame, E. M., 4040
Estacio y Calanog, C. I., 2599
Estarellas Ripoll, J., 900
Estaville, L. E., 4896
Estavillo, F. H., 5348
Esterly, V. J., 3364
Estes, C. S., 1402
Estrada, G. E., 957
Estrellas, A. R., 2733
Estridge, M. P., 3182
Etheridge, T. H., 901
Ettenson, R. J., 5134
Etter, C. L., 2373
Eusden, R. A., 5031
Evans, G. M., 5104
Evans, H. L., 902
Evans, M. P., 958
Evans, O. M., 4041
Evans, P. M., 3877
Evenson, A. B., 727
Everett, C. W., 4042
Ewan, J. D., 1584
Ewing, R. H., 1985
Eybers, E., 504
Eyler, M. H., 3878
Ezell, P. H., 5349

F

Factora, A. Q., 2600

Fadipe, N. A., 466
Fafunwa, A. B., 454
Fahnbulleh, E. O., 443
Fahs, L. S., 585
Fairbank, M. L., 1986
Fairfield, W. C., 1585
Faldwell, M. P., 3476
Fam, Y., 404
Fan, C. T., 1403
Fan, I. C., 1404
Fan, T. C., 1405
Fang, T. Y., 1406
Fanning, M. W., 4414
Fargo, A. F., 2170
Farmer, W. A., 5350
Farr, H. L. K., 4043
Farrell, R. A., 4473
Farrell, R. F., 222
Farrington, F. E., 3382, 4474
Faryar, A., 2146
Fastenberg, R., 3183
Fath, J. J., 4044
Faunce, L. W., 5351
Fausold, C. D., 59
Faust, A. F., 1199
Favriano, S. F., 736
Fawcett, K., 4665
Fawcett, W. B., 5372
Fawell, W. C., 1987
Fay, T. P., 4475
Feehan, J. F., 959
Feely, G. M., 2317
Feldman, E., 60
Feldstein, L. K., 2734
Feliciano y Romas, J., 2735
Fellenbaum, E. H., 333
Felt, N. M., 1988
Feng, H. Y., 1586
Feng, P. Y., 3717
Feng, R. T. Y., 1587
Feng, Y. T., 12
Fenn, W. P., 1306
Fenton, D. M., 4045
Fenton, E. J., 3184
Fenton, E. L., 4046
Ferges, M. L., 5352
Ferguson, E. C. D., 3718
Ferguson, R. H., 728
Fernandez, M., 4368
Fernando, S., 1989
Feroze, 2566
Ferrer, A. R., 2601
Ferrier, W. K., 586
Ferrigno, J. M., 3477
Ferring, C. A., 3719
Fick, M. L., 505
Fidelma, M., 251
Field, E. B., 1588
Fierro, V. N. D., 2736
Filbeck, O., 3185
Filella, J. F., 1264
Filipino, R. F., 3365
Fine, E. M., 4047
Fineberg, S. A., 2211
Fink, T. R., 13
Finlay, P. R., 131
Finley, E. M., 132
Finley, G. E., 4048
Finley, R. J., 4759
Finn, T. G., 587
Finnan, M. R., 4476
Fischbacher, T., 2249

Fischer, A., 4854
Fischette, R. M., 729
Fisher, A., 4897
Fisher, G. H., 903
Fisher, J. E., 2492
Fisher, O. M., 730
Fishman, A. T., 1857
Fite, G. K., 3720
Fitzgerald, D. T., 133
Fitzjohn, W. H., 486
Fitzpatrick, D., 4049
Fitzpatrick, D. C., 5353
Fitzsimons, I., 4050
Fjeld, K., 4598
Flack, H. W., 3082
Flaherty, P. F., 4760
Flanagan, M. M., 4051
Flanagan, T. E., 223
Flather, D. M., 588
Fleming, D. J., 1897
Fleming, R. L., 5115
Fleming, W. C., 61
Fleming, W. J., 4477
Flockhart, L. L. W., 4052
Flores, D., 224
Flores, M. S., 2737
Flores, R. W., 2738
Flores, T. W., 2739
Flores, Z. K. J., 5354
Floreza, F. A., 2740
Flower, B. E., 2549
Fodor, R., 4617
Fody, M., 960
Foley, F. C., 3186
Foley, R., 134
Follmer, M. E., 4053
Folsom, M. G., 225
Font, R. O., 1112
Foo, T. S., 1407
Foote, F. P., 2374
Forbes, J. M., 1990
Ford, Eddy Lucius, 1408
Ford, Eudora Lorene, 4761
Ford, E. M., 1991
Fores-Ganzon, G., 2741
Forest, J., 731
Forstat, R. E., 4988
Fosbrink, R. H., 1228
Foster, C. L., 3721
Foster, J. E., 589
Foster, M. N., 226
Fournadjieff, K. Z., 4727
Fowler, F. S., 4478
Fox, H. F., 2602
Fox, J. H., 590
Fox, J. T., 4479
Frabbito, P. F., 4480
Francis, C. A., 1169
Francisco, F. V., 2742
Franck, G. P., 4898
Franey, J. T., 3187
Frank, R. C., 2375
Franke, C. E., 3722
Franke, V., 3478
Franklin, L. M., 2250
Franklin, M. R., 1229
Franklin, S. P., 4899
Franz, N. A., 4054
Franz, R. C., 227
Franzblau, R. N., 3083
Fraser, A. M., 591
Fraser, H. G., 4582

Frawley, J. J., 2251
Frazier, A. C. M., 3188
Frech, F. P., 5355
Frederick, L. M., 904
Frederick, L. R., 3479
Free, L. F., 3383
Freeburg, R. E. W., 135
Freedman, A. E., 3723
Freehill, A. M., 3033
Freeman, A. T., 4055
Freeman, G. H., 5168
Freeman, H., 14
Freeman, W. F., 3480
Freitag, C. R., 4728
Freitag, H. T., 15
Freitag, M. C., 3724
Freitas, W. J., 1230
Freivogel, E. E., 3189
French, C. M., 1858
French, L. H., 3084
French, W. H., 4056
Frenoy, F. C., 3481
Frenzel, R. E., 5356
Frenzkem, L. E., 228
Frerichs, R. M., 5357
Friedenberg, J., 3384
Friedland, D. K., 3725
Friedmann, E. M., 3726
Friedrich, R., 3482
Friesenhehn, M. H., 3727
Frink, L. M., 537
Fritchley, N. H., 2212
Fritz, J. C., 5358
Frost, F. H., 4057
Frost, H. H., 3313
Fuentes, F. S., 2743
Fugh, P. C., 1409
Fujikawi, F. M. C., 2376
Fujimoto, E., 2377
Fujiyoshi, D. H., 5169
Fukuda, H., 2378
Fukuyama, Y., 2969
Fullwood, R. J., 5359
Fultz, M. C., 2379
Fuoss, D. E., 16
Furie, W. B., 4610
Furnadjieff, V. D., 3226
Furnivall, F., 961
Fuss, J., 5656
Fussell, W. D., 5360
Fynes, H. M., 3728

G

Gabbard, A., 4058
Gage, B., 1410
Gagneron, M., 879
Gagon, G. S., 2161
Galang, R. C., 2744
Gale, E., 1992
Gallagher, A. M., 4375
Galloway, B. O., 5361
Galt, H. S., 1411
Galt, R., 371
Galz, A., 3190
Gamarra, T. V., 1276
Gamble, J. C., 2745
Gamboa, E. M., 843, 846
Gammon, W. H., 1231
Gamoran, E., 3085
Gandara, M. A., 1113

Gandia, R. D. C., 1114
Ganja, R. S., 5696
Gant, L. S., 5362
Garber, H. L., 136
Garcia, A. S., 2746
Garcia, D. A., 4641
Garcia, E. E., 962
Garcia, F. A., 2747
Garcia, G. M. D., 1115
Garcia, L. C., 2748
Garcia, M., 1053
Garcia Deere, C. P., 1116
Garcia-Hernandez, L., 1117
Garcia-Palmieri, R. A., 1118
Garcia Ruiz, F., 963
Gardner, A. E., 4989
Gardner, D. A., 2380
Gardner, E. A., 3086
Garey, W. F., 4331
Gargle, I. N., 4059
Garner, V. B. R., 5363
Garnett, H. M. B., 5364
Garniss, G. W., 856
Garrard, J. L., 905
Garretson, O. K., 5365
Garza, E. D., 5366
Garza, G. J., 5367
Garza, M. A., 5368
Gascoigne, S., 544
Gates, G. G., 5107
Gates, I. M., 4900
Gates, W. D., 3191
Gauche, W. J., 372, 405
Gaudin, A. C., 3385
Gaut, G. F., 5369
Gauthier, E. H., 4901
Gaylord, M. L., 326
Gebre-Hiwet, M., 430, 3878a
Geil, M. G., 732
Geis, G. L., 4902
Geldenhuys, F. E., 506
Gelinas, M. D. L., 3483
Gelston-Gelles, R. H., 137
Gemarino, R. G., 2603
Geng, G. Y. H., 1412
Genova, V. O., 4481
Geoffrey, J. R., 3192
George, K. K., 1859
George, R. C., 3729
George, R. C. L., 5170
Gephart, M. L., 4957
Geraty, T. S., 229, 1298
Gerawi, N., 406
Gerdine, C., 3193
Gergawi, N., 419
Gerhardt, H. W., 964
Germaney, R. T. H., 733
Gershom, B. S., 1993
Getty, O. M., 1994
Ghalib, H., 2542, 2550
Ghent, E. C., 965
Ghiizai, G. F., 1325
Ghormley, N. B., 327
Ghosh, P. K., 1995
Giadrides, G. E., 4332
Gibson, A. S., 3194
Gibson, C. M., 4060
Gibson, G. D., 592
Gibson, M. E., 5370
Gibson, W., 5371
Giddings, E. M., 966
Gideon, S. S., 1860

Gifford, R., 4333
Gifford, W. J., 3730
Gilbert, A. M., 3879
Gilbert, E. E., 4762
Gilbert, F. G., 5372
Gilbert, W. R., 138
Gilito, D., 2749
Gill, B. J., 3087
Gill, C. C., 906
Gill, E. P., 4851
Gill, M. S., 5373
Gillespie, E. D., 593
Gillett, C. S., 2318
Gillette, G. C., 5374
Gilliland, A. M., 4061
Gillman, V., 3484
Gilmer, W. E., 734
Gilroy, Bro., 3437
Gin, D. S., 5070
Ginsburg, H. H., 4573
Girard, M. M., 4482
Girard, R. S., 3195
Giron-Tupas, A., 2750
Gish, W. K., 735
Gladney, K. M., 5375
Glahn, M., 3485
Glass, M. R., 4483
Glatstein, H., 230
Glavas, C. B., 4334
Glazier, K. M., 594
Glinz, L. A., 595
Gloria, P. M., 2751
Gloyn, C. K., 3880
Glynn, E. V., 4387
Glynn, M. A., 3486
Glynn, M. V., 4484
Godard, L. F., 4062
Goddard, I., 4676
Goduco, A. M., 2752
Goedecker, M. L., 4063
Goedertier, J. M., 231
Goehegen, G., 3487
Goelman, E., 139
Goerner, W. J., 3610
Goetzinger, H., 3731
Gogate, R. V., 1996
Goldat, G. D., 4302
Golden, M. E., 5376
Goldfinger, M., 1281
Goldman, C. R., 4064
Goldman, L. Y., 2213
Gomez, L., 1054
Gomez, L. R., 5377
Gonzales, A. M., 5378
Gonzales, M., 967
Gonzales, M. U., 2753
Gonzalez, A., 968
Gonzalez, A. Q., 2754
Gonzalez, E. B., 2604
Gonzalez, E. L., 1250
Gonzalez, T. F., 4903
Gonzalez, W., 1119
Gonzalez de Davila, C., 1055
Gonzalez de Gueits, F., 1120
Gonzalez de los Santos, M. D. J., 5379
Good, M. E. S., 2381
Good, M. M., 1997
Gooden, H. B., 140
Goodnough, R. L., 4065
Goodrich, L. C., 1589
Goodwin, M. F., 2517

Goozee, E. S., 4485
Gordon, D. S., 1998
Gordon, G. R., 3337
Gordon, L. M. J., 4812a
Gordon, W. E., 1999
Gore, W. R., 5380
Gorman, M. J. T., 4415
Gorman, M. R., 4303
Gorman, N., 4486
Gormley, C. L., 2957
Gormley, S. F. F., 736
Gosen, M. D. S., 232
Goss, G. E., 2605, 3034
Gott, M. E., 5381
Gottleib, J. G., 3488
Gottshall, N. T., 233
Goulard, S. E., 5171
Gould, B., 5382
Gould, M. F., 4487
Goulter, O. J., 62, 1590
Gowen, M. R., 63
Gowin, L. E., 3881
Goyenechea, F. C., 2755
Graalfs, M., 5071
Graefe, E. W., 1203
Graf, R. M., 3386
Graham, C. A., 4904
Graham, G., 4958
Graham, G. A., 737
Graham, H., 4388
Graham, L. R., 5383
Graham, M. A., 3489
Grajewski, H. C., 4618
Grant, H. E., 596
Grant, I. M., 1170
Grantham, G. C., 5090
Grantham, H. H., 597
Graves, A. N., 467
Graves, F. P., 3387
Graves, R., 4066
Graves, S. M., 2606
Gray, D., 4488
Gray, G., 4763
Gray, R. F., 4905
Gray, W. H., 738
Graybill, H. B., 1591
Graziani, G., 4489
Green, A. E., 4067
Green, A. S., 3732
Green, B. A., 1171
Green, E. J., 407
Green, E. K., 5697
Greenberg, G. I., 2252
Greene, A., 3733
Greene, H. H., 4906
Greene, O., 64
Greenspoon, B., 4764
Greer, V. D., 3490
Gregg, A. H., 1413
Gregorio, H. C., 2756
Gregorovic, M. C., 5684
Gregory, M. A., 3491
Greiner, W. E., 4490
Griebling, F. G., 3196
Griffith, H. E., 2319
Griffiths, W. G., 2000
Grillo, F. C., 4491
Grimes, E. T., 4068
Gross, C. H., 598, 3197
Gross, S. M., 5384
Grossman, M., 3388
Grout, P. A., 5385
Grove, E. E., 496

Gruener, J. R., 4069
Grueser, F. T., 4335
Grusendorf, A. A., 5386
Gryte, C. A., 739
Grzybowska, Z., 3198
Gualandris, P. J., 3492
Guardia, L. R., 1215
Guerra, E. L., 4416
Guess, B. L., 350
Guiang, P. G., 2607, 2757
Guinan, A., 3088
Guindon, F. X., 3389
Guinid, M. N., 2758
Gukich, D., 4990
Gulentz, A. B., 4070
Gulley, E. E., 2759
Gundersheimer, E. M., 3611
Gunkel, N. L., 3612, 3734
Gunn, E. L., 5387
Guo, L. R. W., 1414
Gupta, P., 2001
Gushue, W. J., 599
Gustafson, G. J., 4071
Guterl, L. F. X., 3199
Guyer, C. R., 4072
Guyette, G. F., 5105
Gwinn, A. E., 2382
Gwynn, I. R., 4073

H

Haake, H. B., 3735
Haan, L. R., 5093
Haar, E. C., 3882
Haas, F. L., 65
Habermacher, A. L., 5388
Habito, C. P., 2608
Hackett, P. R., 1335
Haddock, H., 1121
Hafidh, N. A. S. al-, 2171
Hagenhoff, M. P., 3613
Haggerty, R. L., 4389
Hagstolz, H. B., 3883
Hague, D. W., 234
Hahn, W., 3614
Haines, J. H., 2557
Hainline, M. L., 4074
Hakkak, H. J. al-, 2196
Haklai, M. D., 2214
Halbert, A. E., 3089, 3200
Halder, R. M., 2002
Hale, C. A., 907
Hale, H. M., 4991
Halim, B., 2970
Hall, C. J., 2558
Hall, E. S., 4075
Hall, J., 436
Hall, J. S., 4492
Hall, M. B., 969
Hall, M. E., 2383
Hall, R. K., 1185, 1204
Hall, R. S., 3201
Hall, W. W., 3324
Halliday, E., 4701
Halloway, F., 3390
Halnon, W., 141
Halpin, M. J., 3202
Haman, M. H., 4493
Hamdani, M. S. T., 1861
Hamel, Albert, 2559
Hamel, Bro. Albert, 3493

Hamilton, E. F., 5389
Hamilton, J. M., 3736
Hamilton, L. D., 600
Hamilton, O. F., 5390
Hamilton, T. G., 970
Hammer, E. L. V., 142
Hammer, H. B., 5391
Hammerman, D., 3494
Hamner, H. N., 3884, 4076
Han, C. L., 1415
Hancock, M., 5392
Hancock, T., 2215
Handloser, E., 4077
Handy, S. S., 4078
Hannan, J. E., 3203
Hannum, R. H., 2003
Hansell, S. G., 2384
Hansen, C., 3737
Hansen, R. E., 4593
Hansome, M., 143
Hanson, E. J., 971
Hanson, R. M., 5213
Hao, P. T. Y., 5035
Hara, M., 2385
Harada, K. G., 5172
Harada, M. F. M., 4079
Harbin, T. A., 5393
Harbourt, J. A., 3204
Harding, M. I., 444
Harding, P. K., 2147
Hardy, B. A., 4080
Hari-Narain, A., 2004
Haring, D. G., 2386
Harkins, B. S., 5394
Harlow, R. F., 3738
Harper, H. R., 4959
Harper, I. M., 2005
Harr, W. C., 468
Harrel, B. J., 5395
Harrell, M., 972
Harrington, G. A., 4081
Harris, C. V., 373
Harris, G. G., 1592
Harris, I. B., 3495
Harris, I. J., 3310
Harris, J. K., 5396
Harris, P., 4619
Harris, R. S., 601
Harris, S., 5397
Harrison, D. C., 5398
Harrison, B. G. M., 1172
Harriss, V. M., 5399
Harsky, J. E., 4765
Hart, J. R., 3885
Hart, N., 4082
Hart, R. N., 5400
Hartman, J., 3496
Hartshorne, E. Y., 3615
Hartung, H., 3616
Hartz, A., 235
Hartzler, O. L., 315
Harvey, H. B., 4083
Harvey, M., 144
Harvey, T. M., 3497
Hascall, T. B., 17
Hase, H. Y., 2387
Hasegawa, S., 2388
Haselden, J., 3319
Hashimi, K. M., el-, 2172
Haskins, F. H., 4494
Hassan, N. M., 408
Hasselbalch, H., 1276

Hassun, A. R. I. al-, 2173
Hastings, M. B., 4390
Hastings, M. P., 3035
Hatch, W. M., 3739
Hatcher, M. L., 3391
Hattersley, L. W., 1336
Hau, G. W., 3740
Hauck, A. A., 602
Haueisen, A. F., 66
Haug, A., 4599
Haven, S. E., 4992
Haverkamp, F. W., 2253
Hawes, H. H., 145
Hawes, V. L., 3741
Hawke, J. R., 880
Hawkes, L. R., 4417
Hawkins, D. C., 1217
Hawkins, E. I., 236
Hawkins, O. R., 973
Hawver, C. F., 4084
Hay, F. H., 3329
Hayashida, A., 5173
Hayden, J., 974
Hayden, J. R., 4867
Hayes, E. D. L., 4689
Hayes, J. J., 2971
Hayes, R. W., 5174
Haynes, A., 2760
Haynes, A. F., 3742
Hazard, E. J., 237
Hazarika, B. K., 1862
Hazlett, C. H., 2006
Hazlett, W. W., 4085
Head, W. O., 4086
Healy, E. E., 4495
Healy, M. M. I., 2254
Heasley, J. I., 4087
Heaton, C. L., 2255
Heavin, A. W., 4088
Hedges, H. G., 740
Heffernen, A. J., 238
Hefley, J. L., 4336
Heflin, C. E., 2609
Hegarty, M. E., 3498
Hegland, M., 3354
Heh, G. P., 4496
Hein, N. J., 1863
Heininger, A. D., 1593
Heinrich, D. L., 5121
Heinrich, M. P., 3090
Heins, C. P., 2007
Heller, H. F., 3886
Helmke, W. R., 5401
Helms, J. E., 908
Helser, A. D., 455
Heltibridle, M. E., 239
Hempfling, M. L., 3499
Hendershot, V. E., 2553, 4337
Henderson, A. L., 3205
Henderson, V. L., 67
Heneise, H. K., 881
Hengehold, R., 3500
Hennessey, M. O. S. P. O. A., 3501
Henry, A. I., 1173
Henry, R. F., 5402
Hensel, J. E., 240
Hepworth, T. S., 4813
Herak, M. H., 3743
Herbans, L. L., 1122
Herkness, W. W., 3617
Hernandez, A., 5403

Hernandez, C., 1056
Hernandez, N. M., 1123
Herndon, C. A., 4089
Herndon, S. M., 1594
Herr, S. E., 5214
Herron, F. H., 5404
Hershey, P. R., 1193
Hertzler, V. B., 5175
Hess, A. M., 497
Hess, C., 3338
Hess, L. C., 241
Hester, M. G., 874
Heth, E. L., 1057
Hetler, L., 4729
Hewatt, V. E., 1205
Hewitt, I. J., 5117
Heyman, K. S., 4090
Hickman, G. A., 603
Hidalgo, J. T., 5405
Higashiuchi, A. H., 5182
Higginson, J. J., 3887
High, N. H., 604
Highbaugh, I., 1416
Highland, H. J., 3888
Higley, J. K., 5406
Hileman, E. M., 4857
Hill, A. T., 3889
Hill, B. B., 5407
Hill, B. O., 857
Hill, C. L., 3618
Hill, H. S., 5122
Hill, J. W., 5408
Hill, K. F., 506a
Hill, M. W., 5409
Hill, T. B., 2008
Hill, W. B., 4702
Hillis, M. C., 3036
Hillsen, H. H., 5410
Hindal, B., 4600
Hine, M., 4642
Hines, B. B., 5411
Hines, J. M., 4091
Hinn, H. T., 1232
Hinton, H. E., 1337
Hintz, C. W. E., 3091
Hippaka, T. A., 3369
Hirabayashi, G. K., 5176
Hirose, H., 2320
Hirota, D., 2389
Hissong, M. C., 4418
Ho, C. S., 2518
Ho, D. P. D., 1595
Ho, P. Y., 5036
Ho, S. O., 2554
Ho, T. C. K., 68
Ho, Y. S., 1596
Hoban, J. H., 3092
Hobart, K. G., 1299
Hobbs, C. C., 1338
Hobson, G. R., 3370
Hockin, K. B., 1417, 1597
Hodgen, M. T., 3890
Hodges, L. H., 5412
Hodson, J. E., 2009
Hoesch, A. C., 469
Hofer, M. R., 3206
Hoff, E. P., 445
Hoffman, B. M., 5110
Hoffman, B. P., 2390
Hoffman, M. L., 2256
Hoffman, M. W., 4419
Hoffman, T. M., 3744
Hoffmeister, M., 2010

Hoffsomer, W. E., 2321
Hogan, E. W., 4497
Hogan, M. A. V. V., 5413
Hoh, D. L., 1598
Hoh, Y. T., 1418, 1599
Holaday, B. E., 3619
Holbrook, S. V. V., 4498
Holcombe, W. M., 5414
Holden, G. K., 242
Holden, J. F., 1194
Holden, M. A., 4993
Holden, R. A., 1419
Holder, H. L., 5415
Holland, O. L., 2011
Hollar, E. C., 4092
Holler, M. O., 1600
Holley, T., 4994
Hollowood, M. F., 2012
Holmes, C. W., 3093
Holmes, K., 5416
Holmes, K. L., 243
Holsinger, C. W., 18
Holtrop, W. F., 4574
Holzschuh, A., 3745
Holzwarth, W. G., 4093
Honjo, Tomoko, 2391
Hood, A. L., 975
Hooley, M. E., 4094
Hooshmand, F. A., 2148
Hoover, M. V., 4095
Hopkins, T. F., 4907
Hopkins, T. W., 4960
Hopkinson, S. L., 5177
Hopman, A. N., 3746
Hopper, W. R., 4908
Horan, M. A., 4365
Horan, W. C., 3037
Horkan, V. J., 4420, 4583
Horner, L., 2392
Horner, N. A., 357
Horning, M. E., 1601
Horton, A. G., 4766
Houde, M. O. S. J. A., 5106
Houghton, A. B., 3620
Houghton, C. W., 741
Houle, B. E. T., 5215
Houlne, A. M., 3502
Hountras, P. T., 4961
House, H. L., 5178
Householder, E., 1602
Houston, N. B., 2393
Howard, A. W., 1864
Howard, C. W., 374
Howard, D. S., 5417
Howard, J. G., 3747
Howard, J. W., 605
Howard, M. D., 5418
Howard, N. C., 2257
Howard, P. P., 3891
Howard, R. G., 5419
Howe, A. L., 5420
Howell, J. M., 1200
Howrani, R. F., 2899
Howsam, R. B., 606
Hoy, G., 1603
Hoye, E. G., 3207
Hoyo, P., 4499
Hoyt, N. D., 3892
Hrvol, A. E., 3208
Hsia, J. C., 1604
Hsiao, T. E., 1420
Hsieh, C. S., 1421

Hsu, C. J., 1606
Hsu, C. P., 1605
Hsu, H. L., 1607
Hsu, J., 1422
Hsu, M., 1608
Hsu, P. S. S., 1609
Hsu, T. Y., 1610
Hsueh, H. C., 1611
Hsung, Y. N., 1612
Hu, C. H. J., 1423
Hu, C. W., 1613
Hu, I., 1424, 1614
Hu, S., 1425
Hua, A. C. T., 1615
Huang, C. S., 1426
Huang, C. S. N., 1616
Huang, J. C., 1617
Huang, L., 5037
Huang, S. F., 1618
Huang, T. C., 1619
Hubbard, M. E., 1620
Huber, M. A., 4500
Huber, M. C., 4703
Huddle, B. P., 2322
Hudli, V. J., 1865
Hudson, V. D., 2610
Huebsch, A., 3392
Huertas, M. C., 3320
Huff, E. M., 1181
Huffert, A. M., 4704
Huffman, V. B., 4868
Hughes, L., 3209
Hughes, L. S., 5421
Hughes, M. M., 5216, 5422
Hughes, N L., 607
Hughes, R. C., 4995
Hull, F. L., 858
Hume, L. N., 4096
Hume, M. M., 244
Hummel, W. F., 1621
Humphrey, L. R., 1622
Hung, K. W., 1623
Hung, M. E., 1624
Hung, W., 1625
Hunkin, A. T., 742
Hunt, E. L., 1339
Hunt, M. G., 3210
Hunt, R. B., 2394
Hunter, J. J., 608
Hunter, R. V., 4097
Huntington, S. D., 1206
Hurbli, A., 2895
Hurst, G. H., 1233
Hurst, W. J., 5423
Hussey, J. M., 743
Hussong, H. L., 3371
Hutchins, B. C., 4869
Hutchins, M., 4098
Hutchison, C., 976
Hutchison, S. B., 4767
Huttenhauer, H. G., 245
Hutton, H. K., 609
Hwang, F., 1626
Hwang, W. Y., 1627
Hyde, H. I., 4996
Hyer, J., 19

I

Iamsakun, P. P., 2928
Iballo, A. L., 2761

Ibanez, D. M., 2323
Ibanez, J. C., 2762
Ibrahim, A. F., 375
Ibrahim, F. S., 409
Idao, L., 2763
Iga, M., 5155
Iglehart, C. W., 2324
Ike, N., 2325
Im, Y. B., 246
Imoh, B. U., 470
Imperial, B. M., 2764
Ing, Z. T., 1628
Ingenhuett, A. H., 1195
Ingle, P. S., 5072
Ingram, D. B., 4338
Ingrum, D. L., 977
Inomata, H. B., 2395
Inouyne, I., 2396, 2397
Inshup, L. H., 3209
Inwright, H. M., 4099
Iobst, R. A., 538
Ioki, T., 2398
Irish, B. H., 5424
Irizarry, J. Y., 1124
Irons, H. M. C., 1125
Irvine, W. B., 4962
Irwin, H. N., 2972
Isaiah, S., 2013
Isarabhakdi, R., 2929
Isarasena, T., 2906
Ishizaka, M., 2326
Isidro y Santos, A., 2611, 2765
Ismail, S. K., 2174
Istavridis, V. T., 376
Itzkowitz, B., 2258
Ivey, A. J., 5425
Iyengar, N. S., 146

J

Jaarsma, C. R., 4575
Jack, H. A., 147
Jackiewicz, M. A., 4100
Jackman, C. F., 3748
Jackson, B., 3211
Jackson, D. E. G., 5426
Jackson, G., 4643
Jackson, L. L., 3094
Jackson, L. P., 5427
Jackson, M. B., 4501
Jacksteit, B., 3749
Jacob, T. N., 1866
Jacobs, S. V., 515
Jacobsen, J. V., 909
Jacquet, M. A., 1629
Jafar, N., 2175
Jafferi, G. H. A. O. K., 2567
Jahoda, G., 3339
Jalali-Shirazi, M., 2149
Jalili, A. R. al-, 2176
Jamali, M. F., 2177
James, E. G., 1168
James, E. J., 2014
James, H. M., 4909
James, H. N., 5428
Janes, H. E., 5030
Janney, R., 69
Jannuzi, L. F., 3503
Jansen, T. D., 4601
Janssen, A. M., 3095
Jaracz, M. D., 4611
Jarrett, E. A., 3504

Jarvis, J. A., 4705
Jauckens, A., 978
Jeha, A. M., 1307
Jellinek, H. J., 3621
Jen, N. Y. Y., 1630
Jen, P. T., 1631
Jenkins, R. E., 979
Jenkins, S., 5661
Jenkins, W. E., 4101
Jennings, H. C., 3893
Jensen, A. R., 5685
Jensen, A. S., 4594
Jensen, C. R., 5429
Jensen, J. C., 744
Jensen, J. M., 5430
Jensen, K. R., 446
Jenssen, H., 4602
Jerden, C. M., 5431
Jesena, F. M., 2612
Jewel, E. F., 867
Jewell, D. W., 19a
Jha, S. N., 1867
Ji, W. Y., 3621a
Jibiya, P. F., 1282
Jiggetts, J. I., 2216
Jiminez, C. T., 2613
Jira, J., 3340
Jiron, M. J., 5432
Jivanayakam, D., 1868
Job, C. C., 3505
John, T. T., 1869, 2015
Johns, C. G., 5433
Johns, R. J., 745
Johnson, B. W., 4102
Johnson, C. G., 5434
Johnson, C. L., 1340
Johnson, D. O., 5179
Johnson, E. L., 4677
Johnson, E. R., 4391
Johnson, E. W., 3212
Johnson, F. B., 4997
Johnson, G. B., 20
Johnson, H. D., 5435
Johnson, H. L., 4339
Johnson, J. C., 247
Johnson, L. E., 4103
Johnson, M. M., 5436
Johnson, R., 3728
Johnson, R. M., 5437
Johnson, T. C., 4104
Johnson, T. J., 5438
Johnson, T. W. D., 490
Johnson, V. L., 5217
Johnson, W. H. E., 4730
Johnson, W. R., 1632
Johnston, C. H., 4105
Johnston, P. B., 5180
Johnston, P. B., 5180
Jonason, J. C., 610
Jonata, C., 4502
Jones, C. H., 5135
Jones, D. D., 3894
Jones, D. J., 4106
Jones, E. R., 4107
Jones, F. A., 746
Jones, G. M., 3750
Jones, H. L., 5439
Jones, J. M., 4690
Jones, K. G., 5440
Jones, K. M., 248
Jones, L. C., 249
Jones, R. M., 70

AUTHOR INDEX

Jones, U. R., 1633
Jones, W. C., 5441
Jonsdottir, A., 4374
Jordan, R. H., 4963
Jordan, T. F., 4706
Jorgensen, P., 5091
Jorgensen, S., 3355
Joseph, K. D., 2016
Josif, G. D., 1326, 1341
Jover, A. M., 2766
Joyce, L. D., 611
Juan, K. C., 1427
Juan, V. C., 2767
Judd, A. R., 4108
Juliano, J. P., 2768
Jurado, L. M., 2614
Jurczak, C. A., 4620
Juviler, P. H., 4768

K

Kaapu, M. K., 5181
Kabat, G. J., 3393
Kabat, G. L., 71
Kachelhoffer, S. C., 516
Kaderli, A. T., 5442
Kaderli, J. N., 5443
Kadhim, A. H., 2178
Kahan, N. N., 3751
Kahn, H. P., 3213
Kahn, R. I., 3752
Kain, C. M., 1196
Kainer, M. C., 3753
Kaiser, A. L., 3895
Kajava, K. S., 3096
Kakouris, N. K., 4340
Kalathiveetil, T. K., 1870, 2017
Kalibala, E. B., 499
Kallio, R. I., 3754
Kamal, M., 410
Kamalanathan, G. S., 2930
Kambara, A. H., 5182
Kamber, F. R., 3506
Kammerer, V. G., 980
Kandaradally, J., 2018
Kandeel, S. D., 377
Kandel, I. L., 3623
Kandil, I. H., 378
Kane, J. I., 250
Kane, T. J., 2217
Kani, A., 2150
Kano, M., 2399
Kao, C. C., 1634
Kao, L. Y., 5038
Kao, W. C., 1635
Kar, A. L., 4612
Karbe, W. W. H. K., 3755
Kardos, L. I., 4369
Karlsen, B., 4910
Karnes, T. L., 531
Karoblis, A. K., 4503
Karp, B., 21
Karunyavanij, L. O., 2931
Kaser, L. S., 4341
Kashiwa, Y. I., 5183
Kasir, D. S., 2151
Kasman, S., 3097
Kasuya, Y., 148
Katzin, S., 3098
Kauffman, A. E., 4707
Kaul, J. N., 1871, 2019

Kavanagh, R. V., 4109
Kavetsky, J., 1058
Kawachi, R., 2327, 2400
Kay, G. M., 4998
Kay, L. O., 4708
Kayeum, A., 1323
Kayser, E. L., 3341
Kazamias, A. M., 1354, 3896
Kazem, M. I., 379
Keane, H., 4504
Keaney, L. E., 251
Keans, L. A., 2020
Kearney, M., 4110
Kearney, M. A., 3038
Kearney, M. W., 3214
Kearney, R., 4911
Kee, L. S., 252
Keelan, J. A., 3507
Keele, J. H. S., 5444
Keen, M. S., 5445
Keenan, M. E., 3215
Kehoe, C. T., 3099
Kehoe, T. R., 3099
Keim, C. Z., 4342
Keithahn, R. R., 4111
Kelleher, E., 3039
Kelley, C. A., 5446
Kelley, R. S., 4112
Kelley, W. A., 3624
Kelly, D. K. B., 253
Kelly, E. J., 4845
Kelly, K. L., 4769
Kelly, L. A., 4113
Kelly, M. E., 4114
Kelly, M. G., 747
Kelsey, J. M., 149
Kelsey, R. M., 5136
Kelty, O. B., 4999
Kemal, A., 2973
Kemper, H. D., 5137
Kendrick, A. C., 748
Kendrick, I. W., 3897
Kenefick, R. M., 5447
Kennedy, C. D., 2021
Kennedy, G., 4115
Kennedy, N., 3216
Kennedy, R. L. I., 5448
Kennedy, W. F. R., 612
Kenney, C. B., 3756
Kenny, J. P., 4505
Kenny, R. H., 22
Kent, J. L., 5449
Keown, S. F., 3217
Kerekes, J., 4366
Kerlinger, F. N., 2328
Kern, C. H., 72
Kessler, J. S., 323
Kettelkamp, G. C., 3625
Kettley, D. L. M., 517
Keyes, G. L., 4421
Keys, J. N., 1636
Keyser, E., 5000
Khaddouri, R. K., 2179
Khair, G. S., 1872
Khalid, A. R. M., 2180
Khan, M. I., 1873
Khanna, S., 2022
Khauli, B. K., 2974
Khouri, H. A., 1308
Khoury, J. F., 2551
Khury, L., 2479
Kiang, W., 1637

Kiang, Y. C., 1428, 1638
Kibitz, A., 4770
Kidd, J. R., 613
Kidder, J. E., 3757
Kidess, A. A., 2259
Kiefer, M. P., 2260
Kiefer, O. H., 254
Kiell, N. T., 4964
Kiernan-Vasa, H. C., 5001
Kilander, H. F., 4666
Kilani, S. F., 411
Kilcoyne, F. P., 3898
Kilfoyle, J. G., 5450
Killeen, S. M., 3508
Killelea, M. E., 1182
Killingsworth, M. L., 1639
Kim, D. S. C., 2563
Kim, H., 2519
Kim, H. C., 2494
Kim, H. K., 2493
Kim, I. S., 2520
Kim, S. J., 2521
Kimball, E. P., 3899
Kimball, L. E., 4644
Kimball, L. J. T., 2023
Kimmel, H., 4116
Kimura, Y., 2401
Kinberg, H. H., 1295
Kindard, E. W., 5451
Kindem, I. E., 4603
King, B. M., 2024
King, D., 749
King, D. A., 4117
King, E. M., 5452
King, G. N., 5453
King, H. B., 614
King, J., 2218
King, J. R., 5454
King, K. V., 750
King, R. P., 1640
King, S. C. L., 1641
Kingman, G. D., 3218
Kingshill, K., 2907
Kingsley, E. H., 3758
Kingson, W. K., 616
Kini, K. N., 1874
Kinnear, E. L., 3759
Kinney, M. A., 4506
Kinsey, L., 5455
Kippes, M. E., 4771
Kirby, C., 4507
Kirk, R. G., 3314
Kirkpatrick, L. H., 3509
Kirkpatrick, W., 4508
Kirkwood, K. M., 4118
Kirschenbaum, D., 5674
Kirwan, E. J., 4392
Kistler, R. B., 615
Kitajima, T., 2402
Kitchen, L. C., 1875
Klaeger, M. L., 3626
Klasek, C. B., 3760
Klavon, M. V., 73
Kleinas, J., 2403
Kleinjans, E., 2329
Kline, F. J., 1876
Klineberg, N. V., 5138
Kloyda, M. T. K., 3100
Knaggs, G. A., 3900
Knauer, J. E., 3761
Knecht, A. L., 3510
Knechtel, E. A., 2522

Kneller, G. F., 3627
Kneller, H. S., 2219
Knight, J., 5218
Knoflach, A., 4422
Knopf, A. C., 5456
Knott, W. W. D., 751
Knox, A., 3511
Knox, P. L., 2025
Knudson, E. R., 150
Knudson, R. B., 5002
Knudten, R. C., 2404
Kobuski, A. M., 4119
Koch, A. M., 1283
Kochanski, S. W., 3219
Koenig, J. C., 2026
Koenig, V. H., 4120
Kohake, C. P., 3628
Kohl, M. J., 1251
Koilpillai, R., 2027
Kohkba, M., 2220
Kolk, R. F., 2769
Koncevicius, J. B., 4570
Kono, A., 5184
Koo, D. C., 1642
Koons, M. L., 3220
Kopf-Seitz, C. E., 4423
Korb, E. A., 4912
Kosaki, M. D., 5185
Kosh, M., 4121
Kosmak, K., 4122
Kotb, Y. S. E., 380
Kouatly, M. A. H., 2896
Koury, E. M., 2181
Kowalski, A. N., 3221
Kraemer, D., 3222
Kraft, M. E., 3629
Kramer, K., 4576, 4584
Kramer, R., 4731
Kramme, C. I., 5457
Kreidler, C. W., 5662
Kreiner, L. M., 3040
Krishnayya, S. G., 1877
Krolikowski, W. P., 3366
Kroll, F. I., 3512
Kropf, L. I., 5458
Kruatrachue, F., 2908
Krulevitch, W. K., 616
Krumtum, J. C. M., 1186
Ku, P. S. Y. C., 3223
Kuan, M. J., 1643
Kuan, T. C., 1644
Kuehner, R. L., 4123
Kuh, K. N., 1429
Kuist, H. T., 2221
Kuki, B. I., 5156
Kumano, K., 2405
Kumarappa, J. M., 1841
Kundak, S. S., 2975
Kung, P. S., 1645
Kung, S. S. S., 5039
Kuo, P. W., 1430, 1646
Kurke, G. S., 3224
Kusuma Na Agudhya, T., 2932
Kustoff, A. P., 4645
Kutlug, B. R., 2976
Kuzhandavelu, K., 2028
Kwei, J. C. B., 1647
Kwei, M. T. H., 1648
Kwoh, E. S. U., 5040
Kwoh, Y. Y., 1649

L

Laboy, M. J., 859
Lacusta y Gascon, M., 2615
Lacy, C., 1650
Lacy, C. B., 1431
Lado, R., 5219, 5459
LaFlamme, M. D. J., 752
La Fontainerie, F. D., 3394
La Grone, E. R., 5460
Lah, K. H., 2495
Lahey, H. C., 3305
Lai, K. P., 5073
Laine, I., 3762
Lal, P. C., 1878
La Malfa, J. J., 4424
Lambe, B. M., 3763
Lambert, P. D. R., 617
Lambie, M., 74
Lanausse, E. Y., 1126
Lancaster, C. F., 618
Lancione, A. M., 4509
Lander, G. C., 497
Landon, K. P., 2909
Landon, M. A., 3513
Landschoof, J. A., 3630
Lane, I. C., 5461
Lane, L. S., 4124
Lang, R. A., 3395
Lange, F. C., 535
Langford, H. D., 619
Langley, G. J., 620
Langmack, C. J., 1234
Langsam, K. H., 3764
Langsam, W. C., 3765
Lanigan, E. M., 4393
Lanza, A. R., 2958
Lao Sunthara, S., 2910
Lapati, A. D., 5100
Lardizabal, A. S., 2616
Larimore, E. R., 3901
Larmore, J. C., 4125
Laroco, G. L., 2770
Larrabee, H. C., 3514
Larry, E. C., 4965
Larsen, J. E. A., 4678
Larson, H. R., 2029
Larson, K. E., 5099
Larson, P. M., 3356
Larson, V. C., 621
Larudy, F., 2162
La Russo, D. A., 4425
La Russo, W. A., 328
Lateef, N. A., 2261
Lathrop, J. C., 151
Latona, L., 5139
Latourette, K. S., 2498, 2505
Latshaw, M. L., 4126
Lau, K. C., 1360
Lauer, J. Q., 3225
Laurel, M., 2771
Laurie, E. E., 4127
Lavell, C. F., 4304
Lavernvich, A., 787
Lavigne, D. M., 753
Law, N. R., 622
Lawler, M. C., 4913
Lawler, M. I., 4510
Lawrence, H. S. S., 1879
Lawson, A. M., 754
Laya, J. C., 2772
Layague, E. C., 2773

Lazaro, F. M., 2774
Lazenby, J. C., 4914
Leaf, C. T., 255
Lear, E. N., 2617
Learned, W. S., 3631
Leary, D. B., 4732
Leasure, N. N., 316, 344
Leavell, U. W., 1651
Lebeque, D. E., 75
LeBlanc, E., 3226
Le Blanc, R., 755
Leckie, G. W., 3227
LeComte, M. V., 4128
Ledesma, M. M., 1127
Leduc, R. J., 756
Lee, A., 4129
Lee, B. D., 1652, 4130
Lee, C. H., 2406
Lee, D. R., 3101
Lee, H., 1518
Lee, K. C., 2523
Lee, K. H., 2524
Lee, K. Y., 2525
Lee, L. A., 1653
Lee, M. B. T., 5075
Lee, M. O., 757
Lee, M. S., 5074
Lee, M. S. L., 1654
Lee, P. C., 1432
Lee, P. H. H., 1433
Lee, S., 1300
Lee, S. D., 5076
Lee, S. H., 2496
Lee, T., 4915
Lee, W. C. C., 1433a
Lee, Y. D., 2527
Lee, Y. S. S., 2526
Leech, L. M. S., 4131
Leedy, F. A., 4772
Leete, W. R., 2030
Le Fever, L., 3228
Lefforge, R., 1434
Leger, S. H., 1435
Lehman, M. M., 3515
Lehman, V. B., 5462
Lehrman, I., 2262
Lei, S. C., 1655
Leibell, H. D., 152
Leibell, J. F., 152
Leipziger, E. W., 2263
Leis, M. C., 153
Leis, W. W., 5463
Leiter, R. G., 4966
Lemmo, C. E., 4132
Lemon, H., 981
Lenaway, M. A., 3396
Lenhart, M. S. M., 4511
Lennon, G., 3516
Lennon, M. L., 3041
Leo, V., 4133
Leonard, M. J., 982
Leopold, Bro., 3042
Leopold, M., 4134
Lerner, R. S., 3397
LeSourd, G. Q., 3902
Leszynsky, H. L., 3229
Leuchs, F. A. H., 3767
Leung, F. Y., 1357
Levai, B., 4967
Levin, N. B., 5675
Levine, A. J., 3398
Levine, V., 4916

Levirs, F. P., 758
Levison, M. E., 23
Levit, M., 4733
Levit, M. A., 3517
Levitas, A., 4773
Levitt, M., 3306
Levitz, J., 910
Levoniam, L. J. K., 2977
Lew, T. T. F., 1436
Lewis, I. B., 1437
Lewis, J. L., 3043
Lewis, L. B., 4512
Lewis, L. J., 3102
Lewis, V., 787
Lexau, K. J., 3230
Li, A. C., 1656
Li, A. F. F., 1657
Li, C. H., 1438
Li, C. L., 1658
Li, C. M., 1652
Li, G. F., 1659, 1660
Li, M. Y., 1439
Li, Pao-chen, 1432, 1661
Li, Pei-chao, 5041
Li, S. F. A., 5077
Li, T. L., 1662
Li, Y. C., 1440
Liao, P. K., 1663
Libby, M. R. S., 3399
Licari, J. J., 4135
Liddle, H. V., 2031
Lide, J. W., 1664
Lieb, T. J., 3231
Liebman, R. R., 3632
Liefield, M. C., 983
Lien, M. E., 3103
Light, J. K., 3633
Light, J. T., 5157
Lighton, E. W., 5464
Lilge, F., 3634
Limcaco, E. R., 2618
Limper, H. W., 2264
Lin, E. C., 1441
Lin, J. S., 1442
Lin, S. S. C., 1443
Linares, S. M., 860
Lindel, B. N., 4136
Lindeman, C. V., 256
Lindemann, E., 3768
Linder, E., 1342
Linderfelt, F. M., 5186
Lindquist, R. M., 5003
Lindsay, O. C., 2407
Lindsey, E. P., 2032
Lineberger, E. R., 3232
Linehan, M. S. P., 3233
Ling, C. L., 1665
Ling, C. S. H., 1738
Ling, H. D., 1666
Ling, H. T., 1309
Ling, P., 154
Lingenfelter, L. S., 3903
Link, S. G., 3904
Linskey, C. J., 76
Linthicum, J. B., 5465
Lintner, M. C., 4837
Lipp, S., 155
Liptzin, S., 2408
Lister, F., 759
Lister, R. W., 760
Lit, M. D., 77
Littell, H., 24

Little, A. M., 761
Little, D. R., 4343
Littlethun, C. C., 4621
Liu, C. E., 1667
Liu, C. F., 1669
Liu, Chi-hung, 1668
Liu, Ching-ho, 5042
Liu, F. J., 5043
Liu, H. C., 1445
Liu, H. C. E., 1444
Liu, I. H., 1670
Liu, K. S., 1672
Liu, K. Y. C., 1671
Liu, L. C., 1673
Liu, M. Y., 1674
Liu, Pao-chin, 1446
Liu, Pei-chang, 1675
Liu, P. S., 1676
Liu, S., 1678, 1679
Liu, S. D., 1677
Liu, T. F., 1436
Liu, Y. C., 1680
Liu, Y. S., 5044
Lively, M. U., 2775
Livingston, P. Y., 3769
Llera, A., 5466
Llombart, R. M. C. D., 5467
Llorens, J., 1207
Lloyd, E., 257
Lloyd, E. T., 3518
Lo, H., 1681
Lo, R. Y., 1447, 1682
Lo, T. C. Z., 1683
Lo, Y. I., 1684
Lobingier, J. L., 5094
Loboyko, G. J., 2978
Lock, E. D., 3104
Lodge, H. M., 5676
Lodge, M., 3234
Loewenheim, F. S., 4709
Loftin, J. O., 5468
Logan, C. E., 3635
Logan, L. M., 911
Logan, L. P., 5469
Logan, R. W., 882
Logan, V. G., 912
Loh, L. S., 1448, 1685
Loh, W. P., 1686
Lommen, H. L., 2138
London, R. E., 5140
Long, M. E., 3327
Loomis, C. D., 2409
Loomis, N. H., 5220
Loosley, E. W., 762
Lopes, S., 1128
Lopez, M. L., 5471
Lopez, M. S., 5470
Lopez, R. M., 984
Lopez, R. S., 156
Loram, C. T., 507
Loram, J. M., 518
Lorimer, W. C., 623
Losier, S. M., 624
Lotfi, M. K., 381
Lougheed, V. R., 4870
Loughery, M. B. F., 3044
Lovell, O. E., 519
Lowe, E. R., 5078
Lowrey, S. G., 4917
Loyes, M. E., 4622
Lozano, A. A., 5472
Lozier, G. C., 3400

AUTHOR INDEX

Lu, H. C., 1687
Lu, P. C. C., 1688
Luben, B. M., 2410
Lubovich, G. V., 4774
Lucas, J. A., 4679
Luddy, M. A., 258
Luebeck, B. H., 3770
Luhmer, N., 2411
Luis, A. N., 2776
Lujan, J. R., 5473
Luke, O. S., 4968
Luker, H. G., 4513
Lund, R. C., 1449
Lunden, W. A., 157
Lung, C. F., 1450, 1689
Lunt, O. A., 5474
Luqueer, F. L., 3636
Luse, E. M., 3771
Lutz, J. G., 1451
Lutz, M. L., 1310
Lyall, J. C., 2033
Lynch, J. J., 4137
Lynch, R. F., 3235
Lyngdoh, H., 2034
Lynn, J. F., 4514
Lynn, K., 5221
Lynn, W. C., 4775
Lyon, E. S., 3519
Lyon, L. L., 5475
Lyon, S. S., 78
Lyon, W. B., 2528
Lyons, C. M., 763
Lyrner, A., 5695
Lyrner, P. J., 5695

Mac, Mc

MacArthur, A. I., 625
McAulliffe, J. O., 4515
McBride, R. W., 4138
McCaffery, E. M., 4139
McCain, P., 1452, 1690
McCain, R., 3105
McCalib, R. D., 5476
McCall, H. F., 626
McCall, L. E., 2933
McCammon, E. L., 5477
McCandliss, T. R., 1691
McCants, M. D., 4516
McCarthy, D. C., 3520
McCarthy, E. J., 985
McCarthy, J. P., 627
McCarthy, M. H., 4776
McCarthy, M. K., 158
McCarty, G., 2265
McCarty, M. B., 4394
McCauley, J. A., 3521
McCaw, W. R., 628
McClatchy, V. R., 259
McClean, V. P., 5478
McClimans, G. B., 4918
McCloughan, E., 4830
McConaughy, G., 3045
McCooey, D. L., 4919
McCorkle, F. M., 260
McCorkle, T. S., 4344
McCormack, M. B., 764
McCormick, H. P., 471
McCormick, J. W., 4140
McCormick, P. J., 3106, 4517
McCoy, B. B., 986

McCrainie, J., 5479
McCready, R. H., 331
McCue, G. S., 4141
McCullough, V. T., 5480
McCully, B. T., 1880
McCutcheon, W. W., 629
McDaniel, G. D., 5481
McDaniel, O., 5482
McDermott, J. C., 3905
McDill, W. A., 765
McDonald, B., 4142
MacDonald, H. E., 2777
MacDonald, J. L., 3522
McDonough, J. A., 4143
McDonough, O. G., 1167
MacDougall, J. I., 630
McDougall, W. D., 631
McDowell, B. C. F., 340
McDowell, E. G., 4814
McDowell, M. R. C., 4144
McEachern, A., 766
McElhaney, J. H., 2412
McElligott, T. E., 432, 3236
McElroy, A. P., 4646
McElroy, H. C., 3906
McElroy, P. S., 412
McElroy, R. L., 1129
McFarland, C. G., 3237
McFarlane, A. B., 767
MacFarlane, R. M., 768
McGavran, D. A., 1881
McGeehan, M. E., 4395
McGehee, E., 4145
McGehee, L. V., 5483
McGilliard, V. D., 358
McGivern, E. D., 4146
McGlynn, J. F., 3238
McGoldrick, K. A., 4920
McGovern, D. A., 4518
McGovern, J. R., 2330
McGrath, E. M., 261
McGrath, M. M., 4519
McGrath, P. O. T. C., 3046
McGraw, J. L., 4345
MacGregor, H. A., 632, 769
McGregor, R. P., 5484
McGuffin, R. L., 1311
McHenry, W. J., 2035
McHugh, H. V., 3047
McHugh, J. J., 987
McInnes, J. R., 5658
McIntosh, L., 159
McKay, B. R., 988
MacKay, V. A., 25
McKay, W. C., 989
McKee, W. J., 1882
McKenna, B. A., 4520
McKenna, D. L., 2266
MacKenzie, T. F., 4815
MacKenzie, W. H., 633
McKibben, C. R., 1692
McKinley, J. F., 2778
McKinney, E. R., 3342
McKinney, M. G., 990
McKinney, R. E., 1235
McKinnon, A., 770
MacKinnon, G. W., 771
McKnight, R. K., 5187
McKoy, C. F., 2222
McLarty, M. A., 4147
MacLatchy, J. H., 772
McLaughlin, M. M., 3401

MacLaurin, D. L., 634
McLean, D. A., 635, 773
McLees, W., 1312
McLellan, F. A., 774
MacLennan, D. G., 4710
McLennan, L., 5485
MacLeod, A. B., 2267
MacLeod, N. B., 636
McLeran, R. L., 4521
McMahon, C., 4396
McMahon, C. A., 4148
McMahon, C. P., 3907
McMullen, R. J., 1453, 1693
McMurray, H. B., 262
McMurry, D., 3637
McMurry, R. E., 3402
McMurtry, A., 263
McNiel, G. B., 5222
McNutt, T. E., 2779
McParlan, F. C., 3523
McPherson, R. G., 3908
McQueen, J., 775
McRae, W. A., 79
MacRury, N. O., 3524
McTaggart, E. L., 4806

M

Ma, F., 1694
Ma, K. Y., 1695
Ma, T. Y., 1696
Ma, Y. Y., 1697, 5045
Maas, A. H., 4711
Maass, E., 1313
Macalinao-Solis, M., 2619
Maceda, C., 2780
Maceda, D. S., 2781
Maceda, W., 2782
Macel, M. G., 5486
Machlin, E. L., 637
Macias, A. C., 991
Mack, E. C., 3909
Macmillan, C. J., 638
Maddalun, D. A., 992
Maddock, S. P., 1201
Maddux, H., 5487
Madison, B. Q., 3315
Madkin, N. H., 5488
Madrinan, C. M., 2783
Mafrige, X., 264
Magbanua, F. R., 2784
Mager, J. F., 4839
Magleo y Galecia, R., 2785
Magsarili, M. R., 2786
Magtira y Clemente, C., 2787
Maguire, D. C., 4149
Maguire, M. I., 4150
Magyar, F., 3638
Mahdesian, R., 1208
Maher, C. H., 3107
Mahone, L. L., 3525
Mahoney, J., 3471
Mahood, M. H., 1197
Majid, H. A., 2182
Majumdar, P. S., 2036
Majumder, K. B., 1883
Makarasara, C. K., 2934
Makary, E. S., 413
Makris, A. J., 4346
Malan, J. R., 508

Malan, W. D. V., 509
Malcolm, F. C., 341
Malefyt, P., 4712
Malherbe, E. G., 510
Malik, A. K., 1884
Malin, W. E., 3403
Mall, W. K., 2574
Malleis, E. F., 257
Maller, J. B., 2223
Malms, C. W., 5489
Maloney, C. L., 4151
Maloney, M. V., 2788
Malovich, B., 3772
Mamulu, M. M., 447
Manacop, C., 2789
Manalaysay, R. S., 2620
Manalo, I., 2790
Maness, M. M., 4152
Mangahis y Caro, E., 2791
Mangum, R. M., 2037
Manikam, D. J., 2038
Manikam, R. B., 1885
Maniti, V. R., 2792
Manley, M. F., 4153
Manley, M. O., 2039
Mann, C. W., 4855
Mann, L. M., 5490
Mann, L. T., 3239
Manning, J. J., 2413
Manosalva, M. M., 1252
Manson, A. M., 265
Mansoury, I. M., 382, 414
Manzo, R., 5491
Mao, P. H., 1698
Marcella, C., 5686
Marchese, A. H., 1130
Marciano, L. P., 1209
Marczynski, R., 4623
Marder, L., 3910, 4154
Mardiah, 2139
Maretzki, T. W., 4850
Margoshes, S., 3639
Mariano, P. P., 2621
Mariano y Romeroso, H., 2793
Mariano y Tiongco, A., 2794
Marique, P. J., 3316
Mark, L. E., 80
Mark, S. G., 1699, 1700
Market, J. C., 3526
Markham, L. C., 4522
Markham, R. F., 2959, 2979
Markowski, A. J., 4921
Marks, L., 3773
Marks, T., 4155
Marraro, H. R., 4523
Marsh, I. T., 266
Marsh, J. S., 317
Marsh, R. C., 3911
Marsh, T. H., 539
Marsh, V., 1131
Marshall, D. W., 3912
Marshall, E. A., 3527
Marshall, E. L., 5004
Marshall, F. L., 5492
Marshall, H., 4156
Marshall, M. V., 639
Marshall, T. F., 3048
Martel, J., 4632
Martin, A. Q., 1132
Martin, C. V., 3640
Martin, D., 2622, 2795
Martin, E. E., 4485

Martin, F. D., 776
Martin, G. R., 5493
Martin, R. P., 4969
Martinez, A. L. R. D., 1133
Martinez, A. S., 5494
Martinez, D., 5495
Martinez, I. W. D., 1134
Martinez, J. N., 1059
Martinez-Acevedo, R. I., 1060, 1135
Martinez-Alvarado, M., 2796
Martinez y Malaya, J. I., 2623
Martin-Valdes, M., 2624
Martyn, F. H., 1314
Martz, E., 4157
Maruyama, K., 2331
Marx, M., 5496
Mascarino, M. C., 3240
Mascord, E. F., 3774
Mason, D. E., 3528
Mason, M. E., 5005
Mason, M. G., 5677
Mason, M. P., 4524
Massari, G. C., 4922
Massey, S. G., 2575
Masso, G., 1136, 3108
Master, I. V., 267
Math, H. M., 4777
Mather, A. J., 4846
Mathew, C. C., 1886
Mathew, M., 1887, 2040
Mathis, M. J., 1454
Mathis, W. S., 3009
Matsumiya, K., 2414
Matsumoto, T., 2332, 2415
Matthews, A. P., 3775
Matthews, J. C., 640
Matthews, R. D., 3913
Matthews, W. C., 3049
Matthewson, M. E., 2416
Mattingly, A. S., 3914
Mattson, O. F., 4923
Matzigkeit, W. W., 5497
Mauch, E. A., 4347
Maurice, M., 4496
Maurin, R. B., 4778
Mavis, W. C., 2268
Mavises, S., 2935
Maxwell, A. B., 4158
Mayans, F., 5663
Mayer, H., 3241
Mayer, L. C., 5498
Mayer, L. V., 3641
Mayer, M. H., 3242
Mayer, M. M., 4159
Mayer, O., 682
Mayers, V., 5499
Maynard, J. A. F., 2224
Mayne, M. D., 4348
Mayo, J. N., 4713
Mead, D. E., 5141
Meader, E. B. G., 3915
Meagher, J. W., 641
Mecredy, M. F., 4633
Meebold, L., 1701
Meehan, C. R., 4160
Meesook, A. J., 2911
Mefort, C. J., 3776
Mehok, W. J., 4161
Mehra, L. C., 2041
Mei, C. Y., 1702
Melconian, V. D., 2269

Melegrito, G. G., 2797
Mellado, R. A., 1061
Mellein, M. F., 5500
Mellenbruch, J. I. K., 5501
Mellinger, A. W., 1991
Melrose, A. M., 1703
Melvin, A. G., 642
Mendenhall, W. O., 5502
Mendes, L. N., 4162
Mendez, A. M., 1062
Mendez, N., 1137
Mendez, P. P., 2625
Mendiones, R. C., 2912
Mendoza, A. C., 1063, 1138
Mendoza, O., 885
Menon, K. A., 1315
Menon, N. P., 2042
Mensendiek, C. W., 1455
Mensing, C. F., 3109
Menzel, E. W., 2043
Meras, E. A., 3404
Mercado, G. S., 2798
Mercer, O. R., 5503
Merchant, L. K., 5504
Meredith, B. H., 4163
Merideth, D. M., 4426
Meroney, G. M., 4376
Merill, A. F., 351
Merryweather, R., 5505
Meshizuka, T., 2333
Metal, J. I. R., 4831
Metaweh, I. E., 383
Metzger, D. E., 3777
Meurman, J. C., 2626
Meyer, A. E., 3642
Meyer, H. H., 3330
Meyer, W. T., 3643
Meyering, H. R., 268
Mialil, K., 2044
Miao, C. S., 1456, 1704
Miao, E., 1705
Michaelides, G. P., 4305
Michaelides-Nouaros, A., 4306
Michaels, L., 993
Michea, C. A., 5506
Mierzwa, D. R., 4970
Miester, A. R., 4164
Mikaelian, L., 2980
Mikami, K., 2417
Mikhail, H., 415
Mikus, F. P., 3778
Milanovich, A., 4802
Miles, D. W., 3405
Miles, G. W., 777
Miller, B. B. M., 5507
Miller, C. W., 1347
Miller, E. A., 778
Miller, E. E., 1888, 2045
Miller, E. M., 1139
Miller, G. A., 4165
Miller, G. C., 4166
Miller, H. E., 643
Miller, J. C., 644, 779
Miller, Leota Agnes, 4167
Miller, Louisa A., 2046
Miller, Margaret Elizabeth, 3050
Miller, Margaret Evelyn, 2956
Miller, N. B., 2270
Miller, R. I., 160
Milligan, C. I., 5508
Milligan, R. W., 5509

Millindra, C., 2936
Mills, H. A., 1174
Mills, H. R., 5510
Milmoe, M. F., 4525
Milor, J. H., 913
Mims, N. R., 269
Min, C. H., 2529
Minkler, H. A., 81, 82
Minogue, W. J. D., 3916
Minor, M. M., 3529
Minsky, H. S., 4691
Miranda, C. M., 5678
Misaki, H., 5188
Misawa, T., 3110
Mita, S., 2334
Mitchell, A. J., 5511
Mitchell, C. T., 3779
Mitchell, D. D., 4807
Mitchell, F. F., 5512
Mitchell, I. W., 4168
Mitchell, M. J., 3780
Mitchell, M. M., 5006
Mitchell, Q. B., 5513
Mitchell, T. C., 4349
Miyamoto, S., 5189
Mizuno, T., 2418
Mo, E. C. W., 1706
Mochizuki, K., 2419
Modell, D. A., 4779
Moe, K. O., 2799
Moe, K. O., Jr., 4858
Moffat, C. S., 2047
Moffatt, E. M., 1889
Moffatt, R. J., 4350
Mohanty, G. S., 1889a
Mok, P. K., 1457
Molefe, G. B., 520
Molinary, S., 1140
Molphy, R. T., 3530
Mone, S. S., 1890
Mongkollugsana, C., 2937
Monica, M., 4427
Monikura, S., 2420
Monleon, P. O., 2800
Montana, E. F., 2801
Monteiro, M. K., 1707
Montemayor-Magsanoc, B., 2802
Montgomery, C. M., 3531
Montier, E. W., 3781
Moomaw, I. W., 1891
Moon, C. W., 2913
Moon, S. E., 352
Mooney, A. A., 3244
Mooney, G. X., 914
Mooney, P. A., 994
Moore, B. G., 1141
Moore, B. M., 5514
Moore, D. E., 1202, 1289
Moore, E. C., 4307
Moore, F., 3782
Moore, F. G., 4971
Moore, I. M., 353
Moore, J. A., 5007
Moore, J. M., 1236
Moore, J. S., 5108
Moore, L. E., 354
Moore, M. A., 995
Moore, M. E., 3532
Moore, T. G., 4169
Moorhead, S. A., 3917
Moorman, R. H., 3406

Moos, H. J., 2048
Morales Rivera, M., 1142
Moran, M. B. S., 5515
Morelli, C. A., 4526
Moreno Marrero, J. A., 1064, 1143
Morgan, E. A., 5516
Morgan, G., 4924
Morimoto, S., 5190
Morishita, S., 5191
Morkovsky, J. L., 996
Morlan, G. K., 3918, 4170
Morphis, J. W., 997
Morris, B. J., 4171
Morris, E. N., 4780
Morris, J. G., 1458
Morris, R. P., 780
Morrison, A. B., 645
Morrison, C. A., 5517
Morrison, G. W., 433
Morsi, S. A. H., 416
Mortensen, R., 177
Morton, C. M., 1144
Morton, H. A., 2271
Morton, M. M., 5518
Moses, I. E., 2272
Moses, J., 2981
Moses, J. T., 270
Mosher, A. W., 83
Moskowitz, L., 4647
Mosston, M., 2273
Mostocky, V., 3343
Motmal, J. T., 2803
Motomiya, I. Y., 2421
Motoyama, E. C., 5079
Mott, I., 2049
Mott, J. R., 2505
Mottershead, N. F., 161
Moussouros, B. G., 4351
Moustafa, M. F. O., 417
Mow, A. C., 2050
Mowat, G. L., 646
Mower, A. P., 3245
Mowry, M. D., 5519
Moyer, E. S., 162
Moyers, R. A., 915
Mozia, P. A. A., 472
Mudge, R. B., 4781
Mueller, C. A., 3246
Mueller, J. F., 1065
Mueller, M., 3402
Mueller, W. A., 3111
Muerman, J. C., 1145
Mukaida, S. N., 4856
Mukerjee, R. K., 2051
Mukerji, S. N., 1892
Mukoyama, K., 2422
Mulcahy, M. N., 781
Mulder, R. L., 162a
Mulhearn, J. J., 1146
Mulhern, J. A., 4397
Mullen, M. F., 3533
Mulvehill, W., 4925
Mulvihill, D. J., 916
Muniz, A. C., 1147
Munoz, M. L., 1066
Munoz, R. F., 5520
Munro, K., 4308
Munro, M. G., 998
Munro, N. G., 3534
Munroe, J. F., 3247
Murdock, M. L., 4527

AUTHOR INDEX

Murphy, A. E., 1708
Murphy, B. M., 4172
Murphy, C. M., 1284
Murphy, J. X., 3535
Murphy, M., 1067
Murphy, M. J., 4528
Murphy, M. M., 5687
Murray, K. H., 782
Murray, R. A., 2335
Murray, W., 431
Murray, W. E., 3248
Musella, G., 4529
Muuss, R. E. H., 3112
Myers, M. M. P., 999
Myers, W. F., 2982

N

Nabholz, J., 3644, 3783
Nadkarni, V. M., 2052
Naftzinger, H. J., 3784
Nagano, S., 2423
Nagle, J. S., 1301
Najarian, P. H., 2543, 2552
Najjar, F. J., 2544
Nakamura, T., 2424
Nakano, A., 2425
Nakosteen, M. K., 2152
Nannar, B. T., 2938
Nanny, O. E., 5521
Naoi, J. Y., 2336, 2426
Naor, Z. S., 2274
Napaha, S., 2275
Napier, A., 418
Nardelli, W., 4352
Nardi, N., 2225
Nash, M. R., 1459
Nash, W. L., 1068
Nasir, M., 2183
Nason, C. D., 5109
Nasr, R. T., 2545
Nassim, G., 419
Nasution, S., 2140
Natesh, A. M., 1893
Nauer, H. L., 3785
Naugle, H. E., 1894
Naumann, T., 3786
Naval e Israel, M. G., 2804
Navales, F. C., 2805
Nazazario de Lopategui, M., 1069
Ndamse, C. M. C., 521
Neal, W. D., 4816
Nee, N. V. C., 1358
Neely, A. E., 5008
Neely, M. T., 1000
Neemuchwala, N. P., 2576
Negehi, M. L. el-, 384
Negi, L. S., 2053
Neider, M., 4173
Neil, L. D., 3051
Nelson, C. C., 2054
Nelson, F. B., 1895
Nelson, G., 5522
Nelson, J. M., 2337
Nelson, J. S., 4428
Nelson, L. A., 1460
Nelson, L. M., 4680
Nelson, N. K., 329
Nelson, S. F., 2276
Nelson, W. M., 844

Nemetz, M. G., 3113
Nesa, A. U., 2577
Nesbitt, P. B., 1001
Nestico, R. F., 3407
Nethercott, J. P. S., 783
Nettings, D., 84
Neubauer, G. W., 1237
Neuenschwander, M. H., 3645
Neufeld, H. V., 784
Neuman, S., 3249
Newberry, J., 1002
Newcomer, R. S., 647
Newick, C. R., 4847
Newman, B., 4648
Newton, D. M., 785
Newton, M. E., 3919
Newton, M. M., 4174
Neyhouse, D. A., 3536
Neysari, S., 2153
Ni, H. R. Y., 1709
Niblo, W. P., 872
Nice, M. D., 3537
Nicholas, C. K., 1316
Nichols, E. G., 2055
Nichols, G. C., 5523
Nicholson, E. S., 2056
Nicholson, J. H., 3787
Nickson, T. B., 1003
Nicola, P. C., 5524
Nicoll, J., 5526
Nicoll, J. S., 5525
Nicoll, M., 1004
Niebuhr, A., 3788
Niebuhr, H. E., 3344
Niehoff, M. A., 4649
Niemeyer, E. H., 5527
Nilam, N., 1350
Nilodom, A. T., 2939
Nilsen, F. R., 1710
Nilson, M., 4175
Nilson, P. E., 2983
Ninneman, W. D., 1711
Nir, A., 2277
Nish, D. L., 786
Nishimoto, M., 2427
Nishimura, S., 2428
Nishiyama, S., 2338
Nobis, G. E., 4176
Nobleza, E. M., 2806
Noce, L., 5142
Noguchi, H., 2429
Noguera, R., 2627
Nolasco, D. F., 5095
Nold, D. S., 5528
Nolting, E. L., 2057
Noonan, W. M., 3538
Nordgaard, M. A., 163
Norman, A., 3789
Norman, E. A. S., 4681
Norman, L. C., 448
Norman, J. S., 2226
Norman, J. W., 3920
Normington, L. W., 3790
Noronha, G. E., 1896
North, W. E., 3250
Nosser, M. A., 2984
Nothdurft, I. H., 1277
Nothomb, M. E., 3408
Novaes, I. R., 1238
Novelli, F., 4530
Nowlan, I. S., 5111
Nugent, J. I., 4531

Nusbaum, A. S., 4650
Nutt, M. C., 85
Nuttall, A. R., 3921
Nuxoll, M. I., 4532
Nyberg, P., 3646
Nyquist, F. V., 3114

O

Oates, M. D., 1253
Obama, S., 2430
Obara, K., 2431
Ober, E. T., 271
Oberst, M. S., 3052
O'Brien, J. R., 4926
O'Brien, M. C., 4398
O'Brien, M. E., 26
O'Brien, M. R., 5529
O'Bryant, H., 5530
Oca, A. S., 2807
Ocampo, P. S., 2628
Ochoa, H., 5531
Ochse, G. H., 272
O'Connell, G., 4399
O'Connell, J. F., 86
O'Connor, M. J., 2985
Odenthal, J. W., 5532
O'Donnell, C. A., 4400
O'Donnell, J. D., 4927
Oechsner, M. L., 3791
Oechsner de Coninck, E. G., 318
Oetjen, C. E., 5657
Offenkrantz, F. M., 87
Ogden, R. C., 273
Ogunsanya, J. O., 473
Oguzkan, A. T., 2986
O'Hara, O. M. F., 1005
Ohberg, H. G., 4682
O'Hern, E. P., 4533
Ohno, K., 5192
Ojeda, P., 1006
Oka, W. M., 5193
Okeke, U., 456
Okongwu, N. J., 457, 474
Okonkwo, O., 475
Oktavec, F. L., 3647
Olcott, M., 1897
Olesen, E. W., 5009
Oliphint, H. L., 5533
Olivar, C. B., 2808
Olive, L. B., 1712
Oliver, E. L., 3922
Olmstead, C. E., 1343
Olney, P., 787
Olson, A. H., 3251
Olson, D., 3357
Oltmans, S. C., 2432
O'Meara, D. C., 334
O'Neil, A. J., 335
O'Neil, J. F., 4534
O'Neil, M. E., 4177
O'Neill, F. M., 648
Onishi, K., 5194
Opdycke, J. B., 4178
Oppe, H. W., 3792
Oravinen, L. O., 3372
Ordona, A. O., 2809
Ordonez, D. E., 2810
O'Reilly, C. T., 4429
Orellana, M., 1254

Oren, F. F., 3539
Orjala, P. R., 883
Orlandi, L. E., 1148
Orozco, J. E., 1007
Orr, M. T., 2339
Orr, W. T., 3345
Ortinez, J., 4651
Orvis, S. W., 2987
Osato, T., 3540
Osborne, C. B., 2811
Osepoff, V. G., 4782
Osgood, R. G., 1713
Osgood, S. M., 4179
Osgood, W. C., 1898, 2058
Osswald, E., 3648
Ostergren, D. L., 4667
Ostman, K., 4683
Osuna, J. J., 1070
Oswald, E. H., 5534
Otake, M., 2340
Otani, Y., 2433
Otis, A. O., 2590
Otomo, S., 2341, 2434
Overman, M. L., 3793
Overmyer, B. B., 4180
Overzet, C., 1317
Oviatt, D. T., 649, 788
O'Yang, S., 1461, 1714
Ozaki, T. C., 2435
Ozdil, I., 2960
Ozer, C. L., 3358

P

Pableo, D. B., 2629, 2812
Pablo, S. V., 2813
Pacana, C., 2814
Packer, B. K., 2278
Padolina, P. F., 2815
Paelian, G. H., 4734
Page, G. A., 5535
Pages, C., 847
Pagtanac, J. G., 2816
Paiewsky, I., 4182
Paik, H. K., 2497
Paik, L. J. G., 2498
Pak, M. H., 2530
Palace, A. L., 5536
Palacpac, L. A., 2817
Paley, D. E., 274
Pallay, M. E., 4370
Pallikunnen, E., 2059
Palm, R. A., 1008
Palmer, B. S., 2818
Palmer, C. W., 275
Palmer, M. E., 3115
Palmer, P. B., 1009
Palmer, P. E., 2060
Palminteri, P. J., 1010
Palsson, K. F., 4684
Pan, W. T. S., 1715
Panchaud, F. L., 3794
Pandit, H. R., 2061
Pandit, K. S., 2062
Pandya, T. R., 1899, 2063
Panganiban, F. C., 2819
Panish, K. S., 2914
Panlasigui, A. G., 2820
Paolino, V. A., 4536
Paolucci, H., 4183
Parada, S. G., 5537

Paras, F. G., 5113
Pardeshi, M. G., 2064
Pardi, C. F., 4537
Paredes, L. B., 2821
Parham, C., 319
Parikh, A. K., 1900
Parisi, A. G., 3252
Park, R. E., 1218
Park, Y. H., 5538
Parke, F. Y., 5539
Parker, A. V., 4184
Parker, B., 3307
Parker, L., 1302
Parker, L. E., 1267
Parker, R. L., 4185
Parker, V. W., 5540
Parks, H. A., 5010
Parks, V. E., 2065
Parr, E. E., 5541
Parr, J. B., 5542
Parry, E. L., 5543
Pascaul, M. C., 2822
Paschang, J. L., 3116
Pascua, E. G., 2823
Pastor, A., 1071
Patial, M. E., 2066
Patrice, A., 3253
Patterson, H. M., 3053
Patterson, L. P., 650
Patterson, V. C., 88
Patterson, V. K., 2436
Patton, W. B., 4685
Pau, R. M. K., 5080
Paul, G. C., 4353
Paul, H. H., 4186
Paul, M. D., 1901
Paulino, S., 2824
Pavamani, V. G. M., 1902
Pavda, M. J., 4538
Pavlak, M. C., 4187
Pawley, A., 2437
Payne, B. R., 3117
Peacock, A. E., 491
Peak, G. J., 5544
Peake, C. H., 1462, 2438
Pearce, C. S., 2279
Pearce, G. M., 2825
Pease, K. E., 1716
Pebworth, V. M., 5545
Peck, J. S., 3795
Peck, M. L., 789
Pedraza, R., 917
Peek, E. M., 1351
Peerman, E. L., 2531
Peet, A. L., 1255
Peffer, T. G., 3254
Pelletier, T. J., 3541
Pemberton, J. S., 276
Peninger, N., 5546
Penner, E. N., 868
Perada Oviedo, A., 1256
Peralta, C. G., 2630
Peralta, M. C. A. D., 2631
Perez, O. E., 5547
Perez, P. T., 2632
Perez, S. L., 1149
Perkins, E. S., 1717
Perlow, B. D., 3649
Perpetua, M. A., 4188
Perron, D. F., 2826
Perry, E. A., 1011
Perry, G. V., 3346

Perry, I. G., 4189
Perry, N. C., 5011
Person, P. P., 5693
Perz, J. R., 4634
Peters, F., 5143
Peters, M. M., 5548
Petersen, C. E., 5549
Peterson, A. E., 5012
Peterson, A. G., 4668
Peterson, B. O., 2827
Peterson, C. S., 4190
Peterson, H. H., 2560
Peterson, I., 5550
Peterson, L. D., 790
Peterson, R. A., 3796
Pettit, G. A., 532
Pfeffer, M. L., 3797
Pfeifer, E. J., 3923
Pflaum, G. R. R., 3255
Pfrommer, V. G., 869
Phabhavi-Vadhana, P., 2940
Phan, F. T., 2997
Pheley, G. E., 2280
Phemister, B. B., 4191
Phifer, J. V., 876
Philip, D. V., 1175
Philips, D. J., 1176
Philleo, H. I., 277
Phillips, B. L., 3542
Phillips, C. J., 164
Phillips, E. A., 875
Phillips, L. M., 2067
Pian, J. H. C., 5081
Pickard, E. E., 918
Pickett, D. R., 89
Pidduck, H. E., 4783
Pierce, L. E., 2988
Pierson, R. D., 1218
Pieters, M., 3543
Pietsch, D. J. S., 3798
Pihlblad, M., 3799
Pilch, J., 4735
Pimpalkhare, M. H., 2068
Pineda, J. C., 2633, 2828
Pinero, F. N., 2634
Pinga, E. G., 2829
Pithon Pinto, A., 1239
Pitt, M. L., 1177
Pittard, M., 4192
Pitts, R. S., 3256
Place, P. A., 2439
Plach, M., 5688
Planadeball, M. J., 1072
Plantinga, C. A., 3800
Plewes, D. W., 651
Plumb, C., 2281
Plummer, R. N., 4193
Poblador, H. G., 2830
Pockrose, F. M., 4784
Poladian, T. V., 2961
Poland, E. B., 5551
Policarpio-Mendez, P., 2635
Policastro, S., 4928
Pollock, M. D., 4194
Ponce, J. A., 1150
Poncel, J. A., 5552
Pond, E. A., 4929
Ponterotto, I. L., 1287
Poole, C. P., 4736
Poonpanich, R. R., 2941
Poos, F. W., 2342
Pope, R. V. D. P., 1210

Popkin, D. J., 4930
Poplofsky, S., 4195
Porrata, O. E., 1073, 1151
Port, G. E., 1012
Porter, E. O., 919
Porter, L., 5553
Porter, R. W., 5046
Portre-Bobinski, M. A. G., 5101
Poshakrishna, T., 2942
Post, G., 3118
Pott, J. H., 5082
Potter, R. E., 5013
Potter, W. S., 791
Potts, A. H., 1718
Poulter, M. W., 4817
Pousson, L. B., 165
Pousson, R. O. L., 4652
Povish, K. J., 3801
Powell, L. J., 3544
Powell, L. S., 4196
Powell, S. R. G., 5554
Power, H. C., 1013
Powers, F. J., 90
Powers, K. E. G., 3257
Powers, L. K., 4197
Powers, M., 2831
Powers, M. E., 5195
Prasad, R. L., 2069
Pratoomratha, Z. V., 2915
Pratt, E. C., 3258
Precise, A. E. P., 2070
Predmore, R. L., 5014
Preece, W. E., 3802
Preisinger, C. V., 3545
Prentice, J. W., 2071
Price, C. N., 5196
Price, F. W., 1463
Priest, B. J., 2636
Prince, J. W., 3924
Pritchard, D. L., 792
Prudell, H. O., 4198
Prudenciado, S. L., 2636a
Prudencio y Benitez, C., 2832
Przedpelski, B. J., 4614
Puderer, F. C., 3259
Pugh, G. T., 1014
Pugh, T. B., 5144
Pugh, W. R., 5197
Pumphrey, F., 91
Purcell, C. F., 5118
Purtell, A., 3546
Pushpanathan, M., 2072
Putnam, B. J., 92
Putnam, H. L., 5223
Putong, C., 2637
Pyatt, C. L., 2227
Pyke, L. T., 278

Q

Qadry, H. T., 2184
Qaysi, A. W. A., 2184a
Quintero, A. G., 1074
Quirante, L. L., 2638
Quraishi, R. A., 1903
Quraishi, Z., 2568

R

Raab, L., 3311

Rabenort, W. L., 4577
Rabuka, M. M., 4785
Rabus, M., 4309
Radner, S. R., 4199
Radwad, A. A. A., 385
Raeppel, J. E., 279
Raheem, A. H. al-, 2185
Rai, D. M., 2073
Raichur, S. S., 1904
Rainbolt, H., 5555
Rainbow, E. L., 4200
Rainwater, V. B., 4201
Rajamanickam, I. J., 2074, 2075
Ramaila, H. S., 522
Ramanjulu, V., 2076
Ramaseshan, P. H., 2077
Ramirez, E. C., 2639
Ramirez, H., 1257
Ramirez, M. D. C., 4653
Ramirez, M. M., 1152
Ramirez, S. L., 5556
Ramirez-Lopez, R., 1075, 3260
Ramoran, Q., 2833
Ramos, A. C., 2834
Ramos, G. C., 1153
Ramras, J., 3803
Ramsay, M. P., 3547
Ramsey, K. H., 3548
Ramsey, L. S., 5557
Ranasinghe, V. S. A., 1296
Randall, D. F., 280
Randall, H. M., 1293
Randall, J. D., 4585
Randals, E. H., 5558
Randel, M. C., 5559
Randell, A. R., 2282
Randels, G. B., 3650
Randen, G. V., 4586
Rao, N. S. S., 1918
Rapier, C. E., 476
Rappaport, M. E., 4202
Raquel, M. R., 2835
Raqueno, P. G., 2836
Raquiza, P. F., 2837
Rasco, L. S., 5560
Rascoli, J. M., 2163
Rashid, R. J., 2569
Ratanakul, S., 2916
Ratcliffe, R. S., 3925
Rathburn, L. M., 4714
Ratikanoke, T., 2943
Ratkovich, M. M., 4803
Rauwolf, H. L., 4203
Raval, S. N., 2078
Raven, L. M. L., 5561
Rawi, M. H. al-, 2197
Rawlinson, K., 5562
Raymond, S. P., 2079
Rayner, S. A., 4818
Rayos, B. F., 2838
Read, E. A., 652
Read, G. H., 851, 861
Ream, G. O., 5563
Reaman, G. E., 4871
Reardon, P. A., 3804
Rearick, E. C., 4367
Reary, H. S., 5112
Reasby, H. V., 523
Reasoner, E. M., 1240
Rectenwald, J. W., 540

AUTHOR INDEX

Rector, L. E., 3409
Reddy, D., 2080
Reddy, E. C., 2081
Redick, J. P., 281
Redmond, C. F., 3410
Redmond, J., 3411
Reed, A. M., 4654
Reed, C. A., 1303
Reed, D., 5123
Reed, G. S., 4786
Reed, M. D., 5564
Rees, R. E., 653
Reese, S. R., 4787
Reeve, W. D., 3946
Reeves, A. W., 654
Reeves, G. E., 5565
Reeves, W. A., 5566
Regenstreif, I., 4204
Rehnstrom, A. E. A., 4669
Reich, S., 3000
Reichmann, L. D., 4539
Reid, A. W., 4540
Reid, C. F., 166
Reid, J. I., 4831
Reid, P. M., 4931
Reid, W. D., 793
Reilly, J. J., 4832
Reilman, A. H., 4205
Reinemund, G., 4655
Reiner, R. O., 2532
Reinert, P. C., 3549
Reithmeier, A., 862
Rejebian, S. M., 2989
Rempel, A. M., 4872
Renner, R. R., 5224
Renson, R. P., 3321
Rentsch, H. J., 4206
Reo, C. E., 4541
Repp, A. C., 4310
Resanontha, P., 2944
Ressing, C. P., 3119
Resume, R. G., 1015
Retief, M. W., 310
Reuthinger, H., 5567
Rex, F. J., 5225
Rex, M. B., 3926
Reyes, F. S., 2839
Reyes, J., 5096
Reynolds, J. P., 4788
Rhoten, W. G., 2840
Ribeiro, L. D., 1905
Ricciardi, M. W., 1016
Riccio, R. A., 1076
Rice, B. L., 3550
Rice, G. P., 3927
Rice, L. E., 794
Rice, R. F., 93
Rice, T. D., 5568
Richard, Bro., 4207
Richard, E., 3120
Richard, I., 795
Richards, G. P., 2082
Richards, M., 1216
Richardson, F. E., 4932
Richardson, J. M., 5198
Richardson, M. F., 4542
Richardson, W. L., 655
Richmond, S. A., 4543
Richter, M. A., 3054
Riddick, M. L., 3928
Rider, L. A., 3929
Ridha, M. J., 420

Ridley, H. G., 27
Riebe, C., 3055
Rieger, E. L., 2283
Riese, R. I., 3261
Riger, L. D., 4208
Riggenbach, J. B., 4354
Riggins, R. T., 5569
Riley, M. W., 3121
Riley, V. L., 4209
Rim, H. Y., 2499
Rimawi, Q. M. el-, 386
Rinden, A. O., 1464
Rios, A. J., 4838
Rios-Castro, R., 1258
Ripoll, J. E., 900
Ritchie, M. H., 656
Ritter, D., 4210
Rivera, R. O., 1268
Rivera, V. L., 3262
Rivera, Z. N., 1154
Rives, F. V., 4211
Rizk, R. G., 387
Roach, J. W., 5570
Robb, J. A., 796
Robbins, C. L., 3651
Robert, F. D. C., 797
Roberts, E. C., 3412
Robertson, C. R., 5571
Robertson, E. I., 657
Robertson, M. B., 3805
Robertson, T. A., 1017
Robinson, C. M., 4833
Robinson, G. A., 5664
Robinson, G. C., 658
Robinson, G. E., 483
Robinson, H. C. S., 4819
Robinson, J. M., 3263
Robinson, K. E., 543
Robinson, M. S., 3551
Roche, M. L., 3264
Rochedieu, C. A. E., 3413
Rochester, L. M., 3010
Rochester, V. W., 1178
Rockefeller, J. D., 2346
Rockett, R. H., 3265
Rockey, C. D., 1906, 2083
Rockoff, G., 4737
Rodd, W. G., 1355
Roden, P. B., 5572
Rodewig, F., 4212
Rodil y Reyes, D., 2841
Rodney, T. C., 3806
Rodriguez, A., 1077
Rodriguez, O., 1078
Rodriguez Bou, I., 533
Rodriguez Diaz, M., 1079, 1155
Rodriguez Robles, J., 1080
Rodutskey, J. A., 3266
Roe, C. Y., 2500
Roebrocks, P. J., 4544
Roeder, W. S., 4430
Rogan, M. J., 4213
Rogers, B. B., 1719
Rogers, F., 437
Rogers, J. C., 3122
Rogers, M. E., 2084
Rogers, M. J., 1318
Rogers, M. K., 5573
Rogers, R. A., 798
Rogers, S. P., 438
Rogerson, J. B., 5015

Rojas, P. M., 1081
Rolland, W. A., 1720
Rollins, E. L., 5574
Rollins, W. B., 4214
Rolls, H. M., 5016
Rolls, R. L., 799
Romanow, C., 5145
Rongione, L. A., 336
Roniger, S. M., 4545
Ronning, E. G., 1721
Ronquillo, B. P., 1319
Rontas, K., 4933
Root, W. D., 2440
Roots, F. E., 5575
Roque, W. P., 4546
Rosa, A. C., 1352
Rosado, H., 920
Rosales, V. Z., 2842
Rosario, O. A. D., 2640
Rose, C. R., 863
Rose, G. H., 2843
Rose, H., 3807
Rose, M. J., 659
Roseman, N., 4547
Rosen, L., 3808
Rosenbaum, M. W., 4738
Rosenberg, L. W., 3552
Rosenberg, M. J., 2284
Rosenbluth, M., 1018
Rosenthal, A. G., 5665
Ross, D. L., 864
Ross, G. J., 660
Ross, M. A., 3930
Ross, N. F., 4548
Ross, R., 320
Ross, V. R., 5158
Rosselot, G. T., 492
Rosser, F., 3809
Rossi, M. A., 4431
Rossi, V. L., 5083
Rossiter, R. D., 421
Rosvall, T. D., 3810
Roth, A. S., 2228
Roth, J. B., 28
Roth, R. D., 2844
Rothstein, B., 4656
Rotimi, B. O., 477
Rotz, H. W., 2641
Roub, C. A., 94
Roucek, J. S., 3347
Rowland, C., 2439
Rowland, E., 4401
Rowland, W. M., 4215
Rowles, E. C., 661
Rowlett, J. D., 95
Rowntree, M. L., 3811
Roy, B., 1907
Royal, R. F., 3123
Royer, M. N., 2085
Royer, N. S., 1019
Royster, S., 4216
Rubenstein, D. H., 524
Ruby, J. L., 41
Rude, P., 1291
Rueff, M. E., 3267
Rugh, A. D., 1465
Ruhland, D., 3553
Ruiz, C., 1272
Ruiz, L. T., 5097
Ruiz, R. E., 921
Ruiz, V. B., 2845
Ruiz Bueno, M., 2846

Ruland, D. R., 282
Rung, J. R., 211
Runkel, V. M., 3268
Russell, C. P., 388
Russell, D. S., 4848
Russell, J. L., 4217
Russell, M. C., 3056
Russell, W. H., 2285
Rutherford, S., 3057
Rutland, L. G., 2642
Ruttenberg, J., 3414
Ryan, A. L., 2847
Ryan, J. D., 800
Ryan, J. Joseph, 4432
Ryan, John Joseph, 3931
Ryan, L. T., 5666
Ryan, M. B., 3812
Ryan, S. J., 4065
Ryan, S. N., 1020
Ryan, T. A., 4549
Ryan, W. M., 801
Rychlak, J. F., 5199
Ryder, S. W., 2343

S

Sabella, R. H., 2643
Saber, N., 422
Sacay, F. M., 2644, 2844
Sacks, M. L., 1320
Sadiq, I. K., 2154
Sadler, D. G., 4834
Saenz, A. N., 5226
Saenz, E. P., 5576
Saenz de Santa Maria, C., 873
Saez, F., 1082
Sagar, W., 2086
Sahai, P. N., 2087
Sahba, H., 2164
Saidla, L. E., 3269
Saito, M., 2344
Sakdapolrak, B., 2945
Saksena, B., 2088
Salandra, F., 5146
Salas-Diaz, D. E., 1244
Salas Silva, I., 1245
Saldanha, M. A., 1908
Salem, M. M., 389
Salemi, A. R., 4789
Salzman, S., 4218
Samaan, S. H., 390
Samaan, W. H. I., 391
Samonte, S. E., 2645
Sampson, A. H., 3813, 3932
Samuel, G. R., 2089
San Agustin, L. R., 2849
San Diego, S. M., 2851
Sanborn, M. L., 3270
Sanchez, C., 2850
Sanchez, E. B., 4657
Sanchez, G. I., 5227, 5577
Sanchez, L. G., 5228
Sanchez, P. C., 4804
Sandercock, G. A., 5147
Sanders, W. J., 3652
Sandhu, J. K., 1908a
Sandhu, S., 2090
Sandiford, P., 3933
Sandler, J. M., 4790
Sandy, G. H., 1198
Sanford, A. L., 2091

Sandguinet, E. N., 2646
Sanguinetti, C. S. B., 5667
Sanjume, J., 5200
Sanjurgo, G. H., 1198
Sanmann, M. S., 4972
Sano, C., 2441
Santayana, S. G., 4433
Santi, E., 4434
Santiago, A. A., 2647
Santos, A. P., 2852
Santos, F. A., 2853
Santos, P. V., 2854
Sapra, K., 2092
Saradatta, L., 2917
Sarafian, K. A., 2962
Sarhan, E. D. A. M., 392
Sarthou-Agoncillo, F., 2855
Sassani, A. H. K., 2155
Satakopochari, P., 2093
Sathranon, S., 2946
Saturen, P. I., 4219
Satvedi, H. G., 1909
Saunders, M. P. P., 5578
Saunders, R. J., 802
Sausjord, R. I., 167
Saute, A. E., 3554
Savi, B. P., 2963
Savran, W. S., 4791
Savvidis, A. P., 4311
Sawin, P. Q., 3653
Sayili, A. M., 168
Sayler, T., 5579
Saymon, I., 169
Scafati, G. D., 3124
Scaife, D. P., 5580
Scalisi, V. F., 4792
Scarpitto, M., 3415
Schacht, F. E., 3654
Schaefer, A. H., 2947
Schaefer, C. S., 803
Schaeffer, G. E., 5148
Schanzer, L. B., 4371
Schatnizky, S., 4220
Schemel, M. C., 922
Scherrer, G., 3058
Scherzer, A. L., 170
Schewel, H. H., 4658
Schick, S., 96
Schille, N. J., 3555
Schmerler, S., 4715
Schmid, R. C., 3655
Schmid, W. D., 4716
Schmitthenner, S. W., 97
Schmitz, M. F., 3656
Schmuller, A. M., 3657
Schnaper, M., 4221
Schneider, V., 5581
Schnepel, E. P., 3814
Schoenchen, G. G., 3308
Schooff, R. L., 3556
Schrader, A. F., 98
Schreiber, M., 4222
Schreiber, R. G., 3059
Schroeder, R. J., 2286
Schroer, C. R., 2442
Schroer, G. W., 2345, 2443
Schroff, R., 5582
Schubert, J. V., 3658
Schueler, H., 4717
Schuette, M., 5583
Schuetz, J. J., 99, 3125
Schuetz-Harkanyi, A., 4372

Schuiteman, R. A., 5229
Schulte, M. G., 2287
Schumacher, M. I., 4550
Schuster, E. B., 4223
Schutter, C. H., 1187
Schwantes, R. S., 2346
Schwartz, B. G., 4793
Schwartz, E., 3815
Schwartz, G. C., 423
Schwehm, E. F., 3816
Sciarillo, L. P., 4659
Scifres, M. L., 4224
Scott, A. S. W., 4973
Scowins, M. E., 4225
Scudder, E. D., 5149
Scully, G. M., 4974
Seago, E. B., 3817
Sebastian, M. P., 2856
Sec, F. F., 1722
Seda, A. L., 1083
Seda, J. I., 1156
Seeck, M., 1723
Seel, E. G., 1259
Seeman, L. W., 3271
Segal, A., 2288
Seguel, L. F., 1246
Sehapayak, S., 2948
Seidlin, J., 4794
Seip, W. H., 3659
Seitz, R. W., 1724
Sellers, G. H., 100
Semilla, F. D. J., 2857
Semmens, L. A., 1327
Semmes, C., 4873
Semprasat, A., 2949
Senn, P. P. L., 1725
Seppi, R. H., 3373
Serisawa, K., 5201
Serrano, J. T., 4551
Seto, Y. S., 1466
Sevilla, G. J., 2858
Shafi, R. S., 2094
Shah, L. K., 1910, 2095
Shahan, J. B., 4805
Shaltout, A. F. M., 393
Shanahan, S. J., 3272
Shanahan, S. T. O. C., 4226
Shane, M. L., 3416
Shanley, M. J., 3060
Shannon, K. C., 3818
Shannon, W., 1911
Shantappa, B., 2097
Shanthamallappa, B. L., 1912
Shanthappa, P., 2098
Shao, L. C. S., 1467
Shapiro, J., 2229
Shapleigh, M., 3819
Sharify, N., 2155a
Sharkey, C. W., 804
Sharma, G. C., 1913
Shastry, S., 2099
Shaver, F. E., 3557
Shaw, A., 2100
Shaw, A. H., 2444
Shaw, E. T., 1726
Shaw, G. J., 2101
Shaw, Job Chia-kwang, 1727
Shaw, Joel Chia-kwen, 1728
Shaw, L. J., 171
Shaw, S. C., 3273
Shea, E. A., 330
Shealy, K., 4552
Sheevers, H. P., 4227

Sheffield, B. N., 3274
Shehab, I. K., 394
Sheldon, A. B., 101
Sheldon, M., 2102
Sheldon, W. H., 5584
Sheley, C. F., 3417
Shen, E., 5047
Shen, K. C., 3820
Shen, W. C., 1468
Shen, Y., 1469
Shen, Y. C., 2533
Shen, Y. K., 5047
Shephard, W. H., 852
Shepherd, F. M., 1914
Sheppard, A., 4578
Sheppard, D. I., 3275
Shereshevsky, E., 3418
Sheridan, L. J., 4624, 4626
Sherman, C. L., 3660, 3934
Sherman, M. F., 4228
Sherry, M. E., 4553
Sherwood, M. R., 3558
Shew, L. L., 1729
Shibles, B. H., 4934
Shidler, W. L., 2445
Shih, C. K., 1730
Shih, H., 1425
Shih, H. J., 5048
Shih, P. S. T., 1731
Shikamura, A. H., 5202
Shilotri, P. S., 1915
Shimamura, Y., 2446
Shipley, C. M., 662
Shipp, F. T., 2534
Shipstone, R., 2103
Shive, J. W., 1021
Shively, B. F., 2447
Shklanka, E., 805
Shodhan, N. G., 2104
Shopland, S., 806
Shore, M. J., 4739
Shores, L. S., 3276
Shrader, R. R., 1732
Shridevi, S., 1916
Shrimali, K., 1917
Shropshire, O. E., 3935
Shuman, W. L., 807
Shumsky, A., 2230
Shute, C. W., 4312
Shutler, M., 283
Shuwarger, M., 5017
Si, M. K., 1344
Sian, R. S., 2859
Sibley, H., 4229
Siddalingaiya, M., 1918
Siddique, H., 2578
Sides, A. C., 3419
Sidhanta, R., 1919
Sidhu, H., 1920
Siegl, M. H., 3309
Siegmeister, W., 3661, 4795
Sies, R. W., 3936
Sievert, J., 102
Silberberg, I. L., 3662
Silos, D. G., 2860
Silva, W. H., 4230
Sima, B., 5585
Simms, E. P., 284
Simon, J. R., 4796
Simon, L., 4377
Simonaitis, J. J., 4571
Simonds, C. A., 3937

Simons, L. G., 2105
Simpson, C. M., 4718
Simpson, G., 2313
Simpson, H. F., 4231
Simpson, M. A., 4232
Sinclair, C. C., 4935
Singer, E. A., 29
Singer, F. K., 3938
Singer, L. M., 3559
Singh, H. K., 2106
Singh, R. K., 1921
Singhabhandhu, S., 2950
Sion, A. P., 5586
Sisson, E. O., 3663
Sisto, T. J., 1022
Sitasuwana, R., 2951
Skelton, J. W., 3420
Skillman, J. H., 2347
Skuly, J. A., 3560
Slattery, C. J., 4233
Slavitchek, M. G. W., 5587
Sledd, G., 3277
Sleeth, E. H., 2107
Sleven, N., 3278
Slifer, L. W., 2108
Smiley, V. B., 1269
Smith, Abraham, 3664
Smith, Autrey, 3821
Smith, A. D., 5588
Smith, A. H., 2990
Smith, A. M., 4234
Smith, B. A., 2289
Smith, C. A., 4235
Smith, C. D., 923
Smith, C. P., 4236
Smith, C. S., 1470
Smith, D. C., 663
Smith, D. M., 1733
Smith, E., 3561
Smith, E. C., 5589
Smith, E. K., 4355
Smith, E. N., 4237
Smith, Γ. E., 3279
Smith, Florence W., 1734
Smith, Frank W., 172
Smith, G. B., 4238
Smith, H. F., 1471
Smith, H. F. A., 808
Smith, H. H., 1735
Smith, H. R., 924
Smith, I. E., 1023
Smith, I. G., 5590
Smith, J. A., 3280
Smith, J. L., 4554
Smith, J. M., 4313
Smith, M. D., 925
Smith, M. E., 1736
Smith, M. J., 5159
Smith, M. V., 2501
Smith, P., 4239
Smith, P. A., 2448
Smith, R. K., 2449
Smith, S., 4797
Smith, S. I., 5591
Smithananda, P., 2952
Smulker, F., 5592
Smuts, A. J., 511
Smuts, M. N., 173
Snapp, C. R., 5689
Snider, W. D., 809
Snodgrass, C. B., 4240
Snow, L. J., 424

AUTHOR INDEX

Snowden, A. A., 3665
Snowdon, H. A., 810
Snyder, M. E., 3281
Soden, A. M., 2450
Sohns, H. W., 5018
Sokalska, M. A., 4241
Solis-Cohen, R. T., 3939
Solomon, G., 2109
Solomon, R. J., 2110
Somers, E A., 4936
Song, U. S., 2348
Sonn, M., 4242
Sonnack, I. A., 1737
Soo-Hoo, C., 1738
Soong, R. J., 5084
Soran, M. R. T., 1024
Soriano, D. G., 2648
Soriano, L. B., 2649
Sorscher, L., 2290
Sosin, G., 4798
Soudah, P. E., 285
Souri, J. D., 2111
Southwood, H. D., 3126
Southworth, J. V. D., 4243
Sowers, L. E., 5019
Spadaro, L., 3562
Spae, J. J., 2349
Spalding, M. R., 3282
Sparby, H. T., 664
Sparkman, C. F., 174
Sparks, G. T., 5593
Spaulding, D. M., 1025
Spaulding, S. J., 534
Spear, W. D., 4555
Speare, N. P. T. A., 449
Speas, G. M., 1026
Specton, S. H., 3939a
Speer, M. B., 1739
Speer, M. R., 3563
Speers, J. M., 1740
Speicher, N. F., 4556
Spell, L. M. H., 535
Spence, R. E., 665
Spencer, D. L., 2451
Spencer, E. R., 4244
Spencer, H. N., 286
Spencer, M., 3127
Sperry, M. G., 4245
Spicer, E. A., 4557
Spicer, S. T., 811
Spock, M., 3822
Spratt, M. C., 287
Sprinkle, E. C., 5594
Sprott, S. E., 3940
Spurgin, E. C., 4937
Sritanyaratana, S., 2953
Staats, P. G., 30
Stabell, C. C., 355
Stabler, E., 3941
Stack, J. H., 4246
Stackhouse, D. M., 5020
Stader, A. M., 3061
Stafford, D. K., 3666
Staines, R. G., 31
Stamper, A. W., 174a, 3062
Stanley, J. W., 926
Stannard, E. M., 1741
Stansell, S. S. S., 812
Stanton, G. E., 4247
Stanton, V. K., 4248
Stappert, M. P., 3823
Starmer, G. L., 2452

Starr, J. M., 4435
Stautland, S., 4604
Stavridou, H. P., 4938
Stayer, J. L., 3824
Stearns, V. H., 425
Steed, E. M., 1027
Steele, C. W., 4635
Steele, E. S., 1028
Steere, J., 288
Steeves, J. M., 2112
Stefan, M. L., 5690
Stegenga, P. J., 5092
Stein, H. F. A., 4436
Steiner, R. L., 356
Steinhart, H., 3825
Stenius, A. C., 3128
Stephan, L. V., 3826
Stephens, M. A., 289
Stephens, S., 4939
Sterck, L. C., 3322
Stevdi, H. G., 1921a
Stern, R., 525
Steven, W. T., 1742
Stevens, J. H., 5595
Stevens, W. A., 4249
Steward, A. K., 5596
Stewart, C. D., 865
Stewart, C. T., 4627
Stewart, E. E., 813
Stewart, H. W., 2923
Stewart, J. A., 814
Stewart, K. P., 290
Stewart, M. V., 290
Steytler, J. G., 479
Stidham, K. H., 4940
Stine, D. P., 32
Stoaks, C. E., 3564
Stob, G., 33
Stob, R., 3129
Stockdale, H. I., 4941
Stohl, D. D., 5597
Stoker, S. L., 175
Stolz, A. L., 5598
Stoltzfus, W. A., 2900
Stone, M., 4849
Stone, M. E., 3063
Stoner, S. L., 2113
Storch, M. F., 291
Stoughton, M. V. B., 439
Stout, K. D., 34
Stout, M. E., 103
Stoutemyer, J. H., 176
Stoval, F. L., 536
Stover, W. B., 2114
Stowe, A. R. M., 3942
Stowe, E. M., 1472
Stowe, G. H., 2453
Stranler, M. W., 2115
Stratemeyer, C., 3667
Straus, M. A., 1348
Strege, A. H., 292
Strelow, T. P., 3827
Strevig, J. M., 666
Strickland, A. E., 4250
Stright, H. L., 2291
Striker, E. P., 4356
Strong, N. B., 1743
Strub, H., 4558
Struck, J. W., 2186
Stryker, R. F., 3283
Stuart, H. F., 2650
Stuart, W. H., 1473

Stubbins, D. G., 5021
Stueckler, P., 293
Stuerm, F. H., 3011
Stueve, B. C., 815
Stump, L. M., 2861
Su, T., 1474
Subbukrishnaiya, E., 2116
Suchoff, L., 2292
Sudershahanan, R., 1921b
Suganthy, I., 2117
Suggs, W. A., 3828
Suh, D. S., 2350
Suh, W. S., 2535
Suhr, M. W., 2502
Suleyman, Z., 2991
Sullivan, A. S., 4437
Sullivan, M., 5022
Sullivan, M. A., 3565
Sullivan, V. F., 4660
Summers, G. E., 2293
Summers, G. V., 2561
Summers, H., 5599
Sumner, M. L., 4251
Sun, C., 3284
Sun, E. C. Y., 1744
Sun, H. C., 1475
Sun, P. F., 1745
Sung, D. N. N., 1746
Sung, K., 1476, 1747
Sutherland, M. M., 4808
Sutton, R. B., 3130
Swalestuen, E. D., 5600
Swanson, A. M., 2992
Swanson, E., 2454
Sweeney, J. A., 816
Sweeney, M., 3566
Swift, R. D., 2562
Sykes, N. J., 3285
Synan, M. B., 337
Szabo, S., 4373

T

Taai, W. K., 1477
Taam, C. W., 1478
Taam, T. T., 5085
Tack, M. P., 5601
Tadena, T. P., 2651
Tadmor, S., 2231
Taffel, A., 3567
Tagore, R., 1878
Taher, M. T., 2480
Tai, Chen-hwa, 1479
Tai, Chin-hsieo, 1480
Tai, S. C., 1748
Tait, J. W., 5124
Tait, M. J., 2118
Tait, R. R., 5602
Tajima, M. H., 2455
Takaki, T., 5160
Takayama, K., 2351
Takayama, W. K., 2456
Takenaka, J., 2457
Takeuchi, M. M., 2458
Takht Singh, P., 1922
Takla, A. I., 426
Talbott, G. A., 4252
Tamayo, M. L., 1285
Tan, C. Y., 1478
Tan, F. C., 2862
Tan, G. L., 1328

Tan, H., 2964, 2993
Tan, J. M., 1481
Tan, S. L., 1749
Tanaka, J., 2459
Tandler, F. M., 4740
Taneji, V. B., 1923
Tang, C. H., 1750
Tang, M. R., 1751
Tang, T. W., 1752
Tangco, C. G., 2863
Tantawi, A. M. O., 395
Tappert, E. E., 177
Taraki, M. R., 1324
Taraska, M. I., 4559
Tarcher, M., 4438
Tarrou, D. I., 4357
Tata, L. P., 5603
Tateossian, A., 2994
Tatnall, E. C., 2198
Tavel, D. Z., 1188
Taw, F. M., 1329
Taylor, C. R., 1029
Taylor, D. M., 2460
Taylor, E. M., 104
Taylor, G. B., 1211
Taylor, H. F., 5604
Taylor, J. F., 5605
Taylor, J. H. R., 4942
Taylor, J. W., 3668
Taylor, M. C., 5606
Taylor, M. R., 1030
Taylor, N. P., 1330
Taylor, P. V., 1482
Taylor, W. S., 3286
Teasdale, R. H., 105
Tefft, L. G., 3568
Tegner, O. H., 4670
Tehie, J. T., 3331
Tejada, M. C., 1286
Teller, J. D., 4253
Ten Brinke, D. P., 4254
Teng, T. C., 178
Terman, E. L., 35
Terner, H., 3569
Terry, W. R., 3516
Terry, Z., 1241
Thaung, M. B., 1331
Thearle, B. J., 4255
Theno, E. C., 3317
Thibault, M. O. B., 4358
Thibeau, P. W., 667
Thoburn, I., 1924
Thom, E. W. C., 1483
Thomas, A. M., 4943
Thomas, D. F., 4256
Thomas, H. H., 493
Thomas, M. E., 4605
Thomas, R. L., 5607
Thomas, R. M., 3287
Thomas, R. M. H., 1753
Thomas, W. T., 2352
Thompson, D. F., 3943
Thompson, F. J., 4378
Thompson, K. L., 3012
Thompson,, M. A., 3829
Thompson, M. C., 427
Thompson, M. M., 4439, 4944
Thompson, M. S., 870
Thompson, S. H., 3288
Thomson, M. C., 1754
Thomson, M. U., 3367
Thomson, R. H., 5161

Thomte, R., 3359, 3368
Thorndike, E. L., 3013, 3064
Thornton, E. W., 2864
Thurber, C. H., 3131
Thurston, H. H., 3289
Thwe, M. K., 1345
Tibesar, A. S., 1278
Tien, S. K., 1755
Tierney, M. C., 4560
Timmons, H. P., 817
Tinder, C. E., 5608
Ting, I., 1756
Tinsley, A. I., 4561
Tint, M. S., 1346
Tiojanco, L., 2865
Tiro, A. A., 2652
Tirona, R. S., 2866
Tjolle, R., 3323
Tobey, C. S., 4257
Tobin, F. A., 4359
Tobin, M. A., 4258
Todd, A. J., 179
Todd, H. J., 818
Toddhunter, L. E., 5609
Toews, E. O., 3669
Togashi, T., 2461
Tolbert, G., 4259
Toledo, M., 2867
Tolman, L. E., 4260
Toma, S., 2188
Toma, S. J. al-, 2187
Tomlinson, L. L., 3570
Tomoyose, E., 4852
Tompkins, A. E., 3421
Tong, S. F., 1757
Tooker, D. B., 3014
Tormay, M. C., 1031
Torrance, A. F., 2653
Torre, C. A., 3290
Torregrosa Rivera, F. M., 1157
Torrijas, F., 2868
Tossas de Irizarry, L. V., 1084
Totah, K. A., 180
Touchstone, M. M., 4874
Touhey, M. E., 5679
Tovey, G. V., 3944
Townsend, E. B., 927
Tracey, H. A., 3830
Traina, S., 1158
Trainor, J. C., 928
Tramel, L., 5610
Trauger, W. K., 3945
Trautwein, M. C., 4945
Treff, S. L., 5611
Treick, E. L., 3831
Tremain, M. A., 2462
Treschman, H. F., 2536
Trevino, E., 1292
Triantafyllou, T. T., 4360
Trillo de Garriga, A. M., 1159
Trinidad, T. M., 2869
Trinidad, V., 2870
Triplett, W. G., 5612
Tronvold, H. L., 4606
Troth, D. C., 2871
Troxel, M. J., 2537
Trueman, G. J., 668
Trummer, W., 3832
Trzebiatowski, M. W., 4562

Tsai, J. Y., 1484
Tsai, Mark, 1484
Tsai, Mildred, 106
Tsakova, V. I., 2294
Tsang, C. S., 1485
Tsang, J. W., 1758
Tsang, Y. Y., 1759
Tsao, J. T. K., 1760
Tseng, M. H. S., 1761
Tseng, T. C., 1486, 1762
Tseu, T. M., 1763
Tsou, G. Y. C., 5086
Tsu, Y. H., 1764
Tsunekawa, Y., 2463
Tsuru, H., 2353
Tu, H. T. C., 1487, 1765
Tu, T. H., 1766
Tuan, R. D. S., 1488
Tuan Kwei, M. C., 1767
Tuason, R. C., 2872
Tubbs, L. L., 5613
Tuck, D. I., 1160
Tucker, A. R., 2464
Tucker, F. I., 2295
Tumbagahan, T. J., 2654
Tung, D. C. T., 1768
Tung, L. H. W., 2465
Tung, T. F., 1769
Tuohy, J. W., 294
Tupper, L. A., 819
Turechek, A. A., 3348
Turenne, M. O. B., 820
Turk, L. H., 1260
Turner, A. R., 4261
Turner, A. V., 821
Turner, H., 3349
Turner, I. S., 3946
Tuttle, L. J., 1770
Twersky, J., 3132
Twinem, J. M., 1771
Twiss, G. R., 1489
Twist, F. J., 822
Ty, E. F., 2654a
Tyer, M. C., 295
Tyler, B. B., 4262
Tyrrell, M. I., 3291
Tzeng, J., 1359
Tzovas, C., 4314

U

Udick, B., 1261
Udin, S. A., 4799
Uesugi, S., 2466
Uhl, C. A., 3571
Uhlenkott, M. S., 4263
Uka, N., 478
Ukeje, O., 458
Ukpaby, E. N., 459
Ulin, R. O., 5125
Ullah, S., 1925
Ulmer, F. M., 5614
Ulrey, D. L., 1032
Underwood, E. V. W., 2538
Underwood, H., 3572
Underwood, H. H., 2503, 2539
Underwood, M. L., 5615
Unger, S. E., 296
Unoura, K., 5203

Untalan, P. P., 2655
Upadhyay, S. N., 1926
Upadhyaya, H. L., 2119
Uprichard, E. M., 823
Urgell, F. C., 1085, 1161
Urnauer, M. F., 3833
Usdane, W. M., 3947
Utzinger, A. D., 3292
Uy, J. T. U., 2873

V

Vafa, J., 2156
Vakharia, P. H., 1927
Valencia-Vasquez, H. G., 1265
Valle, A. J., 886
Valle, R. H., 535
Vallejos, G. Y., 2874
Vallve, G., 866
Van, A. L., 1772
Van Camp, R., 3948
Van Doren, A. B., 2120
Van Graan, L. R., 512
Van Hook, J. O., 1773
Van Lierop, P., 2504
Van Putten, J. D., 1490
Van Reeth, M. E., 3573
Van Vliet, M. L., 669
Van Winkle, H., 2875
Van Zyl, A. J., 513
Van Zyl, H., 3949, 4587
Vance, F., 3834
Vanderbie, J. H., 3293
Vander Weele, E. J., 824
Vandraegen, D. E., 3950
Vangsnes, J., 107
Varias, J. R., 2876
Varis, F., 2995
Varki Varki, K., 1928
Varney, W. D., 2121
Varon, E. J., 3574
Varona, A., 2877
Varona, C. L. F., 1086
Vasa, V., 3350
Vaswani, H. V., 4975
Vazquez, H., 1087
Vazquez-Torres, E., 1162
Vedanagagam, E., 2122
Vee, L. N., 1774
Vega, M. D. L., 5616
Vega Brau, I., 1163
Vegher, M. R., 5023
Velasco, M. D. C., 297
Velasco, V. A., 2878
Velasquez, M. A., 2656
Velder, E., 3015
Velder, M., 4264
Veloria y Fernandez, P., 2879
Venugopal, K., 2123
Vergara, F. C., 2880
Vergara, J. R., 2881
Veringa, G. H., 4588
Vermald, V. F., 3065
Verno, C. A., 5680
Vernon, V. O., 1242
Vertanes, C. A., 108
Vetters, A. H., 5617
Vevier, E. I., 4265
Viado-Tuazon, R., 2882
Viault, B. S., 3835

Vicente, J. A., 2883
Vickland, E. E., 2124
Viets, W. T., 4266
Vijaya, S., 2954
Villacorta y Luna, E., 2884
Villanueva, P. C., 2885
Villareal, J. J., 5230
Villariba, C. A., 2657
Vincent, A. M., 1929
Vincent, H. H., 5618
Vincenty, N. I., 1088
Violanda, F. T., 2886
Viray, B. V., 2887
Vishnoi, S. L., 2125
Vlassis, G. D., 298
Voeller, J. B., 5024
Voight, H. W., 109
Voight, W. W., 4361
Von Mohrenschildt, D. S., 3133
Von Wenck, K., 3351
Von Winning, H. L., 299
Votaw, P. D., 359
Vu, I. T., 2998
Vu, Y. T., 1321

W

Wachs, W., 5231
Wackerbarth, A. M., 1033
Wade, H. A., 3294
Wade, N. A., 3951
Wager, C. E., 5619
Wagner, M. B., 2126
Wahl, C. A., 526
Waide, F. G., 670
Waits, L. A., 5620
Walberger, K. L., 3575
Walch, H. J., 4267
Walch, M. R., 4692
Walcott, F. G., 3952
Waldman, M., 300, 2232
Waldron, R. E., 1775
Waldstein, D., 2233
Wales, B. E., 671
Wales, L. F., 2296
Walker, B. E., 672
Walker, Elita,
Walker, Evelyn, 3422
Walker, L. A., 4268
Walker, M. R., 825
Walker, T. A., 4269
Walkwitz, R. W., 110
Wallace, C. J., 3296
Wallace, E. W., 111, 1364
Wallace, F. M., 826
Wallace, M. A. L., 5621
Wallack, S. I., 5150
Wallens, J. W. S., 827
Walling, L. E. M., 4563
Wallis, E. S., 4719
Walls, F. W., 929
Walrath, P. L., 4661
Walsh, F. X., 828
Walsh, J., 3576
Walsh, M. C., 1034
Walsh, M. F., 4564
Walsh, T. S., 2888
Walsh, W. J., 4270
Walt, E. B., 3577
Walter, G., 1930
Wang, B. P. Y., 1776

AUTHOR INDEX

Wang, F. C., 1492
Wang, F. G., 1491, 1777
Wang, K. R., 1778
Wang, L. Y. L., 1779
Wang, M. S., 829
Wang, P. H. F., 1781
Wang, P. Y., 1780
Wang, S. C., 1782
Wang, S. K., 1783
Wang, Tung, 112
Wang, Tung-chi, 1495
Wang, Te-chung, 1493
Wang, Tsi-chang, 1494
Wang, Y. C., 1496
Wang, Y. K., 1784
Wang, Z., 1785
Ward, A. V., 830
Ward, P. A., 113
Wardwell, W. D., 1931
Ware, W. R., 4565
Warmer, G. A., 4589
Warner, K. P., 3297
Warner, L. V. A., 831
Warner, M., 2127
Warratie, S., 494
Warren, L. Z., 3836
Warren, M. W., 301
Wasson, A. W., 2505
Waterfall, E. A., 3953
Watson, G. M., 3670
Watson, H. T., 2467
Watson, H. V. R., 3066
Watt, M. E., 1262
Wattawa, V., 3298
Watts, A., 4271
Way, R. V., 5622
Wear, R. E., 181
Weatherby, L., 5623
Weathington, D. T., 5624
Webb, A. H., 2297
Webb, A. M., 4272
Webb, H. F., 2354
Webb, J. H., 1035
Webb, R. F., 5625
Webb, R. K., 4273
Webber, C. L., 541
Weber, D. A., 5681
Weber, M. A., 302
Webster, F. C., 3578
Webster, J. B., 1497
Wee, K. A., 1498
Weefur, M. K., 450
Weeks, H. L., 673
Wei, W. S. S., 1499, 1786
Wei, Y. C., 1500
Wei, Y. T., 1787
Weible, G. M., 2468
Weibusch, M., 5626
Weil, T. T., 3299
Weinbaum, L. L., 5682
Weiner, M. M., 114
Weir, E. G., 3954
Weir, M. B., 4274
Weir, W. W., 1353
Weiss, D., 3837
Weitzdorfer, R., 3838
Weitzel, E. J., 3579
Weitzel, T. R., 5627
Wekel, M. F., 832
Welch, M. M., 1788
Weller, E. D. H., 1179
Wellman, C. R., 1089

Wellons, R. D., 182, 303
Wells, G., 5628
Wells, G. A., 4720
Wells, W. M., 674
Wellworth, M. G., 4275
Welsheimer, E. L., 4276
Welty, F. A., 2298
Wen, L. C., 1789
Wentworth, E., 304
Werner, E. E., 4946
West, A. M., 1790
West, G. A., 5629
West, N. E. D., 4947
West, R. E., 2469
West, R. L., 4948
Westerberg, I. S., 4671
Westergaard, H. C., 5630
Westerman, W. A., 4820
Westphal, M. E., 3839
Wetzel, M. L., 5631
Whalen, J., 5632
Whatley, A., 2299
Wheaton, D. D., 3580
Wheen, G. A., 4821
Whelan, J. F., 4721
Whitby, H. R., 1036
White, A., 833
White, A. E., 5633
White, C. F., 5634
White, E. M., 834
White, F. L., 2897
White, G. C., 4278
White, G. M., 4277
White, L. C., 1037
White, M. I., 5635
White, P. W., 1791
White, R. F., 4566
White, R. M., 1792
White, W. B., 115
Whited, H. C., 5636
Whitelaw, J. A., 835
Whiteley, B. R., 4279
Whitfill, A. L., 5691
Whitford, R. L., 4822
Whiting, E. L., 2128
Whitsett, M. B., 4280
Whittle, H. D., 836
Whittle, M. A., 2129
Whitwell, C. G., 2658, 2889
Whitwell, I. M., 5637
Whyman, H. C., 5694
Whyte, J. P., 4835
Wiant, B. M., 1501
Wicks, R. H., 5638
Wiggin, G. A., 675
Wiksten, F. A., 3840
Wilbur, E. M., 2300
Wilcox, A. C., 5025
Wilcox, G. M., 4315
Wilde, A. H., 3423
Wilder, G. E., 116
Wilkins, C. J., 676
Wilkinson, R. C., 3841
Will, F. L., 4281
Williams, C. H., 5639
Williams, C. S., 3300
Williams, F. G., 1932
Williams, G. P., 5204
Williams, H. V., 5232, 5233
Williams, J. H., 5640
Williams, J. R., 3424
Williams, L., 3426

Williams, L. D., 5641
Williams, Lida Myrtle, 117
Williams, Lois Marietta, 1243
Williams, L. P., 3425
Williams, M., 4362
Williams, M. L., 3842
Williams, M. O., 1502
Williams, N. B., 1038
Williams, R. E., 36
Williams, R. I., 930
Williams, S. H., 3301
Williams, W. E., 5642
Williams, W. H., 4282
Willingham, D. A., 4722
Willis, J. L., 1793
Williston, H., 2470
Wilson, B. A., 305
Wilson, F., 4949
Wilson, H. A., 4283
Wilson, H. T., 837
Wilson, I., 931
Wilson, I. C., 838
Wilson, J. A. R., 677
Wilson, J. H., 5643
Wilson, M. E., 2301
Wilson, R. D., 839
Wilson, R. N., 1164
Wilson, S. M., 1794
Wilwers, N., 3843
Windham, M. E., 2130
Wingard, E. S., 2302
Winger, O., 4363
Winicov, W. R., 3844
Winn, J. C., 5644
Winn, R. H., 4800
Winsted, H. L., 3302
Winston, M. E., 306
Winter, C. E., 1795
Winter, J. E., 183
Winters, A., 2303
Wintrup, M., 1165
Wise, J. E., 184
Withers, C. D., 5645
Witherspoon, R. P., 4646
Wittenberg, M. E., 3581
Wittenbrink, B. L., 3845
Witucki, M. A., 4284
Woelfel, L. S., 3955
Woellner, A. L., 5026
Wojcicki, A. B., 4615
Wolf, F. E., 1332
Wolfe, A. D., 1796
Wolfe, A. W., 1039
Wolfe, J. R. M., 4836
Wollstein, R. H., 3582
Wong, C. H. S., 5087
Wong, F. F. Y., 1503
Wong, G. D., 1797
Wong, H. K., 1798
Wong, H. W. C., 4950
Wong, P. H., 1504
Wong, S. C. P., 1799
Wong, V. L., 1800
Wong, W., 1801
Woo, G. Y., 1802
Wood, L. F., 345
Wood, M. L., 4285
Wood, N. N., 3956
Woodard, W., 2471
Woodford, B. H., 3303
Woodhull, A. S. H., 185

Woodring, E. O., 1322
Woodruff, H. E., 4286
Woods, B. M., 2131
Woods, D. S., 678
Woods, M. F., 848
Woolcock, C. W., 3957
Wooton, F. C., 3958
Worthington, R. A., 37
Wright, C. J., 4823
Wright, D. G., 4163
Wright, Edwin M., 2165
Wright, Eleanor M., 1803
Wright, E. S. J., 3583
Wright, H. E., 2890
Wright, M., 1040
Wright, S. T., 4287
Wright, V. K., 4853
Wu, C. K., 1505
Wu, K. T., 1506
Wu, W. C. J., 1804
Wuensch, O. A., 5647
Wukitsch, E. O., 4288
Wulfeck, D. F., 307
Wunderlich, H. J., 2355
Wyatt, M., 4289
Wyburn, M. A., 4875
Wyeth, E. R. H., 4824
Wylie, J. F., 3671
Wynn, C., 3067
Wytrwal, J. A., 5655a

X

Xuto, P., 2955

Y

Yale, J. R., 1933
Yamagata, R., 2472
Yamamoto, S. P. A., 2473
Yanagimachi, N., 5205
Yancy, M. G., 451
Yang, C. I., 1805
Yang, E. H. P., 1806
Yang, L. K., 1507, 1807
Yang, S. C., 1808
Yang, S. H., 1508
Yang, T. W. H., 1809
Yang, Y. C. Eo-, 1583
Yap, D. M., 2891
Yasin, M. H., 2189
Yates, B. F., 5648
Yaukey, J. B., 1810
Ybarra, J. R., 5649
Yeager, B. A. S., 5650
Yearsley, R. E., 481
Yee, A. A., 5088
Yen, W. Y., 1811
Yeung, K. T., 5089
Yieh, T. K., 1812, 5049
Yin, C., 1509, 1813
Ying, K. S., 1814
Ylagan, F. R. O., 2892
Yoh, P. L. M., 1815
Yokogawa, Y., 2474
Yoo, H. J., 2506
Yoo, Y. S., 2540
Yoon, S. S. S., 2541
Yorke, G. C., 1189
Yoshikawa, T., 2475

Yoshino, I. R., 2356
Yosohachi, Y., 2476
Yost, J. W., 1816
Young, A., 5651
Young, B. L., 118
Young, C. I., 1180
Young, D. E., 4859
Young, D. T., 2477
Young, F. A., 3959
Young, H. B., 2166
Young, J., 2893
Young, M. W., 5652
Young, R. E., 4290
Young, S. S., 1817
Young, W. G., 4291

Youngs, J. P., 3063
Younis, H., 2190
Yousef, M. F., 396
Yousuf, A. M., 2234
Yowell, W. M., 4951
Yu, C. F., 1818
Yu, S. T., 1819
Yu, S. W., 5050
Yuan, P. Y., 1820
Yuhas, T. F., 3960
Yurgutis, M. A., 5654

Z

Zabriskie, E. C., 4292

Zachar, I. J., 4293
Zacofsky, W. J., 308
Zafar, S., 2579
Zaki, E. G., 397, 428
Zaki, E. M., 398
Zanelli, L. J., 4567
Zanfagna, M. L., 4440
Zangle, F. L., 5206
Zapata Rivera, L., 1090
Zearing, S. F., 4294
Zechman, H. W., 2304
Zeiders, C. E., 3672
Zeiger, C. E., 5653
Zeligs, D. F., 2235
Zellner, A. A. J., 1934, 2132

Zemel, H., 849
Zia, Z. K., 1821
Zieroth, E. H., 3846
Zimmer, S. R., 1822
Zimmerer, M. F., 3847
Zimmerman, C. E., 2133
Zimpfer, D. G., 4568
Ziprick, E. H., 4952
Zischke, J. B., 2478
Zobaie, A. J. al-, 2191, 2199
Zollinger, E., 1017
Zollo, R. P., 4295
Zook, L. M., 932
Zuniga-Tristan, V., 850
Zyl, A. J. V., 513

GENERAL INDEX

Includes names and addresses of all institutions in the United States at which doctor's dissertations or master's theses were written; previous names of these institutions, when different from present names; names of all countries and other political subdivisions concerning which theses have been written; organizations, institutions, and individuals referred to in titles of these or in notes on them; books and periodicals (with addresses) in which theses or abstracts of them have been published except abstract series issued by the institutions at which they were written; and miscellaneous topical and other references.

All references are to numbered theses, not to pages.

A

Abelard, P., 3048, 3534
Abendgymnasium, 3803
Abeokuta, Nigeria, 466
Abitur, 3710
Academic freedom, 2350, 3088, 3130, 3401, 3537
Accreditation, 2865
Acerca, G. M. S., 4660
Activity school, 3079, 3089, 3124, 3167, 3308, 3762. See also Dewey, J.
Adams, H., 3376
Adams, Sir J., 3928, 3960
Adams State College, Alamosa, Colorado. Master's thesis, 1216, 5432
Addison, J., 4232
Adelphi College, Garden City, New York. Master's theses, 2106, 3061, 3334, 3835, 5679. Other references, 3068, 4938
Aden, 226
Adler, A., 3698
Administration and Organization, 111, 119, 141, 171, 182, 303, 391, 470, 477, 546, 551, 589, 590, 593, 606, 608, 610, 619, 620, 622, 626, 632, 633, 640, 644, 645, 647, 652, 653, 654, 655, 663, 672, 680, 682, 684, 707, 727, 732, 737, 784, 788, 789, 791, 807, 816, 824, 838, 898, 906, 937, 939, 965, 1001, 1025, 1073, 1082, 1101, 1129, 1136, 1140, 1168, 1200, 1241, 1243, 1265, 1315, 1327, 1377, 1378, 1394, 1414, 1415, 1423, 1438, 1453, 1474, 1475, 1483, 1493, 1507, 1538, 1556, 1565, 1637, 1651, 1675, 1681, 1697, 1701, 1712, 1720, 1729, 1768, 1814, 1825, 1903, 1935, 1937, 1981, 1984, 2038, 2045, 2124, 2146, 2155, 2176, 2275, 2309, 2311, 2328, 2335, 2375, 2400, 2460, 2482, 2532, 2535, 2582, 2586, 2588, 2619, 2634, 2638, 2677, 2683, 2709, 2732, 2789, 2821, 2830, 2854, 2881, 3098, 3131, 3505, 3653, 3819, 3824, 3875, 3876, 3893, 3958, 3995, 4159, 4296, 4477, 4663, 4742, 4870, 4927. See also Financing of education; Supervision; Teachers salaries
Administrators, Education of, 4599
Adult education, 6, 14, 69, 143, 146, 161, 397, 398, 428, 476, 534, 648, 671, 675, 693, 817, 866, 1058, 1108, 1117, 1129, 1257, 1333, 1373, 1383, 1384, 1412, 1462, 1464, 1504, 1571, 1581, 1598, 1613, 1628, 1644, 1653, 1680,

Adult education (Cont'd.), 1686, 1754, 1774, 1853, 1862, 1898, 1905, 1945, 2009, 2051, 2088, 2103, 2111, 2231, 2337, 2565, 2572, 2608, 2960, 2963, 2986, 3126, 3164, 3662, 3746, 3890, 3947, 3988, 4010, 4155, 4160, 4190, 4615, 4670, 4740, 4743, 4861, 4882, 4904, 4905, 4922, 4945, 4947, 4980, 5001, 5052, 5120, 5219, 5231, 5351, 5402, 5514, 5551, 5565. See also Immigrant education; Literacy education; Women and girls, education of
Adventist education. See Seventh-day Adventist education
Aesthetic education, 136, 3213, 3645
Afghanistan, 1323-1325, 4972, 4975
Agricultural and Mechanical College of Texas, College Station, Texas. Master's theses, 1150, 5642.
Agricultural and Technical College of North Carolina, Greensboro, North Carolina. Master's thesis, 55
Agricultural education, 6, 69, 193, 382, 429, 431, 506, 629, 632, 675, 694, 932, 963, 1045, 1060, 1076, 1117, 1135, 1137, 1140, 1150, 1162, 1173, 1175, 1179, 1228, 1367, 1574, 1741, 1806, 1865, 1886, 1891, 1994, 2123, 2130, 2374, 2483, 2608, 2637, 2644, 2671, 2756, 2767, 2768, 2840, 2842, 2848, 2944, 3925, 4168, 4346, 4614, 4806, 4858, 5523, 5642
Ahmednagar College, India, 1944
Air Force schools, 212, 1109
Akron, University of. See University of Akron
Alabama, University of. See University of Alabama
Alabama Polytechnic Institute, Auburn, Alabama. Master's thesis, 3696
Albania, 3304, 5001, 5027
Albert, Saint, 4446
Albert the Great, 3812
Alberta. See preceding No. 545
Alberti, L. B., 4433, 4444
Albion College, Albion, Michigan. Master's thesis, 1531
Alcohol education, 586
Alcuin, J., 3168, 4102, 4120, 4151
Alexeev, C. S. See Stanislavsky
Alfred the Great, 3921, 3937, 4179
Algebra, Teaching of, 263, 781, 1152, 1923, 2151, 3100, 3512, 3600, 3886, 4069, 4195, 5490, 5543, 5600. See also Mathematics education
Algeria, 331-337

Allahabad Bible Seminary, India, 1980
Alleghany College, Meadville, Pennsylvania. Master's theses, 57, 973, 1549, 3338
Alliance Francaise, 3562
Al-Nashr, L. A. A., 369
Amado, R. R., 4652
American Annals of the Deaf, Faribault, Minnesota. 265, 3063
American Baptist Foreign Mission Societies, 1340, 1985
American Board of Commissioners for Foreign Missions, 164, 268, 514, 2310, 2318, 2969, 2984, 3324
American College, India, 2057
American Expeditionary Force, Education in, 3029, 3455
American Friends Service Committee, 869
American Institutes of Bolivia, 1212, 1214
American International College, Springfield 9, Massachusetts. Master's thesis, 4881
American Journal of Theology, University of Chicago, Chicago, Illinois. 3423, 3663
American Occupation of Japan. See Occupation of Japan.
American Political Science Review, Washington, District of Columbia, 2311
American Samoa, 4804-4808
American University, Washington 16, District of Columbia. Doctor's dissertations, 2181, 2207, 2494, 2643, 4409. Master's theses, 74, 981, 1356, 1357, 2022, 2078, 2088, 2157, 2158, 2444, 2940, 2942, 3714, 4040, 4238, 4463
American University at Cairo, Egypt, 374
American University of Beirut, Lebanon, 217, 1303, 2547
Americanization. See Immigrant education
Amin, A., 369
Andover Newton Theological School, Newton Center, Massachusetts. Master's theses, 116, 1551, 1642, 1944, 2067, 2826, 2988
Angela, Saint, 4476
Angola, 338-341
Annals of the American Academy of Political and Social Science, Philadelphia, Pennsylvania, 2311, 3615
Antoniano, S., 4440, 4466
Aoyama Gakuin University, Japan, 2469

Appalacian State Teachers College, Boone, North Carolina. Master's thesis, 3775
Apprenticeship education, 222, 765, 1891, 2119, 3020, 3043, 3058, 3156, 3278, 4101
Arabia. See Saudi Arabia
Arabic, Teaching of, 2187
Araki, General, 2470
Arbeitschule, 3734
Argentina, 1199-1211, 4969, 4970, 4975
Aristophanes, 4349
Aristotle, 3112, 3127, 3168, 3224, 3227, 4312, 4323, 4327, 4330, 4338, 4352, 4363
Arithmetic, Teaching of, 263, 326, 463, 611, 792, 1300, 1310, 1561, 1603, 2011, 2087, 2274, 2589, 2712, 2939, 3094, 4576, 4931, 5240, 5375, 5380, 5392, 5491. See also Mathematics education
Arizona, University of. See University of Arizona
Arizona State College (formerly Arizona State Teachers College), Flagstaff, Arizona. Master's theses, 2374, 4194, 4915, 5242, 5246, 5252, 5279, 5310, 5348, 5424, 5474, 5534, 5619, 5626, 5627
Arizona State College (formerly Arizona State Teachers College), Tempe, Arizona. Master's theses, 66, 204, 936, 1610, 2425, 2577, 4619, 5163, 5341, 5440, 5520, 5579, 5603
Armenia, 2961, 2989, 2994, 5030
Armenian Church education, 2961
Army education, 416, 1317
Arnold, M., 3194, 3866, 3872, 3904, 3905, 3952, 3984, 4004, 4021, 4028, 4063, 4066, 4067, 4078, 4082, 4099, 4110, 4135, 4184, 4239, 4247
Arnold, T., 4004, 4035, 4174
Art education, 271, 274, 411, 424, 568, 570, 776, 802, 863, 902, 930, 935, 956, 958, 1036, 1064, 1112, 1142, 1143, 1161, 1163, 3114, 3311, 3337, 3626, 3764, 3842, 3975, 4062, 4226, 4292, 4309, 4370, 4790, 5310, 5361, 5598
Aruba, 293, 4969
Arya Samaj, 2041
Asbury Theological Seminary, Wilmore, Kentucky. Master's theses, 957, 2086
Ascham, R., 3201, 3962, 4097
Ashkenazic schools, 3015
Atheism, 4782
Athletics. See Physical education, and Recreation
Atlanta University, Atlanta, Georgia. Master's theses, 473, 879
Auburn Theological Seminary. See Union Theological Seminary
Audio-Visual education, 47, 97, 197, 202, 399, 410, 589, 616, 656, 659, 696, 702, 774, 887, 981, 1086, 1276, 1357, 1404, 1488, 1576, 1686, 1862, 1946, 1967, 2028, 2033, 2048, 2066, 2094, 2193, 2201, 2364, 2385, 2497, 2512, 2518, 2566, 2573, 2640, 2651,

Audio-Visual education (Cont'd.), 2672, 2813, 2874, 2937, 2955, 3128, 4243, 4613, 4856, 5363, 5459, 5478, 5481
Auer, L., 3140
Augustine, Saint, 183, 184, 189, 191, 203, 284, 286, 294, 331, 332, 333, 334, 335, 336, 337
Augustinian education, 196, 985
Augustus Caesar, 4550
Australia, 4809-4836, 4956, 4957
Austria, 3305-3311, 4959, 4963, 4975, 4985, 5001, 5020, 5083
Aztec education, 299, 897
Azuela, M., 936

B

Babylonia. See Iraq
Baccálaureate degree, 3025, 3256
Bach, J. S., 3763
Bachelor of Divinity theses, 47, 69, 80, 94, 97, 102, 292, 313, 346, 348, 355, 356, 431, 494, 516, 949, 1227, 1692, 1944, 2067, 2130, 2293, 2368, 2396, 2705, 2921, 2969
Bachi, P., 4537
Bacon, F., 245, 286, 3168, 3901, 3944, 4079
Bacon, R., 4288
Bahama Islands, 542
Bain, A., 4138
Bakafu, 231
Bank Street College of Education, New York 14, New York. Master's theses, 2928, 5307, 5674
Bantu education, 312, 317, 318, 338, 357, 503, 520, 521
Baptist education, 123, 346, 472, 657, 881, 992, 1217, 1253, 1293, 1299, 1326, 1336, 1340, 1374, 1985, 2067, 2121, 2680, 2826, 3005, 5282, 5398
Barat, S. M. S., 3546
Barbarin, E. G., 4642
Barnard, H., 3739
Barnard College, New York, 4950
Barth, K., 3111, 3218
Bartok, B., 4364, 4365
Basedow, J. B., 3110, 3174, 3630, 3721
Basic education, 903, 1862, 1884, 1900, 1909, 1921a, 1976, 2019, 2022, 2078, 2082
Basic English, 45
Basil, Saint, 2985
Bavinck, H., 4575
Baylor University, Waco, Texas. Master's theses, 945, 5386
Becher, J. J., 3684
Bede, J. A., 3569
Bedouin education, 2177
Belgian Congo, 342-356
Belgium, 3312-3323, 4957, 4970, 4975
Bellamy, E., 245, 286
Bellisle, Father, 729
Bello, A., 1260
Beloit College, Beloit, Wisconsin. Master's thesis, 3180
Benedict, Saint, 4468, 4471
Benedictine education, 3016, 3022, 3377, 4473, 4528

Bentham, J., 3906, 4042
Beontes, 3166
Bergson, H., 3378, 3383
Berkeley Baptist Divinity School, Berkeley 4, California. Master's theses, 104, 201, 202, 243, 346, 355, 881, 969, 1654, 1705, 1994, 2091, 2130, 2276, 2364, 2459, 2676, 2680, 2921, 4900, 5282
Berlioz, H., 3195
Bermuda, 147, 543, 544
Bernhardt, S., 3216
Bethel College and Seminary, St. Paul 1, Minnesota. Master's theses, 94, 431
Bible, College of the. See College of the Bible
Biblical Seminary in New York, New York 17, New York. Master's theses, 51, 228, 349, 356, 1229, 1235, 1240, 1271, 1571, 1581, 2133, 2300, 2301, 2360, 2379, 2526, 2947, 3182, 4245, 4897, 5087
Bilingualism, 20, 500, 505, 1091, 1104, 1141, 1159, 1328, 2187, 4717, 4865, 4867, 4868, 4896, 4920, 4921, 4931, 4934, 4935, 4976, 5014, 5066, 5072, 5079, 5083, 5088, 5103, 5119, 5122, 5133, 5138, 5207, 5209, 5227, 5304, 5346, 5436, 5496, 5511, 5520, 5592
Billiart, J., 3397, 3574
Binet, A., 3397, 3574
Binet-Simon Intelligence Test, 2751, 3572, 5005
Biology, Teaching of, 147, 389, 1632, 2674, 2776, 2851, 3091, 4728, 4838
Birmingham-Southern College, Birmingham 4, Alabama. Master's thesis, 3487
Black Death, 3007
Blake, W., 4017
Blind, Education of, 1893, 2002, 2016, 2243, 2461, 2546, 2807, 3132, 3292
Bloch, E., 4691
Blow, S. E., 4499
Bode, B. H., 2175
Boeckh, A., 3733
Boethius, A. M. S., 4456
Boletin Litino-Americano de Musica, Montevideo, Uruguay. 535
Bolivar, S., 223, 1182
Bolivia, 1212-1216, 4975
Bonheur, R., 3216
Bonsai, 2374
Booker T. Washington Agricultural and Industrial Institute, Liberia, 447
Borneo, 104, 179, 301, 1309, 2894, 4956
Borromeo, C., 4511
Bosco, G., 4423, 4442, 4451, 4455, 4457, 4460, 4475, 4484, 4496, 4522, 4525
Boston College, Chestnut Hill 67, Massachusetts. Doctor's dissertations, 26, 3099, 5100. Master's theses, 43, 828, 1012, 2473, 3202, 3365, 3464, 3483, 3538, 3706, 3741, 3756, 4011, 4027, 4051, 4143, 4160, 4352, 4380, 4385, 4390, 4393, 4398, 4441, 4455, 4636, 4776, 4832, 4913, 5056, 5103

GENERAL INDEX

Boston University, Boston 15, Massachusetts. Doctor's dissertations, 362, 376, 561, 599, 1188, 1189, 1297, 1434, 1904, 2212, 3921, 4365, 4610, 4669, 4867. Master's theses, 40, 41, 211, 261, 284, 308, 330, 542, 544, 705, 747, 787, 804, 837, 1009, 1092, 1160, 1311, 1515, 1554, 1560, 1570, 1576, 1602, 1629, 1659, 1660, 1675, 1723, 1725, 1751, 1764, 1788, 1790, 1821, 1963, 1964, 1991, 2002, 2016, 2066, 2070, 2081, 2094, 2097, 2271, 2291, 2294, 2397, 2402, 2439, 2454, 2516, 2521, 2546, 2754, 2935, 3024, 3050, 3138, 3154, 3175, 3179, 3189, 3218, 3219, 3265, 3279, 3292, 3300, 3304, 3325, 3360, 3448, 3471, 3477, 3514, 3524, 3534, 3561, 3578, 3700, 3705, 3716, 3725, 3728, 3758, 3825, 3830, 4055, 4065, 4130, 4139, 4174, 4179, 4217, 4283, 4295, 4354, 4453, 4485, 4491, 4589, 4676, 4681, 4840, 4841, 4882, 4922, 4926, 5106, 5145, 5339, 5658

Boswell, J., 3211

Bowling Green State University, Bowling Green, Ohio. Master's theses, 1043, 1283, 4084, 4093, 4877, 5585

Boxer Indemnity Remissions, 1418

Boy Scout Movement, 216

Bradley University, Peoria 5, Illinois. Doctor's dissertation, 459

Brahminic education, 1913

Brahms, J., 3195

Brazil, 1217-1243, 4970, 4975, 4988

Brazilian Naval Academy, 1230

Brethren in Christ education, 567

Brethren of the Common Life education, 99

Brigham Young University, Provo, Utah. Master's theses, 785, 786, 2161, 4902, 5436

Brightman, E. S., 3622

British Columbia. See preceding No. 545

British Columbia Schools, Vancouver, British Columbia, Canada, 597

British West Indies. See West Indies

Broadcasting. See Radio education

Bronte, C., 4264

Brooklyn College, Brooklyn 10, New York. Master's theses, 274, 5668, 5671

Brotherhoods, Teaching, 3125

Brothers of the Christian Schools, 367, 717

Brougham, Lord, 3879

Brown, T. E., 3986

Brown University, Providence 12, Rhode Island. Doctor's dissertation, 3923. Master's theses, 276, 3704, 4149, 4546, 4673, 4901, 5129

Browne, Tom, 3940

Browning, E. B., 3179

Browning, R., 4089, 4136, 4194

Bruno, G., 4448

Bryn Mawr College, Bryn Mawr, Pennsylvania. Doctor's dissertations, 3893, 3897, 4419

Bucknell University, Lewisburg, Pennsylvania. Master's thesis, 2844

Buddha, G. 1302. See also Buddhist education

Buddhist education, 233, 1296, 1305, 1320, 1335, 1352, 2360, 2458

Buffalo, University of. See University of Buffalo

Bugenhagen, J., 3769

Buildings, School, 2950, 3881, 4240, 5057

Bukh, N., 3363

Bulgaria, 3224-3227

Bulletin of the Department of Secondary School Principals, National Education Association, Washington, D. C., 4057

Bulwer-Lytton, E. G. E. L., 245

Burger, E., 3308

Burma, 1326-1346, 4956, 4957, 4970, 4975

Burt, C. L., 4109

Burton, R., 4202

Busby, R., 4277

Bushnell, H., 2419

Business education, 10, 60, 257, 307, 673, 768, 800, 918, 1092, 1106, 1147, 1283, 2196, 2484, 2540, 2786, 2924, 2934, 2958, 3217, 4217, 4238, 5297

Butler, S., 245, 4049, 4169, 4293

Butler University, Indianapolis 7, Indiana. (Formerly Butler College). Master's theses, 436, 1698, 1960, 4038, 4488

Byron, G. G., 3993

Byzantine education. See Turkey

C

Cadet training, 605

Calasanctian method, 3253

Calasanctius, J., 4651

California, University of. See University of California

Calvin, J., 3185, 3279, 4688, 4690, 4695, 4702, 4710, 4712

Cameroons, 357-359

Campan, Madame H. G., 3499

Campanella, T., 245, 286

Canada, 545-839, 4970, 4988

Canadian Broadcasting Corporation, 616

Canadian Citizenship Council, 613

Canadian Historical Review, Toronto, Ontario, Canada. 535

Canisius, P., 3706

Canisius College, Buffalo 8, New York. Master's theses, 822, 831, 1031, 2997

Canon law, 4543

Canonesses, 3090

Canterbury Pilgrims, 4211

Canton Union Theological College, China, 1699

Cantus Planus, 3006

Cape of Good Hope, 501, 504, 526

Cape Sable Island, Canada, 549

Capital University, Columbus 9, Ohio. Master's thesis, 102

Cappodocian Fathers, Education by, 2981

Carlyle, T., 1519, 4234, 4282

Caroline Islands, 4859

Carthage, Tunisia, 284

Casotti, M., 3124, 4486

Cassian, Saint, 183

Cassiodorus, F. M. A., 4467, 4520

Caste, 1996

Cathedral schools, 3042, 3514

Catholic education, 43, 76, 283, 289, 357, 600, 635, 695, 714, 718, 722, 725, 736, 743, 747, 763, 773, 820, 825, 828, 948, 955, 968, 987, 996, 998, 1015, 1019, 1065, 1122, 1146, 1181, 1454, 1589, 1656, 2018, 2044, 2079, 2450, 2580, 2612, 2997, 3019, 3035, 3037, 3052, 3056, 3059, 3063, 3067, 3090, 3099, 3106, 3116, 3125, 3150, 3187, 3196, 3215, 3253, 3312, 3318, 3381, 3432, 3440, 3446, 3486, 3526, 3785, 3797, 3823, 3847, 3855, 3867, 4068, 4161, 4188, 4415, 4508, 4533, 4535, 4541, 4549, 4747, 4826, 5100, 5684. See also Encyclicals; Popes; Theological education; Augustinian; Benedictine; Brethren of the Common Life, Brothers of the Christian Schools, Congregation of Notre Dame, Congregation of the Sisters of the Holy Humility of Mary, Daughters of Charity, Dominican, Franciscan, Jesuit, Lorettine, Maryknoll, Religious of the Sacred Heart of Mary, Sisters of the Sacred Heart, Sisters of Notre Dame de Namur, Society of the Divine Word, Ursuline education; Catholic colleges listed in the United States; Catholic colleges listed in this index under "Higher Education"

Catholic Educational Review, Catholic University of America, Washington, District of Columbia. 158, 232, 262, 421, 635, 667, 764, 801, 1296, 1975, 2044, 2257, 2336, 2395, 2426, 2965, 3059, 3075, 3106, 3378, 3396, 3475, 3496, 3613, 3801, 3865, 3867, 4128, 4159, 4198, 4235, 4375, 4420, 4482, 4524, 4551, 4570, 4583, 4607, 4608, 4649, 4652, 4653, 4692, 4693, 5313, 5486, 968, 2435, 4467

Catholic Historical Review, Catholic University of America, Washington, District of Columbia. 535

Catholic Sisters College of the Catholic University of America, Washington 17, District of Columbia. Doctor's dissertations, 158, 4303. Master's theses, 52, 218, 337, 2985, 3016, 3020, 3035, 3046, 3052, 3056, 3282, 3476, 3515, 3690, 3727, 3812, 4284, 4511, 4550

Catholic University of America, Washington 17, District of Columbia. (Microfilm copies of master's theses may be obtained through the interlibrary loan department of the University

Catholic University of America, (Cont'd.), library. Information on costs will be sent on request). Doctor's dissertations, 158, 165, 372, 635, 667, 1063, 1278, 1454, 1896, 2336, 3069, 3074, 3075, 3088, 3090, 3092, 3106, 3109, 3116, 3125, 3312, 3377, 3378, 3396, 3411, 3613, 3855, 3865, 3867, 4375, 4410, 4414, 4420, 4423, 4428, 4437, 4440, 4607, 4608, 4631, 4634, 4692. Master's theses, 68, 73, 76, 99, 100, 196, 200, 216, 220, 232, 238, 254, 258, 262, 294, 334, 335, 336, 405, 421, 540, 690, 695, 700, 710, 714, 725, 731, 743, 752, 753, 755, 763, 764, 773, 781, 797, 801, 815, 817, 825, 832, 845, 934, 955, 959, 968, 985, 987, 996, 998, 1105, 1114, 1122, 1138, 1146, 1177, 1196, 1225, 1226, 1266, 1296, 1314, 1318, 1568, 1579, 1656, 1975, 2044, 2079, 2138, 2257, 2285, 2287, 2369, 2376, 2395, 2426, 2435, 2450, 2468, 2524, 2748, 2771, 2800, 2877, 2888, 2965, 2971, 3019, 3025, 3026, 3033, 3037, 3042, 3044, 3054, 3058, 3059, 3137, 3150, 3156, 3162, 3169, 3174, 3184, 3186, 3187, 3198, 3203, 3215, 3243, 3247, 3250, 3271, 3291, 3318, 3322, 3323, 3340, 3343, 3428, 3442, 3443, 3451, 3453, 3456, 3457, 3462, 3467, 3472, 3475, 3485, 3492, 3496, 3498, 3499, 3500, 3502, 3507, 3508, 3520, 3521, 3526, 3533, 3535, 3541, 3545, 3553, 3555, 3556, 3560, 3563, 3576, 3583, 3675, 3719, 3724, 3753, 3778, 3785, 3791, 3793, 3797, 3801, 3823, 3843, 3845, 3847, 3990, 4044, 4068, 4071, 4128, 4133, 4140, 4150, 4151, 4159, 4187, 4198, 4203, 4207, 4223, 4231, 4235, 4241, 4270, 4288, 4335, 4347, 4368, 4399, 4447, 4456, 4459, 4467, 4468, 4477, 4481, 4482, 4486, 4490, 4493, 4497, 4499, 4503, 4505, 4507, 4510, 4515, 4516, 4517, 4520, 4524, 4531, 4533, 4534, 4551, 4556, 4558, 4559, 4562, 4564, 4570, 4583, 4622, 4625, 4637, 4641, 4649, 4652, 4653, 4657, 4693, 4697, 4699, 4706, 4711, 4747, 4771, 4778, 4826, 4911, 5027, 5102, 5117, 5118, 5313, 5486, 5500, 5656, 5684, 5690
Catholic University of the Sacred Heart, Italy, 4481
Celleni, B., 3211
Censorship of books, 1028
Central American University, 529, 531
Central Baptist Theological Seminary, Kansas City 2, Kansas. Master's thesis, 2451
Central Philippine College, 2591, 2592
Central Washington College of Education, Ellensburg, Washington. Master's thesis, 3831
Ceylon, 1347-1352
Chadwick, E., 3894
Chaminade, W. J., 3560
Champagnat, Father, 3493
Chang, C., 1395
Character education. See Moral education

Charlemagne, 3048, 3421, 3423, 3465, 3466
Charles V., 188, 4547
Charter schools, 4379
Charterhouse program, 2084
Chaucer, G., 4090, 4137, 4248
Chemistry, Teaching of, 103, 1694, 2406, 2948, 3729
Chesterfield, P. D., 3966, 4003
Chesterton, G. K., 4051
Chicago, University of. See University of Chicago
Chicago Lutheran Theological Seminary, Maywood, Illinois. Master's thesis, 4166
Chicago Musical College of Roosevelt University. See Roosevelt University.
Chicago Theological Seminary, Chicago 37, Illinois. Master's thesis, 2969
Chico State College (formerly Chico State Teachers College), Chico, California. Master's theses, 2570, 3028, 3230, 5629. Other reference, 3028
Chile, 1244-1262, 4957, 4970, 4975, 4990
China, 1362-1822, 5032-5089
Chinese Federation of Educational Associations, 1479
Chinese Industrial Cooperation Movement, 1504
Chinese language, 1362
Chivalry, 3046
Chopin, F. F., 3195
Chosen Christian College, Korea, 2484
Christ. See Jesus Christ
Christian education, 8, 17, 38, 62, 63, 79, 81, 82, 84, 94, 97, 102, 105, 109, 112, 145, 153, 158, 191, 193, 199, 201, 202, 233, 314, 318, 319, 320, 325, 339, 345, 348, 350, 354, 461, 468, 492, 494, 522, 538, 1232, 1338, 1352, 1374, 1402, 1417, 1421, 1433, 1434, 1451, 1452, 1458, 1464, 1467, 1472, 1473, 1490, 1497, 1498, 1511, 1514, 1517, 1518, 1521, 1530, 1546, 1548, 1551, 1554, 1570, 1575, 1581, 1593, 1597, 1602, 1629, 1632, 1643, 1644, 1645, 1650, 1651, 1655, 1670, 1671, 1683, 1690, 1693, 1705, 1708, 1712, 1734, 1735, 1751, 1806, 1810, 1814, 1830, 1857, 1859, 1860, 1869, 1894, 1906, 1942, 1953, 1955, 1959, 1971, 1972, 1980, 1982, 1990, 2003, 2005, 2015, 2076, 2083, 2086, 2091, 2162, 2243, 2314, 2324, 2326, 2330, 2340, 2352, 2360, 2364, 2373, 2385, 2387, 2402, 2407, 2415, 2416, 2419, 2421, 2422, 2442, 2451, 2454, 2458, 2459, 2460, 2471, 2472, 2484, 2526, 2534, 2549, 2641, 2676, 2706, 2777, 2792, 2847, 2893, 2921, 2923, 2933, 2947, 2988, 3017, 3123, 3124, 3134, 3182, 3502, 3534, 3560, 3827, 3863, 3865, 4215, 4245, 4347, 4355, 4376, 4398, 4432, 4457, 4482, 4492, 4495, 4754, 4821, 4825, 4897, 4900, 5050, 5085, 5087, 5169, 5282, 5397, 5596, 19a. See also Catholic education; Protestant education

Christian Reformed education, 33
Chrysostom, St. John, 2965, 2978, 4310, 4335
Chu, H., 1568
Chulalongkorn University, Thailand, 2928, 2934
Church of Christ education, 2443, 2927
Church of England education, 618, 3084, 5031
Church of the Brethren education, 162
Cicero, M. T., 184, 3168, 4464, 4474, 4488, 4521, 4553, 4563
Cincinnati, University of. See University of Cincinnati
City College of New York. See College of the City of New York
Civic education. See Social science education
Cizek method, 3337
Claparede, J. L., 4700
Claremont College. See Claremont Graduate School
Claremont Graduate School (formerly Claremont College), Claremont, California. Master's theses, 61, 214, 478, 961, 974, 984, 1016, 1022, 1040, 1279, 1775, 1776, 2423, 2578, 3295, 3361, 3731, 4118, 4599, 4626, 4742, 4746, 5177, 5257, 5317, 5324, 5400, 5409, 5430, 5447, 5454, 5462, 5495, 5523, 5526, 5562, 5565
Clark University, Worcester, Massachusetts. Doctor's dissertations, 7, 11, 144, 154, 176, 2215, 2218, 2584, 3002, 3110, 3131, 3585, 3598, 4686. Master's theses, 48, 86, 217, 240, 1793, 2008, 2267, 2363, 2474, 2476, 3372, 3543, 3726, 3754, 3762, 3789, 3810, 3961, 4359, 4677. Other reference, 3726
Classics, Teaching of, 3236, 3265, 4118
Clausura of Religious Women, 3056
Clement of Alexandria, 421
Clemson Agricultural College, Clemson, South Carolina. Master's thesis, 683
Coleridge, J. D. C., 3880, 3993
Colet, J., 3864, 4185
Colgate Rochester Divinity School, Rochester 20, New York. (Formerly Colgate Rochester Theological Seminary). Master's thesis, 1338
Colin, J. C., 3464, 3507
College de France, 3474
College education. See Higher education
College of Idaho, Caldwell, Idaho. Master's thesis, 2394
Colleges of Priests, Italy, 4419
College of St. Rose, Albany 3, New York. Master's thesis, 820
College of the Bible, Lexington, Kentucky. Master's thesis, 348
College of the City of New York, New York 31, New York. (Name changed to City College in 1929). Master's theses, 192, 1010, 1166, 2245, 2252, 2258, 2273, 2764, 3148, 3181, 3241, 3276, 3310, 3429, 3484, 3517, 3518, 3552, 3559, 3562, 3567, 3569, 3673, 3682, 3751, 3764, 3772, 3803, 3808,

GENERAL INDEX

College of the City of New York (Cont'd.), 3815, 3837, 4010, 4018, 4035, 4059, 4090, 4135, 4173, 4182, 4195, 4220, 4222, 4239, 4293, 4465, 4567, 4617, 4647, 4648, 4656, 4700, 4704, 4715, 4717, 4987, 5134, 5148, 5682

College of the Pacific, Stockton 4, California. Master's theses, 933, 1139, 3164, 3170, 3254, 4604, 5063, 5070, 5164

College of William and Mary, Williamsburg, Virginia. Master's thesis, 3022

Colombia, 1263-1269, 4956, 4969, 4975, 4990, 5229

Colonna, A., 3184

Colorado Agricultural and Mechanical College. See Colorado State University

Colorado College, Colorado Springs, Colorado. Master's theses, 212, 5280, 5653

Colorado State College, Greeley, Colorado. (Formerly Colorado State Teachers College, to 1935; and Colorado State College of Education, to 1957). Abstracts of all doctoral dissertations are published and copies of original dissertations are available on microfilm from University Microfilms, Ann Arbor, Michigan. Doctor's dissertations, 5217, 5232, 5233. Master's theses, 275, 286, 288, 295, 777, 935, 1142, 1143, 1261, 1281, 1577, 1802, 2389, 2675, 2689, 3141, 3440, 3479, 3510, 4262, 4650, 4660, 4879, 4890, 4907, 4908, 5142, 5178, 5278, 5311, 5452, 5468, 5487, 5498, 5583, 5608

Colorado State College of Agriculture and Mechanic Arts. See Colorado State University.

Colorado State College of Education. See Colorado State College.

Colorado State University, Fort Collins, Colorado. (Formerly Colorado State College of Agriculture and Mechanic Arts, to 1945; Colorado Agricultural and Mechanical College, to 1957). Master's theses, 688, 716, 745, 765, 776, 1096, 1121, 5238, 5267, 5287, 5329, 5390, 5483, 5546, 5553, 5555, 5593

Colorado, University of. See University of Colorado.

Columbia Bible College, Columbia, South Carolina. Master's theses, 88, 103, 110, 320, 1269, 2136, 2159, 2893

Columbia University, New York 27, New York. Doctor's dissertations, 2, 10, 14, 15, 16, 23, 31, 130, 132, 134, 137, 142, 143, 148, 151, 160, 163, 166, 170, 180, 182, 322, 339, 342, 343, 344, 360, 361, 364, 368, 370, 371, 375, 380, 382, 384, 385, 386, 389, 390, 392, 394, 395, 396, 398, 452, 455, 458, 486, 500, 501, 502, 503, 507, 508, 509, 510, 511, 513, 549, 565, 566, 568, 570, 571

Columbia University (Cont'd.), 573, 577, 581, 582, 583, 585, 591, 593, 596, 602, 603, 611, 612, 613, 619, 620, 623, 625, 631, 633, 636, 637, 640, 642, 643, 644, 645, 648, 650, 651, 661, 662, 665, 668, 676, 869, 872, 888, 891, 907, 914, 931, 1044, 1047, 1049, 1050, 1051, 1053, 1054, 1057, 1058, 1061, 1062, 1065, 1066, 1067, 1068, 1070, 1071, 1072, 1076, 1078, 1082, 1083, 1084, 1086, 1087, 1089, 1090, 1183, 1201, 1245, 1246, 1263, 1273, 1277, 1326, 1329, 1330, 1347, 1353, 1360, 1363, 1365, 1367, 1368, 1369, 1370, 1372, 1375, 1379, 1380, 1381, 1383, 1385, 1386, 1387, 1389, 1390, 1393, 1394, 1395, 1397, 1398, 1400, 1403, 1407, 1412, 1413, 1417, 1418, 1422, 1425, 1426, 1427, 1428, 1430, 1432, 1435, 1436, 1437, 1438, 1440, 1442, 1443, 1444, 1445, 1452, 1453, 1457, 1459, 1462, 1469, 1471, 1472, 1479, 1483, 1485, 1489, 1498, 1500, 1502, 1503, 1508, 1826, 1827, 1829, 1830, 1832, 1834, 1836, 1837, 1839, 1841, 1845, 1850, 1851, 1858, 1860, 1862, 1866, 1868, 1873, 1874, 1876, 1877, 1878, 1879, 1880, 1881, 1882, 1884, 1885, 1886, 1887, 1890, 1892, 1893, 1897, 1899, 1901, 1911, 1915, 1916, 1917, 1918, 1922, 1923, 1925, 1928, 1930, 1932, 2142, 2146, 2147, 2151, 2154, 2167, 2168, 2171, 2177, 2178, 2179, 2180, 2182, 2183, 2189, 2200, 2201, 2206, 2211, 2219, 2220, 2225, 2226, 2230, 2231, 2233, 2235, 2313, 2315, 2317, 2318, 2320, 2321, 2332, 2343, 2349, 2350, 2353, 2354, 2482, 2492, 2493, 2495, 2497, 2499, 2544, 2564, 2569, 2591, 2593, 2609, 2613, 2615, 2617, 2621, 2623, 2625, 2635, 2646, 2648, 2649, 2657, 2894, 2895, 2897, 2901, 2905, 2908, 2916, 2917, 2959, 3001, 3007, 3013, 3077, 3079, 3081, 3083, 3085, 3094, 3096, 3103, 3108, 3117, 3133, 3307, 3309, 3331, 3354, 3375, 3376, 3382, 3384, 3385, 3386, 3387, 3388, 3390, 3394, 3399, 3401, 3402, 3405, 3422, 3584, 3586, 3587, 3595, 3599, 3600, 3607, 3608, 3623, 3636, 3637, 3647, 3651, 3665, 3667, 3668, 3849, 3860, 3861, 3874, 3876, 3880, 3886, 3887, 3889, 3899, 3909, 3910, 3915, 3918, 3920, 3926, 3933, 3935, 3936, 3940, 3942, 3943, 3944, 3946, 3951, 3953, 4296, 4304, 4312, 4314, 4315, 4364, 4367, 4412, 4413, 4417, 4434, 4438, 4572, 4577, 4591, 4592, 4609, 4614, 4615, 4662, 4663, 4666, 4667, 4668, 4723, 4730, 4731, 4732, 4740, 4809, 4814, 4816, 4817, 4820, 4821, 4822, 4823, 4856, 4862, 4866, 4869, 4875, 4955, 4956, 4957, 4959, 4964, 4965, 4970, 4973, 4974, 5033, 5038, 5039, 5040, 5041, 5042, 5050, 5119, 5123, 5124, 5151, 5210, 5225, 5663, 5667, 5698, 19a, 174a, 506a, 1889a, 2155a. Master's theses, 44, 50, 62, 63, 78, 79, 87, 101, 107, 111, 208, 231, 263, 264, 271, 273, 300, 316, 351, 423, 424, 460, 466, 474, 487, 490, 499, 514, 518, 520, 522, 526, 692, 719, 721,

Columbia University (Cont'd.), 723, 768, 775, 778, 779, 780, 783, 809, 819, 827, 834, 855, 1018, 1037, 1097, 1127, 1153, 1158, 1172, 1180, 1206, 1207, 1224, 1257, 1259, 1284, 1295, 1322, 1351, 1352, 1514, 1519, 1530, 1533, 1537, 1538, 1542, 1555, 1572, 1573, 1575, 1588, 1589, 1591, 1592, 1597, 1605, 1619, 1621, 1625, 1628, 1632, 1633, 1645, 1646, 1647, 1650, 1653, 1657, 1669, 1688, 1693, 1699, 1700, 1717, 1722, 1724, 1726, 1733, 1735, 1739, 1754, 1761, 1770, 1774, 1791, 1792, 1796, 1799, 1800, 1801, 1803, 1810, 1811, 1813, 1815, 1816, 1817, 1935, 1948, 1959, 1967, 1982, 1983, 1998, 2005, 2007, 2013, 2015, 2021, 2030, 2038, 2049, 2057, 2060, 2063, 2105, 2108, 2111, 2117, 2120, 2121, 2129, 2165, 2166, 2198, 2238, 2242, 2243, 2255, 2292, 2361, 2366, 2383, 2386, 2398, 2408, 2409, 2420, 2424, 2427, 2428, 2433, 2438, 2440, 2447, 2456, 2457, 2462, 2477, 2515, 2522, 2684, 2778, 2831, 2843, 2870, 2873, 2899, 2966, 2974, 2977, 2979, 2981, 2990, 3000, 3040, 3048, 3062, 3064, 3134, 3151, 3152, 3163, 3165, 3178, 3183, 3191, 3194, 3196, 3201, 3234, 3261, 3269, 3270, 3283, 3285, 3288, 3301, 3327, 3433, 3447, 3449, 3474, 3478, 3480, 3488, 3503, 3511, 3513, 3537, 3540, 3558, 3564, 3566, 3582, 3684, 3686, 3697, 3698, 3702, 3708, 3709, 3712, 3715, 3722, 3730, 3740, 3742, 3765, 3766, 3767, 3768, 3773, 3774, 3779, 3787, 3802, 3819, 3822, 3839, 3962, 3963, 3964, 3971, 3972, 3986, 3991, 3993, 3994, 3995, 3996, 3998, 3999, 4001, 4016, 4017, 4021, 4022, 4023, 4042, 4043, 4045, 4049, 4050, 4054, 4060, 4061, 4064, 4074, 4075, 4078, 4081, 4082, 4087, 4094, 4098, 4099, 4105, 4113, 4121, 4122, 4125, 4129, 4142, 4144, 4152, 4154, 4155, 4157, 4158, 4162, 4170, 4175, 4178, 4183, 4185, 4190, 4191, 4197, 4199, 4202, 4204, 4212, 4213, 4216, 4236, 4243, 4249, 4251, 4257, 4259, 4269, 4272, 4273, 4278, 4280, 4292, 4316, 4317, 4327, 4330, 4334, 4349, 4356, 4361, 4371, 4384, 4444, 4474, 4478, 4483, 4502, 4523, 4527, 4529, 4537, 4547, 4598, 4602, 4628, 4629, 4639, 4644, 4654, 4658, 4694, 4701, 4743, 4750, 4754, 4763, 4766, 4768, 4770, 4772, 4779, 4790, 4794, 4798, 4799, 4834, 4880, 5068, 5097, 5133, 5137, 5138, 5143, 5149, 5592, 5620, 5670, 5678. Other references, 3000, 3513, 4956, 4970, 5038, 5225

Comenius, J. A., 210, 261, 3110, 3122, 3127, 3141, 3168, 3189, 3205, 3221, 3224, 3277, 3329, 3333, 3334, 3344, 3345, 3349

Commercial education. See Business education

Communal education, 1921

Communism, 313, 1366, 1431, 1541, 1781, 3835, 3956, 4607, 4726, 4739, 4754, 4757, 4760, 4775

Community colleges. See Junior colleges
Community education. See Rural education
Comparative education, 924, 1397, 2911, 4319
Composite. General, 119-308; America, North, 527-541; America, South, 1183-1198; Asia, 1297-1322; Europe, 3068-3303; United States, 4953-5026
Compte, A., 3433
Compulsory education, 1321, 1813, 1992, 2400, 3235, 4824
Concordia Seminary, St. Louis 5, Missouri. Doctor's dissertation, 3621a. Master's theses, 292, 2705, 3621a
Condorcet, M. J. A. N. C., 3394, 3484, 3528, 3550
Confucian education, 1407, 1456, 1652, 1763, 1821, 2996. See also Confucius
Confucius, 208, 231, 246, 1297, 1447, 1625, 1682, 1700, 1728, 2500
Congo. See Belgian Congo
Congregation of Notre Dame, 550, 687, 736
Congregation of the Sisters of the Holy Humility of Mary, 3532
Congregational education, 164, 268, 514, 2310, 2318. See also American Board of Commissioners for Foreign Missions
Connecticut, University of. See University of Connecticut
Connelly, C., 3973, 4225
Constantinople Women's College, Turkey, 217
Contemporary Japan, Tokyo, Japan, 2314
Continuation schools, 3912, 3953, 4160, 4351
Convent schools, 3410
Cooperative education, 747, 2622
Copernicus, N., 4448
Coptic education, 413
Coraes, A., 4305, 4332
Cornell University, Ithaca, New York, Doctor's dissertations, 6, 147, 479, 506, 512, 564, 604, 605, 629, 841, 920, 1079, 1324, 1378, 1409, 1416, 1439, 1451, 1476, 1493, 1838, 1849, 1883, 1903, 2152, 2543, 2565, 2567, 2568, 2604, 2614, 2641, 2644, 2907, 3353, 3380, 3414, 3425, 3628, 3927, 4728, 4871. Master's theses, 83, 89, 237, 435, 757, 769, 859, 886, 1102, 1155, 1173, 1175, 1176, 1178, 1215, 1228, 1272, 1308, 1350, 1526, 1574, 1612, 1681, 1743, 1747, 1753, 1947, 1969, 2036, 2123, 2125, 2194, 2359, 2552, 2579, 2742, 2798, 2815, 2819, 2842, 2848, 2854, 2892, 2926, 2930, 2952, 3255, 3258, 3574, 3733, 4024, 4119, 4168, 4351, 4504, 4539, 4555, 4586, 4827, 4836, 4893, 5009.
Corporal punishment, 3239
Correspondence education, 563
Costa Rica, 840-850, 4957, 4975
Costs of education. See Financing of education

Counseling. See Guidance
Counts, G. S., 4776
County colleges, 3912
Courts, 660
Cowper, W., 4191
Craig, C. E., 4534
Creighton University, Omaha, Nebraska. Master's theses, 2260, 2686, 3060, 3067, 3465, 3981, 4458
Crete, 226
Crippled children, 705. See also Handicapped children.
Croce, B., 4445
Cuba, 851-866, 4957, 4969, 4975, 5530
Curie, M., 3216
Curriculum study and revision, 311, 355, 385, 455, 502, 649, 672, 699, 735, 739, 759, 763, 830, 1010, 1039, 1132, 1172, 1174, 1201, 1223, 1246, 1329, 1331, 1354, 1379, 1403, 1452, 1460, 1469, 1471, 1476, 1530, 1542, 1560, 1608, 1673, 1715, 1731, 1743, 1746, 1748, 1753, 1769, 1779, 1788, 1807, 1808, 1866, 1872, 1882, 1884, 1906, 1920, 1931, 1932, 2004, 2034, 2075, 2099, 2102, 2114, 2123, 2140, 2167, 2174, 2185, 2216, 2219, 2320, 2351, 2421, 2424, 2433, 2447, 2480, 2485, 2548, 2623, 2629, 2631, 2646, 2666, 2726, 2747, 2754, 2763, 2809, 2864, 2880, 2889, 2896, 2904, 2908, 2920, 2926, 2952, 3044, 3117, 3391, 3510, 3639, 3748, 3957, 4271, 4286, 4300, 4317, 4320, 4409, 4829, 5248, 5251, 5283, 5308, 5552, 5622, 5632. See also various subject matter fields
Curry, 4724
Cusa, 4448
Cypriots, 4975
Cyprus, 1353-1354, 4975
Cyril, Saint, 183, 2293
Czechoslovakia, 3328-3351, 5683-5691

D

Dalcroze, E. J., 4714
Dallari, U., 4483
Dallas Theological Seminary and Graduate School of Theology, Dallas, Texas. Master's thesis, 539
Dalton plan, 3917
Dancing, 585, 914, 953, 979, 1002, 1004, 1014, 1234, 2774, 2839, 3036, 3351, 4348, 4350, 4367, 4847, 4857, 5447. See also Music education; Recreation
Dante, A., 4408
Danzig, 119
Dartmouth College, Hanover, New Hampshire. Master's theses, 3519, 4758
Darwin, C., 3248, 3923, 4071
Daughters of Charity Schools, 2603
Davidson, T., 3961, 4056
Dawn Institute, Canada, 839
Day, T., 3285, 4117
Day care centers, 2892
Deaf, Education of the, 265, 1893, 1949, 2862, 3063, 3292, 3314, 3542
Deans of women, Training of, 4372

Debussy, C. A., 3195
Decroly, O., 3319
Defoe, D., 3963, 3985, 4244
Degrees, Meaning of, 3256
Delaware, University of. See University of Delaware
Demiashevich, M. J., 4771
Denmark, 3352-3368, 5090-5091
Dental education, 3737, 4684,
Dental status, 2930
Denver, University of. See University of Denver
De Paul University, Chicago 1, Illinois. Master's theses, 1359, 1541, 1561, 1615, 1763, 1809, 1989, 2059, 2254, 2769, 2788, 2978, 3173, 3332, 3579, 3732, 4506, 4518, 4528, 4919, 4931, 4933, 5688
Dependent schools in Europe. See Occupied Europe, American education in
De Sauze, E. B., 3374
Descartes, R., 3406
Detroit, University of. See University of Detroit
Dewey, J., 304, 2500, 2552, 3089, 3205, 3221, 3233, 3275, 3306, 3308, 3392, 3487, 3526, 3548, 3597, 3640, 3652, 3670, 3738, 3762, 3828, 3868, 3871, 3916, 4012, 4013, 4079, 4136, 4218, 4313, 4333, 4337, 4353, 4619, 4651
Dhahabi, M. I. A. al-, 1295
Dickens, C., 3970, 4005, 4019, 4022, 4029, 4050, 4052, 4073, 4091, 4113, 4146, 4158, 4197, 4237, 4287
Diderot, D., 3394
Didymus the Blind, 372, 405
Dietitians. See Home economics education.
Discipline, School, 42, 498, 3012, 3093, 4472, 5196
Dissertation Abstracts, Ann Arbor, Michigan. (Formerly Microfilm Abstracts), 3, 23, 25, 28, 31, 32, 37, 127, 131, 138, 140, 145, 146, 149, 159, 181, 357, 369, 375, 379, 383, 390, 393, 394, 429, 454, 456, 457, 459, 485, 531, 551, 557, 558, 559, 564, 576, 601, 616, 617, 620, 621, 628, 646, 664, 671, 672, 840, 871, 892, 895, 904, 907, 916, 924, 1055, 1056, 1069, 1075, 1080, 1185, 1270, 1287, 1300, 1332, 1348, 1367, 1368, 1385, 1395, 1407, 1449, 1451, 1457, 1505, 1823, 1824, 1844, 1845, 1846, 1847, 1861, 1864, 1865, 1869, 1871, 1894, 1895, 1902, 1909, 1912, 1916, 1929, 2142, 2143, 2145, 2153, 2155, 2156, 2170, 2172, 2173, 2180, 2181, 2184, 2186, 2190, 2203, 2205, 2207, 2213, 2216, 2228, 2234, 2306, 2307, 2309, 2312, 2328, 2330, 2333, 2334, 2342, 2344, 2350, 2354, 2481, 2483, 2491, 2501, 2504, 2542, 2545, 2583, 2585, 2588, 2595, 2597, 2601, 2604, 2608, 2616, 2617, 2618, 2619, 2620, 2627, 2628, 2632, 2641, 2642, 2645, 2647, 2651, 2655, 2896, 2902, 2904, 2907, 2910, 2912, 2918, 2958, 2964, 3009, 3070, 3072, 3080, 3095, 3096, 3112, 3113, 3121, 3126,

GENERAL INDEX

Dissertation Abstracts, (Cont'd.), 3130, 3306, 3328, 3331, 3400, 3401, 3407, 3624, 3626, 3671, 3853, 3863, 3870, 3873, 3874, 3875, 3877, 3878, 3884, 3889, 3900, 3910, 3914, 3923, 3925, 3926, 3940, 3944, 3947, 3949, 3955, 4298, 4300, 4302, 4377, 4419, 4421, 4424, 4425, 4429, 4576, 4592, 4612, 4635, 4665, 4667, 4687, 4728, 4731, 4804, 4818, 4861, 4862, 4863, 4867, 4870, 4872, 4874, 4953, 4956, 4961, 4969, 4971, 5028, 5029, 5035, 5042, 5043, 5092, 5160, 5207, 5209, 5210, 5219, 5220, 5224, 5226, 5229, 5655a, 5662, 5664, 5665, 5697, 162a, 506a, 599, 641, 1188, 1265, 1908, 2155a, 2184a, 2329, 2347, 2496, 2615, 2902a, 3871, 842, 1849, 1900, 1908a, 2636a, 3878a, 4812a, 5655a.

Distributive education, 2755
Doctoral dissertations. See under names of individual institutions
Doctoral Dissertations in the Field of Religion, 1940-1952. Published by Columbia University Press for the Council on Graduate Studies in Religion in Cooperation with the National Council on Religion in Higher Education, 1954. 561, 1382, 1863, 1904, 4669
Dolls, Educational uses of, 239
Dominican education, 2877, 3026
Dominican Republic, 867
Dominici, G., 4410
Dominicis, S., 4462
Doshisha University, Japan, 2310
Drake University, Des Moines 11, Iowa. Master's theses, 498, 824, 1042, 1552, 1582, 1594, 2031, 3710, 3841, 4584, 4853
Drama, Teaching of. See Speech and dramatic education
Drew University, Madison, New Jersey. Doctor's dissertations, 1388, 1421, 2324. Master's theses, 278, 1231, 1671, 1696, 1767, 1806, 2075, 2126, 2792
Drexel Institute of Technology, Philadelphia 4, Pennsylvania. Master's theses, 708, 2093
Dropsie College for Hebrew and Cognate Learning, Philadelphia 32, Pennsylvania. Doctor's dissertations, 139, 910, 2210, 3358, 3418, 3596, 3611, 3649, 4735
Duff, A., 1950
Duke University, Durham, North Carolina. Doctor's dissertations, 373, 647, 1274, 4690. Master's theses, 1268, 3800
Dupanloup, F. A. P., 3396, 3443, 3467
Durkheim, E., 3525
Dutch. See Netherlands
Dutch Reformed Church education, 5094

E

East India Company, 1843
East Tennessee State College, Johnson City, Tennessee. Master's thesis, 988
East Texas State College, Commerce, Texas. (Formerly East Texas State Teachers College). Master's theses, 994, 2779, 3027, 3185, 3720, 4279
Eastern Baptist Theological Seminary, Philadelphia 31, Pennsylvania. Doctor's dissertation, 2204. Master's theses, 105, 495, 497, 1342, 1518, 1971, 2012, 2076, 2286
Eastern New Mexico University, Portales, New Mexico. Master's theses, 3736, 5259
Eastman School of Music. See University of Rochester
Economics, Teaching of, 137, 2812
Ecuador, 1270-1272, 4975
Edgeworth, M., 4384
Education, Boston, Massachusetts, 3663
Educational Administration and Supervision, Baltimore, Maryland. 5115
Educational finance. See Financing of education
Educational guidance. See Guidance
Educational ladders, 229
Educational legislation. See Legislation, Educational
Educational legislation, Effect of teacher's association on, 551
Educational organizations. See Teachers organizations
Educational philosophy. See Philosophy of Education
Educational psychology, 126, 204, 210, 223, 262, 272, 308, 392, 393, 394, 396, 436, 665, 934, 1088, 1120, 1148, 1294, 1348, 1399, 1436, 1540, 1566, 1713, 1777, 1850, 1887, 2029, 2089, 2380, 2452, 2513, 2584, 2659, 2669, 2695, 2758, 2783, 2834, 3083, 3205, 3619, 3698, 3784, 4109, 4170, 4225, 4327, 4424, 4471, 4631. See also Guidance; Tests, Standardized
Educational publicity. See Publicity, Educational
Eells, W. C., 1300, 2306, 2312, 2313, 2314, 2317, 2319, 2323, 2325, 2332, 2336, 2339, 2346, 2350, 2355, 2395, 2426, 2468
Eggersdorfer, F. X., 3793
Egypt, 360-428, 4956, 4970, 4975, 4990
Einheitsschule, 3620
Ekken, K., 2428
Elementary education, 135, 141, 167, 215, 253, 274, 297, 326, 395, 469, 471, 476, 486, 506, 512, 547, 649, 651, 670, 683, 690, 714, 725, 740, 794, 796, 812, 823, 843, 846, 943, 976, 978, 1018, 1040, 1046, 1048, 1054, 1056, 1065, 1071, 1131, 1143, 1151, 1206, 1225, 1240, 1246, 1252, 1266, 1289, 1292, 1331, 1344, 1409, 1448, 1461, 1471, 1534, 1544, 1545, 1564, 1568, 1603, 1615, 1623, 1665, 1667, 1707, 1714, 1725, 1731, 1748, 1778, 1808, 1849, 1861, 1866, 1882, 1909, 1918, 1921a, 1925, 1940, 1962, 1984, 2005, 2010, 2023, 2027, 2035, 2050, 2058, 2072, 2073, 2087, 2099, 2102, 2114, 2115, 2133, 2140, 2145, 2148, 2161, 2167, 2179, 2192, 2199, 2205, 2210, 2220, 2247, 2277, 2303, 2348, 2351, 2359, 2369, 2386, 2424, 2428, 2433, 2446, 2485, 2514, 2587, 2601, 2602, 2619, 2621, 2645, 2652, 2655, 2668, 2678, 2682, 2686, 2692, 2711,
Elementary education, (Cont'd.), 2715, 2716, 2737, 2746, 2785, 2811, 2828, 2846, 2850, 2860, 2863, 2867, 2868, 2880, 2886, 2888, 2906, 2908, 2914, 2917, 2919, 2920, 2931, 2936, 2950, 2970, 2980, 2995, 3069, 3117, 3167, 3197, 3277, 3281, 3309, 3312, 3323, 3349, 3372, 3382, 3398, 3429, 3523, 3531, 3540, 3545, 3547, 3566, 3567, 3584, 3586, 3623, 3637, 3651, 3667, 3707, 3748, 3765, 3817, 3849, 3881, 3884, 3915, 3922, 3942, 3949, 4014, 4047, 4048, 4111, 4124, 4147, 4239, 4267, 4271, 4314, 4360, 4370, 4382, 4452, 4529, 4539, 4573, 4606, 4628, 4645, 4647, 4648, 4663, 4668, 4674, 4713, 4727, 4745, 4770, 4780, 4785. See also Kindergarten education. (Note: Theses from Nos. 4860 to 5698 not indexed under this heading)
Eliot, G., 3216, 3998, 4246
El Salvador, 868-870, 4969, 4975
Elyot, T., 4177
Emerson College, Boston 16, Massachusetts. Master's thesis, 2576
Emory University, Emory University, Georgia. Master's theses, 1223, 1227, 1548, 1616, 1692, 2293, 2362, 2368, 2396, 2519, 2559, 3193, 3445, 4076, 4782
Encyclicals, 203, 4432, 4458, 4493, 4503, 4505, 4524, 4538, 4541, 4558
English, Teaching of, 14, 64, 159, 305, 480, 575, 601, 704, 833, 837, 860, 1049, 1051, 1062, 1072, 1086, 1123, 1129, 1141, 1153, 1159, 1255, 1259, 1262, 1311, 1363, 1364, 1381, 1442, 1443, 1445, 1457, 1508, 1569, 1600, 1607, 1618, 1630, 1636, 1639, 1719, 1722, 1724, 1739, 1802, 1833, 1914, 1942, 1961, 2006, 2100, 2190, 2220, 2329, 2377, 2379, 2391, 2423, 2440, 2449, 2453, 2516, 2545, 2571, 2599, 2611, 2662, 2702, 2727, 2736, 2745, 2762, 2772, 2828, 2829, 2836, 2855, 2922, 2935, 2946, 2949, 3733, 4060, 4157, 4216, 4295, 4373, 4704, 4715, 4871, 4873, 4878, 4886, 4887, 4889, 4891, 4907, 4917, 4926, 4930, 4934, 4939, 4942, 4943, 4944, 4950, 4965, 5010, 5016, 5022, 5026, 5054, 5064, 5066, 5072, 5146, 5181, 5190, 5192, 5206, 5219, 5235, 5244, 5311, 5323, 5348, 5368, 5369, 5380, 5394, 5402, 5406, 5420, 5422, 5424, 5432, 5451, 5467, 5471, 5472, 5512, 5517, 5527, 5531, 5545, 5575, 5583, 5626, 5641, 5657, 5662, 5663, 5666, 5671, 5689
Erasmus, D., 3168, 3238, 4563, 4578, 4582, 4583, 4585
Erigena, J. S., 3931
Eritrea, 226, 322
Ernest, Duke, 3769
Eskimos, 532
Estonia, 119, 147, 161, 226
Ethics, University of Chicago, Chicago, Illinois. 3652
Ethiopia, 429-431
Eurhythmics, 4714
Euthenics program, 1911
Evaluative Criteria, 387, 1839

Evangelical Church education, 883, 1583
Evangelical Seminary of Puerto Rico, 1082
Ewha Woman's College, Korea, 2516, 2530
Ewing Christian College, India, 1860, 2006
Examinations, 427, 685, 701, 755, 826, 832, 1372, 1566, 1925, 2761, 2857, 3265, 5389, 5519
Exceptional children, Education of, 364
Exchange programs. See Teacher exchange programs; Student exchange programs
Experimental education, 173, 453, 974, 2007, 3096, 3397, 3594, 3606, 3612, 3621, 3638, 3642, 3662, 3737, 4117, 4632, 4797
Extension education, 841, 886, 920, 1093, 1149, 1176, 1178, 1215, 1272, 1806, 1838, 1886, 2036, 2120, 2123, 2125, 2194, 2798, 2815, 2819, 2902, 2952, 4168, 4412, 4614, 4836, 5241
Extra-Curricular activities. See Student activities
Eymiue, A., 3434

F

Fairbairn, A. M., 3857
Family relations courses. See Home economics education
Faraday, M., 3248
Far Eastern Quarterly (Later, Journal of Asian Studies), Ann Arbor, Michigan, 2346
Fascism, 4402, 4431, 4489, 4508, 4512, 4515, 4566
Federation of Catholic Guides, 722
Felbiger, J. I., 3727
Fellenberg, P. E., 4706
Feltre, V., 4470, 4495, 4517, 4555, 4559
Fenianism, 4378
Fenlon, F., 3162, 3263, 3435, 3443, 3489, 3498, 3501, 3506, 3515, 3530, 3554, 3582
Ferrer, F., 4632, 4661
Ferry, J., 3567, 3575
Festival, School, 730
Fichte, J. G., 3110, 3608, 3742
Fiji Islands, 179, 4855, 4858
Filipino groups, 5095-5097
Financing of education, 283, 388, 450, 614, 668, 678, 785, 818, 824, 1200, 1387, 1415, 1536, 1657, 1825, 2071, 2581, 2684, 2697, 2854, 3223, 3949, 3955, 3999, 4104, 4123, 4812, 4828, 5393, 5570
Finland, 3369-3373, 5098-5099
Fisk University, Nashville 8, Tennessee. Master's thesis, 1169
Flattich, J. F., 3753
Fleury, C., 3582
Florida, University of. See University of Florida
Florida State University, Tallahassee, Florida. Master's theses, 1124, 1262, 4719

Floyd, A. C., 2519
Foerster, F. W., 3613, 3678, 3692, 3719
Fordham University, New York 58, New York. Doctor's dissertations, 128, 184, 367, 550, 624, 1264, 1484, 1848, 2580, 2603, 2612, 3305, 3864, 3885, 3905, 4415, 4432, 4611, 4865, 4873, 5114, 5659. Master's theses, 687, 722, 736, 2719, 3023, 3030, 3045, 3155, 3272, 3320, 3432, 3463, 3493, 3501, 3523, 3977, 3987, 3992, 4100, 4117, 4225, 4226, 4386, 4392, 4460, 4476, 4514, 4545, 4549, 4571, 4588, 4620, 4678, 4775, 5132, 5654, 5676, 5680
Foreign language education, 127, 922, 2153, 2187, 3008, 3032, 3240, 3272, 3374, 3402, 3460, 3479, 3518, 3542, 3617, 3682, 3708, 4677, 4784, 4920. See also Arabic; French; Greek; Hebrew; Japanese; Latin; Spanish; Thai
Formosa (Taiwan), 1355-1359
Forster, W. E., 4086
Fort Hays Kansas State College, Hays, Kansas. Master's thesis, 1354
Foster, S., 3195
France, 3374-3583, 5100-5106
France, A., 3412, 3459, 3503
Francis de Sales, Saint, 200, 4697, 4699
Franciscan education, 528, 938, 955, 959, 1031, 1278, 3500, 4415, 4560
Franck, C., 3195
Francke, A. H., 3610, 3844
Franklin, F., 4000
French, Teaching of, 3510, 3513
French Equatorial Africa, 164, 185, 327
French Revolution and education, 3414, 3419, 3425, 3430, 3439, 3480, 3482, 3516, 3544, 3545, 3564
French West Africa, 323
Fresno State College, Fresno 26, California. Master's thesis, 2090
Freud, A., 3113
Freud, S., 3112, 3306
Froebel, F. W., 3110, 3127, 3141, 3167, 3174, 3189, 3205, 3221, 3275, 3301, 3595, 3670, 3720, 3732, 3739, 3742, 3762, 3774, 3780, 3787, 3804, 3829
Fulbright programs, 34, 1332, 3781
Fundamental education, 106, 534, 2033, 2104, 2566
Furdek, S., 5690
Furman University, Greenville, South Carolina. Master's theses, 353, 1607, 1630

G

Galdos, P., 4635, 4654
Gallaudet College, Washington 2, District of Columbia. Master's theses, 265, 1949, 3063, 3542
Galsworthy, J., 3898
Gambia, 324

Gandhi, M. K., 198, 1917, 1975, 2061, 2078
Garjan Memorial School, India, 1997
Gaskell, Mrs., 4032
Gates Silent Reading Tests, 5340
Gaudig, H., 3734, 3772, 3794
General education, 601, 1074, 2059, 2900
Genlis, Madame de, 3270
Gentile, G., 3271, 4407, 4439, 4514, 4529, 4544
Geography, Teaching of, 255, 1638, 1736, 2495, 3859, 4494
Geometry, Teaching of, 263, 3062, 3077, 3153, 4301, 4302, 174a. See also Mathematics education
George Peabody College for Teachers, Nashville 5, Tennessee. Doctor's dissertations, 871, 915, 1046, 1501, 1914, 2502, 3082, 3405, 3413, 3416, 3417, 3904, 4691, 5101. Master's theses, 194, 209, 269, 301, 418, 471, 956, 1220, 1236, 1511, 1600, 1609, 1639, 1640, 1651, 1694, 1712, 1731, 1936, 1978, 1997, 2025, 2082, 2085, 2100, 2103, 2160, 2253, 2384, 2406, 2422, 2472, 2530, 3188, 3208, 3212, 3244, 3346, 3557, 3750, 3818, 4057, 4193, 4268, 4338, 4341, 4348, 4350, 4464, 4469, 4494, 4501, 4548, 4605, 4762, 5104, 5303, 5441
George Washington University, Washington 6, District of Columbia. Doctor's dissertations, 119, 1362, 2626, 3093. Master's theses, 239, 416, 858, 986, 1035, 1118, 1145, 1234, 2032, 2073, 2713, 2853, 2885, 2891, 3041, 3341, 3350, 3491, 3572, 3744, 3746, 4070, 4095, 4126, 4208, 4645, 4844, 5001, 5065, 5241, 5527
George Williams College, Chicago 15, Illinois. Master's theses, 53, 1995, 2110, 2399
Georgetown University, Washington 7, District of Columbia. Doctor's dissertations, 152, 873, 3605
Georgia, University of. See University of Georgia
Gerbert, 3298
German East Africa, 327
Germany, 3584-3867, 5107-5112
Gerson, J., 3389
Gesell, A., 3112
Ghana, 432-435
Gifted children, Education of, 1469
Gilbert Islands, 4859
Gild schools, 4133, 4581
Gilson, E. H., 3207
Giner, F., 4656
Girard, J. B., 4711
Goethe, J. W., 185, 3604, 3735, 3777, 3798
Gold Coast. See Ghana
Goldsmith, O., 1405
Goncharov, I. A., 4738
Gonzaga University, Spokane 2, Washington. Master's theses, 3237, 3973, 4263, 4400, 4659
Goodenough Intelligence Test, 2043
Gordon Divinity School, Beverly Farms, Massachusetts. Master's thesis, 80

GENERAL INDEX

Gouin, F., 3404
Grammar, 2425
Granbery College, Brazil, 1223
Great Britain, 3848-4295, 4957, 4959, 4963, 4970, 4975, 4978, 4985, 4989, 5006, 5013, 5020, 5025, 5031, 5698
Greece, 4296-4363, 4954, 4956, 4957, 4975, 4982, 4985, 5006, 5113
Greek, Teaching of, 1595, 4122
Greenland, 122, 147, 212, 271, 532
Gregg, R. T., 2405, 2418, 2448, 2821, 3168, 3473, 3694, 4046, 4244, 4904
Gregory, St. of Nyssa, 2371
Grocyn, W., 4185
Group dynamics, 2204
Grundtvig, N. F. S., 3352, 3356, 3357
Guam, 4837-4838
Guarino da Verona, 4517, 4559
Guatemala, 871-875, 4957, 4969, 4975
Guidance, 394, 426, 524, 596, 677, 681, 691, 741, 783, 786, 808, 842, 845, 1053, 1083, 1101, 1103, 1180, 1264, 1286, 1307, 1360, 1459, 1606, 1714, 1723, 1732, 1842, 1844, 1845, 1846, 1850, 1927, 1955, 1978, 1983, 1990, 2002, 2018, 2023, 2044, 2068, 2082, 2090, 2097, 2122, 2127, 2241, 2257, 2266, 2277, 2353, 2395, 2427, 2511, 2515, 2527, 2547, 2580, 2583, 2585, 2591, 2597, 2612, 2613, 2618, 2624, 2627, 2652, 2654a, 2665, 2691, 2716, 2773, 2807, 2832, 2835, 2876, 2882, 2932, 2938, 2964, 2976, 2993, 3222, 3241, 3407, 3415, 3583, 3602, 3753, 4240, 4372, 4455, 4564, 4810, 4811, 4816, 4818, 4827, 4848, 4864, 4869, 4870, 5060, 5324, 5409, 5423, 5476, 5593, 5659. See also Educational psychology; Tests, standardized
Guilds, Mediaeval, 3020, 3043, 4101, 4133, 4581
Gumbel, E. J., 3615
Guru Principle, 1933

H

Hadassah Medical Organization, 2238
Haiti, 876-883, 4970
Hajime, K., 2342
Haldane, J. S., 3932
Hall, G. S., 3110
Hall, T., 4121
Hampton Institute, Virginia, 2131
Handel, G. F., 3591
Handicapped children, Education of, 2863, 3024, 3296, 3947
Hardin-Simmons University, Abilene, Texas. Master's theses, 5276, 5399, 5469, 5492, 5590, 5631
Harrington, J., 245, 286
Harris, W. T., 3089, 3110
Hartford School of Religious Education. See Hartford Seminary Foundation
Hartford Seminary Foundation, Hartford 5, Connecticut. (Includes Hartford Theological Seminary, Hartford School of Religious Education, and Kennedy School of Missions). Doctor's dissertations, 338, 357, 369, 433, 1482, 1497, 1856,

Hartford Seminary Foundation, (Cont'd) 1869, 1875, 2345, 4305, 5108. Master's theses, 64, 186, 199, 226, 312, 315, 319, 325, 340, 341, 441, 496, 521, 883, 1144, 1181, 1527, 1593, 1627, 1644, 1658, 1664, 1691, 1708, 1721, 1771, 1818, 1822, 1951, 1986, 2020, 2270, 2289, 2414, 2442, 2443, 2517, 2531, 2720, 2956, 2980, 4266
Hartford Theological Seminary. See Hartford Seminary Foundation
Hartmann, N., 3738
Harvard Report, 4274
Harvard University, Cambridge 38, Massachusetts. Doctor's dissertations, 155, 157, 164, 168, 323, 365, 391, 505, 543, 572, 578, 590, 600, 618, 627, 638, 639, 658, 673, 897, 900, 1088, 1303, 1396, 1405, 1411, 1480, 1840, 1843, 1905, 1907, 1921, 1926, 2187, 2227, 2308, 2346, 2506, 2599, 2606, 2650, 2996, 3071, 3114, 3115, 3118, 3381, 3389, 3423, 3424, 3631, 3634, 3646, 3654, 3656, 3663, 3666, 3859, 3892, 3896, 3911, 3912, 3941, 3945, 3959, 4311, 4593, 4630, 4813, 5125, 5693. Master's theses, 3192, 4948. Other reference, 4537
Hauptmann, G., 3688
Hawaii, University of. See University of Hawaii
Health education, 87, 170, 213, 227, 308, 363, 422, 518, 612, 651, 697, 715, 1007, 1258, 1684, 1740, 1947, 1962, 2052, 2203, 2238, 2259, 2267, 2538, 2738, 2844, 2879, 2930, 2945, 3017, 3353, 3737, 3894, 4318, 4623, 4684, 4762, 4807, 5243, 5253, 5286, 5316, 5371, 5428. See also Nursing education; Physical education
Hearn, L., 2408, 2436, 2477
Hebrew, Teaching of, 139, 2283, 3474
Hebrew education. See Jewish education
Hebrew Union College -- Jewish Institute of Religion, Cincinnati 10, Ohio. Master's theses, 2239, 2250, 2262, 2263, 2288, 2303, 3752
Hebrews, Epistle to, 2300
Hegel, G. W. F., 3110, 3622, 3636, 3652, 3697, 3748
Helvetius, 3388
Hennon-Nelson Test of Mental Ability, 5559
Herbart, J. F., 3110, 3127, 3141, 3193, 3205, 3221, 3275, 3595, 3632, 3637, 3640, 3650, 3666, 3672, 3683, 3685, 3694, 3696, 3697, 3700, 3771, 3773, 3782, 3809, 3828, 3834, 3841
Herder, J. G., 3249, 3585, 3740, 3766
Hesse, H., 3758, 4687
Hexateuch, 2246
Higher education, 25, 149, 155, 156, 157, 168, 182, 220, 303, 307, 384, 418, 454, 464, 472, 529, 540, 573, 594, 601, 637, 662, 674, 709, 724, 738, 741, 743, 747, 751, 755, 757, 760, 797, 809, 873, 916, 963, 964, 1031, 1236, 1244, 1250, 1298, 1303, 1410, 1422, 1428, 1431, 1451, 1453, 1461, 1490, 1498, 1507, 1519, 1522, 1525, 1541, 1569, 1610, 1613, 1618,

Higher education (Cont'd) 1656, 1679, 1693, 1737, 1781, 1788, 1806, 1830, 1851, 1855, 1873, 1885, 1889, 1892, 1907, 1908, 1911, 1916, 1920, 1982, 2024, 2028, 2032, 2037, 2057, 2062, 2071, 2076, 2092, 2141, 2164, 2183, 2306, 2307, 2333, 2340, 2350, 2353, 2358, 2379, 2402, 2450, 2499, 2507, 2537, 2540, 2550, 2568, 2569, 2629, 2640, 2730, 2812, 2876, 2952, 2957, 3018, 3025, 3044, 3060, 3067, 3070, 3076, 3080, 3088, 3098, 3116, 3118, 3119, 3130, 3186, 3202, 3256, 3258, 3276, 3339, 3364, 3365, 3367, 3395, 3522, 3552, 3580, 3592, 3615, 3634, 3641, 3644, 3706, 3783, 3851, 3926, 4006, 4045, 4057, 4081, 4118, 4135, 4161, 4228, 4274, 4391, 4519, 4558, 4607, 4763, 4793, 4799, 4864, 4869, 4870, 4874, 4938, 4950, 4952, 4954, 4956, 4957, 4958, 4961, 4964, 4967, 4970, 4971, 4972, 4974, 4975, 4977, 4978, 4988, 5002, 5003, 5006, 5008, 5040, 5049, 5114, 5165, 5176, 5186, 5187, 5202, 5223, 5395, 5429, 5516, 5639, 5693, 5697. See also Legal, Medical, Nursing, Professional, Theological education; all American higher educational institutions listed; and Ahmednagar College, American College, American University at Cairo, American University of Beirut, Aoyama Gakuin University, Brazilian Naval Academy, Canton Union Theological Seminary, Catholic University of the Sacred Heart, Central American University, Central Philippine College, Chosen Christian College, Chulalongkorn University, College de France, Constantinople Women's College, Doshisha University, Ewha Woman's College, Ewing Christian College, Hokkaido University, Huachung University, Imperial University of Peking, Inter-American University of Puerto Rico, Kobe College, Kyoto University, Lady Irwin College, Lingnan University, Lucknow University, Meiji Gakuen University, National Central University, National Peking University, Osmania Agricultural College, Peiping National Teachers College, Philippine College of Commerce, Philippine Normal College, Philippine Union College, Philippine Women's College, Philippine Women's University, Polytechnic Institute of Puerto Rico, Robert College, Royal University, Saint Christopher Training College, Seiwa Woman's College, Shantung Christian University, Silliman University, Soochow University, Teachers College of Thai, Tokyo University, Yale-in-China, Yenching University; and Universities of Berlin, Bologna, Budapest, Cambridge, Central America, Cheeloo, Edinburgh, Halle, Mexico, Moscow, Oslo, Oxford, Paris, Prague, Puerto Rico, Philippines, Salerno, Sydney

Hindu education, 1347, 1850, 1856, 1863, 1881, 1963, 1996, 1999, 2000, 2049, 2105, 2116
Hippaka, T. A., 3369
Hiroshima Girl's School, Japan, 2422
Hirsch, S. R., 3611
Hispanic American Historical Review, Durham, North Carolina, 535
Hispano-Americans. See Latin-Americans
History, Teaching of, 190, 194, 255, 805, 1035, 1756, 1778, 2575, 3171, 3268, 3439, 3637, 3765, 3779, 3795, 3835, 3935, 3939, 4059, 4139, 4182, 4196, 4208, 4243, 4700, 5160, 5466
Hitler, A., 3589, 3715, 3776, 3846
Hoelderlin, J. C. F., 3833
Hoffding, H., 3360
Hokkaido, Japan, 2306, 2471
Hokkaido University, Japan, 2306
Holland. See Netherlands
Home and School Association, 762
Home economics education, 235, 242, 249, 269, 311, 525, 549, 625, 661, 688, 698, 721, 728, 754, 767, 796, 831, 853, 859, 1000, 1078, 1093, 1096, 1100, 1102, 1108, 1113, 1115, 1116, 1121, 1122, 1124, 1126, 1128, 1133, 1134, 1154, 1284, 1345, 1350, 1968, 1976, 1977, 2062, 2065, 2077, 2080, 2093, 2098, 2139, 2201, 2238, 2442, 2568, 2579, 2604, 2625, 2635, 2690, 2781, 2796, 2798, 2802, 2806, 2849, 2874, 2903, 2975, 3101, 3103, 3353, 4320, 4507, 4586, 4875, 4957, 5003, 5015, 5020, 5070, 5204, 5238, 5258, 5267, 5270, 5287, 5329, 5390, 5546, 5555, 5615, 5637
Homer, 3177
Honduras, 884-886, 4956, 4969, 4975
Hong Kong, 1360, 1361, 4956
Hood Theological Seminary, Livingstone, North Carolina. Master's thesis, 97
Hope College, Michigan, 5092
Horace, 4552
Horne, H. H., 3271
Hospital dietitians, 3353
Hostos, E. M., 224, 540
Houston, University of. See University of Houston
Hovre, F. D., 3321
Howard University, Washington 1, District of Columbia. Master's theses, 491, 711, 1956
Howells, W. D., 245
Hsuntzu, 1386
Huachung University, China, 1363
Hugo of Saint Victor, 3155, 3845
Humanities, 1076
Humboldt, W., 3593, 3686
Hungary, 4364-4373, 4970, 4975, 4980, 4981, 4985, 4992, 5014, 5020, 5021
Hunter College of the City of New York, New York 21, New York. Master's theses, 90, 411, 1013, 1131, 2290, 3339, 3494, 4127, 4526, 4709, 4793, 4928, 5673
Hutchins, R. M., 3481, 4033, 4263
Huxley, A., 4084, 4259
Huxley, T. H., 3853, 3902, 4008, 4030, 4063, 4081, 4253

Huysmans, C. M. G., 3440
Huysmans, J. K., 3440

I

Ibsen, H. J., 4605
Iceland, 4374, 4975
Idaho, College of. See College of Idaho
Idaho, University of. See University of Idaho
Igorots, 2710
Illinois, University of. See University of Illinois
Illinois State Normal University, Normal, Illinois. Master's theses, 444, 445, 448, 449, 450, 451, 3166 4479, 4857
Illinois Wesleyan University, Bloomington, Illinois. Master's thesis, 2507
Illiteracy. See Literacy education
Immaculate Heart College, Los Angeles 27, California. Master's theses, 3273, 4274, 4473, 4484, 4560, 4651, 5325
Immigrant education, 4861, 4862, 4879, 4880, 4888, 4890, 4897, 4904, 4905, 4909, 4923, 4929, 4933, 4945, 4947, 4951, 4981, 5017, 5021, 5633, 4870a
Imperial University of Peking, 1449
Inca education, 299
India, 1823-2133, 5114-5115
Indiana State Teachers College, Terre Haute, Indiana. Master's theses, 197, 2556, 3536, 3974, 4184, 4252, 4802, 4924, 4936, 4941, 4993, 4999
Indiana University, Bloomington, Indiana. Doctor's dissertations, 5, 24, 25, 120, 141, 363, 378, 397, 530, 589, 674, 922, 1048, 1077, 1276, 1404, 1474, 1835, 1900, 1920, 2153, 2156, 2234, 2486, 2582, 2589, 2595, 2620, 2627, 2633, 2634, 2640, 2647, 2651, 2655, 2910, 2918, 2963, 4306, 4953, 1921a, 2902a, 2636a. Master's theses, 303, 305, 399, 428, 439, 803, 1111, 1545, 2573, 2875, 2922, 2931, 2936, 2938, 2939, 2941, 2946, 2950, 3345, 3748, 4088, 4104, 4201, 4224, 4363, 4540, 4833. Other references, 25, 4953
Indo-China, 147, 226, 308, 2996, 2997, 2998. See also Viet-Nam
Indonesia, 2134-2140
Industrial education, 234, 716, 745, 748, 756, 777, 880, 893, 902, 904, 970, 1036, 1098, 1111, 1112, 1142, 1149, 1161, 1163, 1358, 1900, 1969, 2019, 2186, 2509, 2713, 3043, 3058, 3103, 3431, 3587, 4062, 4675, 4708, 5353, 5528. See also Technical, Trade, Vocational education
Infant schools. See Kindergarten education
Intelligence tests. See Tests, Standardized
Inter-American tests, 533, 536, 5479
Inter-American University of Puerto Rico, 1084
International African Institute, 339

International education, 3, 5, 9, 12, 16, 19, 25, 32, 34, 35, 40, 57, 68, 73, 74, 77, 84, 85, 89, 98, 101, 107, 113, 115, 118, 143, 146, 150, 151, 161, 175, 177, 214, 225, 236, 240, 241, 261, 277, 366, 575, 602, 679, 924, 1306, 1332, 1407, 2053, 2456, 3003, 3091, 3175, 3518, 4026, 4700, 4860, 4872, 4959, 4967
International Vocational Guidance Association, 3230
International YMCA College. See Springfield College
Iowa, University of. See State University of Iowa
Iowa State College of Agriculture and Mechanic Arts, Ames, Iowa. Doctor's dissertation, 429. Master's theses, 193, 256, 728, 754, 963, 1000, 1116, 1128, 1134, 1149, 1179, 1540, 2671, 2781, 5002, 5204. Other reference, 5002
Iowa State Teachers College, Cedar Falls, Iowa. Master's theses, 523, 2087, 2747, 2786, 2883, 2948, 3713, 4200
Iran (Persia), 2141-2166, 4956, 4970, 4975, 4977, 5116
Iraq, 2167-2199, 4956, 4970, 4975, 4977, 4990
Ireland, 4375-4401, 5117-5118
Ireland, Northern, 4092, 4144
Islamic education. See Muslim education
Isle of Pines, 865
Isocrates, 4342
Israel, 2200-2304, 4956, 4957, 4970, 4975, 4977
Italy, 4402-4568, 5119-5150
Ivrit B'Ivrit, 139

J

Jacks, L. P., 4128
Jahn, F. L., 3814
Jamaica. See West Indies
James, W., 3127
Jan H. Hofmeyer School of Social Work, 506a
Janet, P., 3441
Jankola, M., 5684
Japan, 2305-2478, 5151-5206
Japan Christian Quarterly, Tokyo, Japan, 2340
Japanese, Teaching of, 2441
Japanese language schools, 5172, 5194
Jefferson, T., 3550
Jerome, Saint, 183, 2260, 2285, 2287
Jesuit education, 86, 576, 592, 909, 2363, 2719, 3010, 3014, 3023, 3030, 3039, 3050, 3061, 3165, 3199, 3706, 3973, 4392, 4721
Jesus Christ, 246, 254, 291, 1297, 1302, 1650, 2202, 2204, 2207, 2212, 2215, 2222, 2227, 2240, 2241, 2243, 2244, 2249, 2251, 2254, 2255, 2265, 2266, 2267, 2270, 2271, 2276, 2278, 2281, 2282, 2286, 2295, 2296, 2299, 2301, 3553
Jewish education, 139, 230, 910, 1320, 2200-2304, 2999, 3000, 3015, 3085, 3418, 3596, 3611, 3639, 3649, 3752, 3808, 4609, 4610, 4617, 4735, 4861,

GENERAL INDEX

Jewish education (Cont'd.), 4888, 5107, 5121, 5132, 5140, 5150, 5195
Jewish Education, New York, N. Y., 910
Jewish Institute of Religion. See Hebrew Union College -- Jewish Institute of Religion
Jewish Theological Seminary of America, New York 27, New York. Doctor's dissertations, 2223, 3639
Jinsai, I., 2349
Joan of Arc, 3179
Jocist method, 220, 815
John, Saint, 2268
John of Salisbury, 3497, 4205
Johannesburg, 506a
Johns Hopkins University, Baltimore, Maryland. Doctor's dissertations, 898, 1301, 1402, 2209, 2325, 2326, 3015, 3601, 3632, 3882, 3907, 3908, 4739. Master's theses, 245, 333, 2460, 3257, 3550
Johnson, S., 4003, 4173
Jordan, 2479-2480
Journal of Home Economics, Washington, D. C., 661
Journal of Negro History, Washington, D. C., 882
Journal of Race Development, Worcester, Massachusetts, 176
Journal of Religious Psychology, Worcester, Massachusetts, 144, 176
Jouvancy, J., 3400
Jowett, B., 4007
Juarez, B., 952
Judaeus, P., 2237
Julien, 261
Junior colleges (community colleges), 709, 751, 1902, 2379, 3126, 3163
Juvenal, 4552

K

Kagawa, T., 2368
Kairis, T., 4305
Kansas, University of. See University of Kansas
Kansas State College of Agriculture and Applied Science, Manhattan, Kansas. Doctor's dissertation, 2335
Kansas State Teachers College, Emporia, Kansas. Master's theses, 794, 2009, 3228, 3809, 4047, 5405
Kansas State Teachers College, Pittsburg, Kansas. Master's theses, 2102, 4939
Kant, I., 3110, 3191, 3601, 3633, 3660, 3702
Kautz, H., 3797
Kavirondo school, Kenya, 437, 438
Kawakami, H., 2342
Keller, G., 3656
Kellner, L., 3724
Kennedy School of Missions. See Hartford Seminary Foundation
Kent State University, Kent, Ohio. Master's theses, 795, 983, 1006, 3539, 5315

Kentucky, University of. See University of Kentucky
Kenya, 436-439
Kerschensteiner, G. M., 3612, 3669, 3673, 3734, 3751
Keyserling, H., 3662
Kibbotrim, 2239
Kidd, B., 4044
Kierkegaard, S., 3213, 3359, 3362, 3366, 3368
Kilpatrick, W. H., 361
Kindergarten, Pre-School, and Nursery school education, 449, 651, 911, 1224, 1416, 1612, 1691, 1744, 1887, 2418, 2526, 2676, 2747, 3167, 3322, 3539, 3787, 3829, 4409, 4463, 4472, 4534, 4542, 4622, 4800, 4865, 5079, 5080, 5214, 5222, 5307, 5369, 5471, 5493, 5610, 5665. See also Froebel; Montessori
Kingsley, C., 3996, 4280
Kitsilano High School, Canada, 774, 792
Kiwanis International, 679
Kiyotaka, K., 2306
Klein, M., 3113
Knox, J., 4025
Kobe College, Japan, 2453
Koheleth, 300
Kondratier, Mr., 4794
Koraes, A., 4305, 4332
Korea, 2481-2541, 4956, 4970, 4972, 4979, 5013
Korzybski, A., 4619
Krause, K. C. F., 3742
Krumbacher, A., 3255
Kyoto University, Japan, 2342

L

Labor movement, 2258, 4010
La Chalotais, L. R. D., 3394, 3350, 3577
Lady Irwin College, India, 1968
La Habra Experiment, 974
Laicism, 3411
Lakanal, J., 3436
Lama education, 2956
Lancaster, J., 4209
Lanfranc, Archbishop, 3555
Lanne, A., 3502
Larsson, G., 4676
Latin, Teaching of, 3208, 3236, 3265, 3283, 3303, 4046
Latin-American, 5207-5653
Latvia, 119, 147, 226, 4975
Laubach, F. C., 102, 124, 228, 278
Laurie, S. S., 4009
Law, Canon. See Canon law
League of Nations, 3, 30, 44, 87, 177, 1819
League of United Latin-American Citizens, 5366
Leasuretime activities. See Recreation.
Lebanon, 2542-2552, 4957, 4970, 4975, 4977
Lee, F. C., 1822
Legal education, 4449
Legislation, Canon. See Canon Law.
Legislation, Educational, 551, 766, 772, 773, 928, 1438, 1757, 2610, 2814, 3045, 3768, 3947, 4048, 4124, 4143, 4178, 4588, 4591, 4791, 4927

Leiter International Performance scale, 73, 4966, 5166, 5171, 5309, 5506
Leland Stanford Junior University. See Stanford University.
Leo XIII, 4458, 4477, 4493, 4562
Leopold, G. A. J., 3140
Lessing, G. E., 3749, 3767
Lewin, K., 3112, 4719
Lewis, S., 484
Liberal Arts, 184, 3001, 3042, 3065
Liberia, 440-451
Libraries, 279, 562, 708, 780, 809, 892, 1006, 1177, 1198, 1478, 1506, 1605, 1647, 1657, 1761, 1799, 1800, 1801, 1811, 1815, 2465, 2850, 2887, 3071, 3178, 3198, 3340, 3343, 3449, 3744, 4098, 4213, 4501, 4598, 4602, 4743, 4778, 4799, 4835, 5315
Libya, 120, 212, 226, 322
Lietz, H., 3588
Linacre, T., 4185
Lind, J., 3216
Lindworsky, J., 3291
Lingam Middle School, Hong Kong, 1360
Lingnan University, China, 1370
Linguistics, General, 3375
Literacy education, 70, 93, 102, 121, 124, 228, 278, 313, 430, 494, 495, 982, 1242, 1373, 1888, 1894, 2017, 2094, 2572
Literature of Japanese Education, 1945-1954, Hamden, Connecticut: Shoe String Press, 1955. viii, 210 p., 1300, 2306, 2312, 2313, 2314, 2317, 2319, 2323, 2325, 2332, 2336, 2339, 2346, 2350, 2355, 2395, 2426, 2468
Lithuania, 4569-4571, 4985, 4987, 4992, 4993, 5001, 5003, 5020, 5654
Livingstone, D., 327
Livingstone, R. W., 4198
Locke, J., 3110, 3112, 3143, 3149, 3157, 3168, 3188, 3205, 3209, 3224, 3259, 3865, 3977, 4000, 4024, 4092, 4103, 4112, 4116, 4153, 4163, 4193, 4245, 4275
Lolo of China, 1586
Lombardo-Radice, G., 4416
Lorettine education, 1024
Louis XIV, Education of, 3488
Louisiana State University and State Agricultural and Mechanical College, University Station, Baton Rouge, Louisiana. Doctor's dissertations, 2483, 5221. Master's theses, 874, 1676, 3297, 3436, 4180, 4552, 4980, 4983, 5144
Louisville, University of. See University of Louisville
Louisville Presbyterian Theological Seminary, Louisville 2, Kentucky. Master's thesis, 1233
Loyola College, Baltimore 10, Maryland. Master's theses, 3427, 3806
Loyola University, Chicago 11, Illinois. Doctor's dissertation, 1870. Master's theses, 943, 944, 1321, 2017, 3214, 3240, 3321, 3967, 4258, 4703, 4920
Lucknow University, India, 1911
Lucretius, 3135
Luis de Leon, 4644

Luther, M., 3146, 3624, 3699, 3703, 3705, 3728, 3736, 3747, 3754, 3769, 3790, 3796, 3805, 3806, 3826, 3827, 3621a

Lutheran education, 292, 446, 1894, 2108, 2133, 2322, 3084, 3703, 3709, 3806, 5111

Luxembourg, 3198

Lyly, J., 4053

M

McAuley, C., 3486, 4387, 4395

McCormick Theological Seminary, Chicago 14, Chicago, Illinois. (Formerly Presbyterian Theological Seminary until 1943; includes also Presbyterian College of Christian Education, which was absorbed in 1949, and with which the Seminary had cooperated closely in earlier years). Master's theses, 38, 84, 682, 854, 2525, 2923, 5372, 5623, 5696

McDowell, E. A., 3195

Mabillon, J., 3377

Macauley, T. B., 2021, 4236, 4285

Machiavelli, N., 3263, 4502

Macrakis, A., 4305

Madagascar, 308

Madigas, 1857

Magdalen College, England, 4172

Magellan, F., 2775

Magic, Study of, 3013, 3064, 3399

Maine, University of. See University of Maine

Malaya, 2553-2562, 4975

Malta, 142, 164, 226

Manchuria, 2563

Manhattanville College of the Sacred Heart, Purchase, New York. Master's theses, 3207, 4013

Manitoba. See preceding No. 545

Maintenon, Madame de, 3463, 3483, 3489, 3504, 3530, 3582

Majuro, 4856

Malory, T., 3177

Manila, University of. See University of Manila

Manjon, A., 4641

Mann, H., 1186, 1195, 3739

Mannheim, K., 3646, 3671

Mannheim school system, 3606

Mantovani, J., 1202

Mariana Islands, 4859

Marionettes, 5416

Maritain, J., 3207, 3408, 3420, 3475, 3481

Marlowe, C., 3922

Marlowe, J., 3216

Marquesas Islands, 4856

Marquette University, Milwaukee 3, Wisconsin. Master's theses, 1562, 2018, 3242, 3284, 3333, 3546, 4394, 4513, 4618, 5113

Marshall College, Huntington 1, West Virginia. Master's thesis, 4083

Marshall Islands, 4859

Mar Thoma Syrian church education, 1859, 1869

Martin, M. S. J., 4507

Martineau, H., 4075, 4273

Martinique, 147

Marx, K., 3835

Mary of the Incarnation, 718

Maryknoll schools, 1318

Maryland, University of. See University of Maryland

Masaryk, T. G., 3331

Mason, L., 4698

Mass Education Movement, China, 1504

Massachusetts, University of. See University of Massachusetts

Massachusetts Agricultural College. See University of Massachusetts

Massachusetts Institute of Technology, Cambridge, Massachusetts. Master's thesis, 1258

Massachusetts State College. See University of Massachusetts

Massachusetts State Teachers College, Boston 15, Massachusetts. Master's theses, 2365, 4073, 4389

Massachusetts State Teachers College, Fitchburg, Massachusetts. Master's theses, 1182, 4760

Massachusetts State Teachers College, Hyannis, Massachusetts. (Discontinued 1944, Library combined with that of Massachusetts State Teachers College, Bridgewater.) Master's thesis, 4884

Massachusetts State Teachers College, North Adams, Massachusetts. Master's thesis, 3039

Master's theses. See under names of individual institutions

Mathematics education, 15, 129, 163, 263, 418, 463, 513, 574, 793, 821, 822, 1095, 1197, 1355, 1543, 1555, 2105, 2195, 2252, 2479, 2510, 2766, 2787, 2794, 2916, 2937, 2951, 3244, 3406, 3538, 3756, 3861, 3946, 4027, 4039, 4061, 4144, 4249, 4323, 4324, 4334, 4494, 4866, 4883, 5271, 5295, 5647. See also Algebra; Arithmetic; Geometry; Trigonometry

Mathura, 1863

Mauriac, F., 3432

Maurus, R., 3472, 3628, 3675, 3676, 3690, 3801, 3825

Maya education, 299

Mead, G. H., 3112

Measurements, Educational. See Tests, Standardized

Mechanical drawing, Teaching of, 5648

Medical education, 58, 3004, 3017, 3379, 4449, 4483

Meiji Gakuen University, Japan, •2332

Melanchthon, P., 3618, 3691, 3728, 3769

Mendelssohn, M., 2288, 3808

Mental hygiene, 1059, 2000, 3848

Mentally retarded, Education of, 408, 4360

Mercier, Cardinal, 3320

Meredith, G., 4199

Merici, A., 4427, 4564

Merimee, P., 3416

Methodist education, 267, 327, 848, 919, 951, 997, 1089, 1236, 1408, 1548, 1622, 1696, 1720, 1818, 1930, 2070, 2505, 2519, 2557, 2559, 2823, 4821, 4823, 5126, 5127, 5182, 5205, 5398, 5538, 5694

Metric weights and measures, 1189

Meumann, E., 3664

Mexican-Americans. See Latin-Americans

Mexico, 887-1040, 5207, 5653

Meysenbug, M., 3295

Miami University, Oxford, Ohio. Master's thesis, 1001

Michigan, University of. See University of Michigan.

Michigan State College of Agriculture and Applied Science. See Michigan State University of Agriculture and Applied Science

Michigan State University of Agriculture and Applied Science, East Lansing, Michigan. (Formerly Michigan State College of Agriculture and Applied Science). Doctor's dissertations, 145, 621, 840, 2334, 2597, 3329, 5043, 5220. Master's thesis, 1547

Microfilm Abstracts. See Dissertation Abstracts

Micronesia, 4858, 4859

Middle schools. See Secondary education

Miguel de Cervantes Laovedra, 4658

Military Science and Tactics, 1068

Mill, J. S., 3918, 3929, 4099, 4170

Mills College, Oakland 13, California. Master's thesis, 2763

Milton, J., 208, 3168, 3964, 3974, 3977, 3987, 4055, 4193, 4201, 4252, 4260, 4261

Ministers, Education of. See Theological education

Ministries of education, National, 119, 917, 947, 1356, 1749

Minnesota, University of. See University of Minnesota

Minnesota State Techers College, Mankato, Minnesota. Master's thesis, 4606

Miskito Indians, 538

Missionary education, 6, 38, 47, 51, 62, 63, 69, 75, 80, 83, 88, 93, 94, 97, 103, 104, 110, 111, 116, 123, 130, 144, 162, 164, 182, 193, 197, 211, 228, 233, 268, 303, 309, 320, 339, 342, 349, 350, 351, 352, 353, 359, 365, 423, 431, 461, 481, 491, 492, 493, 497, 514, 519, 539, 666, 852, 948, 955, 977, 987, 996, 1019, 1217, 1229, 1232, 1233, 1235, 1253, 1269, 1273, 1278, 1293, 1299, 1318, 1326, 1336, 1351, 1365, 1402, 1413, 1431, 1455, 1466, 1512, 1513, 1589, 1592, 1667, 1693, 1701, 1703, 1723, 1741, 1775, 1790, 1791, 1794, 1795,

GENERAL INDEX

Missionary education (Cont'd.), 1825, 1828, 1858, 1885, 1961, 1964, 2023, 2029, 2050, 2056, 2085, 2126, 2130, 2159, 2308, 2318, 2330, 2343, 2352, 2363, 2379, 2492, 2536, 2671, 2705, 2898, 2959, 2979, 2991, 4596, 5115. See also Catholic, Christian, Protestant, Religious education
Mississippi, University of. See University of Mississippi
Missouri, University of. See University of Missouri.
Mistral, G., 1261
Mizrachi education, 2214
Mo, T., 1527
Mohammedan education. See Muslim education
Moliere, J. B. P., 3477, 3489
Monaco, 147, 226
Monastic schools, 3541, 3852, 4189, 4207, 4226, 4385, 4388, 4393, 4400
Monitorial system, 1649
Montagu, M. W., 3976
Montaigne, M., 3221, 3409, 3437, 3476, 3495, 3496, 3551
Montana State University, Missoula, Montana. Master's thesis, 1106
Monte Cassino, 4532
Montessori, M., 3089, 3167, 4409, 4463, 4472, 4479, 4480, 4499, 4533, 4534, 4542
Moore, G. E., 4012
Moore, T., 4140
Moral education, 108, 174, 183, 208, 218, 233, 404, 722, 1302, 1407, 1524, 1568, 1642, 1704, 1725, 1785, 1812, 1821, 1875, 1999, 2227, 2253, 2367, 2381, 2389, 2401, 2430, 2463, 2556, 2765, 2923, 2966, 2983, 3030, 3398, 3434, 3678, 3685, 3692, 3700, 3719, 3751, 4194, 4225, 4268, 4269, 4304, 4321, 4533, 4652, 4731, 4761, 4840, 5281
More, H., 3971
More, T., 245, 286, 3888, 3969, 4072, 4125
Moro, 2653
Morocco, 212, 226
Morris, W., 245, 286, 3880, 4242
Morrison, H. C., 3176
Morsabre, J. M., 3485
Moses, 2208, 2269
Moslem education. See Muslim education
Mount Holyoke College, South Hadley, Massachusets, 4950
Mount Saint Joseph Teachers College, Buffalo, New York. Master's theses, 718, 3031, 3253, 4188, 4976
Mozart, W., 198, 3140
Mulcaster, R., 4002, 4235
Munich method, 258
Municipal University of Wichita, Wichita, Kansas. Master's theses, 257, 1631, 3303, 3717
Music education, 2, 18, 27, 37, 52, 61, 72, 134, 135, 150, 205, 252, 282, 295, 437, 535, 542, 565, 591, 638, 798, 850, 868, 914, 946, 1057, 1066, 1171, 1234, 1318, 1429, 1432, 1501, 1503, 1539, 1570, 1654, 1661, 1775, 2298, 2302, 2334, 2378, 2507, 2508,

Music education, (Cont'd.), 2780, 3006, 3009, 3051, 3055, 3072, 3076, 3102, 3121, 3173, 3190, 3264, 3281, 3317, 3348, 3355, 3591, 3607, 3624, 3763, 3799, 3811, 4070, 4186, 4200, 4308, 4344, 4348, 4365, 4597, 4603, 4640, 4691, 4698, 4714, 4783, 4801, 4803, 4937, 4968, 4985, 4989, 4991, 4997, 5158, 5352, 5358, 5362, 5434, 5453, 5489, 5522, 5539, 5597, 5601, 5603, 5604, 5655. See also Dancing
Musical Quarterly, New York, New York, 535
Muslim education 130, 186, 233, 2159, 2165, 2172, 2549, 3196
Mussolini, B., 4509
Mysticism, 2030

N

Nagle, N., 4390
Napier, J., 4027
Napoleon I., 198, 223, 3511, 3564
Natal, 327, 502, 514
Natarp, P., 3616
National Central University, China, 1804
National Intelligence Test, 5250
National ministries of education, 119
National Peking University, China, 1480
National Union of Teachers, 3891, 3948
Nauru, 247
Nazarene Theological Seminary, Kansas City, Missouri. Master's thesis, 47
Nebraska, University of. See University of Nebraska
Negro education, Canada, 711, 839, 1877
Netherlands, 4572-4589, 5092-5094
Nevius Missionary Method, 359, 2489
New Brunswick. See preceding No. 545
New Guinea, 160, 179, 195, 247, 275, 308, 4839
New Jersey State College, Newark 4, New Jersey. (Formerly New Jersey State Teachers College, to 1958). Master's theses, 118, 328, 329, 442, 2467, 2811, 3816, 4124, 4851, 5669, 5677
New Jersey State College, Upper Montclair, New Jersey. (Formerly New Jersey State Teachers College, to 1958). Master's theses, 4242, 4777
New Life Movement, China, 1504
New Mexico, University of. See University of New Mexico
New Mexico Highlands University, Las Vegas, New Mexico. (Formerly New Mexico Normal University). Master's thesis, 5369
New Mexico Historical Review, Sante Fe, New Mexico. 535
New Mexico Normal University. See New Mexico Highlands University
New Mexico State Teachers College. See New Mexico Western College

New Mexico Western College, Silver City, New Mexico. (Formerly New Mexico State Teachers College). Master's theses, 4943, 5285, 5330, 5493, 5519, 5545, 5618
New School for Social Research, New York 11, New York. Doctor's dissertations, 1927, 4403. Master's thesis, 2999
New South Wales, 4815, 4820, 4821, 4829, 4830, 4831, 4834
New York State College for Teachers at Albany, Albany, New York. Master's theses, 332, 800, 3038, 3209, 3468, 3470, 3516, 3735, 3795, 4097, 4146, 4275, 4553, 4712, 4888, 4909, 4989, 4998, 5016, 5135
New York University, New York 3, New York. Doctor's dissertations, 17, 27, 35, 126, 129, 131, 136, 140, 169, 173, 174, 321, 331, 374, 454, 456, 457, 504, 547, 552, 553, 556, 569, 615, 616, 666, 670, 876, 930, 1045, 1055, 1059, 1080, 1168, 1244, 1270, 1287, 1302, 1332, 1384, 1392, 1420, 1423, 1429, 1446, 1466, 1477, 1499, 1507, 1509, 1823, 1828, 1853, 1854, 1855, 1861, 1872, 1888, 1894, 1895, 2141, 2143, 2202, 2203, 2205, 2216, 2217, 2221, 2222, 2224, 2232, 2331, 2338, 2351, 2484, 2491, 2503, 2583, 2605, 2653, 2896, 2915, 2958, 2961, 3006, 3010, 3011, 3012, 3014, 3072, 3084, 3086, 3089, 3098, 3105, 3107, 3111, 3113, 3120, 3122, 3124, 3127, 3132, 3308, 3316, 3328, 3352, 3359, 3374, 3383, 3391, 3392, 3397, 3398, 3404, 3409, 3419, 3421, 3588, 3594, 3597, 3602, 3604, 3606, 3612, 3616, 3620, 3621, 3622, 3624, 3630, 3635, 3638, 3642, 3644, 3658, 3660, 3661, 3662, 3664, 3670, 3848, 3852, 3856, 3857, 3863, 3875, 3888, 3898, 3902, 3929, 3931, 3934, 3937, 3938, 3947, 4299, 4309, 4377, 4378, 4406, 4407, 4408, 4411, 4416, 4422, 4430, 4433, 4436, 4575, 4578, 4632, 4665, 4725, 4734, 4737, 4738, 4815, 4960, 5035, 5120, 5121, 5156, 5231, 5660, 5661, 5664, 5665, 5666, 5694. Master's theses, 58, 96, 224, 279, 306, 446, 749, 839, 979, 1147, 1156, 1306, 1313, 1320, 1608, 1634, 1695, 1740, 1742, 1758, 1794, 1950, 1965, 1970, 1981, 2000, 2040, 2045, 2237, 2244, 2268, 2269, 2272, 2284, 2299, 2430, 2431, 2437, 2469, 2538, 2539, 2973, 3034, 3147, 3157, 3160, 3200, 3213, 3224, 3260, 3287, 3299, 3336, 3337, 3347, 3351, 3368, 3441, 3469, 3522, 3691, 3734, 3737, 3747, 3769, 3780, 3783, 3794, 3807, 3975, 3976, 3984, 3989, 4020, 4039, 4052, 4080, 4103, 4176, 4210, 4218, 4246, 4318, 4332, 4343, 4360, 4452, 4454, 4462, 4480, 4498, 4512, 4661, 4675, 4764, 4773, 4784, 4792, 4795, 4797, 4878, 4889, 5053, 5080, 5086, 5128, 5146, 5681
New Zealand, 4840-4849, 4957, 4975
Newfoundland. See preceding No. 545
Newman, J. H., 184, 3207, 4006, 4013, 4033, 4063, 4081, 4099, 4148, 4161, 4174, 4228, 4260, 4263, 4274, 4283

Newton, I., 3861
Niagara University, Niagara University, New York. Doctor's dissertations, 3314, 3589. Master's theses, 434, 799, 816, 3235, 3969, 4461
Nicaragua, 119, 126, 133, 190, 205, 215, 226, 256, 260, 307, 528, 529, 530, 531, 537, 538, 539, 541, 4970
Nietzsche, F. W., 3679, 3813
Nigeria, 452-478, 4956, 4970
Night schools, 927, 4905
Nightingale, F., 3179, 3216, 3919
North Carolina, University of. See University of North Carolina
North Carolina Agricultural and Technical College. See Agricultural and Technical College of North Carolina.
North Carolina College at Durham, Durham, North Carolina. Master's thesis, 443
North Dakota, University of. See University of North Dakota
North Texas State College, Denton, Texas. (Formerly North Texas State Teachers College, to 1949). Master's theses, 95, 252, 970, 1038, 3043, 3431, 3821, 4322, 4362, 4708, 5010, 5264, 5320, 5322, 5334, 5373, 5428, 5433, 5522, 5587, 5651
Northeast Missouri State Teachers College, Kirksville, Missouri. Master's theses, 2196, 2727, 2729, 2797, 2812, 2837, 4852
Northeastern University, Boston 15, Massachusetts. Master's thesis, 3460
Northern Baptist Theological Seminary, Chicago 12, Illinois. Doctor's dissertation, 1293
Northern Ireland, 4092, 4144
Northwestern University, Evanston, Illinois. Doctor's dissertations, 18, 146, 150, 575, 622, 628, 653, 659, 1408, 2228, 2344, 3095, 3097, 3356, 3395, 3877, 3914, 3950, 4425, 4724, 4969, 4972, 5034, 5209, 5230. Master's theses, 205, 233, 732, 798, 954, 1193, 1243, 1343, 1580, 1596, 1665, 1667, 1672, 1728, 1768, 1812, 2083, 2114, 2137, 2236, 2264, 2509, 2528, 2536, 2558, 2562, 2706, 2827, 2847, 3570, 3703, 3798, 4014, 4684, 4899, 4927, 4985, 5126, 5127, 5141
Norway, 4590-4606, 4957, 4963, 4970, 4971, 4975, 4978, 4985, 4988, 5023, 5025, 5655, 5683
Notre Dame, University of. See University of Notre Dame
Nova Scotia. See preceding No. 545
Nunn, P., 3878a
Nursery school education. See Kindergarten and Nursery school education
Nursing education, 132, 407, 710, 713, 731, 752, 753, 763, 797, 832, 1105, 1114, 1196, 1314, 1528, 1832, 2748, 2750, 3520, 3576, 4303
Nyasaland, 479-481

O

Oberlin College, Oberlin, Ohio. Master's theses, 461, 488, 734, 761, 1546, 1559, 1585, 1620, 1635, 1643, 1661, 1683, 1805, 2023, 2163, 2401, 2419, 2455, 2458, 2927, 3836, 4294, 5077
Oblates of St. Francis de Sales, 200
Occidental College, Los Angeles 41, California. Master's thesis, 4079
Occupation of Japan, Effect on education of, 2305, 2307, 2311, 2312, 2313, 2361, 2328, 2336, 2337, 2339, 2353, 2355, 2359, 2365, 2370, 2371, 2375, 2392, 2393, 2394, 2403, 2411, 2412, 2413, 2426, 2429, 2473, 2478
Occupied Europe, American education in, 3057, 3170, 3598, 3602, 3605, 3641, 3648, 3680, 3681, 3701, 3707, 3717, 3718, 3725, 3731, 3741, 3746, 3755, 3760, 3761, 3789, 3816, 3831, 3840, 4518
Oglethorpe University, Oglethorpe University, Georgia. Master's thesis, 3829
Ohio, University of. See Miami University, Ohio State University, Ohio University
Ohio State University, Columbus 10, Ohio. Doctor's dissertations, 124, 366, 534, 598, 843, 851, 919, 1265, 1461, 1891, 1909, 1921a, 1931, 2172, 2175, 2188, 2542, 2566, 2622, 2639, 2903, 2960, 3070, 3128, 3355, 3420, 3618, 3619, 3645, 3871, 3884, 3916, 3957, 4418, 4635, 4805, 162a. Master's theses, 241, 358, 409, 417, 430, 447, 463, 525, 713, 807, 830, 846, 861, 863, 877, 885, 1117, 1141, 1163, 1170, 1190, 1213, 1250, 1280, 1285, 1310, 1345, 1714, 1720, 1756, 1766, 1789, 1977, 1979, 2014, 2028, 2033, 2048, 2051, 2062, 2064, 2068, 2072, 2074, 2140, 2193, 2385, 2412, 2449, 2480, 2512, 2527, 2550, 2755, 2762, 2829, 2840, 2881, 2890, 2924, 2932, 2934, 2937, 2951, 2955, 2986, 3143, 3216, 3239, 3248, 3267, 3459, 3506, 3528, 3683, 3721, 3776, 3814, 3842, 4019, 4031, 4101, 4123, 4156, 4205, 4240, 4253, 4271, 4281, 4324, 4341, 4357, 4756, 4796, 4830, 4990, 4992, 5020, 5187, 5199, 1908a, 3878a. Other references, 2072, 4990
Ohio University, Athens, Ohio. Master's theses, 282, 1119, 1539, 2773, 2816, 4370, 4903, 4938, 5013. Other references, 4903, 4938
Okinawa, 4850-4853
Oklahoma, University of. See University of Oklahoma
Oklahoma Agricultural and Mechanical College. See Oklahoma State University of Agriculture and Applied Science
Oklahoma State University of Agriculture and Applied Science, Stillwater, Oklahoma. (Formerly Oklahoma Agricultural and Mechanical College, until 1957). Master's theses, 219, 249, 1214, 1288, 1291, 3145, 3177, Oklahoma State University of Agriculture and Applied Science (Cont'd.), 3226, 3826, 4002, 4041, 4091, 4336, 4561
Olave, F., 535
Oliver Twist, 1739
Olympic Games, 16
Omar Khayyam, 2151
Ontario. See preceding No. 545
Open air schools, 3302
Orange Free State, 510, 512
Oregon, University of. See University of Oregon
Oregon State College, Corvallis, Oregon. Doctor's dissertations, 584, 586, 626, 632, 656, 671, 677, 1898. Master's theses, 681, 694, 756, 767, 1680, 1686, 1744, 2058, 2370, 2513, 3687, 3701, 3786, 4062, 5196, 5353
Organization. See Administration
Organization of American States, 859
Origen of Alexandria, 373
Orlando di Lasso, 3317
Ortega y Gasset, J., 4653, 4655
Osaka Civil Affairs team, 2305
Osmania Agricultural College, India, 2123
Otis Classification Test, 5435
Otto, B., 3815
Otto, E., 3594
Ottoman Empire. See Turkey
Overseas teaching, 114
Owen, R., 4134, 4265
Ozanam, F., 3451

P

Pacific, College of. See College of the Pacific
Pacific Islands, 4857-4859
Pacific School of Religion, Berkeley 9, California. Master's theses, 482, 709, 1309, 2246, 2417, 4829, 5012, 5085, 5182, 5191, 5203, 5205
Pacific Union College, Angwin, California. Master's theses, 483, 1029, 1595, 1760, 2027, 2035, 2039, 2548, 3790, 4120, 4355, 4596
Pacific University, Forest Grove, Oregon. Master's theses, 1556, 2034
Pagan education, 17, 122, 153, 164
Pakistan, 2564-2579, 4956, 4957, 4964, 4967, 4970, 4977, 5026
Palace school, 3466
Palaus, 4856
Palestine. See Israel
Palma, R., 1281
Panama, 1041-1043, 4970, 4975
Pan-American conferences, 277
Papal encyclicals. See Encyclicals
Paraguay, 1273, 4957
Pasteur, L., 198, 3248
Paul, J., 3625
Paul, Saint, 191, 2217, 2218, 2221, 2242, 2257, 2289
Paulsen, F., 3722, 3739
Payne, J., 4132
Payot, J., 3291

GENERAL INDEX

Peabody College. See George Peabody College for Teachers
Pearse, P. H., 4386, 4394
Pedagogical Seminary, Worcester, Massachusetts, 7, 11, 1487, 2584, 3002, 3131, 4855
Pedro de Gante, 535
Peiping National Teachers College, China, 1432
Pennsylvania, University of. See University of Pennsylvania
Pennsylvania State College. See Pennsylvania State University
Pennsylvania State University, University Park, Pennsylvania. (Formerly Pennsylvania State College to 1953). Abstracts of all doctoral dissertations are published and copies of original dissertations are available on microfilm from University Microfilms, Ann Arbor, Michigan. Doctor's dissertations, 171, 609, 641, 932, 1060, 1073, 1085, 2186, 3903. Master's theses, 190, 311, 802, 880, 1112, 1135, 1140, 1148, 1154, 1161, 1162, 1516, 2698, 2767, 2768, 2806, 2849, 3286, 4320, 4326, 4696, 4885
Pensions, 1099, 2735, 3936, 4088, 4587
Pentateuch, 2269
Pepys, S., 3211
Persia. See Iran
Personnel services. See Guidance
Peru, 1274-1286, 4957, 4970, 4975, 4990
Pestalozzi, J. H., 3110, 3127, 3138, 3141, 3168, 3174, 3193, 3200, 3205, 3221, 3245, 3817, 4686, 4689, 4692, 4693, 4694, 4696, 4698, 4701, 4705, 4707, 4708, 4709, 4713, 4718, 4719, 4720, 4722
Ph.D. programs, 3070
Philippine College of Commerce, 2755
Philippine Evangelical education, 2777
Philippine Normal College, 2597, 2623, 2655, 2685, 2872, 2882, 2883, 2636a
Philippine Union College, 2620
Philippine Women's College, 2613
Philippine Women's University, 2627
Philippines, 2580-2893, 5095-5097
Philippines, American school system in, 2600, 2602, 2616, 2626, 2643, 2673, 2677, 2681, 2693, 2698, 2717, 2718, 2732, 2759, 2770, 2796, 2814, 2830, 2843, 2844, 2871, 2875
Philippines, Japanese Occupation of, 2617, 2686, 2795
Philippines, University of the. See University of the Philippines
Phillips University, Enid, Oklahoma. Master's thesis, 2461
Philosophy of Education, 11, 125, 165, 198, 221, 238, 266, 296, 361, 390, 599, 1047, 1202, 1359, 1386, 1389, 1396, 1411, 1450, 1482, 1499, 1541, 1592, 1672, 1689, 1763, 1854, 1907, 1915, 1963, 2030, 2061, 2078, 2079, 2166, 2175, 2213, 2275, 2278, 2348,

Philosophy of education (Cont'd.), 2351, 2372, 2373, 2411, 2475, 2500, 2543, 2552, 2604, 2803, 2878, 2978, 3069, 3074, 3092, 3097, 3122, 3149, 3159, 3185, 3205, 3220, 3224, 3227, 3233, 3242, 3251, 3271, 3291, 3308, 3329, 3378, 3383, 3388, 3389, 3392, 3403, 3406, 3408, 3431, 3433, 3444, 3454, 3467, 3481, 3485, 3501, 3571, 3613, 3618, 3622, 3627, 3645, 3652, 3654, 3660, 3671, 3672, 3673, 3677, 3693, 3702, 3709, 3714, 3730, 3736, 3757, 3778, 3780, 3790, 3800, 3810, 3815, 3829, 3832, 3856, 3857, 3860, 3865, 3871, 3880, 3885, 3899, 3905, 3911, 3916, 3919, 3929, 3932, 3934, 3939a, 3978, 3987, 4005, 4009, 4012, 4013, 4019, 4024, 4033, 4037, 4044, 4056, 4072, 4085, 4097, 4116, 4135, 4138, 4141, 4148, 4210, 4218, 4219, 4223, 4239, 4252, 4258, 4260, 4263, 4307, 4310, 4325, 4330, 4354, 4404, 4418, 4435, 4439, 4451, 4486, 4506, 4514, 4536, 4544, 4638, 4646, 4708, 4745, 4771, 4819. See also individual educational philosophers, especially Aristotle, Arnold, Augustine, Bacon, Bode, Carlyle, Chrysostom, Comenius, Condorcet, Confucius, Dewey, Erasmus, Feltre, Fenlon, Froebel, Gandhi, Hegel, Herbart, Hutchins, Huxley, Jerome, Kant, Locke, Maritain, Maurus, Mill, Milton, Montaigne, Newman, Nietzsche, Pestalozzi, Plato, Rabelais, Rousseau, Ruskin, Russell, Socrates, Spencer, Tagore, Thomas Aquinas, Tolstoy, Vives, Wells, Wesley, Whitehead
Physical education, 16, 90, 92, 181, 219, 288, 378, 422, 518, 612, 641, 651, 669, 686, 715, 726, 733, 750, 760, 782, 811, 835, 836, 856, 984, 1068, 1157, 1221, 1238, 1279, 1344, 1361, 1376, 1498, 1505, 1678, 1679, 1684, 1687, 1706, 1758, 1804, 1826, 1855, 1864, 1895, 1920, 1928, 1940, 1941, 1946, 1957, 2042, 2047, 2069, 2092, 2143, 2259, 2273, 2333, 2466, 2569, 2584, 2601, 2605, 2687, 2688, 2689, 2714, 2723, 2738, 2805, 2808, 2837, 2838, 2841, 2886, 2915, 3033, 3034, 3082, 3087, 3139, 3177, 3206, 3212, 3219, 3231, 3280, 3293, 3355, 3363, 3371, 3599, 3647, 3750, 3775, 3776, 3817, 3818, 3878, 3900, 4036, 4057, 4326, 4329, 4331, 4489, 4664, 4679, 4683, 4741, 4756, 4765, 4830, 4892, 4996, 5013, 5063, 5078, 5302, 5316, 5327, 5388, 5439, 5457, 5525 5561. See also Health education; Recreation
Physical therapy education, 58
Physics, Teaching of, 2663, 2787, 4095
Piarist Fathers, 3253
Piccolomini, A. S., 4428, 4433
Pinocchio, 4417
Pittsburgh, University of. See University of Pittsburgh
Pittsburgh-Xenia Theological Seminary, Pittsburgh 6, Pennsylvania. Master's thesis, 4695

Pius XI, 4482, 4541
Pius XII, 4441, 4500, 4531
Plato, 136, 184, 245, 286, 3086, 3112, 3127, 3129, 3141, 3152, 3168, 3205, 3224, 3226, 3254, 3260, 3287, 4299, 4313, 4316, 4318, 4322, 4328, 4331, 4333, 4337, 4339, 4343, 4347, 4353, 4354, 4355, 4356, 4361, 4362
Plautus, 3101
Pliny, 4540
Plutarch, 3211
Poland, 4607-4623, 5656-5657
Polytechnic Institute of Puerto Rico, 1057
Ponape, 4856
Popes, 3116, 3118. See also Leo XIII; Pius XI; Pius XII; Encyclicals
Poppe, Father, 3323
Port Royalists, 3442
Portsmouth, Canada, 564
Portugal, 4624-4627, 4965, 4968, 4975, 4991, 5013, 5658
Portugese East Africa, 327
Postage stamps in education, 226
Post-Primary education. See Secondary education
Post-Secondary education. See Higher education
Presbyterian College of Christian Education. See McCormick Theological Seminary.
Presbyterian education, 38, 84, 854, 1240, 1373, 2107, 2489, 2504, 2522, 2528, 2728, 2897, 4121, 5398, 5623, 5696
Presbyterian Theological Seminary. See McCormick Theological Seminary
Pre-School education. See Kindergarten education
Priestly, J., 3982, 4037
Primary education. See Elementary education
Primitive education, 7, 41, 42, 52, 59, 65, 72, 79, 90, 95, 122, 129, 169, 172, 176, 179, 195, 247, 259, 262, 275, 287, 299, 306, 308, 315, 317, 318, 329, 438, 455, 532, 538, 897, 1293, 1988, 2653, 2710, 2758
Prince Edward Island. See preceding No. 545
Princes, Education of, 3054, 3263, 3590, 4559
Princeton Theological Seminary, Princeton, New Jersey. Doctor's dissertations, 33, 844, 1859. Master's theses, 93, 359, 413, 538, 1203, 1232, 1349, 1703, 1942, 2162, 2549, 2557, 5397
Princeton University, Princeton, New Jersey. Doctor's dissertations, 2488, 4421
Principalships, Improvement of, 395, 444, 791, 1054, 1565, 2169, 2715, 2846
Principles of education. See Philosophy of education
Professional education, 1829, 1920, 3629, 4054, 4449, 4527
Progressive education, 2007, 2575, 3254, 3344, 3458, 3612, 3751, 4469, 4555, 4632. See also Dewey, J.

Protestant education, 164, 270, 303, 313, 351, 353, 357, 539, 594, 596, 629, 650, 682, 733, 761, 780, 844, 908, 949, 954, 1082, 1122, 1183, 1203, 1229, 1231, 1309, 1365, 1412, 1413, 1431, 1455, 1470, 1498, 1512, 1521, 1656, 1737, 1788, 1828, 1850, 2037, 2314, 2352, 2385, 2416, 2458, 2487, 2498, 2525, 2671, 3111, 3651, 3663, 3769, 4366, 4434, 4580, 5087, 5127, 5151, 5397, 3621a. See also Theological education; Armenian Church, Baptist, Brethren in Christ, Christian Reformed, Church of Christ, Church of England, Church of the Brethren, Congregational, Dutch Reformed, Evangelical, Lutheran, Mar Thoma Syrian, Methodist, Philippine Evangelical, Presbyterian, Protestant Episcopal, Reformed Church in the United States, Seventh-day Adventist, United Brethren, United Church of Canada education; Protestant colleges listed in the United States; Protestant colleges listed in this index under "Higher Education"

Protestant Episcopal education, 2728
Proverbs, Book of, 2253
Proverbs, Mexican, 994
Psalms, 2256
Pseudo-Boethius, 3492
Publicity, Educational, 703, 2016, 3119
Public relations. See Publicity, Educational
Puerto Rico, 1044-1165, 5659-5682
Purdue University, Lafayette, Indiana. Doctor's dissertations, 1056, 1069, 4954. Master's theses, 2065, 2975, 4988. Other references, 4954, 4988
Putney Graduate School of Teacher Education, Putney, Vermont. Master's thesis, 5695
Pythagoras, 4341

Q

Quebec. See preceding No. 545
Queensland, 4813, 4818, 4824, 4836
Querbes, L., 3579
Quick, R. H., 4085
Quintilian, M. F., 184, 3127, 3168, 3224, 3254, 3255, 4405, 4406, 4436, 4450, 4453, 4459, 4469, 4504, 4546, 4548, 4561, 4563, 4568

R

Rabelais, F., 3221, 3437, 3468, 3471, 3554
Radcliffe College, Cambridge 38, Massachusetts. Doctor's dissertations, 2911, 4854. Other reference, 4950
Radio education, 197, 616, 659, 887, 981, 1488, 2193, 2385, 2490, 2955, 3128, 4243. See also Audio-Visual education
Raikes, R., 4065
Ramus, P., 3387

Ranschburg, P., 3638
Rashi, S. I., 3418
Ratio Studiorum. See Jesuit education
Ratke, W., 3221
Rauch, F. A., 3784
Ravel, M., 3195
Reading, Teaching of, 167, 358, 381, 451, 574, 676, 725, 742, 944, 978, 990, 1011, 1033, 1058, 1081, 1104, 1170, 1220, 1270, 1363, 1372, 1375, 1424, 1478, 1492, 1531, 1534, 1537, 1563, 1614, 1688, 1748, 1759, 1765, 1776, 1816, 2026, 2035, 2046, 2100, 2341, 2386, 2423, 2488, 2521, 2539, 2561, 2593, 2664, 2682, 2721, 2746, 2818, 2869, 2914, 2941, 2946, 3914, 3950, 4295, 4479, 4606, 4685, 4837, 4868, 4885, 4894, 4895, 4915, 4921, 4931, 4983, 4999, 5019, 5067, 5083, 5143, 5259, 5298, 5312, 5313, 5331, 5340, 5380, 5381, 5387, 5399, 5412, 5438, 5448, 5452, 5460, 5461, 5469, 5486, 5488, 5493, 5515, 5529, 5550, 5557, 5564, 5580, 5594, 5607, 5612, 5651, 5654, 5656, 5669
Realschule, 3711
Rebsamen, H. C., 1017
Recreation, 65, 122, 149, 187, 301, 340, 400, 415, 422, 577, 585, 612, 627, 651, 674, 760, 984, 1156, 1342, 1578, 1709, 2404, 2714, 2839, 3033, 3036, 3066, 3139, 3206, 3297, 3755, 3838, 4186, 4682, 4859, 5061, 5074, 5123, 546a. See also Dancing; Physical education
Reddie, C., 3938
Redlands, University of. See University of Redlands
Reed College, Portland, Oregon. Master's thesis, 5096
Reformed Church in the United States education, 1482, 2343
Rein, W., 3788
Religious education, 5, 17, 41, 62, 82, 108, 116, 117, 131, 176, 218, 226, 232, 233, 243, 266, 310, 314, 315, 351, 362, 482, 488, 489, 493, 520, 594, 618, 682, 690, 709, 722, 761, 778, 799, 815, 817, 819, 834, 857, 957, 1078, 1083, 1144, 1181, 1233, 1277, 1334, 1335, 1347, 1349, 1370, 1382, 1388, 1417, 1456, 1463, 1472, 1482, 1502, 1518, 1527, 1530, 1539, 1546, 1560, 1567, 1572, 1576, 1580, 1583, 1592, 1593, 1601, 1616, 1620, 1621, 1627, 1654, 1655, 1658, 1659, 1660, 1667, 1675, 1691, 1693, 1703, 1705, 1713, 1718, 1721, 1725, 1726, 1733, 1742, 1752, 1754, 1764, 1771, 1788, 1805, 1818, 1821, 1863, 1885, 1904, 1944, 1947, 1965, 1986, 2005, 2051, 2055, 2075, 2084, 2109, 2113, 2116, 2133, 2137, 2202, 2242, 2255, 2268, 2290, 2320, 2332, 2345, 2357, 2362, 2368, 2390, 2396, 2397, 2404, 2414, 2415, 2417, 2431, 2455, 2458, 2462, 2463, 2469, 2489, 2505, 2517, 2519, 2522, 2525, 2530, 2531, 2536, 2556, 2558, 2588, 2706, 2726, 2823, 2826, 2827, 2861, 2897, 2980, 2982, 2987, 3015, 3138, 3154, 3169, 3187,

Religious education (Cont'd.) 3203, 3218, 3312, 3323, 3326, 3330, 3359, 3360, 3372, 3381, 3442, 3453, 3543, 3563, 3583, 3624, 3663, 3703, 3705, 3757, 3770, 3791, 3819, 3884, 3892, 3924, 3954, 4047, 4076, 4103, 4107, 4130, 4137, 4175, 4231, 4305, 4368, 4434, 4510, 4533, 4554, 4580, 4589, 4625, 4640, 4669, 4681, 4716, 4726, 4813, 4821, 4840, 4841, 5012, 5062, 5102, 5108, 5126, 5141, 5191, 5203, 5212, 5372, 3621a. See also Christian, Missionary, Brahminic, Buddhist, Confucian, Coptic, Hindu, Jewish, Muslim, Shinto education
Religious Education, New York, N. Y., 556, 566, 573, 1471, 1859, 1860, 1904, 2204, 2208, 2210, 2228, 2340, 2603, 3015, 3400, 3596, 3611, 3621a, 3649, 3663, 3863, 4726, 4823, 5151, 5212, 5692
Religious of the Sacred Heart of Mary, 251, 290
Remplein, H., 3112
Research, Educational, 2683, 2854, 3091
Research in Industrial Education, 1930-1955, Washington: U. S. Department of Health, Education, and Welfare; Office of Education, 1957. 527 p. (Vocational Division Bulletin No. 264; Trade and Industrial Series No. 65). 75, 95, 447, 716, 744, 745, 765, 777, 880, 902, 1085, 1107, 1111, 1142, 1161, 1237, 1912, 1931, 1969, 2753, 2881, 3043, 3431, 3602, 3947, 4062, 4574, 4675, 4708, 4852
Retarded children, 628
Revista de Rivistas, Madrid, Spain, 535
Revista Rotaria, 85
Rhetorical education, 3095, 3395, 4425, 4436, 4443, 4447, 4504
Rhode Island College of Education, Providence 8, Rhode Island. Master's thesis, 3554
Rhodes, 147
Rhodesia, 482, 483
Rice, E. I., 4382
Richardson, S., 4220
Richmond, University of. See University of Richmond
Richter, J. P. F., 3625, 3654
Ritschl, A., 3757
Rivier College, Nashua, New Hampshire. Master's thesis, 3452
Rizal, J., 2803, 2852
Robert College, Turkey, 217, 2990
Roberval, G. P., 3422
Rochester, University of. See University of Rochester
Roerich, N., 4734
Rollin, C., 3385
Roman Catholic education. See Catholic education
Roman Empire, Rome. See Italy
Romania, 4628-2629, 4956, 4963, 4970, 4975
Roosevelt University, Chicago 5, Illinois. Doctor's dissertation, 3591
Rosetti, C., 3216

Rosmini-Serbati, A., 4404
Rotarian, 85
Rotary International, 85
Rouse, R., 4215
Rousseau, J. J., 3086, 3089, 3110, 3112, 3127, 3141, 3143, 3146, 3149, 3157, 3159, 3160, 3168, 3174, 3183, 3185, 3188, 3193, 3200, 3205, 3209, 3211, 3224, 3226, 3228, 3234, 3245, 3246, 3249, 3259, 3261, 3275, 3279, 3285, 3287, 3301, 3390, 3392, 3413, 3431, 3437, 3448, 3450, 3458, 3469, 3487, 3506, 3519, 3526, 3548, 3549, 3554, 3570, 3571
Royal Ambassador Organization, 123
Royal Commission on Education in Ontario, 740, 813
Royal Institute Scholarships, 814
Royal University, Thailand, 2905
Rundle, R. T., 561
Rural education, 382, 383, 397, 508, 548, 566, 629, 644, 648, 712, 725, 770, 779, 786, 811, 840, 851, 858, 869, 921, 926, 943, 991, 1005, 1009, 1026, 1027, 1030, 1032, 1036, 1055, 1067, 1077, 1079, 1080, 1097, 1125, 1155, 1219, 1240, 1275, 1308, 1348, 1377, 1403, 1409, 1421, 1440, 1463, 1471, 1571, 1601, 1612, 1613, 1620, 1632, 1696, 1725, 1743, 1747, 1753, 1767, 1806, 1824, 1827, 1831, 1838, 1873, 1876, 1877, 1878, 1882, 1886, 1892, 1894, 1897, 1906, 1917, 1932, 1951, 2013, 2031, 2050, 2051, 2055, 2060, 2085, 2095, 2096, 2099, 2102, 2111, 2117, 2120, 2126, 2131, 2146, 2161, 2261, 2356, 2486, 2493, 2497, 2551, 2567, 2630, 2660, 2753, 2815, 2907, 3925, 4351, 4412, 4594, 4620, 4814, 5560, 2654a
Rusk, R. R., 3271
Ruskin, J., 3862, 3883, 3980, 4165, 4210, 4233, 4258, 4292
Russell, B., 3871, 3911, 4039, 4218, 4223, 4281, 4286
Russia. See Union of Soviet Socialist Republics (USSR)
Rutgers University, New Brunswick, New Jersey. Doctor's dissertations, 918, 927, 2309, 5122. Master's theses, 517, 1958, 3222, 4346, 4935, 5014
Ryerson, E., 560

S

Sacramento State College, Sacramento 19, California. Master's thesis, 3245
Sacred Congregation for the Propagation of the Faith in China, 1454
Sa'di, the Persian, 2166
Sadler, M. E., 4187, 4206
Sadoleto, J., 4487, 4556
Saint Bonaventure, 4506
Saint Bonaventure University, St. Bonaventure, New York. Master's theses, 1034, 3065, 3568, 4323, 4720
Saint Christopher Training College, India, 2072
Saint Francis, 4490, 4510
Saint Jane Frances, 3563
Saint John Baptist de la Salle, 3428, 3453, 3470, 3529, 3553, 3561

Saint John College of Cleveland, Cleveland 14, Ohio. Master's theses, 283, 289, 4466, 4500, 4535, 4538
Saint John's College, Annapolis, Maryland, 3044
Saint John's University, Brooklyn 6, New York. Doctor's dissertation, 22. Master's theses, 251, 290, 938, 941, 3167, 3221, 3238, 3438, 3486, 3530, 4387, 4442, 4496, 4522, 4525
Saint Louis University, St. Louis, Missouri. Master's theses, 189, 203, 2796, 3176, 3199, 3225, 3233, 3366, 3434, 3446, 3497, 3549, 3676, 3685, 3692, 3695, 4006, 4063, 4153, 4161, 4265, 4325, 4379, 4448, 4487, 4544, 4638, 4721
Saint Paul's School, England, 3930
Saint Peter Canisius, 3706
Saint Rose, College of. See College of St. Rose.
Saint Scholastica's College, Manila, Philippines. Master's thesis, 188
Saint Sulpice, 3456
Saint Vincent de Paul, 3454, 3520, 3533, 3576
Saipan, 4856
Salaries, Teachers, 142, 2703, 2858, 4088
Sam Houston State Teachers College, Huntsville, Texas. Master's thesis, 5533
Samoa. See American Samoa, Western Samoa
San Diego State College, San Diego 15, California. Master's theses, 1174, 2278, 5381, 5532
San Francisco State College, San Francisco 2, California. Master's theses, 114, 1129, 1317, 1325, 1974, 2164, 2520, 2672, 2690, 2807, 2855, 2929, 5072
San Francisco Theological Seminary, San Anselmo, California. Master's theses, 70, 2387, 2777
San Jose State College, San Jose, California. Master's theses, 953, 5377, 5480. Other reference, 5202
Sanderson, F. W., 304
Sandiford, P., 4719
Santals, 1875
Sapparo Agricultural College, Japan, 2306
Sarawak, 104, 179, 301, 1309, 2894, 4956
Sarmiento, D. F., 281, 1184, 1186, 1190, 1193, 1194, 1195, 1205, 1211
Saskatchewan. See preceding No. 545
Saudi Arabia, 120, 169, 212, 215, 308, 4970, 4975, 5028, 5029
Saussure, F., 3375
Scarritt College for Christian Workers, Nashville 5, Tennessee. Master's thesis, 848
Schelling, F. W. J., 3742
Scheubel, J., 3600
Schiller, J. C. F., 3213, 3730
Schleiermacher, F. D. E., 3677
Scholae Cantorum, 3150
Scholarships, 643, 814
Scholastic Commentary, 3035

Scholasticism, 3041
School and Society, New York, N. Y., 2346
School of Wisdom, 3662
School Review, University of Chicago, Chicago, Illinois, 3643
School service bureaus, 1052
School surveys, 1883
Schoolships, 3994
Schopenhauer, A., 3635
Schubert, F. P., 3195
Schulze, R., 3621
Schumann, F., 3195
Schweitzer, A., 185
Science education, 380, 389, 409, 452, 574, 580, 588, 597, 769, 1040, 1330, 1355, 1489, 1615, 2014, 2072, 2180, 2192, 2537, 2550, 2649, 2667, 2883, 2970, 3031, 3080, 3081, 3135, 3399, 3425, 3659, 3872, 4254, 4338, 4446, 4666, 5667. See also Biology; Chemistry; Physics
Scotland, 3867, 3951, 3958, 4025, 4168
Scotus, D., 4231
Scranton, University of. See University of Scranton
Scribes, Education of, 2198
Seattle Pacific College, Seattle 99, Washington. Master's thesis, 347
Secondary education, 15, 84, 128, 140, 148, 151, 172, 257, 298, 360, 363, 375, 377, 378, 387, 400, 409, 412, 418, 425, 426, 427, 448, 456, 460, 477, 478, 489, 498, 506, 509, 513, 515, 557, 568, 569, 570, 574, 575, 578, 582, 588, 590, 595, 597, 599, 624, 627, 629, 630, 651, 658, 665, 672, 674, 676, 685, 686, 688, 694, 697, 704, 733, 735, 739, 742, 743, 754, 755, 758, 774, 781, 782, 785, 787, 788, 792, 793, 799, 800, 810, 811, 818, 821, 822, 833, 835, 845, 922, 925, 950, 972, 975, 986, 1012, 1042, 1050, 1064, 1065, 1069, 1087, 1090, 1092, 1095, 1101, 1113, 1118, 1122, 1131, 1132, 1147, 1157, 1175, 1185, 1188, 1201, 1204, 1213, 1221, 1222, 1226, 1245, 1248, 1249, 1251, 1256, 1263, 1264, 1265, 1266, 1280, 1283, 1284, 1285, 1307, 1329, 1360, 1379, 1406, 1417, 1460, 1469, 1472, 1475, 1476, 1477, 1481, 1483, 1517, 1518, 1539, 1541, 1545, 1556, 1560, 1566, 1572, 1574, 1577, 1582, 1585, 1593, 1597, 1606, 1608, 1611, 1627, 1636, 1638, 1640, 1665, 1673, 1677, 1698, 1705, 1706, 1710, 1715, 1726, 1745, 1760, 1766, 1769, 1779, 1782, 1790, 1797, 1807, 1808, 1814, 1818, 1820, 1826, 1828, 1835, 1836, 1839, 1844, 1855, 1867, 1870, 1872, 1873, 1879, 1881, 1890, 1901, 1914, 1923, 1925, 1928, 1929, 1931, 1936, 1939, 1946, 1952, 1955, 1974, 1979, 1987, 1989, 1993, 2014, 2018, 2024, 2027, 2032, 2042, 2044, 2052, 2063, 2064, 2065, 2068, 2074, 2077, 2081, 2093, 2127, 2138, 2158, 2169, 2173, 2185, 2189, 2190, 2195, 2206, 2318, 2321, 2359, 2367, 2374, 2377, 2384, 2395, 2401, 2405, 2406, 2415, 2416, 2417,

Secondary education (Cont'd.), 2422, 2423, 2440, 2449, 2479, 2480, 2486, 2511, 2520, 2533, 2541, 2570, 2577, 2582, 2585, 2607, 2615, 2622, 2628, 2635, 2640, 2647, 2657, 2660, 2672, 2674, 2681, 2686, 2689, 2690, 2699, 2702, 2706, 2724, 2725, 2731, 3736, 2741, 2754, 2757, 2762, 2763, 2766, 2776, 2781, 2787, 2797, 2801, 2809, 2810, 2816, 2821, 2829, 2836, 2837, 2855, 2859, 2884, 2891, 2896, 2897, 2904, 2905, 2910, 2918, 2925, 2926, 2932, 2935, 2946, 2953, 2958, 2993, 3081, 3093, 3136, 3158, 3163, 3192, 3203, 3224, 3229, 3240, 3268, 3272, 3280, 3300, 3307, 3310, 3335, 3350, 3352, 3355, 3361, 3372, 3402, 3405, 3431, 3490, 3523, 3557, 3559, 3578, 3609, 3614, 3617, 3626, 3631, 3643, 3651, 3659, 3682, 3704, 3725, 3729, 3760, 3775, 3820, 3823, 3830, 3873, 3896, 3913, 3920, 3930, 3939, 3946, 3951, 3957, 3965, 3992, 4031, 4057, 4059, 4060, 4114, 4131, 4135, 4139, 4149, 4196, 4217, 4227, 4231, 4254, 4289, 4294, 4306, 4334, 4374, 4397, 4398, 4491, 4526, 4528, 4539, 4560, 4566, 4597, 4603, 4624, 4626, 4634, 4637, 4663, 4666, 4667, 4668, 4673, 4683, 4728, 4745, 4810, 4814, 4816, 4817, 4820, 4834, 4838, 4842, 4849, 4881. (Note: Theses from Nos. 4860 to 5698 not indexed under this heading)

Seiwa Woman's College, Japan, 2320

Selected Graduate Theses in Religious Education (1933-38); Selected Doctoral Theses in Religious Education (1939-42), International Council of Religious Education, 203 N. Wabash Ave., Chicago, Illinois. (Mimeographed). 5, 488, 682, 1382, 1464, 1467, 1620, 2324, 2368, 2390, 2401, 3921, 4215, 4690, 5694

Serra, J., 1034
Seven Cardinal Principles, 2809
Seven Liberal Arts, 184, 3001, 3269
Seventh-day Adventist education, 852, 1191, 1192, 2039, 2697
Sevigne, Madame de, 3581
Shakespeare, W., 3910, 4058, 4083, 4154
Shantung Christian University, China, 1573
Shaw, G. B., 3939a, 4377
Shields, T. E., 2376
Shikoku, Japan, 2328
Shinto, 2330
Shushin, 2367, 2446
Siam. See Thailand
Sibelius, J. J., 3195
Sidney, P., 4096
Sierra, J., 894, 1022, 1034
Sierra Leone, 484-494, 4856
Silliman University, Dumaguete, Negros Oriental, Philippines. Master's thesis, 2667. Other references, 2609, 2654, 2726, 2728, 2806
Simons, M., 4579
Simpson, T., 3861
Singapore, 164, 226, 1299, 1300

Sisters of Mercy education, 764, 3486
Sisters of Notre Dame de Namur, 2376, 2435, 3322
Sisters of the Sacred Heart, 4415, 4545
Sistine Chapel, 4554
Sloyd system, 4675, 4676
Smith, T., 3870
Smith College, Northampton, Massachusetts. Master's theses, 92, 106, 823, 1238, 1254, 1307, 1344, 1697, 1819, 1973, 2004, 2092, 2728, 2945, 2970, 2991, 4108, 4541, 4714, 4800, 4895, 4950, 5022, 5140, 5147. Other reference, 4950
Smollett, T. G., 3854
Social science education, 360, 375, 441, 574, 587, 627, 719, 762, 787, 823, 864, 872, 972, 1188, 1247, 1323, 1516, 1533, 1542, 1870, 1871, 1919, 1936, 1938, 1958, 2081, 2173, 2264, 2289, 2294, 2502, 2664, 2744, 2931, 3350, 3725, 4250, 4272, 4430, 4497, 4538, 4585, 4725, 4777, 4781, 4817, 4879, 4887, 5023, 5266, 5292, 5462, See also Economics, History, Sociology, Social Work education
Social studies. See Social science education
Social work education, 749, 1634, 1641, 2387, 3315, 4678, 506a
Society of Jesus education. See Jesuit education
Society of the Divine Word education, 2769
Sociology, Teaching of, 3313, 3347, 3525, 3646, 3899, 4462
Sociology and Social Research, Los Angeles, California, 4988
Socrates, 254, 291, 3141, 4336
Sokol movement, 3346
Somaliland, 322, 326
Soochow University, China, 1502
Sophistic education, 4359
Sorbonne. See University of Paris
South Africa. See Union of South Africa
South Carolina, University of. See University of South Carolina
South Dakota, University of. See University of South Dakota
Southeastern Baptist Theological Seminary, Wake Forest, North Carolina. Master's thesis, 2933
Southern Baptist Theological Seminary, Louisville 6, Kentucky. Doctor's dissertations, 310, 1433, 1458. Master's theses, 354, 1242, 1253
Southern California, University of. See University of Southern California
Southern Methodist University, Dallas 1, Texas. Master's theses, 246, 248, 260, 857, 950, 972, 989, 990, 1027, 1192, 2010, 2099, 2868, 3210, 3211, 3571, 3699, 3804, 3827, 3834, 3983, 4008, 4066, 4102, 4112, 4261, 4287, 4344, 4718, 4745, 4751, 4994, 5290, 5316, 5344, 5345, 5376, 5383, 5411, 5431, 5538, 5628, 5691

Southwest Texas State Teachers College, San Marcos, Texas. Master's theses, 967, 1014, 1030, 2240, 2925, 3344, 3788, 5244, 5251, 5286, 5318, 5319, 5323, 5356, 5362, 5366, 5367, 5392, 5412, 5415, 5460, 5471, 5503, 5508, 5510, 5524, 5537, 5539, 5554, 5610, 5641, 5648
Southwestern Baptist Theological Seminary, Fort Worth 15, Texas. Doctor's dissertations, 123, 657, 1217, 1374, 2208, 3005, 3123, 4726, 5212
Southwestern University, Georgetown, Texas. Master's theses, 267, 2377, 2571, 2572, 2575
Soviets. See Union of Soviet Socialist Republics (USSR)
Spain, 4630-4661, 5013, 5417, 5547, 5592
Spanish, Teaching of, 891, 5317, 5472, 5576, 5618
Spanish-Americans. See Latin-Americans
Spearman, C., 4109
Speech and drama education, 558, 637, 794, 795, 829, 912, 1255, 1798, 1863, 2344, 2404, 2521, 3255, 3380, 3384, 3858, 3869, 3877, 3915, 3927, 4171, 4285, 4405, 4729, 4798, 4877, 4922, 5112, 5174, 5585, 5617, 162a.
Spelling, Teaching of, 2729, 3979, 4279, 4295, 5091, 5106, 5279, 5444, 5535
Spencer, H., 3127, 3135, 3152, 3160, 3191, 3885, 3899, 3934, 3975, 3978, 3983, 4203, 4230, 4275, 4278
Spenser, E., 3887, 4041
Spinoza, B., 4577
Sports. See Physical education; Recreation
Spranger, E., 3112, 3714
Springfield College, Springfield, Massachusetts. (Formerly International YMCA College, until 1954). Master's theses, 112, 187, 234, 400, 414, 415, 686, 733, 750, 760, 782, 811, 856, 1007, 1221, 1361, 1678, 1706, 1755, 1785, 1940, 1941, 1946, 1957, 2042, 2047, 2259, 2688, 2714, 2774, 2841, 2886, 3142, 3293, 3681, 3838, 4036, 4329, 4489, 4600, 5193
Sriniketan, India, 1878
Stanford Achievement test, 5250
Stanford University, Stanford, Palo Alto, California. Doctor's dissertations, 4, 28, 30, 135, 175, 432, 531, 551, 563, 579, 580, 587, 595, 597, 646, 649, 654, 664, 672, 842, 926, 1401, 1491, 1824, 2173, 2184, 2307, 2319, 2342, 2355, 2490, 2586, 2596, 2616, 2618, 2619, 2630, 2654, 2957, 3102, 3426, 3850, 3868, 3917, 3919, 3954, 3958, 4405, 4431, 4804, 4855, 4958, 5032, 5047, 5152, 5154, 5157, 5161, 5213, 5216, 4812a. Master's theses, 56, 113, 115, 221, 222, 236, 712, 727, 730, 751, 788, 812, 838, 864, 995, 1211, 1230, 1294, 1558, 1563, 1564, 1569, 1598, 1599, 1611, 1618, 1623, 1626, 1638, 1663, 1674, 1715, 1730, 1749, 1777,

Stanford University (Cont'd.), 1779, 1786, 1807, 2452, 2478, 2514, 2533, 2534, 2752, 2795, 2801, 2804, 3017, 3047, 3049, 3172, 3223, 3236, 3251, 3263, 3274, 3373, 3466, 3504, 3509, 3531, 3580, 3581, 3688, 3689, 3718, 3763, 3820, 4012, 4015, 4053, 4096, 4282, 4383, 4443, 4643, 4655, 4672, 4741, 4748, 4781, 4849, 4886, 4916, 4918, 4929, 4979, 4995, 5030, 5052, 5054, 5059, 5060, 5069, 5083, 5089, 5098, 5162, 5179, 5180, 5188, 5197, 5202, 5327, 5328, 5335, 5384, 5464, 5549, 5606, 5609, 5625, 5686. Other reference, 5202

Stanislavsky (stage name of C. S. Alexeev), 4724, 4729

State aid for private schools, 283, 289, 302, 600

State College of Washington, Pullman, Washington. Master's theses, 438, 735, 737

State University of Iowa, Iowa City, Iowa. Doctor's dissertations, 149, 167, 617, 1300, 1376, 1382, 1487, 1919, 1934, 2333, 2601, 2610, 3087, 3643, 3872, 3894, 4313, 4576, 4590, 4872. Master's theses, 85, 470, 960, 1036, 1248, 1637, 1736, 1765, 1938, 1961, 1962, 2046, 2127, 2132, 2441, 2563, 2681, 2726, 2810, 3018, 3029, 3036, 3311, 3348, 3363, 3482, 3771, 3777, 3796, 3979, 4029, 4110, 4137, 4277, 4285, 4508, 4521, 4595, 4597, 4752, 4845, 5025, 5078, 5091, 5093, 5250, 5552, 5564

Statistics, Teaching of, 2937

Steiner, R., 3661, 3737, 3822

Stern, W., 3642, 3800

Stetson University, De Land, Florida. Master's thesis, 427

Stoicism, 4325

Stout Institute. See Stout State College

Stout State College, Menomonie, Wisconsin. (Formerly Stout Institute). Master's theses, 75, 744, 1237

Straits Settlements. See Malaya, Singapore

Stuart, J., 3498

Student activities, 818, 1360, 1677, 2347, 2480, 2603, 2660, 2722

Student exchange programs, 113, 151, 4026, 4918, 4964

Student movement. See Youth movements

Student opinions, 1075, 1122, 1588, 1881, 2054, 4429, 5660

Student personnel services. See Guidance

Student self-government, 2731

Student Volunteer Movement, 63, 112

Sturm, J., 3151, 3769, 4563

Sudan, 308, 495, 496

Sukuma tribe, Tanganyika, 497

Sul Ross State College, Alpine, Texas. (Formerly Sul Ross State Teachers College). Master's theses, 3057, 3811, 4780, 5347, 5391, 5451, 5461, 5559, 5580, 5614, 5634

Sulzer, J. G., 3645

Sumatran education, 2137

Summer schools, 4665

Sumu Indians, 538

Sun, Y. S., 1495

Sunday schools, 618, 657, 854, 1521, 2083, 2447, 2458, 2528, 2778, 2847, 4065

Superintendent of schools, 606, 653

Supervision, 377, 517, 548, 583, 626, 698, 770, 1137, 1426, 1513, 1665, 1671, 1730, 1814, 1884, 2520, 2633, 2778, 2824, 2867, 2881, 2902, 2929, 3560, 3667, 4317, 5652

Surinam, 147

Sweden, 4662-4685, 5683, 5692-5694

Swift, J., 4229,

Switzerland, 4686-4722, 4957, 4959, 4970, 4975

Syracuse University, Syracuse 10, New York. Doctor's dissertations, 546, 567, 608, 1391, 1447, 1908, 2311, 2347, 5159. Master's theses, 59, 477, 515, 691, 698, 796, 1157, 1305, 1315, 1346, 1550, 1565, 1587, 1606, 1624, 1652, 1682, 1702, 1727, 1752, 1780, 1797, 1945, 1976, 2080, 2098, 2101, 2139, 2241, 2759, 2789, 3450, 3729, 3759, 4163, 4333, 4557, 4921, 5006

Syria, 2895-2900, 4956, 4970, 4975, 5696

T

Tagore, R., 136, 304, 1841, 1878, 2079

Taiwan. See Formosa

Talmud Torah, 2262

Talmudic education, 2262, 2263, 2303

Tanganyika, 160, 195, 247, 327, 497

Tao, H. C., 1393

Tasmania, 4814, 4822

Teacher education, 74, 141, 178, 257, 342, 347, 353, 365, 375, 383, 389, 395, 409, 422, 439, 443, 445, 462, 464, 472, 474, 477, 483, 526, 540, 544, 545, 554, 558, 559, 572, 603, 609, 623, 631, 636, 639, 641, 642, 657, 662, 716, 719, 723, 744, 746, 749, 757, 777, 819, 841, 846, 871, 877, 885, 983, 1029, 1043, 1044, 1084, 1089, 1096, 1106, 1110, 1119, 1150, 1173, 1210, 1233, 1238, 1244, 1250, 1309, 1324, 1325, 1341, 1404, 1432, 1452, 1471, 1500, 1553, 1557, 1577, 1602, 1622, 1646, 1661, 1669, 1708, 1729, 1756, 1772, 1813, 1823, 1827, 1836, 1852, 1868, 1879, 1897, 1901, 1903, 1922, 1926, 1942, 1968, 1973, 1977, 2025, 2036, 2056, 2058, 2082, 2087, 2089, 2120, 2138, 2139, 2142, 2147, 2157, 2160, 2167, 2169, 2171, 2172, 2178, 2182, 2184, 2188, 2199, 2319, 2327, 2334, 2366, 2407, 2429, 2434, 2468, 2471, 2491, 2512, 2525, 2542, 2544, 2550, 2564, 2589, 2596, 2597, 2609, 2614, 2615, 2619, 2620, 2621, 2628, 2630, 2642, 2645, 2647, 2655, 2656, 2675, 2676, 2678, 2679, 2685, 2700, 2703, 2749, 2761, 2767, 2768, 2772, 2784, 2804, 2817, 2835, 2853, 2857, 2870, 2884, 2895,

Teacher education (Cont'd.), 2905, 2910, 2912, 2917, 2918, 2928, 2995, 3115, 3136, 3192, 3240, 3305, 3382, 3393, 3402, 3523, 3586, 3623, 3626, 3647, 3830, 3889, 3933, 3946, 4038, 4088, 4099, 4340, 4599, 4601, 4604, 4668, 4730, 4796, 4808, 4821, 5429

Teacher exchange programs, 34, 114, 138, 3687, 4034, 4126, 4214

Teacher load, 569, 630, 2607, 2668, 2711, 4088

Teacher opinion, 473, 1075, 1154, 2598, 3943, 4088, 5629

Teachers College, Columbia University. See Columbia University

Teachers College Journal, Terre Haute, Indiana, 197, 2556, 3536, 4184, 4252, 4924, 4936, 4999

Teachers College of Thailand, 2915

Teachers College Record, Columbia University, New York, New York, 395, 398, 566, 591, 611, 623, 636, 1183, 1417, 1827, 1851, 1930, 2179, 2233, 2317, 2332, 2564, 2591, 3665

Teachers organizations, 551, 706, 1479, 2370, 3891, 3943

Teachers pensions. See Pensions

Teachers salaries, See Salaries, Teachers

Teachers status and problems, 622, 806, 1075, 2184, 4088

Teaching techniques, 1849, 2197

Technical education, 775, 776, 893, 1264, 1931, 2134, 2629, 2797, 2881, 4748, 4769. See also Industrial education

Television education, 5363

Temple, W., 1405, 3863, 4100

Temple University, Philadelphia 22, Pennsylvania. Doctor's dissertations, 893, 2322, 3617, 3659, 2932. Master's theses, 65, 213, 230, 272, 296, 481, 2574, 3435, 3577, 3813, 3844, 4007, 4009, 4030, 4037, 4056, 4085, 4132, 4134, 4138, 4165, 4219, 4234, 4353, 4646, 4791, 5150

Tennessee, University of. See University of Tennessee

Tennessee Agricultural and Industrial State University, Nashville 8, Tennessee. Master's theses, 472, 3828

Tennyson, A., 4094, 4152, 4284

Terman Group Test of Mental Ability, 5250

Tests, Standardized, 352, 584, 683, 793, 971, 1056, 1088, 1372, 1399, 1444, 1923, 2043, 2122, 2144, 2191, 2510, 2578, 2590, 2625, 2635, 2709, 2751, 2790, 2890, 2941, 2968, 3572, 3836, 4109, 4855, 4901, 4973, 5005, 5103, 5135, 5188, 5250, 5255, 5277, 5301, 5340, 5374, 5518, 5534, 5572, 5618

Texas, University of. See University of Texas

Texas Agricultural and Mechanical College. See Agricultural and Mechanical College of Texas

Texas Christian University, Fort Worth 9, Texas. Master's theses, 949, 992, 997, 2535, 3490

Texas College of Arts and Industries, Kingsville, Texas. Master's theses, 948, 2135, 2375, 2943, 3781, 5090, 5234, 5243, 5247, 5248, 5249, 5254, 5261, 5262, 5263, 5266, 5268, 5270, 5272, 5273, 5284, 5288, 5289, 5294, 5312, 5352, 5355, 5370, 5371, 5375, 5385, 5388, 5389, 5393, 5395, 5407, 5408, 5418, 5423, 5438, 5448, 5457, 5470, 5489, 5504, 5509, 5521, 5528, 5542, 5547, 5551, 5560, 5566, 5570, 5573, 5574, 5576, 5589, 5591, 5602, 5612, 5624, 5638, 5640, 5647, 5652

Texas School of Mines and Metallurgy. See Texas Western College

Texas State College for Women. See Texas Woman's University.

Texas Technological College, Lubbock, Texas. Master's theses, 242, 1126, 2296, 3548, 5283

Texas Wesleyan College, Fort Worth 5, Texas. Master's thesis, 1017

Texas Western College (of University of Texas), El Paso, Texas. (Formerly Texas School of Mines and Metallurgy to 1949). Master's theses, 293, 5235, 5240, 5535

Texas Woman's University, Denton, Texas. (Formerly Texas State College for Women, to 1957). Master's theses, 54, 67, 297, 1004, 2510, 4769, 5359, 5458, 5514

Textbooks, 167, 194, 255, 381, 441, 462, 575, 805, 823, 854, 976, 978, 990, 1011, 1028, 1033, 1035, 1058, 1081, 1090, 1220, 1270, 1300, 1462, 1473, 1530, 1531, 1666, 1711, 1776, 1919, 2026, 2046, 2348, 2355, 2365, 2386, 2425, 2446, 2495, 2502, 2593, 2664, 2682, 2694, 2702, 2721, 2746, 2818, 2822, 2851, 2880, 2923, 2970, 3000, 3094, 3148, 3175, 3204, 3208, 3479, 3512, 3835, 3886, 4046, 4059, 4069, 4182, 4196, 4250, 4417, 4558, 4891, 4917, 5160, 5231, 5612

Thai language, Teaching of, 2936

Thailand, 2901-2955, 4956, 4957, 4970, 4977, 4990

Theological education, 325, 343, 376, 556, 573, 607, 780, 848, 1223, 1343, 1435, 1470, 1699, 2562, 2894, 3207, 3649, 3991, 4549, 4829

Thomas a Kempis, 4589

Thomas Aquinas, Saint, 184, 203, 294, 3069, 3074, 3092, 3109, 3137, 3169, 3173, 3176, 3186, 3187, 3203, 3225, 3233, 3242, 3243, 3247, 3251, 3266, 3273, 3282, 3284

Thompson, G. H., 3271

Thompson, J., 4183

Thorndike, E. L., 4109

Tibet, 1305, 2956

Tichnor, G., 3802

Tilton, J. W., 4109

Togoland, 247, 498

Tokyo University (formerly Tokyo Imperial University), Japan, 2477

Tolstoy, L., 3172, 3183, 4951, 4779, 4792

Totalitarianism, 3082

Toth, T., 4368

Trade education, 95, 256, 716, 776, 1098, 3278. See also Industrial, Technical, Vocational education

Transportation, Pupil, 646

Transvaal, 505, 510

Trigonometry, Teaching of, 4018. See also Mathematics education

Trinity College, Washington 17, District of Columbia. Master's theses, 4148, 5357

Trinity University, San Antonio 12, Texas. Master's theses, 469, 3805, 5299, 5557, 5646, 5649

Trollope, A., 4272

Truk, 4854, 4856

Tsai, Y. P., 1480

Tschaikowsky, N. V., 3195

Tufts College. See Tufts University

Tufts University, Medford, Massachusetts. (Formerly Tufts College). Master's theses, 210, 1256, 4472

Tulane University of Louisiana, New Orleans 18, Louisiana. Master's theses, 45, 810, 2992, 3259, 3290, 3481, 4086, 4164, 4949, 5110, 5236

Tulsa, University of. See University of Tulsa

Tung-lin Academy, China, 1368

Tunisia, 147, 184, 226, 284

Turgot, A. R. J., 3394

Turkey, 2957-2995, 4970, 4972, 4975, 4977, 4988, 5697

Turnvereine, 209

U

Uganda, 195, 326, 327, 330, 499

Unamuno, M., 3260, 4646

Underprivileged boys, 414

UNESCO (United Nations Educational, Scientific, and Cultural Organization), 4, 12, 21, 22, 23, 43, 48, 50, 56, 60, 66, 67, 69, 71, 91, 100, 106, 120, 124, 261, 903, 929, 988, 2104, 3055

Union of South Africa, 500-526, 4956, 4957, 4970, 4975

Union of Soviet Socialist Republics, 4723-4800, 4963, 4970, 4975, 4978, 4985, 4987, 5001, 5013, 5015, 5017, 5020, 5021, 5024

Union Theological Seminary, New York 27, New York. (Includes Auburn Theological Seminary). Doctor's dissertations, 343, 1078, 1277, 1452, 1455, 2332, 2959. Master's theses, 108, 318, 412, 468, 520, 522, 1622, 1690, 1734, 1772, 2055, 2057, 2084, 2281, 2304, 2407, 2415, 2778, 3326, 4580, 4716, 5596

United Brethren education, 492

United Church of Canada education, 566, 607, 734, 827, 2522

United Nations, 3, 31, 160, 929. See also UNESCO

United Theological Seminary, Dayton, Ohio. Master's theses, 69, 494

Universal language, 45

University education. See Higher education

University of Alabama, University, Alabama. Master's thesis, 4891

University of Akron, Akron, Ohio. Master's theses, 4005, 4803

University of Arizona, Tucson, Arizona. Master's theses, 250, 2733, 3444, 3743, 4189, 4947, 5057, 5239, 5255, 5260, 5265, 5281, 5342, 5349, 5351, 5358, 5453, 5455, 5491, 5512, 5540, 5544, 5569, 5607

University of Berlin, Germany, 3070

University of Bologna, Italy, 3070, 3119, 3202, 3250, 4483

University of Budapest, Hungary, 4372

University of Buffalo, Buffalo 14, New York. Doctor's dissertations, 185, 2624, 3119, 3895. Master's theses, 98, 524, 1003, 2416, 2734, 4289, 4509, 4568, 4755, 4789, 4887, 5130, 5139

University of California, Berkeley 4, California. Doctor's dissertations, 161, 532, 592, 606, 909, 921, 925, 1328, 1460, 1825, 2174, 2581, 2587, 2636, 2914, 3073, 3078, 3313, 3379, 3403, 3408, 3609, 3851, 3881, 3890, 3956, 4824, 4968, 4975, 5045, 5048, 5107, 5211, 5227. Master's theses, 207, 684, 942, 951, 982, 1026, 1247, 1304, 1543, 1729, 1738, 1769, 1996, 2041, 2247, 2470, 2743, 2830, 3229, 3364, 3755, 3792, 3846, 4543, 4905, 4975, 5075, 5076, 5095, 5206, 5477, 5633. Other references, 4975, 5202

University of California, Los Angeles, California. Doctor's dissertations, 663, 669, 913, 1202, 1433a, 3669, 3960, 4574, 4810. Master's theses, 426, 993, 1005, 1249, 1289, 1685, 2104, 2249, 2302, 2813, 2920, 3161, 3252, 3275, 3761, 4177, 4206, 4214, 4470, 4601, 4674, 5306, 5548, 5599

University of Cambridge, England, 3070, 3887, 3908, 3993, 4023, 4074, 4152, 4221, 4280

University of Central America, 529, 531

University of Cheeloo, China, 1488

University of Chicago, Chicago 37, Illinois. ("We regret that we cannot lend on inter-library loan University of Chicago theses written after 1947. Beginning with 1948, the University has required only one typewritten copy of M.A. and Ph.D. theses from candidates for degrees. These unique copies cannot be spared for off-campus lending. No microfilm copies of such theses are housed in the library, but our laboratory has a non-circulating negative microfilm of Ph.D.'s written after 1947, and of M.A.'s written after June 1952, so they can prepare positive microfilm reproductions of these at cost. Order from Department of Photographic Reproduction, Swift Hall Basement, Box 132, University of Chicago." -- Librarian). Doctor's dissertations, 8, 21, 36, 122, 345, 381, 388, 528, 554, 562, 607, 655,

GENERAL INDEX

University of Chicago (Cont'd.), 660, 678, 1074, 1187, 1212, 1218, 1364, 1366, 1371, 1424, 1448, 1456, 1478, 1490, 1492, 1494, 1496, 1506, 1906, 1910, 2144, 2316, 2341, 2489, 2505, 2598, 2602, 2611, 2631, 2637, 2909, 3003, 3004, 3008, 3091, 3129, 3315, 3415, 3615, 3930, 4307, 4733, 5037, 5046, 5049, 5115, 5153, 5215. Master's theses, 117, 270, 403, 489, 492, 519, 679, 680, 685, 699, 738, 739, 746, 762, 772, 805, 991, 1039, 1099, 1136, 1151, 1204, 1319, 1334, 1335, 1336, 1340, 1341, 1517, 1521, 1522, 1524, 1525, 1553, 1557, 1566, 1567, 1601, 1604, 1614, 1636, 1677, 1701, 1704, 1718, 1732, 1741, 1746, 1748, 1750, 1778, 1795, 1937, 1953, 1972, 1985, 1999, 2003, 2050, 2056, 2071, 2096, 2107, 2109, 2115, 2116, 2118, 2124, 2131, 2283, 2357, 2358, 2367, 2404, 2410, 2434, 2446, 2453, 2463, 2465, 2466, 2471, 2537, 2547, 2679, 2692, 2725, 2730, 2737, 2814, 2864, 2967, 2968, 2972, 2983, 2984, 2987, 3032, 3204, 3770, 4004, 4048, 4116, 4554, 4585, 4587, 4640, 4831, 4835, 4839, 4914, 4940, 5003, 5008, 5031, 5062, 5064, 5067, 5084, 5094, 5111, 5354, 5422, 5499, 5541, 5550, 5687, 5689

University of Cincinnati, Cincinnati 21, Ohio. Doctor's dissertations, 3400, 3672, 4404. Master's theses, 833, 1107, 1109, 1312, 1337, 1980, 2279, 2953, 3149, 3158, 3195, 3296, 3532, 3573, 3832, 3965, 3997, 4211, 4228, 4286, 4451, 4530, 5099

University of Colorado, Boulder, Colorado. Doctor's dissertations, 9, 20, 178, 557, 1064, 1475, 1831, 2134, 2592, 2654a, 5222. Master's theses, 198, 281, 425, 870, 1194, 1205, 1666, 3220, 4028, 4032, 4141, 4290, 4345, 4449, 4757, 4761, 4774, 4986, 5005, 5018, 5170, 5275, 5401, 5511, 5584

University of Connecticut, Storrs, Connecticut. Doctor's dissertations, 2481, 3407, 3873, 4300, 4860

University of Delaware, Newark, Delaware. Master's theses, 1125, 1165, 2523

University of Denver, Denver 10, Colorado. Doctor's dissertations, 12, 917, 1323, 1331, 1488, 2554, 2652, 4729, 4868. Master's theses, 225, 266, 865, 946, 1333, 2282, 2380, 2392, 2560, 2823, 3256, 4710, 4978, 5136, 5380, 5414, 5417, 5435, 5439, 5518, 5529, 5568, 5604

University of Detroit, Detroit 1, Michigan. Master's theses, 302, 324, 729, 1015, 2411, 3982, 4391, 4707

University of Edinburgh, Scotland, 3897

University of Florida, Gainesville, Florida. Doctor's dissertations, 902, 2642, 2902, 3009, 3126, 5697. Master's theses, 253, 862, 958,

University of Florida (Cont'd.), 1103, 1197, 2673, 2822, 2995, 5516, 5530. Other references, 5516, 5697

University of Georgia, Athens, Georgia. Doctor's dissertation, 1846. Master's theses, 1210, 2919, 4559

University of Halle, Germany, 3070

University of Hawaii, Honolulu, Territory of Hawaii. Master's theses, 206, 255, 1290, 1798, 2799, 3144, 3159, 3294, 4806, 4807, 4808, 4858, 4883, 4991, 4997, 5003, 5066, 5073, 5079, 5088, 5172, 5173, 5174, 5181, 5183, 5184, 5185, 5186, 5189, 5190, 5194, 5200

University of Houston, Houston 4, Texas. Doctor's dissertations, 32, 2312, 3900, 5226. Master's thesis, 4446

University of Idaho, Moscow, Idaho. Master's theses, 758, 790, 1532, 2856, 2874, 4532, 4749, 5446

University of Illinois, Urbana, Illinois. Doctor's dissertations, 3, 37, 2656, 2912, 3112, 3412, 3625, 3629, 3671, 3862, 3878, 3922, 4818. Master's theses, 1198, 2001, 2197, 2405, 2413, 2418, 2448, 2821, 2954, 3051, 3168, 3362, 3473, 3694, 4046, 4244, 4250, 4759, 4904

University of Indiana. See Indiana University

University of Iowa. See State University of Iowa

University of Kansas, Lawrence, Kansas. Doctor's dissertations, 379, 2337, 3104, 4811. Master's theses, 493, 1260, 2077, 2372, 2677, 2693, 2721, 2756, 2809, 2851, 3264, 3439, 3679, 4000, 5026, 5513, 5601. Other reference, 4860

University of Kentucky, Lexington 29, Kentucky. Doctor's dissertations, 923, 2629, 4819. Master's theses, 850, 1649, 1773, 2297, 2432, 2998, 3227, 3319, 3458, 4221

University of Louisiana. See Louisiana State University and State Agricultural and Mechanical College

University of Louisville, Louisville, Kentucky. Master's theses, 978, 2274, 2775, 4196

University of Maine, Orono, Maine. Master's theses, 4934, 5105, 5112

University of Manila, Manila, Philippines. Master's thesis, 2668

University of Maryland, College Park, Maryland. Doctor's dissertations, 559, 675, 852, 1275, 2169, 2170, 2190, 2348, 2638, 2964, 3393, 3641, 3925. Master's theses, 71, 91, 408, 849, 1286, 1529, 2277, 2551, 2993, 4209, 4248, 4255, 4264, 4395, 4627, 4767

University of Massachusetts, Amherst, Massachusetts. (Formerly Massachusetts Agricultural College, to 1931; Massachusetts

University of Massachusetts (Cont'd.), State College, to 1947). Master's theses, 3249, 3437, 4788, 4984

University of Mexico, 964, 999, 1006, 1020

University of Michigan, Ann Arbor, Michigan. Doctor's dissertations, 159, 181, 183, 485, 601, 892, 916, 924, 1081, 1185, 1414, 1505, 1833, 1842, 1844, 1847, 1864, 1871, 1912, 2328, 2329, 2545, 2585, 2904, 3100, 3121, 3306, 3853, 3854, 3949, 3952, 4298, 4424, 4612, 4687, 4861, 4961, 4967, 5044, 5092, 5160, 5219, 5229, 5662, 2184a. Master's theses, 268, 285, 326, 420, 715, 740, 741, 808, 813, 1095, 1104, 1132, 1534, 1535, 1536, 1578, 1613, 1673, 2019, 2192, 2266, 2702, 2976, 3055, 3262, 3455, 4682, 4683, 4842, 5058, 5061, 5081, 5082, 5467. Other references, 4961, 5044, 5061, 5082

University of Minnesota, Minneapolis 14, Minnesota. Doctor's dissertations, 383, 574, 576, 906, 1415, 1865, 2145, 2590, 2608, 2628, 2632, 2645, 3080, 3626, 4426, 4963, 4971, 5692. Master's theses, 352, 766, 784, 2429, 2541, 2709, 2900, 3302, 4254, 4388, 4932, 4981

University of Mississippi, University, Mississippi. Doctor's dissertation, 377

University of Missouri, Columbia, Missouri. Doctor's dissertations, 440, 895, 905, 1399, 2155, 3130, 4674. Master's theses, 977, 3289, 4092, 4328

University of Moscow, USSR, 4738

University of Nebraska, Lincoln 8, Nebraska. Doctor's dissertations, 172, 1200, 2500, 3883, 3901, 4297. Master's theses, 464, 475, 1091, 1101, 1191, 1987, 2029, 2054, 2128, 2561, 2661, 2707, 3760, 4910, 4946, 5685. Other reference, 4910

University of New Mexico, Albuquerque, New Mexico. Master's theses, 962, 1008, 1024, 1028, 4227, 4276, 5277, 5301, 5361, 5429

University of North Carolina, Chapel Hill, North Carolina. Doctor's dissertations, 13, 903, 2150, 2339, 4689. Master's theses, 467, 1239, 1648, 2479, 3139, 4145, 4147

University of North Carolina Record, Chapel Hill, North Carolina, 13

University of North Dakota, Grand Forks, North Dakota. Doctor's dissertations, 868, 1377, 5655. Master's theses, 42, 215, 726, 1710, 3512, 4267, 4374, 4744, 5021, 5024

University of Notre Dame, Notre Dame, Indiana. Doctor's dissertations, 529, 1913, 2588, 4427, 4429. Master's theses, 291, 717, 2251, 2256, 3231, 3266, 3278, 4033, 4319, 4358, 4382, 4396, 4471, 4475, 4616, 4623, 5404

University of Oklahoma, Norman, Oklahoma. Doctor's dissertations, 1186, 1852, 5029. Master's theses, 223, 1952, 2760

University of Oregon, Eugene, Oregon. Doctor's dissertations, 545, 610, 652, 1867, 3317, 4376, 4812. Master's theses, 836, 1641, 2391, 2717, 2753, 2808, 2333, 3197, 3371, 3978, 4106, 4229, 4232, 4828, 4843, 5449, 5482, 5517

University of Oslo, Norway, 4592, 4602

University of Oxford, England, 3070, 3119, 3202, 3250, 3908, 3990, 4011, 4023, 4068, 4157, 4172, 4221

University of Paris, France, 3070, 3073, 3119, 3202, 3250, 3401, 3447, 3478, 3513, 3514, 3535, 3537, 3558, 3568

University of Pennsylvania, Philadelphia 4, Pennsylvania. Doctor's dissertations, 29, 387, 453, 560, 1184, 1406, 1441, 1468, 1481, 2330, 3410, 3650, 3870, 3879, 3913, 3939, 4624, 5109. Master's theses, 1586, 1603, 1820, 3824, 4397

University of the Philippines, Manila, Philippines. Master's theses, 1617, 1808, 2659, 2662, 2663, 2664, 2665, 2666, 2669, 2670, 2678, 2682, 2683, 2685, 2687, 2691, 2694, 2695, 2697, 2700, 2703, 2704, 2708, 2711, 2712, 2715, 2716, 2722, 2723, 2731, 2735, 2736, 2738, 2739, 2741, 2744, 2746, 2750, 2751, 2758, 2761, 2765, 2766, 2772, 2782, 2783, 2784, 2785, 2787, 2790, 2793, 2794, 2802, 2803, 2818, 2820, 2824, 2825, 2828, 2832, 2834, 2836, 2838, 2839, 2845, 2846, 2850, 2857, 2859, 2860, 2861, 2863, 2865, 2866, 2869, 2872, 2879, 2880, 2882, 2884, 2887. Other references, 2618, 2624, 2651, 2663, 2687, 2688, 2700, 2722, 2723, 2739, 2782, 2805, 2820, 2841, 2859. See note on availability of these theses preceding No. 2580

University of Pittsburgh, Pittsburgh 13, Pennsylvania. Doctor's dissertations, 153, 1373, 2148, 2149, 2229, 2496, 2504, 3906, 4366, 4688, 4962. Master's theses, 81, 406, 419, 1707, 2006, 2265, 2298, 2745, 3281, 3489, 3495, 3749, 3757, 3784, 3833, 4077, 4115, 4131, 4186, 4340, 4342, 4372, 4373, 4581, 4582, 4765, 4912, 4917

University of Prague, Czechoslovakia, 3341

University of Puerto Rico, 1047, 1052, 1053, 1062, 1068, 1072, 1074, 1076, 1087, 1148

University of Redlands, Redlands, California. Master's theses, 2122, 4937, 5410

University of Richmond, Richmond, Virginia. Master's thesis, 1787

University of Rochester, Rochester 20, New York. (Includes Eastman School of Music). Master's theses, 2508, 2780, 3190, 5131

University of Salerno, Italy, 3119

University of Scranton, Scranton 3, Pennsylvania. Master's theses, 1130, 1209, 3529, 4457

University of South Carolina, Columbia 1, South Carolina. Master's theses, 3232, 3349, 4025

University of South Dakota, Vermillion, South Dakota. Master's theses, 2701, 4026, 4114

University of Southern California, Los Angeles 7, California. Doctor's dissertations, 125, 890, 896, 1298, 1327, 1450, 1504, 1933, 2176, 2191, 2323, 2327, 2356, 2553, 2594, 2600, 2913, 2962, 3640, 3657, 3928, 4439, 4633, 4664, 4670, 4966, 5036, 5158, 546a. Master's theses, 46, 60, 77, 191, 195, 227, 229, 235, 244, 280, 299, 304, 327, 401, 402, 410, 437, 480, 537, 541, 696, 835, 847, 867, 875, 940, 966, 971, 980, 1019, 1020, 1025, 1032, 1208, 1282, 1316, 1523, 1544, 1584, 1662, 1670, 1679, 1684, 1689, 1709, 1711, 1716, 1757, 1782, 1783, 1784, 1804, 1939, 1988, 1990, 1993, 2011, 2024, 2037, 2052, 2053, 2061, 2089, 2113, 2199, 2280, 2371, 2373, 2388, 2390, 2400, 2403, 2436, 2475, 2518, 2529, 2532, 2540, 2660, 2674, 2696, 2740, 2749, 2776, 2817, 2852, 2949, 3053, 3066, 3146, 3206, 3280, 3342, 3367, 3370, 3461, 3527, 3674, 3677, 3693, 3707, 3723, 3739, 3745, 3799, 4034, 4067, 4072, 4089, 4109, 4136, 4167, 4233, 4260, 4337, 4339, 4369, 4381, 4401, 4445, 4536, 4603, 4621, 4679, 4680, 4753, 4783, 4787, 4801, 4838, 4848, 4894, 4896, 4925, 4930, 4944, 4945, 4996, 5000, 5011, 5015, 5017, 5019, 5023, 5051, 5055, 5074, 5166, 5167, 5168, 5169, 5171, 5198, 5201, 5253, 5258, 5274, 5298, 5304, 5308, 5309, 5326, 5336, 5340, 5346, 5350, 5374, 5382, 5394, 5402, 5406, 5413, 5434, 5456, 5463, 5465, 5466, 5475, 5478, 5484, 5488, 5490, 5496, 5497, 5502, 5505, 5506, 5525, 5536, 5558, 5581, 5582, 5586, 5594, 5600, 5605, 5611, 5616, 5622, 5632, 5635, 5637, 5645. Other references, 1804, 5051

University of Sydney, Australia, 4809

University of Tennessee, Knoxville, Tennessee. Doctor's dissertation, 34, 2185, 3068. Master's theses, 350, 1100, 1108, 1113, 1115, 1133, 1358, 1513, 1955, 1968, 2261, 3217, 3547, 4003, 4058, 4107, 4230, 4492

University of Texas, Austin 12, Texas. Doctor's dissertations, 19, 121, 127, 527, 533, 535, 536, 887, 889, 894, 899, 901, 908, 1075, 1929, 2501, 2658, 3610, 3955, 5028, 5208, 5214, 5218, 5223, 5224, 5228. Master's theses, 39, 247, 259, 287, 853, 860, 866, 937, 947, 952, 964, 975, 976, 999, 1002, 1011, 1033, 1094, 1098, 1120, 1123, 1152, 1159, 1164, 1195, 1222, 1241, 1267, 1292, 1510, 2195, 2248, 2393, 2876, 2889, 3135, 3140, 3153, 3551, 3565, 3678, 3711, 3738, 3817, 3966, 3985, 4192, 4563, 4565, 4722, 4942, 4951, 5007, 5237, 5256, 5269,

University of Texas (Cont'd.), 5271, 5291, 5292, 5293, 5295, 5296, 5297, 5300, 5302, 5305, 5314, 5321, 5332, 5333, 5337, 5338, 5343, 5360, 5363, 5364, 5365, 5368, 5378, 5379, 5387, 5396, 5398, 5403, 5416, 5419, 5420, 5421, 5425, 5426, 5427, 5437, 5442, 5443, 5444, 5445, 5459, 5472, 5473, 5479, 5481, 5485, 5494, 5501, 5507, 5515, 5531, 5543, 5556, 5561, 5567, 5571, 5572, 5575, 5577, 5578, 5588, 5597, 5598, 5613, 5615, 5617, 5621, 5639, 5643, 5650, 5675. Other reference, 5639

University of Tulsa, Tulsa 4, Oklahoma. Doctor's dissertation, 133

University of Utah, Salt Lake City, Utah. Doctor's dissertations, 1052, 1199, 3614, 5155, 5207. Master's theses, 2069, 2770, 3205, 4847, 4982, 5165, 5450. Other reference, 5165

University of Vermont and State Agricultural College, Burlington, Vermont. Master's thesis, 4698

University of Virginia, Charlottesville, Virginia. Master's theses, 3136, 3680, 4237

University of Washington, Seattle 5, Washington. Doctor's dissertations, 138, 548, 588, 614, 630, 634, 905, 928, 929, 1449, 1465, 1486, 1889, 1902, 2607, 3593, 4308, 4435, 4594, 4671, 4736. Master's theses, 49, 72, 407, 465, 689, 697, 701, 702, 703, 704, 706, 707, 720, 724, 742, 759, 770, 771, 774, 789, 791, 792, 793, 806, 814, 818, 821, 826, 939, 965, 1167, 1251, 1339, 1520, 1528, 1668, 1745, 1759, 1762, 1781, 1954, 1966, 2112, 2295, 2381, 2382, 2445, 2464, 2555, 2699, 2718, 2724, 2757, 2835, 2867, 2871, 2878, 3171, 3525, 3840, 3988, 4291, 4450, 4569, 4642, 4713, 4846, 4952, 5071, 5175, 5176, 5195, 5595, 5630. Other references, 2835, 5176

University of West Virginia. See West Virginia University

University of Wisconsin, Madison 6, Wisconsin. Doctor's dissertations, 156, 555, 558, 911, 912, 1348, 2305, 2485, 2906, 3101, 3369, 3653, 3655, 3858, 3869, 4302, 5683. Master's theses, 277, 298, 829, 1219, 1252, 1255, 1943, 2119, 2732, 2994, 3021, 3268, 3298, 3575, 4171, 4786, 4923. Other reference, 5683

University of Wisconsin, Milwaukee Campus, Milwaukee, Wisconsin. (Formerly Wisconsin State Teachers College, Milwaukee). Master's theses, 462, 5672

University of Wyoming, Laramie, Wyoming. Master's theses, 422, 3980, 4898, 5331

Ursuline education, 4441, 4476

Uruguay, 1287-1289, 4957

Utah, University of. See University of Utah

Utah State Agricultural College. See Utah State University of Agriculture and Applied Science

GENERAL INDEX

Utah State University of Agriculture and Applied Science, Logan, Utah. (Formerly Utah State Agricultural College, to 1957). Master's theses, 2278, 2805, 2944, 4256, 4977, 5116, 5644. Other reference, 4977
Utopias, 54, 96, 245, 3274, 3888

V

Vacation school, 2012
Vaishnava dramatic traditions, 1863
Vanderbilt University, Nashville 5, Tennessee. Master's theses, 307, 516, 3430, 3544
Varela, J. P., 1287
Vartapet, 2961
Vassar College, Poughkeepsie, New York. Master's thesis, 4542. Other references, 4950
Vegio, M., 4414, 4420, 4437, 4516
Venezuela, 1290-1292, 4969, 4975, 4988
Veracruz, A., 899
Vergerio, 4487
Vermont, University of. See University of Vermont and State Agricultural College
Vetable, F., 3474
Victoria, Australia, 4810, 4825, 4827, 4828
Viet-Nam, 2996-2998
Villanova College. See Villanova University
Villanova University, Villanova, Pennsylvania. (Formerly Villanova College, to 1954). Master's theses, 693, 3454, 4495, 4519
Vincent of Beauvais, 3556
Virgin Islands, 1166, 1167, 4970
Virginia, University of. See University of Virginia
Virginia Polytechnic Institute, Blacksburg, Virginia. Master's theses, 1093, 1137, 4837
Vittorino da Feltre, 4470, 4495, 4517, 4555, 4559
Vives, J. L., 3162, 4563, 4630, 4631, 4633, 4636, 4638, 4639, 4644, 4649, 4659
Vocational education, 256, 264, 447, 465, 581, 627, 700, 775, 776, 880, 1019, 1085, 1107, 1111, 1121, 1169, 1254, 1358, 1550, 1585, 1685, 1723, 1829, 1874, 1893, 1912, 1949, 2119, 2186, 2629, 2650, 2657, 2661, 2753, 2825, 2858, 2910, 2918, 3049, 3078, 3230, 3288, 3316, 3602, 3868, 4115, 4527, 4574, 4750, 4848. See also Agricultural, Home Economics education
Vocational guidance. See Guidance
Voltaire, F. M. A., 3399, 3536
Vrindaban, 1863

W

Wake Forest College, Winston-Salem, North Carolina. Master's theses, 2710, 3277
Wales, 3946, 4088, 4106, 4217, 4227, 4289, 5698
Wallstonecraft, M., 4094, 4212
War, Effect on schools of, 154
Ward, L. F., 3899, 4462
Wardha scheme, 1917
Washington, State College of. See State College of Washington
Washington, University of. See University of Washington
Washington University, St. Louis 5, Missouri. Doctor's dissertations, 1041, 1495, 3590, 4310. Master's theses, 476, 1984, 2026, 2043, 2862, 3246, 3968, 4169, 4172, 4876
Watts, I., 4001
Waxweiler, E., 3313
Wayne State University, Detroit 1, Michigan. (Formerly Wayne University, to 1956). Doctor's dissertations, 393, 2213, 3939a, 4863, 4864, 4870. Master's theses, 1110, 1171, 2858, 4566, 4705, 5657
Webb, B., 3941
Webb, S., 3941
Wechsler-Bellevue Intelligence Scale, 2578
Wellesley College, Wellesley 81, Massachusetts. Master's theses, 1687, 3505, 4069. Other references, 1687, 4950
Wells, H. G., 286, 3172, 3888, 3968, 3989, 4108, 4219
Welsh, 5698
Wesley, J., 3138, 3874, 3924, 4080, 4130, 4166, 4266
Wesseley, N. H., 3358
West Indies (British), 1168-1180, 4970, 4975
West Texas State College, Canyon, Texas. Master's theses, 2511, 5245, 5636
West Virginia University, Morgantown, West Virginia. Master's theses, 3782, 4892, 4906
Western Australia, 4816
Western Illinois State College. See Western Illinois University
Western Illinois University, Macomb, Illinois (Formerly Western Illinois State College). Master's thesis, 1021
Western Reserve University, Cleveland 6, Ohio. Doctor's dissertations, 484, 1355, 1924, 3357, 3948. Master's thesis, 3335
Western Samoa, 195, 247
Western State College of Colorado, Gunnison, Colorado. Master's thesis, 4785
Western Theological Seminary, Pittsburgh 12, Pennsylvania. Master's theses, 82, 4702
Western Washington College of Education, Bellingham, Washington. Master's thesis, 748
Wheaton College, Wheaton, Illinois. Master's theses, 313, 884
Whitehead, A. N., 3856, 3916, 4150
Whittier College, Whittier, California. Master's theses, 4685, 5192
Wichita, University of. See Municipal University of Wichita
Wieland, C. M., 3263
Wiener Schulreife tests, 3836
Wilderspin, S., 3959
William and Mary, College of. See College of William and Mary
Williams College, Williamstown, Massachusetts. Master's thesis, 882
Willman, O., 3597, 3778, 3847
Wisconsin, University of. See University of Wisconsin
Wisconsin State Teachers College, Milwaukee. See University of Wisconsin, Milwaukee Campus
Wittenberg College, Springfield, Ohio. Master's thesis, 4321
Woman's Movement, China, 1504
Women and girls, Education of, 51, 78, 148, 152, 180, 199, 244, 250, 288, 403, 422, 496, 516, 650, 691, 806, 884, 1116, 1180, 1217, 1235, 1236, 1261, 1271, 1319, 1365, 1422, 1437, 1483, 1504, 1511, 1571, 1581, 1598, 1602, 1643, 1664, 1675, 1676, 1687, 1709, 1710, 1723, 1729, 1754, 1786, 1788, 1790, 1827, 1842, 1856, 1895, 1896, 1911, 1916, 1930, 1941, 1948, 1953, 1954, 1960, 1966, 1971, 1991, 2024, 2032, 2037, 2040, 2070, 2092, 2106, 2118, 2128, 2168, 2184, 2292, 2320, 2358, 2376, 2382, 2384, 2402, 2416, 2417, 2422, 2437, 2439, 2444, 2451, 2453, 2472, 2474, 2476, 2516, 2524, 2530, 2580, 2612, 2613, 2624, 2632, 2665, 2670, 2689, 2696, 2752, 2805, 2837, 2896, 2994, 3038, 3056, 3075, 3087, 3158, 3162, 3179, 3216, 3236, 3237, 3270, 3280, 3287, 3297, 3364, 3443, 3463, 3477, 3498, 3499, 3506, 3515, 3517, 3524, 3530, 3581, 3582, 3971, 3976, 3981, 3992, 4040, 4054, 4064, 4083, 4094, 4142, 4162, 4167, 4180, 4192, 4212, 4241, 4284, 4372, 4496, 4644, 4660, 4957, 5006, 5053, 5068, 5297, 5305, 5322, 5553, 5567, 5593. See also Home Economics education
Woodstock School, India, 2113, 5115
Wooten, M. L., 535
Wordsworth, W., 3993, 4016, 4020, 4119, 4129, 4156, 4224, 4262
Workers' education, 3890, 4010, 4155, 4740
Workingmen's College, 4155
World's Student Christian Federation, 4215
Writing education, 46, 1762, 1777, 2144, 2539, 3290
Wuertemberg, 3665, 3680
Wyoming, University of. See University of Wyoming

X

Xenophon, 3201

Y

Yale-in-China, 1410, 1419
Yale University, New Haven, Connecticut. Doctor's dissertations, 1, 162, 177, 179, 309, 594, 1299, 1410, 1419, 1431, 1463, 1464, 1467, 1470, 1473, 1857, 1863, 2306, 2310, 2314, 2340, 2352, 2487, 2498, 3076, 3324, 3330, 3592, 3603, 3627, 3633, 3648, 3652, 3866, 3891, 3924, 4301, 4402, 4573, 4727, 4850.
Master's theses, 109, 314, 317, 404, 878, 1023, 1512, 1583, 1590, 1655, 1713, 1719, 1737, 1814, 1992, 2275, 2421, 2898, 2982, 2989, 3970, 4111, 4215, 4247, 4579, 4825, 5563

Yap, 4856
Yemen, 2216, 2999, 3000
Yen, Y. C. J., 278
Yenching University, China, 1459
Yeshiva University, New York 33, New York. Doctor's dissertation, 2214
YMCA education, 53, 1007, 1505, 1566, 1755, 1995, 2110, 2399, 2534, 3034, 4600
Youth movements, 280, 1390, 1494, 1662, 1780, 1803, 3107, 3161, 3182, 3294, 3655, 3668, 3689, 3712, 3713, 3723, 3750, 3781, 3786, 3792, 3846, 4465

Yugoslavia, 4801-4803, 5684-5691
Yuth Dzar Academy, China, 1642
YWCA education, 78, 1675

Z

Zanzibar, 327, 330
Zinzendorf, L. N., 3330
Zionism, 2225, 2275
Zollinger, E., 1017
Zulus, 502, 514, 524
Zumarraga, J., 916

Copy Preparation By:
WALTER CONWAY & ASSOC., INC.

Offset Printed By:
KIRBY LITHOGRAPHIC CO., INC.
Washington, D. C.